PHILIPPIANS

VOLUME 33B

THE ANCHOR YALE BIBLE is a project of international and interfaith scope in which Protestant, Catholic, and Jewish scholars from many countries contribute individual volumes. The project is not sponsored by any ecclesiastical organization and is not intended to reflect any particular theological doctrine.

THE ANCHOR YALE BIBLE is committed to producing commentaries in the tradition established half a century ago by the founders of the series, William Foxwell Albright and David Noel Freedman. It aims to present the best contemporary scholarship in a way that is accessible not only to scholars but also to the educated nonspecialist. Its approach is grounded in exact translation of the ancient languages and an appreciation of the historical and cultural context in which the biblical books were written, supplemented by insights from modern methods, such as sociological and literary criticism.

John J. Collins
GENERAL EDITOR

THE ANCHOR YALE BIBLE

PHILIPPIANS

◆

A New Translation
with Introduction and Commentary

JOHN REUMANN

THE ANCHOR YALE BIBLE

YALE UNIVERSITY PRESS
New Haven and London

Printed in the United States of America.

Library of Congress Control Number: 2007942902
ISBN 978-0-300-14045-3 (cloth : alk. paper)

A catalogue record for this book is available from the British Library.

The paper in this book meets the guidelines for permanence and durability
of the Committee on Production Guidelines for Book Longevity
of the Council on Library Resources.

This paper meets the requirements of ANSI/NISO Z39.48-1992 (Permanence
of Paper). It contains 30 percent postconsumer waste (PCW) and is certified
by the Forest Stewardship Council (FSC).

10 9 8 7 6 5 4 3 2 1

CONTENTS

◆

THE BODY OF THE LETTER, 1:12–4:20

LETTER B, BODY, 1:12–3:1

PREFACE

◆

Reading and research for this commentary began in 1973 when I received the Anchor Bible assignment for Philippians. Originally Prof. Krister Sendahl was to do Paul's epistles in the format of "translation" for an "interfaith Bible" along with *brief* notes and comment. I planned a volume on the grand scale that the AB had by then become, beginning with a treatment of Paul and Philippi in Acts 16 and 20. (AB 31 by Johannes Munck was by then considered all too brief; far more can be said about the founding mission and Paul's subsequent contacts with Philippi.) A draft of over 1200 pages was completed on Acts.

Despite teaching and administrative duties at the Lutheran Theological Seminary in Philadelphia and church and ecumenical commitments, especially in the U. S. Lutheran-Roman Catholic dialogue, I hammered out an approach to Philippians in the 1980s and 1990s, articulated in Reumann 1987, 1993a, and 1996, with attention to methodologies (INTRO. IX bibl.). Paul writes "to the Philippians," but the house churches in his favorite congregation made significant contributions to the Pauline mission and early Christianity, including the piece about Christ and God in 2:6–11, designed by the Philippians for mission in the Roman world of the day. The letter(s) to Philippi are part of a dialogue. Paul responds to the story in 2:6–11 with support and corrective as part of that dialogue. Views were explored and tested in seminary classrooms, with pastors' groups, in learned societies, and private discussions over the years.

Leisure to complete the draft came with retirement from full-time teaching in 1995. The first draft ran over 2800 pages (plus 1200 on Acts, which dropped out of the AB picture with publication of *Acts* by Joseph Fitzmyer, AB 31, 1998). I hope to publish my treatment of 16:11–40 and 20:1–6 elsewhere. In 2002, the commentary on Philippians was revised for consistency and cut to 2400 pages. What I regarded as a well-balanced treatment, the publisher insisted had to be cut to 1250 manuscript pages; the result may be a more focused treatment. This final revision was carried out while the author was receiving radiation and other treatment for cancer. Some materials thus omitted I hope to publish in a separate volume, referred to in this commentary as *Philippian Studies*.

Over the years, I am grateful for help to the staff of the Krauth Memorial Library, Lutheran Theological Seminary, Philadelphia, especially David Wartluft, Harry Jackson, Lillian Scoggins, Ron Townsend, and Karl Krueger; Westminster Theological Seminary Library; the Kirchliche Hochschule, Neuendettelsau, Bavaria, Pfarrer Folkers Freimanis; the University Libraries at Tübingen, Hamburg, Leipzig, Cambridge, Oxford, and Sheffield. Editors at Doubleday, most recently

Andrew Corbin, provided liaison with the publisher. David Noel Freedman, editor of the Anchor Bible, has been a special support and advisor, reading every one of more than 4000 manuscript pages through 2002 and offering wise counsel on major issues and endless details with patience and clarity. He has not read the final revised version. Donald Deer (Claremont, California), shared analyses he and his wife did of text and translations for Philippians. Profs. Edgar Krentz (Chicago) and Frederick Danker (St. Louis) read portions of the drafts. Dr. Erik Heen (Philadelphia) helped on materials in Swedish. Contents and wordings are my responsibilities.

I dedicate this volume to my wife, Martha Brobst Reumann, without whose encouragement, support, and love, the labor and joy of learning that a commentary represents would never have been possible. She is Euodia, Syntyche (Phil 4:2–3) and Lydia, without controversy.

USING THIS COMMENTARY

Just as other volumes in the Anchor Yale Bible divide the Scripture into segments for purposes of commentary, this volume is divided into seventeen such segments. For each of the seventeen pericopes of scripture, TRANSLATION is followed by NOTES and COMMENT. The NOTES survey and report the varied opinions of commentators, lexica, and other resources on philological, grammatical, literary, rhetorical, historical, and other matters, often without reaching any conclusion. The NOTES are raw material for exposition. In the COMMENT, section A deals with sources and forms that shape the pericope. In light of this evidence, conclusions are finally reached in section B of the COMMENT, where the aim is to present what Paul meant, and the interpretation given to his words by the Philippians and others since then.

Throughout the text there are cross references to NOTES or COMMENT outside the pericope currently being read. The number before the reference indicates the pericope where the note or comment can be found.

On most points ample documentation is provided in English and German works. It is hoped that those studying Philippians with this commentary will regularly check in one of the works cited. Commentators with whom there is frequent dialogue are often referred to by an abbreviation of the author's name, as given in the bibliography of Select Commentaries (pp. 43–49).

Since this is a volume in the Anchor Yale Bible commentary series, an effort has been made to draw on other volumes in the series, but these vary considerably over the forty-year period in which they were produced.

> John Reumann,
> Ministerium of Pennsylvania Professor, emeritus,
> Lutheran Theological Seminary at Philadelphia
> 5 May, 2008

ABBREVIATIONS

◆

The SBL Handbook of Style, ed. P. H. Alexander et al. (Peabody, MA: Hendrickson, 1999) is used, and, where necessary, S. Schwertner, TRE Abkürzungsverzeichnis (Berlin/New York: de Gruyter, 1976), and RGG⁴. For classical authors, OCD, BDAG. See also General Bibliography.

AB, *ABD*	Anchor Bible, *Anchor Bible Dictionary*
ANRW	*Aufstieg und Niedergang der römischen Welt: Geschichte und Kultur Roms im Spiegel der neueren Forschung*, ed. H. Temporini/W. Haase. Berlin/New York:de Gruyter, 1972–
APOT	*The Apocrypha and Pseudepigrapha of the Old Testament*, ed. R. H. Charles. 2 vols. Oxford: Clarendon, 1913.
ATR	A. T. Robertson, *A Grammar of the Greek New Testament in Light of Historical Research*. London: Hodder & Stoughton/New York: George H. Doran, 1914, 3rd ed., 1919.
BAGD	W. Bauer, W. F. Arndt, F. W. Gingrich, F. W. Danker, *A Greek-English Lexicon of the New Testament and Other Early Christian Literature*. Chicago: Univ. of Chicago, 1979.
BCH	*Bulletin de correspondance hellénique*
BDAG	W. Bauer, F. W. Danker, W. F. Arndt, F. W. Gingrich, *A Greek-English Lexicon of the New Testament and Other Early Christian Literature*. Chicago: Univ. of Chicago, 2000. Cited, as in BDAG, **boldface roman type** for word meanings, ***boldface italic*** for formal equivalents.
BDF	F. Blass, A. Debrunner, tr. R. W. Funk, *A Greek Grammar of the New Testament and Other Early Christian Literature*. Chicago: Univ. of Chicago, 1961.
BDR	F. Blass, A. Debrunner, rev. F. Rehkopf, *Grammatik des neutestamentlichen Griechisch*. Göttingen: Vandenhoeck & Ruprecht, 17th ed. 1990.
Burton, *MT*	E. de Witt Burton, *Syntax of Moods and Tenses in New Testament Greek*. Chicago: University of Chicago Press, 1893.
CRINT	Compendia rerum iudaicarum ad Novum Testamentum.
DA	*A Discourse Analysis of Philippians*, see Reed, J. T., 1997, in Gen. Bibl.
DDD	*Dictionary of Demons and Deities in the Bible*, ed. K. van der Toorn et al. Leiden: Brill, 1995.
DPL	*Dictionary of Paul and his Letters*, ed. G. F. Hawthorne/R. P. Martin. Downers Grove, IL/Leicester: InterVarsity, 1993.
EC	*The Encyclopedia of Christianity* (based on *EKL*), ed. E. Fahlbusch et al. Grand Rapids: Eerdmans/Leiden: Brill, 1999– .

ECC   Eerdmans Critical Commentary (Grand Rapids).
EDNT   *Exegetical Dictionary of the New Testament*, ed. H. Batz/G. Schneider.
                       3 vols. Grand Rapids: Eerdmans, 1990–93. Ger. 1980–83.
ER   *The Encyclopedia of Religion*, ed. M. Eliade. 16 vols. New York, 1987.
García Martínez, F.   *The Dead Sea Scrolls Translated*. Leiden: Brill, 1994.
GGBB   *Greek Grammar Beyond Basics*, by D. B. Wallace. Grand Rapids:
                       Zondervan, 1996.
GNTG   *A Grammar of New Testament Greek*. Edinburgh: T & T Clark. Vol. I.
                       J. H. Moulton, 1906; II. J. H. Moulton and W. F. Howard, 1919–29;
                       III. N. Turner 1963.
Goodwin   W. W. Goodwin, *Syntax of the Moods and Tenses of the Greek Verb*.
                       Boston: Ginn Brothers, 5th ed. 1874.
Goodwin/Gulick   W. W. Goodwin/C. B. Gulick, *Greek Grammar*. Boston: Ginn, 1930.
Hatch-Redpath   E. Hatch/H. A. Redpath, *A Concordance to the Septuagint*. . . . 2 vols.
                       Oxford: Clarendon, 1897. Supplement 1906. Repr., Graz: Akade-
                       mischer Druck, 1954.
HCNT   *Hellenistic Commentary to the New Testament*, ed. M. E. Boring/
                       K. Berger/C. Colpe. Nashville: Abingdon, 1995.
HSNTApoc   E. Hennecke, W. Schneemelcher, *New Testament Apocrypha*, ed.
                       R. McL. Wilson. 2 vols. London: Lutterworth/Philadelphia: Westmin-
                       ster, 1963–65 (Ger.1959, 1964). Rev. ed., Louisville: Westminster John
                       Knox, 1991–92.
IDB, IDBSup   *The Interpreter's Dictionary of the Bible*, ed. G. A. Buttrick. 4 vols.
                       Nashville: Abingdon, 1962. *Supplementary Volume*, ed. K. Crim,
                       1976.
Jastrow   M. Jastrow, *A Dictionary of the Targumim, the Talmud Bibli and Yerush-
                       almi, and the Midrashic Literature*. New York/Berlin: Verlag Choreb/
                       London: Shapiro, Vallentine & Co., 1926. Repr. Peabody, MA: Hen-
                       drickson, 2003.
JE   *The Jewish Encyclopedia*, ed. I. Singer. 12 vols. New York: Funk &
                       Wagnalls, 1925.
KlPauly   *Der kleine Pauly*, ed. K. Ziegler/W. Sontheimer. 5 vols. Stuttgart:
                       Druckenmüller, 1964–75. Cf. now *Brill's New Pauly*, ed. H. Cancik/
                       H. Schneider (Leiden, 2006–).
LAE   *Light from the Ancient East: The New Testament Illustrated by Recently
                       Discovered Texts of the Greco-Roman World*, by A. Deissmann. Lon-
                       don: Hodder & Stoughton, 1927.
Lausberg   H. Lausberg, *Handbook of Literary Rhetoric: A Foundation for Literary
                       Study* (Ger. 1960; 2nd ed., 1973), ed. D. E. Orton/R. Dean Anderson.
                       Leiden: Brill, 1998.
Louw/Nida   J. P. Louw/E. A. Nida et al., *Greek-English Lexicon of the New Testa-
                       ment Based on Semantic Domains*. 2 vols. New York: United Bible So-
                       cieties, 1988.
LSJ   H. G. Liddell, R. Scott, new ed. H. S. Jones with R. McKenzie, *A
                       Greek-English Lexicon*. Oxford: Clarendon, 1925–40, repr. 1966. Sup-
                       plement 1968.
MM   J. H. Moulton/G. Milligan, *The Vocabulary of the Greek New Testa-
                       ment*. London: Hodder & Stoughton, 1914–29. Repr., Peabody, MA:
                       Hendrickson, 1997.

Moule, *IB*	C. F. D. Moule, *An Idiom Book of New Testament Greek.* Cambridge: Cambridge Univ. Press, 1953. 2nd ed., 1959.
NewDocs	*New Documents Illustrating Early Christianity,* ed. G. H. R. Horsley/ S. Llewelyn. North Ryde, N.S.W., 1981– .
NIDNTT	*New International Dictionary of New Testament Theology,* ed. L. Coenen et al., ET ed. C. Brown. 3 vols. Grand Rapids: Zondervan, 1975–85. Ger., *TBLNT,* 1967–71.
NIDOTTE	*New International Dictionary of Old Testament Theology and Exegesis,* ed. W. A. VanGemeren. 5 vols. Grand Rapids: Zondervan, 1997– .
OCD³	*The Oxford Classical Dictionary,* 3rd ed., ed. S. Hornblower & A. Spawforth. Oxford/New York: Oxford Univ. Press, 1996. 1st ed, 1949. 2nd ed., 1970.
OEANE	*The Oxford Encyclopedia of Archaeology in the Near East,* ed. E. M. Meyers. Oxford: 1997.
OTP	*Old Testament Pseudepigrapha,* ed. J. H. Charlesworth. 2 vols. Garden City: Doubleday, 1983.
PG	Patrologia Graeca = Patrologiae cursus completus: Series graeca, ed. J.-P. Migne, 162 vols. Paris, 1857–86.
PGL	*Patristic Greek Lexicon,* ed. G. W. H. Lampe. Oxford: Clarendon, 1961–68.
PL	Patrologia latina = Patrologiae cursus completus: Series latina, ed. J.-P. Migne, 217 vols, Paris, 1844–64.
PRE, PW	*Paulys Real-Encyclopädie der classischen Altertumswissenschaft,* ed. G. Wissowa. Stuttgart: Metzler/Munich: Druckenmüller, 1893–1978. *Supplement,* 1903ff. New ed., Munich 1980– .
RAC	*Reallexikon für Antike und Christentum,* ed. T. Klausner et al. Stuttgart: Hiersmann, 1950– .
RGG	*Die Religion in Geschichte und Gegenwart,* 3rd ed., ed. K. Galling. Tübingen: Mohr Siebeck, 1957–65. 4th ed., ed. H. D. Betz et al., 1998–2005.
Rice/Stambaugh	*Sources for the Study of Greek Religion,* ed. D. G. Rice and J. E. Stambaugh. SBLSBS 14. Missoula, MT: Scholars Press, 1979.
Rienecker	F. Rienecker, *A Linguistic Key to the Greek New Testament,* tr. ed. C. L. Rogers, Jr. 2 vols. Zondervan: Grand Rapids, 1976. Ger. 1938.
Smith, *Dictionary*	*A Dictionary of Greek and Roman Antiquities,* ed. W. Smith. London: John Murray, 1878.
Spicq or *TLNT*	C. Spicq, *Theological Lexicon of the New Testament,* tr. J. D. Ernst. 3 vols. Peabody, MA: Hendrickson, 1994. French, *Notes de lexiographie néo-testamentaire,* OBO 22/1–3 (Fribourg: Editions Universitaires/Göttingen: Vandenhoeck & Ruprecht, 1978–82).
Str.-B	(H. Strack and) P. Billerbeck, *Kommentar zum Neuen Testament aus Talmud und Midrasch.* 6 vols. Munich: Beck, 1926–63.
SVF	*Stoicorum Veterum Fragmenta,* ed. H. von Arnim. 4 vols. Leipzig: Teubner, 1903–24. Repr. Stuttgart: Teubner, 1968.
TCGNT	*A Textual Commentary on the Greek New Testament,* by B. M. Metzger. London/New York: United Bible Societies, 1971.
TDNT	*Theological Dictionary of the New Testament,* ed. G. Kittel/G. Friedrich. Grand Rapids: Eerdmans, 1964–76. Tr. of *ThWNT* (Stuttgart: Kohlhammer, 1932–79).

TDOT	*Theological Dictionary of the Old Testament*, ed. G. J. Botterweck/ H. Ringgren. Grand Rapids: Eerdmans, 1974– . Tr. of *ThWAT* (Stuttgart: Kohlhammer, 1970–2006).
THAT	*Theologisches Handwörterbuch zum Alten Testament*, ed. E. Jenni/ C. Westermann. 2 vols. Munich: Kaiser/Zürich: Theologischer Verlag, 1971–76. Tr. *Theological Lexicon of the Old Testament* (Peabody, MA: Hendrickson, 1997).
TLG	Thesaurus Linguae Graece CD ROM, volume E. University of California, Irvine.
TLNT	*Theological Lexicon of the New Testament*. See Spicq, above.
TPTA	*The Theology of Paul the Apostle*, by J. D. G. Dunn. Grand Rapids: Eerdmans, 1998.
TRE	*Theologische Realenzyklopädie*, ed. G. Krause et al. (Berlin: de Gruyter, 1977–).
TWNT	*Theologisches Wörterbuch zum Neuen Testament*, see TDNT, above.
WDNTECLR	*The Westminster Dictionary of New Testament and Early Christian Literature and Rhetoric*, ed. D. E. Aune. Louisville: Westminster John Knox, 2003.
ZAPNTG	M. Zerwick, *Analysis Philologica Novi Testamenti Graeci*, SPIB 107. Rome: Pontifical Biblical Institute, 1953.
ZBG	M. Zerwick, *Biblical Greek*, SPIB 114, tr. J. Smith. Rome: Biblical Institute, 1963.
ZG	M. Zerwick/M. Grosvenor, *A Grammatical Analysis of the Greek New Testament*. Rome: Pontifico Instituto Biblico, 1996

BIBLE TRANSLATIONS

Brackets, as in [N]RSV, = RSV *and* NRSV; [N]JB = JB *and* NJB.

Barclay	William Barclay, New Testament, 1969
CEV	Contemporary English Version, NT 1991, *Bible for Today's Family* 1995
Confraternity Version	Roman Catholic revision of Rheims-Douai version, 1952
ERV	English Revised Version (of KJV), 1881, 1885
EÜ	*Die Bibel, Einheitsübersetzung* (Freiburg: Herder, 1980)
GNB	Good News Bible, 1976–79, 1992 (American eds.)
Gdsp.	E. J. Goodspeed, *The Complete Bible: An American Translation*, 1927, 1931
JB	Jerusalem Bible, 1966 (La Sainte Bible 1956; one vol. ed., Le Bible de Jérusalem, 1961); see Bibliography: Commentaries, s.v. "Benoit, P."
Jeh. Wit.	*New World Translation of the Christian Greek Scriptures* (Brooklyn: Watchtower Bible and Tract Society, 1950)
KJV	King James Version, 1611; 1873 printing in *The New Testament Octapla*, ed. L. A. Weigle (New York: Nelson, 1962), as are other older Eng. trs.
Knox, R.	Ronald Knox, NT, 1947, OT 1958
LB/NLT	Living Bible 1967–76, New Living Translation 1996
Moffatt	James Moffatt, *The New Testament: A New Translation*, 1913, 1924
NAB	New American Bible, 1970; NAB[RNT] = 1970 and 1986 revision
NABRNT	New American Bible Revised New Testament, 1986

NEB	New English Bible, 1961–70
NIV	New International Version, 1973–78
NJB	New Jerusalem Bible (Le Bible de Jérusalem, 1975), 1985 © 1985 by Darton, Longman & Todd, Ltd., and Doubleday, a division of Random House, Inc. Reprinted by permission
NKJV	New King James Version, 1982
NRSV	New Revised Standard Version © 1989 by the National Council of the Churches of Christ in the USA, used by permission
Phillips	J. B. Phillips, *The New Testament in Modern English*, 1952–58
REB	Revised English Bible, 1989
Rheims	Rheims NT, 1582 (in Weigle, *Octapla*, see KJV above)
RSV	Revised Standard Version (1946–52, 1960, 1971 year cited where editions differ) © by the National Council of the Churches of Christ in the USA, used by permission
RV	Revised Version (of KJV), ERV and/or American Standard RV (1901)
Schoder	R. V. Schoder, S. J., *Paul Wrote from the Heart, Philippians, Galatians in Straightforward English* (Oak Park, IL: Bolchazy-Carducci, 1987)
TEV	Today's English Version 1966 (later "Good News Bible")
Tyndale	William Tyndale, NT 1525, 1535 (in Weigle, *Octapla*, see KJV above)
Weymouth	R. F. Weymouth, *The New Testament in Modern Speech*, 1903

GRAMMATICAL AND OTHER TERMS

abs.	absolute	def.	definite
abstr.	abstract	dem.	demonstrative
acc.	accusative	diss.	dissertation
act.	active	ed.	edited (by), editor(s)
adj.	adjective, adjectival	Eng.	English
adv.	adverb, adverbial	esp.	especially
aor.	aorist	ET	English translation
Aram.	Aramaic	et al.	*et alii*, and others
art.	article	fem.	feminine
art. infin.	articular infinitive	f(f).	and the following one(s)
attrib.	attributive	fig.	figurative(ly)
b.	born	fl.	floruit, flourished
bibl.	bibliography	frg.	fragment
bis	twice	FS	Festschrift
ca.	circa, about	fut.	future
cent.	century	gen.	genitive, genitival
cf.	*confer*, compare	Ger.	German
ch(s).	chapter(s)	Gk.	Greek
circumst.	circumstantial	GS	Gesammelte Schriften, collected essays
cj.	conjecture (on uncertain reading)	Heb.	Hebrew
cl.	clause	ibid.	*ibidem*, in the same place
col(s).	column(s)	imperf.	imperfect
conj.	conjunction	impers.	impersonal
Copt.	Coptic	impv(s).	imperative(s)
d.	died	indef.	indefinite
dat.	dative	indic.	indicative

indir.	indirect	pl.	plural (or plate)
infin(s).	infinitive(s)	pred.	predicate
interrog.	interrogative	prep.	preposition(al)
intrans.	intransitive	pres.	present
Lat.	Latin.	pron.	pronoun
lit.	literal(ly)	Ps.	Pseudo-
loc. cit.	*loco citato*, in the place cited	ptc.	participle, participial
LXX	Septuagint (Gk. OT tr.)	re	regarding, with reference to
m(-p)	middle (-passive) voice	rel.	relative
m.	Mishna (tractate named)	repr.	reprinted
masc.	masculine	rev.	revised (by)
mg	in margin (note) of tr.	sg.	singular
MS(S)	manuscript(s)	subj.	subjective (gen.)
MT	Masoretic Text	subjunct.	subjunctive
n(n)	note(s)	subst.	substantive
N.B.	*nota bene*, note carefully	suppl.	supplement(ary)
n.d.	no date	s.v.	*sub voce*, under the word
neg.	negative	Syr.	Syriac
neut.	neuter	T.	*Testament (of)*
no(s)	number(s)	tech.	technical (term)
nom.	nominative	Tg.	Targum
n.p.	no place, publisher, or page	TR	Textus Receptus, received text
NS	new series (any language)	tr.	translator, translated by
NT	New Testament	trans.	transitive
obj.	object	txt	in the text of the translation
opt.	optative	v(v)	verse(s)
OT	Old Testament	vb.	verb
p(p).	page(s)	Vg	Vulgata, Vulgate
pap.	papyrus	v.l.	*varia lectio*, variant reading
par(r).	parallel(s)	voc.	vocative
pass.	passive	vol(s).	volume(s)
passim	there and there	vs.	versus
per.	person	x	no. of times a form occurs
pf.	perfect		

INTRODUCTION

◆

Traditionally, the Introduction to a commentary discusses in depth topics such as are listed in the outline that follows. In reality, users, checking a passage or theme, may go directly to it, without working through the Introduction. Accordingly, the findings of this Introduction, presupposed throughout the volume, are summarized here.

Paul writes to Christian house churches at Philippi **from Ephesus in 54–55.*** The canonical four-ch. Phil contains **parts of three letters** from Paul:

- **Letter A.** 4:10–20 expresses thanks for the Philippians' concern for him and joy at their relationship; he describes some of his situation (no indication he is imprisoned). A.D. 54.
- **Letter B.** 1:1–3:1, likely parts of 4:1–9, 4:21–23, late 54 or early 55, while Paul is imprisoned in Ephesus. Joy and appreciation at their sharing in the gospel, including the ministry of a Philippian, Epaphroditus. Paul tells of his dire situation and the more positive prospects for the gospel's progress, urging unity in the face of opposition.
- **Letter C.** 3:2–21, perhaps parts of 4:1–9, A.D. 55; no evidence that Paul is still jailed. A polemical letter to warn against enemies, with concern over doctrine, ethics, and unity.

Letters B, C, and A were **combined A.D. 90–100,** probably in Philippi, to preserve Paul's words to his favorite congregation for Christians elsewhere.

There are many purposes to Phil because it combines letters for different situations. The commentary must treat each section in its original setting *and* further meanings in the redacted epistle. While I prefer thorough presentation of options on questions an Introduction should take up, limitation here on pages makes that impossible. Arguments are therefore condensed in each section, with some Bibliography.

I. PHILIPPI AND ENVIRONS

The approach in this commentary will not be understood unless it is grasped that Philippi was almost unique among cities Paul addressed in his letters: it differed from other places he evangelized because of its "Roman-ness" and lack of a Jewish community. It was twice founded as a Roman *colonia* (Acts 16:12), first by Gaius Octavian (later Augustus Caesar) and Mark Antony after a double battle there in 42 B.C. when they defeated Cassius and Brutus and ended the Roman Republic; and then, after the defeat of Anthony and Cleopatra in 31 B.C., as *Colonia Iulia Augusta Philippensis.* This "little Rome" had legal status as if in Italy, with some 10,000 inhabitants, many of them citizens, in a walled city of 167 acres plus over 700 square miles around it. Philippi reflected Thracian underpinnings, Hellenistic culture, but dominant *Romanitas.* Its religions included classic Greco-Roman gods and goddesses, Thracian deities, and Oriental cults (Isis). The dominant new

---

* Boldface type indicates key points.

factor was Imperial religion and the Emperor cult, the faith of some fifty million people, more or less, with rituals and celebrations that touched most of life. Acts 16 and archeology report no synagogue (at best, a "place of prayer" for a few women like Lydia, a convert). On women in these cults, see Marchal 73–90. Phil may echo but never overtly quotes (OT) Scripture ([4] COMMENT A.1). Jews were negligible or nonexistent (Bockmuehl 9) in Roman Philippi. See further *Philippian Studies.*

SELECT BIBLIOGRAPHY ON PHILIPPI (see also General Bibliography and Commentaries)

Barr-Sharrar, B., and E. N. Borza, eds. 1982. *Macedonia and Greece in Late Classical and Early Hellenistic Times.* Studies in the History of Art 10, Symposium Series I. Washington, DC: National Gallery of Art.

Brunt, P. A., and J. M. Moore, eds. 1967. *RES GESTAE DIVI AUGUSTI: The Achievements of the Divine Augustus.* London: Oxford Univ. Press.

Cassidy, R. J. 2001b. *Christians and Roman Rule in the New Testament. New Perspectives.* Companions to the New Testament. New York: Crossroad.

Collart, P. 1937. *Philippes, ville de Macédoine, depuis ses origines jusqu'à la fin de l'époque Romain.* École française d'Athènes: Travaux et Mémoires 5. 2 vols. Paris: Boccard.

Elliger, W. 1978. *Paulus in Griechenland. Philippi, Thessaloniki, Athen, Korinth.* SBS 92/93. Stuttgart: KBW; repr. 1987 (cf. *TLZ* 113 [1988] cols. 441–42; Pilhofer 1:36 n 112).

Ferguson, E. 1993. *Backgrounds of Early Christianity.* Grand Rapids: Eerdmans, 2nd ed.

Harrison, J. R. 2002. "Paul and the Imperial Gospel at Thessaloniki," *JSNT* 25/1:71–96.

Helgeland, J. 1978. "Roman Army Religion," ANRW 2/16:2:1470–1505.

Jewett, R. 1986. *The Thessalonian Correspondence: Pauline Rhetoric and Millennial Piety.* Philadelphia: Fortress.

Koukouli-Chrysantaki, C. "Colonia Iulia Augusta Philippensis," in Bakirtzis/Koester 5–35.

Krentz, E. 2001. "De Caesare et Christo," *CurTM* 28:341–45.

MacMullen, R. 2000. *Romanization in the Time of Augustus.* New Haven: Yale.

Price, S. R. F. 1984a. *Rituals and Power: The Roman Imperial Cult in Asia Minor.* Cambridge: Cambridge Univ. Press, repr. 1996.

Raaflaub/Toher = *Between Republic and Empire: Interpretations of Augustus and His Principate,* ed. K. A. Raaflaub and M. Toher. Berkeley: Univ. of California, 1990.

RoR = *Religions of Rome, Vol. 1: A History; Vol. 2, A Sourcebook,* ed. M. Beard, J. North, and S. Price. Cambridge: Cambridge Univ. Press, 1998.

Sakellariou, M. B., ed. 1983. *Macedonia: 4000 Years of Greek History and Civilization.* Greek Lands in History. Athens: Ekdotike Athenon (Gk. ed. 1982).

Schowalter, D. N. 1993. *The Emperor and the Gods: Images from the Time of Trajan.* HDR 28. Minneapolis: Fortress.

Turcan, R. 1996. *The Cults of the Roman Empire.* Tr. A. Neill. Oxford: Blackwell.

Vittinghoff, F. 1952. *Römische Kolonisation und Bürgerrechtspolitik unter Caesar und Augustus.* Mainz, Akademie der Wissenschaft und der Literatur, Abhandlungen der Geistes- und Socialwissenschaftlichen Klasse Jahrgang 1951, Nr. 14. Wiesbaden: F. Steiner Verlag.

Zanker, P. 1990. *The Power of Images in the Age of Augustus.* Ann Arbor: Univ. of Michigan Press.

II. PAUL AND PHILIPPI IN ACTS: THE FOUNDING MISSION AND SUBSEQUENT VISITS (ACTS 16:11–40; 20:1–6)

Philippians has long been treated in light of the Apostle's visits to the city as reported in Acts. Luke may have good source materials for chs. 16 and 20, perhaps even "information concerning Philippi . . . from an eyewitness of the Pauline mission" (Haenchen, *Acts* 503, cf. 86–87; Lüdemann 1989b:181–84, 222–25), behind his eight units:[1] (1) Travel Itinerary, from Troas to Philippi (Acts 16:11–12a); (2) The First Converts, Lydia, with her household (16:12b–15). A "house church" results when Lydia "was baptized and her household" (*oikos*, children, slaves, extended family), the first of several in Philippi.[2] (3) Exorcism of a Python-spirited slave girl (16:16–18); (4) The Sequel to the Exorcism: Paul and Silas beaten and jailed by the Philippian authorities (16:19–24); (5) The Further Sequel: an earthquake frees the prisoners, the jailer and his household are converted (16:25–34); (6) The Next Day: Paul and Silas get public apologies, but are asked to leave Philippi (16:35–40). Paul invokes his Roman citizenship in 16:37; that he possessed citzenship has sometimes been denied, but it is likely historical.[3] (7) A Second Possible Visit by Paul to Philippi (20:1–2); (8) Paul's Final Visit to Philippi (20:3–6).

SELECT BIBLIOGRAPHY ON ACTS, including Commentaries (cited by author's name; plus, if necessary, *Acts* or (Ger.) *Apg.*; year or series added, if necessary)

BC = *The Beginnings of Christianity. Part I. The Acts of the Apostles*, ed. F. J. Foakes-Jackson/ K. Lake, 5 vols. London: Macmillan, 1920–33; repr., Grand Rapids: Baker, 1979.

Conzelmann, H. 1987. *Acts of the Apostles: A Commentary* (Ger. 1963, 2nd ed.1972). Hermeneia. Philadelphia: Fortress.

Fitzmyer, J. A. 1998. *The Acts of the Apostles: A New Translation* with Introduction and Commentary. AB 31. New York: Doubleday.

Haenchen, E. 1971. *The Acts of the Apostles: A Commentary* (Ger. 1965). Philadelphia: Westminster/Oxford: Blackwell.

---

[1] For this commentary a full treatment of the Acts vv was prepared because J. Munck (AB 31, 1967) was so brief. The Fitzmyer AB vol. on Acts (1998) is more detailed, but more can be said than its limited space permitted. It is hoped that my treatment, with excursuses, will appear elsewhere.

[2] For "the church [or assembly] in the house of so-and-so" (*hē kat' oikon* + gen. *ekklēsia*), cf. 1 Cor 16:19; Rom 16:5 (AB 33:736); Phlm 2 (AB 34C:89–90); Banks 1980/1994; Klauck 1981; Matson 136–68; *EDNT* 2:501–2. Was Lydia patron, leader (in hospitality, worship?), and even *episkopos* (Phil 1:1) of such a group? *RoR* 2:10–13 (INTRO. I Bibl.) sketches examples of house churches. A second house church emerged for Philippi at 16:32–24, the jailer and his *oikos*. R. W. Gehring, *House Church and Mission: The Importance of Household Structures in Early Christianity* (Peabody, MA: Hendrickson, 2004). Cf. (1) COMMENT B.5, Bibl. **overseer.**

[3] Tarsian citizenship (Acts 21:39) could also be involved (BC 4:201;5:309–12). Jews could hold Roman citizenship and often did (S. Appelbaum, "The Legal Status of Jewish Communities in the Diaspora," in CRINT 1:420–63). Saul may have had it by birth (22:28; F. F. Bruce, *New Testament History* [London: Nelson, 1969; Garden City, NY: Doubleday, 1971] 235). A citizen might carry a small wooden diptych copy of birth registration, cf. F. Schulz, "Roman Registers of Birth and Birth Certificates (i)," *JRS* 33 (1942) 78–91 and (ii) 33 (1943) 55–64; Sherwin-White 1963:148–46; Tajra 28, 81–89. See further, (3) COMMENT B.3.j, n 39; (4) COMMENT A.7; (16) COMMENT B.1.a.

Jervell, J. 1998. *Die Apostelgeschichte.* KEK 3, 17th ed. Göttingen: Vandenhoeck & Ruprecht.

Levinskaya, I. 1996. *The Book of Acts in Its Diaspora Setting.* BAFCS 5. Grand Rapids: Eerdmans/Carlisle: Paternoster.

Matson, D. L. 1996. *Household Conversion Narratives in Acts: Pattern and Interpretation.* JSNTSup 123. Sheffield: Sheffield Academic Press.

Matthews, S. 2001. *First Converts. Rich Pagan Women and the Rhetoric of Mission in Early Judaism and Christianity.* Contraversions: Jews and Other Differences. Stanford, CA: Stanford Univ. Press. Pp. 51–100.

Munck, J. 1967. *The Acts of the Apostles.* AB 31. Rev. W. F. Albright & C. S. Mann. Garden City, NY: Doubleday.

Tajra, H. W. 1989. *The Trial of St. Paul: A Juridical Exegesis of the Second Half of the Acts of the Apostles.* WUNT 2/35. Tübingen: Mohr Siebeck.

Weiser, A. 1981. *Die Apostelgeschichte.* ÖTK 5/1–2. Gütersloh: Mohn/Würzburg: Echter-Verlag, 2nd ed. 1985.

III. THE LETTER(S) "TO THE PHILIPPIANS" (*PROS PHILIPPĒSIOUS*)

A. *Outline.* In light of content (logical or thematic development; Lft.), epistolary approaches (J. L. White, Doty), and rhetoric (Garland 1985), the following outline fits the four chs. as a whole:

1:1–2   Opening salutation or address (sender, addressees, greeting).

1:3–11   Thanksgiving and prayer (report on how Paul prays) for the community.

1:12–26   Paul's situation in imprisonment: prospects for the gospel and for himself.

1:27–2:18   Exhortation to the Philippian community in its situation: unity, fearlessness, harmony, traditionally "humility" has been emphasized, love for others, and witness in the world.
            2:6–11   the "Christ hymn" or "story of salvation," among other gospel incentives (2:1,5).

2:19–30   News and plans about Timothy, Paul, and Epaphroditus.

3:1   Rejoice!

3:2–21   Warnings against "dogs" and "enemies of Christ's cross," with references to the righteousness of God, Christ's death and resurrection, Paul as pattern, future eschatology.

4:1   Stand firm!

4:2–9   Admonitions to individuals (vv 2–3) and the community at Philippi (vv 4–7, 8–9).

4:10–20   Thanks, sort of, for gifts from Philippi to Paul.

4:21–23   Conclusion: greetings (vv 21–22), benediction (v 23).

B. *Purposes,* in part noted above (p. 3), are detailed in (1) COMMENT B.2. The eight purposes suggest several letters; the several problems addressed point to how the document(s) arose.

C. *Communications Between Paul and Philippi.* The number of trips between Macedonia and the city of Paul's imprisonment is a factor in reconstructing the situation behind Phil, for determining its place of composition (VII.A, below), and hence an overall chronology (VIII). The chart below sketches likely contacts between Paul and the Philippians.

CHART 1: Communications between Paul and Philippi, including his three letters.

A.D. 54   **EPHESUS**   **PHILIPPI**

Word about Paul's situation in Ephesus
reaches the Philippians —————————————————————————→

←————————————————————— Aid (financial) is sent via Epaphroditus

Paul writes a note of thanks (Letter A, 4:10–20) —————————————→

News that Epaphroditus has been taken ill
reaches Philippi ————————————————————————————→

(The news about Paul may or may not have included his imprisonment, since it is unclear in 4:10–20 whether he is in jail as yet; by the time of Letter B, Paul is under guard, 1:12–14)

←————————————————————— Paul hears that the Philippians are
disturbed at Epaphroditus' illness (2:26,
Epaphroditus is distressed too)

Epaphroditus returns home (2:25–30)
with Letter B (1:1–3:1) ——————————————————————→

←————————————————————— Paul, released from prison, is able to send
Timothy to Philippi (2:19,23)

A.D. 55

Paul hears about "the enemies," possibly soon to threaten Philippi
←—— (news from Galatia, or events in the Ephesus area, or tidings from Philippi?) ——→

Paul sends Letter C (3:2–21) from
somewhere near Ephesus ———————————————————————→

Paul expects the following contacts *in the future:* (1) Timothy will go to Philippi (2:19a) as soon as Paul sees how his own situation will turn out (2:23). (2) He looks for Timothy to come back and report firsthand on matters in Philippi, thus cheering Paul with news about the Philippians (2:19b). (3) Paul expects "deliverance" (1:19); then he will come to Philippi again, indeed "shortly" (1:16; 2:24), details that fit Ephesus better than Caesarea or Rome.

IV. TEXT, GLOSSES, AND INTERPOLATION THEORIES

A. *Text.* Our tr. and commentary are based on the 27th ed. of Nestle-Aland et al., *Novum Testamentum graece* (Stuttgart: Deutsche Bibelgesellschaft, 1993; hereafter NA[27]), with occasional references to its earlier editions, the UBSGNT, and

WH = B. F. Westcott/F. J. A. Hort, *The New Testament in the Original Greek* (Cambridge/London 1881). The judgment of Vincent (xxxvii) in 1897, "The epistle presents no textual questions of importance," found assent by Bockmuehl 40 a century later. Textual matters are regularly taken up in the NOTES, often, because of constraints of space, by referring to NA[27], though one would like to spell out for the general reader MS names, dates, etc. The critical principle of preferring the shorter reading is reconsidered in (13) NOTE on 3:12b, *or . . . justified.*

B. *Glosses and Interpolations.* Most such (19th-cent.) notions of later additions (cf. Moffatt, *Intro.* 172) have long since been forgotten. Recent commentators agree there are no interpolated passages in Phil. But note W. Schmithals; J. C. O'Neill 1988 (Section 7 Bibl.); NOTES on 1:1 *episkopoi kai diakonois;* 1:17 *ouch hagnōs;* (3) COMMENT B.2 n 22.

SELECT BIBLIOGRAPHY ON TEXT, GLOSSES, AND INTERPOLATIONS

Aland, K. 1963. *Kurzgefasste Liste der griechischen Handschriften des Neuen Testaments,* vol. 1: *Gesamtübersicht.* ANTF 1. Berlin/New York: de Gruyter.
Clemen, C. 1894. *Die Einheitlichkeit der paulinischen Briefe an der Hand der bisher mit Bezug auf sie aufgestellten Interpolations- und Kompilationshypothesen.* Göttingen: Vandenhoeck & Ruprecht.
Silva, M. 1982. "The Text of Philippians: Its Early History in the Light of UBSGNT[3]." AAR/SBL Abstracts 1982, p. 158, SBL no. 59, reflected in Silva's *Phil.* 1988:25 n 28.
Walker, W. O., Jr. 2001. *Interpolations in the Pauline Letters.* JSNTSup 213. London/New York: Sheffield Academic Press.

V. AUTHORSHIP

Phil says it is by Paul and Timothy (1:1). On co-senders, see (1) COMMENT B.4.c. Polycarp's Letter to the Philippians (A.D. 115–135) expressly states Paul wrote to Philippi and contains echoes of his letter(s). Though 19th-cent. criticism (Tübingen School) sometimes denied Paul wrote Phil (Moffatt, *Intro.* 165, 170–72; 165), today, "authenticity of Philippians is not seriously challenged" (L. T. Johnson 1999:369), even from computer research in the 1960s.

VI. PARTITION THEORIES AND THE UNITY (INTEGRITY) OF THE DOCUMENT

"Unity" implies Paul composed all four chs. of Phil as one letter and sent it on a single occasion. Some speak of "integrity," a somewhat loaded term, as if composite letters lack integrity.

A. *External Evidence in Antiquity.* Polycarp, Phil 3.2, recorded that Paul, "when he was absent, wrote to you letters" (*epistolas;* "them," pl.; cf. 11.3, *epistulae*);

some seek to explain away the pl. (Hartog 224–25; Berding 62–63). It has been argued that the "Epistle to the Laodiceans" (*ABD* 4:231–33; HSNT*Apoc* 2:128–32) used a version of Phil that lacked 3:2–4:3 and 4:10–20 (Sellew; contrast Holloway 1998). There is thus some ancient outside support for partitioning (Bockmuehl 22, "corroborating evidence"). The view rests mainly on what is in Phil.

SELECT BIBLIOGRAPHY ON POLYCARP AND LAODICEANS

Berding, K. 2002. *Polycarp and Paul: An Analysis of their Literary and Theological Relationship in Light of Polycarp's Use of Biblical and Extra-Biblical Literature*. VCSup 62. Leiden: Brill.

Hartog, P. 2001. *Polycarp and the New Testament. The Occasion, Rhetoric, Theme, and Unity of the Epistle to the Philippians and its Allusions to New Testament Literature*. WUNT 2/134. Tübingen: Mohr Siebeck.

Holloway, P. A. 1998. "The Apocryphal *Epistle to the Laodiceans* and the Partitioning of Philippians," *HTR* 91:321–25.

Sellew, P. 1994. "*Laodiceans* and the Philippians Fragments Hypothesis," *HTR* 87:17–28; cf. 91 (1998) 327–29.

B. *Internal Evidence in Philippians.* The case for one or more letters in Phil is cumulative.

1. 3:1–2 represents an abrupt shift in mood and content, followed by polemical invective in 3:2–21. Ch. 3 was starting point for theories of a letter within canonical Phil. Cf. below, (10), (11).

2. 4:10–20, where Paul seems finally to thank the Philippians for their support but never quite says "thank you," is buried late in the four-ch. letter. It could be the body of a note written to the Philippians promptly upon receipt of their gift. Cf. (16) COMMENT A.1.

Partition theories go back to 19th -cent. German scholarship (not to Le Moyne in 1685; so D. Cook). In 1914 Symes argued for *five* letters by Paul to Philippi! In general, a case for *two* letters was common by 1940 (3:1–2 as dividing line; e.g., Gnilka). After 1945 *three* letters became more common (e.g., Rahtjen, Schmithals, Beare). Space does not permit listing arguments here or supporters for each view or for the unity of Phil. By 1978 a considerable consensus could be claimed, at least in German scholarship, for partitioning.[1] But some, esp. in the Anglo-Saxon world, never were convinced and defended the unity of Phil. In particular there has been appeal to *rhetorical* analysis[2] to support a four-ch. letter. Rhetorical anal-

---

[1] Schenke-Fischer 1:125, 132 n 2.

[2] **Rhetorical approaches:** On application of classical rhetoric to the NT, see G. A. Kennedy 1984; B. Mack, *Rhetoric and the New Testament* (Minneapolis: Fortress, 1990); F. W. Hughes 13–50; on the "New Rhetoric," Marchal 3–11. Terms in Lausberg; *WDNTECLR* 357–59. Swift combined some rhetorical aspects with epistolary terms. Garland 1985 regarded 1:27–4:3 as a literary unity, with the appeal to Euodia and Syntyche in 4:3 "climactic" (173); 3:1–21 a digression, but deliberate rhetorically, "to affect his audience prior to the direct, emotional appeal in 4:2." Robuck ([7] Bibl.) 156–74, *salutatio* (1:1–2), *captatio benevolentiae* (1:3–11), *narratio* (1:12–3:21), *petitio* (4:1–20), and *conclusio* (4:21–23), with 2:5–11 as *exemplum* (194). Watson 1988b, deliberative rhetoric (not epideictic, as

ysis can also be enlisted in support of more than one letter to Philippi (Pesch). The rheotorical approach is important enough to summarize examples in n 2, to which reference will be made throughout the commentary. Much the same is true of appeal to *chiastic* or concentric structure as a key (Wick),[3] and to the principle of

---

Kennedy 1984:77 held, but cf. Watson 60, Phil 2:19–30 is epideictic): *exordium* (1:3–26); *narratio* (1:27–30); *probatio* (2:1–3:21), with three developments of the proposition, in 2:1–11, 2:12–18, and 3:1–21 (2:19–30 is *digressio*); *peroratio*, 4:1–20. So Geoffrion 21, 160–61; Fields (see below [12] COM- MENT A.1); Sisson 246–48. Critique of Watson in Reed 1993 (JSNTSup 90) 314–23. Watson 1997 in- tegrated epistolary and rhetorical structure, followed by D. K. Williams 2002:89–90. Schoon-Janßen 141, the rhetorical outline Watson employed for all four chs. was used by Schenk as rhetorical struc- ture for his Letter C (*exordium*, 3:2–4; *narratio*, 3:5–7; *propositio*, 3:8–11; *argumentatio*, 3:12–14; and *refutatio*, 3:15–21; cf. Reumann 1991a). Wick 163 concludes that the rhetorical method produced no clarity on the unity question. Bloomquist 119–38, Paul's letter is deliberative but with forensic and epideictic elements (120); 1:3–11 = *exordium*; 1:12–14 *narratio*; 1:15–18a *partitio*; 1:18b–4:7 = *argu- mentatio*, with 1:18b–26 *confirmatio*, 1:27–2:18 *exhortatio* concluding the *confirmatio*, 2:19–30 *exem- pla*; 3:1–16 *reprehensio*; 3:17–4:7 *exhortatio*, concluding the *reprehensio*; and 4:8–20, *peroratio*. 1:1–2:30 presents "all of the component parts of a non-literary papyrus letter" (116), with 3:1–4:7 mir- roring 1:15–2:18 (111) and 4:8–20 providing a third section of epistolary "body"; thus there could be three letter bodies (though Bloomquist opts finally for an integral letter, 117). Black 1995:48, 1:1–2 = epistolary prescript; 1:3–11 *exordium*; 1:12–26, *narratio*; 1:27–3:21, *argumentatio*, involving a *proposi- tio* in 1:27–30, *probatio* in 2:1–30, and *refutatio* in 3:1–21; the *peroratio* consists only of 4:1–9, for 4:10–20 is again *narratio*; 4:21–23, epistolary postscript. Primarily deliberative rhetoric (16; but cf. 46 on "judicial" rhetoric; "friendship" is minimized for any macrostructure, n 46); epistolary categories (22–44) like "body opening"; "Philippians is best understood as a hybrid letter in which the epistolary body contains a deliberative heart," 49. J. Walker, *Rhetoric and Poetics in Antiquity* (New York: Oxford, 2000), epideictic discourse had more importance in antiquity than is often assumed, compared with civic, "pragmatic" oratory. D. K. Williams 2002:78–105 stresses "rhetorical arguments using theologi- cal language" (82). C. W. Davis 1999 injects "principles of orality" into the question of literary struc- ture in Phil (see n 3 below). Brucker ([7] Bibl.): 1:3–11 *exordium*, 1:12–26 *narratio*, 1:27–30 *propositio*, 2:1–3:21 *probatio*, 4:1–20 *peroratio*. Edart 290–300, 1:3–11 *exordium*, 1:12–26 *narratio*, 1:27–30 *prop- ositio*, 2:1–18 first *probatio* (12–19 = *peroratio*), 2:19–30 + 3:1a + ch. 4 *digressio* (4:1–9 = *recapitulatio*, 4:10–23 *peroratio*, with two *propositiones*); all this is Text A; 3:2–16 is a separate letter; see n 7 below. For Bittasi, see n 3. R. D. Anderson, *Ancient Rhetorical Theory and Paul*, CBET 18 (Kampen: Kok Pharos, 1996; rev., Leuven: Peeters, 2000) and others conclude that Paul knew little about, and did not conform to, ancient rhetorical theories. Bockmuehl 39, this "frenzy of scholarly activity" is a dangerous "pan-rhetoricism."

[3] **Chiastic structures:** Rolland 1990 found a relatively simple structure: 1:1–11 goes with 4:10–23, 1:12–2:18 has parallels with 3:1–4:20; 2:19–30 is "interlude." P. Aspen, 1992 diss. (cf. Pretorius 1995: 273–75, 277–84), proposed a chiastic, or better concentric, reading where 2:6–11 is the center of a letter that excludes 3:2–4:1 and 4:10–20. His "main letter" runs: Phil 1:1–2 = Greetings; 4:21–23 = Final salutation

1:3–11	A[1]	Gospel-*koinōnia*, the central concern of the letter
1:12–26	B[1]	Paul's trials
1:27–2:5	C[1]	Exhortation to "one mind, one spirit"
2:6–11	Center	Hymn
2:12–18	C[2]	Exhortation to obedience
2:19–3:1	B[2]	Epaphroditus' trials
4:2–9	A[2]	Summons to *koinōnia* for Euodia and Syntyche, the specific concern of this letter.

P. Wick 1994, without noting Aspen's proposal, laid out blocks of parallel material (depending chiefly on vocabulary links), with the hymn as center, but for all four chs.:

Prescript, 1:1–2   Prooimium, 1:3–11   Postscript, 4:21–23

Einheit A (theme: friends and enemies, in a self-report; salvation; "death," "flesh," 243 and 250 words)

a[1] = 1:12–26   (see box on p. 43; Greek printout 205)   a[2] = 3:1–16 an *inclusio*, two references serving as brackets for a passage or document (e.g., "grace" at 1:2 and 4:23; "peace" 1:2, 4:7, cf. 4:9). Such analyses vary and often contradict each other. L. Alexander sees a Hellenistic "family letter"—1:1–2, 1:3–11, 1:12–26 (reassurance about the sender); 1:27–2:18 (request for reassurance

Einheit B (theme: walk/conduct, opponents; admonition, warning; *politeuesthai, politeuma*, 82/90 words)

    b^1 = 1:27–30   (box on p. 45; Greek, 206) b^2 = 3:17–21

Einheit C (theme: the same mind, joy; *parakalein* words; (be)love(d); 5 items in 2:1 and 4:1; 58/53 words)

    c^1 = 2:1–4 (+ 5–11)   (box on p. 47; Greek, 207) c^2 = 4:1–3

         2:5–11, the hymn relates to all units (Einheiten)

Einheit D (theme: awe and joy at salvation; rejoice 2x, always; series of terms in 4:6, 8; 115/101 words)

    d^1 = 2:12–18   (box on p. 51; Greek, 208) d^2 = 4:4–9

Einheit E (theme: [epistolary] correspondence; joy, need, send, lack, Epaphroditus; 173/169 words)

    e^1 = 2:19–30   (box on p. 53; Greek, 209) e^2 = 4:10–20.

Wicks' proposal has received some support (e.g., Pretorius 1998), but critique in Reed, *DA* 292–93, 361–64, cf. 292–93 and 255 n 372.

Different again is Luter/Lee 1995:92; their center is 2:17–3:1b, not 2:6–11:

1:1–2 *Opening Greetings*, previewing "partnership" theme, emphasizing servant-leadership.

  A. 1:3–11 *Prologue*, "Partnership in the Gospel" theme, introduced with prayerful gratitude.

    B. 1:12–26 *Comfort/Example*: Paul's Safety and Right Thinking in the Midst of a Difficult 'Guarded' Situation.

      C. 1:27–2:4 *Challenge*: Stand Fast and Be United, Fulfilling Paul's Joy!

        D. 2:5–16 *Example/Action*: Christ's Example of Humility and Suffering before Glory, then Related Behavioral Instructions.

          E. 2:17–3:1a *Midpoint*: Caring Models of Gospel Partnership, Two of Which Are Sent to Help Immediately.

        D′. 3:1b–21 *Example/Action*: Paul's Example of Humbling and Suffering before "Upward Call"/Transformation, then Instructions.

      C′. 4:1–5 *Challenge*: Stand Fast and Accentuate Existing Joy by the Reconciliation of Two Past Gospel Partners!

    B′. 4:6–9 *Comfort/Example*: The Philippians' 'Guarded' Peace of Mind and Right Thinking in the Midst of an Anxious Situation.

  A′. 4:10–20 *Epilogue*: Partnership from the Past Renewed, with Expressed Gratitude.

4:21–23 *Closing Greetings*: Reviewing Partnership Theme, Emphasizing Oneness of the Saints. Severe critique by Porter and Reed 1998, and on Wick's use of Qoh 1:3–3:15, 2 Sam 9–20, and 1 Kgs 1–2 to provide evidence for parallelisms in a Pauline letter. *WDNTECLR* 358, either Wick or Luter/Lee or both "manipulated the data." C. W. Davis is similar to Luter/Lee (Phil 2:19–30 as "center," D. F. Watson's "digression") but differs on the number and scope of concentric units:

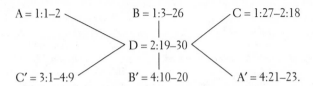

$$A = 1:1{-}2 \qquad B = 1:3{-}26 \qquad C = 1:27{-}2:18$$
$$D = 2:19{-}30$$
$$C' = 3:1{-}4:9 \qquad B' = 4:10{-}20 \qquad A' = 4:21{-}23.$$

Bittasi 210–11, cf. 206: two halves around 2:19–30: 1:1–2 *praescript*, 1:3–11 *exordium*, with 1:9–11 as *propositio* → 1:12–26 → *exhortatio* 1:27–30 → 2:1–18 the example of Christ Jesus; the center of the letter = 2:19–30 Timothy and Epaphroditus; 3:1 hesitation and reception formula → 3:2–16 the example of Paul → 3:17–4:1 exhortation → 4:2–9 particular exhortations → 4:10–20 final thanks → 4:21–23 *postscriptum*. J. W. Welch ([12] Bibl.) 226 concluded Phil "contains no overall chiastic structure"; the small chiastic patterns are "relatively insignificant and unremarkable." For a possible chiastic structure in Letter B, see (5) COMMENT A.1.

about the recipients); 2:19–30; 4:10–20, thanks; 4:21–22 (greetings), 4:23; 3:1–4:9 breaks the pattern to deliver a "sermon at a distance." Holloway 2001:7–34 takes Phil as a unity in his effort to show that the entire document is a "letter of consolation."[4] Similarly, West, in stressing "dying for friends" as part of the *philia topos*.[5] Arguments have also claimed Phil as a "letter of friendship"; e.g., Fee 23, cf. 3–4, is dubious for the letter in its entirety, but elements from this topos work well in Letter A (4:10–20; see [16] COMMENT A.2). Witherington, in spite of his title *Friendship . . . in Philippi*, does *not* go the route of *philia*, but instead invokes a presumed *rhetorical* structure (27–28, cf. 11–20). Epistolary and rhetorical analyses were applied by R. Pesch 1985 in a three-letter hypothesis.[6] Edart prefers a rhetorical over an epistolary model, with 3:2–16 as a separate letter.[7]

Arguments exist, along various lines, for Phil as a unitary letter or a combination of two or three letters. Note esp. Schenk's text-linguistic, as well as traditional and rhetorical, arguments for three letters. We are impressed with a broad trend toward three letters, but this carries the obligation to provide a "double exegesis," the sense in Letter A (or B or C) and in the redacted document we possess. Hence the working hypothesis outlined on p. 3, above, for three letters by Paul to Philippi.

---

[4] Holloway 2001 "seeks to understand" Phil "as an ancient letter of consolation" (p. 1). "Consolation" = not just as "sympathy" but considerable admonition ("tough love"). Philosophical theories in Cic., *Tusc.* 3.31.76. It was common to distinguish "what really matters" from *adiaphora* and to emphasize joy ("you must . . . learn how to rejoice," Seneca, *Ep.* 23.3). Overall, Holloway's attempt at genre does not convince, but instances of consolation in some passages (not always in Holloway) will be examined in context.

[5] Dying for friends was a frequent, though varied, theme in the ancient world (West 32–130; cf. Rom 5:8, 1 Thess 5:10, and 1 Cor 15:3). But the "hymn to Christ" in 2:6–11 (133–54) lacks any *hyper* phrase ("for us"), and so West is reduced to arguing that "[r]eaders in a Greco-Roman city" could have understood the hymn thus, "based on their cultural context" (135–36; 152 n 66). The attempt to find "eschatological proof" in 2:9–11 of "vindication that will be shared at the Day of the Lord by those who suffer for the sake of the gospel" (153) faces the difficulties that these vv lack any parousia reference and speak of all "in heaven, on earth, and under the earth," not suffering Christians.

[6] *Letter A*, prescript and possible *exordium* are missing; the body (4:10–20) is a *narratio*. For *Letter B* see Doty 43, Schenk 68–249, as well as Pesch: prescript (1:1–2), *exordium* (1:3–11), *narratio* (1:12–26, about Paul), with thesis for the congregation (1:27–30), proofs (*probatio*) and paraenesis woven in (2:1–18). Then travel plans (2:19–30), followed by concluding admonitions (3:1, possibly 4:4–7) and doubtless greetings and benediction in a postscript (not extant). *Letter C*: prescript and *exordium* not preserved, the body (3:1b or 2–21) is a warning, with *narratio* about Paul (3:4–14), which provides proofs (*probabtio*, 3:8b–11, eschatologically oriented), admonitions, and *peroratio* (3:20), possibly including 4:1–3 and 8–9. Any greetings and benediction are lost. For *Letter C*, see also Reumann 1991a ([11] Bibl.) 137: 3:2–3 = *exordium*, sharp antithesis between "true circumcision" and "mutilation," with warning against the (negative example) "evil workers" who trust in the flesh. Transition in 3:4 to autobiography ("I"), with 5–6 a *narratio* about Paul's way of life under the Law (negative example) and then 7–11 as positive example, *narratio* becoming *argumentatio*. *propositio* in vv 9–10, on righteousness and faith and knowing Christ (resurrection and sufferings). Paul's personal testimony continues through 12–14, as *argumentatio*. Vv 15–21 are direct *refutatio* of those warned against in v 2. Vv 20–21 cite as climax and future promise a "song of confidence in Christ's power." 4:1–3 and 8–9 can then be taken as *peroratio*.

[7] Edart 15–41 and 210–75; see above, n 2. Letter B stresses justification, which is not referred to in 1:1–3:1a or 3:17–4:23. 3:11, 12b (perfection) 13b, 14 (the prize) are redactoral (261), from the perspective of a Stoic sage (266–71), with Luke the probable redactor (273–75). Eckey concludes for three letters.

The proof of any theory is how it works out in practice and enables readers to see things in the text. Letters to Philippi from different settings contrasts with the tradition that all the "imprisonment epistles" (Phil, Col, Phlm, Eph) are of a piece, from one place.

SELECT BIBLIOGRAPHY ON UNITY (INTEGRITY) AND PARTITIONING OF PHILIPPIANS (see also General Bibliography)

Bell, G. 1914. "The Epistle to the Philippians: A Reply [to K. Lake]," *Exp*, 8th Series, Vol. 8: 143–54.

Benoit, P. *La Sainte Bible. Les épîtres de Saint Paul aux Philippiens, à Philemon, aux Colossiens, aux Éphésiens*. 2nd rev. ed. Paris: Les Éditions du Cerf, 1953, p. 19, cf. 31; 1956 one-vol. ed, p. 1487. The Eng. tr. does not reflect this view. See *JB*, ed. A. Jones (1966) (NT) 260–61, 341 note on 3:1, where 3:1ff. is taken as a "postscript." On the relationship of *JB* to the French *Bible de Jérusalem* (originally *La Sainte Bible . . .*), and *JB*'s general conservatism, cf. B. Vawter in *The Duke Divinity School Review* 44 (1979) 94–96.

Cook, D. 1981. "Stephanus Le Moyne and the Dissection of Philippians," *JTS* 32:138–42.

Jones, M. 1914. "The Integrity of the Epistle to the Philippians," *Exp*, 8th Series, Vol. 8:457–73.

Koperski, V. 1992. "Text Liguistics and the Integrity of Philippians: A Critique of Wolfgang Schenk's Argument for a Compilation Hypothesis," *ETL* 68:331–67.

———. 1993. "The Early History of the Dissection of Philippians," *JTS* 44:599–603.

Lake, K. 1914. "The Critical Problems of the Epistle to the Philippians," *Exp*, 8th Series, Vol. 7: 481–93.

Michael, J. H. 1920. "The Philippian Interpolation—Where Does It End?" *Exp*, 8th Series, Vol. 19:49–63.

———. 1922–23. "The First and Second Epistles to the Philippians," *ExpTim* 34:106–9.

Müller-Bardorff, J. 1957–58. "Zur Frage der literarischen Einheit des Philipperbriefes," *Wissenschaftliche Zeitschrift der Friedrich-Schiller Universität Jena* 7, Gesellschafts- und sprachwissenschaftliche Reihe 4, 591–604.

Symes, J. E. 1914. "Five Epistles to the Philippians," *The Interpreter* 10.2:167–70.

VII. THEORIES ON PLACE AND DATE OF WRITING FOR THE (THREE) LETTERS AND THEIR REDACTION

A. *Places and Dates for the Letter(s) by Paul to Philippi.* The traditional answer was *Rome* (Acts 28 or at a later imprisonment there). As the 19th cent. dawned, *Caesarea* in Palestine was proposed (Acts 23:33–27:2); late in the 19th cent., *Ephesus*, where Paul ministered for two years or more (Acts 19:1–22). *Corinth* has been suggested, esp. since 1973. Generally those who favor Rome also champion the unity of Phil (Beare is an exception: Rome, but three letters). R. P. Martin 1976:56 declared "an impasse" on place.

Patristic views are mixed (cf. Curran 200, *"there was really no ancient tradition on the subject"*) but eventually came down for Rome, a position that continued into the 19th cent. and beyond (e.g., Schinz 1833; H. G. A. Ewald 1857; K. Barth 1927). *Caesarea Maritima* was esp. championed by Lohmyer (1930 KEK; 1956 ed., pp. 3–4; Schmauch, Beiheft 12–13; Reicke 1970). *Ephesus*, first advanced by H. Lisco, then Deissmann, received major support in Feine 1916 and G. S. Duncan. On *Corinth*, see S. Dockx.

For each site, reconstruction of events is necessary. Arguments involve (1) distance and travel time for trips between Philippi and the place of Paul's imprisonment (see III.C, above; Ephesus comes off well); (2) the meaning of Praetorium (see on 1:13, possible for all sites); (3) "those of the Emperor's household" (4:22, people found in all four places); (4) Paul's collection project for the saints at Jerusalem (completed by the time Paul was in Caesarea or Rome; Philippi was likely much involved); (5) the serious nature of Paul's incarceration (Phil 1:20–23, death possible; hardly the freedom "without hindrance" at Rome in Acts 28); (6) identity of the brothers and sisters with Paul (Phil 4:21b; see [17] COMMENT B.3); (7) references to Paul visiting Philippi and travel references in 1 Cor like 4:17. Each site continues to have champions (often less firm than in the past, with perhaps increasing support for Ephesus). An Ephesian provenance explains more for and about Phil than any other theory. Once place is agreed on, dating follows (VIII, below).

SELECT BIBLIOGRAPHY ON PLACE AND DATE (see also Commentaries)

Albertz, M. 1910. "Über die Abfassung des Philipperbriefes des Paulus zu Ephesus," *TSK* 83:551–94.

Bowen, C. R. 1920. "Are Paul's Prison Letters from Ephesus?" *AJT* 24:112–35, 277–87.

Curran, J. T. 1945. "Tradition and the Roman Origin of the Captivity Letters," *TS* 6:163–205.

Deissmann, A. 1923. "Zur ephesinischen Gefangenschaft des Apostle Paulus," in *Anatolian Studies presented to Sir William Mitchell Ramsay*, ed. W. H. Buckler/W. M. Calder (Manchester: Manchester Univ.) 121–27.

Dockx, S. 1973. "Lieu et date de l'épître aux Philipiens," *RB* 80: 230–46, repr. in his *Chronologies néotestamentaires et Vie de l'Église primitive: Recherches exégétiques* (Paris: Duculot, 1976) 89–105; cf. also 119–280 on chronology.

Duncan, G. S. 1929. *St. Paul's Ephesian Ministry. A Reconstruction with special reference to the Ephesian origin of the Imprisonment Epistles*. London: Hodder & Stoughton/New York: Scribners, 1930. Also *ExpTim* 43 (1931–32) 7–11; 46 (1935–36) 293–98; 67 (1955–56) 163–66; and *NTS* 3 (1956–57) 211–18.

———. 1958–59. "Chronological Table to Illustrate Paul's Ministry in Asia," *NTS* 5:43–45.

Feine, P. 1916. *Die Abfassung des Philippersbriefes in Ephesus mit einer Anlage über Röm 16,3–20 als Epheserbrief*. BFCT 20/4. Gütersloh: Bertelsmann.

Lisco, H. 1900. *Vincula Sanctorum. Ein Beitrag zur Erklärung der Gefangenschaftsbriefe des Apostels Paulus*. Berlin: J. Schneider & Co. (H. Klinsmann).

Manson, T. W. 1939. "St. Paul in Ephesus: (1) The Date of the Epistle to the Philippians," *BJRL* 23:182–300, repr. in and cited from Manson's *Studies in the Gospels and Epistles*, ed. M. Black (Manchester: Manchester Univ. Press/Philadelphia: Westminster, 1962) 149–67.

Michaelis, W. 1925a. *Die Gefangenschaft des Paulus in Ephesus und das Itinerar des Timotheus. Untersuchungen zur Chronologie des Paulus und der Paulusbriefe*. NTF I. Reihe, 3. Heft. Gütersloh: Bertelsmann. Chronological Table, 188–89.

————. 1928a. "The Trial of St. Paul in Ephesus," *JTS* 29:368–75.

————. 1933. *Die Datierung des Philipperbriefes.* NTF I. Reihe, 8. Heft. Gütersloh: Bertelsmann.

Reicke, B. 1970. "Caesarea, Rome and the Captivity Epistles," in *Apostolic History and the Gospel. Biblical and Historical Essays Presented to F. F. Bruce,* ed. W. W. Gasque/ R. P. Martin (Exeter: Paternoster/Grand Rapids: Eerdmans) 277–86; repr. 2001, *Re-examining Paul's Letters. The History of the Pauline Correspondence,* ed. D. P. Moessner/I. Reicke (Harrisburg, PA: Trinity Press International, 2001).

Schmid, J. 1931. *Zeit und Ort der paulinischen Gefangenschaftsbriefe.* Freiburg-im-Breisgau: Herder.

Thielman, F. S. 2003. "Ephesus and the Literary Setting of Philippians" in FS Hawthorne (General Bibliography, under "Hansen") 205–23.

Thiessen, W. 1995. *Christen in Ephesus. Die historische und theologische Situation in vorpaulinischer und paulinischer Zeit and zur Zeit der Apostelgeschichte und der Pastoralbriefe.* TANZ 12. Tübingen/Basel: Francke.

B. *The Redaction of the Three Letters.* Local congregations (Mowry), some individual (like Onesimus, later bishop of Ephesus; Goodspeed 1933), or a Pauline "school" (Schenke 1975) have been proposed for putting together letter fragments and a Pauline corpus. More recently, Trobisch suggested Paul himself began the task while in Ephesus (Phil deserves more discussion, 137). Most likely Christians in Philippi were responsible for combining Letters B, C, and A (in that order), A.D. 90–100 (Bornkamm 1962; Gnilka 17–18; Bormann 1995:133–36). Letter A comes last because of its "personal character" or its length (shortest last), or to close the redacted epistle on a note of *ad maiorem Philippensium gloriam,* "to the greater glory of Philippi," a natural theme in the Roman *colōnia* (Vielhauer 1975:162, cf. Walter 20). Thus another contribution of the church, to be added (Bormann 1995:136) to those in Reumann 1993.

SELECT BIBLIOGRAPHY ON REDACTION (see also General Bibliography)

Bornkamm, G. 1962. "Der Philipperbrief als paulinische Briefsammlung," in *Neotestamentica et Patristica,* FS O. Cullmann, NovTSup 6 (Leiden: Brill) 192–20; repr. in Bornkamm's *Geschichte und Glaube:* GA 2/4, BEvT 53 (Munich: Kaiser, 1971) 195–205.

Gamble, H. 1975. "The Redaction of the Pauline Letters and the Formation of the Pauline Corpus," *JBL* 94: 403–18.

Goodspeed, E. J. 1933. *The Meaning of Ephesians.* Chicago: Univ. of Chicago Press.

Harnack, A. 1926. *Die Briefsammlung des Apostels Paulus und die anderen vorkonstantinischen christlichen Briefsammlungen: Sechs Vorlesungen aus der altkirchlichen Literaturgeschichte.* Leipzig: Hinrichs.

Hartke, W. 1917. *Die Sammlung und die älteste Ausgabe der Paulusbriefe.* Bonn: C. Georgi.

Mowry, L. 1944. "The Early Circulation of Paul's Letters," *JBL* 63:73–86.

Schenke, H.-M. 1975. "Das Weiterwirken des Paulus und die Pflege seines Erbes durch die Paulus-Schule," *NTS* 21:505–18 = Schenke/Fischer, *Einl.* (1978) 233–47.

Schmithals, W. 1960. "Zur Abfassung und ältesten Sammlung der paulinischen Hauptbriefe," *ZNW* 51:225–45, repr. in *Paulus und die Gnostiker* (1965), cited from

Gnostics (1972), "On the Collection and Earliest Composition of the Major Epistles of Paul," 239–74.

Trobisch, D. 1989. *Die Entstehung der Paulusbriefsammlung: Studien zu den Anfängen christlicher Publizistik.* NTOA 10. Freiburg: Universitätsverlag/Göttingen: Vandenhoeck & Ruprecht.

———. 1994. *Paul's Letter Collection: Tracing the Origins.* Minneapolis: Fortress.

Zahn, T. 1888–92. *Geschichte des neutestamentlichen Kanons.* 4 vols. Erlangen: Deichert. Repr. Hildesheim/New York: Georg Olms, 1975.

VIII. CHRONOLOGY ON PAUL AND PHILIPPI (A.D. 48–57)

The three letters from Paul to Philippi and three possible visits he made to the city according to Acts (II, above) may be integrated into an overall chronology, using dates in agreement with a majority of recent interpreters, not the proposed "early chronologies" of J. Knox or Lüdemann.

CHART 2: Paul and Philippi: An Attempt at Chronology and Critical Coordination

---

Apostolic Conference (Acts 15), variously dated by scholars to A.D. 43, 46, 47, 48, 49

So-Called Second Missionary Journey (Acts 15:36–18:22)
  Antioch → Syria, Cilicia (Tarsus? 15:41) → Lystra (+ Timothy, 16:1–4). 16:5 = fourth "summary statement" in Acts (cf. 6:7; 9:31; 12:24; 19:20; 28:30–31). → Phrygia, Galatia, (16:6) → Mysia and Troas (vision of man of Macedonia, 16:9–10).

A.D.	"We"-section (16:10–17 or 18) → Neapolis, PHILIPPI (16:12)

48–49   FOUNDING MISSION AT PHILIPPI (Acts 16:12–40, above, II), several months duration = **Visit 1** by Paul (and team) to Philippi

49   Paul goes to Thessalonica, Beroea, and Athens. The Philippians send aid to Paul in Thessalonica at least twice (Phil 4:16)

50   Arrival in *Corinth*, extensive ministry there 50–51 (or 52, Marxsen, *Intro.*, others). Writes 1 THESSALONIANS (and 2 Thess, if genuine). Contacts with Philippi?? — unknown.

51   Hearing before Gallio, proconsul from summer 51 till summer 52 (Riesner 206–7, e.g.)

        Paul leaves Corinth, by ship, via Ephesus, and goes to Jerusalem (Acts 18:22). Apostolic Conference (account in Acts 15), if identified with this visit (so J. Knox, Jewett, e.g.)

        Winter of 51/52, at Antioch (Acts 18:22b–23a) (conflict with Peter, Gal 2:11ff.)

52   So-called Third Missionary Journey (Acts 18:23–21:17), goes through Galatia and Phrygia, to Ephesus

53–54   Paul settles in *Ephesus*, eventually locating his ministry in the hall of Tyrannus, for two years, perhaps 27 months (19:10). Planning further missionary work, he sends, perhaps at this time, Timothy and Erastus to Macedonia (Acts 20:22).

1 CORINTHIANS written, before Pentecost, perhaps in 54 (1 Cor 16:9). = Letter A in the sequence to Corinth. A "previous letter" (cf. 1 Cor 5:9) is likely lost (some see it at 2 Cor 6:14–7:1, but others claim that frg. is related to Qumran or is an *anti-Pauline* frg. from Paul's opponents). Collange and others put Phil A and B before 1 Cor, but does 1 Cor suggest any imprisonment experience? At 1 Cor 16:5, Paul notes that he intends to pass through Macedonia on the way to Corinth.

GALATIANS was written sometime in this period (A.D. 52–54, Jewett 1979:50–55, H. D. Betz, *Gal*; unless it is fitted into the Corinthian sojourn in 56–57 when Paul writes Rom; Wedderburn 2002:108, before 1 Cor).

During this Ephesian period, the congregation in Philippi hears of Paul's situation (from Timothy and Erastus?) and sends aid, presumably with their congregational *apostolos* and *leitourgos*, Epaphroditus. See Chart 1, in III.C, above, on these and other contacts between Philippi and Paul.

Paul writes **LETTER A TO PHILIPPI** (4:10–20), a note of thanks; he may not as yet be imprisoned; cf. 4:14 *thlipsis*, however.

54–55   Paul *imprisoned in Ephesus*—cf. Duncan's "first crisis": charged by Jews with temple-robbery (Acts 19:9; 20:19 and 3; 19:37 *hierosulos*; Paul had effects not only on the pagan temple of Artemis but also on the temple-tax for the Jewish cult center in Jerusalem).

Writes **LETTER B TO PHILIPPI** (1:1 or 1:3–2:30 or 3:1, plus perhaps parts of the present 4:1–9 and 21–23)

Sometime during this period Titus was sent to Corinth concerning Paul's "collection project" for the Jewish-Christian poor in Jerusalem.

55   Paul released (cf. Acts 20:21). Riot of the silversmiths (19:23–41, if not earlier or later). Paul in Asia Minor (province of Asia, outside Ephesus). Imprisoned again? (cf. 2 Cor 1:8)—PHILEMON written.

Writes **LETTER B TO CORINTH,** an apologia for his ministry, seeking to win the Corinthians over, in the face of unsettled conditions in the church there (= 2 Cor 2:14–6:13, 7:2–4), from the Ephesus area.

LETTER C TO PHILIPPI (3:2–21), the polemic. Is the same group as, or one similar to, the opponents in Galatia, or those who are being encountered in Corinth?

(June)—"Painful Visit" to Corinth, a quick trip across the Aegean; Paul humiliated (trip unrecorded in Acts, but cf. 2 Cor 2:4, 9; 7:12; 12:14; 13:1).

LETTER C TO CORINTH, the "Letter of Tears" (so called from 2 Cor 2:4, "I wrote you with many tears"; some compare Phil 3:18 "with tears") = 2 Cor 10–13; from the Ephesus area. 2 Cor 11:8–9 notes how Christians from Macedonia had supplied Paul's needs when he was in Corinth.

Sometime thereafter, Titus was dispatched to Corinth (so Marxsen, among others, assuming that 2 Cor 12:18 refers to an earlier visit).

A possible Asian imprisonment that led Paul to despair of life itself (2 Cor 1:8–11). Jewett places it at the end of the winter of 55–56, actually in 56.

After release or when circumstances permitted, Paul travels overland to Troas and, not finding Titus there (after his trip to Corinth), goes on to *Macedonia* (Acts 20:1; 2 Cor 2:12), where he meets Titus and learns that reconciliation has been achieved with the Corinthians. Did this take place at *Philippi* or Thessalonica?

= **Visit 2** by Paul to Philippi.

LETTER D TO CORINTH, the "Reconciliation Letter," 2 Cor 1:3–2:13, 7:5–16, from Macedonia (7:5–6). If 2 Cor 8 was a separate letter, it was dispatched soon afterwards to Corinth, and ch. 9 just after that, to Achaia, from Macedonia. Both concern the collection, the latter being more positive on its progress. Some take as part of a single letter, with 1–8 or portions thereof.

56–57,   winter—Paul in *Corinth* (Acts 20:2–3)—ROMANS written, copies possibly also to churches in the East.

57   Trip back through Macedonia, including *Philippi* (Acts 20:6) = Paul's **third and last visit** there, according to Acts. → Troas, Miletus (contact with elders from Ephesus), arrival in Jerusalem in June. Arrest.

57–59   Imprisonment, mostly in *Caesarea.*

59–60,   winter—Voyage to Rome, shipwreck in Malta. ————→ Rome in early A.D. 60.

SELECT BIBLIOGRAPHY ON CHRONOLOGY (see also General Bibliography)

Dockx, S. 1971. "Chronologie de la vie de Saint Paul, depuis sa conversion jusqu'à son séjour à Rom," *NovT* 13:261–304, repr. in 1976 (INTRO. VII.A, under 1973) 45–87.

———. 1974. "Chronologie Paulinienne de l'année de la grande collecte," *RB* 81:183–95, repr. in 1976 (INTRO. VII.A, under 1973) 108–18.

Donfried, K. 1992. "Chronology: New Testament," *ABD* 1:1011–22.

Georgi, D. 1965. *Geschichte der Kollekte des Paulus für Jerusalem.* TF 38. Hamburg-Bergstedt: Reich, Evangelischer Verlag. Cited from tr., *Remembering the Poor: The History of Paul's Collection for Jerusalem.* Nashville: Abingdon, 1992.

Hurd, J. C. 1976. "Chronology, Pauline," *IDBSup* 166–67.

Jewett, R. 1979. *A Chronology of Paul's Life.* Philadelphia: Fortress.

Knox, J. 1950. *Chapters in a Life of Paul.* New York/Nashville: Abingdon. Rev. ed., ed. D. R. A. Hare. Macon: Mercer, 1987.

———. 1983. "Chapters in a Life of Paul—A Response to Robert Jewett and Gerd Luedemann," in *Colloquy on New Testament Studies: A Time for Reappraisals and Fresh Approaches,* ed. B. C. Corley (Macon: Mercer) 339–64.

Lüdemann, G. 1984. *Paulus der Heiden Apostel. I. Studien zur Chronologie.* FRLANT 123. Göttingen: Vandenhoeck & Ruprecht, 1980. Cited from tr., G. Luedemann, *Paul Apostle to the Gentiles: Studies in Chronology.* Philadelphia: Fortress.

———. 1983. "A Chronology of Paul," in *Colloquy,* ed. B. C. Corley (cited above under Knox, J., 1983) 289–307.

Ogg, G. 1968. *The Odyssey of Paul: A Chronology.* Old Tappen, NJ: Fleming H. Revell, 1968. = *The Chronology of the Life of Paul.* London: Epworth.

Scriba, A. 2001. "Von Korinth nach Rom: Die Chronologie der letzten Jahre des Paulus," in F. W. Horn, ed., 2001:157–73.

Suhl, A. 1995. "Paulinische Chronologie im Streit der Meinungen," *ANRW* 2.26/2:939–1188.

Wedderburn, A. J. M. 2002. "Paul's Collection: Chronological History," *NTS* 48:95–110.

IX. METHODS AND APPROACH IN THIS COMMENTARY

Methodology calls for more attention than space here permits.[1] In general, the recognized steps in historical-literary-critical approaches have been followed (cf. L. E. Keck/G. M. Tucker, "Exegesis," *IDBSup* 296–303, esp. 299–301; Reumann 1969, 1978). Of so-called new methods (cf. Reumann 1992), rhetorical and social-world approaches have proven helpful but not so definitive as some hoped. One can applaud the desire for "historically grounded theological exegesis" (Bockmuehl 43), but within the confines of space and human frailty, an eclectic approach often results, fitting for Phil. See further, *Philippian Studies.*

SELECT BIBLIOGRAPHY ON METHODS AND APPROACH (see also General Bibliography)

Reumann, J. 1969. "Methods in Studying the Biblical Text Today," *CTM* 40: 655–81.
———. 1978. "Exegetes, Honesty, and the Faith . . . ," *CurTM* 5: 16–32.
———. 1992. "After Historical Criticism, What? Trends in Biblical Interpretation and Ecumenical, Interfaith Dialogues," *JES* 29: 55–86.

X. THEOLOGY IN PHILIPPIANS

Commentators sometimes produce a treatment of theology in Phil only; e.g., Fee 46–53; U. B. Müller 25–31; Hawthorne 1987; Reumann 1987; I. H. Marshall 1993; Fowl 2005:205–35, theology of friendship. More commonly Phil is treated as part of Pauline or NT theology, often minor in comparison with Gal or Rom. E.g., *TPTA*, Bultmann. See further, *Philippian Studies.*

SELECT BIBLIOGRAPHY ON THEOLOGY, esp. NT and Pauline (see also General Bibliography)

Beker, J. C. 1980. *Paul the Apostle: The Triumph of God in Life and Thought.* Philadelphia: Fortress.
Bultmann, R. 1951, 1955. *Theology of the New Testament.* 2 vols. New York: Scribner/London: SCM.
Caird, G. B. 1994. *New Testament Theology,* completed and ed. by L. D. Hurst. Oxford/New York: Clarendon.
Conzelmann, H. 1969. *An Outline of the Theology of the New Testament.* New York: Harper & Row/London: SCM.
Dunn, J. D. G. 1977, 1990. *Unity and Diversity in the New Testament.* London: SCM/Philadelphia: Westminster, 1977. 2nd ed., SCM/Philadelphia: Trinity Press International, repr. 2005.
Eichholz, G. 1972. *Die Theologie des Paulus im Umriss.* Neukirchen: Neukirchener Verlag.

---

[1] For experiences and reflections in writing AB Phil, see my address at the 1997 SBL/AAR Lutheran Professors and Graduate Students breakfast, "Serving Two Masters: Teaching and Writing Between Academy and Church," *Intersections* (ELCA Division for Higher Education and Schools) 9 (2000) 23–33.

Fitzmyer, J. A. 1967. *Pauline Theology: A Brief Sketch.* Englewood Cliffs, NJ: Prentice-Hall = *JBC* (1968) #79.

———. 1989. *Paul and His Theology: A Brief Sketch.* Englewood Cliffs, NJ: Prentice-Hall = *NJBC* (1990) ##79 and 82.

Goppelt, L. *Theology of the New Testament* (Grand Rapids: Eerdmans), vol. 1. *The Ministry of Jesus in its Theological Significance* (1981); 2. *The Variety and Unity of the Apostolic Witness to Christ* (1982).

Hawthorne, G. F. 1987. *Philippians.* Word Biblical Themes. Waco, TX: Word.

———. 1993. "Philippians, Letter to the," *DPL*, 712–13, "Theological Themes."

Kümmel, W. G. 1973. *The Theology of the New Testament According to Its Major Witnesses: Jesus-Paul-John.* Nashville: Abingdon.

Marshall, I. H. 1993. "The Theology of Philippians," in *The Theology of the Shorter Pauline Letters*, with K. P. Donfried. New Testament Theology series. New York: Cambridge Univ. Press. 115–95.

Morris, L. 1986a. *New Testament Theology.* Grand Rapids: Zondervan, Academie Books.

Richardson, A. 1958. *An Introduction to the Theology of the New Testament.* London:SCM/ New York: Harper.

Ridderbos, H. 1975. *Paul: An Outline of His Theology.* Grand Rapids: Eerdmans.

Schoeps, H. J. 1961. *Paul: The Theology of the Apostle in the Light of Jewish Religious History.* London: Lutterworth/Philadelphia: Westminster.

Stauffer, E. 1955. *New Testament Theology.* London: SCM/New York: Macmillan.

Stewart, J. S. 1935. *A Man in Christ: The Vital Elements of St. Paul's Religion.* London: Hodder & Stoughton/New York: Harper; repr., London, paperback, 1974.

TPTA = *The Theology of Paul the Apostle*, Dunn, J. D. G., 1998, General Bibliography

GENERAL
BIBLIOGRAPHY

◆

Aasgaard, R. 2002. "'Role Ethics' in Paul: The Significance of the Sibling Role for Paul's Ethical Thinking," *NTS* 48:513–30.

———. 2003. *'My beloved brothers and sisters!' A Study of the Meaning and Function of Christian Siblingship in Paul, in Its Greco-Roman and Jewish Context*. London: Continuum/T&T Clark.

Abrahamsen, V. A. 1988. "Christianity and the Rock Reliefs at Philippi," *BA* 51:46–56.

———. 1995. *Women and Worship at Philippi. Diana/Artemis and Other Cults in the Early Christian Era*. Portland, ME: Astarte Shell.

Aland, K. 1968. "The Relation between Church and State in Early Times: A Reinterpretation," *JTS* 19:115–27. Cf. ANRW 2.23.1 (1979) 60–246.

———, ed. 1991. *Text und Textwert der griechischen Handschriften des Neuen Testaments. II. Die paulinischen Briefe*. Band 3, *Galaterbrief bis Philipperbrief*. ANTF 18. Berlin: de Gruyter.

Alexander, L. 1989. "Hellenistic Letter-Forms and the Structure of Philippians," *JSNT* 37: 87–101, repr. in *The Pauline Writings* (Sheffield: Sheffield Academic Press, 1995) 232–46.

Alvarez Cineira, D. 1999. *Die Religionspolitik des Kaisers Claudius und die paulinische Mission*. Herders Biblische Studien 19. Freiburg: Herder.

Ascough, R. S. 2003. *Paul's Macedonian Associations: The Social Context of Philippians and 1 Thessalonians*. WUNT 2/161. Tübingen: Mohr Siebeck.

Aspen, P. F. 1992. "Towards a New Reading of Paul's Letter to the Philippians in the Light of a Kuhnian Analysis of New Testament Criticism." Diss., Vanderbilt Univ.

Aune, D. E. 1987. *The New Testament in Its Literary Evironment*. LEC 8. Philadelphia: Westminster.

Bakirtzis, C., and H. Koester. 1998. *Philippi at the Time of Paul and after His Death*. Harrisburg, PA: Trinity International Press.

Banker, J. A. 1996. *A Semantic and Structural Analysis of Philippians*. Dallas, TX: Summer Institute of Linguistics. Earlier draft by K. A. Heyward, SIL, n.d.

Banks, R. 1980. *Paul's Idea of Community: The Early House Churches in Their Historical Setting*. Grand Rapids: Eerdmans. Rev. ed., Peabody, MA: Hendrickson, 1994.

Barclay, J. M. G. 1987. "Mirror-reading a Polemical Letter: Galatians as a Test Case," *JSNT* 31: 73–93.

Barrett, C. K. 1957. *New Testament Background: Selected Documents*. New York: Macmillan; rev. eds., London: SPCK, 1987; San Francisco: HarperCollins, 1995.

———. 1962. *From First Adam to Last: A Study in Pauline Theology*. New York: Scribner's.

Bash, A. 1997. *Ambassadors for Christ: an Exploration of Ambassadorial Language in the New Testament*. WUNT 2/92. Tübingen: Mohr Siebeck.

Bateman, H. W. 1998. "Were the Opponents at Philippi Necessarily Jewish?" *BSac* 155:39–61.

Baumbach, G. 1971. "Die von Paulus im Philipperbrief bekämpften Irrlehrer," *Kairos* 13: 252–66, repr. in *Gnosis und Neues Testament: Studien aus Religionswissenschaft und Theologie*, ed. K.-W. Tröger (Gütersloh: Gütersloher Verlagshaus Gerd Mohn, 1973) 293–310.

———. 1977. "Die Zukunftserwartung nach dem Philipperbrief," in *Die Kirche des Anfangs*, FS H. Schürmann, ed. R. Schnackenburg/J. Ernst/J. Wanke (ETS 38, Leipzig: St. Benno Verlag, 1977; Freiburg/Basel/Wien: Herder, 1978) 435–48.

Baumert, N. 1973. *Täglich Sterben und Auferstehen. Der Literalsinn von 2 Kor 4,12–5,10*. SANT 34. Munich: Kösel-Verlag.

———. 2001. *Studien zu den Paulusbriefen*. SBAB 32. Stuttgart: Katholisches Bibelwerk.

Baumgarten, J. 1975. *Paulus und die Apokalyptik. Die Auslegung apokalyptische Überlieferungen in den echten Paulusbriefen*. WMANT 44. Neukirchen-Vluyn: Neukirchener Verlag.

Berger, K. 1980. "Die impliziten Gegner. Zur Methode des Erschliessens von 'Gegnern' in neutestamentlichen Texten," in *Kirche* (FS G. Bornkamm), ed. D. Lührmann/G. Strecker (Tübingen: Mohr Siebeck) 373–400.

———. 1984a. *Formgeschichte des Neuen Testaments*. Heidelberg: Quelle & Meyer.

———. 1984b. "Hellenistischen Gattungen im Neuen Testament," *ANRW* 2.25.2:1031–1432.

Beyer, K. 1962. *Semitische Syntax im Neuen Testament I.1*. SUNT 1. Göttingen: Vandenhoeck & Ruprecht.

Bieringer, R., V. Koperski, B. Lataire, eds. 2002. *Resurrection in the New Testament: Festschrift J. Lambrecht*. BETL 165. Leuven: University Press, Peeters.

Bittasi, S. 2003. *Gli esempi necessari per discernere: Il significato argomentativo della struttura della lettera di Paolo ai Filippesi*. AnBib 153. Rome: Editrice Pontificio Instituto Biblico.

Black, D. A. 1995. "The Discourse Structure of Philippians: A Study in Textlinguistics," *NovT* 37:16–49.

Blomqvist, J. 1969. *Greek Particles in Hellenistic Prose*. Lund: C. W. K. Gleerup.

Bloomquist, L. G. 1993. *The Function of Suffering in Philippians*. JSNTSup 78. Sheffield: JSOT Press.

Blumenfeld, B. 2001. *The Political Paul: Justice, Democracy and Kingship in a Hellenistic Framework*. JSNTSup 210. Sheffield: Sheffield Academic Press.

Bockmuehl, M. 1995. "A Commentator's Approach to the 'Effective History' of Philippians," *JSNT* 60: 57–88.

Boers, H. 1976. "The Form-Critical Study of Paul's Letters: I Thessalonians as a Case Study," *NTS* 22:140–58.

Bonhöffer, A. 1911. *Epiktet und das Neue Testament*. RVV 10. Giessen: Töpelmann; repr. Berlin: Töpelmann, 1964.

Bormann, L. 1995. *Philippi: Stadt und Christusgemeinde zur Zeit des Paulus*. NovTSup 78. Leiden: Brill.

Branick, V. P. 1989. *The House Church in the Writings of Paul.* Wilmington, DE: Glazier.

Braun, H. 1966. *Qumran und das Neue Testament.* Tübingen: Mohr Siebeck.

Brändl, M. 2006. *Der Agon bei Paulus: Herkunft und Profil paulinischer Agonmetaphorik.* WUNT 2/222. Tübingen: Mohr Siebeck.

Brown, R. 1994. *The Birth of the Messiah.* New York: Doubleday.

Buchanan, C. O. 1964. "Epaphroditus' Sickness and the Letter to the Philippians," *EvQ* 36:157–66.

Buls, H. H. 1988. *Notes on Philippians and Colossians.* Fort Wayne, IN: Concordia Theological Seminary Press, rev.

Bultmann, R. 1910. *Der Stil der paulinischen Predigt und die kynisch-stoische Diatribe.* FRLANT 13. Göttingen: Vandenhoeck & Ruprecht.

———. 1956. *Primitive Christianity in Its Contemporary Setting.* New York: Meridian Books.

CAH. 1934. *The Cambridge Ancient History.* Vol. X, *The Augustan Empire 44 B.C.–A.D. 70,* ed. S. A. Cook/F. E. Adcock/M. P. Charlesworth. Cambridge: Cambridge Univ. Press.

CAH.[2] 1996. *The Cambridge Ancient History,* 2nd ed. Vol. X, *The Augustan Empire,* 43 B.C.–A.D. 69, ed. A. K. Bowman/E. Champlin/A. Lintott. Cambridge: Cambridge Univ. Press.

Capper, B. J. 1993. "Paul's Dispute with Philippi: Understanding Paul's Argument in Phil 1–2 from His Thanks in 4:10–20," *TZ* 49:193–214.

Carr, W. 1981. *Angels and Principalities: The Background, Meaning and Development of the Pauline Phrase Hai Archai Kai Hai Exousiai.* SNTSMS 42. Cambridge: Cambridge Univ. Press.

Carrington, P. 1940. *The Primitive Christian Catechism: A Study in the Epistles.* Cambridge: Cambridge Univ. Press.

Cassidy, R. J. 2001a. *Paul in Chains: Roman Imprisonment and the Letters of St. Paul.* New York: Crossroad.

Chapple, A. L. 1984. "Local Leadership in the Pauline Churches: Theological and Social Factors in Its Development: A Study Based on 1 Thessalonians, 1 Corinthians, and Philippians." Diss., Durham Univ.

Childs, B. S. 1984. *The New Testament as Canon: An Introduction.* Philadelphia: Fortress.

Clarke, A. D. 1993. *Secular and Christian Leadership in Corinth: A Socio-Historical and Exegetical Study of 1 Corinthians 1–6.* AGJU 18, Leiden: Brill.

Collins, R. F. 2000. "'I Command That This Letter Be Read': Writing as a Manner of Speaking," in Donfried/Beutler (see below) 319–39.

Combrink, H. J. B. 1989. "Response to W. Schenk, Die Philipperbriefe des Paulus," in *Reader Perspectives on the New Testament,* ed. E. V. McKnight, *Semeia* 48 (Atlanta: Scholars Press) 135–46.

Cruz, H. 1990. *Christological Motives and Motivated Actions in Pauline Paraenesis.* European University Studies, Series XXIII Theology, 396. Frankfurt/Bern/New York/Paris: Peter Lang.

Cullmann, O. 1964. *Christ and Time. The Primitive Christian Conception of Time and History.* Tr. F. V. Filson. Philadelphia: Westminster, rev. ed.

Culpepper, R. A. 1980. "Co-workers in Suffering: Philippians 2:19–30," *RevExp* 77:349–58.

Cuss, D. 1974. *Imperial Cult and Honorary Terms in the New Testament.* Paradosis 23. Fribourg: Fribourg Univ. Press.

Dalton, W. J. 1979. "The Integrity of Philippians," *Bib* 60:97–102.

Danker, F. W. 1982. *Benefactor: Epigraphic Study of a Greco-Roman and New Testament Semantic Field.* St. Louis: Clayton Publishing House.

Datiri, D. C. 1999. "Finances in the Pauline Churches: A Social-Exegetical Study of the Funding of Paul's Mission and the Financial Administration of His Congregations." Diss., Sheffield.

Davies, W. D. 1948. *Paul and Rabbinic Judaism.* London: SPCK/Philadelphia: Fortress, 4th ed. 1981.

Davis, C. W. 1999. *Oral Biblical Criticism: The Influence of the Principles of Orality on the Literary Structure of Paul's Epistle to the Philippians.* JSNTSup 172. Sheffield: Sheffield Academic Press.

deSilva, D. A. 1994. "No Confidence in the Flesh: The Meaning and Function of Philippians 3:2–21," *TJ* 15: 27–54.

———. 2000. *Honor, Patronage, Kinship & Purity: Unlocking New Testament Culture.* Downers Grove, IL: InterVarsity.

de Vos, C. S. 1999. *Church and Community Conflicts: The Relationships of the Thessalonian, Corinthian, and Philippian Churches with Their Wider Civic Communities.* SBLDS 168. Atlanta: Scholars Press.

De Witt, N. W. 1954. *St. Paul and Epicurus.* Minneapolis: Univ. of Minnesota Press.

Dickson, J. P. 2003. *Mission-Commitment in Ancient Judaism and in the Pauline Communities. The Shape, Extent and Background of Early Christian Mission.* WUNT2/159. Tübingen: Mohr Siebeck.

Dodd, B. 1999. *Paul's Paradigmatic 'I': Personal Example as Literary Strategy.* JSNTSup 177. Sheffield: Sheffield Academic Press.

Donaldson, T. L. 1997. *Paul and the Gentiles: Remapping the Apostle's Convictional World.* Minneapolis: Fortress.

Donfried, K. P., and J. Beutler, eds. 2000. *The Thessalonians Debate: Methodological Discord or Methodological Synthesis?* Grand Rapids: Eerdmans.

Dormeyer, D. 1989. "The Implicit and Explicit Readers and the Genre of Philippians 3:2–4:3, 8–9: Respose to the Commentary of Wolfgang Schenk," *Semeia* 48 (above, under "Combrink") 147–59.

Doty, W. G. 1973. *Letters in Primitive Christianity.* GBS. Philadelphia: Fortress.

Doughty, D. J. 1995. "Citizens of Heaven: Philippians 3.2–21," *NTS* 41:102–22.

Downing, F. G. 1999. "'Honor' among Exegetes," *CBQ* 61:53–73.

Dunn, J. D. G. 1975. *Jesus and the Spirit. A Study of the Religious and Charismatic Experience of Jesus as Reflected in the New Testament.* NTL. London: SCM.

———. 1990. *Jesus, Paul and the Law: Studies in Mark and Galatians.* London: SCM/Louisville: Westminster.

———. 1998. *The Theology of Paul the Apostle.* Grand Rapids: Eerdmans. (= TPTA)

———. 1999. "Who Did Paul Think He Was? A Study of Jewish Christian Identity," *NTS* 45:174–93.

Ebner, M. 1991. *Leidenslisten und Apostelbrief: Untersuchungen zu Form, Motivik und Funktion der Peristasenkataloge bei Paulus.* FB 66. Würzburg: Echter.

Edart, J.-B. 2002. *L'Épître aux Philippiens: Rhétorique et Composition Stylistique.* Etudes Biblique 45. Paris: Gabalda.

Elliott, J. H. 1981. *A Home for the Homeless: A Sociological Exegesis of 1 Peter, Its Situation and Strategy.* Philadelphia: Fortress.

Elliott, N. 1994. *Liberating Paul: The Justice of God and the Politics of the Apostle.* Maryknoll, NY: Orbis/Sheffield: Sheffield Academic Press, 1995.

Engberg-Pedersen, T. 1995. "Stoicism in Philippians," in *Paul in His Hellenistic Context,* ed. T. Engberg-Pedersen (Minneapolis: Fortress) 256–90.

———. 2000. *Paul and the Stoics.* Edinburgh: T&T Clark/Louisville: Westminster John Knox.

Everts, J. M. 1985. "Testing a Literary-Critical Hermeneutic: An Exegesis of the Autobiographical Passages in Paul's Epistles." Diss., Duke Univ.

Exler, F. X. J. 1923. *The Form of the Ancient Greek Letter: A Study in Greek Epistolography.* Washington, D.C.: Catholic Univ. of America.

Fatehi, M. 2000. *The Spirit's Relation to the Risen Lord in Paul: An Examination of Its Christological Implications.* WUNT 2/128. Tübingen: Mohr Siebeck.

Fears, J. R. 1981. "The Cult of Virtues and Roman Imperial Power," *ANRW* 2.17.2:827–948; cf. 736–826, "The Theology of Victory at Rome: Approaches and Problems."

Fee, G. D. 1994. *God's Empowering Presence. The Holy Spirit in the Letters of Paul.* Peabody, MA: Hendrickson.

Fendt, L. 1931. *Die Alten Perikopen für die theologische Praxis erläutert.* HNT 22. Tübingen: Mohr Siebeck.

Ferrari, M. Schiefer. 1991. *Die Sprache des Leids in den paulinischen Peristasenkatalogen.* SBB 23. Stuttgart: KBW.

Fields, B. L. 1995. "Paul as Model: the Rhetoric and Old Testament Background of Philippians 3:1–4:1." Diss., Marquette Univ.

Fitzgerald, J. T. 1988. *Cracks in an Earthen Vessel: An Examination of the Catalogues of Hardship in the Corinthian Correspondence.* SBLDS 99. Atlanta: Scholars Press.

———, ed. 1996. *Friendship, Flattery, and Frankness of Speech: Studies on Friendship in the New Testament World.* NovTSup 82. Leiden: Brill.

———. "Philippians in the Light of Some Ancient Discussions of Friendship," in Fitzgerald, ed., 1996:141–60.

———, ed. 1997. *Greco-Roman Perspectives on Friendship.* SBLRBS 34. Atlanta: Scholars Press.

Fleury, J. 1963. "Une société de fait dans l'Eglise apostolique (Phil. 4:10 à 22)," in *Mélanges Philippe Meylan*, vol. 2, *Histoire du Droit* (Lausanne: Université de Lausanne) 41–59.

Forbes, C. 1986. "Comparison, Self-Praise and Irony: Paul's Boasting and the Conventions of Hellenistic Rhetoric," *NTS* 32:1–30.

Fortna, R. T. 1990. "Philippians: Paul's Most Egocentric Letter," in *The Conversation Continues: Studies in Paul & John*, ed. R. T. Fortna/B. R. Gaventa, FS J. Louis Martyn (Nashville: Abingdon) 220–34.

Fowl, S. E. 1990. *The Story of Christ in the Ethics of Paul. An Analysis of the Function of the Hymnic Material in the Pauline Corpus.* JSNTSup 36. Sheffield: JSOT Press.

Francis, F.O./Sampley, J. P. *Pauline Parallels.* NT FF. Philadelphia: Fortress, 2nd ed., 1984.

Fredrickson, D. E. "*Parrēsia* in the Pauline Epistles," in Fitzgerald, ed., 1996:163–83.

Fridrichsen, A. 1994. *Exegetical Writings: A Selection.* Ed. C. C. Caragounis/T. Fornberg. WUNT 76. Tübingen: Mohr Siebeck.

Friedrich, G. 1978. "Der Brief eines Gefangenen: Bemerkungen zum Philipperbrief," *MPTh* 44 (1955) 270–80, repr. in *Auf das Wort kommit es an*, GS, ed. J. H. Friedrich (Göttingen: Vandenhoeck & Ruprecht) 224–35.

Froitzheim, F. 1982. *Christologie und Eschatologie bei Paulus.* FB 35. Würzburg: Echter Verlag, 2nd ed.

Fuller, R. H. 1965. *The Foundations of New Testament Christology.* New York: Scribner's.

Funk, R. W. 1966. *Language, Hermeneutic, and Word of God. The Problem of Language in the New Testament and Contemporary Theology.* New York: Harper & Row.

Furnish, V. 1963–64. "The Place and Purpose of Phil. III," *NTS* 10:80–88.

———. 1968. *Theology and Ethics in Paul.* Nashville: Abingdon.

Galitis, G., et al. 2001. *Per Me Il Vivere è Cristo (Filippesi 1,1–3,21).* Benedictina, Sezione Biblico-Ecumenica, 14. Rome: Benedicina, Abbazia di S. Paolo.

Garland, D. E. 1980. "The Defense and Confirmation of the Gospel: Philippians 1:1–26," *RevExp* 77:327–36.

———. 1985. "Composition and Unity of Philippians: Some Neglected Literary Factors," *NovT* 27:141–73.

Garnsey, P. 1970. *Social Status and Legal Privilege in the Roman Empire.* Oxford: Clarendon.

Geoffrion, T. C. 1993. *The Rhetorical Purpose and the Political and Military Character of Philippians: A Call to Stand Firm.* Lewiston/Queenston/Lampeter: Mellen Biblical Press.

Georgi, D. 1964a, 1986. *Die Gegner des Paulus im 2. Korintherbrief: Studien zur Religiösen Propaganda in der Spätantike.* Neukirchen-Vluyn: Neukirchener Verlag. Cited from tr., *The Opponents of Paul in Second Corinthians* (Philadelphia: Fortress, 1986).

————. 1991. *Theocracy in Paul's Praxis and Theology.* Tr. D. E. Green. Minneapolis: Fortress.

Glombitza, O. 1962. "Der Schritt nach Europa: Erwägungen zu Act 16, 9–15," ZNW 53:77–82.

Gnilka, J. 1965. "Die antipaulinische Mission in Philippi," *BZ* 9:258–76.

————. 2001. "Die Kehre des Paulus zu Christus (Phil 3,2–21)," in Galitis et al., 2001:137–52, with responses 152–60.

Goodspeed, E. J. 1945. *Problems of New Testament Translation.* Chicago: Univ. of Chicago Press.

Grabner-Haider, A. 1968. *Paraklese und Eschatologie bei Paulus: Mensch und Welt im Anspruch der Zukunft Gottes.* NTAbh N.F. 4. Münster: Aschendorff.

Grayston, K. 1986. "The Opponents in Philippians 3," *ExpTim* 47:170–72.

Gunther, J. J. 1972. *Paul: Messenger and Exile: A Study of the Chronology of His Life and Letters.* Valley Forge, PA: Judson.

————. 1973. *St. Paul's Opponents and Their Background. A Study of Apocalyptic and Jewish Sectarian Teachings.* NovTSup 35. Leiden: Brill.

Guthrie, G. H. 1995. "Cohension Shifts and Stitches in Philippians," in Porter/ Carson, eds., JSNTSup 113:36–59.

Güttgemanns, E. 1966. *Der leidende Apostel und sein Herr. Studien zur paulinischen Christologie.* FRLANT 90. Göttingen: Vandenhoeck & Ruprecht, 1966.

Hainz, J. 1972. *Ekklesia. Strukturen paulinischer Gemeinde-Theologie und Gemeinde-Ordnung.* Münchener Universitäts-Schriften, Katholisch-Theologische Fakultät. Regensburg: Pustet.

Hansen, G. W. 2003. "Transformation of Relationships: Partnerships, Citizenship, and Friendship in Philippi," in *New Testament Greek and Exegesis: Essays in Honor of Gerald F. Hawthorne,* ed. A. M. Donaldson/T. B. Sailors (Grand Rapids: Eerdmans) 181–204.

Harnisch, W. 1999. "Die paulinische Selbstempfehlung als Plädoyer für den Gekreuzigten. Rhetorisch-hermeneutische Erwägungen zu Phil 3," in *Das Urchristentum in seiner literarischen Geschichte,* FS Jürgen Becker, ed. U. Mell/U. B. Müller, BZNW 100 (Berlin: de Gruyter) 133–54.

Hartman, L. 1974. "Some Remarks on 1 Cor. 2:1–5," *SEÅ* 39:109–20.

————. 2001. "Overseers and Servants—For What? Philippians 1:1–11 as Read with Regard to the Implied Readers of Philippians," in Galitis et al., 13–43, with responses 43–51.

Harvey, J. D. 1998. *Listening to the Text: Oral Patterning in Paul's Letters.* Grand Rapids: Baker.

Hellerman, J. H. 2005. *Reconstructing Honor in Roman Philippi. Carmen Christi as Cursus Pudorum.* SNTSMS 132. Cambridge: Cambridge Univ. Press.

Hengel, M. 1974. *Judaism and Hellenism: Studies in their Encounter in Palestine during the Early Hellenistic Period.* Ger., 2nd ed. 1973, tr. J. Bowden. 2 vols. Philadelphia: Fortress.

————. 1981. *The Atonement: The Origins of the Doctrine in the New Testament.* Tr. J. Bowden. Philadelphia: Fortress.

————. 1983b. *Between Jesus and Paul: Studies in the Earliest History of Christianity.* Philadelphia: Fortress.

————. (with R. Deines). 1991. *The Pre-Christian Paul.* London: SCM/Valley Forge, PA: Trinity Press International.

————. (with U. Heckel). 1991. *Paulus und das antike Judentum.* WUNT 58. Tübingen: Mohr Siebeck.

Holladay, C. R. 1977. *Theos Aner in Hellenistic Judaism: A Critique of the Use of This Category in New Testament Christology.* SBLDS 40. Missoula, MT: Scholars Press.

Hollingshead, J. R. 1998. *The Household of Caesar and the Body of Christ: A Political Interpretation of the Letters from Paul.* Lanham: University Press of America.

Holloway, P. A. 2001a. *Consolation in Philippians: Philosophical Sources and Rhetorical Strategy.* SNTSMS 112. Cambridge: Cambridge Univ. Press.

Holmberg, B. 1978. *Paul and Power: The Structure of Authority in the Primitive Church as Reflected in the Pauline Epistles.* ConBNT 11. Lund: Gleerup.

Holmstrand, J. 1997. *Markers and Meaning in Paul: An Analysis of 1 Thessalonians, Philippians and Galatians.* ConBNT 28. Stockholm: Almqvist & Wiksell.

Hooker, M. B. 2002. "Philippians: Phantom Opponents and the Real Source of Conflict," in *Fair Play: Diversity and Conflicts in Early Christianity: Essays in Honour of Heikki Räisänen,* ed. I. Dundenberg/C. Tuckett/K. Syreeni, NovTSup103 (Leiden: Brill) 377–95.

Horn, F. W. 1992. *Das Angeld des Geistes. Studien zur paulinischen Pneumatologie.* FRLANT 154. Göttingen: Vandenhoeck & Ruprecht.

————, ed. 2001. *Das Ende des Paulus. Historische, theologische und literaturgeschichtliche Aspekte.* BZNW 106. Berlin/New York: de Gruyter.

Horsley, R. A., ed. 1997. *Paul and Empire: Religion and Power in Roman Imperial Society.* Harrisburg, PA: Trinity Press International.

————, ed. 2000. *Paul and Politics: Ekklesia, Israel, Imperium, Interpretation.* FS K. Stendahl. Harrisburg, PA: Trinity Press International.

————, and N. A. Silberman. 1997. *The Message and the Kingdom: How Jesus and Paul Ignited a Revolution and Transformed the Ancient World.* New York: Grosset/Putnam, Penguin Putnam.

Horst, P. W. van der. 1980. *Aelius Aristides and the New Testament.* SCH 6. Leiden: Brill.

Hübner, H. 1987. "Paulusforschung seit 1945, Ein kritischer Literaturbericht," ANRW 2.25.4: 2649–2840.

Hughes, F. W. 1989. *Early Christian Rhetoric and 2 Thessalonians.* JSNTSup 30. Sheffield: Sheffield Academic Press.

Jegher-Bucher, V. 1991. *Der Galaterbrief auf dem Hintergrund antiker Episto-*

lographie und Rhetorik. Ein anderes Paulusbild. Zürich: Theologischer Verlag.

Jeremias, J. 1971. *New Testament Theology. Part One: The Proclamation of Jesus.* London: SCM.

Jewett, R. 1970a. "The Epistolary Thanksgiving and the Integrity of Philippians," *NovT* 12:40–53.

———. 1970b. "Conflicting Movements in the Early Church as Reflected in Philippians," *NovT* 12: 362–90.

———. 1971. *Paul's Anthropological Terms. A Study of Their Use in Conflict Settings.* AGSU 10. Leiden: Brill.

———. 2007. *Romans: A Commentary.* Hermeneia. Minneapolis: Fortress.

Johanson, B. C. 1987. *To All the Brethren: A Text-Linguistic and Rhetorical Approach to 1 Thessalonians.* ConBNT 16. Stockholm: Almqvist & Wiksell.

Jones, D. L. "Christianity and the Roman Imperial Cult," ANRW 2.23.2:1023–54.

Joubert, S. 2000. *Paul as Benefactor: Reciprocity, Strategy and Theological Reflection in Paul's Collection.* WUNT 2/124. Tübingen: Mohr Siebeck.

Joüon, P. 1938. "Notes philologiques sur quelques versets de l'épître aux Philippiens (1,21; 2,5.12.13.20; 3,1.5.10.11.15.17.19; 4,9–19)," *RSR* 28:89–93, 223–33, 299–310.

Kähler, C. 1994. "Konflikt, Kompromiss und Bekenntnis. Paulus und seine Gegner im Philipperbrief," *KD* 40:47–64.

Keller, N. 1995. "Choosing What Is Best: Paul, Roman Society and Philippians." Diss., Lutheran School of Theology, Chicago.

Kennedy, G. A. 1984. *New Testament Interpretation through Rhetorical Criticism.* Chapel Hill: Univ. of North Carolina Press.

Kim, S. 1981. *The Origin of Paul's Gospel.* WUNT 2/4. Tübingen: Mohr Siebeck.

———. 2004. *Paul and the New Perspective: Second Thoughts on the Origin of Paul's Gospel.* Grand Rapids: Eerdmans.

Kittredge, C. B. 1998. *Community and Authority: The Rhetoric of Obedience in the Pauline Tradition.* HTS 45. Harrisburg, PA: Trinity Press International.

Klauck, H.-J. 1981. *Hausgemeinde und Hauskirche im frühen Christentum.* SBS 103. Stuttgart: Katholisches Bibelwerk.

———. 1982. *Herrenmahl und hellenistischen Kult. Eine religionsgeschichtliche Untersuchung zum ersten Korintherbrief.* NTAbh N. F. 15. Münster: Aschendorff, 2nd ed. 1986.

———. 2003. *The Religious Context of Early Christianity. A Guide to Graeco-Roman Religions.* Tr. B. McNeil. Studies of the New Testament and Its World. Edinburgh: T&T Clark, 2000/Minneapolis: Fortress, 2003.

Klein, G. 1989. "Antipaulinismus in Philippi: Eine Problemskizze," in *Jesu Rede von Gott und ihre Nachgeschichte im frühen Christentum. Beiträge zur Verkündigung Jesu und zum Kerygma der Kirche,* D.-A. Koch/G. Sellin/ A. Lindemann, eds., FS W. Marxsen (Gütersloh: Mohn) 297–313.

Kleinknecht, K. T. 1984. *Der leidende Gerechtfertigte: Die alttestamentlich-jüdische Tradition vom 'leidenden Gerechten' und ihre Rezeption bei Paulus.* WUNT 2/13. Tübingen: Mohr Siebeck.

Klijn, A. F. J. 1965. "Paul's Opponents in Philippians iii," *NovT* 7:278–84.

Koester, H. 1961–62. "The Purpose of the Polemic of a Pauline Fragment (Philippians iii)," *NTS* 8: 317–32.

———. 1979. "1 Thessalonians—Experiment in Christian Writing," in *Continuity and Discontinuity in Church History,* FS G. H. Williams, SHCT 19, ed. F. F. Church and T. George (Leiden: Brill) 33–44.

———, ed. 1995. *Ephesos, Metropolis of Asia: An Interdisciplinary Approach to its Archaeology, Religion, and Culture.* HTS 41. Valley Forge, PA: Trinity Press International.

Konstan, D. "Friendship, Frankness and Flattery," in Fitzgerald, ed., 1996:7–19.

Koskenniemi, H. 1956. *Studien zur Idee und Phraseologie des griechischen Briefes bis 400 n. Chr.* Suemalaisen Helsinki: Tiedeakatemian Toimituksia, Sarja B, 102, 2. Suomalainen Tiedeakatemia.

Kraus, W. 1996. *Das Volk Gottes: Zur Grundlegung des Ekklesiologie bei Paulus.* WUNT 85. Tübingen: Mohr Siebeck. Paperback study ed., 2004.

Krentz, E. M. 1993. "Military Language and Metaphors in Philippians," in *Origins and Method: Towards a New Understanding of Judaism and Christianity,* FS J. C. Hurd, ed. B. H. McLean, JSNTSup 86 (Sheffield: Sheffield Academic Press) 105–27.

———. 2003. "Paul, Games, and the Military," in Sampley, ed. (below), 344–83.

Lampe, P. 2003. "Paul, Patrons, and Clients," in Sampley, ed. (below), 488–523.

Larsson, E. 1962. *Christus als Vorbild. Eine Untersuchung zu den paulischen Tauf- und Eikonentexten.* ASNU 23. Lund: Gleerup/Kopenhagen: Munksgaard.

Lincoln, A. 1981. *Paradise Now and Not Yet: Studies in the Role of the Heavenly Dimension in Paul's Thought with Special Reference to His Eschatology.* SNTSMS 43. Cambridge: Cambridge Univ. Press.

Lohmeyer, E. 1919a. *Christuskult und Kaiserkult.* Sammlung gemeinverständlicher Vorträge und Schriften aus dem Gebiet der Theologie und Religionsgeschichte 90. Tübingen: Mohr Siebeck.

Lohse, E. 1991. *Theological Ethics of the New Testament.* Minneapolis: Fortress.

Longenecker, B. W., ed. 2002. *Narrative Dynamics in Paul. A Critical Assessment.* Louisville: Westminster John Knox.

Lüdemann, G. 1989a. *Opposition to Paul in Jewish Christianity,* tr. M. E. Boring (Ger. 1983). Minneapolis: Fortress.

———. 1989b. *Early Christianity According to the Traditions in Acts: A Commentary,* tr. J. Bowden (Ger. 1987). Minneapolis: Fortress.

Lund, N. W. 1942. *Chiasmus in the New Testament.* Chapel Hill: Univ. of North Carolina Press.

Lütgert, W. 1909. "Die Vollkommenen im Philipperbrief und die Enthusiasten in Thessalonich," *BFCT* 13 (Gütersloh: Bertelsmann) 547–654.

Luter/Lee = Luter, A. B., and M. V. Lee, "Philippians as Chiasmus: Key to Structure, Unity, and Theme Questions," *NTS* 41 (1995) 89–101.

Lyons, G. 1985. *Pauline Autobiography: Toward a New Understanding.* SBLDS 73. Atlanta: Scholars.

Mackay, B. S.1960–61. "Further Thoughts on Philippians," *NTS* 7:161–70.

MacMullen, R. *Enemies of the Roman Order: Treason, Unrest, and Alienation in the Roman Empire.* London: Routledge, 1966/Cambridge: Harvard, 1967, repr. Routledge 1992.

Malherbe, A. J. 1970. "'Gentle as a Nurse': The Cynic Background of 1 Thess. 2," *NovT* 12:203–17 = 1987 (below) 35–48.

———. 1977/1988. "Ancient Epistolary Theorists," *Ohio Journal of Religious Studies* 5:3–77, rev. as *Ancient Epistolary Theorists*, SBLSBS 12 (Atlanta: Scholars Press, 1988).

———. 1983. *Social Aspects of Early Christianity.* Philadelphia: Fortress, 2nd ed.

———. 1986. *Moral Exhortation: A Greco-Roman Sourcebook.* LEC 4. Philadelphia: Westminster.

———. 1987. *Paul and the Thessalonians: The Philosophical Tradition of Pastoral Care.* Philadelphia: Fortress.

Malina, B. J. 1981. *The New Testament World: Insights from Cultural Anthropology.* Atlanta: John Knox, 1981; 2nd ed., Louisville: Westminster John Knox; 3rd ed., 2001.

———, and J. H. Neyrey. 1996. *Portraits of Paul: An Archaeology of Ancient Personality.* Louisville: Westminster John Knox.

Marchal, J. A. 2006. *Hierarchy, Unity, and Imitation. A Feminist Rhetorical Analysis of Power Dynamics in Paul's Letter to the Philippians.* SBL Academia Biblica 24. Atlanta: SBL.

Marshall, J. W. "Paul's Ethical Appeal in Philippians," in Porter/Olbricht 1993 (below) 357–74.

Marshall, P. 1987. *Enmity in Corinth: Social Conventions in Paul's Relations with the Corinthians.* WUNT 2/23. Tübingen: Mohr Siebeck.

McDonald, J. I. H. 1980. *Kerygma and Didache: The Articulation and Structure of the Earliest Christian Message.* SNTSMS 37. Cambridge: Cambridge Univ. Press.

Mearns, C. 1987. "The Identity of Paul's Opponents at Philippi," *NTS* 33:194–204.

Meeks, W. A. 1983. *The First Urban Christians: The Social World of the Apostle Paul.* New Haven: Yale.

Meggitt, J. J. 1998. *Paul, Poverty and Survival.* SNTW. Edinburgh: T&T Clark.

Mengel, B. 1982. *Studien zum Philipperbrief: Untersuchungen zum situativen Kontext unter besonderer Berücksichtigung der Frage nach der Ganzheitlichkeit oder Einheitlichkeit eines paulinischen Briefes.* WUNT 2/8. Tübingen: Mohr Siebeck.

Merk, O. 1968. *Handeln aus Glaube. Die Motivierung der paulinischen Ethik.* Marburg: Elwert.

Mihoc, V. 2001. "L'Hymne christologique de l'Epître aux Philippiens dans son contexte (Phil 1,27–2,18)," in Galitis et al., 89–122, with responses 122–36.

Minear, P. S. 1990. "Singing and Suffering in Philippi," in FS Martyn (above, under "Fortna") 202–19.

Mitchell, A. C. 1992. "The Social Function of Friendship in Acts 2:44–47 and 4:32–37," JBL 111:255–72.

Mitchell, M. M. 1992. *Paul and the Rhetoric of Reconciliation: An Exegetical Investigation of the Language and Composition of 1 Corinthians.* Louisville: Westminster/John Knox.

Montague, G. M. 1961. *Growth in Christ. A Study of Saint Paul's Theology of Progress.* Kirkwood, MO: Maryhurst Press/Fribourg: Regina Mundi.

Moule, C. F. D. 1982. *The Birth of the New Testament.* San Francisco: Harper & Row, 3rd ed.

Müller, M. 1997. *Vom Schluss zum Ganzen: Zur Bedeutung des paulinischen Briefkorpusabschlusses.* FRLANT 172. Göttingen: Vandenhoeck & Ruprecht.

Müller, U. B. 1975. *Prophetie und Predigt im Neuen Testament. Formgeschichtliche Untersuchungen zur urchristlichen Prophetie.* SNT 10. Gütersloh: Gütersloher Verlagshaus Gerd Mohn.

——. 1999. "Der Brief aus Ephesus. Zeitliche Plazierung und theologische Einordnung des Philipperbriefes im Rahmen des Paulusbriefe," in FS Jürgen Becker (above, under "Harnisch") 155–72.

Murphy-O'Connor, J. 1983. *St. Paul's Corinth: Texts and Archaeology.* Wilmington, DE: Glazier.

Niebuhr, K.-W. 1992. *Heidenapostel aus Israel: Die jüdische Identität des Paulus nach ihrer Darstellung in seinen Briefen.* WUNT 62. Tübingen: Mohr Siebeck.

Oakes, P. 2001. *Philippians: From People to Letter.* SNTSMS 110. Cambridge: Cambridge Univ. Press.

——. 2002. "God's Sovereignty over Roman Authorities: A Theme in Philippians," in *Rome in the Bible and the Early Church,* ed. P. Oakes (Carlisle: Paternoster/Grand Rapids: Baker Academic) 126–41.

Ollrog, W.-H. 1979. *Paulus und seine Mitarbeiter: Untersuchungen zu Theorie und Praxis der paulinischen Mission.* WMANT 50. Neukirchen: Neukirchener Verlag.

Park, J. S. 2000. *Conceptions of Afterlife in Jewish Inscriptions with Special Reference to Pauline Literature.* WUNT 2/121. Tübingen: Mohr Siebeck.

Patte, D. 1983. *Paul's Faith and the Power of the Gospel: A Structural Introduction to the Pauline Letters.* Philadelphia: Fortress.

Peifer, C. J. 1985. "Three Letters in One," BiTod 23:363–68.

Peres, I. 2003. *Griechische Grabinschriften und neutestamentliche Eschatologie.* WUNT 157. Tübingen: Mohr Siebeck.

Perkins, P. 1987. "Christology, Friendship and Status: The Rhetoric of Philippians," *Society of Biblical Literature 1987 Seminar Papers.* SBLSPS 26. Atlanta: Scholars Press. 509–20.

————. 1991. "Theology for the Heavenly Politeuma," *PT* 1:89–104.

Peterlin, D. 1995. *Paul's Letter to the Philippians in Light of Disunity in the Church.* NovTSup 79. Leiden: Brill.

Peterman, G. W. 1997. *Paul's Gift from Philippi: Conventions of Gift-exchange and Christian Giving.* SNTSMS 92. Cambridge: Cambridge Univ. Press.

Pfitzner, V. C. 1967. *Paul and the Agon Motif.* NovTSup 16. Leiden: Brill.

Pilhofer, P. 1995. *Philippi. Band I. Die erste christliche Gemeinde Europas.* WUNT 87. Tubingen: Mohr Siebeck.

————. 2000. *Philippi. Band II: Katalog der Inschriften von Philippi.* WUNT 119. Tübingen: Mohr Siebeck.

————. 2002. *Die frühen Christen und ihre Welt: Greifswalder Aufsätze 1996–2001.* WUNT 145. Tübingen: Mohr Siebeck.

Pohill, J. B. 1980. "Twin Obstacles in the Christian Path: Philippians III," *RevExp* 77:359–72.

Pollard, T. E. 1966–67. "The Integrity of Philippians," *NTS* 14:57–66.

Popkes, V. 2002. "Zum Thema 'Anti-Imperiale Deutung neutestamenticher Schriften,'" *TLZ* 127:850–62.

Portefaix, L. 1988. *Sisters Rejoice: Paul's Letter to the Philippians and Luke-Acts as Received by First Century Philippian Women.* ConBNT 20. Stockholm: Almqvist & Wiksell.

Porter, S. E. 1993. "Word Order and Clause Structure in New Testament Greek. An Unexplored Area of Greek Linguistics Using Philippians as a Test Case," *FiloNT* 6:177–205.

————, ed. 1997. *Handbook of Classical Rhetoric in the Hellenistic Period 330 B.C.–A.D. 400.* Leiden: Brill.

————, and T. H. Olbricht, eds. 1993. *Rhetoric and the New Testament: Essays from the 1992 Heidelberg Conference.* JSNTSup 90. Sheffield: JSOT Press.

————, and T. H. Olbricht, eds. 1997. *The Rhetorical Analysis of Scripture: Essays from the 1995 London Conference.* JSNTSup 146. Sheffield: Sheffield Academic Press.

————, and J. T. Reed. 1998. "Philippians as a Macro-Chiasm and its Exegetical Significance," *NTS* 44:13–31.

Preisker, H. 1933. *Das Ethos des Urchristentums.* Gütersloh: Gütersloher Verlagshaus Gerd Mohn; repr. Darmstadt: Wissenschaftliche Buchgesellschaft, 1968.

Pretorius, E. A. C. 1995. "New Trends in Reading Philippians: A Literature Review," *Neot* 29:273–98.

————. 1998. "Role Models for a Model Church: Typifying Paul's Letter to the Philippians," *Neot* 32:547–71.

Price, J. D. 1987. "A Computer-Aided Textual Commentary of the Book of Philippians," *Grace Theological Journal* 8:253–90.

PT 1 = *Pauline Theology, Volume I: Thessalonians, Philippians, Galatians, Philemon,* ed. J. M. Bassler (Minneapolis: Fortress, 1991).

PT 2 = *Pauline Theology, Volume II: 1 & 2 Corinthians,* ed. D. M. Hay (Minneapolis: Fortress, 1993).

PT 3 = *Pauline Theology, Volume III: Romans,* ed. D. M. Hay/E. E. Johnson (Minneapolis: Fortress, 1995).

PT 4 = *Pauline Theology, Volume IV: Looking Back, Pressing On,* ed. E. E. Johnson/ D. M. Hay, SBLSS 4 (Atlanta: Scholars Press, 1997).

Radl, W. 1981. *Ankunft des Herrn. Zur Bedeutung und Funktion der Parusieaussagen bei Paulus.* BBET 15. Frankfurt/Bern/Cirencester: Peter D. Lang.

Rahtjen, B. D. 1959–60. "The Three Letters of Paul to the Philippians," *NTS* 6:167–73.

Ramsaran, R. 2005. "In the Steps of the Moralists: Paul's Rhetorical Argumentation in Philippians 4," in *Rhetoric, Ethic, and Moral Persuasion* (below, under "Sisson, R. B. 2005") 284–300.

Ramsay, W. M. 1896. *St. Paul the Traveler and the Roman Citizen.* London: Hodder & Stoughton/New York: G. P. Putnam's Sons; repr. Grand Rapids: Baker, 1960.

Rapske, B. 1994. *The Book of Acts and Paul in Roman Custody.* The Book of Acts in Its First Century Setting, vol. 3, ed. B. W. Winter et al. Grand Rapids: Eerdmans/Carlisle: Paternoster.

Reed, J. T. 1993. "Using Ancient Rhetorical Categories to Interpret Paul's Letters: A Question of Genre," in Porter/Olbricht, 1993:292–324.

———. 1997. *A Discourse Analysis of Philippians: Method and Rhetoric in the Debate over Literary Integrity.* JSNTSup 136. Sheffield: Sheffield Academic Press. = *DA.*

———. 2000. "Language of Change and the Changing of Language: A Sociolinguistic Approach to Pauline Discourse," in *Diglossa and Other Topics in New Testament Linguistics,* ed. S. E. Porter, Studies in New Testament Greek 6 (Sheffield: Sheffield Academic Press) 121–53.

Refshauge, E. 1972. "Litterærkritische overvejelser til Filipperbrevet, i," *Dansk teol. Tidsskr.* 35: 186–205.

Reitzenstein, R. 1978. *Die hellenistischen Mysterienreligionen.* Leipzig: Teubner, 3rd ed. 1927. Cited from *Hellenistic Mystery-Religions.* PTMS 15. Pittsburgh: Pickwick Press.

Reumann, J. 1957. "The Use of *Oikonomia* and Related Terms in Greek Sources to about A.D. 100 as a Background for Patristic Applications." Diss. Univ. of Pennsylvania. Subsequently published in *Ekklēsiastikos Pharos* 60, 3–4 (1978) 482–579; 61, 1–4 (1979) 563–603; and *Ekklēsia kai Theologia/ Church and Theology* 1 (1980) 368–430; 2 (1981) 591–617; 3 (1982) 115–40; section 4 and "results" not published.

———. 1966–67. "*Oikonomia*-Terms in Paul in Comparison with Lucan *Heilsgeschichte,*" NTS 13: 147–67.

———. 1985. *The Supper of the Lord: The New Testament, Ecumenical Dialogues, and Faith and Order on the Eucharist.* Philadelphia: Fortress.

———. 1987. "The Theology of 1 Thessalonians and Philippians: Contents,

Comparison, and Composite," *SBL 1987 Seminar Papers*, SBLSPS 26, ed. K. H. Richards (Atlanta: Scholars Press) 521–36.

————. 1989. "Justification and the *Imitatio* Motif in Philippians," in *Promoting Unity: Themes in Lutheran-Catholic Dialogue*, FS J. Willebrands, ed. H. G. Anderson/J, R. Crumley, Jr. (Minneapolis: Augsburg) 17–28.

————. 1991a. "Christology in Philippians, Especially Chapter 3," in *Anfänge der Christologie*, FS F. Hahn, ed. C. Breytenbach/H. Paulsen (Göttingen: Vandenhoeck & Ruprecht) 131–40.

————. 1993a. "Contributions of the Philippian Community to Paul and to Earliest Christianity," *NTS* 39:438–57.

————. 1996. "Philippians, Especially Chapter 4, as a 'Letter of Friendship': Observations on a Checkered History of Scholarship," in Fitzgerald, ed., 1996:83–106.

————. 2003. "Correcting a Flaw in the 'Christ Hymn': The Judgment Theme in Philippians," in *Apokaradokia: Zborník pri prílezitosti sedemdesiakty Doc. ThDr. Jána Greša*, ed. O. Prostrednik/F. Ábel (Bratislava: Evanjelická bohoslovecká Univerzity Komenského v Bratislave) 97–104.

Reimer, R. H. 1997. "'Our Citizenship Is in Heaven': Philippians 1:27–30 and 3:20–21 as Part of the Apostle Paul's Political Theology." Diss. Princeton Theological Seminary.

Richardson, P. 1969. *Israel in the Apostolic Church*. SNTSMS 10. New York: Cambridge Univ. Press.

Richter Reimer, I. 1995. *Women in the Acts of the Apostles: A Feminist Liberation Perspective*. Minneapolis: Fortress.

Riesner, R. 1998. *Paul's Earlier Period: Chronology, Mission Strategy, Theology*. Grand Rapids: Eerdmans.

Rigaux, B. 1968. *The Letters of St. Paul. Modern Studies*. Chicago: Franciscan Herald.

Ringgren, H. 1963. *The Faith of Qumran: Theology of the Dead Sea Scrolls*. Tr. E. T. Sander. Philadelphia: Fortress. Repr. New York: Crossroad, 1995.

Robinson, J. A. T. 1952. *The Body: A Study in Pauline Theology*. SBT 5. London: SCM/Chicago: Henry Regnery; rep. Bristol, Ind.: Wyndham Hall Press, 1989.

Rolland, P. 1990. "La structure littéraire et l'unitié de l'Épître aux Philippiens," *RSR* 64:213–16.

Roloff, J. 1965. *Apostolat – Verkündigung – Kirche. Ursprung, Inhalt und Funktion der kirchlichen Apostelamtes nach Paulus, Lukas und den Pastoralbriefen*. Gütersloh: Gütersloher Verlagshaus Gerd Mohn.

Ruppert, L. 1972a. *Der leidende Gerechte. Eine motivgeschichtliche Untersuchung zum Alten Testament und zwischentestamentlichen Judentum*. FB 5. Würzburg/Stuttgart.

————. 1972b. *Jesus als der leidende Gerechte? Der Weg Jesu im Lichte eines alt- und zwischentestamentlichen Motivs*. SBS 59. Stuttgart: KBW.

Russell, R. 1982. "Pauline Letter Structure in Philippians," *JETS* 25:295–306.

Sampley, J. P. 1977. "Societas Christi: Roman Law and Paul's Conception of the

Christian Community," in *God's Christ and His People*, FS N. Dahl, ed. J. Jervell/W. A. Meeks (Oslo/Bergen/Tromsö: Universitetsforlaget) 158–74.

————. 1980. *Pauline Partnership in Christ: Christian Community and Commitment in Light of Roman Law*. Philadelphia: Fortress.

————. ed. 2003. *Paul in the Greco-Roman World: A Handbook*. Harrisburg, PA: Trinity Press International.

Sanders, E. P. 1977 = *PPJ*. *Paul and Palestinian Judaism: A Comparison of Patterns of Religion*. Philadelphia: Fortress.

————. 1983 = *PLJP*. *Paul, the Law, and the Jewish People*. Philadelphia: Fortress.

Schenk, W. "Der Philipperbrief in der neueren Forschung (1945–1985)," ANRW 2.25.4:3280–3313.

Schillebeeckx, E. C. F. 1979. *Jesus: An Experiment in Christology*. New York: Seabury.

Schlosser, J. 1995a. "La Figure de Dieu selon l'Épître aux Philippiens," NTS 41:378–399.

Schmithals, W. 1972. "Die Irrlehrer des Philipperbriefes," ZTK 54 (1957) 297–341, repr. in Schmithals' *Paulus und die Gnostiker. Untersuchungen zu den kleinen Paulusbriefen* (TF 35; Hamburg: Herbert Reich Evangelischer Verlag, 1965) 47–87. Cited from *Paul & the Gnostics*, tr. J. F. Steely (Nashville/New York: Abingdon, 1972) 65–122.

Schneider, N. 1970. *Die rhetorische Eigenart der paulinischen Antithese*. HUT 11. Tübingen: Mohr Siebeck.

Schöllgen, G. 1988b. "Hausgemeinden, *oikos*-Ekklesiologie, und monarchischer Episcopat," JAC 31: 74–90.

Schoon-Janßen, J. 1991. *Umstrittene "Apologien" in den Paulusbriefen. Studien zur rhetorischen Situation des 1. Thessalonicherbriefes, des Galatersbriefe und des Philipperbriefes*. GTA 45. Göttingen: Vandenhoeck & Ruprecht.

Schrage, W. 1961. *Die konkreten Einzelgebote in der paulinischen Paränese: Ein Beitrag zur neutestamentlichen Ethik*. Gütersloh: Gütersloher Verlagshaus Gerd Mohn.

————. 1988. *The Ethics of the New Testament*. Philadelphia: Fortress. Ger. 1982.

Schürer, E. *History of the Jewish People in the Age of Jesus Christ*, rev. ed., ed. G. Vermes et al. III.1 (Edinburgh: T&T Clark, 1986).

Schüssler Fiorenza, E. 1983. *In Memory of Her. A Feminist Reconstruction of Christian Origins*. New York: Crossroad.

Schuster, J. P. 1997. "Rhetorical Situation and Historical Reconstruction in Philippians." Diss., Louisville Southern Baptist Theological Seminary.

Schütz, J. H. 1975. *Paul and the Anatomy of Apostolic Authority*. SNTSMS 26. Cambridge: Cambridge Univ. Press. Repr., with new Introduction by Wayne Meeks, New Testament Library, Louisville: Westminster John Knox, 2007.

Segal, A. F. 1998. "Paul's Thinking about the Resurrection in its Jewish Context," *NTS* 44:400–419.

Seidensticker, P. 1954. *Lebendiges Opfer (Röm 12,1): Ein Beitrag zur Theologie des Apostels Paulus.* NTAbh 20. Münster: Aschendorff.

Sherwin-White, A. N. 1963. *Roman Society and Roman Law in the New Testament.* Oxford: Clarendon, 1963. Repr., Grand Rapids: Baker, 1978.

———. 1972. "The Roman Citizenship: A Survey of Its Development into a World Franchise," *ANRW* 1.2:23–58.

Simonis, W. 1990. *Der gefangene Paulus. Die Entstehung des sogenannten Römerbriefs und anderer urchristlicher Schriften in Rom.* Frankfurt/Bern/New York/Paris: Peter D. Lang.

Sisson, R. B. 2003. "A Common *Agōn*. Ideology and Rhetorical Intertexture in Philippians," in *Fabrics of Discourse: Essays in Honor of Vernon K. Robbins,* ed. D. B. Gowler/L. G. Bloomquist/D. F. Watson (Harrisburg, PA: Trinity Press International) 242–63.

———. 2005. "Authorial *Ethos* in Philippians: The *Agōn* Topos in Paul and the Hellenistic Moralists," in *Rhetoric, Ethic, and Moral Persuasion in Biblical Discourse: Essays from the 2002 Heidelberg Conference,* ed. T. H. Olbricht/A. Eriksson, Emory Studies in Early Christianity (New York/London: Clark), 238–54.

Smith, Y. W. 2004. "Lament, Consolation and the Structure of Philippians 3," *SBL International 2004* (Groningen) 27–10, Abstract p. 93.

Snyder, G. 1985. *Ante Pacem: Archaeological Evidence of Church Life before Constantine.* Macon, GA: Mercer Univ. Press. Repr. 1991.

Snyman, A. H. 1993. "Persuasion in Philippians 4:1–20," in Porter/Olbricht 325–37.

Son, S.-W. (A). 2001. *Corporate Elements in Pauline Anthropology. A Study of Selected Terms, Idioms, and Concepts in the Light of Paul's Usage and Background.* AnBib 148. Rome: Editrice Pontifico Insituto Biblico.

Sonntag, H. 2000. *Nomos Sōtēr. Zur politischen Theologie des Gesetzes bei Paulus und im antiken Kontext.* TANZ 24. Tübingen: Francke.

Soulen, R. N. 1976. *Handbook of Biblical Criticism.* Atlanta: John Knox. 3rd ed.

Spencer, A. B. 1984. *Paul's Literary Style. A Stylistic and Historical Comparison of II Corinthians 11:16–12:13, Romans 8:9–39, and Philippians 3:2–4:13.* Evangelical Theological Society Monograph Series. Jackson, MS: Evangelical Theological Society.

Spicq, C. 1965. *Théologie morale du Nouveau Testament.* Paris: Gabalda. Vol. 1.

Stagg, F. 1980. "The Mind in Christ Jesus: Philippians 1:27–2:18," *RevExp* 77:337–48.

Standaert, B. 2001. "'Prenez garde aux chiens!' A la recherche des opposants visés par Paul en Philippiens 3," in Galitis et al., 161–80.

Stanley, D. M. 1961. *Christ's Resurrection in Pauline Soteriology.* AnBib 13. Rome: Pontifical Biblical Institute.

Steen, H. A. 1938. "Les Clichés épistolaires dans les Lettres sur Papyrus Grecques," *Classica et Mediaevalia* 1:119–76.

Stegemann, W. 1987. "War der Apostel Paul ein römischer Bürger?" ZNW 78:200–29.

Stendahl, K. 1963, 1976. "The Apostle Paul and the Introspective Conscience of the West," HTR 56:199–215, repr. in Ecumenical Dialogue at Harvard 236–56 and his Paul among Jews and Gentiles (Philadelphia: Fortress, 1976) 78–96, from which references are cited.

Stirewalt, M. L., Jr. 1993. Studies in Ancient Greek Epistolography. SBLRBS 27. Atlanta: Scholars Press.

———. 2003. Paul, the Letter Writer. Grand Rapids: Eerdmans.

Stowers, S. K. 1986. Letter Writing in Greco-Roman Antiquity. LEC 5. Philadelphia: Westminster.

———. 1991. "Friends and Enemies in the Politics of Heaven: Reading Theology in Philippians," PT 1:105–21.

Strack, W. 1994. Kultische Terminologie in ekklesiologischen Kontexten in den Briefen des Paulus. BBB 92. Weinheim: Beltz Athenäum.

Strecker, C. 1999. Die liminale Theologie des Paulus: Zugänge zur paulinischen Theologie aus kulturanthropologischer Perspektive. FRLANT 185. Göttingen: Vandenhoeck & Ruprecht.

Studiorum Paulinorum Congressus Internationalis Catholicus 1961. Simul Secundus Congressus Internationalis Catholicus de Re Biblica. Completo Undevicesimo Saeculo post S. Pauli in Urbem Adventum, Vol. I and II. AnBil 17–18. Rome: Pontifico Instituto Biblico, 1963.

Suhl, A. 1975. Paulus und seine Briefe. Ein Beitrag zur paulinischen Chronologie. SNT 11. Gütersloh. Cf. further http://cit.uni-muenster.de/Paulus/Pls-Uebersicht.htm, esp. 323, Die Gaben der Philippi für Paulus.

Sumney, J. L. 1990. Identifying Paul's Opponents: The Question of Method in 2 Corinthians. JSNTSup 40. Sheffield: JSOT Press.

———. 1999. 'Servants of Satan,' 'False Brothers,' and Other Opponents of Paul. JSNTSup 188. Sheffield: Sheffield Academic Press.

Swift, R. C. 1984. "The Theme and Structure of Philippians," BSac 141:234–54.

Tannehill, R. C. 1967. Dying and Rising with Christ. A Study in Pauline Theology. Berlin: Töpelmann.

Tellbe, M. 1993. "Christ and Caesar: The Letter to the Philippians in the Setting of the Roman Imperial Cult." Unpublished M. Th. Thesis, Regent College, Vancouver.

———. 1994. "The Sociological Factors Behind Philippians 3:1–11 and the Conflict at Philippi," JSNT 55: 97–121.

———. 2001. Paul between Synagogue and State: Christians, Jews, and Civic Authorities in 1 Thessalonians, Romans, and Philippians. ConBNT 34. Stockholm: Almqvist & Wiksell.

Theissen, G. 1982. The Social Setting of Early Christianity: Essays on Corinth. Philadelphia: Fortress.

Thielman, F. 1994. Paul and the Law: A Contextual Approach. Downers Grove IL: InterVarsity.

Thom, J. C. 2003. "'The Mind is Its Own Place:' Defining the Topos," in Early

Christianity and Classical Culture: Comparative Studies in Honor of Abraham J. Malherbe, ed. J. T. Fitzgerald/T. H. Olbricht/L. M. White, NovTSup 110, FS Malherbe (Leiden/Boston: Brill) 555–73.

Thomson, I. H. 1995. *Chiasmus in the Pauline Letters*. JSNTSup 111. Sheffield: Sheffield Academic Press.

Thraede, K. 1970. *Grundzüge griechisch-römischer Brieftopik*. Zetemata 48. Munich: C. H. Beck.

Thrall, M. E. 1962. *Greek Particles in the New Testament. Linguistic and Exegetical Studies*. Leiden: Brill.

Thurén, L. 2002. *Derhetorizing Paul. A Dynamic Perspective on Pauline Theology and the Law*. WUNT 124. Tübingen: Mohr Siebeck, 2000. Repr., Harrisburg, PA: Trinity Press International.

Thüsing, W. 1965. *Per Christum in Deum: Studien zum Verhältnis von Christozentrik und Theozentrik in den paulinischen Hauptbriefen*. NTAbh, NF 1. Münster: Aschendorf.

Tomson, P. J. 1990. *Paul and the Jewish Law: Halakha in the Letters of the Apostle to the Gentiles*. CRINT III, 1. Assen/Maastricht: Van Gorcum/ Minneapolis: Fortress.

Turner, N. 1980. *Christian Words*. Edinburgh: T&T Clark.

Unnik, W. C. van. 1962. *Tarsus or Jerusalem: The City of Paul's Youth* (London: Epworth), repr. in his GS, *Sparsa Collecta: The Collected Essays of W. C. van Unnik*, 1 (NovTSup 29, Leiden: Brill, 1973) 259–320, + "Once Again, Tarsus or Jerusalem?" 321–27.

Vallotton, P. 1960. *Le Christ et la foi*. Geneva: Labor et fides.

Vielhauer, P. 1975. *Geschichte der urchristlichen Literatur. Einleitung in das Neue Testament, die Apokyphen and die Apostolischen Väter*. Berlin/New York: de Gruyter.

Vollenweider, S. 2002. *Horizonte neutestamentlicher Christologie. Studien zu Paulus und zur frühchristlichen Theologie*. GS. WUNT 144. Tübingen: Mohr Siebeck.

Volz, P. 1934. *Die Eschatologie der jüdischen Gemeinde im neutestamentlichen Zeitalter. Nach der Quellen der rabbinischen, apokalyptischen und apokryphen Literatur*. Tübingen: Mohr, 2nd ed.; repr., Hildesheim 1966.

Vos, G. 1961. *The Pauline Eschatology*. Princeton: Princeton Univ. Press, 1930, cited from repr., Grand Rapids: Eerdmans.

Vos, J. S. 2001. "Phil 1,12–26 und die Rhetorik des Erfolges," in Galitis et al., 53–87, with responses 78–87. Eng., "Philippians 1:12–26 and the Rhetoric of Success," in *Rhetoric, Ethic and Moral Persuasion* (above, under "Sisson, R. B. 2005") 274–83.

———. 2002. *Die Kunst der Argumentation bei Paulus. Studien zur antiken Rhetorik*. WUNT 149. Tübingen: Mohr Siebeck.

Wansink, C. S. 1996. *Chained in Christ: The Experience and Rhetoric of Paul's Imprisonments*. JSNTSup 130. Sheffield: Sheffield Academic Press.

Ward, R. B. 1967. "The Opponents of Paul," *ResQ* 10:186–89.

Ware, J. 1996. "'Holding Forth the Word of Life': Paul and the Mission of the

Church in the Letter to the Philippians in the Context of Second Temple Judaism." Diss., Yale Univ.

———. 2005. *The Mission of the Church in Paul's Letter to the Philippians in the Context of Ancient Judaism.* NovTSup 120. Leiden/Boston: Brill.

Watson, D. F. 1988a. *Invention, Arrangement, and Style. Rhetorical Criticism of Jude and 2 Peter.* SBLDS 104. Atlanta: Scholars Press.

———. 1988b. "A Rhetorical Analysis of Philippians and Its Implications for the Unity Question," *NovT* 10:57–88.

———. 1997. "The Integration of Epistolary and Rhetorical Analysis of Philippians," in Porter/Olbricht, 399–426.

———. 2003. "A Reexamination of the Epistolary Analysis Underpinning the Arguments for the Composite Nature of Philippians," in FS Malherbe (above, under "Thom") 157–77.

Watson, F. 1986. *Paul, Judaism and the Gentiles. A Sociological Approach.* SNTSMS 56. Cambridge: Cambridge Univ. Press.

Weder, H. 1981. *Das Kreuz Jesu bei Paulus. Ein Versuch, über den Geschichtsbezug des christlichen Glaubens nachzudenken.* FRLANT 125. Göttingen: Vandenhoeck & Ruprecht.

Weima, J. A. D. 1994. *Neglected Endings: The Significance of the Pauline Letter Closings.* JSNTSup 101. Sheffield: JSOT Press.

Weiss, J. 1897. "Beiträge zur paulinischen Rhetorik," in *Theologische Studien Herrn Wirkl. Oberkonsistorialrath Professor D. Bernhard Weiss zu seinem 70. Geburtstag dargebracht . . .* (Göttingen: Vandenhoeck & Ruprecht) 165–247.

West, A. L. S. 2001. "Whether by Life or by Death: Friendship in a Pauline Ethic of Death and Dying." Diss., Duke Univ.

Westerholm, S. 1988. *Israel's Law and the Church's Faith: Paul and His Recent Interpreters.* Grand Rapids: Eerdmans.

———. 2004. *Perspectives Old and New on Paul: The "Lutheran" Paul and His Critics.* Grand Rapids: Eerdmans.

White, J. L. 1971a. "Introductory Formulae in the Body of the Pauline Letter," *JBL* 90:91–97.

———. 1972. *The Form and Function of the Body of the Greek Letter: A Study of the Letter-Body in the Non-literary Papyri and in Paul the Apostle.* SBLDS 2. Missoula, MT: SBL.

———. 1978. "Epistolary Formulas and Cliches in Greek Papyrus Letters," *SBLSP* 2:289–391.

———. 1984. "New Testament Epistolary Literature in the Framework on Ancient Epistolography," *ANRW* 2.25.2: 1730–56.

———. 1986. *Light from Ancient Letters.* FF. Philadelphia: Fortress.

White, L. M. 1990. "Morality Between Two Worlds: A Paradigm of Friendship in Philippians," in *Greeks, Romans, and Christians. Essays in Honor of Abraham J. Malherbe,* ed. D. L. Balch/E. Ferguson/W. A. Meeks (Minneapolis: Fortress) 201–15.

———. 1995. "Visualizing the 'Real' World of Acts 16: Toward Construction of a Social Index," in *The Social World of the First Christians: Essays in Honor of Wayne A. Meeks*, ed. L. White/O. L. Yarbrough (Minneapolis: Fortress) 234–61.

Wick, P. 1994. *Der Philipperbrief: Der formal Aufbau des Briefs als Schlüssel zum Verständnis seines Inhalts.* BWANT 7/15 (135). Stuttgart/Berlin/Köln: Kohlhammer.

Wiles, G. P. 1974. *Paul's Intercessory Prayers. The Significance of the Intercessory Prayer Passages in the Letters of Paul.* SNTSMS 24. Cambridge: Cambridge Univ. Press.

Wiles, V. 1993. "From Apostolic Presence to Self-Government in Christ. Paul's Preparing of the Philippian Church for Life in his Absence." Diss., Univ. of Chicago.

Williams, D. J. 1999. *Paul's Metaphors: Their Context and Character.* Peabody, MA: Hendrickson.

Williams, D. K. 2002. *Enemies of the Cross of Christ: The Terminology of the Cross and Conflict in Philippians.* JSNTSup 223. London/New York: Sheffield Academic Press.

Winter, B. W. 1994. *Seek the Welfare of the City: Christians as Benefactors and Citizens.* FCGRW. Grand Rapids: Eerdmans/Carlisle: Paternoster.

Winter, S. F. 1998. " 'Worthy of the Gospel of Christ': A Study in the Situation and Strategy of Paul's Epistle to the Philippians." D. Phil. diss., Oxford.

Wolff, H. W. 1974. *Anthropology of the Old Testament.* Philadelphia: Fortress. Ger. 1973.

Wright, N. T. 1991. *The Climax of the Covenant: Christ and the Law in Pauline Theology.* Edinburgh: T&T Clark/Minneapolis: Fortress, 1993.

———. 2000. "Paul's Gospel and Caesar's Empire," in Horsley, ed. 2000, 160–83.

———. 2003. *The Resurrection of the Son of God. Christian Origins and the Question of God*, Vol. 3. Minneapolis: Fortress. Pp. 225–36.

Select Commentaries on Philippians

Cited by author (or abbreviation), plus, where necessary, "*Phil.,*" date, and/or series.

Alford, H. (1845–60). *The Greek Testament.* Cambridge: Deighton, Bell & Co./ London: Longmans, Green & Co.; repr., rev. Everett F. Harrison (Chicago: Moody, 1958). 3:152–95.

Aquinas, Thomas (1225–74). *In omnes D. Pauli Apostoli Epistolas Commentaria* (Paris: L.Vives, 1874) 2:318–55. Tr. F. R. Larcher/M. Duffy, *Commentary on Saint Paul's First Letter to the Thessalonians and the Letter to the Philippians* (Albany, NY: Magi, 1969).

Barclay, W. 1957. *The Letters to the Philippians, Colossians, and Thessalonians.* Daily Study Bible. Edinburgh: Saint Andrews Press/Philadelphia: Westminster. Repr., The New Daily Study Bible (Louisville: Westminster John Knox, 2005).

Barth, Gerhard. 1979. *Der Brief an die Philipper.* Zürcher Bibelkommentare NT, 9. Zurich: Theologischer Verlag.

Barth, Karl. 1962. *The Epistle to the Philippians*, tr. J. W. Leitch. London: SCM/ Richmond: John Knox. 40th Anniversary Edition, Introductory Essays by B. L. McCormack, F. B. Watson (Louisville: Westminster/John Knox, 2002), iv-li. Ger., *Erklärung des Philipperbriefes* (Zurich-Zollikon: Evangelischer Verlag, 1927; 6th ed. 1947).

Beare, F. W. 1959. *A Commentary on the Epistle to the Philippians*. Black's/ HNTC. London: A. & C. Black/New York: Harper & Brothers, 2nd ed. 1969, 3rd ed. 1973.

Beet, J. A. 1890. *A Commentary on Paul's Epistles to the Ephesians, Philippians, Colossians, and to Philemon*. London: Hodder & Stoughton.

Bengel, J. A. (1687–1752). *Gnomon Novi Testamenti*. Tübingen: J. G. P. Schramm, 1742; 3rd ed. 1855; 765–82; tr., ed. A. R. Fausett, *Gnomon of the New Testament* (Edinburgh: T&T Clark, 1858–59; tr., ed. Blackley and Hawes, Intro. by R. F. Weidner, *Gnomon of the New Testament* (New York: Fleming H. Revell, 1893) 2:662–90.

Benoit, P. 1949. *Les Epîtres de saint Paul aux Philippiens, à Philemon, aux Colossiens, aux Ephesiens* (Paris: Les Editions du Cerf); part of *La Sainte Bible* traduite en français sous la direction de l'Ecole Biblique de Jérusalem (Paris: Les Editions du Cerf, 1949, 2nd ed. 1953, 17–27; 3rd ed. 1959); tr. ed. A. Jones, *The Jerusalem Bible* (Garden City, NY: Doubleday, 1966) 260–61, 338–43; rev. ed. *La Bible de Jérusalem* (Paris: du Cerf, 1973), tr. *The New Jerusalem Bible* (Garden City, NY: Doubleday, 1985) 1858–59, 1940–44.

Bittlinger, A. 1970. *Ratschläge für eine Gemeinde: Der Brief des Paulus an die Philipper*. Schloss Craheim: Rolf Kühne Verlag.

Bockmuehl, M. 1998. *The Epistle to the Philippians*. Black's NTC. Peabody, MA: Hendrickson.

Bonnard, P. 1950. *L'épître de saint Paul aux Philippiens . . .*, CNT 10 (Neuchâtel: Delachaux et Niestlé) 5–82.

Boor, W. de. 1962. *Die Briefe des Paulus an die Philipper und an die Kolosser, erklärt*. Wupperthaler Studienbibel. Wupperthal: Brockhaus, 3rd ed. 1974.

Bouwman, G. 1965. *De Brief van Paulus aan de Filippiërs*. Het Nieuwe Testament uitgelegd. Roermond: J. J. Romen.

Bruce, F. F. 1983. *Philippians*. Good News Commentary. San Francisco: Harper & Row. Peabody, MA: Hendrickson, 1989.

Byrne, B. 1990. "The Letter to the Philippians," in *The New Jerome Biblical Commentary* (Englewood Cliffs, NJ: Prentice-Hall) #48, 791–97.

Caird, G. 1976. *Paul's Letters from Prison*. New Clarendon Bible (Oxford: Oxford Univ. Press) 95–154.

Calvin, John (1509–64). *Epistola Pauli ad Philippenses* (1539), CR. *J. Calvin*, 52:5–76; cited from: tr. J. Pringle, *Commentaries on the Epistles of Paul the Apostle to the Philippians, Colossians, and Thessalonians* (Edinburgh: Calvin Translation Society; Grand Rapids: Eerdmans, 1948); tr., ed. T. H. L. Parker, *The Epistles of Paul the Apostle to the Galatians, Ephesians, Philippians, and Colossians* (Grand Rapids: Eerdmans, 1965).

Chrysost. = Johannes Chrysostomus (347–407). *In Epistolam ad Philippenses commentarius*, PG 62:177–298; tr., NPNF, 1st Series, 13:173–255.

Clark, G. H. 1996. *Philippians*. Hobbs, NM: Trinity Foundation.

Collange, J.-F. 1979. *The Epistle of St. Paul to the Philippians*. London: Epworth. Tr. A. W. Heathcote, from the French, *L'épître de saint Paul aux Philippiens*, CNT 10A (Neuchâtel/Paris: Delachaux & Niestlé, 1973).

Craddock, F. B. 1985. *Philippians*. IBC. Atlanta: John Knox.

Dib. = Dibelius, M. 1925. *An die Thessalonischer I II. An die Philipper*. HNT 11. Tübingen: Mohr, 1913; cited from 2nd ed., 50–76; 3rd ed. 1937, 59–98.

Dietrich, S. de. 1942. *L'épître aux Philippiens*. Paris: Cahier Biblique 1; Publications du Conseil Protestant de la Jeunesse, 1946. Tr. *Toward Fullness of Life: Studies in the Letter of Paul to the Philippians*. Philadelphia: Westminster, 1966.

Eadie, J. 1859. *A Commentary on the Greek Text of the Epistle of Paul to the Philippians*. London: Richard Griffen, 2nd ed., Edinburgh: T&T Clark, 1884.

Eckey, W. 2006. *Die Briefe des Paulus an die Philipper und an Philemon. Ein Kommentar*. Neukirchen-Vluyn: Neukirchener.

Egger, W. 1985. *Galaterbrief, Philipperbrief, Philemonbrief*, Der Neue Echter Bibel (Würzburg: Echter Verlag) 45–73.

EGT = Expositor's Greek Testament. See Kennedy, below.

Ellicott, C. J. 1857. *A Critical and Grammatical Commentary on St. Paul's Epistles to the Philippians, Colossians, and to Philemon*. Ellicott's Commentaries, Critical and Grammatical, on the Epistles of Saint Paul, with Revised Translations, 2,1. London: Parker, often repr.; cited from Andover: Warren F. Draper, 1872, xv–xvi, 17–115; 5th ed. 1888, 233–55.

Erasmus, Desiderius (ca. 1466–1536). "Adnotationes in Epistolam Pauli ad Philippenses" (Basel: Froben, 1518); *Opera omnia* (repr. London: Gregg, 1962) 6:861–80; "Paraphrases in Epistolam Pauli ad Philippenses," 7:991–1004.

Ernst, J. 1974. *Die Briefe an die Philipper, an Philemon, an die Kolosser, an die Epheser*. RNT. Regensburg: Pustet.

Ewald, H. G. A. 1857. *Die Sendschreiben des Apostels Paulus*. Handbuch des Neuen Bundes 3/1 (Göttingen: Verlag der Dieterischen Buchhandlungen) 431–57.

Ewald, P. 1908. *Der Brief des Paulus an die Philipper ausgelegt*. T. Zahn's Kommentar zum Neuen Testament 11. Leipzig: Deichert; see "Wohl." = G. Wohlenberg for rev. ed.

Fabris, R. 2000. *Lettera ai Filippesi—Lettera a Filemone. Introduzione, versione, commento*. Scritti delle origini cristiane 11. Bologna: EDB.

Fee, G. D. 1995. *Paul's Letter to the Philippians*. NICNT. Grand Rapids: Eerdmans.

Fitzmyer, J. A. 1968. "Philippians," *Jerome Biblical Commentary* (Englewood Cliffs, NJ: Prentice-Hall) 2:247–53 = #50:1–27.

Fowl, S. E. 2005. *Philippians*. The Two Horizons NT Commentary. Grand Rapids: Eerdmans.

Friedrich, G. 1962. "Der Brief an die Philipper," in *Die kleineren Briefe des Apostels Paulus*, NTD 8 (Göttingen: Vandenhoeck & Ruprecht) 92–129; 10th ed., 1965, 92–130; 16th ed., 1985, 125–75.

Gnilka, J. 1968. *Der Philipperbrief*. HTKNT 10/3. Freiburg: Herder, 2nd ed., 1976; cited from 3rd ed. 1980.

Grayston, K. 1957. *The Epistles to the Galatians and to the Philippians*. Epworth Preacher's Commentaries. London: Epworth.

————. 1967. *The Letters of Paul to the Philippians and to the Thessalonians*. Cambridge Bible Commentary. Cambridge: Cambridge Univ. Press.

Grotius, Hugo (1583–1645). "Annotationes in Epistolam ad Philippenses" (Paris, 1644), *Opera omnia Theologica* (Amsterdam: J. Blaev, 1679; Basel, 1782) 3:908–21.

Hargraves, J. 1983. *A Guide to Philippians*. TEF Study Guide 18. London: SPCK.

Haupt, E. 1902. "Die Brief an die Philipper," in *Die Gefangenschaftsbriefe*. MeyerKEK. Göttingen: Vandenhoeck & Ruprecht, 6th ed 1897; 7th ed. cited.

Hawth. = Hawthorne, G. F. 1983. *Philippians*. WBC 43. Waco, TX: Word.

Hendricksen, W. 1962. *Philippians*. New Testament Commentary. Grand Rapids: Baker. 2nd ed. 1979.

Hofmann, J. C. K. von. 1871. *Die Briefe an die Philipper*. Die Heiligen Schrift Neuen Testaments 4/3. Nordlingen.

Hooker, M. D. 2000. "The Letter to the Philippians," in *The New Interpreter's Bible* (Nashville: Abingdon) 11:467–549.

Horn, E. T. 1896. "Annotations on the Epistle to the Philippians," in *The Lutheran Commentary*, ed. H. E. Jacobs (New York: Christian Literature Co.) 9:119–92.

Houlden, J. H. 1970. *Paul's Letters from Prison: Philippians, Colossians, Philemon, and Ephesians*, Pelican New Testament Commentaries (Harmondsworth, England/Baltimore, MD: Penguin; Westminster Pelican Commentaries, Philadelphia: Westminster, 1977) 29–116.

Jer. = Jerome (342–420). *Commentarii in Epistolam ad Philippenses*, PL 30:841–52.

Johnstone, R. 1875. *Lectures (Exegetical and Practical) on the Epistle of Paul to the Philippians*. Edinburgh: T&T Clark; repr. Grand Rapids: Baker, 1955; Minneapolis: Klock & Klock, 1977.

Jones, M. 1918. *The Epistle to the Philippians, with Introduction and Notes*. Westminster Commentaries. London: Methuen.

Kennedy, H. A. A. 1900. "The Epistle to the Philippians," *The Expositor's Greek Testament* (= EGT), ed. W. R. Nicoll. London: Hodder & Stoughton; repr., Grand Rapids: Eerdmans, 1976. 3:397–473.

Klöpper, A. 1893. *Der Brief des Apostels Paulus an die Philipper*. Gotha: F. A. Perthes.

Koenig, J. 1985. *Philippians, Philemon*. . . . Augsburg Commentary on the New Testament 11 (Minneapolis: Augsburg) 119–82.

Lenski, R. C. H. 1937. *The Interpretation of Paul's Epistles to the Galatians, to the Ephesians, and to the Philippians* (Columbus, OH: Lutheran Book Concern) 691–911.

Lft. = Lightfoot, J. B. 1868. *Saint Paul's Epistle to the Philippians*. The Epistles of Paul 3/1. London: Macmillan; 2nd ed. 1869; 3rd ed. 1873; 4th ed. 1878, with additions 1881; with slight alterations 1885, 1913, subtitled "A Revised Text with Introduction, Notes, and Dissertations"; repr. Grand Rapids: Zondervan, 1953; Wheaton, IL: Crossway, 1994.

Linton, O. 1964. "Pauli brev till filipperna," in *Pauli Mindre Brev*, Tolkning av Nya Testamentet IX (Stockholm: Verbum/Kyrkliga Centralförlaget) 148–205.

Loh. = Lohmeyer, E. 1930. *Die Briefe an die Philipper, an die Kolosser und an Philemon*. MeyerKEK 9/1. Göttingen: Vandenhoeck & Ruprecht, 9th ed. 1953; 13th ed. 1964; 14th ed. 1974. See also below under "Schmauch."

Loh/Nida = Loh, I-Jin, & E. A. Nida. 1977. *A Translators* [sic] *Handbook on Paul's Letter to the Philippians*. Helps for Translators 19. Stuttgart/New York: United Bible Societies.

Marshall, (I.) H. 1992. *The Epistle to the Philippians*. Epworth Commentaries. London: Epworth.

Martin, R. P. 1960a. *The Epistle of Paul to the Philippians*. Tyndale Bible Commentaries, NT Series 11 (Grand Rapids: Eerdmans); rev. ed., Tyndale New Testament Commentaries, 1987.

———. 1976. *Philippians*. New Century Bible. London: Oliphants/Greenwood SC: Attic Press; Grand Rapids: Eerdmans, 1980; 2nd ed. 1987. With G. Hawthorne, WBC 43, rev., Nashville: Nelson Reference, 2004.

Mayer, B. 1986. *Philipperbrief, Philemonbrief*, Stuttgarter Kleiner Kommentar, Neues Testament 11 (Stuttgart; Katholisches Bibelwerk) 1–73.

Melick, R. R., Jr. 1991. *Philippians, Colossians, Philemon*. New American Commentary 32. Nashville: Broadman.

Meyer, F. B. 1952. *The Epistle to the Philippians*. London: Marshall, Morgan & Scott.

Meyer, H. A. W. 1847. *Die Briefe Pauli an die Philipper, Kolosser und Philemon*. MeyerKEK 9/1. Göttingen: Vandenhoeck & Ruprecht, 2nd ed. 1859; 3rd ed. 1865; 4th ed. 1874; tr. J. C. Moore, rev. W. P. Dickson, notes to the American ed. by T. Dwight, *Critical and Exegetical Hand-Book to the Epistles to the Philippians and Colossians and to Philemon* (New York: Funk & Wagnalls, 1889).

Michael, J. H. 1928. *The Epistle to the Philippians*. MNTC. London: Hodder & Stoughton/New York: Harper, 1929.

Michaelis, W. 1935. *Der Brief des Paulus an die Philipper*. THKNT 11. Leipzig: Deichert.

Morlet, R.-M. 1985. *Epître de Paul aux Philippiens*. Vaux-sur-Sein, France: Edifac.

Motyer, J. A. 1984. *The Message of Philippians: Jesus Our Joy*. The Bible Speaks Today. Leicester, England/Downers Grove, IL: InterVarsity.

Moule, H. C. G. 1897. *The Epistle to the Philippians.* Cambridge Greek Testament. Cambridge: Cambridge Univ. Press.

Müller, J. J. 1955. *The Epistles of Paul to the Philippians and to Philemon,* NICNT (Grand Rapids: Eerdmans) 13–156.

Müller, U. B. 1993. *Der Brief des Paulus an die Philipper.* THKNT 11/1. Leipzig: Evangelische Verlagsanstalt, 2nd ed. 2002.

O'B = O'Brien, P. T. 1991. *The Epistle to the Philippians. A Commentary on the Greek Text.* NIGTC. Grand Rapids: Eerdmans.

Osiek, C. 1994. "Philippians," in *Searching the Scriptures,* Volume Two, A Feminist Commentary, ed. E. S. Fiorenza (New York: Crossroad) 237–49.

———. 2000. *Philippians, Philemon.* Abingdon NT Commentaries. Nashville: Abingdon.

Perkins, P. 1992. "Philippians," in *The Women's Bible Commentary,* ed. C. Newsom/S Ringe (Louisville: Westminster/John Knox) 343–45.

Pesch, R. 1985. *Paulus und seine Lieblingsgemeinde: Paulus—neu gesehen. Drei Briefe an die Heiligen von Philippi.* Freiburg: Herder.

Plummer, A. 1919. *A Commentary on St. Paul's Epistle to the Philippians.* London: Robert Scott.

(Ps.)-Oec. = attributed to Oecumenius, Bishop of Tricca, Thessaly, 10th cent. *Pauli Apostoli ad Philippenses Epistola,* PG 118:1255–1326.

Robertson, A. T. 1917. *Paul's Joy in Christ: Studies in Philippians.* New York: Fleming H. Revell.

Schenk, W. 1984. *Die Philipperbriefe des Paulus. Kommentar.* Stuttgart: W. Kohlhammer.

Schmauch, W. 1964. *Beiheft* to E. Lohmeyer, *Die Briefe an die Philipper.* . . . Göttingen: Vandenhoeck & Ruprecht.

Schmitz, O. 1922. *Aus der Welt eines Gefangenen: Eine Einführung in der Philipperbrief.* Die urchristliche Botschaft, 11. Berlin: Furche-Verlag, 5th ed. 1934.

Scott, E. F. 1955. "The Epistle to the Philippians," *The Interpreter's Bible* (New York/Nashville: Abingdon) 11:1–129.

Silva, M. 1988. *Philippians.* Wycliffe Exegetical Commentary. Chicago: Moody Press; repr., Baker Exegetical Commentary on the New Testament, Grand Rapids: Baker, 1993, 2nd ed. 2005.

Synge, F. C. 1951. *Philippians and Colossians.* London: SCM. 2nd ed. 1958.

Thdrt. = Theodoret of Cyrrhus (393–466). *Interpretatio in Epistolam ad Philippenses,* PG 82:557–90.

Theo. Mop. = Theodore of Mopsuestia (350–428). PG 66:921–26. *Theodori Episcopi mopsuesteni in Epistolas b. Pauli commentarii,* ed. H. B. Swete (Cambridge: Cambridge Univ. Press, 1880–82).

Thielman, F. 1995. *Philippians.* The NIV Application Commentary. Grand Rapids: Zondervan.

Thurston, B. B./J. M. Ryan. *Philippians and Philemon.* Sacra Pagina 10. Collegeville, MN: Liturgical Press, 2005.

Tillmann, F. 1917. "Der Philipperbrief," in *Die Gefangenschaftsbriefe des heili-*

gen Paulus. Die Heilige Schrift des Neuen Testaments, ed. H. Meiner/ F. Tillmann (Bonn: Hanstein, 4th ed. 1931) 7:121–62.

Vincent, M. R. 1897. *Critical and Exegetical Commentary on the Epistles to the Philippians and to Philemon.* ICC. Edinburgh: T&T Clark/New York: Scribner's, repr. 1922.

Walter, N. 1998. *Die Briefe an die Philipper, Thessalonischer* (E. Reinmuth) *und an Philemon* (P. Lampe), NTD 8/2 (Göttingen: Vandenhoeck & Ruprecht) 9–101.

Weiss, B. 1859. *Der Philipper-Brief ausgelegt und die Geschichte seiner Auslegung kritisch dargestellt.* Berlin: W. Hertz.

Wesley, John (1703–91). *Explanatory Notes upon the New Testament* (1818, often repr., New York: Carlton & Parter, 10th ed. 1856) 505–15.

Wette, W. M. L. de. 1843. *Kurze Erklärung der Briefe an die Colosser, an Philemon, an die Ephesier und Philipper.* Kurzgefasstes exegetisches Handbuch zum Neuen Testament 2/4 (Leipzig: Weidmann, 2nd ed. 1847) 173–231.

Wettstein, Johann Jakob (1693–1754). *Hē Kainē Diathēkē: Novum Testamentum graece* (Amsterdam: Dommer, 1751–52; repr., Graz, Austria, 1962) 2:262–80.

Wiesinger, J. C. A. 1850. *Die Briefe des Apostels Paulus an die Philipper, an Titus, Timotheus und Philemon.* Biblischer Commentar über sämmtliche Schriften des Neuen Testaments . . . , ed H. Olshausen/J. H. A. Ebrard/ A. Wiesinger, 5/1. Königsberg: Unzer. Tr. J. Fulton in Olshausen's *Biblical Commentary on St Paul's Epistles* (Edinburgh: T&T Clark, 1851; New York: Sheldon, Blakeman & Co., 1858) 5:1–143.

Witherington, Ben, III. 1994. *Friendship and Finances in Philippi: The Letter of Paul to the Philippians.* Valley Forge, PA: Trinity Press International.

Wohl. = Wohlenberg, G. P. Ewald's *Der Brief des Paulus an die Philipper ausgelegt,* rev. 3rd ed. 1917; 4th ed.1923.

Wuest, K. S. 1942. *Philippians in the Greek New Testament.* Grand Rapids: Eerdmans.

Select Introductions to the New Testament

Broer, I. 2001. *Einleitung in das Neue Testament. II. Die Briefliteratur.* . . . Würzburg: Echter.

Brown, R. E. 1997. *An Introduction to the New Testament.* New York: Doubleday.

Johnson. L. T. 1986. *The Writings of the New Testament: An Interpretation.* Philadelphia: Fortress. Rev. ed., with T. C. Penner, 1999.

Koester, H. 1982. *Introduction to the New Testament,* Vol. 2, *History and Literature of Early Christianity* (Philadelphia: Fortress/Berlin & New York: de Gruyter) 130–34.

Kümmel, W. G. 1975. *Introduction to the New Testament.* Rev. ed. tr. H. C. Kee. Nashville/New York: Abingdon. Ger. 1973.

Marxsen, W. 1968. *Introduction to the New Testament: An Approach to its Problems.* Philadelphia: Fortress. Ger. 1964.

Moffatt, J. 1921. *An Introduction to the New Testament.* New York: Scribner's.

Perrin-Duling = Perrin, N., *The New Testament: An Introduction,* 2nd ed., with D. C. Duling (New York: Harcourt Brace Jovanovich, 1982).

Schenke, H. M., K. M. Fischer. 1978. *Einleitung in die Schriften des Neuen Testaments. I. Die Briefe des Paulus.* . . . Gütersloh: Gütersloher Verlagshaus Gerd Mohn.

Schnelle, U. 2000. *Einleitung in das Neue Testament.* Göttingen: Vandenhoeck & Ruprecht, 4th ed.

TRANSLATION, NOTES, COMMENT, AND SECTIONAL BIBLIOGRAPHIES

◆

LETTER OPENING, 1:1–11

◆

1. *Prescript (Address, Salutation), 1:1–2*

TRANSLATION

1:1 Paul and Timothy, slaves of Christ Jesus,
  to all the saints in Christ Jesus who are in Philippi,
      together with overseers and agents;
  2 grace to you   and peace
    from God   our Father
    and Lord   Jesus Christ.

NOTES

1:1. *Paul.* First word in all 13 Pauline letters, + *apostolos* in 8 of them (chart in *WDNTECLR* 373). *Paulos* (Lat. *Paul[l]us*) in inscriptions, papyri, literary sources; Sergius Paulus, Acts 13:7. Romans generally used three names, *praenomen*, *nomen*, and *cognomen*, e.g., Lucius Aemilius Paullus. "Paul[l]us" was a well-known Lat. *cognomen* (BDAG 787; Balz, *EDNT* 3:59). Some see a "hypercoristic" or by-name (*supernomen* or *signum*; *BC* 4:145; G. H. R. Horsley, *ABD* 4:1011–17, B.1 and D.5): Saul, his "synagogue name," from birth; Paul, his name in the Gentile world. Harrer: Paul's father, a freed slave, took the *praenomen* and *nomen* of his former master plus his own slave name as *cognomen* ("Marcus Tullius Tiro," freedman and secretary of Marcus Tullius Cicero). Paul's letters never use "Saul," but he was of the tribe of Benjamin (Phil 3:6) and could have had the name of the tribe's greatest king as *signum*; cf. Cranfield *Rom.* 48–50, Fitzmyer *AB* 33:230–31. Jerome claims he had been born in Gischala in Galilee, but when the legions of Varus crushed a rebellion there ca. 4 B.C. the family was removed to Tarsus (*Comm. on Phlm* v. 23, re Phil 3:5, PL 26:617; *Vir. ill.* 5, PL 23:615). On his career, see COMMENT B.4.a; Chart 2, INTRO. VIII.

Timothy. Gk. "(one who) honors God," frequent from Aristoph. and Xen. on; LXX, 1 Macc 5:6–44, e.g.; inscriptions and papyri (BDAG 1006; MM 635). Co-sender, see COMMENT B.4.c; 2:19–22, highly praised, sent to Philippi till Paul can come (2:23–24). Schenk 272, Timothy is to help Euodia and Syntyche resolve their conflict; NOTE and COMMENT on 4:3. He is "our brother" (*ho adelphos,*

1 Thess 3:2, etc.). Ellis (1970–71:445–51 = 1978:13–22, cf. *DPL* 183–84) refers the term (esp. in the pl. and with the art.) to "a relatively limited group of *workers*, some of whom have the Christian mission and/or ministry as their primary occupation" (447 = 15), with a "structured, i.e. appointed role" (451 = 22). But the entire congregation is addressed as *adelphoi* (Phil 1:12; 3:1,13,17; 4:1,83; Ollrog 78 n 9). Timothy = "coworker" (Rom 16:21). Among the "apostles of Christ" (1 Thess 2:7), commissioned missionary-preachers, a group larger than "the twelve" (1 Cor 15:5, 7), more significant than "congregational apostles" like Epaphroditus (Phil 2:25). Cf. Kertelge 1972: 83–84, 95–96. But not an apostle like Paul (Ollrog, 22 n 78). Paul converted him (1 Cor 4:17, BDAG *teknon* 3.b; cf. Acts 14:5–7, 16:1; Schmithals, *RGG*³ 6:903); Ollrog 20–21, 67–68 thinks conversion came later; cf. Cohen, C. Bryan, Fitzmyer AB 31:574–575. A "troubleshooter" for Paul (1 Thess 3:1–6; 1 Cor 4:16–21). Some think "Paul had misgivings about his young colleague" (1 Cor 16:10–11); a "failure" in Corinth (Kee, *IDB* 4:650–51; below, [9] COMMENT B.1.a). But no indication that Timothy needed "rehabilitation" (Furnish, *2 Cor*, AB 32A:105). Claims: Timothy wrote Col, while Paul was imprisoned in Ephesus (Ollrog 219–33, 236–42); the "we"-sections in Acts or a diary behind these vv. Some correct traditions on him in the Pastorals (Quinn/Wacker, *1 and 2 Tim.*, ECC 581–83). Cf. Acts 16:1–3; 17:14–15; 18:5; 19:22; 20:4; 1, 2 Tim; Heb 13:23; Furnish, AB 32A:103–6; Kee, Trummer, Gillman. Later traditions (bishop of Ephesus, Eus. *HE* 3.4.5) in *The Oxford Dictionary of the Christian Church*, ed. F. L. Cross (London: Oxford University Press, 2nd ed., 1974) 1378.

slaves of Christ Jesus. Three Gk. words, "a semantic unity" (Schenk 77); gen. is subj. or possession ("belong to Christ"), but objective gen. cannot be excluded, "slaves for Christ Jesus."

Christ Jesus. "Jesus Christ" in some MSS (KJV; Silva 42). Sanday/Headlam (*Rom.* 5th ed. 1902, p. 3), only early letters (1 Thess, 2 Thess, Gal) had "Jesus Christ." Cerfaux, **Christ*** 501–5, 508: "Jesus Christ" = the man Jesus; "Christ Jesus," the preexistent one. By the time of Phil, (the) Christ, Christ Jesus, and Jesus Christ "all mean the same thing" (*TDNT* 9:553). W. Kramer, **Christ** 204–6, with statistics, "*Jesus Christ* in the nominative case, but in the oblique cases . . . *Christ Jesus*," for clarity (grecized Semitic names lack case endings). Here not "messiah."

slaves. Trs. tone down *doulos* to "servant" (*TLNT* 1:380); [N]RSV-mg, rightly, "slaves." Ownership of human beings existed throughout the ancient Near East, Israel, even Qumran (CD11:12, 12:10–11; I. Mendelsohn, *IBD* 4:383–91; W. Zimmerli, *IDBSup* 829–30); in Judaism (Str-B 4:698–744; H. H. Cohn, *EncJud* 14:1655–60; Flesher); the Greco-Roman world (*OCD*³ 1415–17; Barrow; Finley 1974, 1987; Callahan et al., eds., *Semeia* 83–84; Glancey 9–38, 99). Aristot.: a slave is "a living tool" (*Eth. Nic.* 8.11.6), property with a soul (*Pol.* 1253b32), a "thing" (Lat. *res*), under the master's control. At times, a "benevolent" institution

---

* Boldface as in Sectional Bibliography headings below on specific terms.

(Vogt; contrast Bradley). Ideology enters into many modern assessments (Finley 1980; O. Patterson).

The Christian movement included slave-owners (Philemon) and slaves (Onesimus), though not "the lowest menials," working in mines as near Philippi (Moule 1982:209). Perhaps a third of the people in Corinth were slaves, another third ex-slaves (J. Murphy-O'Connor, *1 Corinthians*, NT Message 10 [Wilmington: Glazier, 1979] xi). For terms involved, legal details, manumission practices, and early Christian attitudes, see Bartchy; *IDBSup* 830–32; Lyall 1970–71, 1984:27–46; Fitzmyer, *Phlm.* AB 34C:25–33; "social-world," literary approach to Onesimus, N. R. Petersen, **slaves,** esp. 93–102, 163–70, 206–15. Roman law sometimes ameliorated conditions. Stoics promoted egalitarianism. Only the Essenes launched "a programmatic denunciation of institutionalized slavery" (Philo, *Prob.* 79 = LCL *Philo* 9:56–57; *IDBSup* 831). But by and large slavery "was never really questioned in antiquity. . . . Almost no one, slaves included, thought to organize society any other way"; slaves sometimes had slaves (D. B. Martin 42, cf. 7 and 31).

In Paul, "slave(ry)" can describe the human condition prior to salvation (Gal 4:1–9, 24–25; 5:1; Rom 8:12–23) or Christian obedience (Rom 6:16–22; Gal 5:13; M. R. Harris 2001). A nonreligious use (BDAG *doulos* 1) is rare (1 Cor 7:21), as a contrast to "free person" (Gal 3:28; cf. 1 Cor 12:13) or "lord"/master (Col 3:22; 4:1; Sass). Gk. sources seldom spoke of slaves to some deity (D. B. Martin xv); "*doulos* . . . of a god is radically non-Greek," simultaneous freedom and bondage "unthinkable" (Conzelmann, *1 Cor.* 128 and n 32). *slaves of Christ Jesus* suggested to converts Oriental, ancient Near Eastern backgrounds (D. B. Martin 56). Explanations proposed for NT use include the following:

(1) The presence of slaves in Hellenistic-Roman life accounts for "servile imagery in the NT" (*IDBSup* 832). Cf. Hawth. 4–5; O'B 45; Bockmuehl 50; Harris 2001; Collange 36; Silva 40–41.

(2) Near Eastern praxis (Sass, summary in Best 1968:375; cf. K. C. Russell; *Semeia* 83–84:67–111): slaves to a king or deity (1 Sam 29:3; 2 Kgs 5:6; BDAG 2.b); in Israel *'ebed YHWH* (LXX *doulos*), for leaders like Moses, Joshua, David, the prophets (Amos 3:7; Jer 7:25), the *pais* or "servant (of the Lord)" (Isa 42:1), God's people (Isa 45:4), worshipers generally (Ps 34 [33]:22 , etc.). NT carryover for prophets (Rev 10:7), apostles (Acts 4:29), and "God-fearing people" (Luke 2:29; Rev 2:20); BDAG *doulos* 2.b.β; Gnilka 31. Is Paul then on the same level as all Christians? No, he does not apply *doulos* to all believers (Gnilka 30). Really a "concept of office" (Sass), its antonym Christ, meaning christologically derived (2:7); cf. 2:22; Schenk 77; DA 186–88 and n 125. Asserts "apostolic authority" (R. P. Martin 1976:60; cf. D. B. Martin 55–56), an honorific title of some significance (Sass; G. Barth 14; *EDNT* 1:352; Edart 46–47; Hooker, NIB 11:480, like Phil 2:11, not 2:7).

(3) "Biblical theology": all Christians = *douloi Christou* (TDNT 2:273–79; K. C. Russell; *NIDNTT* 3:596–97). Christ took the form of a *doulos* (Phil 2:7; John 13). His cross (Gal 3:13; 4:4–5) sets people free (1 Cor 7:23; Gal 5:1) but obligates them as *douloi* (1 Cor 7:22b; Rom 6:16b–19; 14:18), after a "change of masters," "slaves of the Slave Jesus Christ." One may (Sokolowski) or may not

(Bartchy 1973:121–25; Combes 84–87) invoke parallels in "sacred manumission," a practice at Greek temples (Deissmann, *LAE* 326–30; *Paul* 172–76; texts in Barrett 1957:52–53). A freed slave *(libertinus)* might have to perform certain services *(operae)* for his patron (Lyall 1984:43–45). Cf. Combes, Byron, below.

(4) Social-history lines: *doulos* = a *title of honor* (D. B. Martin; cf. Bartchy, *ABD*; Laub; *DA* 309). In a tiered hierarchy among slaves, "middle-level" *douloi* with managerial skills (as in Matthew's parables) could control property and achieve upward social mobility and status by association with the upper class in a patron–client system. "Slavery to *Christ*" brings status and a kind of derived authority (1–49). Paul was "Christ's managerial slave" (1 Cor 9:19–23). But contrast Fields 48–55; Rollins 1987. B. Dodd 148 (re Gal 1:1), "slave of Christ" was "a metaphor of power by affiliation with the most important person in the cosmos, much as a member of the *familia Caesaris* [cf. on Phil 4:22] might claim his or her unique social status as Caesar's slave." The *doulos* of Caesar has a stake in the Imperial household (M. J. Brown). *DA* 187 n 127, it implies power. A significant term for Philippi.

(5) Revisionist social history (O. Patterson, cf. Finley; Callahan et al. 1998, *Semeia* 83/84; Glancey 27–29, 114): Most NT treatments of slavery come from classicists who reflect "modern humanism"; they make the practice too benign. For most slaves, no "upward mobility" (cf. Meggitt, contra Weaver [(17) Bibl.], Meeks 1983). Not an appropriate figure for salvation (contra D. B. Martin); = "social death," maintained by "institutional violence" (Patterson), hand in hand with Empire, class structure, degradation, dehumanization, and humiliation (Horsley 1998a:38). Manumission (of old worn-out slaves) was "incentive for obedient servitude" (53). Horsley 1998b, Paul reflects a "counter-imperial mission" and "alternative society" (176). "Slave-like humiliation" in 2:6–11 "does not indicate that Paul thought of the status or role of believers as that of a slave of Christ" (171, contra N. Petersen, **slaves,** 240–42). Slave language in Paul is "overemphasized and inappropriately valorized" (175). Cf. Ascough 2003:122–23. At best, for Paul, "semi-titular . . . as a 'slave of Christ'" (176). Wire (*Semeia* 83/84) questions Pauline "opposition to Roman imperial structures" (288, 290); similarly Stowers (ibid. 302, cf. 308–10), "slaves of Christ" is a "plastic metaphor," used in many ways.

Combes 72–94 rejects (2) and (4), OT prophet and "manager slave," in favor of a metaphor for all Christians (cf. above [3] and in [5] Patterson). Bryon considers only OT-Jewish background (15–16). In Israel since the exodus all were "slaves of God" (in MT, only at Ezra 5:11; LXX Jonah 1:9 "*doulos kyriou* I am"). A pattern "sin-exile-return" is claimed in *Bar.* and *Par. Jer.* (*4 Bar.*), and "humiliation-obedience-exaltation" in Jdt (7:27; 8:23–27; 6:19, etc., 9:11), the pattern he sees in Phil 2:6–11 (see [7] Exc. B, II.D.10), in light of which Byron views Phil 1:1 and all slavery references in Gal, Rom, and 1 Cor. From Christ, "the paradigmatic slave of God," stems an "implicit call" to all Philippians "to act as slaves of Christ" (178); Paul and Timothy are so named specifically (1:1, cf. 2:2); "emblematic status" for association with Christ (263). But if OT, why only in letters to Roman cities? Derivation of 1:1 from *doulos* at 2:8 is questionable, evidence for the claims limited. Hellerman 117–21, Greco-Roman background, not OT. See further in COMMENT B.4.d below.

Jesus. (ho) Iēsous, Heb. Joshua ("Yahu is help, Yahweh saves"; *yĕhôsūa'*; after the exile, usually *yēšûa'*; AB 6:120); Joshua son of Nun and others in the OT (1 Sam 6:14,18; 2 Kgs 23:8), common among Jews until the 2nd cent. A.D. (Foerster, *TDNT* 3:285; K. H. Rengstorf, *NIDNTT* 2:331). Cf. Acts 7:45; Heb 4:8; Luke 3:29; Matt 27:16 (MSS; NRSV) "Jesus Barabbas"; Bar-Jesus (Acts 13:6); Jesus called Justus (Col 4:11). For Paul's readers, any etymological sense (Matt 1:21, Jesus "will *save* his people from their sins") was probably unknown. 22x in Phil; only at 2:10 without some added term like *Christos.*

Christ. Christos, from *chriein,* to anoint. LXX, for Heb. *māšîah,* "anointed one." In OT, of anointed kings and high priests; occasionally, prophets (1 Kgs 19:16), patriarchs (Ps 105:15); Cyrus as Yahweh's agent (Isa 45:1); cf. *TDNT* 9:497–509; S. Szikszai, *IDB* 1:138–39; E. Jenni, *IDB* 3:360–65; S. E. Johnson, *IDB* 1:562–71; K. H. Rengstorf, *NIDNTT* 3:335–37; M. de Jonge, *ABD* 4:777–81. Varied views in Judaism and Jesus' cautious reaction to the term (Mark 8:27–29 parr.; 14:61–62 parr.; *TDNT* 9:509–27, 537–40; *NIDNTT* 3:340–42; Hahn 1969:136–60; Fuller 1965:109–11) are background for (post-Easter) assertion, "Jesus is the Christ" (Acts 5:42; 9:5; 17:3; 18:5,28; 1 John 5:1; Mark 8:29). Gk.-speaking Jewish Christians employed *Christos* with OT backgrounds in mind, in faith statements ("*pistis*-formulas," W. Kramer, Christ) about Jesus' death and resurrection (e.g., 1 Cor 15:3–5), for mission proclamation and baptism. "Christ crucified" and risen was associated with the blessings of salvation. Believers belong to Christ, united "with Christ" and "in Christ" by baptism, in the "body of Christ" (1 Cor 12:12–13,27; Rom 6:3–11; Schreiber 2000:408–10), with implications for living in and conforming to Christ (Rom 15:2–3,7), while awaiting his parousia and judgment before Christ (2 Cor 5:10). Paul took over and deepened ideas about Christ (W. Kramer). 2 Cor 5:14–21 = a "summary of Paul's own theology" centered in Christ (*TDNT* 9:545). Phil abounds with "Christ statements."

Paul knew the Semitic background of *Christos* (2 Cor 1:21–22). Gentile converts might be taught some of the titular meaning as "messiah" (*TPTA* 197–99), but *Christ* was more a second personal name, Jesus' *cognomen* (Hahn 193; Bockmuehl 52, with bibl.; Hengel 1962:67–69, comparing *Caesar Augustus*), its meaning from proclamation about Christ (Hengel 1962:77).

to all the saints in Christ Jesus who are in Philippi. Indir. obj. of vb. (understood), "Paul and Timothy [write]" (cf. 3:1; Johanson 60); or, possibly, "[say] (*legousin,* cf. 3:18; 4:11; ATR 394) to all . . . in Philippi." Some paraphrase, "From Paul and Timothy . . . to . . ." (NEB/REB). A two-part description, "to all the saints *(tois hagiois)* in Christ Jesus,/ the ones-who-are *(tois ousin)* in Philippi." An *ekklēsia* (4:15). On house churches there, see COMMENT B.5.a. *Saints* occurs for addressees in 1 Cor, 2 Cor, and Rom.

all. BDAG *pas, pasa, pan* 1.b.β + art. + pl. noun = "all," in the sense of "every saint in Christ Jesus" (4:21). Unusual in Paul's prescripts (Rom 1:7; Col, Eph). Lft. 83 saw "studied repetition of the word 'all,'" 1:4, 7 ("you all" twice), 8,25; 2:17,26; 4:21, cf. 22 and 23 (MSS); *all* exhorts to unity. Hawth. 5, against "dissension in Philippi," disunity that Peterlin carried to extremes (Fee 66 n 41). Esp. characteristic of Letter B (cf. Gnilka 31).

the saints. hagiois (dat. pl.), "the holy ones" (NABRNT). Also at Phil 4:21, an *inclusio?* Lat. *sanctis* led to "saints" in KJV, [N]RSV. NEB/REB, GNB, "God's people." Adj. *hagios, -ia, -ion,* **dedicated or consecrated to the service of God** (BDAG 1). BDAG 2.d.β *believers, loyal followers, saints.* BDAG employs **boldface roman type** for word meanings, ***boldface italics*** for formal equivalents, as below s.v. 1:1 *agents.*

Oriental/OT background was more decisive for NT meaning. Heb. *qādôš* (LXX *hagios*), often cultic, "separation" (from what is impure), encounter with God's awesome power (Muilenberg; Seebass 224). Hence consecrated, sanctified persons (Num 6:1–5) and places (Ps 24:3[4]). God's holiness or "holy name" (Amos 2:7; 4:2; Lev 20:3; Ezek 36:20–23), Yahweh as "the Holy One (of Israel)" Isa 40–55, in contrast with what is human and creaturely (Hos 11:9; Isa 6:3). Lev 17–26, "You shall be holy, for I the Lord your God am holy" (Lev 19:2; 20:7; cf. 1 Pet 1:15–16; 2 Cor 6:14–7:1). Hence "a people holy to the Lord your God" (Deut 7:6; 14:2,21; 26:19), i.e., elect, separated from pagan practices (7:2–5; 14:1,21), a "holy nation," corporate, through covenant-relationship with Yahweh (Exod 19:6; Fee 64–65). For individuals as saints, cf. Dan 7:18,22; Wis 18:1,9; *Pss. Sol.* 8.34 (OTP 2:660, "the devout," *hosioi*); 9.6 (= 9.3b); 10.7 (= 10.6). In the Maccabean period, remembering and honoring holy persons of the past (*hăsîdîm*, the "pious"), esp. martyrs, grew (Fitzmyer 1991). Qumran spoke of God's "holy people" (1QM 14.12) and "the saints of his people." Angels = "holy ones" at Zech 14:5; Job 5:1 LXX; Deut 33:2; Ps 89:5,7; 1QM 6.6, etc.;1 Thess 3:13.

Paul used "holy" for Israel (Rom 11:16–24) and "saints" for the Jerusalem Christian community (1 Cor 16:1; 2 Cor 8:4; Rom 15:25–26), as well as his own congregations (1 Cor 1:2; 2 Cor 1:1; Phil 1:1) and other churches (Rom 1:7). Holiness grounded in Christ (1 Cor 1:30) led to the call (*klētoi*) "to be saints" (1 Cor 1:2; Rom 1:7), to lead godly lives (1 Thess 4:3–8), a holy living sacrifice of self to God for the neighbor daily (Rom 12:1; 15:16). The community, "churches of the saints" (1 Cor 14:33), "God's temple" where "God's Spirit dwells" (1 Cor 3:17; 2 Cor 6:16), is the sphere or zone of God's rule or lordship. Ollrog 136–38: holiness is needed in it (1 Cor 5), holiness through baptism and the Spirit (1 Cor 6:11). 1 Cor 1:2 (which Phil 1:1 echoes), "the church of God" = "those who are sanctified in Christ Jesus, those called (to be) saints," "individualisation" of the holy assembly of the OT (*klētē hagia,* Exod 12:16; Lev 23:2,4; Proksch 107). Asting 133–48 saw in Paul (1) a "theocratic-eschatological" concept of the church as people of God, heirs of Israel according to the promise, the "true circumcision" (Phil 3:3; cf. Rom 2:28–29; 9:24–31); and (2) a "mystical-ethical" aspect (be "holy and blameless" (Phil 2:15; Eph 1:4; 5:27). For *hagios* in Mediterranean culture, see Malina 1981:143–52; 1993 ed. 149–62.

in Christ Jesus. Double name again (see above on *Christ* and *Jesus*) in dat. + *en.* The phrase sets forth many aspects of Pauline theology but "utterly defies definite interpretation" (BDF #219[4]). No need to repeat the art. *tois* before *in Christ Jesus* (ATR 783); it is attrib. in effect, "the saints who are in Christ Jesus." Variations (data in N. T. Wright 1991:44–45; *TPTA* 396–98; Son 187–90) include in Phil: "in Christ Jesus," 1:1,26; 2:5; 3:3,14; 4:7,19,21; "in Christ," 1:13; 2:1; "in him," 3:9; "by Christ [Jesus]," 3:12; "in the Lord" *(en kyriō[i])*, 1:14; 3:1; 4:1,2,4,10; "in the Lord Jesus," 2:19; "in (with) the affection *(en splanchnois)* of Christ Jesus," 1:8; "in the name of Jesus," 2:10; cf. "in the One who strengthens me," 4:13. Cf. "with Christ" (1:23). Textual variants common (cf. 3:12). Phil has the "in Christ" theme 11 to 14x, plus "in the Lord (Jesus)" 7x, the highest concentration per page in any letter by Paul except for Phlm, exceeded in the Deutero-Paulines only by Eph.; tables in Deissmann 1892:1 and Bouttier 1962:24 n 2.

History of interpretation (Neugebauer 18–33; Bouttier 1962:5–22; Best 1955:8–19; *TPTA* 390–412; W. B. Barcley 5–19; C. Strecker 189–92):

(1) Deissmann 1892, *en Christō[i]* is a tech. formula (cf. Sanday/Headlam, *Rom.* 161; J. Stewart [INTRO. X Bibl.] 154–73). (a) Coined by Paul, 165x in his writings + Phil 4:13. Never "in Socrates"; "in Moses" (1 Cor 10:2) is "analogy to Christian phraseology" (AB 32:245). 2 Sam 19:44, "in David," corrupted Heb. text, expanded in the LXX (P. K. McCarter, Jr., *II Sam.*, AB 9:419). To trace "in Christ" to Jesus, Matt 18:20 ("two or three gathered together in [*eis* + acc.] my name") or John 15:14 ("abide in me"), is highly improbable. (b) "In Christ" connected Paul with a living person he met on Damascus road at conversion (sketched in Deissmann *St. Paul* 128–32). Paul's vbs., "be found in Christ" (Phil 3:9), "stand firm in" (4:1), "be confident in" (1:14), or "hope in" (2:19) (more in BDAG 328), are dynamic, not static. More controversially, (c) *en* has a local sense: "Christ" is the redeemed person's habitat, dwelling place, sphere, or atmosphere, the air the person breathes (J. Stewart [INTRO. X Bibl.] 157; Nock [(1) Bibl. **Paul**] 150). (d) To be "in Christ" = be "in the Spirit" (cf. 2 Cor 3:17). A mystical relationship, "Christ mysticism," "reacting" to what God has first done; leads to fellowship *(communio)*, not oneness *(unio)*, with God *(Paul* 147–54). A long influential view. Later a synthesis resulted: an ecclesiological sense for "in Christ" + "body-of-Christ"; then connection with baptism that puts a person *en Christō[i]* (Neugebauer 21–28). Catholic interpreters (Prat, Wikenhauser) welcomed Deissmann's Christ mysticism and the ecclesial-sacramental emphases; cf. Neugebauer 21–30; Bouttier 1962:8–10. For others, "Christ-mysticism" was pushed "much too far" (Fee 65; Son 23–25; cf. Fatehi 273).

(2) Schweitzer 1931: Jewish apocalyptic expectations, "solidarity of the elect to the Messiah" (Dan 7:27, *1 En.* 38:1–5; 62:7,8,14,15). To be "in Christ" ("eschatological mysticism") is to partake of God's reign, in the church, through baptism and the Lord's Supper, sufferings, and the Spirit—concluding with the parousia. Union now with Christ is sacramental and physical, the ethical side is devalued. Cf. Son 25–26.

(3) Neugebauer's salvation-history interpretation emphasized the event of Christ's cross and resurrection as determinative for those "in Christ" (his body, through baptism and the Spirit). An adverbial or adjectival phrase. Cf. Goppelt 1982 (INTRO. X Bibl.) 2:105–6; Son 26.

(4) Lohmeyer (1929:139–46; *Phil.* 133–38, esp. on 3:9, and 78 on 1:29), a "metaphysical" interpretation: "in Christ" contrasts with *en nomō[i]* ("under

Law"; cf. Phil 3:3–11). Not mystical but from eschatological revelation of God in Christ in time and history, a *Christusmetaphysik*, of "eschatology, martyrdom, knowing, and faith" (*Phil.* 135; 1929:145; Bouttier 1962:10–11; cf. Schmauch 66, 102, 135). Cf. Neugebauer 30–32; Bouttier 12; critique in Best 1955:30–32.

(5) Bultmann: *ecclesiological* ("body" of Christ = the church), *eschatological* ("the eschatological event has been inaugurated," 1956:197). Baptism brings one into the body of Christ as "a new creation" (2 Cor 5:17); "in Christ" interchanges with "in the Spirit" (1951:311). The believer's existence is realized in "walk" or conduct. Paul is "completely determined by the salvation-occurrence" of Jesus' death and resurrection (Phil 3:8–11). The life of faith, in Christ, thus becomes the new historical possibility.

(6) Büchsel's "'dynamic' conception" (Bouttier 1962:17–18) allowed *en* a variety of meanings: instrumental (Phil 1:1, Christ's lordship makes them "saints"), modal (Phil 3:9), or local. Believers are "en route," not at their goal (3:12–13); hence constant exhortations "in the Lord" (from the LXX? 1 Cor 1:31 = Jer 9:23–24). Others appeal to the Heb. prep. *bĕ*; Best 1955:32–33.

(7) T. Preiss: a "mystical-juridical" and eventually, from justification, an ethical side to life "in Christ," as in Phlm (Bouttier 1962:18–20).

(8) "Christ as a universal personality" (Oepke, *TDNT* 2:542), the second Adam (1 Cor 15:22, 45–49; Rom 5:12–21), makes *en Christō[i]* cosmic and eschatological. "Corporate personality" (in OT studies, H. Wheeler Robinson; repr., FBBS 11 [1964]; contrast G. M.Tucker, in 1980 repr. [Philadelphia: Fortress] 10–13) was applied by E. Best (1955:203–7, cf. 19–30); Christ "includes his community in himself." Best sought what Büchsel abandoned, a "unitary exegesis" for all 165 occurrences of *en Christō[i]*, "held together" by Christ "who in his own person gained the salvation of believers, and of whose personality they are members" (29). Cf. Son 27, 38, 75–79 178–86, "the corporate dimension of human existence." But note J. R. Porter, "The Legal Aspects of the Concept of 'Corporate Personality' in the Old Testament," *VT* 15 (1965) 361–80; J. W. Rogerson, "The Hebrew Conception of Corporate Personality: a Re-examination," *JTS* 21 (1970) 1–16, *ABD* 1:1156–57; cf. Wedderburn 1985:52 and n 52 on limitations; and S. E. Porter, "Two Myths: Corporate Personality and Language/Mentality Determinism," *SJT* 43 (1990) 289–307. Moule 1967:26–27 preferred "inclusive personality"; N. T. Wright 1991:46, "representative figure." Moule endorsed the distinction (Bouttier) that "in Christ (Jesus)" goes with the indic. for "the *fait accompli* of God's saving *work*"; "in the Lord," with the impvs. for human conduct.

(9) Bouttier: "in Christ" is an overarching phrase with a variety of references (contra Deissmann): (a) Jesus' historical ministry (1962:98–116), Phil 2:5–11; 1 Cor 15:35–55; Rom 5:12–21, the "heavenly Man," incarnation, etc., resurrection. (b) The living Lord's present ministry (122–33), mediator at God's right hand, presiding over the evangelization of the world through his body the church, via the Spirit. All Christians are "alive to God 'in Christ Jesus'" (Rom 6:11); Paul seeks to be found "in him" (Phil 3:9). (c) Future reference (116–22) to the consummation; "'in Christ' shall all be made alive" (1 Cor 15:22); Paul hopes to attain to the resurrection of the dead in Christ (Phil 3:9,11,20–21). "In Christ"

refers to what Jesus Christ has done, is doing, and will do for us. Not mystical but *heilsgeschichtlich*, ecclesiological, and eschatological. See further on 1:23 *with Christ* and, for his own summary, Bouttier 1966, esp. 32–52, 59–71, 118–19. Berger 1971 ([1] **Christ**) 403–8 saw OT roots (2 Sam 22:29–30); Wedderburn 1985, Gen 12:3, 18:18, Gal 3:8, picked up in Gal 3:14, "that *in Christ Jesus* the blessing of Abraham might come to the Gentiles." Barcley derives four categories from W. Grudem, *Systematic Theology: An Introduction to Biblical Doctrine* (Grand Rapids: Zondervan, 1994) 840–47, an overlap with "Christ in you" (a phrase not found in Phil).

(10) C. Strecker combines features of the mystical (Deissmann, Schweitzer) or "participatory" model (E. P. Sanders 1977 *PPJ*: 458–61), the ecclesiological (Bultmann), and the "heilsgeschichtlich-historisierende" (Neugebauer) in the "Christuscommunitas," anchored in the ritual of baptism (Gal 3:26–28; Rom. 6:11). Cf. Victor Turner (cultural anthropology) and "liminality," the transitional stage "betwixt and between" separation (from one group) and incorporation (into another group), via "rites of passage" and a communitas that is "antistructural" re the society out of which one comes (*ER* 12:382–86; "liminal" from the Lat. for "threshold," passing through a door). Cf. Meeks 1983:88–90; S. C. Barton, *DPL* 989–99. N. R. Petersen, **slaves,** 151–70, "if Turner had not created the concepts of structure and antistructure we would have had to invent them . . . to account for what we see in Paul's letters" (197 n 165). For Strecker's application to "the liminal theology of Paul" and his "initiation process" of transformation (83–157), see on 3:2–21; Christ's "transformation," under 2:6–11, is an "initiation into office." Baptism as rite of passage puts people "in Christ," into the Christuscommunitas, connected with Heilsgeschichte (Neugebauer, rightly). Societal barriers are transcended (Gal 3:26–28; Rom 12:4–5; 1 Cor 1:30; Gal 5:6); everyday thinking, feelings, and actions become part of a world wherein one lives "in Christ." Persons "transcend the individual self" and are linked together "into enduring and true forms of community" (E. M. Zuesse, *ER* 12:406). A. F. Segal **Paul** 262: "in Christ" represents Paul's "closest approximation of a definition of community."

No one view has carried the day or fits every passage. M. J. Harris (*NIDNTT* 3:1192) lists seven options. For 1:1 Bockmuehl 52–53 narrows it down to "corporate, modal, and instrumental"; cf. Seifrid, *DPL* 433–36. C. Strecker 152, "in Christ" is not a formula. Fatehi 274, in the sphere of Christ's lordship, living by the Spirit. See COMMENT B.5.a.

who are in Philippi. Art. + ptc. in attrib. position (dat. pl., modifying *the saints*) + prep. phrase *in Philippi.* Parallelism and, in the two phrases beginning with "in," possibly a contrast (cf. 3:20–21):

to all the saints	in Christ Jesus,
the ones-who-are	in Philippi.

On the ptc., lit. "being," see BAGD *eimi* I.2 ("live"), 3 ("reside") and III (with prep.) 4 (+ *en* + dat., of place); BDAG 4 and 3.a. Cf. in prescripts 1 Cor 1:2; 2 Cor 1:1; esp. Rom 1:7.

Philippi. Pl., like *Athēnai* (Athens) and *Thēbai* (Thebes). Renamed for Philip of Macedon (Diod. S. 16.3.7; 8.6). See INTRO. I.

together with overseers and agents. syn + dat. Two nouns, no art., "bishops and deacons" (KJV), "overseers and helpers" (NRSV-mg). B, D, both in a corrector's hand, etc., *synepiskopois,* "fellow-bishops" (with Paul and Timothy? O'B 43); BDAG 969, "'co-supervisor' . . . apparently an error"; Hooker, NIB 11:480, by a scribe worried about hierarchy. Cf. *PGL* 1323; Lft. 96 n 2. *syn-* has "no appropriate reference," "the letter is . . . for the whole community" (*TCGNT* 611).

together with. Associative; BDAG *syn* 1.a.γ; Grundmann, *"syn-meta,"* *TDNT* 7:770–71; M. J. Harris, *NIDNTT* 3:1206–7; "together with, including" (O'B 48; Fee 67; U. B Müller 34). Or *syn* "nearly equivalent to *kai,*" "and," as in "Peter with John" (Acts 3:4); BDAG *syn* 3.a.β; BDF #221, 1 Cor 1:2 (but cf. *DA* 191 n 142). Then "bishops and deacons" are a second entity in the church (Ewald 31), distinguished from "the saints" (E. Best 1968:374). Therefore Schenk 78–79, a later *gloss;* Walter 32–33, redaction 40 years later. Contrast Fee 66 n 43; U. B. Müller 34; *DA* 191. Skeat (*NovT* 37 [1995] 12–15 = Skeat's *Collected Biblical Writings,* ed. J. K. Elliott [Leiden: Brill, 2005] 258–60) measured the gap in P⁴⁶; difficult to decide whether *episkopois kai diakonois* were there; *DA* 190 n 137. Are leaders part of the local congregation or do they stand apart from the saints? To use "including" or "and" tilts the issue. *together with* allows both possibilities. See COMMENT. Edart 51–52, *syn* is a key term in Phil 1–2; 1:1, it values each group.

overseers and agents. episkopois kai diakonois, Lat. *episcopis et diaconibus,* long tr. in light of later "threefold ministry" as "bishops and deacons" (KJV, [N]RSV, NEB/REB). But "'bishop' is too technical and loaded with late historical baggage" (BDAG 379). So "overseers and ministers" (NABRNT); "superintendents and assistants" (Gdsp.); "church leaders and helpers" (GNB). Space limits preclude citing here much of the evidence; see *Philippian Studies.*

overseers. episkopos, skopein + prep. prefix *epi,* "look upon, inspect; . . . visit" (*TDNT* 2:600–601; LSJ 657). LXX, for Heb. *bāqar,* "inspect, look at, look after, take care of," and other vbs. Classical Gk., *episkopos* = (a) one who watches, hence protector or patron; (b) title for officers in government, voluntary associations, and societies (*TDNT* 2:608–14; *RAC* 2:394–99). For NT *episkopoi* many backgrounds have been proposed.

A. Most likely Gk. background: a "function or a fixed office of guardianship within a group" (BDAG *episkopos* 2; *TDNT* 2:611–14; *RAC* 2:394–99; *KlPauly* 2:323; Merkle 59–61).

1. State officials: (a) Supervisor(s) sent by a city-state to dependent cities to oversee agreements (*TDNT* 2:611–12). (b) A college of officials in independent cities (*TDNT* 2:611–14; *RAC* 2:395–96). Cf. U. B. Müller 34–35; Krentz 2003:360, military usage.

2. Officials in various societies exercising supervision and control (Ascough 2003: 80–81, 130–32, voluntary associations). Deissmann, "a technical sacral sense in pre-Christian times"; *TDNT* 2:612–13. Pilhofer 1:140–47 parallels *procuratores* in the organization of devotees of the "Thracian Rider" and *episkopoi* for Christian groups, both only in Philippi at this time (244).

3. Cynic-Stoic philosophers: Georgi 1986:29–31, 61–62 nn 16–20: a developing tradition where *episkopein* interprets the older *kataskopos*, "scout" (n 17; Epict., *Diss.* 1.24.6; 3.22.24–25, 38, 69, 77, 79, 97; Diog. Laert. 6.102); the closest parallel in the Greco-Roman world to the NT "apostle" (Rengstorf, *TDNT* 1:408–13). At Phil 1:1 both *episkopoi* and *diakonoi* refer to Cynic itinerants, "(missionary) proclaimers present or living in Philippi" (30, cf. n 18). G. Barth 16. See COMMENT B.5.b; NOTE on 1:15 *are proclaiming Christ*.

B. Some point to OT-Jewish backgrounds. Cf. Hawth. 8; O'B 47; "tenuous" (Bockmuehl 54).

1. LXX: *episkopos* 14x; Merkle 56–57. A Gk. mistranslation of Isa 60:17, "I will appoint Peace as your overseer *(pĕqudātēk)* and Righteousness as your taskmaster," appears in *1 Clem.* 42:5, "I shall establish their *episkopoi* in righteousness and their *diakonoi* in faith" (cf. *TDNT* 2:92). Slim grounds for NT *episkopos*. Greco-Roman use influenced Philo, Jos., and the LXX.

2. *Synagogue* (Farrer 142–70; Shepherd, *IDB* 1:442; *RAC* 2:399–400): *episkopos = ḥazzān* (Str-B 4/1:145–49; Sonne, *IBD* 4:489–90) or (Burtchaell 240–44, 306–12) *archisynagōgos*, community chief, a term perhaps borrowed from the Gk. guild (Schrage, *TDNT* 7:844–47).

3. *Damascus Document* (CD): Jeremias 1929 = 1969a, the Essene *mĕbaqqēr*, "supervisor" of a "camp," was model for the (etymologically equivalent) Christian *episkopos* (1969:259–62; *TDNT* 2:618–19; *IDB* 1:442; cf. Quinn/Wacker, *1, 2 Tim.* ECC, 267–71). Thiering 70–74, *mĕbaqqērîm* became *episkopoi* away from Jerusalem; a farfetched theory. Merkle 57–58.

Most likely background for *episkopoi* in Philippi: the Greco-Roman world, the ubiquitous overseer/supervisor in government, guilds or associations, possible Cynic influence. See COMMENT on 1:1.

agents. To tr. *diakonos* as "deacons" is often determined by later ecclesiastical polities. Under the influence of J. N. Collins 1990, *diakonos* is totally recast in BDAG 229: (1) **one who serves as an intermediary in a transaction**, *agent, intermediary, courier*; (2) **one who gets someth[ing] done, at the behest of a superior**, *assistant*. We place Gk. backgrounds for *diakonoi* into the setting Collins provided, thus modifying previous word studies. (His evidence must be weighed for pertinency, for passages long *after* Paul may be cited with earlier texts.)

A. General Gk. background: a "go-between" in commerce, civic life, or between gods and humans (Collins 87–88). (i) Courier with a message (cf. Hermes; Collins 90–92; 100–4; 152). (ii) Agents who transmit something or effect some deed. (iii) Attendants in a household, at table, on a staff. 2 Cor 6:4, Thuc. 1.133, Pollux 8.137–38 ("ambassador") are figurative (Collins 169).

1. *Diakonoi* = officials in Gk. guilds, societies, or religious associations (*TDNT* 2:91–92; Collins 1990 passim; Ascough 2003:82–83, 131–33).

2. The Cynic philosopher as *diakonos* of God. Georgi 1964a: opponents in 2 Cor 11:23 *(diakonoi Christou)* = Hellenistic Jewish Christian wonderworkers, cf. AB 32A:49–54, 502–5, opponents perhaps reflected in Phil 3. Cf. Gnilka 39.

B. OT-Jewish proposals—For Deut 16:18 (Lemaire 1971:99–103), see COMMENT B.5.b.

1. *LXX: diakonos* only 7x, all with a "secular sense." Less LXX background than for *episkopos* (Brandt 166–67 n 2).

2. *Levites* in the Jerusalem temple (*RAC* 2:903–4; Str-B 2:63–66; *NIDNTT* 3:33–34; R. Meyer, *TDNT* 4:239–41). For Levites in *1 Clem.* 42:5, see above, *overseers*, B.1. Unconvincing.

3. *Committees of seven* (*parnāsîm*, "shepherds, directors") for civil affairs in Jewish communities (Jeremias 1929). Caution is called for (Haenchen, *Acts* 263; Lüdemann 1989b:74–79; Fitzmyer, AB31: 345,349). Acts 6:1–6 does not use *diakonoi*.

4. *Synagogue: ḥazzān* (Gk. *hyperētēs*) (*RAC* 3:904–5; Hainz 1976:97–98). Burtchaell 246–49, 317–32: the synagogue "assistant to the community chief." Christian deacons are not likely taken over from the synagogue (Hainz 1976:98).

5. *Qumran origins* (Colson 1960 and 1962) appear less often than for *episkopoi*. Collins 44; *TRE* 8:623; Hainz 1976:98–102.

6. *The NT gospels*: Jesus = one who serves (Luke 22:26–27; Mark 10:43–45). Contrast Collins 245–52. No direct line to Phil.

Most likely background: the Gk. world; the Cynic preacher is closest analogy. *agent* (Collins) is the least tendentious rendering today. *episkopoi* and *diakonoi* do not appear together in any proposal above. Are they paired here for the first time?

and. kai could indicate hendiadys (BDF #442[16]), "overseer-agents," "*episkopoi* who serve." COMMENT B.5.b rejects Lemaire's attempt to apply hendiadys here.

1:2. *grace to you and peace. charis . . . kai eirēnē*, salutation in all Pauline letters. Outside the NT, only *1 En.* 5.7a and there uncertainly (Berger 1974:197–98, esp. n 32; Schnider/Stenger 26). "Mercy and peace" in *2 Bar.* 78.2 (APOT 2:521; OTP 1:648 "grace and peace"). To some "mercy and peace" suggest benedictions (cf. Gal 6:16) like *Shemonêh Esrê* 19, "Bestow peace (*šalôm*), happiness, and blessing, grace (*ḥēn*), and lovingkindness (*ḥesed*) and mercy (*raḥămîm*) upon us and upon all Israel, your people" (cf. H. D. Betz, *Gal.* 321–22; Martyn, AB 33A:566). Other (reconstructed, sometimes later) texts in Berger 1974:191 n 10, 197 n 31. Elephantine texts (Egypt, 5th cent. B.C.) seem too remote and inexact. On NT letter salutations and liturgical origins (Champion, Loh.), see COMMENT A and B.2. Meaning is affected by Paul's general use of "grace" and "peace" and that the two gifts are *from God our Father and Lord Jesus Christ*.

grace. Characteristic of Paul, even if an earlier formula (COMMENT A and B.6, below). *charis* sets the tone for all his letters. About two-thirds of 155 NT examples occur in the Pauline corpus (66x in acknowledged letters; Phil, only here, 1:7 a prayer, and 4:23 a benediction). Vb. *charizesthai*, 16 of 23 NT examples in the Pauline corpus, 10x in acknowledged letters; Phil 1:29, 2:9. *charisma*, "grace-gift," is not in Phil. The related *chairein/chara*, "rejoice/ joy," are frequent (see NOTES on 1:4 and 18; *sugchairein*, "rejoice with," 2:17, 18). Cf. *eucharisteō*, 1:3, "I give thanks," and *eucharistia*, 4:6, "thanksgiving." *TDNT* 9:359–415 groups *chara* and *charis* together; etymology, 360 n 3 and 373 n 1. Note substitution of *charis* for the infin. *chairein*, with which a Gk. letter normally began, "hail, greetings" (BDAG 1075, *chairō* 2.a and b; Acts 15:23; 23:26; Jas 1:1). An "imperatival infin.," or supply *legei*, "So-and-so [tells you] to rejoice," or *euchetai* "[prays] greeting to so-and-so." Cf. BDF #389, 480.5; Moule *IB* 126; *TDNT* 9:360 n 9 and 367. Though often connected with OT ḥesed ("lovingkindness"), *charis* in Paul is better viewed against "Greco-Roman *benefaction*" as backdrop, reciprocity its ethos, the *charites* (favors) of the gods, and esp. "the Augustan age of grace" (J. R. Harrison; earlier, Wetter, Spicq, deSilva 2000). Harrison connects *charis* with "covenant-grace" as a unilateral act of God (2003:100, cf. 113 n 80), but the point is compromised by "hellenistic reciprocity ideology" in Jos., Philo, and LXX (106–10, 128–33, 140–46).

Classical Gk. *charis* = "that which brings joy or delight," **graciousness, attractiveness, charm** (BDAG 1). "Favor" of the gods, in Eur. *Bacch.* 535; Aeschyl. *Ag.* 182, 581; Dio Chrys. 30.41; J. R. Harrison 2003:53–57, 184–90. Hence, benefits, love, leading to gratitude (*TLNT* 3:501–3). Moffatt 1931:29 saw "supernatural" grace in an inscription, "May *Charis* and Health watch over *(episkopoiē)*" (Ditt. *SIG*² no. 891 = *SIG*³ 1240; J. R. Harrison 2003:34). Reciprocity led to use of *charis* to express thanks to the gods (PPetr 1.292.2; cf. Rom 6:17; "*charis* . . . always begets *charis*," Soph. *Aj.* 522). It became a term for a ruler's favor (e.g., "of the deity Claudius"; the Caesars bestow divine *charis*, Wetter 15–19; Harrison 48–49, 61–62) and the gracious disposition (or *philanthrōpia*) of the ruler. Aristot. (*Rhet.* 2.7.2; Boers 1997:703), *charis* is "that according to which the one who has it is said to render favor to the one who needs it, not for something [in return], nor for the sake of the one who renders it, but for the sake of the other." Not esp. used in religion, but note favors *(charitas)* of God (Epict. 1.16.15); divine favor *(charis,* Lat. *gratia;* Stoic optimism). In the Hellenistic world, "power in a substantial sense" (cf. Wetter 40–46), streaming "down from the world above" (Conzelmann, *TDNT* 9:376; *Poimandres; Asclepius* Epilogue 41b; *Nag Hammadi Codices*, ed. J. M. Robinson 1988, VI.7.63.33–65.7), "Thanks *([ch]arin)* we render to thee, O Most High, . . . for by thy grace alone *(. . . monon chariti)* we have reached this light of knowledge." Cf. MM 684–85; Moffatt 1931:21–36, 52–55; *TDNT* 9:373–76; analogues, not sources, for the NT (cf. *ABD* 3:156–57). A "secular word . . . suited for . . . [Christian] theological meaning"; "its nuances made sense to new converts" (*TLNT* 3:500), esp. in the Augustan era (Harrison 2003).

OT: 190x in the LXX, only about 75 have a Heb. equivalent; ḥēn in 61 of these; ḥesed is usually rendered by the Gk. *eleos* or "mercy" (*NIDNTT* 2:116). Conzelmann (*TDNT* 9:391), "to refer to the OT ḥēn . . . does not help much in determining the sense in the NT," except in Luke (cf. 1:30; 2:40, 52). "Nor does ḥesed . . . help much, since it points us to *eleos*." Paul "never quotes a single phrase about 'grace' from the OT" (Moffatt 1931:39). Moffatt's "antecedents of grace" came more from Philo, the Hermetica, mystery religions, and "religious philosophy" like Stoicism (45–67), a "rich soil of grace-interest" between 150 B.C. and A.D. 150; God graciously befriends those who carry out the revealed divine will (69–70). On ḥēn/ḥesed see *TDNT* 9:376–87 (Zimmerli); *NIDNTT* 2:116–17; W. L. Holladay, *IDBSup* 375–77, supplementing Mitton, in *IDB*, who, not incorrectly, says little about OT backgrounds. Not, then, an OT-LXX "concept" that could be taken over into Christianity.

1:2 and 4:23 seem "a fresh form of greeting" and "a fresh conclusion to the Christian letter," (Moffatt 1931:137, 141–43), but see COMMENT A (preformed Christian material), epistolary forms shared with Christians of the day. Paul emphasized, "All is of grace, and grace is for all" (Moffatt 1931:131), a term prior even to faith (Doughty). Grace "abounds" (Rom 5:17, 20; Theobald; cf. Phil 1:9, 26), a free gift, from God, through Christ (2 Cor 13:14), in his becoming poor (2 Cor 8:9), expiation for our redemption/justification (Rom 3:24–25). Thus salvation by grace (Rom 5:15), in which we stand, possessing peace (Rom 5:1–3). It reigns "through justification, leading to eternal life" (Rom 5:21). Actualized in Paul's life and sufferings (Phil 1:7). Pauline *charis* can be presented topically (Mitton), as "event" (Bultmann 1951 [INTRO. X Bibl.] 288–92; *TPTA* #13.2; "the structure of the salvation event," Conzelmann, *TDNT* 9:394–96); or chronologically (Moffatt 1931:156–296): less explicit in "Macedonian letters" to Thessalonica and Philippi; more developed in Gal (cf. Burton, *Gal.* 423–24), Rom, 1–2 Cor (Boers 1997). Eastman studies passages showing "dependence on God" (10); for Phil (189–206), dependence + "human responsibility"; 1:2, 4:23 not treated. In Paul's apostleship (*charin kai apostolēn*, Rom 1:5, hendiadys; Rom 1:1, cf. Phil 3:4–14), Satake sees *charis* embodied; contrast Ollrog 176 n 67.

to you. Pl., *all the saints . . . in Philippi, together with overseers and agents.* The word order (no vb.) holds in all Pauline salutations: indir. obj. between "grace" and "peace," the two gifts.

peace. eirēnē, 26x in Paul's uncontested letters, 3x in Phil (4:7, 9, blessings or promises). Content usually said to be from the Heb. *šālôm* (Foerster, *TDNT* 2:411; Mitton, *IDB* 3:706; critique in Brandenburger 16). Paul's own usage as well as early Christian formulas of greeting and blessing like 1:2 must be considered.

Gk. *eirēnē* denoted absence of war, tranquility (Hom. *Il.* 2.797; OGI 763.12). One could "make peace" (Xen. *Cyr.* 3.2.12). Its blessings (Philemon of Syracuse, ca. 368–263 B.C.) = "marriages, festivals, kinsfolk, children, friends, wealth, health, grain, wine, pleasure" (*CAF* 2:496–97, frg. 71); quiet or rest, law and order, not strife or disturbance (*TLNT* 1:424–25), as in the NT: a God "not of confusion (*akatastasias*) but of peace" (1 Cor 14:33). Could involve an attitude of mind: "peace toward one another and kindliness (*philophrosynē*)" (Plat. *Leg.* 1.628c); "peace with all persons" (Epict. *Diss.* 4.5.24), esp. among Stoics, a gift from God. Epict., "the peace proclaimed not by Caesar but by God through reason," for "all things are full of peace" (3.13.12–13). Hence, *harmony* in society and self (BDAG 287, sense 1.b), but hardly what we call "peace within" (*TLNT* 1:426; that's *euthymia,* "feeling good," cf. AB 37A:329 on Jas 5:13).

In NT times, publicly the *pax Romana* or *pax Augusta,* pacification of the known world by Roman arms, imposition of Rome's law and culture, an economic "common market," Rome as "vicar of the gods" in a Golden Age (Wengst 1987:7–54), its architectural symbols the Ara Pacis (Rome 9 B.C., under Augustus) and Templum Pacis under the Flavian emperors in A.D. 75. Literary monuments: the *Index rerum a se gestarum* or "Things done" (*Res gestae*) by Augustus, surviving most completely in an inscription in Ancyra, Galatia (Monumentum Ancyranum; OCD[3] 1309; *pax* results from the *Victoria Augusta;* Brunt/Moore, INTRO. I Bibl.);

Virgil's Fourth Eclogue, about a Golden Age; orations like Aelius Aristides' *Eulogy of Rome*. Coins promoted universal peace and prosperity under Rome. Central themes: *Securitas, Salus, Concordia,* and *Libertas,* security, safety, concord, and freedom (Tellbe 2001:31, 202–3). Early Christians (Wengst) sometimes adapted to Caesar's rule (Luke-Acts, *1 Clem.*), sometimes resisted it (the Book of Revelation). Paul's stance is complex. "Our citizenship is in heaven" eschatologically (Phil 3:20; NOTES on *politeuma* and *sōtēr*). Paul and the Philippians suffer at the hands of government officials (1 Thess 2:2; Acts 16:23; 2 Cor 11:23, 25–26; 2 Cor 6:5; Phil 1:13,20,28). Nonetheless, be subject to the authorities (Rom 13:1–7, full of Hellenistic administrative language). Believers, at peace with God (Rom 5:1–5), are to "overcome evil with good" (1 Thess 5:15; Rom 12:17–21), though some (false prophets) claim there is already "peace and security" (1 Thess 5:3; versus Imperial Roman ideology, Wengst 1987:18–20, 76–79; Tellbe 2001:123–26; Popkes 854–55; Harrison 2002 [INTRO. I Bibl.] 86–87). Paul had "sorry experiences" with the *pax Romana* and benefits from it. *Eirēnē/pax* entered into Greco-Roman cult chiefly through the universal political peace brought by the Emperor and ultimately the gods *(pax deorum).*

The OT reflects a different world. *šālôm* is a gift of Israel's God (*TLNT* 1:426–38), well-being, often quite material (Judg 19:20; 2 Sam 18:28–29), health, prosperity (examples in Burton, *Gal.* 425; *NIDNTT* 2:777–78). OT references can be organized historically (*TDNT* 2:403–6, von Rad) or catalogued as "secular" or "religious" peace, re individuals or community (Good 705–6). Peace relates to the covenant (Josh 9:15; Isa 54:10; Ezek 37:26). Not "peace *with* God" but a blessing *from* God now and in the future.

Pertinent for 1:2 is *šālôm* in greetings (Gen 29:6; 2 Sam 20:9–10), a practice continued orally, in rabbinic writings (*šālôm 'ālêkā, TDNT* 2:408), and in letters. Early Christians translated this Jewish usage into Gk. (BDAG, *eirēnē* 2; *TDNT* 2:411 n 60). Aramaic letters, Fitzmyer 1974:214–15. Num 6:24–26, the Aaronic priestly benediction, is perhaps echoed (AB 33:228). The LXX does not use *eirēnē* for *šālôm* in greetings but Gk. idiom: Gen 29:6 *hygiainei;* "Is he well?" for *šālôm; TDNT* 2:408. Reed (*DA* 195–96), OT "well-being" is close to *hygiainein,* in the salutation reflected at 2 Macc 1:10, "Greetings and good health." For inscriptions, see Park 87–112, 183–84.

NT *eirēnē* (BDAG 287–88) = (1) **a state of concord, *peace, harmony*;** (2a) **a state of well-being,** Heb. *šālôm,* salutations fit here; (2b) (messianic) salvation. Foerster *(TDNT)* gives a "biblical theology approach"; Mitton *(IDB),* a primarily Pauline picture of peace as the "restored relationship" with God and, more debatable, "peace of mind" (see NOTE on Phil 4:7). To read all the OT and NT concepts of "peace" into Paul's salutations (O'B 51) is "illegitimate totality transfer" (*DA* 196 n 155). For a Pauline view re the peace Rome brought, see Wengst 72–89; Brandenburger provides early Christian concepts of peace in Paul's theology (51–60), then Pauline paraenesis on peace (61–65), with an apocalyptic frame of reference (cf. Isa 11:1–9; 2 Esdr 7–8; 2 *Bar.* 29 and 73; Rom 16:20; 14:17). "Cosmic peace" under Christ the Lord appears in hymns like Phil 2:6–11 and Col 1:15–20 (Brandenburger 17–32).

Paul combined apocalyptic hopes and the results of Christ's death in "justification" (Rom 3:21–4:25), resulting in peace with God (5:1–21; *TLNT* 1:432), access
to ongoing grace, boasting amid sufferings, endurance, character, and hope, plus
exhortations to peace (1 Cor 7:15;1 Cor 14:33; Rom 14:1–15:13). Paul could have
had such emphases in mind at Phil 1:1, known to the Philippians from Paul's oral
teaching, but *eirēnē* will appear in Phil only in formulas.

Schenk (*Phil.* 85–87) separates "peace" at 1:2 from "fashionable misuse of the
Jewish *šālôm*-greeting" and provides structural analysis of Rom 5:1–5: "access to
God" (Thüsing 1965:183–90), fellowship with God. Fee 71 n 62 sees (1) peace
with God, (2) within the believing community, and perhaps (3) inner peace (Walter 33 is doubtful, rightly). Final decision depends in part on origins of the salutation formula. See COMMENT on 1:2.

from God our Father and Lord Jesus Christ. Prep. *apo.* The source of *grace . . .
and peace* is God and Jesus Christ (mentioned for the third time in 1:1–2). Each is
identified by a title, to show which god and the authority of Jesus Christ as *Lord.*
kyrios, lord, is a key term, paralleling God in the Gk. word order, perhaps accounting for the shift from "Christ Jesus" (1:1 bis) to "Jesus Christ" (cf. 2:11). W. Kramer,
Christ 42b–e, pp. 151–54: Paul added reference to God and Christ, making *grace
and peace* specifically Christian; "our" *(hēmōn)* goes with "Lord" as well as "Father," omitted for stylistic reasons, to achieve structural balance, in Gk.,

charis hymin kai eirēnē   apo theou patros hēmōn   kai kyriou Iēsou Christou.

Not "unequivocal proof that Paul believed in the deity of Christ" (Silva 43); that
depends on vv like Rom 9:5 (see NRSV-txt and -mg; R. Brown 1965). Normal
Pauline usage is "from *(apo)* God" but "through *(dia)* Christ," God as source,
Jesus as mediator (W. Kramer 19a–f, pp. 84–90, esp. 19f, 4; Thüsing 164–237;
Schenk 87–88, *dia* omitted for style and structure). In salutations of all acknowl-
edged letters except 1 Thess.

God. theos, 24x in Phil (compare *Christos* 37x), 430x in the acknowledged letters (266x for "Christ"). Often overlooked, compared with Christology. Treatments may bring out only aspects like "wrath" or "the righteousness of God"
(Ridderbos, INTRO. X Bibl.) or a general NT composite (Stauffer *TDNT* 3; Moule
IDB 2; J. Schneider *NIDNTT* 2). Emphasis on "God" in Paul is rare (but see Althaus; L. Morris 1986a [INTRO. X Bibl.] 26–38; 1986b; *TPTA* 25–38); in summaries of Phil, infrequent (but see Hawthorne 1987 [INTRO. X Bibl.] 21–39).
Experience of God by Paul is often organized around categories from later theology. BDAG 451 itemizes *theos* with the art. (3.a, Phil 1:8) or without it (3.b, 1:11;
3:9); + gen. (3.c, to show relationship, "my God," 1:3, 4:19); + "father" (3.d, as
here, 2:11, and 4:20); or (3.e) + gen. to show what God brings about ("the God of
peace," 4:9).

Paul's view was shaped by Israel's experiences, faith, and Scriptures: God as
deliverer and presence, the holy and righteous One who elected and entered into
covenant with a people (Rom 9:4–5). The "living and true God" (1 Thess 1:9) is
judge, before whom all are accountable (Rom 2:2; 3:19; 14:10). "OT view of
God": Argyle 9–34; Anderson; Quell, *TDNT* 3:79–87; J. Schneider 67. Paul con-

tinued to confess the *shema* (Deut 6:4, expanded as in 1 Cor 8:6) and to recount stories about Abraham's faith, Moses' glory, and Israel's time in the wilderness (Rom 4, 2 Cor 3, and 1 Cor 10, respectively). Cf. Stauffer/K. G. Kuhn, *TDNT* 3:90–94, 96–100; J. Schneider, *NIDNTT* 2:71–72. Heb. *elohim* = *theos* in the LXX. God's name YHWH was avoided; 4 Macc used Gk. *theion*, "the divine," or "divine Providence" (*theia pronoia*, 4 Macc 17:22). God was regarded as transcendent, communicating with the world by angels, the word, wisdom, and spirit. Israel's traditional "One God" proved a "stone of stumbling" to the Hellenistic-Roman world (Amir). Qumran saw God as sovereign, who battles against enemies in the world (1QM 10.12; 11.1–3; Ringgren 47–67); new stress on divine grace and saving righteousness (Braun 2:166–72).

To *theos* Paul's hearers might bring backgrounds from Gk. religions, philosophy, Oriental or mystery cults, or Roman state religion—Zeus, Apollo, Athena; One who brings "order"; divinized human beings (Hom. *Il.* 5.440; 5.78); a divinized world ("all things are full of God," Thales; "the whole world is God's being," or body, Stoics said). Only Epicureans doubted one could know about god(s). To offer grace and salvation was the gods' primary function; they were to be properly thanked in doxologies. Hellenistic ruler cults used divine titles, an eastern practice that spread westward in the Roman Empire. Oriental religions filled the void for some. Greek and foreign gods readily fused; syncretism came easy. 1 Cor 8:6 and Rom 11:36 use Stoic phrases about God ("from whom, through whom, and to whom are all things"). Cf. Kleinknecht, *TDNT* 3:67–79; *NIDNTT* 2:85.

Christianity held that the God of the Heb. Scriptures had sent Jesus and, after the cross, raised him to exaltation, presaging the climax of all history. Jesus' proclamation of God's reign continued in Paul (1 Cor 6:9–10, 15:24,50; Rom 14:17), seen now in light of the Easter event. The God-concept was shaped by past heritage, new experiences, and hopes; theoultimate, even when speaking enthusiastically about Christ (Phil 2:11). God (Phil 2:9; 1:28) continues to work among the Philippians (2:13, 27). Doxology, giving glory to God for gifts (1:2), appears in 1:11; 2:11; and 4:20—the link = prayer, thanksgiving (1:3) and petition (1:9).

our father. patros (gen.) *hēmōn*, "father of us." Not "of us and of the Lord Jesus Christ"; *kyriou* depends on *from* (*apo* + gen.). All nouns, *God, father*, and *lord* (*Jesus Christ*), are anarthrous, as is characteristic of formularies; see *TDNT* 5:1006–7; BDF ##252, 254, 257(3).

father/parent (BDAG 6), of God, had a somewhat parallel development in ancient Near Eastern-Israelite and Greco-Roman thought. In both, "father language" for God arose out of a patriarchal society (*TDNT* 5:948–51, 959–65; *NIDNTT* 1:615–16, 617). Head of the family (*paterfamilias*), with supreme authority over wife, children, their spouses, and their children (*patria potestas*), part of the Roman legal structure and everyday life. For a city or empire, "father" went with "benefactor," "savior" or "preserver" (*sōtēr*, cf. 3:20), for a hero or (deified) ruler bringing peace and well-being (Cuss 63–67; Dion. Hal. *Ant. Rom.* 4.32.1; 10.46.8; Plut. *Cam.* 10.6). In Greece, Zeus was "father of gods and men" (*Od.* 1.28; *Il.* 1.544); Lat. *Juppiter* (= *Zeu pater*), father of heaven. Plato and the Stoics fused father as creator with ruler in a household as king (BDAG 6.a). Cf. "We are offspring of yours" (Cleanthes' *Hymn to Zeus*; Stob. *Ecl.* 1.25.3 = SVF 1.121.37); Aratus, *Phaenomena* 5 (Acts 17:28), "We too are his offspring." Epict. sounds almost Christian: Zeus "is the Father who cares for all"; Odysseus "thought of him as his own father and called on him and always looked to that one in everything he did" (3.24.16).

Invocation of God as Father was also common in Assyria, Babylonia, and Israel (*TDNT* 5:951, 965–66). The "father concept" was imported into Yahwehism (967), without notions that God begets the nation or individuals. OT references to God as father are therefore relatively rare (Burton, *Gal.* 384; *NIDNTT* 1:617): Deut 32:6 (creator); Isa 63:16, 64:8 (of the people); Mal 1:6, 2:10; or, of the king, 2 Sam 7:14; Ps 89:26. Rarely of individuals (Ps 68:5, so Burton), if at all (Hofius 617–18; 68:5 refers to Israel). Never in the OT for Yahweh's relationship with all humankind (ibid 617); Ps 103:13 refers to Israel. God's authority as father of Israel, in a filial relationship, with a trend toward greater universality (cf. Jer 3:19), was a "supreme insight of biblical faith" (Quell 971–74). Mystery cults used "father language" (Osiris, Mithras, *Hēlios* [the sun]). In Cybele cult, cries of "*Atte pappa*," "Attis, father!" Hermetic mysticism and gnosticism; cf. *TDNT* 5:953–54, 958–59; *Gos. Truth* 1.16.31–33. Use of "father" grew in Judaism too in this period, probably influenced by Gk. practice. Cf. *TDNT* 5:978–82; Burton, *Gal.* 384–85.

The gospel tradition was a factor in Christian use. One view: Jesus experienced God as "*abba*" and addressed God with this intimate, filial term, teaching his disciples to pray, "(Our) Father . . ." (Mark 14:36; Luke 11:2 par. Matt 6:9; G. Kittel, *TDNT* 1:5–6; Jeremias 1966, 1967; AB 28A: 898–903; Hawth. 11, Phil 1:2 echoes it). Paul's Gk.-speaking churches used Aramaic *abba* (Gal 4:6; Rom 8:15). Alternative view: from pagan use, as in the Cybele cult (above), into the Gk.-speaking church; retrojected onto Jesus' lips in the gospels. Cf. Conzelmann 1969 (INTRO. X Bibl.) 101–6; AB 27:590; Käsemann, *Rom.* 228. Likely the historical Jesus used "father," perhaps *abba*, of God, but he does not join with the disciples in saying "Our Father" (Matt 6:9 is how Jesus' disciples are to pray.) See *TDNT* 5:982–1003. The gospels use "Father" for God more than the epistles. Not related to Jesus as "Son" so often in the letters as in the gospels but rather with Christ as "Lord" (e.g., Phil 1:2; 2:11; Berger 1971 [(1) **Christ**] 422).

In Phil 1:2, not "Father of (our Lord) Jesus Christ" or "Father of the world or universe" (cf. Hawth. 22), but "Father of us" = those who believe (BDAG *patēr* 6.c.β). Paul's "Father concept" (lordship and the gift of grace [*TDNT* 5:1010–11]) is well borne out by Phil. 1:2, *grace and peace* come *from the Father*. 2:11, even Christ's lordship is to "the glory of God the Father," as is 4:20, a doxology to "our God and Father."

Lord Jesus Christ. As regularly, Paul's salutations (except 1 Thess) mention *Jesus Christ* with *God our Father* as source for *grace and peace* (Christ the mediator through whom such benefits come, Schenk). *God* and *Christ* are in parallel; the relationship is enhanced and clarified by *Lord* for Jesus, not God. Shift from "Christ Jesus" (twice in 1:1) to "Jesus Christ" may be stylistic. Perhaps for Gk. readers *cognomen* and *supernomen*. Not likely "messiah," although Paul could have instructed them that *Christos* was originally a title. See above on 1:1 *Christ* and *Jesus*.

Lord. kyrios, from the adj. "possessing power" (BDAG 576), hence "important, principal" (person), master or lord (*TDNT* 3:1041–42), "in control" over things or persons, in contrast to *doulos, diakonos* (Burton, *Gal.* 399–400). **owner** (BDAG 1; Matt 20:8; Gal 4:1), extended to God/gods, deified or earthly rulers, and eventually Jesus (BDAG 2). In Paul, Rom 14:8, 12, "we are the Lord's" ("owner, master"); 1 Cor 3:23, cf. 1 Cor 11:3. The term helps work out Christ's exaltation within the oneness of God. 1:2 involves traditions Paul inherited and his own experience "in Christ Jesus" (Hawth. 1987:52–59).

In the Gk. world, applied to gods and rulers: Zeus (Pindar, *Isthm.* 5.53); Isis and Sarapis, *kyria* and *kyrios* (CIG 4897a; *TDNT* 3:1052, additional examples 1051; *TLNT* 2:344–45). Foerster, *TDNT* 3:1048–49, differentiates Gk. and oriental views: Gk gods and humans are "organically related," destiny *(heimarmenē)* or fate *(moira)* are equal with Zeus or over him; "for Orientals the gods are lords of reality. Destiny is in their hands." Apart from *kyrios* + gen., "never used of gods or rulers prior to the 1st cent. B.C.," and then from "non-Greek usage" (Egypt, Syria; ibid. 1049–51). "Lord" for personal relationship to a deity appears esp. in prayers, thanksgivings, and vows. "Lordship cults," (deified) rulers, = an eastern practice spreading westward into the Roman Empire by the time of Augustus and Tiberius Caesar, encouraged from Nero on (ibid. 1054–55; INTRO. I; Cuss 53–63); in Lat., *dominus* (e.g., Stat. *Silv.* 4 praef. 27; 4.2.6), *dominus et deus* (Suet. *Dom.* 13.2). CIG 4923 (text repr. in *TDNT* 3:1056), "To Caesar, ruler of the sea and holding sway over boundless lands, Zeus, from Father Zeus, . . . [who] arose (as) great Savior Zeus." Cf. Acts 25:26, "our sovereign" (NRSV, Gk. *tō[i] kyriō[i]*; BDAG 2.b.β; *TLNT* 2:346; Wlosok). Christians faced martyrdom to combat this claim.

OT background: *'adôn*, LXX *kyrios*. The vowels from *'ădōnāy* (lit., "my lords") were read (6,156 times) with the tetragrammaton YHWH; YHWH entered into most LXX MSS (4th/5th cent. A.D.) as *kyrios*; but see below. For Yahweh (Exod 3:14; Deut 6:4), see *TDNT* 3:1062–81; *NIDNTT* 2:511–12; *IDB*, "Lord," "Jehovah," and "God, Names of" (2:409–11). Aramaic *mārê'*, like *'adôn* and *kyrios*, an epithet (*TDNT* 3:1053, citing Baudissin). In rabbinic use, divine reign over the universe, lord and judge over individuals (*TDNT* 3:1085).

In the gospels, Jesus is frequently addressed with the voc. *kyrie* (Aram. *mārê'*), "sir" (Mark 7:28; Luke 7:6 NEB; *EDNT* 2:329). After the resurrection, apostolic proclamation asserts that God has made Jesus "both Lord and Christ" (Acts 2:36); the risen Christ is addressed as lord (Acts 1:6; 7:59, 60; 22:19, in Paul's vision). John 20 reflects both "Sir" (v 15) and "the Lord" (v 18). Thereafter *kyrios* is widely applied to Jesus as perhaps the basic christological assertion: "Jesus is Lord" (1 Cor 12:3; Rom 10:9; cf. Phil 2:11).

Bousset (1913; Eng. tr. 1970:119–52): absolute use of *kyrios* for Jesus (no qualifiers, like "lord of heaven and earth") arose after Easter, in the Hellenistic church, specifically Antioch, by analogy with *kyrios* for gods and rulers in the eastern Mediterranean world. So (INTRO. X Bibl.) Bultmann 1951:51–52, 124–26, Conzelmann 1969:82–84, and others. Contrast G. Vos; Hurtado; *NIDNTT* 2:514–16,

C. Brown. The Achilles' heel of Bousset's theory was 1 Cor 16:22, the formula "Our Lord, come!" *in Aramaic* (*Marana tha* NRSV-mg). Cf. K. G. Kuhn, *TDNT* 4:466–72; K. Berger 1971 ([1] **Christ**) 413–22; G. Schneider, *EDNT* 2:385. Since Bousset's day, MSS from the Judean desert show absolute usage of "Lord" in Aramaic for God (Fitzmyer 1975, 1981b; *EDNT* 2:330). Thus origins at least in Jewish Christianity, reflected in 1 Cor 16:22. Fitzmyer: "the Palestinian Jewish community in Jerusalem," perhaps Caesarea (*NJBC* 82:53).

Some (see above) had traced *kyrios* to the LXX; use for the tetragrammaton YHWH led to application of OT passages about Yahweh to Jesus (Capes). Then Phil 2:11, Jesus Christ is *kyrios*, puts him on a par with Yahweh. But LXX MSS using *kyrios* are later ones copied by *Christian* scribes. Texts copied by *Jewish* scribes (PFuad 266; 8 Hev XIIgr) do not translate the tetragrammaton but insert it into the Gk. text in Aramaic "square" characters or paleo-Hebrew. Perhaps a Jew, reading in Gk., said or thought *kyrios* at that point, but evidence for that is lacking. Cf. *NIDNTT* 2:512; G. Howard, "The Tetragram and the New Testament," *JBL* 96 (1977) 63–83; AB 28:201; Fitzmyer 1981b:221; *EDNT* 2:330; *TPTA* 247–48.

Kyrios, therefore, came into early Christian usage not from the LXX, not by analogy to Greek cult, but from Jewish-Christian origins, from *mar* as "sir" to *mar/ kyrios* as lord. So also the "New Religionsgeschichtliche Schule" (Zeller 2001:315–24), though the Greco-Roman setting of Philippi plays a role in use of *kyrios*; see on 2:11b *Lord*. W. Kramer, **Christ**, ##15–23 finds in the Pauline corpus (*TPTA* 244 n 47 lists various combinations) three categories: (1) *Kyrios* used of God ("Tetragrammaton *kyrios*"), esp. in OT quotes (1 Cor 3:20; 2 Cor 3:16–18; not in Phil, unless 4:5 = Ps 145:18; see NOTE on 4:5 *The Lord is near*). (2) *Mare-Kyrios*, the Aramaic petition, 1 Cor 16:22, above (cf. Rev 22:20, Gk. example), for Jesus' future coming or as an invocation for presence (epiclesis) at the Lord's Supper. (3) Acclamation-*Kyrios*, Jesus (Christ) hailed as Lord, enthroned in heaven (Phil 2:11; 1 Cor 12:3), Hellenistic Gentile church. All three uses are pre-Pauline. Paul developed *kyrios*-language, in particular "in the Lord," usually with impvs. (list in *TLNT* 2:330), Phil 1:14; 2:19,24,29; 3:1; 4:1,2,4,10; a reflex of "in Christ (Jesus)" (see NOTE on 1:1 *in Christ Jesus*).

In Phil, some take 3:20 as part of a hymn, like 2:11; 4:23 as inherited liturgical benediction; 1:2, part of a salutation form. Only 3:8, "knowing Christ Jesus my lord," is clearly Paul's own composition. Thus he takes over but develops lordship language about Jesus, so as to speak "from tradition and from personal experience" (Hawth. 1987:53).

Charts on *Superscriptio* = Sender(s), Titles (*Intitulatio*), and Descriptions; *Adscriptio* = Addressee(s) with titles and further descriptions; and *Salutatio* = salutation, wish of blessings, are omitted here for reasons of space; summaries available in WDNTECLR, 373–76. See for 1:1–2, pp. 73–74.

COMMENT

Paul begins with a Christianized form of greetings common to ancient letters. The senders are briefly identified, those addressed described more fully (14 of 32 Gk. words, just 6 on the senders). A greeting follows, in 12 words, combining Greco-Roman and Semitic-Jewish elements, unmistakably Christian by the third reference in two vv to Jesus Christ. Structure and much phraseology are inherited, with little room for creativity.

A. FORMS, SOURCES, AND TRADITIONS

Letters of Paul's day shared a general structure (Stowers, Pardee, Dion; M. M. Mitchell 1998), developed in the Gk. world over the previous four cents. or so, with parallels in the ancient Near East. Knowledge of Gk. letters was greatly enhanced by discovery in Egypt, in the late 19th cent., of thousands of papyrus examples, especially private and business letters (J. L. White 1986, Stowers 1986 provide examples). Deissmann *LAE* and others popularized such nonliterary backgrounds for the NT, Paul's writings as real letters, not literary "epistles." By the 1970s form-critical analysis developed, for parts within the letter-form (Doty). "Friendship" came to be stressed; letters = communication of friends talking with each other; cf. Ign. Eph. 9.2; *ABD* 5:320. Stirewalt sees "official correspondence" as a greater influence on Paul than personal letters; this undercuts appeal to "personal friendship letters,"[1] but Paul is no authoritarian figure in Phil.

Paul's letters were to be read aloud to assembled recipients (1 Thess 5:27; cf. Col 4:16; oral aspects in Stirewalt 2003:5, 13–18). A form of "apostolic speech" (Berger 1974), involving rhetoric. Modern rhetorics, literary theory, and text-linguistics have been applied to them as "creative acts" in a "practical process of communication" (e.g., Johanson). 1:1–2 will be considered in the framework of ancient letters, which Paul took over but changed (Reed 2000).

Letters included a prescript, "body," and letter-closing (Doty; Johanson 59–67), with more agreement on letter-opening and closing (in Phil, 4:20 or 21 to 4:23) than on content in between. Lat. terms are often employed for the three parts of the opening: *superscriptio* ("Paul and Timothy, slaves of Christ Jesus"); *adscriptio* ("to all the saints in Christ Jesus who are in Philippi," to which a second *adscriptio* is added, "together with overseers and agents"); *salutatio* ("grace to you and peace from God our Father and Lord Jesus Christ"). Wording is relatively uniform in NT letters for senders and their titles or *intitulatio*; addressees with *intitulatio*; and

---

[1] Stirewalt 2003:81–84; 128–29; 46, 89–91: the apostle was an "official" in the "religious citizenry" of "councils" and "people" in his network of assemblies (29; 60 n 5; Welles No. 15). L. Hartman 2001:16–17 appeals to "official letters to a community," e.g., "Tiberius Caesar . . . to the overseers (*ephorois*, in Spartan cities, *epi + horaō*) and the city." (SEG vol. 11, 922; three other inscriptions; 2 Macc 1:10; Jos. *Ant.* 20.1.1). Unlike Phil 1:1, five of these six examples list officials first, then people. Hartman's limited data should be integrated into Stirewalt 2003.

salutatio or wish of blessings to recipients (Murphy-O'Connor 1995a:45–55; WDNTECLR 373–76; Lat. terms in Schnider/Stenger 5–6).

Paul had a set form. 1 Thess may be an initial formulation[2] subsequently expanded (Schrenk, *TDNT* 5:1007; Vielhauer 1975:65) or truncation of a longer original formula (Schenk 83; Johanson 60). Paul's creation (Koester 1979) or from predecessors? Champion, Loh., and others see, esp. in the salutation, "Grace and peace . . . ," liturgical usage Paul did not create. Senders had only to decide on description of themselves and the recipients, plus here *overseers and agents*.

In developing a discourse, Aristot. (*Rhet.* 3.13–19) and other rhetoricians referred first to *heuresis* (Lat. *inventio*), the "finding" of material.[3] For Phil 1:1–2, structure and about two-thirds of the wording were at hand in set formulas. Arrangement and style were the next steps.[4] For prescripts some appeal to Hellenistic royal and diplomatic correspondence (Welles), literary letters or epistles (Traede), rhetoricians and epistolary theorists (Malherbe 1977/1988), and later letters, as well as papyrus letters (Probst 56–105).

A Gk. nonliterary papyrus letter usually began "A (sender) to B (recipient), greeting *(chairein)*."[5] So Acts 23:26; Acts 15:23; Jas 1:1. It has been widely held (e.g., AB 34:71–75, esp. 71 and 73) that Paul substituted for *chairein* a similar-sounding word *charis*, "grace," and added the Jewish greeting, "peace (be) to you" (NOTES on 1:2 *grace* and *peace*); cf. DA 196. Cf. Num 6:24–25, "The Lord . . . be gracious to you . . . and give you peace."[6]

That Paul himself first combined *grace* and *peace* is dubious. They occur in letters not by Paul (*WDNTECLR* 376: 1 Pet, 2 Pet, Jude, Rev 1:4b–6); "mercy and peace" appears in Semitic sources.[7] The combination may be non- and pre-Pauline. There was also an "Oriental" form of salutation (Taatz), "A to B," + 2nd per., "rejoice(-ye)" or "health to you." E.g., Dan 4:1 (Aram. 3:31, Gk. *eirēnē hymin plēthuntheiē*). Fitzmyer 1974:214–16, nine examples in Aramaic letters besides Dan 4:1 and (NRSV) 6:25, plus "To B, *salôm*" (Ezra 4:17).

Loh. 1927c argued that Paul followed Oriental and Jewish forms, without

---

[2] No title for Paul, without "from God the Father and the Lord Jesus Christ" in 1:1c (correct WDNTECLR 376).

[3] On *heuresis/inventio*, see G. A. Kennedy 1984:14–23 and 1963:87–103; Lausberg #260; Watson 1988a:13–20; Heath, in Porter, ed., 1997:89–119; D. K. Williams 2002:84–85.

[4] Thuc. 2.60 and 8.68, *heuresis* and *lexis* or *elocutio* (expression, presentation) are the two parts of a speech. Aristot. added *taxis*, arrangement; Quint., *inventio*, then *dispositio* (*Inst.* 3.3.1ff.) or *oikonomia*; cf. D. K. Williams 2002:85–92. For orators "delivery" and "memory" entered in a way they do not for letters. Cf. Reumann 1958:348–61 = *EkT* 3 (1982) 115–24; Lausberg ##443–45 and ##453–1082. "Delivery" for a letter involves how its messenger (for Letter B, Epaphroditus?) or a local leader would read (and comment on) it for the house churches; cf. J. D. Harvey 1–34.

[5] Variations tabulated by C.-H. Kim 9–21; cf. Roller 46–91, the opening = "Protokoll" from Gk. for the first sheet of a papyrus roll (*proto* = first + *kollon, kollēma*, that is which "glued together"), the ending "Eschatokoll," last sheet.

[6] Cf. W. Schenk, *Der Segen im Neuen Testament* (see [2] Bibl. **Prayer Forms**) 80–84. Fitzmyer, *Rom.* AB 33:228, is iffy on the point.

[7] 2 *Bar.* 78.2; cf. the opening blessing in 1 Tim, 2 Tim, 2 John; see the NOTE on 1:2 *grace and peace*; Berger 1974: 199, esp. nn 9, 10; U. B. Müller 36.

deserting the Gk. prescript style: sender(s) with descriptive attributes, as in Oriental examples; a co-sender (contrast Roller 58–59, 99–102, 164–68); "grace and peace," liturgical character, which Friedrich 1956 rightly disputed. That nouns in 1:2 lack arts. can be explained in other ways (cf. BDF 259[1], "fixed prepositional phrases"). Paul transformed "mercy" (with "peace" in Jewish letters, *2 Bar.* 78.2) into "grace" (*charis,* echoing the sound of *chairein,* though Schenk 84 thinks this unlikely); Paul added "from God our Father and Lord Jesus Christ" (Friedrich 97; Vielhauer 1975:64–65). On "grace . . . peace" as Pauline, see Schenk 85–86, and below, B. 6, and NOTE on 1:2 *peace.* Hence the judgment, the Pauline prescript "is derived from the oriental epistolary formula, but has been developed further" (Conzelmann, *1 Cor.* 19). But "Hellenistic and even Pauline developments should not be overlooked" (H. D. Betz, *Gal.* 37; Heckel [(17) Bibl.] 281–88). *apo* ("from") is used by Paul to refer to the divine source of gifts; in secular Gk. letters the prep. *apo* (or *para*) is used, if at all, with the name of the human sender of the letter (Berger 1974:202). *charis* in Paul's formulation is not then simply a substitute for *chairein* but a blessing from God, as in Jewish texts and other Gattungen (Berger 1974: apocalypses, Rev 1:4b–5, 22:21; the "testament" form, Deut 33:1; *1 En* 1.1, "the [word of] blessing of Enoch"); "apostle and congregation" like "father and children" (1 Cor 4:14–15; Phil 2:22; cf. 3:17). *grace to you and peace,* like the report on Paul's thanksgiving prayers in 1:3–11, produces *captatio benevolentiae*—captation, appeal for, gaining of the hearers' good will. Cf. also Schnider/Stenger 3–4, 25–33.

Malherbe 1977/1988 drew attention to rhetorical treatments on letter-writing.[8] Betz's 1979 commentary on *Gal.*, reflecting Luther's awareness (via Cicero) of classical rhetoric in Paul's letter (p. 14 n 97), opened new vistas for seeing entire documents under a rhetorical *Gattung,* with rhetorical subsections. But rhetorical criticism is less convincing re the prescript.[9] The prescript has many similarities to letter-openings, few to the way an orator began an address. 1:1–2 = "epistolary praescript."[10] Paul writes *real letters* with *rhetorical features.*

In summary, Paul inherited from his Jewish and Gentile worlds the letter-opening formula "A (with description) to B (with description)," plus a greeting form. The Jewish "mercy and peace" became "grace and peace" at least by the time Paul wrote 1 Thess, and thereafter the significant phrase "from God the Father and Lord Jesus Christ" was regularly added. This Paul (and Timothy) now adapted to the situation in Philippi.

---

[8] Handbooks: *Typoi Epistolikoi* (21 types of letters, 3rd cent. B.C.–3rd cent. A.D.), *Epistolimaioi Characteres* (4th–6th cents. A.D.); treatises *On Style,* e.g., Demetrius (*De Elecutione*); discussions in the rhetorician Julius Victor (4th cent. A.D.), and a papyrus collection (PBononiensis I) of 11 sample letters in Lat. and Gk. (3rd–4th cents. A.D.).

[9] H. D. Betz viewed Gal 1:1–5 as an *epistolary* prescript, separable from the rhetorical letter. Others put the opening vv in a Pauline letter in the *exordium* (Gk. *prooimion*) that introduced the rhetor and his subject; Jewett 1986:72, 1 Thess; Hughes 51–52, 2 Thess; Watson 1988a:40–43, Jude 1–2 a "quasi-Exordium," 2 Pet 1:1–2 (95–96).

[10] D. F. Watson 1988b:65; Witherington; Black 1995; Bittasi 17–20. D. F. Watson 1997:409 shifted to *exordium*; D. K. Williams 2002:107, like an *exordium*; contrast Edart 44–45.

B. MEANING AND INTERPRETATION

1. *Methods, Ancient and Modern.* People look in commentaries for "meaning" and "interpretation." What did *Paul* mean? How have readers *interpreted* his meaning? From materials at hand (A, *heuresis*), we shall treat in COMMENT B arrangement and expression by Paul (see n 4 above; Murphy-O'Connor 1995a:72–73; Edart 37–41; WDNTECLR 62–64). In modern terms, the writing/editorial process *(Redaktionsgeschichte)*, the author as a creative, often theological, mind adapting materials to situation(s) addressed. For letters, more authorial responsibility is often involved than for NT gospels or Acts, not just stringing together inherited units (though this can occur, in paraenesis) or adding phrases here and there (Phil 2:8c, *on a cross*). The letter writer(s) seek(s) appropriate, persuasive words for matters at hand, in a laborious (and not inexpensive) process of writing things down to be read to others with whom they cannot personally be present.

Ancient rhetoricians spoke also of *stasis* (Lat. *status* or *constitutio*), a term apparently from Hermagoras of Temnos[11] about 150 B.C., how one "stands," posture, position; state or condition, status. "Stasis theory," on which there were many variations (Quint. 3.6.22), sought to articulate the basic question(s) (Gk. *hypothesis*) at issue, questions of fact, concerning persons, time, etc. *Stasis* shaped how one developed a case. Cf. Watson 1988a:11–13; Lausberg ##79–138, esp. 80, 96; 1246, French *situation*. G. A. Kennedy 33–38 makes *stasis*, the question(s) on which the matter turns, one of his steps for rhetorical methodology re NT texts today.

A letter was "one of the two sides of a dialogue" (Artemon, who edited the letters of Aristot.); it should be studied even more than a dialogue, for it is written (not just extemporaneous) utterance and "sent as a gift" to others (Demetrius, *Eloc.* 223–24; Malherbe 1977/1988:19). From rhetorical principles came Greco-Roman epistolary theory, with emphasis on the letter as "the heart's good wishes *(philophronēsis)*," as if the writer(s) were present, in appropriate language and style, adapted to circumstances and the mood of the addressees but reflecting also the character of the writer(s) (Malherbe 1977/1988:15–17, summarizing Gk. and Lat. rhetoricians and letter writers). Paul appropriates and modifies the *prescript* form (DA 181–97).

Under *Meaning and Interpretation*, we treat how Paul put together any source materials or traditions (e.g., from the OT), forms from his day or as form critics identify them, in light of concerns addressed *(stasis)* and his own theological stance. Therefore *heuresis* under COMMENT A; matters of style, in A or the NOTES; situation, arrangement, amplification, and (rhetorical) effect, generally under COMMENT B. Thus G. A. Kennedy's rhetorical criticism will be applied.

In terms of modern criticism, the NOTES treat textual, grammatical, philological, and many historical details, as well as word studies; COMMENT A, source and form criticism; COMMENT B, redaction, Paul's intention, how he wrote, and the

---

[11] See OCD³ 689; R. Volkmann, *Hermagoras, oder Elemente der Rhetorik* (Stettin: Th. von der Nahmer, 1865); PW 8:692–95; Reumann 1957:350–55 = *EkT* 3:117–19; WDNTECLR 213, 449.

place of the unit in the apostle's overall argument and thought. Lack of space eliminated treatment on *Nachwirkung*, subsequent "working" of the text over the centuries, beyond a few sentences at the end of B.

Paul writes to a specific audience, the house churches at Philippi, to move them to certain responses. Exegesis must pay some attention to those Paul addresses. We hear their views or words only indirectly. But to ask about Philippian reactions, a reading beyond Paul's own, is a first step toward subsequent interpretation. Space will not permit carrying through the model of communication proposed by Johanson.[12]

Hartman 1986 argued Paul's rhetorical care suggests he intended his letters "to be read and reread in the communities to which they were addressed, and in others as well" (136). Cf. INTRO. VII.B, Trobisch on Paul as redactor; a "Pauline school" that preserved and spread Paul's work (Berger 1974:215–16). Paul had "two intentions" re "what the text meant" or means: "specific occasion and, secondly, . . . more general meaning" (Hartman 145). We seek Paul's meaning and how he was possibly heard by the recipients (at points reheard and interpreted later).

2. *The Prescript and Purposes of the Letter(s) to Philippi.* The eight purposes for the four chs. of Phil (INTRO. III.B) can be related to one (or more) of the three letters (INTRO. VI.B) thus:

1. to express joy over the mutual relationship of Paul and the Philippians: Phil A (4:10–20), B (esp. 1:3–11, 18bc, 25–26; 2:2, 17–18, 28–30);
2. express thanks for gifts: Phil A (4:10–20) (and possibly B, 1:3–5, 7–8);
3. secure a welcome for Epaphroditus at Philippi: B (2:25–30);
4. warn against various "enemies": C (3:2–21) and possibly B (1:27–30, not 1:15–17);
5. urge unity in the house churches: B (esp. 1:27, 30; 2:2–4, 14–16) and C (3:15–17, 20–21);
6. help clarify ethical matters: B (1:27–2:5, 12–16) and C (3:10, 12–17); including the problem of suffering, stressed by Loh., Bloomquist, N. Keller, among others;
7. inform Philippians of Paul's situation: A (4:10–13, 17–19) and B (1:12–26, 30; 2:17, 19–30);
8. promote mission, progress of the gospel: A (4:14–17) and B (1:5–7, 12–18b, 25, 27–30).

None of these aims is alien to the prescript, but none is clearly indicated in 1:1–2.

3. *With Which Letter to Philippi Does the Prescript in 1:1–2 Go?* As the text stands, 1:1–2 is the prescript for all four chs. Each of the three letters to Philippi

---

[12] His three aspects, text-syntactic, text-semantic, and text-pragmatic, were applied by Schenk (cf. 13–28).

would have had a prescript. Pesch 1985 reconstructed one for each supposed letter. Usually 1:1–2 is related to our Letter B, chs. 1–2.[13] Fitzmyer, however, takes 1:1–2 with 4:10–20 (Letter A), assuming the "bishops and deacons" in 1:1 were leaders in gathering the gifts sent to Paul (4:10–20). Appeal to *in Christ Jesus* in 1:1 is indecisive; the phrase appears in all three letters, A at 4:10 and 19 and C at 3:3,9,12,14.

Prescripts for the three letters to Philippi would have been very similar (true for all Paul's letters). To B, as base, a redactor could have added the reference to "overseers and agents" (originally in A, re financial help; and/or in C, because of leaders' responsibility to oppose false teachers; Schmithals 1972:76–77 n 47). We shall treat 1:1–2 as reflecting the prescripts to all three letters, and as the opening for the entire redacted text. The *episkopoi*-and-*diakonoi* reference most likely went originally with Letter A (Marxsen, *Intro.* 61–62).

4. The Co-Senders. The two "main participants" are immediately mentioned (DA 386), Paul, then Timothy, but both on the same level, with the title *slaves of Christ Jesus* (Byrskog 246).

a. *Paul.* He likely dictates to an unnamed scribe or scribes who had access to him while he was imprisoned (so Letter B; cf. 1:7, 13–17; no evidence on a "secretary"; cf. E. R. Richards 1991: 189–90, 201). Death is an imminent possibility (1:20–24), yet Paul hopes he will be released and come to his beloved Philippians (1:25–26; 2:24). For Ephesus as place of imprisonment and 54–55 the date for writing the three letters to Philippi, see INTRO. VII.A. Paul was about fifty years of age when he wrote,[14] a Christian for over twenty years, a missionary most of that time, in charge now of his own mission team. He, Silvanus (Silas), and Timothy had evangelized in Philippi and Thessalonica shortly over five years before. Corinth was his base of operations A.D. 50–51, Ephesus from at least 53 till the time he writes (see Chart 2). He was an artisan (Hock 1980) and a Roman citizen ([3] COMMENT B.3.j, n 38).

---

[13] Michael, Friedrich, Gnilka, Doty, assuming two letters; Beare, Collange, G. Barth, Schenk, Pesch, Byrne, assuming three letters. Pesch 1985:59, 68, 95 prints 1:1–2 with Letter B, supplies the same wording for Letter C (including the reference to "bishops and deacons"); he appends the identical prescript, minus "and Timothy" and "with the bishops and deacons," to Letter A, thus an initial note of thanks from Paul alone to the Philippian congregation, with no reference to congregational leaders there, the reverse of Fitzmyer's position.

[14] If Jerome is correct that Paul was born before 4 B.C. (see NOTE on 1:1 *Paul*), or Jeremias ("War Paulus Witwer?" ZNW 25 [1926] 310–12 and 28 [1929] 321–23) that he was a rabbi (forty years old to be ordained) and so he was born 10 B.C. or earlier, then in A.D. 55 he was in his late fifties or mid-sixties. Ogg (1968 [INTRO. VII Bibl.] 1–10, 200, esp. 7 n 27) makes him younger (born between A.D. 5 and 14). If one combines Luedemann's "low" chronology (which dates Paul's career much earlier) with A.D. 10 for Paul's birth, the apostle would have been forty or younger when he wrote Phil during an Ephesian imprisonment (Luedemann 1984 [INTRO. VII Bibl.] 262–63). If Caesarea or Rome is the place of origin for Phil, Paul would have been three to six years older when he wrote. He was, we conclude, about fifty, vigorous, though scarred by missionary labors and persecution (2 Cor 11:24–27).

During the years at Ephesus,[15] Paul engaged in correspondence with Galatia and Corinth, as well as Philippi, and with Philemon in the nearby Lycus Valley. Only Romans, among his extant letters, lay ahead. His mind was on the collection project for Jerusalem, with its theological vision for church unity. Beyond that, a trip to Rome, proposed base for a proposed mission campaign in Spain (Rom 1:10–13; 15:15–29), perhaps inspired by experiences with Roman Philippi. In the Ephesian period Paul faced opposition—in Galatia, from Jewish Christians; Corinth was a hotbed of cliques and party spirit (1 Cor 1–4) and later the target of outside agitators (2 Cor 11). Onesimus, whom Paul had brought to faith in prison, had to be eased back to life with his master as now a "beloved brother," though still legally slave property. In Ephesus there were preachers who did not see eye to eye with Paul and selfishly proclaimed Christ so as to increase Paul's suffering (Phil 1:15–17). Hence, "daily pressure because of my anxieties for all the churches" (2 Cor 11:28). The Philippians were a bright spot. Contacts with them are called "the beginning of the gospel" (4:15), as if a new start had been made at Philippi in his work.

Theologically Paul had by this time integrated much from his Jewish, Gk., and Christian backgrounds, commitments, and environments. Proclamation about Jesus Christ, often involving inherited formulas, creedal slogans, and hymns from those "in Christ" before him, had become his own gospel. He had developed themes like righteousness/justification, reconciliation, and being "in Christ." Paul's understanding of the human situation in the world, under the Law, but in sin; the work of Christ, to redeem; the power of the Spirit; the role of the Law to point out sin and lead to Christ; the response of faith, and an ethic of God's will for holiness and for love toward one another had emerged through teaching, debate, and pastoral care. Particularly in the concurrent visits and letters to Corinth, Paul was forging his theology of "Christ crucified" (1 Cor 1:23). This he applied in new and growing ways to his own life and apostleship, "the weakness of the cross" as a lifestyle (D. A. Black 1984 [(9) Bibl.] 239; cf. J. Becker 1993 [INTRO. X Bibl.] 187–239; R. P. Martin, WBC 2 Cor. lix–lxi, *theologia crucis*). Not all these motifs will be heard in Phil; occasions do not call for them. The mature but embattled Paul of the Corinthian correspondence and the Letter to Galatia, the pastor who addressed Philemon, writes Phil. "Images" or "(self-)portraits" of Paul have been sketched from various angles.[16] He reveals much about himself in Phil 3. Cf. Hultgren 1991 on Paul's self-definition and his communities.

---

[15] Bibl. in VII.A, esp. Duncan 1929 and Thiessen 90–142, who places Phil during imprisonment in Ephesus; J. Becker 1993:151–85; W. Elliger, *Ephesos—Geschichte einer antiken Weltstadt*, Urban-TB 375 (Stuttgart: Kohlhammer, 1985) 137–48, esp. 144 (Phil was written in this period); R. Schnackenburg, "Ephesus: Entwicklung einer Gemeinde von Paulus zu Johannes," BZ 35 (1991): 41–64, esp. 34–49; Koester 1995, ed., 119–24, the place where "most of the Pauline correspondence originated," including Phil. On later conflict with Rome, see E. Faust, *Pax Christi et Pax Caesaris: Religionsgeschichtliche, traditionsgeschichtliche und sozialgeschichtliche Studien zum Epheserbrief*, NTOA 24 (Fribourg: Universitätsverlag/Göttingen: Vandenhoeck & Ruprecht, 1993).

[16] S. E. Porter, *The Paul of Acts*, WUNT 115 (Tübingen: Mohr Siebeck, 1999) = *Paul in Acts* (Peabody, MA: Hendrickson, 2001); M. Wiles; A. Lindemann 1979a; M. de Boer, "Images of Paul in the Post-

b. *Timothy.* As the co-sender, Timothy is the second most important individual in the letter. He and Silvanus had been with Paul on the missionary journey into Europe and set forth the gospel in Philippi,[17] where they were "shamefully treated" by the authorities (1 Thess 1:1; 2:2). They then evangelized in Thessalonica (1 Thess 1:5–6; 2:1,5–12). Later sent back by Paul to Thessalonica, evidently from Athens, to aid and exhort converts there (1 Thess 3:1–2). Himself converted by Paul (see NOTE on 1:1 *Timothy*), he shared in responsibility (Ollrog 22), not simply as "helper" like John Mark (Acts 13:5; Hadorn 70 inferred from Acts 16:3 and the order of names in 2 Cor 1:19 that Timothy began as an assistant but moved into the role of missionary). With Paul most of his known career, he never returned to his home area, Lystra (Acts 16:3; or possibly Derbe).

In Corinth, Timothy joined in sending 1 Thess (cf. 1:1); in Ephesus, he was involved as co-author or -sender of Phil, 2 Cor, and Phlm. The nature of Gal. and of Rom explains the absence of Timothy's name as sender (but cf. Rom 16:21, Timothy sends greetings). Lacking at 1 Cor 1:1 because he was already en route to Corinth ("when Timothy comes," RSV, not "if"; Furnish AB 32A:104–5). May have later visited Philippi with Paul on the way from Corinth to Jerusalem (20:3–6). Paul's praise and titles for Timothy are cited in the NOTE on 1:1 *Timothy.* In him "Paul found the co-missionary whom he . . . had sought in vain in Barnabas and Silvanus, . . . a Christian only of the second generation, . . . , not fully Jewish," but who became "the unique missionary partner of Paul" (Ollrog 22).

In Phil, Timothy looms large. Paul hopes to send him to the congregation until he himself can come; see on 2:19–24. Loh. (119–20) inferred that Timothy was "the chosen successor of the apostle," as Paul contemplated death (Ollrog 23). Timothy could be the "true yokefellow" of 4:3; see NOTES and COMMENT on 4:3.

c. *Co-Senders, not Co-Authors (The Problem of "We" and "I").* Does "we" include Timothy, or is it a pl. of majesty, just Paul (Bryskog 232)? At one extreme, Timothy as co-author (Zahn, *Intro.* 203, 209–11, passim; for Phil, 538–39). Or "subordinate *joint-writer*" (Meyer, *Phil.* 8). Or secretary or amanuensis who wrote what Paul dictated (Ewald 21–22, 30–31; Michaelis 9–10; Bruce 1; O'B 44; Fee 61, Timothy concurs). Or part of a Pauline "school" of wisdom (Ellis 1970–71:452 = 1978:22; *DPL* 188; *synergoi*; cf. E. R. Richards 1991:153–58). But no evidence Timothy was one of Paul's secretaries (Hawth. 3; Schenk 76, "sheer speculation"; the scribe's name in Rom 16:22 is at the end of the letter, not in the opening

---

Apostolic Period," *CBQ* 42 (1980) 359–80; G. Lohfink et al., *Paulus in den Neutestamentlichen Spätschriften* (QD 89, Freiburg: Herder, 1981); S. G. Wilson, "The Portrait of Paul in Acts and the Pastorals," *SBLSP* 1976:397–412; J. Roloff, "Die Paulus-Darstellung des Lukas: Ihre geschichtlichen Voraussetzungen und ihr theologisches Ziel," *EvT* 39 (1979) 510–31, tr. "Luke's Presentation of Paul," *TD* 29 (1981) 49–52; R. F. Collins, "The Image of Paul in the Pastorals," *LTP* 31 (1975) 147–73; P. Trummer, *Die Paulustradition der Pastoralbriefe* (BBET 8; Frankfurt: Lang, 1978); Col-Eph, M. Y. MacDonald 1988 ([1] **overseers**) 123–26; "the Paul of the Pastorals," 203–7; Gnostic views: *JAC* 22 (1979) 123–38. That in 1 Thess is esp. relevant; R. F. Collins, "Paul as Seen through His Own Eyes," *LS* 8 (1980–81) 348–81 = *Studies on the First Letter to the Thessalonians* (BETL 66; Leuven: Leuven Univ. Press/Peeters, 1984) 175–208.

[17] His involvement in Acts 16:12–40 has been inferred from 16:1–3, 17:14–15, and use of "we" in the narrative.

salutation). Or that Paul talked over the contents first with Timothy (Gnilka 29; Murphy-O'Connor 1995a:33–35) or introduced his name to show Timothy concurred with the censure that the letter will contain (Michael 2).

At the other extreme, "we" as a "literary pl." (Dick; BDF 280); Paul was simply courteous in mentioning Timothy (Caird 105; Bruce 1, "a gesture of friendship"; Bockmuehl 40, "to raise his status"; Walter 31). Hawth. 4, Paul teaches "the Philippians a lesson" about "humble equality" (Collange 36, who adds Paul is moving Timothy from an assistant's role to that of "his plenipotentiary"). Martin 1976:60, because of "his association with Paul in his imprisonment"; Silva 39, "a link that bonded the apostle with his Macedonian congregation" as "a corroborating witness of the truth he expounds." U. B. Müller 32, with Ollrog 36, "joint responsibility" for what Paul writes. Reed (*DA* 185), "Paul is 'portrayed' as the implied author, whether Timothy actually contributed to the letter writing process or not."

Inclusion of Timothy is not casual or condescending. Paul's salutations (except for Gal and Rom) normally have co-senders, reflecting the specific relationship between the Pauline missionary team and the local congregation (Craddock, 11, rightly), and the authority Timothy possesses as "co-worker for God" (1 Thess 3:2). Roller 153–87 provided detailed statistical analysis of Paul's use of "I" and "we" re co-senders. The co-sender's role receded in the face of the apostle's developing independence (174). By the time of Phil, Paul's role has become more prominent. Emphasis in Phil on Paul through use of an autobiographical 1st per. sg. and the paucity of "we" references to include his assistants or even co-sender with him are striking. Statistical analysis gives little comfort to Timothy as a real joint-author, though he was a highly involved colleague of Paul's with the Philippians and appropriate co-sender.

Bryskog was intrigued with Roller's theory of "development" (250), but critical of overstress on the independence of the "late Paul" based in part on "un-critical acceptance" (231) of the Pastorals (and Heb at times). Bryskog opts for Paul as the leader of a "school" (so H. Conzelmann, *NTS* 12 [1965–66] 231–44; cf. T. Schmeller, *Schulen im Neuen Testament? Zur Stellung des Urchristentums in der Bildungswelt seiner Zeit*, HBS 30 [Freiburg: Herder, 2001] 15–27, 92–182, no single model), associates with whom he worked things through. But Malherbe concludes (with Dick) for a literary pl. for 1 Thess, partly on the basis of some of Seneca's Epistles in Lat. (AB 32B:88). We conclude with Bryskog 247, Timothy is nowhere co-author for Phil; with Malherbe, one reason for including a co-sender was that Timothy had been involved in the founding mission. 1:1 is particularly appropriate for Letter B, where Timothy's imminent visit to Philippi is proposed (2:19–23). Stirewalt 2003:37–44 sees co-senders as "informed participants in the letter-event."

d. *The Co-Senders' Self-Description.* Paul and Timothy are *slaves of Christ Jesus,* using a term *(douloi)* common in the world of the day. *slaves* draws its meaning from their relation to their Lord, though some see humility in a counterpoise to apostleship (e.g., O'B 45; contrast Parkin); others, an emblem for all Christians (Byron). To be slaves of a deity hinted for Greeks at eastern origins of Christianity.

Given various theories about NT use of the term (see NOTE on 1:1 *slaves*), we conclude for more than reflection of the ubiquity of slaves in the Greco-Roman world, not *doulos* in biblical theology, but an understanding contextual to a Roman urban area like Philippi. It makes an assertion of authority.

slaves of Christ, here for Paul (cf. Rom 1: 1; Gal 1:10) and Timothy (cf. 2:22), is elsewhere used for followers of Jesus (Matt 21:34–36, etc.), but never in Paul for believers in general; church leaders (Luke 12:41–46; 17:7–10; Acts 16:17; 20:19; cf. AB 28A:989); God's servants (Rev 1:1, etc.) and prophets (10:7, etc.); and in other prescripts (Jas 1:1; 2 Pet 1:1; Jude 1; Titus 1:1). It likely reflects older practice (D. B. Martin 51–55; but not from Phil 2:8, as Byron claims).

With the phrase Paul asserts a particular authority. He is in the same class as OT leaders like Moses and prophets, slaves of Yahweh. He claims the authority of the Lord Jesus, as "slave *of Christ*." Cf. the Jewish principle re *apostolos*, "the one sent by a man is as the man himself" (*Ber.* 5.5; *TDNT* 1:415–16). Slaves as managerial agents in the Greco-Roman world had the authority of the upper-class person whom they represented.[18] Cf. D. B. Martin, 56–59, "patronal structure" (contrast [3] COMMENT B.1, n 11, below). "Slave of Christ" could be a symbol of salvation itself. "The Lord ransoms the lives of his slaves" (Ps 34:22 = 33:23 LXX); they look to God for deliverance (Ps 143 [LXX 142]:12; 122:2 LXX). Paul finds power by association with his lord, whose tattoo or brandmark he bore (Gal 6:17, possibly scars from persecution). To call himself a slave means solidarity with other such slaves, but also reflects the hierarchy among slaves of the day. Power came from appointment by, and association with, an overlord. People sometimes voluntarily continued or even entered into slavery, to link them to powerful people (D. B. Martin 48). Deissmann was correct, even if analogy to sacred manumission decrees at Delphi was inexact: when purchased (*ēgorasthete*) by Christ for freedom at a price, you belong to Christ (1 Cor 7:23; cf. Gal 5:1,13; Martin 63, 65, xix).

Though a free person in terms of social status, Paul had become "a slave to all" (1 Cor 9:19), in service to his converts. As "slave of Christ," he has higher status than the slaves of anyone else; he possesses a commission (to preach the gospel 9:17). "Paul sees himself as a free man, working voluntarily, with apostolic authority," under "the sort of compulsion and necessity that is laid on an *oikonomos*, one who fills the steward's role in a Greek household—an office usually held by a slave" (Reumann 1966–67:159). In teaching without payment and working with his own hands, Paul did something shocking to the upper classes in Greco-Roman society but readily acceptable to persons of low estate (D. B. Martin 117–35), attracting both groups.[19] Is *slaves of Christ* at 1:1 an attempt to prod the Philippians with a model of humility? Many think so, but this contrasts with D. B. Martin's stress on the "authority" aspect of the term. Using *douloi*, omitting *apostolos*, and

---

[18] Cf. Alexander Pope's couplet for the collar of the Prince of Wales' dog, "I am his Highness' dog at Kew; Pray tell me, sir, whose dog are you?"

[19] Martin 130–31 would tie this christologically to the downward/upward movement of Jesus as first *doulos*, then *kyrios* in Phil 2:6–11. But in Philippi there seems to have been no social conflict involving "strong" and "weak" Christians (Rom 14; Corinth). Paul's manual labor is not at issue in Philippi, and the Philippians have been supporting his mission work.

addressing the *episkopoi* and *diakonoi* all model a "reversal of Roman honor practices" (Hellerman 162).

All in all, remembering the cautions in *Semeia* 83/84 (NOTE on *slaves* [5]), one may see here a set formula for himself as leader that Paul employs elsewhere, perhaps implying "staunch financial independence" (Meggitt 77 n 11, not paid by someone else, dependent on God; cf. Phil 4:11–13). Whatever else *douloi Christou* conveyed to the Philippians, it could, for Paul, be a title of authority. Being a slave, *if* it was "of *Christ Jesus*," was a status symbol, showing Paul's "social network (i.e., to whom he belongs)" (*DA* 188). Apostles are *slaves of Christ Jesus* in a particular sense as proclaimers of the gospel (2:22).[20]

5. *The Addressees in Philippian House Churches*.[21] Paul usually addressed "the church," at Thessalonica, Corinth, or "churches of Galatia." At 4:15 he speaks of the Philippian believers as a church. 1:1 provides rich theological identity, *to all the saints in Christ Jesus*, and geographical identity, *who are in Philippi*. Plus a secondary group of addressees, *together with overseers and agents*,[22] a group of leaders or officials. Co-senders and addressees are brought together by dual references to Christ Jesus, the former as Christ's slaves, the latter as "holy ones in Christ Jesus."

a. *All the Saints in Christ Jesus*. The community is described in its totality *(all)*, status and identity *(in Christ Jesus)*, and nature, composed of *saints* (the "group identifier," *DA* 185). Despite the absence of the word "church" in 1:1, Phil is nonetheless a source for Pauline ecclesiology.[23] Some call Phil "less official . . . than Galatians, Corinthians, or even 1 Thess"; it is directed to "every single member of the community personally . . . and yet . . . a letter to all as a community" (Schnider/Stenger 15,18, cf. 20). See NOTE on 1:1 *all*. Repeated use of "all" and "each" throughout chs. 1–2 and 4:21–22 (Letter B) can suggest need for unity, "all together" (Peterlin), but also that considerable ecclesio-social cohesion exists.

Paul's chief term of address is "the holy ones" (pass. sense, "sanctified by God," U. B. Müller 33). See NOTE on *the saints* for OT background and corporate sense, later applied to individuals within the people of God; God as holy leads to holiness through Christ, extended to those called, justified, baptized, and sanctified (Rom 8:28–30; 1 Cor 6:11), "who have been and are sanctified in Christ Jesus,

---

[20] Schnider/Stenger 10, citing Michei, *Rom.* (KEK 4, 1978) 65–66, Rom 1:1–5, as structured by Schnider/Stenger 13. The *intitulatio* in Phil does not include the term "prisoner" *(desmios)* for Paul, as in Phlm 1, though 1:7–2:24 will refer to Paul's imprisonment. Not need at 1:1, his audience knew of his captivity. Paul was a prisoner at the writing of Letter B, not A or C; an editor could have dropped the term as not pertinent to the redacted totality.

[21] Brief papyrus letters usually had just the recipient's name (Deissmann, *LAE* 154, 162, 164; Kim, 11; White 1986: ##1–4, 5–26 to Zenon, etc.).; sometimes a further description (Deissmann, *LAE* 151; J. L. White 1978. esp. 291).

[22] Papyrus letters might include several addressees (cf. Deissmann, *LAE* 151; White ##56, 88; #33). 1 Cor, 2 Cor, and Phlm have a second *adscriptio*. Stirewalt 2003:44–46 finds multiple recipients more characteristic of official than of personal letters, to "people" and "council" (60 n 5); above, n 1.

[23] Cf. R. F. Collins 1984 (above, n 16) 285–98, "The Church of the Thessalonians" on the basis of 1 Thess.

called to be saints" (1 Cor 1:2; G. Barth 14–15). "Theocratic" (because holiness comes from God), "eschatological" (in the "last times"); here not "mystical" or an "ethical" call (impvs. follow in 2:14–15; 4:8–9; cf. Asting, in NOTE). Paul and other Christians think of each other as "saints" (4:21–22), but he never uses it in direct address, like *adelphoi* or "beloved."

Use of *hagioi* for "the saints" in Jerusalem (1 Cor 16:10; 2 Cor 8:4; 9:1,12; Rom 15:25–26, 31) suggests a pre-Pauline, Jewish background (Schenk 69; Schnider/ Stenger 15; cf. Acts 9:13, 32,41; 26:10) and continuity with Israel in the Jerusalem community to which Paul links his churches in ecclesial solidarity (prescripts to Corinth and Rome, God's "dedicated people," AB 33:239). "Saints" (holy ones, sanctified, consecrated, set apart) denotes a communal relationship with God through Christ and the Spirit; cf. 1 Cor 1:2; Rom 15:16, "the community of the Christ who is risen and present" as "the Spirit"[24] or simply God's people. The sg. at Phil 4:21 has a corporate context.

The other identifying phrase is *in Christ Jesus*. In Paul, frequently at the end of a sentence or construction, with rhetorical weight, esp. in a prescript re the church (W. Kramer, **Christ**, #36a, p. 141; 36g, p. 145; nn 505, 510). See NOTE on this theme in its several forms, so prominent for Phil and Pauline theology. None of the 10 proposals for interpreting *en Christō[i]* fits every passage. As a comprehensive reference to the ministry of Jesus culminating in the cross, his present risen lordship, and future parousia, "in Christ Jesus" serves as an umbrella for other phrases like "with Christ" (1:23).

In 1:1, the first and obvious way to take the phrase is with the preceding words, "to (the) saints (who are) in Christ Jesus." Instrumental or causal dat. (Büchsel), it tells how those in Philippi came to be "saints," namely, "by (the work of) Jesus Christ"; cf. Neugebauer 1957–58:131. Further, that they are now "holy" by Christ's sustaining them, and where they exist as holy people, namely, in union with Christ, in the sphere of his reign and power, spatially. Ecclesial, not individualistic. Christ Jesus provides the basis for their relation to God, "glue" for their connections with each other, the sphere for their life and endeavors together, and in Philippi the locale that distinguishes them from others as "Christ's saints." A shorthand expression of identity for the community of those being saved and their belonging to it (C. Strecker 206), it is ecclesiological and spatial. Who Christ is and what Christ has done (as in 2:6–11) will be brought out later as basis for the community (2:1–5). Thus the view of the church is "christologized."

The Christian community in Philippi, as elsewhere, consisted of several *house churches*. The Jewish synagogue, Gk. philosophical schools, and voluntary associations in Hellenistic cities[25] have all been considered as backgrounds for Pauline congregations; Meeks 1983:84 concluded for the household as "basic

---

[24] Cf. Schenk 69, 75, 89 on the circumlocution.

[25] Ascough 2003:10, 114, 160–61, features of religious voluntary associations (*ABD* 1:117); 3–13 on history of research; 20–24, not burial associations, less likely professional associations for Philippi (*thiasai, collegia*, guilds are difficult to distinguish); 110–61, Philippi. J. Harrison, "Paul's House Churches and Cultic Associations," *RTR* 58 (1999) 31–47, charismatic, not cultic, in Corinth.

context"; cf. Klauck 1981; Reumann 1998b, among others. See INTRO. II n 2 on *oikos* assemblies in the households of Lydia and the jailer (Acts 16:15 and 34–35). Till mid-2nd cent., most Christians met in private houses, with little or no building-renovation for religions needs; thereafter, some examples appear of re-modeling (Dura-Europos) and eventually new construction; in the Constantin-ian age, massive building operations (in Philippi, Basilicas A and B; Bakirtzis/Koester; *ABD* 5:316–17). Cf. Klauck 1981:77–81; Murphy-O'Connor 1983; Branick 1989:38–42; L. M. White 1990, 1992 ([16] Bibl.); *OEANE* 3:118–21; Krautheimer; G. Snyder 1985. Not "house tenements" in Rome, nor villas like those in Pompeii, but much humbler buildings, without atrium setting for a eu-charistic liturgy (from Hippolytus).[26] The notion (Affanasieff) of "one church, one Eucharist" in a city is dubious (Malherbe 1983:101 n 30; Meeks 1983:221 n 7; Reumann 1998b:114–15). Christians in Corinth or Philippi may at times have all assembled together (1 Cor 14:23, "the whole *ekklēsia*," "into one place" KJV), not just for a communion service but "service of the word" activities listed in 1 Cor 14:26 (W. Bauer 1930), to discipline someone (1 Cor 5:4), or hear a letter from Paul. But each house church likely carried out every type of ecclesial activity (Klauck 1981:35–39; Branick 97–116; Reumann 1998b:111–12). They "net-worked" (Branick 22), perhaps through periodic meetings of patrons, *episkopoi*, or a council of leaders. Assemblies in homes permitted worship and fellowship apart from temples (in Jerusalem or pagan ones in Philippi) or synagogues and empha-sized the family unit (Filson) and with it the *paterfamilias* and patron–client struc-tures of the day, so that the early church was not entirely "a poor man's organization." Multiplicity of house churches helps explain tendencies "to party strife" (empha-sized in Philippi by Peterlin; Reumann 1998b:112–14). House churches provided leadership from household leaders and could offer hospitality. Cf. Banks 1980/1994; Doohan; M. Y. MacDonald, "institutionalization" of the "community-building" type. Christianity's ability to attract Imperial freedmen and slaves (in Philippi, see 4:22) brought people with organizing skills into the community (Kyrtatas).

How many house churches there were in Philippi and environs relates to the size of the total Christian community there (see INTRO. I) and of each house church.[27] Two noted above rest on Acts 16. Epaphroditus, Euodia, Syntyche, Clement, and perhaps the "loyal companion" in Phil 4:2–3 may have each headed house churches. Size of each? Guesses range from 10 to 50 (Banks 1980:34–42;

---

[26] G. Dix, *The Shape of the Liturgy* (London: Dacre Press, 1941, 2nd ed. 1945) 19–35; rev. ed. (New York: Seabury, 1982), where P. V. Marshall pp. 766–77 modifies Dix's claims; Dix's ground plan of a Roman villa (1945) has been removed, under R. Krautheimer's influence, *Early Christian and Byzan-tine Architecture* (Baltimore: Pelican, 1975).

[27] For Rome, P. Lampe ([17] NOTE on *Extend greetings*) finds five groups in Rom 16:5, 10, 11, 14, 15 and conjectures two more circles, plus those around Paul, Acts 28:30–31. Jewett 2007:61–70, four of the five "tenement churches" were without patrons and reflected "agapaic communalism." For Thes-salonica, Malherbe speaks of "a number of house churches, each consisting of not more than a couple of dozen members" (AB 32B:344–45; cf. 63). For Philippi, Peterlin 125–26; Portefaix 137 (over 100 members); P. Oakes 2001:177; Tellbe 2001:224 n 63 (between 30 and 100).

Murphy-O'Connor 1983:156–58); Klauck (1981:100–1), 10–30 for effective group interaction. Peterlin 169–70 conjectures four, up to 30 people each; de Vos 261 n 103 supposes 33 as total if "Clement, Lydia, Epaphroditus, Syntyche, Euodia and the gaoler all had 'average' size families [spouse, two children]." 1:2 greets such house churches They provide the setting in which to view *episkopoi* and *diakonoi*.

b. *Leaders in the Philippian Community*. No other Pauline *adscriptio*[28] lists a second group as co-addressees. To some, *syn episkopois kai diakonois* seems a later addition (Schenk 78–82, Schneider/Stenger 23), though no MS or ancient version lacks the words (O'B 50 n 25). At issue: can such organization have developed in a church of Paul's by A.D. 55 or so?

No, if read as later threefold ministry, bishop, presbyters, and deacons. Phil 1:1 has *episkopoi* (pl.) and *diakonoi*, but no *presbyteroi* (true in all Pauline letters except the Pastorals, where *presbyteroi* = the same group of ministerial leaders for which *episkopos* is used, Merkle). To tr. "bishops and deacons" concedes too much to later developments.

Yes, in the text's historical-societal environment. NOTES outline backgrounds proposed for each term. Those from the OT and Judaism are not convincing for Greco-Roman Philippi. For *episkopoi*, examples exist for state officials of varying sorts (A[1]) and officers in guilds and societies (A[2]); for *diakonoi*, (A[1]); for both, Cynic itinerant preachers (A[3] and A[2], respectively) comparable to Christian missionaries. The titles were widespread in the Greco-Roman world for persons with responsibilities in government, social, or religious groups (cf. Hainz 1976:84–102), like "director," "manager," "assistant," or "agent" today, but no clear area of responsibility is discernible from the words themselves. Perhaps an *ad hoc* pairing here. Georgi's interpretation of Cynic texts comes closest to uniting them (*overseers* A[3], *agents* A[2], but contrast Collins).

Some (Hainz 1972:20–28, Hainz 1976:91–107) take *episkopois kai diakonois* as a hendiadys, "'bishops' who serve"; see NOTE on 1:1 *and*. Lemaire 96–103, 186 explored the phrase (as part of the letter frg. now in Phil 3) in light of *Didache* 15.1 and *1 Clement*.[29] Hendiadys is possible grammatically, the connotations for "bishops" post-Vatican II attractive, but the appeal to Syrian origins[30] for an institution

---

[28] There is no real analogy in 1 Cor 1:2 (*syn* refers to Christians elsewhere) or Phlm 1-2 (two persons and a house church appended to the individual addressed).

[29] *Did.* 15.1: "Elect (*cheirotonēsate*) for yourselves therefore *episkopous kai diakonous* . . . for you the ministry (*leitourgian*) of the prophets and teachers." 1 *Clem.* 42.1,2,4–5: "The apostles . . . appointed (*kathistanon*) their first fruits . . . as *episkopous kai diakonous* of those who were going to believe. . . . Scripture somewhere says [cf. Isa 60:17 LXX], 'I shall establish (*katastēsō*) their *episkopous* in righteousness and their *diakonous* in faith.'" 1 *Clem.* 43.1; 44.1 and 4, contention over *episkopē* that "our apostles" knew would arise. Herm. *Vis.* 3.5.1, "the apostles and *episkopoi* and teachers and *diakonoi* who . . . oversee (*episkopēsantes*) and teach and serve (*diakonēsantes*)"; Schweizer 1961:18c (p. 159) sees the last three as real "officers" in contrast to "apostles" in this passage.

[30] For Lemaire, *episkopoi kai diakonoi* recalled Deut 16:18, "You shall appoint judges and officials (LXX *kritas kai grammatoeisagōgeis*) . . . , in all your towns," responsible for justice. From Exod 18:13–27, Deut 19:9–18 (on judges), and Num 11:16 ("elders of the people and officers," LXX *presbyteroi tou laou kai grammateis*), the conclusion was drawn that "elders" (*presbyteroi*) and "judges and officials"

in Philippi dubious. *episkopoi* and *diakonoi* occur in three documents of scattered origins, but closer examination makes the theory questionable (O'B 48 n 21; Fee 66 n 43; U. B. Müller 36 n 16).[31]

On methods and conclusions below, see Reumann 1993a:446–50 and 1993b. Such references as exist in Paul's letters to local leaders[32] show *no uniformity* but instead an *ad hoc* development. Leadership structures developed in each congregation, not from a blueprint Paul brought from Antioch (let alone Jerusalem), but locally, from people with certain talents and abilities and gifts of grace and the Spirit (cf. Brockhaus; Dunn 1990:#29.1; G. Barth 15).

Variety in congregations and lack of uniform officials in Paul's letters refute any notion he imposed a plan for church organization on converts. So do the apostle's imminent eschatology, the vivid manifestations of the Spirit in Corinth, and opposition in Galatia (Paul must defend his apostolic authority; structures of local leadership are not an issue). He cared little more for congregational organization than he did for baptizing (cf. 1 Cor 1:17). There were baptisms, but Paul did not do them all himself or impose a standard model for ministering.

Likely, *the Philippians themselves developed for their church the leadership of episkopoi kai diakonoi* ("a local idiosyncrasy," Campenhausen 1969:69). Terms came from Greco-Roman civic and societal life. Roman officials would view Christian groups in Philippi like clubs or guilds. Paul, when he wrote, may not have known precisely what these local officials did. After the three letters to Philippi were combined, perhaps the sense shifted toward a later, more formal view of "bishops and deacons" (Pesch 1985:120).

Best 1968 argued Paul quotes the phrase from a Philippian letter to him. Paul rebukes their overstress on "office" by omitting his own title of "apostle" and substituting *doulos* to teach humble service (cf. 2:1–11).[33] This "first case of the desire

---

are parallel expressions for community authorities. Rabbinic references led Lemaire (98 n 84) to posit a tradition in Syria based on Deut 16:18 to justify a tribunal in each village. Hence the recommendation in *Did.* (of Syrian provenance) for *episkopoi kai diakonoi*. These vague Gk. terms are taken to designate, like *presbyteroi*, those responsible for a local church, "presbyters" among Jewish Christians, *episkopoi-kai-diakonoi* in Gentile congregations. In Philippi, local leaders (Lemaire 99), among them, Epaphroditus, "Clement and . . . my co-workers" in 4:3. Lemaire compared the Syriac tr. of Phil 1:1 (cf. Lft. 97 n 2), and Chrysost. (*Hom. in Phil.* 1.1 = PG 62:183 = LNPF 13:184): "the presbyters used to be called, of old, '*episkopoi kai diakonoi* of Christ,' and the *episkopoi* 'presbyters'"; cf. also Thdrt. on 1 Tim 3:8 (PG 82:803–804). Cf. Collange 41. Hawth. 9–10 adds Pol. *Phil.* 5:2–3, *tois presbyterois kai diakonois* (hendiadys) = "presbyters-who-serve."

[31] A major problem is the jump from judicial authorities in a Jewish community (to judge cases? apply Torah?) to authorities (esp. for finances and preaching?) in a Greco-Roman Christian missionary community.

[32] Thess, *proïstamenoi* (5:12, "those who labor among you and care for you and admonish you," AB 32B: 310–11, not "have charge of you," NRSV); cf. Rom 12:8, "the leader" (*ho proïstamenos*). 1 Cor, re spiritual or grace-gifts, "apostles, prophets, teachers" and then various functions, including "forms of leadership" (NRSV 12:28 *kybernēseis*). Gal 6:6, a teacher supported by those taught. Phlm depicts a house church; Phil, *episkopoi + diakonoi*.

[33] For Best the sg. at 4:21, "Greet every saint," raises the question for each person "whether he belongs to the category 'saint' or not—for Paul everyone does but do the bishops and deacons count themselves differently?"

for ecclesiastical position" Paul corrects with "a little mild irony" (375–76). Best's oversubtle, combative view is not readily apparent in the letter (cf. Ollrog 184 n 108; Edart 51). The *episkopoi* (and *diakonoi*) are not villains; growth of the church led to the need for such offices (Portefaix 137).

We cannot determine what each group of Philippian leaders did.[34] They were part of the congregation, "saints" too ("inclusive" sense for *syn;* see NOTE on 1:1 *together with overseers and agents*). Women could have been included (particularly if a *prostatis*, "patron, benefactor," Rom 16:2; Schüssler Fiorenza 1983:176–84; but BDAG 885, "not to be confused w[ith] the Rom[an] patron–client system"). For *diakonos*, note Phoebe (Rom 16:1); for *episkopos*, Lydia in Acts 16:14–15,40 (if patroness of a house church in Philippi, "oversight" would be involved; Pilhofer 1:238 speculates she is not named in Phil because she was away at the time on business or as a Christian missionary).

Why mention *episkopoi* and *diakonoi* in 1:1? In which letter did the phrase originally appear or to which portion(s) of the four chs. does it relate? Guesses (O'B 49–50) range from rebuke to *captatio benevolentiae* (he is "pleased with them"). To bolster them in the face of opponents (ch. 3; Letter C)? Because of splits in the congregation (chs. 1–2, 4; Letter B)? Because the leaders were part of the problem (haughtiness and pride, chs. 1–2, 4; Letter B)? Because they were imprisoned (in Philippi, persecution had broken out; Loh. 12–13)?

From Gk. backgrounds, most likely *episkopoi* and *diakonoi* had to do with financial matters (Loh. 12; Fitzmyer *JBC* 50:10; Byrne, *NJBC* 48:12; Hooker, NIB 11:481), as with *episkopoi* in government and guilds. Here, the gifts sent for Paul's missionary work (4:10–20, Letter A; Fitzer; *EDNT* 2:36). One area of organization to which Paul gave attention was choosing congregational agents to deliver the collection to Jerusalem (1 Cor 16:3–4; Acts 20:4). To attribute the gifts to the entire congregation (as do the thanks in 4:10–20) or stress Epaphroditus who brought the aid (4:18; 2:25; Rohde 1976:55–56 and Schenk 81) does not exclude a role for agents and overseers in the congregation, or Epaphroditus as one of these officials.

Georgi stresses preaching: *episkopoi* and *diakonoi* as terms from the Cynic tradition (NOTES on 1:1 *overseers* A[3] and *agents* A[2]) for religious propagandists

---

[34] E. von Dobschütz, KEK *Thess* (1910:216–17), lists (5:12) actions by the *proïstamenoi* (numbered as in Holmberg 1978:102, cf. H. O. Maier, *The Social Setting of the Ministry as Reflected in the Writings of Hermes, Clement and Ignatius*, DSR 1 [Waterloo, Ont.: Wilfrid Laurier Univ. Press, 1991] 36–37): (1) "provide the locale for the community assembly, (2) perhaps also establishing the necessary order or arrangements (*Ordnungen*) for it; (3) lead prayers, (4) readings, (5) singing; (6) provide quarters and support for traveling brothers; (7) support the poor; (8) put up bail (cf. Jason, Acts 17:9); (8) advocacy before the courts (as patron); (10) trips in the interests of the congregation; . . . all the duties that later fell to the leader (*Vorsteher*), the bishop, but . . . voluntary . . . without legal commission, without salaried compensation." Theissen 1982:73–96, "influential church members" in Corinth, active in civic or religious office (synagogue, perhaps *collegia*, guilds, etc.), possessing a house, providing services to Paul and/or the community, and perhaps making trips for the cause; leadership was not "purely pneumatic." Holmberg sees "a certain degree of wealth and social standing" for leaders performing many of the actions in von Dobschütz's list. Preaching, teaching, "sacraments," and discipline for members are not listed but were part of assembly life.

(cf. "proclaimers of foreign deities," Acts 17:18), used by non-Pauline preachers in Corinth (2 Cor 11:23).[35] The leaders are called by Cynic-Stoic terms but not necessarily from the group mentioned in 2 Cor.

In summary, the *overseers and agents* were leaders developed by the Philippian congregation (invented by them, Reumann 1993a:449–50; 1993b:88–90; Pilhofer 1:140–47; Bormann 1995: 210–11; "possible . . . speculative," Bockmuehl 54, but hardly "from silence"; *DA* 190 n 137). In connection with and out of the house churches (Dassmann 1984; Dassmann/Schöllgen, *RAC* 13:886–901; Schöllgen 1988b). Terms come from their world of government, society, and (to a minor extent) religion. Unclear are their duties or distinctions between *episkopoi* and *diakonoi.* Not two levels, above "the saints."[36] Bockmuehl 54–55, "under the umbrella of apostolic oversight" but with "Paul's extended absence . . . an increasing role of local church leadership." L. Hartman 2001:38–39, "wider, pastoral tasks" beyond "financial and social responsibilities."[37] We include financial administration, gathering funds and distributing them to Paul's missionary team, possibly to *apostoloi* like Epaphroditus, and for the collection for Jerusalem; preaching and teaching in Philippi and as missionaries elsewhere (cf. Ollrog 85 n 116; 223 n 84; Gnilka 39); promoting faith and unity, in the face of threats from persecutors and false teachers from outside the community; liaison with Paul and among house churches in Philippi and elsewhere. No evidence for Philippi at this date as to what, if anything, *episkopoi* and *diakonoi* did in cult. To read in later notions of deacons caring for the poor, or *episkopoi* supervising presbyters goes beyond the evidence. Phil 1:1 is one of several roots for later developments in Christian ministry, already "institutionalized," in a rudimentary way, but activities not yet fixed (Ollrog 74 n 63; cf. M. Y. MacDonald). Philippian *episkopoi* and *diakonoi* could have been part of the problem of disunity, divisiveness, pride, and self-interest along with the rest of the congregation. See further, *Philippian Studies.*

6. *The Salutation.* Paul and Timothy wish their audience *grace . . . and peace,* not from themselves but *from God our Father and the Lord Jesus Christ,* vb. form to be

---

[35] That *episkopoi* and *diakonoi* in Philippi *originated* from usage by Paul's opponents in 2 Cor faces the chronological question whether, before Paul wrote to Philippi, his converts there had adopted a term from missionaries who had not yet appeared in Philippi (see COMMENT on Phil 3). Presumably the Cynic *diakonos* and *episkopos* was one and the same person. But *episkopois kai diakonois* in 1:1 is no hendiadys. The pl. suggests a body of persons, not the Cynic-Stoic individual. Georgi's case would be stronger if 1:1 said *"episkopoi kai diakonoi* of God or of Christ." Connected by *syn* ("with") to *the saints . . . in Philippi,* the combination seems more a creation of the congregation than one from Cynic-Stoic self-understanding.

[36] Holmberg 1978:101–2, two groups, "leading" and "serving." Collins 1990:235–37, "agents" subordinate to the "overseers." Fee 68–69, *overseers* "looking after" or "caring for the people"; for deacons, "deeds of service."

[37] Hartmann 2001 concludes this from the needs of the (reconstructed) "implied readers" in Phil, assuming the "overseers and servants" of 1:1 "replaced him and did what Paul himself would do among the Philippians" (39) in "continuous pastoral work." Respondents (47, 49–50, cf. 45, 43) were not all in agreement. 4:3 (not discussed by Hartman) is an acid test: Paul's *faithful partner,* not the overseers, is asked to assist Euodia and Syntyche.

supplied.[38] Not part of Greco-Roman oratory, it reflects the Gk. "A to B, *chairein* (greetings)," but owes more to Oriental-Jewish background. Modifications from typical Gk. forms (evidence from papyrus letters in P. Arzt-Grabner, *Philemon*, Papyrologische Kommentare zum Neuen Testament 1 [Göttingen: Vandenhoeck & Ruprecht, 2003] 109–23) draw "the reader into a letter with different aims than those to which they were accustomed" (DA 193).

For pre-Pauline form see COMMENT A. The Jewish formula "mercy and peace" was changed to *grace and peace* at least by the time 1 Thess was written. Thereafter, + *from God our Father and the Lord Jesus Christ*, a set piece to open every Pauline letter; see WDNTECLR 376; AB *Rom.* 33:227–28, *Thess.* 32B:101–3. That Paul developed the wording (perhaps by combining *charis* and *eirēnē*) puts the terms within Paul's own theology. A liturgical phrase is unlikely.[39]

The words are *captatio benevolentiae* (DA 351) to capture the audience's goodwill. But more, they extend *charis* and *eirēnē* from God and Christ. Given Paul's concept of "the word," possibly "Grace and peace *are* yours" (supply an indic. form of the vb.).[40] Grace as divine gift undergirds all that follows. One could well repeat the point "Grace is yours, from God and Christ; therefore . . ." as presupposition for every paragraph in what Paul writes.

Berger 1974:192–93 goes further: grace implies "revealed knowledge."[41] As "apostolic speech," the salutation stamps the whole letter: the contents are knowledge from God and Christ, via the apostle. Cf. 1 Cor 15:1–11; 1 Cor 11:23; 1 Thess 4:15. Paul does communicate "a [revealed] mystery" at points (1 Cor 15:51; Rom 11:25); he is one to whom God "revealed" the gospel (Gal 1:12,15–16), through whom the Lord speaks (1 Cor 7:10,12,25; cf. Rom 15:15–16). Cf. Phil 3:15b, *this too God will reveal to you*. *grace and peace* (salvation) *from God and Christ* casts the power and authority of God through Christ over all that follows in the letter (Berger 197). Fee (62; cf. Schoon-Janßen 136–37, 145) minimizes apostolic authority here by appeal to Phil as a "letter primarily of friendship and exhortation," but the language of 1:2 is scarcely that of *philia*; see Reumann 1996; Bockmuehl 54–55; U. B. Müller 33. Berger's thesis[42] cannot apply to all parts of a Pauline letter (Schnider/Stenger 27–28); e.g., travel plans or thanks for

---

[38] Perhaps *eiē*, "May there be . . ." (opt. of wish; cf. in 1 Pet 1:2, 2 Pet 1:2, and Jude 2 *plēthuntheiē*, aor. pass. opt., "May [grace and peace] be multiplied to you"), or *estō* (3rd sg. impv., "Let there be . . . ," Johanson 1987:60).

[39] With Friedrich and Fitzmyer AB 33:228, against Loh. 14 and Champion 25–34. Cf. Mullins 1977; G. P. Wiles 1974 ([2] Bibl.) 108–14, O'B 50–51; Jewett 1969:31; DA 194 n 150. Malherbe AB 32B:100 is open to *use* of 1:1–2 in a communal, worship setting for reading the letter, if not to liturgical *origins*.

[40] So W. C. van Unnik for "The Lord (be)/(is) with you," Christ eschatologically manifested "in the Spirit." See "*Dominus vobiscum*: the Background of a Liturgical Formula," in *New Testament Essays*, FS T. W. Manson, ed. A. J. B. Higgins (Manchester: Manchester Univ. Press, 1959) 270–305.

[41] Cf. Ps 143 (LXX 142):8; 119:76 LXX; 2 *Bar.* 81.4, cf. 44.13–14, 49.1; 1QH 7.27; 1 QS 2.1–4; 1QH 10,14–16; 12.12–14; *1 En.* 71, and *T. Dan.* 5.9.

[42] A problem is that grace as "revealed knowledge" and *peace* as promise and formula of blessing are found *separately* in intertestamental literature. Schenk 85, no prehistory of the terms *together* as greeting, wish of blessing, let alone revelation-formula; together they are *Pauline* terms. Schnider/Stenger

financial support. But some autobiographical sections in Phil 3 reveal through Paul's experiences what the apostle wishes his readers or hearers to live by. God's revelation is not only to Paul but also through him (Gal 1:16, *en emoi*, NRSV-txt and -mg). Again, cf. Phil 3:15b.

As Paul wrote the salutation, thoughts he expressed elsewhere on grace and peace may be reflected, addressees were familiar with some of these ideas. *Grace and peace* in Paul's sense of the words set the tone. Grace is not a disposition of God but (cf. *TPTA* 322–23) a striking *gift* seen in the eschatological *action* of *God's* setting forth Christ as expiation for sin (Rom 3:24–25; 5:15–16). Grace, from the Judge, abounds through justification, leading to eternal life through Christ (Rom 5:17–21). When the good news about God's grace is preached, a new time and new situation result (2 Cor 6:1; "a new epoch," *TPTA* 317). The individual is called to Christ's grace (Gal 1:6), stands in it (Rom 5:2), and, as participant with others (Phil 1:7), lives under grace (Rom 6:14–15). One can fall from it (Gal 5:4). What God gives, suffices (2 Cor 12:9; "you will get no more, you need no more," *TDNT* 9:315). God's grace is actualized in the lives of believers in the church (grace, unilaterally God's extraordinary action, "begets grace," *TPTA* 323, and therefore thanksgiving) through, e.g., the collection project, which grace enables (2 Cor 8:1); through suffering (Phil 1:28–29); through Paul's apostolic ministry and speech (Rom 1:5; 12:3; 15:15), and for all Christians in grace-gifts (1 Cor 12; Rom 12:6).

peace, while not without reference to OT "well-being," is an eschatological result of justification. From God, through Christ, it means peace with God (Rom 5:1) and life through the Spirit (Rom 8:6); indeed, a fruit of the Spirit (Gal 5:22), characteristic of the kingdom (Rom 14:17). God's peace "keeps (or guards) the hearts and minds" of Christians (Phil 4:7). That is as close as Paul comes to "peace of mind," so popular in American religion in the 1960s. Peace has more of a place in paraenesis than references to grace do (cf. 1 Cor 7:12–17; 14:26–33; Rom 14:1– 15:13, often together with *oikodomē*, upbuilding the community; Brandenburger 61–65).

Is *grace* a given, but *peace* a goal to be striven after, as Rom 14:19 may suggest? No, for all believers whom Paul addresses already have *grace and peace*. The salutation coordinates the two terms. Schenk's analysis of Rom 5:1–5 (see NOTE on 1:2 *peace*) views peace with God as a result of justification, which is by prior grace. Yet it is "grace all the way," for continuing access is needed to God's grace, "in which" and by which "we stand." The sequence *grace and peace* is probably no accident. Not *šālôm* first, then what sounds like Gk. *chairein*; but grace first, as in the Jewish formula "mercy and peace." Cf. Fee 70. Like all wishes, "May grace and peace be yours" is future-oriented; dependable because *from God*, who will do it (cf. 1 Thess 5:24), the real sender of the gifts in 1:2, along with Christ, through the apostle (Berger 1974: 202–3; n 55).

For *Father* or *Lord* we need not claim so specifically a Pauline sense. Both terms

---

28 agree. The Pauline nature of *charis* (see NOTE on 1:2 *grace*, esp. Moffatt, Doughty, Zeller 1990, and Boers 1997) strengthens the point.

had widespread use for God in Judaism and earliest Christianity; see NOTES on each. *Father* did not raise in Paul's day concerns that feminist theology today might see (but cf. Bockmuehl 56–57). Even in the patriarchal society and language of the Jewish and Greco-Roman worlds, "father" and "mother" functioned as honorifics to present the deity as deliverer, creator, sustainer, or powerful one and judge. Here it is "Father of us" who believe, God as the One who raised up and exalted Jesus (2:9) and from whom our salvation comes (1:28).[43]

The epithet *Father* for God will appear later in Phil only in hymns or formulas (2:11; 4:20). *Lord* for Jesus will appear more prominently. Each term serves to identify: God, as Father of believers; Christ as Lord, on a par with, not identified as but individuated from, God (AB 33:113); see NOTES on each term; with *TPTA* 83, against Capes. For more precise distinction between God the Father and Jesus the Lord, see on 2:11. The prescript, through the term *Lord*, speaks "of Jesus' unique role and privileged position with respect to mediating God's blessings to the churches concerned," the apostle's letter "channeling grace and peace from God and Christ" (Kreitzer 1987:19).

In 1:1–2 a number of themes occur *in dyads* (indicated by brackets; cf. Edart 43, 8 cola), with particular emphasis on *Christ* (boldface):

$$\left.\begin{array}{l}\text{Paul +}\\\text{Timothy}\end{array}\right\} \longrightarrow \left\{\begin{array}{l}\text{to all saints in Christ Jesus who are in Philippi}\\\text{together with overseers and agents:}\end{array}\right.$$

slaves of **Christ Jesus**

$$\left.\begin{array}{l}\text{grace +}\\\text{peace}\end{array}\right\} \text{ to you}$$

$$\text{from} \left\{\begin{array}{l}\text{God our Father +}\\\text{Lord Jesus Christ.}\end{array}\right.$$

SELECT BIBLIOGRAPHY, (see also General Bibliography and Commentaries). For 1:1–2 generally, then by word, phrase, or theme. *Letters*: P. E. Dion, "Letters (Aramaic)," *ABD* 4:285–90; D. Pardee, "Letters (Hebrew)," *ABD* 4:282–85; S. K. Stowers, "Letters (Greek and Latin)," *ABD* 4:290–93; M. M. Mitchell 1998, "Brief," *RGG*[4] 1:1757–62.

Affanasieff, N. 1974. "L'assemblée Eucharistique unique dans l'Église ancienne," *Kleronomia* 6:1–36.

Berger, K. 1974. "Apostelbrief und apostolische Rede/Zum Formular frühchristlicher Briefe," *ZNW* 65: 190–231; repr., *The Thessalonian Correspondence*, ed. R. F. Collins (Leuven: Leuven Univ. Press/Peeters, 1990) 190–231.

---

[43] Such functions could be attributed to a god via "father"-language (Zeus as "father of gods and human beings") or to a goddess via "mother"-language (Cybele = Gk. Demeter as "mother of gods," and *magna mater*, men as well as women being caught up into her cult); or to a pair of deities like Cybele and Attis or Isis and Osiris. As the one with "countless names," Lady Isis might even be addressed with masc. epithets, indicating her functions, including (in an "invocation of Isis," POxy 11.1380) *theos* (lines 77 and 107) as well as *thea* (fem.); or "lawgiver" (*thesmophoros*) and "lord (*kyrios*) of rainstroms" in an Isis aretalogy (*BCH* 51 [1927] 380; in F. C. Grant, *Hellenistic Religions* [Library of Religions; New York: Liberal Arts Press, 1953] 128, 133). Note, in Apuleius, Isis's self-description as *deorum dearumque facies uniformis*, "the one form that fuses gods and goddesses" (*Met.* 11.4).

Brockhaus, U. 1972. *Charisma und Amt: Die paulinische Charismenlehre auf dem Hintergrund der frühchristlichen Gemeindefunktionen.* Wuppertal: Theologischer Verlag Rolf Brockhaus.

Byrskog, S. 1996. "Co-Senders, Co-Authors and Paul's Use of the First Person Plural," ZNW 87:230–50.

Champion, L. G. 1934. *Benedictions and Doxologies in the Epistles of Paul.* Diss. Heidelberg. Oxford: Kemp Hall Press, n.d.

Dick, K. 1900. *Der schriftstellerische Plural bei Paulus.* Halle: Ehrhardt Karras.

Fitzmyer, J. A. 1974. "Some Notes on Aramaic Epistolography," *JBL* 93:201–25.

Friedrich, G. 1956. "Lohmeyers These über das paulinischen Briefpräscript kritisch beleuchtet," *TLZ* 81:343–46, repr. in his GS, *Auf das Wort kommt es an* (Göttingen: Vandenhoeck & Ruprecht, 1978), 103–6.

Hartman, L. 1986. "On Reading Others' Letters," in *Christians Among Jews and Gentiles: Essays in Honor of Krister Stendahl on His Sixty-Fifth Birthday,* ed. G. W. E. Nickelsburg/G. W. MacRae (Philadelphia: Fortress) 137–46.

Hultgren, A. 1991. "The Self-Definition of Paul and His Communities," *SEÅ* 56:78–100.

Jewett, R. 1969. "The Form and Function of the Homiletic Benediction," *ATR* 51:18–43.

Kim, Chan-Hie. 1972. *Form and Structure of the Familiar Letter of Recommendation.* SBLDS 4. Missoula, MT: Scholars Press.

Lohmeyer, E. 1927c. "Probleme paulinischer Theologie. I. Briefliche Grussüberschriften," ZNW 26:158–73.

Mullins, T. Y. 1972. "Formulas in New Testament Epistles," *JBL* 91:380–90.

———. 1977. "Benedictions as a NT Form," *AUSS* 15:350–58.

Murphy-O'Connor, J. 1995. *Paul the Letter-Writer: His World, His Options, His Skills.* GNS 41. Collegeville, MN: Glazier/Liturgical Press.

Parkin, V. 1986. "Some Comments on the Pauline Prescripts," *IBS* 8:92–99.

Probst, H. 1991. *Paulus und der Brief. Die Rhetorik des antiken Briefes als Form der paulinischen Korintherkorrespondenz (1 Kor 8–10).* WUNT 2/45. Tübingen: Mohr Siebeck.

Richards, E. R. 1991. *The Secretary in the Letters of Paul.* WUNT 2/42. Tübingen: Mohr Siebeck.

———. 2004. *Paul and First-Century Letter Writing: Secretaries, Composition and Collection.* Downers Grove, IL: InterVarsity.

Roller, O. 1933. *Das Formular der paulinischen Briefe: Ein Beitrag zur Lehre von Antiken Briefe.* Stuttgart: Kohlhammer.

Schnider, F./W. Stenger. 1987. *Studien zum neutestamentlichen Briefformular.* NTTS 11. Leiden: Brill.

Taatz, I. 1991. *Frühjüdische Briefe. Die paulinische Briefe im Rahmen der offiziellen religiösen Briefe des Frühjudentums.* NTOA 16. Fribourg: Universitätsverlag/ Göttingen: Vandenhoeck & Ruprecht.

Welles, C. B. 1934. *Royal Correspondence in the Hellenistic Period.* New Haven: Yale Univ. Press.

Paul: H. Balz, *EDNT* 3:59–62; H. D. Betz, *ABD* 5:186–201; G. Bornkamm 1961, *RGG*³ 5:166–90; A. C. Purdy, *IDB* 3: 681–704; S. Vollenweider, *RGG*⁴ 6 (2003) 1035–66.

Becker, J. 1993. *Paul: Apostle to the Gentiles.* Louisville: Westminster John Knox. Ger. 1989.

Bornkamm, G. 1971. *Paul,* tr. D. M. G. Stalker (New York: Harper & Row), esp. 78–79, 99–103.

Cony.-Hows. = Conybeare, W. J./J. S. Howson. 1897. *The Life and Epistles of St. Paul.* 2 vols. (New York: Scribner's), esp. 1:285–319; 2:202–4, 422–35.

Deissmann, A. 1912. *St. Paul: A Study in Social and Religious History*, tr. William E. Wilson. London: Hodder & Stoughton; 2nd ed.,1927; New York: Harper Torchbooks, 1957; repr. Gloucester, MA: Peter Smith, 1972.

Harrer, G. A. 1940. "Saul who is also called Paul," *HTR* 33:19–33.

Hock, R. F. 1980. *The Social Context of Paul's Ministry. Tentmaking and Apostleship.* Philadelphia: Fortress.

Lindemann, A. 1979a. *Paulus im ältesten Christentum: das Bild des Apostels und die Rezeption der paulinischen Theologie in der frühchristlichen Literatur bis auf Marcion.* BHT 58. Tübingen: Mohr Siebeck.

Murphy-O'Connor, J. 1996. *Paul: A Critical Life.* Oxford: Clarendon.

Nock, A. D. 1937. *St. Paul.* New York: Harper & Brothers; Torchbooks, Harper & Row, 1963.

Segal, A. F. 1990. *Paul the Convert: The Apostolate and Apostasy of Saul the Pharisee.* New Haven: Yale Univ. Press.

Wiles, M. 1967. *The Divine Apostle: The Interpretation of St. Paul's Epistles in the Early Church.* New York: Cambridge Univ. Press.

Timothy: J. Gillman, *ABD* 6:558–60; H. C. Kee, *IDB* 4:650–51; W. Schmithals, *RGG*[3] 6:903; P. Trummer, *EDNT* 3:359–60; Ollrog (Gen. Bibl.) 20–24, 93–5, 241–5, passim; G. Häfner, *RGG*[4] 8:414.

Bryan, C. 1988. "A Further Look at Acts 16:1–3," *JBL* 105:292–94.

Cohen, S. D. 1986. "Was Timothy Jewish (Acts 16:1–3)? Patristic Exegesis, Rabbinic Law, and Matrilineal Descent," *JBL* 105:251–68.

Ellis, E. E. 1970–71. "Paul and his Co-Workers," *NTS* 17: 437–52, repr. in Ellis, GS *Prophecy and Hermeneutic in Early Christianity: New Testament Essays* (WUNT 18; Tübingen: Mohr Siebeck/Grand Rapids: Eerdmans, 1978) 3–22. Cf. "Coworkers, Paul and His," *DPL* (1993)183–89.

Hadorn, W. 1992. "Die Gefährten und Mitarbeiter des Paulus," in *Aus Schrift und Geschichte. Theologische Abhandlungen*, FS A. Schlatter (Stuttgart: Calwer Vereinsbuchhandlung) 65–82.

slaves *(douloi)*: S. Bartchy, *ABD* 6:65–73 (Bibl.); K. H. Rengstorf, *TDNT* 2:261–80; W. G. Rollins, *IDBSup* 830–31; R. Tuente/H. G. Link, *NIDNTT* 3:592–98; A. Weiser, *EDNT* 1:349–52; *TLNT* 1:380–89.

Barrow, R. H. 1928. *Slavery in the Roman Empire.* New York: Dial Press; repr. New York: Barnes & Noble, 1968.

Bartchy, S. S. 1973. *Mallon Chrēsai: First-Century Slavery and the Interpretation of 1 Corinthians 7:21*, SBLDS 11 (Missoula, MT: SBL) 37–125.

Bradley, K. R. 1984. *Slaves and Masters in the Roman Empire: A Study in Social Control.* Brussels: Latomus; New York: Oxford Univ. Press, 1987.

———. 1989. *Slavery and Rebellion in the Roman World, 140 B.C.–70 B.C.* Bloomington: Indiana Univ. Press.

———. 1994. *Slavery and Society at Rome.* New York: Cambridge Univ. Press.

Brown, M. J. 2001. "Paul's Use of *doulos Christou Iēsou* in Romans 1:1," *JBL* 120:723–37.

Byron, J. 2003. *Slavery Metaphors in Early Judaism and Pauline Christianity: A Traditio-Historical and Exegetical Examination.* WUNT 2/162. Tübingen: Mohr Siebeck.

Callahan, A. D., R. A. Horsley, A. Smith, eds. 1998. *Slavery in Text and Interpretation.* Semeia 83/84.

Combes, I. A. H. 1998. *The Metaphor of Slavery in the Writings of the Early Church: From the New Testament to the Beginning of the Fifth Century.* JSNTSSup 156. Sheffield: Sheffield Academic Press.

Finley, M. I. 1980. *Ancient Slavery and Modern Ideology.* New York: Viking Press.

————, ed. 1974. *Slavery in Classical Antiquity: Views and Controversy.* Cambridge: W. Heffer.

Fleshner, P. V. M. 1988. *Oxen, Women or Citizens? Slaves in the System of the Mishnah.* Atlanta: Scholars Press.

Glancey, J. A. 2002. *Slavery in Early Christianity.* Oxford: Oxford Univ. Press.

Harrill, J. A. 2006. *Slaves in the New Testament: Literary, Social, and Moral Dimensions.* Minneapolis: Fortress.

Harris, M. J. 2001. *Slave of Christ: A New Testament Metaphor for Total Devotion to Christ.* NSBT 8. Downers Grove, IL: InterVarsity; Leicester, UK: Apollos, 1999.

Horsley, R. A. 1998a. "The Slave Systems of Antiquity and Their Reluctant Recognition by Modern Scholars," in Callahan et al., eds., *Semeia* 83/84:19–66.

————. 1998b. "Paul and Slavery: A Critical Alternative to Recent Readings," in Callahan et al., *Semeia* 83/84:153–200.

Kyrtatas, D. J. 1987. *The Social Structure of Early Christian Communities.* New York: Verso.

Laub, F. 1982. *Die Begegung des frühen Christentums mit der antiken Sklaverei.* SBS 107. Stuttgart: Katholisches Bibelwerk.

Lyall, F. 1970–71. "Roman Law in the Writings of Paul—The Slave and the Freedman," *NTS* 17:73–79.

————. 1984. *Slaves, Citizens, Sons: Legal Metaphors in the Epistles.* Grand Rapids: Zondervan.

Martin, D. B. 1990. *Slavery as Salvation: The Metaphor of Slavery in Pauline Christianity.* New Haven: Yale Univ. Press.

Patterson, O. 1982. *Slavery and Social Death: A Comparative Study.* Cambridge: Harvard Univ. Press.

Petersen, N. R. 1985. *Rediscovering Paul: Philemon and the Sociology of Paul's Narrative World.* Philadelphia: Fortress.

Rollins, W. G. 1987. "Greco-Roman Slave Terminology and Pauline Metaphors for Salvation," *SBLSP 1987*, ed. K. H. Richards (Atlanta: Scholars Press) 100–10.

Russell, K. C. 1968. "Slavery as Reality and Metaphor in the Pauline Letters." Diss. Pontifical Univ., Rome.

————. 1972. "Slavery as Reality and Metaphor in the Non-Pauline New Testament Books," *RUO* 42:439–69.

Sass, G. 1941. "Zur Bedeutung von *doulos* bei Paulus," *ZNW* 40:24–32.

Sokolowski, F. 1954. "The Real Meaning of Sacral Manumission," *HTR* 47:173–81.

Vogt, J. 1975. *Ancient Slavery and the Ideal of Man.* Oxford: Basil Blackwell, 1974/ Cambridge: Harvard Univ. Press.

Christ: W. Grundmann, *TDNT* 9:493–580, esp. 527–28, 540–56; F. Hahn, *EDNT* 3:478–86; M. de Jonge, *ABD* 1:914–21; Hawthorne, *Phil* (WBT) 48–51; M. Karrer, *RGG*⁴ 2 (1999) 273–88; K. H. Rengstorf, *NIDNTT* 2:334–43; E. de W. Burton, "III. *CHRISTOS*," in "Detached Notes . . . , III. Titles and Predicates of Jesus," in *The Epistle to the Galatians* (ICC; Edinburgh: T&T Clark, 1921) 395–99.

Berger, K. 1971. "Zum Traditionsgeschichtlichen Hintergrund Christologischer Hoheitstitel," *NTS* 17:391–425.

Cerfaux, L. 1959. *Christ in the Theology of Saint Paul.* New York: Herder & Herder.

Fitzmyer, J. 2007. *The One Who Is to Come*. Grand Rapids: Eerdmans.

Fuller, R. H. 1965. *Foundations* (see General Bibliography), esp. 23–31, 63–64, 109–11, 158–60, 191–92.

Hahn, F. 1969. *The Titles of Jesus in Christology: Their History in Early Christianity* (New York: World) 136–222.

Hengel, M. 1962. "'Christos' in Paul" = "Erwägungen zur Sprachgebrauch von *Christos* bei Paulus und in der 'vorpaulinischen' Überlieferung," *Paul and Paulinism*, FS C. K. Barrett, ed. M. D. Hooker & S. G. Wilson (London: SPCK) 135–59, cited from *Between Jesus and Paul: Studies in the Earliest History of Christianity*, tr. J. Bowden (London: SCM/Philadelphia: Fortress, 1983) 65–77.

Kramer, W. 1966. *Christ, Lord, Son of God*. SBT 50. London: SCM. ##2–14, 31–41, 60–65, pp. 19–64, 133–50, 203–14. Ger. 1963.

Schreiber, S. 2000. *Gesalbter und König. Titel und Konzeption der königlichen Gesalbtenerwartung in frühjüdischen und urchristlichen Schriften*, BZNW 105 (Berlin/New York: de Gruyter) 405–20.

Zeller, D. 1993. "Zur Transformation des *Christos* bei Paulus," *JBT* 8:155–67.

Jesus: W. Foerster, *TDNT* 3:284–93; B. F. Meyer, *ABD* 3:773–96; K. H. Rengstorf, *NIDNTT* 2:330–32; J. Roloff/P. Pokorný, *RGG*[4] 4 (2001) 463–70; G. Schneider, *EDNT* 2:180–84; E. de W. Burton, "II. *IESOUS*," in ICC *Gal.* (cited above, under **Christ**) 394.

saint(s): H. Balz, *EDNT* 1:16–20; G. W. H. Lampe, *IDB* 4:164–65; J. Muilenburg, "Holiness," *IDB* 2:616–25; O. Procksch/K. G. Kuhn, *TDNT* 1:88–115; H. Seebas/C. Brown, *NIDNTT* 2:223–32; J.-W. Taeger, *RGG*[4] 3 (2000) 1532–33; D. P. Wright/R. Hodgson, Jr., *ABD* 3:237–54, esp. 250–51.

Asting, R. 1930. *Die Heiligkeit im Urchristentum*. FRLANT 46, NF 29. Göttingen: Vandenhoeck & Ruprecht.

Fitzmyer, J. 1991. "Biblical Data on the Veneration and Intercession of Holy People," in *The One Mediator, the Saints, and Mary*, ed. H. G. Anderson/F. J. Stafford/J. Burgess, Lutherans and Catholics in Dialogue 8 (Minneapolis: Augsburg) 135–48.

"In Christ (Jesus)": G. F. Hawthorne 1987, *Phil* (WBT) 48–51; M. A. Seifrid, *DPL* 433–36.

Barcley, W. B. 1999. *"Christ in You." A Study in Paul's Theology and Ethics*. Lanham/New York/Oxford: University Press of America.

Best, E. 1955. *One Body in Christ: A Study in the Relationship of the Church to Christ in the Epistles of the Apostle Paul* (London: SPCK) 1–33.

Bouttier, M. 1962. *En Christ: étude d'exégèse et de la théologie paulinennes*. Paris: Presses Universitaires de France.

———. 1966. *Christianity according to Paul*. SBT 49. French, *La condition chrétienne selon saint Paul* (Geneva: Labor et Fides, 1964), tr. F. Clark. London: SCM.

Büchsel, F. 1949. "'In Christus' bei Paulus," ZNW 42:141–58.

Deissmann, A. 1892. *Die neutestamentliche Formel "in Christo Jesu."* Marburg: N. G. Elwert.

Lohmeyer, E. 1929. *Grundlagen paulinischen Theologie*, BHT 1 (Tübingen: Mohr Siebeck) 139–46.

Moule, C. F. D. 1967. *The Phenomenon of the New Testament. An Inquiry into the Implications of Certain Features of the New Testament*. SBT 2/1. Naperville, IL: Allenson.

Neugebauer, F. 1957–58. "Das paulinische 'in Christo,'" *NTS* 4:124–38.

———. 1961. *In Christus, en Christō[i]: eine Untersuchung zum paulinischen Glaubens-*

verständnis. Berlin: Evangelische Verlagsanstalt/Göttingen: Vandenhoeck & Ruprecht.

Prat, F. 1926–27 (French). *The Theology of Saint Paul*, tr. J. L. Stoddard. London: Burns, Oates, and Washbourne/Westminster, MD: Newman Bookshop, 1945. 2:391–95.

Preiss, T. 1952. *Life in Christ*. French, *La Vie en Christ*. Neuchâtel: Delachaux et Niestlé. Tr. of sections by H. Knight, SBT 13 (London: SCM, 1954) 32–42.

Schmauch, W. 1935. *In Christus: eine Untersuchung zur Sprache und Theologie des Paulus*. NTF 1/9. Gütersloh: C. Bertelsmann.

Schmitz O. 1924. *Die Christus-Gemeinschaft des Paulus im Lichte seines Genitivgebrauchs*. NTF, Reihe 1, vol. 2. Gütersloh: Bertelsman.

Schweitzer, A. 1931. *The Mysticism of Paul the Apostle*. Ger. 1930, tr. W. Montgomery. London: A. & C. Black, New York: Henry Holt, 1931; repr. New York: Seabury, 1968.

Wedderburn, A. J. M. 1985. "Some Observations on Paul's Use of the Phrases 'in Christ' and 'with Christ,'" *JSNT* 25:83–97.

Wikenhauser, A. 1960. *Pauline Mysticism: Christ in the Mystical Teaching of St. Paul*. Ger 1928, rev. ed. 1956, tr. J. Cunningham. New York: Herder & Herder.

with *(syn)*: W. Grundmann, *TDNT* 7: 766–97, esp. 770–71; W. Elliger, *EDNT* 3:291–92; M. J. Harris, *NIDNTT* 3:1206–7; G. Otto, diss. Berlin 1952, see *TLZ* 97 (1954) 12–15.

overseer *(episkopos)*: R. J. Banks, *DPL* 131–37; H. Bellen, *KlPauly* 2:323; H. W. Beyer, *TDNT* 2:599–622; H. W. Beyer/H. Karpp, *RAC* 2 (1954):394–407; L. Coenen, *NIDNTT* 1:188–201, esp. 188–92; M. Dibelius, *An die Philipper*, 3rd ed. (1937) 60–62; J. Rohde, *EDNT* 2:35–36; G. Schöllgen, *RGG*[4] 1:1614–15; E. Schweizer, *ABD* 4:835–42; M. H. Shepherd, Jr., *IDB* 1:441–43. *House churches*: INTRO. II, n 2.

Bauer, W. 1930. "Der Wortgottesdienst des ältesten Christen," repr. in his GS, *Aufsätze und kleine Schriften* (Tübingen: Mohr [Siebeck] 1967) 150–209.

Best, E. 1968. "Bishops and Deacons: Philippians 1,1," *SE IV* (= TU 102) 371–76.

Burtchaell, J. T. 1991. *From Synagogue to Church: Public Services and Offices in the Earliest Christian Communities*. New York: Cambridge Univ. Press.

Campenhausen, H. von. 1969. *Ecclesiastical Authority and Spiritual Power in the Church of the First Three Centuries*. Stanford: Stanford Univ. Press.

Dassmann, E. 1984. "Hausgemeinde und Bischofsampt," in *Vivarium*, FS T. Klauser, JAC Ergänzungsband 11 (Münster: Aschendorff) 82–97.

Doohan, H. 1984. *Leadership in Paul*. GNS 11. Wilmington: Michael Glazier.

Farrer, A. M. 1946. "The Ministry in the New Testament," in *The Apostolic Ministry: Essays on the History and the Doctrine of Episcopacy*, ed. K. E. Kirk (London: Hodder & Stoughton) 113–82, esp. 142–70.

Filson, F. V. 1939. "The Significance of the Early House Churches," *JBL* 58:105–12.

Fitzer, G. 1975. "Die Entstehung des Vorsteheramtes im Neuen Testament," *Pro Oriente* 1 (Innsbruck/Vienna/Munich: Tyrolia) 91–109.

Hainz, J. 1976. "Die Anfänge des Bischofs- und Diakonenamtes," in *Kirche im Werden: Studien zum Thema Amt und Gemeinde im Neuen Testament*, ed. J. Hainz (Munich/Paderborn/Vienna: Schöningh) 91–107, esp. 94–102.

Jeremias, J. 1969a. Ger. 1929, II.B.1, 130–40; 3rd ed. (1962) 294–303, tr. F. H./C. H. Cave, *Jerusalem in the Time of Jesus: An Investigation into Economic and Social Conditions during the New Testament Period* (Philadelphia: Fortress) 259–67.

Kertelge, K. 1972. *Gemeinde und Amt im Neuen Testament*. Biblische Handbibliothek X. Munich: Kösel.

————, ed. 1977. *Das Kirchliche Amt im Neuen Testament.* Wege der Forschung 189. Darmstadt: Wissenschaftliche Buchgesellschaft. Reprints H. Lietzmann 1917, "Zur altchristliche Verfassungsgeschichte," *ZWT* 55:97–153, and Dibelius 1937, on pp. 93–143 and 413–17, respectively.

Lemaire, A. 1971. *Les Ministères aux origines de l'église: Naissance de la triple hiérarchie: évêques, presbytres, diacres,* LD 68 (Paris: Les Editions du Cerf) 27–31. Cf. *BTB* 3 (1973) 133–66, esp. 144–48.

Lohse, E. 1980. "Die Entstehung des Bischofsamtes in der frühen Christenheit," *ZNW* 71:57–83.

MacDonald, M. Y. 1988. *The Pauline Churches: A Socio-Historical Study of Institutionalization in the Pauline and Deutero-Pauline Writings.* SNTSMS 60. New York: Cambridge Univ. Press.

Merkle, B. L. 2003. *The Elder and Overseer: One Office in the Early Church.* Studies in Biblical Literature, 57. New York: Peter Lang.

Reumann, J. 1993b. "Church Office in Paul, Especially Philippians," in FS Hurd (Gen. Bibl., under "Krentz 1993") 82–91.

————. 1998b. "One Lord, One Faith, One God, but Many House Churches," in *Common Life in the Early Church: Essays Honoring Graydon Snyder,* ed. J. V. Hills et al. (Harrisburg, PA: Trinity Press International) 106–17.

Rohde, J. 1976. *Urchristliche und frühkatholische Ämter: Eine Untersuchung zur frühchristlichen Amtsentwicklung im Neuen Testament und bei den apostolischen Vätern.* ThA 33. Berlin: Evangelische Verlagsanstalt.

Schweizer, E. 1961. *Church Order in the New Testament.* SBT 32. London: SCM.

Thiering, B. E. 1981. "*Mebaqqer* and *Episkopos* in the Light of the Temple Scroll," *JBL* 100:59–74.

agent *(diakonos):* H. W. Beyer, *TDNT* 2 (1935) 81–93; M. Dibelius, *Philipper*[3] (1937) 61–62, repr. in Kertelge, ed., 1977, 414–17; K. Hess, *NIDNTT* 3:544–53, esp. 544–49; Th. Klauser, *RAC* 3 (1957) 888–909; T. Kramm, *RAC* Sup 3 (1985) 350–401, esp. 358–60; C. Osiek, *RGG*[4] 2 (1999) 783–84; P. Philippi, *TRE* 8 (1981) 621–44; M. H. Shepherd, Jr., *IDB* 1:785–87; A. Weiser, *EDNT* 1:302–4.

Brandt, W. 1931. *Dienst und Dienen im Neuen Testament.* NTF 2/5. Gütersloh: Bertelsmann; repr. Münster: Antiquariat Th. Stenderhoff, 1983.

Collins, J. N. 1974. "Georgi's 'Envoys' in 2 Cor. 11:23," *JBL* 93:88–96.

————. 1990. *Diakonia: Re-interpreting the Ancient Sources.* New York: Oxford University Press. © John N. Collins, cited by permission of Oxford University Press.

Colson, J. 1960. *La fonction diaconale aus origines de l'Eglise.* Paris/Bruges: Desclée.

————. 1962. "Der Diakonat im Neuen Testament," *Diaconia in Christo: Über die Erneuerung des Diakonates,* ed. K. Rahner and H. Vorgrimler, QD 15–16 (Freiburg/ Basle/Vienna: Herder) 3–22.

Uhlhorn, G. 1882. *Die Christliche Liebesthätigkeit,* 3 vols. Stuttgart: D. Gundert, 2nd ed. 1895; repr. Neukirchen-Vluyn, 1969. Tr., *Christian Charity in the Ancient Church.* New York: Scribner's, 1883.

grace *(charis):* K. Berger, *EDNT* 3:457–60; H. Conzelmann/W. Zimmerli, *TDNT* 9:359–415; H.-H. Esser, *NIDNTT* 2:115–24; W. L. Holladay, *IDBSup* 375–77; C. L. Mitton, *IDB* 2:463–68; *TLNT* 3:500–6; D. Sänger, *RGG*[4] 3 (2000) 1025–27; *TPTA* 319–23. E. de W. Burton, "VII. CHARIS," in *Gal.* (above under **Christ**) 423–24.

Boers, H. 1997. "*agape* and *charis* in Paul's Thought," *CBQ* 59:693–713.

Doughty, D. J. 1972–73. "The priority of *Charis*: An Investigation of the Theological Language of Paul," *NTS* 19:163–80.

Eastman, B. 1999. *The Significance of Grace in the Letters of Paul.* Studies in Biblical Literature 11. New York: Peter Lang.

Harrison, J. R. 1999. "Paul's Eschatology and the Augustan Age of Grace," *TynBul* 50:79–91.

———. 2003. *Paul's Language of Grace in its Graeco-Roman Context.* WUNT 2/172. Tübingen: Mohr Siebeck.

Moffatt, J. 1931. *Grace in the New Testament* (London: Hodder & Stoughton/New York: Ray Long & Richard R. Smith, 1932) esp. 21–72 and 131–77.

Satake, A. 1968–69. "Apostolat und Gnade bei Paulus," *NTS* 15:96–107.

Theobald, M. 1982. *Die überstromende Gnade: Studien zu einem paulinischen Motivfeld.* FB 22. Würzburg: Echter Verlag.

Wetter, G. P. 1913. *Charis: Ein Beitrag zur Geschichte des ältesten Christentums.* UNT 5. Leipzig: O. Brandstetter.

Zeller, D. 1990. *Charis bei Philon und Paulus.* SBS 142. Stuttgart: Katholisches Bibelwerk.

peace *(eirēnē):* H. Beck/C. Brown, *NIDNTT* 2:776–83; G. Delling, *TRE* 11 (1983) 613–18; E. Dinkler/E. Dinkler-von Schubert, *RAC* 8 (1972) 434–505, esp. 460–66; G.von Rad/ W. Foerster, *TDNT* 2:400–20; E. M. Good/C. L. Mitton, *IDB* 3:704–6; V. Hasler, *EDNT* 1:394–97; *TLNT* 1:424–38; K. Wengst, *RGG*⁴ 3 (2000) 360; E. de W. Burton, "VIII. *EIRĒNĒ*," in *Gal.* (above under **Christ**) 424–26.

Brandenburger, E. 1973. *Frieden im Neuen Testament: Grundlinien urchristlichen Friedensverständnisses.* Gütersloh: Gerd Mohn.

Stuhlmacher, P. 1970. "Der Begriff des Friedens im Neuen Testament und seine Konsequenzen," in *Historische Beiträge für Friedensforschung,* Studien zur Friedensforschung 4, ed. W. Huber (Stuttgart: Ernst Klett Verlag/Munich: Kösel-Verlag) 21–69.

Wengst, K. 1987. *Pax Romana and the Peace of Jesus Christ.* Philadelphia: Fortress.

God *(theos):* B. W. Anderson, *IDB* 2:417–30; H. D. Betz, *EDNT* 2:140–42; D. Guthrie/ R. P. Martin, *DPL* 354–68; H. Kleinknecht,/G. Quell/E. Stauffer/K. G. Kuhn, *TDNT* 3:65–123; A. Lindemann, *RGG*⁴ 3 (2000) 1104–8; C. F. D. Moule, *IDB* 2:430–36; J. Schneider/C. Brown/J. S. Wright, *NIDNTT* 2:66–90; *TPTA* 27–50.

Althaus, P. 1941. "Das Bild Gottes bei Paulus," *TBl* 20:81–92.

Amir, Y. 1987. "Das jüdische Eingottglaube als Stein des Anstosses in der hellenistischen-römischen Welt," in *Der eine Gott der beiden Testamente,* Jahrbuch für Biblische Theologie 2 (Neukirchen-Vluyn: Neukirchener Verlag) 58–75.

Argyle, A. W. 1965. *God in the New Testament.* Knowing Christianity. London: Hodder & Stoughton.

Brown, R. E. 1965. "Does the New Testament Call Jesus God?" *TS* 26:545–73, repr. in Brown's *Jesus God and Man: Modern Biblical Reflections* (New York: Macmillan, 1967) 1–38.

Kreitzer, L. J. 1987. *Jesus and God in Paul's Eschatology.* JSNTSup 19. Sheffield: Sheffield Academic Press.

Morris, L. 1986b. "The Apostle and his God," in *God Who Is Rich in Mercy,* FS D.B. Knox, ed. P. T. O'Brien/D. G. Peterson (Homebush West, Australia: Lancer Books, Anzea Publishers/Grand Rapids: Baker) 165–78.

Father *(patēr)*: B. W. Anderson, *IDB* 2:415; J. M. Bassler, *ABD* 2:1054–55; O. J. Baab, *IDB* 2:245, point 6; O. Michel, *EDNT* 3:53–57; O. Hofius, *NIDNTT* 1:615–21, cf. also 2:71, 75–76; G. Quell/G. Schrenk, *TDNT* 5:945–1014; J. Schlosser, *RGG*⁴ 8:891–92; E. de W. Burton, "II. PATĒR as applied to God," in *Gal.* (above under **Christ**) 384–91.

Jeremias, J. 1966. "Abba," in *Abba: Studien zur neutestamentliche Theologie und Zeitgeschichte* (Göttingen: Vandenhoeck & Ruprecht) 15–66.

———. 1967. *The Prayers of Jesus*, SBT 2/6 (London: SCM/Naperville, IL: Allenson) 11–65.

Lord *(kyrios)*: B. W. Anderson, *IDB* 2:409–11; 817; 3:150–51; H. Bietenhard/C. Brown, *NIDNTT* 2:508–19; J. A. Fitzmyer, *EDNT* 2:328–31; S. E. Johnson, *IDB* 3:151; G. Quell/ W. Foerster, *TDNT* 3:1039–98; D. Zeller, *DDD* 2nd ed. 1999:492–97; *TLNT* 2:341–52; *TPTA* 244–52; C. Perrot, *RGG*⁴ 4:1921–24; E. de W. Burton, "IV. KYRIOS," in *Gal.* (above under **Christ**) 399–404.

Bousset, W. 1913. *Kyrios Christos: Geschichte des Christusglaubens von den Anfängen des Christentums bis Irenäus*. FRLANT NS 4. Göttingen: Vandenhoeck & Ruprecht, 2nd ed. 1922; tr. J. E. Steely from 5th ed. (1964) with introduction by R. Bultmann, *Kyrios Christos: A History of the Belief in Christ from the Beginnings of Christianity to Irenaeus*. Nashville/New York: Abingdon, 1970.

Capes, D. B. 1992. *Old Testament Yahweh Texts in Paul's Christology*. WUNT 2/47. Tübingen: Mohr Siebeck.

Fitzmyer, J. A. 1975. "Der semitische Hintergrund des neutestamentlichen Kyriostitels," in *Jesus Christus in Historie und Theologie*, FS Conzelmann, ed. G. Strecker (Tübingen: Mohr Siebeck) 267–98 = "The Semitic Background of the New Testament *Kyrios*-Title," in Fitzmyer's GS, *A Wandering Aramaean: Collected Aramaic Essays* (SBLMS 25; Missoula, MT: Scholars Press, 1979) 115–42.

———. 1981b. "New Testament *Kyrios* and *Maranatha* and Their Aramaic Backgrounds," in Fitzmyer's GS, *To Advance the Gospel: New Testament Studies* (New York: Crossroad, 1981) 218–35.

Hurtado, L. W. 1979. "New Testament Christology: A Critique of Bousset's Influence," *TS* 40:306–17.

———. 1988. *One God, One Lord: Early Christian Devotion and Ancient Jewish Monotheism*. Philadelphia: Fortress. Repr., New York: T&T Clark, 2003. 104–7.

Vos, G. 1915. "The Continuity of the Kyrios Title in the New Testament," *PTR* 13:161–89.

———. 1917. "The Kyrios Christos Controversy," *PTR* 15:21–89.

Wlosok, A., ed. 1978. *Römischer Kaiserkult*. WdF 372. Darmstadt: Wissenschaftliche Buchgesellschaft.

Zeller, D. 2001. "New Testament Christology in its Hellenistic Reception," *NTS* 47:312–33.

2. *Prooimion (Prayer Report, Thanksgiving and Intercession), 1:3–11*

TRANSLATION

[1:3] I thank my God because of your every remembrance of me, [4] always, in every entreaty of mine for all of you, making entreaty, with joy, [5] because of your sharing in the gospel from the first day until now, [6] since I am confident about this point, that the One who inaugurated a good work among you will bring it to completion by the Day of Christ Jesus.

[7a] It is indeed right for me to think about all of you in this way because you have me in your heart, [b] both in my imprisonment and in the defense and confirmation of the gospel, [c] you all sharing, as you do, with me in this gracious opportunity of mine. [8] For God is my witness that I long for you all with the affection of Christ Jesus.

[9a] So this is what I am praying:
[b] that your love may continue to grow still more and more in perception and discernment in every situation, [10a] so that you may keep on appreciating the things that are best;
[b] I pray that you may be flawless and unfailing [c] for the Day of Christ, [11a] because you have been filled with fruit of righteousness, [b] the fruit that comes through Jesus Christ [c] for God's glory and praise.

NOTES

1:3. *I thank my God. eucharistō* + dat., the first two units in Schubert's "thanksgiving period"; see COMMENT A.2. On *God*, see NOTE on 1:2 *God. my* God, only here, Phlm 4, Rom 1:8, and 1 Cor 1:4 (MSS); *mou* for "a special relationship" between apostle and God (BDAG 451, *theos* 3.c); cf. 4:19. U. B. Müller (1975:231–32; *Phil.* 40), Paul carries on the intercessory function of OT and early Christian prophets. A few Western text MSS read "*I thank our Lord*" (*egō . . . tō[i] kyriō[i] hemōn*); Silva 23–24; H. Conzelmann, *TDNT* 9:413. *God* is customary in opening thanksgivings (O'B 56).

thank. Classical Gk. *eucharistein,* "show a favor" to someone, imposing an obligation of thanks or gratitude; hence "be thankful" (BDAG *eucharisteō* 1); "give thanks, return/render thanks" (BDAG 2, regularly in Pauline letter introductions). Can be directed to human beings or (papyrus letters) god(s); + *epi* (with gen. or dat.) to indicate the reason. Also in civic decrees of honor; religious use in the ruler cult and thanksgivings for healing miracles (*TDNT* 9:407–9).

Hebrew "has no equivalent" for *eucharistō*-terms (*TDNT* 9:409), but cf. thanksgiving psalms of the individual (Ps 116) and of the community (136); thank-offering or *tôdâ* ceremony (T. H. Gaster, "Sacrifices and Offerings," A.l.d, "Thanksgiving," *IDB* R-Z 149); Qumran Thanksgiving Hymns or *Hôdāyôt* (Audet, J. M. Robinson 1964). LXX *eucharistein*-terms, only at Prov 11:16 ("a gracious [*eucharistos*] woman") and in apocryphal books under Hellenistic influence (e.g., 3 Macc 7:16; 2 Macc 1:11, in a letter, "we thank God greatly"). Therefore (H.-H. Esser, *NIDNTT* 3:818) no "specific theological colouring from the OT'"; reasons for thankfulness seem drawn esp. from God's current activity. Philo shows Gk. influence, with *euchar*-words frequent for thanks to God; not a human work, God brings it about (*TDNT* 9:410; see below, on "infused prayer").

In the NT, employed esp. by Paul (37x in the corpus, out of 54 in the NT). For thanks at meals (Mark 8:6), in the Upper Room (Mark 14:22–23 parr.; 1 Cor 11:24; Luke 22:17, 19). Tech. sense, "celebrate *eucharistia*," is post-NT (*TDNT* 9:412, 414–15). In Paul, "grace" at meals (1 Cor 10:30, cf. 31; Rom 14:6), thanks to God as creator (Rom 1:21), and appreciation due coworkers (Rom 16:4). Part of the "service of the word" (1 Cor 14:16–17; W. Bauer 1930, ch. 1 Bibl. **overseer**); the will of God in all circumstances (1 Thess 5:18). *eucharistia*, a gift for the collection (2 Cor 9:11–12), producing "thanksgiving to God" and "glory." Theory (cf. 1 Thess 3:9; 2 Cor 1:11; 4:15; 9:11–12): grace given by God flows back to the deity in praise and glory, "infused" as in Hellenistic speculative philosophy (so Boobyer); cf. 1 Chr 29:14 ("all things come from you, and of your own we have given you"), possibly developed in liturgy (cf. Aus 1973 [**thank**]; Malherbe AB 32B:382–83). *eucharistō* occurs in the prooimion to most Pauline letters; see COMMENT A.1–4; B.3, reasons for thanking God vary.

because of your every remembrance of me. epi pasē[i] tē[i] mneia[i] hymōn, usually tr. "in all my remembrance of you" (RSV, etc.), *epi* temporal, *hymōn* obj. gen. ("whenever I think of you," NEB). So Gnilka 42–43; Hawth. 15–17; Wiles 1974:205 n 4; *DA* 200–1; Fee 78–80; Bockmuehl 58; U. B. Müller 39; Holloway 2001a:88–89 and 2006, reflecting letters of consolation. L. Hartman 2001:18–19. The alternative, in the TRANSLATION, takes *epi* as causal (BDAG *eucharisteō* 2; *DA* 209, 325), *hymōn* as a subj. gen., "I thank my God for all your remembrance of me" (Moffatt; Michael, MNTC 10, argued against it; Schubert 74; Jewett 1970a:53; O'Brien 1977:23, 41–46; Schenk 94; Leivestad, *EDNT* 2:434; Peterman 1997:93–99; Witherington 38; Fee 78 n 29; Martin 1976:64; O'B 56, 58–61; Peng). ATR 604, 1:3 "wavers between occasion and time." *GNTG* 3:207 (intentional?) ambiguity. Cf. Omanson 1978a; Bittasi 24 n 23. Final decision involves reconstruction of the situation.

remembrance. mneia, from *mimnēsomai*, "I remember," = (1) remembrance or (2) mention (BDAG; O. Michel, *TDNT* 4:678–79; K. H. Bartels, *NIDNTT* 3:230–32 on classical use; 240–42, 246; R. Leivestad, *EDNT* 2:434; *TLNT* 2:496). *mneian poieisthai* was an idiom in prayers, "make mention" of someone (MM 414; *TLNT* 1:32 n 5; 2:496), 4x in Pauline thanksgivings, unit (5) in Schubert's Type Ia thanksgiving periods; usually ptc. (1 Thess 1:2; Phlm 4; Rom 1:9 indic.; cf. Eph 1:16). Phil 1:3 is complicated by the fact that unit 5 (Phil 1:4) has a different noun, *tēn deēsin*, "making the entreaty," because Paul has injected into 1:3, between Schubert's units (2) and (3), the phrase under discussion. The meaning of *mneia* in v 3 cannot be determined (as by Collange 45) through appeal to the usual phrase in a thanksgiving period, *mneian poioumenous*. Leivestad 434, 1:4 *(deēsin)* provided the model for 1:3 *(mneian)*. Paul has thrust it into prominence earlier in the sentence, for emphasis; COMMENT A.2 on such additions in 1:3–5.

Against "as often as you make mention (of me)," Michael 10 objects "the words *of me* are not in the Greek"; but two genitives, "of me" (obj. gen.) and "of you" (subj. gen.), would have been awkward. The art. *tē[i]* makes the noun specific, with the immediately preceding *mou*, "*the* mention" is "of me," in the Philippians' prayers for Paul (cf. 1:19). Does *mneia* have a more tangible sense, "a little remembrance (gift) for you"? So O'Brien 1977:23, 45–46, more from the situation than texts in antiquity. Re Vincent (a subj. gen. after *mneia* is "against usage"), cf. *2 Bar.* 5.5, "rejoicing that God has remembered them" *(chairontas tē[i] tou theou mneia[i])*.

Three points are debated.

(1) *epi* + dat. is usually *temporal* (BAGD *epi* II.2, citing specifically 1:3; BDAG 18.b). But in 1:3, *epi* + dat., different in its location from Schubert's unit (5), can be causal (BAGD *epi* II.1.b.γ; BDAG 6.a,c; BDF #235.5, citing 1:3, cf. #196; Phil 3:9 "on the basis of [*epi*] faith"; 3:12; 4:10, *eph' hō[i]* = because; 2:17?; in thanksgiving sections, 1 Cor 1:4 "because of God's grace given you"; 1 Thess 3:9). On Phil 1:5, *epi* as causal, see NOTE below. Cf. O'Brien 1977:43; DA 199–200; Fee 78–79; Peterman 1997:95–96.

(2) Lft., the art. *tē[i]* after *pasē[i]* implies " 'in *all* my remembrance,' not 'on *every* remembrance,' " which would call for *epi pasē[i] mneia[i]*, no art., and would imply "isolated, intermittent acts." But if subj. gen., "your every remembrance of me," "isolated, intermittent acts" fits well for Philippian aid to Paul. Generally *pas* + sg. noun without an art. = "every" (cf. 1:4); with a noun + art. (as here), "all" (BAGD 631, *pas, pasa, pan* 1.a and c; BDAG 1.a and b). But the distinction is notoriously difficult to carry through (Moule, *IB* 93–95; GNTG 3:200, "not very clear in NT"). Grammatically possible are "in all remembrance," "in every remembrance," or "in any and every remembrance." Schenk 94, "all that remembrance of yours," a totality of money and continuing intercessions for Paul.

(3) On the overload of cls. in 1:3–6, whether *temporal* phrases or *causal*, and the circumstances involved (as in O'Brien 1977:44–46 or *Phil.* 60–61), see COMMENT B, in light of A.2 on form. The usual interpretation has three *temporal* phrases in 3b–4a (italicized); v 4 is parenthetical (Gnilka 42): [3] I thank my God *every time that I remember you —* [4] *always, in every prayer of mine,* I pray for you all with joy — [5] because of your fellowship in the gospel . . . (NAB). We prefer three *causal* phrases (in italics): [3] I thank my God *because of your every remembrance of me,* [4] always, in every prayer of mine making entreaty for you all with joy, [5] *because of your fellowship in the gospel . . . ,* [6] *because I am confident of this,* that. . . .

1:4. *always. pantote* (19x in Paul's acknowledged letters), the third of Schubert's seven units; with v 3, "I always thank my God." Alliterative ("every time," NRSV) with *pasē[i]* in v 3 ("at every remembrance"), *pasē[i]* and *pantōn* in v 4 ("every prayer," "every one of you"). Schenk 94–95, asyndeton (no "and"; BDF ##458,

460, 494), *pantote en pasē[i] deēsei. always* = "in every prayer of mine," not "uninterrupted praying." O'B 56–58 takes *pantote* with *eucharistō* (so Schubert) but (with Schenk) it is "further explained" by the next phrase *(en pasē[i] deēsei mou)*. Some take *pantote* to imply regular hours for prayers (Jeremias 1967; Gebauer 137 and n 209).

in every entreaty of mine for all of you, making entreaty, with joy. Ptc. + three prep. phrases.

for all of you (without exception), the fourth of Schubert's seven syntactical units. *hyper* + gen. also at 2 Cor 1:11 (twice in most MSS, "for us"); Col 1:9; Eph 1:16, but Paul's usual prep. at this point is *peri* + gen. (1 Thess 1:2; 3:9; 1 Cor 1:4; Rom 1:8; cf. also 2 Thess 1:3,11; 2:13; Col 1:3). *hyper* = "on behalf of, for the sake of"; *peri* designates those for whom petition is made (BAGD *hyper* 1.a.α; BDAG A.1.a.α; *peri* 1.f; BDF ##231 and 229.1). They overlap (M. J. Harris, *NIDNTT* 3:1174 [I.B.f], cf. 1196–97 *hyper*; 1203 *peri*).

you (pl.) + *all* (with *hyper*) occurs in Pauline thanksgiving periods only here; part of the *pas*-cluster of vocabulary in 3b–4a (see NOTE on *always*). Schubert 66–68 takes the phrase with the words that follow; see COMMENT A.2.(4).

making entreaty = tēn deēsin poioumenos. poioumenos mneian, "making mention" or "remembrance," is Schubert's fifth unit (NOTE on 1:3 *remembrance*). Manner ("I thank my God . . . by making entreaty . . ."), or temporal, "when I make entreaty" (Schubert, NEB). Paul replaces *mneia* with *deēsis* (employed in v 3). Western text adds *kai* before *tēn deēsin*; cf. Silva 23.

entreaty. deēsis (twice in v 4; 1:19; 4:6) primarily a Pauline term (7x in acknowledged letters). Vb. *deomai* = "lack," then "request" or "beseech." The noun, regularly in the LXX, always in the NT, for address to God; hence "prayer," "entreaty" (BDAG *deēsis*, with ptc. from *poieisthai*, in the papyri). *(pros)euchesthai* is the primary Gk term for "pray" (H. Greeven, *TDNT* 2:775–808). *deomai/deēsis* suggest petition, asking in prayer (806–7). *deomai* may trail off into a "courtesy formula," "I beg you," "please" (Acts 21:39). In Paul cf. 2 Cor 5:20; 1 Thess 3:10; Rom 1:10; noun, Rom 10:1. Words for prayer are difficult to distinguish. BDAG 213: *deēsis* is "more specif[ic] supplication," *proseuchē* "the more general term"; cf. Phil 4:6 NRSV, "By prayer *(proseuchē)* and supplication *(deēsis)* with thanksgiving *(eucharistia)* let your requests *(aitēmata)* be made known." At 1:4 prayer with intercession for *all of you*, but no content given, unless (until) at vv 9–11. Cf. Greeven, *TDNT* 2:40–41; H. Schönweiss, *NIDNTT* 2:860–61.

in every entreaty of mine. pas, no art., "in any prayer of mine"; cf. 1:3 *every remembrance*.

with joy. As at 2:12, 29, and 4:6, *meta* for means (DA 360) or attendant circumstance (BDAG A.3.a). Unparalleled in other Pauline thanksgiving periods. "Joy" *(chara)* has been called "the key-note of Philippians" (A. T. Robertson 1917:56). Terms from the vb. *chairein* appear 16x in Phil (noun here, 1:25; 2:2,29; 4:1; vb., including compound *sugchairein*, 1:18 bis; 2:17 bis; 2:18 bis; 2:28; 3:1; 4:4 bis; 4:10). Doubled use of "rejoice" in four vv is impressive; absence of the terms from ch. 3 (Letter C), striking. Cf. also "I thank" *(eucharistō)* 1:3, *eucharistia* 4:6, and "grace" 1:2; *chara* relates etymologically to *charis*; see NOTE on 1:2 *grace*.

In the NT, *chara/chairein, sugchairein* appear esp. in Paul (50x in acknowledged letters), in Phil 16x. Gulin studied "joy" in Paul's theological ideas; Plenter, exegetically, esp. in Phil; Backherms, its sources ("objective" ones: Christ, the Spirit; "subjective": faith, hope, love); Meitzen, "levels" of feelings, phenomenologically; Baskin, causes for joy in Paul and Philo; R. D. Webber, contextual meanings set in emotion or affections; Fatum: eschatological joy "in the gospel" has concrete paraenetic consequences, even in the face of opponents; Morrice, NT terms for joy.

Classical Gk. *chairein,* "rejoice" or "be merry," became a greeting, as in papyrus letters (see NOTE on 1:2 *grace*). The noun designated an action, "rejoicing." In the philosophers, an object of reflection (Aristot. *Eth. Nic.* 2.5, 1105b 19ff.); in Stoicism, negatively as an affection, positively as a "good mood" of the soul, for the wise, the *telos* (goal or supreme good) in life, grief or pain *(lypē)* the supreme evil, brought about, respectively, by practical wisdom or folly. In Hellenistic religious texts, festal joy (mystery cults, expectations of a wonder-child who would rule the world, Verg. *Ecl.* 4.48–52). *Word studies:* H. Conzelmann, *TDNT* 9:360–62; O. Michel, *RAC* 8:348–418 (bibl.), esp. 350–71; *TLNT* 3:498–99.

In the OT (Heb. vb. *śāmaḥ,* noun *simḥâ,* and other roots): rejoicing over food and wine (Ps 104:14–15), wise children (Prov 23:25), a wedding (Jer 25:10), good things God gives in life (Ps 84:2 Heb 3]); joy to God for divine acts of deliverance (Exod 18:9; Ps 33:1, 21) and the gift of Torah (Neh 8:10,12; Ps 119:14; cf. the festival *simḥât tôrâ,* "rejoicing in the Law"); cultic rejoicing, esp. at harvest. In the exile and later periods, rejoicing was often projected into the future as a hope (Isa 35:10 = 51:11; 65:17–19; Zech 2:10 [Heb 14]; 8:19; Joel 2:21). *Word studies:* *TDNT* 9:362–63; E. Beyreuther/G. Finkenrath, *NIDNTT* 2:356–57; E. Ruprecht, *THAT* 2:828–35; E. Otto/T. Schramm, *Festival and Joy;* M. A. Grisanti, *NIDOTE* 3:1251–54.

In the LXX, generally *euphrainō* and *agalliaomai; chairein* chiefly in later, deuterocanonical books under Hellenistic influences (Wis, 1–4 Macc). Rabbinic literature continued OT emphases, not just joy in the Law (so Conzelmann). Qumran stressed eschatological and "everlasting" joy; cf. Bockmuehl 59. Philo embraced Hellenistic senses, joy as intoxication (with God), virtues give joy to God *(Spec.* 1.271); *TDNT* 9:365–66.

Jesus depicted joy eschatologically (Matt 5:12 par Luke 6:23; Luke 15:7,10; cf. Matt 18:13). Joy is particularly strong in Luke (1:14; 2:10; 19:6, 37; 24:41 and 52) and Acts (5:41; 8:8, 13:48, 52). "Festive joy" at worship, Acts 2:46, especially the agape (Reicke 1951 [1] Bibl. **agent;** du Toit 1965) seems less well supported in the NT than the "charismatic and experiential *(enthusiastisch)* character" of joy (Berger, *EDNT* 3:451, 454).

In Paul, joy *(chara;* never *agalliasis; euphrainein* in OT quotes at Gal 4:27 and Rom 15:10, otherwise only at 2 Cor 2:2) comes with the gospel through the Spirit; it parallels "progress" in faith (Phil 1:25) and connects with hope (Rom 12:12; 15:13). For the present, believers must live with afflictions, grief, or pain (1 Thess 1:6; 2 Cor 2:3; 7:4–16; 8:2; Phil 1:17–18; 2:28), paradoxically (1 Cor 7:30; 2 Cor 6:10; 13:9). "Rejoice!" (impv.) is often connected with "in the Lord," esp. in Phil

(3:1; 4:4,10), so an ecclesiological dimension (see COMMENT on *en kyriō[i]* in 3:1, etc.), a reciprocal matter (Rom 2:15) between apostle and congregation (1 Thess 3:9; Phil 2:17–18, 28–29; 2 Cor 1:24; Rom 15:32). It marks Paul's outlook and style of speech ("I rejoice," Phil 1:18; 2:17; Rom 16:19; 1 Cor 16:17). His congregations are his joy (Phil 4:1), expected to "stand" at Christ's parousia (1 Thess 2:19–20). "I rejoice . . ." re a congregation serves to gain the goodwill of the addressees (Berger 1984b:1082; 2 Cor 2:3; 7:7,9,13,16; Phil 4:10).

Rejoicing was often a feature in the Gk. letter. See NOTE on 4:10 *I rejoiced* and (16) COMMENT A.4 on the "epistolary rejoicing formula" (Webber 96–156; J. L. White 1971a:95–96; 1986:201), "exclamation of joy at receipt of a letter." The rejoicing formula (Webber 174) was "more widespread in the papyri than is the thanksgiving"; where both occur, "the rejoicing formula dominates." Phil 1:4, *with joy* is not "epistolary rejoicing" (164–67) but a temporal reference to Paul's prayers and feelings about the Philippians, from a relationship of longer duration and deeper than receipt of a letter.

1:5. *because of your sharing in the gospel from the first day until now.* Schubert's unit 6, causal, why Paul makes entreaty with joy (1:4) and gives thanks (1:3). See COMMENT A.2.(6). Connection with *eucharistō* in v 3 (Schubert; Omanson 1978a) was well brought out by Moffatt, 1:3 "I thank my God for all your remembrance of me . . . ," 1:4–5 "I always pray with a sense of joy for what you have contributed to the gospel. . . ." Two phrases provide the *termini a quo* ("the first day") and *ad quem* ("until now") that overarch the community's life.

because of. epi + dat., as in 1:3 (see NOTE on *because of your every remembrance of me*), causal, giving a reason for prayer (NEB, NIV, NABRNT, NRSV).

your sharing. gen. *hymōn,* "of you," generally taken as subjective (Hauck, *TDNT* 3:798, following Seesemann 16–17), i.e., "the Philippians' share in the gospel."

sharing. koinōnia, a word in which NT "authors expressed the essence of Christianity" (Panikulam 1), of "central significance" in Paul (Schattenmann, *NIDNTT* 1:641, 643), 13x in acknowledged letters (19x in NT). Vb. *koinōnein* (4 in Paul, 8 NT examples), noun *koinōnos* (5x out of 10 NT instances), + compounds *sugkoinōnein* (Phil 4:14) and *sygkoinōnos* (1:7), 4 out of 7 examples. Gk. background, not OT. Trs. vary at 1:5, KJV "fellowship"; RSV "partnership"; NEB "the part you have taken"; Moffatt "what you have contributed"; NRSV "your sharing."

The adj. *koinos* meant "common," "communal" (in contrast to "private"), hence "public"; *to koinon,* common property, the community, the state (cf. "commonwealth"). *koinōnos* = participant, one who shares in something with others. Vb. *koinōnein* (Hauck, *TDNT* 3:797), "1. 'to share with someone . . . in something which he has,' 'to take part,' 2. . . . 'to have a share with someone in something which he did not have,' 'to give a part,' 'to impart.'" BAGD/BDAG *koinōnia*: 1. **close association involving mutual interests and sharing,** *association, communion, fellowship, close relationship:* Phil 2:1 and 1:5; 2. **attitude of goodwill that manifests an interest in a close relationship,** *generosity, fellow-feeling, altruism:* perhaps 2:1; 3. abst. for concrete, **sign of fellowship, proof of brotherly**

unity, even **gift, contribution;** 4. **participation, sharing** (+ gen.) **in someth[ing]:** 3:10. A bewildering variety of renderings!

Gk. philosophers used *koinon*-vocabulary re the social order (Hauck, *TDNT* 3:791–96; *NIDNTT* 1:640). In Acts 2:44, the community has "all things in common *(koina)*"; 4:32; cf. the Pythagorean maxim, friends have all things in common *(koina ta philōn;* Diog. Laert. 8.1.10; "amity is parity [*philia isotēs*]"); from *koinōnia,* etc. Phil is claimed as a letter of friendship (L. M. White 1990; Ebner 1991:345–64, on Phil 4:10–20; J. T. Fitzgerald, *ABD* 5:230 and 1996:83–160). Some city states (Sparta) had a communal economy and equality *(isotēs)* for citizens. Pythagoras taught a communal order (derived from the order of the *kosmos*), all held in common. Plato's ideal republic had communal, not private, property *(Resp.* 3.416E; 4.457C; cf. *Critias* 110). Behind visions of an ideal society lurked the notion of a "golden age" (Hesiod, *Op.* 109ff.) and tales about ideal communities (Diod. Sic. 2.55–60, esp. 58.1; 5.45.4–5; 6.1.4–5). Cynic teachers aimed at no property, just an itinerant's sack; Stoics, a consortium of gods and humans, a brotherhood with equality; also Neo-Pythagoreans like Apollonius of Tyana (Philosotratus, *Vit. Apoll.* 3.15). Luke's account of the Jerusalem church in Acts 2–5 suggests "the ideal which the Greeks sought with longing was achieved in the life of the primitive community" *(TDNT* 3:796; A. C. Mitchell 1992).

In the Greco-Roman world, concord sometimes involved eating at the table of the god(s) (Eur. *El.* 637; Plato *Sym.* 188b); hence the invitation, "Chaeremon asks you to dine at the table of Lord Sarapis at the Sarapeum tomorrow" (POxy 1.110 = *LAE* 351 n 2; cf. 1 Cor 10:18–22,27). Epict., "fellowship with [*koinōnia pros* + acc.] Zeus" (1.19.27). In some cults, perhaps union sexually with the deity *(TDNT* 800 nn 20,24). The LXX never uses such "sacral" speech re Yahweh (Hauck 799–801), but cf. Deut 32:17, 37–38, re *other* gods (eating in the presence of YHWH, Exod 24:9–11; Isa 25:6–8, is unusual). *koinon*-words are rare in the LXX, chiefly in later, deuterocanonical books, under Hellenistic influence *(koinōnia* only at Wis 6:23, 8:18, and 3 Macc 4:6; *TDNT* 3:790–91, 800–3). The Heb. root thus rendered is usually *ḥābar,* "to join together" *(TDOT* 4:193–97); cf. *ḥăbûrôt* in rabbinic lit., tech. term for a society of Pharisees (R. Meyer, *TDNT* 9:16–20). Jos. a bit and Philo considerably use Hellenistic *koinon*-terms *(TDNT* 3:795–96, 800–3; *NIDNTT* 1:640–41).

In the NT used chiefly by Paul. Interpretation as "participation" (Seesemann, J. Y. Campbell) shifted toward eucharistic, ecclesiological emphases (Hainz *EDNT* 2:304; Hainz 1994). Earlier Protestant treatments may minimize ecclesial emphasis; more recent ones may overstress church and eucharist. Cf. Schenk's criticism (95 n 29) of Hainz's "Wortfeld" in *EDNT*. Each use by Paul is best considered in the context of each letter (Hainz 1972, 1982; Dewailley 1973). 1 Cor 10:16 is likely the earliest (Hellenistic) Christian use, a pre- or non-Pauline formula about the Lord's Supper, from Gk. terminology for social meals (Klauck 1982:261; cf. McDermott 232; Bori 111–12; Hainz 1982:203). The group is the church *not only* when it eats, or *because of,* the Lord's Supper, but because of God's call (1:9), justification, reconciliation, and sanctification through Christ's cross (1:17,18,30). The Corinthians were called into "an association/

partnership belonging to Jesus Christ" (possessive gen.; Yamsat, cf. 1:9, 10:20). Cf. J. Reumann 1985:14–15, 41–43; AB 32:250–53; Conzelmann, *1 Cor* 171; Fee, *1 Cor.* 467–69.

Paul employed *koinōnia* for the fellowship with God's Son to which the Corinthians were called (1 Cor 1:9; cf. Phil 3:10); "the right hand of fellowship," a sign of agreement in the gospel (Gal 2:9; cf. Phil 1:5); mutual sharing between teacher and those being taught the word (Gal 6:6; cf. Phil 4:15; reciprocity in Rom 15:27); sharing in the collection (*koinōnia*, 2 Cor 8:4; 9:13; cf. Rom 12:13). 2 Cor 13:14, possibly traditional, a benediction, "sharing in the Holy Spirit," "the communion of the Holy Spirit," or "the fellowship created by the Holy Spirit"; cf. Phil 2:1. Phlm 6, "the sharing of your faith," like Phil 1:5 and 1 Cor 1:9, in the introduction to a letter.

Hainz 1994:388–89 regards 1:5 as key to Phil (Bormann 1995:161–205, 4:10–20 is key): Paul and the Philippians shared a common gospel. Baumert 2003:200–2, 502, 525: they shared financial support for gospel preaching. *sharing*, in the TRANSLATION of 1:5, fits with the subj. gen. *your* and the dynamic nature of the phrase that follows, *eis to euangelion*.

in the gospel. BAGD/BDAG *eis* 4.c.β, for the goal of an action; *koinōnia* 1, but cf. 4, **sharing**, as in 2 Cor 8:4. An obj. gen. could have been used, *tou euangeliou*, "sharing the gospel," but the subj. gen. *hymōn* calls for a different construction. *eis* suggests movement, action, proclaiming the good news. De Boor, *Phil.* 42, proof the Philippians were active in its spread; cf. Gnilka 45 n 24; Ware 1996:171–72; Schenk 95 (Rom 15:26; 2 Cor 9:13); *ZBG* #107, cf. 108–9; O'B 62.

gospel. euangelion. In Paul, 48 out of 76 NT occurrences. 9x in Phil (1:5,7,12,16,27 [bis]; 2:22; 4:3,15), a tie with the much longer Rom. Vb. *euangelizesthai*, not in Phil. Paul "established the term *euangelion* in the vocabulary of the NT" (U. Becker, *NIDNTT* 2:110), but it was used in Christian circles prior to Paul, with roots in both the Greco-Roman and OT worlds. Cf. *TPTA* #7. For Paul, oral proclamation, involving content and action; *euangelion* as "gospel *book*" is later (Friedrich, *TDNT* 2:735–36; U. Becker, *NIDNTT* 2:113–14).

Gk. background: from *angelos* ("messenger") came *euangelion*, reward to a messenger who brings good news (Homer, *Od.* 14.152,166); then the message itself, e.g., of victory (30 cases in Schniewind 1927:130 n 2; *TDNT* 2:710–11). Usually good news, but the information may prove false. Vb. "announce as good news," + dir. obj. like deliverance *(sōtēria)* or good fortune *(eutychia)*. Some stress application to (1) a divinized person *(theios anēr)* like Apollonius of Tyana (Philosotratus, *Vit. Apoll.* 1.28); or (2) a Hellenistic ruler or the Roman Emperor, cf. inscriptions, Priene 9 B.C. ("ruler cult"), "the birthday of the god" Augustus "was the beginning of good tidings *(euangeli[ōn])* for the world" (OGIS 458; *TDNT* 2:724; *TLNT* 5:85–86; Klauck 2003:297–98); a "new era" connected with a ruler's deeds (16 annual Augustan festivals, listed in Klauck 2003:320–21). The *euangelion* of Jesus Christ contrasts with political claims about the Emperor as lord (*TDNT* 2:725; HSNTApo 1:72–73, "Hellenistic Christianity took over the term . . . from Hellenistic piety especially . . . in the Imperial cult"; rev. ed. 1991:78–79 cites Stuhlmacher 1968 and Strecker, *EDNT* 2:71; Koester, *Intro.* 2:92). Texts in Klauck 2003:252–88, esp. 255.

Appeal to OT sources often assumes Jesus used Heb. *běśôrâ* or some Aramaic equivalent. But Markan examples seem redactional (Mark 1:15; 8:35; 10:29; 13:10; 14:9; *EDNT* 2:71; from Paul, avoided by Luke? cf. Fitzmyer, *Luke* AB28:173); Luke has *euangelizesthai*, never the noun. At issue: Luke 4:18 (= Isa 61:1); 7:22 par Matt 11:5 (cf. Isa 35:5–6; *euangelizesthai* = Heb. *biśśar*).

OT development of *biśśar* parallels *euangelizesthai* in Gk.: "bring news" (sometimes + the adj. *tôb* = good, 1 Kgs 1:42), of battlefield success (2 Sam 4:10; 1 Sam 31:9); deliverance by Yahweh (Ps 40:9, Heb. 10); with future reference (Isa 52:7–10; 40:9). Such passages influenced, if not Jesus, at least the early church; cf. Rom 10:15 = Isa 52:7, applied to Christian missionaries. The LXX has the noun, always in the pl., *euangelia*, for *běśôrâ*, at 2 Sam (2 Regn) 4:10; 18:20, 22; and 2 Kgs (4 Regn) 7:9. G. Dalman 1898 held Jesus likely had *not* used the term "gospel"; M. Burrows 1925, Jesus derived it from Second Isaiah. Schniewind 1927, 1931 gathered source materials used by Molland to argue the Pauline concept was not Hellenistic, though understandable from usage in the Emperor cult; Rom 10:15 reflects rabbinic tradition, not LXX (Molland 37–38; cf. Str-B 3:282–83). Stuhlmacher's "prehistory" of the Pauline gospel (1968: 204–6) opposed Hellenistic influences. Pre-Pauline are 1 Thess 1:9–10, 1 Cor 15:3–8; with less unanimity, Matt 28:16–20 par Mark 16:9–20; Mark 1:14–15; Luke 4:16–30 *(euangelizesthai);* Matt 11:5–6 par Luke 7:22; Rev 14:6–7. *euangelion* was used within an eschatological framework (cf. Rom 11:28; Mark 13:10 par Matt 24:14; also Rom 1:3b–4a, *euangelion* at 1:1 and 9, Strecker, *EDNT* 2:71). Cf. Schütz 54–71. Dickson 153–77 sees gospel, from Isa (esp. 40:9, 52:7, and 61:1) and Jesus, as "authorized speech" in Paul. Some who see the primary basis in Hellenistic ruler cult allow that OT-Jewish elements are involved (Strecker, *EDNT* 2:71).

For Paul (cf. O'Brien 1986:213–16) "gospel" involves action (with vbs. like *katangellein,* "announce," 1 Cor 9:14; *gnōrizein,* "make known," Gal 1:11); preaching the good news (Phil 4:3, cf. 15; 1 Cor 9:14b,18b) ". . . in power and in the Holy Spirit" (1 Thess 1:5). For Paul, like Peter, the content and purpose of apostleship (Gal 2:7–8; 1 Cor 1:17). The sequence "sent," "proclaim," so that people "hear," "believe," and "call upon" the Lord (Rom 10:13–17) reflects OT prophetic vv (Joel 2:32; Isa 52:7; and 53:1). The gospel leads to faith (Rom 10:17; Phil 1:27). Hence, one proclaims "the faith" (Gal 1:23, the content and result of the gospel). Gospel (Gal 4:13) also stresses "promise" (Gal 3:14,16,17,18,21,22,29, *epangelia;* cf. Acts 13:32–33; *TDNT* 2:720; J. Schniewind/G. Friedrich, *"epangellō,* etc.," *TDNT* 2:576, 579 ["a complement of *euangelion*"], 581–84).

Its content (stressed by Burton, *Gal.* 422–23) is "of [i.e., about] Christ" (1 Thess 3:2, etc.) who is also source (i.e., subj., rather than obj., gen.), Rom 15:18. In 1 Cor, "Christ crucified" (1:23), exalted as lord (1 Cor 15; 2 Cor 4:5; Phil 2:8–11), hence the glory of Christ (2 Cor 4:4). The gospel is christocentric, but from and about God, at work in Christ, making known the divine will and glory (1 Thess 2:2,8,9; 2 Cor 11:7, cf 4:3–6; Rom 1:1–5; 15:16). It originates with God's action, exhibited as grace and gift (2 Cor 9:13–15), light and revealed knowledge (2 Cor 4:4–6), power for salvation (Rom 1:16; 1 Cor 15:2; cf. Phil 1:27b–28). Various images suggest the contents and results: justification (Reumann 1982:

##58–76; see NOTE on 1:11 *righteousness*; cf. 3:6–11), reconciliation (Reumann, "Reconciliation," *IDBSup* 728–29; formulas in 2 Cor 5:19–21; Rom 11:15; Col 1:15–20; Eph 2:15–16; R. P. Martin, *Reconciliation: A Study of Paul's Theology* [Atlanta: John Knox, 1981; repr. Grand Rapids: Eerdmans, 1989] 80–89, 93–97, 114–17, 172–76), life, peace, and love; *NJBC* 82:67–80, "Effects of the Christ Event."

"*my* gospel" (Rom 2:16; 16:25; Schütz 71–78) or "*our* gospel" (1 Thess 1:5, etc.) imply not an idiosyncratic message, but that Paul made the gospel his own. Synonyms include "the word of the cross" (1 Cor 1:23, cf. *logos* at Phil 1:14; 2:16), "word of life"; "the truth (of the gospel)" (Gal 2:5, 14), and "Jesus," a shorthand reference (2 Cor 11:4), sometimes + "Christ" or other titles (Rom 4:25; 1 Cor 1:30). Strecker (*EDNT* 2:72) traces letter-by-letter emphases. Fitzmyer 1979: 152–58, the Pauline gospel is revelatory or apocalyptic (Rom 1:17; cf. Stuhlmacher), dynamic (Rom 1:16, *dynamis theou*), kerygmatic (1 Cor 15:1–7), normative (Gal 1: 6–9), promissory (Rom 1:2, "promised beforehand"), and universal (Rom 1:16, Jew and Greek = all the world).

In Phil, use is shaped by Paul's relationships (1:5; 2:22; 4:3, 15 their partnership); imprisonment (suffering "serves the expansion of the gospel," 1:12); and pressures on the community. It is "norm for the Church's conduct and safeguards the unity of the faith (1:27)" (Strecker, *EDNT* 2:72). At 1:5, its content can be assumed as familiar (no explanatory phrases, *TDNT* 2:729). The action aspect = sharing in missionary proclamation (Schniewind 1910:94–95; Molland 49–50; Ware 1996:169; O'Brien 1986:216–28). Dickson attempts to limit proclamation to apostle and colleagues, but admits 1:5 "comes quite close" to showing converts as "personally engaged" (128–29; cf. *TDNT* 2:732).

from the first day until now. tēs is omitted before *first day* in Western uncials and the Majority text, but occurs in P⁴⁶ ℵ A B D, etc.; cf. Silva 23. The art. may be omitted with ordinal numbers like "first" that designate time (Lft. 83; BDF #256; Acts 20:18).

Two preps., *apo* (BDAG II.2.b.β) and *achri* (BDAG 1.a.α), both + gen., provide time limits, forward and backward. A further temporal phrase comes in v 6, *by (achri) the Day of Christ Jesus* (cf. v 10, *for [eis] the Day of Christ*). *Day* in vv 6 and 10 refers to the parousia; v 5 *hēmera* = a period of time (BDAG 2.c).

first (protos, ē, on; BDAG 1.a, "first, earliest" or even "initial"), when the Philippians heard the gospel from Paul and shared in it by believing, "an objective, communal fact" (Collange 45). Baumgarten 69–70, "a metaphor for the beginnings of the Philippian congregation"; not a single date on the calendar but protological analogy to the eschatological "Day of the Lord," 1:6.

now. nyn, here, without a noun, subst., "(the) present time" (BAGD *nyn* 3.b; BDAG 1.a.β.‌ℶ; *TDNT* 4:1107, 1110; papyri, inscriptions, LXX, Mark 13:19 par Matt 24:21). = the time when Paul wrote or when the Philippians received the letter.

1:6. *since I am confident about this point. pepoithōs*, masc. nom. sg. ptc., agrees with the subj. in v 3, *I thank.* Schubert, O'Brien 1977:22–23; *Phil.* 63, and others, see a third reason why Paul thanks God (unit 6), paralleling *because of your every* *remembrance of me* (3b) and *because of your sharing in the gospel* (5). Circumst. ptc. of cause. *since* to distinguish it from the other two (*epi* + dat.). Some ([N]RSV, NEB) begin a new sentence with v 6, less connected with v 3. Paul's confidence ("God active among you") is further *captatio benevolentiae* (Berger 1974 [section 1 Bibl.] 220; 1984b:1047–48).

Ptc. from *peithō*, "convince, persuade," 2nd pf. with pres. meaning (BDF #341); pf. pass. *pepeismai* = "I have been persuaded and therefore am convinced"; pf. act. *pepoitha*, "depend on, trust in" and therefore "be sure, certain" (BDAG *peithō* 2.a and b); confidence that is certitude (*TLNT* 3:76). Usually "God" is assumed as basis (as in the OT, e.g., Ps 25 [LXX 24]:2), cf. 2 Cor 1:9, but Loh.19–20 suggests "you" Philippians.

this point. Obj., neut. acc. sg., dem. pron. *houtos, hautē, touto,* "this," BDAG 1.b.β, with reference to what follows; so Gundry Volf 47 n 230; BDF #290 hesitates, perhaps v 5 and the constancy described there; cf. BDAG 1.a.β and ε and 1.b.α and Phil 3:7; 4:8, 9, but all these examples have a rel. pron. preceding *tauta,* and at 1:22 there is an art. infin. What Paul is confident about will be expressed in the *hoti* cl. that follows (Fee 85 n 62); acc. + *hoti* is common in Paul (1 Cor 1:12, etc.); Phil 1:25, *touto pepoithōs oida hoti,* "since I am confident of this, I know that. . . ." With *pepoithōs, touto* can be a "cognate acc. of inner content" (ATR 478; BDF #154, "in just this confidence"). Paul likes using with *touto* the neut. of the intensive pron. *autos, ē, o* (BAGD 1.h/BDAG 1.g, "even, very"; "this very thing"; "just this," or "precisely this"). *auto touto,* Rom 9:17; 13:6; 2 Cor 7:11 (ATR 686, 705). As introduction to what follows, *point* has been supplied.

that the One who inaugurated a good work among you will bring it to completion by the Day of Christ Jesus. God will perfect at the parousia the divine deed inaugurated when they accepted the gospel. Subst. ptc. with its own obj., vb. fut. tense, prep. phrase for the eschatological *terminus ad quem.* If *this point* in 6a refers backward (see above on *touto* in BDF #290.4), then *hoti* can = "because": "I am confident about this point (your sharing in the gospel), because God . . . will complete the good work begun among you. . . ."

the One who inaugurated a good work among you. Subst. ptc. *ho enarxamenos,* masc. nom. sg., aor. *enarchomai,* strengthened form of *archō,* in the m., "begin." Aor. = action prior to the main vb., "began." Possible cultic overtones to *enarchomai* (Eur. *Iph. Aul.* 1470, ". . . begin [*enarchesthō*]" the sacrifice, BDAG 331) and *epileleō* (Lft. 84; *Gal.* 135, on 3:3) find little resonance in subsequent discussion. See Ewald 44 n 2; Wohl. 52 n 1; Michael 12–13; H. D. Betz, *Gal.* 133 n 57. Dib. 53 compared 2 Cor 8:6, 10, beginning and completing the collection (*proenarchomai* and *entelein*), and suspected proverbial language (Radl 1981:43). Loh. 20–21, festal tone and liturgical style, like God as beginning and end (Rev 21:6; Wis 7:18); Baumgarten 71 rightly questions such evidence for a "Beginning-Completion" schema of tradition. Loh., the beginning and end of faith (cf. Heb 12:2), but would Paul speak of the "work" of faith? (See NOTE on 1:6 *a good work,* observations [3] and [4].) Loh., "a pre-Pauline tradition" during persecution, expressing trust that they are under God's care. Schenk 99–100, a "faithful saying" (*Treuesprüche* or *Gewissheitssprüche,* "saying of certainty"), perhaps beginning,

"God is faithful" (*pistos ho theos*, 1 Cor 10:13b; cf. 1:8–9; Rom 8:38–39; 2 Cor 1:18), + vb. fut. tense. Cf. P. von der Osten-Sacken, *Römer 8 als Beispiel paulinischer Soteriologie* (FRLANT 112; Göttingen: Vandenhoeck & Ruprecht, 1975) 42–45; Osten-Sacken, "Gottes Treue zur Parousie: Formgeschichtliche Beobachtungen zu 1 Kor 1,7b–9," *ZNW* 68 (1977) 176–99. *Pirke Aboth* 2.18 (*Mishnah*, ed. Danby, 'Abot 2.14) is cited because of the presence of "work" (1:6b), "Faithful is he, the Lord of your work, who will pay you the reward of your labor." Final decision depends on analysis of *work* and exegesis of the whole v.; see COMMENT A.2.b.

Commentators are virtually unanimous, "he who began a good work in you" (RSV) = God (Schlosser 1995a:379; DA 378, cf. 381). Pelagius (*Exp.* 388,19–389,2, ed. A. Souter, TS 9:1) applied it to Paul; cf. Gal 1:6, Betz (*Gal.* 48), but Paul used such phrases for God (cf. Gal 1:15; 1 Thess 5:24; Phil 2:13). Here, *will bring it to completion by the Day of Christ Jesus* cannot apply to an apostle in prison who faces death any day, prior to the parousia (1:7, 19–24).

among you. en + dat.; "in you" (KJV, RSV, NEB) may suggest God's activity in individual hearts. *hymin* is pl., the context is corporate or communal. So Gnilka 46; Schenk 98; cf. BAGD *en* I.4.a/BDAG 1.d; Moule, *IB* 75. NRSV "among."

a good work. agathos, ē, on, good, (a) fit, capable, useful, or (b) morally, of inner worth (Rom 5:7; 7:12; 1 Thess 3:6); with *ergon*, 2 Cor 9:8, you "share abundantly in every good work"; BAGD 1.a.,b.β; BDAG 1.a, 2.a.β. Attrib., even without an art. (ATR 776).

work. ergon, from *ergazomai*. On one hand, of *God's work* in creation (Gen 2:2, 3, etc.) and salvific activity (Exod 34:10; Ps 76 [77]:12; Isa 28:21; esp. John, 5:17, 36; 10:32 *kala erga*, etc.). For Paul, the community of believers is the "work of God" (Rom 14:20; 1 Cor 9:1). Cf. E. Peterson 1941; Kitzberger 206–8; H.-C. Hahn, *NIDNTT* 3:1151, "through the apostles." On the other hand, of *human work*, a task given by God with positive meaning (Gen 2:15; Isa 28:23–29; John 3:21; *TDNT*). In Paul, "work with your hands" (1 Thess 4:11); "work the good" (Gal 6:10; cf. Rom 2:10); "work out your salvation" (Phil 2:12). Work will be examined at the final judgment (1 Cor 3:11–13a, etc.). BDAG *ergon* 1.c.β puts Phil 1:6 under "the deeds of humans."

1:6 is "*crux interpretum*" (Gundry Volf 33), singular but not unique among 47 instances of *ergon* in Paul's undisputed letters (3 in Phil). Some claim "traditional material" (Radl 1981:43). (1) *a good work* in 1:6 is not a contrast to, or reflection of, Paul's battle with those in Galatia who stressed "the works of the Law," *erga nomou* (2:16; 3:2,5,10; cf. 5:19), always pl., + a gen. (likely of source). Here sg., modified by *good*, no inkling of "Law." When Paul discusses Law in Phil 3:5–9, *ergon* does not appear. (2) *ergon* is positive at 1:6, as elsewhere in Phil (1:22 "fruitful labor," *karpos ergon*; 2:30 "the work of Christ"). God began and will complete this "good work." (3) 1:6 relates to three other passages using *agathon ergon* (cf. also Col 1:10; Eph 2:10 and 1 Tim 2:10): Rom 13:3, "good conduct" in the state. Rom 2:7, eternal life "to those who by patiently doing good seek for glory and honor and immortality" (NRSV); faith, if Christians are meant, or God judges "well doing" in an impartial way; cf. Reumann 1982: ##125–29 and 390. 2 Cor

9:8 some make decisive: God provides blessings "so that you may share in every good work." H. D. Betz calls *agathon ergon* here, re the collection, "more Hellenistic than Jewish"; "wealth is a divine gift" that "enables the human recipient to share with others" (2 *Cor* 8–9: 110; cf. AB 32A:447). (4) In Paul's earliest letter, the Thessalonians' "work of faith *(tou ergou tēs pisteōs)* . . ." (1 Thess 1:3) is likely a "deed arising out of faith" (subj. gen. or gen. of source; unless a gen. of quality, therefore "work of God or Christ"), possibly missionary work, healings, and other results of faith (cf. 1 Cor 13:2; 12:9; E. Best, *1 Thess.* 68; Malherbe, AB 32B:108, 124, preaching; J. Ware 1996). Paul continued to speak of missionary labor (*kopos*, 1 Thess 3:5; 1 Cor 3:8, etc. vb. *kopian* Phil 2:16; Gal 4:11; 1 Cor 16:16), but "in the later letters, when the problem of the Judaizers has surfaced, *pistis* is never again so related to *ergon*, and *ergon tēs pisteōs* is studiously avoided—undoubtedly because of the connotation that *ergon* has by then acquired because of *erga tou nomou*, 'deeds of the law' (Rom 3:28) or even *erga* alone (Rom 4:2)" (Fitzmyer in Reumann 1982: #337, cf. 83). Nonetheless, (5) 1:6 relates *agathon ergon* to (a) the vbs. *inaugurated* and *will bring it to completion;* (b) a temporal reference, from the time when God *inaugurated* this *work* until *the Day of Christ*, including the period mentioned in v 5 *from the first day until now;* (c) *among you*, work common to all in the community. (6) It can be taken as a *nomen resultantum*, the result from what God (or a community) does. Or (Schenk 97) *nomen actionis*, working (= *ergazesthai*, as in Gal 3:2), *ergon* as an action, cf. vv with the same syntagma (2 Cor 9:8, Phillips "giving away to other people"; Rom 2:7 "well-doing"; 13:3 "do right," NIV), and from the use of *epitelein* at 2 Cor 8:6,11; Rom 15:28, "completing" the collection; cf. 2 Cor 7:1, a parallel in content, "making holiness perfect" *(epitelountes hagiasynēn)*. (7) This reason for Paul's giving thanks relates to those in v 3 *your remembrance of me* and v 5 *your sharing in the gospel* (Schubert; O'Brien 1977:22–26). Interpretive options:

(A) *ergon agathon* as the **work of God**—God is the subject who *inaugurated a good work among you* and *will bring it to completion.* Cf. TDNT 2:643; 4:722; Gundry Volf 39–40; Fee 86–87. (A.1) "Salvation"—cf. Michael 13; Martin 1976:65; their faith (Loh. 20); reconciliation (K. Barth 16); sanctification (Wohl. 54; Gundry Volf 47; cf. Silva 52; Caird, Bruce 32). (A.2) Creation was "good" (Gen 1; I. H. Marshall 11), therefore God's new creation (2 Cor 5:17; 4:6; cf. 1 Cor 15:38 with Gen 1:11–12). Martin 1976:66; Gnilka 46; Radl 1981:44; Hawth. 21; G. Barth 18; O'Brien 1977:27 and *Phil.* 64–65, creation and calling; Schenk 98–99, calling is an act of creation; U. B. Müller 41. Silva 51–52, at best "secondary and indirect"; similarly Melick 58 n 15. (A.3) God's almsgiving—Gundry Volf 42–44, an older "tradition of good works" (cf. Heiligenthal), used by Paul "to denote God's salvific activity" in 2 Cor 8:9 and here (cf. 46). Their "good works" (*sic* pl.), almsgiving, assumes "God's prior, saving work in their lives." This position edges away from (A.2) toward (B.5).

(B) *ergon agathon* as **the work of God and the Philippians**—God began and will complete it, but it is in or among the Philippians and involves them. Cf. 2:12–13 and Gundry Volf 39–42; Lft. 84; Bertram, TDNT 2:640; Bockmuehl 61. (B.1) The *living Christianity of the Philippians (Glaubenstand*, Gnilka 46), expressed in action (Michaelis 14; Melick 58); the church (Craddock 17; Heiligen-thal:137; Kitzberger 206–7); Merk 1968:14, "the totality of the transactions of the justified." Loh. 19–21, U. B. Müller 41, faith. Walter 35, 36: participation in God's love, expressed toward the neighbor. (B.2) *Evangelization* or *missionary advance*—Hawth. 21; Schlosser 1995a:380. (B.3) *Furtherance of the gospel*, more broadly (cf. 1:12,25)—O'Brien 1977:26, cf. 24; Meyer, *Phil.* 13; Vincent 8; Collange 45; Fee 85: the "broader sense" is "their relationship to Christ and the gospel," par-ticipation and sharing; Hartman 2001:21. (B.4) *Cooperation with and affection for Paul*— Lft. 84; Bonnard 16; Michaelis 14. (B.5) *Financial gifts*, for Paul or the collection (Fee 85, the narrower sense of the phrase)—Zahn 1895:191–92; Koenig 136. Gundry Volf 1990:42 n 207 lists variations re material aid.

(C) *ergon agathon*, as a **human activity** (cf. BDAG). The Philippians are the ones engaged in the good work of 1:6. (C.1) *Financial gifts*, noted in (B.5). (C.2) Doing *good in general*—Zahn 1895:192, including their "citizenship" in the Roman *colonia* and God's kingdom (1:27). Schenk 97 develops a strong case for *nomen actionis* and the doing of good (128, cf. 2 Cor 9:8 and 1 Cor 15:58). Human works (Heiligenthal), in Gk. literature, exhibit a person's character and provide the basis for judgment. In early Christianity, deeds functioned as witness in mis-sionary endeavor, exhibiting social significance (1 Pet 2:12; Matt 5:13–16; Rom 13:2–4), and before God in the judgment (Gal 5:19–26; 2 Cor 5:2–10; Rom 2:1–11).

To tr. as *a good work* is standard, open to most of the possibilities above. Final decision involves situation, structure, possible tradition and Paul's use of it. See COMMENT A.2.b and B.3.

will bring it to completion. epiteleō, fut.; see NOTES on *the One who inaugurated a good work among you* and *a good work* (6). From *teleō*, "bring to an end, com-plete, accomplish" (cf. *telos*, "end," "goal"), *epiteleō* occurs in the NT only 10x, in letters, 7x by Paul. BDAG 383 (1) "end, bring to an end, finish," 2 Cor 8:6,11a and b and Rom 15:28. G. Delling, *TDNT* 8:61–62, no cultic sense; 1:6 = God carries out in the congregation "the exclusive work of God . . . right up to the *parousia*," with "transition from the congregation to the individual in v. 7" (62 n 5). Burton, *MT* #60, a "progressive future"; Moule, *IB* 10, is less convinced about any linear nature. Vincent 8, "will carry it on toward completion, and finally complete," which O'Brien 1977:28 approves. Cf. Louw/Nida 68:22. With the phrase that fol-lows, completion dominates (Schenk 100).

by the Day of Christ Jesus. Prep. *achri*, see v 5 *until* (BDAG 1.a.α), where *hēmera* has a sense different from "parousia" here. KJV, "will perform *it* (dir. obj. sup-plied) until the day of Jesus Christ." RSV "at," only on that Day will God complete the work, "salvation." *by* (NEB, NRSV) is truer to the sense of *achri* as "until" (cf. 1:5; 1 Cor 4:11) and to *ergon agathon* as action (doing good, evangelizing, etc.) continuing "until" the parousia but not "at" the judgment.

the Day (BDAG *hēmera* 3.b.β) appointed for God's judgment; OT *yôm YHWH* (Amos 5:18, 20, etc.); "the Day of the Lord" (Mal 4:3), cf. "in that day," Zech 12:3,6,11, etc.), intensified in apocalyptic literature. On the lips of Jesus (Matt 10:15 = Luke 10:12; Mark 13:32; Matt 12:36). His image of the thief at night

(Matt 24:43–44 par Luke 12:39–40) also appears in Paul (1 Thess 5:2). Imminence of the judgment is often stressed: "the Day is near" (Rom 13:12; cf. Phil 4:5b). Judgment of all people, with wrath for some (Rom 2:5); re believers, 1 Cor 1:8; 3:13; 5:5; Phil 1:10 and 2:16. Terminology varies: "Lord's Day" (1 Thess 5:2); "Day of the Lord" (1 Cor 1:8, etc.); "Day of our Lord Jesus Christ" (1 Cor 1:8); *hē hēmera tou kyriou* (1 Cor 5:5); or simply "The Day" (1 Thess 5:4, etc.). Only in Phil but consistently, "Day of Christ" (1:10; 2:16); 1:6, *Day of Christ Jesus* (names reversed in some MSS). Because 1:6 is different, do we have earlier tradition in 1:6 (Loh. 21)? Or is it characteristically Pauline to replace "of the Lord" with "of Christ (Jesus)"? "Christ" is used more frequently than "Lord" in Phil (21:5 ratio) and reflects "fading of the original meaning of christological titles" (Kramer [(1) Bibl. **Christ**) pp 140–41, 173–76). Schenk 100, "Christ" may occur under the influence of "gospel" (v 5), call and completion, not judgment, in v 6; Jesus Christ as deliverer (1 Thess 1:10), not the Lord as judge here. On "Day (of the Lord)," see E. Jenni, *THAT* 1:707–26, esp. 723–26; G. Delling, *TDNT* 2:944–48, 951–53; G. Braumann, *NIDNTT* 2:887–88, 892–93, 894–95; W. Trilling, *EDNT* 2:121 (3b); *TPTA* 254–55, 308–9; Baumgarten 64–65; Radl 1981:181–85; L. J. Kreitzer 1987 ([1] Bibl. **Jesus**) 112–29. Froitzheim 14–17: the goal of Christian existence, the future event central in Pauline eschatology.

Christ Jesus. See Notes on 1:1 *Christ Jesus,* 1:2 *Lord Jesus Christ.* On "Jesus Christ" (v.l.) see Silva 23. Kramer ([1] Bibl. **Christ**) 204–5, *Christ Jesus* is Paul's normal order in the gen.

1:7a. *It is indeed right for me to think about all of you in this way.* Loh. 22 complains of lack of rhythm and order in 7–8 (in contrast to couplets he supposed in the rest of the prooimion). Hawth. 22, ambiguous Gk., a section "difficult . . . to translate." V 7 = impers. vb. + suppl. infin.; then art. infin. in a causal construction (*dia* + acc.), two prep. phrases describing Paul's imprisonment and trial, + a further reference to the Philippians, with attached ptc. V 8 is an oath about the apostle's longing for those with whom he can be present only through writing. Vv 7–8 function as *captatio benevolentiae* (Schenk 101); vocabulary links within vv 7 and 8, *right for me* and *God is my witness*; connectives, *kathōs* (7) and *gar* (8), lit. "just as" and "for." Vv 7 and 8 are not intrusive, no more (or less) "personal" than the rest of 1:3–11.

it is right. Impers. vb.; BDAG 2, *dikaios, a, on* 5, neut., **obligatory in view of certain requirements of justice;** cf. G. Schneider, *EDNT* 1:324–25. Loh. 22 n 2, "an everyday sense, without religious or ethical weight"; *TLNT* 1:323 n 18. First appearance in Phil of *dikaio-*, the root for *dikaiosynē,* righteousness/justification, 1:11, 3:6 and 9. No need to relate 1:7 to Paul's view of righteousness (Reumann 1982: #108; *DA* 360); otherwise, R. Jewett 1971a:324 n 1, versus the heretics in Phil 3.

indeed. kathōs, causal conjunction, **since** or **in so far as** (BDAG 3), common at the beginning of a cl. (BDF #453.2; Fee 88 n 76 objects, v 7 continues the sentence started in v 3, but note his tr., p. 74). Cf. 1 Cor 5:7; Gal 3:6; Rom 1:23; 1 Cor 1:6 (prooimion). Contra Loh. 22 n 1, form-critical analyses have not made *kathōs* cls. a feature of the Pauline prooimion. Hawth. 22, no correlative like *houtōs* ("just as . . . , so") follows in any of these passages; he adapts NEB's "It is indeed only right that . . . ," which adds "only," and expresses *kathōs* by "indeed" (so TRANSLA-TION). Many trs. ignore *kathōs* (Moffatt, [N]RSV, etc.). U. B. Müller, a new beginning but continuity with *all of you* (4). *for me* is emphatic, perhaps "right for me (not for others)" (Theo. Mop., PG 66:921); Ewald 48–49 related *emoi* to *hymas* in v 7, "*you* as partners"; "right for me in light of Philippian gifts."

to think. Infin. *phronein*, pres. act., possibly linear "continue to think." Vb. (26x in the NT) 22x in Paul's acknowledged letters, 10x in Phil (only 9 in Rom). Of major importance in Phil. BDAG: 1. *think, form/hold an opinion, judge:* Phil 1:7; 4:10 (bis); 3:15 (bis); 2:2b; 3:16 v.l.; 4:2; 2:2d; 2. *set one's mind on, be intent on:* 3:19; . . . 3. *develop an attitude based on careful thought, be minded/disposed:* 2:5. Difficult to tr., exact sense often disputed. 1:7 is relatively straightforward. The stem *phrēn* (vb. from Homer on) meant "mind, understanding, consciousness." With Plato and Aristot. (L. T. Johnson 2003:221–25) *phronēsis* came to mean "practical wisdom," reckoned with virtues like wisdom (*sophia*), justice, and courage; a gift of God, moral insight. No single Heb. term for which *phrēn*-derivatives are used in the LXX; often *lēb*, "heart" (see below), *hākām*, "be wise." Esp. in the wisdom literature, then in Philo and Jos. See *TDNT* 9:220–30 (Bertram) on this background. For the NT, *TDNT* 9:232–33; Goetzmann, *NIDNTT* 2:617–18, reflecting Bultmann 1951 (INTRO. X Bibl.) 214. Jewett 1971a:323–27 treats *phronein* in connection with *kardia* (see NOTE on *heart*) and the heretics in ch. 3 (see NOTE on 1:7 *it is right*); this approach sometimes sways his decisions; O'B 67–68 rightly doubts reading so much into the introductory thanksgiving.

For Paul, the mind (Gk. *nous*, sometimes *kardia*, "heart"; cf. Heb. *lēb, lēbāb*) within the human being as a person capable of having a relationship with self as well as with others (and with God)—i.e., as part of *sōma* (body, the whole person)—involves "the knowing, understanding, and judging which belong to man as man and determine what attitude he adopts" (Bultmann 1951:211; Ger. *Mensch* = human being). Includes volition and intent, "what one has a mind to do"; "the real self." In Paul's analysis, under Sin's dominance and the rule of the flesh (*sarx*). *phronein* "means one's 'attitude' in which thinking and willing are done" (214). Paul will urge Philippian believers to "think the same thing" or "the one thing," i.e., have the same or a common attitude (2:2; 3:16; 4:2); to "think this" re Christ, self, and others (2:5; 3:15); and not to think "earthly" but "heavenly" things (3:19). See NOTES on these vv and 4:10, where Bultmann takes *phronein* as "be helpfully concerned. . . ." The content of *phronein* is not always immediately clear, but "the way one thinks is intimately related to the way one lives" (*NIDNTT* 2:617).

At 1:7 is *phronein* cognitive-intellectual ("think," KJV, NRSV) or a matter of feeling ("feel like this about you," RSV, NEB)? The prep. phrase that follows, *hyper* + gen. (*pantōn hymōn*), BDAG 1065 takes as "think or feel in a certain way" *about all of you*, cf. 4:10; BDAG *hyper* A.1.a.δ; ZBG #96; Moule, *IB* p 65; H. Riesenfeld, *TDNT* 8:508, "be concerned about," cf. *TDNT* 9:233; Paulsen, *EDNT* 3:439. Some count it as "friendship language" (DA 268–69).

in this way. touto. Can point forward or backward (see NOTE on 6 *this point*; BDAG *houtos* 1.b.β and 1.b.α). Probably not forward because a causal cl. follows (*dia to* etc.), probably not back to all of 3–6 (so Wohl. 56–59; Gnilka 48 n 1) but to Paul's confident hope about the Philippians in v 6 (*DA* 206 n 195; 315; Fee 89, vv 3–5 esp.). Schenk 102–3: 4:10, "your concern for me *(to hyper emou phronein)*" was the Philippians' description of their actions supporting Paul. Paul used the phrase in Letter A (4:10) and now echoes it in Letter B (1:7). He reciprocates with concern for them, not simply feeling but a judgment theologically based on knowledge of God's faithfulness and what Paul sees happening through the Philippians (v 6). *in this way* reflects (with Schenk) v 6, *I am confident that God . . . among you will bring it to completion.*

because you have me in your heart. dia + acc. + art. infin. (BAGD *dia* B.II.3; BDAG B.2.c), common in the NT (32x; ATR 966; BDF #402.1, cf. 398–409). Usually prep. *(dia)* and art. (here *to*) + infin. *(echein)*, + subj. of the infin. in the acc. (here *me*), any additional phrase, such as "in the heart" *(en tē[i] kardia[i]*, no personal pron., "my" or "your," to tell whose heart is meant), + the dir. obj. of the infin. (here *hymas*). = "because I have you in my heart" (KJV; RSV; NRSV-mg; many commentators, Chrysost. [therefore L. Hartman 2001:19]; Loh. 23 n 2; Collange; Martin; O'B; Fee 90; *DA* 380; U. B. Müller 42–43; Bockmuehl 63; Silva 56–57, but "earlier commentators" took it as "you have me in your heart"). *me* after *echein* can be obj. of the vb., the subj. "you" understood *(hymōn*, "all of you" has occurred just before *dia; hymas* appears at the end of the construction, after "heart," as delayed subject to clinch the sense). NRSV, "because you hold me in your heart"; NEB-txt; Hawth. 23; Witherington 38; Schenk 104 (the alternative, "to think about you all because I think about you in my heart," is a tautology). Studied ambiguity by Paul? *dia to echein* cls. in the NT have the subj. acc. later about as often as directly after the infin. (Hawth. 23; contrast Silva 56). Paul's feelings *(right for me to think about you in this way)* root in reciprocity with Philippi. V 7b reiterates what 3b said.

heart. kardia, BDAG (1) the "seat of physical, spiritual and mental life," more specifically (a) "the center and source of physical life," (b) "center and source of the whole inner life, w[ith] its thinking, feeling, and volition," with 1:7 listed under (ζ) "esp. also of love." In Eng., "heart," a symbol of (sentimental) love, may mislead and influence tr. of *phronein* in 7a as "feel" (concern). *Word studies* (F. Baumgärtel/J. Behm, *TDNT* 3:605–13; T. Sorg, *NIDNTT* 2:180–84; A. Sand, *EDNT* 2:249–51; cf. H. Schlier 1962, Jewett 1971a:305–33, history of research) rightly conclude NT use of *kardia* agrees with OT understanding of *lēb* (from Isa. on, *lēbāb*), as the center of inner life, including emotions, understanding and knowledge, and will. M. S. Smith 432 n 27, heart = thought as well as emotions because "Hebrew had no word for brain." "Heart" functioned as "a comprehensive term for the personality as a whole" (W. Eichrodt, *Theology of the Old Testament* [Philadelphia: Westminster] 2 [1967] 143). On *kardia*, Paul remained "a Hebrew of the Hebrews" (H. Wheeler Robinson, *The Christian Doctrine of Man* [Edinburgh: T&T Clark, 1911; 3rd ed. 1958] 104), though Bultmann 1951 (INTRO. X Bibl.) 220–23 moves closer to making *kardia* synonymous with *nous*. If *nous* is "the thinking I," Dunn calls *kardia* "the experiencing, motivating I" (*TPTA* 75). If *kardia* is the center for knowledge and understanding, not just emotions, is "heart" the right tr.? Use "mind"? Cf. 1 Kgs 3:12; 4:29 (Heb. 5:9); Matt 24:48; Rom 10:6; Acts 7:23; *TDNT* 3:612 point b. The TRANSLATION keeps *heart*, but it involves the intellect, not just emotions. See Ewald 52–53 on "hold dear" versus "have before one's eyes, know." *heart* (sg.) is used corporately (Semitically, *GNTG* 3:23), of the Philippian community. In Eng., emphasize *you*, the last word in the Gk. unit, not *me*.

1:7b. *both in my imprisonment and in the defense and confirmation of the gospel.* Two prep. phrases with *en*, "in my bonds" and "in the defence [sic] and confirmation of the gospel" (KJV). The latter phrase has just one art. in Gk., hendiadys (BDF #442.16). The two prep. phrases are linked by *te . . . kai*, "both . . . and," "not only . . . but also" BDAG *te* 2.c. Gen. *mou* occurs only with "bonds," but context and the art. *tē[i]* with "defense and confirmation" make it clear *Paul's* defense and confirmation for the gospel is meant. Some MSS lack *en* before *defense* (cf. Silva 23).

imprisonment. desmos, dat. pl. after *en*, bond or fetter (BDAG), "chains" (Cassidy 2001). Pl. in Acts 16:26, Paul jailed at Philippi; 4x in Phil 1–2 of Paul's imprisonment (1:7, 13, 14, 17; cf. also Phlm 10 and 13). NEB, "when I lie in prison."

On *gospel*, see NOTE on 1:5; BDAG *euangelion* 1.b; oral, dynamic missionary proclamation.

defense and confirmation ([N]RSV; NIV "defending and confirming") Lft. 85 took in a general sense, "all modes of preaching and extending the truth"; Phillips, "in prison as well as when I was out defending and demonstrating the power of the gospel"; similarly GNB. This introduces a temporal contrast between imprisonment now and a time when Paul went about unhindered. Most commentators since Deissmann (1909 [(1) Bibl.] 104–6, from the papyri) see "defense and confirmation" as semi-tech. law court terms, referring to Paul before a magistrate.

defense. apologia (BDAG, 2.b), a speech of defense in court (Acts 22:1; 1 Cor 9:3) or the entire court process (2 Tim 4:16). Occurs in papyri, MM 66, Loh. 24 n 2. Gnilka 49, most NT uses have to do with defense before a court (1:7, 16), with a touch of apologetic for the gospel (1 Pet 3:15). Cf. U. Kellermann, *EDNT* 1:137.

confirmation. bebaiōsis (BDAG 173). A tech. legal sense (MM 108) at Heb 6:16 is "still discernible" in Phil 1:7. Jeh. Wit.: "legally establishing" the good news. Cf. H. Schlier, *TDNT* 1:600–3; H. Schönweiss, *NIDNTT* 1:658–60; A. Fuchs, *EDNT* 1:210–11; *TLNT* 1:280–83. Lft. 85, *apologia* "implies the negative or defensive side of the Apostle's preaching," removing obstacles; *bebaiōsis* "the positive or aggressive side, the direct advancement and establishment of the Gospel," is cited with approval by Schenk 106. Paul says he was appointed to make the gospel known, even before the authorities (1:16); NEB, "when I . . . appear in the dock to vouch for the truth of the Gospel." Message and apostle intertwine. Hawth. 24, 35 hints at converting hearers in the courtroom (cf. 1:13, 18). CEV narrows the sense, "as I defend the good news and tell about it here in jail." Paul was a witness not only in the dungeon but also in the courtroom.

1:7c. *you all sharing, as you do, with me in this gracious opportunity of mine.* Noun "partakers" + gen. *mou* ("of me"), another gen. "of the grace" (with art.), and in the acc. "you all" + the ptc. "being" (*ontas*, from *eimi*, acc. masc. pl., pred. position, circumst. use). Lit., "you all being my co-sharers of (the) grace." Agrees with *hymas* at the end of the causal cl. *you have me in your heart.* May be explanatory of *hymas* (repetition in 7c is then pleonastic, Ewald 53, *ontas* an attrib. ptc.; cf. Loh.); or causal ptc. (Hawth. 23, "because all of you are sharers together with me in the privilege [*charitos*] that is mine ..."); or even an acc. abs., "you all being co-sharers ..." (but should involve a neut. ptc., of an impers. vb., cf. BDF #424). NEB, attrib. ptc. in its note, "as those who ... all share in the privilege that is mine"; causal in the text, "because ... you all share. ..." Trs. often make a separate cl. out of 7b and c and may reverse them, RSV "for you are all partakers with me of grace, both in my imprisonment and in the defense and confirmation of the gospel"; cf. NRSV. Phillips makes 7c the main cl., with 7b subordinate.

you all (not U.S. southern idiom but KJV "ye all," RSV, [N]JB, NEB/REB) echoes emphasis on the Philippian community, every member of it (1:1 *to all the saints;* 1:4 *all of you;* 1:7a *all of you*). *sygkoinōnos,* acc. pl., variously rendered "partner" (RSV), "participant," or "sharing in," is *syn* "with" + masc. subst. from *koinōnein;* see NOTE on 1:5 *sharing. syn* may strengthen *koin-* in the stem (Baumert 2003:109). "Business partner" (Sampley) is unlikely; see COMMENT B.2. "Have a share," not "give a share." Horizontal or vertical? "co-sharers *with me* in a privilege that is mine" (to testify to the gospel), or "co-sharers *of grace* with me" or even "of my grace"? Baumert 2003: 108–11, 502, 508, 523, comrades for me in my grace, not "God grant you some of my grace." The key word is the gen. of *charis,* tr. "grace" (KJV, [N]RSV) or "privilege" (Gdsp., NEB, GNB).

this gracious opportunity. See NOTE on 1:2 *grace.* Eberhard Nestle's cj. *chreias,* "(my) need," is rightly dismissed by O'B 65. *charis* here is grace or favor God has made known through Christ to all who respond in faith and obedience (BDAG 2.c, 3.b), "a power" that "actualizes itself" in the church community (*TDNT* 9:395). Bultmann (1951 [INTRO. X Bibl.] 291), "the shared grace of suffering bestowed upon both Paul and the Philippians." Cf. Martin 1976:66; Bloomquist; Oakes 1998, 2001: economic suffering. Silva 53–54, "shared suffering" is not "fully convincing" but *charis* connects with gospel ministry (1 Cor 9:23) that "entails suffering." (1) O'B 70 prefers *mou* with *sygkoinōnous* (n 36; "partakers with me in God's grace"); cf. Fee 91 n. 88; Walter 33; Bockmuehl 63; Baumert 2003:108–11, 502, 523. (2) To take *mou* with *tēs charitos,* "co-sharers in the grace of me" (*charitos* obj. gen. after *sugkoinōnous*), relates "grace" to Paul's apostleship (Satake; see on 1:2 **grace**). So Hainz 1982:199–200, 1994:389; cf. Loh. 26, Silva 53, Collange 47, Eastman ([1] Bibl.) 194. Hawth. 23; Paul is graced. (3) *charis* (BDAG 4) = "**exceptional effect produced by generosity, favor** ... beyond those associated with a specific Christian's status," Paul's call (Gal 2:9), grace as a hallmark of his apostolic existence (2 Cor 12:9), or *charismata.* Note art., "*the* grace," something specific in the situation just described in 7b, something in which the Philippians also share. I. H. Marshall 6, both "share with me" and "the grace God gives me."

Loh. 24–27 invoked 4:14: you Philippians "share my distress" (same vb., *sygkoinōnēsantes mou tē[i] thlipsei*); 1:7 = "comrades in my 'grace,'" i.e., the chains given him for the gospel (not noticed by Cassidy 2001). Then 1:7–9 apply also to the Philippians, martyrdom for them as well as Paul. Verse 7c = "you who have, together with me, partnership in my 'grace.'" But, Hainz 1982: 119–20 objects, 4:14 is *sygkoinōnēsantes + dat.*; 1:7 is *sygkoinōnous + gen.* Loh.'s *syn emoi* is problematic as a representation of *mou.*

Schenk 105 relates 1:7 to 1:4, *every entreaty of mine for all of you*. "Grace" + the art. refers to Paul's imprisonment situation; *mou* goes with "grace," in the sense of 1:29–30, God "has graciously granted you the privilege *(echaristhē)* . . . of suffering," the same struggle Paul faces. In 7b, *defense and confirmation of the gospel* gets the emphasis; *imprisonment* is subordinated. Semantically "grace" is less adequate here as a tr. than is "solidarity." So Schenk 74 on 4:23, *charis* as "the solidarity of God with God's people till the end," following N. Glueck, H̲esed in the Bible, tr. A. Gottschalk (Ger. 1927; Cincinnati: Hebrew Union College Press, 1967), but allowing a more Hellenistic sense in Paul. In 1:7, then, *charis* denotes Paul's God-given situation. Gnilka 48: Paul's present situation of suffering; Friedrich 139, to be permitted to suffer and have chains are signs of grace; U. B. Müller 43–44.

Verse 7c has a studied ambiguity about it. All the Philippians are "sharers with Paul in God's grace." They shared gifts with him in the past (4:14,16). Will they now share in a stand for the gospel in the face of enemies, as a unified community (1:27–2:4)? Oakes 1998:161–64, "suffering" of one sort or another, but some may have heard *sharing* as "financial support"; see COMMENT B.4 n 33 for his reader-response approach.

The TRANSLATION emphasizes in 7c *you all*, picking up *all of you* in 7a. The ptc. *ontas* has been combined with *sugkoinōnous*, "being co-sharers"; *sharing as you do* ("participants as you are"). From the prefix s̲ugkoinōnous comes the phrase *with me*, for *mou* just after "co-sharers." *mou* goes with *charitos*, for which we attempt to preserve the root idea as more than "privilege" but not equating it with "grace." The Gk. art. *tēs* = *this*. One could put *gracious opportunity* in quotation marks, but it is not ironic for Paul.

1.8. *For God is my witness that I long for you all with the affection of Christ Jesus.* Oath form, involving God, to show how Paul's entreaty for (v 4), and thought about (v 7a), the Philippians reflect intense yearning for them, at the level of Christ's own love. *gar* is explanatory (DA 330).

For God is my witness. God, last mentioned in v 6 *(the One who inaugurated a good work among you)*, is the Father to whom Paul gives thanks (v 3). See NOTE on 1:2 *God. witness* is followed by gen. *mou*, "of me," in most MSS. Some (א^c vid D F G etc.) read "God is witness to me" *(moi; Silva 23)*. P^46 and OL MS a omit any pronouns, "God is witness." No vb. (P^46 א original hand, B etc.), though some MSS have *estin*, "is" (א 2nd corrector, Majority text).

witness. martys is used figuratively of God (BDAG 2.a), in a formula re Paul's relationship to a congregation (cf. Rom 1:9; 2 Cor 1:23; 1 Thess 2:5 and 10). Not rabbinic (for God is named), but OT parallels ("God is *martys* between you and me," Gen 31:44 LXX; 1 Regn [Heb. 1 Sam] 12:5–6, etc.; cf. Str-B 3:26 and 1:330–

32). KJV "God is my record" is from Tyndale. *Word studies:* H. Strathmann, *TDNT* 4:491; L. Coenen, *NIDNTT* 3:1043; J. Beutler, *EDNT* 2:394; *TLNT* 2:447.

that. In classical Gk. the cl. that follows was commonly introduced by *hōs,* "how"; later by *hoti,* "that." Cf. ATR 1032. Most trs. continue KJV's "how greatly I long after you all" ([N]RSV, etc.; Loh. 22; Silva 50). But BAGD IV.4 (BDAG 5) takes *hōs* after vbs. of knowing, saying, and hearing, as equivalent of *hoti* = that, citing 1:8. Cf. BDF #396. Similarly Hawth. 24 (content, rather than degree of yearning); O'Brien 1977:214 and *Phil.* 71 n 41; Schenk 106, with analogy to v 6 *confident . . . that (hoti);* U. B. Müller 44. Hence Moffatt, GNB, "God is my witness that . . . ," and our TRANSLATION. The choice of "how" is influenced by the vb. that follows.

I long for. epipotheō. 7 of 9 NT examples are in the Pauline corpus, 6 in acknowledged letters; *epipothētos,* brothers and sisters "longed for," Phil 4:1. *NIDNNT* 1:458: "desire and longing in a good sense"; also at Phil 2:26; 1 Thess 3:6, etc. Eng. trs. from Tyndale through the 1881 RV used "long after"; RSV "yearn for" (as in Moffatt and Gdsp.); NRSV went (back) to "long for." GNB, "my deep feeling for you." Spicq, "cherish" with tender affection (*TLNT* 2:60; *RevistB* 64 [1957] 184–95). Reed (*DA* 206) sees a "'desire' to *visit*" the Philippians.

you all. As in 7c *you all (pantas hymas,* same Gk.) cf. 4 and 7a *all of you.* The community, including every member.

with the affection of Christ Jesus. Prep. phrase (*en* + dat.), manner (*DA* 327). See NOTES on 1:1 and 2 *Christ Jesus.*

affection. In many languages, emotions are expressed by reference to organs of the body like the heart (1:7a; Louw/Nida 288 n 1). Heb. *raḥămîm* ("innards, bowels, affection, compassion, mercy," Hos 2:21), Gk. the pl. of *splanchnon.* Cf. H. Köster, *TDNT* 7:548–59; H.-H. Esser, *NIDNTT* 2:599–600; N. Walter, *EDNT* 3:265–66; *TLNT* 3:273–75. *splanchna* first meant "the nobler parts" of a sacrifice (heart, liver, etc.); then, the "inward parts" of a human being (a boy ate too much *splanchna* at a sacrificial feast: "'O mother, I'm throwing up my innards.' 'Not yours, child, but what you ate,'" *Corpus Fabularum Aesopicarum* 47.1 [ed. A. Hausrath, 1.1 (Leipzig: Teubner, 1940) 64–65]). Might refer to womb, loins, procreation, and even children. Then for passions like anger, desire, and love ("my *splanchna* swelled with *erōs,*" Aeschyl. *Cho.* 413). Thus "the centre of personal 'feeling,'" "affections like love and hate, courage and fear, joy and sorrow," though, Köster cautions, never mercy (549).

LXX usage is rare (noun 15x), with no specific Heb. term behind *splanchna* (*raḥămîm* is usually *oiktirmoi,* "mercies"). Note Prov 12:10 and 17:5. In *T. 12 Patr.,* striking and consistent use of *splanchna* occurs for the inward parts of human beings as "the seat of feelings." Cf. 1QS 2.1 and 1.22; *TWNT* 7:552. In the gospels, this usage continues: *splanchnizomai* in Jesus' parables (Matt 18:27; Luke 15:20; 10:33, be moved with pity, compassion) and for Jesus' attitude toward the multitude (Mark 6:34; 8:2 par) and suppliants (Mark 1:41; 9:22, etc.). Dunn thinks "Jesus' emotional response at various points during his ministry" can lie behind 1:8 (*TPTA* 193 n 55).

Paul uses only the noun *splanchna*, 7x (3 in Phlm; in Phil, here + 2:1 with *oiktirmoi*), out of 11 NT examples (Col 3:12 is likely modeled on Phil 2:1). Like *kardia*/"heart," re the whole person (Köster 555), a "typically Pauline change," not a "natural emotion" but the Christian experiencing personal liking and love for other Christians. Cf. 2 Cor 7:15; 2 Cor 6:12. Through Philemon "the hearts *(ta splanchna)* of the saints" (v 7) and that of Paul (v 20) are refreshed. Onesimus is Paul's own "heart" *(splanchna)*. On Phil 2:1 see NOTE below. At 1:8, "personal love" or "affection" (BDAG *splagchnon* 3). KJV's literal rendering, "in the bowels of Jesus Christ" (cf. OED "bowel," sb. 3), was subsequently avoided through paraphrase, "affection" (Moffatt, RSV); "compassion" (NRSV); or "deep yearning" (NEB/REB), a shift so successful that people under forty have scarcely heard "bowels" language.

the affection of Christ Jesus masks a problem. Is *Christou Iēsou* a *genitivus auctoris*, showing source (Köster 556; Michaelis 16; Gnilka 50; U. B. Müller 44) or gen. of quality, the sort of affection involved (Ewald 57; Wohl. 65, "in [i.e., with] a Christ-Jesus-heart"; contrast Schenk 109)? "Christ-mysticism" is often invoked. Louw/Nida 25.49, "ambiguous." *en* shows the realm where God's love can be found, with a gen. of quality, like *agapē Christou* at 2 Cor 5:14, "Christ-love urges us on." Jesus is not model but basis for the gospel (Schenk 109). Paul longs for the Philippians with affection such as Christ Jesus has shown and shows for Paul and them. Not just "affection flowing from the heart" (Jewett 1971a:324) but Christ-compassion.

1:9a. *So this is what I am praying.* Vv 9–11 is a prayer report about Paul's intercessions for the Philippians, indicated in two *hina* cls., 9b and 10b. V 11 can be explanatory of 10b or grounds for the petition(s), "because you have been filled...." Others (Gnilka 51, citing Loh.; Collange 49) see all three cls. (9b, 10b, 11) completed by the *eis* construction (10a) + 10c "... to the Day of Christ," and 11c "to God's glory and praise." *Captatio benevolentiae* ("he cares about us so as to pray thus for us") and ethical admonition ("our love should abound and be discerning ... pure"). 10c is an eschatological climax, 11c, doxological conclusion in most trs.; they stand over 9–11 and 3–11.

I am praying. Pres., *proseuchomai*, linear, continuing action. Parallels 1:3, *I thank my God*; no designation of the deity need be repeated. Schubert 1939b:54–55, cf. 60, syntactical unit #5, normally a temporal ptc.; here finite vb., after vv 7–8, "to complete the initial *eucharistō*-period" (60). A new beginning; thanksgiving leads to intercessory petitions (O'Brien 1974 [cf. H. D. Betz, review in *JBL* 98 (1979) 304]; *Phil.* 73, recalling v 4 *entreaty* + the outlet Godward of the feelings mentioned in 7–8). *euchomai*, "pray," + prefix *pros* is common in Koine Gk. (BDF #202; cf. 187.4); + *hina* + subjunct. (BDF #392.1.c). *euchomai* in Paul only 3x; *proseuchomai*, 12x in acknowledged letters (in Phil, here only); *proseuchē* 6x (in Phil, at 4:6). See H. Greeven, *TDNT* 2:775–808, prayer in the Gk. world, OT (J. Herrmann), and NT; H. Schönweiss, *NIDNTT* 2:855–86, 861–64; H. Balz, *EDNT* 3:164–69 (bibl.), esp. 168.

Dir. obj. *touto*, lit. "I pray this (to God), that ... ," points to what follows (with O'B 73, contra DA 206, 383), as in 1:6. The TRANSLATION paraphrases as *This is what I am praying;* cf. NRSV. Resumptive after *eucharistō* in v 3 *I thank my God,* giving content to Paul's *entreaty* (v 4), without repeating the vb. there *(tēn deēsin poioumenos);* Paul varies vocabulary. Prayer-report style like vv 3–6, 1st per. as in vv 7–8. So is the link to 7–8 (and 4b and 3a; cf. BAGD *kai* 2.f/BDAG 1.b.ζ, result from what precedes; Gnilka 51).

1:9b. *that your love may continue to grow still more and more in perception and discernment in every situation.* Syntactical unit #7 in Schubert's thanksgiving periods; *hina* + subjunct., equivalent to an explanatory cl. after *touto* ("I pray this, namely, that . . ."; BAGD *hina* II.1.e/BDAG 2.e; BDF #394; Moule *IB* 145–46 notes Phil 2:2). *your love (hymōn* subj. gen.), *agapē* for the first time in Phil. Pres. subjunct., *perisseuō,* continuing, linear action, *may continue to grow.* For "grow more," see 1 Thess 4:10 *(perisseuein mallon).* 1:9 makes a double comparison (ATR 663): *still* (Gk. *eti,* BDAG 2.b, nontemporal, "in addition," "more, also") and *more and more* (comparative of adv. *mala,* "much, very," *mallon* = "more, to a greater degree" [BDAG 1], doubled, *mallon kai mallon,* "more and more"). *perception* and *discernment* are key words for the sort of love sought.

love. agapē (75 of 116 NT examples are in the Pauline corpus, 47 in acknowledged letters) the unmerited love from God revealed in Christ (BAGD *agapē* I.2/BDAG 1.b; Bultmann 1951 [INTRO. X Bibl.] 291–92). In Phil (1:9, 16; 2:2; possibly 2:1, see NOTE), "human love" (BAGD I.1/BDAG 1.a), *agapē* of believers for each other, though reflecting God's love in Christ; see NOTE on 1:8 *the affection of Christ Jesus.* The source of such love does not have to be spelled out for the Philippians, nor the object of their love delineated. *agapaō* (vb.) does not occur in Phil. On *agapētoi* see NOTE on 2:12 *beloved* and 4:1 (bis). Attestation to *agapē* prior to the LXX remains disputed (literature in *EDNT* 1:9; *TLNT* 1:14–19 for the texts; Wischmeyer; Söding 1992a; BDAG 6–7). NT *agapē* is basically in continuity with the OT concept of love via the LXX, but it does not erect impossible barriers to pagan religion and philosophy (Söding 1992a).

TDNT 1:21–55 takes a "biblical theology" approach: *'ăhăbâ* as God's (suffering) love, in contrast to Gk. *erōs* and *philia.* W. Gunther/H.-G. Link, *NIDNTT* 2:538–51, add other Gk. terms (even "Philippians" at 4:15 because derived from Philip, lit. "lover of horses"). *philia* material (2:547–49; *TDNT* 9:113–71, G. Stählin) is pertinent to theories of Phil. as a letter of friendship, although no term from the root is used in Phil. Spicq (2:276–84) terms Phil 1:9–11 "the New Testament's most profound and precise statement about the influence of *agapē* from the intellectual and moral point of view, in this world or in the next"; eight words show "the extent of its domain: knowledge, insight [v 9], judgment [10 NRSV "what is best"], uprightness, blamelessness [10 NRSV "pure and blameless"], holiness [11 NRSV "righteousness"], glory, and praise of God." This defines *agapē* from context, but overlooks the sense it already had in Paul. For that, see Furnish (1968:199–203), in a Pauline ethics grounded in his theology: "not just an aspect of the Christian's new life, but its whole content and mode. The believer *is* 'love,'" one "overtaken by love" (Phil 3:12), whose faith is expressed in loving, urged on by being loved by God (Gal 5:6; 202–3; cf. Spicq 2:218–22). Cf. G. Schneider, *EDNT* 1:8–12, esp. 3b; *TLNT* 1:8–22, Spicq summarizes and updates; bibl. 19–

22). Most see more than material gifts from the Philippians to Paul (cf. 4:14–16). González-Ruiz 323, a term for the community or church; rejected by most who have come across it (Thierren 1973:169 n 4). *agapē* here means "the Christian life," pure and simple, the capacity for service (Schenk 110; U. B. Müller 45).

grow. perisseuō = "be abundant, rich" (BDAG 1.a.δ, intrans., "grow," Acts 16:5). *perisseuē[i]*, pres. subjunct. "keep on growing." MSS B D etc., *perisseusē[i]*, aor. subjunct. not repeated action; cf. Silva 23. Continuing growth fits better; the Philippians long expressed love; their *agapē* must "grow richer and richer" (O'B 72; Therrien 1973:171–72; BDF #318.2). See further on 4:12 bis, 18 (Letter A), and 1:26 for this somewhat favored term in Paul (24x in acknowledged letters, of 39 NT examples). Word studies: F. Hauck, *TDNT* 6:58–63; T. Brandt, *NIDNTT* 1:728–31; G. Schneider, *EDNT* 3:76–77. No widespread or significant LXX usage. For the NT, "an eschatological catchword," for "a fulness present and proclaimed in the age of salvation as compared with the old aeon" or "a new standard . . . required in this age" (*TDNT* 6:59); God's grace abounds, believers rejoice in response, and, re the collection (2 Cor 8:2,7,14; 9:8), overflow with thanksgivings to God (9:12; 4:15; cf. Rom 3:7 and Boobyer, in NOTE on 1:3 *thank*). In Paul's prayers, here and at 1 Thess 3:12. + *en* + dat. Calvin 27,31, a Hebraism "with" (Lat. *cum*), "unless . . . by, . . . the instrument or formal cause." Many trs. have "in," mode (Söding 1995:169 n 27), effect, or the domain within which love operates (Spicq 1965, 2:278; Theobald 1982 [(1) Bibl. **grace**] 318: sphere). *en* exhibits qualities or spheres in which the Philippians should grow. Cf. 1:26, *en Christō[i] Iēsou, en emoi*; 1 Cor 15:58; Rom 15:13, and 2 Cor 8:7. Are *epignōsis* (perception) and *aisthēsis* (discernment) philosophical or biblical terms? Speculative and practical knowledge (cf. Gnilka 52)? A binominal expression of synonyms (cf. Loh. 32 n 1)? At issue are the force of *epi* in *epignōsis* and relationship of knowledge to love (Therrien 1973:172).

perception. epignōsis (acknowledged letters 6x), only here in Phil. *gnōsis*, "knowledge," only at 3:8 (otherwise in Paul's letters 20x, esp. 1 and 2 Cor; 23 times in the Pauline corpus). Vb. *ginōskō*, Phil 1:12; 2:19,22; 3:10; and 4:5 (43x in acknowledged letters); *epiginōskō*, not in Phil (10x in acknowledged letters). *epignōsis*, "knowledge, recognition" (BDAG 369, "limited to transcendent and moral matters") draws meaning in 1:9 in relation to *discernment* (aisthēsis) that follows.

No word study (Therrien 1973:172 n 4) can overlook backgrounds in Heb. *yādaᶜ* (noun *daᶜat*; cf. J. Bergmann/G. J. Botterweck, *TDOT* 5:448–81) or use in Gk. philosophical thought and gnosticism (O. A. Piper, *IDB* K–Q 42–48; W. Baird, *IDBSup* 524–25; Qumran and Nag Hammadi documents add new source materials). Some bypass gnosticism (E. Schütz, *NIDNTT* 2:391, but cf. 401–5; C. Brown, even "incipient gnosticism," 401). The debate is pertinent to opponents in Phil 3.

Bultmann (*TDNT* 1:689–719, esp. 703–4, 707 on *epiginōskō*): *ginōskō* = knowledge derived from *nous, logos*, or "revelation," contrast *aisthēsis*, "sensual perception" (689–90). May be gnostic (692–96), contrast the OT (696–701). Hellenistic background (cf. Epict. 2.20.21; 702–3, 707; U. B. Müller 45–46). But early Christian usage approximates the OT view (Bultmann 704–8): "insight into the will of God" (Rom 3:17; 10:19), knowing about God (Rom 1:18–32; 1 Cor 8:4–6; Rom 11:34, and 1 Cor 2:16 = Isa 40:13). God elects (one "is known by God," Gal 4:9; 1 Cor 13:12); this leads to service (in love, to build up the community, 1 Thess 1:9b; 1 Cor 8:1–3). "Knowledge of God," through the triumph of Christ (2 Cor 2:14; 4:6; 10:5), may reflect the "Jewish concept of *da{^{c}}at*" (706). "Un-Stoic" (Bonhöffer, *Epiktet* 105; Söding 1995:169).

epiginōskō-terms can scarcely be distinguished at times from *ginōskō* ones (*TDNT* 703; cf. Rom 1:21 and 1:28). But *epignōsis* becomes "almost a technical term for the decisive knowledge of God . . . implied in conversion to the Christian faith" (707; 1 Tim 2:4; cf. 1 Thess 1:9b; Gal 4:8–9), in contrast to pagan ignorance; cf. Therrien 1973:175. At Phil 1:9, not theoretical knowledge, but practical consequences stand out: "reflective inquiry . . . grounded in love," leading to right action (708; cf. Phlm 6, AB 34C:93). Mostly "determined by the OT" (707), even if developed in conflict with gnostics in Corinth and Philippi (3:8ff., 710). See further Bultmann 1951 (INTRO. X Bibl.) 318–19, 326–28: faith and knowledge "are identical as a new understanding of one's self." Knowledge, as a gift of the Spirit, is "capable of further development" as a task for believers (citing Phil 1:9–10). E. D. Schmitz, *NIDNTT* 2:397, adds Qumran; W. Hackenberg, *EDNT* 2:24–25; Dupont 1949, 1960: 13, 43, 47–48, 410–11; K. Sullivan, a "strictly Semitic" concept in Paul. Is *epi* intensive (Lft. 138: larger knowledge), directive (toward an object, J. A. Robinson, *Eph.* [1928] 249), or "decorative" (typically Hellenistic, Bultmann)? González-Ruiz 325 finds "growth of love in 'knowledge'" an "unintelligible paradox"; this overlooks Paul's understanding of such perception as a divine gift, of edificatory value (Rom 15:14). Therrien, *epignōsis* is "knowledge of God and his will revealed in Jesus Christ . . . leading to a moral life worthy of the Lord" (1973: 176). Merk 1968 1968:207–8: "ethical perception."

The TRANSLATION *perception* distinguishes *epignōsis* from *gnōsis* and over-intellectual understandings that "knowledge" (KJV, [N]RSV) might suggest. Cf. BAGD 25, "intellectual perception" for *epignōsis*, s.v. *aisthēsis*; BDAG 29 "insight."

discernment. aisthēsis, only here in the NT; vb. at Luke 9:45; *aisthēterion*, Heb 5:14, "faculties trained . . . to distinguish good from evil," a sense (ethical discernment) also present in Phil 1:9 (v 10, love sharpened by *epignōsis* and *aisthēsis* is to "approve what is excellent and be pure and blameless" (RSV). Hence BDAG 29, **"capacity to understand, discernment** . . . denoting moral understanding." In Gk., originally "sensual perception"; in Stoic and LXX usage, reliable and even intellectual understanding. Cf. Epict. 1.26.15; 2.18.8. Equated with *da{^{c}}at* (in 25 of 27 LXX examples), *aisthēsis* takes on a sense of wisdom and (moral) judgment; e.g., Prov 1:7 LXX (22 LXX examples are in Prov); Jer 4:19; 4 Macc 2:22. Schenk 113: LXX, empirical experience, individualizing of knowledge. Cf. G. Delling, *TDNT* 1:187–88, cf. 1:690 n 2; E. Schütz, *NIDNTT* 2:391. Trs. vary: KJV "judgment," R[S]V "discernment," NEB, NIV "insight"; NAB "wealth of experience." Louw/Nida 32.38, noting *pasē[i]*, "complete capacity for understanding"; this raises *aisthēsis* above *epignōsis* more than NT evidence warrants. For the practi-

cal, less intellectual sense of *aisthēsis,* related to broader *perception,* anticipating v
10, the TRANSLATION uses *discernment.*

in every situation. pasē[i]. BAGD *pas* 5 "every kind of, all sorts of," a distributive
sense, rather than elative, for the adj. without an art. (cf. B. Reicke/G. Bertram,
TDNT 5:888). Spicq 1965:279, "circumstances of everyday life where 'knowledge' gives no definite rule but where a loving heart instinctively senses what to
do." Similarly Therrien 1973:177. Contrast KJV-NRSV, "full insight" (attainable
in this life?). Better: realistic concern in a mission church for application of discerning love to all sorts of situations for which there are no rules or distinct *charismata.*

1:10a. *so that you may keep on appreciating the things that are best.* To the *hina*
cl. in v 9, Paul attaches 6 Gk. words: *eis* + art. infin. in the acc. *(to dokimazein),* +
subj. acc. *you (hymas)* + dir. obj. *ta diapheronta.* Can express purpose ("in order
that"; O'B 77) or result ("so that"; Spicq 1965: 280; RSV); BDAG *eis* 4.f; BDF
#402.2; ATR 1071–72. The TRANSLATION takes 10a as a result following from the
gift of *love* that continues *to grow . . . in perception and discernment* applied in
various situations. Cf. *GNTC* 3:143. In Paul, *eis* + art. infin., 50x (Rom 3:26; 8:29;
1 Thess 3:10; common in the papyri). Can occur with a *hina* cl. following, Rom
1:11; or preceding, Rom 7:4.

Both infin. and ptc. have at least two meanings. In BAGD/BDAG, *dokimazein*
= (1) put to the test, examine; (2) accept as proved, approve. For *diapherō* (behind
the subst. ptc. *ta diapheronta)* "differ, be different" or "be superior" to others from
which a thing differs (BAGD 2.a and 2.b; BDAG 3, 4). Hence four possible construals: (a) *examine* the things that *differ* (cf. NEB-txt., "bring you the gift of true
discrimination"; Moffatt, "enabling you to have a sense of what is vital"; cf. Gdsp.);
(b) *examine* the things that are *superior* (cf. NEB-mg, "teach you by experience
what things are most worth while"; NRSV, "help you to determine what is best";
NIV, "discern what is best"); (c) *approve* the things that *differ* (too obvious, too
ambiguous to attract trs.); (d) *approve* the things that are *superior* (KJV, "approve
things that are excellent"; RSV). Among many interpretations (Therrien 1973:178;
TLNT 1:422 n 13): ability to distinguish heresy from authentic doctrine (church
fathers; re Phil 3, O'B 78); teach affection for those worthy, not love for heretics
and their spurious doctrines (cf. Chrysost.); distinguish essentials from what is
secondary or quibbling over words (K. Barth 21–22, we must not fall for catch-
words); know the fundamentals of the gospel and live the life of love (Loh. 32
quotes Augustine, "Love and do what you want"). See below.

keep on appreciating. Pres. act. infin., *dokimazō,* linear or durative (BDF #318).
Word studies: W. Grundmann, *TDNT* 2:255–60; H. Haarbeck, *NIDNTT* 3:818–
10; G. Schunack, *EDNT* 1:341–43; Spicq, *TLNT* 1:353–57, in light of Therrien
1973. The adj. *dokimos,* "tested," "proven," "valuable," gave rise to the vb. used for
"test" and then recognize the results as proved, approved. Applications in the Gk.
world (Therrien 10–15), esp. in business and law. In the LXX (56 examples of the
word family), for *bāhan* and *bāhar,* test, prove, Jer 17:9–10; 9:7 [LXX 6], cf. 6:27–
30. Hellenistic Judaism (Therrien 26 30–31) inherited this biblical, eschatological sense.

dokimazein occurs 13x in Paul's acknowledged letters (in Phil, only here). Grundmann provides a biblical-theology composite, Therrien a doctrinal synthesis (239–301), dual senses, "test" and "approve." Eschatological testing and approval in the judgment by God are prominent (any clash with justification by faith is minimized; cf. Reumann 1982: ##125–29). The "moment of truth" at the final judgment underlies the impvs. for the Christian life. Authentic life in the community "in via" takes specific form in testings and discernments that must continually be made. Applies to Paul and other leaders (1 Thess 2:4). *dokimazein* roots in faith, baptism, and the gift of the Spirit, leading to a new existence marked by love and knowledge (Phil 1:9–10, p. 273). It involves mind (*nous,* Rom 12:2), conscience (*syneidēsis,* Rom 2:14–15; 1 Cor 8:7–13), and heart (*kardia,* Rom 2:15) in (Jewett 1971a:447–48, 450–51, 458–60), respectively, paraenesis, ethical questions, and as the center from which thoughts and desires flow. Therrien stresses discernment within the concrete realities of the community's situation till the judgment and confirms (303) the conclusion of Cullmann (1964:228) that *dokimazein* as "testing" is *"the capacity of forming the correct Christian ethical judgment at each given moment,"* and so "the key of all New Testament ethics."

Trs. vary. W. R. Forrester (*ExpTim* 36 [1924–25] 285) wrote, "[W]e have in English a word . . . to 'appreciate' which means both to distinguish and to approve or value after due deliberation." Hence, with Therrien 138, *appreciating,* to express both judging and esteeming.

the things that are best. Neut. pl. ptc., either "the things that differ" or "the things that are superior" (that "excel"). *diapherō* (K. Weiss, *TDNT* 9:62–64; L. Oberlinner, *EDNT* 1:315) has many meanings, "excel" (positive sense; *diapherei,* "it matters"), (negative) "be less." The ptc., as a noun, = "difference" or "things that are significant," neut. pl. a Stoic-Cynic philosophical term. *adiaphoron* (sg.) = "something that does not matter" (Epict. 1.20.12), tech. term for what is neither virtue nor vice, standing between good and evil (Diog. Laert. 6.9.105). No LXX use. Likely in the Hellenistic synagogue from popular philosophy and hence to Paul (so U. Wilckens, EKK *Röm.* 1:148 n 380; Fitzmyer, AB 33:316).

Rom 2:18, ERV 1881, poses alternative trs.: margin, "the things that differ" (Sanday-Headlam, *Rom.* 65); text, "the things that are excellent" (Lft., most Eng. trs.); the trend has been toward the latter. Likewise Phil 1:10, KJV-NRSV tradition (NIV "what is best"). Bengel: "Not merely the good in comparison with the bad, but the best among the good, the excellence of which no one except those more advanced discern." Hawth. 27–28, to distinguish "things that differ significantly is a relatively easy task. But great powers of insight and perception are needed 'to decide with sureness what things are really excellent and worthy of adoption in practice' (Plummer)." Similarly BDAG 239; Wiles 1974:209; Collange 49; O'B 77; Schenk 112; Holloway 2001:94–99. *the things that are best* suggests what is excellent among good things, not just in contrast to evils.

1:10b. *I pray that you may be flawless and unfailing* ᶜ *for the Day of Christ.* Like 9b, *hina* + subjunct. Depends on *proseuchomai* in 9a, repeated in the TRANSLATION as *I pray,* to show the two *hina* cls. are parallel; 10b is not a second ramification, along with 10a, of Paul's prayer *that your love may continue to grow* but rather a further prayer request alongside it. *ēte* is pres. subjunct., *eimi*, possibly, "continue to be," but few press it (*eimi* has no aor. subjunct.). Philippian believers are *flawless and unfailing*; 10b prays they will continue thus until the parousia of Christ.

flawless. Adj. *eilikrinēs*, in the NT only at 1:10 (pl.) and 2 Pet 3:1. Noun *eilikrineia* 3x in Paul (1 Cor 5:8; 2 Cor 1:12; 2:17). Compound, said to derive from *heilē*, "the sun's warmth" (cf. *hēlios*), + *krinō*, "test"; therefore "sunlight-tested." Cf. *TLNT* 1:420. That the Philippians or Paul were aware of such etymology is dubious (BDAG 282; Schenk 121 n 191). Moral sense as early as Plato. In inscriptions and papyri (MM). LXX only at Wis 7:25. Eng. NT trs. for 1:10 include "sincere" (KJV, = "unadulterated"); "pure" ([N]RSV); "flawless" (NEB); "that you may be transparent" (Moffatt); "transparent character" (Gdsp.); Louw/Nida 88.41 n 7, "with clean lives." *Word studies:* F. Büchsel, *TDNT* 2:397–98; H. Goldstein, *EDNT* 1:391; *TLNT* 1:420–23.

unfailing. *aproskopos* (BDAG "undamaged, blameless," here pl.), from vb. *proskoptō*, "strike against, stumble," then "give or take offense" (BDAG 882). Cf. G. Stählin (*TDNT* 6:745–58) for a framework into which terms from the vb. can be arranged. Adj. with *alpha*-privative (BDF #177.1) in the NT at 1 Cor 10:32, Acts 24:16, and here. (1) "without blame, free from spot" (Loh. 33 n 6; cf. [N]RSV). Or (2) "without offense" (KJV) toward God, i.e., pleasing God (1 Cor 7:32, etc.; see NOTE on Phil 4:18 *acceptable, well-pleasing to God*), or toward human beings (so Chrysost., below). Or (3) "without falling," from grace till the goal is reached. Not to "stumble . . . on the path of faith" (*TDNT* 756). Cf. those "being saved," 1 Cor 1:18. Lft. 87, "without stumbling." *NIDNTT* 2:707 reflects all three senses. Chrysost. took *eilikrineis* as "sincere *before God*," *aproskopoi* as "without offense *before human beings*" (PG 62:191 = NPNF 13:189). Collange 50, "without reproach," i.e., without becoming stumbling blocks; Moffatt, "no harm to anyone." Gnilka 52, a positive and a negative, "pure and blameless." Schenk 120, a semantically unified, single expression, "perfection" (earlier, Loh. 33); 128 "as perfect as possible"; cf. "perfection"/"maturity," *teleios* terms, 3:12,15, Paul denying he possesses it as yet. Perhaps, "that you may test 'pure' and prove surefooted." *flawless and unfailing* tries to catch some overtones, be open to others, without defining whether *unfailing* toward God, the life of faith, or others.

1:10c. *for the Day of Christ.* *hēmeran Christou.* P⁴⁶ adds *tēn*, "the"; cf. Silva 23. Eng. calls for an art. See NOTE on *Day* at 1:6. For *Christ*, NOTE at 1:2 and 1:6 *Day of Christ Jesus. Day of Christ,* only in Phil, here and at 2:16. Cf. Kreitzer 1987 ([1] Bibl. **Jesus**) 163; Radl 1981:46–47. *eis*, lit. "into," BDAG 2.a.α, of time, "until." ATR 594, "marks either the limit or accents the duration expressed by the accusative." KJV has the former sense ("till the day of Christ"), RSV the latter ("for the day of Christ"). Cf. *TDNT* 2:426–27. Kept *flawless and unfailing* until the parousia or for the judgment then? "Perfected" at the Day of Christ, or do they achieve purity and blamelessness (before God? before the world?) en route to that Day? Cf. *TDNT* 6:756 n 63. Some paraphrase: "Then on the Day of Christ you will be flawless and without blame" (NEB, cf. NRSV), the goal achieved or apparent at the parousia. Cf. 1:6 NOTE *will bring it to completion.* Others, "progress in sanctification . . . in preparation for the day of Christ," *eis* = "for" (Gundry Volf 44 n 216; Silva 61; Gundry Volf adds, completion of "entire sanctification" by God comes on the day of Christ (45), God doing "a good work" (v 6) in them (47).

In Koine Gk., *eis* can = *en*, therefore "in the day of Christ" (BAGD *eis* 9/BDAG 1.a.δ, but usually of place, not time; O'Brien 1977:57–58). O'B 79 rejects "until" in favor of "'in preparation for' or 'against' the day of Christ." Schenk (114–15, 121, 128) suggests "for Jesus' appearance that brings fulfillment," the parousia is completion of God's work. Paul therefore prays that the Philippian believers, in their continuing growth (v 6), *may be flawless and unfailing* not simply in *the Day of Christ* but *for* it (Fee 102 n 23; cf. 2:16), indicating the extent of the process (*DA* 316; note the ptc. *peplērōmenoi* in 11a).

1:11a. *because you have been filled with fruit of righteousness,* b *the fruit that comes through Jesus Christ* c *for God's glory and praise.* The ptc., "having been filled," agrees with *you* in 10b, the Philippian believers. Its object is "fruit (sg., no art.) of righteousness," modified by a prep. phrase *through Jesus Christ* attached to "fruit" (by the art. *ton* in Gk.). Then a final phrase, usually understood as "glory and praise for God."

On connection of v 11 with 9b and 10b, see NOTE on 1:9a *So this is what I am praying.* (1) Some connect v 11 with 10b as explanatory expansion of the second petition (Silva 57, 59–60, "pure and blameless . . . , that is, filled with the fruit of right conduct"). Hawth. 14, 28–29 sees three adjs., "pure and harmless . . . filled with the fruit of righteousness" (O'B 79), supplying "that is" or "and" and overlooking *for the Day of Christ* between the two pred. adjs. and the ptc., though the phrase should go with all three. Or (2) the TRANSLATION takes v 11 as the grounds for what Paul prays in 10b: "I pray that, *because* you have been filled with the fruit of righteousness . . . you may be flawless. . . ." So KJV, [N]RSV. Or (3) 1:11 provides grounds for both petitions: *peplērōmenoi* agrees grammatically with *you* in the *hina* cl. of 10b, but also fits with *your love* in 9b; "I pray that, *because* you have been filled with fruit of righteousness, your love may continue to grow . . . and that you may be flawless and unfailing. . . ." Schenk 121, a contextual synonymy. Or (4) emphasize the two *eis* phrases (10c, 11c) and *eis to dokimazein* in 10a, *so that you may keep on appreciating. . . .* Gnilka 51, Collange 49, "I pray that your love may grow . . . (9b), that you may be flawless and unfailing . . . (10b), (that you may be) filled with fruit of righteousness . . . (11a)." Loh.'s attempt (30) to get three-line units (9b–10b; 10c–11) is reflected (consciously?) in TEV and CEV. There is no connective—"and," "so that," or "because"—at the beginning of v 11, so decision rests with how the ptc. is taken.

because you have been filled with. Perf. m.-pass. ptc., *pleroō*, "fill." Masc. nom. pl., to agree with *you* in the vb. *ēte* (10b). In pred. position, the ptc. could be taken after the vb., "that you may be flawless and unfailing (and) filled," but a connective to the preceding pair of adjs. is lacking. To say this, Paul could have used *plēreis* (an adj. not found in his letters) or the subjunct. (to continue the *hina* construction in 10b), namely *hina ēte . . . kai plērōthēte* (as at Eph 3:19) or *peplērōsthe*. To take the ptc. as circumst., expressing cause (BDF #418.1; ATR 1128; *GNTG* 3:157) is preferable to a temporal sense ("after you have been filled"); the temporal aspect is carried by the tense of the ptc. Means cannot be ruled out ("flawless . . . by being filled . . ."), but that aspect is carried by the voice and other indications that the filling is God's work; see NOTES on 1:6 *a good work* and 1:11 *God's glory and praise*. Pf. tense indicates action in the past, with results continuing into the present (BDF ##318.4, 340, 342; GNTG 3:81–85). An eschatological term here (Söding 1995:172); cf. 4:18–19 (an *inclusio* via 2:2 is doubtful); Rom 13:8–11; 15:13–14.

Occasionally taken as m. voice; Caird 10, Beare: "bringing forth a full harvest of righteousness," though Beare explains that "the right relationship with God" or being justified is what "produces the harvest" (54–55); hence NEB, virtually act. voice (cf. BDF #316.1; GNTG 3:55), "reaping the full harvest of righteousness" (changed by REB to "yielding the full harvest"). But most take it as pass. voice, "having been filled and so being filled" (BDAG *plēroō* 1.b; O'B 79–80; Schenk 122 n 195), implying "by God" (TDNT 6:291; 9:551 n 371). To connect 'being filled" with opponents in ch. 3 is speculative (Collange 50, claiming a contrast to Christ "emptying" himself in 2:7).

plēroō = "fill" things or persons; "bring to fullness" or completion (Phil 2:2; 4:19). 4:18 is idiomatic (NRSV "paid in full"). Thus 4 examples in Phil of the 13 in acknowledged letters. In classical Gk., a variety of senses. In the LXX some 70x, usually for the Heb. *mālē'* (Loh. 34 n 1, Pss 16:11 LXX ; 20:4 [LXX 19:5]; Jer 23:24; Wis 1:7). God as One who richly gives spiritual gifts (cf. 1:9b *that your love may continue to grow*) stands behind the picture here. With the pass. voice, "by God" may be supplied (BDF #130.1, 342.1). With *plēroō* an acc. of reference is possible, as at Col 1:9; BDAG 1.b; BDF #159.1; TDNT 6:291 n 24; GNTG 3:232–33, 247. In Eng. one must say *filled with*. *Word studies:* G. Delling, TDNT 6:286–98, esp. 291; R. Schippers, NIDNTT 1:733–41, esp. 739; H. Hübner, EWNT 3:256–62.

fruit. Instead of "fruit (acc. sg.) of righteousness which (is) . . . (*karpon . . . ton*)," Ψ, the Majority text, etc. read gen. pl., "fruits of righteousness which (are) . . . (*karpōn . . . tōn*)." Data in Aland 1991:568–71. The gen. is normal after a vb. of fullness like *plēroō*, but the acc. of reference (in the sg.) is well supported here (P⁴⁶ ℵ A; B without *ton*; D F G [Western text], etc.; O'B 72).

Gk *karpos* and Heb. *pĕrî* (*karpos* most frequently in the LXX) were used lit. for "fruit" from trees or the earth or animals or persons, and then metaphorically for the "product" or "result" of an action (BDAG 3). E.g., M. Ant. 6.30.4; Hos 10:13; Jer 17:10; Wis 3:15. *karpos dikaiosynēs*, "fruit of righteousness," occurs at Prov 3:9; 11:30; 13:2 LXX; thus (DA 291) OT language embedded in Paul's argument. Amos 6:12 LXX is regularly cited, as is a frg. (#519) from Epicurus, "The greatest fruit of justice (*dikaiosynēs*) is absence of disturbances (*ataraxia*, calm)." BDAG 248 adds Apc Sed 12:5. Here, product, result, or outcome (BAGD 2.a/ BDAG 1.b). Cf. Heb 12:11; Jas 3:18. At Phil 1:22 *karpos ergou* (NRSV "fruitful labor") applies to Paul's missionary work (which produces fruit for the apostle, 1 Cor 9:7); 4:17, *karpon* in a financial sense ("profit, interest"); see NOTES on these vv. Behind most applications lies Paul's understanding of the Holy Spirit as the source of fruit (*karpos*, sg.) in the lives of believers as love, joy, peace, etc.

(Gal 5:22). For those justified or freed "in regard to righteousness" the fruit or "advantage" (NRSV Rom 6:22, cf. 20–21) is sanctification *(hagiasmon)*. Some treat *karpon* in 1:11 as if a pl. (Jones, *Phil.* 8; Loh. 30, 34; KJV, RSV; Ziesler 1972:203, despite 151). The sg. (not a collective here or in Gal 5:22) denotes an eschatological outcome (Schenk 122, with Loh. 34 n 1). *Word studies:* F. Hauck, *TDNT* 3:614–16, bibl. *TWNT* 10/2:1135; R. Hensel, *NIDNTT* 1:721–23; H.-T. Wrege, *EDNT* 2:251–52.

righteousness. dikaiosynē, 4x in Phil; see NOTE on 1:7 *It is indeed right.* Can be expressed in Eng. by justice/justify/justification (from the Lat.) or righteousness/ "rightwise" (from the Anglo-Saxon). *dikaio-*terms 93x in acknowledged letters (chart in Reumann 1982: p. 42; *ABD* 5:747). Impact of the theme is often dissipated by separate articles ("justification," "righteousness") in Eng.-language wordbooks (so *ABD*), though the same Gk. terms are involved for both, as in Heb., *sdq*, *sĕdāqâ.* Paul's thought on *dikaiosynē* has unity, well developed by the time he wrote Phil. A rich OT background; inherited early Christian formulas. While writing Phil in Ephesus, juridical and eschatological aspects were prominent in the thought of the imprisoned apostle. Phil 1:11 is often taken in a moral sense, *"righteousness, uprightness* as the compelling motive for the conduct of one's whole life" (BAGD 2.b/BDAG 3 "produce of uprightness"), in contrast to *dikaiosynē (theou),* "the (saving) righteousness (of God)" and its implications. *Research reports:* Ziesler 1972:1–16; Brauch; C. Brown, *NIDNTT* 3:371–77; C. Müller, 5–27; Stuhlmacher 1965:11–73; Wilckens, *Röm.* 1:223–33 (each characterized in Reumann 1982: p. 9 n 11; cf. 10 n 14). *Word studies: TDNT* 2:174–224 (G. Quell/G. Schrenk); *NIDNTT* 3:352–71 (H. Seebass, additions by C. Brown); *EDNT* 1:325–30 (K. Kertelge, cf. his 1967 treatment); *ABD* (Scullion, Hays, Reumann). Literature in Reumann 1982; *ABD* 5:749–73. S. Westerholm 2004:262–96 speaks of "dikaioness."

In the Greco-Roman world (often overlooked), *dikaiosynē* ("justice") was a cardinal virtue, with prudence or practical wisdom *(phronēsis),* temperance or moderation *(sōphrosynē),* and courage *(andreia);* see NOTE on 4:8. Some in his audience may have heard Paul in light of this background. *dikaio-*terms commonly referred to what was "right" or "just" in human relationships, in the state (Plato, *Resp.* books 1–4; Aristot., esp. *Eth. nic.* book 5) and among friends, particularly equals, involving equality and fairness *(epieikeia;* cf. 4:5, NRSV "gentleness"). "Distributive justice" (rightly or fairly distributing honor and goods in the community) and "corrective justice" were philosophical and practical concerns. The Stoics held God (Zeus, nature, or fate) provides justice as a norm for society through reason and law. The earth itself "teaches *dikaiosynē,* for the more she is served, the more good things she gives in return" (Xen. *Oec.* 5.12). A tradition about human righteousness or benevolence and its fruit may be reflected in 2 Cor 9:10 (cf. H. D. Betz *2 Cor* 8–9:115; applied to Philippi by Reumann 1993:450–54, an idea that Paul got from his converts there). Connections also exist between *dikaiosynē* and *pistis* or belief/faith, esp. in connection with friendship (*Eth. nic.* 8. 1155a–63b), leading to reverence toward God and piety, benevolence, and *dikaiosynē* toward others (Dobbeler [(4) Bibl. **faith**] 102–14; *RAC* 10:238–50). See

NOTES on *dikaiosynē* and faith in 3:6,9; Reumann, "Righteousness, Greco-Roman World," *ABD* 5:742–45.

Biblical backgrounds in outline: *sĕdāqâ* shaped OT views of human life and reflected Heb. views of God even more than *dikaio*-terms did in the Gk. world. Over 500 examples of *sdq*-terms, treated in *TDNT* 2:174–78; *NIDNTT* 3:354–58; E. Achtemeier; Ziesler 17–127; K. Koch, *THAT* 2:507–30; H. Ringgren/B. Johnson, *ThWAT* 6:898–924; *TDOT* 12:239–64; J. Scharbert, *TRE* 12 (1984) 404–11; and J. Scullion. References can be organized around *sdq* as (1) the activity of human beings and (2) the activity of God (so Ziesler 23–32); or around divine order in the world and God's just reign; Yahweh's salvatory activity; and how one "stands" before God and the covenant Law in a legal, forensic sense (Scullion 725–27, 735–36). Little agreement on a single "master theme" behind all these references. Biggest difference from the Greco-Roman concept of *dikaiosynē*: God's righteousness as deliverance, working vindication for the oppressed (Ps 103:6), far beyond notions of distributive justice ("to each his or her own"). Note also the "righteous sufferer," corporate or individual, in 2 Isa (ch. 53), the Pss (22, 64), possibly relevant to Phil 2:6–11, Paul, and the community at Philippi.

In the LXX, *sdq*-terms are rendered usually, but not always, by *dikaio*-vocabulary. C. H. Dodd 1935:42–53 saw a narrowing toward Gk. (distributive) justice; similarly Olley. Contrast Ziesler 52–69 (a covenantal setting remains). For Judaism, see A. Cronbach's composite. From the Apocrypha and Pseudepigrapha, Ziesler 73–85 concluded the vb. *dikaioō* is "almost entirely forensic" but the noun *diakaiosynē* "almost entirely ethical." See Reumann, *ABD* 5:736–42 for further references. The Dead Sea scrolls, with their heightened sense of human unrighteousness in contrast to God's righteousness (1QH 1.16; 4.29–31), have been taken as an anticipation of Paul's view of salvation and indeed of justification (*mišpāt*, 1QS 11.5,12); but "faith" is not emphasized as in Paul, and key vv like Hab 2:4 are differently treated. Cf. Ziesler 85–94; E. P. Sanders 1977:239–328, esp. 305–12; Przybylski 13–38; *ABD* 5:738. Rabbinic literature has forensic and ethical meanings for *sdq*.

E. P. Sanders found in Jewish sources 200 B.C. to A.D. 200 a "pattern of religion" for Palestinian Judaism that he termed "covenantal nomism": "one's place in God's plan is established on the basis of the covenant and . . . the covenant requires as the proper response . . . obedience to its commandments, while providing means of atonement for transgressions" (*PPJ* [1977]:75, cf. 236). On this pattern in contrast to Pauline righteousness/justification, see Reumann 1982: ##217–22, 408 (Fitzmyer); J. Neusner's review of *PPJ* in *HR* 18 (1978) 177–91; Seifrid 1992 esp. 46–77; Stuhlmacher 2001 (and D. Hagner). Sanders would fit Phil 1:9–11 into his picture of Pauline soteriology as an example of how "in their present life the Christians have been *sanctified* in the sense of *cleansed* (1 Cor 1.2), and Paul urges them to remain *pure and blameless* until the Day of the Lord" (1977:450–51, italics his; similarly Sanders 1983:94).

Jesus did not use *sdq*/*dikaiosynē* terms significantly in our sources (Reumann 1982:##49–54; *ABD* 5:749–52, part c). The starting point for Christian use lies in some seven confessional formulas *(homologiae)* about the meaning of Jesus' death

(Kertelge 1967; Seifrid 1992:176–80, an "initial stage"): 1 Pet 3:18; 1 Cor 1:30; 2 Cor 5:21; Rom 3:24–26a; Rom 4:25; 1 Cor 6:11; 1 Tim 3:16; cf. Reumann 1982: ##58–76, 368–75; *ABD* 5:752–54.

Paul's usage: Ziesler 148–51 takes up Phil first among all the Pauline letters. Phil 3 is a good starting point, about Paul autobiographically, but he used *dikaiosynē* prior to writing Phil. (a) Paul reflects OT-Jewish roots, the early Christian formulas, and possibly Gk. senses of *dikaiosynē*. (b) Modest use of the terms in 1 Thess and 1–2 Cor, great escalation in Gal in the dispute with the "Judaizers" over two contrasting kinds of righteousness, by Law or by faith; cf. on Phil 3: 6,9. (c) This dispute was prior to writing Phil, a period in Ephesus (54 or 55–56) during which the thoughts that would appear in Rom (from Corinth in 56–57) were taking shape. (d) *dikaiosynē* has christological, soteriological, eschatological aspects—as in the earlier formulas—but also communal/ecclesiological (as in 1:11), or ethical ones. See *ABD* 5:758–63 on factors and features; for letter-by-letter development, Reumann 1982: ##82–162; *ABD* 5:763–67. In letters roughly contemporary with Phil, Gal, 2 Cor, and later Rom, references to God's saving righteousness or justification predominate.

The gen. *dikaiosynēs* may be (1) gen. of apposition (Hawth. 29; BDF #167; epexegetical gen., ATR 498–99; *GNTG* 3:214–15; *TDNT* 2:210; Ziesler 1972:151; Silva 60, cf. Gnilka 53; Söding 1995:172 n 45; O'B 80, "gen. of definition"), fruit that consists of righteousness; "fruit, i.e., righteousness." (2) gen. of quality (BFD #165, like an adj.; ATR 496–97, "attributive gen."; Silva 60, "Semitic-like"; *GNTG* 3:212–13; cf. Gnilka 53; *TDNT* 2:210; Wohl. 70; Söding 1995: 172 n 46), righteous fruit, fruit well-pleasing to God. (3) gen. of origin (Silva 60, "subjective [indicating origin]"; Haupt 17, cf. 18 n 1 gen. of authorship; Schenk 122; U. B. Müller 46; BDF #162.7; *GNTG* 3:210–12, subj. gen. indicating the source; Ziesler 151; Kertelge 1967:259, under indic. and impv.; Wiles 1974:212 n 3, but also an obj. gen., "fruit resulting from and demonstrating righteousness"; O'B 80, "the sense is much the same"; denied by Gnilka 53 n 16. So Spicq; Michael 25; Beare 53; Reumann 1982:#108; Schlosser 1995a:389.

Thus 1:11 could be forensic, ethical, or any or several of the gen. types. Pauline usage suggests ethical fruit, with God-given righteousness or justification as source (*TDNT* 2:210). Schenk 122–23: *genitivus auctoris* (origin), above (c), our preference: (i) Synchronically, the passage joins *dia Iēsou Christou* in attribut. position after *ton* to a noun without art. (*karpon*) to make *dikaiosynēs* more precise, "righteousness through Jesus Christ." Cf. Phil 3:6, "as to righteousness, that which is under the Law (*kata dikaiosynēn tēn en nomō[i]*)"; 1 Cor 2:7; Gal 3:2; Rom 1:18; 2:9,14; 9:30. Cf. BDF #412.3. (ii) Elsewhere in Paul a gen. with *karpos* is a gen. of origin (Haupt 17). Phil 1:22; Gal 5:22 "fruit of the Spirit" (the decisive parallel, Beare 55); Rom 6:22; cf. Eph 5:9. (iii) OT-LXX character is established from Amos 6:12; Prov 11:30; in LXX vv without Heb. counterparts, Prov 3:9 and 13:2 (both, "fruits of righteousness"), gen. of authorship. Cf. Ziesler 151; O'Brien 1977:36 and *Phil.* 80; Jas 3:18. Righteousness as proper fellowship with God provides fullness of fruit or results in daily life, toward the perfection of the eschaton. Cf. Thüsing 182, cited below in the NOTE on 1:11 *through Jesus Christ*.

1:11b. *the fruit that comes through Jesus Christ. ton,* agreeing with *karpon,* puts what follows in attribut. position, *dia* + gen. The TRANSLATION repeats *the fruit* to make the antecedent clear. Some ptc. is understood, *onta,* "fruit that is" (KJV), or *erchomenon,* "fruit that comes . . ." ([N]RSV, TRANSLATION). Paul likes to add a clarifying phrase in attribut. position after a noun without the art.; see NOTE on 1:11 *righteousness,* Schenk's point (i). *dia* + gen. indicates the person through, or by means of, whom something occurs (BAGD *dia* III.2.a and b.γ; BDAG A.4.a., b.β).

On *Jesus Christ,* see NOTES on 1:2; 1:1 *Christ Jesus,* bis, as also at 1:6 and 8; 1:10 *Day of Christ.* Kramer ([1] Bibl. **Christ**) #37 thinks the title used in 1:6 and 8 was determinative for v 11, i.e., without the usual "Lord." Because *through Jesus Christ* explicates *righteousness* (cf. Schenk), the reference is to Jesus' cross and exaltation (so Harder 110). But righteousness/justification is not limited by Paul to a past event. It involves the power of God at work in the present and for future fulfillment and consummation (Reumann 1982:##141, 142, 147, 397–98). Hence (Thüsing 181–83), the work of the Spirit of the exalted Lord; cf. Rom 7:4; Rom 6:22, *karpos eis hagiasmon,* justification and sanctification occurring "in Christ." Less persuasive is Thüsing's suggestion (181–82) that *through Jesus Christ* be taken with *for God's glory and praise* (no comma in NA²⁵), "the fruit that is through Jesus Christ to the glory of God." KJV, RSV, NEB, REB all have a comma in v 11, NIV a dash, as if to make the doxological climax more emphatic. NRSV, no punctuation; deliberate decision or policy of using fewer commas? Thüsing's interpretation depends on a traditional understanding of v 11c as doxology to God; an alternative will be suggested below.

1:11c. *for God's glory and praise.* Two nouns, the first more frequent and important in Phil and in biblical Gk. generally; concluding gen., "of God," which emerges as ambiguous; initial *eis* + acc., aim or purpose (GNTG 3:206; cf. BDAG *eis* 4.d and f); "to" in RSV, NEB; "for" in NRSV.

glory. doxa. The meaning of this Gk. word was totally changed by the LXX. From Homer on, "opinion" (or "reputation, renown"). Cf. G. Kittel, *TDNT* 2:233–36; E. F. Harrison 1950. In the LXX, of some 280 places where *doxa* appears, 180 represent the Heb. *kābôd,* "glory, honor," which is regularly the sense of *doxa* in the NT. Carrez believed Paul chose to use *doxa* in part because of the Hellenistic milieu in which his audience lived.

For OT *kābôd,* see G. von Rad, *TDNT* 2:238–42; C. Westermann, *THAT* 1:794–812; M. Weinfeld, *ThWAT* 4:23–40. Used esp. of God (*kābôd YHWH*), "the luminous manifestation of his person, his glorious revelation of himself" (S. Aalen, *NIDNTT* 2:45), "the basic nature of God . . . in his revelation" (H. Hegermann, *EDNT* 1:346). Manifested in creation (Pss 19:1, etc.), acts of salvation (Exod 14:17–18, etc.), in the sanctuary (Exod 40:34–35; Ps 63:2, etc.), and in the "last days" (Isa 60:1–2; Ezek 39:21–22). LXX *doxa* is primarily God's glory, honor, or power. Sometimes ascribed to human beings; e.g., Ps 8:5; Prov 11:16 LXX, "A gracious woman"; Sir 3:11 LXX (*TDNT* 2:242–45). Both senses are expanded in Jewish literature, including Qumran (*NIDNTT* 2:45).

NT *doxa* regularly reflects this OT sense of "glory." But another background, in the magical papyri, Hellenistic "mysticism," and the mystery religions, possibly also influenced NT meaning (*TDNT* 2:252–53; denied in *NIDNTT* 2:46). The structure in the BAGD entry (203–4; BDAG 257–58) reflects this theory: 1. *brightness, splendor, radiance,* lit. (citations from the magical papyri; Phil 3:21 and 4:19) or applied to Christ or disciples (2 Cor 4:17); 2. *magnificance, splendor;* 3. *fame, recognition, renown, honor, prestige,* including Phil 3:19 (prestige), 4:20 (praise), and the phrase "to the praise of God," at 1:11. *TLNT* 1:372, "homage to the almighty and faithful God." On "glory" of God as a substance of "light," increased by thanksgivings, cf. Boobyer 7–14, 35–72, esp. 56–62 on the praise (*ainesis*) of God as "shining substance" (citing Hab 3:3–4; Pss 66(65):2; 71(70):8; 1 Chr 16:27), and the NOTE on 1:3 *thank.*

doxa is distinctively Pauline (57x in acknowledged letters). 6x in Phil: 2:11 and 3:21, as here, at the end of a section; once in describing the opponents (3:19); in a doxology (4:20), as well as at 4:19. Schlier 1963 stressed *heilsgeschichtlich* usage in the NT, not backgrounds. Phil 1:11, fruit from justification for glory, fits with appeals to give glory to God by ethical actions. For Paul, his congregations could mean "glory and joy" for him at the Lord's parousia (1 Thess 2:20). Cf. H. Hegermann, *EDNT* 1:346–47.

and praise of God. kai epainon theou (in most texts). D in Gk. + one cursive have "praise *of Christ*" (the abbreviation for God ϑ̄Ῡ read as X̄Ȳ); in some Vg. MSS "praise of him" (= Christ). More striking, F and G in the Gk. + one OL MS + Ambrosiaster read: "for glory and praise *to me*" (*kai epainon moi*); P⁴⁶ has "to the glory of God and praise *to me*" (*theou kai epainon emoi*). Metzger, *TCGNT* 611, these last variants are "very remarkable" and have "no parallel in Paul." Bockmuehl 70 conjectures that ϑ̄Ō̄Ῡ was read as MOY, "corrected" to MOI. The sense of "(glory and) praise to Paul" picks up the Pauline idea that his converts are his joy and crown (4:2) and provide him eschatological grounds for boasting (2:16; cf. 1 Cor 4:5; 1 Thess 2:20). J. D. Price (note the "partial skepticism" of Silva 22–27 on the approach) quantifies readings: "and praise of God," 0.96 certainty, extremely high on his scale; "praise of Christ" and "praise to me," 0.02 each, and "(glory) of God and praise to me" and "praise of him [= Christ]" 0.0 each. But P⁴⁶ represents a very early text and is likely based on awareness of Paul's sense of eschatological boasting, even if one prefers the text in NA²⁷ and UBSGNT. Full data in Aland 1991:571–74.

J. M. Ross, esp. 70, made a case for F and G as original, "to my glory and praise," a reading misunderstood as egotistical; toned down by P⁴⁶ to "the glory of God and my praise"; other MSS avoid any reference to Paul and make the words solely a doxology to God. Silva 64, "the reading of P⁴⁶ accounts most easily for the history of the text," but he "hesitates to adopt such a jarring variant when it is found in this lone witness." Collange 48, 50, calls P⁴⁶ "surprising enough in character to be original," apologetic for Paul and polemic against the Philippians: let them live "so that he may not have run or laboured in vain" (2:16). But that destroys any *captatio benevolentiae* and contrasts with the mood of 1:3–11 and picture of the community in what follows. One cannot solve such problems on textual evidence. See NOTES on *praise* and *God's.*

praise. epainos, 11x in the NT, 9 of them Pauline, 6x in 1–2 Cor, Phil, and Rom. In Phil also at 4:8, "anything 'worthy of praise.'" Many in antiquity cherished praise as a goal, desiring to be acknowledged and given respect. An orator "wants to be praised" (Epict. 2.16.6). Stoic philosophy sought to free a person from dependence on such appreciation. The LXX used *epainos* more for praise to God, esp. in the Pss (35 [LXX 34]:28, etc.), but also for praise of righteous individuals by the community (Sir 44:8,15) or by God (H. Schultz, *NIDNTT* 3:817).

In the NT, Phil 4:8 reflects classical Gk. "praiseworthy." BDAG (p. 357): (1) approval or recognition (a) coming from (α) others in the community (Rom 13:3; 2 Cor 8:18); or (β) from God, esp. eschatologically (Rom 2:29; 1 Cor 4:5); or (b) praise toward God, as in the Pss, only Phil 1:11 is cited (but cf. Eph 1:6,12,14, "to the praise of God's glorious grace"), with a cross-reference to 1.a.β, "praise to humans from God." Most assume Phil 1:11 denotes praise to God (H. Preisker, *TDNT* 2:588; *NIDNTT* 3:817). But *epainos* can express "approval of man by God" (*TDNT* 2:587; O. Hofius, *EDNT* 2:16–17).

God's. theou, usually taken as obj. gen., "glory and praise of (i.e., for) God." A certain uneasiness about this appears in the comments above from Collange and Silva (NOTE on *and praise of God*) because of the striking variants (P⁴⁶ F G). Alternative: take *theou* as subj. gen., "God's glory and praise" given to Paul and the Philippians by God, as in these variants. Schenk 123–26 has developed most fully the case for this; contrast Schlosser 1995a:390–92. The groundwork has been laid in NOTES above on *glory* and *praise.* (a) "Doxology" (O'B 82; Gnilka 53, among others) does not fit here, even "the *report* of a doxology" (O'Brien 1977:37; *Phil.* 82, italics added). Most Pss passages cited refer to an obligation or wish to offer *future* praise (Pss 21:13; 35:28; 45:17; 145:21; 2 Sam 22:50 = Rom 15:9; Pr Man 15). Others say "Blessed be God . . ." (Pss 41:13; 66:20; 72:18–19; 89:52; 106:48) or "Praise the Lord" (Ps 150). Sir 39:10, "the congregation will proclaim his praise," refers not to God but to a man who devotes himself to the study of the Law! 1QSb 4.25 ("you shall hallow [God] and glorify his name and his holy ones") is scarcely an exact parallel. (b) The five Gk. words at the end of 1:11 are too brief to match stylistic criteria for a doxology. Champion ([1] Bibl.), cf. p. 33, made no form-critical claim for a benediction here. (c) 1:11 is the only such conclusion in an introductory prayer report in a letter by Paul; it is singular, not a "form." Eph 1:6,12,14 and 1 Pet 1:7 may depend on Phil 1:11, rather than on a doxological form behind all these passages (Schenk 124). (d) It is misleading to speak of a "change of style . . . to the doxology" through the phrase *eis doxan,* as Käsemann (*Rom.* 384) does re Rom 15:7, where "glorify God," 15:6, 9, cf. 11, interprets *doxan tou theou;* not so in Phil 1:11. (e) Five Pauline and two Qumran passages have been used to argue at 1:11 for *theou* as an obj. gen. (1 Cor 10:31; 2 Cor 4:15; 1:20; Rom 3:7; Phil 2:11; 1QS 10.9 "to the glory of God"; 1QSb 4.5). Such evidence proves irrelevant when *peplērōmenoi* in 11a is not taken as middle voice and a *human* action of "bringing forth a harvest of righteousness" (Beare), but instead as an eschatological understanding of *God's* action. (f) The OT, far from providing examples of doxological application of the phrase Godward, employs *eis doxan* re God's addressing a warning to King Uzziah, "This will not be to you for honor from the Lord God" (2 Chr [Paralip] 26:18, *eis doxan para kyriou theou*). Indeed, most passages involving *eis* (or *pros*) *doxan* have human beings or sites on earth as the object of glory or honor from God: e.g., Exod 28:2,40 (Aaron); 2 Chr 3:6 (the temple); Sir 45:23 (Phinehas). (g) The v.l. (see NOTE on *and praise of God*), "glory and praise to me," F and G; P[46], "God's glory and praise to me," are evidence for how certain scribes (correctly) understood the subj. gen. use of *theou* (Walter 37). (h) *eis epainon kai doxan kai timēn* in the prooimion of 1 Peter, "so that the genuineness of your faith . . . may be found to result in praise and glory and honor when Jesus Christ is revealed" (1:7), "signifies the acceptance or approval of the righteous by God . . . in the last judgment" (H. Preisker, *TDNT* 2:587); E. G. Selwyn, *First Peter* (1952) 130, "Primarily the praise, etc. bestowed by God upon man," comparing Phil 1:11. J. H. Elliott, AB 37B:340–42, "be found worthy of praise and glory and honor at the revelation of Jesus Christ." (i) *theou* in 1:11 as a subj. gen. can be supported by the two pertinent uses of *epainos* in Paul: 1 Cor 4:5, when the Lord comes, each person will receive *epainos* (NRSV "commendation") from God (corresponding to his or her fidelity, v 3); Rom 2:29, "praise not from others but from God." Similarly with *doxa*: Rom 2:7,10, the norm at the judgment will be "glory and honor and peace to everyone who does good." Pauline use elsewhere of *praise* and *glory* re the final hope and eschatological completion of Christians supports a subj. gen. at 1:11. (j) Both nouns in 1:11 are actions by God, the equivalent of active vbs. with God as subj. (Schenk). The parousia is completion and perfecting by God, not simply judgment or *dies irae*. The Philippians' gifts in support of Paul, their activity for the gospel, and their solidarity with the imprisoned Paul are evidence of their relationship to God through Christ.

The TRANSLATION suggests the subj. gen. through the phrase *God's glory and praise*, without specifying "to me (Paul)," as in a few MSS, or "to us," including the Philippians. See COMMENT.

COMMENT

"Prayer" and "thanksgiving" for the Philippians have long been the headings for 1:3–11, at times + "intercession" or "petition." Or a Lat. rhetorical term, *prooemium* (Gk. *prooimion;* Loh., Michaelis, Mengel; Vielhauer 1975:65–66) or *exordium* (Swift; D. F. Watson 1988b, for 1:3–26).[1] Craddock: thanksgiving in the past (1:3–6), the present (1:7–8), and the future (1:9–11). Russell: a "thanksgiving formula," with "eschatological climax" *(Day of Christ)* (Doty, J. L. White 1971a). Some divide into 1:3–7 and 8–11 (Michael, Fitzmyer, Byrne, Bockmuehl). It is claimed 1:3–11 sets up themes for the letter that follows, even thankfulness for financial support. The section is also about Paul (cf. L. Alexander 1989:95): imprisoned (1:7), he

---

[1] Or "body opening" (Black 1995:25; contrast *DA* 130 n 15). Schenk (ANRW 2.25.4:3282) used "Proömium," but in *Phil.* 90 "Dank- und Fürbittebericht"; Alexander 1989: "prayer for recipients"; *DA* 197, thanksgiving and prayer.

prays and hopes (1:3,4,6,9).[2] Better, Paul, the Philippians, and God (Bittasi 240). Saul the Pharisee knew how to pray. Paul was indebted also to Hellenistic prayer practices, from Tarsus; Gk.-speaking Jewish Christians; his mission in the Greco-Roman world; desires to connect with the Philippians. Some see Jesus' teaching and practice of prayer as an influence. For *prooimion* texts, see F. O. Francis/J. P. Sampley #2, cf. 238, without reflecting Schubert's form-critical findings.

A. FORMS, SOURCES, AND TRADITIONS

Several factors are involved as Paul moves from salutation to letter body. He was jailed (1:7), something un-Roman (Bormann 1995:135). How will the Roman Philippians take this?

1. *Private Letters in the Papyri as a Factor.* Ancient letters, after the salutation, often had a wish or prayer for health, thanksgiving, blessing, "I thank the gods. . . ." Cf. Deissmann; J. L. White 1986 200–2; Murphy-O'Connor 1995a ([1] Bibl.) 55–57; Jewish Hellenistic letters (2 Macc 1:10b–11, but not Acts 23:26; 15:23). Prayer wishes seem to have dropped from Gk. letters in the 1st cents. B.C. and A.D., reemerging in the 2nd and 3rd cents. A.D. (Rigaux 1968:121).[3] At least in the 2nd cent. A.D., a *mneia* (or remembrance) motif appeared (Koskenniemi 128–48). Pauline "thanksgiving periods" (always after the salutation) differed (Schubert) in wording (Paul, *eucharistein* in the 1st per.), the god addressed, and reasons for thanksgiving and invocation.[4] Vielhauer 1975:66 correctly concluded that the prooimion is not simply taken over in Paul's letters from secular epistolary forms. Stylization may have been Paul's own work.

2. *Form Criticism.* Schubert 1939b, Wiles 1974, and O'Brien 1977 provide major studies.[5]

a. The "thanksgiving period"[6] appears regularly in Pauline letters, fixed in 1 Thess, with little variation thereafter. Of Schubert's two types of thanksgiving periods (cf. *TDNT* 9:412), Phil 1:3–11 fits under type Ia (with Phlm, 1 Thess),

---

[2] 1st per. sg. pron. 6x (vv 3,4,7 thrice, 8), 1st per. sg.vbs. in 3, 8, and 9, + ptcs. in vv 4 and 6 that refer to Paul.

[3] Cf. P. Artz, 1994:24–46; Reed 1996; P. Artz-Grabner, *Philemon* ([1] COMMENT B.6, p. 90), 124–35.

[4] In the papyri, the health of the individual recipient(s), delivery from some calamity; in Paul, for the community's perseverance and growth and mission advance, surprisingly *not* thanksgiving for the Christ event or personal deliverance from danger (except 2 Cor 1:3–11).

[5] Brief accounts on thanksgiving and intercession in Doty 31–33; Stowers 1986:21–22, papyrus examples 73, 88; O'Brien 1977:4–15; Gebauer 184–89; C. Wolff, *ABD* 6:437–38; *DA* 203–7; Murphy-O'Connor 1995a ([1] Bibl.) 56–59; Edart 57; *WDNTECLR* 458–59. Fee (72 n 3) is dubious about such formularies.

[6] Schubert 43–82. Schubert 171, concluded, with Deissmann, that *eucharistein tois theois* represented "the direct antecedent, i.e., the prototype of the Pauline epistolary thanksgiving formula." Cf. H. Conzelmann, *TDNT* 9:407–15; BAGD/BDAG *eucharisteō*; Mullins 1972 ([1] Bibl.). *Usages outside the Thanksgivings* (82–93) include IVb. Practical religious—i.e., paraenetic—instruction, e.g., Phil 4:6, *prayer and entreaty, with thanksgiving.*

seven units (Schubert 43, 56–71) in 1:3–6; ##5 and 7 also in 1:9–11. Schubert laid out a detailed structure and then a basic pattern.

(1) Main vb. = "I (or "we") thank" (1:3 *eucharistō*). (2) Personal object: "God," 1:3 *tō[i] theō[i]*, + the suffix "of me." (3) Temporal phrase: most commonly *pantote* = "always" (1:4), with *eucharistō* (68). (4) Pronominal obj. phrase: prep., *peri* (8x) or *hyper* (5x, including Phil 1:4), + 2nd pl. pron., gen., for "the persons . . . 'about whom' the thanksgiving is offered to God or 'in whose behalf' the intercessory prayer is made" (Schubert 59). In Phil, "for you *all*" goes with the ptc. that follows (". . . for you all making my prayer with joy," RSV; Schubert 66–68); temporal, "I thank (my) God always, as often as I think of you in my (daily) prayers, when making intercession for you all with joy" (1 Thess 1; Phil, Phlm, Col [cf. 1:9]; cf. Eph and Rom 1:8,10). (5) Ptc. + a temporal adverbial phrase, Phil 1:4 "in every prayer of mine" (*en pasē[i] deēsei mou*). Usually *mneian poioumenos* ("making mention," 1 Thess 1; Phlm; Eph; cf. Rom 1:10); Phil 1:4, *tēn deēsin poioumenos* ("making entreaty"), "is only a . . . slight variation." Schubert 60 placed Phil 1:9 ("this I pray," *touto proseuchomai*), "in this same syntactical unit . . . to complete the . . . initial *eucharistō*-period," interrupted by vv 7–8. The "participial construction [in 1:4] . . . invariably expresses *intercessory* prayer" for the addressees (60). Thanksgiving and intercession are thus mixed (Schenk 91–92). (6) Causal ptc. construction (1 Thess 1, double example; Phlm; Col) or causal adv. phrase with *epi* (1 Thess 3; 1 Cor; cf. 2 Cor): In Phil, both forms occur, the adv. phrase with the prep. *epi* twice, 1:3 *epi pasē[i] tē[i] mneia[i] hymōn*, 1:5 *epi tē[i] koinōnia[i] hymōn . . .*, plus 1:6 *pepoithōs auto touto*, "confident of this." 1:3 = "for each occasion when you remember me" (Schubert 61, *hymōn* subj. gen., cf. *koinōnia[i] hymōn* v 5). 1:5 goes with 1:3, "I thank my God . . . for the cooperation you manifest in the gospel" (so Gdsp., Dib., Loh.). Unit #6 gives the reason Paul thanks God. The vbs. are ones of "learning"—because I hear, remember, know, am sure. 1 Thess, Col, Phil, and Phlm contain this second causal ptc. and use *mneian poioumenos*, "making mention," just before it (slight variation in Phil); "a single, rigidly fixed structural pattern" in these four letters (62). (7) Concluding subordinate cl., "final" (*hina* or *hopōs* usually in type Ia, "[in order] that") or "causal" (*hoti* in type Ib). Phil, like 1 Thess 1, is "mixed": *hoti* in v 6, that God will complete the good work begun; *hina* and *eis to* + infin. in 1:9 and 10, "that your love may overflow . . . so that you may approve . . . and be. . . ." Here "the specific epistolary situation" influences the earlier "rigidly fixed structural pattern" (ties to the letter body that follows?). Schubert used his "fixed structural pattern" to settle debated points, though variations can exist (63–64).

Basic pattern: (1) *eucharistō*, temporally defined by (2) a ptc. "expressing the fact that the author offers an intercessory prayer in behalf of the addressees"; causally defined by (3) a second ptc., "expressing some knowledge which the author has obtained"; completed by (4) a final or telic cl. giving "the content of the intercessory prayer" (66,67). If there was "syntactical queerness" in this final cl. depending on the first ptc.—in Phil, "making prayer in every prayer of mine (*deēsis* really = intercession, 1:4) . . . that your love may overflow, etc. (1:9)"—there was

"no logical queerness" for readers. For them and Paul, thanksgiving and intercessory prayer were "two inseparable aspects of the same religious or liturgical act."
"In a wider sense, the final clause modified the entire principal clause (cols. 1–6)"
(67). Thus, "thanksgiving" provides "the spirit in which all prayer (*proseuchē*) and
all petitions (*deēsis*) are offered" (cf. Phil 4:6), an understanding developed from a
"*eucharistia*-concept . . . in Hellenistic religious thought and practice,"[7] i.e.,
Boobyer's "*eucharistō* speculation."[8] Paul was in prayer "a Hellenist of the Hellenists" (183).

Phil 1:3–11 is "the most verbose" of all Schubert's thanksgiving periods (71–
82). Compared with the "norm" in Phlm 4–5, certain "added" phrases stand out
in 1:3–11: the normal model runs,

#1 I thank	#5 praying	#5 in every prayer	confident of this,
#2 my God	#4 for all of you	of mine	#7 that . . . (v 9)
#3 always,			

Additions in Phil:

#6 at every remembrance of you (v 3) *epi pasē[i] tē[i] mneia[i] hymōn*	with joy (v 4) *meta charas*	#6 at your sharing in the gospel from the first day until now (v 5) in Gk.: *epi tē[i] koinōnia[i] hymōn eis to euangelion apo tēs prōtēs hēmeras achri tou nyn*

Syntactical inversion from the "norm": #6 comes before the normal unit #3; #5
comes between *pantote* and unit #4, *hyper pantōn hymōn*. These variations
Schubert took as a triple reference to the Philippians' gifts to the apostle. Paul
thanks God (a) 1:3, "for every expression of your remembrance of me" (#6; 73–
74), perhaps (74 n 1, 77) from the congregational *episkopoi* and *diakonoi*, 1:1.
Hence Paul prays "with joy" (v 4; pp. 78–79, 82). (b) 1:5, "for your cooperation
in the gospel. . . ." (#6), expanded in 1:7b, "both in my imprisonment and in
the defense and confirmation of the gospel," which in turn announces 1:12–2:30
(77 n 2); parallel in 4:14–15, the Philippians' share with Paul ([*syg*]*koinōnein*)
in his affliction by giving and receiving. (c) 1:6, "confident of this, that the One
who began a good work (*ergon agathon*) among you will bring it to completion
by the day of Jesus Christ" (#6). *ergon agathon* alludes to their "money gift" to
Paul.

Dubious is Schubert's contention that a Pauline thanksgiving announces or

---

[7] Schubert 68; cf. 122–78, esp. 122–31 on Philo. Cf. Epict. and the early Stoics. Andronicus, "Gratitude (*eucharistia*) is the science of to whom and when thanks should be given and how and from
whom it should be accepted" (SVF 3:67, No. 273); 142–78, inscriptions and papyri show that "to
thank (*eucharistein*) the gods" represented "a religious concept universal in Hellenistic life," 171.
[8] The theory in Boobyer was that the thanksgiving of Christians leads to "an actual material increase"
of the glory of God (4); cf. 2 Cor 1:11; 4:15; 9:11–12; AB 32A: 125, 147, 203, 261, 287, 451.

summarizes the theme(s) of the letter that follows (24, 77),[9] like the "thankless thanks" in 4:10–20, opponents in ch. 3. Mullins 1972 ([1] Bibl.) 387 well argued that thanksgiving formulas do not necessarily introduce or "prefigure" the "writer's mainline of thought." So Reed (*DA* 202–3, 210); Murphy-O'Connor 1995a:63. 1:3–11 is pertinent to Letter B, but does not introduce all the themes for all four chs.

Wiles 1974 (194–215 on Phil 1:3–11) reworked Schubert's form criticism. "Prayer *report*" is preferred for vv 4 and 9–11. Schubert's triple reference to the Philippians' gifts shrinks to "an oblique allusion" in *koinōnia* at 1:5 (206) and in v 11, "fruit of righteousness" (212). Thus a *divided* prayer *report*, v 4, "always in every prayer of mine for you all, making my prayer with joy," and vv 9–11, the longest such report in any letter by Paul. 1:9–11, is a "supplication" containing two balanced sections, each introduced by *hina* and concluding with an *eis* construction:

> 9 that *(hina)* your love may abound more and more,
> with *(en)* knowledge and all discernment,
> so that *(eis to)* you may approve what is excellent,
> 10 so that *(hina)* you may be pure and blameless for the day of Christ,
> 11 filled *(peplērōmenoi)* with the fruits of righteousness which come
> through Jesus Christ to *(eis)* the glory and praise of God (203–4).

Wiles is more interested in relating this intercessory prayer report with the three chs. that follow than in depicting form and function. Thus he sees allusions in 1:3–11 to ch. 3 (197, 200, 209), e.g., in 1:6 that "only at the parousia" will they "be made perfect" (3:12, 20–21).

For O'Brien 1977, Phil 1:3–11 exhibits epistolary, didactic, paraenetic, and pastoral functions for the entire letter (37–41; 38, 91). It reflects Schubert's type Ia, but with a different arrangement: (1) that your love may overflow . . . (v 9, *hina* to express content; *eis to dokimazein* in 10a gives the purpose of this love); (2) that you may be pure and blameless . . . (10b, *hina* to express purpose and result); (3) that you may be filled . . . (11, *peplērōmenoi*).[10] In his 1991 commentary, O'B 54–55 lists Schubert's sevenfold framework as adopted from a "Hellenistic epistolary *model*" but filled with OT/Jewish *contents* (similarly J. M. Robinson 1964; Audet 1959; Delling 1962a:51–52; *JBC* 47:6–8; *NJBC* 45:6–8).

Arzt 1994 examined many more Gk. papyrus letters than Schubert. A wish for health and well-being (*formula valetudinus*; cf. J. L. White 1986:200–1) that "is extended by a thanksgiving seems to be limited to the third century BCE" (45; cf. Rigaux 1968:21), therefore not contemporary to Paul. In Paul, we have no "introductory thanksgiving" but a "report of prayer" and "motif of remembrance" with

---

[9] Cf. Wiles 1974:204; O'Brien 1977: 12–13, 37–40; Edart 57–63. U. B. Müller 47, 1:9–11 point to 1:27–2:18, esp. 2:14–16, vv 9–11 correspond to 4:10–20 with the themes of joy, *koinōnia*, and *phronein*; but these are links that some connect with other parts or all of Phil. Bittasi 23–24.

[10] *proseuchomai* in v 9 is taken to refer back to v 4, *tēn deēsin poioumenos*, not (as in Schubert 14) to *eucharistō* in v 3, as well as to 4 and 5; i.e., "I pray" (v 9), "making petition" (v 4), rather than "I pray" (v 9) as a reflection of "I give thanks, make petition, and am confident."

thanksgiving to God (44). Reed 1996 (cf. *DA* 197–98) is critical, but allowed that Paul "employs the formula in the opening of his letter, though his thanks for the deity seem to be occasioned more by the well-being of his recipients than by his own welfare."

b. Possible proverbial, perhaps liturgical language and a "confidence formula" about God's faithfulness behind v 6: see NOTE on *the One who inaugurated a good work* . . . ; Radl 1981:43; U. B. Müller 41–42 (*Treuesprüche;* "the One who calls you is faithful and will do this," 1 Thess 5:24; J. Becker 1993 ([1] Bibl. **Paul**) 316, cf. 131–32, 135). A tradition behind *a good work* (1:6, see NOTE) is difficult to demonstrate. Perhaps a *pothos*-motif in 1:8, the writer "desires" to be with friends.[11]

Conclusion on form criticism: Schubert's judgments have not always been sustained. His exclusive reliance on a *Hellenistic* background for *eucharistō* material and limited non-NT data limit the work. But his (seven-part) analysis of thanksgiving periods in the NT, including intercessions, must be reckoned with. Cf. Boers 1976:141–45; Schnider/Stenger 1987 ([1] Bibl.) 42–49; Gebauer 1989:50–53, 184–86. "Prayer *report*" is a more accurate description.

3. *Rhetoric as a Factor.* Influences from Greco-Roman rhetoric on 1:3–11 have been claimed (Schubert; Holloway 2001a:87–100, consolation as an expression of sympathy and affection in 1:7–8, "the things that matter" v 10). Orators might commence a speech with a reference to prayer; Dem., *Cor.* 18.1; Aratus, *Phaen.* 1. *De Corona* 18.324 concluded with a prayer.[12] *prooemium* was used by Loh. and others for 1:3–11, *exordium* by H. D. Betz, G. A. Kennedy, D. F. Watson 1988b: 61–65, Bloomquist, Bockmuehl 57; Edart 63 sees some characteristics; Bittasi 17–33, 9–11 = *propositio,* "introduction," a prelude or prologue.[13] To make the audience well disposed to what follows.[14] But parallels are overstated (Fee 73 n 8). Some enfold the epistolary salutation into the "exordium" (so Hughes 34–36, 51–56, cf. 117 n 3), or extend the *exordium* for the putative situation that has been reconstructed (so D. F. Watson 1988b:61–62, Phil 1:3–26). The case would be strengthened if one knew Paul opened his sermons with prayer (Rigaux 1968:121–22) or employed "homiletical benedictions" (Jewett 1969 [(1) Bibl.]), but convincing proof for each is lacking. Paul's sections are prayer *reports,* not invocations of a god. Is the *exordium* a "table of contents" for the letter (Hughes 52)? Better:

---

[11] Thraede 1970; Schoon-Janßen 137, Phil 1:3–4; 4:1 (*epipothētai*); and 2:19; Perkins 1987:513; U. B. Müller 44.

[12] Also Dem., *Ep.* 1; Cicero, *Inv.* 1.22. Berger 1974 ([1] Bibl.) 224 n 162, Plat., *Tim.* 27BC, reflected in Philo, *Aet.* 1; Iamblichus, *Vit. Pyth.* 1.1; Quint. 10.1.48, with reference to Homer; (225 n 33) Diogn. 1. Delling 1962a:52 claimed "the *eucharistō* prayer, with such Hellenistic roots, belongs to the Pauline-primitive-Christian service" *of worship.*

[13] Cf. Lausberg ##262–88. G. A. Kennedy 1984 prefers "proem" (23–24, 142, 148 [on Gal 1:6–10], 153).

[14] Aristot., *Rhet.* 1.1.9 [1354b]; 3.14 [1415a.7]; *Rhet. ad Her.* 1.4.6–7,11; Cicero, *Inv.* 1.15.20–17.25; Quint. 4.1.1–79, esp. 61–62; D. F. Watson 1988a: 35–36. On the *exordium* preparing an audience for deliberation, cf. Watson 1988a:34, 61; H. D. Betz, *Gal.* 44–45; Hughes 32–36, 51–56; Lausberg ##263–88.

thanksgiving-intercession periods share common themes *with each other,* but are not a full listing of topics that this letter will take up. From Phil 1:3–11 could one predict the attention to be given to unity/humility, or "the enemies" in 3:2–21?

4. *Enthymemes?* The term[15] is used of 1:3–6 (Debanné) and elsewhere.[16] Often defined as an abbreviated or incomplete syllogism. Treated in Aristot., but definitions are unclear, his *Ars Rhetorica* was little known in the Roman period, and subsequent developments varied. Quint. 5.10.1–3 has five meanings, Demetrius *De elocutione* 30–33, four. Cf. Lausberg #371, 356.2, 875, 879; Holloway 2001b:335, "a brief pointed argument drawn from contraries," often as a rhetorical question. Debanné claims nineteen enthymemes in Phil 1, convertible into syllogisms; the "silent premise" we tease out can amount to a text beneath the visible text. E.g., Major Premise, "God brings to completion any good work that he begins among you [as believers]," 1:6; suppressed Minor Premise, "Your sharing in the gospel from the first day until now [1:5] is [clearly] a good work begun by God among you"; Conclusion, "[God will bring to completion your sharing in the gospel from the first day until now.] I thank my God every time I remember you . . . because of [it]" (1:3a). Such reconstructions include subjective judgments (on "[clearly] a good work") and too easily assume truncated syllogisms (*WDN-TECLR* 157 = Aune 2003:319). Promising, problematic.

5. *Liturgical Elements?* Some suggest 1:3–11 incorporates phrases from public worship. Did Paul follow such prayer traditions or was he more charismatic, praying in the Spirit, or both? Schubert 1939:95–114: the thanksgiving-periods root in Hellenistic religiosity; Wiles 23–27, OT and synagogue liturgy, as well as Hellenistic prayer style. O'Brien, 11b "liturgical style" (*Phil.* 82; 1977:36). R. Russell (1982:298–99), "Jewish custom . . . through the eucharist of the early church"; this too easily combines Jewish expressions of "thanks" (cf. Matt 11:25) and post-NT use of *eucharistia* for the patristic eucharist.

The intercessions and doxology (1:9–11 and 11b traditionally interpreted) are what the Philippian community might have prayed. But we lack evidence churches then prayed thus in liturgy. "I thank (my) God" (1:3) is age-old prayer-language (2 Sam 22:50; Pss 18:49, etc.), "for the glory and praise of God" (11c) typical laud to a deity, but neither is necessarily liturgical. The "doxology" at the end of v 11 proves uncertain when examined; see NOTES on *God's glory and praise.*

---

[15] M. J. Debanné, "An Enthymematic Reading of Philippians: Towards a Typology of Pauline Arguments," in Porter/Stamps (eds.) 2002:481–503. *WDNTECLR* 150–57; cf. D. E. Aune 2003, "The Use and Abuse of the Enthymeme in New Testament Scholarship," *NTS* 49:299–320; D. Hellholm, "Enthymenic Argumentation in Paul: The Case of Romans 6," in Engberg-Pedersen (ed.) 1995a:119–79; P. A. Holloway 2001b, "The Enthymeme as an Element of Style in Paul," *JBL* 120:329–42.

[16] Phil 1:27–30, (5) COMMENT A.1; 2:12–13, (8) COMMENT A.3; 3:2–4, (11) COMMENT A.1; 3:17–19, 20–21, (14) COMMENT A.1 n 1.

6. "Apostolic Speech." Paul's letters express what the apostle would say if present in person (Berger 1974 [(1) Bibl.]); "apostolische Rede" appeared in the address ([1] COMMENT A). Phil 1:3–11 follows Hellenistic convention (location after the salutation) but not re form, content, or function (Berger 219–24). As with *grace* in 1:2 (it grants "revealed knowledge," see [1] COMMENT B.6), Berger 220 finds thanks for "revelation and insight granted by God" (1:6). From 1 Cor 1:4–5 ("grace has been given you . . ." ; cf. 1:8–9), Phlm 4, and other passages, Berger argues for a pattern where blessing conveys revelation or authority.[17] Thanksgiving is for the faith and love of those addressed (perhaps under "thanksgiving for election," cf. 1 Thess 1:4; Berger 220 n 140). An author seeks goodwill by referring to his/her own person (*captatio benevolentiae a nostra persona*, Lausberg #275); thus Phil 1:7. Mutuality ("you share in God's grace with me"), Paul as "brother, not teacher." Johanson ([1] Bibl.) 71 prefers *philanthrōpia* ("goodwill") in the thanksgiving, following Koskenniemi (35ff.) and Boers 1976:147. But goodwill already existed with the Philippians; Paul may assert his (apostolic) (spiritual) authority in the face of possible objection to his prisoner status. Prayer, particularly intercession, was part of his missionary responsibility (Hamman 301; O'Brien 1977:13–14; D. M. Stanley 1973:32), apostolic concern for converts in the gospel's advance.

7. The Old Testament and Other Possible Traditions. No OT phrases, apart perhaps from *fruit of righteousness* in v 11.[18] Wiles 159–60, Paul's prayer parallels Jewish liturgical practices (cf. O'Brien 1977:217). Wick, an OT context (177–78), but this underestimates the Gk. evidence at hand (*DA* 203 n 181). Jewish *hodaya* formulas (J. T. Sanders 1962) are not pertinent to Phil (*DA* 203 n 184).

Boobyer and others have spoken of a Hellenistic speculative philosophy behind the term "glory"; see n 8, above, and NOTES on 1:3 *I thank* and on 1:11 *glory*.

On "inaugurate" and "complete" as cultic, proverbial, pre-Pauline tradition, perhaps a "faithful saying," see NOTE on 1:6 *One who inaugurated* and A.2.b, above. On Webber's "rejoicing formula," see NOTE on 1:4 *with joy*. 1:10 *the things that are best* is Stoic-Cynic language.

To find reflections of the phrases of opponents in ch. 3 (see NOTES on 1:7 *it is right* and 1:10a *so that you may keep on appreciating the things that are best*) assumes Paul knew of these people when writing the prooimion but nonetheless burst out abruptly as he does in 3:2. Unlikely.

8. Conclusions. As a thanksgiving, prayer report, and intercessions section to build goodwill on the part of the readers, Phil 1:3–11 reflects many elements familiar to author and audience—thanksgiving to the gods at the start of papyrus letters, perhaps an orator's opening-prayer allusion, age-old phrases in prayer piety and liturgy ("I thank God" and "to the glory and praise of God," if v 11 is so interpreted).

---

[17] *T. Sol.* Prologue; *Mart. Ascen. Isa.* 6.9; 8.22; 11.36, cf. Matt 9:8; 2 Chron 2:12 (Heb. 11) and *T. Sol.* 22.1 (*OTP* 1:983; *captatio benevolentiae!*).

[18] See NOTE on the phrase. E. E. Ellis 1957; Koch 1986; Hays 1989 (all in [4] Bibl. OT) do not treat 1:11.

But it conforms to none of these. The vv are reports, not prayers, not phrases out of liturgies. Paul has welded together various elements into a whole that reflects mission concern for the advance of the gospel in the lives of those addressed. This style of thanksgiving report had been worked out by Paul by the time he wrote 1 Thess. He conforms to the basic seven-unit structure in his other letters. Significant additions in Phil 1:3–11 are *because of your remembrance of me* (v 3), *with joy* (v 4), and *because of your sharing in the gospel from the first day until now* (v 5).

B. MEANING AND INTERPRETATION

For 1:3–11, *heuresis* or invention of material involves a thanksgiving-and-intercession pattern employed in Paul's letters for several years (A.2.a, above), expanded to secure the ear of the Philippians for the body of the letter. Which letter? See 1, below. The Philippians and Paul are "partners" (*sugkoinōnous*, 1:7); a legal, business partnership? See 2, below. COMMENT then turns to Paul's meaning in 1:3–6, 7–8, and 9–11.

1. With Which Letter to Philippi Does the Prooimion in 1:3–11 Go? If three letters are posited, Letter B (chs. 1–2 and parts of 4; Beare, Collange, G. Barth, Schenk, Pesch, Fitzmyer, Byrne). If two letters, the longer one (chs. 1–2 and 4; Michael, Friedrich, Gnilka, Doty, and J. L. White). Pesch prints 1:3–11 after 1:1–2, leading into 1:12–3:1 as the bulk of Letter B.[19] We make no effort to carve Phil 1:3–11 into phrases from three letters. Contents fit chs. 1–2 and parts of 4 well.

Letter A (see 4:10–20) earlier thanked the Philippians for gifts of money and a helper, Epaphroditus. There is no need to strain for references in 1:3–11 to Paul's thanks for the Philippians' gifts. He may allude to them in 1:3 *because of your remembrance of me*; 1:5 *your sharing (koinōnia)*, but addition of *in the gospel* implies a wider reference than just financial gifts; 1:6 *a good work* also has a broad sense.

To take 1:3–11 as part of Letter B has two implications. (a) One can appeal to 4:10–20 (Letter A) in understanding 1:3–11. No need to try to explain why thanks for gifts from Philippi are delayed so long in the letter (DA 138). (b) No need to try to find veiled allusions in 1:3–11 to the opponents in ch. 3.[20] O'B 1991:12, if Paul "had already sent a note of thanks, the allusions to the community's generosity in a subsequent letter (1:3–11 and 2:25–30) would be more understandable" but (16) "the apostle . . . introduced motifs that he later takes up" in ch. 3, e.g., *phro-*

---

[19] Letter A (4:10–20) likely had a thanksgiving (Pesch 59); C, an introduction after the Prescript (95). For A, cf. the typical prayer of thanks in papyrus letters or Phlm 4–7, with "philophronetic" phrases between friends (61–63): "I thank my God always when I remember you in my prayers, that you stand fast in faith in Jesus the Lord and in love to all the saints. And I pray that you may become richer in all perception and insight that Christ provides." Perhaps Letter C had no thanksgiving (99). Cf. Gal 1:6, Paul has little about which to be thankful! The situation in Philippi seems less far gone; then Paul included a brief thanksgiving report to seek goodwill. Pesch leaves the matter open.

[20] O'B; Collange 50; see NOTE on 1:11 *because you have been filled with*; in Patte's "second reading," 1983:176–82, 3:17 is the clue to understand 1:3–11 (Letter A = 3:2–21; B = 4:10–20; C = 1:1–3:1 + 4:2–9, 21–23, an unusual reconstruction of sequence).

nein (1:7; 3:15—which appears in all 4 chs.; see above on Letter A). If Paul had ch. 3 in mind from the outset, the abruptness of 3:2 and its vehemence are hard to explain (cf. 352, 357). In making the opponents "Judaizers" (357, 33–34), O'B and others forget that in his letter against such opponents in Galatia, Paul provided no thanksgiving period.

Others appeal to a rhetorical *inclusio*: 1:3–11 and 4:10–20 (*exordium* and epilogue), or 1:9–11 and 4:19–20 (cf. Swift 249–50; Dalton 101; Wiles 1974: 104–5). O'B 18, 4:19–20 provides "the answer to Paul's intercessory prayer (1:9–11)." But 1:9–11 needs no such answer. 1:9–11 in Letter B may just as well echo 4:19 in Letter A. What balances what in a chiastic outline is disputed (see INTRO. VI.B, nn 2, 3). Pesch sees Phil *redacted* as a "ring composition," 4:10–18 balances 1:3–11; 4:19–23 is the postscript in tandem with 1:1–2 as prescript. Arguments from proposed rhetorical or chiastic structures are precarious.

1:3–11 functions well as thanksgiving- and intercession-report for Letter B, fairly well but not perfectly for the redacted letter. Meaning in Letter B holds generally for the redacted letter.

2. Prior Relationships: Did Paul and the Philippians Have a Business Tie or a Contractual, Legal Ecclesiology? Fleury claimed a business arrangement (see [16] COMMENT B.1.[A]1), which Sampley 58–60 rejected. More significantly, Sampley ([16] COMMENT B.I.[A].2) argued Paul used the Roman legal concept of "consensual *societas*," an "artificial consortium" of persons "drawn together by some mutually valued goal or purpose" (12), "persons of different social strata," even slaves, but "equal partners" (17), with strong mutual obligation. Such a *societas* "was termed *koinōnia* in Greek" (12). (1) Paul and Barnabas entered into such an arrangement with Peter, James, and John at Jerusalem ("the right hand of *koinōnia*," Gal 2:9). (2) Paul had a consentual *societas* with the Philippians, and only with them among all his churches. (3) He used "*societas* partnership language" with Philemon (v 17) and may have had "a formal *societas*" with him.

Questions: (1) Consensual *societas* seems oriented to financial matters (18 n 10, cf. 13–14). Are there Roman examples in religious matters? (2) Does an "artificial consortium" of nonfamily members fit house-church structure at Philippi? Datiri 31 emphasizes how "the family provided a social model for the finances of the Pauline churches." (3) Admittedly, "*koinōnia* is 'ambiguous' when referred to Greek associations" (18 n 7; cf. p. 29). One looks for evidence (which 45 n 26 does not provide) that *koinōnia* = *societas*, and *koinōnos* = *socius*. The Gk. *koinōnia* = Lat. *participatio* and *communio*, not necessarily *societas* (Hahn 1979 and others).[21] N. R. Petersen ([1] NOTE on 1:1 **slaves**) 103–9, re Phlm 17 (*koinonos* as "partner"), denies equality, Paul writes as "senior partner"; Sampley's views (cf. 177 n 31) are little employed by Petersen. (4) Would Roman authorities have allowed such status for the (Philippian) church in Roman law? More likely they were viewed as a guild or *collegia* (Meeks) or persecuted like other eastern cults.

---

[21] The chief deficiency (G. R. Horsley, ed., *NewDocs* 3:4) is the inability to show Lat. *societas* = Gk. *koinōnia*.

(5) Some legal aspects of a *societas* (Sampley 12–17) would have been awkward. It "lasts as long as the parties remain of the same mind [*in eodem sense*]" (15, Gaius, *Inst.* 3.151, 2nd cent. A.D.). Was this mind already shattered at Phil 2:2, 4:2? It lasts until any individual partner dies (15). Therefore reconstituted each time a Philippian believer died? And if legally binding and court suits were brought (13–14), would Paul (cf. 1 Cor 6:1–8) have encouraged going to court? Would Philippian Christians have gone into a Roman court to "legalize" their association, given their struggle with authorities indicated in 1:27–30? (6) Is "*societas Christi*" warranted for a partnership involving *Paul and the Philippians*? If this second leg of the argument for *societas* in Phil (60–62, cf. 103–4, 106–7) poses questions, so also does the first point, that 4:10–20 is a "receipt" (52–60). (7) Is the case overstretched by having to take *doma* in 4:17 as "gift" *and* "payment," and *chreia* (4:16; 2:25) as both "need" *and* "request" (54–55)? Would the long inactivity of the Philippians (4:10) not have put an end to the agreement? (8) The third supporting leg to the argument suggests that *in eodem sensu* of a *societas* means the same as *to auto phronein* in Phil 2:2, 4:2 (62–70, 105–6), cf. 2:2,5. But did all the Philippians and Paul "think the same thing"? On Sampley's view re Letter A, see (16) COMMENT B.1.(A).2.

Subsequent treatments moved away from Sampley's *societas* to the *topos* of "friendship." See (16) COMMENT B.1.(A).3, on 4:10–20, esp. v 15; P. Marshall 1987:157–64, 257. L. M. White 1990, the "semantic field" should be broadened beyond the "quasi-legal" setting of contractual *societas*. "Partnership" is a sign of friendship, the larger theme (Marshall). Hospitality, letters of recommendation, and patronage/benefaction are grounded in *philia* (210–11; 214 n 59). Hainz 1994:385 and Bormann 1995:226–32 reject Sampley's consensul *societas*. Finally there are reservations about an ecclesiology—which is what *societas Christi* involves—for one Pauline church only. A *societas* relationship of Roman legal, contractual nature was not involved in Phil.

3. Paul and the Philippians: Introductory Prayer Report of Thanksgiving and Intercession (1:3–6).

1:3–11 is a unity (Schenk 109; see NOTES on 1:7 *It is indeed right . . .* , and on 1:9 *I am praying*), built around characteristic features of Paul's *eucharistō* period or thanksgiving formula (all 7 features in vv 3–6, two of them repeated in vv 9–11).[22] We follow most commentators in dividing it 1:3–6, 7–8, 9–11: "I" statements, vv 3–6 (*I thank*); impers. and oath constructions in vv 7 and 8 (*It is indeed right . . . ; God is my witness*); back to prayer report in vv 9–11. 1:7–8 are not intrusive or an aside but part of a unit about past relations, the present situation, and future hopes.

Paul reports how he thanks God and makes entreaties for his converts. His ac-

---

[22] The unit may exhibit a caesura (break) between 3–8 and 9–11, where *I am praying* in v 9 resumes vv 3–6 (Beare, Fitzmyer, Byrne, Schenk 109–10, Bockmuehl), or between vv 3–7 and 8–11, a shift from Paul's prayer report to his yearning and hopes for the Philippians (Michael; Chrysost., Aquinas, vv 1–7, 8–17). Silva: 3–5, 6–8, 9–11. Refshauge, two "preambles," 1:3–6 and 7b–11, joined by a redactoral bridge in 7a.

tual prayers must be reconstructed (Orphal). Within this prooimion Paul moves
from thanksgiving to intercession (e.g., O'Brien 1977), from indic. to impv. (Furnish 1968:224–27). Yet intercession begins in v 4 (*entreaty* 2x). Paul speaks and
prays as an individual before God (U. B. Müller 39, contrast 1 Thess 1:2 "we").[23]
There is a personal tone to the prooimion, "about me," Paul. At the same time,
1:3–11 is very much about the Philippians (2nd per. pl.).[24] Thus apostle and community in their mutual relationship before God. It arouses interest in what Paul
will say to them and sympathy for him as their apostle in bonds.

Focus is increasingly on the Philippians, esp. in vv 9–11. No word of complaint
about Paul's plight or petition for his personal future (unless 11c that *God's glory
and praise* may be his at the Day of the Lord, as a few MSS suggest). Yet not simply
"flash thoughts" running through his mind or meditation in prison about Philippi.
Social-world analysis of NT prayer stresses its oral and communal character.[25]
People prayed aloud (Acts 16:25; Mark 14:32–41 parr.; Mark 15:33,37 parr.). The
individual was embedded in the group. People never prayed "apart from the context of the community to which they belonged and to which they were closely
bound for a sense of their own identity" (Osiek 147).

I thank my God (1:3) links the prooimium to *God our Father* in v 2. *my God* suggests identity of the ancestral deity of Saul (and Israel) with the God about whom
the Philippians have heard in the gospel of Christ. It reminds them of Paul's particular and personal relationship with this God, different from god(s) mentioned
in most letters the Philippians received (*DA* 207)! *I thank* (see NOTE on 1:3) employs a term of gratitude also found in papyrus letters and orations. In Hellenistic
speculation, "thanksgiving" may have suggested a response prompted by God-
given favor. In Christian letters, it was often reflective of God's current activity
with those who pray and their community, their election (1 Thess 1:4), grace-gifts,
faith, and mission (1 Cor 1:4; Phlm 4–5; Rom 1:8); here, support for Paul (Phil
1:3b) and the missionary advance of the gospel (1:5,12,25). Nothing liturgical
here, let alone eucharistic; thanksgiving was due God at many times and places
(1 Cor 10:30–31; 14:16–17). To thank God was not strange to Paul's hearers,
whether as Greeks, Jews, or Christians.

Three reasons follow for thanksgiving by Paul the prisoner at this grim point in
his life (usually at least one in a Pauline prooimion, unit #6). The three reflect
Paul's circumstances and positive relationship with the Philippians. Two have to

---

[23] See NOTES on frequent use of the 1st-per. sg. pron. and vbs. (v 3 *I thank my God;* "*remembrance* 'of
me'"; 4 *entreaty of mine, making entreaty;* 6 *I am confident;* 7 *right for me, you have me in your heart;
my imprisonment,* implying [*my*] *defense and confirmation of the gospel; sharing . . . with me;* 8 *my witness, I long;* 9 *I am praying*). "I" form, in spite of Timothy as co-sender; see (1) COMMENT B.4.

[24] 1:3 *your every remembrance of me;* 4 *for all of you;* 5 *your sharing in the gospel;* 6 *among you;* 7 *to think
about all of you; you have me in your heart; you all sharing, as you do, with me;* 8 *for you all;* 9 *that your
love may continue;* 10a *that you may keep on appreciating . . . ;* 10b *you may be flawless and unfailing;*
11 *you have been filled,* and 11c *God's glory and praise* (for the Philippians).

[25] Osiak 146, with B. J. Malina, "What Is Prayer?" *TBT* 18 (1980) 214–20, esp. 218–19; "The Individual and the Community—Personality in the Social World of Early Christianity," *BTB* 9 (1979) 126–38;
Malina 1981:51–60.

do with Philippian involvement in the Pauline mission for Christ. The third is a response encouraged by this history of goodwill, as well as by the gospel itself. Thanks for (1) Philippian remembrance of him (v 3b); (2) their sharing in the gospel from conversion till the present (v 5); (3) grounds for the sure hope he voiced about them in v 6: Paul trusts God's promises, he sees and hears of the Philippians' life in Christ, and so is confident about their future. An exceptional number of causal statements in a prooimion, but warranted by the apostle's ties with Philippi and with God, rounded out by a beginning of petitions to God in v 4.[26] They structure 1:3–6.

The key word in 1:3 is their *remembrance*, praying for Paul, maintaining solidarity with him in his imprisonment and possibly imminent death, including financial gifts and personnel sent from Philippi to Paul. In Letter B, a deft reminder of the gift previously acknowledged in Letter A (4:10–20). In the redacted letter, reference here to financial help is less apparent; cf. O'B 60–61, "not . . . the most important reason for [Paul's] thanksgiving." The Note on *pasē[i]* in v 3, the first of five Gk. words beginning with the letter "*p*" in vv 3b–4 (*pantote, pasē[i]* again, *pantōn*, and *poioumenos*; cf. v 20), suggests "any and every," the totality of, your *remembrance*, a sequence of prayers and examples of solicitude for Paul.

1:3 may be termed simply good manners (Robertson 1917:59), to build goodwill (*captatio benevolentiae*). O'Brien (1977:13–15; 37–41; 262–63) sees this first reason as *apostolic*; *epistolary* (reflecting Gk. letters); *pastoral* (concern for him); perhaps *paraenesis*, encouraging further support. (But 4:10–20 did *not* do that, speaking instead of Paul's self-sufficiency in God.)

V 4 is not a parenthetical aside (Gnilka, many trs., NRSV), but is closely linked to v 3. It advances the presentation. When and how does Paul give thanks? *always* (alliteration in Gk.) goes with *I thank my God* but is explained by *in every entreaty of mine . . . .* Unit #3 in Paul's thanksgiving periods. Not "prayer unceasing" (1 Thess 5:17; Rom 12:12, talking to God without respite, cf. 2 Macc 13:12); it reflects "the style of ancient letters" and literary hyperbole (O'B 57–58).[27] One can paraphrase, "I always, when I make entreaty for you . . . , thank my God."

Paul prays with inclusive emphasis on each and every member of the Philippian community (*all of you*, syntactical unit #4; *pantōn* is alliterative), *with joy* (one of Paul's additions to his usual prooimion structure; see COMMENT A.2). It reflects his happy relations with Philippian Christians. *with joy* (*charas*) links verbally with *grace* (*charis*) in 1:2 (see NOTE on 1:4, re the thematic importance of the Gk. terms *chara/chairein* in Phil).[28] "Joy vivifies prayer" (Bengel). Prayer is

---

[26] On three *causal* units, rather than *temporal* interpretations, see NOTES on 1:3 *remembrance*; 1:5 *because of*; 1:6 *since I am confident on this point*; COMMENT A.2 (Schubert on syntactical unit #6; O'Brien); Gebauer 1989:196–98.

[27] Less likely, regular hours for prayer, three times a day (at sunrise, 3 p.m., sunset; Dan 6:11,14; *Did.* 8.3), possibly using the Lord's Prayer, cf. "Abba" in Gal 4:6 and Rom 8:15–16; Jeremias 1967 ([1] Bibl. **Father**) 66–81, 81 re Phil 1:3–6, *mneia*.

[28] But scarcely "*announces* one of the *most obvious* subthemes of the letter" (Black 1995:30), emphasis added by Reed, who comments, "This is the type of indiscriminate lexical paralleling that single-letter theorists must avoid," DA 198 n 163; 414–15. L. Hartman 2001:36 rejects connection of joy with per-

"the line of communication with the base of supplies."[29] The Hellenistic nature of rejoicing and the OT focus in it on God as object of joy are pointed out in the NOTE, plus NT connection with Jesus and its charismatic or grace-gift nature. As part of the "fruit of the Spirit" (Gal 5:22), an expression of God's reign in believers' lives (Rom 14:17), joy marked early Christian life and mission. Not simply from a "rejoicing formula" in Gk. letters (Webber), it stems from the experience of God's presence through the Spirit manifested in life together. Paul's joy and that of the Philippians flow through Letter B (16 references in the NOTE), "in the midst of sadness, affliction, and care" (*NIDNTT* 2:359), even prison; "a defiant 'Nevertheless'" (K. Barth 120).

All this grounds the initial intercessions by Paul for the Philippians (more in vv 9–11, v 4 *every entreaty of mine for all of you*). Instead of his usual word at this point (*mneia*, used in v 3, *remembrance*), Paul twice employs in v 4 *deēsis, entreaty*, asking, petition, or specific intercession (at 1:19, Paul will ask their prayers for his court proceedings; 4:6, let their supplications be known to God). "Thanksgiving" in 1:3–6 includes intercession as part of Paul's report.

The second reason for Paul's joyous thanks (1:3) and intercession for the Philippians (1:4) is their *sharing in the gospel from the first day until now* (v 5). The structure builds chronologically around two decisive moments (*kairoi*): first, when people in Philippi heard the gospel and believed, then the present moment, as Paul faces trial and possible death and the Philippians face opponents who could divide them. Paul does not begin here with Christ or the cross, God's plan, or Israel's history, but the Philippians and their Christian experience. There is also a third decisive moment to come (v 6) — who knows when? — Christ's parousia, final judgment and completion of God's work. Thus: gospel heard and believed → now → the Day of Christ. This "existential salvation history" is marked by *sharing in the gospel*, receiving and passing it on.

The NOTE on *gospel* brings out its Gk. and Pauline nature, a concept developed particularly in the Hellenistic Jewish church, an eschatological, even apocalyptic, term, for what God has wrought at the end of the ages in Jesus' death and resurrection. In Paul's day, oral proclamation, promised in the Scriptures, addressed to all, to Jew and Greek alike, norm for faith and life. To preach the gospel is apostolic activity (Schütz 35–53). For Paul, power, from God, denoting action, a missionary term. No need of definition at 1:5 for Paul's converts, though the apostle elsewhere fills out the sense, sometimes against opponents ("Christ crucified," in Corinth; "righteousness by faith" [not Law; Kertelge 1996], Gal. Phil 3).

The other important term introduced in v 5 is *koinōnia, sharing.*[30] Four occurrences in Phil, plus a compound 1:7; see NOTE. It means "have a share in some-

---

secution (Loh.) or imitation of Christ (Wick 82–85); most likely, joy over the advancement of the gospel (Hofius; 36 n 74).

[29] A. T. Robertson 1917:61 = C. G. Baskerville, *Side-Lights on the Epistle to the Philippians* (London: Nisbet, 1914).

[30] Eichholz 1965:142, the key concept in 1:3–11; others (Swift 236, Wick 142–48), for the entire letter. L. Hartman 2001:33 n 66 cautions against "presupposing too quickly that a Pauline letter necessarily has one given theme."

thing or someone," "give a share," and then participation, fellowship, or communion, ecclesially. What one shares in includes the gospel (Phil 1:5), faith (Phlm 6), the Son of God (1 Cor 1:9), the body and blood of Christ (1 Cor 10:16–17), sufferings (Phil 3:10–11), the collection (2 Cor 8:4; 9:13), the Spirit and a fellowship created by the Spirit (2 Cor 13:14, cf. Phil 2:1). See NOTE on pre-Pauline formulas, development in Paul's letters, and a certain consensus for "participation" or "communion" grounded in participation in certain "goods" (good things) granted by God. It has vertical and horizontal aspects:

Spiritual aspects:	participation in the Son, Spirit, etc.

$$\downarrow \quad \uparrow$$
$$\downarrow \quad \uparrow$$
$$\downarrow \quad \uparrow \qquad \text{fellowship created}$$

Social aspects:	← believer(s) → in the gospel, faith, and sharing all one has

But every passage about *koinōnia* needs examination in context. At 1:5, an initial and continuing "sharing in" the gospel that nurtures the Philippians, plus "sharing of" the gospel with others (Fee 84); "mission," broader than just financial contributions to Paul (O'Brien 1977:25; U. B. Müller 40; contrast Mengel 227–28). For Philippians *koinōnia* could imply friendship, client–patron obligations, communal relations, and even political identity (cf. *DA* 207–8).

A third reason for thanksgiving (1:6): Paul is sure *that the One who inaugurated a good work among you will bring it to completion by the Day of Christ Jesus.* The parousia is terminus and goal of Paul's vision, concluding counterpart to *the first day* the gospel was preached in Philippi and the present moment *now* (sketched above). "Inaugurate" and "complete" may reflect proverbial, cultic use (though no exact analogue; Loh., God as Beginning and Ending). Better: God's activity all the way, in the gospel process of bringing the Philippians to faith and sustaining them until God's work with them is completed.[31] Divine fidelity all along the way, until the consummation.[32] God works through human agents like Paul, but *the One who inaugurated* the gospel and faith among the Philippians is God. The process of salvation involves "eschatological tension" (*TPTA* 461–98).

a good work is debated. See NOTE on *work* re (A) *God's work* of salvation, the new creation, community (cf. *koinōnia* in v 5), or divine "almsgiving"; (B) *God and the Philippians* working together re their Christianity, mission work, achievements for the gospel, cooperation with Paul, or financial gifts to him; or (C) *the Philippians'* activities, through their gifts or generally. For Paul, the apocalyptic horizon frames his meaning: he expects the End, if not in his lifetime, certainly in the generation then living. A positive sense, *"good* work." Not like the Judaizers' use in Galatia, "works *of the Law*" (or opponents in Phil 3), but as Paul uses *ergon agathon* elsewhere, a "good work" done by human beings (Rom 13:3; 2:7; 2 Cor 9:8), what *Christians* do as the result of faith (1 Thess 1:3). A tradition about God's

---

[31] Schlosser 1995a:378–88 couples 1:6 with 2:12–13 to lift up the activity (*energeia*, cf. the vb. in 2:13) of God, acting now in the community. At 1:11 (and 2:11) God stands at the end of everything.

[32] Janzen finds in the beginning/completion process or narrative pattern macrocosmically an encouragement to Christians to plan and bring to preliminary completion microcosmic tasks (42).

salvific "work" or the "mission work" of Christians is difficult to pin down. Paul employs language of his own, thought not unparalleled in other letters.

Reference here to (financial) gifts from the Philippians (see COMMENT B.1) is in Letter B unnecessary. Broader activity is meant, including prayers for, and involvement in, the gospel's spread. Many interpretations involving work by the Philippians or with God (B and C, above) guard against human presumptions through the understanding that all is God's doing among them (2:13). Interpretations that speak of God's work (A, above) must not be separated from actual results among the Philippians in their life and witness. 1:9–11 will provide further views on this *good work* as growth in discerning love, perceptive ethical decisions, and lives filled with fruit from justification by God. 1:6 may not be clear till we read on. Paul may have meant God's saving work, carried through to completion (cf. 2:12–13); they may have heard mission work and support. Or vice versa: Paul is confident they will continue the work God intends, as they look to the gospel and faith as God's work among them. Neither aspect can be excluded in an ambiguous phrase.

4. Paul and the Philippians: Introductory Report about Himself and His Affection for Them (1:7–8). The apostle, on trial for the gospel, longs for the Philippians. The prayers in vv 3–6 and 9–11 grow out of experiences (D. M. Stanley 1973), some reflected here. 7a, 7c–8 are about Paul and the Philippians, the apostle's current situation sandwiched in between (7b). The whole is quite moving; Paul arouses good feelings by pouring out the emotions of his heart. The affection and longing may reflect the friendship *topos* (Stowers 1986:60; Berger 1984b:1389; DA 170–72). Paul may here be presented as a model in prayer, attested by the witness of God (1:8, Marchal 127f.).

In a few words Paul sketches his situation (7b). He is in fetters,[33] awaiting a court appearance (*defense and confirmation*, hendiadys of tech. terms), in Ephesus. Vv 13–26 will tell more about him, the Imperial guard (or "the Praetorium"), jailed "for Christ" (1:13), and local Christian rivalry making life difficult for him (1:15–17). The legal outcome is uncertain; death, a possibility (1:20–24). Meanwhile Paul witnesses, in prison and courtroom; his legal process is a "defense and confirmation *of the gospel*," apologia and positive presentation, wherever possible, even among his guards (v 13), with a ripple effect in spreading the word (v 14).

On Paul and the Philippians, v 7 speaks most positively about *all* Christians in Philippi; they in their hearts deal lovingly with him. No need to read into the phrase *it is . . . right* any contrast to a "heretical theology" in ch. 3 (so Jewett; contrast O'B

---

[33] A metaphor for imprisonment ("confined by walls or fetters" [*Digest* of Justinian, 6th cent.] 4.6.9). Fee 92, "literally chained to his guards." Discussions (Rapske [INTRO. II Bibl.] 25–38; D. J. Williams 152 and n 91; Cassidy 2001:36–43, types of incarceration include "prison," "military custody," and "free custody," *OCD*³ 1248, 1278–79) envision mostly prison sites *in Rome.* Whether any chains on Paul were attached to prison walls (as at Philippi, Acts 16:24,26) or to a guard (Eph 6:13–17) is unclear. The phrase has been downplayed by some in reaction to Loh.'s martyrological interpretation (Fee 92 n 94), but revived in different ways by Bloomquist and Cassidy 2001. Loh.'s view (martyrs + a quasi-mystical concept of "grace," v 7) is rightly rejected by most, e.g., Walter 36.

68), or to sense (OT) Law or righteousness/ justification. How fitting, Paul says, to be so minded about the Philippians. *in this way* points backward to the hope just expressed. Paul thinks about them as he does, *because you have me in your heart*, a fourth reason for mutuality with the Philippians. See NOTE on this rendering (with NRSV, against many other trs.). To say, traditionally, "I think about you so optimistically because I hold you in my heart," is not profound. Rather, "I think optimistically because *you* still hold me in *your* heart," prisoner that I now am. Some in Philippi, like some in Ephesus (cf. 1:14–18), might disparage Paul because he is jailed and over how he proceeds with his legal case. His experience of their love is in v 7 further grounds for the hope just expressed. God continues a *good work* among the Philippians toward Paul; it is in order for him *to think* as he does.

The TRANSLATION "to have . . . in the heart" is lit., not quite "to love" (Paul can use *agapē*, v 9). *heart* (see NOTE) is center of the inner life (OT sense, understanding, knowledge, and will, as well as emotions). Conversely, *to think* (see NOTE on *phronein*) has a sense beyond the intellect (as in the Eng. "think"), "feel" and "judge"; a major term in Phil (10x), involving "heart" *(kardia)* and "mind" *(nous)*, the "real self" of attitudes and will. Fee 89: "mindset." Schenk: the Philippians had employed *phronein* when they sent funds to Paul, to show their "concern" toward him. The apostle used it in writing thanks (Letter A, 4:10, "your concern for me," *to hyper emou phronein*). Now in Letter B he picks up the phrase, *phronein hyper pantōn hymōn* (see NOTE on 1:7 *right for me to think about all of you*), a counterpart in solidarity to how *you have me in your heart*. (It can be a Philippian term even if one does not accept a multiple-letters theory.) V 7 grounds experientially the assertion in v 6 of theological confidence (based on the known character of God). Thus a faith-statement about God and personal experience in community.

heart refers to the Philippian community corporately. *you all* in v 7c picks up individuals as well as the house churches in their totality. They and Paul are drawn together by *sharing, as you do, with me in this generous opportunity of mine.* *sugkoinōnous*, "co-sharers," is the second example of "sharing" language in the passage, after *koinōnia* in v 5. We reject theories (COMMENT B.2; [16] COMMENT B.1.[A].1,2) that Paul and the Philippians shared in a business venture or a contractual Roman legal *societas* agreement, or (Loh.) that members of the Philippian church were imprisoned and facing martyrdom like Paul, in a "common fate." The imprisonment is Paul's *(mou)*, not the Philippians (O'B 70).[34] What unites them is *the gospel* and *defense and confirmation* of it, in Ephesus and Philippi, respectively.[35] These God-given situations Paul will further describe in 1:12–26 and 1:27–30, respectively; "the same struggle" in both places, in different

---

[34] Ambiguity in 1:3–11, esp. v 7, is suggested in the reader-response treatment by Oakes 1998. He creates two "readers" in Philippi who hear what Paul wrote in very different ways, due to each one's particular circumstances (2001:89–96).

[35] Philippi was not the only Pauline community that suffered under pagan oppression. Cf. T. Söding, "Widerspruch und Leidensnachfolge. Neutestamentliche Gemeinden in Konflikt mit der paganen Gesellschaft," *MTZ* 41 (1990) 137–50. On Ephesus as a place of opposition to Christianity, see INTRO. VII.A and (1) COMMENT n 15.

forms, just as in Philippi on that *first day* (1:30), when the missionaries came (Acts 16:19–39).

sharing (1:7c) means share in witnessing. Schlosser 1995b calls the community there "co-responsible" with Paul for their mission. "Grace" (NRSV and many trs., but a special usage here) is taken (see Note) not as sharing in the grace of Paul's apostleship (cf. Rom 1:5), or as "sharers together in God's grace" (though that is true), but as the exceptional *gracious opportunity* granted Paul in Ephesus. He is "put here for the defense of the gospel"; what has happened has actually helped its spread (Phil 1:12–16). The Philippians showed they stand in solidarity with him by their aid to him; he is convinced they will stand firm amid future perils in Philippi.

Paul's intense yearning for the Philippians, to be with them (cf. 2:24), bursts forth in the oath of v 8. *God* who sees them all through to the end (v 6) is invoked as *witness*, to affirm Paul's longing for them with *the affection of Christ Jesus*. Sentiments of a piece with Paul's entreaties (v 4) and thoughts about them (vv 6–7a), but grounded in their remembrance of him (3b,7a) and sharing in the gospel (vv 5,7c). Emotive language. The Gk. (see Note on *affection*) = "deep, inner feeling." Literally the "nobler viscera (heart, liver, lungs, etc.)," the seat of emotions in the "stomach-brain" (Robertson 1917:65–66); metaphysically, the seat of feelings. Prominent in the gospel tradition, then used to express feelings of Christians for other Christians. Christ is the source or basis of the affection that here wells up, but many also find a particular quality or kind of love ("Christ-like"). Paul goes on to report what he prays to God for the Philippians, on the basis of their relationship in Christ and their current needs.

5. Paul and the Philippians: Introductory Prayer Report on Intercessions (1:9–11).

A new beginning with the words *I am praying* (prayer formula, DA 203) reflects Paul's starting point in v 3, *I thank my God*. Schubert form-critically classifies the opening in v 9 with v 4 (his syntactical unit #5, *making entreaty*). But *I am praying* in v 9 is a finite vb., v 4 a ptc. Only v 4 really fits the "temporal participial clause" category. (Unit #7 will occur in 10b.) *So this is what I am praying* does pick up v 4, and 9–11 expand the *entreaty* for the Philippians mentioned there. *So* (Gk., *kai*; NRSV resumptive "and") links what follows with v 4 esp., thus entreaties Paul makes *with joy*. The Notes (cf. esp. Wiles for decisions summarized above) indicate other possible interconnections in this unified report, e.g., how 9–11 fill out reference in v 6 to the ongoing work that God guides among the Philippians. In this skeletal structure,

> *I thank my God* (v 3)   paralleled by   *I am praying* (v 9)
>   in lieu of being there (v 8);
> *making entreaty* (v 4), expanded and explained
> within the hope of v 6,   in vv 9b–11,   the intercessions in 9–11 are twofold:
> (1) *that your love may continue to grow still more and more in perception and discernment in every situation* (v 9b), with the further result, *that you may keep on appreciating the things that are best* (v 10a);
> and (2) *that you may be flawless and unfailing for the Day of Christ* (v 10b).

The reason for such optimism is stated in v 11, *because you have been filled with fruit of righteousness, the fruit that comes through Jesus Christ.* Notions of discord in Philippi should not be overdone (Söding 1995:167), as in Jewett 1970b or Black 1995:28, "I pray that your love [for one another] may become . . . sincere and blameless conduct [toward one another]" (*DA* 414 n 25). The "mutual exhortation" in 1:9a may be a sign of friendship (L. M. White 1990: 211–12). 1 Thess 3:12 is the closest Pauline parallel. The key phrase may be *more and more.*

for God's glory and praise (11c) provides an "eschatological climax" to 9–11, indeed all of 3–11. References to *the Day of Christ Jesus* (v 6) and *for the Day of Christ* (10b, stressed by Merk 1986) are part of the apocalyptic outlook or "future reservation" that regularly marks Paul's paraenesis (Grabner-Haider 85–86; here, "future assurance"). 11c as doxological conclusion ("fruit to bring glory and praise to God") has been interpreted differently in the NOTES; the TRANSLATION points to God's glorifying and praising the Philippians and Paul at the consummation. 11c thus goes with the causal construction in v 11a and Paul's positive hope about the outcome at the End. (Alternative understandings of the structure in 9–11 are presented in the NOTES.)

V 11 amounts to a fifth reason for Paul's joyful, hopeful statements about the Philippians. Along with (1) *your every remembrance of me* (v 3b), (2) *your sharing in the gospel* (v 5), (3) his confidence God the inaugurator will complete *a good work among you* (v 6), and (4) the fact, verified by experience, that *you have me in your heart* (v 7), Paul now adds (5) *because you have been filled with fruit of righteousness . . . through Jesus Christ.* The result of justification grounds the petitions in 9b and 10a. *Captatio benevolentiae.* Paul is concerned *(phronein)* about readers in a positive way; his prayer is stimulus to continuing response and growth, to live up to what is prayed and "become what you already are" as justified saints. Paul hopes to "visit the Philippians so that he may actively participate in their Christian development" (*DA* 210; cf. Rom 1:10–11; Phil 2:24).

9b and 10b are the heart of Paul's intercessions for the Philippians. First, that their *love may continue to grow still more and more.* Not that the Philippians had no *agapē* (though L. Hartman 2001:34 speculates their love had stagnated or grown cold); he prays for its *increase* among them (Bockmuehl 66). That he prays God for it means it is a gift from God (Söding 1995:168). A not unusual request by Paul for converts.[36] In Phil, and generally in Paul, the reference is to life within the community, *agapē* toward other believers, not the world or to God (Paul's term toward God is "faith"; yet note 1 Cor 16:22). On what he wishes for Philippian Christians re the *polis,* see 1:27.

love (see NOTE) involves here the horizontal, ethical side, as in Jesus' "call to love." It is the NT's "most profound and precise statement" on *agapē* in the moral sense (Spicq). God's love, exhibited in Christ, stands behind all Paul says (Rom 5:8; cf. Phil 2:1), but most references in Phil and Paul generally are to love by be-

---

[36] Cf. 1 Thess 3:12; 1 Cor 12:31–14:1. In Gal 5:22 *agapē* heads the list of characteristics making up the fruit of the Spirit. Genuine love, mutual affection, and love for one another and others ("the neighbor") are urged in Rom (12:9; 13:8–11) as fulfilling the Law.

lievers, esp. for each other. The church is to be a community of love, though *agapē* is not a name for the church. "Love" is not limited to the material gifts to Paul, but covers a wide range of relationships among and with the saints in Christ. No object is mentioned, to specify or limit love's outreach, but it is communal (2:2 and elsewhere).

Spicq lifts up eight words that define love here and show its domain: *perception* and *discernment* in 9b; a third in v 10 on what growth in love means. The other five aspects in the second petition of Paul's prayer actually describe Christians, not love. Montague 1961:112 limits himself to five items ("knowledge, discernment, purity, blamelessness, fulfillment") but sees them (as in some later spiritualities) as "a chain of ultimate perfections of the Christian life." The text employs but two nouns to define *agapē* for Christian life, in surprisingly intellectual ways; then two other phrases for where and how such love operates.

Paul does not encourage "sloppy *agapē*," sentimental, undisciplined.[37] Maturity in Christ means love grows in *perception and discernment*, terms with good backgrounds in Gk. moral philosophy (Dib. 54; Gnilka 51–52; U. B. Müller 45; Fee 99). The latter *(aisthēsis)* suggested apprehension of data through the senses, the former *(epignōsis)* knowledge or understanding that takes such data and goes deeper in comprehension, intelligent appropriation in one's mind or inner being. *epignōsis (perception)* is the more common term in Paul and the NT generally; OT roots, "the decisive knowledge of God" and insight into the will of God, knowledge *(gnōsis)* God gives in Christ (2 Cor 4:6; cf. 2:14; Bultmann *TDNT* 1:707).

One might expect the reverse order, "love marked by apprehension through the senses, then divine knowledge and understanding." Bengel 664 called the second term the "genus"; the first, "species." Paul's word order suggests love marked by God-given knowledge or understanding, applied in terms of what the senses perceive in specific situations. The words are the bane of trs. (terms in Eng. could be reversed, and sometimes are). Schenk 128, "ability to know and judge." Revealed understanding and practical application, both necessary. Love marked by knowledge of God and the divine will in Christ, leading to vital moral engagement in daily life (Therrien 176). A dynamic concept, love continuing *to grow*, with *perception and discernment* so that proper appreciation (10) results, of what is right and good, for God's judgment. Discernment (cf. Rom 12:2) becomes a key in the Christian's moral life (Helewa).

Such discerning, discriminating love holds *in every situation*, esp. where rules, knowledge, or spiritual gifts (1 Cor 12) do not fit or suffice. Where there is not full insight amid life's ambiguities, love decides, perceptively and discerningly. Such love that makes judgments with discernment must continue growing in the community. Its presence and increase are possible only because of the new eschato-

---

[37] Fee 99: "a sober kind of love." W. Schrage, "Zum Verhältnis von Ethik und Vernunft," in *Neues Testament und Ethik,* FS R. Schnackenburg, ed. H. Merklein (Freiburg/Basel/Wien: Herder, 1989) 482–503, spontaneous, intuitive but tied to reason, "an enlightened, intelligent, and clear-sighted love"; Schrage 1988:216–17, "the supreme . . . but not the only criterion."

logical situation since the death and exaltation of Jesus, grace abounding, setting forth new expectations of love abounding with discernment among Christians. Not anything and everything goes in the name of love. The cross and the judgment at the Day of Christ set parameters. God-given knowledge or perception plus practical observation or discernment by our common senses shape the praxis of loving, a community task ("you" pl., "you all").[38]

An immediate outcome of growth is stated as a further aim: *that you may keep on appreciating the things that are best* (10a). Again, continuing and refining the practice of the Christian life. Not a "once and for all times" morality, for new ethical situations keep arising. Paul puts this result of discerning love in Stoic-Cynic terms, a pleasant touch for the Philippians. The NOTES outline two possible meanings for each term. *dokimazein:* "examine, test," or "recognize and approve," brought together in the TRANSLATION by the vb. "appreciate" — to come to approval of something by examining it. *ta diapheronta:* "things that differ" or "things that are excellent" or superior. To pick out differences is easy. More difficult is to discern the better or best thing to do. Hence discerning what is *best.* Perceptive love about "God's will in each new situation . . . what is best at any given moment" (Schrage 1988 [n 31 above] 198). It counterbalances glib understandings of love from 1 Cor 13:7 as bearing, believing, hoping, and enduring *all* things. Discerning love does not put up with everything; it makes judgments about, among, or between possibilities. Cf. Dunn, *TPTA* 648. Not the task of a few elite but of each believer and the whole community. Resources exist in the gospel, in love that makes distinctions, growth in the Christian life, and the use of human abilities.

The second petition (10b), *that you may be flawless and unfailing for the Day of Christ*, Roberts regards as "eschatological climax" and transition to the letter body (cf. 1 Thess 1:1, 1 Cor 1:7–8, 2 Thess 1:6–11). Paul assumes that they are "pure and blameless" (NRSV), but could exhibit flaws, even fatal ones, and fail; hence reminders of God's care and their goal at *the Day of Christ*. The NOTES describe meanings and imagery in *flawless* and *unfailing*. To some the first suggests an object tested in the bright light of the sun, revealing no flaws or spots. But in v 11, persons are involved. In moral metaphor, "transparent" in character. For the second term, "not falling" or *unfailing* re the eschatological goal involved. To make the first "relationship with God," the second, "relations with other human beings," is unlikely, for the second, *(aproskopoi)* could be used to suggest "without offense" toward God. Similarly with a positive and a negative ("with sincerity, without blame," cf. KJV). Schenk paraphrases "as perfect as possible."

Introductory intercessions seeking the goodwill of the listeners are not the place to strike a note of warning, as in 1 Cor 10:12, but rather promise (1 Cor 1:9, "God is faithful, by whom you were called into *koinōnia* with his Son . . ."). Without using "sanctification" language in Phil 1:10–11, Paul looks for the advance of

---

[38] Cf. 1 Thess 5:21; Rom 12:1–2; H. Schürmann, "Die Gemeinde des Neuen Bundes als der Quellort des sittlicher Erkennens nach Paulus," *Catholica* 26 (1972) 15–37, repr. in his GS, *Studien zur neutestamentlichen Ethik*, ed. T. Söding, SBAB 7 (Stuttgart: Katholisches Bibelwerk, 1990) 17–48, esp. 24–27; G. Barth 22; Schrage 1988:198.

those righteous/justified, in faith, toward the Day when what each is will become apparent and God's plan for perfection for each saint will be fulfilled. V 10 is not teaching about the coming of the Lord but paraenesis within the horizon of the parousia (Radl 1981:47).

Why Paul can pray with such hopes is set forth in v 11a, *because you have been filled with the fruit of righteousness . . .*, a fifth causal construction in 1:3–11 that helps explain the other four. The Philippians share the gospel (v 5), have Paul in their heart (v 7), remember him (v 3), and take part in a good work (v 6) because they are filled with the result of justification through Jesus Christ. This foundational statement in v 11 is typically Pauline (they share in the gospel, v 5); it clarifies the process God inaugurated among the Philippians and will complete at the End.

No "and" links v 11 with what precedes; see NOTES on a causal explanation here of why Paul looks for the believers' love to grow and they themselves to prove flawless and unfailing: because they have been and are filled by God with the fruit or result of justification, an eschatological outcome to be seen in the very things for which continuing petitions are made. This "filling" Paul likely understands to involve the Spirit and gifts of grace (Gal 3:2,5; 5:22; Rom 5:1–5; 8:9,23,29–30; 1 Cor 6:11, baptism; 12:13; unspoken here). Only "glorification," as part of the chain of results (cf. Rom 5:2, 8:30), will be reflected, in *God's glory* (for believers). It is not language from opponents; for *filled with,* cf. Rom 15:13. Nor need *fruit of righteousness* be derived from any specific source (Gk. and LXX examples cited in the NOTE). Paul might have been conscious for *karpos dikaiosynēs* of Prov 3:9 or Amos 6:12. A Philippian with an ear for Epicurus might have found the phrase familiar, but such speculations are dubious. Philippians more likely heard *righteousness* (justification) with Pauline usage in their minds. Cf. 3:6–9, Letter C; Fee 101, 104 on 3:1–11 and 1:11, "righteousness under the Law" and "righteousness based on faith." The phrases about the Law may be associated in ch. 3 with teachers who threaten Philippi and the gospel, but the Philippians likely knew the term righteousness/justification from Paul's own story, how he came to faith, and from *dikaiosynē* formulas Paul taught them (see NOTE on *righteousness*).

The NOTE sets forth two lines of interpretation for *dikaiosynē* at 1:11, a Gk. virtue from a Heb. term for salvation (deliverance) and in morality: God's saving righteousness or right (upright) conduct. Paul's letters exhibit many christological, soteriological, eschatological, and ecclesiological applications, but a relative paucity of moral or ethical uses. Justice was a cardinal virtue in the Hellenistic world. Some see the noun expressing right behavior (Ziesler); but examples are limited (1 Thess 2:10 adv.; 1 Cor 15:34 adv.; 2 Cor 9:9 [= Ps 112:9] and 10, "benevolence," in connection with the collection; 2 Cor 6:7). For God's righteousness that delivers or justifies at the judgment cf. 1 Cor 1:30; 6:11; 2 Cor 5:21; 3:9; and 11:15. Many references in Rom reinforce this sense. Gal 5:5 ("in the Spirit, by faith, we eagerly wait for the hope of righteousness") is debated, like Phil 1:11, re the gen. "hope *of righteousness,*" "fruit *of righteousness*"; for "hope which springs from righteousness," now and at the judgment, see Reumann 1982: #104; cf. Dunn, *TPTA* 708. At 1:11 (see NOTE) "fruit that results from righteousness," i.e., the outcome of justification, a sense suggested esp. by the phrase Paul appends to *fruit, through Jesus Christ,* supported also by "fruit" + a gen. elsewhere in Paul and in the LXX. Cf. Jesus' saying about the tree made good by God bringing forth good fruit (Matt 7:16–20 par Luke 6:43–45). Justification from God is the origin or source. Ethical concern is not to be seen in righteousness (*dikaiosynē* as "upright conduct") but in the *fruit* or result with which the Philippians are filled.[39] Justification = a process involving the believer in the past, present, and future; it includes upright conduct as the impv. that follows the indic. (Reumann 1982: ##141–42, 147, 149, 173; cf. ##397–98, Fitzmyer). 1 Cor 6:11 sets baptism, justification, and sanctification side by side; they are simultaneous (1982:##64–65). On the Spirit behind Phil 1:11, cf. Thüsing's comments in the NOTE on v 11 *Jesus Christ.*

1:11c, *for God's glory and praise,* is usually taken to show Paul's theocentricity or theoultimacy (Thüsing 181–82; Söding 1995:172–73), an "eschatological climax." Cf. 1 Thess 1:10 and 1 Cor 1:9. But the entire content and structure of 1:3–11 is eschatological, beginning with the new age that dawned for the Philippians *the first day* the gospel was preached to them, stretching *until now* (v 5) and to *the Day of Christ (Jesus)* (1:6,10). Better, 11c is the finale to all this eschatology. "The Day" has been mentioned in vv 5 and 10; Paul reiterates the theme here. Not for judgment or wrath but completion (v 6), goal (v 10), and in 11c commendation by God. Cf. Artz 1992b.

1:11c is not human praise of God (doxology) but praise and glory given to human beings by God at the End, commendation of believers. See NOTE on *God's,* a subj. gen. Then the reading in a few MSS, including P⁴⁶, can be understood as accurate interpretation, "for the glory (of God) and praise *to me.*" God will grant glory and give praise to Paul! This is what the apostle expected, his mission work and congregations will be his "glory and joy" at the parousia (1 Thess 2:20; cf. Phil 4:1, *my joy and my crown*). *praise* comes from God at the judgment (1 Cor 4:5; Rom 2:29), as does *glory* (Rom 2:7,10; cf. 1 Pet 1:7). Paul expected Philippian Christians to receive God's praise and glory too, growing, *flawless and unfailing because . . . filled with the fruit of righteousness.*

To receive *praise* is a human goal. To receive *glory* takes one into the realm of God (cf. the OT sense of *kābôd*). A Gk. audience might have read into *doxa* "radiance" and even "light" that surrounds deity. This considerable and weighty expectation Paul holds out to the Philippians. Cf. 2:15–16, "that you may be blameless and innocent, children of God without blemish in the midst of a crooked and perverse generation, in which you shine like stars in the world. It is by your holding fast to the word of life that I can boast on the day of Christ that I did not run in vain or labor in vain" (NRSV). Who, knowing this, would not bend every effort to keep on moving toward such a goal, given what the saints in Philippi have already attained (cf. 3:16 NOTE on *stoichein;* Gal 5:25 for such paraenesis).

---

[39] D. F. Watson, "Why We Need Socio-Rhetorical Commentary and What It Might Look Like," in Porter/Stamps, eds., 2002:151 suggested titling 1:3–11 "Thanksgiving for Participation in an Alternative Culture of Righteousness."

The prooimion seeks goodwill, but Paul is interested in more, their salvation (2:12–13). His introductory words make them eager to hear to what else their apostle has to say. He will not, till 1:27–30, get into how the congregation, in the face of the final judgment, is to authenticate its faith in everyday life (Merk 1968:175). He has whetted their appetite to know about himself and his imprisonment (v 7). To such matters the body of the letter will now turn.

The prooimion contains theologically and ethically important terms like *gospel* and *agapē*, but almost never is 1:3–11 the starting point or the decisive passage in their interpretation. Long church use in the Roman Missal, 1:6–11 for the 21st Sunday after Trinity (Pentecost 22); in the Book of Common Prayer and Lutheran lectionaries, 1:3–11 for the following Sunday (Fendt 1931:207). In the Roman *Ordo*, 1:4–6, 8–11, the 2nd Sunday in Advent, Year C; in "daughter versions" 3–5 (6–11). 1:3–11 played "a germinal role" in the "tradition of prison literature,"[40] with "models from Boethius through Dostoevsky . . . and Bonhoeffer," not to mention Martin Luther King, Jr., in Birmingham jail.

SELECT BIBLIOGRAPHY (see also General Bibliography and Commentaries)

Artz, P. 1992b. *Bedrohtes Christsein. Zu Eigenart und Funktion eschatologisch bedrohlicher Propositionen in den echten Paulusbriefen*. BBET 36. Frankfurt/Berlin/Bern: P. Lang.

Dewailley, L. M. 1973. "La part prise à l'Évangile (Phil I.5)," *RB* 80:247–60.

Dupont, J. 1949. *Gnosis: la connaissance religieuse dans les Épitres de Saint Paul*. Bruges: Desclée de Brouwer. 2nd ed., Louvain/Paris: E. Nauwelaerts, 1960.

Eichholz, G. 1962. "Bewahren und Bewähren des Evangeliums: der Leitfaden von Phil 1–2," in *Hören und Handeln*, FS E. Wolf, ed. H. Gollwitzer/H. Traub (Munich: Kaiser); repr. in Eichholz's GS, *Tradition und Interpretation: Studien zum Neuen Testament und zur Hermeneutik*, TB 29 (Munich: Kaiser, 1965) 136–60.

Helewa, G. 1994. "Carità, discernimento e cammino cristiano: Una lettura di Fil 1,9–11," *Teresianum* 45:363–404.

Holloway, P.A. 2006. "Thanks for the Memories: On the Translation of Phil 1.3," *NTS* 52: 419–32.

Janzen, J. G. 1996. "Creation and New Creation in Philippians 1:6," *HBT* 18:27–54.

Johnson, L. T. 2003. "Transformation of Mind and Moral Discernment in Paul," in FS Malherbe (Gen. Bibl., under "Thom, J. C.") 215–36.

Oakes, P. 1998. "Jason and Penelope Hear Philippians 1:1–11," in *Understanding, Studying and Reading: New Testament Essays in Honour of John Ashton*, ed. C. Rowland/ C. H. T. Fletcher-Louis JSNTSup 153 (Sheffield: Sheffield Academic Press) 155–64.

Omanson, R. L. 1978a. "A Note on the Translation of Philippians 1,3–5," *BT* 29:244–45.

Peng, K.-W. 2003. "Do We Need an Alternative Rendering for Philippians 1:3?" *BT* 54:415–19.

Reed, J. T. 1991. "The Infinitive with Two Substantive Accusatives, An Ambiguous Construction," *NovT* 33:1–27.

---

[40] D. Gioia, *Incarnation: Contemporary Writers on the New Testament*, ed. A. Korn (New York: Viking, 1990) 187.

Roberts, J. H. 1986. "The eschatological tensions in the Pauline letter body," *Neot* 20:29–35.

Ross, J. M. 1983. "Some Unnoticed Points in the Text of the New Testament," *NovT* 25:59–72.

Schlosser, J. 1995b. "La communauté en charge de l'Évangile. A propos de Ph 1,7," *PHPR* 75 (FS E. Trocmé) 67–76.

Smith, M. S. 1998. "The Heart and Innards in Israelite Emotional Expressions: Notes from Anthropology and Psychobiology," *JBL* 117:427–36.

Sullivan, K. 1963. "Epignosis in the Epistles of Paul," *Studiorum Paulinorum Congressus* (Gen. Bibl.) 2:405–16.

Therrien, G. 1973. *Le Discernment dans les écrits pauliniens*, EBib (Paris: Librairie Lecoffre, J. Gabalda) 166–86.

Zahn, T. 1895. "Altes und Neues zum Verständnis des Philipperbriefes," *ZWL* 6:192.

Paul and Prayer Forms (Thanksgiving and Petition): K. Berger 1984b, "Gebet. IV. Neues Testament," *TRE* 12:47–60; R. Gebauer 2000, "Gebet, III. Neues Testament," *RGG⁴* 3:487–91; W. B. Hunter, "Prayer," *DPL* 725–34; C. W. F. Smith, "Prayer," *IDB* K-Q 857–67.

Arzt, P. 1994. "The 'Epistolatory Introductory Thanksgiving' in the Papyri and Paul," *NovT* 36:29–46.

Audet, J.-P. 1958. "Esquisse historique du genre littéraire de la 'bénédiction' juive et de l'eucharistie' Chrétienne," *RB* 65:371–99.

Boobyer, G. H. 1929. *"Thanksgiving" and the "Glory of God" in Paul.* Diss., Heidelberg; Borna- Leipzig: Robert Noske.

Delling, G. 1962a. *Worship in the New Testament.* Philadelphia: Westminster.

Gebauer, R. 1989. *Das Gebet bei Paulus: Forschungsgeschichtliche und exegetische Studien.* Giessen/Basel: Brunnen Verlag.

Hamann, A. 1959. *La Prière. I. Le Nouveau Testament*, Bibliothèque de Théologie (Tournai: Desclée & Cie) 245–337.

Harder, G. 1936. *Paulus und das Gebet.* NTF 1/10. Gütersloh: C. Bertelsmann.

Mullins, T. Y. 1962. "Petition as a Literary Form," *NovT* 5: 46–54.

O'Brien, P. T. 1977. *Introductory Thanksgivings in the Letters of Paul.* NovTSup 49. Leiden: Brill.

———. 1980. "Thanksgiving within the Structure of Pauline Theology," in *Pauline Studies*, FS F. F. Bruce, ed. D. A. Hagner/M. J. Harris (Grand Rapids: Eerdmans) 50–66.

Orphal, E. 1933. *Das Paulusgebet: Psychologisch-exegetische Untersuchung des Paulus-Gebetslebens auf Grund seiner Selbstzeugnisse.* Gotha: Leopold Klotz Verlag.

Osiek, C. 1988. "Paul's Prayer," in *Scripture and Prayer: A Celebration for Carroll Stuhlmueller*, ed. C. Osiek/D. Senior (Wilmington, DE: Glazier) 145–57.

Reed, J. T. 1996. "Are Paul's Thanksgivings 'Epistolary'?" *JSNT* 61: 87–99.

Robinson, J. M. 1964. "Die Hodajot-Formel in Gebet und Hymnus des Frühchristentums," *Apophoreta*, FS E. Haenchen, ed. W. Eltester/F. H. Kettler, BZNW 30 (Berlin: Töpelmann) 194–235.

Sanders, J. T. 1962. "The Transition from Opening Epistolary Thanksgiving to Body in the Letters of the Pauline Corpus," *JBL* 81:348–62.

Schenk, W. 1967. *Der Segen im Neuen Testament: Eine begriffsanalytische Studie.* Theologische Arbeiten, 25. Berlin: Evangelische Verlagsanstalt, 1967.

Schubert, P. 1939. *Form and Function of the Pauline Thanksgivings.* BZNW 20. Berlin: Töpelmann.

Stanley, D. M. 1973. *Boasting in the Lord: The Phenomenon of Prayer in Saint Paul.* New York: Paulist.

1:3 **thank** *(eucharistō)*: H. Conzelmann, *TDNT* 9:407–15; H.-H. Esser, *NIDNTT* 3:817–20; H. Patsch, *EDNT* 2:87–88; A. Stuiber, *RAC* 6:900–928; C. Wolff, "Thanksgiving," *ABD* 6:435–38.

Aus, R. D. 1973. "The Liturgical Background of the Necessity and Propriety of Giving Thanks According to 2 Thes 1:3," *JBL* 93:432–38.

1:3 **remembrance** *(mneia)*: O. Michel, *TDNT* 4:678–79; K. H. Bartels, *NIDNTT* 3:230–32, 240–42, 264; R. Leivestad, *EDNT* 2:434; *TLNT* 2:496.

1:4 **joy** *(chara)*: H. Conzelmann, *TDNT* 9:359–72, bibl. *TWNT* 10:1290; E. Beyreuther/ G. Finkenrath, *NIDNTT* 2:356–61; K. Berger, *EDNT* 3:454–55, cf. 451–52; *TLNT* 3:498–99; O. Michel, *RAC* 8:348–418; A. B. du Toit, *TRE* 11:584–86; T. Schramm, *RGG*[4] 3:347–48.

Backherms, R. E. 1963. *Religious Joy in General in the New Testament and Its Sources in Particular.* Diss., Fribourg, Switzerland: St. Paul's Press.

Baskin, J. R. 1966. "Words for Joy and Rejoicing in the Writing of the Apostle Paul and Philo Judaeus." Diss., Princeton Theological Seminary.

du Toit, A. B. 1965. *Der Aspekt der Freude im urchristlichen Abendmahl.* Winterthur-Zürich: P. G. Keller.

Fatum, L. 1975. "Den eskatologiske glæde, et ledenmotiv i Filipperbrevet," in *Hilsen til Noack*, FS B. Noack (København, G. E. C. Gad, 1975) 42–64.

Gulin, E. G. *Die Freude im Neuen Testament.* 2 vols. Helsinki: Druckerei-A.G. Der Finnischen Literatur-Gesellschaft. AASF 26/2 (1932); 37/3 (1936).

Lohse, E. 2006. *Freude des Glaubens. Die Freude im Neuen Testament.* Göttingen: Vandenhoeck & Ruprecht.

Meitzen, M. O. 1960. "Christian Joy in Contemporary Theology." Diss., Harvard Univ.

Morrice, W. G. 1984. *Joy in the New Testament.* Grand Rapids: Eerdmans.

Plenter, J. D. 1953. *De Blijdschap in Paulus' Brieven: Een Studie met diens Brief aan de Filippenzen als Uitgangspunt.* Groningen: Van Gorcum.

Webber, R. D. 1970. "The Concept of Rejoicing in Paul." Diss., Yale Univ.

1:5 **sharing** *(koinōnia)*: F. Hauck, *TDNT* 3:789–809, bibl. *TWNT* 10/2:1145–460; J. Schattenmann, *NIDNTT* 1:639–44; J. Hainz, *EDNT* 2:303–5; cf. *TLNT* 2:478–82; V. Popkes, *RAC* 9:1100–1145; *TPTA* 561–62, 616–17, 709; J. Reumann, *EC* 3 (2003) 134–36. Bibl. to 1993 in Reumann 1994 (below).

Baumert, N. 2003. *Koinonein und Metechein—synonym? Eine umfassende semantische Untersuchung.* SBB 51. Stuttgart: Katholisches Bibelwerk.

Bori, P. C. 1972. *Koinōnia. L'idea della communione nell'ecclesiologia recente e nel Nuovo Testamento.* TRSR 7. Brescia: Paideia.

Campbell, J. Y. 1932. "KOINŌNIA and its Cognates in the New Testament," *JBL* 51:352–82; repr. in Campbell's *Three New Testament Studies* (Leiden: Brill, 1965) 1–28.

Hahn, F. 1979. "Einheit der Kirche und Kirchengemeinschaft in neutestamentlicher Sicht," in F. Hahn/K. Kertelge/R. Schnackenburg, *Einheit der Kirche: Grundlegung im Neuen Testament*, QD 84 (Freiburg: Herder) 9–51.

Hainz, J. 1982. *Koinonia: "Kirche" als Gemeindschaft bei Paulus*. BU 16. Regensburg: Pustat, 1982. Pp. 89–94; 206–70 on church usages ecumenically.

———. 1994. "KOINŌNIA bei Paulus," in *Religious Propaganda and Missionary Competition in the New Testament World*, FS D. Georgi, ed. L. Bormann et al., NovTSup 74 (Leiden: Brill) 375–91.

McDermott, J. M. "The Biblical Doctrine of KOINŌNIA," *BZ* 19 (1975) 64–77 and 219–33.

Panikulam, G. 1979. *Koinōnia in the New Testament: A Dynamic Expression of Christian Life*. AnBib 85. Rome: Biblical Institute Press.

Reumann, J. 1994. "Koinonia in Scripture: Survey of Biblical Texts," in *On the Way to Fuller Koinonia*, ed. T. F. Best/G. Gassmann, Faith and Order Paper No. 166 (Geneva: WCC) 37–69.

Seesemann, H. 1933. *Der Begriff KOINŌNIA im Neuen Testament*. BZNW 14. Giessen: Töpelmann.

Suggs, J. M. 1984. "Koinonia in the New Testament," *Mid-Stream* 23:351–62; cf. *NovT* 4 (1960–61) 60–68.

Yamsat, P. 1993. "The Ekklesia as Partnership: Paul and Threats to Koinonia in 1 Corinthians." Diss., Sheffield.

1:5 **gospel** *(euangelion)*: G. Friedrich, *TDNT* 2:707–37; U. Becker, *NIDNTT* 2:107–15; G. Strecker, *EDNT* 2:70–74; *TLNT* 2:82–92; O. Michel, *RAC* 6:1107–60; *TPTA* 164–69, 177–79, 206, 232–33, 572–74, see index; H. Koester, *RGG*[4] 2 (1999):1735–42; Dickson (Gen. Bibl.) 86–132, 153–77.

Burrows, M. 1925. "The Origin of the Term 'Gospel,'" *JBL* 44:21–33.

Dalman, G. 1898. *Die Worte Jesu* (Leipzig: Hinrichs, 2nd ed. 1930, repr. Darmstadt), tr. *The Words of Jesus*. Edinburgh: T&T Clark, 1902.

Fitzmyer, J. A. 1979. "The Gospel in the Theology of Paul," *Int* 33: 339–50; repr. in his GS, *To Advance the Gospel: New Testament Studies* (New York: Crossroad, 1981) 149–61.

Molland, E. 1934. *Das paulinische Evangelion: Das Wort und die Sache*. ANVAO NF 1934 no. 3. Oslo: Jacob Dybwad. Cf. O. Michel, *TLZ* 60 (1935) 141–42.

O'Brien, P. T. 1986. "The Importance of the Gospel in Philippians," in *God Who Is Rich in Mercy*, FS D. B. Knox ([1] Bibl. **God**, under "Morris, L.") 213–33.

Schniewind, J. 1910. *Die Begriffe Wort und Evangelium bei Paulus*. Diss., Bonn: Carl Georgi.

———. 1927, 1931. *Euangelion. Ursprung und erste Gewalt des Begriffes Evangelium*. BFCT 2/13 and 25. Gütersloh: Bertelsmann; repr. Darmstadt: Wissenschaftliche Buchgesellschaft, 1970.

Stuhlmacher, P. 1968. *Das paulinische Evangelium, I. Vorgeschichte*. FRLANT 95. Göttingen: Vandenhoeck & Ruprecht.

1:6 **work** *(ergon)*: G. Bertram, *TDNT* 2:635–55, bibl. *TWNT* 10/2:1084–85; H.-C. Hahn, *NIDNTT* 3:1147–52; R. Heiligenthal, *EDNT* 2:49–51.

Gundry Volf, J. M. 1990. *Paul and Perseverance: Staying In and Falling Away*. Louisville: Westminster/John Knox.

Heiligenthal, R. 1983. *Werke als Zeichen: Untersuchungen zur Bedeutungen der menschlichen Taten in Frühjudentum, Neuen Testament und Frühchristentum*. WUNT 2/9. Tübingen: Mohr Siebeck.

Kitzberger, I. 1986. *Bau der Gemeinde: Das paulinische Wortfeld* oikodomē/(ep)oikodomein. FB 53. Würzburg: Echter Verlag.

Peterson, E. 1941. "ERGON in der Bedeutung 'Bau' bei Paulus," *Bib* 22:439–41.

1:7 **think** *(phronein)*: G. Bertram, *TDNT* 9:220–35, bibl. *TWNT* 10/2:1289; J. Goetzmann, *NIDNTT* 2:616–20; H. Paulsen, *EDNT* 3:438–39. For **grace** *(charis)* see (1) Bibl.

1:9 **love** *(agapē)*: G. Quell/E. Stauffer, *TDNT* 1:21–55, bibl. *TWNT* 10/2:948–51; W. Günther, H.-G. Link, C. Brown, *NIDNTT* 2:538–51; G. Schneider, *EDNT* 1:8–12; *TLNT* 1:8–22, bibl. supplements Spicq's earlier vols. 1963–66 and H. Riesenfeld in ConBNT 5 (1941) 1–27; O. Wischmeyer, *TRE* 21 (1991):138–46; K. D. Sakenfeld/W. Klassen, *ABD* 4:375–96; *TPTA* 733.

González-Ruiz, J. M. 1959. "Sentido comunitario-eclesial de algunos sustantivos abstractos en San Pablo," *Sacra Pagina: Miscellanea Biblica Congressus Internationalis cathlici de re biblica*, ed. J. Coppens et al. Paris: Gabalda/Gembloux: Duculot. 2:322–26.

Moffatt, J. 1929. *Love in the New Testament*. London: Hodder & Stoughton/New York: R. R. Smith, 1930.

Söding, T. 1992a. "Das Wortfeld der Liebe im paganen und biblischen Griechisch. Philologische Beobachtungen an der Wurzel AGAP-," *ETL* 68:284–330.

———. 1995. *Das Liebesgebot bei Paulus: Die Mahnung zur Agape im Rahmen der paulinischen Ethik*. NTAbh N.F. 26. Münster: Aschendorff.

Spicq, C. 1963–66. *Agape dans le Nouveau Testament. Analyse des textes*, EBib, 3 vols. (Paris: 1958–59) 233–43. Cited from tr. by M. A. McNamara/M. H. Richter, *Agape in the New Testament*, 3 vols. (St. Louis: Herder), esp. 2 (1965):276–84.

Wischmeyer, O. 1978. "Agape in der ausserchristlichen Antike," *ZNW* 69:212–38.

1:11 **righteousness/justification** *(dikaiosynē)*: G. Quell/G. Schrenk, *TDNT* 2:174–225, bibl. *TWNT* 10/2:1048–53; H. Seebass/C. Brown, *NIDNTT* 3:352–77; K. Kertelge, *EDNT* 1:325–34; A. Dihle, *RAC* 10: 233–360; E. and P. Achtemeier, *IDB* R-Z:80–99; G. Klein, *IDBSup* 750–52; J. J. Scullion, *ABD* 5:724–36; R. B. Hays, "Justification," *ABD* 3:1129–33; J. Reumann, *ABD* 5:736–73 (bibl.)

Brauch, M. 1977. "Perspectives on 'God's Righteousness' in Recent German Discussion," in E. P. Sanders 1977:523–42.

Cronbach, A. "Righteousness in Jewish Literature," *IDB* R-Z:85–91.

Dodd, C. H. 1935. *The Bible and the Greeks*. London: Hodder & Stoughton.

Kertelge, K. 1967. *"Rechtfertigung" bei Paulus: Studien zur Struktur und zum Bedeutungsgehalt des paulinischen Rechtfertigungsbegriffs*. NTAbh NS 3 Münster: Aschendorff.

———. 1996. "Gottes Gerechtigkeit – das Evangelium des Paulus," in *Der Lebendige Gott: Studien zur Theologie des Neuen Testaments*, FS Thüsing, ed. T. Söding, NTAbh NF 31 (Münster: Aschendorff) 183–95.

Müller, C. 1964. *Gottesgerechtigkeit und Gottes Volk*. FRLANT 86. Göttingen: Vandenhoeck & Ruprecht.

Olley, J. W. 1979. *"Righteousness" in the Septuagint of Isaiah*. SBLSCS 8. Missoula, MT: Scholars Press.

Przybylski, B. 1980. *Righteousness in Matthew and His World of Thought*. SNTSMS 41. Cambridge: Cambridge Univ. Press.

Reumann, J. 1982. With J. A. Fitzmyer and J. Quinn. *"Righteousness" in the New Testament: "Justification" in the United States Lutheran-Roman Catholic Dialogue*. Philadelphia: Fortress/New York: Paulist.

Seifrid, M. A. 1992. *Justification by Faith: The Origin and Development of a Central Pauline Theme.* NovTSup 68. Leiden: Brill.

Stuhlmacher, P. 1965. *Gottes Gerechtigkeit bei Paulus.* FRLANT 87. Göttingen: Vandenhoeck & Ruprecht.

———. 2001. *Revisiting Paul's Doctrine of Justification: A Challenge to the New Perspective.* Downers Grove, IL: InterVarsity. Pp. 75–105, D. Hagner, "Paul and Judaism: Testing the New Perspective."

Ziesler, J. A. 1972. *The Meaning of Righteousness in Paul: A Linguistic and Theological Enquiry.* SNTSMS 20. Cambridge: Cambridge Univ. Press.

1:11 **glory** *(doxa)*: G. von Rad/G. Kittel, *TDNT* 2:233–55; S. Aalen, *NIDNTT* 2:44–48; H. Hegemann, *EDNT* 1:344–49; *TLNT* 1:362–79; *RAC* 4:210–16 (A. Stuiber, "Doxologie"); 11:196–225 (A. J. Vermeulen, "Gloria").

Carrez, M. 1965. *De la souffrance à la gloire: La DOXA dans la pensée paulinienne.* Bibliothèque théologique. Neuchâtel/Paris: Delachaux & Niestlé.

Harrison, E. F. 1950. "The Use of *Doxa* in Greek Literature with Special Reference to the New Testament." Diss., University of Pennsylvania.

THE BODY OF THE LETTER, 1:12–4:20

◆

LETTER B, BODY, 1:12–3:1

3. *Narratio (Paul Describes the Situation Where He Is), 1:12–18c*

TRANSLATION

1:12 I wish you to come to know, brothers and sisters, that events affecting me have actually resulted in progress for the gospel. 13 The results are first that in Christ it has become clear in the whole Praetorium and to all the rest that my bonds are for Christ; 14 second, that most of the brothers and sisters, having become confident in the Lord through my bonds, are so much the more daring fearlessly to speak the word. 15 Some are proclaiming Christ, indeed on account of envy and strife, but others indeed on account of goodwill. 16 The latter, out of love, set forth Christ in preaching, because they know that I am put here for defense of the gospel. 17 The former, out of self-interest, set forth Christ in preaching, not with a pure motivation, because they suppose thereby to stir up trouble for my imprisonment. 18a What then? Simply that, in every way, either under pretense or in truth, Christ is being set forth in preaching. So over this fact I rejoice.

NOTES

1:12. *I wish you to come to know.* Emphasis is on the infin. *(to come) to know*, the first word in the v, signaling discontinuity and the start of a new thematic unit (*DA* 118–19).

I wish. boulomai (pres. act. indic., no subject pron. or emphasis on "I"), conscious volition as a result of deliberate reflection (BDAG 2.a.δ. + acc. + infin.); therefore "wish, want" ([N]RSV). In the NT period, crowded out by *(e)thelō* (207x, *boulomai* 37x). *TDNT* 1:629–33, esp. 632 n 52 (G. Schrenk); *NIDNTT* 3:1015–18 (D. Müller); *EDNT* 1:225–26, point 2 (H.-J. Ritz).

to come to know. Infin. after a vb. of wishing, BDF #392 (1)(a). Pres. act., *ginōskō*; BDAG 6.c, **have come to know** that + *hoti* + indic. Bultmann (*TDNT* 1:703), here "learn," as at Phil 2:19. Similarly Burdick 353, cited by O'B 89, "'come to know' something they had not previously known." Schmithals, *EDNT* 1:248, "I want to *communicate* to you . . . ," comparing Roller ([1] Bibl.) 67–68 (correct to 65–66) and the formula, "I do not want you to be ignorant *(agnoein)*, brothers" (not found in Phil). *de* links v 12 to 1:3–11 (Meyer *Phil.* 21, "the *de* of continuation"); *DA* 328; Ware 1996:179, "transition . . . to the body of the letter." Most trs. omit. KJV "But. . . ."; Phillips "Now. . . ." On a possible "disclosure form," see COMMENT A.2.

   brothers and sisters. adelphos, voc. pl. BDAG 2, for members of a religious community (the Essenes, the Serapeum at Memphis, Egypt; cf. Harland, esp. pp. 507–9); by Jesus (Mark 3:35 parr.); Christians for each other (1 Cor 5:11; Rom 8:29), sometimes + a proper name "to indicate membership in the church," Phil 2:25, "Epaphroditus the brother. . . ." Ascough 2003:76–77, in associations. Cf. NOTE on 1:14, *adelphoi* in the city where Paul is imprisoned. Voc. pl. at 3:1, 13, 17; 4:1, 8, and here. *adelphoi* with Paul send greetings, 4:21. Cf. *TDNT* 1:145–46, H. F. von Soden; *NIDNTT* 1:254–58, W. Günther. + *agapētoi* ("beloved"; Phil. 4:1). J. Beutler, *EDNT* 1:30, in Paul, "fellow Christians" is the "prevailing sense," as here. Part of the "family of Christ" (*DA* 169), within which the letter provides exchange of information (Alexander 1989). On "sibling terms," see COMMENT B.1, n 11. Paul used the fem. *adelphē* in the sg. (1 Cor 9:5, a Christian wife) but followed the general rule, in Gk. as in Eng. (until recently), masc. pl. for a group of men and women. Phil 4:1 *adelphoi* clearly includes women (two named at 4:2). "Inclusive language" trs. often employ *brothers and sisters* (NRSV), not "modernizing" but clarity for a congregation where women are mentioned (Walter 38). NEB "Friends" at the start of 1:12 (more prominence than in Gk.) too easily suggests "letter of friendship." REB, regularly "My friends." At 1:12 (like 3:17; 4:1, 8) a transitional marker (*DA* 262 n 397; 378; Banker 1984; E. Rogers 1984).

   that events affecting me have actually resulted in progress for the gospel. hoti (recitative function, *DA* 324) + indic. *elēluthen + eis +* acc. *mallon, actually,* hints at a result some did not expect. The *events* can be ascertained only by reconstructing the situation; see COMMENT B.1.

   events affecting me. ta kat' eme, lit., "the (neut. pl.) things concerning me." BDAG *egō,* p. 275, col. a, bottom; BDF #279, emphatic pron. form after prep. *kata +* acc., "with respect to, in relation to" (BDAG B.6). *ta,* from *ho, hē, to* (BDAG 2.e), makes subst. the prep. phrase that follows, "the (things, circumstances) regarding me." Classical and papyrus examples (BDAG *kata* B.6); LXX, Schenk 134; Col 4:7 + "parallel" Eph 6:21 (echoing Phil 1:12?). "what concerns me" (GNTG 3:15), "what has happened to me" (RSV, NIV; cf. KJV); "my circumstances" (Lft. 87); "my affairs" (Michael 27); "this business of mine" (NEB). From *ta kata ton Paulon* (Acts 25:14), "Paul's case," Turner (*GNTG* 3:15) suggested "my lawsuit" (so O'B 89). *events affecting me* brings out the pl. + Paul as object. Schenk 129 thinks *eme* emphatic, *inclusio* with *emēs* in 1:26; Ware 1996:180, not emphatic, cf. *mou* in 13 and 14 (where *emou* is unlikely, BDF #278).

   have resulted in. . . . 2nd perf. act indic., *erchomai* (BDAG 5), "come," + *eis,* "result in furthering (the gospel)." Neut. pl. subject with 3rd sg. vb. (BDF #133). To see "abiding character" and "providential ordering of events" (Ware 1996:181; Eadie 25–26) is forced (Silva 67).

actually. Adv. *mallon* (see NOTE on 1:9 *more and more*), comparative, **to a greater or higher degree,** *more* (BDAG 1; cf. 1:25; 3:4), more than might have been expected (by whom?). Ware 1996:181 n 34, more progress for the gospel; *DA* 318, "*more* than if he had not been imprisoned," but cf. 329. Could also mean (BDAG 2) *for a better reason,* **rather** (2:12); so KJV, NEB ("helped on, rather than hindered"), Omanson 1978b, etc. Lft. 87, "'*rather*' than the reverse, as might have been anticipated"; hence, "'instead,'" O'B 90, cf. 2:28 and other vv in Paul with comparatives, but none use *mallon.* RSV (cf. Fee 110), "really"; NRSV "actually."

progress for the gospel. See NOTE on 1:5 *gospel,* shared vocabulary with the Philippians. Here, the 3rd of 6 occurrences in ch.1, in the absolute, "the gospel," no modifying phrase, just as at 1:5 and 7 and almost half the references in the Pauline corpus (Friedrich, *TDNT* 2:729 n 65). In the gen., dependent on another noun (BDAG 1.a.β; 1:7 and 16). 1:7, 16 *defense . . . of the gospel,* 12 *my imprisonment* show Paul's situation and make the noun *progress* here the more surprising. Subjective gen., equivalent of "the gospel progresses." 1:12 relates well to 4:15 (Letter A), on the beginning of the gospel in Macedonia, the gospel now advancing (O'Brien 1986 [section 2 Bibl. **gospel**] 222–23). 1:14 will use as synonym "a more traditional term borrowed from the Old Testament," *the word* (of God) (Fitzmyer 1979 [(2) Bibl. **gospel**] 151).

progress. prokopē, **progress, advancement, furtherance** (BDAG), 3x in NT, two of them in Phil, 1:12, 25 ("your progress and joy in faith"). Thus a/the key word for 1:12–26. Extensive Gk. usage, esp. philosophical; see *Philippian Studies.* Summary below in COMMENT B.1. Stählin 1957:24–25: the individualistic concept of progress in the Hellenistic world appears in the NT in modified form (Luke 2:52, 1 Tim 4:15); a more-than-individual ("collective") sense (2 Tim, of false teachers; Phil 1:12, 25); serviceable even within the NT's eschatological thinking. Possibly "Paul himself . . . coined" 1:12, 25, using a term, *prokopē,* shared with the Philippians, who brought the theme out of the Greco-Roman world into fuller use re the gospel and themselves.

1:13. *The results are first that. . . . hōste* (conj., 39x in Paul), **so that** (BDAG 2.a.β), + acc. + infin., result. Classical Gk. distinguished actual result (*hōste* + indic.) from possible outcome (+ infin.); the NT uses the infin. for both (Moule *IB* 141; BDF #391 [2]; *GNTG* 3:136); indic. at Gal 2:13, but the infin. is more common. Phil 2:12 and 4:1, *hōste* + impv. Here, *genesthai* = aor. m. infin., *ginomai,* "be(come)." V 13 has "explanatory force" (Vincent 16), "a more precise statement" of how progress came about (Meyer 22). Silva 69–70, "epexegetical"; Schenk 133–34, U. B. Müller 50, explicative. Collange paraphrases, "that is to say." Gnilka 55, "of such a sort that"; colon at the end of v 12 to point to the results in 13. Two acc. + infin. statements follow, v 13 *tous desmous . . . genesthai,* 14 *tous pleionas . . . tolman* (*DA* 212). Some number them "First . . . Second" (Schenk 142; cf. Silva 67; Phillips). Sequence of tenses (*elēluthen* perf., 12; *genesthai* aor.,

13; *tolman . . . lalein* pres., 14) suggests the first is already so, the second continues to occur.

in Christ. See NOTE and COMMENT on 1:1 *in Christ Jesus.* Here, *en Christō[i]*, as at 2:1. Taken usually as a formula (W. Kramer [(1) Bibl. **Christ**] 143–44, in "theological argument," to describe "persons, circumstances, and actions"). But the "formula" is hard to pin down precisely. At issue is construal in the cl. Possibilities include:

(1) With *desmous*, "my bonds in Christ" (KJV). *TDNT* 2:43 n 1: "bonds for Christ's sake," cf. ps.-Pauline *Laodiceans* 6 (HSNTApoc 2:132). ZG; Bockmuehl 75, "**imprisoned in Christ** . . . as his prisoner . . . like Jeremiah in the pit (Jer. 38.6ff.,22) . . . under divine coercion." But (Ewald 65 = Wohl. 73 and others) such an interpretation is "put out of court by the order of the Greek" (Michael 31). Not *tous desmous mou tous en Christō[i]* but *phanerous en Christō[i]*. Yet Fee 113, "in chains because I am a man *in Christ*"; cf. Hawth. 32, 34; NASB. Was it a crime to be a Christian, when Paul wrote?

(2) With *phanerous*, "manifest in Christ" (ERV 1881). Bonds "seen in their relation to Christ" (Lft. 88). The spirit in which Paul endured imprisonment (Ellicott; Michael 32). Loh. 39–40, a martyriological sense: Paul's bonds = "a revelation in Christ," who is glorified in Paul's body; the apostle suffering "in Christ" is a bearer of Christ's revelation, a witness to others (*martys* = witness and suffering-unto-death). Not what Paul is but what he has, namely bonds. Gnilka 56–57: *en Christō[i]* occurs between *phanerous* and *genesthai*, to show it goes with "manifest," not after *genesthai* (where it should stand, "become 'in Christ' manifest") since two more phrases with *en* follow, "in the Praetorium and all the rest." This goes partway with Loh. but not on Paul as bearer of "divine revelation." Cf. 1 Cor 11:19 (Gnilka), divisions made clear who "the genuine" members were (*phaneroi genōntai*). Paul's bonds will serve the gospel when he makes a defense that could win court personnel or soldiers to the faith. The sequence would happen "in Christ" (cf. 2 Cor 2:12, "in the Lord"; 1 Cor. 15:58; Haupt 19). Many endorse "manifest-in-Christ" (Dib. 64, "known 'in the Christian sphere'"; Friedrich 101; Ware 1996:183–84, agency; U. B. Müller 50); some, with or without acknowledging Loh., argue for participation in Christ's sufferings "from the *nature* of discipleship" (Fee 113; cf. 112 n 29, O'B 92, they appeal to Phil 3:10; Bruce 41; Silva 68). Cf. *TDNT* 2:541, s.v. "*en*" (Oepke), a local sense of membership.

(3) Take "in Christ" adverbially, with the entire cl. Plummer 18–19, "in the power of Christ." Neugebauer ([1] Bibl.) 121; cf. Jewett 1970b:366–67, 1:13 shows Christ's saving activity (death and resurrection) by which the lives of Paul and other followers are now determined. Paul's imprisonment "conforms to Christ"; it manifests Christ's saving activity, and thus contributes to the gospel's advance. Cf. G. Barth 25; Walter 39. O'B 92 doubts the phrase here can support such a weight, but his linkage with "sharing Christ's suffering" applies "death and resurrection" not just to Christ but also Paul (cf. 3:10). Grundmann (*TDNT* 9:550–51) reflects Neugebauer, "salvation is operative in the field of force of Christ." Bouttier 1962 ([1] Bibl.) 28, 88, 130, Paul's chains are an "authentic manifestation in Christ," part of his "apostolic conscience"; cf. 2 Cor 4:10. Bouttier 1966 ([1] Bibl.) 79, cf. 2

Cor 4:12, "In this intense struggle . . . in Ephesus, where death was hanging over him, the life of Christ shines in his threatened person with an intensity never known before, and at the same time it spreads to the whole body." But Paul's ordeals carry no "redemptive value" (78; contrast Thielman 59, like Christ's, 68–69). Schenk 134: *en Christō[i]* = "gospel of Christ" (*Christusnachricht*, 142). Not a "formula" (so C. Strecker; contrast W. Kramer) but a synonym for the "progress of the gospel" (v 12), "speak the word" (14), "Christ" (15, 16, 17, and 18), a metonym for the contents of what is proclaimed. Paul's imprisonment has its basis in the proclamation of Christ. Cf. 2 Cor 2:14 and 4:10–11 (correcting Schenk's 4:4). Emphasized is "the effect upon onlookers" (W. Kramer [(1) Bibl. **Christ**] 145 n 524). 1:20 provides further support for a metonymous synonym for "gospel": "Christ will be magnified" by Paul's life or death. Not (*GNTG* 2:463) "causal use of *en*."

Interpretation (1) limps on grounds of word order. Choice lies between (2), *en Christō[i]* with *phanerous*, and (3) with the entire cl. There is some overlap between the sphere or spirit of his captivity and the gospel because of which Paul is jailed but which is being advanced by his witness. [N]RSV recasts, to make the phrase the climax of the v (which it is), "it has become known . . . that my imprisonment is for Christ."

it has become clear . . . that my bonds are for Christ. Noun in the acc. (subject of the infin.) + infin. + pred. adj. (also in the acc.). On *bonds*, see NOTE on 1:7 *imprisonment*. The second of four examples of the pl. noun in Phil. The masc. *ho desmos* can yield a neut. pl. nom. and acc. *desma* (Acts 16:26) or a masc. acc. *desmous*, as here (the only clear NT example, *GNTG* 2:121–22; *ATR* 262). *desma* as "actual bonds," *desmoi* as "bondage" (*GNTG* 2:122) do not hold up for the NT. The notion of Reitzenstein (1978:241–48, 258; *TDNT* 2:43), that Paul saw his imprisonment as preparation for the final stage of being with Christ (1:23), akin to detention in the Serapeum and possession by the god, can safely be set aside. Schenk 134: *my bonds* parallel *ta kat' eme* in v 12 and indicate what is meant by the *events affecting me*. The infin. 2nd aor. m. infin., *ginomai* (BDAG 5.b), = *become* (a change in state, not *eimi*, DA 301; Ware 1996:185 n 46, resultant aor.). + adj. (cf. 1 Cor 3:13; 14:25) *phaneros*, **visible, clear, plainly to be seen . . . evident, known** (BDAG), thus "come to light, become known" (Bultmann/Lührmann, *TDNT* 9:3; not a theological term, U. B. Müller 50 n 13, not Loh.'s religious revelation from God; BDAG *phaneroō* 1.a.β, *be revealed*). See NOTE on 1:13 *in Christ*, above (little support for Paul's bonds as a revelation). No need to supply a ptc., *ontas*, with *en Christō[i]* (so Hofmann), "manifest as being in Christ," rejected by Meyer 22, rarely noted today.

The TRANSLATION, like (N)RSV, etc., recasts to emphasize *in Christ:* at the outset to show it stands over the entire cl., a second time with *phanerous* at the end, the bonds are *for Christ*, i.e., senses (2) and (3) above. Having one's cake and eating it too? Cf. JB, "My chains, in Christ, have become famous." *phanerous* we take as *clear*, re the Christ-caused and -oriented nature of Paul's imprisonment. The concluding phrase in Gk., about the *praitōrion* and "all the rest," has been moved up to indicate to whom the point of Paul's jailing has become clear.

in the whole Praetorium and to all the rest. en + dat. *praitōriō[i]* shows place where (BDAG 1.a); Fee 112 n 25, "locative"; "the *extent* to which" the result has been manifested, throughout the whole group. *all the rest* can be obj. of the same prep. (cf. Rom 1:19b; then tr. "among," NEB), but *kai tois loipois pasin* is better taken as dat. after *phanerous* (BDAG *phaneros* 1). KJV took both as locations ("in all the palace and in all other *places*"). Most trs. vary the wording "throughout . . . and to . . ." ([N]RSV); "to . . . and among" (NEB); "throughout . . . among" (REB). Each noun is modified by an adj., *praitōrion* by *holos* ("whole, entire, complete"; in the NT, always in pred. position, BDF #275.2), "the others" by *pas*, "all." Each involves hyperbole.

Praetorium. praitōrion, a loan-word from Lat. (BDF #5.1), *praetorium*, originally the tent of the praetor (general who led the army, *prae-itor*), then the area surrounding it. In Republican Rome, praetors administered justice for the city (*praetor urbanus*) and with foreigners (*praetor peregrinus*); as military magistrates, they served in the provinces. Cf. OCD³ 1240–41. From bodyguards (*cohors praetoria*) for a general arose the "Praetorian Guard" (Benoit 1952 = 1973: 169, examples in n 1). After the battle of Philippi in 42 B.C., 8000 veterans were organized into Praetorian cohorts for the triumphant Anthony and Octavian. The latter in 27 B.C. created a permanent corps of 9 cohorts, 500 or 1000 men each, a military elite (later 12 cohorts). Under Augustus, only 3 cohorts were in Rome at any one time. Under Tiberius, the commander of the Praetorians, the infamous Sejanus, concentrated all the cohorts at a single barracks (*castra praetoris*), northeast of Rome, near the Porta Viminalis (Tac. *Ann.* 4.2). Praetorians made Claudius Emperor in 41 and often thereafter were king-makers. They could serve on field campaigns. Cf. OCD³ 1241; L. Keppie, *ABD* 5:446–47. By extension, *praetorium* could be used for the residence of a ruler or governor, e.g., the palace of Hiero in Syracuse (Cic. *Verr.* 2.133, etc.); Egypt (BGU 1.288.14, etc.; MM 532); quarters for officials (*praetoria*, BCH 22, p. 491, 246ff., Antinopolis; more in Dib. 65); an imperial villa (*CIL* 3.5050; Suet. *Tib.* 39, etc.), villa of a private person (Epict. 3.22.47, "I sleep on the ground, no wife, no children, no *praitōridion*").

In the gospels, *praitōrion* = where the Roman governor resided and held court when in Jerusalem, probably the Herodian palace near the Jaffa Gate; see AB on Matt 27:27; Mark 15:16; John 18:28; P. Benoit 1952 = 1973; R. E. Brown, *The Death of the Messiah* (New York: Doubleday, 1994) 1:705–10; G. Schneider, *EDNT* 3:144–45; B. (V.) Pixner, *ABD* 5:447–48. At the trial of Jesus *praetorium* fits the judicial role of praetors (Benoit 171–72). MM 532: "'palace' or 'official residence' of a Governor" is the regular sense in the NT—except at Phil 1:13.

For Phil 1:13, if written in Rome, "the whole *praitōrion*" has been explained as (1) the palace or imperial residence on the Palatine Hill (a patristic view; KJV "in all the palace"); (2) a small praetorian barracks attached to the Palatine palace; (3) the Praetorian camp outside the Colline Gate or Porta Viminalis (B. Weiss 77), all rejected by Lft. 99–102. He settled on (4) a body of elite soldiers, the Praetorian Guard (Tac. *Hist.* 4.46; Suet. *Nero* 9; Macedonian inscription about "a veteran who served in the Guards," *en praitōriō[i]*, texts in MM 533). Then "all the rest" = a "far wider circle" than the Imperial Guard. For Lft., Praetorian Guards took turns watching Paul in his "hired house" (Acts 28). So RSV, many commentators (Dib. 65; Reicke 1970 (INTRO. VII.A Bibl.) 282–83; cf. BDAG 859). Hyperbole if 9000–10,0000 guardsmen are involved. This interpretation also meant Praetorium (guards) could be found outside Rome; it fits Caesarea or Ephesus (Michael 29–30, for Ephesus; Beare 57–58; O'B 93–94; Fee 113; Silva 70). Ware 1996:184–85, praetorian guard is "most probable," imperial palace "more suited" for Rome.

If Caesarea, cf. Acts 23:35 ("Herod's *praitōrion*"), the palace of Herod the Great, become residence and administrative center of the procurator (AB 31:227; Rapske 155–58; the "Promentory Palace," *BAR* 19 [1993] 50–57, 76). Cf. Loh. 40–41; Hawth. 35.

For Ephesus, as for Caesarea, the governor's palace (BDAG). NEB-mg "the Residency"; NEB-txt "headquarters here"; Gnilka 58; Schenk 134, 142; Dib. 65: the inhabitants of the governor's palace; *EDNT* 3:145; Walter 39. "Praetorian Guard" was bolstered by a funeral inscription in Ephesus (J. T. Woods, *Discoveries at Ephesus* [Boston: Osgood, 1877], Appendix No. 2, p. 4): a *praetorianus* in 3 Lat. inscriptions (*CIL* 3.6085, 7135, 7136) later discharged police duties as a *stationarius* on a Roman road; Bruce *Phil.* xxii would make him "a *former* member of the praetorian guard" (like Roman veterans settled in Philippi?). Coins from Philippi (COHOR[s] PRAE[toria]) suggest colonists from a Praetorian cohort (Krentz 2003:360, citing Collart). See COMMENT B.1 below.

The argument against Ephesus, "no known instance in imperial times" of *praetorium* "for the headquarters of a proconsul, the governor of a senatorial province such as Asia was at this time" (Bruce, *Phil.* xxii, repeated by O'B 20–21, cf. 93, and others) does not reckon with the evidence cited in U. B. Müller 52 n 25, including Cic., *Verr.* 4.65 and 5.92, praetorium as the dwelling of the governor in Syracuse, in the senatorial province of Sicily (or is that ruled out as "pre-Imperial" times?). J. L. Jones, in *The Catacombs and the Colosseum* (Valley Forge, PA: Judson, 1971) 199, "the military detachment assigned to security duties at the headquarters" in a provincial capital, "even though it was not part of the Praetorian Guard." Further, F. Lemmert, *PRE* 22 (1954) 2535–37; W. Schleiermacher, *PRE Suppl.* 9 (1952) 180–81; R. Egger, "Das Pratorium als Amtssitz und Quartier römischer Spitzenfunktionäre" (SÖAW. PH 250, 4 Abh., Vienna, 1966); W. Thiessen (INTRO. VII.A Bibl.) 118–19.

and to all the rest. Dat. (*kai tois loipois pasin*) after *phanerous* (see above). *loipos* is subst. (BDAG 2.b.a), "the others," modified by "all." If neut., "all other places," with *praitōrion* taken as "palace" (KJV); Chrysost., Thdrt., Moffatt ("everywhere else"). But as opinion on *praitōrion* shifted to "imperial guards," *loipois* was taken as masc., other persons; so already Lft. Who? (1) Other people at the place of Paul's imprisonment. Cf. 4:23; Michael 30–31; Gnilka 58 "a broader circle"; Hawth. 35 "the surrounding community"; O'B 94; Silva 67; Schenk 134–35. (2) Those connected with Paul's hearing, esp. "officials charged with preparing his case for hearing before the emperor" (Bruce 41; Rome or Caesarea). Cf. Loh. 41; B. W. Winter 1994:96, "the bureaucracy of Rome"; Beare 58; Fee 144. (3) A vague phrase, all others who come into contact with Paul besides guards or court personnel, but not Christians of any sort. Thus B. Weiss 77; Meyer 23; Lft. 88;

Vincent 17, "the city at large"; Ware 1996, "the pagan populace" (182), "outsiders," non-Christians (185); his proposed chiasm—"(a) *en holō[i]* (b) *tō[i] praitōriō[i]* (c) *kai* (b′) *tois loipois* (a′) *pasin*"—does not help interpretation. See COMMENT B.1.

1:14. *second, that most of the brothers and sisters . . . are . . . daring . . . to speak the word.* Subject acc. + infin., dependent on *hōste* at the beginning of v 13, another positive result of Paul's imprisonment. For *second,* cf. BDAG *kai* 1.b.ζ; Phillips; Ware 1996:186 "a second effect."

The subject acc. = *tous pleionas,* from *pleiōn, pleion,* comparative of the adj. *polus, pollē, polu,* BDAG I.b.β.ℵ (subst. use), "the majority, most" (NRSV; Hawth. 35; O'B 94; a countable number, DA 314); possibly 1.b.β.ℶ, "the others, the rest," in contrast to a majority. KJV "many." Cf. BDF #244.3; Gnilka 58 n 27. Since 13 has *all the rest* and vv 15–17a *Some . . . others,* avoid "others" or "the rest" here. Paul differentiates the group in vv 14–17 from those of the Praetorium and all the others in v 13 by adding in v 14 *brothers and sisters* with *tous pleionas.* See the NOTE on 1:12 *brothers and sisters* for inclusive use of *adelphoi.* Many, the majority of Christians where Paul is, are emboldened to preach more fearlessly. Possibly *tous pleionas* for the whole group, but not every last individual in it. Cf. 2 Cor 9:2 and 2:6, with BDAG *polus* I.b.β.ℵ and ℶ and the NOTES in AB 32A:155–56 and 426. Fee 115 n 43 well rejects for 1:13 *adelphoi* as a tech. term for a group with ". . . ministry as their primary occupation" (E. E. Ellis 1970–71[(1) Bibl.] 445–52 = 1978:13–22), but cf. Silva 69 and Dickson 144–50. To limit *adelphoi* to professional leaders or salaried evangelists makes the group quite small.

are daring. Infin., pres. act. (continuing action), *tolmaō,* BDAG 1.a, *dare, have the courage, be brave enough;* G. Fitzer, *TDNT* 8:181–86, "'the courage of confession"; *NIDNTT* 1:365. + *lalein,* again pres. act. (BDAG *laleō* 2.b, *speak, assert, proclaim*), + "the word" as obj., a tech. term in early Christianity (Mark 8:32; John 12:48; Acts 4:29, 31; cf. 1 Thess 2:2). *logos* is frequent in Paul for the message about Christ (BDAG 1.a.β 599–600). Cf. G. Kittel, *TDNT* 4:114–16; Schniewind 1910; R. Asting, *Die Verkündigung des Wortes im Urchristentum* (Stuttgart: Kohlhammer, 1939); R. Bultmann, *Faith and Understanding I* (New York: Harper & Row, 1969) 286–312, esp. 297–308; *NIDNTT* 3:1110–13 (B. Klappert); *EDNT* 2:358 (H. Ritt).

having become confident in the Lord through my bonds. Ptc. *pepoithotas,* from *peithō,* "persuade, be convinced"; see NOTE on 1:6 *since I am confident. . . .* Again 2nd perf., "having been convinced, therefore certain, confident"; BDAG *peithō* 2.a. NIV's "have been encouraged" is criticized by Fee 115 n 41. Acc. masc. pl. ptc. agrees with *tous pleionas;* it tells more about the majority of Christians where Paul is. Pred. position, no art. *tous* in front of it, so circumst., "because they have become confident." Cf. Moule *IB* 45–46, "*having grown confident* **as a result of— encouraged by the witness of**—*my imprisonment*" (italics and boldface in original).

tois desmois mou, dat., same phrase as the subject (acc.) in v 13; see NOTES on *it has become clear . . . that my bonds . . .* and 1:7 *imprisonment.* Here, dat. of cause (ZG, confident "because of my bonds"; RSV, NIV) or instrument ("by my bonds,"

KJV, NRSV; Vincent 17; O'B 95; Fee 116 "the means God has used" to make the *adelphoi* confident). Ware 1996:189, not the object of confidence. Silva 70, the type of dat. "makes no substantive difference." A problem is how the next phrase with *en* in Gk. fits in (Fee).

in the Lord. See NOTES on 1:2 *Lord,* 1:1 *in Christ Jesus,* 1:13 *in Christ* (question, as here, with what the phrase is to be taken). *en kyriō[i]* also at Phil 3:1; 4:1, 2, 4, and 10. Does it go (a) with the *most of the brothers and sisters* (KJV "brethren in the Lord," NIV), or (b) with *pepoithotas,* "confident in the Lord" (RSV)? If with *pepoithotas,* how do "confident *en kyriō[i]*" and "confident with respect to/by/through my bonds" relate? (a) is supported by Gk. word order. Against it: no art. *tōn* before "in the Lord," to show attrib. position, "brethren the ones (who are) in the Lord." Is the art. to be supplied (Moule *IB* 108; *GNTG* 3:221–22)? Then *pepoithotas* and *tois desmois mou* go together: "brothers in the Lord," "confident because of my imprisonment" (*GNTG* 3:242). So Oepke (*TDNT* 2:541): *adelphoi* + "in the Lord" = "membership" in the church; Loh. 42; Beare 59; cf. Kramer ([1] Bibl. **Christ**) 178. Against (a): *tōn adelphōn* already "designates the Christian brotherhood," no need to add "in the Lord." See NOTE on 1:12 *brothers and sisters* for this "prevailing" sense in Paul. Lft. 88, instances claimed for "brothers in the Lord" do not stand up (Col 1:2, 4:7; Eph 6:21, all deutero-Pauline). The "parallels" are muddy, many rule them out of the argument (Lft.; cf. Fee 116 n 48). (b) For "confident in the Lord," cf. *peithō* + *en* + dat., *adelphoi* suffices to designate Christians. So ATR 540; Gal 5:10; Rom 14:14; 2 Thess 3:4; and, particularly pertinent, Phil 2:24 ("trust in the Lord") and 3:3, 4 ("confidence in the flesh"). Hence von Soden (*TDNT* 1:144 n 1) "*en kyriō[i]* belongs to *pepoithotas*"; "'brothers in the Lord' . . . is to be rejected" (145 n 9). So Ewald 66 = Wohl. 74; Haupt 21; Gnilka 59 n 29; Hawth. 35; ZG; O'B 94–95; Ware 1996:187, "not the *ground* but the *sphere* of this confidence"; Fee 116, "all the other modifiers in this clause also stand in emphatic first position" (*perissoterōs* before *tolman; aphobōs* before *lalein*). O'B 95, Fee 116, and Bockmuehl 76: "in the Lord" = *ground* of confidence, Paul's "bonds" = the *instrument* used by God to generate this confidence.

The trend has been toward (b) (O'B 94), but the exegetical problem (ATR 784) is not solved by grammar or arguments that "cancel out each other" (Silva 70). Schenk 135–36 mounts six points in favor of (a), but each can be countered. He poses the question E. E. Ellis raised (without mentioning him): only certain leaders or the majority of the community (Schenk, in Ephesus)?

The TRANSLATION takes *en kyriō[i]* with *confident,* of certain Christians (in Ephesus) who continue to speak out what they believe. *in the Lord* stands over what they do as sphere of outlook and activity (Ware 1996:188); it occupies a central but ambiguous place in v 14, as *in Christ* does in v 13. Perhaps rhetorical variation. They do not suggest "indic." and "impv." Outsiders see Paul's imprisonment to be *in Christ*; Christians gain confidence to continue to preach *in the Lord,* even with Paul in prison.

so much the more . . . fearlessly. Two advs., *perissoterōs* before *tolman, aphobōs* before *to speak the word.* The first is comparative degree of *perissōs,* **exceedingly, beyond measure** (from the adj. *perissos,* **extraordinary, abundant**), a "colloquial substitute for *mallon*" (ATR 279; BDF #60,3), which occurred in 1:12 (see NOTE on *actually*; cf. 1:9 *more and more*). Can have an intensifying sense, *(even) more, so much (the) more* (BDAG 806). Trs. often take it with *pepoithotas*, "are much more bold" (KJV, RSV), "with greater boldness" (NRSV).

aphobōs, "not fearing," **fearlessly** (1 Cor 16:10, Luke 1:74). Some trs. take the two advs. together, NEB "fearlessly and with extraordinary courage," NRSV "with greater boldness and without fear." Schenk 136–37, with Loh. 42–43, a threefold emphasis on the courage of Christians: they are confident *(pepoithotas)*, they dare or venture *(tolman)*, they do so fearlessly *(aphobōs)*. They were witnesses for Christ before Paul's imprisonment, now (taking *perissoterōs* with *pepoithotas*) more confident. Paul's boldness emboldens them (Ware 1996:189).

to speak the word. ton logon lalein, P⁴⁶ (but most of [*ton logo*]*n* must be supplied), D (2nd corrector), K, Majority text. UBSGNT, {D} level, "very high degree of doubt." ℵ, A, B, etc. have *ton logon tou theou*, "the word of God." Aland 1991 (3:574–77) lists for "of God" 99 witnesses, 444 without it. KJV followed the short form. ERV 1881, RSV, NEB, and NIV adopted "word of God." NRSV-txt "speak the word," a tech. missionary term (Loh. 43 n 6), in Acts (4:20, 31, etc.) more than in Paul (cf. 1 Thess 2:2, *lalēsai . . . to euangelion tou theou*).

1:15. *Some . . . , but others. . . .* New sentence; in (N)RSV a new paragraph. Two indef. subjects share the same vb., *kēryssousin* (+ *ton Christon*), *are proclaiming Christ,* at the end of the cl. *tis, ti,* masc.-fem. nom. pl., as a noun = "some, a number of" (BDAG 1.a.α.ℵ). *men* (affirmative) and *de* (a common connective; thus far in Phil. only *de* has occurred, at 1:12; BDF #447.2) separate the two groups; "some" and "others" (BDAG *men* 1.c). Both particles are post-positive (cannot stand first in a cl.). *tines* is enclitic (normally no accent, not a word to lead off a cl.). But occasionally, as here, the enclitic pron. begins a sentence (BDF #301; Moule *IB* 125). Paul contrasts two groups who do the same thing, but with differing motives. *men/de* and similar word order will occur in 16–17. For accent in such situations, cf. *GNTG* 2:54.

are proclaiming Christ. 3rd pl. pres. act. indic., only example in Phil. of *kēryssein* (or its noun *kērygma*), a concept prominent in 1 and 2 Cor (11x, "we preach Christ crucified," 1 Cor 1:23, etc.) and basic to Paul's gospel (Gal 2:2). Very much a Gk. term (*EDNT* 2:288), "proclaim aloud" as by a herald. Of religious proclamation by Greco-Roman philosophers (Epict. 3.13.12) or OT prophets (Jonah 1:2 and 3:2 LXX; Jos. *Ant.* 9.214 = 9.10.2); "contemporary proclaimers . . . of the great deeds of the gods" (BDAG *kēryssō* 2.b.β). Of false prophets (JW 6.285 = 6.5.2), or "preaching Moses" (Acts 15:21; cf. Rom 2:21, a Jewish missionary). Most common in NT for "proclamation of the Christian message." Content, G. Friedrich, *TDNT* 3:710–12; reconstructions of kerygma *NIDNTT* 3:57–67; *EDNT* 2:288–89; J. Schniewind, *TDNT* 1:71, "language of mission."

Philippians were familiar with proclamations by a herald *(kēryx)*; announcements of victors at athletic games, honors conferred by a city, publicly declared at assembly, marketplace, or theater (e.g., about a benefactor; examples in *TDNT* 3:698 n 11). Cf. further *TDNT* 3:683–94, 697–98. Also Cynic street preachers who regarded themselves sent by Zeus as messengers, heralds comparable to the *kēryx* in the ancient Eleusinian mysteries (Epict. 3.21.12–16; *TDNT* 3:692–93; *NIDNTT* 3:50). See (1) NOTES ON 1:1 *overseers* A (3) and *agents* A.2. 1 Thess 2:3–12 may distinguish Christian missionaries from such heralds (Malherbe 1987:21–33; AB 32B:156–63). *kēryssein* occurs re the mighty acts of the god Imouthes-Asclepius in an aretalogy or recitation of such virtues (cf. D. L. Tiede, *ABD* 1:372–73), POxy 11.1381 (pp. 223–34), and in the Hermetic Corpus (*TDNT* 3:699; tr. in Barrett 1957: #89, pp. 88–89). Such texts illustrate a religious milieu, proclamation by missionaries of various types. Cf. R. Reitzenstein, *Poimandres* (Leipzig: Teubner, 1904; repr. Darmstadt: Wissenschaftliche Buchgesellschaft, 1966); J. A. Trumbower, "Hermes Trismegistos," *ABD* 3:156–57; Ferguson 1993 (INTRO. I Bibl.) 294–95. NT usage, G. Friedrich, *TDNT* 3:683–718; L. Coenen, *NIDNTT* 3:48–57; O. Merk, *EDNT* 2:288–92. In the TRANSLATION, the vb. has been moved up, after the first of the two subjects it serves.

Christ. See NOTE on 1:1 *Christ.* Here + art. *(ton),* first time in Phil, lit. "the Christ" or anointed one. But no indication a title, "the messiah," is meant; see BDAG *Christos* 1; BDF #260; Kramer ([1] Bibl. **Christ**) #62, esp. d., pp. 206–12; Schenk 130. *Christos* with or without the art. means the same (Grundmann, *TDNT* 9:541; contra Loh. 44 n 2). Almost all trs. have simply "preach Christ," kerygmatic content; Gnilka 60; Kramer #8 b.3–g, pp. 40–44.

Some . . . indeed on account of envy and strife, but others indeed on account of goodwill. dia + acc (BDAG B.2.a, to indicate motives). *kai* appears in each cl., after *tines men* and *tines de,* before *di(a);* more than "and" or "but" (BDF #442). Silva 71, the initial *kai* has "a transitional but emphatic force." 1:15–17 are not an excursus (A.7.a); on the groups involved, see B.3.

The double *kai* can have a strong sense: "some indeed . . . some also" (KJV); "And yet some . . . but surely some" (Hawth. 32, 36, within the double chiasm that he finds in vv 15–18a [see COMMENT A.7], "connective . . . expressing surprise at something unexpected or noteworthy"). Cf. BDAG *kai* 1.b.ζ; BDF #442.1. Not "both . . . and" (BDAG 1.f, Phil 2:13; 4:12 and 16), either for the two groups in 15a and 15b or with the two reasons given for the preaching of the first group ("both on account of . . . and [on account of] . . ."). *kai* in 15a is often taken as an adv. with ascensive force (BAGD *kai* II.2; BDAG 2.b, cf. 1.c), "even" or "indeed" (RSV, NEB). In 15b, the second *kai* can be taken the same way ("others indeed . . ."). But often regarded as pleonastic (BAGD II.3; BDAG 2.c, assuming a contrast) and so omitted ([N]RSV). Renderings can suggest a concession on Paul's part, "It is true that some . . . , but others . . ." (NIV; Fee 119 n 9; REB; Phillips). The sense of *kai* can be settled only by reconstructing the situation. Do the two groups in v 15 belong, as is assumed in the COMMENT, to the *brothers and sisters* in v 14? What is the degree of opposition against Paul in v 15? Schenk 138, the motives stated in the v are secondary to the "confidence in the Lord" in v 14 (Dib. 65); contra Loh. 44, *kai* strengthens a contrast. Beare 21 is evenhanded, "Some, it must be said . . . , but some also . . ." (56). The TRANSLATION uses *indeed . . . indeed.*

indeed on account of envy and strife. The first group in v 15 is motivated by these two factors (hendiadys? Edart 71, 78). dia + acc., **because of, for the sake of,** or *out of* (BDAG *dia* B.2.a; KJV "of"). Construction repeated re the second group in

15b. On *kai*, see above, *indeed*. Both nouns, *phthonos* and *eris*, are in the list of vices at Rom 1:29 (AB 33:289; cf. 274–75). *phthonos* is the more consistently negative, even nasty, term, *eris* suggests the outcome as strife.

envy. *phthonos*, **envy, jealousy** (BDAG; *NIDNTT* 1:557–58, and esp. *TLNT* 3:434–35); Gal 5:21 (pl., in a vices catalogue); cf. Titus 3:3 (AB 35:190–91); 1 Tim 6:4; 1 Pet 2:1; James 4:5, + Mark 15:10 par. Matt 27:18, jealousy against Jesus (AB27:633 "malice"). Vb. *phthoneō*, Gal 5:26, Christians "envying one another." The 4 LXX uses of *phthonos* (Wis 2:24; 6:23; 1 Macc 8:6; 3 Macc 6:7) have no basis in Heb.; cf. D. Lührmann 1978:364. A thoroughly Gk. term, in classical sources and the papyri (MM 667–68). Spicq 3:434, "always pejorative"; James 4:5 is too uncertain to allow claim for a "good sense" there (*NIDNTT* 1:558; AB37A:281–82, "crave enviously," of the human spirit, Hellenistic background in "the *topos* of envy," "*always* a vice."

phthonos was "widely prevalent in Greek society, engrained in Greek life" (Walcot 7, 101; Hesiod, *Op.* 195–201, *Theog.* 383ff.). Walcot explores "envy of the gods" toward the powerful, like Agamemnon; envy of eastern potentates, like Croesus the Lydian king. A factor in politics of the city-state, 5th and 4th cents. B.C. (Walcot 52–76). Aristot. (*Rhet.* 2.11.1387b–88b): *to phthonein* is "the base passion of base people"; *zēlos* (zeal, emulation), "the honest passion of honest people." A feature in Hellenistic diatribes (*TLNT* 3:435 n 3; note *T. Sim.* 4.7, *Aristeas* 224).

In Plut.'s treatise "On Envy and Hatred" (*Peri phthonou kai misous, Mor.* 536E–538F = LCL 7:94–107), both are contrary to goodwill (*eunoia*) and friendship (*to philein*) (536F), but dissimilar (chs. 2–8). People hate someone who is bad or when they think they have been wronged. Prosperity ("doing well" in life) attracts envy, which has no bounds (though hated does, 537A). Envy occurs only on the part of a person toward another human being (537B). The two passions differ in intent (ch. 8). Those who hate aim to injure (*kakōs poiēsai*); envy aims to "reduce one's neighbor to equality with oneself" (p. 93). Stobaeus (5th cent. A.D.) collected some 59 sayings on envy (*Ecl.* 3.38 = vol. 3, pp. 708–21 ed. C. Wachsmuth/ O. Hense [Berlin: Weidmann, 1884–1912]), a well-known topic. #4, "*phthonos* is the most unjust thing of all"; #15 "it rejoices at evils and pains the good"; #48, "Socrates said *phthonos* is a wound of the soul" (possibly authentic gnomic material, Walcot 75).

Spicq characterizes *phthonos* as "malevolent envy." "The worst of all evils" (Menand., in Stob. 28.29 = 3.713); "the hater of good" (Philo, *Leg.* 3.3 = LCL *Philo* 7:476–77). None of our good feelings is strong enough to hold out against *phthonos* (Jos., *JW* 1.77 = 1.3.4). Sadness at good things happening to friends (Ps.-Plato, *Def.* 416; Diog. Laert 7.111), rejoicing at evils they experience (Plato, *Philebus* 49C–D). The Edomites (Num 20:14–21) rejoiced at the Hebrews' misfortunes (Philo, *Moses* 1.247 = LCL *Philo* 6:404–5). *phthonos* will "defile and denigrate" success (Heraclitus, *All.* 6.3) and slander a person in authority (Jos., *Life* 80 = LCL 1:32–33). More examples in Spicq 435–36 n 7.

Envy could show itself in lawsuits (papyrus examples in MM 667–68, Spicq 436 n 8) or in political life, leading to rivalries, strife in the city-state, division among countrymen (examples in Spicq 435 n 6 esp. from Plut.). Contrast 1 Macc 8:16, Roman senators show "no envy or jealousy"; Wis 7.23–24 (AB 43:160) cf. 2:24. Spicq (434 n 2) relates envy to demons, Fortune, and the evil eye (cf. Gal. 3:1). Cf. *Vita Caesaris* by Nicolaus of Damascus (1st cent. B.C.; *FGrH* ii A, p. 324; C, p. 229; ed. W. Witte 1900; Spicq 436): "Some, in order to please Caesar, heaped honors upon him, while others, in their perfidy, approved and proclaimed these extravagant honors only in order that envy *(phthonos)* and suspicion might make Caesar hateful to the Romans"—the latter group hoped envy of the honors would lead to opposition to Caesar. B. W. Winter 1994:93–94 connects *phthonos* and local politics *(politeia,* cf. on 1:27 below) and desire to harm Paul when he comes to trial. 1 Clem. 3.2; 4.7,13; and 5.2 trace "jealousy and envy" through history (Cain and Abel; Deut 32:15, Israel against God; David; in the deaths of Peter and Paul; current troubles in the church at Corinth, where new presbyters have ousted the older ones); what does not fit the author's view of order (or God's order), is the result of envy.

   strife. Attic acc. sg. form, *erin,* instead of *erida* (ATR 265; BDF #47.3), from *hē eris, eridos* (BDAG **Engagement in rivalry, esp. w. ref. to positions taken in a matter, strife, discord, contention**). In Paul's vice lists (Rom 1:29; 1 Cor 3:3; 2 Cor 12:20; Gal 5:20). 1 Cor 1:11, "divisions *(erides)* among you." Rom 13:13, life together should be characterized "not by quarreling *(eridi)* and jealousy *(zēlō[i],* pls. in some MSS)." Titus 3:9; 1 Tim 6:4 (vice list). Thus all 9 NT examples are Pauline. Word studies (*NIDNTT* 1:106, 535, 558; 2:587; 3:544; *TLNT* 2:69–72; *EDNT* 2:52–53, H. Giesen) find no OT background. Just 3 LXX occurrences, all in vice lists, Sir 40:4 (NRSV 5), 9; 28:11. Quinn AB 35:237 adds LXX Ps 138 (Eng. 139):20, pl., if accented with an acute. *Aristeas* 250; Philo 12x; occasionally in the papyri (MM 254; BDAG).

   "Greeks divinized Dispute or Emulation, which they considered the energizing spirit of the world and one of the primordial forces" (*TLNT* 2:71, citing Antoninus Liberalis, 2nd cent. A.D., *Metamorphoses* 11.3). Personification of Strife is common, in Homeric battle scenes (*Il.* 4.440–41) or Hesiod (*Theog.* 225ff., the mother of battles). *Eris* stirred up the quarrel over whether Hera, Athena, or Aphrodite was most beautiful, leading to the Trojan War (*Cypria*; Hyginus, *Fab.* 91, reflecting a Gk. source of Paul's day; OCD 328, cf. "Paris" 647–48 = 2nd ed. 781–82; 3rd ed. 1113, cf. 531). "Eagerness for competition" marked chariot races or battles (Jos. *Ant.* 14.470 = 14.16.2; *TLNT* 2:71 n 12). Often coupled with *phthonos* in vice lists, a factor in church life. 1 Clem. uses *eris* 9x: rivalry and strife run through biblical history and live in the house churches of Corinth and Rome in the 90s A.D. G. Delling, discussing *stasis* or "discord, rebellion," sees vocabulary from the political sphere (*TDNT* 7:571; B. W. Winter 1994:95). Corinthian Christians (46.5), like Israel in Deut 32:15, are accused of "jealousy and envy *(phthonos),* strife *(eris),* and dissension," disorder and even war, in replacing former presbyters with new ones (3.2; 4:7,13; 5.2,5; 6.4; 9.1; 14.2; 35.5; cf. 46.5; 54.2). A classic Gk. vice persisting in NT churches, *"disputes* that endanger the Church," its peace and unity, as in contemporary society (*EDNT* 2:52).

   but others indeed on account of goodwill. The second group *(tines de)* is also described by *dia* + acc., preceded by *kai*. BDAG *men* (1.c, with *de*), "some . . . but still others . . . ," heightens the force of *de*, perhaps too much. Paul writes even-handedly. KJV took *kai* as "even," then here as "also." NRSV omits *kai* each time. The TRANSLATION indicates *kai* each time by *indeed*.

eudokia, **state or condition of being kindly disposed**, *good will* (BDAG 1; KJV through RSV; NRSV "goodwill") moves the second group. *Word studies*: G. Schrenk, *TDNT* 2:738–51, esp. 746–47; H. Bietenhard, *NIDNTT* 2:817–18; R. Mahoney, *EDNT* 2:75–76; *TLNT* 2:99–106. From vb. *eudokeō*, "consider good, be (well) pleased with," often with a legal sense "accept, approve"; cf. MM 260 and *TLNT* 2:99–101. The "noun is not completely unknown in secular Greek" (Spicq 103 n 26), but examples are few. In Jewish as well as Christian sources (MM; *EDNT* 75) for the goodwill of God or of humans. In the LXX, vb. 60x, noun 25x, esp. in later sections, for a number of Heb. terms (often *rāsôn*, "good pleasure, good will"). The LXX has a theological sense when applied to God's acceptance, e.g., of burnt offerings or praise (119 [118]:108); God pleased to deliver someone (Ps 40:13 [39:14]; 51:18, 19 [50:20, 21]); showing favor (77:7b [LXX 76:8b]; 85:1 [84:2]). Spicq maintains "the LXX uses *eudokia* only with re-gard to God" (*TLNT* 2:104; Ps 5:12, 106:4 [LXX 105:4], etc.). More examples in *TLNT* 2:101–2, 104, + Qumran (vb. *rāsāh*, as in CD 2.15). In Sir 11:17, God's *eudokia* (NRSV "favor"), in parallel with "gift"; but 1:27 what is pleasing to the Lord (1:27; more in *TLNT* 2:104 n 28).

In the Synoptic Gospels, *eudokeō* 6x and *eudokia* 3x (11x and 6x in the Pauline corpus; the rest of the NT, vb. 3x in Heb [10:6, 8, 38], 2 Pet 1:17, all in OT quota-tions). Five of the six Synoptic vb. uses are from Isa 42:1, ". . . my servant . . . my chosen in whom my soul delights" (Matt 12:18; Mark 1:11 parr. Matt 3:17, Luke 3:22; Matt 17:5). Luke 12:32, "It is your Father's good pleasure *(eudokēsen)* to give the kingdom" to the little flock, is full of OT echoes (AB 28A:980), something true also of Matt 11:26 par. Luke 10:21, about God's "gracious will" *(eudokia)* to reveal hidden things to infants (AB 26:144–45; 28A:868–69, 873–74). Luke 2:14, *en anthrōpois eudokias* (Qumran evidence) means "people whom he [God] favors" (AB 28:410–12).

Paul uses *eudokeō* for how God "was pleased" (NRSV "decided") to save those who believe the kerygma (1 Cor 1:21); the Lord was displeased with rebellious Is-raelites (10:5). God was pleased to reveal Christ to Paul (Gal 1:15); the apostle was pleased (NRSV "determined") to share the gospel with the Thessalonians (1 Thess 2:8). The vb. characterizes his mission work; cf. 2 Cor 12:10 (AB 32A:531); 1 Thess 3:1–2; Rom 15:26–27. With *mallon* at 2 Cor 5:8 (on whether to continue on earth or be fully with the Lord; cf. Phil 1:20–24), it expresses human preference, "we, rather, are resolved . . . to get on home" (AB 32A:273–74). See also 2 Thess 2:12 (vb.) and Eph 1:5, 9; 2 Thess 1:11 (noun).

eudokia, 3x in Paul's undisputed letters, reflects both aspects noted above. Phil 2:13 — traditionally, to will and do God's good pleasure or will — is God's *eudokia*, but human performance of it; but cf. on 2:13. Rom 10:1, Paul's *eudokia*, "desire," that his Jewish brothers and sisters "may be saved" (AB 33:582). 1:15, what pleases or is decided upon by certain preachers in the town where Paul is imprisoned, but over it hangs a suggestion that the *eudokia* is more than their own, it is under God (Bockmuehl 79, "**for the sake of** the divine will"). *eudokia* at 1:15 is then not just a matter of sincerity or goodwill toward Paul (though both things may be true). It involves orientation to God and the gospel. Not here "*God's* good purpose" (Schrenk, *TDNT* 2:746; Ware 1996:206), but the goodwill *of Christians*, toward Paul, possibly with "a Godward reference" as well (O'B 99–100). More than "weak feeling" (*EDNT* 2:75) or "favorable sentiments" (*TLNT* 2:106), but not clear notions of fitting into a divine plan. Paul himself further defines what he means in v 16.

1:16–17. *The latter, out of love, set forth Christ in preaching. . . . The former, out of self-interest, set forth Christ in preaching. . . .* Some MSS (full list in Aland 1991 [3:577–80]) reverse the cls., to read (as in KJV), "¹⁶ The one [group, *hoi men*] preach Christ of contention, not sincerely, supposing to add affliction to my bonds: ¹⁷ But the other [*hoi de*] of love, knowing that I am set for the defence of the gospel." This keeps the sequence as in v 15, "Some indeed preach Christ even of envy and strife; and some also of good will" (AB, AB sequence). The vast majority of earlier MSS (P⁴⁶, ℵ, A, B, D original hand, etc.), the Lat. tradition, and other versions have the order found in (N)RSV and most modern trs., an ABB'A' chiastic structure:

A (some, from envy and strife, v 15)⟍⟋ B (others, of goodwill)
B' (the latter, out of love, v 16)⟋⟍ A' (the former, out of partisanship, v 17)

Thus in trs. from ERV 1881 on, usually without a note; cf. UBSGNT punctuation apparatus; unmentioned in *TCGNT*. Silva 74, KJV's order is "not attested earlier than the sixth century"; Fee 117 n 1, "one of the few major transpositions of this kind in . . . the Pauline corpus."

1:16. *The latter, out of love.* hoi men, balanced by *hoi de* in v 17. The def. art. serves as a dem. pron. (BDAG *ho, hē, to* 1.b; GNTG 3:36) with *men* and *de* (see 1:15 *Some . . . but others*). Refers back to *tines men* and *tines de* in v 15. In Eng., "the latter" and (v 17) "the former" (RSV); or "these" in v 16, for the group just mentioned in 15b, "the others" in v 17 for those described in 15a (NEB, NRSV). On *ex agapēs*, see NOTE on 1:9 *love*. Here, human love (BDAG *agapē* 1.a.α) on the part of Christians, those preaching Christ in the city where Paul is jailed. No object of their love indicated, whether God, Christ, or Paul (O'B 99). Gen. after *ek* (*ex* because *agapē* begins with a vowel). Cf. BDAG *ek* 3.e, origin, cause, motive, reason. KJV's "of love" does not pick up *ek* very well. Possibly the full subject in v 16 is *hoi men ex agapēs*, "some who (act) out of love" (v 17 "others who (act) out of contention") (so ZG). Then *set forth Christ in preaching* is the entire predicate. Most (Gnilka 61), however, take *hoi men* and *hoi de* as subjects; the prep. phrase modifies the vb. RSV "the latter do it out of love."

set forth Christ in preaching. Supplied from v 17, *katangellousin + ton Christon.* As in v 15, moved up for clarity in Eng. *katangellō* (1:17, 18, by implication v 16; cf. 1 Cor 2:1; 9:14; 11:26; Rom 1:8; plus Col 1:28) is a strengthened form of *angellō*, sometimes termed "sacral" language from the Hellenistic world. Equivalent to *ton Christon kēryssousin* (1:15) and *euangelizesthai* (*TDNT* 1:70–72).

Some see a sense of "promise" in *angelia*-words (cf. U. Becker/D. Müller, *NIDNTT* 1:44–48). Likely rhetorical variation in "vbs. of proclamation" and "missionary preaching" in 1:14–18. Cf. I. Broer, *EDNT* 2:256. That B, etc., omit *ton* before *Christon* is secondary, of no significance (Fee 117 n 2).

because they know that I am put here for defense of the gospel. Ptc. perf. act. nom. pl. *eidotes*, from *oida*, "know," perf. of the stem *eid-* (as in *eidon*), lit., "I have seen," with a pres. sense, "I know." + *hoti* + indic., for what they know (BDAG *oida* 1.e). Causal (ZG; O'B 101; U. B. Müller 49), but seldom brought out (Gdsp., Phillips, "for they know"). Contrasts with *oiomenoi* (17), "supposing" (Fee 120 n 17; O'B 101; Collange 57).

I am put here. keimai, BDAG 3.a, *be appointed, set, destined.* Pres. and imperf. only, in the NT; serves as perf. pass. for *tithēmi*, "be placed, put, appointed" (ATR pp. 316, 357, 813; 1 Thess 3:3, "this is what we are destined for," NRSV). Often a spatial sense (F. Büchsel, *TDNT* 3:654); hence RSV adds "here." Paul often uses *tithēmi* "to describe God's work" (1 Thess 5:9, "God has destined us . . . for . . . salvation"; cf. Luke 2:34); hence, "I am where I am" (NEB) because God has put me there (C. Maurer, *TDNT* 8:157; S. Wibbing, *NIDNTT* 1:471; R. Schippers, *NIDNTT* 2: 809; H. Hübner, *EDNT* 2:280, "*be destined for* [by God]; Ware 1996:212 *"commissioned"* for "missionary defense of the gospel," cf. Isa 49:6); Silva 72, a "predestinarian motif" as in Gal 1:15–16 (Paul's call). O'B 101, "originally a military term" (evidence?), Paul "under orders, issued by God." But *defense* is rhetorical/legal, not military. Trs. prefer a less theological rendering than O'B's "divinely appointed" (97). RSV-NRSV: *put here.*

for defense of the gospel. apologia, see NOTE on 1:7 *defense. eis* (+ acc.), purpose or goal of Paul's imprisonment (cf. BDAG *eis* 4d; *keimai* 3; cf. 4:16 *for my needs*). Unlike 1:7, *defense and confirmation, apologia* here has no def. art. and is not paired with another noun. defense-*of-the-gospel*, not (Eadie 32) of himself before the judgment seat of God (Chrysost.). BDAD (2)(b) an eagerness to defend the gospel. Kellermann (*EDNT* 1:137), "an unexpected opportunity for missionary proclamation." Ware 1996:209–12, a "protreptic aspect" to confirm or corroborate the gospel. On *euangelion* see NOTES on 1:5, 7, 12, and 4:15 *gospel.*

1:17. *The former, out of self-interest, set forth Christ in preaching. hoi de,* see NOTE on 1:16, *The latter.* . . . Vb. + object, see NOTE 1:16, *set forth Christ in preaching* (inferred for v 16 from Gk. here). The significant phrase is *ex eriteias, ek (ex)* + gen., as in v 16 *out of love. eritheia* (*erithia* in some MSS and WH; *GNTG* 2:57), 7x in the NT, 5x in Paul, 2x in Phil (also at 2:3). Two lines of interpretation: "contention" (KJV, Vg *contentio*) or "selfish ambition" (NRSV). The first relates it to Gk. *eris*, "strife, discord" (Phil 1:15, see NOTE on *strife*), two terms found together in vice lists: 2 Cor 12:20 (*eris, zēlos, thymoi, eritheiai*, NRSV "quarreling, jealousy, anger, selfishness"); Gal 5:20 (same four Gk. terms, same order, NRSV "strife, jealousy, anger, quarrels"). Since *eris* and *eritheia(i)* occur in the same lists, each may have a different sense.

Prior to the NT, *eritheia* is found only in Aristot., *Pol.* (text in *TDNT* 2:660), seek political office by suspect means like "election intrigue *(dia te tas eritheias),* . . . people used to elect those who canvassed *(eritheuomenos)*" (5.2.8–9, 1303a 14–

21; LCL tr. by H. Rackham, *Politics*, p. 385). Cf. also 5.2.3, 1302b 4–5, causes of party friction *(staseis)* and revolutions in polity include "election intrigue" *(eritheia)* (LCL pp. 379, 381). Büchsel,"illegal manipulation" (2:660). Cf. *TLNT* 2:70, *aneritheutos* (Philo, *Legat.* 68) = government "without factions" or "intrigue." B. W. Winter 1994:95 connects the term with *politeia*. How do the references in the *Pol.* apply to 1:17?

The dominant rendering now (NRSV) derives *eritheia* from *eritheuomai*, "work for hire," *erithos* "worker for hire"; in a derogatory sense "mercenary." *Selfishness* rather than *factiousness* "was the original meaning, labouring for one's own interests rather than devotion to public service [as in Aristotle]. So in the 3 NT passages" (*GNTG* 2:339). Ware 1996:213, "gain disciples for themselves." Haupt 24 and H. A. A. Kennedy (*EGT*) long ago adopted "selfishness" at 1:17. Cf. (H. Giesen, *EDNT* 2:52) Jas 3:14, 16 and Rom 2:8 (KJV "contentious," NRSV "self-seeking"; AB33:302, "selfishly disobey the truth"). Neither etymology nor usage and context solve the matter, but the tendency has been away from *eris*, "strife," toward self-interest, selfishness, base self-seeking ("baseness," Büchsel). But "strife, contentiousness" has supporters (BDAG 392 cites Dib.), because popular etymology may have made connection with *eris*. At the least, self-interest ("What's in it for me?" *TLNT* 2:70), perhaps leading to open contention.

not with a pure motivation. ouch (before a word beginning with vowel and rough breathing) to negate a single word; *no* "but (also) . . ." follows. *hagnōs*, adv. from *hagnos*, adj. at 4:8 (NRSV "pure"); cf. *hagioi*, holy ones or saints, 1:1 and 4:21 (*TDNT* 1:88, 122). The adv., only here in the NT (not in LXX), = "holily, purely, sincerely," therefore "(not) *from pure motives*" (BDAG), "mixed" (ZG) or "unhallowed motives" (Beare 56, 59; Schenk 139). *TDNT* 1:122, Gk. inscriptions, "blameless discharge of office"; MM 5. Some link it to *oiomenoi*, "with ulterior motives imagining . . ." (Collange 52, 57), but most take it independently (set off by commas, NA[26,27]; Fee 117, 121) or with *katangellousin* (BDAG *hagnōs*; O'B 101, against Collange). Juxtaposition with *set forth Christ in preaching* is striking.

because they suppose thereby to stir up trouble for my imprisonment. Circumst. ptc., causal, like *eidotes* in v 16; from *oiomai (think, suppose, expect)* + infin., no art., as dir. obj. (*GNTG* 3:137; *EDNT* 2:505). MM 444, EGT *Phil.*, "purposing." The Translation adds *thereby* to make explicit that the group hopes to add to Paul's afflictions.

to stir up trouble for my imprisonment. Infin. *egeirein*, pres. act., *egeirō*, "raise up, rouse" (from sleep); fig. sense, **bring into being, cause** (BDAG 5). Cf. Lucian, *Syr. Dea* 18; Luke 1:69, "raise up (a horn of salvation)" (ZG). The dir. obj. in these instances is not a person but a thing (Oepke, *TDNT* 2:334). NA[26,27] note *epipherein* in some MSS, "to add affliction to my bonds" (KJV v 16), rather than "to raise up affliction." Aland 1991 (3:580–84): only 14 cursives use a form of *-pherein*. Fee 117 n 3 cannot imagine how "*epipherein* . . . would have been changed (so early and so often)" to the more striking *egeirein*. Read *egeirein*. The crucial and difficult word is the dir. obj., acc. sg. of *thlipsis*, "pressure," fig. **oppression, affliction, tribulation,** (1) from outward circumstances, or (2) mental and spiritual affliction of mind (BAGD; BDAG "inward experience"; both place 1:17 here). Usually "inner distress and sorrow" (H. Schlier, *TDNT* 3:147). Some add theological significance from the affliction of Israel or the righteous remnant (Schlier 142) and eschatological overtones as in Mark 13:19, 24, etc. (Schlier 144–46). In Paul, frequently persecution (1 Thess 1:6; 3:3) or connected with God's judgment (Rom 2:9, distress for evildoers). Court 1982 claimed a NT pattern of *thlipsis*, labor pains (1 Thess 5:3 only), and *telos*, the End, Phil 3:19. But "affliction" takes many forms. The common denominator Schlier saw was "death at work" (2 Cor 1:8–9; 4:8–12; Phil 3:10). Accepting *thlipsis*, by faith, Christians promote edification of the community (1 Thess 1:6–7; 2 Cor 1:4–7). Similarly *NIDNTT* (R. Schippers 2:807–9). J. Kremer (*EDNT* 2:152–53), "persecution as eschatological *thlipsis*," at 1:17 "*affliction* in addition to his chains." But what and how? Theories vary with how the "rival preachers" (Phil 1:15–17) are viewed; COMMENT B.3.

At 1:17 *thlipsis* may simply mean "trouble," as in the papyri (MM 292), which the activity of Christian preachers brings on for Paul. At Phil 4:14 Paul notes how Philippian Christians have shared with him in his *thlipsis*; see NOTE on *in my affliction*. (Hardly evidence for a single-letter theory; Paul may face the same or a similar situation as he writes two letters, DA 361.) At 1:17 more than mental anguish may be involved, just as at 4:14 more than finances and outward help.

for my imprisonment (tois desmois mou). See NOTES on 1:7 *imprisonment*, 1:13 *it has become clear . . . that my bonds . . .* , and 1:14 *through my bonds* (all pl., dat. pl. at 1:7 and 14). At 1:17, not instrumental ("make use of my imprisonment to stir up fresh troubles," NEB-mg), as Silva 74 observes. Indir. obj. (ATR 538, cause trouble to my bonds) or dat. of reference (with regard to my imprisonment). Lft. 90 rendered rather freely, "to make my chains gall me."

1:18a. *What then?* Some Gk. text eds. and trs. make a break here. Nestle[25], a space after v 17, with 18–26 as a paragraph. NA[26,27], space after v 17, with 18abc (*Ti gar . . . chairō*) a conclusion to vv 12–18; then 18d (*alla kai charēsomai*) begins a new paragraph through 1:26. UBSGNT, two paragraphs, 12–14, 15–26, no extra space in 17–18. We follow NA[26,27] and (N)RSV. The opening question is elliptical. Neut. sg., interrog. pron. *tis, ti* (BDAG 1.a.β.ח) + conj. *gar* ("continuative," DA 330), indicating a cause or reason, "for," as often in questions (BDAG *gar* 1.f., transitional). *gar* may be omitted in Eng. or expressed by *then* or "Pray, what?" Loh. 47 n 2, "a formula from cultured diction." Cf. Rom 3:3, "What then is the situation?" "What difference does it matter?" (BDF #299.3), "What are we to think?" (O'B 106), or even "Well, what of it?" Cf. Thrall 1962:44. *gar* connects 18a "in a sort of 'explanatory' way, 'For (even in light of those mentioned in v 17) what does it matter?' " (Fee 124 n 36).

1:18b. *Simply that, in every way, either under pretense or in truth, Christ is being set forth in preaching.* Depends on the elliptical question in 18a. Complicated by textual variants (see end of this note) and the adv. *plēn*, here a conj. (rendered *Simply*), + *hoti, that*, to introduce the content of Paul's conclusion. Basically meaning "only," *plēn* (see J. Blomqvist 1969:75–100) can stand at the beginning of a cl. as here (ATR 1187, cf. 646). It can have an adversative sense (BDAG 1.a; Luke 22:22, "but woe . . ."); Thrall 1962:20–21; Fee 124 n 36, but he allows

"In any case" or NIV's "The important thing is . . . ," *plēn* breaks off a discussion and emphasizes what is important, 1 Cor 11:11; Phil 3:16, 4:14 (on which, see NOTES); BDAG *plēn* 1.c for these passages and "perhaps" 1:18. Cf. ZG; ATR 1187; BDF #449.2; DA 329, "a marker of contrast . . . to correct possible misunderstandings." O'B 97 prefers "The significant thing is that. . . ." Under 1.d, *plēn hoti*, BAGD opts for "except that," as at Acts 20:23 and "perhaps" Phil 1:18, "What then will come of it except that . . . ?" K. Beyer 122 n 2 suggests "an emphatic *hoti*," as at 3:12; here, "What then? In any case, it is so, that. . . ." Textually, *plēn hoti*, read in many MSS, is adopted by Nestle[25], NA[26,27], and UBSGNT (no note). MS B and Sy[p] read *hoti* by itself. D Ψ the Koine tradition Sy[h], *plēn* alone (hence KJV, "notwithstanding"). *plēn hoti* could conflate the two readings, but more likely each variant has omitted one word from the original *plēn hoti*. The TRANSLATION conveys Paul's focus on his conclusion by *Simply* (NRSV "Just this, that Christ is proclaimed . . .").

in every way. panti tropō[i], dat. sg., *pas* (BDAG 5), "every kind of," cf. 1:9; + dat. sg. of *tropos*, "manner, way, kind, guise," dat. of manner, ATR 530, cf. 487; BDF #198.4, cf. 160; GNTG 3:241, a stereotyped phrase; perhaps even "in any and every way" *Christ is being set forth in preaching* (same vb. as in v 17, implied in v 16; see NOTE there). Two ways are indicated for the two groups in vv 15–17: they preach *either* in one way *or* another. On *eite . . . eite* see BDF #446; 454.3; BAGD *ei* VI.13; BDAG 6.o. *ei* ("if") + *te* (enclitic "and") (P[46] actually reads *ei . . . eite*), in classical Gk., the papyri, and LXX, "if . . . if," "whether . . . or," often without a vb. (GNTG 3:333; 1 Cor 8:5; 2 Cor 5:10; in a sequence of more than two items, 1 Cor 3:22; Rom 12:6–8).

under pretense. Dat. of manner (ATR 530), from *prophasis* (once each in Mark, Luke, Acts, and John, plus 1 Thess 2:5 and here in the NT). A classical Gk. term, not in the LXX but common in the papyri (MM 555), from vb. *prophainō*, "show forth, declare," for an actual motive or reason (BDAG 1); in medical writers, "(initial) manifestation, cause" (TLNT 3:204 n 2; 206 n 10). Cf. John 15:22. More commonly a **falsely alleged motive, *pretext, ostensible reason, excuse*** (BDAG 2). Five of the 6 NT examples (plus textually secondary Matt 23:14) fit here. All dat., adverbial (manner, circumstance), pejorative: Mark 12:40 par Luke 20:47; Acts 27:30; Paul and his mission team did not come to the Thessalonians "with a pretext for greed" (*prophasei pleonexias*, 1 Thess 2:5). In 1:18 those who preach with impure motivation act "under pretext." TLNT 3:204–6, "This dichotomy between true and false motives is classical" (Dem. Cor. 225; 206 n 8). To speak with pretended motives is often linked with jealousy and envy (v 15); examples in Spicq n 7, the purpose in Phil 1 was "to make the apostle's chains heavier . . . to supplant him and undermine his authority." See (3) COMMENT n 21.

in truth. The second group preaches *in truth*, dat of manner, from *alētheia*, 47x in the Pauline corpus. = (1) "truthfulness" (1 Cor 5:8); (2) "truth," in opposition to falsehood, a designation of the gospel (Gal 2:5,14; 5:7); (3) reality, in contrast to appearance (BDAG puts 1:18 here, along with Rom 2:2). Bultmann (TDNT 1:232–51) and others make much of etymology (*alpha* privative [BDF #117.1] + *lanthanō/lēthō*, a vb. that means "hide"; therefore, "not hidden," "what is seen, expressed, or disclosed"), plus the Heb. background in *'ĕmeth*, "truth, faithfulness, reliability." Paul, it is claimed, was true to a Hebraic sense, not a Gk. philosophical one (T. Boman; D. J. Theron). Challenged by A. C. Thiselton (*NIDNTT* 3:874–902) on etymology (875) and *'ĕmeth* (880). Cf. also H. Hübner in *EDNT* 1:57–60; *TLNT* 1:66–86. *alētheia[i]* at Phil 1:18 needs little such analysis, the only instance of *alēth*-terminology in Phil., except for the adj. at 4:8 (see NOTE on the Greco-Roman moral sense there). In 1 Thess, only the adv. occurs ("really God's word," 2:13). The three references in Gal (above) are to the Pauline gospel as "truth." The terms are frequent in 1 and esp. 2 Cor, in Rom primarily in 1:18–3:20 (see Hübner 59–60 on chronological development). At Phil 1:18 "'sincerity' or 'honesty'" on the part of the preachers (cf. 2 Cor 7:14); it reveals the "real state of affairs" (*TDNT* 1:243), "honestly" in contrast to "hypocritically" (*prophasei, TLNT* 1:74 and n 35). Hence Hübner: "the *truthfulness* of the one who proclaims, . . . contrasted with subterfuge" (1:59). Cf. Thuc. 6.33.2. The focus "is on the different ways in which Christ is proclaimed (the topic of vv. 15–17)" (*DA* 382).

1:18c. *So over this fact I rejoice. kai*, "and" (KJV, [N]RSV), may have a stronger sense: BDAG *kai* 1.c, *and so*, to explain or comment on what has gone before (BDF #442.2), or something "surprising or unexpected or noteworthy" (BDAG *kai* 1.b.η). Cf. ATR 1182–83; Phil 4:7. P⁴⁶ adds *alla* before *kai*, from 18d *alla kai charēsomai* (Gnilka 63 n 29; Fee 117 n 4).

over this fact. en toutō[i], neut. of *houtos*, to refer to what precedes (BDAG 1.b.α; *DA* 258 n 381). Supply *fact*, i.e., that Christ is proclaimed (O'B 106 n 46; Ware 1996: 216 n 120; KJV "herein"; RSV, NRSV "in that"). *en* + dat. can, after *chairō*, mean "rejoice over" (BAGD 873, col. a; BDAG 1074) or, less likely, be connected with 18b and 19, "I rejoice . . . that this will turn out for my deliverance" (873 col. b; 1074); cf. 4:10 *I rejoiced . . . that now . . . you have revived your concern for me. . . .* Not like the *en kyriō[i]* construction at 3:1; 4:4a and 10. *chairō* + *epi* is more common than *chairō* + *en* (otherwise only at Col 1:24 in the Pauline corpus; 4 examples with *epi* in acknowledged letters; references in BDAG *chairō* 1); Webber ([2] Bibl. **joy**) 286 n 53, "This [use of *en*] probably denotes the more general situation that gives rise to joy, rather than the immediate event." Rejecting Loh.'s martyrdom theory, Webber 287 concludes Paul rejoices "simply that Christ is proclaimed."

I rejoice. See NOTE on 1:4 *with joy; chairō*-terms 16x in Phil. First instance of the vb. in the canonical letter, but in Letter A at 4:10 (1st per.; "epistolary rejoicing"). The basic sense is "rejoice, be glad" (BDAG). Not Loh.'s "joy in martyrdom" but "a Church basis . . . growing out of the fact that Christ is proclaimed" (Conzelmann *TDNT* 9:369); 18d, *I shall rejoice*, "directs our gaze to the future judgment and the account . . . to be given, 2:16; 4:1 . . . not just preliminary joy" but "future experience as joy in the present." "Salvation does not depend on Paul's human destiny" (369–70 n 97). 18c deals with present fact, Christ is being proclaimed. Paul rejoices.

COMMENT

Phil 1:12–26 begins the body of Paul's letter (B and canonical four-ch. Phil). It describes his situation in prison in Ephesus (INTRO. VII.A), specifically the prospects for the gospel (1:12–18c) and for himself, a matter of life or death (1:18d–26). 1:12–26 begins and ends with the key term *progress* (1:12, 25). 1:12–18c is a subunit (so, e.g., Schenk 129–43). For parallels see Francis/ Sampley #239, p. 278. For how editors of the Gk. text and trs. paragraph a break at or in v 18, see the NOTE on 18a *What then?* The most difficult issue is the identity of those in vv 15–18 who *set forth Christ in preaching* but with varying motivations; see B.3, below.

A. FORMS, SOURCES, AND TRADITIONS

1. *Body Opening.* Following the Prescript (Phil 1:1–2; [1] COMMENT A) and *Prooimion* (Phil 1:3–11; [2] COMMENT A) comes the letter *body.* "Body-opening" is appropriate for 1:12–18a (J. L. White 1972:73, cf. 77–79, 87–88; Doty 43), perhaps "body-closing" for 2:19–30, but "body-middle" (for Phil 1:18b–2:18) is more vague.[1] L. Alexander 1989:88 suggested simply "the topics covered"; 1:12–26 = "Reassurance about the sender." But the topics cover more than that. Cf. Murphy-O'Connor 1995a ([1] Bibl.) 64–65; J. L. White 1971a ([2] Bibl.); *WDNTECLR* 270–71.

2. *"Disclosure Form"?* Phil 1:12 has been called a "disclosure form(ula)," *I wish (boulomai) you to come to know, brothers and sisters, that . . .* (Mullins 1964; White 1971a:93); Roller ([1] Bibl.) 65–66, 467 n 301, "Kontexteingang" (10 papyrus examples, *thelō* "I wish" + *ginōskein*). In response to J. T. Sanders 1962 ([2] Bibl.) on transition from thanksgiving to letter body, Mullins (from a hint in Exler) examined some nineteen papyrus examples of (1) *thelō* ("I wish") + (2) the person addressed, (3) a vb. like "know" in the infin., (4) information introduced by a *hoti* cl. (cf. MM 286 and 115), and (5) a voc. like *adelphoi.* Mullins concluded these elements appear in a fairly rigid order in nonliterary papyri, but the NT was less rigid. The "disclosure" or "petition" form (Mullins 1962 [(2) Bibl.]) seemed a clue that the "thanksgiving" in a letter was completed.[2] Application to the NT was less successful. Paul's closest example with *thelō* is 1 Cor 11:3, *not* following an epistolary thanksgiving. Phil 1:12 with *boulomai* is singular. Mullins' formula is lacking in 1

---

[1] Bloomquist 117 has 1:15–2:18, 3:1–4:7, and 4:8–20 as body-middles. White 1972 treated only Phil 1–2 (thus unsatisfactory for the four-ch. letter and most partition theories). To suggest that 1:18 *What then?* provides "background" (72–74) to 1:12–18a is misleading; 18abc is a conclusion about the situation sketched there. D. F. Watson 2003 sought to set aside possible epistolary "conventions and formulas" as "misidentified" or too restricted, and (inadvertently) showed how frail markers for a "middle" are.

[2] Gk. texts and trs. in Hunt/Edgar, *Select Papyri* (LCL 1) ##111, 120, 125, 126, 134, the first and last of which are given in Fee 106 n 2: "I wish you to know, mother, that I arrived in Rome . . ." (2nd cent. A.D.), and ". . . in Alexandria, safe and sound" (3rd cent. A.D.; all examples seem from these cents.).

Thess 2:1, where it might have been expected. 1 Cor 1:10 has *parakalō* + *hina*. "Disclosure form" can sound overly theological, suggesting revelation, or "rather trite" (Collange 63; contrast O'B 89). There is also a formula (MM), "I do not want you not to know" (*agnoein*, BDAG 1), 1 Thess 4:13; 1 Cor 10:1, cf. 20; 12:1; 2 Cor 1:8 ("we"); Rom 1:13 and 11:25; cf. 2 Cor 2:11; + Col 2:1. Mullins found 9 NT instances of "disclosure" only by claiming examples from this list plus 1 Thess 2:1.

The "disclosure form" met with considerable acceptance (White 1972:121–22; 1984:1743–44; R. P. Martin 1976:71; Edart 75). Was Paul "establishing a new model" that 2nd- and 3rd-cent. letter-writers would follow? No, Hawth. 33 decided, he was "adhering to a standard formula seemingly characteristic only of personal, intimate letters written in the first century or earlier." Cf. Silva 69; O'B 86, esp. n 4. Schenk 132–33 prefers "opening formula" transmitting news. It comes directly after a prayer report only here in Phil 1:12. 2 Cor 1:8 is the closest parallel as to position, after a prayer (1:3–7), but reads, "We do not wish you to be ignorant. . . ." *I want you to come to know . . .* at 1:12 does make a transition. To call it a form-critical category, the "disclosure formula," over-identifies it. Fee 106, the words reflect "letters of friendship" or how a client informs patrons of circumstances (110 n 4); but Mullins' papyrus examples do not fit that elusive letter-type; no claim for the phrase in Fitzgerald *ABD* 5:320 or 1996, except that friends would "provide information about their own situation (1:12–26)" (320a). The "form" remains debated.

3. Autobiography. 1:12ff. is characterized by *1st per. sg.* (vb. 1:12, 18, *I wish, I rejoice*, an *inclusio*; "my" 1:13, 14, 17), on into 1:18d–26; hence, "first person singular narrative" (Fee 106 n 1), in contrast to 1:27ff., 2nd pl., impv. (Schenk 129). Or "autobiography" (Rigaux 1968:122); *peri-auto-logia*, self-praise (Bittasi 34). Plut. *Mor.* 539A–547F). "I/me" here is not paradigmatic, but Paul may be preparing the way for what he will say to the Philippians about the "struggle" (*agōn*) in 1:27–30. Cf. *WDNTECLR* 68–70.

4. Rhetorical Factors. Russell 1982:299–301 saw 1:12–2:30 as "the body," begun with a "disclosure formula" (1:12), but allowed that "[t]here is almost as much irregularity as regularity in 'the Pauline letter form' " (306). Swift 241–43 took 1:12–26 as "biographical prologue" or "biographical narrative," *narratio* (from H. D. Betz, *Gal.* 14–15, 58–62, for Gal 1:12–2:14). Thus rhetorical terminology began to enter into outlines for 1:12ff. Cf. Witherington 42, Edart 75–77. Watson 1988b:61–65, 1:3–26 is *exordium; narratio* comes in 1:27–30. L. G. Bloomquist 124–25, 147–51: 1:12–14 is *narratio*, 15–18a *partitio*,[3] + double *propositio* (on

---

[3] Does 1:15–18a fit Cic. (*Inv.*1.31–34) on *partitio* (clarifies a controversy by showing agreements and disagreements with opponents and explaining topics concisely)? Quintillian's understanding (enumeration of propositions in a lucid order, *Inst.* 4.5)? Cf. *Rhet. ad Herennium*; F. Hughes 38–40. *partitio* moves from deliberative to forensic rhetoric; this Bloomquist says Paul did "wittingly or unwittingly." Cf. Bittasi 36–37 n 58.

two kinds of preaching). Murphy-O'Connor 1995a ([1] Bibl.) 65–83, esp. 73–74, speaks of "misuse of rhetorical schema." Perhaps "a secretary composed 1:1–2:30, while the hand of Paul added the subscription of 3:1–4:23" (Bahr [(16) Bibl.] 300). Lack of agreement is apparent.[4] Cf. *WDNTECLR* 312, 416–18.

1:12–18c can be described as *narratio* (Gk. *diēgēsis*, [Ps.-]Oecumenius for 1:12–26); 1:18d–26 partakes more of *pathos* (Watson 1988b). Paul departs from his usual letter form in that he presents current circumstances up front, rather then later, because of the grave charges he faces (Bockmuehl 71–72). He writes to a *public* (the house churches), not an individual, and reflects *speech forms* (rhetoric), to create an ethos for hearing.[5] 1:12–30 can be termed "epistolary self-recommendation," providing at the outset the apostle's function and brief presentation of his gospel, with rejection of opposing views.[6] Contrast letters in antiquity from prisoners asserting their innocence, needs, etc. (Michaelis 1925; G. Friedrich 1978:225; U. B. Müller 51, citing PPetr. 3:36 = Rapske 1994:213, 327). Further details about Paul's situation could have been provided orally by Epaphroditus (2:25–30), the bearer of Letter B, or by Timothy (Walter 38).

5. Vocabulary from Missionary Preaching. 1:12–18c has no OT material, no early Christian liturgical tradition. Phrases about *the word* (14; Loh. 44), *Christ* (15), and *preaching* (17, 18, implied in 16) are "expression of the kerygma" or *the gospel* (1:12, 16), "the central object of expression" in the section, set forth in an eight-fold way[7]; 12–18c is a self-enclosed, unified subtext (Schenk 129–30), focused on proclamation. From that and the *progress* of the Philippians in (the) faith will arise admonitions for a unified community in the face of opposition (1:27–30).

6. Greco-Roman Terminology. Much of the vocabulary is from the Greco-Roman world. See NOTES ON *progress* (1:12); *envy* and *strife* (v 15); *self-interest* (v 17);

---

[4] Against notions of 1:12–14 as "the rhetorical heart of the letter," see Oakes 2001:122–23. Holloway 2001: 102–8 finds five *"topoi* from contemporary consolation": "things that matter" (1:10) are illustrated by "the progress of the gospel" (and his own chains); "misfortunes often advance the cause of things that really matter"; "hardship enhances one's reputation" (1:13); "misfortune makes one an example to others" (1:14); joy "in the midst of crisis." J. S. Vos 2001:59–60, 83 extends the idea of military language in 1:27–30 (see [5] COMMENT A.4.b) to 1:12–26; 2002:141–42, the rhetoric of success or victory covers a weak position with hyperbolic speech about present and future success (1:12–18a, 18b–26). Respondents questioned this emphasis (2001:78, 80–81, 86).

[5] Schnider/Stenger ([1] Bibl.) 50–59; K. Berger, ANRW 2.25.2:1353–54; 1984a:268–71, 273, "Apostolikon," with "I"-style, on Christian existence and suffering; a "speech act," R. F. Collins 2000, in light of 1 Thess 5:27.

[6] Schnider/Stenger ([1] Bibl.) 52–53; Berger, ANRW 2.25.2:1353; U. B. Müller 48; cf. Rom 1:13–15; Gal 1:8–11; 1 Thess 2:1–12; Phlm 7–8; for Harnisch's use of a similar phrase for 3:2ff., see (12) COMMENT B.

[7] 1:12 progress for *the gospel*; 1:13 *in Christ* it has become clear; 1:14 to speak *the word*; 1:15 are proclaiming *Christ* (an abbreviated metonym); 1:16 for the defense of *the gospel*; 1:17 set forth *Christ* in preaching (like 15, a metonym); 1:18 *Christ* is being set forth in preaching (pass. voice); 1:18 over *this fact* (*toutō[i]*, anaphoric summary). Fee 111, "the language of evangelism." Cf. also 1:25 "progress and joy in *faith.*"

pretense (v 18b); *goodwill* in v 15 is not a "purely Biblical word" (Vincent 19). On honor/shame aspects, see B.1, n 12, below. Were some terms derived from his audience or the "rival preachers"?

7. Chiastic Structures. For Ware's AB(C)B′A′ form in 1:13, see NOTE on *and to all the rest.* For vv 15–17, see NOTE on 1:16–17 (Jeremias 1958:147 = *Abba* 279; Bloomquist 151; Richards 1991 [(1) Bibl.] 208), A-B-C-C′-B′-A′ chiasmus in 1:15–17. Hawth. 36 a double chiasmus:

v 15	A envy	B goodwill
vv 16–17	B′ love	A′ self-interest
v 18a	A pretense	B truth To that could be added, as pendants,
vv 16–17	B because they know . . .	A because they suppose . . .
	I am put here	to stir up trouble
plus in v 17		A not with a pure motivation

The (negative) description of group A is fuller than that for group B.

More elaborate are O'B 87, 97–98 (antithetical parallelism, chiasmus, and an *inclusio*); Ware 1996:198 on 15 and 18; H. J. Rose (see [15] NOTE on 4:7), rhythmic *clausulae* in the antithetical parallelism, 15–18 (BDF 487: such a search "is a needless waste of time," but cf. 489–91 and Lausberg #985–1052); and Schenk 131–32, 138–41, six negative themes (envy and strife, self-interest, not with a pure motivation, trouble, pretense) and four positive ones (goodwill, love, defense [of the gospel], truth); U. B. Müller 53: v 16 = positives; 17, negatives. Schoon-Janßen 143 was content to speak of antitheses in 1:15ab and 1:16–17, typical of the diatribe style; *DA* 261 n 395. Cf. Edart 71.

a. *Vv 15–18, an Excursus?* Some see 15–18c as an aside. Thus Vincent 18; Dib. 65–66, the two groups in 15–18 had nothing to do with *the brothers and sisters* in v 14, but rather reflect experiences with other people in various places over the years. So K. Barth 29–30; Gnilka 59–60 (a caesura after v 14); Hendriksen 71; Bruce 19; and, among others, Schmithals 1972:75 n 45. But Hawth. 36 finds no grammatical reason for a break at 15 (*tines* refers back to *adelphōn* in 14); J. S. Vos 62–63; Fee 118; Edart 78 n 26. *most of the brothers and sisters* may have become confident in their witness, but "a minority has remained unmoved." The two groups are probably "subsections of the majority" (O'B 98). Ware 1996:199–200, *tines men* of 1:15 is a "group excepted from" the majority. Fee 119, 124, v 15 strikes an "unexpected note," 15–17 are "something of an aside," but the vv too interconnected with the context to be an excursus (123 n 32). Schenk 141–42 concludes 15–18a is better called a "supplementary report" (additional information, 137; U. B. Müller 53), not about groups in Philippi (so Schmithals 1972:74–75 n 45), but information shared by Paul about Ephesus to explain his joy (v 18) and thanksgiving.

b. *Other Structures?* Schenk 130–31 analyzed v 14 as three lines in Gk., each with 13 syllables, if *tou theou* is read in the final line; he then rejected this as an argument for reading *tou theou*; the context is not "elevated prose." Edart 64–66, 71 lists possible literary devices.

8. *Macrostructure?* Do notions of a chiastic macrostructure for Phil (INTRO. VI.B n 3) shed light on 1:12–26? P. Wick organized a concentric structure around 2:5–11, including (p. 62, Gk. on 204–9):

> A. 1:12–26 (block a¹)   Theme: Rejoice!   3:1–16 (block a²)

The key (39–41) was the *chara/chairō* terminology ("rejoice!") and references to opponents in a¹ and a²; cf. Wick pp. 41–43, 69–73, 85–101. "Joy" appears at 1:18 and 3:1. Some vocabulary like *adelphoi* is used in both passages. But his list on 42–43 is not impressive for 1:12–18c.[8] Wick's section on the relation of the hymn to 1:12ff. yields little,[9] his treatment of 1:12–18 does not provide impressive support for his overall theory. Luter/Lee (see INTRO. VI.B n 1) parallel B (1:12–26 "Comfort/Example") with B′ (4:6–9 "Comfort/Example"), unconvincingly[10]; Bittasi 210, 1:12–26 with 4:2–9; C. W. Davis, 1:3–26 with 4:10–20. Such proposals are generally contradictory, the results meager (Murphy-O'Connor 1995a [(1) Bibl.] 86–95).

For Letter B, a chiastic structure (cf. Aspen) will be proposed in (9) COMMENT A.2: 1:12–26 (A) relates to 2:19–30 (A′), news about Paul (*ta kat' eme,* 1:12) and hoped-for news about the Philippians (*ta peri hymōn,* 2:19); the gospel's progress + mission plans = common denominator.

9. *Summary.* Paul, using the vocabularies of mission preaching and the Greco-Roman world, narrates his current situation. The opening of the body of the letter employs an initial phraseology not uncommon in papyrus letters and his own idiom, though not exactly a "disclosure formula." The artfully constructed section is framed by the words *I wish* and *I rejoice* (1:12, 18b) and in its larger scope by the term *progress* (1:12, 25).

---

[8] E.g., *alla* at 1:18 and 3:7, 8; *ginesthai* at 1:13 "become clear" and 3:6 "being blameless"; each unit is a "self-report" by Paul. But in 1:12ff. "events affecting me" have to do with the progress of the gospel as currently preached by others, whereas in 3:4–16 (+ 17?) the account is about Paul's own experience with the gospel as faith-righteousness. 3:2ff. lacks any reference to Paul's imprisonment, as Wick admits (89). As to "opponents" (*Gegner*) in each passage, those in 1:14–17 are nothing like the "dogs" of 3:2ff. Wick speaks for 1:14–17 of "brothers" (86, 87) and distinguishes them from opponents elsewhere in the letter (91 point 4). He offers nothing on the identity of those in 1:14–18. For the opponents of 3:2–16 he inclines to "Judaizing Christians" (with Mearns, who, however, draws on all of 3:1–21, not just vv 1–16), but they play only a secondary role in the letter (91), exemplifying "negative patterns" (100) for the Christian life. Schoon-Janßen 192 spoke of a 'negative example" in 3:2–11, but in contrast to the positive ones in 2:19–30.

[9] Paul's bonds in 1:13 remind Wick 70 of "unfree 'slaves'" (2:7?). Christ's lordship (2:11) as Paul's "ground for joy (1,18)" (70) ignores the reason stated in 1:18c, proclamation of Christ by "other preachers."

[10] Their "center" point (2:17–3:10) is different from that of Wick. Length and analysis of units vary considerably. To claim that their B-B′ layer "describes the results of Paul's partnership with the Philippians" (92; *koinōnia* as theme) misses the involvement of those preaching Christ where Paul is imprisoned. The only link suggested (93) is that "[p]erhaps Paul's time in prison gave him the idea of having the peace of God 'guard' (*phroureō*; i.e., in a military or custodial manner) their hearts and minds (4.7)." But that would be possible at any point in an imprisonment epistle, without invoking chiasm.

B. MEANING AND INTERPRETATION

Material for 1:12–18c *(heuresis)* comes out of the Greco-Roman world and Paul's missionary experience, esp. recent events during imprisonment. The chief difference between reading 1:12–18c as part of Letter B and taking them as part of a four-ch. letter is that, for the latter, one must explain why Paul delays thanking the Philippians for their recent gifts till much later (see [16] COMMENT on 4:10–20, B.3 and A.3 "thankless thanks"). We assume Paul has dealt with that in Letter A, the renewal of Philippian friendship through gifts to him and the question of "patron and client" thereby raised (see [16] COMMENT B.2, and B.1.(A) 3 [d]). In Letter B the apostle takes up his own situation and the threat of death (1:19–24), yet how he rejoices that the gospel goes forward. 1:12–18c is commonly divided into two parts (so [N]RSV; text segmentation in Schenk), vv 12–14 and 15–18c (1 and 2 below). 15–18 are not an excursus (COMMENT A.7.a, above). The identity of the two groups of preachers in Ephesus will be treated in 3 below.

1. *Paul Reports How, During and Despite Imprisonment, the Gospel Goes on Advancing (1:12–14).* A shift from what Paul prays for the Philippians (1:3–11) to information about himself, *events affecting me,* not so much a narration about what's been happening as a positive assessment of *progress for the gospel* (12; cf. 7) in a twofold way. First, it is clear to those who encounter Paul that his *bonds are for Christ* (13); second, most believers there are *daring fearlessly to speak the word.* In both ways there is witnessing. We learn here more about *the word* and results *in Christ* than about the legal process and how dire the threat of death (1:20–23).

Signs of transition from the *prooimion* and a major break between v 11 and v 12 (Black 1995:18–19; Fee 109–10) include the "I" form (above, A.3, yet with 1:9, cf. 7–8) and address of the Philippians as *adelphoi.*[11] The shift is from *prooimion* or *exordium* to *narratio* or *diēgēsis,* from introduction to the body of the letter-oration; from sharing thanks and hope to imparting information; from praying about the future (*the Day of Christ,* v 10) to interpreting what is happening now *in Christ. I wish you to come to know . . .* parallels phraseology in papyrus letters after the thanksgiving and is akin to Paul's frequent phrase "I do not want you to be ignorant . . . ," an "opening formula" readers in Philippi would recognize, where the writer discloses what is going on currently (see A.2, above). *de* (KJV "but"), connecting v 12 with 11 (see NOTE; first occurrence in Phil), serves as transition (Loh. 39). *events affecting me* is a "topic marker or shifter" (Porter 1993 [Gen. Bibl.] 195). "I want you to know" (NRSV) is equivalent to "Now hear this. . . ."

The first word in Gk. is the infin., "To know, I want you to . . . ," as in the papyri (A.2). Pres. tense, "keep on knowing" or "learn." "Contrary to rumors" (Bengel).

---

[11] Evidence in associations is considerable (Harland). Much has been made of Paul's sibling language as a vision of equality, in contrast to patriarchy (Sandnes 1997; Bartchy 1999; Aasgaard 2002, 2003; Horrell), often fictive siblings. (But in Phil actual households were likely involved.) The address *adelphoi* promotes solidarity and mutual regard, challenging lack of community (among house churches?). Contrast D. B. Martin in (1) COMMENT B.4.d.

More than just hearing news. What Paul reports the Philippians need to ponder. Interpreted news: what's happening to him has *actually resulted in progress for the gospel.* Can they comprehend the startling results? *to know* (1:12 *ginōskein*) picks up *epignōsis* in the prayer of 1:9 for *perception (and discernment in every situation).* Paul perceives for them the significance of events, he *"reflects a knowledge that is his"* for the Philippians to acquire and *do* (Engberg-Pedersen 2000:110, italics his).

To what precise trouble does Paul allude in 17 *thlipsis* and *bonds?* "One wishes that Paul had been more specific" (Hawth. 33). Rapske 298 thinks Paul addresses "shame concerns" from imprisonment,[12] but there is little of this in what Paul writes, perhaps only in v 20 (NRSV "that I may not be put to shame in any way"). Many see *a turn in Paul's juridical process* and so reconstruct the situation. Gnilka 55, *a new stage in the court case.*[13] Michaelis 19, Jewish opponents in Ephesus had presented his preaching as a menace to the state (cf. Acts 17:5–6; 18:13). Similarly Walter 39, for Ephesus (2 Cor 1:8–10; Acts 19). Perhaps the hearing was delayed, but now the apostle has an opportunity to give his witness. Grounds for such a reconstruction: *the defense and confirmation of the gospel* (1:7) and how it has become publicly apparent that Paul's *bonds are for Christ* (1:13). Michaelis (18), the court and wider circles recognize that Paul is "a prisoner in Christ."

Other reconstructions (cf. Hawth. 34): The events refer to his destiny *(Geschick)* and fate *(Schicksal),* martyrdom and witness through sufferings in 1:12–26 (Loh. 38–39, cf. 36–37); cf. vv 20–23, Paul's desire "to depart and be with Christ." Loh.'s massive thematizing has generally been rejected. Others, Paul's *"determination to secure release* for himself, a change of mind that may have angered and alienated his radical followers (Collange)" (Hawth. 34, italics added). Cf. vv 24–26 ("I will remain . . . with all of you"). Paul has taken the initiative during his legal process in Ephesus of revealing his *Roman citizenship* to the authorities (Collange 51–53;

---

[12] Rapske 298–312 treats "shame concerns in Acts" re bonds, esp. for Philippi (16:37–39) and cites 2 Tim 1:8, 11–12, 16 and 2:9 (cf. Rom 1:16, not ashamed of the gospel). In contrast with Tajra (INTRO. II Bibl.) 28 (Paul appeals to the Valerian and Porcian laws of 509 and 248 B.C., respectively, on treatment of Roman citizens) and Haenchen 1971:503–4 (Lucan apology), Rapske has Paul protesting "procedural irregularities" (302) as he tries to "claw back some dignity after having been deeply shamed" (303). This shame still existed as he wrote 1 Thess 2:2. But cf. Malherbe on 2:1–2, AB 32B, esp. 143 and 157. Possible honor-and -shame terms in Phil include *aischynē,* shame (3:19); *aischynomai,* be put to shame (1:20); *doxa,* BDAG 3 **honor as enhancement or recognition of status or performance,** praise (1:11; 2:11; 4:20), prestige (3:19), cf. 3:21; 4:19; *epainos,* praise (1:11; 4:8); *kauchomai, kauchēma,* boast (vb. 3:3; noun 1:26; 2:16). Note Downing's cautions on some treatments. See (9) NOTES on 2:29b.

[13] Gnilka cites esp. Ewald 65 = Wohl. 73. Less clearly Vincent 16; Tillmann, J. J. Müller, Beare 57, and Hawth. 34. According to Ewald 63–65 and 17–19 = Wohl. 71–73, 20, the pl. in v 12, *events,* refers to his legal process and what has resulted (*elēlythen,* perf. tense), a move after two years in a hired house (Acts 28:30) to a praetorian barracks on the Palatine [see NOTE on 1:13 *Praetorium;* this interpretation had already been abandoned by Lft.] and an imminent hearing where the apostle can speak out. Similarly Kennedy EGT 423; cf. Lüdemann 1989 (INTRO. II Bibl.) 266–67. But this "beloved . . . explanation" is more than the text states (Phil 1:12–26 is not *custodia libera et aperta,* Paul under arrest but "free and unhindered"; U. B. Müller 50–51, Paul looks to a [public] juridical session where the theme of the gospel can enter in).

we agree), just as he did in Acts 16:37 in Philippi. He was confident he would be released. This step irked detractors (group A among those proclaiming Christ), who saw in Paul's conduct "an attitude of infidelity to the Cross," indeed of "cowardice" (51), their "[r]adical, doctrinaire commitment" versus Paul's "'realistic,' opportunistic commitment" (52). This explanation assumes the Acts tradition (16:35–40; 22:25–28). Rapske 83–112 agrees Paul possessed Tarsian and Roman citizenship ("entirely defensible," 108), as does Tellbe 2001:76. O'B 90, Collange's view is "highly suggestive but difficult to prove." See below, 3.j, esp. n 39.

Hawth. 34 claims Paul faced "a *lengthy prison term*"; cf. Walter 39. Against this view: Paul talks of dying soon (1:20–23), but expects to come to the Philippians again (1:25–26; 2:23–24)—neither fits a long period in jail. Neither Acts nor Phil refer to a "lengthy prison term." (The two years at the end of Acts 28 do not involve a prison sentence.) This view and Loh.'s martyrdom theory can be safely set aside. A new stage in the judicial process and/or specific appeal to his Roman citizenship remain possibilities.

Paul says little or nothing in what follows about "what has happened to me" (NRSV). He dwells instead on interpreting the outcome positively for the gospel. "To the question . . . how it is with *him* an apostle *must* react with information as to how it is with the *Gospel*" (K. Barth 26, seconded by Gnilka 56). Paul's words exemplify "apostolic speech"; see (2) COMMENT A.5, apostleship and message (gospel, grace) as in Rom 1: 1, 5, 16–17. The information and reflection in Phil 1:12b–18c are chiefly about *the gospel*.

Reconstructing the situation involves how one takes *mallon* in v 12; see NOTE on *actually*. To render "rather" (KJV) implies people were "looking for bad news" (Kennedy, EGT 423). To render "more" suggests some expected him to embrace suffering (Collange 51) and martyrdom (Loh.) more than he did. Or was Paul's imprisonment hindering mission work more, nullifying an agreement with the Philippians ("contractual agreement" theory, discussed and rejected in COMMENT B.2 on 1:3–11)? Or was there a rift between Paul and the Philippians? So Capper 208–9: Paul was "in breach of contract." But Paul argues his imprisonment actually serves the gospel. "'[M]irror-reading' of a most unfortunate kind," Fee 111 n 18, cf. 7–8 and 436 n 4; Bockmuehl 72. The contractual and rift theories can be set aside.

Paul's words are an attention-getting cliff-hanger. 1:12 suggests, "To know, I want you to, brothers and sisters, that events affecting me have to a greater degree. . . ." As we read on, the sense is ". . . have *actually* . . . turned out for . . ." (*mallon*, contrary to expectations, in a positive way). The surprising shift is from his own prospects to those of the gospel; the word *progress* is unexpected.

In treating 1:12 (and 25), forget modern ideas of "progress." *prokopē* was thoroughly Gk., philosophical, a tech. term in Stoicism. No Heb. equivalent, the few LXX examples chiefly under Hellenistic influence (Sir 51:17; 2 Macc 8:8). The Gk. term was taken over by Jos. and esp. Philo;[14] it became a loan-word in the rab-

---

[14] S. K. Stowers, *A Rereading of Romans: Justice, Jews, and Gentiles* (New Haven: Yale, 1994) claims Philo presents the Jews as a people who have mastered "the sort of virtues valorized in the Augustan

bis. It referred (1) to the *individual's moral progress in virtue*, as in treatises on *prokopē* by Plut. and Epict. Advancement from folly and vice to wisdom and virtue stemmed from one's disposition, will, choices, instruction from philosophy teachers, and influences and examples from friends. In earlier Stoicism one either had certain virtues or did not, often as a result of sudden change. Later Stoicism laid emphasis on progressing toward virtue, Keep on advancing! (There could be regressing too.) The widely known question-and-answer dialogue on the *Tabula of Cebes*[15] depicted moral progress, though it does not employ the term *prokopē*. Such ideas were likely known in Philippi and may be pertinent to what Paul says in Phil 3:13–14 about pressing forward and upward to the goal. *prokopē* also applied (2) to *progress in Greek science, technology, and culture* and *the rise to power by Rome*, progress based on Roman valor and divine fortune, part of a supposed administration (*oikonomia*) of the universe by Zeus and the gods for good. (There also existed protests against such deification of Roman hegemony.[16]) Early Christian attitudes toward the Roman Empire varied from the positive view in Rom 13:1–7 (reflecting the OT; cf. Jer. 29) to the negative assessment in apocalyptic writings like Rev 13. Philo's extensive use of *prokopē*-terms reflects the first sense, "the person who progresses," and probably also (*Exsecr.* 164–72 = LCL 8:388–423) the broader sense of betterment of the world and the whole human race.

Paul used the term for how he once had been "making progress in Judaism" (Gal 1:14), a Gk. concept to describe his zeal as a Pharisee. Rom 13:12a, "the night has progressed, the day is near," applied the vb. to the Christian's situation eschatologically.[17] In Phil see also 1:25, *your progress and joy in faith* and COMMENTS on 2:12–14 and 3:11–14. At 1:12 Paul likely picks up a concept familiar to his audience. When he says *events have actually resulted in progress . . .* , the Philippians might have expected "*prokopē* in Paul's moral development through imprisonment or suffering." Or their own advance, ethically; he had prayed in 1:9–11 for their abounding in knowledge and discernment with regard to things that matter. Paul speaks of advance not in his own spirituality (through prison and suffering) or in virtues for the Philippians or advance of Rome to dominance but of the progress of the gospel. This progress will be the topic through v 18c, and later too.

Paul gives two reasons in vv 13–14 why he concludes events about him have turned out, rather surprisingly, for the advance of the *euangelion* in Ephesus, where he is imprisoned. The vv state results of Paul's imprisonment *and* explain

---

ideology" of the Empire (57, citing *Leg.* 13–14, 143–44). For Stowers, Paul's Letter to the Romans also teaches self-mastery, beyond the Law, of the Augustan "gospel" of virtues, justice, and piety.

[15] *The Tabula of Cebes*, ed. J. T. Fitzgerald/L. M. White, SBLTT 24, Graeco-Roman Series 7 (Chico, CA: 1983), deals with a temple painting about how some in life pursue betterment and virtue and others drift from the upward path into pleasures, false education, and disaster. K. Seddon, *Epictetus' Handbook and the Tablet of Cebes* (London: Routledge, 2005).

[16] Cf. H. Fuchs, *Der geistige Widerstand gegen Rom in der antiken Welt* (Berlin: de Gruyter, 1938, 2nd ed. 1964). E.g., Tac., *Agr.* 30 = LCL *Tacitus . . . Agricola* 219–21, "To plunder, butcher, steal, these things they misname 'empire'; they make a desolation and they call it 'peace'"; Sen., *Clem.* 1.3.5.

[17] See also Luke 2:52; 1 Tim 4:15 (individual progress); 2 Tim 2:16; 3:9, 13 (the advance of heresy).

the *prokopē* of the gospel. 1:13 concerns non-Christians; 1:14, believers. See NOTES on 13 *The results are first that . . .* and 14 *second, that most of the brothers and sisters. . . .*

The massive unity that runs through vv 12–18 about proclaiming *gospel/Christ/ the word* ("missionary preaching vocabulary," A.5, above) is least specific in v 13. But *in Christ* is a functional synonym for "gospel" (Schenk 134; see NOTE on 1:13 *in Christ*, which functions more flexibly than a Pauline "formula" *en Christō[i]* that is often hard to classify). Similarly with *in the Lord* (v 14; see the NOTE about debate over exact meaning). A rule of thumb on "in Christ" + the indic. and "in the Lord" + the impv. does not hold up here; Paul may be using familiar phrases with a certain rhetorical freedom. *in the Lord* may belong with the eight ways in which Paul's central theme is set forth. The gospel word about Christ the Lord dominates all that is said. In v 13 *en Christō[i]* (see NOTE on 1:13 *in Christ*) is taken in the TRANSLATION both as *in Christ*, overarching all of v 13, and as climax of the sentence, *my bonds are for Christ.*

The first outcome is the perception of those in the *Praetorium* and *all the rest:* Paul's *bonds are for Christ.* The same pl. Gk. term appears for *bonds* in vv 13 and 14 and in vv 7 and 17 *imprisonment.* Paul "is silent about himself" (Friedrich NTD 15th ed. 1981:225), not pushing pathos or depicting squalid conditions that prisoners complained about in antiquity.[18] His imprisonment was not apparent in Letter A (4:10–20). The term here *(desmoi)* Paul otherwise employs only in Phlm (vv 10, 13), among the acknowledged letters. But he does not call himself here "a prisoner *(desmios)* of Christ Jesus," as in Phlm 1 and 9. Phil 1 fits with "imprison-ments" *(en phylakais)* mentioned in the catalogues of hardships (see [16] COM-MENT A.4.e, on 4:10–20) in 2 Cor 6:5 and 11:23 ("in prisons, more frequently"). In vv 12–18c, *bonds* is the second most frequent concept after *gospel/Christ/word.* How the two relate is much debated.

The NOTE on *in Christ* discusses reasons for taking *my bonds* not with *en Christō[i]*, but with *it has become clear* "in the Christian sphere" or with the entire cl. ("in the realm of the Christ event," U. B. Müller 50). The trend has been away from KJV's "my bonds in Christ," but trs. still relate *en Christō[i]* with Paul's bonds, though now as predicate and subject: (N)RSV, "my imprisonment is for Christ"; Fee 109; O'B 91–92. To connect *clear* with "in Christ" should not imply a new revelation, shining forth from Paul in his cell (Loh. 40, whoever endures suffering "in Christ" is "bearer" of the revelation of the Crucified yet Risen One; cf. grace, 1:7; the martyr is "a special bearer of God's revelation before public authorities," L. G. Bloomquist 51). If the theme of suffering is brought in (often under a "mysti-cal" sense of "in Christ"), some caveat is needed that sufferings by Jesus' disciples are not "redemptive." But neither Paul's sufferings nor revelations through his

---

[18] In PPetr 3.36 the prisoner Posidonius petitions an official, "I am now completely worn down in prison, I'm dying of hunger. . . . Therefore I ask you, beseechingly: do not let me perish of hunger in prison" (verso lines 27–29). Or again, "The need is very great. To have to live under such straits! And to have death before one's eyes, lying in prison, with great want. . . . No one can be worse off than I am. . . . Not once do I have the necessities. I therefore ask you, free me from my needs. You can do it and will also rescue me" (recto lines 4–9, 18–23). U. B. Müller comments, "Not so Paul" (51).

imprisonment surface in vv 12–14, let alone a reference to believers in Philippi being in the same straits. (Cf. discussion on 1:30 *the same contest*, as to opponents and whether imprisonment is involved.)

Exegesis in v 13 has often spoken about Paul's bonds being *for Christ*. In the overlap of meanings, to take "in Christ" with the entire cl., so that this "sphere" stands over all that Paul says, is attractive but almost untranslatable in Eng. A difficulty is that, whether with the entire content of v 13 or with "manifest (in Christ)," the phrase deals with what non-Christians (*in the whole Praetorium and . . . all the rest*) have come to perceive about Paul. Presumably Paul speaks "in Christ"; he understands, from a Christian point of view, that it is apparent to unbelievers his bonds have significance due to the Lord Paul serves, and not for some other reason. Hence his hope: as events unfold, in his bold witness and person "Christ will be magnified" (1:20).

the whole Praetorium has occasioned much discussion. For imprisonment in Rome, there are problems, more opinions than for Caesarea or Ephesus. Though a place or building can be meant, the phrase stands for the people stationed or located there; in Ephesus (or Caesarea), the governor's palace, a residency or headquarters, but really the people there, even members of the Imperial or Praetorian Guard. Paul and the Philippians know who was involved; we do not, precisely. The "*whole* Praetorium" may be hyperbole. It fits easier re a detachment of Praetorians in Ephesus (or Caesarea) than 10,000 troops in Rome. The phrase *clear . . . to all the rest* has prompted debate too. Again, people, not "places" (which KJV added); "(Roman) legal staff," "broader circles" connected with the Praetorium, the general populace of the city (again easier for Ephesus than for Rome), or a vague phrase, as the TRANSLATION *all the rest* acknowledges. Paul seems to have in mind a "ripple effect": his current imprisonment for the gospel is becoming apparent to wider circles of non-Christians in Ephesus, beginning with those involved in his imprisonment and trial. Paul is a "Trojan horse" (Houlden 58) in Caesar's system (Fee 114).

The second outcome (v 14) concerns fellow Christians, *brothers and sisters*, in Ephesus. Some see Christians beyond the city of Paul's captivity (Martin *Phil.* 72, without saying where, or how Paul knew so much about their motives). Fee 115 denies believers in Corinth, Thessalonica, etc., are in view. *adelphoi* in Philippi? So Schmithals 1972:74–75; rightly rejected by Bruce 1989:45 and Fee 115 n 44 (it reflects Schmithals's theory that group A of these preachers = the "dogs" of 3:2, already in Philippi). The *adelphoi* of 1:14 are in the place of Paul's imprisonment, Ephesus. Hence he knows about them, data he proceeds to share with the Philippians.

The main point, surprising, is that *brothers and sisters* in Ephesus are, in the face of Paul's captivity, *daring fearlessly to speak the word*. In this way too the gospel advances. These witnesses are variously motivated (15–18). Paul's Gk., *most of* the Christians in Ephesus, poses a problem. A majority but not all believers in the area seem involved. "Majority," not in contrast to the hyperbolized "*whole* Praetorium and *all* the rest" in v 13; 13–14 involves classes of people (nonbelievers, Christians), not the percentages of each involved. Fee 115 n 45 suggests "popular language"; Paul "has not counted noses" in each house church.

adelphoi in v 14 does not refer to Christians generally or a smaller group of church workers or leaders (see NOTE on *second, that most of the brothers and sisters . . .*) but Christians in the house churches of Ephesus. They do this, *confident in the Lord*, with *daring* or at a venture, *fearlessly.* These three phrases, plus *so much the more* than before, characterize the widespread proclamation that makes Paul rejoice (18c). Great courage is being shown by Christians in Ephesus. Paul observes the effects but does not laud human resolve. It is confidence *in the Lord*, not (see NOTE) KJV's tautology, "brethren in the Lord" or (Schenk) "active *(in-the Lord)* Christians." The activity is *speaking the word*, "proclaiming Christ." No need to explicate the gospel Philippians and Christians in Ephesus know well. It is "the gospel that he gospeled" to the Corinthians and elsewhere, the core of which is Christ crucified and risen (1 Cor 15:1, 3–4; Rom 1:2–4; Fitzmyer 1979 ([2] Bibl. **gospel**), esp. pp. 151–52).

Paul's *bonds* have provided a new impulse for such witnessing in Ephesus. The imprisonment that officials and others in v 13 begin to see as *for Christ* moves Christians to new confidence to preach. The Lord (Jesus) is the object and grounds for confidence, Paul's bonds an occasion for new activity. O'B 95 and Fee 116 distinguish "*ground* of confidence" and bonds as an *instrument* used by God toward it. Did Ephesian Christians seek to take up the slack in public witnessing while Paul was out of circulation? Did his heroic example spur them on? Is it because Paul survives that they take up proclamation anew, without fear, because Paul isn't being prosecuted for such activity under criminal law? The text doesn't say (15–18c may shed more light).

What Paul writes concerning *gospel* and his *bonds* rests on witnessing to Christ as characteristic of Christianity and, underlying it, "the victory of Jesus Christ" who is to be magnified (1:20). Even in the face of the *imperium Romanum*, with its courts and soldiers, believers dare to speak anew about their joy (Eichholz [(2) Bibl.] 145–47). 1:12–14 is not apologetic (in the face of a "right" Paul's patrons have to be informed about the progress of his work) but paradigmatic and paraenetic for the Philippians, to encourage readers boldly to set forth the gospel message (Ware 1996:195–97).

2. Paul Elaborates, from Prison, on How He Rejoices That Christ Is Proclaimed, Even If the Motives of the Preachers Vary (1:15–18c). With a new Gk. sentence and a new (unnecessary) paragraph in some trs. (including [N]RSV), Paul goes on about the *brothers and sisters* in Ephesus who are spreading *the word* all the more during his imprisonment (v 14). Not an "excursus" to separate the groups in 15–18b from the Christians described in 14 (see above, A.7.a). The *narratio* continues. Paul interprets what he narrates (perhaps a *partitio*, A.4, above). "Additional information" beyond vv 12–14 (Schenk 137; U. B. Müller 53), to expand on and nuance what was said in v 14 about gospel advance through evangelistic preaching. The motives of two groups come out vividly, though how group A (marked by *envy, strife*, impure motives) can cause joy to Paul puzzles interpreters. The identity of these *brothers and sisters proclaiming Christ* will be discussed in 3, below. The subunit extends three-quarters of the way through v 18; see NOTE on 18a *What then?* and COMMENT A.1.

Verse 1:15 links with 1:14. The groups described in 15–18c are among the confident *brothers and sisters* in v 14, used as evidence that the gospel is advancing; see NOTE on 1:15 *Some . . . , but others . . . are proclaiming Christ.* Efforts to separate 15–17 (or –18b) from 14 end up with an abstract picture of Christians all over the map, not related to the people mentioned in 14.[19] Vv 15–18c present Christians where Paul is, in Ephesus, who are preaching the gospel of Christ (Ewald 68 = Wohl. 76; Michaelis 20–21; Gnilka 59–60; U. B. Müller 53; Hawth. 36; O'B 98, but Silva 69, v 14 = Christians generally, 15–17 = church leaders).

The most frequent theme continues to be *proclaiming Christ/set forth Christ in preaching,* cf. *gospel* (v 12, now also at 16) and *speak the word.* See A.5, above. *my bonds* (13, 14) continues in v 17, *my imprisonment* (same word), a circumstance also hinted at when Paul says *I am put here for the defense of the gospel* (16). Another theme occurs at the very end, in 18c, *I rejoice* (for prior references to *joy,* see NOTES on 18c *I rejoice* and 1:4 *with joy*). Rejoicing will introduce the next unit, in the fut. tense, at 18d. Paul's *defense of the gospel* thus relates to its *progress* or advance, as will also be true for the Philippians (v 25; Bockmuehl 74).

Proclamation *(kērygma)* would have been familiar to Philippians and Ephesians from the world of the day. The herald *(kēryx)* was well-known from athletic events and urban life. So were religious proclaimers about the gods, their mighty acts, and how to live; e.g., on Asclepius or by Hermetic missionaries (see NOTE on 15 *are proclaiming Christ*). What distinguished Paul and other Christian evangelists from such street preachers was their message, about *Christ.*

Paul's additional information is artfully conveyed—parallelism, antithesis *(some, others; the latter, the former; because they know, because they suppose),* and chiastic structure. See COMMENT A.7, and the NOTE on 1:16–17. Earlier MSS allow us to correct the KJV sequence to that in almost all recent trs. Vv 15–17 (cf. Schenk 131–32) show an ABB'A' chiasm for the two groups of persons proclaiming Christ:

15 (A)   Some *(tines men),* indeed on account of envy and strife,
   (B)   but others *(tines de)* indeed on account of goodwill, are proclaiming Christ.
16 (B') The latter, out of love,
         = because they knew that I am put here for the defense of the gospel;
17 (A') The former, out of self-interest, set forth Christ in preaching
         not with a pure motivation
         = because they suppose thereby to stir up trouble for my imprisonment.

The subjects in v 15, *Some . . . , others . . . ,* are Gk. indef. prons., followed "with an article (1.16–17) and zero-anaphora (1.17b,c)" (DA 379, cf. 94 on *ouch hagnōs, oiomenoi*). Use of *tines* (or *tis*) is characteristic of Paul to refer to those with whom he is not in agreement (Gal 1:7; 2:12; 2 Cor 2:5; 10:7 NRSV "you"; 11:21). He probably knows more about the identity of the person(s) than he lets on. A gesture

---

[19] The "excursus" theory (A.7.a) did just that, as did notions that one group of preachers in vv 15–18, inclined to self-interest and strife, were unbelievers and/or Jews (Chrysost., PG 62:193 = NPNF 13:191; B. Weiss 82; Suhl 170–71).

of courtesy and his goodwill? In 16 and 17 *hoi men* and *hoi de* (*latter* and *former*) are no more precise.

The two groups we may align in Paul's terms, both characterized by "preaching Christ":

Group A	Group B
They are proclaiming Christ	
on account of envy and strife (15 *phthonos, eris*)	on account of goodwill (15 *eudokia*)
They set forth Christ in preaching	
out of self-interest (17 *eritheia*)	out of love (16 *agapē*)
not with a pure motivation (17 *ouch hagnōs*)	
because they	
suppose thereby to stir up trouble for my imprisonment;	know that I am put here for the defense of the gospel (16)
under pretense (18b *prophasis*)	in truth (18b *alētheia*).[20]

Group A is more fully characterized. Does Paul know more about them? Is he more stung by their activity? Or is bad easier to depict than good? The weight is carried by the nouns, only once the *via negativa* (*not with a pure motivation*) and then without saying that group B has pure motives. For group B, *goodwill* implies good pleasure (toward Paul), favorable sentiments toward the apostle and his gospel. *love* = a feeling of self-giving on the part of Christians toward others (Loh. 44–45 "abandon"), human love but modeled after God's (Rom 5:8). Since Paul does not use *agapē* for response toward God, it must be love for those to whom they preach or love for Paul (O'B 99). *in truth* suggests witnessing done "honestly," "with sincerity," "in reality." The underlying reason for preaching thus is *because they know that I am put here for the defense of the gospel.* Paul credits them with a discerning knowledge (1:9), they perceive his imprisonment has to do with the gospel cause, indeed that God's hand is in Paul's current circumstances (see Note on 16 *I am put here* and the overtones to *eudokia*; 1:19 will speak of the holy Spirit). 16b helps one decide that the *goodwill* and *love* involved are directed toward Paul. All in all, an admirable group of preachers, perceptive, sincere, pro Paul! 1:7 had commended the Philippians for empathy in his *imprisonment* and *opportunity in the defense and confirmation of the gospel.* Some in Ephesus exhibit this position in the way they preach.

Group A is described in greater detail, often using Greco-Roman terminology. *envy and strife*, found in NT "vice lists," have to do with disposition toward, and relations with, others. No Heb., OT background. Both are characteristic Gk. passions. *envy* was "the base passion of base people" (Aristot.), worse than hatred (see Plutarch's treatise), "the worst of all evils" (Stobaeus, in the Note). Philo found

---

[20] J. A. Smith, *Marks of an Apostle: Deconstruction, Philippians, and Problematizing Pauline Theology,* Semeia Studies 53 (Atlanta: SBL, 2005) makes 1:18b epicenter (128), Trojan logic (1), and fracture for 1:15–17, which it governs. Proclamation, gospel in its iterability, not who proclaims it, is the point (158); "the text deconstructs itself while leaving the ethical imperative of proclamation unscathed" (1). On Paul and psychagogy (guiding souls in moral philosophy), see 76–86; on pretext (*prophasis*) and truth 83–84, 131–34.

examples in the Bible; Jos., in his own day; 1 Clem., from Genesis to Peter and Paul in Rome and dissension in the church at Corinth about A.D. 95. Envy esp. took deadly aim at leaders; some perfidiously heaped honors on Caesar to make Romans envy and hate him (text in the NOTE). M. M. Mitchell 1992:81–82, *eris* in Gk. literature esp. refers to "political strife and its causes," part of a *topos* on how "factionalism is a 'human' failing" (cf. Phil 2:2 and the contrast in 1:16–17 with *eritheia*, Mitchell 168 and n 625).

strife (eris), often personified, was said to stir up emulation and quarrels. In the NT, "Paul virtually holds the copyright" on its use (Schütz 161) for church divisions and controversies. In 1 Clem., like envy, a vice in Israel's history and church life (references in NOTE). In v 17 *eritheia* (cf. W. Barclay, *New Testament Words* [Philadelphia: Westminster, 1964] 99–100) was formerly tr. "contention," a sense close to "strife"; there has been a move (see NOTE) away from this toward *self-interest*, self-seeking, baseness on the part of a person, out for oneself.

not with a pure motivation (adv. *hagiōs* + a negative, "not in a holy way") is the one characteristic for group A not paralleled for group B. "Mixed motives." Juxtaposition with *set forth Christ in preaching* is jarring.[21]

The final telling phrase about group A is (18b) that they act *under pretense*. Gk. *prophasis* usually had to do with a pretext, ostensible reason, alleged motive, which turns out to be false, often contrasted with true motives or sincerity.[22] Hypocrisy is implied for group A.[23]

They speak and act thus *because they suppose thereby to stir up trouble for my imprisonment*. Not *believe* as in the case of group B, but *suppose. oiomenoi* suggests purpose, at least in their own minds, to bring new worries to the imprisoned apostle. Some interpreters see apocalyptic pressures or affliction in missionary work, but such connections need not be in the picture here when *trouble* is men-

---

[21] Rose 1924 ([15] NOTE on 4:7) 37 n 1 inclined to remove *ouch hagnōs* on rhythmic grounds, cf. J. Weiss, "Is it a gloss?" Edart 79, cf. 332–33, calls the phrase *commoratio*, rhetorically an idea on which one lingers (Lausberg #830, 835). Ewald 68 = Wohl. 76 saw a strict parallelism that was ruined by the *ouch hagiōs* phrase; therefore Ewald wanted to apply *not with a pure motivation* to *both* groups, with the vb.-phrase that it follows (C and C' below):

  A The latter, out of love,   B The former, out of self-interest,
  A' because they know that I am put here for the defense of the gospel
            C set forth Christ in preaching,
            C' not with a pure motivation
                  B' because they suppose thereby to stir up trouble for
                     my imprisonment

Both groups act "not with pure motives." How so for group B? They proceeded out of love *for Paul*, not out of zeal *for the gospel*. It would explain why there is no corresponding phrase for *ouch hagiōs*. But Wohl. termed Ewald's concept of the parallelism and chiasm (which is certainly skewered) "too pedantic."

[22] Examples from Dem. in the NOTE on 18b *under pretense*; MM 555, Loh. 48 n 1 (but no example with both *prophasis* and *alētheia*), most post-NT. *prophasis* is not common in the church fathers, PGL 1190.

[23] Bockmuehl 80–81 remarks on **Pure motives or false** that, while "'[p]ost-modern sensibilities tend to balk at this polarity'" (whose motives are ever unmixed?), there is "a common-sense distinction between sincerity and duplicity of behaviour" and here "the truth of God" was involved.

tioned. O'B 102, "some inward annoyance . . . perhaps by bringing 'home to him the limitations and restraints of his condition . . . as contrasted with their own unfettered freedom'" (citing Michael 42, the words in single quotes above; cf. Baumert 1973:312–13). H. C. G. Moule 21, "Anti-Paulines" tried to prevent "the access of enquirers or converts to the imprisoned Apostle; a severe test to his faith and patience"; G. H. Clark 29 well asked, "[S]evere enough to provoke Paul's remark?" Loh. 45, Paul's phrase does not say, "*thlipsis* for me" but as in v 13 "for *my bonds* or *imprisonment*." The aim of group B must have something to do with Paul's being jailed and with the Roman authorities. Discussion of *thlipsis* has oscillated between mental anguish for Paul (he must worry about the motives of some preachers)[24] and external pressure (by the authorities or in God's eschatological scenario).

Group B is an unattractive bunch of preachers. Yet Paul employs exactly the same phrases for what they do as for the witnesses he has lauded. Both *are proclaiming Christ*; by both, *Christ is being set forth in preaching*. How and why Paul can speak thus of group A as well as of group B can be answered only by conjecture about the situation as Paul writes. See 3, below.

The presentation in vv 15–17 is broken off with the elliptical question in 18a, *What then?* It is connected with the pervious vv by *gar* ("*for* what [of it]?"). 18a moves toward a conclusion for the subunit. 18b will sum up on the groups with the phrases *under pretense or in truth*. The conclusion is, *Simply that, in every way, . . . Christ is being set forth in preaching*. Surprising, but the apostle has already said this in vv 15 and 16–17. "Opponents" (Loh. 44, an overstatement) and "friends" are put in the same category on witnessing to the gospel. Thus 1:18a is "a discourse marker"; "Paul raises the question . . . ('what do I make of those who are preaching the gospel so as to increase my suffering?') and then proceeds to answer it himself ('as long as Christ is proclaimed I am glad . . . ')—a . . . diatribal use of the interrogative (cf. Rom. 3.3)" (*DA* 348–49).

Paul can say *I rejoice* (18c) over the fact that the word goes forth. He returns to the theme articulated in 1:4. Can Paul begin a letter to Philippi without rejoicing? 1:18c is another of the 16 instances of *joy* in Phil. It will loom over the grim discussion of Paul's immediate prospects in 18d–26, "Yes, and I will continue to rejoice" (NRSV). Here at 18c, not just spontaneous but a consequence of the apostle's will and reflection (Gulin [(2) Bibl. *joy*] 251 n 1), a disposition "that can be elicited by many events and circumstances, and can be ultimately destroyed by none" (R. D. Webber [(2) Bibl. **joy**] 287). 1:18c stems specifically from conditions in Ephesus, including the work of other preachers, not as in 4:10 from the Philippians' solidarity with him. Concentration by Paul on his own person in 1:16–18 is not egocentrism (Fortna 1990 overlooked the passage) or apologetic, but (like

---

[24] Ware 1996:213–16 claims a "rhetorical pattern" behind 1:17; cf. 1 Thess 2:17–3:10; Gal 4:12–20; 2 Cor 2:1–4; 6:11–7:16, *how* his churches obey affects the Apostle's emotional wellbeing. 1:17 is not "a description of the actual *avowed aim*" but a subjective *effect* on him. But the "intent clause" *(because they suppose)* must then be explained as an effort "to further their own factious interests," not to "save souls." Paul's *trouble* in prison is not explored.

1:12–14) paraenetic, paradigmatic encouragement for the Philippians to preach (Ware 1996:216–19).

3. Identifying "the Other Preachers" of 1:14–18c. Debate over who "the rival preachers" are in 1:14–18c intertwines with where they were located (and, in turn, the city from which Paul writes) and whether they are opposed to Paul or something else. He is imprisoned by Roman authorities *in Ephesus* (INTRO. VII.A), a site compatible with *the whole Praetorium* in 1:13 and, given the varying views on Paul in 1:15–18b, with the different types of Christianity in Ephesus in Paul's day, Pauline, Jewish-Christian, and perhaps Johannine and other communities.[25] The *persons described in 1:14–18b* are also to be located in "the city of Paul's imprisonment" (Fitzgerald, *ABD* 5:323). That means *in Ephesus*.[26]

What Paul says is sometimes taken as a *general description* of preachers Paul experienced in many places, but nowhere specific (a view prior to efforts to make opponents in Phil 3 a "literary composite"). Thus Martin 1976:72. But the vividness of vv 14–18 and the fact that Paul is sharing information to support the current *progress of the gospel* make reference to experiences elsewhere in the past unlikely. The two groups of preachers are more than rhetorical examples, positive and negative (J. S. Vos 2002:144–46).

Do the Ephesian preachers in 1:14–18b relate to *references elsewhere in Phil*?[27] Like 3:2–21, "the dogs, evil workers, who mutilate the flesh"? These "enemies of

---

[25] On *Ephesus*, cf. Koester, *Intro.* 2:114–36, 250–55; R. E. Oster, Jr., *ABD* 2:548–49; W. Thiessen (INTRO. VII.A Bibl.) esp. 111–28: Paul spent the longest period of his (known) missionary career here, including an Ephesian imprisonment, and wrote most of his extant letters from Ephesus. There existed in Ephesus "a dynamic pluralism of coworkers with various interests and points of view" (128; against Gnilka 64, who assumed an apostle was the recognized authority in a place). M. Günther, *Die Frühgeschichte des Christentums in Ephesus*, 2nd ed. (AGSU 1; Tübingen: Mohr Siebeck, 1998). Walter 40, Christian groups in Ephesus included Jewish Christians (cf. Rev 2:1–7); groups from Apollos or with an independent notion of baptism (Acts 18:24–27; 19:1–7); plus Johannine Christianity. A Pauline group was not, as in Thessalonica or Philippi, the "original community."

[26] For recent discussion see Ollreg 193–94; W. Thiessen (INTRO. VII.A Bibl.) 111–18, not in Philippi (as claimed by Schmithals, Baumbach 1971:296–97, and O. Merk 1968:188; noted above in A.7.a, end; cf. also Silva 72 n 3 and Hargraves 30) or in Corinth (T. W. Manson 1962 [INTRO. VII.A Bibl.] 149–67 [originally 1939]: Paul, freed from prison in Ephesus, reflects on factions in Corinth, later described in 1 Cor 1–4; O'B 102 regards this as unlikely). To place the *brothers and sisters* of 1:14–18b in some other place than where Paul is makes it difficult to explain how Paul knows as much as he does about them. To put them in Philippi makes it awkward for having Paul tell the Philippians about them and assumes he knows from afar more about the motives of these preachers than Christians in Philippi do. The description he gives, if of people in Philippi, would likely (further) polarize readers there (even though the apostle seems to bless both groups, his descriptive nouns would not help matters); Phil 1:27–2:4 aims to strengthen church unity in Philippi. Many theories noted below assume Rome or Caesarea, rather than Ephesus; some of their arguments may, however, apply to the Ephesian hypothesis as well.

[27] C. Kähler, e.g., distinguishes those in 1:14–18 (in Ephesus) from the menacing group in 3:2–21, as well as those in Philippi disturbing the church from outside (1:28). He also brings in Euodia and Syntyche (4:2–3) as an instance of internal problems in Philippi. The redacted epistle instructs the church over "a) personal, non-dogmatic (daily life) conflicts and b) conflicts of confession" where compromise is impossible.

the cross of Christ" (3:18), we shall conclude, have nothing to do with the "rival preachers" of 1:14–18b. That those who proclaim Christ in 1:14–18b were *later* identified by Paul as "dogs" after he learned more about them is unpersuasive. What of *1:28–30*, "intimidating opponents" in a struggle with the Philippians? These opponents in Philippi do not *proclaim Christ*, they menace salvation. They are the Roman authorities in Philippi ([5] COMMENT B). Finally, *2:21*, where Paul criticizes coworkers, "All of them are seeking their own interests, not those of Jesus Christ." To "seek their own interests" *(ta heautōn zētousin)* sounds like the *self-interest (eritheia)* of group A in 1:17.[28] But 2:21 speaks of "all of them," 1:17 refers only to some of *most of the brothers and sisters* in 1:14. There are closer matches (e.g., 2:4) than 1:17 to "seeking one own interests." 2:21 refers to people on Paul's mission team whom he might have sent to Philippi instead of Timothy. Paul's staff thus included people who at times put their own interests ahead of those of Christ or of the Philippians, but v 21 does not castigate them the way group A is criticized in 1:15–18b. The preachers in Ephesus, even in group B, were not at Paul's beck and call to send to Philippi. 2:21 sheds no light on those proclaiming Christ in 1:14–18b.

The following proposals, often drawing on *other letters*, exist on the nature and identity of the other preachers in 1:14–18b (cf. Schenk ANRW 2.25.4:3294–99; Mearns; O'B 102–5):

a. *Pagan agitators* who preached Christ *under pretense* (18b), to stir up the authorities (in Rome) against Paul.[29]

b. *Jews*, similarly, calling attention to the gospel only to discredit it. B. W. Winter 1994:96–97, "The Jewish 'lobby' "; cf. Suhl 170–71; contrast U. B. Müller 53 n 28. Neither group could have preached Christ in a way that made Paul rejoice.

c. *Judaizing Christians* (many variations).[30] It is inconceivable that a "gospel" so differing (in Gal) from Paul's own could be involved. That they rightly "preach the word" means they cannot be Judaizers (Michael 41; Beare 59; O'B 103).

d. *Zealot Christians*, preaching political revolt against Rome.[31] Martin 1976:73 was somewhat attracted to this view, but finally settled for opposition to Paul, not to the Roman imperium. The view has little following (Edart 78 n 26).

e. *Christians jealous of Paul.* Esp. in Rome, Paul, an intruder (Hendriksen 72), upset local relationships. Martin 39; Beare 17; O. Cullmann, *Peter* (Philadelphia: Westminster, 1953) 104–9 = 1962:105–10; Bockmuehl 78: personal animosity, "to rub salt" in Paul's wounds, citing rabbinic sources for "mixed motives"; Hooker

---

[28] So Friedrich NTD *Phil.* 1961:114, but not 16th ed. 1985:157; Jewett 1970b: 369–70; contrast Vincent 74, Dib. 85, Michaelis 50.

[29] Thus Chrysost. (PG 62:192 = NPNF 13:190); cf. Vincent 18; Gnilka 59 n 1.

[30] Vincent 19; Jewett 1970b:365 n 2; Ollreg 195 n 165. Lft. 88–89, they sought converts for the Law (cf. Phil 3:2ff.), jealous of Paul's influence; O'B 103 n 31; Ware 1996:219–22; Silva 73; Fee 122–23; Tellbe 2001:267.

[31] A. S. Way, *The Letters of St. Paul* (London: Macmillan, 1906) 155; T. Hawthorn 1950–51: the groups were attacking the civil authorities who had imprisoned Paul, one group by preaching divine "vengeance to come," the other a "God who controls all history" and "can turn the bonds of Paul to the furtherance of the gospel."

2002:385, 394. Applicable to Caesarea (Loh. 46–47), Corinth (T. W. Manson [INTRO. VII.A Bibl] 161–62; cf. Beare 59; O'B 102, "hardly . . . correct"), or Ephesus. For many,[32] the most likely explanation. K. Barth 31, *"personal* unfriendliness," *"articuli* NON *fundamentales," non*fundamental points of doctrine.

f. "[*I*]*tinerant Christian missionaries with a divine-man theology* similar to that which appears in II Corinthians," Jewett 1970b:371 (italics added), "a different understanding of the Christian life than . . . Paul" (Martin 39; 73–74). Jewett depended on the "divine-man" as developed by Georgi, *Opponents* (Ger. 1964; but cf. Georgi 1986:30 and n 19). Upon scrutiny,[33] the "divine man" *(theios anēr)* seems dubious, application to Phil 1:15–18 ill-founded; Ollreg 195–96 n 165; O'B 104–5 raises penetrating questions.

g. *Gnostic Christians.* Schmithals (but little about 1:15–18).[34] Perhaps Jewish Christian gnostics.[35] Since the 1950s and 1960s,[36] there is greater reticence to see "gnostics" all over Paul's world (AB 32A:48–54; Machalet). There are few links between Phil 3 and Nag Hammadi documents, let alone with the *envy, strife, self-interest,* or *pretense.* Cf. O'B 103.

h. F. C. Synge 1951:124–25: *the preachers* of 1:14–18 *were denouncing the Jews* who had secured Paul's imprisonment; lacks "substantial exegetical support from the text" (O'B 103).

i. Paul is *imprisoned for some crime of his own* (O. Linton 1937, summary in Jewett 1970b: 364–65; cf. Ollreg 198 n 177). Linton could not say what Paul's "private crime" was. J. Munck 1954 (Eng. 1959:323–25, re Acts 28, Paul in Rome; no ch. on Philippi in Munck): perhaps "profanation of the temple in Jerusalem" (cf. Acts 21:28) or "not unassailable conduct during his journeys in the east" (324; cf. Acts 24:5).[37] Walter 38, damage in Ephesus to business (of the silversmiths) or rioting (Acts 19:23–40). Cf. Thiessen 100–8, 119–28. The proposal has not gotten very far.

j. Collange (*Phil.* 9–10, 51): *Paul has appealed to his Roman citizenship.* Some

---

[32] Vincent 19; E. F. Scott *IB* 11:32; Beare 59–60; K. Barth 29–30; Hawth. 38; O'B 105; cf. Schenk 140 and U. B. Müller 54, following Haupt 23.

[33] Cf. H. Kee, "Divine Man," *IDBSup* 243 (critical of the concept); D. L. Tiede, "Aretalogy," *ABD* 1:372–73, and *The Charismatic Figure as Wonder Worker* (SBLDS 1; Missoula, MT: SBL, 1972), a "conceptual umbrella" (254) to be "used with great caution"; C. R. Holladay 1977, "too vague" for organizing christological evidence, "the blind leading the blind, so to speak" (*JBL* 98 [1979] 608); Furnish, *2 Cor.*, AB 32A: 243–45, 501; de Vos 266 n 119

[34] 1:15–17 "is on circumstances in Philippi . . . not yet . . . precise. . . . Only in the next epistle [C] does he call them *dogs"* (74–75 n 45). Schmithals thinks the Philippians would have gotten the point in an earlier letter.

[35] Gunther lists R. B. Ward 1967:185–95; Marxsen, *INTRO.* 63–64; and Müller-Bardorff (INTRO. VI Bibl.).

[36] See, e.g., E. H. Pagels, "Gnosticism," *IDBSup* 364–68; K. Rudolph, "Gnosticism," *ABD* 2:1033–40.

[37] Munck added, often "the Church is tempted to leave its leaders in the lurch when . . . accused of criminal offenses and not for the Gospel's sake." Cf. Linton's 1964 commentary (160–62): *Paul's preaching of the gospel got him into trouble, not Paul's preaching of the gospel.* "Why should Paul take the whole church down with him?" (160, tr. E. Heen). See Spicq, *Agape* ([2] Bibl. **love**) 2:244–45 n 4 = 1965 2:285–86.

Christians in Ephesus feel he should not have done this. Doctrine is not at stake but how to defend the gospel. He claims status and freedom to preach; this may help the gospel cause. But some Christians object; missionary life should involve suffering. There is jealousy over Paul's citizenship and use of it in Ephesus (it is "outside the capital" that "the apostle's Roman citizenship would protect him from any death sentence," 10).

Paul did appeal to citizenship at Caesarea (Acts 25:11–12); at Acts 22:25 to escape a flogging; in Philippi (Acts 16:37). In his letters[38] Paul never states he is a citizen of Tarsus or of Rome. If a Roman citizen,[39] he could well have invoked his rights at Ephesus, as elsewhere. But some Christians there felt him a coward, fleeing "the true vocation for a disciple . . . and an apostle . . . ," martyrdom (p. 9). Christians at Ephesus, at first paralyzed by his incarceration, regained courage to witness to their faith (v 14). They preached Christ, but some with envy and contentiously over Paul's appeal to his citizenship: he shouldn't have done it! Hawth. 37–38 refers to Collange's theory only in the form of the question. O'B 105, "difficult to prove or disprove" (an odd response if Acts is credited with historical accuracy). Morlet 72–73 mentions it, while admitting our ignorance about the historical context.

How would Paul's appeal to Roman citizenship fit with *patron–client relationships* (see [16] COMMENT, B.1.(A).3d)?[40] In Roman Philippi Paul's converts would likely have understood and approved. In Ephesus a patron–client relationship between Paul and Christian groups is unlikely, unless in house churches where he was founder or friend. Bormann 1995:214 thinks Paul was left on his own by friends as well as opponents in Ephesus. Isolation from the local community could have encouraged appeal to his citizenship. Paul needs to explain to the Philippians why he played his citizenship card. He does so in 1:18d–26, without referring to the appeal directly. Threat of death and desire to remain in service to and with

---

[38] That he was thrice flogged by lectors (2 Cor 11:25) has been used to deny his citizenship, since a citizen was not to be flogged. But this provision was often ignored by authorities (AB 32A:516).

[39] Only some representative literature on Paul's citizenship can be cited here. Cf. INTRO. II n 3; (4) COMMENT A.7; and (14) COMMENT 3, on 3:20 *governing civic association*. Acts references (16:37–38; 22:25–29; cf. 23:27; 21:39 [Tarsus]; 25:10–11; 28:19) are often ascribed to Lukan tendentiousness; cf. Haenchen 504; Schmithals, *Apg.* 153, Conzelmann 133; Alvarez 348–70. Contrast Munck, AB 31:163, 220; Fitzmyer, AB 31:144–45, 589–90; Jervell, *Apg.* 430–31. For arguments against citizenship for Paul, see W. Stegemann 1987:200–29; Pilhofer 2002:154; Alvarez 348–70 (old literature in n 23). For his citizenship, Lüdemann 1989 (INTRO. II Bibl.) 240–41; Rapske 1994:71–112; M. Hengel 1991: 193–208; P. van Minnen, "Paul the Roman Citizen," *JSNT* 56 (1994) 43–52, contra Stegemann 1987; Riesner 1998:148–56; J. H. Neyrey, in FS Robbins (Gen. Bibl. under "Sisson") 161–64, Luke may well be right, considering Paul's social location and rhetorical-educational level.

[40] Bormann 211 sees a contradiction between Phil 1:12–17 and Acts 16: in the letter the apostle seeks a *public* context for presenting the gospel, while according to Luke he *avoided* public proclamation "within the *pomerium* of Philippi," preaching outside the city (Acts 16:13), baptizing inside private houses (16:15, 32). But the Jewish meeting place where he preached was of necessity outside the town; the exorcism of the slave girl was "public," as was Paul's demand for an apology from the authorities. Bormann ignores the reference to Roman citizenship in 16:37. Moreover, in the Acts passage Paul is newly arrived in a Roman city in Europe and, though a free man, proceeds cautiously; in Phil 1, the apostle has little choice but a public hearing to change his status as a prisoner.

them accounts for the appeal, though he was also trying to help them grow to a certain maturity (see 4:10–20), to be, in Bormann's phrase, "emancipated clients." Bormann's suggestion of an anti-government or revolutionist stance on the part of Paul and Philippian Christians (224) seems unlikely. Antagonism with the authorities (1:27–30), but scarcely warfare in Paul's day. Formal persecution in Philippi remains doubtful.[41]

k. Influence from *contemporary concepts of friendship and enmity*.[42] "Using typical vocabulary of friendship and enmity, 1:15–18 compares [*sygkrisis?* cf. (4) COMMENT A.4] the reactions of friends and enemies to his misfortune" (Stowers 1991:114), with *agapē* substituted for *philia* (1:16; cf. 1 Thess 4:9, re "love of the brothers and sisters *(philadelphia)* . . . you yourselves have been taught by God to love *(agapan)* one another" (NRSV; AB 32B:243–44, 255–60). For group A, note v 15, *envy*, often linked with "enmity" (P. Marshall 49–50; NOTE on 1:15 *envy*); *strife* (*eris*/contentio, part of a *topos* related to friendship and factionalism);[43] and *eritheia*, "self-interest" (see NOTE on 1:17; political connection in Aristot.).[44] Group A reflects Gk. factionalism that often beset the Christian movement, cliques of non-Pauline house churches arrayed against those regarding Paul as founder or friend in Ephesus. Paul responds with a frank comparison of those friendly and those hostile to him. Could such rhetoric help the group to reconsider its hostility? The rhetoric allows Paul to affirm both groups, A and B, they preach the word about Christ, the gospel norm, to which apostle and all preachers are subordinate (Schütz 160–65). Christ is being preached, a note of victory (J. S. Vos 2002:146).

Summary—Some theories can be set aside: (a) pagan agitators, (b) Jews, (d) Zealot Christians, (f) missionaries with a divine-man theology, (g) gnostic Christians, (h) preachers denouncing the Jews, (i) Paul jailed for some crime of

---

[41] Portefaix 140, "the Philippian Christians were regarded with suspicion"; cf. 138–41. Pilhofer (1:135) speaks of an "un-Roman-ness" about Christians. He sees (204–5) a Lukan construct in Acts 16:37–40. Were Christians at this time "enemies of the Roman order" (MacMullen)?

[42] See COMMENT A.4 for rhetorical terms applied to 1:14–18. 1:15, 17 may exemplify "frank speech" (*parrhēsia*), connected with Greek *philia*; candor, criticism assumed among friends (Konstan; Fredrickson 165–70; Fitzgerald 1996:155). Enmity was treated "as a brief adjunct to friendship" (Plut. *Mor.* 86B–92F; Arist. *Rhet.* 2.4.30–32; P. Marshall 35–69); "*philia*/amicitia presupposes *echthra*/inimicitia," enmity and friendship in a reciprocal relationship, "inseparable from public and social life" (278, 279). Sometimes with exaggeration (279–81). Paul showed "distaste for relations of this kind which constantly dogged him in his work" (P. Marshall 152, citing Phil 1:15,17 in n 105); hence ethical injunctions against such hostility, often a concomitant of *philia* (151; cf. 1 Thess 5:15; Rom 2:14,17,19–21).

[43] Stowers 1991:113–14; M. M. Mitchell 1991:81 nn 90, 94; 150 n 509, a political term; *topos* = a "region" from which arguments are drawn, not a literary form, 67 n 8. Dio Chrys. (*Or.* 34.19) catalogued as "civil ills" *phthonos*, greed, contentiousness (*philoneikia*), and seeking to promote one's own welfare; he listed gods like *Homonoia*/ Concordia and prayed *eris* and *philoneikia* might be cast out of a city (39.8). See further the NOTE on 1:15 *strife*.

[44] P. Marshall 27–28 connects "friendship for utility" with "being entirely self-interested." Fitzgerald 1996:157–60, Paul in 4:8–20 sought to lift the Philippians' understanding of *philia* from the utilitarian type to "character friendship" based on virtue (see NOTE and COMMENT on 4:8). Is a move of the same sort involved in 1:15–17 with the two types of preachers?

his own. Paul's bonds were *for Christ, for the defense of the gospel* (cf. also 1:7); in his opinion all in Ephesus who are preaching the word really do proclaim Christ. That some in group A who discomfort Paul were (c) Jewish Christians is possible, but not like the Judaizers in Galatia. (e) Jealousy toward Paul cannot be excluded. But there must be something specific, having to do with *trouble* for Paul in prison. (j) Appeal to his Roman citizenship is the item some thought unwise or, worse, betrayal of what a mission leader should be. That caused *envy and strife*, mixed motives in preaching, *self-interest*, and even *pretense*. Christians often differ over *the how*, not *the why*, in mission work. (k) Greek factionalism may be involved, enmity as concomitant of friendship; Paul reacts with a possibly exaggerated division into two groups, friends and those envious of the apostle. Use of his citizenship seems the likely catalyst for their resentment. How, in the face of possible death, he will explain his hopes for renewed life in the cause of Christ, makes 1:18d–26 necessary, a poignant continuation of the narrative with comments.

Not much use has been made over the centuries of 1:12–18c for its most prominent theme, speaking *the word* (1:14) = proclaim *Christ*; or of *progress* (but cf. Beardslee, Montague on "growth"). Paul's *bonds* (vv 13, 14, 17) are part of a history of prisoners and martyrs for the faith (Hargraves 26–27), including victims in Nazi concentration camps (Dietrich Bonhoeffer, Alfred Delp, S.J.;); Martin Luther King, Jr.; and oppression in South Africa. The passage was not assigned for Sunday use in traditional pericopes or the *Ordo's* three-year cycle.[45] Portraits of Paul in these vv range from "a completely defeated man" (R. R. Wicks, *IB* 11:28) to one stamped by "greatness" (B. Mayer 22).

SELECT BIBLIOGRAPHY (see also General Bibliography and Commentaries)

Banker, J. 1984. "The Position of the Vocative *adelphoi* in the Clause," *Selected Technical Articles Related to Translation* 11:29–36.

Bartchy, S. S. 1999. "Undermining Ancient Patriarchy: The Apostle Paul's Vision of a Society of Siblings," *BTB* 29:68–78.

Benoit, P. 1952. "Praetorium, Lithostraton, and Gabbatha," *RB* 59:531–50, repr. in his *GS, Exégèse et Théologie* (Paris: Editions du Cerf, 1961), cited from his *Jesus and the Gospel*, Vol. 1 (London: Darton, Longman & Todd/New York: Seabury, 1973) 167–88.

Boman, T. 1960. *Hebrew Thought Compared with Greek*. London: SCM.

Burdick, D. W. 1974. "*Oida* and *ginōskō* in the Pauline Epistles," in *New Dimensions in New Testament Studies*, ed. R. N. Longenecker/M. C. Tenney (Grand Rapids: Eerdmans) 344–56.

Court, J. M. 1982. "Paul and the Apocalyptic Pattern," in *Paul and Paulinism: Essays in honour of C. K. Barrett*, ed. M. D. Hooker/S. G. Wilson (London: SPCK) 57–66.

Harland, P. A. 2005. "Familial Dimensions of Group Identity: 'Brothers' (*Adelphoi*) in Associations of the Greek East," *JBL* 124: 491–513.

Hawthorn, T. 1950–51. "Philippians i.12–19. With Special Reference to vv 15.16.17," *ExpTim* 62: 316–17.

---

[45] Sporadic use, in some German Protestant lectionaries: 1:15–21 for Laetare, the Fourth Sunday in Lent; 1:12–21 for Sexagesima, just prior to Lent. Hence R. C. H. Lenski, *The Eisenach Epistle Selections Made Ready for Pulpit Work* (Columbus, OH: Lutheran Book Concern, 1914) 338–56.

Horrell, D. G. 2001. "From *adelphoi* to *oikos theou*: Social Transformation in Pauline Christianity," *JBL* 120:293–311.

Jeremias, J. 1958. "Chiasmus in den Paulusbriefen," *ZNW* 49:145–56 = *Abba* (GS 1966) 276–89.

Johnston, L. T. 1983. "James 3:13–4:10 and the Topos *peri phthonou*," *NovT* 25: 327–47.

Linton, O. 1937. "Zur Situation des Philipperbrief," *AMNSU* 4 = *Coniectanea Neotestamentica II. Adolf Jülicher zum achzigjährigen Geburtstag am 27. Januar 1937* (Uppsala) 9–21.

Lührmann, D. 1978. "De invidia et odio (Moralia 536E–538E)," in *Plutarch's Ethical Writings and Early Christian Literature*, ed. H. D. Betz, SCHNT 4 (Leiden: Brill) 363–66.

Machalet, C. 1973. "Paulus und seiner Gegner. Eine Untersuchung zu den Korintherbriefen." *Theokratia, Jahrbuch des Institutum Judaicum Delitzschianum* 11, 1970–72 (Rengstorf Festgabe), ed. W. Dietrich et al. (Leiden: Brill) 183–203.

Michaelis, W. 1925. "Die Gefangenschaftsbriefe des Paulus und antike Gefangenenbriefe," *NKZ* 36:586–95.

Mullins, T.Y. 1964. "Disclosure. A Literary Form in the New Testament." *NovT* 7: 44–50.

Munck, J. 1959. *Paul and the Salvation of Mankind*, Ger. 1954, tr. F. Clarke (London: SCM).

Omanson, R. L. 1978b. "A Note on the Translation of Philippians 1:12," *BT* 29:446–48.

Rogers, E. 1984. "Vocatives and Boundaries," *Selected Technical Articles Related to Translation* 11:4–29.

Sandnes, K. O. 1997. "Equality within Patriarchal Structures: Some New Testament Perspectives on the Christian Fellowship as a Brother- or Sister-hood and a Family," in *Constructing Early Christian Families*, ed. H. Moxnes (London/New York: Routledge) 150–65.

Theron, D. J. 1954. "*ALĒTHEIA* in the Pauline Corpus," *EQ* 26:3–18.

Walcot, P. 1978. *Envy and the Greeks: A study of human behaviour*. Warminster, England: Aris & Phillips Ltd. Annotated bibl. pp. 103–106.

1:12, 25 **progress/advance** *(prokopē)*: G. Stählin, *TDNT* 6:703–19; bibl. *TWNT* 10:1249; W. Bauder/D. Müller, *NIDNTT* 2:128,130,131; W. Schenk, *EDNT* 3:157–58; *TLNT* 3:185–88; K. Traede, *RAC* 8 (1972) 141–82; *OCD*[3] 102–3; H. Cancik, *RGG*[4] 3 (2000) 202–4. Additional bibliography in *Philippian Studies*, consulted but not listed here.

Beardslee, W. A. 1961. *Human Achievement and Divine Vocation in the Message of Paul*. SBT 31. London: SCM.

Stählin, G. 1957. "Fortschritt und Wachstum. Zur Herkunft und Wandlung neutestamentlicher Ausdrucksformen," in *Festgabe Josef Lortz*, ed. E. Iserloh/P. Manns, Vol. 2 *Glaube und Geschichte* (Baden-Baden: Bruno Grimm) 13–25.

4. *Narratio, Continued (Paul's Expectations, as He Weighs the Balance: To Stay on in Service), 1:18d–26*

TRANSLATION

1:18d Not only this, but I shall also continue to rejoice. [19] For I know that "this will lead to deliverance for me" through your entreaty and Jesus Christ, whom the Spirit supplies, [20] in accord with my expectation and hope; that I shall not be disgraced in any way, but in a totally free and open way, as always, so now, Christ will be made great through my own self, whether by life or by death. [21] For to me to live, Christ, and to die, gain. [22a] But if "to live" in the flesh, [b] this implying fruitful missionary labor for me, [c] what then shall I choose? I do not know. [23] But I am betwixt and between the two. If I have the desire to depart and be with Christ—for that is much better by far . . . , [24] but to continue to stay on in the flesh is more necessary on your account. [25] And since I am confident of this, I know that I shall stay, and stay on in the service of you all, for your progress and joy that arise from your faith, [26] in order that your grounds for boasting may continue to abound in Christ Jesus, in me, through my coming again to you.

NOTES

1:18d. *Not only this, but I shall also continue to rejoice. charēsomai*, from *chairō* (see NOTES on 18c *I rejoice* and 1:4 *with joy*), fut. m. deponent (BDF #77; GNTG 2:264). Doubled use of *chairō* also at 2:17,18 (+ *synchairō*), and 4:4. Here, linear action (Moule *IB* p. 10; ATR 889, "progressive future," MT #60, p. 32), "I am going to . . ." or "shall continue to rejoice"; cf. O'B 107; NRSV. KJV "I will rejoice" shows determination but is stronger "than the original justifies," Lft. 90.

alla kai, "(not only this, just mentioned) but also" (BDF #448.6; GNTG 3:330; cf. 2 Cor 11:1; Phil 3:8). *alla* (BDAG 3), not adversative but progressive or ascensive with *kai* (Hawth. 39; O'B 108); cf. sixfold *alla*, 2 Cor 7:11. Thrall 13–16. Paul's rejoicing is heightened, as the *gar* cl. in v 19 indicates (Schenk 144). NA[26,27] put a period after 18c (NRSV, NEB), only a comma after 18d, which begins a new paragraph (RSV period after 18d, renumbered as 19[a]). Most see a new beginning in 18d (Gnilka 63; Hawth. 39, O'B 108; Fee 126; U. B. Müller 57), but Collange 59, continuity. Silva 75–80 takes 1:18–20 as a unit.

1:19. *For I know that . . . gar*; a few MSS read *de* (P[46] B etc.). Fee 127 n 5, "most likely the *de* is secondary." *oida*, repeated in 1:25 (+ ptc. "being convinced, sure," which Schenk 144 would supply here also), 4:12 bis (*I know how*), 4:15; ptc. at 1:16, *because they know* . . . , all pf. tense, "I have seen," pres. sense "I know." + *hoti* (recitatival, *DA* 324), *know that* (BDAG *oida* 1.e; BDF #397.1) for the content of what is known (O'B 108). A second, parallel *hoti* cl. will occur in v 20. *oida*, know by seeing (with the mind's eye), intuitively, is often contrasted with *ginōskō*, come to know, learn; see NOTE on 1:12 *to come to know*. *oida*, knowledge based on observation, complete and final; *ginōskō*, knowledge incomplete and developing (Burdick [(3) Bibl.] 344). 1:19, "the knowledge of intuition or satisfied conviction or absolute knowledge" (Vincent 23). Similarly A. Horstmann, *EDNT* 2:494; Burdick 354–55. Hawth. 39 doubted "such fine distinctions. . . . Paul . . . uses them synonymously"; at times NT " 'knowing' and 'believing' are interchangeable" (John 14:7, 10; AB 29: 513–14). Bultmann, Phil 1:19, "knowledge which discloses itself to faith as a new self-understanding" (*TDNT* 6:218; Rom 5:3, etc.). Loh. 51 n 3, *oida* as religious certainty usually occurs in the pl., except in Phil (sg., 1:19, 25; 4:12).

    "this will lead to deliverance for me." Five Gk. words, Job 13:16a LXX verbatim; see COMMENT A.1. *touto* = neut. nom. sg., *houtos*. Could refer back to *en toutō[i]* in 18c, proclamation of Christ (Eadie 42; Bonnard 26); see NOTE there on *over this fact*; G. H. Clark, *Phil*. 30, "this [preaching by the 'rival preachers'] will result toward salvation" for their converts. More commonly (Lft. 91; O'B 109), Paul's situation in 1:12–18 (*ta kat' eme*); see NOTE on 1:12 *events affecting me. moi*, unemphatic, dat. of advantage or reference. *apobēsetai*, fut., deponent, m. voice, *apobainō*, BDAG 2, **turn out, lead (to)**, "eventuate," Luke 5:2; John 21:9; Luke 21:13, "this will eventuate to you [disciples hauled before the authorities] for witnessing (*eis martyrion*)," unmentioned by Loh. for 1:19. *eis* + acc., "with a view to, resulting in" (*IB* 70).

    deliverance. sōtēria, traditionally "salvation" (KJV, NAB, NIV-mg), fut. eschatological redemption (Vincent; Beare; Collange; O'B; cf. Bockmuehl 83). *deliverance*, release (Moffatt) from prison, has been adopted by RSV, NEB/REB, GNB ("I shall be set free"); cf. Hawth. (contrast Dailey 20). Some offer both (NIV-txt "deliverance," mg "salvation"). Others, a general sense of well-being (Gdsp. "highest welfare," CEV "will keep me safe"). BDAG (2) **salvation** with "transcendent aspects"; "exclusively . . . God's saving activity" (J. Schneider, *NIDNTT* 3:214). K. H. Schelkle (*EDNT* 3:327–29) sketches the secular Gk. sense of deliverance "from human beings or from natural circumstances," hence "welfare, well-being" re Paul's "present distress"; *TLNT* 3:345–49, without citing 1:19. B. W. Winter 1994:96, "the successful outcome" of Paul's trial; Holloway 2001:108–9, deliverance "from cowardice and shame"; J. S. Vos 2002:147, for his missionary work.

    sōtēria had an initial sense in Job, a further sense for Paul. Possibly the Philippians heard deliverance from mortal danger or a mystery-religions sense (Julius Firmicus Maternus, "Be of good cheer, you initiates, because the God is saved, *sōtēria* will come to us out of toils," *Errore Profanarum Religionum* 22.1; cited in *TDNT* 7:969; *EDNT* 3:327; *TLNT* 3:351; about A.D. 335). See COMMENT A.1 and B.1. The TRANSLATION (*deliverance*) allows for both aspects.

    through your entreaty and Jesus Christ, whom the Spirit supplies. Lit., "the supplying of the Spirit, of Jesus Christ." *dia* + gen. governs both *entreaty* and *supplying*, each + a gen. BDAG *dia* A.3.a., **by, via, through**, means or "intermediate agency" (*DA* 326). Possibly causal, "because you are praying for me" (NEB/REB, Schenk 164). For *deēseōs*, see on 1:4 *entreaty*. Gen. pl. *hymōn* (BDAG *su* 3, for the possessive pron.) stands between the art. *tēs* and its noun (as at 1:25 *tēn hymōn prokopēn*), distinguishing the Philippians' prayer from "the supply of the Spirit of Jesus Christ." *deēseōs* is a "distributive singular" (Fee 132 nn 26, 27), thus "prayers" [N]RSV). *hymōn*, subjective gen., not "prayer for you" or gen. of source. O'B 111, united prayer. U. Schoenborn, *EDNT* 1:286–87, "*intercession* of the church."

For *entreaty* and *supplying* with a single art. *tēs* (hendiadys), cf. 1:7 *defense and confirmation of the gospel*; 1:20, 1:25; 2:17. Cf. *ZBG* #184 (do "the prayers of the faithful" = "help which has as its object the Spirit of Jesus Christ"?); BDF #442.16, *kai* coordinates so as to avoid a series of genitives, "your prayer for [of] the supply of the Spirit of Jesus Christ."

supplies. epichorēgia, only here and Eph 4:16. BDAG **assistance, support;** *epichorēgeō* (3) **provide what is necessary for the well-being of another, support** (in the NT, only at Col 2:19). *chorēgeō* classical sense, "defray the cost of a chorus" at a public drama festival in Athens, a rich person's *leitourgia*; hence "provide money for something," then "grant, furnish." (*epi-* scarcely implies a *generous* supply, cf. Fee 132 n 28.) R. Mahoney (*EDNT* 2:45), "simply *help*." Is it act., supplying of the Spirit (Gk. fathers), or pass., that which the Spirit supplies (Chrysost.; Thdrt., the Spirit given to Paul)? Schenk 147, *nomen actionis*, God's providing the Spirit of the risen Lord; but Louw/Nida 35.31, "what the Spirit of Jesus Christ will provide for." NEB-txt, "the Spirit of Jesus Christ" was given to Paul as support; NEB-mg, "the Spirit of Jesus Christ supplies me with all I need." Fee 133 traces how "help" has evolved into a popular tr. (RSV, Gdsp.; NIV; JB) — without "evidence for such a meaning in the Greek materials"!

pneumatos after *epichorēgias* can be subjective, "from the Spirit" (NAB, GNB, CEV) or "by the Spirit" (NIV; O'B). Or obj. gen. (KJV; "I am provided with the Spirit"; Moffatt; Hawth., Bockmuehl 84). Lft. 91, "the Spirit of Jesus" is "both the giver and the gift." Or epexegetical, "Spirit" in apposition to "supply": the help is the Spirit of Jesus Christ. Fatehi 224 n 62 allows obj. or subj. gen. See below for a decision.

the Spirit. First of five instances of *pneuma* in Phil. Here "a supernatural non-material being" (*DA* 300); elsewhere possibly the "inner being" of the Philippians (*DA* 300), cf. 4:23; 1:27, like 2:1 and 3:3, is disputed. 1:19 (BDAG *pneuma* 5b) = the divine Spirit, of Christ, but "Spirit of Christ" is rare in Paul (E. Schweizer, *TDNT* 6:419 n 570), only Rom 8:9c, Gal 4:6, perhaps 2 Cor 3:17–18. Dunn, *NIDNTT* 3:703, "the Spirit for Paul" is "constitutively stamped with the character of Christ," who has by the resurrection become "a life-giving Spirit" (1 Cor 15:45), "the medium of union between Christ and the believer (1 Cor. 6:17)."

On *Jesus Christ* (MSS D, etc., reverse the order), see NOTES on 1:1 *Jesus* and *Christ* (1:14, 15, 17, 18; 20, 21, 23, and 26). See further the NOTE on 1:1 *in Christ Jesus* and EXC. A. Many regard "Christ," "the Christ," "Jesus Christ," and "Christ Jesus" (1:26) as interchangeable (Grundmann, *TDNT* 9:542–43; 553). The gen. at 1:19 is variously construed: source (Eadie 38); subjective gen. (majority view; Ewald 74 = Wohl. 82; Vincent 24; Michael 49; Gnilka 67; Collange 60,

O'B 111–12), "the Spirit from or sent by Jesus Christ," cf. Luke 12:11–12 par. Matt 10:19–20 (but in Paul the Spirit is usually said to be given by God the Father, 1 Cor 6:19; 2 Cor 1:21–22; 5:5; Gal 3:5; etc.); or apposition, "the Spirit, i.e., Jesus Christ." So Fee 134–35, "This is how Christ lives in him . . . , Christ resident in him by the Spirit." Schenk 146, an "epexegetical, qualifying attributive gen."; "the Spirit . . . as the risen, present Lord whom God has given us." Fatehi 225, "*the living Christ himself . . . at work . . . through 'the Spirit of Jesus Christ.'*" Hence, "the supplying of the Spirit, Jesus Christ," i.e. the Christ whom the Spirit supplies; smoothed out in Translation as *Jesus Christ, whom the Spirit supplies.*

The chiastic structure noted by Schenk 146 (Comment A.3, below) parallels *deēseōs* and *epichorēgias, hymōn* and *tou pneumatos,* but how prayer and the Spirit relate here is a further exegetical matter (Comment B, below). Many tr. literally, "of the Spirit of Jesus Christ"; the reader must unscramble. We regard *hymōn* as subjective gen. (prayer by the Philippians); similarly *pneumatos* (supplying from the Spirit); *Iēsou Christou* is explanatory. Both phrases introduced by *dia* can be moved up earlier in the sentence ([N])RSV, etc.) to explain why Paul thinks things will turn out for his salvation, but the Translation preserves the Gk. sequence.

1:20. *in accord with my expectation and hope.* Prep. phrase + *hoti* cl. for the content of his hope. To begin a new sentence (NIV, JB, GNB, NABRNT) separates this phrase from what it modifies in v 19 and is "conceptually misleading (. . . Paul expected 'deliverance,' v. 19), but hoped . . . that Christ might be magnified, v. 20)" (Fee 130 n 137). Loh. 51, hope is a further reason for his assurance that things will lead to his salvation; cf. Schenk 144–45, *kata* in v 20 is "identical" with *gar* in v 19; the *hoti* cl. in v 20 then depends, like the one in v 19, on *oida.* The apostle thus introduces readers to more that he knows surely. *kata* + acc. (BDAG B.5.a.δ) = *in accordance with* or "as a result of, on the basis of"; cf. Phil 4:11 . . . *being in need,* and 4:19 *in accord with the divine riches;* cf. DA 325.

expectation. apokaradokia (BDAG *eager expectation;* MSS F G read *karadokia*), in the NT here only and Rom 8:19, the "eager longing" of the creation. Coined by Paul? or (Chang) from the Gk. OT tradition, (Aquila Pss 38:8, 129:6; Prov 10:28)? Older interpreters drew on a "picturesque etymology of the word" (O'B 112–13): to watch (*dokein*) with the head (*kara*) turned away from (*apo*) other interests, therefore outstretched; thus "look forward with the head." Martin 1976:76, one "strains forward as with outstretched head . . . , a positive attitude," synonymous with "hope" (*elpis*). But Bertram 1958 saw uncertainty and even doubt (cf. Jos. *JW* 3.264 = 3.7.26, "await the hail of arrows" in a battle.; O'B 113 n 31). Theo. Mop. took *apo* negatively, lack of certainty. Denton 1982 (cf. Schenk 145) found no negative sense of uncertainty (cf. Morlet 75) or emotional tensions within Paul. *Wordbooks* vary between optimism (Delling, *TDNT* 1:393; Fee 135, "hope-filled expectation" for the hendiadys) and anxious anticipation (E. Hoffmann, *NIDNTT* 2:444–45). The Translation keeps *expectation,* without "earnest" (KJV) or "eager" ([N]RSV). On the hendiadys, see on 1:19 *entreaty and* "supplying of the Spirit."

hope. elpis, an important Pauline term; only here in Phil.; vb., 2:19, 23. BDAG 1.b.β, Christian hope (Rom 5:2, 4–5; 1 Thess 1:3, etc.); contrast Gk. "hopes" re death (Peres 274–61). Bultmann (*TDNT* 2:517–35), "the NT concept" is "essentially determined by the OT," *bātaḥ* and other terms, "confidence in God's help and protection," "expectation of good . . . linked with trust" (522–23). *bātaḥ* may also be rendered by *pepoithēsis* terms; cf. Phil 1:25 *pepoithōs oida*, "know confidently." Bultmann 531 saw three elements in NT hope: expectation of the future, trust in God, patience in waiting; echoed by Gnilka 67 and *DPL* 415. "Boldness" (1:20 *parrhēsia*) and "boasting" (*kauchēsis*, 1 Cor 1:12, etc.; *kauchēma* Phil 1:26) "are grounded in it"; waiting "effected by the Spirit" (cf. 1:19). With faith, *elpis* "constitutes Christian existence." Bultmann 1951 (INTRO. X Bibl.) 319–22: hope is faith pointing toward the future, grounded in God's grace (Gal 5:5; Rom 5:1–2); "freedom for the future" and "openness toward it" (320). Its correlative is fear. This situation leads not to "wavering between hope and fear" (which many find in 1:20–24) but to self-examination, the discrimination Paul recommended in 1:10 for the Philippians. "Existence in faith, then, is a movement between 'no longer' and 'not yet'" (322) for those who have "such a hope" and confidence and boldness (2 Cor 3:12). In 1:19 *elpis* expresses "sure confidence" (*TDNT* 2:531). Word studies: E. Hoffmann, *NIDNTT* 2:238–44; *TLNT* 1:489–90; J. M. Everts, *DPL* 415–17; Conzelmann 1969 (INTRO. X Bibl.) 184–90.

that I shall not be disgraced in any way. Most take the *hoti*-cl. to provide the content of Paul's expectation and hope in 20a; so (N)RSV; Ewald 74 = Wohl. 83; Fee 135; O'B 113. Or a more precise definition for *eis sōtērian* (1:19), "deliverance" = Paul's "not being put to shame." Or it parallels v 19, both cls. depend on *oida*. Cf. Michaelis 22–23; Hawth. 42; Schenk 143–44, 147–48; Gnilka 65 (67 to the contrary), O'B 107 (113 to the contrary); see chart in Fee 128–29, and below under COMMENT B.1. Schrenk's structural analysis is persuasive: "that I shall not be disgraced in any way" is synonymous with "this will lead to *sōtēria* for me," negative statement followed by a positive one, ". . . Christ will be magnified. . . ." To take *hoti* as "for" or "because" (Eadie 47; cf. DA 324, NEB) has little support; the fut. tense is against it, Loh. 53 n 2.

I shall not be disgraced in any way. en (BDAG 11, manner) + *oudeni*, dat. neut. sg., *oudeis* (BDAG 2.b.γ), "in nothing" (KJV), therefore "not . . . in any way" (NRSV, NABRNT). Some make it "never" (NAB, [N]JB), periphrasis for an adv. *aischynō*, in NT, only in the pass., **be put to shame, disgraced** (BDAG 2; 2 Cor 10:8); *TDNT* 1:190 saw merely "being disillusioned." Likely *passivum divinum*, "put to shame *by God*" (Hawth. 42; Collange 60 n 2). A contrast with "boldness" in the next cl. (Vincent 26; Craddock 28); better, with "Christ be magnified" (Fee 135–36; Schenk 148). Many stress OT coloring to the vb. (Gnilka 67; Hawth. 42; e.g., Pss 25:3; 69:7; 119:80, 116; 1 QH 4.23–24, etc.; [6] COMMENT A.1). Cultural anthropology contrasts shame with trust in God and "a sense of security that allows a person to act with great boldness (2 Cor 3:12), without fear of being shamed (Phil 1:20)," J. J. Pilch/B. J. Malina, eds., *Biblical Social Values and Their Meaning: A Handbook* (Peabody MA: Hendrickson 1993) 180.

but in a totally free and open way, as always, so now. alla introduces a contrast (BDAG 1.a); with a new cl. (BDAG 2) **the other side of a matter or issue, but.** Cf. DA 327, 328. en + *pasē[i]* *parrhēsia[i]*, manner (BDAG *en* 11 *freely, openly*; DA

327) or modal (Fee 136 n 52, citing Wedderburn 1985 [(1) Bibl. **in Christ**] 85). The modifier from *pas* (BDAG 3) suggests "all," in the highest degree, "full, supreme, total, greatest" (Reicke, *TDNT* 5:888, "elative").

parrhēsia is elusive. Only here in Phil; 2 Cor 2:12; 7:4; Phlm 8; more frequent in John, 1 John, Heb, and esp. in Acts 2:29; 4:13, 29, 31; 28:31 as "(Christian) boldness." Vb. in Paul, only at 1 Thess 2:2. Prominent in the Gk. political sphere for free and open speech by freeborn, male citizens, and among friends (Plut. *Adulator* 51C = LCL 1:276–77, the language of *philia*), and then as a moral concept; for Cynics "freedom of speech" was "the most beautiful thing in the world" (Diog. L. 6.69; outspokenness, verging on license in public; the LCL tr. of Aristophanes *Thesm.* 541 keeps part of the passage in Lat. because of its "scabrous nature"; Marrow 435, the Cynics' "dogged insolence"). Holloway 2001:110, a *topos*. Rare in the LXX (12x), but "the Gk. and Hell[enistic] understanding of *parrhēsia*" came over into Jewish literature. Word studies: H. Schlier, *TDNT* 5:871–86; H.-C. Hahn, *NIDNTT* 2:734–37; H. Balz, *EDNT* 3:45–47; E. Peterson 1929; Marrow 1982; van Unnik 1980.

BDAG lists (1) **speech that conceals nothing and passes over nothing,** *outspokenness, frankness, plainness;* (2) *openness to the public,* "before whom speaking and actions take place" (Phil 1:20); (3) *courage, confidence, boldness, fearlessness* (Acts 4:29), which trs. have preferred at 1:20 ("boldness," KJV, NRSV; "courage," RSV, NIV, JB, Marrow 445; "confidence" NAB; "fearlessness" NJB; "brave" CEV). For "Semitic background" (van Unnik 1980), Marrow 437–38 pointed chiefly to Lev 26:13 LXX and Ps 94 (LXX 93):1; Loh. 54, to Jewish wisdom literature, Prov 13:5 LXX; cf. 2 Esdras 7:87, 98. At the parousia Christians will not be shamed but exhibit *parrhēsia*. Schenk 148 terms Loh.'s statement the clearest semantic definition formulated, "This openness is the free courage of confession that expresses its firm conviction, all external opposition to the contrary." For Loh., the joy of public witness (cf. Ps. 119:46; Wis Sol 5:1), plus Loh.'s "martyr" theme; both "objective" (speak or act in public) and "subjective" (speak boldly, with trust in God). Paul's use reflects his apostolic authority (2 Cor 7:4; Phlm 8), with eschatological flavor (cf. Schütz 1975:223). Cf. Balz, *EDNT* 3:46, drawing on E. Peterson, van Unnik, and Malherbe 1970: "subjective interpretation of *parrhēsia* ('confidence') is not possible here"; rather "the glorification of Christ in oneself" (missionary activity or, with Loh., a public martyr's death, 4 Macc 10:5).

Malherbe furthered investigation of "frankness of speech," esp. re friendship and flattery. Cf. Fitzgerald 1996; Fredrickson 163–84, background in Gk. politics, rhetoric, and philosophy (overstated, Bockmuehl 85). 1:20 = "free speech" on the part of Paul and "the brothers and sisters" (1:14), the gospel "entering and shaping the public realm" (172) — paradoxically "through the suffering and shameful position of Christ, Paul, and the church." Vorster 1971, "conviction," but A. C. Mitchel (in Fitzgerald 1996: 211 n 27) thinks courage "fits the context better." Rhetorical analysis allows at 1:20 both "frank speech" and public setting. Cf. O'B 115. Schütz 1975:223 lamented, "no single English word . . . translates" all the nuances "with equal success." Most Eng. trs. take it subjectively, Paul's courage or confidence, commentators incline more to the open public arena where he will witness

(K. Barth; Morlet 75; Bormann 1995:217; Bockmuehl 85; Walter 41) or the frank character of his words. The TRANSLATION paraphrases, *in a totally free and open way*; the exact sense depends on how the situation is reconstructed.

as always, so now. hōs (BDAG 2.b) introduces a comparison (*DA* 315, 316), with *kai* (BDAG 2.c, like an adv., *so, so also*), as at Phil 2:7, 12, 15. On *pantote*, see 1:4 *always*; alliteration, *pasē[i] parrhēsia[i]*. *nyn* (BDAG 1.b) refers to "time shortly before or shortly after the immediate pres[ent]," *now*, possibly (BDAG 1.a.β.ג) *kai nyn*, "even now," in Paul's imprisonment. GNB, "especially right now." Most trs. have "now as always" ([N]RSV).

Christ will be made great through my own self. Vb. + *Christ* (no art., as in vv 13, 18, and 19) + "in my body." Cf. *DA* 381 on word order. *megalynthēsetai*, fut. pass. indic., root from *megas*, "great" (adv. at Phil 4:10 *greatly*). Hawth. 43, pass. not merely to parallel *aischynthēsomai* or "to keep the sounds agreeably similar" or because both occur in the Psalms (35 [LXX 34]:26–27; etc.) but "because he cannot bring himself to say, '*I* will magnify Christ.'" *megalynō* (in Paul, only here and 2 Cor 10:15, Furnish, AB 32A:473, 482) has a Gk. heritage; LXX, esp. for the Heb. *gādôl*, stressed by Loh. 55–56; see COMMENT A.1.(6) below. *Wordbooks:* W. Grundmann, *TDNT* 4:453, cf. 10:1172; F. Thiele, *NIDNTT* 2:424–27; *EDNT* 2:399; *TLNT* 2:459–60 ("no meaningful pagan parallel to the biblical *megalynō*," confess that God is great, exalt or celebrate God). Vg *magnificabiter Christus*, hence (Tyndale through ERV) "Christ shall be magnified." RSV "will be honored" (NRSV "exalted"; (N)JB "glorified"). NEB "the greatness of Christ will shine out clearly in my person" (cf. REB, "display his greatness in me"), sounds like Loh., "revelation" expressed through the martyr (56–57). BDAG 2, fig., "*exalt, glorify, magnify, speak highly of* . . . the prestige of Christ will be advanced in connection with me"; cf. Luke 1:46b. Perhaps it is *passivum divinum*, glorified *by God*, through Paul's body (cf. Hawth. 43). Schenk 148–49 argues against "glorified"; Paul knows no doxologies of Christ. LXX background permits "enlarge"; cf. Matt 23:5. Decisive is the only other Pauline passage, 2 Cor 10:15, the apostle's mission is to grow or be increased (BDAG *megalynō* 1), not "attaining to a greater worth" but "mastering of greater tasks" in mission (Bultmann, *2 Cor.* 197, cf. 196; see also Martin, WBC 40:322–26). Schenk connects this with 1:12, "the advance of the gospel," equated with "Christ being proclaimed" 1:18. That "the news about Christ may be spread widely through me" (Schenk's paraphrase, 164) is a synonym for the gospel's progress. The TRANSLATION *Christ will be made great* seeks to express this extension of his work and person through the missionary message.

through my own self. en tō[i] sōmati mou, first of only three instances in Phil of an important Pauline term sōma, "body" (2x at 3:21). *en* + dat., instrumental (BDAG *en* 5; W. Grundmann, *TDNT* 4:543; *DA* 326, 344, dat. of means), possibly locative (cf. BDAG 8, the object in which something shows itself; and 2.b, state or condition). *mou*, enclitic gen., "of me." *sōma* here is anthropological; BDAG 1.b, *the living body*, as "instrument of human experience and suffering" (Gal 6:17; 2 Cor 4:10), "organ of a person's activity" (1 Cor 6:20; cf. Rom 12:1, ta sōmata hymōn, "your very selves"), the great term of continuity in Paul's anthropology. As equivalent of Heb. *bāśār*, it can suggest the universality of sin

(J. A. T. Robinson 1952:17–33; Rom 6:6), but also the human body as wholly destined for God (ibid. 31–32 n 1). The "mortal bodies" of Christian believers are
made alive through (Christ's) indwelling Spirit (Rom 8:11). The body is thus "for
the Lord, and the Lord for the body" (1 Cor 6:13). The "physical body" (*sōma
psychikon*) will become a "spiritual body" at the resurrection (*sōma pneumatikon*,
1 Cor 15:44). Paul does not use *psychē* ("soul") at any point in Phil 1:20–23. This
twin aspect of *sōma* — dedicated to God (cf. 1 Cor 6:11–20) in Christ's service as a
vehicle for witness; fut. personal expression of Paul in the resurrection — allows
"through my body" to refer either to further missionary preaching by Paul or to
what happens to Paul's body in death (martyrdom) and then resurrection; or both.
How what follows is interpreted, "whether through life or through death," also is a
factor. Cf. E. Schweizer, *TDNT* 7:1064. Bultmann 1951 (Intro. X Bibl.) 195–96,
Paul "can expand *himself* for Christ."

Traditionally "body" (KJV, [N]RSV, NIV, etc.). Or "my person" (NEB) or "me"
(NAB, REB; Hawth.). Gdsp., "I shall do Christ credit" (cf. LB, CEV) loses Paul's
shift to Christ as subject and the modest emphasis on "of me." Some paraphrase,
Paul's "whole being" (GNB; Collange 60; Martin 1976:76, "his total life";
O'B 115; Bockmuehl 85). Against "person," Silva 80, following Gundry 1976:37,
insists on a presence that "is specifically physical"; similarly Fee 137 n 57. Dunn,
TPTA #3.2, argues that Gundry concentrates too narrowly on "physical body," but
Robinson 1952:28–29 went too far with *sōma* as a modern concept "personality."
Dunn suggests "embodiment" or "corporeality"; 1:20, "more than . . . physicality,"
namely "his witness as embodied" (p. 8).

whether by life or by death. Two *dia* (+ gen.) phrases (BDAG A.3 and 4, instrument, agency), + *eite . . . eite* ("if" + enclitic *te*, "and"), "if . . . if," "whether . . . or"
(BDAG *ei* 6.o.β). No vb.; KJV supplied "whether *it be. . . .*" *zōē* and *thanatos* omit
the art., like other pairs of words like "heaven and earth," 1 Cor 8:5; ATR 793(f),
794(k). *zōē* (Paul does not use *bios*) 26x in acknowledged letters; in Phil, also at
2:16 "word of life" and 4:3 "book of life." Vb. *zaō* 1:21, 22. BDAG (1) **life in the
physical sense,** the opposite of "death," so here, cf. Rom 8:38 and 1 Cor 3:22,
contrasting terms in rhetorical lists; or (2) **transcendent life** from God and Christ,
for believers "in the future, but which they also enjoy here and now" (BAGD; cf.
BDAG; Rom 6:4; Phil 2:16; 2 Cor 2:16). "Life of the new age," already present in
Paul? *Word studies:* von Rad/Bertram/Bultmann, *TDNT* 2:832–75; Bultmann
1951:203–10, esp. 209–10; H.-G. Link, *NIDNTT* 2:474–84; L. Schottroff, *EDNT*
2:105–9; J. J. Scott, Jr., *DPL* 553–55; Eichholz 1962 ([2] Bibl.) 149; Scott, *DPL*
553; Vollenweider 1994:99. Most refer 1:20 to "natural life" (*TDNT* 2:861 n 242).
EDNT 2:106, U. B. Müller 59, 1:21 overshadows or relativizes the phrase at 1:20.

thanatos = "(natural) death"; BDAG 1.a; Bultmann, *TDNT* 3:14; W. Schmithals,
NIDNTT 1:440; *EDNT* 2:129–33; *ABD* 1:110–11. In Phil 5x (1:20; 2:8, 27, 30;
3:10).

The Translation uses *whether by life or by death* and *sōma* as the equivalent of
"self"; "me myself" overemphasizes *mou.* my own self brings out concreteness as
human being and apostle.

1:21. *For to me to live, Christ, and to die, gain.* The Gk. conceals problems beyond grammar and philology. On chiastic, structural features, see COMMENT A.3. O'B 119–22 and Vollenweider 99 n 29 rightly reject 21a as protasis for a conclusion in 21b ("if . . . , then . . ."; Schenk 152, 164).

For to me. gar (1:18a, 19a) links 21 with 20: *Christ will be made great* by Paul's *life* or *death* (DA 324). The link may be with the last phrase of v 20 (Loh. 57; P. Hoffmann 1966:293–94; Gnilka 69; Fee 139–40), all of v 20 (Ewald 75–76 = Wohl. 84–85; Jones 20; Bonnard 28), vv 19–20 (Michaelis 24, grounds for Paul's knowledge that events will lead to his salvation), or 18d–20 (grounds for Paul's joy 18d, B. Weiss; Haupt 36–37, 18c–20). (N)JB takes *gar* as general reinforcement, "of course"; BDAG *gar* 3, **marker of inference, *certainly, by all means, so, then.*** The Moffatt NT omits *gar*; no close connection with what precedes (Michael 53). Unlike Nestle[25] and UBSGNT, NA[26,27] introduce a space between 20 and 21, as between 18c and 18d.

to me. Dat. sg. *emoi,* emphatic form, first in the cl.; dat. of advantage (BDF #188, for whose interest is affected; Edart 81) or respect (DA 345). Dat. of possession if *Christ* is the subject of the sentence (see below). Continues the 1st per. in vv 13, 14, 17, 18, 19, and 20. Many infer "'to me,' whatever it may be to others" (Lft. 92), as with *hēmōn* at 3:20; Paul sees differently than others do (Ewald 76 = Wohl. 85); "personal confession" (Schmitz 161).

gain (kerdos). Loh. 57 n 5 and Friedrich 144–45 cite parallels: "death . . . a wonderful gain," Plato, *Apol.* 40D = HCNT #792; "for someone to die well is gain," Pausanias, 4 *Messenia* 7.11; "How does dying not bring gain?" Soph. *Ant.* 462–64, cf. Antin and *El.* 814–22; "what gain is living further for me?" Eur. *Med.* 145, cf. 798 and *HF* 1301–1302; "gain if one would die, to live, misfortune," Jos. *Ant.* 15.158 = 15.5.5, *JW* 7.358 = 7.8.7; Aelian, *VarHist* 4.7, "Dying was not gain for the evil"; Aeschyl. *PV* 747 (cf. Palmer 208), "What way is living for me gain?" Ael. Arist. 51, 56, in van der Horst 1980:63. Palmer 208–16; Aeschyl. *Pro.* 747, 750f.; Soph. *Ant.* 462–64.; Vollenweider in COMMENT A.4 below. A Greco-Roman commonplace, *death is gain* because one thus escapes life's troubles (Palmer 218). Loh., *to me* distances Paul from such *communis opinio.* O'B 118 denies contrast to views of "others." Vollenweider 1994:98, *emoi* is part of the *sygkrisis* form Paul employs; COMMENT A.4, below.

to live. Art. infin., *zaō,* pres. act. A "continuous present" (Vincent 26), contrast aor. "to die" (single action). Fee 140–41 n 9, "the natural 'tenses' . . . in Greek"; DA 389, "two different topics are set apart with different tense-forms," "to live" and "remain" (in vv 24, 25) in contrast with "die" and "depart." No one bothers to render, "keep on living." BDAG 2.b.α, **live in a transcendent sense,** "the sanctified life of a child of God . . . in the glory of the life to come" (Rom 8:13b; cf. Phil 1:19). The art. infin. occurs more in Paul (106x in the Pauline corpus) than in the rest of the NT; ATR 1426–27; *to zēn* 1:22; *to de epimenein* 24; *to . . . pisteuein . . . paschein* 29; 2:13 (twice). Here for something previously mentioned (BDF #399.1), "life" *(hē zōē)* in v 20 (Loh. 57 n 4, papyrus examples, *zōē* is identical with *to zēn*). Most take *to live* as subject (ATR 1059; as the art. suggests; ZBG 174, cf. 175), *Christ* as pred. nom. (DA 424; Moule *IB* 115–16 on Colwell's rule, but far from certain here due to the absence of a vb.). See below, on *Christ.*

Whether *zēn* = physical existence here on earth (in contrast to death) (B. Weiss; O'B119; J. S. Vos 2002:150) or supernatural life of the new age in Christ (cf. BDAG *zaō* 1 and 2) now or in the fut., or both (Haupt, Schmitz, Dib., Hoffmann 1966, Gnilka, Walter 42; in Exc. A, Hanhart Siber 88–89) cannot be settled on philological data or even Pauline usage, but only from context and Paul's thought. From the *sygkrisis* form, Vollenweider 1994:99 concludes for "earthly life."

estin is sometimes supplied (MSS F G^gr, etc.), most trs., "to live *is* Christ" (KJV, italics = what the trs. supplied; [N]RSV, etc.); "means Christ" (BDAG *eimi* 2,c.α, explanatory) in Moffatt, Gdsp., etc. BDAG, "life is possible for me only where Christ is" (*zaō* 2.b.α, citing Schmitz), but noting, "Another common interpr[etation] is *for me to live is Christ*, i.e., while I am alive I experience real life in connection with Christ; w[ith] death comes life in all fullness in the presence of Jesus." The TRANSLATION omits any vb.

Christ. Christos, no art., as in vv 20, 19 (with "Jesus"), 18, and 13 ("in Christ"). See NOTE on 1:1 *Christ*. Usually taken as pred., after *estin* (supplied), "to live is (or "means") Christ," "to me life is Christ" (NEB/REB; [N]JB; GNB). Others see (mission) purpose: LB "living means opportunities for Christ" (cf. CEV, NLT); Schmitz, "while I am alive I work for Christ"; Bultmann, *TDNT* 2:868, s.v. *zaō*, with 1:22. ZBG #173, his fruit is "'Christ' because Paul's life-work is 'building up of the body of Christ'" (but Phil does not use *sōma Christou*). Giglioli's emendation, *chrēstos*, "for me to live is profitable" (cf. Phlm v 11)—Collange 61; Bockmuehl 88, "life is good"—may be ignored. Droege/Tabor 1992:120–21, "cannot be sustained," but wordplay is suggested (*Christos* should be *chrēston* [neut.] to agree with *to zēn*, 1988:280 n 61).

Christos was treated as subject by Chrysost. (K. Barth 37); some medieval exegetes; Luther; Calvin 41–42 (others cited by B. Weiss 102 n 1), "I . . . make Christ the subject . . . so that he is declared to be gain for him both in life and death." The art. infins. are then acc. of respect, BDF #160; or supply *pros* (Schmitz 155). Tyndale's "For Christ is to be me lyfe" continued through the Bishops' Bible; KJV followed the Rheims NT, "to live is Christ" (Vg *Mihi enim vivere Christus est*). Since 1611 no Eng. tr. seems to have *Christ* as anything but pred. Hofmann revived the alternative interpretation (Schmitz 155). The Ger. Catholic EÜ (1980) continues the Luther-Calvin tradition ("for me, Christ is life"), influenced by Gal 2:20, "no longer I, but Christ lives in me"; cf. Col 3:4, "Christ our life." The same effect results if *to live* is subject, defined by the pred. *Christ* so comprehensively that *Christos* is in effect subject, Christ-life now but also after death (BDAG 2.b.α, see above on *to live*). So Ewald 76 = Wohl. 85; Schmitz 163; Dib. 67–68; K. Barth 37; Hoffmann 1966:292–95, esp. 294; Siber (Exc. A) 88–89; Gnilka 71; U. B. Müller 59. Not an assertion about earthly existence but the second alternative in v 20, *death*. Christ means life for Paul (life of the new age during the time he lives in the flesh); death is a further gain (Schreiber 2003:339), Paul's *expectation and hope* (v 20, Schmitz 161). Contrast Loh. 58 n 1. Against taking *to live* in v 21 as a reference to life after death: v 22 will specify *to live in the flesh* (Baumbach 1977 [(Exc. A)] 453).

O'B 119–21 explores five arguments for *to zēn* as life of the new age (the Luther-

Calvin view) and counterarguments to each (against which further points can be raised), before concluding for the "traditional view," living on earth, but "Christ-centered." Fee 141 n 10 finds the Luther-Calvin view theologically attractive but goes with O'B's "refutation" of it. Cf. Schenk 151; Vollenweider 1994:99. Though Eng. trs. favor "to live is Christ," it cannot be excluded that "Christ" colors (rules?) "living" as a Christian for Paul. See COMMENT B.2, below.

and to die. kai connects two cls., "to live, Christ, and to die, gain"; in the Calvin interpretation (above), two nouns, "Christ is gain in regard to living and dying." *kai* puts both on the same level. Not either/or (Loh. 57) or "but rather" *(kai mallon)* (O'B 121), though *kai* can suggest something "surprising or unexpected or noteworthy," BDAG *kai* 1.b.η, "and yet"; 2.c (= BAGD II.3), *also, so.* Eng. trs. usually have *and*; NAB "hence"; [N]JB "but then."

die. Art. infin (see on *to live*), aor. act., *apothnēskō,* BDAG 1.a.α, natural death. 42x in the Pauline corpus, 23x in Rom; in Phil, only here. Aor., single action, is to be expected. Some see the "*act* of dying" (contrast "*process* of living," *to zēn*); Hawth. 77, the fate of martydom (Loh.); Schenk 149, instantaneous; all of this Silva 82–83 rightly denies. Others, the aor. "denotes . . . the consequence of dying, the state after death" (Lft. 92); Vincent, "complete union with Christ"; Melnick 85 ("see" and "enjoy" the Lord). GNB: "Death, then, will bring more." Confusion (Silva 83)! If any of this is present, it comes from v 23 *with Christ,* not an aor. tense, to die.

gain. Pred. after "is" (understood). *to kerdos,* 3x in the NT (Phil 1:21, 3:7 pl., Titus 1:11 "sordid gain"). Vb. *kerdainō,* 6x in Paul, 5 of them in 1 Cor 9:19–22, "gain converts," a missionary term; Phil 3:8, see NOTE on *gain Christ* in contrast to "loss of all other things." Commercial background is apparent at 3:7 and 8; cf. Mark 8:36 parr., "gain the whole world"; Matt 25:16, 17, 20, 22, gain money by trading. *TDNT* 3:672–73 (H. Schlier) gives classical Gk. background; on death as a gain, see NOTE on 1:21 *For to me.* Schlier 673 and B. Siede (*NIDNTT* 3:136–38) weave references in Phil together, the latter to attain "a positive understanding of gain"; "gain for the gospel," rather than for Paul (so Bonnard 28), Gnilka 71–72 n 11 rejects this. Dailey 24, no art., so death is "a gain."

1:22. Literally, 22a, "But if to live in (the) flesh" (often with some vb. added, such as "If it is to be life in the flesh" [RSV] or "If I am to live in the flesh" [NRSV, cf. KJV, NIV]), is clearly the protasis of a conditional sentence. 22b, "this for me (is, KJV) (or "means," [N]RSV) fruit of labor," may be conclusion (or apodosis) of the conditional sentence or part of the *if*-cl. 22c, "and what I shall choose, I do not know," the conclusion, or a separate sentence, or two sentences ("What shall I choose? I do not know"). The following combinations are possible (see UBSGNT apparatus on punctuation after *en sarki, karpos ergou,* and *hairēsomai*):

I. Traditional and quite common, "But if (it is to be) life in the flesh, this (means) fruitful labor for me. And what I shall choose I do not know." (a) protasis, (b) apodosis, and (c) a separate sentence. Lat. fathers generally (B. Weiss 103 n 1); TR (therefore KJV); Moffatt, [N]RSV, etc. Variations include a semicolon after (b), as in NRSV or a dash after (b), so WH, NAB.

II. (a) protasis, (b) apodosis, and then (c) two statements, the first usually punctuated as a question. NIV, "If I am to go on living in the body, this will mean fruitful labor for me. Yet what shall I choose? I do not know." So REB, NLT.

III. (a) and (b) are an incomplete conditional sentence, (c) a separate sentence or sentences. Lft. 92–93, his second choice and third explanation: the *if*-cl. is "elliptical, the predicate being suppressed," or the *if* "implies an interrogation": "but what if my living in the flesh will bear fruit, etc.? In fact what I shall choose I know not" (cf. Lft.'s expanded paraphrase at the top of p. 92, col. 1). So NEB, "but what if my living in the body may serve some good purpose? Which then am I to choose? I cannot tell."

IV. Most frequent, apart from I, is (a) and (b) protasis, (c) conclusion or apodosis. Gk. fathers generally (B. Weiss 103 n 1); JB, "if living in this body means doing work that is having good results—I do not know what I should choose"; cf. NJB, Gdsp., GNB, LB. ERV-txt, two *if* cls.: "if to live in the flesh, —*if* this shall bring fruit." We shall adopt IV, with modification.

V. Some renderings are free and hard to classify. CEV = (c), then (a) (b) as a complete, nonconditional sentence. On the history of exegesis, see B. Weiss 103–4 n 1. No interpretation "can claim to be quite satisfactory" (Michael 56); Paul wrote simply (*ExpTim* 1923), "And which to choose I cannot tell" (22c). 22a and b = later marginal comments. Gnilka 72 n 19 rejects this: it interrupts progression in Paul's thought from "to live" to "live in the flesh."

1:22a. *But if "to live" in the flesh. ei de.* P⁴⁶ D, *eite,* "if" + the enclitic connective *te,* "and if" (P⁴⁶ *epei,* "since," BFD #442.8, Collange 61); O'B 124 n 39. Gnilka 72, Schenk 151 regard *de* as adversative (a different possibility than "death" or "gain"; contrast *gar* in v 21); so KJV, JB, NEB, "but"; or even "on the other hand," NAB, NJB. Fee 143–44, *de* "signals a progression of thought, not a contrast" to v 21, "Thus: '*now* if "to live" in the flesh is what transpires.' " We take *de* to continue the thought (*DA* 327) and expand on what was said of life in vv 20 and 21 (*DA* 356). ZBG #173, "illative." Introduces a condition (O'B 124). Vincent 27, syllogistic: if (a) is true; then (b) follows. The protasis is assumed to be true, the conclusion is also true.

"*to live.*" Art. infin. *to zēn,* repeated from v 21; hence quotation marks. BDAG *zaō* 1.c, "physical life," + "the sphere" where it is lived ("*in the flesh* in contrast to the heavenly life"), citing Gal 2:20c. BDAG too easily made v 21 "the life to come"; "physical life here" is too one-sided. Gal 2:20 speaks of "the life I now live in the flesh," but life "by faith" in Christ, who "lives in me."

in the flesh. First of five occurrences in Phil of the important Pauline and biblical term *sarx* (1:24; 3:3; 3:4 bis; 72x in acknowledged letters). *Word studies: TDNT* 7:98–151 (E. Schweizer et al); *NIDNTT* 1:671–82 (H. Seebass/A. C. Thiselton); *EDNT* 3:230–33 (A. Sand); *TLNT* 3:231–39; Bultmann 1951 (Intro. X Bibl.) 232–46; R. J. Erickson, *DPL* 303–6, esp. 304; Dunn, *TPTA* #3.3; Sand 1967; Jewett 1971a:49–166; Gundry 1976:147–56. Like "flesh" in Eng., often a negative connotation. Bultmann treats *sarx* with "sin" and "world" in Paul. But *sarx* has a range of meanings in the NT. For Heb. *bāśār* (H. W. Wolff, "frail man" in OT use), "the human being in weakness," compared to God (Isa 31:3; 40:6–7; Gen 6:3, etc.). Qumran literature heightened this sense (R. Meyer, *TDNT* 7:110–14). Cosmological aspects at times, *sarx* in contrast to God's Spirit, as a principle like Sin. Sin operates in the flesh and finds its beachhead there for an assault on all of human life (Rom 7:8, 11). Flesh becomes a power like Sin (Bultmann 1951:245; criticized in T. W. Manson's review, *JTS* 50 [1949] 205).

In Paul, *sarx* ranges in meaning from neutral to negative. Spicq, a "neutral" and a "pejorative nuance," and then "[i]t gets worse" (*TLNT* 3:236–37). Well illustrated in BAGD (revised in BDAG): (1) "the material that covers the bones of a human . . . body," 1 Cor 15:39a; (2) the physical body, Gal 4:13–14, bodily illness; (3) humans as "flesh (and blood)," Gal 1:16; (4) human/mortal nature, earthly descent, Rom 4:1; (5) life here on earth, marked by physical limitation(s), corporeality, 1 Cor 7:28; 2 Cor 4:11; Phil 1:24, 22; Gal 2:20, but inserted by BDAG under 2) above, as b]; (6) the external side of life, 1 Cor 1:26; Phil 3:3–4 [BDAG 5]; (7) "the willing instrument of sin," so that "no good thing can live in the *sarx*," Rom 7:18, in BDAG as 2.c.α; and BAGD (8) "the source of the sexual urge" = BDAG 2.c.β.

Verse 22 fits in the middle of this continuum, human existence as earthly and limited, not corrupted or corrupting, simply corporeal. Neither hostility to God (Rom 8:6–8) nor negative ethical aspects (Gal 5:19–21) are apparent here. All human life is existence "in the flesh" (Gal 2:20; 2 Cor 5:9), but need not mean living "according to the flesh" (*kata sarka*, 2 Cor 10:3). Christian life is not yet the full *zōē* of the new age (Bultmann, *TDNT* 2:863). Hence Schweizer: "earthly life in its totality" but "not in any way disparaged" (*TDNT* 7:126). To live or remain (1:23) "in the flesh" is simply "'to remain alive'—alive in the sphere of earthly life," where people, Christians too, lead their lives (Bultmann 1951:233, 235). Sand (*EDNT* 3:231), "sounds Hellenistic" but "agrees with the OT view"; in the "Greek understanding the soul can indeed be in the body, but not the human being in the *flesh*." The justified-but-not-yet-perfected Paul (3:12–14) reflects on continuing in the flesh. Cf. *GNTG* 3:264, a "peculiarly Christian" usage. *NIDNTT* overstates, "the flesh is . . . so vanquished, that . . . it is all one whether he lives or dies" (1:676, Seebass) and (with Jewett) Paul writes here against "a false type of 'enthusiasm'" (679, Thiselton). Some question the tr. "flesh" (KJV tradition), old-fashioned, too negative (*TPTA* p. 11). But "body" ([N]JB, NIV, NEB/REB) suggests *sōma*; Gdsp.'s "here" lacks specificity. Dunn 70 concludes, "best translated consistently by the same term, 'flesh.'" *en* + dat. is local (Wedderburn 1985 [(1) Bibl. **in Christ**] 87).

1:22b. *this implying.* Dem. pron. *touto*, neut. nom. sg.; refers to the art. infin. in v 22a, *to zēn en sarki*; cf. BDAG *houtos, hautē, touto* 1.a.ε; Phil. 3:7; 4:8, 9. One could render, "But if this living on in the flesh (implies) . . . ," *to zēn* + *en sarki* (without repeating the art. *to*, to indicate second attrib. position) + the dem. pron.; unusual (though in Paul *houtos* does often come after the subst., BDAG 2.b). For the punctuation in the TRANSLATION, cf. ZBG #459, *ei de to zēn en sarki touto moi* *karpos ergou, kai ti hairēsomai;* Cf. BDF #442.8 (p. 229); GNTG 2:422. *estin,* must be supplied at least once, perhaps twice, in 22a and b. We assume it after *touto,* rendered as "implies." If *estin* is added after *zēn,* "But if it is life in the flesh," or "If to live means (living) in the flesh," then 22b becomes apodosis (so Fee 144, esp. n 25) or an awkward continuation of the *if* cl. — "But if it is life in the flesh, this (being) fruitful labor for me" ([N]JB, Gdsp., NEB).

fruitful missionary labor for me. moi karpos ergou, lit., "for me fruit of work." For *karpos* see NOTES on 1:11 *fruit of righteousness* and 4:17 *profit,* agricultural and commercial senses. Here, **advantage, gain, profit** (BDAG *karpos* 2). On *ergon,* see NOTE on 1:6 *a good work.* Here, positive, as always in Phil (1:6; 2:30); **work, occupation, task** (BDAG 2). The debate noted at 1:6 ("work of God," "human work") surfaces at 1:22 in comments about "God's work" (Loh. 60); "the divine work goes forward" (*TDNT* 2:643). But there is wide agreement (F. Haupt, *TDNT* 3:615) that "the work of the apostle" is involved here. "The results of the missionary are his fruit" (B. Weiss 104), fruits of which he may partake (Rom 1:13; 1 Cor 9:7), but the Philippians also benefit (1:6; 4:17). Similarly, *NIDNTT* 1:723 (R. Hensel), 3:1151 (H.-C. Hahn); H. Th. Wrege, *EDNT* 2:251–52. O'B 125, "fruitful missionary work in the future."

The gen. *ergou* is variously explained: epexegetical (ZG; ZBG #45); apposition (BDF #167)—Paul's fruit is the work itself, *erga* = *karpos* (*TLNT* 1:57 n 12); gen. of quality (Ewald 78 n 3 = Wohl. 87–88 n 4; cf. BDF #165), "work-fruit." *karpos* is sometimes taken as an adj., "fruitful labor" ([N]JB, NIV, NAB). Less likely, subjective gen., "fruit (or results) from my work" (Ewald/Wohl.; TC, "brings me fruit from my labors").

The dat. *moi* goes with the subst., not the assumed vb. (ATR 537); i.e., my fruitful labor (KJV, [N]RSV), not just "it means for me. . . ."

1:22c. *what, then, shall I choose?* Interpretation Number IV above, *kai ti hairēsomai* as apodosis, taken as a question. *kai* = *then* at the start of the conclusion (Fee 144, esp. n 25, Paul "shifts gears"—anacoluthon). If *kai* introduces a new sentence (RSV, NIV; O'B 126 n 53, "Yet"; DA 326, 328), it introduces "an abrupt question, which may often express wonder . . . incredulity, etc." (BDAG *kai* 1.b.θ; BFD #442.8; GNTG 2:422; ZBG #459). DA 349, the interrog. form highlights Paul's dilemma.

The interrog. *ti,* neut. sg. *tis, ti,* = *which of two* (BDAG 1.a.α.ℷ), i.e., "life" or "death" in v 20. Cf. O'B 127, "*ti* is used in place of *poteron,* 'which of two'"; ZBG #153; BDF 65.

Most MSS have fut. m. deponent, *haireō,* BDAG 2, **choose, prefer.** P[46] B cursive 2464 (10th cent.) read subjunct. *hairēsōmai* (deliberative, BDF #336), "What am I to choose?" The fut. indic. can have a deliberative sense (Schreiber [(1) Bibl. **Christ**] 339 n 10). In 22c taken as one sentence ("I do no know what I shall choose"), an indic. is possible in an indirect question (BDF 366.2, 368, 442.8; GNTG 3:117; ZG, cf. ZBG #341, ATR 875).

For Paul, "selective preference . . . between two possibilities" (H. Schlier, *TDNT* 1:180; cf. G. Nordholt, *NIDNTT* 1:533–35). Loh.'s "martyrdom" theory (60–61) sees no real choice for Paul (these are internal musings); what Paul says about "fruit" tests the Philippian community facing its own martyrdoms. Gnilka 72 and O'B 127 stress Paul standing before God. Collange 63, such views not convincing; *haireō* = "'take into one's hands, to seize' in a very realistic way, and in the middle 'to take for oneself, to choose,'" Paul plans to exercise his Roman citizenship in court; see COMMENT A.7. O'B 126–27, would avoid "this very concrete or realistic way," but ends up, "Yet what shall I choose?" On "chose" as the preferred rendering, cf. Wansink 97–102.

I do not know. ou *gnōrizō*, a separate sentence. Also at Phil 4:6. BDAG (1) **to cause information to become known:** *make known, reveal* (Rom 9:22–23, etc., Phil 4:6); (2) **be knowledgeable . . .** *know* (Phil 1:22). 1:22 could be (1), causative (BDF #108.3; GNTG 2:408), but most Eng. trs. follow BDAG (2), "I do not know" (NRSV, etc.). But cf. "I cannot tell" (RSV, NEB; Bockmuehl 90). W. Mundle, *NIDNTT* 3:314, lists 1:22 with passages about "immediate proclamations of the divine will." O. Knoch (*EDNT* 1:256), "'I cannot . . . *discern.*" Vincent 27–28, "I have nothing to say as to my own preference"; O'B 128, "nothing to declare (from God)." Fee 145 n 28 with "most interpreters": "I do not know," i.e., "I don't know what to say." See COMMENT A.7.

1:23. *But I am betwixt and between the two. de,* continuative with v 22 (DA 327). Few tr. it. KJV "For," from *gar* in TR. Vincent 28, "an explanation": "I do not declare my preference. Now the reason is that I am in a strait." Similarly ZG; ZBG #467. Voice emphasis, "But I *am* hard-pressed."

synechō, pres. m.-p., = "have together, hold together," (Luke 8:45; 22:63), "impel, seize on, control" (2 Cor 5:14). At 1:23, "be claimed, totally controlled" by two conflicting options and thus divided (H. Koester, *TDNT* 7:883–84). Hence, BDAG 5, pass., *be tormented by, afflicted w*[ith], *distressed by*; "be hard pressed" (to choose) ([N]RSV). The papyrus cited by MM 606, "held in prison" *(synechomenos)*, is no parallel (Koester, 7:878 n 14, 884 n 65). Loh. notes "bound" or imprisoned (62 n 2), but opts for "inner" oppressions. "I am torn" (NEB, NIV, NLT), "pulled" (REB), "caught in this dilemma" ([N]JB), "caught between the two" (NABRNT). Louw/Nida, 30.18, "in the middle between two sets of thoughts" (too cerebral?). *TLNT* 3:338 "be on the horns of a dilemma," as in Lft. 93.

ek tōn duo, gen. pl. of "two" (BDAG *duo*) + art. (neut.) after *ek* (BDAG 3, cause, d.β; possibly g.γ, of the inner life; DA 326, the options faced by Paul). Assumes two opposites and refers back ultimately to *life* or *death* (20).

If I have the desire to depart and be with Christ. Circumst. ptc. *echōn*, "having" (agrees with "I" in the vb. in 23a, *synechomai*), causal or conditional ("if"). BDAG *echō* 7.a.β, *have* as one's own, possess + dir. obj.; "of conditions, characteristics, capabilities, emotions, inner possession." Cf. *DA* 306, 312. That keeps open whether Paul controls the option (suicide; Roman citizenship, see COMMENT A. 6, 7) or it is a matter of inner reflection.

desire. epithymia, here only in Phil, 10x in the acknowledged letters. Usually bad connotations, esp. in Paul, physical, evil cravings (of the flesh) (BDAG 2; KJV, "lust," Gal 5:16, etc.). *sarx*, "flesh," at Phil 1:22 and 24 sometimes carried this negative sense into 1:23. But here *epithymia* has a good sense, as at 1 Thess 2:17 (BDAG 1.b). Loh. 62–63 n 4 provides LXX examples. The art. *tēn* can indicate possession, "my desire" (Vincent 28; [N]RSV). + *eis* + acc. "desire for something" (BDAG 1.b), *to depart* (*to analysai*, art. infin.). BDF #402.2, *eis* + art. infin., purpose or result cl. (1:10 *eis to dokimazein*). Haupt 37, direction toward a goal; *DA* 329, the content of a process. *eis* is omitted in P[46] D E F G (BDF #402.2; GNTG 3:143); O'B 116, left out "to simplify or smooth out the text." Probably apposition to *epithymian*, "my desire, i.e., to depart"; Ewald 79 = Wohl. 89. No matter how construed, the sense is much the same. The TRANSLATION uses the infin.

to depart. Infin., *analyō*, aor. act., single action (cf. ATR 858). BDAG 2, *depart, return.* Used of breaking up an encampment (Polyb. 5.28.8; 2 Macc 9:1), "pull up stakes." Lft. 93, "symbol of man's transitory life on earth" (repeated in Hawth. 48, who adds references to "weighing anchor," Polyb. 3.69.14; our idiom, "sail on"). Reeves 287 uses this ship reference to claim 1:23 = "to be set free from chains," but the parallel with v 21 *apothanein* points to "physical death" (*DA* 302 n 14). Hawth. 48 notes "'solution'" from LSJ, evidently "9. solve the (Indian) problem (Plu[t] 2.133c)"; but cf. also LSJ 4, "investigate analytically" (Aristot. *Nic. Eth.* 1112b20) or "reduce a syllogism" (Aristot., *Logic*). G. M. Lee claimed a Gk. hexameter line behind Phil 1:23 and the Oration of Libanius for the Emperor Julian (the Apostate), "better *(kratton)* to go away *(apelthein)* than to live *(zēn).*" The anti-Christian Libanius would not have quoted St. Paul, so Lee reconstructed a "source" both of them might have used, "My heart now bids me to depart. Better to go away." Unlikely. Vogel 1977, that *analysai* = "depart the body" assumes Paul distinguished "body" and "soul" as in Gr. philosophy; Paul's concept was Semitic/OT.

Good literary koine (ATR 130), Hellenistic (Peres 244), a euphemism, as in Socrates, *Ep.* 27.5. Some cite Lucian, *Philopseudes* 14, "when he was eighteen, he departed" (LCL *Lucian* 3:340–41 A. M. Harmon tr., "he was solving fallacies"; cf. LSJ 9, above); IG XIV 1794 2 (in MM 36, to depart [from] life); Epigr. Graece 340,7 = Schreiber 2003:356, below, next NOTE; Epict. 1.9.16, "Whenever [God] will . . . release *(apolysē[i])* you . . . , then you will depart *(apolyesthe)* to him." Cf. 2 Tim 4:6, "the time of my departure *(analyseōs).*" F. Büchsel, *TDNT* 4:337; *EDNT* 1:84, leave this life. KJV tradition = "depart"; [N]JB: "be gone."

and to be with Christ. art. *to* before *analysai* also serves to make *einai,* "to be," a second art. infin. One art., two nouns; cf. 1:19 *through your entreating and the supplying of;* 1:20 *my expectation and hope.* It binds closely together *to depart* and *to be with Christ.* Gnilka 73, U. B. Müller 63, and Schreiber 2003:340 take *kai* as explicative, "to depart, i.e., to be with Christ." *syn* (BDAG 1.a.γ; cf. 1:1; 4:21; at 2:22, as here, to modify a vb.) suggests accompaniment and association, to be with someone (Xen. *An.* 1.8.26, Luke 24:44). Deissmann, *LAE* 2nd ed. (1927) 303 n 17, reported an Alexandrian *graffito* (Imperial times) about meeting someone after death, "I pray swiftly to be with you *(syn soi einai)*"; Schreiber 2003:356 n 81, a tombstone inscription (2nd/3rd cent. A.D.), "I have departed *(anelysa)* to the gods and am with the immortals *(athanatoisi).*" Quintus Smyrnaeus (4th cent. A.D.), *Posthomerica* epic, Achilles "is with the immortals." Ael. Arist. 50, 52, *syneinai theō[i]* . . . *suggenesthai theō[i],* of Aristides' contact with the god by means of his dreams; van der Horst 1980:63. Cf. *TDNT* 7:783–84. On *Christos*, see NOTES on 1:1, esp. *in Christ Jesus*. On "with Christ," see EXC. A, below.

for that is much better by far. . . . gar, lacking in ℵ D etc., Koine tradition (KJV supplied "which"), Lat., other versions, but present in P⁴⁶ A B C, etc., most eds. and trs.; [N]RSV; CEV "because"; "causal," *DA* 324. Supply a vb., "is," and subject, *that* ([N]RSV) or "which" (NIV).

better. Comparative of *agathos*, "good," *kreittōn, -on* Attic form; *kreissōn, -on*, Hellenistic Koine, generally found in Paul (BDF #34.1, pp.18 and 19; GNTG 2:107; NA²⁷ *kreisson*). BDAG *kreittōn* 2, **more useful, more advantageous, better,** 1:23 *much better indeed.* + dat. sg. neut. *pollō[i]*, from *polus, pollē, polu,* "much, many" (also at Phil 2:12; 3:18), here substantively (BDAG 2.a.β. כ). Dat. of degree of difference, "better by much." Cf. BDF #246; *DA* 360; common in the papyri; GNTG 3:29, *pollō[i]* functions as an adv. On *mallon*, "more," see NOTES on 1:9 *still more and more* and 1:12 *actually.* Cf. 2:12 *pollō[i] mallon*, "much more." The double comparative *mallon kreisson*, "more better" (ATR 278, 546), or triple with *pollō[i]* (Lft. 93; Martin 1976:79), is redundant, but cf. Shakespeare, "most unkindest cut" (Moule *IB* 98).

1:24. *but to continue to stay on in the flesh is more necessary on your account.* As in v 22, *de* is adversative (*DA* 327, 356), *but* ([N]RSV, etc.); KJV "nevertheless"; ERV "yet" (NJB). Again art. infin. as subject (like *to zēn* in 1:21 and 22, BDF #399.1; IB p.127; GNTG 3:140), pres. act., *epimenō*, **stay, remain** (BDAG 1; 7x in acknowledged letters; only here in Phil). in B, a few cursives (NA²⁷; O'B 116), aor. act. infin. *epimenai* to parallel aor. *analysai* in 23 (Collange 61).

in the flesh. en tē[i] sarki (P⁴⁶ B D etc., Koine tradition). ℵ A C etc. omit *en* (homoeoteleuton, *epimenein en?*). UBSGNT, NA²⁷ bracket *en.* On *sarx* (BDAG 2.b), see NOTE on 1:22 *in the flesh;* local again (Wedderburn 1985 [(1) Bibl. **in Christ**] 87). *epimenō* can be followed by *en* + dat. (1 Cor 16:8). But the dat. (without *en*) can depend on *epi* prefixed to the vb.; adding *en* was then a "correction" (Ewald 81 = Wohl. 90; cf. O'B 116). Little difference in meaning, with or, as we prefer, without *en. flesh*, no pejorative sense here. *tē[i]* may be equivalent to a possessive: "(for me) to remain in my flesh." To "remain in prison" (Reeves 286) is forced (*DA* 302–3 n 14).

more necessary. Comparative of the adj. *anagkaios, a, on,* "necessary" (2:25; 2 Cor 9:5). On the comparative *-oteros*, see BDF #61.2. "(It is) necessary" (+ infin.) is common; BDAG 1.

on your account. di' hymas (dia + acc. of the 2nd per. personal pron, pl.); **because of, for the sake of** (BDAG B.2.a) you Philippians. Cf. NOTE on 1:15 *on account of.* It describes "the motive (or reasons) behind a person's actions or decisions" (*DA* 324, "benefaction"). Many trs. (NRSV, etc.) follow KJV, "for you"; or "for your sake(s)" (NEB/REB), "for your benefit" (NABRNT). Gnilka 76 and Schenk 159–60, "you" pl. includes all Paul's congregations, not just that at Philippi.

1:25. *And since I am convinced of this, I know that. . . . kai* (as in 18c and 22c) + *touto* ("this") + *pepoithōs* (2nd pf. act. ptc., *peithō*, BDAG 2.b, **be convinced, sure, certain,** see NOTE on 1:6 *since I am confident*), then *oida*, as in v 19, NOTE on *I know.* Followed by a *hoti*-cl., for the content of what is known. Eds. and trs. have usually (a) placed a comma after *popoithōs*, "And being confident of this, I know that . . ." (KJV-NRSV). Others (UBSGNT punctuation apparatus) have (b) no punctuation after *pepoithōs* but a comma after *oida* (NA[25]), "And being confident I know this, that . . . ," = "This indeed I know for certain" (NEB). Or (c), no punctuation (so WH, NA[27]), let the reader decide. Lft. 94 preferred (b), "Of this I am confidently persuaded, that. . . ." So NAB[RNT], [N]JB. The KJV interpretation (a) is supported by Gdsp. ("I am convinced of this, and so I know . . ."), REB, Vincent, Michael, Hawth. Punctuation and construal affect how *touto* is taken: does it look back to something already said (view [a]), or forward to the *hoti* cl. (view [b])? Cf. Ewald 81 = Wohl. 90–91. We follow view (a).

And since I am confident of this. kai (overlooked in [N]RSV, NIV; Fee 152 n 7) links vv 23–24 to 25 (*DA* 328). Circumst. ptc. *pepoithōs* (referring to Paul), causal sense (NRSV). Its object, *touto* (see NOTE on 1:6), refers back to v 24, more necessary for Paul to remain in the flesh for his communities. So Bultmann, *TDNT* 6:6 n 17; this confidence is "the basis of the knowledge that he will in fact remain"; *pepoithōs oida* = "a non-logical expression" for *eidōs touto* (= v 24), *pepoitha hoti*, "Because I know this (what is better for you), I am confident that I shall remain. . . ." *hoti* recitatival (*DA* 324). Confidence occurs also at 1:6; 2:24; cf. 1:14.

I know that I shall stay, and stay on in the service of you all. oida, see NOTE on 1:19 *I know*, cf. 1:12 *to come to know (ginōskein)*, and (unsuccessful) attempts to distinguish them. Silva 85 and his 1980 article deny *oida* stresses "certainty in contrast to *ginōskō*"; "either verb . . . would indicate Paul's strong conviction." Does Paul speak here like a prophet (so Calvin 44; Bengel; denied by Lft. 94 but echoed by Loh. 66, O'B 138, and others)? Does *I shall stay* contradict Paul's expectation in 1:20? See COMMENT B.3. Ewald 83, 85, cf. Chrysost., proposed reading *ho ti*, neut. *hostis, hētis*, "whatever": "what I shall remain, that I will remain together with you for your progress." But (Wohl. 92 n 1) it should have *touto* (or *ekeino*) in the second cl. ("*that* will I remain"). The proposal is not needed; v 25 does not contradict 20.

Haupt 41–42 argued for 24a as *conditional* ("*if* I continue to live"), parallel to v 23, "if I die . . ." (*echōn* as conditional, "If I have the desire to depart . . ."). In vv 25–26, emphasize the purpose cls. introduced by *eis* (v 25 "for your progress and joy") and *hina* (v 26 "that your boasting may abound . . ."). 25a = "With full confidence I know this"; *touto* refers to what follows: "that if I remain on earth, I shall stay on (to serve) with you all" (KJV; involving more than just the Philippians). When Paul says, "(If) I remain," he already has in mind v 25, "for your progress." Ewald 82–83 = Wohl. 91–92 repeated this interpretation, with *ho ti*, and *paramenō* as "willingly remaining"; cf. Gnilka 93 n 1. Schenk 160 endorsed the conditional-sentence proposal. On lack of *ei*, indicating an *if*-cl., Schenk pointed to K. Beyer 1961 on Semitic syntax in the NT (no page reference; cf. p. 68 on Phil 1:22; 73–74, 233–37, and 259–81; most examples in Beyer are from the Synoptic Gospels, but cf. Rom 13:3; 1 Cor 7:18ab, 21, 27). "(If) I remain, then (*kai* as in 22c) I shall stay on (to serve) you all . . . ," fits Schenk's structural analysis and tr. (160, 164). U. B. Müller 71 states the obvious objection: no explicit evidence in v 25 for a conditional.

I shall stay. menō (circumflex on final syllable, contraction of *e* + *ō*), fut. indic., *menō* (pres. tense, acute on first syllable). BDAG 2.a , ***remain, last, persist, continue to live***; 1 Cor 15:6. Wordplay with *epimenō* (infin.) in v 24 and *paramenō* which follows, ***stay, remain with someone, continue, go on living*** (BDAG 1.b). Trs. seldom capture the wordplay. The TRANSLATION uses "stay" for *menō* and "stay on" for *epimenein. paramenō*, the third expression, poses another problem: besides "stay," it can mean ***continue in an occupation/office***, "serve" (BDAG 2). Cf. MM 487–88; Loh. 67 n 3 gives papyrus evidence for service of slaves; Heb 7:23 priests serving. PPetr. 3.2.21 (B.C. 236), BGU 4.1126.2 (B.C. 8), etc., led to the dictum "*paramenein* . . . is a common euphemism for *serve* [required service]," but MM also provides examples of a manumitted slave staying on in (voluntary) service. *Paramenōn* was a slave's name (Schenk 160). Hence NABRNT, "continue in the service of you all"; Moffatt, Gdsp. ("serve"); "stand by you all" (NEB/ REB, NJB). *symparamenō*, D (2nd hand) etc., Koine MS tradition, "is clearly secondary" (O'B 138). The TRANSLATION takes *paramenō* (+ dat.) as "serve," but to keep the wordplay, *stay in the service of*. . . .

you all. pasin hymin, 4x in 1:3–11; see NOTES on 1:4 . . . *all of you,* 1:7 . . . *you all* and *all of you sharing,* and 1:8 *you all.* As in v 24 (see NOTE *on your account*), some claim *you all* refers to more converts than those in Philippi (Haupt 42; Schenk 160; contrast Loh. 65, 67, whose "martyrdom theme" limits it to Paul and the Philippians, rejected by Gnilka 94 n 7, among others). Fee 152 italicizes "*all* of you" because he sees friction in the congregation. O'B 140 sees pastoral care for "the whole congregation of the Philippians."

for your progress and joy that arise from your faith. eis, purpose (cf. BDAG *eis* 4.a, e, and f; DA 345, though 325 n 39 also suggests "result"), + two terms, *progress* and *joy,* with a single art. *tēn,* "the advance of you and joy of faith"; hendiadys, cf. 1:7 *defense and confirmation;* 1:19 *through your entreaty and the supplying of;* 20 *my expectation and hope;* and 23 *to depart,* NOTE on *and to be with Christ.*

progress. prokopē, a key term and *inclusio* word for 1:12–26. See NOTE on 1:12 *progress* and (3) COMMENT B.1. *your* (pl.) *progress* re faith differs from Gk. examples about moral progress of the individual; it's communal (*TDNT* 6:714–15). Classical sources, notably Polyb., sometimes had a collective sense, progress involving more than individuals, applied to the Principate, notions of a new "Golden Age" and "good tidings" of Caesar's advent. Cf. *Philippian Studies.*

your. Gen. pl. *hymōn* (BDAG *su* c), subjective gen. (your advancing; Ewald 83–84 = Wohl. 93; Loh. 67 n 5), or possession (Eadie 2nd ed. 65), or objective gen. Can go with both *progress* and *faith.* For its position between art. *(tēn)* and noun *(prokopēn),* cf. 1:19 *tēs hymōn deēseōs kai epichorēgias* . . . (art., gen. pl., noun and noun).

and joy. charan, see NOTES on 1:4 *with joy,* 1:18c *I rejoice,* and 1:18d *I shall also continue to rejoice* (vb. *chairein,* twice). Here it parallels "progress . . . in faith."

faith. pistis, also at 1:27; 2:17; 3:9 (twice); vb. at 1:29, an immensely important term in Paul (91x in acknowledged letters). Many nuances in BDAG (references below include all passages in Phil): (1) **that which causes trust and faith:** a. ***faithfulness, reliability, fidelity, commitment*** on God's part (Rom 3:3) or by those in

Christ (Gal 5:22, with other virtues); (2) **state of believing on the basis of the reliability of the one trusted, *trust, confidence, faith,*** believing in a. God (Rom 4:5, 9, etc., of Abraham); b. Christ (Phil 3:9a, but see NOTE there); c. the gospel (Phil 1:27); d. without an object, α, faith as true piety, genuine religion (Phil 1:25; 2:17; 3:9b; often in Rom), the most frequent Pauline sense; γ. as a Christian virtue (1 Thess 3:6; Phlm 5; 1 Cor 13:13; . . . ζ. miracle-working faith (1 Cor 12:9; 13:2); 3) **that which is believed, *body of faith/belief/teaching*** (Rom 1:5; Gal 1:23). Thus Paul has both "faith with which one believes" subjectively (*fides qua creditur*) and "(the) faith content which one believes" objectively (*fides quae creditur*; *TDNT* 6:213–14) (2 and 3 above). BDAG assigns 1:25 and two other of the five references in Phil to 2.d.α, "believing," no specific objects of belief specified. The other two examples (2b and c) specify who or what is believed, 1:27 the gospel, 3:9a Christ (so NRSV-txt, NRSV-mg "the faith of Christ"). *Word studies:* Burton, *Gal.* (ICC 1921) 475–85; R. Bultmann/A. Weiser, *TDNT* 6 (1959) 174–228; Bultmann 1951 (INTRO. X Bibl.) 314–30; O. Michel, *NIDNTT* 1:593–606; G. Barth, *EDNT* 3:91–98; J. Reumann, *IDBSup* 332–35, *EBD* 453–54; *TLNT* 3:110–16; Dunn, *TPTA* 371–79; K. Haacker, *TRE* 13 (1984) 277–304; D. Lührmann, *ABD* 2:749–58.

NT faith roots in the Heb. Scriptures, esp. the vb. *'āman* (330x), hip'il *he'ĕmîn* (51x, "believe, declare God reliable"), and nouns *'ĕmet* (127x, stability), *'ĕmûnāh* 49x, faithfulness), and *'āmēn* (30x, in response to prayers). None coincides fully with NT faith as belief, trust, and obedience, not to mention hope and faithfulness (*TDNT* 6:205–8). Significant OT passages for Paul include Gen. 15:6 (Gal 3:6; Rom 4:3, 9); Hab 2:4 (Gal 3:11; Rom 1:17); Isa 28:16 (Rom 9:33; 10:11) + Isa 8:14 (Rom 9:33). See *TDNT* 6:182–96. Buber 1951 distinguished OT/Judaic, communal trust and faith, based on the covenant, and Christian, Gk. *pistis,* as persuasion or belief in someone or something. Critique in E. Lohse 1977. Attempts to trace NT faith to Gk. origins (*TDNT* 6:182–83, 201, 215–17) prove uncertain. Note Kinneavy, Gk. rhetoric as "persuasion" (cf. *NIDNTT* 1:587–93, "Faith, Persuasion"); Lührmann 1976:751–52, Hellenistic-Jewish links; G. Barth 1982, Hellenistic connections. Spicq finds inner Christian development, little secular parallel (*TLNT* 3:110). Because *pistis* "derives from *peithomai* ('be persuaded, have confidence, obey')" (ibid., cf. 66–79 and 110–16), note at 1:25 *pistis* and *pepoithōs* (NOTES on 1:6 *since I am confident* . . . and 1:14 *having become confident in the Lord* . . .).

Jesus' call for faith and, some say, his own example of trusting God (Jeremias 1971:159–66; Schillebeeckx 1979:194–200; *TRE* 13:292–94; Yeung) may have influenced Christians. Faith in Christ as response to the *kērygma* marks Christianity (*TDNT* 6:208–13; 1 Cor 15:11, etc.). To believe is "mission language." Disciples after Easter are believers (Acts 2:44; Rom 1:16; 3:22), a view inherited by Paul. *pistis* = ongoing believing, trusting, and commitment, a content to be believed and expressed in life. Paul related it esp. to righteousness/justification (Lührmann 754); see below on 3:4b–11.

At 1:25, the believing, trust, piety, indeed religion of the Philippians (and other Christians) that is living, can grow (2 Cor 10:15) and be strong or weak (Rom 14:1;

TDNT 6:212 n 283). *Fides qua creditur* rather than here a content that is believed. The art. (as at 1:27; 2:17; and 3:9b, but not 9a) can suggest "the faith," but more likely specifies whose believing is involved, i.e., "you," Philippians. *pisteōs* (gen.) has been called possessive (Eadie, 2nd ed. 65); subjective (Loh. 67 n 5, a personified power that has joy re impending martyrdom for Paul and the Philippians, cf. 1:27; Gnilka 94 n 4 questions the view); source or origin (O'B 140, "progress and joy which spring from your trust"); objective (in effect *fides quae*; O'B 140, claiming Collange 70). Fee 153 n 15, gen. "of reference," "progress and joy, both with regard to the faith, that is, the gospel." Schenk 161, followed by U. B. Müller 71: causal (or subjective) gen., "joy caused by your believing" (Schenk 164; *nomen actionis,* for *en tē[i] pisteuein,* "in [your] believing"; cf. the noun in v 27, infin. in v 29). Schenk's chiastic structure (COMMENT A. 3) parallels "faith's joy" with "your boasting" in v 26.

Usually taken with both *progress* and *joy* (Vincent, among others). A few, only with *joy* (Gnilka 94 n 5); B. Weiss 113 n 1, with *progress* obj. gen.; with *joy,* subjective gen. Three renderings are possible (O'B 140): "(1) 'for a joyous furtherance of your life of faith' (or 'for a cheerful advance in faith' [so Stählin, *TDNT* 6:715—*charan* functions as an adj. with *prokopēn*]; (2) 'for your progress and joy in the faith' [so O'B; Fee; Hawth. 52; RSV, etc., TC "the Faith"—objective gen., *fides quae*; but Fee 153 n 15 weighs the possibility of a possessive gen., "your faith's progress and joy"; Melick 87 n 102, "progress and joy directed toward their faith"]; (3) 'for your progress and joy which spring from your trust' [*pisteōs,* gen. of source or origin; or subjective or causal gen., Schenk 161, "for your progress," explained—*kai* is epexegetical—by "yes, your believing produces joy"; U. B. Müller 57 *Glaubensfreude*]." The TRANSLATION follows (3), using *faith,* as in most Eng. trs., the art. with *pisteōs* makes specific it is the faith of those addressed (Gdsp., NEB, CEV "your faith").

1:26. *in order that your grounds for boasting may continue to abound. hina* (BDAG 1.a.δ), purpose. Most tr. "so that," which may suggest result. Pres. act. subjunct., *perisseuō,* BDAG 1.a.β, *be present in abundance,* as at 1:9 *may continue to grow* (Loh. 59, 68, growth of the "measure of faith" assigned each one by God, Rom 12:3). As at 1:9, continuing action.

your grounds for boasting. to kauchēma (BDAG 1) **boast,** object of boasting, *the thing of which one is proud* (2:16). Rienecker 202: ground or reason for boasting. Vb. *kauchaomai* at 3:3. Pauline (55 of 59 NT occurrences, 54x in acknowledged letters). OT roots (cf. Jer 9:23 at 1 Cor 1:31). Genths distinguished "grounds for glorying" (pass. 1:26) from "boasting" (act. 1 Cor 5:6, etc.). Word studies distinguish egotistical "boasting" (viewed negatively) from Paul's positive, boasting "in the Lord." Bultmann (*TDNT* 3:645–54) begins with OT admonitions against self-glorying (Prov 21:7; Ps 52:1, etc.) and for exulting in God (Ps 89:16–17; Jer 9:23–24), sometimes eschatologically (Zech 10:7). Paul contrasts with "faith" (Rom 3:27; 4:2) boasting in a negative sense, glorying in the covenant law (Rom 2:17, 23) or in the flesh (see on Phil 3:3–4). People on their own have nothing to boast about (1 Cor 1:25–31; 4:7). But believers can "boast in God through our Lord Jesus Christ" (Rom 5:11), esp. in Christ's cross (Gal 6:14). A particular aspect is "apostolic self-boasting" (esp. 2 Cor 10–12). At the parousia Paul expected his churches to be his grounds for boasting (1 Thess 2:19–20; 2 Cor 1:14; Phil 2:16) and the apostle their grounds for boasting (2 Cor 1:14; 5:12). Christians, like the apostle, can glory amid afflictions (Rom 5:3; 2 Cor 4:7–11; 11:23–30); "sufferings" are "the envelope of the *dynamis* [power] of God" (*TDNT* 3:650). *Word studies:* Bultmann 1951 (INTRO. X Bibl.) 242–43, 281, 300–1, 315, 345; H.-C. Hahn, *NIDNTT* 1:227–29; J. Zmijewski, *EDNT* 2:276–79 ("be ashamed" at 1:20 is an antonym, "be confident" at 1:25 a synonym, as is "trust" or "faith"); *TLNT* 2:295–302; Sánchez Bosch 118–19. Because of negative connotations to "boasting," trs. resort to "Christian exaltation" (Gdsp.), "pride" (NEB/REB), "praise" (JB), "cause to glory" (RSV), "proud confidence" (NASB), or "jubilation" (Bockmuehl 94–95). KJV "rejoicing" wrongly suggests *chara* (Plummer 31; cf. NIV "your joy"). NRSV went back to "boasting," assuming people understand its positive sense.

your. Pl. *hymōn*, could be objective gen., "my boasting about you Philippians." Most take it as subjective gen., "your boasting"; Lft. 94, Vincent 31; Hawth. 52 ("probably"). The Philippians do the boasting, O'B 141; Fee 154 n 19. Of whom or of what do they boast?

in Christ Jesus, in me, through my coming again to you. Three prep. phrases, two with *in. en Christō[i]*, see NOTES on 1:1 *in Christ Jesus*, 1:13 *in Christ*, 1:14 *in the Lord*, and (1) COMMENT B.5.a. *en emoi*, prep. + dat. sg., *egō*, emphatic form (expected after the prep., BDF #279), *emoi* at 1:7 and 21 (*moi* 1:19, 22). MSS F G f g reverse the order, *en emoi en Christō[i] Iēsou*.[N]KJV reverse the names, "in Jesus Christ," without textual evidence. The real problem is with what to connect these two prep. phrases: NEB "your pride (*kauchēma*) in me," REB "pride in Christ Jesus"; cf. [N]RSV; Hawth. Gdsp. "in me fresh cause for Christian exaltation" (*kauchēma* with both phrases), cf. Moffatt, "ample cause to glory in Christ Jesus over me." CEV "pride in Christ Jesus because of me" (txt), "pride in me because of Christ Jesus" (mg).

en emoi might mean "with reference to me" (ATR 588); or dat. of means (*DA* 326, 344). Vincent 31 combines the three phrases, "ground for glorying . . . in Christ, then in Paul as representing Christ; then in Paul's personal presence with them." Loh. 69 n 1, Paul plays with the prepositions, *en, en, dia,* and *pros:* a "time-less" *in Christ,* Paul's time-conditioned "coming again" to the Philippians, escha-tological *en emoi*—the Philippians would become his "joy and crown" (4:1). Schenk 162, "in Christ" = "in the day of Christ Jesus"; cf. 1:10; 1 Cor 15:31; 1 Thess 2:19–20. The word field here and at 1:11 includes eschatological terms: "gain" 1:21, "fruit" 1:11, 22, "glory" 1:11, and "praise" 1:11. Interpretation relates to how *hymōn* gen. pl. is taken. If the Philippians do the boasting (subjective gen.), then boasting or pride over their apostle Paul (NEB; Lft. 94, O'B 141; Vincent 31, Christ the sphere, *en emoi* the immediate occasion; A. Oepke, *TDNT* 2:541). Silva 86, "an unquestionably Pauline concept" (cf. 2 Cor 1:14; cf. Phil 2:16), to which one need not object on "theological grounds"; "in Christ Jesus" with "abound," *en emoi* = "through my ministry." We conclude for "in Christ Jesus" with "abound" (Paul's literal word order; Vincent 31; O'B 141), not with *kauchēma*. But Fee 155 n 21, a "fine distinction"; "it 'overflows in Christ' . . . precisely because he [Christ] is first of all the grounds for any and all such boasting." Things do not fall into place until the final phrase is considered.

through my coming again to you. dia (means, cause or reason, "because of," DA 326) + gen. of *parousia*, modified by the gen. fem. sg. of *emos, ē, on*, possessive pron. used as an adj. (GNTG 3:191; BDAG a.α.ℵ) for the possessive *mou* (1:3, etc.), "my." Stylistic variety or more emphasis here? *palin*, "again," means "back" with vbs. and nouns of coming, etc.; BDAG 1.a, *my return*.

coming. 14 of 24 NT instances of *hē parousia* occur in the Pauline corpus (3x in 2 Thess, never in Col, Eph, or the Pastorals). So associated with the fut. coming of Christ (Matt 24:3, 27, 37, 39; 1 Cor 15:23; 1 Thess 2:19, etc.) that one almost overlooks a general sense "being present, presence" (1 Cor 16:17; 2 Cor 10:10; Phil 2:12) and the "coming" of some human being (BDAG 2.a, 2 Cor 7:6–7, Phil 1:26). For "apostolic parousia," see on 2:12, 19–24. Not used in Phil of Christ's future coming, but see Exc. A; A. Oepke, *TDNT* 5: 858–71, esp. 859 for 1:26; G. Braumann, *NIDNTT* 2:898–901, esp. 899; W. Radl, *EDNT* 3:43–44; *TLNT* 3: 53–55, esp. 53 n 3 (papyrus examples). Discussions on "presence"/"arrival" are sometimes confused over whether the vb. root is (*para* = by the side of +) the enclitic *eimi* = be ("be present") or *eimi* (circumflex accent, first syllable) = go ("go alongside, come near"). Paul's *parousia* (in Philippi) is plainly meant (Loh. 69 n 1), but some see overtones of present with the Philippians at "the End" (martyrdom, Loh.) or Christ's parousia (Schenk, "in Christ Jesus" = the Day of Christ). The TRANSLATION uses *coming* for *parousia* and *again* for *palin* (KJV-NRSV tradition), rather than simply "being with you again" (NAB, NIV) or "through seeing me restored to you" (REB).

to you. pros (+ acc. pl.), BDAG 3.g, *"by, at, near, . . . be (in company) with* someone." Cf. 2 Cor 11:9; Gal 4:18, 20, all with forms of *pareimi*, "be present." *pros* + acc. may suggest motion towards, or be stylistic variety after a vb.-compounded with *para*. Reicke (*TDNT pros*, 6:722), motion *and* ensuing state (of being), "both coming again and staying." Cf. Moule *IB* 52–53, *"position . . . a* more 'punctiliar' sense"; cf. 1 Thess 3:4; *GNTG* 2:467, an Aramaism (for *lĕwāt*) or extension of classical usages. DA 320, 344, spatial distance, as in 2:25, involving travel. Trs. alternate between "to you" (KJV-NRSV) and "with you" (NIV, NAB, JB, Gdsp., NEB), depending on the rendering of *parousia*. Some make "your boasting" the subject (KJV, NEB, NIV, NABRNT) or "you" (the Philippians) (Gdsp., RSV, JB, TC, REB, CEV); others, Paul's being with them (NAB), his ("my) return," or "I" (Paul) the starting point (NJB, LB; NRSV). As often, tr. depends on overall construal and reconstruction of Paul's situation. See COMMENT B.3 for application of our rather literal tr.

COMMENT

Phil 1:18d–26 continue the letter body begun at 1:12. *progress* in 1:12 and 25 provides an *inclusio*. Paul, in prison, turns to his own situation and the Philippians' progress in faith. Commentators speak of agitation, emotion, even suicide, but the passage is artfully written, with a number of literary features (Edart 66–70, 72–73). Some continue from 1:12–18c: *1st per. sg. narratio* (see [3] COMMENT A.3); "I" style in the vbs., 1:20, 22, 23, and 25; 1st per. pron. in vv 19, 20, 21, 22, and 26; *pathos* (or *ēthopoiia*, Edart 80–81; Lausberg #820–22) as Paul faces dying; the vocabulary of missionary preaching ([3] COMMENT A. 5); Greco-Roman terminology, but some phrases have OT backgrounds. 1:19 seems to employ five words out of the Gk. Scriptures. Material in 18b–26 comes from Paul's reflections on his situation.

A. FORMS, SOURCES, AND TRADITIONS

1. *An Allusion to Job 13:16 LXX; the Gk. OT in Phil.* For use of the OT in Phil and this first possible example at 1:19, see Reumann 2006b, here summarized. All OT wordings in Phil are "embedded," not cited.[1] Hays 1989:21–24 took 1:19 as parade example of an OT "echo" (more subtle than an allusion; Oakes 2000:252, "potential echo"), though earlier application by Michael (1924a; MNTC *Phil.* 46–49) to Paul as a Job figure was not noted. (1) The same five Gk. words appear in 1:19 as in Job, but no formula shows Scripture is being quoted. (2) Job 13:16 is subject to interpretation; e.g., Job as righteous, destined to face the divine Judge, thus connections with righteousness in 3:6–11. See (5) below. (3) The phrase at 1:19 may have been proverbial, an optimistic way of saying, "The outcome is up to the gods" (White 1986:55 #28, lines 31–32). Adding *eis sōtērian* produces a positive note, "It will come out OK."[2] We lack evidence the saying was common coin. (4) "Vindication" before a tribunal, divine or Roman, is seen by many as link between the OT words and Paul. Cf. Michael, O'B, Hays (for Paul), Fee 130–31. (5) Some see Job and/or Paul as "righteous sufferer" (Hays; Bockmuehl; L. Ruppert) or the OT "poor man" (Fee). K. T. Kleinknecht offers the fullest case for "the suffering righteous [or justified person] motif" in the OT and Jewish tradition as background for understanding Paul's theology of suffering. Kleinknecht, who regards Ephesus as the place of writing for Phil (p. 305, cf. 321–28), allows (308) for Phil 1:19 "a distinct reference to . . . the suffering righteous one" through the use of Job 13:16. Connection between Paul as "righteous sufferer" and the "poor man" of the Psalms (a wordfield of which Job is a part; denied by J. S. Vos 2001:66, 2002:147) is made through the "the righteousness of God." (6) Several interpreters link Job's "comforters" and the "rival preachers" of Phil 1:15–18 (Bengel; Hays; perhaps Michael). Morlet 74, Job was condemned by his friends, but waited for his justification from God.

---

[1] DA 291 lists 1:11 (Prov 3:9; 11:30 LXX); 2:7 (Isa 53:3,11); 2:10–11 (Isa 45:23 LXX); 2:15 (Deut 32:5; Dan 12:3 LXX); 2:16 (Isa 49:4; 65:23 LXX); 3:19 (Hos 4:7); 3:21 (Ps 8:7 LXX); 4:3 (Ps 69:28); 4:5–6 (Ps 145:18); 4:18 (Gen 8:21; Exod 29:18; Isa 56:7); Minear 1990:213 claims other Isa allusions. For 1:19, Fatehi 222–24 sees echoes of Ps 35 (LXX 34).

[2] Bockmuehl 83 compares Eccl 8:12; Sir 39:25; b. Ber 60 [bar.]; Plato *Resp.* 10.12 (613a), *Ap.* 41D for the general idea, and Nahum of Gimzo, "another 'Jewish Job,'" for the phrase "This too will turn out for good" (b. Ber 60a [bar.]).

In summary, words from Job 13:16 are present at Phil 1:19, but not obviously. Even if proverbial, Paul could have been conscious of use in Job. It is speculative to assume familiarity among the Philippians with the words as Scripture (Bockmuehl 82; Walter 41). To see Paul as a Job-figure is more a matter of biblical theology or reader-response today than verifiable from Paul's own writings. Overtones from Job involve vindication (preservation, Oakes 2000:253), relationship to "friends" (Job's comforters, other Christians in Ephesus), and Paul's understanding of salvation as both present and future for a justified believer facing suffering.

2. Rhetorical/Literary Features. 1:12–26 is a rhetorical unit (INTRO. VI.B n 2). Black 1995, Brucker, Edart 74–76, 84–85 term it *narratio* (Edart, with *dubitatio*[3]), but others *exordium, confirmatio* in *argumentatio* (Bloomquist 126); cf. Bittasi 37–48. Literary features include *inclusio* (*progress* 1:12, 25; 1:14 *having become confident in the Lord* and 1:25 *confident of this*; *alliteration* (1:20, *pasē[i] parrhēsia[i] hōs pantote*). *Wordplay* (perhaps 1:21, *Christos . . . kerdos*[4]; 1:25 *menō, paramenō,* and *epimenein* v 24; *en Christō[i] Iēsou en emoi,* Loh. 69 n 1 1:26). 1:23 is overloaded, *much better by far;* see NOTE. 1:23 *to depart, euphemism?* But 1:20, 21 use *death* and *die* so likely literary variety. For *hendiadys,* see NOTES on 1:19 *through your entreaty and the supplying of the Spirit;* 20 *my expectation and hope;* and 25 *your progress and joy.* The "apostolic parousia" form (discussed re 2:12, 19–24) is reflected in 1:26. On *synkrisis,* see 4, below; Croy 525 n 28 pays little attention to it, the quandry is rhetorical. J. S. Vos claims a "rhetoric of success" in 1:18b–29, from a military sense of victory; little support (78, 80–81). Further, J. S. Vos 2001:70; Edart 73, 76, 82–83, 112–13.

3. Chiastic Structures? *Macrochiastic* proposals for Phil differ considerably from each other and do not prove convincing bases for interpretation.[5] For Letter B, Aspen's linking of 1:12–26 ("Paul's trials") with 2:19–30 ("Epaphroditus' trials") has some plausibility; in both, threat of death (1:21–23; 2:27), hope for, or experience of, deliverance and God's mercy (1:19, 25; 2:24, 27), and confidence in the Lord (1:15; 2:24) are prominent.

---

[3] Uncertainty (over choices), Lausberg #776–78. Croy 525–30, 1:22–24 = "feigned perplexity" (Gk. *aporia* or *diaporēsis;* Lat. *dubitatio*); Paul pretends to be at a loss but knows all along what he intends; the dilemma is not real. J. S. Vos 2002:150.; cf. n 23 below. R. L. Fowler, "desperation speech," "The Rhetoric of Desperation," *HSCP* 91 (1987) 6–38. W. Deming, Stoic indifferents *(adiaphora),* in Sampley, ed., 2003:388–90.; cf. (12) COMMENT n 29.

[4] Fee 140–41 n 8 calls attention to the "assonance between *kerdos* and *Christos,*" *k/ch, r,* and *s* (Edart 67).

[5] See INTRO. VI.B n 3, and (3) COMMENT A.8. Wick takes 1:12–26 as "parallel" to 3:1–16 (note *gain* at 1:21 and 3:7, 8; *death,* 1:20 and 3:10; *in the flesh,* used positively at 1:22, 24, but negatively at 3:3 and 4). Luter/Lee take 1:12–26, "Comfort/Example," as parallel to 4:6–9. This sheds scant light on 1:18d–26 and shows little of the poignancy with which Paul writes in 1:18d–26. Reed (*DA* 292–93, 363–64) finds Wick's work "forced" and Luter/Lee even less persuasive. Rolland aligned 1:12–2:18 with 3:1–4:20; C. W. Davis, 1:3–26 with 4:10–20. K. T. Kleinknecht (above, A. 1. [5]) regards "joy" *(chara/chairein)* as the "red thread" running through Phil; his chart gives a detailed list of correspondences in 1:18b–2:18.

Microchiastic proposals for 1:19–26 esp. involve *to live* and *to die*: v 20 *whether by life or by death*; 21b *to die* parallels *to depart* (v 23); 22*"to live" in the flesh* parallels *to continue to stay on in the flesh* (v 24); 22 *fruitful missionary labor* corresponds to *on your account* (24); 23 *to be with Christ* goes with *to live* (is) *Christ* (21a, though not identical in sense). At the least, antithesis, perhaps diatribe style (Schoon-Janßen 143; *DA* 261 n 395). Standard treatments on NT chiasmus (Lund) or in Paul (I. H. Thomson [(12) Bibl.]) do not cite Phil 1:18–26. Life/death (20c), death/life (21–22) is chiastic. Gnilka 70 found the following interchange (left column); Schreiber 338–39 (right column):

21a *For me to live* (is) *Christ,*	Premise: Life = Christ (21a)
Paul's overarching position	
21b *and to die, gain* — death	A death, gain (21b)
22 *But if "to live" in the flesh* — life	B life, fruit (22ab)
	C indecision (22c)
23 *to depart and be with Christ* — death	C′ indecision (23a)
	A′ death, better (23ab)
24 *to continue to stay on in the flesh* — life.	B′ life, more necessary 24.[6]

Fee 145 n 31 speaks of "a piece of (not pure) chiasmus" (B does not mention "death"):

> A If 'life' in the flesh it is to be, then that means 'fruitful labor,' [22a]
> B which would put me in a real quandary, if I had to choose between the two. [22b]
> B′ If I could choose, it would be 'death,' hands down, [23]
> A′ but since there is no choice (but God's), it means 'fruitful labor' among you." [24]

Schenk 146, citing Haupt 29–30, found a shorter chiastic sequence in v 19:

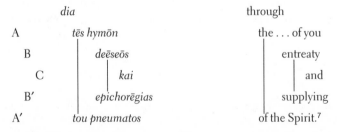

	dia		through
A	*tēs hymōn*		the . . . of you
B	*deēseōs*		entreaty
C	*kai*		and
B′	*epichorēgias*		supplying
A′	*tou pneumatos*		of the Spirit.[7]

Webber ([2] Bibl. **joy**) 216–17 claimed "a chiasmus of thought if not of syntax" at 1:25–26. Schenk 161, a more far-reaching chiasmus in vv 25b–26 (*faith* in v 25 is *nomen actionis* and subjective gen., "your believing"; the Philippians' "progress,

---

[6] Martin 1976:76–77 similarly outlines Paul's "progressive chain of thought," which concludes, "my pastoral responsibility demands my continuing presence"; Hawth. 44; O'B 117; J. S. Vos 2001:70 n 46. Schreiber's is, admittedly, not really a chiasm.

[7] Schenk takes "the Spirit" as subjective gen. and *Jesus Christ* as an epexegetical, qualifying attributive gen., as in Gal 4:6; 2 Cor 3:17; Rom 8:9, the risen, present Lord whom God gives via the Spirit, reflected in our TRANSLATION.

yes your joy from believing," cf. 164). Many proposals, perhaps too many; little agreement.

4. 1:21–26 as Sygkrisis, *Rhetorical "Comparison."* Where many see chiasm, Vollenweider 1994 has persuasively argued for an example of *sygkrisis* (not noted in *WDNTECLR* 110). Bockmuehl 87 and Bormann 2001:319–20 agree. From Gk. *syn + krisis*, vb. *sugkrinein* = "compare."[8] A tech. term, *sygkrisis* (Lat. *comparatio*) was a rhetorical device comparing and evaluating two persons (Ajax and Achilles; Demosthenes and Aeschines) or things (summer and winter; examples in Vollenweider 97–98 n 24). Cf. Plut., *Parallel Lives of Greeks and Romans* (LCL 11 vols.).[9] Johannes Stobaeus collected gnomic material on a "Sygkrisis of Life and Death" (5th cent. A.D., *Florilegium* 4.53, ed. Hense 1097–1112; cf. 4.32). In rhetoric,[10] *sygkrisis* was part of school instruction and the *progymnasmata*.[11] It often followed in a speech after praise *(enkomion)* and blame (Vollenweider 95), in more than one rhetorical genus. Either antithetical or comparative, it may present one point in the comparison as "great," the other "greater," not "bad" versus "good." That fits "Phil 1, 21–24 (/25f.) . . . as a little *sygkrisis* of life and death."[12] The image of "scales in a balance" between life and death has appeared in more than one commentator (e.g., Loh. 62; O. Schmitz, *Phil.* 21).

In 1:21ff., Vollenweider 98 notes (1) the abundance of comparatives (v 23 *much better by far;* 24 *more necessary*) and use of *men* and *de* (vv 22, 23, 24). (2) The alternating sequence of *life* and *death* may reflect a rhetorical rule that the "losing" term is mentioned *first*, in v 20, *"life* or death." Paul's preference will be for death (21b, 23). (3) The emphatic *emoi* (v 21, *For to me*) is "personal evaluation," as in ancient examples of *sygkrisis*. Paul "appears to speak only for his own person." Or does he endeavor to draw the Philippians toward his own preference?

Conclusions[13]: (1) In 21a *life* means *"earthly* life," in which to proclaim the gospel (2:21–22; 3:7), for the benefit of the Philippians (1:24). (2) Paul helps read-

[8] Vb. at 1 Cor 2:13 NRSV-mg and 2 Cor 10:12. *Sygkrisis* was used in connection with friendship and enmity (P. Marshall 53–55); above, (3) COMMENT B.3.k, on the rival preachers of 1:14–18b.

[9] The device took dramatic form in a "battle of words *(agōn logōn),*" as between Homer and Hesiod (LCL *Hesiod, The Homeric Hymns and Homer,* tr. H. G. Evelyn-White, repr. 1950, 566–97) or the allegory about "The Choice of Heracles" at the crossroads of decision in Prodicus. Roots can be claimed in folk culture, Aesop's fables (winter versus summer), or Samson's riddle (Judg 14:14, 18); Vollenweider 94–95.

[10] Quint. *Inst. Orat.* 9.2.100; Lausberg #799; cf. 1130.

[11] D. L. Clark, *Rhetoric in Greco-Roman Education* (New York: Columbia Univ. Press, 1957) 177–212; H. I. Marrou, *A History of Education in Antiquity,* tr. G. Lamb (New York: Sheed & Ward, 1956; repr. Madison: Univ. of Wisconsin Press, 1982) 238–42, 276–77, 288–89, 342, cf. 89; G. A. Kennedy, *Greek Rhetoric under Christian Emperors* (Princeton: Princeton Univ. Press, 1983) 54–73; R. F. Hock/ E. O'Neil, *The Chreia in Ancient Rhetoric, I: The Progymnasmata* (SBLTT 27; Atlanta: Scholars Press, 1986) 9–22.

[12] Vollenweider 96; earlier by A. Klöpper, *Phil.* 1893: 89; cf. Dupont 1952 (Exc. A Bibl.) 175–76.

[13] Vollenweider 99–102. Paul employs *sygkrisis* also at 1 Cor 4:10 (4:8–13a, Fitzgerald 1988:132–48; M. M. Mitchell 1992: 220 nn 180, 181; Ebner 24 n 21; Ferrari 417 n 94, has reservations) and 2 Cor 11:22–23 (cf. 10:12, "We do not dare to classify or compare *(egkrinai ē sygkrinai]* ourselves with some"; C. Forbes 1986:1–30; Ebner 101–3, a "battle of words."

ers follow the *process* of comparison. Both options are made attractive; the apostle is *hard put to decide* (v 23 *betwixt and between*).[14] The introspection and shift from nouns in v 20 to verbal forms in 21–25, *to live, to die*, add to the liveliness of the passage. Notions of "a glimpse into the soul of an agitated apostle" (see 5, below) should be corrected by the fact that we deal with a rhetorical form. (3) Paul's *rhetorical strategy* contrasts something good (earthly life) with something better, departing (21, 23). The *turning point* comes in v 24, *to stay on*, with application to the addressees, *on your account.* No break between vv 24 and 25–26, no need to assume "prophetic revelation" (against Bengel and Loh. 66–67). The form speaks against a Paul who wallows in indecision. (4) Although Paul formulates 1:21ff. very personally, the *pragmatic dimension* is to draw the Philippians as co-participants into his sufferings (1:29–30; cf. 3:17; 4:9), the "same struggle" and same decision for life on behalf of others (2:4, 21–22); Schreiber 357–59, to provoke them to reflect on "with Christ" for this situation. Vollenweider does not claim Paul had a full education in rhetoric (with Stowers 2003:367–68). He limits application to *elocutio*, not *genus* or letter-gattung (101, with Classen 1991, against D. F. Watson 1988a). Paul could have acquired knowledge of rhetoric in a school even in Jerusalem and Gk.-speaking synagogues.[15]

As "building stones" for the *sygkrisis* in Phil 1:21–26 Vollenweider 103–11 lists classical (and some Jewish) texts. For "death as 'gain,'" a starting point lies (1) Telemachus in Homer, *Od.* 20.316–17, "much more a gain *(polu kerdion)* to die," (2) a sentiment often expressed in *gnomic* form (see NOTE on 1:21). (3) In the Gk. tragedians, *personal* emphasis ("I," "me") may be present.[16] A dozen examples present (4) a *choice*, about what is *desirable*, a preference one wishes for. E.g., "Death is more to be chosen than an evil life."[17] Choice is part of the pattern. Often there is (5) a *comparative* (or *superlative*) *aspect*; one thing is clearly "better." Comparatives are piled up, as in Eur. *Hec.* 377–78, "Dying he is much more fortunate than living."[18] Cic. *Att.* 3.19.1, "drag on this miserable life or, what is much better, end it." This sentiment about what is "better" can also be found in (6) *Oriental wisdom literature* (the Heb. *tôb min* construction): "better for one to die than to live" (Jonah 4:3; cf. 1 Kngs 19:4).[19] Preference (to die) is found in (Jew-

---

[14] Cf. Philo, *Mos.* 2:163–65 (LCL *Philo* 6:528–31): Moses must decide whether to stay on Mt. Sinai or "go quickly hence" (Exod 32:7); the crisis over the golden calf settles his dilemma. Cf. also 2 (Syr) Bar 3.3 (*OTP* 1:621).

[15] So M. Hengel/U. Heckel 1991: 177–293, esp. 237–39, 260–65; Hengel/Deines 1991:37–39, 57–61; Meggitt 84–87.

[16] See NOTE on 1:21, *For to me*, Eur. *Med.* 145; Eur. *HF* 1301 ("why then must I live? What gain shall we have?"); Aesch. *PV* 747; a frg. from Soph.; (Ps)Plut *Cons. Ad Apollonium* 2.107B = LCL Plutarch's *Mor.* 2:134–35 (not noted by Holloway 2001a).

[17] Aeschylus [?] in Stob. 4.53.17 = TrGF 3:466); Xen. *Polity of the Lacedaemonians* 9.1, cf. *Cyr.* 3.3.51 and *Mem.* 4.4.14; *Anth. Gr.* 9.359.9 (LCL *Greek Anthology* 3:192–93, "a choice between two things, not to be born or to die immediately upon being born"); Juncus (philosopher, 2nd cent. A.D.?), and Herm. 23.6, "Not to be born would be more desirable for you" (cf. Mark 14:21b).

[18] Cf., e.g., *Eur. Hec.* 214–15; Herodot. *Hist.* 1.31; Soph. (Stob 4.53.11 = TrGF 4:488); Xen. *Apologia Socratis* 33; Plato *Gorg.* 483B; Plat. *HippMinor* 304E; Isoc. *Or.* 6.89 and 10.27; Epict. *Ench.* 12.1.

[19] Cf. Tob 3:6; Sir 30:17 and 40:28; 1 Macc 3:59; 2 Esdras 12:44, "how much better . . . if we also had been consumed in the burning of Zion"; cf. 2 (Syr) Bar 33.3 (*OTP* 1:631–32).

ish) pessimistic wisdom literature; for the Philippians it was "common sense" (Vollenweider 109–10). The christological aspect (v 23) accounts for joy amid sufferings and existence beyond death. Notions of (7) *death as "better"* because of immortality, with the gods, were not unknown in Greek thought.[20] The death of Socrates and Stoic vocabulary (Edart 93–102; Engberg-Pedersen 1995a:45–79) would have been familiar in Philippi. Phil 1:21–26 thus reflects a widely known comparison between life and death, with preference for physical death.

5. Paul's Agitated State. Commentators often remark about intense emotions as Paul writes. "The grammar . . . reflects the conflict of feeling in the Apostle's mind . . . abrupt and disjointed sentences express this hesitation" (Lft. 92, cf. 90, cited with approval by Silva 76, cf. 81). Loh., imminent martyrdom.[21] O'B 147–48 n 38, emotion from Paul's focus on Christ and yearning for "the prize" (3:12–14), and a desire to "rekindle eschatological longings" in the Philippians. Cf. Gnilka 69; Garland 1980 ([1] Bibl.) 334. Lest Paul's words seem contradictory (*I am betwixt and between; I know that I shall stay on*), some assume possibilities in conditional-sentence form (Haupt, Schenk; see NOTE on 1:25 *I know that . . .* , with *ho ti* for *hoti*). Or that Paul's outlook has changed from vv 21–24 to the more positive view in 25–26 through prophetic illumination from God (Loh.), meditation on God's purpose (Bonnard), news from the Roman court (Martin 79; cf. Michaelis 27), or a sense of duty (the Philippians need him, Michael 59–60; Martin 1976:79–80). Vollenweider 100 better explains the passage on the basis of the *sygkrisis* form, not inner uncertainty. Croy 6, a rhetorical device of "figured perplexity." To speak here of "indifference to death" as "the *topos* of things that do not matter" (Holloway 2001:110) minimizes the emotions.

6. Does Paul Contemplate Suicide? Droge (1988:278–85; *ABD* VI:228–29; with Tabor 1992:113–26; cf. Clemons 1990:70–71) argued Paul, "in prison, presumably in Ephesus," though expecting "a favorable verdict (1:25–26)," lusted after death (1:23) and contemplated suicide. Taking one's life was not uncommon in antiquity (Socrates; Plato, *Laws* 873CD; the Cynics; Cassius after the battle of Philippi; cf. the jailer at Acts 16:27). The five cases of self-destruction in the OT (Abimelech, Saul, Samson, Ahithophel, Zimri) were not condemned in biblical accounts. Maccabean martyrdoms were regarded as heroic. Jewish and Christian prohibitions of suicide are post-NT. In Phil 1:21–26, Paul is said to decide that it was "not yet the appropriate time" (1988:283; *ABD* 229). God has not yet sent necessity (*anagkē*; Socrates, *Phaedo* 62C) upon him, though Droge sketches how Paul later did die by suicide. For weaknesses in Droge's case, see Jacquette 1994; cf.1996; Croy 522–25; rejected in Bockmuehl 90–91. Holloway 2001:115 holds "it likely that Paul entertained some . . . idea of forcing his own fate," not by

---

[20] Plato, *Phaed.* 62A; *Ap.* 41A–D, 40DE, 69C, 81A; the *graffito* and text from Quintus Smyrnaeus in the NOTE on 1:23 *and to be with Christ.* PCairZen I. 59060 *syn theois* (J. L. White 1986:#15, p. 38) is not about death.

[21] Bockmuehl 88–89 speaks of Loh.'s "somewhat fanciful and one-sided discussion," in light of Jewish concepts of martyrdom as "ultimate witness." J. S. Vos 2002:153 n 93 questions Loh.'s thesis.

suicide but "perhaps by courageous exhibition of *parrhēsia* in court (cf. 1:20)" (with reference in n 67 to Collange and Paul's appeal to Roman citizenship). See further *Philippian Studies.*

7. Paul's Appeal to the Authorities Based on His Roman Citizenship. The apostle faces death. 1:25–26 expresses the conviction he will stay on as missionary-preacher-pastor in service of the gospel and his converts in Philippi. 1:20 announced in scriptural language that something will lead to "deliverance" for Paul; released from prison, he will come to Philippi again (1:26).

Commentators struggle over possible playacting on Paul's part (cf. Jacquette 1994:183, "figured speech"), anguish (A.4, above). Not suicide (A.6, above); how would quitting life aid the Philippians in their struggle? How would the "rival preachers" react? Those in the Praetorium (1:13) or of Caesar's household (4:22)? Jacquette (1994, 1996) claims a "novel twist": Paul decides *not* to die but to live on and labor for the progress of his Philippian friends. Cf. how Paul reflects Greco-Roman ideas of *philia* and the patron–client system but is critical, as with *progress* at 1:12 and 25 or "friendship," (16) COMMENT A and B. Reeves' reconstruction has the "decisive apostle" refuse to use the money the Philippians sent to "bribe his way out of prison" (287); this reads "much into the text that is not explicitly stated" (DA 214–15 n 228); it badly underplays Paul's expected *parousia* in Philippi (1:26; 287–88).

Better grounded is the proposal that Paul has appealed to his Roman citizenship and so expects to regain his freedom (see [3] COMMENT B.3.j, n 38). Collange worked out application to this passage only partly.[22] Paul's invoking his citizenship caused a split among preachers (and house churches) in Ephesus ([3] COMMENT B.3). Did some think he should have committed suicide? Others took courage from the fact that Paul possessed and used this legal advantage, and might soon go free. When Paul appealed to his rights as a Roman citizen is unclear, but his "disclosure strategy" was often delayed (Rapske 189–91).

In 1:18d–26 Paul touches on his inner feelings about what he has done in asserting citizenship, an action controversial in Ephesus (1:14–18), needing explanation to the Philippians, with their fears for Paul and their own situation. If "figured speech" (Jacquette 1994), there are good reasons for it. The course adopted, *not* death but continued life and service, Paul sees as "looking to the interests of others" (2:4); "standing firm" in the gospel, not intimidated by government authorities (1:27–28); he looks to be present with the Philippians soon again (1:26). Optimistic that his citizenship will be honored (cf. Wansink 123–24), Paul is positive in vv 19 (Job 13:16) and 25–26. But death cannot be excluded. His trump card has been played. Execution weighs on Paul's mind as the alternative.

---

[22] Collange 59: *this*, v 19 *touto*, = "the sequence of events which he has just set in motion"; 60, his hope is on "his anticipated trial," where (61) "the reasons for his long silence on the circumstances of his imprisonment" will come out. Paul has nothing to make known from the Lord (v 22, p. 64), but he expects what he is doing will be "in the best interests of the Philippians" (70). Croy 524, such an appeal by Paul is a way to affect the outcome of his trial. Cf. also Morlet 77–78, 44.

Hence "figured speech," tactfully broaching a sensitive area: vv 20 (death but not disgraced); 21b *to die*; the dilemma when he decided to appeal on the basis of his citizenship—now relived, in the rhetorical question of v 22.[23] Conditions in prison and in the churches (disunity at Philippi, split opinions over Paul in Ephesus) may have helped Paul decide "being with Christ" was best (vv 22–23). But the divine necessity of preaching the gospel (1 Cor 9:16, NRSV "obligation"; Phil 1:24 *more necessary*) dominates in his decision.

This appeal by Paul could not be seen as long as it was assumed Phil was written in Rome; in that scenario, Paul had already asserted his citizenship (Acts 21:39; 22:25–28; 23:27) and previously appealed to Caesar (Acts 25:10–12; 26:32). The great advocate of Caesarea as place of imprisonment, Ernst Lohmeyer, had no interest in such an appeal; everything was in terms of prospective martyrdom. Only when Phil was read from a setting in Ephesus could the Acts references to citizenship be taken into consideration to explain the varied opinions among Christians (in Ephesus) over Paul's action and his own expectation of release, which brackets the passage in 1:19 (= Job 13:16) and 25.

EXCURSUS A: "With Christ" (1:23) and Eschatology

The phrase *syn Christō[i]*, 1:23 *depart and be with Christ*, raises many questions. For fuller discussion, see *Philippian Studies*; on ties to Hellenistic readers, Peres 242–47; for application see COMMENT B.2, below. Main points are summarized here, propositionally.

1. "With Christ" appears in Paul (1) in connection with baptism and the ensuing daily life of the believer (Rom 6) and (2) at the End (of the believer's life, 1:23; of all things, the parousia, 1 Thess 4:17; 5:10). It is to be considered along with the "In Christ" theme (see NOTE on 1:1 *in Christ Jesus* and [1] COMMENT B.5.a), in this way:

$$syn\ Christ\bar{o}[i] \rightarrow en\ Christ\bar{o}[i] \rightarrow syn\ Christ\bar{o}[i]$$

For passages using *syn*, often compounded with vbs., see *TPTA* #15.3 nn 58, 59; Gnilka 76.

2. "With Christ" thus has future eschatological sense (1 Thess 4:17; 5:10; 2 Cor 4:14; Phil 1:23, 3:21; Rom 8:17, 29) and a past-present eschatological sense, the event of baptism and "daily dying and rising" (Baumert 1973; Rom 6:4–8; Gal 2:19; Phil 3:10; cf. 2 Cor 13:4). Bouttier and Neugebauer ([1] Bibl. **in Christ**) show how God has acted through *(dia)* Christ to bring people into *(eis)* Christ, so that they are "with" and "in Christ," and "through" Christ share in the new age, looking to the Day of the Lord when they will finally and fully be "with Christ." Response to God's will "in the Lord" comes in daily life.

3. The origins of "with Christ" remain debated, but are connected with baptism and, for the future sense, Jewish apocalyptic literature.

---

[23] J. S. Vos 2001:82, 1:22 is rhetorically a *dubitato*, in relation to Paul's Roman citizenship; cf. n 3 above.

4. Over against views that Paul's eschatology evolved or "developed" from apocalypticism to a cosmic "realized eschatology,"[24] it is truer to the evidence to see a consistent present-and-future position throughout Paul's career, reflecting local, current factors in each letter.

5. The construals possible for 1:23 (Caird 1994 [Intro. X Bibl.] 272) do not support a special hope only for an apostle (Schweitzer) or for martyrs (Loh. 63–64).

6. An "intermim state" between the individual's death and the general resurrection (Cullmann 1956, 1958; Schreiber 2003:340–41; for martyrs?), in light of Phil 1:23 (cf. 2 Cor 5:1–10), rather than simply "sleep" (1 Cor 15:6, 18, 20, 51 NRSV-mg), has long been debated. What is clear is the continuity of the Christ-relationship for believers that *syn Christō[i]* ties together.

SELECT BIBLIOGRAPHY

Campenhausen, H. F. von. *Die Idee des Martyriums in den alten Kirche.* Göttingen: Vandenhoeck & Ruprecht, 1936, 2nd ed. 1964.

Charles, R. H. 1899. *The Doctrine of a Future Life in Israel, in Judaism, and in Christianity—A Critical History.* London: A. & C. Black, 2nd ed. 1913. Repr. as *Eschatology: The Doctrine of a Future Life in Israel, Judaism and Christianity: A Critical History,* Intro. by G. W. Buchanan. New York: Schocken Books, 1963.

Cullmann, O. 1956. "The Proleptic Deliverance of the Body according to the New Testament," in Cullmann's GS, *The Early Church: Studies in Early Christian History and Theology,* ed. A. J. B. Higgins (Philadelphia: Westminster) 163–73.

———. 1958. *Immortality of the Soul or Resurrection of the Dead? The Witness of the New Testament.* London: Epworth; repr. in *Immortality and Resurrection: four essays,* ed. K. Stendahl (New York: Macmillan).

Dodd, C. H. 1933–34. "The Mind of Paul: I" and "The Mind of Paul: II," *BJRL* repr. in Dodd's GS, *New Testament Studies* (Manchester: Manchester Univ. Press, 1953) 67–128.

Dupont, J. 1952. *SYN CHRISTŌI: L'Union avec le Christ suivant saint Paul.* Louvain: Nauwelaerts, Paris: Desclée de Brouwer.

Giesen, H. 2006. "Eschatology in Philippians," in *Paul and His Theology,* ed. S. E. Porter, Pauline Studies 3 (Leiden: Brill).

Hanhart, K. 1966. *The Intermediate State in the New Testament.* Fraenker: T. Wever.

Lohmeyer, E. 1927a. "SYN CHRISTŌ[I]," in *Festgabe für Adolf Deissmann zum 60. Geburtstag, 7 November 1926* (Tübingen: Mohr) 218–57.

———. 1927b. "Die Idee des Martyriums im Judentum und Urchristentum," ZST 5 (1927) 232–49, French in *RHPR* 7 (1927) 316–29.

Siber, P. 1971. *Mit Christus leben. Eine Studie zur paulinischen Auferstehungshoffnung.* ATANT 61. Zürich: Theologischer Verlag.

---

[24] R. H. Charles achieved this for Phil, which he dated with Col and Eph, only by assigning 3:21 to an earlier period; C. H. Dodd 1933–34, by removing any hint of the parousia from 4:5; see Note on *the Lord is near.*

B. MEANING AND INTERPRETATION

Paul had available for composing 1:18d–26 an OT verse (Job 13:16 LXX = 1:19) and a host of literary devices (A.2; many see chiasms, A.3), including the *sygkrisis* form (A.4). Content derives from personal reflection on life, some of this over the years, with the conviction, "This (event) too will lead to deliverance for me" (v 19). Other aspects arise out of the present situation in an Ephesian jail (Siber 87, 93, among others), including the prospect of imminent death. Paul speaks with emotion (A.5), yet art and skill. His words do not arise solely out of agitation and despair. He did not set out to feign perplexity by using an *aporia* or *dubitatio* form (Croy) or tantalizingly employ "figured speech" (Jacquette 1994; A.6, above). "Death is gain" (v 21) was part of popular wisdom; comparison with "living" was natural, widespread in rhetoric and oratory. Paul likely shaped what he says around the device of "comparison." The Philippians were likely aware of *sygkrisis* and its conventions, e.g., mentioning first what the speaker does *not* prefer (v 20, *life* or *death*). Yet 18d–26 would not have come to expression without Paul's Christian beliefs and heritage. The emphasis so pervasive in 1:12–18c on *Christ* and *gospel* (see [3] COMMENT A.5) continues: *Jesus Christ, whom the Spirit supplies* (v 19), *expectation and hope* eschatologically (20), to be *with Christ* (23); Christ continually magnified (20); life centered on *Christ* (21), *fruitful missionary labor* (22). His convictions were part of the *heuresis*, shaping rhetorical forms and grim prospects into Christian witness, as Paul treats *events affecting me* (v 12) personally.

Phil 1:18d–26 will be treated below in B.1, 2, and 3 as part of Letter B from Paul to Philippi, within the context of 1:1–2:30 (+ 4:1–9, 21–23), after Letter A (4:10–20), the note of thanks. Under B.4, 1:18d–26, as part of the four-ch., redacted letter, where Paul continues to delay clear acknowledgment of the Philippians' gift, even while discussing his fate and his continuing relationship with the Philippian house churches (25–26; cf. 27–30).

1:18d–26 occur within the *inclusio* framed by *progress* in 1:12 (of the gospel) and 1:25 (*progress and joy that arise from your faith*). When he took up *ta kat' eme* (1:12), emphasis was on how the gospel went on advancing (1:12–18). In 1:18d–26 the apostle stresses how, come what may, *Christ will be made great* (v 20), there will be progress and joy in and from the Philippians' faith (25). In vv 15–18c Paul rejoiced over proclamation of Christ by preachers in Ephesus with doubtful motives; in 18d–26 he finds cause for rejoicing in his own prospects, life or death, and in the Philippians' advance.

Commentators vary on how to subdivide and title 1:18d-26.[1] Fairly common is a three-part subdivision: 1:18d-20 (Christ will show himself to be mighty); 1:21–24 (the choice between life and death); 1:25–26 (remaining for the sake of the Philip-

---

[1] Some use a phrase from these vv for all of 1:12–26; K. Barth, "Christ will be magnified," v 20; UBSGNT, "For Me to Live is Christ" for 1:12–30. Others, a phrase from 1:12–18c, like "News about Paul" (1:12, Dib., Hawth.), for 1:12–26. Movement from effects on the gospel's spread (1:12–18) to effects on Paul and the Philippians (1:19–26) is narrowed by U. B. Müller 56 to "The Personal Future of the Apostle"; Beare, "The Apostle's Attitude and Outlook."

pians).[2] Schenk's segmentation differs.[3] His detailed analysis does not always convince,[4] though it offers insights for our subdivisions.

1. Paul Expects Deliverance: The Apostle Will Not Be Disgraced, Christ Will Be Made Great, Whether Paul Lives or Dies (1:18d–20).

Paul's situation was sketched in the COMMENT on 1:12–18c. He turns from how his imprisonment has affected the preaching of the word to its outcome for his own life. The danger is death, execution by Roman authorities. No new turn in the judicial process is indicated in the text. But he has recently appealed to his Roman citizenship, a move that stirred up controversy among Christians in Ephesus (1:14–18; see [3] COMMENT B.1 and 3.j) but provided grounds for hope in 1:26 about *coming again* to the Philippians. This move also undergirds what he will tell the Philippians in 1:27–30 about standing firm in their struggle against opponents. It ties in with his plans for future relations with Philippi, sending Timothy to them (2:19–24), having Epaphroditus return home (2:25–30), trusting he himself "will also come soon" (2:24), "as soon as I see how things go with me" (2:23).

The "I"-form (1:12–14, 16, 17, 18c) goes on, *I shall also continue to rejoice* (18d), shifting from pres. tense, *I rejoice* (18c), to the fut. (18d, 19, 20). Vbs. in 18c and d are connected by *Not only this* (present rejoicing over the advance of the word) *but also* (future gladness, to be indicated). Paul's future joy will involve using his rights as a citizen and theological factors. He returns to the "Christ" theme in vv 20, 21, 23, and, in a pastoral tone, v 26, the Philippians' continuing *to abound in Christ*. Schmitz, who spoke of Christ as "the midpoint of Paul's existence," linked present joy (even in the face of "rival preachers," 1:14–18) and future joy by noting the apostle differed in the generous way he judged others and optimism about his fate (1934:17, 22). 18d states Paul's certainty; it stands over what follows (Schenk 163).

What Paul rejoices over is initially set forth in v 19: *For I know that "this will lead to deliverance of me,"* an explanation for 18d. *oida* is the first of several noetic vbs. (22 *choose, know*; 23 *I am betwixt and between*; 25 *confident of this, I know*; Schenk 144; DA 305 #14). The NOTE cites attempts to view such knowing as based on seeing observable phenomena or on knowledge and certainty in relation to faith (DA 306–7 #16). What Paul knows is set forth in scriptural words from Job 13:16 LXX (in quotation marks, above). See COMMENT A.1 on this embedded echo about an individual who hopes for vindication in the face of a tribunal. Perhaps proverbial, the words may have been ones Paul long employed or thought about amid dangers (as in 2 Cor 11:23–27; cf. Phil 4:11–13). It is less clear the Philippians would have spotted an LXX quotation or seen the apostle as a Job-like figure.

---

[2] Michaelis; Gnilka 65, 69, 93; O'B; Fee, "The Future—for the Glory of Christ and the Good of the Philippians" (1:18d–26, in contrast to 1:12–18c, "The Present"). Collange, 1:12–20 = "The Progress of the Gospel," then 1:21–24 and 1:25–26; Holloway 2001:108–15, 1:18d–21 and 1:22–26, ". . . the Philippians' lack of progress."

[3] Schenk 163, Gk. p. 143. 21–26 unfolds v 20 and in turn 18d (cf. also DA 215).

[4] On positing an *if* cl., see NOTE on v 25 *I know that I shall stay*; Vollenweider 1994: 99 n 29; Silva 78 n 9; 83 and n 17. The proposed chiasmus for 1:25b–26 is far from certain (COMMENT A.3). Rhetorical influence from the *sygkrisis* form is likely (Vollenweider; COMMENT A.4).

The ambiguous *this* from Job does not here refer to the proclamation of Christ in 18c but to the situation he began describing in 1:12, *events affecting me*, and hope in the face of them. These events will result in *deliverance* for Paul. To render as "salvation" suggests eternal deliverance. But the passage has to do with Paul's continuing in service to the gospel and its converts, coming to Philippi again (25–26). West 183–86, "future salvation *and* his present vindication," release from prison, as well as eternal *deliverance* (NRSV; NIV, Thielman 75 to the contrary). *entreaty* to God by the Philippians for Paul (19b) was not about his future salvation but deliverance from his present straits. Perhaps through use of their financial gift to him and help from Epaphroditus in legal matters. What *the Spirit supplies*, namely *Jesus Christ*, refers not just to heaven in the future, but now and here, amid Paul's vicissitudes, "getting through" his time in prison and sustaining his future ministry of service. Earthly deliverance as well as heavenly salvation.

The OT quote reflects "levels of meaning," initially in Job (see COMMENT A.1). But the situations of Job and Paul are by no means parallel (as E. F. Scott thought, *IB* 33–34; contrast O'B 109 n 7). There was a meaning for Paul (see above), and for the Philippians (optimism on Paul's part?). Paul may have seen himself, like Job, a servant of God who would be vindicated, perhaps even a "righteous sufferer" (if the righteousness concept in 3:6–11 is brought into the picture, with Kleinknecht), but the notion of a "second Job" is dubious (ch. 6, COMMENT A.1). To use Scripture, like the reflections of Pss vv in 1:20 *(not disgraced, be made great)*, is an expression of personal faith, whether others grasp it or not (Loh. 50, 53; U. B. Müller 58). 1:19 means more than "this too will turn out for the best."

Paul indicates two means through which events will lead to deliverance, *through your entreaty and Jesus Christ whom the Spirit supplies*. They go with the immediately preceding cl. about *sōtēria*, not how Paul came to this confident assertion. Some trs. move them up ahead of the echo from Job, thus putting a more clearly Christian spin on the (OT) words.

(1) The prayers of the Philippians for Paul are part of a mutual, reciprocal relationship between apostle and congregation (benefaction, a patron relationship? deSilva 2000:132) before the God to whom both pray. Paul's entreaty for them was mentioned in 1:4 (*deēsis*, same word as here), along with his thought for them (1:7a), just as they remember him (1:3) and *have* Paul *in* their *heart, both in* his *imprisonment and in the defense and confirmation of the gospel* (1:7). What Paul asks of God for them was stated in the prayer report in 1:9–11. Now we learn of the Philippians' communal prayer, likely in each house church, for Paul during his imprisonment. Wiles 1974: 276–81 sees in vv 19–20 an indirect request by Paul for (continued) intercessions, petitions perhaps specifically for Christ's presence with Paul through the Spirit (19), that he not be shamed at any judgment, Christ glorified in whatever happens (20). Even that Paul continue in service of the gospel (25) and of them, free to come to Philippi and aid them in their struggle (26, cf. 30).[5]

---

[5] Hardly that Paul corrects the Philippians here for prayers that "were not what they should be" (Holloway 2001:111). One need not speculate either "about whether God could not save if the Philippians had not been there to pray" (Bockmuehl 83).

(2) The second means is the "supplying of the Spirit of Jesus Christ," intimately connected with prayer by the Philippians (through the use of a single art. for both nouns) but distinguished from it. The NOTES on 1:19 make clear why translating *epichorēgia* as "help" has been avoided. Not a matter of aid that the Spirit gives, but the Spirit (him)self, a subjective gen., the preceding noun showing an action, "what the Spirit supplies." Then, with Schenk (see COMMENT A.3 n 7) and Fee, the third phrase in the gen., "of Jesus Christ," is in apposition. The Spirit supplies the presence and person of Christ in the life of believers. The Spirit is the agent for manifesting Christ, of whom Paul has spoken in connection with proclamation in 1:12–18 (= gospel) and will speak of as magnified through witness (1:20), in present life (1:21, 26) and as an ultimate goal beyond (1:23). Through the Spirit, Christ is experienced here and now, the agent through whom, along with prayer, *sōtēria* will come.

Thus far, in a complex sentence,[6] 18d, "I shall rejoice," is an overall assertion about the future, supported by what Paul knows. He knows that (v 19)

(a) *things will lead to deliverance for him,* through
   (1) the prayers of the Philippians and, interrelatedly,
   (2) what the Spirit brings, Jesus Christ.

Now, v 20, Paul goes on about the future: in accord with his expectation and hope, he knows that

(b) *he will not be put to shame* in any way,
   but freely and openly, as always, so now,
Christ *will be made great*
   in Paul's body,
     whether through life or death.

The italicized words reflect OT language (Job 13:16 and Pss) and may illumine each other—*sōtēria* = not being disgraced, Christ magnified; the latter cls. form an antithetical parallelism.

The opening of v 20 is variously construed.[7] The TRANSLATION takes 20 as continuation of 19, the two *hoti* cls. parallel (Schenk's first and second confessions of hope, basis and goal respectively). *in accord with my expectation and hope* relates to both the anticipated *deliverance* and *not* being *disgraced* but Christ magnified.

---

[6] See NOTE on 1:19 *through your entreaty and Jesus Christ,* and COMMENT A.3 n 7; Schenk 144–50, Gk. on 143, cf. 164. Fee 128–30 notes tension between the positive expectation in 19 and the "measure of doubt" at the end of 20, *whether by life or by death,* and decides against NIV, which "solved" things by making vv 19 and 20 into separate sentences (NRSV, not RSV). Thielman 76, v 20 qualifies v 19, but not as a second confession of hope (so Schenk).

[7] Fee, the *hoti* cl. in v 20 *(that I shall not be disgraced)* = the content of Paul's "expectation and hope," rather than dependent on *oida* in v 19 *(I know),* partly on the grounds that there is no *kai* to connect vv 19 and 20. (But the expectation relates also to the first *hoti* cl. and tells more of what Paul knows.) Schenk, the *kata* phrase at the start of v 20 is causal, the equivalent of *gar* ("for") in v 19. O'B 112, like others, simply connects the *kata* phrase with v 19: that "things will turn out for deliverance" is in accord with Paul's future hope and longing or expectation. The connectives (or lack of them) in vv 19–26 are notoriously difficult, sometimes attributed to mental agitation.

"The string of prepositional phrases and a *hoti* clause in vv. 19–20, seemingly cluttered, modify (directly or indirectly)" the main cl. in v 19, about *sōtēria* (DA 212).

The hendiadys *expectation and hope* provides a third characterization about how what Paul knows "will turn out soteriologically."[8] *elpis* is of great significance in Pauline theology, though occurring only here in Phil. OT background includes expectation about the future, trust in God, and patience in waiting. In the NT, part of "existence in faith," applied to as-yet unknown things to come (Bultmann). Leads to boldness and boasting in a good sense (v 26). The quaint etymology of *apokaradokia* ("expectation") aside (see NOTE), there is tension between this term (negative expectations) and biblical hope. The latter overshadows the former here and draws *expectation* into a more optimistic orbit. But the tension will resurface in the words *whether by life or by death* and subsequent comparison between something good and something better.

expectation and hope lead into a further expression of what Paul knows: *that I shall not be disgraced in any way, but . . . Christ will be made great.* The first statement, about Paul, is in the negative; the second, about Christ, positive. Actually, "*not* to be *disgraced*" is litotes, use of a word (often with a negative prefix) that states the opposite of what one desires to say, coupled with a negative, to imply a positive point. In the Pss, "not be put to shame" suggests being "delivered" (25:20; 31:1, 16–17) or "saved" (Ps 22:5; Ps 31:17; Silva 80 n 13; coupled with "speaking of God's decrees before kings" at 119:46).

The pass. voice in 1:20 suggests God as agent (*passivum divinum*),[9] "not be put to shame *by God*," the one invoked to avoid such disgrace, who puts the wicked to shame and delivers those calling upon the Lord (Ps 31:17; Isa 41:11; 65:13, God's servants will rejoice, in contrast to those put to shame, etc.). Shame and disgrace are brought about by divine judgment, which is not what the proud confidently expect (Bultmann, *TDNT* 1:189–90; cf. *NIDNTT* 3:562–63; *IDB* R–Z 305–6). For Paul Christian hope "does not disappoint us" (*kataischynei*, put to shame; Rom 5:5, cf. Ps 22:5; 25:20); one is not ashamed (but proud) of the gospel (Rom 1:16); the believer "will not be put to shame" (Rom 9:33 = Isa 28:16). In Phil 1:20 *not be disgraced* may relate to *parrhēsia* in the next cl., *as in a totally free and open way*, with its connotations of outspokenness and boldness as well as openness to the public. Paul knows, as part of his *deliverance*, he will *not be disgraced in any way* in coming events.

That Christ *will be made great* in whatever happens to his apostle also reflects OT language. Pss speak of "shame" and declare "Great (is) the Lord" (35:26–27;

---

[8] Holloway 2001:109 speaks of a third reason here, after prayers and Christ's spirit, why Paul's salvation will come to pass: his "own ardent desire . . . not to act shamefully." He later adds, fourth, Paul's past record (see below on *always*) and, fifth, conviction that "death is gain."

[9] Cf. Jeremias 1971:9–14; Dalman noted the pass. construction, Billerbeck the avoiding of the divine name. Follows apocalyptic style. Cf. BDF 103.1; 313; 342.1; M. Reiser, "The So-called *Passivum Divinum* or *Passivum Theologicum* and the Eschatological Passive," in his *Jesus and Judgment: The Eschatological Proclamation in Its Jewish Context* (Minneapolis: Fortress, 1997) 266–73; E. M. Sidebottom, "The So-called Divine Passive in the Gospel Tradition," *ExpTim* 87 (1975–76) 200–4.

40:15–16).[10] At Phil 1:20 Paul's "whole life" appears as "a magnifying of Christ," his "death as well" (Grundmann, *TDNT* 4:543), Christ's greatness proclaimed by whatever becomes of Paul; fut. rejoicing, like present joy that Christ is being proclaimed *in every way* (18b). *will be made great* (Paul as agent) parallels *not be disgraced* (God as agent).

The five phrases surrounding *Christ will be made great* explain ways in which, when, and how Paul knows this hope will come about. First, openly (*parrhēsia*, its only occurrence in Phil). No single Eng. term does justice to all nuances, "courage," "boldness" (many trs., KJV-NRSV); "frank speech" (ties to "friendship," *DA* 173, following Malherbe, a feature of epistolary paraenesis); "openness," a public setting for Christ's being magnified by Paul, as in a court hearing. Witness to Christ will come freely, frankly, openly in a public forum, total *parrhēsia* contrasting with "disgraced *in no way*." It has an objective side, in public view, and a subjective one, confidence on Paul's part. The word occurred in philosophy for free speech, but was at home in the church for the courage of confession, all opposition to the contrary (Loh., Schenk, as cited in the NOTE). Paul will profess Christ *in a totally free and open way.*[11]

Second, magnification of Christ *as always* in the past. In Paul's missionary career, Christ was the center of his life and message from the outset (cf. Acts 9:20; 1 Thess 1:10; 1 Cor 2:2; Gal 1:7; 2:20; 3:13). In Phil 1:12–18, Christ and gospel have been the recurrent theme. It characterized the "rival preachers" in Ephesus (1:15, 16, 17). A mark of early Christianity.

The third phrase, "*so now* Christ will be made great," means now as Paul faces possible death. Emphatic, the immediate present and imminent future, "the *kairos* of God's action and human opportunity" (Bockmuehl 86).

The fourth phrase, directly after the vb. and subject (lit., "will be made great, Christ"), is a prep. phrase "in my body," *through* Paul's *own self.* It tells how his Lord will be magnified. Here Paul's physical *sōma*, a body battered and scarred in the service of Christ (Gal 6:17; 2 Cor 11:23–27) but destined to be raised a spiritual body at the last day (1 Cor 15:44). Recent trs., from OT anthropology, speak of Paul's entire "person" or "being." But modern concepts of "person" or ontology should not be read in. *my own self* suggests the personal aspect and totality of Paul's existence. Magnification of Christ will come through Paul, all of him, as embodied witness.

The final phrase, *whether by life or by death*—continued earthly existence or physical death—expands on the means for Paul to set forth Christ's greatness.[12] It points to the two options discussed in 1:21–24, a comparison of death and life. The order "*life* or *death*" indicates, in the style of the *sygkrisis* form (see COMMENT

---

[10] Cf. Pss 48:1; 70:4; 96:4; 145:3; Mal 1:5; R. Mosis, *TDOT* 2: 406–16.

[11] The suggestion (J. S. Vos 2001: 67) that if Christ is magnified *en pasē[i] parrhēsia[i]*, the heavenly *politeuma* of 3:20 is visible on earth misses Paul's "eschatological reserve" (81).

[12] West 171–83 sees Paul choosing life, like Hercules in Euripides' tragedy (55–60), Musonius Rufus, and Cic. (*ad Quintum Fratem* 1.3, pp. 110–13); as metaphor the cross is "a paradigm for the life of faith" (177 n 143, with R. B. Hays, *The Moral Vision of the New Testament* [HarperSanFrancisco, 1996] 27–32).

A.4), that his personal desire is "to depart and be with Christ" (v 23; "life" loses), though his ultimate choice will be to remain alive in the service of the Lord. Existence is already "in Christ"; death would bring him to be more fully "with Christ." He makes great the Lord's name through bonds for Christ (1:13) and, in death, as a blood-witness.

Paul's confession in v 20 contains a chiasm, often unobserved. It is flagged by delay of the subject *Christ* until after the vb. *megalynthēsetai* (as in Pss, "Great [is] the Lord" or "Let-be-magnified the Lord," Heb. and Gk.; e.g., Pss 35 [LXX 34]:27; 40 [LXX 39]:17). Paul knows that

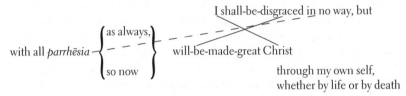

The basic chiasm involves Paul ("I") and Christ, *disgraced* and *made great*; "in no way" and "with all *parrhēsia*" also contrast (broken line). He expects to speak and act with *parrhēsia*. Christ has always been made great in the past; so now too. "through my own self" applies to past witness, but esp. now. One could even infer agency in this structure: "disgraced" (by God), "made great" (through Paul). Paul speaks modestly about himself while looking firmly ahead to *life* or *death*, the pendant at the end of v 20 that sets the theme for the comparison to follow.

2. Weighing the Balance: To Live on in Labor for Christ or to Depart and Be with Christ? (1:21–24).

The Hellenistic flavor to Paul's reflections has become increasingly apparent (Droge; Dailey; Bormann 1995:215 n 25). Vv 21–24 continue the "I" form (*to me*, 21; *for me*, 22; three vbs. 1st per. sg., in 22c and 23, plus a ptc. in 23 rendered *I have the desire to . . .*). This, plus introspection on Paul's part, and broken constructions (v 23) lead commentators to speak of Paul's "agitated state" (see COMMENT A.5). Yet he ends clearly focused on what is *more necessary on* the Philippians' *account* (24). 1:21–24 is not just about Paul, or Paul and Christ (21, 23), but *missionary labor* for the gospel and his converts. Possible chiastic structures find little agreement (COMMENT A.3). Schenk takes vv 21–26 as a third confession of hope, after vv 19 and 20. Paul's expectations are in terms of life and death (21–22), departing and continuing on (23–24).

Identification by Vollenweider 1994 of a rhetorical comparison or *sygkrisis* (COMMENT A.4) means a "rhetorical strategy" that leads on from v 24 to 25–26, increasingly applying what Paul says about himself to the Philippians in their situation (1:27–30 and 2:1–18). Only in Letter C will Paul speak specifically of himself and others as examples (3:17). He employs *sygkrisis* without embracing all its implications, just as (COMMENT on 4:10–20, A.2 and 3; B.1.[A].3) he accepted features of *philia* (friendship) in the Greco-Roman world and of patron–client relationships, but broke with aspects of them (A.2 and 3; B.1.[A] 3). Paul reshapes the *synkrisis* and shatters the bounds of its comparison between what is good and what is better by introducing his relationship with Christ (vv 21, 23), connections with others (24, 25–26, his converts in Philippi), and eschatology (resurrection; "with Christ," 1:23; the Day of Jesus Christ, 1:6, 11).

In the course of the legal process, Paul has invoked his Roman citizenship ([3] COMMENT, B.3.j; [4] A.7, B.1). Hence, the hope and commitment in v 24, *to continue to stay on in the flesh*, in the service of the Philippians (25). But he cannot be sure how things will come out. Will the Imperial system honor his rights? Do delay and uncertainty wear him down? Use of rhetoric cannot mask anguish over eschatological desire versus his task, to proclaim Christ (Gal 1:15–16). How to discern and appreciate what is best (1:9b–10a, applied to Paul)?

Phil 1:21 has been called the central assertion of the passage (U. B. Müller 59), nine Gk. words in a difficult sequence, striking to its original hearers/readers in Philippi (Fee 140, alliteration and assonance; COMMENT A.2, above). Paul wrestles with deep matters of faith, as he begins, *For to me to live, Christ, and to die, gain*. We omit any vb., so as to be as terse as the original.

For indicates that v 21 will explain how *Christ will be made great* by Paul, in *life* or *death* (v 20). He will expound a further part of his *expectation and hope* (v 20). Though no longer introduced by the words *I know* (v 19, assumed in 20b), what follows is a third confession of hope (Schenk), under Paul's basic certainty about the future, "I shall continue to rejoice" (18d).

to me is emphatic in the Gk. What follows holds true "for my person." Personal confession, not in an OT echo (v 19) or language of the Psalms (v 20). Paul formulates his master statement using a Hellenistic commonplace (21b) and a christocentric affirmation (21a). Is he speaking for himself in contrast to others, in opposition to what "to live" means to others? That would make it *statu confessionis*, a statement of belief to the exclusion of other claims. Like *"our* citizenship" (in heaven) in contrast to (Roman or Ephesian, or Tarsus) citizenship in the estimation of others (Phil 3:20; Lft. 92). Cf. 1 Cor 8:6, *"for us* there is one God . . . and one Lord" (though not for others of the day). Paul may have this in mind. But with respect to whom? Hardly the Philippians (unless Paul models a proposition he wants them to adopt as their own). Certainly not the court authorities, who would not speak thus of Christ. The "rival preachers" of 1:14–18? They might not identify their lives so exclusively with Christ as did Paul, but we lack evidence. These preachers in Ephesus might have stressed "(a martyr) death as gain" for Christians and felt Paul wrongly used his citizenship to avoid witness unto death. But *to me* need not demand a contrast, "but not for others." In the *sygkrisis* form "personal evaluation" (Vollenweider 1994:98) makes Paul's *to me* quite natural.[13]

An alternative reading makes "Christ" the subject of the sentence. So Calvin, "To me Christ is gain in life and in death" (*kerdos* as pred. nom.), or "For me Christ is life, and death is gain" (some church fathers, medieval exegetes, Luther,

---

[13] Is Paul thinking of what "thrills him," selfishly "for the benefit and enjoyment of Paul"? "the longer he lives the more opportunity . . . for Christ to show his greatness in him"? This view (I. H. Marshall 27) of a priggish, self-glorifying Paul, from the REB rendering in 1:20, "Christ will display his greatness in me," seems wide of the mark.

Tyndale, much Ger. interpretation, including the 1980 Roman Catholic EÜ). Attractive to Fee (141 n 10). The case for it remains plausible, paralleling Christ as subject in v 20, with analogy to Gal 2:20 and John 14:6 (Christ is life). But already in the 19th cent. B. Weiss 101–2 argued against it, as do O'B, Schenk, and Vollenweider (see NOTE on 1:21 *Christ*). H. C. G. Moule 1897:65 n 1, "untenable, though expressing . . . a deep and precious truth."

A second, more recent proposal (Schenk 152, 164) sees an *if*-cl. and conclusion: "For if for me life is nothing other than the risen Jesus, then on the one hand sacrifice of life is no loss at all, but a win-situation." ("On the other hand" comes in v 22, another condition.) Little support; where discussed, it has been rejected. See the opening NOTE on 1:21.

The starting point lies in the maxim *to die, gain* (cf. Palmer). From Homer on, often using the word found here, *kerdos* (see NOTES and COMMENT A.4); gnomic wisdom on "dying well"; Gk. tragedies, whether "to live is gain for me." Often a choice (*Tabula of Cebes* 38.3), "To die is often more preferred than to live." Comparisons may use "better" (Oriental wisdom literature; occasionally Gk. literature, immortality after death, end of A. 4). Paul likely knew such ideas from school instruction *(progymnasmata)*, the Greco-Roman world, or even Greek-speaking synagogues in Jerusalem (references in A. 4). From such a background, *to die* = physical death.

To this maxim, Paul prefixes a reference to *life* (art. infin., rhetorical variation on *life* and *death* in v 20). Pres. tense for living, aor. for dying, is natural, as in many Gk. statements about death *(to apothanein)*. "Continuing to live" will be brought out in v 24, *continue to stay on. to live* in v 21 means existence as a Christian ("in Christ," by the Spirit; cf. Rom 8:1–2, 4b, 5b, 9–11, 13b) in the present world of legal charges, prisons, and struggle with opponents (1:28–30). And new life in Christ present in the physical existence of believers. "In Christ" and "in the flesh" at the same time mark Christian existence.

Use of *Christ* to define life is not surprising. No art. (1:1, etc.), a personal name, once a title ("Anointed One"), for Paul's risen Lord. *Christos* can have missiological and ecclesial connotations (see NOTE on 1:21 *Christ*), if read in (the former from v 22; "body of Christ" is not in the picture). From interrelation of "Christ" and "gospel" in 1:12–18c, it suggests "the Christ proclaimed in the good news," what living on will mean for Paul (v 25).

All this sheds light on *to die*. In Gk. maxims, death was the end to human existence. Here the person for whom it is "gain" is "in Christ," a believer with hopes and expectations. Death lacks in this passage its frequent sense in Paul of "punishment for sin" (Rom 1:32; 6:23a), a finis that sinning brings (Rom 7:9–10). It fits with passages where Paul contemplates death "with some equanimity" (*TPTA*, Ch. 3, #5.7, p. 19); cf. 1 Cor 9:15; 15:31, "I die every day"; 2 Cor 6:9, "dying, and see — we are alive"; 11:23; Rom 14:8, "whether we live or whether we die, we are the Lord's." *To die* at Phil 1:21 has (cf. C. E. Cranfield, *Rom.* 299–300, re Rom 6:2, "we who died to sin") a future-eschatological sense and (cf. 1:23, "with Christ") connection with baptism (Rom 6:2–4). A believer's death can be "gain" because of "eternal life" through Christ (Rom 5:21; 6:22, 23), life that is already a factor for believers, and that means "'gaining' more of Christ . . . full participation in his resurrection" (Bockmuehl 88). Both *zōē* and *thanatos* belong to the Christian (in Stoicism "all things belong to the person who is wise"), but within "the action radius of faith" (1 Cor 3:22; Conzelmann, *1 Cor.* 80–81).

But if, "to live" in the flesh, this implying fruitful missionary labor for me, what then shall I choose? I do not know is Option IV of five possible construals (see NOTE), a double protasis ("if 'to live' . . ." and "if this implies fruitful missionary labor . . ."; both points taken to be true), and a conclusion, in question form, "what shall I choose?" Then a short statement about not knowing, in contrast to *I know* in v 19 and v 20 (where it can be supplied). This leads to the most poignant expression in the passage, v 23, *I am betwixt and between two possibilities.*

The conditions in 22ab develop the first option in v 21, *to live* (is) *Christ. But (de)* suggests progression of the initial thought. *"to live"* (in quotes to show repetition from v 21) is expanded by *in the flesh.* As with "death" in v 21, not negative, pejorative use *sarx* often has in Paul, but simply the earthly, limited side of life here and now, even for the Christian. Remaining alive, even if "in Christ," is, of necessity, in the world. Not a reason to choose against such existence, but a fact of life in a world that is God's but which has not yet received redemption fully. No vb. is supplied, the TRANSLATION is as terse as Paul's Gk. "To live" implies being "in the flesh."

The second item, equivalent to an "if" cl., consists of five Gk. words, again no vb. *This* (as in v 19 Gk. *touto*) looks back to something just mentioned, "this situation of existence in the flesh." *estin* must again be supplied: "is, means, implies." *for me* is not as emphatic as *emoi* was in v 21, but echoes it. Again, Paul's personal evaluation. It goes with what follows, lit., "fruit of labor" on Paul's part. Previous uses of "fruit" *(karpos)* in Phil point up business and agricultural senses (4:17 *profit*, Letter A; 1:11 *fruit*, respectively). *karpos* can mean "gain" (in financial transactions or growing crops); hence a synonym with *gain* in v 21, "eschatological profit" (Schenk 151). Here "life," not "death," involves such a result. *labor,* "work" *(ergou)*, refers to missionary, pastoral tasks (1 Cor 16:10, Timothy does "the work of the Lord"; 1 Thess 5:13, the work of leaders who "care for" you). Not profit for Paul but for the gospel and the Philippians (1:5–6). I. H. Marshall 28 flirts with the idea Paul thinks "he will have something to show for his labours at the day of judgment" (cf. 1 Thess 2:19–20) but admits it is "not actually said here" (but cf. 105 on Phil 4:1). Missionary labor involves God working through Paul and others (1:6), work for Christ (2:30). Paul considers carefully the challenge of *fruitful missionary labor* on his part.

The second premise, "if this means fruitful laboring for me," has been tr. as an absolute construction, *this implying fruitful missionary labor for me,* a correct condition. Paul's dilemma results, *what then shall I choose?* Which option, gain through death (21) or continuing as apostle/ missionary/pastor (22)? The "Christ" aspect of going on in life has attractions too. *choose* (for myself) implies Paul has some say in the matter. That suicide is contemplated (COMMENT A. 6) will be excluded by what Paul says in 24–26 and his future plans in 2:23–24. It fits, however, with the view that Paul banks on his Roman citizenship (COMMENT A.7). He chose to use it. Is there now some self-doubt? If set free, does he want to face problems in Philippi and his other churches, gathering and delivering the collection to Jerusalem, and going to Rome and beyond?

I do not know is Paul's honest statement. Possibly "I do not cause (you) to know," "I cannot tell" (RSV), "I have nothing to declare (from God, a prophetic word, or personal insight)." See NOTE. B. Weiss 100, 104 n 1, "I do not recognize right now what to choose." In context, most likely "I do not know how things will come out" or "what to say." Discernment is at low ebb.

But I am betwixt and between the two. But (Gk. *de*) continues the sequence of question and comment, 1st per. sg. Paul is claimed and controlled by the two possibilities, tormented, hard-pressed between more missionary labor and death. He "balances *choice* against his *vocation*" (E. T. Horn, *Phil.* 143). Why this is such a predicament is indicated in the next cl., which develops the other horn of the dilemma, *to die is gain* (v 21). The flood of thoughts goes on with *echōn* (ptc. agreeing with "I" in "I am hard-pressed"). Possibly causal, "because I have the desire to depart. . . ." Most make a separate sentence (except KJV in its literalness). Schenk's case (155, 164) for a conditional sense is more likely here than for 21a and matches the clear protasis in v 22 ("*if* 'to live' . . ."), *if . . . to depart*. As part of Paul's *expectation and hope* (1:20), *desire* here is positive. Hence, *If I have the desire to. . . .* The art. *tēn* suggests "my (personal) desire," [N]RSV.

to depart and to be with Christ is not a purpose cl. (some MSS even omit *eis*, placing the two art. infin. in apposition *to desire*, namely, to. . .) but the content of what Paul wants. *to depart* had vivid uses in Gk.: pull up stakes (of tents), weigh anchor, sail on; see NOTE on 1:23. Here a euphemism for "die," with hints of "departing from this life *at a signal from God*" or "departing *to the gods*" ("set free from [prison] chains" reads too much in). The two verbal nouns are closely intertwined through a single def. art., "desire for the departing-and-being-with-Christ." *depart* is explained by *be with Christ*, the fullest assertion of Paul's *expectation and hope* (v 20).

The NOTE on 1:23 and EXC. A treat "with Christ." The prep. *syn* can suggest accompaniment, association, experiencing something with someone, and even intimate union and incorporation (BDAG; *NIDNTT* 3:1206–7). *Christ* is prominent as in the immediately preceding vv (1:19, 20, 21). "With Christ" *(syn Christō[i])* must be considered under the broader theme of being "in Christ" (see NOTE on 1:1 *in Christ Jesus*; EXC. A.1). It occurs at the beginning and end of the believer's relationship *en Christō[i]*. At the outset of the faith journey, following conversion, one is united "with Christ" in baptism (Rom 6:4–8). This incorporation continues in daily existence "as we walk in newness of life" (1 Cor 15:31, Rom 14:8; 2 Cor 13:4; Rom 6:8; 8:29; and Phil 3:10). Some vv, like Rom 8:17, "joint heirs with Christ," point to a future inheritance, "with Christ" as a relationship brought to completion at the Day of the Lord (1 Thess 4:17; 5:10; 2 Cor 4:14; Phil 3:21). The origins of the two "with-Christ" usages root, respectively, in Christian baptism and developments from Jewish eschatology (A.3).

At Phil 1:23 "with Christ" fits with an eschatological event "at the end." "In Christ" may be a "formula," but not "to be with Christ." The only instance of *einai syn Christō[i]* is this one at 1:23; similar phrases, including terms compounded with *syn* (a "theology of with-ness") are so varied that one better speaks of a "motif" or "theme" or characteristic way of expression (Wedderburn, O'B 112), not a formula. The coinage, likely here by Paul himself, with roots in earlier apocalyptic, esp. 1 Thess, differs from most references to being "raised up with Jesus" or "forever with the Lord," in that Paul expects his further union "with Christ" to occur when he departs, i.e., at his individual death, prior to a general resurrection and parousia.

Progressive "stages of development" in Pauline eschatology are unlikely (Exc. A. 4). Consistency (appropriate to situations), rather than evolutionary steps, characterized Paul's view. So, among others, U. Luz, *Das Geschichtsverständnis des Paulus* (BEvT 49, Munich: Kaiser, 1968) 355–57, denying any "development" between 1 Thess 4:13–18 and Phil 1:23: what Paul says in 1:23, about possibly dying before the parousia, arises from the concrete situation in which the apostle finds himself. Was being with Christ at death a privilege reserved for an elite group? Apostles only (Schweitzer)? Martyrs (Loh.)? Neither view is likely (Exc. A.5). But does Paul then envision—instead of waiting in the grave for resurrection day (1 Thess 4:16; 1 Cor 15:52) or, in later theories, "soul-sleep" (when you awaken at the resurrection, no time has passed for you since your death; Silva 82; Kreitzer, *DPL* 440)—an "interim state" of existence (Exc. A. 6)? Beyond physical life and personal death but not yet the fullness of life together in the eternal kingdom (Cullmann)? 2 Cor 5:1–10 must also be taken into consideration (the individual believer becomes further clothed at death with a "heavenly house" over his or her "earthly tent"). At Phil 3:20–21, the apostle, reflecting a more traditional view, will speak of the Savior coming from heaven, where our citizenship is; Christ will transform our body. Is being "with Christ" (in heaven) then something only at "the End"?

"Intermediate state"—not Paul's term—may imply more than he actually says and opens the way to misunderstandings (Schreiber 2003:358–59). But alongside the common NT view of future judgment and all the redeemed entering corporately into the promised realm of heaven, Paul at 1:23 is asserting a continuity of the individual's relationship with Christ that begins with call and baptism. He expects the relationship to continue at death. His phrase for the immortality of the Christ-relationship is *to be with Christ*. Where is not stated. Probably in heaven, where Christ is (3:20–21; "Paradise," Eden, the "Promised Land," E. T. Horn, *Phil.* 144).[14] No details, certainly not golden streets or heavenly banquet feasts. The "no longer–not yet" of the believers' life in the flesh will at death be different from what sinful human life was but not yet the corporate fulfillment of the king-

---

[14] Schreiber 2003 asks how Pharisees would have understood being "with Christ" at death *and* a final general resurrection. He notes Hellenistic ideas of death as gain (see Comment A.4), rejects Jewish "martyr-theology" (Loh., U. B. Müller; 2 Macc 7; 4 Macc) and an abode for "the righteous" in *1 En.* 39:4–8; 51:1–2 (P. Hoffmann, Gnilka), in favor of a theory about Adam (*Apoc. Mos.* 31–43 = OTP 2:287–95, esp. 37:3–5, the Lake of Acheron [! Gk. Hades] and Paradise, the third heaven, plus 41:3 resurrection on the last day) and fathers of Israel like Abraham, Isaac, and Jacob, analogous to Paul as "father" of his converts (1 Cor 4:15).

dom when God will "be all in all" (1 Cor 15:28). Paul has moved beyond the metaphor of "sleeping." The more we grant Paul emphasized being "with Christ" during earthly existence after faith and baptism, the more likely Paul is to have come to a view of being "with Christ" after his death but before the parousia. This hope he sets forth not just for himself but as part of the gospel of Christ to assure the Philippians in their struggle (1:27–30).

What Paul has articulated to explain *to die* as *gain*, namely *to depart and be with Christ*, he declares to be the option that is *much better by far*, the (triple) comparative a feature of the *sygkrisis* form. The construction breaks off and swings back to the other side of the comparison.

1:24 picks up again the theme of *life* (1:20; 1:21, *to live, Christ; "to live" in the flesh, fruitful missionary labor* for Paul, 1:22). Paul takes what seems another zigzag, with a new verbal noun, *stay on*, plus a phrase repeated from v 22 *(in the flesh)*. He brings in the Philippians for the first time since v 12 *(your account)*. His letter let them listen to his soliloquy. It concludes, *but to continue to stay on in the flesh is more necessary on your account. But* is adversative, turning the comparison back along the other track, living, not dying. *to continue to stay on* takes *epimenein* as linear action, with wordplay involving *stay (menein)* and *stay on in the service of . . . (paramenein*, 1:25). *in the flesh (tē[i] sarki)*, even without the textually uncertain *en*, reminds one of *en sarki* in v 22. The local sense suggests where Paul remains, the world of human existence. At the moment, in jail, but prison is not where Paul expects to remain as he stays on in this world. The NOTE mentions taking *tē[i]* to mean "in my flesh" (so Meyer 37); cf. [N]JB, "in this body," cf. *to me* in vv 21 and 22b; so Gdsp., "for me." A nice touch of contrast to *on your account*, but perhaps too subtle.

Again a comparative, *more necessary*, a feature of the *sygkrisis* form. To remain in mission service is more necessary for the Philippians. On their account his final decision is to live on, not death to be with Christ. Does this make Paul a benefactor or patron of the Christians in Philippi? The Philippians might have been inclined to such a view. His role as apostle (not stressed in Phil) and example of service (apparent in 1:1 and what he models) argue against it. So the comparison between living and dying ends, as it began in vv 20 and 21; the emphasis on remaining upon earth, active in apostolic witness.

3. Paul Looks to Stay on in Mission Service, for the Progress of the Philippians, with a Return to Them (1:25–26). The line of thought in vv 20 *(life)*, 21 *(to live, Christ)*, 22 *("to live" in the flesh, fruitful missionary labor)*, and 24 *(continue to stay on in the flesh)* is now carried one step further. This comes in terms of *progress and joy* arising out of the Philippians' *faith* and their continued grounds for abounding, in Christ Jesus—but not without Paul. Emphasis is put sometimes on Paul's certainty about the future, but these vv are far more about the needs of others and *service* to his converts (Schreiber 2003:339–40). This fits how the letter moves from events affecting Paul *(ta kat' eme*, 1:12) and his inner thoughts (1:21–24), to the Philippians and their situation and struggle (1:27–2:18). The narrative looks toward specific encouragement and admonitions for the house churches in

Philippi and plans Paul has for their welfare (*ta peri hymōn*, 2:20). Phil 1:24–26 are, then, not just about "reunion in Philippi" or reassurance concerning their apostle, but pastoral concern for their growth in Christian faith and life. Schreiber 357–59 goes further: Paul "provokes" the Philippians into identification with him and the right priorities for congregational life, "with Christ" on earth.

Paul writes (1:25), *I am confident of this*, namely, "staying on as necessary for the Philippians" (v 24), more necessary than his desire to be with Christ (v 23). He thus links vv 25–26 with the poignant comparison of living or dying in 21–24. *kai* is connective, even if many trs. lack *And*. The causal cl. gives a reason for continuing, *I know that I shall stay* alive and be able *to stay on in the service of you all*.[15] The Gk. ptc. rendered as *confident* appeared at 1:6. It has a range of meanings (see NOTE on 1:6 *since I am confident on this point*), from "be persuaded" to "convinced," therefore "confident," and even "trusting." A theme of some prominence in Letter B (cf. also 1:14 and 2:24), it relates to Paul's faith.

I know has occurred also at 1:19. Two uses of *oida* thus bracket the passage, each followed by a *hoti* cl. (= *that . . .*) stating what Paul knows; here (Loh. 66), the "joy of faith" (1:25, cf. 18d; reiterated by U. B. Müller 70). The letter body has moved from what Paul wants the Philippians to know (1:12) to what he knows, not "of a certainty" (NEB) but from firm conviction. Not prophetic knowledge about the future, some "sure token of God's will" (*certitudo*, so Calvin 44), or (Bengel 668) "prophetic intimation" (Loh. 66–67 "the charism of prophecy"). What Paul knows is simply *I shall stay. . . .* Does that contradict 20, seemingly judgment before God, at his death? No, because Paul also speaks in v 20 of *life* as the other possibility, not his *desire* (v 23, which was to be "with Christ"), but his final preference (*more necessary*, v 24). See COMMENT A.4, on the *sygkrisis* form, the "losing" choice (Paul's personal preference) usually mentioned first, *by life or by death*. Paul preferred to die and to be with Christ, but a turning point came in v 24, he has crossed up the rhetorical pattern with the "Christ" factor, a reflection of his call to save others through the gospel.

Proposed chiastic structures in vv 25–26 (Webber [(2) Bibl. **joy**], Schenk, COMMENT A.3) do not agree with each other or find much support.[16] Paul's presentation of aims begins with wordplay in Gk., brought out as *stay on* (v 24 *epimenein*), *stay* (25, using *menein*), and *stay on in service* (25, *paramenein*).[17] The trend has

---

[15] The NOTES discuss alternate renderings (KJV, [N]RSV, etc.), particularly, "I know for certain" (NEB, NJB) or REB's "I am sure" (I. H. Marshall, *Phil.* 30–31, REB has made "a jump from 'I am sure that this is the more necessary' [v 24] to 'I am sure that this will happen'" in v 25).

[16] Schenk's A-B-C-D-D'-C'-B'-A' chiasmus takes 25a as the protasis of a conditional sentence, "*if* I live on . . . ," ending in v 26, "I then could once more be with you." Cf. in the NOTE Haupt and Chrysost. It would match the clearer "if" statement in v 23, "If (I desire) to die. . . ." Paul then would be pursuing each possibility hypothetically. But this analysis founders on the lack of an "if" in v 25 and the fact that Paul breaks off his speculation in v 24 about "departure to be with Christ," to move on to the option he finds *more necessary* and about which he is *confident* (24–25), the perceived results of which he now is spelling out.

[17] "Bide" and "abide" (Lft. 94) do not quite work because of recent conclusions about the compound vb. *paramenō*. Calvin 45 sought to distinguish the Lat. *manebo et permanebo* as "stay for a little while" and "remain for a long time." Ellicott 44 tried "continue" and "continue here (on earth)." Hoffmann

been to take *paramenein* as "remain in service," "continue in some job or office" (*TDNT* 4:577–78; Gdsp.; Moffatt, "serve," Michael 60). Haupt called notions of Paul looking for "rest and relaxation" with the Philippians (JB; NAB) a "psychological monstrosity." Mission and service in ministry are involved. Schenk 160, *paramenein* in v 25 is synonymous with *ergon* in 22, *mission labor*, an active term.

you all, in whose service Paul expects to continue, has sometimes been taken to refer to all his congregations; that better fits a redacted epistle. In Letter B, *you all* means the totality of, every individual in, the house churches there, like *all* in 1:4, 7, and 8 (toward unity at Philippi).

Paul's purpose in staying is *for your progress and joy that arise from your faith,* the emphasis in vv 25–26 (U. B. Müller 70), not confidence he'll stay on (seen in the vbs.) but purpose (*eis* + acc.), stay on in service, a matter further developed in the purpose cl. of v 26. Such purpose in 1:25, recognized since the church fathers (B. Weiss 114) but not always stressed the way the *inclusio* word *progress* (cf. 1:12) demands, is twofold: "advance" and "rejoicing," closely intertwined, two nouns with a single art., but distinguishable themes.

progress as a term (see NOTE on 1:12) came from the Greco-Roman world, likely familiar to people in Philippi from popular philosophy. From here and Hellenistic Judaism it entered Paul's vocabulary. 1:12 *progress for the gospel* was not a phrase the culture of the day would have employed, but natural for a missionary evangelist, the good news advances. At 1:25, *your progress* is that of the Philippians. Philosophy spoke of the individual's progress in morality and self-development; here *your* is pl., communal, *you all* in Philippi. The word order makes it emphatic: lit., "the of-you progress and joy," NAB "your progress and your joy."

The second aim is the Philippians' *joy* (1:4; vb. *rejoice* 18c and d). They can rejoice over Paul's remaining for service to them. But joy arises also as a result of faith, out of their believing. Is *joy* the real content of the Philippians' advance, not "advance in faith"? So Schenk 161, U. B. Müller 71, "your progress, yes, your joy from faith" (hendiadys; epexegetical *kai*). That may limit the "advance" too specifically. NEB "to help you forward and to add joy to your faith" separates *progress* and *joy* too much, faith a dreary thing to which joy must be added, rather than a source for Christian joy. REB has righted this, "your progress and joy in the faith," but "the faith" sounds too content-oriented (*fides quae creditur*, what one believes).

faith appears here for the first time in the letter (also in 1:27; vb. 1:29). It has (see NOTE) OT backgrounds, Gk. rhetorical connections with "persuasion," and a range of meanings: convinced, confident, trust, belief, obedience. It could mean

---

invented a distinction between "remain alive" and "willingly remain alive" (Meyer 37). Meyer's distinction (38) between "remain" (not be deprived of life) and "continue with you all" (be preserved) has fared little better. The variant, *symparamenō*, "remain with," shows scribes puzzled over the distinction (and solved it with a compound, as some scribes had at 1:1 *synepiskopois*); the variant had a vogue (Tischendorff adopted it), but by Lft.'s time was in the discard pile.

"what is believed" (as REB suggests), but the art. *(tēn pistin)* suggests "that faith of yours," among the Philippians. An action or process, "believing," seems meant here, no object indicated, but "gospel" or "Christ" would be obvious. Bockmuehl 94 sees here both content (the gospel) and "trusting human response" to it.

Out of such believing—religious conviction, confidence, trust in Christ and God—*progress and joy* among the Philippians arise and are nurtured. Of the several options suggested (see NOTE), this particularly fits the context. Paul seeks not to clarify doctrine but to deepen their advance in faith, through his own example, to equip them to stand firm in struggles within the Christian community at Philippi and against state authorities. If a benediction were added here, it might be, "God . . . fill you with all joy and peace in believing, so that you may abound *(perisseuein)* in hope by the power of the Holy Spirit" (Rom 15:13). Instead he uses such language (about converts abounding) to express further his purpose for the Philippians.[18]

1:18d–26 is rounded out in v 26 with a purpose cl. that tells more about what *deliverance* or salvation (1:19) will mean for the believers in Philippi: Paul will stay on in service *in order that your grounds for boasting may continue to abound in Christ Jesus, in me, through my coming again to you*. Thus, *Paul's* deliverance, from prison and at the final judgment (1:19) is related to the *Philippians'* growth up through the Day of the Lord.

grounds for boasting has a positive sense, out of an OT background, "boasting in the Lord."[19] Not human activity, but a *"cause* to glory in Christ Jesus" (RSV), "reason to give praise to Christ Jesus" (JB; cf. REB, Moffatt). The NOTE suggests that, instead of experimenting with other vocabulary in Eng. like "pride," it is best to come to terms with the Pauline sense of boasting.

Whose grounds for boasting are involved? Paul regarded his congregations as grounds for him to boast on the Day of Christ that his mission work was not in vain—if these believers continue to hold fast to the word (Phil 2:16). At 2 Cor 1:14

---

[18] Holloway 2001a:112–14 sees a "current *lack* of 'progress and joy in the faith'" on the part of the Philippians (italics added); then Phil fits his category, "letter of consolation," Paul's rhetorical problem "how to rebuke them for their emotional frailty when what they expect from him is a letter thanking them for their support" (again, the problem of 4:10–20, when delayed till the end of a single letter). 1:25 is said to mean, "I am confident that you will not make progress without seeing me again" (113–14). Implication: an "unflattering comparison" between the progress of the gospel where Paul is imprisoned (1:12–18c) and things in Philippi. We read "progress" as a factor in both Ephesus (1:12) and Philippi; the point of comparison is the *agōn* that both Paul and the Philippians face. Debanné ([2] A.4 n 11) 495 claims an enthymeme in 1:25b–26: silent Premise, "God intends to cause believers' faith to progress through specific joyous occasions which cause boasting in Christ to abound"; Minor Premise, "Paul's return to the Philippians will cause 'boasting in Christ' to abound among the Philippians"; Conclusion, "God intends to cause the Philippians['] faith to progress through Paul's return to them." God's intention, not Paul's (as in Holloway).

[19] Jer 9:23, not about wisdom, might, or wealth, but knowing God and understanding divine love, justice, and righteousness, is cited twice by Paul (1 Cor 1:31, 2 Cor 10:17) and reflected in the Christian definition of boasting, not glorifying self or human achievements (Phil 3:3–4; 2 Cor 11:13, 18) but in the cross of Christ (Gal 6:14, on which H. D. Betz commented, "strictly speaking . . . not boasting at all" but "'doxology' or 'hymn,'" *Gal.* 318). Being confident, having trust or faith (in Christ) (1:25), the opposite of "being put to shame" (1:20).

the congregation and apostle are, for each other, "grounds for boasting" mutually: "on the day of the Lord Jesus we are your boast *(kauchēma)* even as you are our boast." But 1:26 is not like 2:16 (U. B. Müller 71 n 116), the situations are very different, no mutuality. 1:26 refers to the *Philippians'* basis for boasting (subjective gen.), not (Paul's) boasting about them.

Paul desires that the Philippians' boasting *may continue to abound* (pres. tense, linear action), ongoing growth, as in the prayer at 1:9 (that *your love may continue to grow still more and more*). *When?* At least, till Paul comes among the Philippians again. As an eschatological term (2:16, 2 Cor 1:14), till Christ comes at the parousia. *in Christ Jesus* is an abbreviated formula for "in the Day of Christ Jesus" (Schenk 162), the terminus at 1:10 when the Philippians' abounding love, knowledge, and discernment come to fullness. *in Christ Jesus* here, as often, has a certain ambiguity. It could go with *grounds for boasting* ([N]RSV, among many trs.), defanging notions of boasting as a human accomplishment; its sphere is "in Christ." But word order suggests *abound in Christ Jesus*, until and at the Day of Christ as the temporal sphere.

What of *in me*, which follows directly *(en Christō[i] Iēsou, en emoi)*? Paul and his ministry are where the Philippians abound in boasting. Not simply boast over Paul as their apostle (NASB "your proud confidence in me," which Silva 86 defends; cf. 2 Cor 1:4). Nor that the apostle represents Christ, their proper grounds for boasting, and Paul will soon be personally present with them again (Vincent 31). Nor (see NOTE) *en emoi* with both *en Christō[i] Iēsou* and *boasting*. So Gdsp. and Moffatt, "cause to glory in Christ Jesus over me." Michael 61 is on the right track, as "the result of his ministry among them," the Philippians (in a letter of theirs) "may themselves have spoken of the Apostle as the ground of their glorying." Bormann 1995:214–15, 1:26 is anchored in the "patron" theme. We suggest Paul's ministry among the Philippians brought them to *faith*; from their believing arise *progress* and *joy*, and hence *grounds for boasting* eschatologically. Paul's ministry will include admonition (1:27–2:18) to stand firm and live out the faith, holding on to the word of life (2:16). So will they go on abounding, with grounds for proper boasting on their own. Not Paul as an icon of theirs, but their advance and joy, due to faith, from the gospel that Paul brought to them and continues to press upon them. That would be "working out (implications of) their salvation *(sōtēria)*, God working through them to will and work for God's good pleasure" (2:12b–13).

They are to live out the gospel in this way whether Paul is absent or present (2:12a). But at 1:26 the expectation is *my coming again to you.* Paul's return will be a means or cause for their continuing to abound (KJV "by," RSV "because of" Paul's coming there again; NRSV's "when I come" somewhat misses the point that the process can go on apart from, as well as with, Paul present). The oddly phrased Gk. *pros hymas* (see NOTE on *to you*) implies travel to, as well as being there with, them. It anticipates the "apostolic *parousia* form" in 2:12, 19–24. Reed (DA171, 173), following Stowers and Malherbe, sees "presence" and *philophronēsis* (kindliness, an affectionate manner, tenderness), *parousia* reflects the "epistolary paraenesis" of friendship. From *parousia* one should not try to smuggle in Christ's "second coming" or martyriological speculations.[20] No, the aim is to continue equipping the Philippians to abound in their maturity. What Paul has written about life and death for himself, what he will urge in 1:27–2:16 for their communal life, as well as his hoped-for return to Philippi, all contribute to that end. The body of the letter will move on to the situation among the Christians in Philippi, come what may for Paul.

Thus, Paul, in an Ephesian prison, has appealed in court to his citizenship (cf. COMMENT A.7, above). As he writes (dictates) 1:18d–26, he has reason for optimism; he will be let off from all charges and can then travel to Philippi to stand shoulder to shoulder with his beloved converts there amid their adversities.[21] But Paul's case was still undecided; anything can still happen. 2:24 goes on to talk, as here, of coming soon to Philippi, but 2:17 will speak of being a sacrifice and offering of the Philippians' faith (2:17). He knows his role on earth in a "divine economy" is not yet played out (Walter 42; Thielman 77).

In comparing his prospects for life or death (1:21–24), Paul has reflected Gk. forms and sentiments about death as gain, but it is no "figured" rhetorical exercise. The earnest talk about himself models for the Philippians (Thielman 79) faith and joy and advance of the gospel in the individual and the community. The apostle's indirect example of how faith thrives amid threat and adversity will become more pointed admonition and exhortation in what follows after 1:27.

4. Phil 1:18d–26 Within the Redacted, Canonical Letter. Meanings sketched for Letter B hold in the four-ch. epistle. A few aspects call for treatment in a way not needed with 1:3–11 and 12–18c.

a. Identity of 1:19 as *a citation from Job* might have been clearer to readers of Phil as a whole, within a growing canonical setting, than it was for the converts of Paul's day.

b. Michael 56 claims Paul wrote, "For me to live means Christ, to die means gain. And which to choose I cannot tell" (v. 21). Marginal comments were then added: "to live: in the flesh" and "this to me: fruit of work." But (Michael 1922–23) these are scribal glosses here, not an editor at work. The NOTE on 1:22 *and to die* has, with Gnilka, rejected the theory.

c. As the "with Christ" theme in 1:23 was given fuller context than Letter B, the frame for interpretation grew. Once 3:20–21 (from Letter C) was part of the same document, the problem became how to relate departing to be *"with Christ" upon one's death* with transformation only *at the coming of Christ* from heaven. As the Pauline corpus took shape, the question of "development" in Paul's eschatology attracted inevitable attention. See EXC. A.4.

---

[20] Loh. 69–70: for Paul to be put to death in a strange place where he has no congregation (Caesarea) heightens the pathos; an apostle should be united in place with his community, so as "to present you [the community] as a chaste virgin to Christ" (2 Cor 11:2). The latter v is termed by Furnish AB 32A:499 part of "An Awkward Appeal," made more so if one tries to imagine Paul physically present at Christ's parousia with each of his several congregations.

[21] Maybe Epaphroditus, whom the Philippians had sent to be with Paul, was of help in the legal work (see on 2:25–30). We doubt that the money the Philippians had sent was intended as, or was used for, a bribe (as Reeves claims).

d. In the canonical order, Paul's critical engagement with *sygkrisis* may be harder to ferret out. His stance towards elements in Gk. culture is clearer after 4:10–20 (Letter A) has been considered.

e. Suggestions that the Philippians regarded *Paul as "the ground for their glorying"* (Michael 61) or that *the money from Philippi* was a bribe toward Paul's freedom (Reeves 286) seem (even) less likely in the canonical epistle. Yet one could argue that the four-ch. letter wants to discuss his situation apart from any reference to the gift from Philippi, so as to avoid any notion of bribery.

f. The *ongoing relationship* of Paul *with the Philippians* is better grasped when Letter B follows upon the acknowledgment of the Philippians' gift in 4:10–20 and the way in which their care for Paul has but recently revived (4:10).

g. 1:25–26 (*you all, your grounds for boasting,* cf. 24 *on your account*) as references to *all of Paul's congregations* better fit a redacted letter; what was said to one church becomes more broadly meaningful. Paul becomes a general example for all Christians.

Phil 1:21–23 is one of the three most influential passages in the epistle, along with 2:5–11 and 3:20–21. Bockmuehl 1995 used it to illustrate what a commentary should include on the "effective history" *(Wirkungsgeschichte)* of a passage. His commentary, cf. p. 45, like this one, did not allow space of such a "history of interpretation." Only in the 19th cent. did 1:12–21 or 1:15–21 begin to appear in lectionaries; see above, (3) COMMENT B, end. The Roman *Ordo* of 1969 assigned 1:20c (NAB "I have full confidence that now as always . . .")–24, 27a for the first of four readings from Phil (25th Sunday of Year A = Pentecost 18); in other churches, 1:20–27 or, in the Revised Common Lectionary, 1:21–30. The encouragement the Philippians found in Paul's words continued to speak in sermons and hymns like "Christ the Life of all the living."

SELECT BIBLIOGRAPHY (see also General Bibliography and Commentaries)

Antin, P. 1974. "*Mori lucrum* et *Antigone 462, 464*," *RSR* 62:259–60.

Bertram, G. 1958. "*Apokaradokia* (Phil. 1,20)," *ZNW* 49:264–70.

Bormann, L. 2001. "Reflexionen über Sterben und Tod bei Paulus," in F. W. Horn, ed., *Das Ende des Paulus: Historische, theologische und literaturgeschichtliche Aspekte,* BZNW 106 (Berlin/New York: de Gruyter) 307–30, esp. 319–21.

Chang, H. K. 2002. "(apo)karadokia bei Paulus und Aquila," *ZNW* 93:268–78.

Dailey, T. F. 1990. "To Live or Die, Paul's Eschatological Dilemma in Philippians 1:19–26," *Int* 44:18–28.

Denton, D. R. 1982. "*Apokaradokia,*" *ZNW* 73:138–40.

Genths, P. "Der Begriff des *kauchēma* bei Paulus," *NKZ* 38 (1928) 501–21; 39 (1929) 78–82.

Giglioli, A. 1968. "Mihi enim vivere Christus est. Congettura al testo di Phil 1,21," *RivB* 16:305–15.

Gundry, R. H. 1976. *Sōma in Biblical Theology with Emphasis on Pauline Anthropology,* SNTSMS 29 (Cambridge: Cambridge Univ. Press) 147–49, 152–53.

Hoffmann, P. 1966. "Das Mit-Christus-Sein im Tode nach Phil 1,21–26," in his *Die Toten in Christus: Eine religionsgeschchtliche und exegetische Untersuchung zur paulinischen Eschatologie,* NTAbh N.F. 2 (Münster: Aschendorff, 2nd ed. 1972) 286–320 (3rd ed. 1978).

Lee, G. M. 1970. "Philippians I 22–3, *NovT* 12:361.

Marrow, S. B. 1982. "Parrhesia and the New Testament," *CBQ* 44:431–46.

Michael, J. H. 1923–24. "Two Brief Marginal Notes in the Text of Philippians," *ExpTim* 35:139–40.

Nebe, G. 1983. *Hoffnung bei Paulus. Elpis und ihre Synonyme im Zusammenhang der Eschatologie.* SUNT 16. Göttingen: Vandenhoeck & Ruprecht.

Palmer, D. W. 1975. " 'To Die is Gain' (Philippians i 21)," *NovT* 17:203–18.

Peterson, E. 1929. "Zur Bedeutungsgeschichte von *parrhēsia*," in *Reinhold-Seeberg-Festschrift, I, Zur Theorie des Christentums,* ed. W. Koepp (Leipzig: A. Deichertsche Verlagsbuchhandlung) 283–97.

Reeves, R. R. 1992. "To Be or Not To Be? That Is Not the Question: Paul's Choice in Philippians 1:22," *PRSt* 19:273–89.

Sánchez Bosch, J. 1970. *"Gloriarse" según San Pablo. Sentido y teología de* kauchaomai. AnBib 40, Colectanea San Paciano 16. Rome: Biblical Institute/Barcelona: Facultad de Teología.

Sand, A. 1967. *Der Begriff "Fleisch" in den paulinischen Hauptbriefen.* BU 2. Regensburg: Pustet.

Schmitz, O. 1914. "Zum Verständnis vom Philipper 1,21," in *Neutestamentliche Studien. Georg Heinrici zu seinem 70. Geburtstag . . .* (Leipzig: Hinrichs) 156–69.

Schreiber, S. 2003. "Paulus im 'Zwischenzustand': Phil 1,23 und die Ambivalenz des Sterbens als Provokation," NTS 49:336–59.

Silva, M. 1980. "The Pauline Style as Lexical Choice: *ginōskein* and Related Verbs," in *Pauline Studies Presented to F. F. Bruce,* ed. D. A. Hagner/M. J. Harris (Grand Rapids: Eerdmans) 184–207.

Unnik, W. C. van. 1980. "The Christian's Freedom of Speech in the New Testament," *BJRL* 44 (1961–62): 466–88, repr. in van Unnik's GS, *Sparsa Collecta. Part Two,* NovTSup 20 (Leiden: Brill, 1980) 290–306.

Vogel, C. J. de. 1977. "Reflexions on Philipp i 23–24," *NovT* 19:262–74.

Vollenweider, S. 1994. "Die Waagschalen von Leben und Tod. Zum antiken Hintergrund von Phil 1,21–26," ZNW 85:93–115; repr. in Vollenweider 2002:237–61.

Vorster, W. S. 1971. "The Meaning of *parrhēsia* in the Epistle to the Hebrews," *Noet* 5: 51–59.

Job 13:16 (1:19), **the OT in Phil** (COMMENT A.1): M. Silva, *DPL* 630–42; *TPTA* 15–16, 169–73, 237–38, 725–26; Fee 1994:737–38; (7) COMMENT A.1 n 3.

Hays, R. B. 1989. *Echos of Scripture in the Letters of Paul* (New Haven: Yale) 21–24.

Michael, J. H. 1924a. "Paul and Job: a Neglected Analogy," *ExpTim* 36:67–73.

Oakes, P. 2000. "Quelle devrait être l'influence des échos intertextuels sur la traduction? Le cas de l'épître aux Philippiens (2,15–16)," in *Intertextualités: La Bible en échos,* ed. D. Marguerat/A. Curtis, MdB 40 (Geneva: Labor et Fides) 251–87.

Reumann, J. 2006b. "The (Greek) Old Testament in Philippians: 1:19 as Parade Example— Allusion, Echo, Proverb?" in *History and Exegesis: New Testament Essays in Honor of E. Earle Ellis on His Eightieth Birthday,* ed. S. A. Son (New York: T&T Clark International, 2006) 189–200.

faith *(pistis)*(1:25): Wordbook and Bible dictionary articles are cited in the NOTE on 1:25.

Barth, G. 1982. "Pistis in hellenistischen Religiosität," ZNW 73:110–26.

Buber, M. 1951. *Two Types of Faith.* London: Routledge & Paul, New York: Macmillan; Harper Torchbook 1961.

Dobbeler, A. von. 1987. *Glaube als Teilhabe. Historische und semantische Grundlegungen der paulinischen Theologie und Ekklesiologie des Glaubens.* WUNT 2/22. Tübingen: Mohr Siebeck.

Hays, R. B. 1983. *The Faith of Jesus Christ. An Investigation of the Narrative Substructure of Galatians 3:1 — 4:11.* SBLDS 56. Chico, CA: Scholars Press. Repr., with new preface, Grand Rapids: Eerdmans, 2002.

Kinneavy, J. L. 1987. *Greek Rhetorical Origins of Christian Faith: An Inquiry.* New York: Oxford Univ. Press.

Lohse, E. 1977. "Emmua und Pistis—Jüdisches und urchristliches Verständnis des Glaubens," ZNW 68:147–63.

Lührmann, D. 1976. *Glaube im frühen Christentum.* Gütersloh: Gütersloher Verlagshaus Gerd Mohn. Cf. also his "Glaube," RAC 11:48–122; ABD 2:749–58.

Yeung, M. W. 2002. *Faith in Jesus and Paul. A Comparison with Special Reference to 'Faith That Can Move Mountains' and 'Your Faith Has Healed/Saved You.'* WUNT 2/147. Tübingen: Mohr Siebeck.

suicide (COMMENT A.6): A. J. Droge, *ABD* 6: 225–31; M. J. Harren, *ER* 14:125–31. See also *Philippian Studies.*

Clemons, J. T. 1990. *What Does the Bible Say about Suicide?* Minneapolis: Fortress.

Croy, N. C. 2003. "'To Die is Gain' (Philippians 1:19–26): Does Paul Contemplate Suicide?" *JBL*122:517–31.

Droge, A. J. 1988. "*Mori Lucrum:* Paul and Ancient Theories of Suicide," *NovT* 30: 263–86.

———. 1989. "Did Paul Commit Suicide?" *BibRev* 14–21.

——— and J. D. Tabor. *A Noble Death: Suicide & Martyrdom Among Christians and Jews in Antiquity.* San Francisco: Harper & Row, 1992. Esp. pp. 113–28.

Jaquette, J. L. 1994. "A Not-so-Noble Death: Figured Speech, Friendship and Suicide in Philippians 1:21–26," *Neot* 28:177–92.

———. 1996. "Life and Death, Adiaphora, and Paul's Rhetorical Strategies," *NovT* 38:30–54.

Sevenster, J. N. 1961. *Paul and Seneca.* NovTSup 4. Leiden: Brill. Pp. 58, 77, 234–38.

5. *Paraenesis* (Propositio, *with Reasons for the Admonitions*), 1:27–30

TRANSLATION

1:27a This point only: Exercise your citizenship in a manner worthy of the gospel of Christ, b in order that, whether I come and see you or continue to be absent, I may hear the news about you, c that you stand steadfast in one and the same Spirit, d engage together in the struggle for the gospel faith with one soul, 28a and are not intimidated in any way by your adversaries. b This, indeed, is to them a pointer of destruction but of your salvation, c and this, from God, 29a because to you it has been granted by God, for the sake of Christ, b not only to continue to believe in him c but also to keep suffering for his sake, 30a since you are having the same contest b such as you saw in my life and of which you are now hearing in my life.

NOTES

1:27a. *This point only:* Gk. *monon* (no connective), neut., *monos, ē, on,* "only, alone," lit. "the only thing"; BDAG 2.a, in effect an adv. At 2:12 and 27, "not only . . . but . . ."; common with impvs.; cf. Gal 2:10; 6:12; 5:13; 3:2 *touto monon.* A Semitism (cf. K. Beyer 126–29) is unlikely. Holloway 2001:115, "even now." Cf. Steen on epistolary clichés. At 1:27, it emphasizes what follows: "above all" (Gnilka 97; Schenk 167); "one highly significant demand," Watson 1988b: 79; "this one essential thing," V. Wiles 45 n 29; "only one thing (matters)," Black 1995:33–34. Some link it with v 26, "Whatever happens" (Lft. 105; Gdsp., NIV, REB; LB adds "to me") or 27b, "whether I come or not, I have only to say . . ." (Vincent 32). Marks off a unit *(DA* 266).

Exercise your citizenship. Impv. (main vb. for 1:27–30; COMMENT A.1 on structure), 2nd pl. m., *politeuomai;* cf. *polis* = city (state), Rom 16:23; 2 Cor 11:32; 2 Cor 11:26; *politeuma,* Phil 3:20. Vbs. in *-euomai* = "play the part of, act as" (citizen) (GNTG 2:399); LSJ, *politeuō* B. Med.; hence BDAG 1, 2, 3, **be a citizen, administer a corporate body, conduct one's life.** Pl., all Philippian Christians, corporate (Beare 66); pres. tense, continual, habitual action.

(1) Often equated with *peripatein,* "walk" (Phil 3:17–18; 1 Thess 2:12, "walk worthily of God"), for moral conduct (BDAG 2.a). RSV "manner of life"; NIV "conduct yourselves" (but see Thielman 92, who favors [2] below); NRSV "live your life" (Acts 23:1). Beare 66–67; Houlden 66; I. H. Marshall 35; W. A. Meeks, "'To Walk Worthily of the Lord': . . ." in *Hermes and Athena,* ed. E. Stump/ T. P. Flint (Notre Dame, IN: Univ. of Notre Dame Press, 1993) 37–59. *politeuomai* at 1:27 because Paul writes from Rome (Lft. 105), to Philippi, a "little Rome" (Silva 90, 93; Geoffrion 44 n 36). Hence *TLNT* 3:132, = "conduct oneself . . . as a member of a social body." Cf. Pilhofer 1:136–37. The Christian *politeia* or Caesar's or both? Portefaix 136, 139–40, "the Roman state" but realization in the "heavenly Kingdom." Sense (1) is *ethical,* "behave."

(2) A political sense: R. R. Brewer 1954; ERV-mg, ". . . behave as citizens"; Gdsp., "show yourselves citizens" (applauded by R. Roberts); Michael 63, "live as citizen." Brewer: used "by Hellenistic writers" for "one's relationship to some form of government" (77; but only Xen. *Cyropoedia* [*sic*] 1.1.1 is cited). 2 Macc 6:1, cf. 11:25; 3 Macc 3:4; and 4 Macc 2:8, etc., = live according to God's laws or Jewish ancestral customs; cf. Philo, *Conf.* 17. Philippi was "Roman to the core" (hence 1:27 and 3:20); Jesus' lordship (2:9–11) contrasts with Emperor worship. "Continue to discharge your obligations as citizens and residents of Philippi fruitfully and as a Christian should [cf. Rom 13:7]; but do not yield to . . . Nero that which belongs to Christ alone. Remember that while you are members of a Roman colony you are also a colony of heaven." The "primary meaning" is "live as a (free)

citizen" (O'B 146); Geoffrion 43; Loh. 74 n 3, in papyri and inscriptions "almost the only sense." Cf. Gnilka 97–98; B. W. Winter 1994:86–93 (COMMENT A.4.a, below); Krentz 1993:115–17: Brewer is "persuasive"; Tellbe 2001:239–42. Edart 102–11 (cf. Vincent 32) prefers a Stoic *topos, militia spiritualis.*

(3)(a) E. C. Miller, Jr., 1982, moved in a (Hellenistic) Jewish direction. References in Macc. ([2] above) and Philo (+ *Let. Aris.* 31, Jos. *Vita* 12 = 1.2) suggest life lived by Jews "faithfully in the covenant relationship with God as manifested in obedience to Torah" (90; cf. Strathman, *TDNT* 6:526); for Christians, according to Christ, not Torah. Phil 1:27 "marks the point of departure" from Jewish to Christian use (91): ". . . you are the true Israel, people . . . who live a life worthy of the new law which is the Gospel" (94); "the church as the new Israel" (86, cf. 91, 93). Cf. Eph 2:12, "the *politeia* of Israel"; 2:19. (Paul never uses the term "new Israel"; see *EDNT* 2:204; P. Richardson.) Geoffrion 48: "Jewish/Christian identity as a special people of God." Silva 90: Miller's "thesis greatly overloads the verb." O'B 147 balks at "contrasts which Miller has read into the term." Geoffrion must admit Torah and (new) Israel are not in the 1:27 passage. In a city where there was no synagogue, in a letter with no explicit OT quotations! Critique in Engberg-Pedersen 1995a:263 n 12; Tellbe 2001:240–41; Edart 104–5.

(b) P. Perkins 1991:92–94: *politeuma* = Jewish communities in the diaspora (see NOTE on 3:20 *governing civic association,* esp. [a]–[c]). Christians at Philippi sought "synagogue status" as a Jewish *politeuma,* to avoid persecution; Paul rejects such views (1987:516–19; cf. 1991:92–94, 102). Stowers 1991:105–21 did not pick up on her theory. Contrast Blumenfeld 119 n 100.

(c) An *ecclesial* sense (Collange 72,73, following Bonnard 34). A. Schlatter, *Erläuterungen zum Neuen Testament* (Stuttgart: Calwer, 1928) 67, "administer the community"; V. Wiles 44, "govern yourselves." A self-governing community, with *episkopoi* and *diakonoi* (1:1)?

(4) *Both* Greco-Roman *politeia and* Jewish ideas (Hawth. 55–56, citing Lft., "St. Paul and Seneca," esp. 305–8 on the Stoic cosmopolis and the Christian's citizenship): citizens of an earthly state *and* the heavenly Jerusalem, the Christian commonwealth (3:20). Lincoln, a "dual allegiance" (1981:100–1); O'B 147; Geoffrion 45, cf. 38–42; *both* "identity as Roman citizens" or at least residing in "a Roman colony" *and* "Christian identity as citizens of a heavenly commonwealth"; "good citizens in the civil context," applied also to "identity as Christians" (Geoffrion 48). Or are they "un-Roman Christians" (Pilhofer 1:135; MacMullen 1966)? Not from a Roman tribe in Philippi (see on 3:5 *tribe of Benjamin*) or *incolae* of noncitizens in the *colōnia,* but citizens only of a *politeuma* in heaven (151–52).

Wordbooks vary. H. Strathman, *TDNT* 6:534, "no political implications." H. Bietenhard, *NIDNTT* 2:804, follows (1) above; so *TLNT* 3:132. U. Hutter, *EDNT* 3:130, Paul adapts "common usage in the gentile Christian community in Philippi," "*conduct your community life. . . .*" B. W. Winter 1994:93–102, "a constellation of 'political' terms"; Tellbe 2001:243, "distinct civic connotations"; Cassidy 2001:177, "civic living." See further COMMENT A.4.a.

in a manner worthy of the gospel of Christ. axiōs, "worthily," + gen. (ATR 505, 637), like *kata* + acc. (BDAG *kata* B.5.a.α, "the norm which governs something";

usually of Christ, 2 Cor 11:17; cf. Rom 12:6b; Schenk 167), "in a manner worthy of" or "suitable to." In the Hellenistic period perhaps not quite so grand a term as in classical Gk. but *axiōs* continued in inscriptions, "worthily of God and country" (Loh. 74 n 2; MM 51; Deissmann 1909 [(1) Bibl.] 248–49). Pilhofer 1:137 (cf. 2: #689), "*axiōs* of both the king and the citizens" (2:532–37; cf. IG 4.1,22). For Philippi, "in a manner worthy of our *colōnia.*" *of the gospel* is an unexpected turn of phrase, worthy not of forebears or city but of the *euangelion* (137). For fighting "worthily" in battle, see Geoffrion 44–45. Cf. 1 Thess 2:12 *(peripatein . . . axiōs . . .);* Rom 16:2; Col 1:10; Eph 4:1. Cf. Collange 73; Michael 63; Mengel 238, a "norm," political and military language that the "old soldiers in Philippi" would understand (Friedrich 147).

the gospel of Christ. See NOTES on 1:5 *gospel* (Hellenistic ruler cult, Geoffrion 49–52), 1:7, 12, and 16; a central theme in 1:12–26; Holloway 2001a:115 n 69; and 1:1 *Christ* (bis; 17x in ch. 1). BDAG *euangelion* 1.b.β.א; also at 27d (an *inclusio?*). Something one "defends by word, conduct, and action" (*TLNT* 2:90); "criterion of conduct" (*TDNT* 2:734). Krentz 1993:117–18 political/ military implications; *LAE* 370–72; with 2:9–11, resistance to Emperor cult of Nero (Brewer 80, 82) in Philippi (Collart [INTRO. I Bibl.] 412); "Christ instead of Nero" (Geoffrion 53).

of Christ. Obj. gen., "about Christ" (BDAG *euangelion* 1.b.β.א; *TDNT* 2:731 n 71), or subj., "from Christ" (*TDNT* 2:731 n 70). "Christ is . . . the object and the author of the proclamation" (ibid. 731). *TLNT* 2:89, a "'comprehensive' genitive" (n 35). Schmitz 1924 ([1] Bibl. **in Christ**) 45–88, a "neutral genitive." W. Kramer ([1] Bibl. **Christ**) #12 (pp. 50–55) saw in the "*pistis*-formula" (9x) mission language prior to Paul (except at 2 Cor 4:4); on the content of the gospel (pp. 19–44), belief about Christ's death and resurrection as saving acts, 1 Cor 15:3b–5, etc.

1:27b. *in order that, whether I come and see you or continue to be absent, I may hear the news about you. hina,* purpose. A textual problem mars the symmetry. Perfect balance would have two pairs of ptcs., *come and see, be absent* and *hear;* then a subjunct. vb. *(hear)* in the *hina* cl. Lft. 105 suggested *mathō* (aor., *manthanō*), "in order that . . . I may *learn*" the news about you. Others, "that I may *know*" (Gdsp., NEB, JB; NIV, NRSV "I will know"); or "*find* that" (NJB). The best MSS read "in order that . . . I may *hear,*" thus reducing the parallel to simply *be absent* (TRANSLATION). Glossed over in REB and CEV "whether I visit you or not."

hear. Pres. subjunct. (P⁴⁶ א B D etc.), *akouō* (aor. subjunct. *akousō* in A, etc., Koine, correctors in א and D; UBSGNT, NA²⁷ do not report it). Fee doubts the pres. is "meaningful" (158 n 12); not pressed in the TRANSLATION. BDAG 3.c, "hear, *learn someth[ing] about someone.*" With 1:30 implies ongoing exchange of information between Philippi and Paul (DA 308).

whether I come and see you or. . . . eite . . . eite, lit. "if . . . if" (BDAG *ei* 6.o, *whether . . . or*), see NOTE on 1:18b *either . . . or.* Conditional ptcs. (Rienecker 202), agreeing with the subject "I" in *akouō: elthōn* (BDAG *erchomai* I.1.a.ζ, 2d aor. act. masc. sg.), of travel, as at 2:24 (DA 360); *idōn,* 2nd aor. act. *eidon* (BDAG 1.a, "see" + acc. *you* pl.), "meet with," visit" (DA 309), "for . . . 'projected' events" (DA 386 n 120; cf. 389). 1:27–30 uses pres. tense in thematic material (*Exercise your citizenship; stand;* etc.), aor. "in background material." *see* = know by personal presence; *hear,* from other sources, a distinction but no antithesis, *TDNT* 5:341.

or continue to be absent. Ptc., *apeimi,* "be away, absent" (enclitic *eimi* = be). Paraphrased, "in my absence" (NIV); "am kept away" (Gdsp.); "stay at a distance" (JB). Pres. tense (contrast two previous aors., but "background material") since Paul may continue in an Ephesian prison or, released, go elsewhere than Philippi, or be absent due to death (1:20–23).

the news about you. ta peri hymōn = neut. pl. art. + prep. phrase (ATR 766) in subst. usage, "the things concerning you" (pl.). Compare *ta kat' eme,* NOTE on 1:12 *events affecting me.* BDAG *peri* (+ gen.) 1.i, your *circumstances, situation, condition* (2:19, 20 same phrase). NJB "all about you" overdoes it; NAB "your behavior" ethicizes. NEB omits.

1:27c. *that you stand steadfast in one and the same Spirit. hoti* (BDAG 1.b; DA 324, 329; recitative function) + *stēkete,* from the pf. *hestēka* of *histēmi* = stand (GNTG 2:220, 259; BDF #73). In the postclassical period people often avoided *-mi* verbs (TDNT 7:636). "*stēkō* is rare in the LXX" (redactoral?). MM, one citation, 3rd cent. A.D. (?). Hence BDAG 944, "found first in the NT" (cf. BDR #73); 2, **be firmly committed in conviction or belief,** *stand firm, be steadfast.* In Paul, 6x (Phil 4:1; 1 Thess 3:8; 1 Cor 16:13; Rom 14:4, Gal 5:1). *hoti* + indic. has imperatival force, specifying how "*politeuesthe* (an imperative) is meant" (Geoffrion 24, cf. 55). Brevity of speech (Loh. 74 n 5) or a break in construction (Schenk 165; instead of *hina* + subjunct., *hoti* + indic. under the influence of *akouō*). The two ptcs. in 27d and 28 also have imperatival force. Cf. "imperatival *hina*"; Moule *IB* 144–45; Gal 2:10, after *monon;* 145 n 3 suggests Phil 2:2; BDF #383 (3); possibly "Let me hear . . . that you stand firm. . . ." Loh. 75 n 2, "the determination of a soldier who does not budge one inch from his post"; similarly Gnilka 97; Edart 107; Krentz 1993:119–21. Geoffrion's evidence involves *histēmi,* not *stēkō.* Little can be established from *stēkete,* since we lack examples earlier than Paul for its usage. Schenk 167, no grounds for military implications; it expresses "stabilization after initial encounter with the gospel as an ongoing task" (Gnilka 99 n 20). Not "stand pat" but "stand firm" (167), as in [N]RSV, etc. Moral steadfastness (C. R. Erdman, *The Epistle of Paul to the Philippians* [Philadelphia: Westminster, 1932] 64) "assumes more than the word implies"; cf. Silva "spiritual tenacity" (91).

in one and the same Spirit. en + dat. of *pneuma* (see NOTE on 1:19 *the Spirit*) + neut. sg. dat., *heis, mia, hen,* BDAG 2.a, **one and the same.** Manner (DA 327), as at 1:8 *with the affection of Christ Jesus,* 1:20 *in a totally free and open way.* The cardinal numeral "one" (4x in Phil, 1:27, "with one soul"; 2:2 "think one thing"; and 3:13) suggests unity. Cf. Rom 3:30; 15:6, etc. Hence, "a united spirit" (Phillips), "one in spirit" (NEB), taking *pneuma* as "a part of the human personality" (BDAG 3.a), parallel to "with one soul" (27d); human *pneuma* and *psychē* may be synonyms (Schweizer, *TDNT* 6:435; Geoffrion 61), though Vincent 33–34 distinguishes (our "non-earthly" and creaturely sides). Here collective, almost "community spirit" or "team spirit" (Montague 1961:142). Or (2) the Holy Spirit; cf. 1:19; 2:1 "sharing in the Spirit" parallel to "encouragement in Christ." *en* for the agent through whom, or sphere in which, the Philippians will stand firm. (3) A disposition, communicated in Christ, Christians as "spiritual." United with the Lord, one becomes "one spirit with him" (1 Cor 6:17 NRSV), receiving the Spirit at baptism to "walk by the Spirit" (Gal 6:1; 5:16; Ellicott 47). Michael 65 combines all three: the Spirit works with the human spirit to produce the disposition that Paul here describes.

Most commentators favor the human spirit, "one common purpose" (O'B 150, others in n 40, Lft. 104, Loh. 75, Hawth. 56; *TDNT* 6:434–35 "anthropological pneuma"). But Holy Spirit has been favored by some (list in O'B n 39, including Gnilka 99, Martin 1976:83, Collange 74, U. B. Müller 75; Hooker *NIB*; *NIDNTT* 3:702, the "charismatic Spirit" as shared gift). Support for the Holy Spirit at 1:27 involves ecclesiologically the Spirit as the premise of the church community, "the key to unity in the church" (Fee 1994:746); J. Kremer, *EDNT* 3:120; Schenk 168, as at 1:19, "the risen, present Lord as the Christ of the messianic interim period." Fee 163–66: (1) "in one spirit" for a common mind or "esprit de corps" has no parallel in Paul. (2) With "stand firm" the *en* phrase is "inevitably locative" for the sphere of steadfastness (4:1; 1 Thess 3:8; 1 Cor 16:13; Meyer 42). (3) 2:1–4 picks up 1:27 in "*koinōnia* (participation) in the Spirit" (2:1) and "*soul* brothers and sisters" (*sympsychoi*, 2:2). (4) 1 Cor 12:13 uses *hen pneuma* for the common baptismal experience; cf. Eph 2:18; 4:4, communal unity. Fee 1994:744–46 adds (5), 27c and d are not "synonymous parallels" (the second does not "explain" the first) but separate expressions (no *en* in 27d); rhetorical effect but not parallel repetition. Thus capitalize "Spirit" as Paul's intention, even if readers heard simply community disposition or team spirit. *one and the same* as at 1 Cor 12:4, 8, 9, 11, and 13.

1:27d. *engage together in the struggle for the gospel faith with one soul. synathlountes*, ptc., taken as parallel with *stēkete*. Modified by *mia[i] psychē[i]* (after *en heni pneumati*, effective rhetoric, spirit/soul); in the Translation at the end (*for the gospel faith* goes closely with the vb.).

with one soul. Dat., manner (ATR 529), + fem. sg., *heis, mia, hen. psychē* (also at 2:30) = the *soul* as **seat and center of the inner life** in humans, "of feelings and emotions" (BDAG 2.c; *DA* 306). Paul brought a Semitic background from the Heb. *nepeš*, "living being" (Gen 2:7 = 1 Cor 15:45), never *psychē* in the Gk. philosophical sense of "immortal" or "preexistent" soul. The "specifically human state of being alive which inheres in man as a striving, willing, purposing self" (Bultmann 1951 [Intro. X Bibl.] 205), a self in a human body, subject to sin. Like *nepeš* (Gen 12:3, NRSV "my life"; Lev 17:10, NRSV "person"), *psychē* can simply mean "human being" (Rom 2:9; 1 Thess 2:8 "our own selves"). In the OT (H. W. Wolff 10–25), the person "in need" (1 Sam 1:15; Ps 107:5), longing (Ps 42:1–2), able to praise God. For Paul, see *TPTA* 76–78.

Jewett 1971a (history of research, 334–46) finds OT senses in Paul (448–49), but in Phil 1:27 (cf. 2:2 *sympsychoi*; 2:20 *isopsychos*; 2:19 *eupsycheō*) "the basic Judaic uniformity . . . is temporarily broken" (449). Here (348–52) "a socially collective sense," Gk. background, "ecclesiastical unity" (449). Familiar to, probably from, the local congregation. So Jewett.

Renderings vary: "with one mind" (KJV tradition; NABRNT); "one in mind" (NEB, REB); "a single aim" (NJB); "one purpose" (Gdsp.); "one desire" (GNB); "as one man" (NIV). Some see rhetorical variation on "in one spirit" 27c (E. Schweizer, *TDNT* 9:649; 4:435 and 445; A. Sand, *EDNT* 3:501; cf. G. Harder, *NIDNTT* 3:683–84). Eng. trs. often miss the collective sense and Gk. background (also in 2:2, 19, and 20). Aristot. (*Eth. Nic.* 9.8.2 [1168b]) spoke of proverbs, *mia psychē, koina ta philōn* ("all belongings of friends are in common"), *isotēs philotēs* ("friendship is equality"); Pythagoras, in a golden age all would be "of one body and one soul *(mias psychēs)*" (Iambl. *Vit. Pyth.* 30.167). Cf. 1 Chron 12:39 (NRSV v 38, "were of a single mind to make David king"; Gk. *psychē mia*). Acts 4:32, the Jerusalem church was "of one heart and soul *(kardia kai psychē)*," possibly Jewish and Gk. thought, "heart" and "soul" respectively, for the ideal community of Gk. philosophy. Jewett 350–52, *mia psychē* is "one of the earliest expressions for ecclesial unity," used by the Hellenistic church and Paul for "the church as one living organism"; instrumental dat., "with their one unified life."

More recent research relates such references to "friendship" Cf. Fitzgerald 1996:144–45, e.g., friends as alter ego, like Siamese twins (*Diog. Laert.* 5.20); Fitzgerald 1997:37–45 on Aristot. (F. M. Schroeder), and 225–62 on NT evidence (A. C. Mitchell), esp. 233–34 and 238–39. The Hellenistic roots would strike a chord with the Philippians, though Schenk 168 saw a Semitism, "striving in common," cf. H. W. Wolff 17. The literal TRANSLATION seeks to signal kinship to Gk. thought and singularity in Paul.

engage together in the struggle. Ptc., from *athlein* = "compete (in a contest)" + *syn* (in the TRANSLATION, *together*), also at Phil 4:3 (probably not an *inclusio*, Silva 17 n 17; 219–20). Parallel with *ptyromenoi* in 28; can be modal, "*by* striving . . . *by* not being frightened"; better, with *stēkete*, ultimately *politeuesthe*, almost impvs. (BDF #468 [1]; cf. Matt 28:19–20); cf. NEB, NAB[RNT]; Schenk 166, 171–72. Some see athletes in the arena (Lft. 105–6, comparing 3:14; Beare 67–68; Michael 66). Pfitzner treats 1:27–30 under "*Pale* [not "vivid"] Athletic Termini" (109–29, italics added), with Phil 4:3, Rom 15:30 etc.; "most English commentators" have carried "arena" imagery too far. Others seek a military sense (Herodot. 1.67, 7.212; cf. Plato *Tim.* 19C; Geoffrion 60–61, Krentz 1993:122–23, Edart 107–8; Tellbe 2001:246, "assist in battle," overextends the brief entry in *EDNT* 3:296). Evidence is limited. *synathlein* can mean "aid" or "assist" (Diod. Sic. 3.4.1; BDAG 964 starts with this reference). Three of the 4 NT passages with *athlein* terms connect with suffering (1:27–29; Heb 10:32; 2 Tim 2:3–5; *NIDNTT* 1:646). The "athletic arena" background has been overdone, the "military" sense is shaky. *synathlountes* lent itself to struggle for a cause, with coworkers in mission (4:3), in the face of sufferings. *syn* = "partners together" ([N]RSV "side by side"; Vincent 34; Michael 66), not just "together with Paul," or with *faith* (B. Weiss 123–24).

for the gospel faith. tē[i] pistei tou euangeliou. No exact NT parallel. On *pistis*, see NOTE on 1:25 *faith* (the Philippians' faith that gives rise to their *progress and joy*); on *euangelion*, NOTES on 1:5 *gospel* and 27a *the gospel of Christ*. BDAG *euangelion* 1.a.β, "faith in the gospel." BDAG *pistis* 2.c, trust, confidence, faith, believing in the gospel; Schenk 168, *nomen actionis,* tech. sense in mission; *DA* 307, "a religious world view." The art. may suggest "the faith" (obj. sense, *fides quae creditur*) or a possessive, "your faith" (possibly subj., believing on your part, *fides qua creditur*). Thus (obj. sense) "the Faith" personified, Lft. 105, Loh. 75–76 ("unlikely," Schenk 168 n 24; U. B Müller 74–75 n 19). Houlden 66: "a sense approaching 'the Christian religion,'" its distinguishing mark the gospel. Then *tou euangeliou* could be appositional, "the faith, i.e., the gospel." But if "faith" = believing (subjective view), then *tou euangeliou* is obj. gen.,"faith in the good news" (Gdsp.). Geoffrion 63–65 (cf. Krentz 1993:124; Edart 108) saw a "political/ military" sense, *pledge of good faith* (LSJ *pistis* II.1), by God for security, or by the Philippians, "loyalty which will result in their salvation" (64), or both. Possible link to friendship (Reumann, *ABD* 5:745). But Dobbeler ([4] Bibl.) 182–83, a power, if not a weapon (cf. Eph 6:16) for battle. Silva 95 notes (but did not adopt) "faithfulness."

The dat. *pistei* has been called (1) instrumental, "through your faith" (*TLNT* 1:336; BDF #195) or "associative," + vb. compounded with *syn-* (BDF #193; Lft., "in concert with the faith"). Or (2) interest (Vincent 34; cf. 31, "on behalf of the gospel"), dat. of advantage (Pfitzner 116; Loh. 75–76; Gnilka 99; Bockmuehl 99; D. R. Hall, "striving along with the faith of the gospel"; O'B 152; Fee 166 n 47), or *dativus commodi* (Schenk 168). Cf. BDF #188. Or (3) dat. of respect to indicate a circumstance (*DA* 345 ; BDF #187). (2) is preferable.

The gen. of "gospel" has been construed as (1) obj., faith in the gospel (BDAG, above; CEV "believe the good news"; Bultmann, *TDNT* 6:204 n 230; 208 n 258, reception of the message; Schenk 168). Or (2) subj., faith which the good news gives (Pfitzner 116, cf. Rom 10:17; Hawth; "the Faith taught by the Good News," TC; O'B 1986:226). (3) Apposition or epexegetical, the faith which is the gospel (Vincent; cf. Gal 3:23; Silva 95; Fee 167). (4) Collange 74 " 'the Gospel of faith'" (appositional use reversed?). (5) Origen, "the faith which is based on the gospel" (O'B 152); cf. Fee 167, "the faith that is contained in the gospel." "We cannot be sure which use of the genitive Paul has chosen" (Geoffrion 62–63), let alone quite how the Philippians understood it. The TRANSLATION, with NEB/REB, uses *the gospel faith,* for an unusual, ambiguous Pauline phrase.

1:28a. *and are not intimidated in any way by your adversaries.* Ptc. *ptyromenoi,* taken, like *synathlountes,* as a finite vb., with *stēkete.* Two prep. phrases describe the degree to which *(in any way)* and by whom they are not to be scared.

intimidated. ptyrō (only NT occurrence), ptc., + neg. *mē* (BDF #430). Not "Stop being afraid," as if the Philippians were already running scared (*DA* 357). *ptyrō,* not Attic Gk. but dialectic, means "frighten, scare, intimidate." Of a (timid) horse (Lft. 106; Hawth. 58); of "the crowd" re authority in the state (Plut., *Praec. ger. reip.* 800C = LCL *Moralia* 10:168–69; cf. Plut. *Vit.* 175; Diod. Sic. 2.19.2; 17.34.6, etc.). Marcus Aurelius 8.45, of his soul, groveling (*tapeinoumenē,* undergoing humiliation), frightened *(ptyromenē).* Gen 41:8 Aquila, Pharaoh's spirit (LXX *psychē*) "was frightened *(kateptyrē).*" Geoffrion 66–69 (cf. Krentz 1993:124– 25; Edart 109–10) suggests a political-military term; cf. esp. Plut. *Flam.* 2.2–5, 3.1. Holloway 2001a:117–18, a *topos* about panic at unforeseen misfortune, cf. 1 Thess

3:3–4 ("We told you beforehand that you were to suffer persecution"); but is Phil 1:28 unforeseen?

in any way. en (for the sphere involved) + dat. neut. sg., *mēdeis, -mia, -den,* "nothing," used as a subst. (BDAG 2.b.α; cf. 2.b.δ *"in no way"* or *"respect,"* 2 Cor 7:9; 6:3); + *mē*, a double neg., beloved in Gk. (BDF #431). It excludes every type of intimidation.

by your adversaries. Agent after the pass. voice, *hypo* + gen. pl. masc. pres. m. ptc., subst. use, *antikeimai,* "be opposed, be in opposition to" (6x in Pauline corpus: Gal 5:17; 1 Cor 16:9 "many adversaries [*antikeimenoi*]" at Ephesus; cf. 2 Thess 2:4; 1 Tim 1:10, 5:14). *TDNT* 3:655 (Büchsel); *TLNT* 1:129–30, *TDNT* 1:137 compare antagonists "in 4 Macc. and occasionally in the Test. of Job." Geoffrion 59 alludes to "the *topos* of *militia spiritualis*" (38–42; Edart 110; *vivere militare est,* "to live is to engage in battle," Sen. *Ep.* 96.5), but (p. 70) allows *antikeimenoi* is not found in "any Greek account of political or military conflict" (at best, Herodot. 9.39). Geoffrion (cf. Krentz 1993:125) goes to Exod 23:22 LXX as "almost certainly the referent for" 1:28: the Lord "will be an enemy to your enemies" (NRSV, Gk. *antikeisomai tois antikeimenois soi*); "those who oppose God's people are God's opponents and they will be destroyed." Cf. Isa 66:6; U. B. Müller 75 adds 2 Macc 10:26, God "an enemy to their enemies (*antikeisthai tois antikeimenois*) . . . , as the law [Exod 23:22] declares." For opponents of Jesus and of his followers (Luke 13:17, 21:15). "Whether the Philippians would have recognized the parallel terminology and concept" is "immaterial to its value in the military metaphor Paul is creating" on the basis of the OT (Geoffrion 70 n 116)(!).

1:28b. *This, indeed, is to them a pointer of destruction but of your salvation, and this, from God.* Rel. pron. (the TRANSLATION opts for a new sentence, *This . . .*), its antecedent unclear. Textual variants exist on *autois* (dat., *to them*) and *hymōn* (gen., *of you = your*); *de* lacks a corresponding *men*. The cl. is so abrupt that WH put vv 28b–29 in parentheses; then 28a leads smoothly into v 30, *you stand steadfast . . . , engage together in the struggle . . . , are not intimidated . . . ,* and face *the same contest* as Paul. But few have accepted their parentheses.

This (lit., *which*) *is to them . . . but* (of you) *your . . . hētis estin autois . . . hymōn de . . .* (NA²⁷; ℵ A B etc.), "corrected" by scribes to improve parallelism and fit classical idiom by (1) inserting *men* to balance *de* (TR; 499 witnesses in Aland 1991:584–85, plus 62 with variations); (2) gen. *hymōn* (ℵ A B C2 etc.) changed to *hymin* to parallel the dat *autois* (D¹ etc., TR; KVJ; C. H. Clark 42; many treat *hymōn* as if a dat., Beare 67, Schenk 170). The result is "to them, on the one hand . . . , to you on the other. . . ." Most MSS adding *men* shifted the word order (correctly) to *autois . . . estin* (cf. NA²⁷), but this is "scarcely original" (Fee 159 n 15; Lft.106). Hawth. 54, 59–60 uses these variants in his reconstruction, below.

hētis (fem., BDAG *hostis* 3), often used in place of *hos, hē, ho,* can "emphasize a characteristic quality by which a preceding statement is to be confirmed" (BDAG 2.b); "to be sure, indeed, certainly"; BDF #293 (4) mentions Phil 1:27; ATR 728, 412, an "explanatory relative"; cf. Lft. 106. Schenk 166, a "causal relative." Fem.

looks forward to *(hē) endeixis*, "pointer" (*ZBG* 216). But what is the antecedent of *hētis*? The Philippians' fearlessness (28a; Lft. 106; Silva 95)? their *faith* (27d; Hawth. 58–59; Martin 1976:84 "the general idea of the preceding clause" (ATR 729; Melick 90 n 114, the entire content from 27b [*stēkete*] on)?

to them. After *estin* (*DA* 382 n 115), *autois* (possession) goes with the noun *pointer*, not the vb. (ATR 537; cf. 1392), a demonstration to them *only* (H. Paulsen, *EDNT* 1:450; RSV; NEB.

pointer. someth[ing] that points to . . . someth[ing], *sign, omen* (BDAG *endeixis* 1), indication (ZG), not "proof" (BDAG 2; Rom 3:25,26). Hendricksen 90 n 70, "proof . . . with the added touch of prophesy," is too strong, as is "sign" if taken in the sense of *sēmeion* in John. Cf. Stalder 157–58.

destruction. apōleia, 5x in 2 Pet 2–3, 5x in the Pauline corpus, in Phil also at 3:19 (hardly evidence for a single letter, *DA* 361); Rom 9:22; 2 Thess 2:3; 1 Tim 6:9. BDAG 2, **the destruction that one experiences, annihilation . . . ruin,** in contrast to *salvation*; hence "eternal destruction" (Oepke, *TDNT* 1:397). KVJ "perdition"; "doom" (NEB); "be destroyed" (NIV). Lenski 760–61, loss of salvation but not annihilation. KJV does not indicate whose *apōleia*; most trs. have "theirs," but Collange and Hawth. adopt "yours" (see below). Cf. Bultmann, *TDNT* 3:21; Portefaix 149; Mattern 61–62. The gen. can be termed objective after *endeixis*.

but of your salvation. hymōn, "of you," emphatic, at the start of the phrase. *de* is adversative (*DA* 327). On *salvation* see NOTE on 1:19 *deliverance*. Here, salvation, with transcendent aspects (BDAG *sōtēria* 2, as at 2:12), fut. eschatological (Foerster, *TDNT* 9:992; Hawth. 39–40, 60). Geoffrion 58, "eschatological destiny" (with Loh. 77 and n 1), "soldiers/citizens . . . in battle against (or resisting) their adversaries"; Krentz 1993:125–26. Portefaix 149: to women in "Paul's audience . . . deliverance from a restricted earthly existence defined by the female role" in life at Philippi, but "complete realization of citizenship" (3:20–21) only "in the afterlife." Hence *Endvollendung* (Schenk 170), eschatological vindication but possible suffering now (*DA* 215).

Alternative construals: Collange 75, "What ('*hētis*', feminine by attraction to '*endeixis*') is for them ('*autois*') a sign of perdition is your ('*humōn*') salvation, . . . namely, that it is necessary to suffer" (v 29). Fails to deal with *de* in making *hymōn sōtērias* the main proposition (Morlet 86), or the gen. case of "salvation"; cf. Fee 169 nn 53 and 56; Oakes 2001:86, "untenable." Hawth. (1983 = *Phil.* 58–60): (1) the antecedent of *hētis* is the *faith* of the Philippians (27d). (2) Full parallelism:

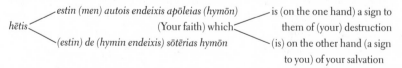

Scribes did add *men*; in line 2 *estin* and *endeixis* can be inferred from line 1. More controversial is taking *hymōn*, in Paul's Gk. directly after *apōleias*, with both nouns, i.e., "your destruction" and "your salvation." Hawth. adds it in parentheses at the end of line 1 and moves it (without parentheses) to the end of line 2. He adds *(hymin)* in line 2 to balance *autois* (so some MSS). Hawth. stresses that no MS ever changed *autois* to *autōn,* "*their* destruction." The contrast is not "*their* destruction" and "*your* salvation," but two perceptions about "the willingness of the Philippians to fight for the faith of the gospel": the adversaries see this as indication of the Philippians' destruction, the Philippians as a sign of their own salvation. (3) *apōleia* and *sōtēria* = not eternal destruction or salvation, but a "lesser sense of 'defeat' or 'victory,'" perhaps wordplay on "the immediate destruction of the body" (in persecution) and "the ultimate salvation of the soul." (4) Hawth. renders, "In no way let your adversaries strike terror in you. For although they see your loyalty to the truth as inevitably leading to your persecution and death *(apōleias),* you see it as leading through persecution to the salvation of your souls." Opponents are not consigned to destruction but understand that what the Christians see as part of "salvation" is a misperceived faithfulness that will result in loss of life for them. Fowl 2003 adopts a version where believers narrate "the stories of martyrs as stories of salvation rather than destruction."

Silva 95 rejected Hawth.'s construal ("the syntax is barely defensible"); cf. O'B 155 n 72; Krentz 1993:126 n 78; Fee 168–69 nn 53, 56; Melick 91. Not in Hawth. 1987. Questionable are (1) referring *hētis* to "faith," rather than to *endeixis* (Fee); (2) the overly precise parallelism, esp. reading back *hymōn* into the first line (Fee); (3) the "weak" and non-eschatological sense of *apōleia* and *sōtēria,* contrary to usual Pauline use (O'B, Fee); (4) contrasting not these terms but *autois* and *hymōn* (O'B); (5) the double use of *hymōn,* given the location of *de.*

1:28c. *and this, from God. kai,* "ascensive" force" (Vincent 35) + *touto* (cf. 1:22), most likely nom. (ATR 487, an adverbial acc.); cf. BDAG *houtos* 1.b.γ "and especially" (BDF #290.5), looking back to what precedes (1.b.α). Rom 13:11. Back to what? *sōtēria* (Calvin 48; Ewald 91 = Wohl. 100)? *pointer* in 28b (Lft. 106; NEB/REB)? The entire cl. beginning with *hētis* (B. Weiss, Vincent 35, Silva 95, O'B 157)? or all of v 28 (Buls)? Not what follows in v 29 (Chrysost.; Ewald 90 = Wohl. 100). Some vb. must be supplied like "comes from. . . ." CEV, "God will make all of this happen," fut. tense from 28b, "you will be saved." *apo* + gen. (BDAG 5.d), cause or originator of an action (1:2 *apo theou;* DA 317, 330). On *God,* see NOTE on 1:2. Lft. 106, "arena language," a "thumbs up" sign from God, not "from the fickle crowd. . . . The great *agōnothetēs* [president or judge of the games] Himself has given him a sure token of deliverance."

1:29a. *because to you it has been granted by God, for the sake of Christ,* [b] *not only to continue to believe on him* [c] *but also to keep suffering for his sake. hoti* is causal (DA 324; Schenk 166, 170, the second of three reasons for the Philippians' stance), not "that," "And this, from God, in view of the fact that . . ." [v. 28a] (Lenski 762).

to you. A few MSS (A 1241ˢ etc.) read "to us" *(hēmin),* Paul and colleagues. But vv 27–29 focus on the Philippians, only v 30 on Paul (cf. Fee 159 n 17).

it has been granted by God. charizomai, "give freely, graciously" (11x in acknowledged letters; also at Phil 2:9), see NOTE on 1:2 *grace,* cf. 1:7. But (Conzelmann, *TDNT* 9:396), "The verb . . . does not have the precise sense of the noun"; basically, "give"; any "Pauline element" is in the context. Aor. pass., "has been given . . . ," supply *hypo tou theou,* "by God," added in the TRANSLATION (*passivum divinum*, [4] Comment B n 9). *to you* can be taken as subject; BDAG *charizomai* 1 "you have (graciously) been granted the privilege of. . . ." Aor., possibly of "timeless events" (*DA* 386 n 120), but more likely (Schenk 170) *charisma(ta)* given at baptism; 1:7, you all share with Paul in his *gracious opportunity* for mission, through God's gifts.

for the sake of Christ. to hyper Christou, art. + prep. phrase, no infin.; then two infins. *to . . . pisteuein* (29b) and *to . . . paschein* (29c), "to believe" and "to suffer." Cf. 1:21, 22, 24 for art. infins. *hyper autou* (= Christ) is repeated with the last infin. *(for his sake)*. BDAG *hyper* A.2 + gen., "because of, for (the sake of)," cause or reason (*TDNT* 8:514), for whom or why believers suffer in Philippi.

Christou, see Note on 1:1 *Christ.* No art., as at 1:10, 18, etc. 2 Cor 12:10 *hyper Christou,* "for the sake of Christ" Paul puts up with insults, hardships, and persecutions. At 1:29 a few MSS (F G) omit *to;* Loh. saw *hyper Christou* a battle-cry or victory cry "For Christ!" (72, 78). Few agree. In the ellipse (sentence "suspended," to be "resumed in *to hyper autou paschein,*" Lft. 107), some add an infin., "to be for Christ" or "serving Christ" (Loh/Nida 43; GNB).

1:29b. *not only to continue to believe in him. not only . . . but also* introduce two art. infins. BDAG *monos, monē, monon* 2, neut. as an adv., *only*, c.α, + neg.; *alla* 1.a; *kai* adv. "also." *mē* might be expected with an infin.; the NT regularly employs *ou* with *monon* (except at 2:12 and Gal 4:18); cf. 1 Thess 1:5; 2:8 *ou monon . . . alla kai,* as here; BDF #448 (1). *to,* repeated, makes clear the initial art. in 27a is being explained; "anaphoric," i.e., parallelism "highlighted by the identity of the initial words in each member" (BDF ##399 [1], 489, 491). *pisteuein* here only in Phil.; see Note on 1:25 *faith.* BDAG 2.a.β, "believe in" or "on" + *eis* + acc., 30x in John, 3x in Paul; cf. Heb. *he'ĕmîn lĕ,* as at Gal 2:16 and Rom 10:14 (*GNTG* 2:463; cf. also Rom 10:10). *eis* indicates "the content of a process" (*DA* 329) and personal relationship (*TDNT* 6:212); pres. infin., repeated action, *continue to believe* (BDF #318). ATR 1424 charts use of the art. infin., Phil 10x: as subject, pres. tense, 1:21, 22, 24, 29 (bis), aor. 1:21 ("to die"); as object, pres., 2:6, 13 (bis), 4:10. Cf. the "*pistis* formula," Note on 1:27a *of Christ, believe in* Christ (W. Kramer p. 46, n 94; Schenk 170). Stalder 81–82, God "works the act of believing."

1:29c. *but also to keep suffering for his sake. alla kai,* see 29b. *hyper autou,* 29a *for the sake of Christ;* closely connected with "suffer" (*hyper autou* comes between art. and *paschein*).

suffering. paschein, only occurrence in Phil, but cf. *pathēmata,* "sufferings of Christ," 3:10. Vb. usually only once in a Pauline letter (7x; 1 Cor 12:26; 2 Cor 1:6; Gal 3:4; 1 Thess 2:14 + 2:2 *propaschō;* 2 Thess 1:5; 2 Tim 1:12). On Gk. background, cf. Comment A.5 and B.2, below. OT views of suffering in W. Michaelis, *TDNT* 5:907–11; Bultmann 1956:26–34; O. Piper, *IDB* R-Z 450–53; Gerstenberger/Schrage; D. J. Simundson, *ABD* 6:219–24, chronological OT development. In the LXX, vb. 21x; *pathēma* not at all; *pathos* once or twice, but 63x in 4 Macc, the *agōn*-motif is prominent. Philo and Jos. reflect "Gk.-Hell[enistic] Philosophy" (*TDNT* 5:909, cf. 906–11, 927, 930). *paschō* is rare in the Pseudepigrapha (Michaelis 5:910). B. Gärtner adds Quman evidence (*NIDNTT* 3:720–21). BDAG *paschō* 3.a.β, "suffer, endure (for)." Pres. infin., repeated action. About possible suffering, Paul must have warned in preaching; at baptism when gifts were granted (1:29a; 1:5, 8; Walter 1979:424). Paul suffered at Philippi (1 Thess 2:2; cf. Acts 16:11–30); 2:14 sufferings in Thessalonica; 2 Cor 7:5, in Macedonia, "disputes" (*machai*, cf. Phil 1:28a "adversaries") and "fears" (*phoboi*, cf. 1:28a "frightened") (Schenk 169). Commentators emphasize "the high privilege of suffering for Christ" (Lft. 106; W. Michaelis, *TDNT* 5:920, cf. 931). Geoffrion 71 notes the citizen who suffers (*kammein* = toil hard) for the *polis* (Pericles' Funeral Oration, Thuc. 2.41.5). Krentz 1993:126, "suffering harm from a military opponent" (Onos. 36.2, cf. 24). On suffering in Phil, see COMMENT A.5, below.

1:30. *since you are having the same contest such as you saw in my life and of which you are now hearing in my life. echontes*, ptc., circumstantial, another reason for the Philippians to stand steadfast: their experience parallels Paul's. *echō* (1:7, 23) BDAG 1.a, "have, own, possess" (*DA* 306); "engaged in" (RSV, NEB); "face." Agrees with "you" in 27c (*stēkete*), taken as a finite vb. (*you are having*). Alternative (BDF #468 [2]; Moule *IB* 31; Moulton's "indicative participle"): "an irregular nominative," with *hymin echaristhē* in 29a (Lft. 107, *stēkete* "is so far distant"). Could be concessive: ". . . although." Paul could have employed a gen. abs. (*hymōn echontōn*) or put the ptc. in dat. pl. (*echousin*, with *hymin*; GNTS 1:225) or added *hoi este* or *kai echein* (B. Weiss 128 n 1). Loh. 79 n 2 unknotted the construction with *hoitines echete*, "(you) who have . . ." (so also U. B. Müller 78). The TRANSLATION takes the text as anacolouthon, the circumst. ptc. as causal, *since*.

1:30a. *the same contest.* Acc. (dir. obj.), *ho agōn, agōnos*, + masc. acc. sg., *autos, ē, o* in first attrib. (or intermediate) position (BDF #270; GNTG 3:185), "same" (BDAG 3.a). *agōn* was used (BDAG) of (1) athletic contests, Heb 12:1; (2) "struggle," "fight," for the gospel (Phil 1:30; 1 Thess 2:2, etc.; Col 2:1, Paul's struggle). Vb. *agōnizomai* only at 1 Cor 9:25 in the acknowledged letters. Tellbe 2001:246–47 connects athletic terms in Phil (*brabeion*, Phil 3:14) with the Imperial games popular at Philippi. Pfitzner traces "the agon motif" in Greek athletics (pp. 16–22) and philosophy (the "struggle of the sage" toward virtue, a battle with oneself to become better, 23–35; Geoffrion 79). Imagery of the boxer, wrestler, runner, and pancration contestant (a sort of boxing-wrestling free-for-all) appears in the moral discourses of Epict., Seneca, Plut., and Marcus Aurelius (29–31). In Philo and Jos., occasionally the LXX (48–57; e.g., 2 Macc 10:28; 14:18; 15:9), esp., under Stoic influence, in 4 Macc (9:23; 11:20, etc.). *T. Job* (1st cent. B.C.-1st A.D., OTP 1:829–86) has "a personal Agon" between Job and Satan (Pfitzner p. 65). Stauffer (*TDNT* 1:136) sees such "martyr theology of later Judaism" as the background for Paul's imagery; cf. Loh. 79 n 1. Sisson stresses "combat sports," esp. the *pankration* (256–60). Esler 2005:381, use for a group is rare in athletics.

1 Cor 9:24–27 is a "self-apology" by Paul in his "*agōn* for the gospel"; cf. Gal 2:2, Phil 2:16. Phil 1:27–30 is among Paul's examples of "contending for the faith" that use "*pale* athletic termini" (Pfitzner 127–29, "*conscious reference to a specific athletic image . . . unlikely*"); Paul's apostolic mission was "an Agon for the Gospel or for the faith," including labor (*kopos*), opposition, and suffering, with "extension . . . to include . . . coworkers, and . . . members of an entire congregation

under special duress (Phil I:27ff.).” But cf. also 3:12–14 below. Pfitzner 158, no “military image” in 1:27–30. But Geoffrion 80–81 (Pfitzner’s data), Krentz 1993:126 (Dion. Hal., *Ant. Rom.* 3.16.2; Onos. 24, vb.; Dib. 1937:71), and Portefaix 140–41 play up “military connotations” of *agōn*; it is “suited the inhabitants of the military colony”; “Paul’s language . . . called to mind” the battle line with its Macedonian Phalanx; all Christians participate (1:30), women (Portefaix) in terms of strife, pangs of childbirth, “fighting females,” like ecstatic women in Eur. *Bacch.* (761ff.), stories of Alexander’s mother (cf. Plut. *Vit. Alex.* 2) participating in battle (Ath. 13.560F); Isis mistress of war; rock carvings at Philippi, Diana with bow and lance (cf. Abrahamsen 1988); the Amazons.

Pfitzner 187–95, Paul is within the traditions of “popular moral philosophy,” but altered. The Stoic “Agon of virtue” and the Hellenistic Jewish “Agon of piety” or “Agon of suffering” (4 Macc) becomes an “Agon of faith” for the gospel through an apostolic life of service. Similarities with the Cynic or Stoic missionary (call, commission, suffering), but also differences (sufferings as “the divine seal of his apostolicity,” not “the toils of the moralist”; the *doulos* is responsible to the Judge on the last day). V. Wiles: an ecclesial realm: a firm, united stance “is dependent on their common identity and purpose that derives from their constitution—the gospel of Christ” (88). *Word studies:* E. Stauffer, *TDNT* 1:134–40; A. Ringwald, *NIDNTT* 1:644–48; G. Dautzenberg, *EDNT* 1:25–27; Danker 1982:365–66, benefactors and “the theme of peristasis [hardships].” On *agōn* in martyrdom and asceticism in the early church, cf. *TDNT* 1:139–40; Pfitzner 196–204.

1:30b. *such as you saw in my life and of which you are now hearing in my life.* Rel. pron., masc. acc. sg., *hoios, a, on,* “of what sort, (such) as”; cf. 1 Thess 1:5. Here, without a correlative *toiautos* (MM 444; BDF 304). BDAG p. 701, *hoion* shows the significance of the *agōn* “in its severity.”

you saw. 2nd aor., *eidon,* BDAG 1.a, **see, perceive;** ptc. in 1:27b. Instead of *eidete* (ℵ A B* etc.), some MSS and correctors read *idete* (Bᶜ Dᶜ etc. TR), “phonetic leveling of *ei* and *i*” in the Hellenistic period, perhaps going back to Paul himself (BDF #23), unless an aor. impv. (“such a struggle see in me . . .”). *kai* after *hoion* (D* etc.) = “which you both saw in me and now hear. . . .”

in my life. en emoi, 2x, with *saw* and *are now hearing.* P⁴⁶ MS 81 omit the second *en emoi* (cf. Fee 159 n 18). BDAG *en* 8, **marker denoting the object in which someth[ing] happens or in which someth[ing] shows itself,** often with vbs.; cf. 1 Cor 9:15; Gal 2:24, “in my case” (Fitzgerald 1988:123 n 18). Oepke, *TDNT* 2:538–39, sees a “spatial sense” mingled with the instrumental; *DA* 319, spatial, locative. KJV “in me” became in RSV “the same conflict which you saw . . . to be mine”; NEB, “you saw me in it once, and . . . I am in it still”; NRSV, *en emoi* as subj., “the same struggle that you saw I had and . . . that I still have.” Both occurrences should be rendered the same way; the TRANSLATION settles for *in my life.* Paul’s missionary career is meant, events of Acts 16:22–39; 1 Thess 2:2 (Loh. 79 n 3; Pilhofer 1:189–99) and now at Ephesus (Phil 4:10–20; 1:12–26). Schenk 171, the second *en emoi* is “stronger than the *hyper emou*” that might have been expected, i.e., “hear about” (BDAG *hyper* A.3). It is part of the “Paul as model” theme.

and of which you are now hearing. hoion carries over as dir. obj. *now,* see BDAG *nyn* 1.a.β.ג, "here and now"; cf. 1:20. The TRANSLATION takes *akouete* (see on 27b) as linear action.

COMMENT

Letter B (and Phil as a whole) moves in 1:27–30 to paraenesis.[1] Markers set off the unit (Holmstrand 100–2; 1:27, like 1:18d, is a new beginning), esp. the impv. *Exercise your citizenship* (27a). Paul moves from the "I"-form in 1:12–26 (*narratio*) to address Philippian Christians in the 2nd pl. 1:30 connects his *agōn* with the Philippians' struggle. Many read 1:27–30 as prelude to 2:1–4 (5–11), on unity through humility (O'B 1986: 224–25) for a disunited community (so Peterlin). V. Wiles 11–18 protested against traditional self-abnegation as a means to unity. Holloway 2001a:116 n 71 links it with 1:12ff., not what follows. The vv are a key within Letter B and all of Phil: Bockmuehl 96, "the centrepiece"; Sonntag 172–75, "the theme of the letter," with 3:20, citizenship; right relations with God (confession) and fellow human beings (concord, kindness).

A. FORMS, SOURCES, AND TRADITIONS

1. Structure and Literary Features. 1:27–30 form a discrete unit, a single Gk. sentence, with one main vb., *politeuesthe* in 27a (Black 34). Schenk 166, one suprenym and three hyponyms:

politeuesthe, Exercise your citizenship (27a)

stēkete (27c)—	*synathlountes* (27d)	— *mē ptyromenoi* (28a),
stand steadfast	engage together . . .	not intimidated . . .

in a manner worthy of the gospel of Christ (27a) parallels *in one and the same Spirit* (27c); in 27 *gospel of Christ = Spirit = gospel* (27d) (= 29 *Christ*). There are three grounds for encouragement (similarly Holloway 2001a:116): (1) new realities from God—the opponents fight for a lost cause, you are on the way to the world's goal or end *(Weltvollendung)*; (2) God's gift is yours, to receive, and suffer for, Christ's gospel (Holloway 2001a:116, suffering "ordained by God"); (3) you face the same battle as I do. The opening *monon* indicates "what is of central importance" (Black; NOTE on 1:27 *This point only*; D. F. Watson 1988b:65). There is "tail-head" linkage, 27b *I see* or *hear*, 30b *you saw* and *are . . . hearing* (Black 31, comparing *prokopē* at 1:12, 25).

Loh. 72 reconstructed 5 three-liners; it gets little support here, more at 2:6–11.[2]

---

[1] A Gk. term used in modern biblical studies for ethical advice (vb. *paraineō* at Acts 27:9, 22). Cf. Grabner-Haider 4–53; Soulen 1976:123–24; Malherbe 1986:24–29 and passim; J. I. H. McDonald 1980:69–100 (paraenesis and catechesis); *DPL* 922–23; *WDNTECLR* 334; A.1, below.

[2] Followed for 1:27–30 only by Michaelis 29; cf. Schenk 166; contrast Gnilka 96–97 and Heriban ([7] Bibl.) 166.

Others claim an *inclusio*.[3] Better: there is repetition of vocabulary, rather than framing of a "unit."

Proposals for larger *chiastic structures* cancel each other.[4] At best, for Letter B (Aspen 238–56), an "epicenter" in 2:6–11, surrounded by a ring of impvs. (C[1], C[2]); B[1] "Paul's trials," B[2] "the Epitome of a Philippian," Epaphroditus, a "Paulist-Christian," and his trials:

Prescript and Prooimion, 1:1–11

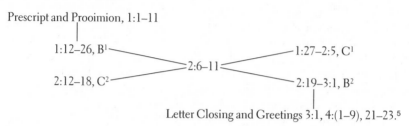

1:12–26, B[1]   1:27–2:5, C[1]

2:6–11

2:12–18, C[2]   2:19–3:1, B[2]

Letter Closing and Greetings 3:1, 4:(1–9), 21–23.[5]

There may be some smaller chiastic patterns.[6] *Antithesis* in 29, "to suffer on behalf of Christ/to believe on him," diatribe style (Schoon-Janßen 143, like vv 23/24); an *enthymeme*[7]; *zeugma* (cf. BDF #479,2) 1:27b: one vb., *hear*, functions in two sentences: "*continue to be absent* (and) *hear*" and "*in order that . . . I may hear. . . .*" Presence/absence is a well-known theme in Gk. letters.

OT material is lacking in 1:27–30; Exod 23:22 LXX might lie behind 28a *by your adversaries. Hellenistic vocabulary* colors 1:27–30 (see A.4, below). For *early Christian tradition*, see the NOTES on 1:27a *of Christ* and 27b *not only to continue*

---

[3] 1:27 and 4:1–3 (Dahl 1995 [(15) Bibl.]; Oakes 2001:124, at most, an echo). 1:27 *politeusthe* and (3:20, Letter C) *politeuma*, plus 4:3 (*the book of life* as a city register), thematic unity around the *polis* concept (E. C. Miller 92–93; 1:27c *stēkete* and 4:1 *stēkete*, 1:27c *synathlountes* and 4:3 *synēthlēsan* (all Letter B). Garland 1985 and G. H. Guthrie 44–45 parallel 1:27 with 3:20–4:3. 1:29b *paschein* and 3:10 *pathēmata*.

[4] Cf. INTRO. VI. B.4 n 3. Wick 45 takes 1:27–30 with 3:17–21 (*politeu-* words, *sōtēr[ia]*, and *apōleia* in each passage); Luter/Lee, 1:27–2:4 with 4:1–5 (*synathlein, stēkete* in each passage); Aspen 239, 1:27–2:5 with 2:12–18 (Paul's presence and absence, athletic language like *agōn* and "run"); C. W. Davis, 1:27–2:18 with 3:1–4:9. Critique in *DA* 292–93.

[5] Cf. Tellbe 2001:232:

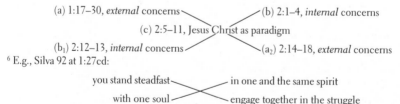

(a) 1:17–30, *external* concerns   (b) 2:1–4, *internal* concerns

(c) 2:5–11, Jesus Christ as paradigm

(b₁) 2:12–13, *internal* concerns   (a₂) 2:14–18, *external* concerns

[6] E.g., Silva 92 at 1:27cd:

you stand steadfast   in one and the same spirit

with one soul   engage together in the struggle

Then "soul" = human spirit. *for the gospel faith* is ignored. Or does this last phrase go with both expressions?

[7] On the term, cf. (2) A.4. D. F. Watson 1988b:66. Geoffrion 24–25, 36, conclusion in 1:27, supporting reason introduced by *hoti* (Kennedy 1984:17) in 29–30, "because God has granted" (but note other causal cls. in 28–30); Debanné ([2] COMMENT A.4 n 14) 496, 1:27c (the Philippians stand firm) is true as he perceives their life, present or past (27b); implied Major Premise ("being a good citizen in Christ's realm involves both faith and suffering"), Minor Premise (God has "graciously granted you the privilege . . . ," 1:29), Conclusion ("live as good citizens," 27a). Edart 91, 110. The examples indicate imprecision and subjective reconstruction in recovering enthymemes.

to believe on him ("*pistis* formula"). Some of the paraenesis may stem from early Christian *catechetical tradition* (1:27a *politeuesthe*, a citizen's relations to the [Roman] state). On 27c *stand steadfast*, cf. the "pattern of early Christian teachings" some see, with the admonition "Stand fast."[8] Selwyn's case "has never been conclusively . . . refuted" or "proved" (M. B. Thompson, *DPL* 922). Cf. Doty 1973:59–60. In connection with *charisma(ta)* at baptism, Paul likely taught suffering might come to believers (Schenk 170–71), along with faith, in a "catalogue of hardships" (see [16] COMMENT A.4.e); cf. 1 Cor 12: 4–11, 26; 1 Cor 4:9–13; 2 Cor 4:8–9; 6:4–10; 11:23–28; 12:10; and 1 Pet 4:10–11 (AB 37B:764–66). J. H. Elliott, for 1 Pet, notes admonitions to house churches, household codes encouraging group solidarity, with linkage to "friendship" themes (1981:145–48; AB 37B:32–34, 35–37; 28–30, 32–34 on baptismal catechesis). Berger 1984a:130–35, "post-conversion discourse" on opposition, military language, "walk" (*peripatein*), eschatology, and "togetherness."

Epistolary analysis recognizes a move from theological to ethical concerns, from "theoretical" to "practical" (J. L. White 1972:71, 112; Doty 37–39, 43), e.g., at Rom 12:1. The shift suggests Letter B was moving to its conclusion.[9] "*Indicative*" *and* "*imperative*" have been used to describe this shift from "What God has done for us" to "What we are to do in response."[10] Cf. Geoffrion 229–34, a "theology of perseverance." Landmesser, "christological performatives."[11]

2. Rhetorical Influences. 1:27–30 is most likely *propositio*,[12] a "thesis for the congregation" (Black 1995:48; Witherington 1994; Tellbe 2001:232; Edart 88–92,

---

[8] P. Carrington's common pattern ran (1) "put off" vices, "put on" virtues; (2) "submit yourselves" to God and to superiors in society (household codes) or to elders in the church community; (3) "watch and pray"; and (4) "resist" the devil and "stand (firm)" (Col. 4:12; Eph 6:11–14; 1 Pet 5:8–12; Jas 4:7) (pp. 40–43, 52–54, 58, 85–87). Phil 1:27 was not mentioned. E. G. Selwyn, *The First Epistle of St. Peter* (London: Macmillan, 1952) 363–466, criticized Carrington's reconstructed catechism, but derived "Watch" and "Stand" from a "persecution-torah," compiled by Silvanus, based partly on words of Jesus. Phil 1:28, "not being frightened," appears in Selwyn's charts as a parallel to 1 Pet 3:14–15, cf. Isa 8:12–13; 1 Thess 3:4–5; and Matt 10:28 (p. 443); 1:27–28 *stēkete* and *endeixis* = *pointer*, to 1 Thess 1:4–5; 1 Pet 4:17 (445); and 1:29 *suffer for* Christ's *sake*, to 2 Thess 1:5; 1 Pet 3:4 and 4:13.

[9] Holloway 2001a:162–63 terms 1:27–30 a "correction" of the consolatory arguments in 1:12–26: the Philippians "should correct their present behavior" (frightened, joyless) *before* they see Paul again.

[10] Cf. Furnish 1968:213, 224–27; Ridderbos 1975 ([1] Bibl. **Paul**):253–58; E. Lohse 1991: 105–13; W. Schrage 1988:167–72. Bultmann (INTRO. X Bibl.) §§ 59–60, pp. 203–31, "the *imperative*, 'walk according to the Spirit,' not only does not contradict the *indicative* of justification (the believer is rightwised [see on Phil 1:11 *righteousness* and 3:9] but results from it" (1951:332).

[11] Landmesser: in Phil 1:27–2:18, after the unity of faith-and-life as gift of God, impvs. follow as "christological performatives," not appelatives (appeals); for those "in Christ" (as "new creation") the language does what it says, as part of "present eschatology," a gift since baptism (575); there is optimism about the power of the word. Cf. H. Umbach, *In Christus getauft—von der Sünde befreit: Die Gemeinde als sündenfreier Raum bei Paulus*, FRLANT 191 (Göttingen: Vandenhoeck & Ruprecht, 1999), esp. 182–96 on Phil.

[12] See INTRO. VI.B n 3; chart in DA 165; critique in Schoon-Janßen 139–43 and Wick 161–73. D. F. Watson 1988b, 1:27–30 is *narratio* ("concerns" and *propositio*); similarly Geoffrion 21–22, 35; cf. O'B 37, contrast Silva 16 and I. H. Marshall xxix. Bloomquist 1993:126–28, 157–60, 1:27–2:18 is *exhortatio*. L. Alexander calls 1:27–2:18 a request for reassurance about the recipients, as in letters of friendship (so DA 168–69). DA 388–90 abandons rhetorical terms; Phil 1:27–30, 2:1–18 are "Re-

vv 27–28; 29–30 = *ratio*), plus "reasons" or "proofs" in support.[13] 1:27a states the purpose of the argument (Geoffrion 23, *politeuesthe*, "political character," 35–82); 28 is deliberative rhetoric, "what is advantageous and harmful, expedient and inexpedient" (p. 30); 29–30 present reasons to stand firm (35, 70–82).

3. The Opponents in 1:28. The *adversaries* (see NOTE on *hoi antikeimenoi*), who are intimidating Philippian Christians but whose *destruction*, from God, is signaled by the Philippians' stance, have sometimes been lumped together with "the dogs, the evil workers" in 3:2–21, whose end is *destruction* (3:19) (Bloomquist 198–201); at times with the "rival preachers" of 1:14–18; + 3:2–21 in a "single-front hypothesis." Cf. Hawth. xliv–xlvii; Collange 75; G. P. Wiles 1974:210; Mearns; Blumenfeld 296–99. Passages in other epistles have sometimes been combined for a global depiction of Paul's opponents. Theories have gone through cycles, Jews, Judaizers, Gnostics, or combinations thereof. See (12) COMMENT A.2.d; (13) COMMENT A.1.b; and ch. 14, COMMENT A.4. The rival preachers of 1:14–18 ([3] COMMENT B.3), Christians in Ephesus who genuinely preach Christ, are not to be identified with those in 1:28 (Peterlin 54; Fowl 1990:78, among others), who are in Philippi. The opponents in 1:28 differ from the group(s) in ch. 3. The former are described in a "vague manner," the latter (in ch. 3) are more "clearly defined"; Paul is "cautious" about problems in 1:27–2:18, "passionate" in ch. 3 (*DA* 135). The adversaries in 1:27–30 are already intimidating Christians in Philippi, producing fear and suffering; the warnings in ch. 3 refer to coming dangers. 1:27–30 and ch. 3 are not to be connected (O'B 153; Fee 7–10).

Those who oppose the Pauline community in 1:28 have been taken as (a) *Jews* (patristic references; Houlden 65; Fendt 1931:71; Fowl 78–79). But Philippi lacked Jews (O'B 153; U. B. Müller 76). Hawth. xlvi–xlvii, 58, Jews from Thessalonica. Oakes 2001:88–89 says "quite implausible." (b) *Judaizers*, as in Gal, in light of Phil 3. (c) *False (Christian) teachers*, as in some theories on Phil 3, but at an earlier stage in ch. 1; Collange 75 (cf. 12–14). Contrast Oakes 2001: 85–87. (d) *Persecutors*, Loh. 4, 76–77, 79, without being specific; G. Barth 37–38; I. H. Marshall 38; cf. Bloomquist 157–60, 103. (e) *Gentiles:* Gnilka 99–100, fellow citizens, but not an official state persecution; Ewald 89 = Wohl. 98; Michael 51; Martin 1976:83; de Vos 1999: 261–65, "ordinary residents of Philippi," adhering to Imperial cult; U. B. Müller 75–76, noting pagan hostility toward converts to Judaism (Tac. *Ann.* 15.44) as analogy. (f) *Non-Christian opponents, Jews and Gentiles:* Vincent 34. (g) *Christians from Ephesus* who left the synagogue under the impact of Paul's preaching but later returned and now appear in Philippi (Suhl 184–85).

Most likely (h) *Roman officials and the populace.* Cf. Paul's run-in with the state in Acts 16:20–39. Johnstone 125–26, "endless annoyances — harassing law-

---

quests/Petitions" after "disclosure" by Paul in 1:12–26. In 1:27–30 Holloway 2001a:115–19 sees "five *topoi* from ancient consolation." Bittasi 48–53, esortazione; 1:9–11 is *propositio.*

[13] Cf. D. F. Watson 1988b:69; Geoffrion 179–82, *ratio* and *narratio*, "to encourage the Philippians" (180).

suits on false accusations, impoverishment of trades-people" on religious grounds and positive dislike, but no edict or formal persecution. Houlden 65, "long drawn-out antagonism" rather than "formal persecution by the Roman authorities." Peterlin 54, "pressure exercised by the secular environment, probably connected in some way with the (Roman) civil authorities, although outright persecution on religious grounds is unlikely." R. P. Martin 1960a:87 and O'B 153, "mob violence." "The authorities" (O'B 153, Bruce 57). The Roman nature of Philippi strengthens the case for Roman officialdom as the adversaries. Cf. Portefaix 138–41, 149–53, God's colony versus the Julian Augustan colony; Bormann 1995:206–24, Christians as "emancipated clients" in conflict with the Roman world; Pilhofer 1:135–39, "UnRoman Christians"; Reumann 1987:527, "the pagan opposition that has jailed Paul and in Philippi threatens the congregation"; Peterlin 54. Fendt 81, "malice" or "spite" is the right term at this stage. Tellbe 2001:232–34 stresses "the civic community and local magistrates";[14] Cassidy 2001:170, 192, Roman authorities. More specifically, de Vos 1999:264–65, "Christian withdrawal from the traditional Greco-Roman cults, especially from the Imperial cult" is the cause of oppressive measures. Oakes, some disturbance caused the *duoviri* to act; perhaps an oath of allegiance was the issue, as at Thessalonica.[15]

The opponents of 1:28, we conclude, involve (h) Roman authorities and some of the populace in Philippi (e, above).

4. The Political, Military, Ecclesial Tone to 1:27–30.

a. *Political Life and Theory.* Gk. political terms appear, beginning with *politeuesthe* in 1:27a,[16] though "political" is variously assessed (V. Wiles 1993; Mihoc 97 n 16). To strike a chord with Philippians in their "little Rome"? Encourage good citizenship by Christians in the Roman *colonia*? Direct attention to their true "commonwealth" in heaven (3:20 *politeia*)? Note also *axiōs* (NOTE on 1:27a

---

[14] Tellbe 2001 theorizes that Paul and his churches operated between synagogue (Jews) and Roman state (civic authorities) in Thessalonica, Philippi, and Rome, admittedly with different dynamics (charts, 280–83). To make the theory work in Philippi, he must import Judaizers (in ch. 3) and assume Christians were seeking Jewish identity to escape suffering for not conforming with Imperial cult. This involves (de Vos 269 n 127) "the non-existent idea of *religio licita*," that Judaism was a legalized religion that had special dispensations from the Roman state on such matters. Tellbe perceives the problem with Judaism as a "legal religion" in the Empire (1994:107 n 46); it is muted in Tellbe 2001. Cf. (14) COMMENT A.1

[15] de Vos 156–57. An oath (preserved from Paphlagonia in northern Asia Minor) to "support Caesar Augustus" and his successors, "in word, deed, and thought," reporting anything "said, planned, or done" against Caesar has sometimes been related to the "decrees of Caesar" (Acts 17:7), contrary to which Paul and Silas are charged with acting; cf. E. A. Judge, "The Decrees of Caesar at Thessalonica," *RTR* 30 (1971) 1–7; Donfried 1985 (INTRO. I Bibl.) = R. A. Horsley 1997:215–23. Bormann 1995:48–50, an oath administered in Philippi at the accession of each Emperor, therefore A.D. 17, 37, 41, 54, and 68–69.

[16] See NOTE on 1:27a *Exercise your citizenship*. Some who take it as "walk" allow coloring from the Roman world. Brewer provides only some of the evidence available from the Greco-Roman world for a "political" sense. Miller's "Israel" reference and notions of Christians seeking a legal status akin to a Jewish *politeuma* are doubtful. Cf. Geoffrion, Krentz 1993, Edart; Tellbe 2001:246–50; D. J. Williams 1999:150; Blumenfeld 11, 138, 182, 293–301, 315 *euangelion* = "a constitution," 298.

in a manner worthy of . . . ; inscriptions, worthy of *polis*, king, or the gods). Philippians might have expected, "citizenship worthy of our *colonia*"; Paul substitutes *the gospel of Christ* (*euangelion* had political connotations in the Emperor cult). 27d, *pistis*: for Philippian ears a sense of "pledge"; see NOTE on *gospel faith*. 28a "not *intimidated*," Plut. *Mor.* 800C re state authority. Perhaps 28 *adversaries*, but examples are lacking. *from God* in 28c may be "arena language" (the Emperor gave the life-or-death verdict for gladiators, Lft. 106). What God graciously grants Philippian believers—faith and suffering (v 29)—contrasts with those in Philippi who do not believe and inflict suffering on those in Christ, i.e., Roman authorities. 1:30 *the same contest*, for Paul and the Philippians the common denominator of the *agōn* was Roman adversaries. Hence B. W. Winter 1994:81–104 treats 1:27–30 under "Civic Responsibility." Amid Roman institutions (Oakes 2001:74–75), social, economic, legal, religious, touching daily life at many points, how shall Philippian Christians live "in the public place (*politeia*)" and its "fairly antagonistic situation" (Winter 84)? "External enemies" (1:27–30) and "internal difficulties" (2:1–4 and 4:2–3) relate, for discord in clubs and associations could spill over into public assemblies (*ekklēsiai*) and life (*politeia*) (85).[17] What strife, envy, and factions produce can be seen at Phil 1:15, 17 (93–97). Paul fears house-church differences (2:3–4; 4:2–3) might "go public" and lead to court cases (1 Cor 6:2, in light of 1 Cor 1:10 and 3:3). Differences from "private matters" can "enter into public life and upset the whole city" (*Mor.* 825A). Thus 1:27 "relates . . . to unity in a community as it strives to give credibility in the public place to the implications of the faith created by the gospel" (103). Paul is concerned about the *politeia* of the house churches and the involvement of Christians in the public assembly (*ekklēsia*). House churches inevitably used the "public space" of a city until able, or forced, to develop their own *politeia* (Engberg-Pedersen 1995a:79–80, 263, 273).

    b. *Military Tone.* Terms appropriate for Roman army veterans in Philippi (Edart 111) can be seen in 1:27–30.[18] 1:27a, perform "worthily" (see NOTE on *in a manner worthy of . . .*) in battle (Herodot. 6. 112; Xen. *Cyr.* 6.4.20); 27c *stand steadfast* (Loh. 75 n 2)[19]; "faith" as "pledge" of loyalty, among soldiers (Geoffrion 64; Dobbeler [(4) Bibl. **faith**] 182–83); *ptyrō*, see on *intimidated* (28a). 28a *adversaries*? Geoffrion turns to Exod 23:22 LXX to account for Paul's usage. *engage together in*

---

[17] Winter notes Plutarch's "Precepts of Politics" (*Praec. ger. reip.*, *Mor.* 798A-825F = LCL *Plutarch's Moralia* 10:155–299)—written for a young man who asked how one deals with "matters of state" (*politikai*) and "public conflicts" (*agōn* in the pl.)—and some of Dio Chrysost.'s thirteen discourses on "concord" (*homonoia*) in public life (pp. 86–93). Households are to show like-mindedness (*homophrosynē*) in the face of strife (*stasis*, 38.15).

[18] Geoffrion; Krentz 1993, 2003:355–56, 363, 1:27–4:1 = "military harangue"; D. J. Williams 1999:265–66 (gladiators) and ch. 10; de Vos 1999:277–79. Pfitzner 158–64, athletic images and military metaphors often intertwine. Some separate "political" and "military" senses; Caird 115. Marchal 29–34; reconsidered from a feminist standpoint, 50–64; the not always happy aspects of military language connect with friendship imagery, 64–68.

[19] That *stēkō* has no demonstrable usage prior to Paul (Schenk 167) undercuts this claim. Geoffrion misses *stēkete* at Exod 14:13 MS A, "Holy War" terminology, but likely Christian redaction for *stēte* in the LXX (*TDNT* 7:636).

the struggle (27d) fits arena athletes more than military usage (Geoffrion 60–61). *contest* (30a) is found more in athletics and moral philosophy than in politics (Pfitzner; see NOTE on *agōn*).

   c. *Ecclesiological Side.* This appears in emphases on Christian oneness, all together. Black 1995:43, "ecclesial unity." See Schlatter, V. Wiles in NOTE on 1:27a *Exercise your citizenship* point (c). Haupt 45–46, "citizenship" in "service" to the "entirety of the total church"; Vincent 32, "the universal Christian commonwealth" (with Lft. 305–8). But Gnilka 98–99, Philippian Christians and their pagan surroundings (plus relationships *within* the Philippian community). E. C. Miller 86, 93–94 rightly to saw ecclesiology in *politeuesthe*. Horsley 1997:205–14, Paul builds "an alternative society" in his *ekklēsiai*, opposing the Roman Imperial order.

   To act "worthily" (1:27a) turns up in Paul re God (1 Thess 2:12) and "the saints" (Rom 16:2). *stand steadfast* (27c) may be catechetical paraenesis (A.1, above). *in one and the same Spirit* (received at baptism by all believers) has to do with remaining together in the church community.[20] 28b, *salvation* relates to God's "celestial colony" at Philippi (the church; Portefaix 149). 29a *it has been granted by God* (see NOTE), grace-gift(s) at baptism, among them belief and suffering. 29b *to continue to believe*, cf. the "*pistis* formula" (NOTE on 1:27 *of Christ*). 29c "to suffer for Christ's sake," likely part of Paul's paraenesis to converts (references in NOTE). V 30 *agōn*, struggle for "(the) faith" (Pfitzner 118, 193–95). Corporate identity and purpose are communal, i.e., ecclesial (V. Wiles 88) in a contest against Roman opponents.

   d. *"Dual Allegiance," State and Gospel.* See Hawth., Lincoln, O'B, Geoffrion, Mihoc 91, Hansen 192–98, and others; NOTE on 1:27a *Exercise your citizenship*. Religious conduct *and* civic conduct of life, outside and within the church, both areas in the sight of God (Aland 1968, 1979). *politeuesthe* may come from the Philippians themselves (*EDNT* 1:130), living in a Roman *colonia*.[21] Corporate life "in the public place *(politeia)*" (B. W. Winter 1994:84) *and* possible discord in their own *politeia*, "their particular associations" (85).

   Paul is concerned about (1) the internal *politeia* of the Christian community, "all the saints" at Philippi, "together with overseers and ministers" ("all," 1:1, 4, 7 bis, 25). Much in 1:27–30 has ecclesiological applicability (4.c, above). Cf. 2:1ff., 4:2–3, working out what their *sōtēria* means (2:12). He was also concerned with (2) relations in the "public space" of the Roman *colonia* and Roman adversaries. Social "givens" included courts, civic officials, economic livelihood, social relations, trade guilds, neighbors of various religions, and a formal state cult (not

---

[20] If "spirit" of the Philippians, a communal understanding. If the Spirit, God's Spirit is the basis for the church in Paul (Fee, W. Kramer, Schenk, cited in the NOTE). Jewett 1971a:449 takes *mia[i] psychē[i]* in 27d in a "socially collective . . . ecclesiastical unity" sense.

[21] "As *milites Caesaris* you [the legionnaires at Philippi] are citizens far from your imperial city of Rome. As *milites Christi* you are citizens of the distant capital and native city where our Lord has his residence [3:20, *politeuma* = fatherland]" (Stauffer 1955 [INTRO. X Bibl.] 296–97 n 518). The "capital or native city . . . keeps the citizens on its registers (Tert. . . .)"; cf. "names in 'the book of life,'" 4:3 (so Caird 150; Pilhofer 1:131–32; see NOTE on 4:3).

yet as in the last years of Nero or Domitian's time, but emphasized more than in any city where Paul previously ministered). Paul knew persecution (2 Cor 11:24–26; 1 Thess 2:14–16). From his Jewish background and concern for stability even under a foreign overlord (Jer 29:1–9, pray for the welfare of Babylon!), Paul used paraenesis as in Rom 13:1–7 (be subject to Imperial authority, instituted by God).[22] In Rom 13:8–14, as in Phil 1:27, Paul gives citizenship a new context: it is measured by "the gospel." Cf. AB 33:661–76. A specific danger was factious Christians calling in pagan judges, to support one group against other believers (1 Cor 6:1–11, B. W. Winter 1994:105–21; Clarke 1993). Paul endorses Christians as citizens, *in a manner worthy of* their new allegiance, *the gospel.* For what this means, see 2:4 (on "the interests of others") and 2:12–15.

5. Suffering. At least some in Philippi were *suffering for the sake of Christ* (1:29; Fee 29–32; *DPL* 921; Güttgemanns 12, suffering reveals the essence of Paul's theology). No evidence any Philippian was in prison or faced death as Paul did (Plummer 36; Houlden 65–66; Michaelis 30; Gnilka 101–2, against Loh. 79, cf. 12, that the *episkopoi* and *diakonoi* of 1:1 were already jailed). The common denominator is "suffering *for Christ*," not the *same kind* of suffering. The suffering is now,[23] not in Philippi six years previously, but suffering shared by other congregations too (Bloomquist 158–59, 1 Thess 1:6; 2:14; 2 Thess 1:5).

Loh. 78–79 tied 1:29–30 into his *martyrdom theory* (Loh. p. 4; also on 3:15; 1:7, 26, 27–28). See (13) COMMENT A.2. Not persuasive (Oakes 2001:79 n 7; Mengel 244–45, 249–50, citing Bultmann's review of Loh. in *DLZ* 51 [1930] col. 777; Bloomquist 50–52; Tellbe 1993:150–53).

For Bloomquist, Christ is not "the exemplary model held up *before* the Christian . . . to imitate" (Ignatius of Antioch, many recent interpreters); "Paul looked *back* over his life, the life of the co-workers and the lives of the Philippians and found mirrored in these lives the experiences of Christ" (194).[24] The method results in "radical Paulocentricity" (Oakes 2001:122; "Christ is personified in" Paul, Bloomquist 135). Rightly criticized (Bockmuehl 23–24, 38–39; DA 158–59, 289 n 494; Fee 16 nn 42, 43; 73 n 8; 106 nn 1,3), not least with regard to 1:27–30. "Paul's suffering . . . mirrored in the Philippians" is overplayed in comparison with "reassurance to the Philippian believers" (Bloomquist 158, 150; Oakes 183).

For forms of suffering besides prison and death, Oakes 2001:96–99 notes torture (Matt 24:9), beatings (1 Cor 4:11; 2 Cor 11:23–25), and exile (Rev 1:9; cf. Suet. *Claudius* 25.4; prominent in letters of consolation, Holloway 2001a:75–

---

[22] Perhaps against Zealot tendencies or Jewish messianic agitators in Rome, M. Borg, "A New Context for Romans XIII," *NTS* 19 (1972–73) 205–18; contrast N. Elliott 1994:219–21 = R. A. Horsley 1997:189; Rom 13:1–7 is advice not called for in Philippi.

[23] With Oakes 2001:176, against Collange 72, 75–76, cf. 12–14 (discussion whether [true] Christians *can* suffer, not a response to *actual* suffering). Silva 92, "Philippian believers did suffer persecution from Gentiles" (9).

[24] See below on 2:6–11, 19–30, and 3:17. But vocabulary in 1:27–30 (*paschein, agōn*) is missing in 2:6–11 re Christ, not the way 1 Pet uses "suffer" for Christ (2:21,23; 3:18; 4:1) and Christians (2:19,20; 3:14,17; 4:1,15,19; 5:10).

77).[25] Also mob violence (Acts 16:19,22, Philippi; 14:19; 17:5–9); plundering of possessions (Heb 10:34). 2 Cor 8:2, "affliction" *(thlipsis)* and poverty *(ptōcheia)*. Oakes 2001:99, cf. 96, sees "a strong economic component" in Philippian suffering. In his reconstruction of society in Philippi (14–54),[26] groups suffered in different ways. Craft workers (with their slaves, 35% of the Christian community) lost business, suffered beatings, were taken before magistrates for abandoning local shrines, engaging in secret associations and in evangelism.[27] Least vulnerable, colonist farming families (19% of the church)—a beating, a night in jail, loss of honor and land; thus debt, dependence on élite landowners. For poor families (25%) work was "affected by any notoriety." Few, if any, of the decurial class were in the church (93), but possibly some citizens.[28] He agrees (93–94) with Portefaix, a Christian woman married to a pagan faced daily tensions (religion was pervasive, no "private realm"); broken marriage meant loss of status, economic suffering. Slaves could purchase manumission, but loss of earnings hurt that hope. It cost to be Christian.

Meggitt 1998 sees a "bleak material existence" (153); only "mutualism," helping each other, provided a "survival strategy" for the dirt-poor (157–63).[29] de Vos (265, with Oakes): those better off may not have been aiding believers of lower social status (see on 2:2–4, below); disunity came over "differing opinions about how to deal with the conflict" with the civic community (266). "Christ and the Emperor" (Oakes 129–74) was an "unstated element" in 1:27–2:4 (205, 207). Suffering could include "withdrawal of facilities by fellow crafts-people . . . violence; summary justice from magistrates; cancellation of tenancy; foreclosure of debt; breaking of patron-client relationships; withdrawal of financial assistance; divorce; repudiation by family; withdrawal of opportunities to earn *pecunium*; being sold" (Oakes 96).

How to relate *paschein* to *adversaries* (who cause the suffering), to "disunity" (overstressed by Peterlin) and "joy" (which Tellbe 230–31 thinks the Philippians have lost, 2:14, but note 4:1, cf. 1:25)? We see the Philippian house churches as a community of joy and faith, facing suffering; not a community overwhelmed by suffering, needing joy and faith. Their encomium (2:6–11) and actions supporting Paul (money and assistance) were ebullient, not dejected. Paul faces a current situation there, of which he knows something and responds accordingly (Oakes 2001: 125).

---

[25] Exile is not in the picture, according to Phil. Paul intends to return to Philippi (1:25; 2:24), as does Epaphroditus, who had access to the apostle, etc., because (Cassidy 2001:166–67 thinks) Epaphroditus was a Roman citizen.

[26] Oakes 55–76 minimizes Romans (40%) and military veterans (contrast Bormann 1995, Tellbe 2001:247–48, yet more Romans than in any church Paul founded), but includes agricultural workers outside town. Several house churches (169–70); see (1) COMMENT B.5.a.

[27] Oakes illustrates with a fictional couple, Simias and Ianthe (89–91), as he had (1998) with a goldsmith and a woman who sells pottery (see [2] COMMENT B.4 n 19).

[28] 2001:65, 147, 177–78; de Vos 287 is more optimistic; Tellbe 2001:223, "primarily . . . citizens," stressing the civic terminology noted in A.4.a, above.

[29] Meggitt 97–128 challenges "the 'New Consensus'" (Theissen 1982, Meeks 1983) that there were *some* people of status and wealth in the church (1 Cor 1:26). Cf. section 6, COMMENT n 19.

B. MEANING AND INTERPRETATION

Letter B turns to paraenesis (ethical admonition, A.2, above; first time in the four-ch. letter). The impvs. (Thielman 91 n 1 lists 19 in all of Phil), beginning with *Exercise your citizenship* (27a), mark a shift from *narratio* (what's happening with Paul, 1:12–26) to the Philippians and the stance Paul hopes for in the future. Rhetorically, 1:27–30 begins an *exhortatio* (through 2:18) with a *propositio* for Letter B: it calls Philippian believers to express in *politeia* (public space) and relationships with one another *(ekklēsia)* what being "in Christ" means. Amid the "you"-pl. language, the "I"-form continues, in 27b (Paul's travel plans) and 30 (*the same contest* as he, with government authorities).

Source material: *the gospel of Christ* preached in Philippi; the *pistis*-formula about faith in Christ (27d, 29b); gospel implications, including paraenesis about baptismal gifts (*charismata*, 29a), standing steadfast (27c), and suffering (29c). *politeuesthe* (27a) might have been applied by Philippian Christians for "living as citizens" in Roman Philippi and life "in Christ." Paul refers to past experiences in Philippi and now in Ephesus (30b). *Heuresis* (material at hand) includes what Paul knows about conditions in Philippi, through Epaphroditus, any letter he may have brought, and news via travelers from Philippi.

Paul's rhetoric (*elocutio* and arrangement) exhibits a literary flair and devices. Proposed chiastic or three-line structures do not convince many (A.1, above). Breaks in style— *hear* in 27b (textual problem too); 28b, the *hētis* cl.; 30a, the ptc.—suggest "syntactical carelessness" (Loh. 72). Concern carries over from 1:20–24, as Paul speaks about his beloved Philippians.[30]

1:27–30 is often overlooked as "introductory summary" or transition, read in light of 2:1ff. (on disunity, the need for humility). Walter 1978, NTD 1998, 1:12–30 presents the theme of Letter B, to *suffer* for Christ's sake, set forth in 1:27–30 with paraenetic undergirding. V. Wiles and Geoffrion make a case for treating vv 27–30 in their own right. The main impv, *Exercise your citizenship*, has "political" connotations, even if many outlines speak primarily in terms of church unity.[31] "Christian Citizenship" (Silva 90, for 1:27–2:4) is on the right track. Both civic and ecclesial aspects appear.

The passage will be treated below as part of Letter B in terms of (1) what Paul looks for in the Philippian house churches externally and internally (27–28a); (2) why they can stand steadfast with Paul in the struggle for the faith (28b–30). Then 3) 1:27–30 in the four-ch. letter.

1. Be Citizens in Philippi and in Christ, Steadfast, Together, Unintimidated by Adversaries (1: 27–28a). Paul moves from his situation (1:12–26, its uncertainties

---

[30] Reed analyzes participants (Paul as "actor," "sensor" 27b, *see, hear,* "carrier" 27b, *be absent*; the Philippians; God), DA 425–26 (charts; terminology, pp. 419–20, ch. 2, 339–41; 381–82). Space prevents noting more of this.

[31] Beare 28; Collange viii; Martin 1976:57. de Vos 275–86, "Paul's response to the relationship" of Christian and civic communities: "Be Good Soldiers for Christ, Accept Suffering, Reject Status and Change Political Loyalties."

still reflected 27b) to the situation in Philippi. He had news through Epaphroditus (deathly ill in Ephesus, 2:27) and a letter with the gift from Philippi (4:10). That gift was acknowledged in Letter A (now at 4:10–20). Perhaps travelers brought additional information. Paul knew Christians could disagree over faith or tactics (the "rival preachers" in Ephesus, 1:14–18) and come afoul of state authorities, as his own case dragged along (1:20–23). Even citizenship did not guarantee immunity from charges, let alone harassment in daily life. By a common struggle or *contest*, Paul has in mind experiences in Philippi that began during the founding mission when he and his missionary team "suffered" *(propathontes)* and were "shamefully treated" *(hybristhentes)* as they declared "the gospel of God in spite of great opposition" (1 Thess 2:2 NRSV, Gk. *en pollō[i] agōni*; Acts 16:19–30). All this was "known history" to the Philippians and Paul.

Paul begins directly. Not "I want you to know . . ." (1:12) or "exhort you to walk worthy of . . ." (Eph 4:1, which Bjerkelund 175 compares), but an impv. + adverbial marker, *This point only*, an essential that matters above all else, a proposal *(propositio)*—"motto," Loh. calls it (74)—standing over all of 1:27–2:18.[32] Abrupt as the opening seems, Paul has assumed in vv 25–26 that the Philippians will progress in Christ Jesus; he and they will find *grounds for boasting* at the last Day (Ewald 85 = Wohl. 94; Loh. 73).

Exercise your citizenship is the one-word Gk. impv. that spreads its aura over three vb. forms that follow in vv 27cd, 28a. *politeuesthe* is addressed to all the Philippian believers, some likely citizens of Philippi and Rome, all baptized members of Christ's community.[33] The vb. had political senses that continued as the *polis* or city-state declined; larger entities, Macedonia, the Roman Empire, or the whole cosmos, came to be regarded as one's *polis*. Not simply an "ethical" term for "walk" or moral conduct, substituted for *peripatein* out of deference for Philippian sensibilities.[34] The Gk. political sense of *politeuomai* (inscriptions, the papyri, Loh. 74 n 3), should not be blunted.

Exercising citizenship suggests first continued involvement in the public life and space of the *colonia*, as each person had participated previously (jailer, pensioned military veteran, civil servant, in the forum, in business) and to whatever degree it continued possible. Compare Erastus as *oikonomos*, probably *aedile*, in Corinth.[35] This aspect has long been overlooked in exegesis (Winter, in A.4.a). Paul, for all his troubles with authorities (2 Cor 11:23–25, 26 "dangers in the

---

[32] Some think the exhortations in 1:27–30 comprise "the same things" that Paul does not weary writing about and that are a "safeguard" for the Philippians (3:1, near the end of Letter B; so Furnish 1963–64:86–87, admonitions to be reiterated orally; *DA* 244; Loh. 73).

[33] Whether Paul has in mind "our *politeuma* in the heavens" (3:20) cannot be established, even if 1:27 and 3:20 are part of one letter—unless 3:20–21 is a hymnic fragment known to Paul and the Philippians (which we shall doubt)—quite apart from what 3:20 means.

[34] At 3:17, in the section where *politeuma* occurs, Paul uses *peripatein*, "observe those who 'walk' thus."

[35] Rom 16:23; AB 33:750; B. W. Winter 1994:179–97, "a Christian of substantial financial means, active in two spheres," civic and missionary, esp. if Acts 19:22 refers to him; otherwise, Meggitt 1998:135–41.

polis," 32–33) spoke positively of government (Nero's!) when violent revolution was the religious alternative (Rom 13:1–7); order and peace were desiderata for the communities of Christ (1 Thess 4:11–12; 1 Cor 7:17–24; Gal 6:10). He drew lines for Christians on litigation before pagan judges about internal factions (1 Cor 6:1–6; B. W. Winter 1994:105–21).

Exercising *politeia* involved, secondly, organization and governance of the cells of believers in Philippi (cf. V. Wiles). Common activities included spreading the faith and providing finance and personnel for Paul's mission work. Coordination of house churches and a "delivery system" were needed. The *overseers* and *ministers* (1:1) likely had a hand in these undertakings. How did a Pauline community, where God is active, work out (2:12–13) internal *politeia* for their "association," after its apostle and his mission team moved on? We do not know in detail, but functions listed at Rom 12:5–8 and 1 Cor 12:27–30a under the *charismata* from God hint at some lines of development. Leaders, benefactors, and hospitality were part of acting "in a manner worthy of God's holy ones" (Rom 16:2; cf. Schenk 167).

Such is Paul's central impv., that and "nothing more, but it encompasses everything" (Michaelis 29, repeated by Merk 175 and U. B. Müller 74). "Dual allegiance" (above, COMMENT A.4.d) implied continuity and break with past life as citizens, sojourners, aliens, or noncitizens in a "little Rome." Working it out called for *discernment* in each household and civic/social/economic venue, determining "what is best" (1:10) in specific situations. Paul asked God (1:3–11) for Philippian *perception . . . in every situation*, with growing *love* amid concrete realities of everyday life (Merk 175; G. P. Wiles 1974:199–200, 208–15; Montague 119–20).

For this undertaking Paul provides criterion and motivation: all is to be done *in a manner worthy of the gospel of Christ*, a norm that is part of the eschatological horizon for Christian life (Grabner-Haider 136). The Philippians knew the *gospel*, from and about *Christ*,[36] whom they learned to believe in and confess at the outset and each one at baptism. The gospel had taken hold, the object and source of sharing since that first day until now (1:5). Paul has referred to the *euangelion* five times thus far in Letter B (1:5, 7, 12, 16; "proclaim Christ" and "the word of God" 1:15–18). The Philippians' particular way of asserting that gospel will be seen in 2:6–11. Missionary language builds and sustains community.

Paul introduces this gospel source and standard with a phrase of political, military overtones: *in a manner worthy of* citizens, suitable to . . . —one might expect "citizens of this *colonia Julia Augusta Philippensis*."[37] Instead Paul makes *the gospel* the norm for church community and Christian public life. For some, *euangelion* conjured up "good tidings" in decrees about an Emperor's birthday (Priene

---

[36] Landmesser 1997:545 would, from 2 Cor 5:17, see Paul's criterion for ethics more specifically in God's saving action in Christ and the new creation. See n 11, above.

[37] R. S. Ascough, "Civic Pride at Philippi. The Text-Critical Problem of Acts 16.12," *NTS* 44 (1998) 93–103, sees pride reflected in the best-attested reading at Acts 16:12, "first city of the district of Macedonia," even if this was not factually correct and the v.l. has been set aside by text critics.

inscription, ca. 9 B.C.),[38] but 1:27–30 do not indicate open conflict as yet between Christ and Caesar in Philippi. *axiōs* at 1 Thess 2:12 and Rom 16:2 = conduct suitable to people called to God's kingdom and glory (*TDNT* 1:380). The gospel is a source for knowledge and discernment, not a "codex of norms or rules" (Hainz 1972:215).

Do this *whether* Paul remains away *or* can soon come to Philippi (27b). The alternatives *(whether . . . or)* replay the possibilities of *life* or *death* in vv 20–25, plus his resolve to stay on in service of the gospel (25) and expectation to come to Philippi (26). Continued absence, if the trial drags on, results turn out badly, or Paul must first go elsewhere (more pressing problems in other churches like Corinth). He hopes to *come and see* the Philippian community. The weight is on hearing *news* about them. 27b *news about you* matches the news about Paul recounted in vv 12–26. Paul was optimistic about *progress for the gospel* in Ephesus (1:12), despite *envy and strife* and *self-interest* among Christians there (1:15, 17). Does he have similar confidence (1:25) about the Philippian house churches?

Paul hopes to hear (and see, God willing) their exercise of *politeia* in three ways: first they *stand steadfast* (27c), secondly *engage together in the struggle* (27d), and thirdly *not* be *intimidated in any way*. This "catalogue of tasks" (Schenk 167) pairs positive and negative examples (*DA* 262) to exemplify what *politeuesthe* means (see chart in A.1 from Schenk 166).

To *stand steadfast* or firm in one spirit (27c) was hardly a fixed military formula. *stēkete* was too new a word to have an established history of meanings, the way *histēmi* did, its source term. Part of Christian catechesis? Paul likely spoke of hardships and even suffering for Christians (A.1), as with proselytes to Judaism (see on 28a, below), part of "stabilization" (Schenk 167) after conversion. The admonition is regularly expressed in impvs. (4:1; 1 Cor 16:13) in the face of threats (Gal 5:1), often with a phrase following that begins with "in" (NOTE on 27c; cf. Rom 14:4. Paul found joy when the Thessalonians stood firm (1 Thess 3:8; cf. 2 Thess 2:15). A stable community is needed for mission work. The "steadfastness" Reed finds (*DA* 141, cf. Geoffrion) "in terms of a political/military concept of citizens/soldiers working together" depends on *politeuesthe* and other terms (A.4, above), not overtones in *stēkete*. Montague's "Progress as Strengthening and Stabilizing" deals not with 1:27–30, but God as Rock, Christ as foundation, and human fidelity. Paul's first expectation becomes more clear through *in one and the same Spirit.* Not (see NOTE) "the human spirit" or *esprit de corps* but God's Spirit, as at 1:19 and 2:1 (Fee 163–66, contrary to most Eng. trs.). Thus an ecclesial, baptismal setting: the Spirit and the gifts *(charismata)* there given equip believers for service in church fellowship and daily life. The Spirit is resource and power for steadfastness.

---

[38] Horsley 1997:3–4, 9–24 lays out "the gospel of imperial salvation" from Augustan Rome and in Imperial cult, with excerpts from (INTRO I Bibl.) S. R. F. Price 1984a:249–74 on "Rituals and Power" and Zanker 1988, "The Power of Images"; note the effects on "civic space" (61–64); for the forum at Philippi, Bakirtzis/Koester 15–17; Bormann 1995:37–54; Pilhofer 1:76–77. For Paul's gospel as "anti-Imperial," see Horsley 1997:140–47, where Phil 3:20–21 is the starting point.

Paul secondly expects the Philippians will *engage together in the struggle for the gospel faith with one soul* (27d), "standing firm" in positive terms, re mission task. Athletic metaphor *(syn-athlein)* is overstressed by some, "suffering" (29c) by others. At 4:3 (Letter B) for women in Philippi who "struggled" beside the apostle "in the work of the gospel," mission proclamation and witness (Schenk 168). Further insight into *the struggle* comes in v 30 *(agōn)*, public witness, suffering, and pagan opposition. *syn-* (= *together*) means solidarity with Paul (an emphasis in Letter A; see COMMENT B.2.a on 4:10–20, and esp. 4:10 *your concern for me*) and, for the Philippians, with one another (brought out by *with one soul*). Others connect *syn* with *tē[i] pistei* (Lft.'s splendidly vague "in concert with the faith"). All three ideas are possible, but emphasis on united together for a struggle is primary.

with one soul is anthropological (not parallel to "with one Spirit"), probably of Gk., Philippian origin (with Jewett, against Schenk's use of Wolff to suggest a Semitism). Communal, social, found in Gk. proverbs reported by Aristot. and the Pythagorean concept of the ideal community. An ecclesial side to "with one mind," from Acts 4:32, etc., is brought out in the NOTE.

the gospel faith brings to the fore terms used at 1:25 and 1:5,7,12,16, and 27d. 1:28 will add more about "believing." Themes heard from the day Paul arrived in Philippi. Of numerous ways to take each term (see NOTE), a dat. of interest (advantage, *commodi*) seems best, the gospel cause, the interests of which are aided by uniting in the struggle; plus gen., obj. and subj. An unusual phrase, what the Philippians struggle for, *the faith*, shaped by and with its object *the gospel*. Possibly "the faith, i.e., the gospel," or "faith" as a weapon for their struggle (cf. Loh. 75–76, rejected by U. B. Müller 75 n 22). Cf. 27a the standard for exercising citizenship.

The third expectation involves a negative: *not* to be *intimidated in any way by adversaries*. Not frightened, like horses shying in battle. Not daunted in any respect. *adversaries* seems not military usage but, at least to Paul, "foes of God" (Exod 23:22 LXX; 2 Macc 10:26; cf. Isa 66:6). External foes, not in the church (see A.3), pagan opponents to the gospel, local and informal; in Paul's case, the Roman authorities in Ephesus. This conclusion, unbelievers (B. Weiss 128), has been strengthened by recent investigation. They sought to destabilize the new community's solidarity by bullying believers (Schenk 169; U. B. Müller 75). Proselytes to Judaism knew such opposition too.[39] Early Christian paraenesis likely included warnings, urged fearlessness, and called on those "in Christ" to welcome

---

[39] Tacitus, *Hist.* 5.5, 15.44. Hence the *topos* in synagogue instruction about proselytes: "Having left native country and friends and kin for the sake of virtue and religion, let them not be denied other city-states *(poleis)* and householders *(oikeiōn;* MSS *oikiōn,* households) and friends, but let them establish places of shelter lying ready for those who flee to piety" (*Spec.* 2.52, tr. JR; = LCL *Philo* 7:128–29; cf. 4.178 = LCL 8:118–19). K. G. Kuhn, "*prosēlytos,*" TDNT 6:731–32, one who has "set himself under the Jewish constitution." See further *Yebamot* 47a bar, time of Hadrian (Str-B 1:110–11; Eng. tr. in I. Epstein, ed., *The Babylonian Talmud, Seder Nashim, Tractate Yebamoth,* tr. I. W. Slotki [London: Socino, 1936], 310–11; repr. in S. W. Baron/J. L. Blau, *Judaism* [New York: Liberal Arts Press, 1954] 163–64): "a proselyte is to be addressed as follows: '. . . do you not know that Israel at the present time are persecuted and oppressed, despised, harassed, and overcome by afflictions?' If he replies, 'I know, and yet am unworthy,' he is accepted forthwith. . . . He is told, . . . 'Be it known to you that . . . Israel at the present time are unable to bear either too much prosperity or too much suffering.'"

others (cf. Rom 15:7). Would Lydia, a Jewish proselyte (Acts 16:14), Paul's convert, have heard of such dangers twice?

2. Grounds for This Stance in the Contest the Philippians and Paul Face (1:28b–30).

Three reasons emerge to stand, struggle, and be unflinching in their exercise of citizenship: effect on themselves and the adversaries (28bc); their own believing and suffering (29); and the commonality of the contest in which apostle and congregation are engaged (30).[40] Paul's *agōn*, in the past (at Philippi) and now (at Ephesus), makes him a partner with his beloved Philippians, though absent. He provides rationale for acting in accord with the *propositio* (Geoffrion's *enthymene*, see A.1, with *ratio* A.2).

Paul's initial reason involves a *pointer* toward *destruction* for the adversaries and *salvation* for the Philippians. Harbingers *from God*, no less! It is so tersely expressed that scribes have made textual alterations (see NOTE on *This* [lit., which] *is to them* . . .), so vigorous that Hawth. has reconstructed it (using scribal variants) to avoid opponents going to "eternal destruction"; instead (Hawth.), the adversaries think the Philippians' obstinacy foolish; it can lead only to death for Christ's followers (Philippian Christians saw their steadfastness leading to salvation). The NOTE on 28b *but of your salvation* gives reasons to reject the proposal (with Fee, against Hawth.). Others seek to limit the sense to "winning and losing." At issue is Paul's view on the fate of "the world" apart from faith.

It is not at first apparent the argument has moved in 28b to reasons for fearless citizenship. *This* seems just explanatory. (But of what?) Ultimately 28b proves the most powerful of the reasons: God is now at work (2:13), who will bring things to completion at "the Day of Jesus Christ" (1:6, 10, cf. 11). Ambiguity stems from Paul's compact style and uncertainty about the antecedent for *This* (fem. because the word for *pointer* is fem.). The closest fem. sg. antecedent is *faith*, eleven words earlier in 27c. Hence some refer *hētis* to the Philippians' intrepidity in 28a (not being intimidated), others to 27c *stand steadfast*; ultimately to exercise of citizenship in 27a. The *politeia* and gospel of the Christians and their bold stance have aroused opposition.

Philippian Christian response to the gospel is a *pointer*, "omen" or "sign" (not a *sēmeion* like those of Jesus in the Fourth Gospel; not a "proof," the way the cross was, Rom 3:25–26). It points Philippian believers to their eschatological *salvation*, at the last Day. Standing steadfast shows they are God's holy ones, to be vindicated at the End, on their way to what Paul prayed for them in 1:6 and 10b–11. The other half of the assertion is unpalatable to some: *to them*, the adversaries, *destruction*. "Doom" catches the sense. Proud expectations will be wiped out, perhaps they themselves. Such judgment is among "unStoic features" in Phil (Engberg-Pedersen 1995a:282).

Thus 1:28a is eschatological, indeed apocalyptic, about the Day of the Lord.

---

[40] *hētis* in 28b can suggest cause. *hoti* 29a is more clearly causal (KJV–NRSV "for"). The ptc. in v 30a we take as causal. WH put parentheses around 28b–29 (*hētis* through *paschein*); v 30 became a fourth statement about engaging in citizenship.

Loh. 76–77 insisted the *pointer* deals with events in time and history, the here and now of divine judgment, an "unbridgeable chasm" between adversaries and the faithful. Paul can use "strong language" (I. H. Marshall 38). 3:19, on the end of the opponents there, also uses "destruction" (*apōleia*, same word). Those who do not heed the message about the cross are "perishing" *(tois apollymenois)*, in contrast to those being saved (1 Cor 1:18; 1:19 God destroys, *apolō*!). Christians are a smell of death to those perishing, of life to those being saved (2 Cor 2:15–16; 4:10, the death of Jesus = putrefaction, *nekrōsis*). Unbelievers are blinded (by the god of, or who is, "this world") to the light of the gospel, things are veiled to those perishing (2 Cor 4:3–4). Paul views "the world" *(kosmos)* and "this age" *(aiōn)* as lost until redeemed.[41]

The stance of the Philippian Christians makes known *destruction to them*, the adversaries, townspeople and Roman authorities who are against Christ's converts. The *pointer* is a revelation to them, a manifestation from God.[42] God wants the adversaries to know they are on the way to destruction, the congregation on the way opened by God to consummation (*deliverance*, 1:19; *salvation*, 2:12). Christians are to follow through, steadfast in mission, leaving the completion (1:6) to (the grace of) God.

A pendant is attached, *and this, from God* (28c). That makes it theological, not the blind play of fate (Walter), the work of a God who is gracious, but also a just Judge. In 28c *this* refers to the entire preceding cl., not just *salvation* (so Ewald 91 = Wohl. 100). To refer *this* to what follows in v 29 (so Chrysost. PG 62:209 = NPNF 13:200), "This is from God, namely, that it was given you . . ." is true but tautological; 29a already implies "given by God"; and 28 is left even more enigmatic. God works both weal and woe (Isa 45:7), *salvation* and *destruction*. To realize their own destiny and the direction in which the opponents in Philippi were going was one reason for the community to continue to stand fast.

Second, gifts God has given (v 29). *it has been granted* implies "by God"; = God "has blessed you" (CEV; *God* as subject can also be inferred from the end of v 28). Paul's choice of the vb. is "scarcely accidental" (Fee 1994:749 n 66). From *charizomai* (vb.) comes *charis*, "grace" (1:7, the Philippians share in Paul's *gracious opportunity* for mission as well as in *grace* from God and Christ that Paul wishes for them all, 1:2). Here aor. for a single past divine action, at baptism, with "grace-gifts" that come to each believer. Cf. 1 Cor 12:8–13; Rom 12:6–8. No list of *cha-*

[41] Cf. H. Sasse, *TDNT* 3:892–94; Bultmann 1951 (INTRO. X Bibl.) 254–59; *NIDNTT* 1:524–25; *EDNT* 2:311–12 (H. Balz). Cf. Matt 10:28; 16:25; Luke 6:9; 19:10; Jas 4:12, the Judge "who is able to save and to destroy" (OT examples for each vb. in AB 37A:294); the principle at 1 Cor 3:17 from "holy law."

[42] So Schenk 170, taking *endeixis* terms at Rom 9:22–23 ("show [*endeixasthai*] wrath," make known power or riches of glory) and 3:25–26 (NRSV "show" God's righteousness, "prove" his righteousness, both *endeixis*) as synonyms for God's righteousness "revealed" (*apokalyptetai*, 1:17–18), righteous judgment revealed (2:5), glory to be revealed (8:18–19), and God's righteousness "disclosed" (*pephanerōtai*, 3:21). That an historical appearance is meant is buttressed by Gal 3:23, parallelism of "before faith came (*elthein*)" and "until faith is revealed (*apokalyphthēnai*)."

rismata occurs in 1:28, but two things are singled out, believing and, surprisingly, suffering.

to you stands in a place of prominence. *Captatio benevolentiae*: Paul calls attention to God's goodwill toward them in gifts their Lord gives from the outset of life in Christ. What gift(s) will he stress? Suspense is heightened by a tantalizing art. infin. (used often in Phil, 10x in Letter B, 6 times in 1:21–29, twice in this v). The art. is followed by *for the sake of Christ*. Not a battle cry, slogan, or motto (Walter 1978:430; 1979:425, contrary to Loh. 78), but a hesitating way (Walter 1978:425, anacolouthon), rhetorically effective, of introducing a crucial phrase, the difficult one for Gk. and Roman minds, *to keep suffering for his sake* (completed only in v 29c with the distasteful vb. *paschein*). Wordplay—*believe on him, suffer for Christ*—links "for Christ" to "with Christ" in v 23.

The correlatives *not only . . . but also* flag the two gifts. *pisteuein*, "have faith," is ongoing action (pres. tense), *to continue to believe*. The only use of the vb. in Phil., but no surprise; 1:25 spoke of the Philippians' *faith*, from which their *progress and joy arise*; 27d, *the gospel faith*, object in their current struggle. *to believe* does not go with the initial phrase ("the matter of . . . [no infin.] *for the sake of* Christ") but is completed with *eis* + acc., to *believe in* or on Christ, an idiom common in the Fourth Gospel. Its other two occurrences in Paul are both connected with the gospel, specifically with justification.[43] Believing the gospel leads to the gift of the Spirit (Gal 3:2); the Spirit in turn makes possible confession of faith in Jesus as Lord (1 Cor 12:3). The linear sense of *pisteuein* is appropriate; continuing trust and obedience, not just initial response, parallel to ongoing suffering (29c). In Paul, *pistis* as faithfulness, fidelity, is the fruit of the Spirit of God (Gal 5:22). On faith as a gift, cf. Rom 4:16; 2 Cor 4:13 (Goppelt 1982 [INTRO. X Bibl.] 2:123; AB 32A:286); Rom 12:3 (AB 33:646, cf. 645, "a gift" that "calls for life together"); 1 Cor 12:7; Eph 2:8. Neugebauer 1961 ([1] Bibl.) 165, Paul never makes faith the object of an impv., "Believe!" but says "Stand fast in the faith" (1 Cor 16:13).[44]

Finally the term fearful to Paul's readers, *suffering*, artfully delayed, a *correctio* (Edart 87) to their thinking. Belief in Christ is a necessary presupposition: it may cause persecution, it helps understand *paschein* as from God. Suffering is a blessing parallel to believing or an even higher privilege (Haupt 49–50; Michaelis 30; U. B. Müller 77). Commentaries call suffering "fellowship with a suffering Christ," sharing "his destiny" (Martin 1976:85; K. Barth 49), "the essence of Christianity" (*TDNT* 5:920). Belief in Christ "is the means of salvation, but suffering is the evident token of salvation" (Eadie 78–79), though to Gk. ears any claim about *paschein* as something good or a divine gift was alien.

How would people in the Hellenistic world have understood *paschein* (Walter

---

[43] Gal 2:16, "we have come to believe (aor.) in Christ Jesus, so that we might be justified by faith in Christ" (NRSV-txt); Rom 10:14, "believe in one of whom they have not heard" (context: faith comes "from what is heard," the word of God, the process of believing and confessing Christ and so becoming justified and saved, 10:10, 17).

[44] J. Becker 1993 ([1] Bibl. **Paul**) 316, with *faith* in 1:27–30 a triad begins: *love* in 2:1–11 and *hope* in 2:12–18. See further ([1] Bibl. **faith**) Lührmann 1976:57–59; G. Friedrich, in F. Hahn/H. Klein 1982:110–13; and Silva 97.

1978, esp. 424–28; 1979:423–25; NTD *Phil.* 47–50)? The Gk meant "experience something," often bad (with *kakōs*), like "undergo" punishment. "Why such experiences?" The common answer: to learn.[45] Affliction was something to be overcome. The Stoics regarded *paschein* as inevitable, throughout the cosmos (cf. Sen., *Ep.* 71.26). Only deity was exempt, "insensible to passion" (*apatheia*). The wise aimed to be free from passion (*apatheia, ataraxia*). To suffer for (the sake of the) god(s) was unthinkable. Cf. the Corpus Hermeticum, *TDNT* 5:904–7 (W. Michaelis), reflected in *NIDNTT* 3:719–20 (B. Gärtner); Malherbe 1986:141–43, cf. 33–34, 88. Danker 1982:409 provides no parallels to "suffering" as a benefit the way it is in Paul.

Greeks were not blind to suffering, but the problem, ultimately one of theodicy, was not connected with the gods and their having to suffer. Fate, Moira, *Heimarmenē, anagkē* (necessity), or a *daimōn* (recall Socrates) controlled human destiny (*OCD*³ 589–90). Cult, astral religion, and magic sought to break their hold. Michaelis (*TDNT* 5:907) wrote of the Hermetic religion, "[O]ne does not learn through suffering, as in tragedy, nor hold *pathē* at bay by *apatheia*, as in Stoicism. One is snatched away from *paschein* by redemption and deification." Philosophy called for *sophrosynē* (moderation, discretion, temperateness); *mēden agan*, "nothing too much" (Diog. L. 1.63), is said to have been carved on the Temple of Apollo at Delphi, the Aristotelian mean between extremes, to avoid the envy or anger of the gods. Cf. Bultmann 1956:136, 147–48, 184–85. "*Good* news" (*euangelion*) that related to suffering was for people in Philippi strange and puzzling (Walter 1978:426; cf. U. B. Müller 79–80).

For the very different senses for suffering in the OT, see Note on *suffering.* For Paul, "suffering for the sake of God as joy" (Walter 1978: 428–31) was familiar from Maccabean times. For those holding fast to Torah, persecution and death were confirmation they belonged to God and thus cause for joy. Hence, blessed those who persevere (Dan 12:12); they are rewarded with resurrection (Dan 12:3, 13); Tobit 13:16, "How happy I will be" to see Jerusalem the golden. In particular, the Maccabean period gave rise to hope for future life and therefore joy amid present sufferings (e.g., the martyrs of 2 Macc 7). W. Nauck, "Freude im Leiden. Zur Problem einer urchristlichen Verfolgungstradition," ZNW 46 (1955) 69–80, suggested this theme came into Christianity via the Beatitudes (Matt 5:10, 11–12); cf. joy at Jas 1:2, 12 (cf. Dibelius-Greeven, *James* 71–72); 1 Pet 3:14 and 4:14; Rom 8:17,18. In Paul, "affliction (*thlipsis*)–glory" at 2 Cor 4:17–18; Rom 8:18–21 (Carrez 1951). Bonds and death are part of the gospel's progress (Phil 1:12) for its messengers and adherents. Suffering is part of being Christ's and serving on Christ's behalf. The apostle was no doubt aware how strange the theme of suffering was for his hearers (Walter 430 n 43, 1 Pet 4:12, "*Stop being surprised* at the fiery ordeal that is taking place"; *thlipsis* and persecution is what those who receive the word

---

[45] The wordplay is common, *patēmata/mathēmata* (Herodot. 1.207, my *experiences* with wretchedness have been my *learnings*, "disaster my teacher"), *pathei mathos*, learn by undergoing affliction, Aeschyl. Ag. 177, 250, "Justice allots to those who suffer to learn," JR tr.; Aesop's fable of the dog and the bone. Gk. tragedies are often more profound than the philosophers.

can expect, Mark 4:14–20). For Hellenistic Christians faith as a gift from God was no problem; *suffering* was the rub. In v 30 Paul will put it in terms of an *agōn*, be active in a contest, not just passively suffering. This "agonal motif" was familiar to Hellenistic self-understanding. Cf. Amir 1978; 1987 (see [1] on 1:2 **God**), and Walter, *Phil.* 49–50.

In Loh.'s martyrdom theory, some in Philippi may have had pride about martyrdom (Loh. 4–5). But his "martyr to martyrs" approach was severely criticized (H. Windisch in *TLZ* 53 [1928] 514); except for Michaelis' commentary, no following (cf. Merk 1968:176, n 11, comment 1; Hainz 1972:216 n 2). But (Walter 1978:418), Loh. rightly saw that "the suffering of Christians for their faith" is an important theme in Phil (for Walter, Letter B, 1:12–30; 1979:423). To make suffering "the *esse* of Christianity and a gift of grace" (*TDNT* 5:931) was startling for the Philippians. Paul has broached it with sensitivity.

Suffering is not being raised by Paul to the Philippians for the first time here. A.1, above, suggests he spoke of it as part of instruction at baptism, as in synagogue instruction for converts to Judaism, a practice (B.1, n 39) of which Paul could have known. His own experiences—a beating and jail in Philippi (Acts 16:23–24), orders to leave town (16:35–39), referred to in the apostle's oldest extant letter, 1 Thess 2:2, as "suffering (-*pathontes*) and being mistreated at Philippi"—were known to the Philippians, as was his present plight (Phil 1:12–26). Cf. 2 Cor 7:5 for terms corresponding to 1:28–29 (Schenk). On suffering or tribulation as part of the Christian life, cf. 1 Thess 3:3–4 ("destined for" persecutions, *keimetha*); Acts 14:22 and 9:16; Rom 8:17, 28–30; 2 Cor 4:10, etc., cited by Silva 96–97.[46] Paul's experiences from his Jewish background, what he underwent in Philippi and now in Ephesus, let him speak of suffering as a gift from God (B. Weiss 119), within his eschatology (Exc.A). The time span till the Day of the Lord and the end of all persecution and tribulation was, for Paul, not long. The relationship now "with Christ" would come to fruition then; that is grounds for joy amid sufferings.

The third reason for standing firm, *since you are having the same contest such as you saw in my life and of which you are now hearing in my life* (30), links apostle and congregation in the struggle together. 28bc connected the Philippians' stance with God and eschatology, 29 with faith in Christ and suffering for him as gifts that go back to baptismal roots. That others have suffered similarly was a widespread argument in antiquity (Holloway 2001a:118–19). *echontes* in 30a is another grammatical break (anacolouthon; see Note), but the sense construction is clear. The Translation takes the circumstance as cause (*since*, NIV, NRSV; "because"). *you are having* means a struggle in which the Philippians are now immersed, though friction has existed in the *colonia* perhaps since the founding mission (1 Thess 2:2; Acts 16:37–39, Paul insisted on his rights as citizen perhaps to gain recognition by the authorities for his converts).

---

[46] U. B. Müller (78–79) objects, something *new* has burst upon the Philippians: Paul compares in v 30 his past *and present* experiences with the contest in which the Philippians are *now* engaged (so Feine 1916 [Intro. VII.A Bibl.] 86). But that presses *echontes* in 30a to exclude Paul's past run-ins with adversaries in Philippi.

Persecutions usually arose first against Paul and his mission team—in Thessalonica from the Jewish community (1 Thess 2:2, 14–16; cf. 2 Thess 1:5); in Macedonia generally from the Greco-Roman (or indigenous) population and authorities (Loh. 79 n 14). The longer the time between "then," when the missionaries first arrived, and "now" (when Paul writes; cf. 30b *you saw . . . you are now hearing*), the greater the likelihood of suffering, as the Christian movement grew. Loh. estimated the time span at six years (for Caesarea; longer, if Rome). If Ephesus (INTRO. VIII, Chart 2), 5–7 years since Paul was first in Philippi (A.D. 48–49) and the writing of Letter B (54–55). Long enough for incidents between believers and neighbors, long enough to attract the attention of authorities, as house churches began to organize like other associations, visible in "public space" *(politeia)*.

The term *contest* puts suffering (and Jewish martyr theology) into an "agonal framework" that readers in Philippi would readily grasp. The word field for *agōn* (see NOTE) can include athletic games and the stadium and, in Gk. philosophy, "struggle" within oneself for virtue and to subdue the passions. OT/Jewish backgrounds added a religious sense, the battle for the One God of Israel against (Seleucid) overlords and struggle against Satan *(T. Job)*. Paul may have known this Jewish background, even if the Philippians did not. Pfitzner sees only "pale" use of "athletic" terminology, not much of the smell of the wrestling palestra. Not much evidence for calling it "military" (hints of Amazons to the contrary; see NOTE on *agōn*); but (Portefaix) *all* the Philippians, women included, were in this struggle. Trs. about "fighting in the battle line" overdo it. The image is "pop" moral theology of the Greco-Roman world, Paul and team somewhat akin to Cynic, Stoic missionaries, but with this difference: such missionaries sought to bring certain people to selfhood individually, the struggle for the gospel faith involves creation of a community involved in the *politeia*. Thus, ecclesial identity is involved (see NOTE on *the same contest*). The Philippians face the *same* struggle Paul does, with *adversaries*, against the state (Cassidy 2001:170, among others), for the *gospel faith*. Paul is model, mentor, and colleague.

The contest is one *such as you saw in my life*, earlier, in Philippi during the founding mission. Some in the house churches had been eyewitnesses, participants in events alluded to at 1 Thess 2:2 and described in Acts 16:12–40: Lydia's household preeminently (16:13–15, 40), the jailer's household most vividly (16:23–36); others, later on (Epaphroditus, Euodia, Syntyche, and Clement, Phil 2:25–30 and 4:2–3). Some Philippian believers may never have seen Paul but heard of him through his converts (1:5, 12). They know his struggle and are being asked to share in it.

The *contest . . . of which you are now hearing in my life* includes his court case, a matter of life and death; judges, jailers, people in the Praetorium and Caesar's household, and others in Ephesus, including various Christian preachers (1:12–26; 4:22). The Philippians heard of Paul's situation in Letter A and now in Letter B; further information from the bearer of this letter, likely Epaphroditus (see on 2:25), and any travelers from Ephesus. Philippian believers face their *struggle* with people in daily business and social life, including the authorities *(politeia)* and in relationships among the house churches (the ecclesial aspect).

Paul writes autobiographically *(en emoi)* re events *in my life,* "then" and "here and now." His life and case become paradigmatic. He associates himself with the Philippians, and they with him—their apostle, in solidarity (4:10; [16] COMMENT)—without using "we." *in my life,* with both *you saw* and *are now hearing,* bridges past and present.

Association of Paul with them in a common struggle is high praise for the Philippians (Chrysost. PG 62:209 = LNPF 13:200), an expression of *captatio benevolentiae* (cf. 1:7; B. Weiss 128). Many speak of "imitation of Paul." *Imitatio Pauli* will come at 3:17 (in Letter C); *mimēsis*-vocabulary does not appear at 1:30. More accurately, Paul is model *(Vorbild)* or co-sufferer in the same *agōn,* an approach stronger than a flat-out apostolic command. It fits with Paul's understanding of "apostolic existence" as "christological proclamation" (Güttgemanns 1966:126–98), without separation between apostle and community (Schenk 171 n 45). Paul can speak thus since his apostolic authority and the authority of the gospel are not at issue in Phil. He can deepen understanding of how gospel and God's gifts involve suffering and struggle along with faith. With 1:30b (about what the Philippians *saw* and *are now hearing* of Paul) a circle is closed, an *inclusio* going back to 1:27 (what Paul would like to *see* and *hear* of the Philippians). They are bound together in *the same contest* for the gospel, past, now, and in the future (Loh. 80).

3. 1:27–30 *Within the Redacted, Canonical Letter.* The unit reads much the same in the four-ch. letter as in Letter B (above). An obvious difference: why not, under 1:27 *news about you* Philippians, mention their recent gift to him? Some reference is in order. He does not lack good will toward them (1:30 is *captatio benevolentiae*). No "crisis" in Philippi is so acute that he must get to it right away (actually 26 vv into the letter). The usual explanations ([16] COMMENT A.3; [2] COMMENT B.1)—earlier veiled reference to the gift (e.g., 1:3 *remembrance;* 1:5 *sharing;* or 1:6 *good work*), he puts off what is for him a difficult matter—can be trotted out (though proponents of a single letter seldom bother at 1:27–30). A specific reason might be that Paul wants to balance *ta kat' eme* at 1:12 with *ta peri hymōn* at 1:27, and Philippian matters immediately involve *adversaries* and "standing steadfast." In light of his own prospects and hopes (for life), he presents his hopes for the Philippians, in *the same contest* that he faces.

Once 1:27–30 was placed in a longer four-ch. letter, its significance diminished, a smaller segment of a bigger whole. It does not stand out as in Letter B. In part because the *adversaries* of 1:28 were often associated with the *dogs* and *evil workers* of 3:2–21 (see A,3 above; e.g., Mearns). They have different profiles, but it is claimed Paul "anticipates" a danger he will discuss in detail later, or become "better informed" with late-breaking news just after he dictated 3:1. In part because *politeuesthe* at 1:27, in a unified epistle, is usually interpreted in light of 3:20 *politeuma,* "citizenship" understood as a "commonwealth" in heaven. The future eschatological side in 3:20–21 pushes away involvement now in the "public sphere" in the *colonia* and an "ecclesial" sense of communal aspects of the house churches. We are left in a unified letter with paraenesis that still ignores the gift(s) from Philippi, though a reflection of their church *politeia* and renewal of support for Paul. A more specific (though conjectural) setting vanishes, as a general setting for an entire epistle takes over (conjectural too, as to where Paul is imprisoned).[47]

Placing 1:27–30 within chs. 1–4 has often led to seeing a fragmented community in Philippi (e.g., Peterlin), blame placed on Euodia and Syntyche (4:2–3). The remedy is then unity in the church, "one spirit" (usually lowercase), "one soul," *together* in v 27, through "humility" (2:3), instead of selfishness (2:4). Be united also because of the opponents profiled in ch. 3. A unified letter views 1:27–30 in light of what follows and so diminishes its importance.

Finally does *the same contest* envision a "worldwide struggle"? Cf. 1 Peter, "the same kind of suffering" that "brothers and sisters in all the world are undergoing," 1 Pet 5:9 NRSV, where they "stand fast in faith," resisting "the devil" as adversary (*antidikos*, 5:8). For Letter B the answer is no. But in a redacted letter, in a canonical collection with 1 Pet, there is impetus to see a broader struggle, but no hint in the vv themselves it is worldwide or involves "the devil."

Political aspects of Phil 1:27–30 have rarely been fully appreciated. Perhaps *suffering* (v 29; COMMENT A.5)[48] and the *agōn* in v 30 have most caught the eyes of readers. 1:27–30 seems never to have been assigned as a lectionary reading, though 1:27–2:4 appeared in the Eisenach Conference series (1896) as Epistle for Septuagesima Sunday, and (part of) v 27 in the *Ordo*.[49]

SELECT BIBLIOGRAPHY (see also General Bibliography and Commentaries)

Aland, K. 1979a. "Das Verhältnis von Kirche und Staat nach dem Neuen Testament und den Aussagen des 2. Jahrhunderts," in his GS *Neutestamentliche Entwürfe*, TB 63 (Munich: Kaiser) 26–123.

Amir, Y. 1978. "Die Begegnung des biblischen und des philosophischen Monotheismus als Grundthema des jüdischen Hellenismus," *EvT* 38:2–19.

Bjerkelund, C. J. 1975. *Parakalô. Form, Funktion und Sinn der parakalô-Sätze in den paulinischen Briefen.* Bibliotheca Theologica Norvegica 1 (Oslo: Universitetsforlaget) 174–76.

Brewer, R. R. 1954. "The Meaning of *Politeuesthe* in Philippians 1:27," *JBL* 73:76–83.

Carrez, M. 1951. "Souffrance et gloire dans les épîtres pauliennes," *RHPR* 31:343–53.

Esler, P. F. 2005. "Paul and the Agon. Understanding a Pauline Motif in Its Cultural and Visual Context," in *Picturing the New Testament: Studies in Visual Images*, ed. A. Weissenrieder et al., WUNT 2/193 (Tübingen: Mohr Siebeck) 356–84, esp. 379–81.

---

[47] The traditional setting in Rome ought to have brought out a "political" meaning for *politeuesthe*, Paul imprisoned there because of his demand, as a citizen, to be heard in Caesar's capital (so Acts—or, if a second imprisonment in Rome, after he has been set free for a while, likely because of his status as a citizen). With Paul as Caesar's prisoner in Caesarea, one might expect some reflection of "political" considerations.

[48] Bloomquist 17–70 gives a *Wirkungsgeschichte* of "how interpreters have understood suffering" in Phil.

[49] Thus Lenski 1914 ([3] COMMENT n 45) 322–37 and L. Fendt, *Die Neuen Perikopen*, HNT (Tübingen: Mohr Siebeck, 1941) 79–82. See (4) COMMENT B, end, on the *Ordo*, though v 27a has often been overlooked or trivialized.

Fowl, S. E. 2003. "Philippians 1:28b, One More Time," in FS Hawthorne (Intro. VII.A. Bibl.) 167–79. Cf. Fowl, *Phil.* 2005:65–68, with Hawth.

Gerstenberger, E./W. Schrage. 1980. *Suffering.* Biblical Encounters Series. Nashville: Abingdon.

Hall, D. R. 1974. "Fellow-Workers with the Gospel," *ExpTim* 85:119–20.

Hawthorne, G. W. 1983. "The Interpretation and Translation of Philippians 1²⁸ᵇ," *ExpTim* 95:80–81.

Landmesser, C. 1997. "Der paulinischen Imperativ als christologisches Performativ. Eine begründete These zur Einheit von Glauben und Leben im Anschluß an Phil 1,27–2,18," in *Jesus Christus als die Mitte der Schrift: Studien zur Hermeneutik des Evangeliums*, ed. C. Landmesser et al., BZNW 86 (Berlin/New York: de Gruyter) 543–77.

Miller, E. C., Jr. 1982. "*Politeuesthe* in Philippians 1.27: Some Philological and Thematic Observations," *JSNT* 15:86–96.

Roberts, R. 1937–38. "Old Texts in Modern Translations: Philippians 1:27," *ExpTim* 49:325–28.

Stalder, K. 1962. *Das Werk des Geistes in der Heiligung bei Paulus.* Zurich: EVZ.

Talbert, C. H. 1991. *Learning through Suffering. The Educational Value of Suffering in the New Testament and Its Milieu.* Zacchaeus Studies. Collegeville, MN: Michael Glazier/LiturgicalPress.

Walter, N. 1978. "Die Philipper und das Leiden. Aus den Anfängen einer heidnischen Gemeinde," in *Die Kirche des Anfangs* (FS H. Schürmann), ed. R. Schnackenburg et al., ETS 9 (Leipzig, 1977, cited from Freiburg: Herder) 417–34

———. 1979. "Christusglaube und heidnische Religiosität in paulinischen Gemeinden," *NTS* 25:422–42.

6. *Paraenesis* (Exhortatio, *with Further Reasons for the Comfort and Admonitions*), 2:1–4

TRANSLATION

2:1a If, then, as we assume, comfort and exhortation in Christ amount to something, b if consolation and encouragement from love amount to something, c if sharing in the Spirit and the fellowship brought about by the Spirit amount to something, d if affections and mercies amount to something, 2a give me further joy b in that you think the same thing, c having the same love, together in soul, d thinking one thing, 3a nothing for self-interest, nor for vainglory. b Rather, in humiliation, consider one another to surpass yourselves, 4a each, regarding not your own interests, b but those of other persons, each of you.

NOTES

2:1–2. *If, then, as we assume, comfort and exhortation in Christ amount to something . . . ,* [2] *give me further joy. . . .* Four *if*-cls. (1a, b, c, and d), *ei* + indef. pron. *tis, ti* = "some one, any (thing)" + noun and a phrase *(in Christ),* gen. *(paramythion* of love, *koinōnia* of the Spirit), or a second noun ("hearts and mercies"). Conclusion (apodosis) in v 2, impv. "fulfil ye my joy" (KJV).

2:1a. *If . . . as we assume.* No vb. The condition, with *plērōsate* (v 2), is "simple particular," reality (BDF ##371–72; Moule *IB* 148), "Class I," assumed to be true; J. L. Boyer, "First Class Conditions: What Do They Mean?" *Grace Theological Journal* 2 (1981) 106; "obviously true," Black 1985:301. "Since" (BDAG *ei* 1.a.α and 3; BDF #372; Martin 1976:86; Schenk 173, 185; Beare 72, citing Plato *Phdr.* 260D; Lft. 107, Virg. *Aen.* 1.603). Cf. Phil 4:8. Paraphrased to show Paul's intent, *If . . . , as we assume* (cf. Black 1985:301).

then. **oun,** normally second in cl., **so therefore, consequently, accordingly, then.** Inferential from what precedes (cf. 2:28 and 29). Cf. BDAG *oun* 2.d; BDAG *ei* 6.k; Phlm 17. Likely refers back to 1:27, *Exercise your citizenship in a manner worthy of the gospel of Christ* (Ewald 97 = Wohl. 107; Vincent 53; Gnilka 103; Schenk 174). If 1:30 (cf. 29), *contest* and *suffering,* then *paraklēsis* = "comfort." Cf. G. P. Wiles 1974:90; Fortna 1990:223–24; V. Wiles 90. J. L. White (1972a:28), *oun* indicates a minor shift in the letter. Some add *moi,* "*paraklēsis* . . . for me (Paul)" (Chrysost; Ewald 94 = Wohl. 103; cf. Walter 52); others, *par' hymin,* "among you," the Philippians and Paul (Ewald 94 and n 2 = Wohl. 103 n 2) or just the Philippians (Schenk 174); as vb., *estin,* "is" (RSV; ZG 595); *estō (ētō),* "let there be" (impv. pres. 3rd sg., *eimi*); *eiē* (opt. pres., 3rd sg.; KJV "If *there be* therefore . . ."; cf. Wohl. 107 n 1); *dynatai* (+ *ti,* acc., supply *poiein*), "able to accomplish anything" (ZBG #9; cf. BDAG *dynamai* 3); or "if therefore any exhortation in Christ is joy . . ." (*gaudium est,* Bengel 797; rejected by Meyer 59–61, Alford 83–84).

something. One expects *tis paraklēsis* (fem.), *ti paramythion* (neut.), *tis koinōnia* (fem.), *tina splanchna* (neut. pl., *oiktirmoi* is masc. pl.). MSS vary (NA[27]). Blass conjectured pred. neut. *ti,* "if *paraklēsis* in Christ (amounts to) something, etc." (BDF #137.2; cf. #131, "stereotyped adverbial *ti*"). Cf. GNTG 1:59, 3:316. *tis* occurs with *paramythion* in D*[c] L 33 2495 (Dib.71; NA[27]); "stereotyped *tis*" 3x. With *splanchna,* NA[26,27] read *tis* (*sigma* by dittography? Edart 115 n 1), a solecism (ATR 130), scribal mistake (ATR 410), or incongruity (Ewald 94 n 1 = Wohl. 104 n 1). K Ψ 81 etc. have *ti* (Blass' consistent solecism; ATR 744); a few MSS, *tina,* correct but unlikely (for "rhythmic considerations," BDF #132.2). Perhaps *ti* 4x; scribes "corrected" Paul's rhetorical style. *ti* suggests "means anything to you" (JB), "anything that will move you" (NJB). Cf. ZBG #9; Hawth. 63; Lft.'s paraphrase 107. The TRANSLATION assumes *ti* 4x. To render "If . . . exhortation, let it therefore be exhortation in Christ, etc." (Hofmann; rejected in Meyer 62 n 2; Ewald 94–96, 97 n 1 = Wohl. 104–106, 107 n 1) implies *paraklēsis not* based on Christ (unlikely). COMMENT A.2 rejects the notion of *ei tis* as adjuration (Köster, "Paul appeals with an oath," i.e., "as sure as there are . . . ," *TDNT* 7:555 n 42).

in Christ. See NOTES on 1:1, 1:26 *in Christ Jesus. DA* 319, locative, "place." "Sphere" or "source" (Eadie 83). Flows out of the Christ event (Neugebauer [(1), Bibl. **in Christ**] 105), with the ecclesial sphere in mind (NEB/REB "our common life in Christ"). Gk. word order discourages taking it with all four phrases, "if you have found in Christ (i.e., in the common life of the church) any encouragement, etc." (Caird 116; cf. NEB).

comfort and exhortation. paraklēsis. BDAG 3, **lifting of another's spirits, comfort, consolation**; BDAG 1, [N]RSV, many trs., **act of emboldening another in belief or course of action, exhortation, encouragement.** Only here in Phil., 19x in unquestioned letters; vb. *parakaleō*, Phil 4:2 twice, 40x in unquestioned letters, esp. 2 Cor. (J. Thomas, *EDNT* 3:23). Vb. (BDAG 1) in etymological sense, "call" *(kaleō)* to one's side *(para)*; (2) "exhort, encourage" Phil 4:2, etc.; (3) "request," 1 Cor 16:12, etc.; (4) "comfort, encourage, cheer up," 2 Cor 1:4b, 2:7, etc.; (5) "speak in a friendly manner, conciliate," 1 Cor 4:13. Rom 12:8. Vb. meanings (2), (3), and (4) = noun (BDAG 1) "encouragement, exhortation," (2) "appeal, request," (3) "comfort, consolation." A word marked by "the company which it keeps" (W. Barclay 1958:40), esp. (2:1b) *paramythion,* "encouragement, consolation"; cf. *TDNT* 5: 779 n 30; Grabner-Haider 7–9, 11–32.

Gk. usage (O. Schmitz, *TDNT* 5:774–76, abbreviated in *NIDNTT* 1:569, G. Braumann): "call in" someone (Xen. *An.* 3.1.32), to help (Herodot. 7:158), as legal advocate (Epict. *Diss.* 1.27.16); the gods as aids (3.21.12); "beseech" (God; *TDNT* 5:775). Often in a military context "exhort" (Polyb. 1.61.1; 3.19.4, etc.). "Comfort" in "times of grief" (limited examples, 776), mainly philosophical: Phalaris, *Ep.* 103, perhaps 5th cent. A.D. (tr. in Stowers 1986:147; Holloway 2001a:152–53 n 39); Dio Chrys. 30.; the Cynic Teles (3rd cent. B.C.), Stob. *Ecl.* 5.990.16–17; Plut. *Otho* 16.2 (I. 1074a), the Roman Emperor encouraged *(parekalei)* his nephew to be brave. Consolation "always contains a note of exhortation" (Braumann 569).

Schmitz contrasted this meager Gk. usage with the LXX where "'to comfort' is by far the outstanding sense" (777); "the comfort of God . . . given to His people when under divine judgment, or to the individual in time of temptation" (778, cf. 776–79, 788–90), in books with a Heb. text *(nāḥam* niphal and piel); in those of Gk. provenance, "exhortation, encouragement" (778–79). Isa 40:1, "Comfort, comfort ye *(parakleite)* my people"; "true consolation" *(paraklēsis,* Isa 57:18c) "comes from God alone" (789), who comforts (51:12) like a mother (66:13). Comfort comes through God's word (Ps 118 [Eng. 119]:50, "in my humiliation [*tapeinōsei*]"), Scripture (2 Macc 15:9), wisdom (Wis Sol 8:9), the prophets (Isa 61:2). Judaism extoled "God as the only true comforter." Philo, "God has sown hope in humankind, that they might have *paramythion* as part of their nature" (*Praem.* 72); comfort = a human endowment. So *TDNT* 5:788–93.

G. Stählin added 779–88 on "the art of consolation" in the Greco-Roman world—for the dying, the elderly, "those left behind at separation," exiles ("consolatory literature," like Plut. *De Exilio*), and victims of injustice and misfortune.

Ways and means to comfort people included "being there" (presence), visits, expressions of sympathy, letters (cf. Stowers 1986:142–52; Malherbe 1986:80, 82; Holloway 2001a:120–21, but his application of this letter form to 2:1–4 is limited); wine and music. Then the contrast: the classical world is "a realm of suffering," "petty and pitiable" compared with "the heavenly comfort of God in Christ" ("something completely new came into the world") — typical *TWNT* biblical theology of that day. Cf. Braumann 570. The indic. of "consolation" was "always more or less plainly accompanied" by the impv. "admonish," and vice versa (779–80); Sen., *Ep.* 95, 65 may distinguish *consolatio* and *exhortatio*, but they often merged in practice.

For the NT, *parakaleō/paraklēsis* "receive their content preponderantly from the NT event of salvation" (Schmitz 793). Exhortation (Acts 13:15; Heb 13:22) is a "type of preaching" urging persistence in faith; cf. J. I. H. McDonald 39–68. Schmitz and Braumann classify Phil 2:1 under exhortation. *EDNT* 3:23–27 notes Gk. rhetoric ("only remotely" related). In 2:1, if "*paraklēsis* in Christ" is connected with "suffering for Christ" (1:29–30), then "comfort" is a natural tr. If with 1:27, exercising citizenship in a manner worthy of the gospel, then "exhortation" makes sense. Some appeal to *paramythion* in 2:1b: if it means "comfort" (Lft. 107), then *paraklēsis* can mean "exhortation." But *paramythion* also exhibits several meanings.

For "comfort" at 2:1: Chrysost.; Calvin; Loh. 80; Gnilka 103, Oakes 2001:179–80 etc.; Vg *consolatio*; KJV "consolation." N. Turner 1980:77, "comfort" is *the* NT meaning, overstates. Glombitza 1959 ([8] Bibl.) 103–4, *paraklēsis en Christō[i]* = messianic exposition of the OT and christological preaching; rejected by Gnilka 104 n 13, but cf. U. B. Müller 1975:120–21.

For "encouragement," cf. Martin 1976:86; Melick 93; (N)RSV, Phillips, NIV, NAB; CEV: "Christ encourages us"; W. Barclay 1958:40, "that which gives a man the ability triumphantly to face a difficult, dangerous, or distressing situation," inserting *moi* (cf. 1:30 *en emoi* twice), "Do you wish to give me strength and courage to face the hardships . . . of my imprisonment?"

Proposals: *paraklēsis en Christō[i]* and *koinōnia pneumatos* are "objective" (Christ and Spirit), *agapē* and "bowels and mercies" (experienced) "subjective" (Meyer 60; Plummer 67). Hawth. 67, the first pair focuses "on the human side of things — Paul's encouragement and love for the Philippians, the second on the divine — the unity . . . created by the Holy Spirit," "God . . . with the warmth of his affection." Wiesinger: (a) and (b) apply to Paul, (c) and (d) to the Philippians. Ellicott 50, all four refer to the Philippians; (Haupt 51, all four to both Paul and Philippian Christians. Hainz 1982 ([2] Bibl. **sharing**) 52, Paul's authority (to exhort) is legitimatized "in Christ" (not an issue in Phil).

The matter remains unsettled. Hawth. 65, with *TDNT*, "exhortation." Silva 103 "comfort/ consolation in Christ," "almost equivalent to 'salvation.'" Fee 179–80, if tied to 1:29–30, "encouragement (comfort)." I. H. Marshall 41, either "comfort" or "exhortation," for Paul probably exhortation. Bjerkelund 1975 ([5] Bibl.) 175, "comfort or consolation" for the noun, "exhort" for the vb.; he raises the issue of indic. and impv. (112–17; Bultmann; Furnish) and ultimately "law and gospel" (cf. W. Joest, *Gesetz und Freiheit* [Göttingen: Vandenhoeck & Ruprecht, 2nd ed. 1956]). Admonition (Schmitz, *TDNT* 5:795) or comfort (Bjerkelund 175) rests on the salvation event *en Christō[i]*, indeed is part of the gospel (cf. G. Friedrich, *RGG*³ 5: cols. 1137–43). But cf. 4:2 *parakalō* + *en kyriō[i]* as admonition (Bjerkelund 175–76). Bjerkelund concludes (188–90; cf. Phlm 8–9), Paul's *paraklēsis*-language is not command or plea, it occurs where his authority is not at issue (hence never in Gal). Schenk 179, 2:1 = "rousing exhortation," *nomen actionis*. Holloway 2001a:120–21, consolation "when the Philippians follow the advice Paul is about to offer," but basis for exhortation. Points (a) and (c) look back to consolatory themes in 1:12–30; (b) and (d) look forward to "fruits of restored unity in the Philippian community." Holloway 163 calls 2:1–4 "Exhortation."

It is likely that, even if Paul had in mind the LXX sense of "comfort" re "suffering" and "struggle," the Philippians would have heard "(ethical) encouragement" or "exhortation." The TRANSLATION uses both *comfort and exhortation*, at which some commentaries hint.

2:1b. *if consolation and encouragement from love amount to anything.* . . . *ei + ti* (pred.), vb. supplied. The new phrase is *paramythion agapēs*.

consolation and encouragement. BDAG *paramythion*: pert[aining] to that which offers encouragement, *consolation, means of consolation, alleviation.* Only here in the NT (*hē paramythia*, 1 Cor 14:3, NRSV "consolation"); vb. 2x, 1 Thess 2:12, 5:14, + John 11:19, 31. Trs. vary: "comfort, consolation" (KJV, NEB/REB, NIV, NRSV); "encouragement, incentive, persuasive power" (RSV, Gdsp., (N)JB); "solace," NAB[RNT]. Etymologically *para* + *mytheomai* (*TDNT* 4:766 n 13) = "speak to," in friendly address; "admonish," "console" (Stählin, *TDNT* 5:816–23). W. Barclay 1958:40, "comfort," with "gentle and loving insistence" (Plato *Phaedo.* 83A; Xen. *On Hunting* 6.25). LXX, only in books of apparently Gk. origin. Attempts to distinguish *paraklēsis* and *paramytheomai* words are not convincing (*TDNT* 5:820–21 n 27). Both express both admonition and comfort. *paramytheomai* etc., never "directly for God's comfort" but mediated through Christian prophets (1 Cor 14:3), Paul's pastoral care (1 Thess 2:11–12; Malherbe 1987:55–58, 75–76), possibly local leaders (1 Thess 5:14 with 5:12), members reciprocally (Phil 2:1–4; 1 Thess 5:14, if addressed to the community). Fits with friendship (Chariton's *Callirhoë*, R. F. Hock, in Fitzgerald 1997:151–54, 156). Stählin, comfort "through the love which derives from God," received in Christ, for "mutual work of consolation" and admonition. G. Braumann, "encouragement" as "expression of love," a "foundation of church life as lived out in the sphere of Christ." Spicq (*TLNT* 3:30–35), "stimulation to love" (obj. gen.) and "love's power to stir to action" (subj. gen.; cf. NEB). Edart 121–22, Philippian love toward Paul (by their gift? *paramythia* can have a financial sense, "compensation," *TDNT* 5:819–20).

agapēs. See NOTES on 1:9 *love* and 1:16 *the latter, out of love.* Here, human love by Christians (BDAG *agapē* 1.a.α) or the love of God and Christ toward human beings (1.b.α), possibly an ecclesial sense (*NIDNTT* 2:546; 1 Cor. 8:1; Phil 2:1f.; Söding 1995 ([2] Bibl. **love**) 180–81, 184); or *agapē* as a virtue, moral conduct (G. Schneider, *EDNT* 1:10). Spicq 1965, 2:291–302 and *TLNT* 1:8–22, Gk.

background and bibl. The following interpretations have been advanced: (1) Paul's love toward the Philippians (Michael 76, cf. Martin 1976:86; Hawth. 65). (2) "[T]he brotherly love of Christians" (Meyer 61), among the Philippians; "for Paul [Eadie 85] or for the Lord" (cf. Martin 1976:86; B. Weiss 132; in effect, Schenk 174, 179–80; cf. U. B. Müller 82–83, with gen. *auctoris*). (3) "[M]utual love" of apostle and believers, Beare 71; Michaelis 31; Collange 78, experienced in communal worship, expressed in "assistance . . . sent to Paul"; Gnilka 104. (4) "Christ's love" (Beare 71; Martin 1976:86, "for the Church"); O'B 172, citing Spicq 1965, 2:294; cf. Morlet 88. NIV, CEV, NLT—a trend, from context? (5) God's love, in a Trinitarian structure of "in Christ, God, and the Spirit"— B. Weiss 132; Loh. 82, as in 2 Cor 13:13 (rejected by Gnilka 104 n 13 and Söding 1995:175 n 58); Schenk 185. Fee 1994:750 n 68 resisted any "divine triad," but later allowed "an intentional Trinitarian substructure" in 2:1, hence "*God's love*" (*Phil.* 179, 180). (6) Glombitza 1959–60 ([8] Bibl.) encouragement expressed in table fellowship (the *agapē*?); cf. Collange, under (3) above. Rejected by Gnilka 104 n 13. The gen. may be subjective, source, or authorship (Loh. 83 n 2; Gnilka 104; Schenk 180; Söding 1995:175); quality (Haupt 54; BDF #165, loving admonition); or obj. gen., "exhortation that leads to love." The TRANSLATION is literal; *paraklēsis = consolation and encouragement*. Precise sense depends on structure (COMMENT A.3 and B.1), whether a triad is involved, and whether Paul uses a *paramythion*-term directly of God (or Christ).

2:1c. *if sharing in the Spirit and the fellowship brought about by the Spirit amount to something. . . . ei + vb. (supplied) + ti(s) as pred., + koinōnia pneumatos.*

sharing . . . fellowship. koinōnia. See NOTES on 1:5 *sharing* (noun also at 3:10) and (vb.) 4:15 *no church shared with me*; compound vb., 4:14 *in sharing together with me* (Letter A) and 1:7 *all of you sharing, as you do, with me (sugkoinōnous).* BDAG classifies 2:1, like 1:5, under (1) **close association involving mutual interests and sharing**, *association, communion, fellowship, close relationship*, or perhaps (2) **attitude of good will that manifests an interest in a close relationship**, *generosity, fellow-feeling, altruism* (cf. 2 Cor 9:13).

For fellowship or *societas* created by the Spirit (BDAG 1, an "ecclesial sense"): W. Barclay 1958:40; Collange 78; Hawth. 66; Silva 103; Schenk 180; U. B. Müller 83; Panikulam ([2] Bibl. **sharing**); GNB-mg: "The Spirit has brought you into fellowship with one another." Di Marco 1980 cautioned not too easily to identify 2:1 with *communio* (contrast Bori). 2:1 (and 2 Cor 13:13) could just as well mean *pneuma koinōnias* ("circularity theory," ambivalence reciprocity; Di Marco 1988); cf. Di Marco 1993 ([12] Bibl.) 484–88, the gen. as both obj. and subj.

For "participation" or "sharing" in the Spirit (B. Weiss' preference, 134), cf. Lft. 107; in (2) Bibl., **sharing,** J. Y. Campbell; Seesemann, *TDNT; EDNT* 2:303, 305; O'B 174; Fee 181; I. H. Marshall 42; Gdsp., [N]RSV; GNB text, "fellowship with the Spirit." Meyer 62 n 2, *koinōnia* with both *pneumatos* and 1d *splanchna kai oiktirmoi*, "*if any fellowship is fellowship of the Spirit, if any* (fellowship) *is cordiality and compassion, fulfill ye* [my joy]." Cf. Ewald 96–97; rejected by Wohl. 107, addition to note 1, "too artful."

Geoffrion 91–92, Paul uses *koinōnia* politically. In Aristot., the village was *prōtē koinōnia*, "primary partnership," the *polis* "perfect partnership" (because it attains *autarkeia*, "self-sufficiency," *Pol.* 1.1252a.1; 1252b.16, 28, 29). The goal of *politikē koinōnia* is "what is of advantage to the state" (*Eth. Nic.* 8.9.4–5). Cf. M. M. Mitchell 1991:136. For Philippian Christians, *koinōnia* stems from their "political identity as citizens of heaven" (Geoffrion re 3:20; cf. 1:27 above). Hansen 189–92, *communio* based on common ownership (of the Spirit).

Decision on how to tr. *koinōnia* is related to how the gen. *pneumatos* is construed.

Spirit. See NOTES on 1:19 *the Spirit* and 1:27 *in one and the same Spirit*, both debated as to divine or human spirit. Most agree, 2:1= the holy Spirit of God (BDAG *pneuma* 5.d.β.; KJV, [N]RSV, most trs., not NAB). Fellowship of spirit and "team spirit" are rare here. Gen., (1) subj. (or source), "the *koinōnia* provided by the Spirit" (W. Barclay 1958: 40; Collange 78; Hawth. 66; Silva 103; CEV; Loh. 138–39; E. Schweizer, *TDNT* 6:434, cf. 3:807; Schenk 180); (2) obj. gen., "participation in the Spirit" (Vincent 54; in [2] Bibl., J. Y. Campbell 25–26; Seesemann 60; Martin 1976:86–87; Gnilka 104; O'B 174; DA 300–301; Fee 181 n 40, "sharing in the Spirit" but then also "with one another"). Dunn *TPTA* 394 n 19; 424, 561, "shared experience" of the Spirit. GNB-txt. Baumert 2003 ([2] Bibl. **sharing**) 216–19, 502, 504–5, 513–14, sharing of the Spirit, from you to me. (3) Hendricksen 98 n 73, obj. and subj., "*adjectival* genitive," "fellowship *with* the Spirit" and "the *gift* of the Spirit"; "*the marvelous Spirit-fellowship.*" Cf. Bori ([2] Bibl. **sharing**): an "attributive" gen. or "gen. of quality," i.e., "spiritual communion." Edart 122, epexegetical, communion = the holy Spirit. Polyvalent, most likely *sharing in the Spirit* on the part of all Christians (*koinōnia* names an activity, as do *paraklēsis* and *paramythion*; *pneumatos* parallels "in Christ" and [God's] love), but also, in the ecclesial context of 1:27–2:4, *the fellowship brought about by the Spirit.* The TRANSLATION incorporates both.

2:1d. *if affections and mercies amount to something. . . . ei + ti(s)* + two pl. nouns (solecism; ATR 130; BDF #137.2) + vb. (supplied). For *splanchna kai oiktirmoi* some claim hendiadys (BDAG s.v. *oiktirmos*; Bultmann, *TDNT* 5:161; Hawth. 67; NJB "warmth of sympathy"), but 1d is not likely a single idea (Köster, *TDNT* 7:555–56; Martin 1976:88; O'B 175; Spicq 1965, 2:297); both terms appear in virtue lists (Collange 78 n 3, citing Wibbing 1959 [(15) Bibl.] 105) and likely have different meanings. Not just subjective aspects (B. Weiss 134; rejected above; cf. COMMENT A.3 and B.1), to which one adds "in you" or "among you" (Calvin 50, Meyer 61).

affections. See NOTE on 1:8 *affection.* Other trs.: "warmth of affection" (REB); "compassion" (NRSV, NAB[RNT]); "tenderness" (NIV, JB, TC); "kindness" (Phillips, GNB). Lft. 108 distinguished *splanchna*, "the abode of tender feelings," from *oiktirmoi* "manifestation . . . in compassionate . . . actions." Others, a general term *splanchna, oiktirmoi* is more specific (B. Weiss 134 n 1). In the LXX (Köster, *TDNT* 7:550; cf. 5:160) Heb. *riham-* is usually rendered by *oiktirmoi* terms, only occasionally by *splanchna* (esp. in 2 and 4 Macc and Sir, 550–51). In *T. 12 Patr.*, *splanchna* terms replaced *oiktirmoi*, etc. (552–53), a usage continued in the NT.

Köster, 2:1d is "a summary" of 1a, b, and c (cf. Schenk 180–81 and COMMENT A.3 and B.1, below), "marks of the life of the Christian community" (555), hence "love" as "the mutual experience and gift among Christians" (556). Cf. NIDNTT 2:598; TLNT 3:275 n 12, "tender compassion" in which "every Christian must be clothed"; Spicq 1965, 2:291–302. Walter (EDNT 3:266), the "readers' predisposition to sympathy" (cf. TDNT 5:161) or Paul's "own heartfeld sympathy for them or (generally) God's compassion as a supporting argument."

Whose affections? The Philippians'? ("you have kindness and compassion for one another," GNB; B. Weiss 134; Michael; W. Barclay 1958:41; TDNT 7:555; more in O'B 175 n 71); they reciprocate Paul's affection for them (1:8, Collange). But 1:8 = "the affections of Christ Jesus." In T. 12 Patr., splanchna was daringly applied to God (T. Zeb 8.1 [OTP 1:807]; T. Ash. 7.7 [p. 818]; T. Zeb. 9.8 [807, reflecting Mal 3:20]; T. Zeb. 8.2, God's compassion, i.e., the messiah [cf. to splanchnon, T. Naph 4.5, T. Levi 4.4]; Gk. in TDNT 7:551–52, perhaps Christian additions to an earlier Jewish text). Mark 6:34; 8:2; 1:41; 9:22 may be not "an emotion" but "messianic characterization" (Köster 554); traceable to Jesus or a characterization growing up in Paul's day? Loh. 84, 2:1 = God's love and mercy (oiktirmoi in Paul of God's love, regularly); similarly Hawth. 67. O'B 175–76, the "'mercy and compassion' of Christ." Paul uses splanchna of himself (Phil 1:8; Phlm 20), Christians like Titus (2 Cor 7:15), and the saints (Phlm 7; 2 Cor 6:12), all "in Christ" (NIDNTT 2:600). Whether splanchnai rest on divine affection or the affection of believers or both depends how all of 2:1 is construed. See COMMENT A.3 and B.1.

mercies. BDAG oiktirmos pity, mercy, compassion—5x in the NT, 3x in acknowledged letters (+ Col 3:12); vb. oikt(e)irō twice in Rom 9:15 = Exod 33:19—usually pl. Heb. raḥămîm "bowels, affections, mercies" (2 Sam [LXX 2 Kgdms] 24:14, etc.; NIDNTT 2:598) or Gk. pl. for abstract concepts (BDF #142; ATR 408). Bultmann's survey (TDNT 5:159–61) remains basic: oiktir-words in the LXX (80x) exhibit senses similar to eleein, "show mercy", sympathy, for the Heb. rḥm, "have compassion," and ḥnn, "be gracious." Deut 4:31, "a merciful (oiktirmōn) God." O'B 175: 23 of 26 LXX references are to God's mercy; + Qumran references (n 67). From the Pss, "Father of mercies" for God was common; 2 Cor 1:3, patēr tōn oiktirmōn (TDNT 5:161), ". . . from whom all compassion comes"; O'B 1977:241–42. Rom 12:1, dia tōn oiktirmōn tou theou summarizes the gospel set forth in chs. 1–8 and "the merciful bounteous acts" of God that are "manifested to Jew and Greek" in chs. 9–11 (AB 33:639); the basis for the ethical appeals that follow (parakalō, 12:1). Many see in 2:1d God's, rather than human, oiktirmoi (Martin 1976:88; Hawth. 67; O'B 176, though Martin called "the Philippians' sympathy" "the common view"; Edart 123). Bockmuehl 107, "the Christian counterpart of a status symbol." See COMMENT A.3.

2:2a. give me further joy. Impv. plērōsate, conclusion after the if- cls. (protasis). bring to completion that which was already begun, complete, finish (BDAG 3); see NOTES on 1:11 because you have been filled with; 4:18 I am filled full; and 4:19 My God will fulfil. . . . Main vb. in 2:1–4, + dir. obj., acc. of chara, BDAG 1.a, the experience of gladness; see NOTES on 1:4 with joy, a "keynote" in Phil, and 1:25 progress and joy. Vb. rejoice in 4:10 (Letter A) and 1:18 (bis).

mou, between vb. and noun, unemphatic gen. of *egō* (as at 1:3, 4, 7 bis, 8, 13, 17, 20 bis), instead of the possessive pron. *emos*; therefore, no special emphasis on *my*. Fee 184 n 52 (a "vernacular possessive" with emphasis) is scarcely convincing. Most (Lft. 108, Schenk 173; contrast Holloway 2001a; Tellbe 2001:230–31) agree joy is already Paul's, re the Philippians and generally (4:18), in how events are turning out for him (1:12–18c) and future hopes (1:18d–26). The Philippians are to add to existing joy, a fine compliment to their potential.

2:2b. *in that you think the same thing. hina* + subjunct. *phronēte*, not purpose (KJV; ATR 992; BDF #369), but content (Paul's further joy; Moule *IB* 145 n 3, "by having the same outlook," cf. RSV, NIV, NEB/REB). *DA* 325 hedges, "for the purpose of thinking the same . . . ," but cf. 330 epexegetical. A weakened sense of *hina*, non-telic; B. Weiss 136 n, Johannine usage (4:34; 8:56, etc., like an epexegetical infin.); G. P. Wiles 1974:92 n 48. Unless imperatival *hina* (Moule *IB* 144–45). NRSV, JB, TEV in effect. Collange 78 n 4, NJB, GNB + (unnecessarily), "I beg you that . . . ," so *hina* does not depend on *plērōsate*.

Pres. tense, "continue to think"; trs. do not try to bring this out. Pres. tense through v 5, with fut. reference, from this moment on (*DA* 386, 390). *phronein*, see NOTES on 1:7 *to think*, 4:10 *your concern for me* and *you were long intent.* Here and 2:2d, BDAG 1, **think, form/hold an opinion, judge.** *phrēn* ("mind, heart," hence "attitude") may suggest intellect, emotions, or both. In Letter A, *to hyper emou phronein* (4:10) = a Philippian phrase, concern for "their apostle." *DA* 268, often in friendship literature.

Trs. vary, depending on how factious or divided the interpreters think the Philippians were and how *to auto* (dir. obj.) is taken. *autos, -ē, -o*, neut., also at 1:6 (NOTE on . . . *this point*). Here, attrib. position, no noun to modify (BDAG *autos* 3.b) = "the same (thing)." Possibly "the same thing" as Paul. More commonly, think "the same thing" among themselves, "be at harmony"; Vincent 55; Loh. 85 n 1. Of a married couple, in a sepulchral inscription (MM 667), "Saying the same things, thinking the same things [*tauta* (= *ta auta*) *phronountes*], we went the road together to Hades"; Deissmann 1909 ([1] Bibl.) 256 supposed it "familiarly used in popular speech." Many trs., "be" + "like-minded" (KJV, NIV); "the same mind" ([N]RSV, NABRNT); "a single mind" (NJB); "unanimity" (NAB); "thinking and feeling alike" (NEB/REB). V. Wiles 94 n 59, 97–99, "perceive." As Pauline idiom, *to auto phronein* means "think in the same way, agree"; Phil 4:2; 2 Cor. 13:11, other closing admonitions ("rejoice"; *parakaleisthe*, NRSV "listen to my appeal"; Rom 12:16; 15:15). See COMMENTS A.3 and B.1.

2:2c. *having the same love. echontes*, ptc., with *phronēte* in 2b, from *echō*; see NOTES on 1:7 *because you have me in your heart*; 1:23 *If I have the desire . . .* ; 1:30 *for you are having the same contest. . . .* Here, **experience someth[ing], have,** of "characteristics, capabilities, emotions, inner possession" (BDAG 7.a.β); cf. 2:27 "have sorrow." Circumst., manner (CEV, "Live in harmony by showing love for each other"). Most parallel the two (RSV "being of the same mind, having the same love"). *agapē*, see NOTES on *love* in 1:9, 16, 2:1b; on *same*, 2:2b. Usually "the same love" toward one another by each individual (BDAG *agapē* 1.a.α), egalitarian, equally intense; perhaps "the same" as Paul for the Philippians; or "the same love" as God to us (Martin 1976: 88).

together in soul. Masc. nom. pl., *sympsychos, -on,* **harmonious** (BDAG), usually set off with commas (NA²⁷; KJV supplies *ontes,* "*being* of one accord"; NEB; NABRNT). Bengel, "that you be *sympsychoi* by thinking one thing," parallel to 2bc "that you think the same thing by having the same love"; then *sympsychoi* to *hen phronountes* explains *to auto phronein;* not different senses for *to auto* and *to hen* (Meyer 63; [N]RSV, [N]JB, "being in full accord and of one mind"; Martin 1976:88: "open in heart with other people, so you will be of one mind with them." Third option: *sympsychoi* with what precedes in v 2bc, the fruit of love or its source (B. Weiss 137).

sympsychoi (*synpsychoi* in some MSS; *syn* + *psychē,* cf. *TDNT* 9:666), BDAG *wholeheartedly* (Fridrichsen 1938a, modern Gk. parallels), **harmonious,** cf. *Declamation* 2.54 by Polemo(n), an orator of the 2nd cent. A.D.: after death, Callimachus was joined (*sympsychos*) to the earth in "solidarity of a natural, physical sort"; Jewett (1971a:350), imagery from Hellenistic pantheism, "the hero . . . of the same nature as the *logos*" of "the universe"; 2:2 "joined together into one living unity." *psychē* terms in Phil indicate "church unity" (Jewett 348–52; Eus. *H.E.* 7.21.3) and bind the Philippians to one another, not Paul "to the audience or to God" (J. W. Marshall 367).

2:2d. *thinking one thing. phronountes,* circumst. ptc., (see 2:2b . . . *think the same thing;* NOTES on *phronein,* esp. 1:7) + *to hen* as obj. Neut. acc. sg., subst., + the art. *to,* "the one (thing)" (BDAG *heis* 2.a, *one and the same,* cf. 1:27), most MSS (P⁴⁶ ℵ² B D etc.). Some (ℵ* A C etc., Vg) have *auto,* from *to auto phronēte* earlier in the v. *TCGNT* 612 gives *to hen* {B}-rating; J. D. Price 277–78, probability of 0.80. *to hen* seems climactic; "the one thing which would make me completely happy" (JB). To parallel *to auto,* "one thing," *hen* no art., would have sufficed (ZBG #170).

2:3a. *nothing for self-interest, nor for vainglory. mēden . . . mēde* (textual details below) + two nouns with *kata* (one used at 1:17, the other related to *glory* at 1:11), no vb. Some add a ptc., *prassontes* (cf. Ign. *Phila.* 8.2) or *poiountes,* "doing nothing . . . ," or understand an impv. (B. Weiss 138 n 1; Lft. 108; KJV, "Let nothing *be done* through strife . . ."; [N]RSV "Do nothing . . ."). Meyer 63–64, Vincent 55, and EGT 433 preferred *phronountes* from v 2d; 3a then shows what *think the same thing* in 2b excludes. NEB/REB, "There must be . . . ," "Leave no room for. . . ." Unnecessary. The prohibitions (DA 398) stand on their own. Ewald 99 = Wohl. 110, with exclamation marks, "Nothing according to *eritheia*! Nor according to *kenodoxia*!"

kata + acc., BDAG B.5.b, *in accordance with, . . . similar(ly) to;* β. For "the nature, kind, peculiarity, or characteristics of a thing (freq[uently] as a periphrasis for the adv. . . .)." *kata logon* = reasonably; cf.1 Cor 7:6 "self-interestedly," or to show motive (B. Weiss 138 n 1). KJV used "through"; [N]RSV, "from"; NIV, NAB[RNT], "out of."

self-interest. 1:17 NOTE on *eritheia* explains the trend away from "strife" (KJV) to "selfish ambition" (NRSV), in light of limited examples (Aristot., political context; J. A. Sanders 1969:285) and etymology; selfishness, not factiousness. V. Wiles 62–63, "intriguing for office" (in the church), as in Aristot. *Pol.* 1302b4, 1303a14.

Cf. Gal 5:20, vice catalogue. Oakes 2001:182–83, "base self-seeking," "being concerned with one's own (social) advantage."

nor. mēde kata kenodoxian (ℵ* A B C etc.), "nor according to vainglory." A shift from *mēden kat' eritheian*, "nothing according to selfishness." Alternatives: omit *mēde*, "nothing according to selfishness, according to vainglory" (P⁴⁶ ℵ² a few other MSS); *ē* ("or vainglory," D etc. [Western witnesses], Koine MSS [hence KJV]); *ē kata* ("or according to . . . ," a few MSS), all "stylistic improvements" (Silva 104) that "do not affect at all the sense." [N]RSV and NIV follow NA²⁶,²⁷, *(mēde kata)*, but render like KJV, ". . . or conceit" (cf. Fee 174). Many paraphrase ("never," NAB; "nothing," NJB). The TRANSLATION takes *mēde* as *nor*, not the same as *mēden nothing*.

vainglory. kenodoxia (only here in the NT, adj. at Gal 5:26), BDAG 1, **a vain or exaggerated self-evaluation,** *vanity, conceit, excessive ambition;* 2:3 *empty conceit; kenos* ("empty," cf. *kenoō* at 2:7) + *doxa*, "glory" (1:11). A vice ("thirst for glory"), *Cebes* 24.2; 4 Macc 2:15; Herm. *Mand.* 8.5.4; cf. Polyb. 3.81.9; 4 Macc 8:19; Vett. Val. 358.31; Ign. *Phld.* 1.1, the ministry of the *episkopos* is "for the common good (*eis to koinon* [a political, social term]), not *kata kenodoxian*." Word studies: A. Oepke, *TDNT* 3:662; E. Tiedke/H.-G. Link, *NIDNTT* 1:546, S. Aalen 2:44, 47 "vain desire for honour"; Bonhöffer 120, 314 compares Epict. 2.23.34; H. D. Betz, *Gal.* 294, from Gk. philosophical tradition. Lucian of Samosata, *ver. hist.* 1.4; *dial. mort.* 10.8; 20.4; *Peregr.* 4, 8, and 23; Lucian maintained Peregrinus' desire to immolate himself was out of "love for glory," *Peregr.* 1.22; cf. H. D. Betz, *Lukian von Samosata und das Neue Testament*, TU 76 (Berlin: Akademie-Verlag, 1961) 201 n 5 and 121–22 n 7. V. Wiles 63–64: "false estimation of one's own importance in the community" (by the *episkopoi* and *diakonoi* of 1:1?); B. Weiss (138), some regarded *kenodoxia* as the mother of *eritheia*; others, two synonymous nouns.

2:3b. *Rather, in humiliation, consider one another to surpass yourselves. alla* introduces a new cl.: ptc. *hēgoumenoi* + dir. obj. *allēlous* + suppl. ptc. *(hyperechontas)* + dependent gen. BDAG *alla* 1.a, "but" (KJV-[N]RSV), "rather" (NAB[RNT]); 1:18d, 20, 29, cf. 2:4. At 3b "contrastive" (DA 328), indeed adversative (356).

consider one another to surpass yourselves. Ptc., with the subj. of *phronēte* in 2b *think* and ultimately *give* in 2a *(plērōsate)*. Circumst. or manner, how the Philippians can make Paul's joy full, by regarding one another in a certain way. Any or all of the three ptcs. can be taken as impv. (BDF #468.2; Moule *IB* 179–80; cf. 1:29, Rom 12:6–21 in paraenesis). Most take *hēgoumenoi* as main vb., impv., "count," "regard others" ([N]RSV, NIV); or (3rd per. impv.), "let each esteem" (KJV, NAB). *hēgeomai*, 8x in acknowledged letters, 6x in Phil (2:6, 25; 3:7 and 8 bis) = (BDAG 2) **engage in an intellectual process,** *think, consider, regard* (1 Thess 5:13; 2 Cor 9:5), often + double acc. (Phil 3:7, 8, "regard all these things as loss"). Cf. *TDNT* 2:907–9 (F. Büchsel); *EDNT* 2:113 (T. Schramm). *hēgoumenos*, subst. ptc., "leader," in Gk. political and religious circles (papyrus examples, MM 277), Hellenistic kingdoms, the OT, Luke 3:1, and for Christian leaders (Heb 13:7, 17, 24; cf. 1 Thess 5:12–13; Spicq, *TLNT* 2:166–70 links Phil 2:3, Luke 22:26, and Acts 7:10 to "one who is [or those who are] in some way superior," 166). It hints at issues of leadership and *politeia* in the house churches; cf. V. Wiles 100–2; COMMENT B.3, end. P⁴⁶ D*ᶜ etc., *prohēgoumenoi*, cf. Rom 12:10, "with regard to honor, preferring [or esteeming more highly] one another" (BDF #150; Fee 174).

one another. Acc. (dir. obj.) of the pl. gen. *allēlōn* (no nom. as a reciprocal pron.), **each other, one another, mutually** (BDAG 46). *allos*, "(an) other," doubled, "one (person) to another," cf. Acts 2:12. In the NT, of peer groups; "within a homogeneous group" for "communication with or, sometimes, negative conduct toward each other," of Paul and believers with some frequency, e.g., Rom 1:12. So H. Krämer, *EDNT* 1:63, who adds, "primarily . . . of the (obligatory) conduct of Christians in the community toward each other, with emphasis on mutuality and culminating in the love commandment: *agapan allēlous*" (1 Thess 3:12), but also "love to all persons" (1 Thess 3:12, cf. 5:15; Gal 6:10, as "top priority"). Many trs. bring out the pl. by use of "others" ([N]RSV); some, the individual nature by "one another" (Gdsp., GNB).

hēgeomai + acc.+ infin. (Phil 3:8) or ptc. acc., here *hyperechontas*. ATR 1123, "indirect discourse"; BDF #416.3, "suppl. ptc." after a vb. of perception, cognition, or opinion, really a pred. acc. (*allēlous* is the subject in the double acc.).

surpass. Compound vb., *hyper* + *echō*, **rise above, surpass, excel** (BDAG 1; GNTG 3:52), fig. in the NT for (2) those who are **in a controlling position,** have **power over,** are **in authority, highly placed** (Rom 13:1); (3) **surpass in quality or value, be better than, surpass, excel,** + gen. (Phil 2:3 and 4:7); cf. "surpassing greatness" (neut. ptc.) 3:8 (BDAG). 3 of the 4 Pauline uses are in Phil; + 1 Pet 2:13, "the Emperor as supreme *(hyperechonti).*" All 5 NT vb. uses are participial. Noun, *hyperochē,* 1 Cor 2:1, Paul did not come as a superior person reflecting loftiness *(kath' hyperochēn)* of reason or wisdom; cf. L. Hartman 1974, Paul as "anti-rhetor"; 1 Tim 2:2. G. Delling, *TDNT* 8:523–24, the vb. in classical sources re political or social position (Aristot. *Pol.* 3.13. 1284a.33; Polyb. 28.4.9, "those who rule," etc.). Usually at 2:3, regard others as one's "betters," better than yourselves (BDAG [3]; Louw/Nida 65.4; KJV-[N]RSV). Gdsp., "your superiors." Oakes 2001: 186, "'more important,' rather than . . . 'more virtuous.'"

Before *hyperechontas,* P⁴⁶ and B add *tous,* "those who are better"; Fee 174, "a patently secondary reading" that particularizes ("those who are better") what Paul "leaves open-ended" ("any and all who are better"). V. Wiles 60, the two MSS understood *hyperechontas* as subst., the "governing authorities" (Rom 13:1; 1 Pet 2:13; BDAG 2; B. Weiss 139). Even without the art., "consider one another superiors or leaders of yourselves" (Wiles 60).

Gen. after *hyperechontas* (ZBG 595, of comparison), *heautōn,* from *heautou,* *-ēs, -ou* (no nom., a reflexive pron), here 2nd per., "yourself, -selves" (ZBG #209), or for *allēlōn,* "regarding one another as surpassing one another," ATR 690; GNTG 3:44. Usually "better than yourselves" ([N]RSV; KJV, NAB, "themselves" because of 3rd per. impv. construction).

humiliation. tapeinophrosynē (BDAG **humility, modesty;** 7x in the NT, Col 2:18, 23; 3:12; Eph 4:2; 1 Pet 5:5; Acts 20:19), only here in Paul's acknowledged letters. Phil 2:3 may be "the first extant occurrence" in Gk. literature (V. Wiles 50,

TLG search). The word field includes *tapeinōsis* (LSJ 3, "humiliation, abasement"; Acts 8:38 = Isa 53:8; Jas 1:10; Phil 3:21, see NOTE there; Luke 1:48); vb. *tapeinoō* (4x in the Pauline corpus, 2 Cor and Phil, see NOTES on 2:8, 4:12 *to be brought low*); adj. *tapeinos*, 3x in Paul (Rom 12:16; 2 Cor 7:6; 2 Cor 10:1); plus *tapeinophōn* (adj., "humble," 1 Pet 3:8). 34 NT examples, 9 in Paul's unquestioned letters.

Word studies: W. Grundmann (*TDNT* 8:1–26) drew on Rehrl and Dihle *RAC* 3 (1956) 735–78. H.-H. Esser (*NIDNTT* 2:259–64) drew on Grundmann. H. Giesen (*EDNT* 3:333–35); C. Spicq 1965 1:160–64; *TLNT* 3:369–71. *caveat lector.* "If Dihle begins with Augustine [as the climax of antiquity], Rehrl begins with Thomas Aquinas" (Grundmann 3 n 4). Patristic views of "(the) virtue(s)" can too easily be woven into the NT (Grundmann nn 6, 11). For Rehrl's critique of Dihle, see *TRE* 8:465. Leivestad: Grundmann orients parts A and B of his article around the Gk. word *tapeinos*, but C, D, and E around "Demut" ("humility" in Ger.) as a later concept, bringing in other Gk. terms like *praüs* ("gentle"). Cf. E. A. Schmidt's critical review of Rehrl in *TRev* 61 (1965) 336–40. On Demut in Ger., cf. Melzer. G. E. Mendenhall (*IDB* 2:659–60) gives some place to OT social setting, but the "vast majority" of the NT references refer to "subjective traits of character." W. Klassen (*IDBSup* 422–23) adds "Greek concepts of humiliation" and "humility as a virtue." Catholic and Anabaptist traditions have often stressed "humility."

BDAG: *tapeinophrosynē* "in our lit[erature] only in a favorable sense . . . **humility, modesty**" but "wrongly directed **Col 2:18, 23.**" Contrast Gk. thought: *tapeiophrosynē* was no virtue but a servile characteristic of inferior classes: Epict. 3.24.56 (JR tr.): [54] "Do not go about humbly *(tapeinōs)* . . ." [56] ". . . where is there . . . a place for *tapeinophrosynē?*" (LCL *Epictetus* 2:203; *TDNT* 8:5, "weakness and pusillanimity," in context, "a mean and petty disposition"); Jos. *JW* 4.494 = 4.9.2, *tapeinophrosynē* = meanness. Not an admirable concept. *tapeino-* terms are rare prior to the NT. *tapeinos* "has almost always a bad meaning, 'groveling,' 'abject.'" Aristot., with "servile" (*Eth. Eud.* 3.3, Lft.; cf. 1231b.9 and 19); Plato, with "not free" (*Leg.* 4.774c); Arrian, with "low-born, ignoble" (Epict. 1.3; cf. Aristot. *Eth. Nic.* 4.8 1124b.22). A low social class, "slave" term. But because of use by Jesus—"I am gentle *(praüs)* and humble *(tapeinos)* in heart" (Matt 11:29); "humble like this child" (Matt. 18:4); "all who exalt themselves will be humbled, and those who humble themselves will be exalted" (Luke 14:11)—and then in 1 Pet, Jas, and Paul, Lft. concluded, the "result of the life of Christ" was "to raise 'humility' to its proper level; and, if not fresh coined for this purpose . . . *tapeinophrosynē* . . . becomes current through . . . Christian ethics"; a Christian virtue, in contrast to antiquity's outlook. But "associations with subservience and servile obedience" make the term "suspect today," not least with women and minorities oppressed patriarchally (Wengst 1988:36). Kittredge 72–73, "the rhetoric of obedience" and a "kyriarchal social system" (re *hypakouein*, Phil 2:12, cf. 2:8 *hypēkoos, hypotassesthai*, 3:21, not *tapeinophrosynē*).

For the pre-Christian negative sense, cf. *TDNT* 8:1–5, people or a state "made lowly, e.g., by the military force and superior power of others," a person "cowed by life" (Aristot. *Rhet.* 2:12.1389a.32); from "the aristocratic culture of ancient

Greece" where "the worth of a [hu]man was determined by his parentage. A noble mind and virtue were inherited" (*TDNT* 8:2; cf. Dihle 738 and the slogan "Know thyself"). Philosophers said "virtue can be taught . . . anyone can attain to a high and free disposition," but *tapeinos* remained a negative term, coupled with "shameful, common, what is worst." Epict. had nothing good to say about being *tapeinos*; the Cynic does not engage in "self-disparagement *(tapeinōsis)*" (Epict. 3.22.104). Cf. 3.24.56. In societal settings, living "in relations that are lowly and bad" *(tapeinos prattein, tapeinōs zēn)*; reduced to petitioning the powerful; speak *tapeina,* "eat humble pie" (Eur. Frg. 181 = *TGF* 384); ostracism humiliated the arrogances *(tapeinōsin ta phronēmata)* of the powerful in Athens and Syracuse (Diod. Sic. 11.87; cf. Plut. *Arist.* 7.2). Be "exalted and not servile" *(hypsēlon . . . kai atapeinōton,* Plut. *Quomodo adol.* 9 = *Mor.* 1.28D; 33D = LCL 1:148–49, 174–75). No Oriental groveling before rulers! Avoid the extremes, arrogance and pride on the one hand, servile conduct and flattery on the other; "the mean" lies between them. See *TDNT* 8:3.

The gods loved to humble human pride and exalt what is lowly (Dihle 737–38; Herodot. 7.10, cf. 1.32; 3.40). Call no one who seems successful "happy—till he dies." A general, celebrating a triumph, had a slave whisper, "Remember, you are mortal" (Epict. 3.24.85). Prometheus was told, Be *tapeinos,* humble, toward the gods (Aeschyl. *PV* 320, cf. 908; *TDNT* 8:4). One might change the mind of the gods by humble petition (Statius *Achilleis* 1.144). Plato (*Leg.* 4.716A), be humble *(tapeinos),* governed by laws originating in Justice *(dikē);* contrast insolence *(hybris).* Plut. saw a positive sense: candidates for office "humbling themselves" *(tapeinountes heautous),* canvassing for votes, no tunic with their toga (*Quaest. Rom.* 49 = *Mor.* 276D, LCL 4:80–81).

Exceptions to the negative meaning of *tapeino*-words did occur (Plato, *Leg.* 4.716, above; the only exception, Dihle 742, cf. 754; the Platonists; Lft. 109; Ortwein 77–84). But people should be brought to obedience *(tapeinounta, Lys.* 210E); cf. *Phdr.* 254E, *Tht.* 191A), "obediently to fit into a given order" (*TDNT* 8:5), *tapeinous* towards a ruler (Isoc. *Or.* 3.56) in army, state, or family. Cf. Xen. *Lac.* 8.2; Plut. *Vit. Dion.* 33. Obedience to, and within, the structures, though not humbling or belittling oneself *(to tapeinoun heauton).* W. den Boer overstates the importance of occasional positive senses and examples (Wengst 1988: 72 n 82; cf. 14–15).

This Gk. view was exacerbated in Roman society with its fixed social order and class distinctions (Dihle 742–43). Lat. *humilis* contrasted with *superbia* ("pride"). *humilator* was "the official designation for the little man" in contrast to his lord *(dominus,* Gk. *despotēs),* or *honestor* (OCD³ 723, a social distinction with increasing legal consequences in the Principate period). In the social pyramid, the underling was "my nothingness" or "most worthless slave." This late-classical social order was the foil for Christian teaching on *tapeinophrosynē.* Cf. LSJ *tapeinos* 2, *abased in power, pride;* adv. *be in low estate, speak in a submissive manner; tapeinōsis* 3, *humiliation, abasement* (Diod. Sic. 2.45.2; Polyb. 9.33.10, Philodemus, *Herculensia Volumina* 1457.4, low birth and *tapeinōsis*).

In the LXX, *tapeino*-terms "are much more common than in Gk. and

Hell[enistic] literature," 270x (vb. *tapeinoō* 165x; adj. *tapeinos* 67x; noun *tapeiōsis* 39x; but not *tapeinophrosynē*), esp. in Isa and Pss (*TDNT* 8:6; Esser 260–61; Dihle 743–48, bibl. with W. Zimmerli). For some 20 Heb. terms, among them '*ānāh*/ '*ănāwāh* "afflict," *šapal* "be abased," and *kāna*' hitpael, "bring low, humble"; cf. Mendenhall; E. Kutsch *RGG*³ 2:77–78; *TDNT* 8:6 nn 14–15. Senses include (a) "humble (someone)," Prov 10:4 LXX; rape a woman, 2 Kgdms = 2 Sam 13:12,14. (b) "Harass, oppress," Gen 15:13; Ps 105 (Heb 106):42b, 43b. (c) "Humble, abase oneself, cast oneself down," Gen 16:9 LXX, "be humbled under her hands"; Prov 22:4, "humility" + "fear of the Lord"; 13:7; 25:7 (cf. Luke 14:7–11, social-economic connotations). Often "humble your souls" (before God) = "fast" (Lev 16:29, 31, etc.; Isa 58:3, 5. Ps 34 [Heb 35]:13–14). (d) *God* is the subject in many OT passages, "The Lord brings low (*tapeinoi*) and lifts up" (1 Kgdms = 1 Sam 2:7). God can humble Israel's enemies; or Israel, Zion, Jerusalem; or individuals. But abasement can lead to salvation; "I was brought low (*etapeinōthēn*), and (the Lord) saved me" (Ps 114 [Heb 116]:6, cf. Ps 17:28 [Heb 18:27]; 118 [Heb 119]:71, 75). Esp. those oppressed by foreign powers (Jdt 16:11; 1 Macc 14:14) or by the rich (Amos 2:7; Isa 58:4). "You will save your humbled people and humble the eyes of the proud" (Ps 17:28 [Heb 18:27]). Yahweh is "the God of the lowly" (*tapeinōn*, Jdt 9:11), who says "on that day" of judgment "I shall leave in you a people humble and lowly (*praün kai tapeinon*, Zeph 3:11,12)." "The Lord is near (*engus kyrios*) [cf. Phil 4:5] to those crushed in heart, and those humble (*tapeinous*) in heart he will save" (Ps 33:19 [Heb 34:18]). 2 Isa stressed during the Exile that God "comforted the lowly (*tous tapeinous*) of his people" (49:13; cf. 54:11; 66:2). 53:8 LXX, "In his humiliation (*tapeinōsis*, the Servant of the Lord) his judgment was taken away" (cf. *TDNT* 8:11; Phil 2:8, Christ "humbled himself," must not be read in). H. D. Preuss: eliminate the Servant and Abraham (Gen 18; Gideon, Judg 6; Jer 1), no Heb. equivalent (*TRE* 8:460). Moses was "very humble" (Num 12:3), but lowly in what? spirit, in society, economically? putting Miriam and Aaron above himself (Dawes 1991b)? submissive to God (Dickson/Rosner)?

Esser 260 procedes by canonical genre; Dihle 744–45, the exilic prophets, wisdom, and Pss ('*ănawîm* circles). Leivestad, *tapeinos* is negative, *tapeinos en kardia[i]* proper, later expressed by *tapeinophrosynē*. Dickson/Rosner, God's people are humiliated but favor is extended to them; hence their submission to God ("theological humility"), not a social virtue of lowering oneself before an equal. Zech 9:9, your king "humble" ('*āni*; AB 25C:127–28) is political humility; he rides for peace, not warfare (Dickson/Rosner). Mathys (*RGG*⁴) 654, a "small and semantically diffuse OT base," never the noun *tapeinophrosynē*. No examples of Yahweh humbling self. Grundmann 11–12 explains the "different estimation" of the word group in Gk. literature (usually negative) "and in the Bible" ("positive") by a "different understanding of man"; "[i]n Israel and post-exilic Judaism, man controlled by God's action." Or is it (also) a different concept of God?

Mendenhall 659, OT "lowliness" is a way of acting toward God; rejection of "pride, arrogance, and violence" is part of Israel's rejection of "aristocratic stratification" in society. The Exodus taught that Yahweh "delivers the humble, but brings down the haughty." The "humble" were originally the poor or afflicted, but later humility was "separated from socio-economic connotations to refer to subjective traits of character," as in the NT (so Mendenhall). Dawes 1991b saw humility as a social virtue in the Heb. Bible, esp. in Sir and Qumran (1QS); the virtue did not, then, arise with Jesus and early Christianity. But his OT examples point to "theological," not "social sins" (Zeph 2:3; Prov 15:33, 18:12, 22:4; Ps 18:35, NRSV "help," act of divine condescension); Ps 45:4, truth, lowliness, righteousness = God-fearing devotion to the right); so Dickson/Rosner. Sir presents humility *(praotēs)* as a theological virtue (in 1:27; 3:17–20; 4:8; 7:16; 10:28–31), but in a social context; the advice to "humble self" *(tapeioō)* begins to appear (3:18; 4:7, "before the city's ruler bow your head," or aristocracy in the synagogue, AB 39:163, 167, cf. 12–13; 7:16; 13:20 *tapeinotēs)*. Advice to show deference seems to reflect the Gk. world.

For Qumran, God = the One who is with the humiliated ('*ănawîm*, 1QH 5.20–22 = 13.20–22, p. 338 in García Martínez), "the poor" ('*ĕbyônîm*), "lowly, afflicted" ('*ănawîm)*, dependent on God's mercy, faithful to the covenant, Torah-observant. Hence, "proper or virtuous humility" (1QS 2.24 '*anĕwat tôb*) in the hierarchical community (Dickson/Rosner, contra Dawes 1991b:39–40, who stresses equality), with "a spirit of humility" (4.3; cf. 5.3, 25). Cf. 1QS 9. 22–23 (García Martínez, p. 14, "like a servant to his master, and like one oppressed before someone domineering him") and 11.1–2 (p. 17, "reply with meekness to the haughty of spirit"—feigned civility, covering hatred? *TDNT* 8:12). In 1QH 5.13–18 = 13.13–18, p. 337, the Teacher of Righteousness evidently presents himself as God's servant, poor and lowly. Humbling self before God likewise appears in *T. 12 Patr.* and apocalyptic passages like 2 Esd (= 4 Ezra) 8:47–54 ("because you have humbled yourself," a future paradise will follow, v 49). Cf. *TDNT* 8:12–13; *NIDNTT* 2:261; *TRE* 8:462 (Awerbuch); Wengst 1988:33–35; V. Wiles 58 n 73.

The rabbis (post-NT) gave an important place to humility, the greatest of all virtues (b. '*Abod. Zar.* 20b), in contrast to Gentile pride (Str-B 1:191–94, esp. 194; *TDNT* 8:13–14; *NIDNTT* 2:261; Reeg *RGG*⁴). One of 48 ways by which knowledge of Torah is acquired (*PAbot* 6.5). Keeping Torah, in turn, leads to humility (b. *Erub.* 54a; '*Abot R. Nat.* 11). God humbles pride (b. *Erub* 13b; Grundmann 13–14). Awerbuch 463 calls attention to passages where God engages in humility. In Hellenistic Judaism, a positive view appears in the *Let. Aris.* 257, 262–63; *OTP* 2:29–30. Jos. used *tapeino*-words "negatively like the G[ree]ks." Philo (Grundmann 14–15) kept "biblical insights" along with "the Gk. sense." *Post.* 46–48 = LCL: 2:352–55 contrasts two kinds of *tapeinōsis*: one produces "dire humiliation" (*Her.* 268 = LCL 4:420–21, cf. Gen 15:13); the other, "noble humiliation" (Gen 16:9, Hagar; *Fug.* 207 = LCL 5: 122–23); "humbling our souls," is enjoined on the Day of Atonement (Lev 23:27), abasement before God in prayer. Dihle 747–48 counts as "positive" only *Fug.* 207 and *Sacr.* 62 (LCL 2:140–41). Not in Philo's virtue lists.

Usually the negative sense of *tapeino*-words in the Gk. world is contrasted with a positive evaluation in OT and NT. The humility of Jesus is seen in what he taught (Matt 23:12; Luke 14:11, 18:14; Matt 18:4); his attitude (Matt 11:29) and actions (John 13, washing the disciples' feet), above all in death (Phil 2:6–11).

Such humility Christians are to exhibit; Phil 2:3 becomes the "locus classicus." So Dihle 749; Rehrl *TRE* 8:464–65; V. Wiles 46–49. The OT played a role through use of Prov 3:34 LXX at Jas 4:6 and 1 Pet 5:5, "God . . . gives grace to the humble." "Humble yourselves before the Lord, and he will exalt you" (Jas 4:10; cf. 1 Pet 5:6; *TDNT* 8:18–19; Luke 1:52, cf. 1 Sam 2:7–8; Sir 10:14; Job 5:11, 12:19; Ezek 21:31 LXX). Be "humble of mind" (*tapeinophaones*, 1 Pet 3:8).

But evidence is not as impressive as appears. The Jesus-references are not from Q or Mark but L or Lukan redaction (14:11; 18:14), M or Matthean redaction (18:4; 23:12). The foot-washing scene does not employ *tapeino*-language (John's Gospel never does). Likewise the "pattern of existence," "humiliation/exaltation," argued as a link between (the historical) Jesus and post-Easter Christology in Phil 2:6–11; J. M. Robinson, "The Formal Structure of Jesus' Message," in *Current Issues in New Testament Interpretation*, FS O. Piper, ed. W. Klassen/G. Snyder (New York: Harper, 1962) 91–100.

Paul was accused of being "humble" (servile, ineffectual, inferior) when face to face, but "bold" when absent (2 Cor 10:1, typically Hellenistic). Paul argues, ironically, he humbles himself that the Corinthians may be exalted (2 Cor 11:7). But he fears fresh humiliation — from God — when he comes to Corinth (12:21). Rom 12:16, not haughty but associate with the lowly (solidarity with the insignificant), reflects OT thought, though the Gk. world also counseled not to vaunt oneself above the crowd. Jas 1:9–10 reflects a social sense, "the believer who is lowly . . . raised up, the rich (believer?) brought low." Cf. *TDNT* 8:17–18, 19–20, 21; *NIDNTT* 2:263; Col 2:18, 23 show an "original derogatory sense," but Giesen 334 takes them positively.

Many Gk. (and LXX) uses of *tapeino*-words cited above reflect a political and social-class setting. Hence Friedrich (on 2:3 in NTD p. 149) and Merk 1968:177–78 (cf. Witherington 63) call attention to the stratification of society. *tapeinophrosynē* does not yet belong to the NT paraenetic tradition but reflects "the concrete situation" in Philippi (Merk 177; U. B. Müller 87), people treated according to their rank in Roman society (Dihle 742–43). Paul argues that, within the church community, believers are not to be disqualified or humiliated by society's valuations of "inferiors" ("no self-interest or vainglory" among themselves, as in that world), but regarded, contrariwise, as one's equal or better. Similarly Mengel 244–45. Dangers in the world's social structures *(politeia)* in Philippi may thus account for the term *tapeinophrosynē*, humiliation.

Wengst (1988, cf. 1986) applied this social-world understanding. In the Greco-Roman setting the terms imply lowly origins for individuals or groups, a lowly disposition expressed often in flattery of others (or insubordination) by insignificant nobodies. Most of the people in that day were from "lower classes," *humiliores* (Wengst pp. 4–8; Alföldy 1988:106, 109). Lowly occupations make one unfit for social position, education, or developing a higher disposition. The way out was upward social mobility. Education or a military career might unlock doors (Ael. Aristid., *Eulogy of Rome* 85). Urban house slaves might hope to be freed at age 30; any child thereafter was freeborn (Wengst 9, but n 36, Alföldy 1988:41 overstates). For those well-born, fate might inflict misfortunes, but the "high-souled" person

will not necessarily fall into the lowly disposition of abject humility. Stoic philosophy (Sen., Epict., cf. 3.24.56), taught how the high-minded person, internalizing
life, could remain free of such "humility," even in adversity (pp. 12–14).

The OT-Jewish tradition likewise knew poverty and humiliation, but its texts
speak from the perspective of the downtrodden, against violence, and of God as
one who reverses such conditions (Wengst 1988:16–35). Cf. Amos 2:6–7, 5:12 the
righteous = the needy, oppressed; Zeph 2:3, 3:11b–13 those oppressed seek righteousness; Ps 37:11–17 "the meek shall inherit the land"; *1 En.* 94:6–104:13, "We
hoped to be the head and have become the tail," Nietzsche's "inversion of values."
But only Zeph 2:3 uses 'ănāwāh, too easily conflated with ' *ᵉbyon* (Dawes 1991a),
and 'ānaw with 'ānî. This reading sees God, through Jesus, in Matt 11:28–30,
identifying in solidarity with those who toil and carry heavy burdens (not Torah),
i.e., the lowest class of manual laborers (Wengst 36–42; people who "suffer under
the violent use of power"; L. Schottroff/W. Stegemann, *Jesus von Nazareth —
Hoffnung der Armen* [Stuttgart: Kohlhammer, 1978] 161–62). That Jesus is *praüs*
and *tapeinos* reflects LXX renderings (Zeph 3:12; cf. Isa 26:6 LXX; Wengst 39);
Jesus promises "rest" (cf. Jer 6:16; Matt 18:4 and 23:11, humbleness and exaltation); an "anti-hierarchical tendency" in a community of "brothers and sisters."
Luke 14:11 and 18:14 reflect pragmatic wisdom for individuals (p. 41). Mary's
Magnificat (1:48 esp.) is a paradigm for how God exalts the humble and casts
down mighty rulers (esp. v 52). Jas (1:9–11; 2:5; 4:6; 5:1–6) deals with reversal for
rich and poor.

Paul is influenced by Gk. as well as OT-Jewish understandings (Wengst 45–53
= 1986:428–39). (a) 2 Cor 10:1, Paul criticized as "servile." He replies (2 Cor
12:7b–10, 20–21), Weakness and abasement are ultimately from God who provides power from Christ to endure. Cf. 7:6, "God who comforts the downcast (Isa
49:13) has comforted us." (b) As matter of principle, he abased self in order to exalt
his hearers, working with his hands to preach the gospel free of charge to converts
(2 Cor 11:7); on 11:8, accepting support from ("robbing") other churches
(Philippi), see Phil 4:10–20, below. Yet (c) "Paul does not invite the better-off
Christians in his community to imitate his way of living" (47 = 432), which is a
matter of *apostolic* existence. His paraenesis urges *tapeinophrosynē* and "solidarity
with the insignificant" (Rom 12:16). Phil 2:3, to the community: Put "one's own
person 'below' that of the other," exactly the reverse of "upward social mobility"
in the society of the early Empire (1986:434–35 draws in more from Alföldy
83–138 [1988:94–156; chart on "Orders-Strata Structure," p. 146] than does
1988:50).

Deutero-Pauline texts make *tapeinophrosynē* a virtue (Col 3:12 influences
Eph 4:1–3). 1 Pet 5:5b–6 puts "reciprocal humility into a hierarchical structure" (Wengst 52–53; AB 37B:849 "acceptance of one's social position"). Humility as "obedient submission to a hierarchical order" becomes *de rigueur* in
1 Clem (2:1; 13:1–19:1; 30:1–8; 56:1, "submit . . ."; 63.1). " 'Humility' . . . serve[s]
the development and establishment of hierarchical structures" (57) in patristic usage; *PGL* 1347, *tapeinophrosynē*, the "fundamental virtue," attainable by
degrees.

V. Wiles (50–70) worked along similar lines, without Wengst's analysis: "Paul's use of the *tapeinos* word-group nowhere intimates that he considers *tapeinos* a virtue" (*praütēs* is his word for that, 57). The terms describe "negative social circumstances or experiences" (51). The Philippians likely heard *tapeinophrosynē* as "humiliation" (56–59). He meant it to refer to their "earthly condition," including suffering (cf. 1:28–30); not a contrast to *eritheia* and *kenodoxia* but the situation of the Philippians as they seek to work out governance among themselves (1:27).

Most trs. take *tapeinophrosynē[i]* as dat. of manner, "in humility" ([N]RSV), or an adverb ("humbly," NEB/REB), or as impv. ("be humble," GNB). The art. is used "possessively, '*your* lowliness' (Lightf[oot])" (Vincent 56); "the well-known humiliation that you experience."

tapeinophrosynē = social-world humiliation that Philippian Christians experienced in daily life from their "betters" in Roman social structures. It also fits in the church community: "Consider (as Christians) one another (in the community) to surpass yourselves"; humiliate self before them, even though you are superior in the world's structures. To tr. *in humiliation* is literal. No indication of humility *before* God or humiliation imposed *by* God.

2:4a. *regarding. skopountes,* circumst. ptc. *skopeō,* **look (out) for, notice, keep one's eyes on.** Vb. 5x in Paul's acknowledged letters, usually admonitory: Phil 3:17, "observe" (in a good sense); Rom 16:17 "keep an eye on those who cause dissensions"; 2 Cor 4:18; Gal 6:1; Luke 11:35. Noun *skopos,* only at Phil 3:14; see NOTE on *goal.* Cf. *kataskopeō* (Gal 2:4 "spy on"), *episkopeō,* "oversee" (NOTE on 1:1 *overseers;* V. Wiles 64 n 94 senses wordplay at Phil 2:4 with 1:1). Classical Gk. *skopeō* came to mean "look critically," as a judge might (Plato *Leg.* 11.925A), a philosopher (Plato *Cra.* 440D), the historian (Thuc. 1.1.3), to discover a propitious time (Thuc. 4.23.2), avoid danger (Aristoph. *Thesm.* 580–81), or accomplish a purpose (Aristoph. *Eq.* 80–81). LXX use is minimal (Gk. *Additions to Esther* 8:12g, ed. Rahlfs 1:968 = NRSV Addition E, 16:7, "can be seen"; 2 Macc 4:5). Cf. E. Fuchs, *TDNT* 7:414–16; *EDNT* 3:255; Louw/Nida 27.36; pres. tense, repeated action, "be continually concerned." Baumert 1973:137: "strive for." Most trs. take it as impv. (BDF #468.2; Moule *IB* 179–80; Lft. 110) or read *skopeite* impv. (not in UBSGNT, *TCGNT;* L ψ Majority Text; KJV "Look . . . !"); K etc., 3rd sg. impv. *skopeitō,* [N]RSV "Let each of you look. . . ." NABRNT ptc., "each looking out. . . ." In the TRANSLATION, *regarding* goes with *consider* (3b); is distinguished from *hēgeomai* (3b, 6); avoids the ambiguity of "look out (for)."

not your own interests. mē (with ptc.) + the first of two dir. objs., *ta heautōn,* "the (neut. pl.) things of (your)selves." For *ta,* see *ho, hē, to,* BDAG 2.g, + gen., to show "a relation of kinship, ownership, or dependence," to someone's advantage; also at 2:21. On the masc. gen. pl. of *heautou,* see NOTE on 2:3 *consider one another to surpass yourselves,* just three words prior in Gk. A prohibition (*DA* 398). For *skopein ta* + gen., cf. Herodot. 1.8 (Ionic spelling), "see what is our own"; Plato *Phdr.* 232D; Thuc. 6.12.2, "his own interest." Neut. pl. (KJV "things"), commonly glossed in Eng. as "interests" [N]RSV, etc.); NJB "selfish interests"; LB "your own affairs; V. Wiles 64 n 96 "your own group." Textual problems enter with *each* (of you) and [*kai*].

each. Sg. or pl. (MSS vary), *hekastos, ē, on,* "each, every," twice in 2:4. Adj. (Luke 6:44 "every tree"), used substantively, of persons (1 Cor 7:7, etc.). Pl. obsolete by NT times (BDF #64.6); in the NT, here and Rev 6:11TR. Earlier instances, Polyb. 1.12.9 (CD-Rom search, 1.7.4.4; etc.; over 80 examples); Diod. Sic. 14.5.4, plus 1.48.3, etc., all dat. pl.; Lucian *Herm.* 68 (plus 26.15, etc.); some authors used the pl. with frequency. Not theologically significant enough to merit wordbook articles, except *EDNT* 1:403–4 (F. G. Untergassmair): = "individual parts of a whole," in comparison with *pas,* "every" (Matt 3:10 par Luke 3:9, "any" [tree], BDF #275.3). *hekastos* suggests not "generality and universality" but "involvement . . . of *each individual,*" making admonitions "more direct and personal" (404), as at 2:4, or in speaking of (spiritual) gifts. Cf. Rom 14:5; Rom 15:2; 1 Cor 3:10, 13; Rom 2:6; 14:12. "Paul addresses everyone in his churches, and with the aid of *hekastos* each is addressed individually."

Text variants: the first *hekastos* is supported by P⁴⁶ ℵ C Majority Text, etc.; but *hekastoi* in A B F G, etc.; Nestle²⁵. Edart 116 n 3, scribal correction. UBSGNT, the sg. is the harder reading (*TCGNT* 612). Fee 175 n 6 argues for "the more difficult plural"; ATR 292, 764, pl. "probably twice" at 2:4. Sg. or pl., the effect is to individualize, every single believer in the Philippian house churches. Hence, *each,* between (in Gk.) *your own* (pl.) *interests* and you (pl.) *regarding.*

2:4b. *each of you.* At the end of 2:4b, NA²⁵,²⁷ UBSGNT have *hekastoi,* {B} level of certainty (P⁴⁶ ℵ A B Dᵍʳ etc.). Sg. *hekastos* in C K Majority Text, etc. (see UBSGNT). MSS F G, etc. omit both (as superfluous). J. D. Price 278 gives *hekastoi* a probability of 0.45; *hekastos,* 0.31; and omission of both, 0.24. Pl. can go with v 5, "(you pl.) each think this. . . ."; so ℵ A etc. (Lft. 110). Fee 175 n 6, against most eds., prefers *hekastoi* each time, so that the pls. balance "the two halves of v. 4." A pl. is hard to express in Eng (Lft. 110, "each *and all*"; NIV "each of you"). Trs. often omit *hekast-* at the end of v 4 (but cf. JB, "nobody . . . everybody") or the beginning of v 5.

those of other persons. Second dir. obj., contrasting with *ta heautōn,* "your own interests," *ta heterōn,* neut. pl. art., "the (interests)," + gen. pl., *heteros, a, on,* "other," BDAG 1.b.ε, more than two; *one's neighbor,* Gal 6:4; Rom 2:1; 13:8; etc.; without the art., Rom 2:21, as here. (MSS D* F G add *tōn* before *heterōn,* correctly; BDF #306.2, GNTG 3:197.) *Mart. Pol.* 1.2 paraphrases Phil 2:4, "not regarding only that which concerns ourselves but also that which concerns the neighbor" (*to kata tou pelas;* adv. *pelas,* "near," = "the near one" or neighbor). Adv. *heterōs,* Phil 3:15. Cf. *TDNT* 2:702–4 (H. W. Beyer); *NIDNTT* 2:739–42 (F. Selter/C. Brown); *EDNT* 2:65–66, K. Haacker, an "abstract concept of the neighbor" at 2:4, but "uncertain" because of the text problem with *kai* (see below). The pl. = other believers in Philippi, perhaps groups of them, or factions. Most trs. (KJV-NRSV) use "others"; JB, "other people's interests." The TRANSLATION *other persons* is open to several interpretations.

but (also). kai after *alla* = "also"; textually disputed; NA²⁷ brackets. Read in P⁴⁶ ℵ A B C D² the Majority text etc., lacking in "Western" witnesses (D*ᶜ F G K, etc.). O'B 164, scribes omitted *kai* "to make the clause consistent with the absolute negation of the first clause," i.e., "not your own concerns . . . but those of others."

Silva 104 "accidental" omission; on the basis of "but also" he supplies, "not [only]" in the first part of the v.; but scribes may have added *kai* lest the injunction not "to look out for one's own interests" sound "too strong." In contrast, Martin 1976:90 rejected "only" in RSV and *kai* in favor of "look not to his own interests but to the interests of others"; Paul corrects "self-centered preoccupations of a perfectionist group in Philippi (cf. 3:12–16)." Witherington 64, "a mollifying addition." If read, *kai* suggests addition rather than contrast (*DA* 327; BDAG *kai* 2 *also, likewise; alla* 3 *but, also,* unless *kai* strengthens the contrast, "but indeed"). Walter 53 keeps *kai* and emphasizes "one's own" and "that of others" coming to fruition together, harmoniously. O'B 164, 185, *kai* softens the contrast. Bockmuehl 113–14, *alla kai* = "but actually, but rather" (cf. LXX Job 21:17; Isa 39:4; 48:6; Ezek 18:11; Wis 14:22). Decision involves MS evidence, situation addressed, and Paul's view of self-interest.

The TRANSLATION, with NRSV, omits *kai* (most Eng. versions, KJV-RSV, include *also*). JB, "so that nobody thinks of his own interests first but everybody thinks of other people's interests instead"; NJB, "not selfish interests but those of others"; and NRSV, "look not to your own interests, but to the interests of others." See COMMENT B. After *alla*, supply *skopountes*, as in 4a.

COMMENT

Ethical paraenesis begun at 1:27–30 continues with four grounds in 2:1 for an appeal in v 2 to *give* Paul *further joy* in at least four ways. V 3 addresses typically Gk. traits, *self-interest* and *glory*-seeking (interior attitude, Edart 129). V 4 (exterior attitude) is advice for Christians about others. 2:5–11 often overshadows 2:1–4, in part through vocabulary links (*vainglory* v 3a **kenodoxian** and **ekenōsen** v 7; *humiliation* 3b **tapeinophrosynē** and **etapeinōsen** v 8), in part because "imitation of Christ" is assumed. But "(be) imitators" does not occur till 3:17, and then imitate Paul and colleagues, not Christ. Emphasis on unity in v 2 has often been attributed to squabbles in Philippi, esp. between Euodia and Syntyche (4:2–3; Gnilka 105; Peterlin), but they are not mentioned in 2:1–4. Much depends on how the situation is reconstructed (*DA* 414 n 25).

2:1–4 is marked off by *oun* (*then; DA* 217, 266) and four conditional cls. ("*If . . .*") in v 1, "a modest new start" (Holmstrand 102). The conclusion of the unit is less clear. Impvs. continue in 2:5 and 12–18. Holmstrand treats 2:1–11 together, but 2:12 draws on 2:6–11 for its exhortation, "Work out your own *salvation.*" Most take 2:1–4 as a unit.

A. FORMS, SOURCES, AND TRADITIONS

1. Literary Features. See Edart 115–18; these include *alliteration* (2:3 *heautōn,* 4 *heautōn hekastos . . . heterōn hekastoi,* Black 1985:303; O'B 166); repetition or *anaphora* (BDF #489, parallelism; cf. #491, #464; O'B 165; J. W. Marshall 368)

2:1, *tis . . . ti . . . tis . . . tis* (MS variations); *asyndeton* (Holmstrand 102; cf. BDF #454.3; 460.2, 494) no connective "and"; *assonance* (O'B 166) *phronein* (2:1) 2x + *tapeinophrosynē* (3b *humiliation*); *homoioteleuton*, same ending (Black 303; O'B 165) v 2 *(echontes, phronontes),* v 3 *(eritheian, kenodoxian)*; *homoioarchton* (same prefix), 2:1 *paraklēsis* and *paramythion.* Chiasm in v 2bcd (Schenk 178; cf. Peterlin 59; Black 1985; see 3, below):

$$
\begin{array}{ll}
\textit{to auto phronete} & \textit{tēn autēn agapēn echontes} \\
\textit{sympsychoi} & \textit{to hen phronountes}
\end{array}
$$

Macro-chiasm theories are contradictory.[1] Rhetorically, 2:1–4, usually analyzed as part of a larger unit, is an *exhortatio* (impv. in 2:2; Bloomquist, 1:27–2:18; Holloway 2001a:163, 2:1–4, 12–18).[2]

2. An Adjuration Form? The *if*-cls. in 2:1 have been taken as an "adjuration"[3]: "By the existence of such graces among you . . . I adjure you that you fulfill my joy" (Eadie 83). Such an appeal brings pressure (Loh. 84). Schenk 173 n 50 calls the term "text-pragmatically false"; the four items are causal, indics. leading to the impvs. ("since . . . , so . . ."). Paul believes his readers agree on the points (Mengel 242). He speaks not as an authority *(amtlich)* but as a brother (Eichholz 1962 [(2) Bibl.] 151, cf. 1:7–8). Probably rightly, "adjure" has fallen into disuse here.

3. Strophic Structure? As with 1:27–30 ([5] COMMENT A.1), Loh. 80 arranged 2:1–4 into 5 three-liners[4]; Collange 77 n 1 and G. Barth 39 reject it. Gnilka found three stanzas (4, 4, 6 lines); Black 1985:300–1, chiastic structure, Stanza III four lines; Stanzas I and III, "based on an OT pattern (parallelism), the second strophe on a Greek one (chiasmus)" (303). They state (I) the grounds for, (II) results of, and (III) expressions of Christian unity. Black 1995:36 modified his structure and concluded 2:1–4 existed "independent of and antecedent to the rest of the epistle" (1985:306; by Paul, "equally applicable to the church in Rome" during his imprisonment there). O'B 1991:164–65 and Witherington 60 followed Black 1985. Silva 1988:99–100, "parallelism" and "strophe quality" akin to Black 1985. Differently for 2:2–4, Heriban ([7] Bibl.) 185. Fee 177 n 15 questions such "literary schemes" ("fails to take seriously either the oral nature of the text . . . or the actual

---

[1] See INTRO. VI.B n 3. Wick 47 parallels 2:1–4 with 4:1–3 *(joy* 2:2a, 4:1; *to auto phronein,* 2:2b, 4:2; *agapē* 2:1, *agapētoi,* 4:1). Luter/Lee match 1:27–2:4 with 4:1–5; C. W. Davis, 1:27–2:18 with 3:1–4:9. Doubts on most macro-chiastic proposals were reinforced by Porter/Reed 1998. For Aspen (1:27–2:5 with 2:12–18), see (5) COMMENT A.1.

[2] See INTRO. VI.B n 2. Some separate 2:1–4 from 1:27–30 as a *probatio* (2:1–3:21, D. F. Watson 1988b; Geoffrion; 2:1–30, Black 1995; 2:1–4:3, Witherington). Watson 68–69 and Edart 117 see *regressio,* reiterating "things that have already been said" and making "distinctions between them" (cf. Quint. 9.3.35–37); Watson's *topoi* from 1:3–26 include in 2:1–4 *agapē, koinōnia, chara,* and *phronein.* Geoffrion 184, 2:1–4 "flows directly from the *narratio*" (1:27–30, with its *propositio* and *ratio)*; 2:1–11 is first development or "proof" (arguments + examples to persuade).

[3] Mengel 242 n 81 *Beschwörung;* Haupt 51; Loh. 84; Michael 74; Gnilka 103, 105, with Euodia and Syntyche in view, 4:2; E. F. Scott 42; noted by O'B 167 n 19; U. B. Müller 81.

[4] Space does not permit reconstructing his Gk. or analysis of his stanzas here.

syntax of the sentence"); the four "if" cls. are protasis, 2a is apodosis ("fulfill my joy"); 2b, explanation ("so that you set your minds on the same thing"); the rest, elaboration (Schenk stresses 2:5 also). Bockmuehl 104 echoes Fee: 2:1–4, no strophes. Schenk 172–78, elevated prose, rhetorically stylized; Loh.'s five three-liners are forced. Strophe structures, let alone a "source," are not convincing for 2:1–4 (with Söding 1995 [(2) Bibl. **love**] 173 n 49).

B. MEANING AND INTERPRETATION

2:1 asserts "indicatives" (what Paul and the Philippians share *in Christ*) as foundation for the advice in 2:2–4 ("indic./impv."; [5] COMMENT A.1). 1:27a, *Exercise your citizenship*, stands over all of 1:27–2:18. Admonitions like 27cd, *stand steadfast in one and the same Spirit . . . with one soul*, echo in 2:2. Not recognizably military language (Krentz 2003:356 offers no real evidence), but political and ecclesial notes are heard. The "dual alliance" (1:27–30) continues: Philippian Christians are citizens, residents, or slaves in a Roman *colōnia* as well as members — their new status — of the *politeia* of heaven, with church structures of their own. For the relation of Christians to the Imperial *politeia*, see B.3 end. 1:27–30 is said to deal with relations "outside," the world and *adversaries* (28a); 2:1–4, "inside" the church community (Gnilka 103, Martin 1976:85; O'B 164, contrast Collange 77). Actually, both internal and external relations are involved in 2:1–4. Conditions in Philippi shape 2:1–4.

Artful rhetoric. In 2:1 Paul may be "casting about for any and every kind of . . . Christian experience to which he may appeal" (Beare 70) and v 3 "begins to get away from him" (Fee 186), but there is structure: four grounds for appeal in v 1, four ways of expressing the unity desired (2bcd), then a pattern "*not . . . rather/but . . .*" (vv 3–4). Paraenesis is often "unsystematic" (Loh. 86). Rhetorically 2:1 provides reasons *(ratio)* for what is enjoined *(exhortatio, 2:1–5, 12–18)*.

Inventio: from Philippian Christians may have come the *phronein* language (Schenk 184; see NOTES on 4:10 *your concern for me* in Letter A, and 1:7 *to think*) and *tapeinophrosynē*, 2:3b "thinking in a humble or humiliated fashion" (cf. 2:8 *etapeinōsen* in their "hymn").[5] No scriptural language, unless *splanchna* and *oiktirmoi* in 1d. *sympsychoi* (2:2c), *eritheia* and *kenodoxia* (3a), and *auto* and *hen* reflect the Greco-Roman world (see NOTES). In 2:1, *paraklēsis* and *paramythion* might stem from Pauline paraenesis (1 Thess 2:12; 5:14; 1 Cor 14:3, though regularly with some third term).

The situation: Paul, in prison, faces death (1:20–23; 2:17), but speaks of release (1:19, 25; 2:24). He has made an appeal on the basis of his Roman citizenship and hopes to be set free in Ephesus, to come to Philippi. The believers in Philippi face

---

[5] If *tapeinophrosynē* appears here for the first time in Gk. literature, it is Paul's creation in light of *etapeinōsen heauton* at 2:8 ("he experienced humiliation on his part," in the Philippians' encomium), *tapeino-* + *phronein* that runs through Phil. There is no prior history of *tapeinophrynosynē* to which one can appeal. The NOTE on *humiliation* and B. 3 below emphasize social-world setting, not later development of "humility" as a Christian virtue.

the same contest as Paul (1:30) with *adversaries* there, local Roman authorities (not "the rival preachers" of 1:14–18, or the "enemies of the cross" in 3:2–21, Letter C). Some make the women at 4:2–3, Euodia and Syntyche, the troublemakers behind disunity perceived in 2:1–4 (so Fee 187, among others), but the text never says that. Philippi is "a healthy church" (Silva 102), "no severity of censure" in 2:1–4, no "divisions or dissension" at "an acute stage" (O'B 167; cf. Michael 74; Bruce 37). Not Galatia or the Corinth of even 1 Cor. (Schenk 181, Bockmuehl 108).

Most outlines for 2:1–4 stress "unity" (+ "humility" as the means to achieve it).[6] Better (Schenk), "Guidelines for the Congregation," 1:27–2:18. No mere "curtain raiser" for 2:5–11, 2:1–4 reflect experiences and concerns among the Philippians (Beare 72; Silva 102).

2:1–4 (Letter B) will be treated in terms of (1) basic experiences of Philippian Christians (2:1) for (2) providing Paul joy through their unitedness (v 2), (3) each and every individual and group rejecting their own interests and glory for the sake of others, in the face of proud egotism and the class humiliation that marked society of the day (vv 3–4). Then (4) 2:1–4 in the four-ch. letter.

1. The Bases in Philippian Experience "in Christ" for Ecclesial "Citizenship Worthy of the Gospel" (2:1).

Four grounds for the appeal in vv 2–4 are presented in compound phrases—*paraklēsis* in Christ, *paramythion* of love, *koinōnia* of Spirit (or spirit), affection and mercies—each introduced by *if*, each with some form of the indefinite pron. *tis, ti* (see NOTE on *something* and the textual problem). *"if* a (b, c, and d) *amount to something,* then. . . ." Paul assumes each item exists significantly among Philippian believers, but each has an ambiguity that makes a precise rendering almost impossible. It is unclear (Hawth. 65), "Who is doing what to whom?" No tr. can convey all Paul likely meant or the Philippians heard in this protasis leading to the conclusion or apodosis in v 2. The *if* construction amounts to "since" (Martin 1976:86; Hawth. 64; Bockmuehl 104; Schenk 173–74, 185, causal). Not "I adjure you" (A.2, above), but *as we assume,* for these correct presuppositions (Fee 177).

then (Gk. *oun*) harks back to 1:27, *Exercise your citizenship.* . . . A minor shift, but not "a completely new start" (K. Barth 51, who regards 2:1–11 as an excursus on *stand steadfast* in 1:27c). On 2:2 paralleling 1:27 (Schenk 174), see below. *oun* is resumptive (BDF #451.1; BDR 451.1, n 2); *epanalepsis* (it takes up a main thought after parenthetical remarks, as at 1 Cor 8:4 and 11:20). Then 1:30 is parenthetical (*suffering* and the *contest* in which Paul and the Philippians are engaged, Schenk 173, against Walter 1977). Paul returns to the crucial matter, togetherness, one in soul.

The four *if*-cls. in v 1 lack vbs. Some propose (see NOTE on *something*), "If there is to be exhortation, let it be in Christ," etc.; the Philippians agree on *paraklēsis,*

---

[6] Beare, Garland; "inner unity" (Loh.); "a call for Unity and Mutual Consideration" (O'B); "unity in humility" (Collange), "unity through humility" (Fee); "harmony and humility" (Hawth.; U. B. Müller). Marchal 91–99 documents as pertinent "unity rhetoric in ancient civic speeches," stressing "concord"; cf. Witherington 13.

paramythion, and *koinōnia*, but Paul insists that it be "in Christ"—unlikely. Better: all four provide grounds for the impvs. in vv 2–4 (e.g., Schenk 174; O'B 176). Fee 176–77, 191 sees "relationship with God" and "relationship with Paul." But "me" in v 2 should not spill over into v 1 (Vincent 53; W. Barclay 1958:4–7, "If you take any account *of me*, received good care *from me* . . . or good at *my* hands," friendship reciprocity). Not Paul's experiences at the hands of the Philippians, but what the Philippians experience from God are the foundations for community (Craddock 37; Silva 99; O'B 174–76). In all four instances, "among you" is to be assumed.

The four items are gifts common to all (Philippian) Christians. *Christ, love* (of God the Father), and *the Spirit* suggest 1abc is "triadic" (Loh. 82) or Trinitarian (Fee 179 n 26, revising 1994:750 n 68; Witherington 1994:61–62; Meyer 61; contrast Bockmuehl 107). Then *affections and mercies* imply the God of salvation history (see NOTE on *oiktirmos*; Rom 12:1). Paul can speak triadically (Christ first, theo-ultimate, the Spirit, 2 Cor 13:13; cf. 1 Thess 1:2–6; 1 Cor 12:5–7), something not necessarily obvious to his audience (as Fee allows, 179 n 26).

Patterns have been proposed for (a) *paraklēsis* in Christ, (b) *paramythion* of love, (c) *koinōnia* of (the) Spirit/spirit, and (d) *affections and mercies*. None has carried the day (O'B 167 n 20).[7] Paul knew what love, the Spirit, and heartfelt mercies mean "in Christ." The Philippians have enjoyed these benefits and so can be called to a response on the basis of them (U. B. Müller 83).

(a) *in Christ* is the obvious starting point (1:1, 13, 26, cf. 1:8, the sphere of Jesus' death and resurrection, spilling over into ecclesial life). *paraklēsis* can suggest *comfort* or "consolation" (KJV) from Christ (O'B 168, 170–71, against "the majority of exegetes"; Turner 1980:77). To Greco-Roman ears, *consolatio* amid the tragedies of life,[8] to which "in Christ" added a new dimension, "almost equivalent to 'salvation'" (O'B 171). In Christian usage, a message of exhortation (*logos paraklēseōs*, Acts 13:15; Heb 13:22) about divine mercy, God's deliverance ap-

---

[7] See NOTE on *comfort and exhortation*. E.g., (a) and (b) refer to the apostle's approach to the congregation, (c) and (d) ties between congregation and apostle (Michaelis 31–32). Seesemann ([2] Bibl. **sharing**) 56–62, (a) and (b) = "what is external to humans" and "what is within them." Or (a) *paraklēsis* governs the other three expressions (Spicq 1965, 2:292–93, but cf. *TLNT* 3:34 n 19; E. F. Scott 42–43). Or (Schenk 180–81) the pl. terms in 2:1d may overarch the prior nouns:

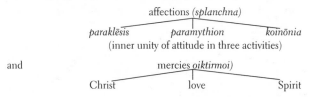

(*oiktirmoi* is the suprenym in a theology of election, shown realized historically)

Fee 178–79: (a) "Christ's comfort," shared by Paul and the Philippians, (b) and (c) focus on the experience of the Philippians, (d) their relationship to Paul.

[8] Holloway 2001a:65–74 summarizes five ancient theories of consolation (Cic., *Tusc.* 3.31.76). It is not clear to which he thinks Paul is closest, or how Paul differs. Linkage is mainly through *topoi*, like "joy."

plied to present needs (O'B 168: "missionary proclamation" and pastoral concerns, citing Grabner-Haider; J. I. H. McDonald 1980: ch. 2). Thus *exhortation* or
encouragement. "The God who comforts" also urges, appeals, and exhorts. See
NOTE on *comfort and exhortation.* Though one might expect "in the Lord" rather
than *in Christ* (cf. 4:2, U. B. Müller 82), most interpreters are not deterred from
taking *paraklēsis* as "encouragement" ([N]RSV, etc.), something "to stir the heart"
(NEB/REB). Schenk 179 sees a *nomen actionis,* admonishing *(ermunternde
Mahnung)* as by prophets at the assembly (1 Cor 14:3, 31; Rom 12:8). The exhortations in vv 2–4 (5), pl., are addressed to the entire community.

Choice between *comfort* and *encouragement* "cannot be answered with any certainty" (Silva 102, cf. O'B 170; Bockmuehl 106, "a false alternative"). Holloway
2001a:120–21, 163, cf. 64 and n 54, intertwines the terms. The TRANSLATION incorporates both, *comfort and exhortation in Christ. en Christō[i]* is a clue to interpreting the third phrase, about the Spirit, and both of these help understand items
(b) and (d).

(b) The second basis is *"paramythion* of love." Alliterative with *paraklēsis,* it too
exhibits dual meanings; see NOTE on 2:1b *consolation and encouragement.* Lack
of LXX use for any Heb. term, lack of other NT use direct attention to its classical
Gk. sense, "what draws the mind aside from care"; "persuasion," JB, TC; "incentive," Moffatt, Gdsp., RSV; the papyri, "solace," MM 488; *NewDocs* 3:79; 4:14
and 166; NAB[RNT]). More a "friendly" word of support than a command to
"buck up." Eng. trs. vary. One could reverse 1a and 1b, "consolation and encouragement in Christ" and "comfort and exhortation of love."

agapēs gen. (see NOTE) can refer to God's *love,* Christ's, Paul's, the Philippians',
apostle and believers mutually, and even the agape table-fellowship. Parallelism
(with *in Christ* and *of the Spirit*) suggests God's love experienced by believers,
which both consoles and encourages (Deut 4:37; 7:13; 10:15; Isa 43:4; Jer 31:1;
Hos 11:1; Rom 8:37; cf. 2 Cor 5:14; 2 Cor 13:13). Likely subj. gen. or source;
"from the *love* of God." Love toward others (2c impv.) is the inner principle that
builds up a community (1 Cor 8–10, 12–14; Söding 1995 [(2) Bibl. *love*] 175).

(c) The third incentive is *"koinōnia* of (the) *pneuma." koinōnia* was "sharing" at
1:5, cf. 1:7, vb. at 4:14 and 15 (Letter A). For Gk. hearers, sharing communal
spirit, in the household or *polis* (Aristot. *Pol.*1.1252a). Paul goes deeper: sharing in
God's Spirit, from baptism on, by all believers (Dunn 1975:260–61). Those in
Christ are also a part of, partners in, a *koinōnia* brought about by the Spirit. The
TRANSLATION brings out both, *sharing in the Spirit* (obj. gen.) by every Philippian
saint, and the corporate result, *the fellowship brought about by the Spirit* (subj.
gen.). Reception of God's greatest charism, the Spirit, and the resulting ecclesial
solidarity (Hainz 1972:327) ground the call to live "worthy of the gospel."

(d) The final basis is *affections and mercies.* Some claim hendiadys, "affectionate mercies" (Dib. 70; Bultmann, "heartfelt sympathy," *TDNT* 5:161; Hawth. 67;
U. B. Müller 83), but trs. avoid this and some (Martin 1976:87–88; O'B 175; Fee
182) reject it. *splanchna* has been used at 1:8. *oiktirmoi* has an OT background for
God's tender *affections.* Some see human feelings (H. C. G. Moule 91), on Paul's
part (Collange 78), or Christian to Christian (Beare 71; GNB, "kindness and

compassion for one another," influenced by 1:8 *I long for you all with . . . affection*; in Paul, *ta splanchna* usually for Christian affection, 2 Cor 6:12; 7:15; Phlm 7, 12, 20). But cf. O'B 175 n 72; Martin 1976:88. *affection of Christ* at 1:8 = Christ's compassion for others, the affection "Christ Jesus has shown and shows." Cf. *mercies* of God (Rom 12:1; cf. 9:15 = Exod 33:19). As "rhythmic parallel to *en Christō[i]*, *agapēs*, *pneumatos*" (Dib. 71; Schenk 181; chart above in n 7), *oiktirmoi* = God's mercies (Rom 9:15), unfolded in Christ, God's love, and the gift of the Spirit. "Root and fruit" (Motyer 104; Fee 182 n 41): the inner heart of God and "emotional reaching out," resulting in *paraklēsis*, *paramython*, and *koinōnia* experience, "eschatological realities" (Jewett 1971a:325), on the basis of which the Philippians are now exhorted.

2. Joy for Paul Through Unity among the Philippians (2:2). Instead of impvs. like 1:27cd, Paul chooses an impv. pointing to himself, in prison: *give me further joy* (2:2a). Joy among friends was part of *philia*.[9] He relates the congregation to himself (Meyer 72; O'B 176) and each other, just as *the same contest* did in 1:30a. The focus is ecclesial and pastoral (Fee 183).

Paul already possesses *joy (chara)*. In Letter A, he *greatly rejoiced in the Lord* (4:10) because Philippian support had revived. Paul prayed for them *with joy* (1:4). Now they are to enlarge his joy, which will reach its goal only at "the Day of Christ Jesus" (1:6, 10b–11). But there is joy now before God (Schenk 174) amid difficulties as the gospel goes forth (1:18bc), and future joy (18d), come what may. What the Philippians are to do (vv 2–4) will carry forward what is already under way, a missing piece they can add, prior to the Last Day as salvation is being worked out (2:12).

2:2a stands out, startling like *Exercise your citizenship* in 1:27a (Schenk 174):

about Paul, the sender	and about the Philippians, the addressees:	
2:2a Give *me* →	2b in that *(hina) you* think →	2:3–4 nothing for self-interest,
further joy	the same thing,	nor for vainglory.
	2c having the same love,	Rather, in humiliation, consider one
		another to surpass *yourselves*,
	together in soul,	each, regarding not *your own interests*, but
	2d thinking one thing,	those [also] of other persons, each of *you*.
↓		↓ (2:2b–4, after *hina* + subj., 4 ptcs.)
		(1:27–28, 1 vb., 2 ptcs.)
= 1:27b that *(hina)* →	1:27a Exercise →	1:27c stand steadfast in one and the same
whether *I* come . . .	*your* citizenship	Spirit, engage together in the struggle
. . . or continue to		for the gospel faith with one soul,
be absent . . .		28a not intimidated in any way . . .

2:2bcd correspond with 1:27c; 2c *together in soul*, with 1:27c *together . . . with one*

---

[9] Fortna 1990 uses 2:2a to claim Phil is egotistical, Paul self-serving. That ignores what apostle and community have in common; it "is quite insensitive" to friendship aspects (Fee 183 n 50; *ABD* 5:320; Reumann 1996:88–89; Malherbe 1996 [(16) Bibl.] 127, "friends rejoice together"). Peterlin 71, 74–75, 102–3 holds that "Paul himself" was "the cause of division" (Euodia and Syntyche split over supporting him); unprovable and unlikely.

soul. "The first continuing task in the congregation" (Schenk 172), "harmonious working together of the various charisms" (1:29 Gk. *echaristhē*, charisms of believing and suffering for Christ), begins to unfold here; other tasks will follow in 2:14 and 15–16a. 2:2a, *give me further joy in that you think the same thing* parallels 2:5 *think this among yourselves,* chiastically:

> 2:1 (four) indics. (*in Christ* 1a) ⟍⟋ 2:2–4 impvs., "you" (pl.)
> 2:5a impv. "among you" (pl.) ⟋⟍ 2:5b–11 indic. (*in Christ Jesus* 5b)

2:2b–4 is introduced by explanatory *hina* (Silva 103). It provides content. Not "I ask that . . . ," or imperatival *hina* (GNTG 3:94–95; NRSV, CEV), but "the method . . . by which Paul's joy is to be made full" (O'B 177). To tr. "by being of the same mind" (RSV, NEB, NIV) may subordinate too much "the main *idea*" (Hawth. 67), complete *joy* when the Philippians *think the same thing.*

2:2b *to auto phronein* reflects a Philippian slogan, their *concern* for Paul and *intent* to aid him (cf. Sampley 1977:167–68; Peterlin 103; discussion of 4:10 in [17].) The apostle reciprocated at 1:7, he thinks constantly about the Philippians. At 2:2 it expresses how they are to continue to think (pres. subjunct.), have a mind-set, not just "cogitate" (Fee 185). *the same* (neut.) implies each Philippian Christian in harmony with other believers there. The standard is "a manner worthy of the gospel of Christ" (1:27a). "Think the same as the good news does." Not the same opinions on everything (Fee 185), people with different spiritual gifts may discern things differently. But "commitment to likeness of aim and purpose" (Bockmuehl 109), in missionary advance and ecclesially. Cf. Rom 15:5. "Thinking the same" was perhaps a phrase in popular speech (see NOTE; Deissmann). Paul amplifies it before returning to *phronein* language in 2d.

2:2c, *having the same love, together in soul,* reinforces the oneness Paul seeks. *agapē* toward one another (NEB/REB) could be a separate impv. (Hawth. 68), but trs. usually keep the participle. Paul prayed (1:9) that the Philippians' *love may continue to grow still more and more* (impv. in a petition). 2:1b premises *consolation and encouragement from love* on God's part. *the same love* in 2:2c likely means the same as God exhibits, now to be expressed toward one another.[10] Cf. 2:5, a mind among yourselves such as you have in your relationship to Christ. Fee 185: "solace from (God's) love," now "one for another," "the same" not necessarily in intensity, but in aim, smoothing over differences in views (Schrage 1961:175).

together in soul (see NOTE) has been taken as a separate characteristic of congregational life ("of one accord," KJV; [N]RSV). Or with what precedes (the *sympsychoi* "have the same love"). Or with what follows in 2d to explain *to hen* in 2d (Vincent 55; Silva 103; Fee 183 n 47, contrast 1994:748), "*how* ('together in soul') they are to 'set their minds on the one thing.'" That destroys the chiasm noted in A.1 (Schenk 178; O'B 165, 177) and the "rhythm of the sentence" (Haupt 56). Does "together in soul" really explain "(the) one thing"? *one (hen)* with the motif-

---

[10] A "sincere love for God" in which all share (Spicq 1965, 2:298, in O'B 178 n 92) is hardly Paul's point in 2:1b and here. Paul usually employs "faith" to express the human response to God, not "love."

word *phronein* is more climactic than a *syn*-compound. With *sympsychoi*, Paul is asking the Philippian Christians to be "fellow souls" (Fitzgerald 1996:145), in contrast to their frequent *humiliation* (3b) in the society of the day.

2:2d *thinking one thing* is often tr. as a noun phrase ("of one mind," KJV-[N]RSV; or "one in . . . purpose," NIV; cf. O'B 179; NAB; NEB; REB; "a mind that is unity itself," H. C. G. Moule 91), rarely as a separate command (CEV). Is Paul talking in a circle, so that *to hen* means nothing more than *to auto* (Vincent 55; Gnilka 105)? But the phrase is different. The definite art. gives Paul's phrase "additional strength" (Lft. 108), "the one thing," "some definite 'one thing' known to him and the Philippians" (ZBG #170). Cf. Heriban ([7] Bibl.) 190–91; W. Barclay 1958:5; Schenk. It could be "mission" (Collange) or (K. Barth 54–55) "grace," seen in the neighbor (2:3). Cf. 2:5, relationship to Christ, played out in relations with one another. In context, it is *the gospel of Christ*, 1:27. How it applies to the *politeia* of the Philippians will become apparent in vv 3–4.

3. Not Self-Interest but Others, amid Humiliation: Social Setting in Philippi (2:3–4).

The injunctions now become prohibitions, *nothing for self-interest, nor for vainglory* (3a), *regarding not your own interests* (4a). The last negative was 1:28a, *not intimidated* by *adversaries*. The adversary now appears among Philippian Christians themselves! Terse, no main vb. impv. till 5a, though ptcs. can serve as impvs. (*consider one another to surpass yourselves* 3b). They are community admonitions, but individualized through sg. and pl. forms of *hekastos* in v 4 (see NOTES on *each, each of you*). The grounds for appeal remain the same (v 1). 2d, *thinking one thing* (cf. 2bc), fulfilling Paul's *joy* (2a), and exercising *citizenship worthy of the gospel* (1:27), stand over vv 3–4. In the TRANSLATION, 3a (Gk., vv 3–4) is separated from 2d by a comma, not a period (most Eng. NTs).

Loh. 86–87 saw a "not . . . but" pattern in vv 3 and 4 *(nothing . . . Rather)*; Peterlin 59, ABAB or antithetical parallelism. Three nouns in v 3 *(self-interest, vainglory, and humiliation)*, then three ptcs. (*hēgoumenoi*, tr. as *consider*; 4a *regarding*, understood in 4b also). Schenk 182–83, "too artful"; 2:2d is the suprenym ("over word"), the ptc. (4a) antithetical hyponyme ("under word"):

$$\text{to think (the) one thing (2d)}$$

not *self-interest* (3a)	for *vainglory*	*regarding your own interests* (4a)

Cf. 1d as key to the phrases in 1abc (Schenk 181; chart on p. 321 n 7); *think one thing* is climax here.

self-interest and *vainglory*, 3a, were typical Greek vices (Edart 126–27), a mindset and path of action *not* wanted in the church. Among you, *nothing* in accord with, out of *eritheia* (see NOTE on 1:17 *self-interest*), a rare word, "selfish ambition" (NIV, NRSV). From a Philippian penchant to advance self or group (or house church), at the expense of others, a norm (*kata* + acc.) by which people operated. In Aristot., intriguing for office in the *politeia*; it possibly carried over into Philippian church life (see NOTE). Faction-mongering was a "spiritual malaise at the heart of the church" there (Martin 1976:89), but pinning this on Euodia and Syntyche (4:2–3; Hainz 1972:218; O'B 187; deSilva 2000:218–19) is dubious.

kenodoxia is desire for honor and glory, leading to conceit ([N]RSV), vanity (Gdsp., NEB), "a cheap desire to boast" (GNB). The word family, for "all kinds of intellectual and moral charlatanism," came from Gk. philosophy into Hellenistic Jewish and early Christian usage (H. D. Betz, *Gal.* 294, Gal 5:26, + "provoking one another, envying one another"). Cf. Martin 1976:69 on *The Cynic Epistles* (ed. Malherbe 1977). The prefix *vain* is a judgment on such quests for self-glory. A nasty word, perhaps referring to false estimations by some Philippian Christians of their importance in the ecclesial *politeia* (V. Wiles 63–64), from their rank in the civic society and the quest there for prestige and power. To "work out salvation" (2:12–13) and live "in Christ" occurs amid such threats (Hainz 1972:22, 2:12 "obeying" Paul may pick up on 2:3–4).

The antidote to such vices comes in 3b: *Rather, in humiliation, consider one another to surpass yourselves.* Usually Paul is said to teach church unity (v 2) via humbleness (v 3) on the part of each Christian (4). The NOTE on *tapeinophrosynē* argues for a sense out of the world of the day, *humiliation* of lower classes in the social pyramid. The rest of 3b is will be treated first.

consider one another in the Christian community *to surpass yourselves.* *hēgoumenoi* could be taken as a fifth way to make Paul's *joy* complete. But most trs. have broken this string at 3a (KJV—[N]RSV) or 3b (JB), ptc. taken as an impv. Fee 188 n 76, "focus on, give due consideration to"; Louw/Nida #31.1, with *phronein:* "have an opinion, hold a view." Schenk 183–84 notes the frequency of *hēgeomai* in Phil (6 of the 8 examples in acknowledged letters; see NOTE) and the likelihood that it relates to *hēgēsato* at 2:6 in the Philippians' hymn.

The first acc. with *consider* is *one another (allēlous)*, members being addressed of house churches. Emphatic (before the ptc.), directly after *in humiliation.* Fee 1994:971–72, "one of the prevailing, but frequently overlooked words in Pauline paraenesis. . . . Everything is done *allēlōn*" (1 Thess 4:9; 5:11; Rom 13:8; 14:19; etc.). *hēgoumenoi* could also mean "leading, guiding (the community)," thus "leaders" (see NOTE); "in your humiliation (in society), with reference to one another, those who are leaders."[11] The surprising turn comes at the end of 3b, *hyperechontas heautōn*, the second acc. after *consider*, "those who surpass," or "as (persons) surpassing," + gen. (BDAG *hyperechō* 2.b), *yourselves.* Thus persons "better than yourselves" ([N]RSV); in the TRANSLATION, *to surpass yourselves.* *hyperechō*, relatively frequent in Phil (3 of the 4 instances in Paul), has a sense of "(those who) rule" (Rom 13:1 "*governing* authorities"; 1 Pet 2:13 the Emperor). On use for prominent, highly placed persons (who may oppress others), see the NOTE. Could (some) Philippians have felt this sense? People who surpassed them in the Roman *politeia* and on the social ladder? Carried over into the house churches, so that patron, head of the house, patriarch (male or female), held power in the church community *de facto*, perhaps inevitably? As *episkopoi* (1:1) in

---

[11] Michael 6 thought Philippian Christians were not showing proper honor and respect to the *episkopoi* and *diakonoi* (1:1). Garland 1980 ([1] Bibl.) 327–28, officials in Philippi sought too much honor; Paul preaches humility to them.

the households? The vocabulary *(hēgoumenoi, hyperechontas, tapeinophrosynē[i])* strengthens the sociological background in Philippi (Merk 1968, O'B 181, among others). But the words *one another* and *yourselves* give the sentence a different twist, "other person-centeredness" (O'B 182), as will become clear in v 4.

A long NOTE on *humiliation* is necessary. Half of U. B. Müller's pages on 2:1–4 are devoted to the term; cf. Walter 53–54. In taking *tapeinophrosynē* as "humiliation," the TRANSLATION breaks with "humility," a virtually unanimous rendering since patristic times, but to be avoided here (Schenk 184–85). Merk 1968's attention to social setting, developed by Wengst and others, offers a new position to which O'B 181–82 was open but Fee 187–88 ignores (Bockmuehl 111, the "humility commended" is not oppressive). The NOTE provides data on the word family and secondary literature. Generally *tapeino*-words had a negative sense in antiquity and often some relation to the social order. The LXX differed in that God may be the subject of the vb. (Ps 18:27 [LXX 17:28]; cf. Jdt 9:11). But Phil 2:3 does not speak of *tapeinophrosynē* before God. The NOTE reexamines the NT picture as Wengst and the newer social-setting approach see it.

Phil 2:3 may be the first occurrence of *tapeinophrysonē* in Gk. (V. Wiles 50). *tapeino*-words often referred to the social order, the context where the new noun emerged. The fixed structures of the Roman world heightened the social pyramid in Philippi (Dihle 742–43). The goal of many was social climbing, upward mobility (Wengst 1988: 4–15; U. B. Müller 85–86, reflecting Alföldy 83–102, 130–38). The Hebrew Scriptures had a different picture of "the poor": they may be victims of violence by the rich, yet are persons whom God delivers, humbling their oppressors, often eschatologically. Cf. Mendenhall; Wengst 1988:16–35.

Traditional presentations of (the historical) Jesus and his teaching, as personification of humility, become less convincing when examined (see NOTE). Not some incident during Jesus' earthly career (like John 13, the foot-washing; cf. J. Ferguson 1971–72), but the christological account in Phil 2:6–11 may be seminal, humiliation (of a heavenly figure) in death, not humbleness during the earthly ministry.

Paul at times was mocked as "humble" (in a bad sense, 2 Cor 10:1). He knew the OT understanding of "God who comforts those humiliated" (2 Cor 7:6). But "a fixed topos in pre-Christian [!] community instruction" (Gnilka 106) or a Jewish-Christian hymn (so Loh.; Ferguson) using the theme are unlikely; *tapeinophrosynē* had no prior demonstrable existence before it turns up in Phil 2:3. Its meaning was not yet fixed, certainly not "humility" in a good sense (Schenk 184). This compound word, *phronein*, so popular with the Philippians (see on 4:10 and 1:7), + *tapeino-*, was not yet a virtue, but a negative, humiliation of self or group, by others, in society, from superiors in the state. Perhaps one should use quotation marks for it as a Philippian word. They knew what it was to be *humiliatores*, "little people." Even if one enjoyed some rank in society and political structures, there was always a person on a higher rung. Such stratification was not likely fully expunged by baptism. It could show up within the church community. "In your 'humiliation,' which you so often experience," Paul writes, "you are nonetheless to regard others among you as your superiors."

tapeinophrosynē has a bite to it: each believer, no matter of what rank socially or in the Roman *politeia*, is to regard every other Christian as superior, rejecting self-ish quests for personal or class glory. Others "in Christ" are your equal (by baptism) and may indeed surpass you (perhaps in spiritual gifts). "Every Christian should regard his brother and sister like a ruling authority in the state"; that person's well-being provides the norm for community relationships (H. W. Bartsch 1974:97–98; cf. Käsemann 1960 = 1964:121).

Later *tapeinophrosynē* took on further senses: Col 2:18, 23 "self-abasement" and "humility" in an erroneous system of piety; Col 3:12, Eph 4:2, one in a series of virtues, like meekness; 1 Pet 5:5–6, something with which all Christians are to clothe themselves in dealing with one another, and as humbleness before God; 1 Clement, "obedient submission" in the church. See NOTE. The stage was thus set for patristic and monastic patterns inculcating submissive humility (Lat. *humilitas*) as *the* Christian virtue for all of life.[12]

At 2:3 the dat. of respect or reference has been kept, *in humiliation*, set off by commas to suggest that *Rather* goes with *consider*. Not the manner in which Christians are to think or act in opposition to *self-interest* and *vainglory* (Silva 101); not a call for self-effacement before God (Loh. 88 and others), *humiliation* reflects things as they are in the world (Schenk 185).[13]

V 4 clarifies v 3 (*DA* 355, 416). Its sgs. and pls. (see textual NOTE on *each*) surface the tension between group and individual (Fee 190): [4a] *each, regarding not your own interests, [b]but those of other persons, each of you*. The structure is *not . . . but . . .* as in v 3. More than repetition of v 3, more than "curtain-raiser" (Martin 1976:90) to 2:5–11. *kai*, bracketed on textual grounds, raises a crucial problem in ethics about self-interest.

regarding (implied also in 4b) is a synonym for *phronein* (Schenk 183); cf. *consider* in 3b. It could be taken as impv. ("Each of you should look," NRSV). Here *skopountes* = "look (critically) at, calculate, weigh the facts." What all the Philippians (see NOTE on *each*; *of you* is added to bring out the pl.) are to look at is expressed by two accs. First, *your own interests (ta heautōn)*, negated by *not*, like *self-interest* and *vainglory* in vv 3–4.[14] A gen. pl. follows, "(things) of yourselves." Supply *interests* (see NOTE), "qualities," "gifts," "possessions," or even "rights" (Bockmuehl 113, with Beare 72–73; rejected by O'B 185 n 146). V. Wiles, "group" (political or ecclesial parties, house churches).

The "positive" dir. obj. is *those* (interests) *of other persons (ta heterōn*, contrast *ta*

---

[12] Oakes 2001:183–85 sees a "trajectory" from 2:3b of "social status," but hesitates (185) "to argue that the word *tapeinophrosynē*, on its own, would be understood unequivocally as relating to social status held by the hearers." If one wants to use the term "trajectory," this is on the right track.

[13] Paul's words *consider one another to surpass yourselves* fall into place without appeal to "grace" (K. Barth 56, critique in Heriban [(7) Bibl.] 198); or perfection (Phil 3:14–15, Loh. 89); or lowliness as "a sense of sinfulness" (Vincent 56); or altruism, disinterested love, and "service" (*diakonia*, Reicke 1962:206–8; Michaelis 32–33; W. Barclay 1958:6–7); or "the impossible," to achieve which "divine assistance" must be invoked (Hawth. 70, who, however, rightly speaks of "proper evaluation of others and of one's self" in light of God, gospel, and Christ; then one can acknowledge gifts and competence in others).

[14] Neut. pl. *ta* recalls 1:12, *events affecting me* and 1:27b *the news about you*; cf. 2:21 "their own interests."

heautōn, BDF #306.2). Others, not we, have priority. Who are (the) *other persons*? Do they perhaps include non-Christians? Primary attention is on Christian groups and individuals (*each* in 4a, *each of you* 4b). Whatever gifts each (group) has are to be employed for others in the church as a whole. A secondary implication may be superiors in the state and social structures.

kai in 4b (brackets in NA[27] ; = *also*; see NOTE on *but*) is more than a matter of Western MSS omitting the word (accidentally, Silva 104). Is Paul is excluding any self-interest (*not your own interests, but those of others*)? Or is it, with *kai*, *not* just *your own interests but also* those of others? Most prefer the "both/and" approach. They read *kai* and even add "not *only*" in 4a (West 244; cf. 179 n 148; RSV; Silva 104; "to forget our own good," G. H. Clark 52, "would be sin . . ."). Martin 1976:90 omits *also* on textual grounds and "only" because it is "not in the Gk. text." Similarly Houlden 83. O'B 184–85 finds this "unsatisfactory." Fee favors "not only/but also" (175 n. 8), but (190–91) do not "push this clause beyond Paul's own intent"; look out for oneself, but orientation to Christ changes things. How much?[15] 2:4a excludes *your own interests*; 2:4b insists on those of the other person (or group) (cf. Schenk 185; U. B. Müller 86–87). The bracketed [*also*] shows how later interpretations began. Paul meant "not this, but that," or, if *kai* is read, "but indeed that" in v 4, as in v 3.

Social Setting in Philippi. Numerous details in 2:1–4 reflect the overall theme of 1:27, *Exercise your citizenship.* The *politeia* is first that of the Roman *colōnia* and then that of the emerging Christian community, thus a dual allegiance for those living *in a manner worthy of the gospel of Christ* (1:27) in society and church. Political and social overtones were noted for *koinōnia* (2:1c); the theme of unity; *self-interest* and *vainglory* (3a; Peterman 1997:113); the ptcs. *consider* and *surpass* in 3b, used of authorities and superiors; *humiliation* (3a) in the social pyramid of superiors and underlings; and looking out for one's *own* or others' *interests* (v 4).

In this sociopolitical setting (Merk 1968, Wengst) and its ecclesial application (V. Wiles), giving Paul *further joy* (2a) should not be limited to settling a spat between Euodia and Syntyche (Peterlin, who recognized something of the social setting, 61). Paul referred to his struggle with the Roman state (1:13, 14; cf. 1:7; *Caesar's household* 4:23) as *the same contest* in which the Philippians are engaged (1:30a). If their acclamation at 2:11, *Jesus Christ is Lord*, aimed at the Caesar cult,

---

[15] The issue is like that of "proper self-love" and Lev 19:18, "love your neighbor *as yourself*" (Schenk 183), often understood as, "First love yourself and gain proper self-esteem; then you can properly love the neighbor; and eventually love for God can follow." Engberg-Pedersen 2003:199–204 justifies the "not-that-but-this" tr. from grammar, context, Stoic and Pauline ethics; Lev. 19:18, "as yourself" = "as one among the others." Contrast G. Bornkamm, *Jesus of Nazareth* (New York: Harper, 1960) 109–17: everyone knows by nature how to love the self. Jesus' use of Lev 19:18 in Mark 12:31 parr. is not commending self-love, but, as in the OT text, setting a standard that no one can evade by asking, "How much must I love the neighbor?" Answer: as much as you love yourself. The other person, not me, is put in the center. God's love engenders love for others, not self-love that characterizes people naturally. Cf. AB27:480–81. Bockmuehl 114 well speaks of "the neo-pagan presupposition that I cannot love others until I love myself," a principle by which "Paul does not operate."

then the struggle involves Emperor and Empire. Paul and the Philippians experience Rome's oppression as well as its benefits

Life in the Greco-Roman *politeia* and life in the community of Christ are vividly pointed up by the antithesis between, on one hand, *self-interest, vainglory*, and the *interests* of individuals or particular groups (negatives) and, on the other hand, (the positives) considering fellow Christians *to surpass yourselves* and regarding the interests of *others*. Features "of the secular *ekklēsia*" were "sadly manifested in its Christian counterpart" (B. W. Winter 1994:98–99). Paul asks Christians to regard each brother and sister as "governing authorities," superior to themselves (H. W. Bartsch). In 3b, *one another* puts the matter to the church, but "the interests of *other persons*" might suggest non-Christian neighbors and even the authorities. How do we live as people of the gospel in such situations?

B. W. Winter 1994:98–104 illustrates with a Christian (faction) bringing another Christian (group) before the magistrates, as in 1 Cor 6:1–8.[16] Paul, in court, appealed to his citizenship (though some in Ephesus disapproved). The problem in Philippi was not the legitimacy of government (Rom 13:1–7), but how the worst practices in the civic-social system could affect Christians in the church.

Bockmuehl 112 (with Pilhofer 1:85–92, 122–39, 142–44) cites aspects of a "social *Sitz im Leben* at Philippi." The population of the *Colonia Iulia Augusta Philippensis* included *cives Romani*. People were proud of positions obtained in an army career or in the *ordo decurionum* (councillors in local government, *honestiores* or upper class in contrast to *humiliores*), or even of their roles as musicians or actors (inscriptions). "[S]uch status considerations . . . would give considerable 'bite' to Paul's call to *consider others better*" (2:3, Bockmuehl 112, noting Bormann and Garnsey 221ff.).[17] Persons of this sort would bring abilities and drive to church life but perhaps also the Gk. proclivity toward factionalism and quest for higher station and glory. Paul's words in 2:3–4 speak sharply to such situations.[18] Paul addresses specific problems in the congregation of a Roman *colōnia* (U. B. Müller 87–88). The very nature of *the gospel of Christ* and its application are being challenged by class practices in the existing *politeiai*. Even if only a few of the converts were powerful or of noble birth,[19] the pervasive mentality was upward social mobility, *self-interest*, party or house and clan partisanship, the quest for *glory*, not the welfare *of others*. Paul's words apply specifically within the

---

[16] Winter 87 ties Phil 2:4 (about *not* looking after personal interests) to Plutarch's criticism of Themistocles, who subordinated public and communal concerns to private interests (*Mor.* 807B, *Praec. ger. reip.*, LCL 10: 204–5).

[17] Example: the Philippian church might have included someone like Erastus, *oikonomos* in Corinth (Rom 16:23). If city treasurer and head of a house church, he would combine power in civic and ecclesial *politeiai*. If a member of some other patron's house church (his father's, e.g.), he might hold lower rank in the church than in the world.

[18] "Tables of household duties" *(Haustafeln)* do not occur in Phil (or any acknowledged Pauline letter), but there was eventually need for paraenesis from the best of Greco-Roman household management and political theory about reciprocal obligations in the church.

[19] 1 Cor 1:26, *dynatoi* = the rich, with social and political power; cf. G. Theissen 1982:69–174; D. Sänger, "Die *dynatoi* in 1 Kor 1:26," ZNW 76 (1985) 285–91; M. Mitchell 1991:94, literature in n 173. Cf. (5) COMMENT n 29.

koinōnia "in Christ"; they could carry over to life in Caesar's *politeia*, for the common good *(ta koina)*.[20]

4. 2:1–4 *Within the Redacted, Canonical Letter.* These verses have much the same meaning as in Letter B, but are less important in a longer letter. Readers may eye 2:6–11 or ch. 3 as "key" to 2:1–4. The redacted letter makes it easier to depict the Philippian community as a fragmented church, threatened with disunity (Euodia and Syntyche, 4:2–3). In a longer letter, it becomes more difficult to explain why Paul puts off till 4:10–20 giving thanks for the gift from Philippi, esp. when he mentions *love* and *sharing* in 2:1b and c, and his *joy* in v 2. The "worldwide struggle" some see at 1:30 ([5] COMMENT B.3) served in a single letter to obscure the local social setting in Philippi sketched above. Paraenesis was generalized. Further, in a unified letter, (a) references to "opponents" (1:14–18; 1:28) are more readily combined and 3:2–21 dominates, linked by the same word, *self-interest*, at 1:17 and 2:3; and by 2:3 *vainglory* to 3:19 ("glory"). (b) The chiastic structure that can be claimed for Letter B ([5] COMMENT A.1) is thrown out of kilter by addition of ch. 3 and 4:10–20. (c) Once 4:10–20 are treated as the final part of the four-ch. letter, Paul's love-hate relationship in these vv with the culture of friendship may disappear as background for reading 2:1–4. A critical approach to Greco-Roman conventions is then harder to see in 2:1–4. In v 3b *tapeinophrosynē* came to be read in light of the virtue of "Christian *humility*," rather than as the *humiliation* of "inferiors" by "superiors" in the social system of Paul's day.

The redacted letter can still be read as asserting what exercising citizenship means in house churches and Roman society. The sociopolitical reading has by no means been developed and accepted only by those who hold partition theories about Phil (cf. O'B 18, 181–82; Bockmuehl 22, 112). 2:1–4 continued to speak against failings in the world of the day that were dangers in church households and *politeia* too. Usually 2:1–4 has been associated with church unity through individual humility as the great Christian virtue, in contrast to Greco-Roman pride. Moses (Num 12:3) and Jesus were regarded as exemplifying humility, a pattern Christians should imitate. Monasticism took up this theme. It became a commonplace (Lat. *humilitas*) in subsequent Christianity. Only recently have feminists and the theologies of liberation protested about humility as an enslaving device. See *TRE* 8:463–68; Wengst, *RGG*[4] 1:657–59, gives a different picture for the NT: "solidarity of the humiliated and with those humiliated" (657).

As a lectionary reading, 2:1–4 has occasionally been assigned along with 1:27–30 ([5] COMMENT B.3 n 40). In the Roman *Ordo*, 2:1–11 (in "daughter versions," 2:1–4 [5–11] or 2:1–13) have been appointed for Year A, Pentecost 19, during insequence reading of Phil.

---

[20] Cf. U. B. Müller 86–88; Walter 52; Oakes 2001:181–87, *economic* help is the issue. Oakes conjectures that some who had suffered little, because of social status and (relative) wealth, did not help financially those poorer and of lower status (96, 99; 1995:220; Peterlin 64). This may too easily relate social status and wealth (de Vos 266 n 117). Meggitt 1998:155–78 spoke of "economic mutualism" as the survival strategy of the poor, more likely in Pauline communities than in urban Greco-Roman or Jewish groups.

Select Bibliography (see also General Bibliography and Commentaries)

Barclay, W. 1958. "Great Themes of the New Testament—I. Phil ii.1–11," *ExpTim* 70:4–7, 40–44.

Bartsch, H.-W. 1974. *Die konkrete Wahrheit und die Lüge der Spekulation. Untersuchung über den vorpaulinischen Christushymnus und seine gnostische Mythisierung.* Theologie und Wirklichkeit 1. Bern: H. Lang, Frankfurt am Main: Peter D. Lang.

Black, D. A. 1985. "Paul and Christian Unity: A Formal Analysis of Philippians 2:1–4," *JETS* 28: 299–308.

Di Marco, A. 1980. "Koinonia – Communio: Flp 2,1," *Laur* 21:376–403.

——. 1988. "KOINŌNIA PNEUMATIOS (2 Cor 13,13; Flp 2,1) – PNEUMA KOINŌ- NIAS: Circolarità e ambivolenza linguistica e filologica," *FilNoet* 1:63–75.

Engberg-Pedersen, T. 2003. "Radical Altruism in Philippians 2:4," in FS Malherbe (Gen. Bibl., under "Thom") 197–214.

Ferguson, J. 1971–72. "Philippians, John, and the Traditions of Ephesus," *ExpTim* 83:85– 87.

Fridrichsen, A. 1938a. "*Sympsychos = holē[i] tē[i] psychē[i],*" *Philologische Wochenschrift* 58:910–12.

Käsemann, E. 1960. "Amt und Gemeinde im Neuen Testament," *Exegetische Versuche und Besinnungen,* I (Göttingen: Vandenhoeck und Ruprecht, repr. 1964) 109–34, esp. 121.

Reicke, B. 1962. "Unité chrétienne et diaconie: Phil 2:1–11," in *Neotestamentica et Patristica: Eine Freundesgabe O. Cullmann,* ed. W. C. van Unnik, NovTSup 6 (Leiden: Brill) 203–12.

Sanders, J. A. 1969. "Dissenting Deities and Philippians 2:1–11," *JBL* 88:279–90.

2:3 **humiliation** *(tapeinophrosynē):* wordbook articles in Note on 2:3; G. Mensching et al., *RGG*[3] 2 (1958) 76–82; G. Gilleman, NCE 7 (1967) 234–36; H. D. Preuss et al., *TRE* 8 (1981) 459–68, 474–88; H.-P. Mathys/G. Reeg/K. Wengst/U. Köpf/O. Bayer, *RGG*[4] 2 (1999) 654–60.

Alföldy, G. *The Social History of Rome,* ed. D. Braund/F. Pollock (Totowa, NJ: Barnes and Noble, 1985; rev. ed., London: Routledge/Baltimore: Johns Hopkins, 1988). Ger. 2nd ed. 1979.

Boer, Willem den. 1983. "*Tapeinos* in Pagan and Christian Terminology," in *Tria corda. Scritti in onore di Arnaldo Momigliano,* ed. E. Gabba (Como: Edizione New Press) 143–62.

Dawes, S. B. 1991a. "Humility: Whence This Strange Notion?" *ExpTim* 103:72–75.

——. 1991b. "'ĂNĀWÂ in Translation and Tradition," *VT* 41:38–48.

Dickson, J. P./B. S. Rosner. 2004. "Humility as a Social Virtue in the Hebrew Bible?" *VT* 54:459–79.

Leivestad, R. 1965–66. "The Meekness and Gentleness of Christ," *NTS* 12:156–64.

Melzer, F. 1973. "Entstehung und Wirksamkeit des christozentrischen Wortschatzes im Deutschen, dargelegt an dem Wort Demut," in *Sprache und Sprachverständnis in religiöser Rede: Zum Verhältnis von Theologie und Linguistik,* ed. T. Michels/ A. Paus (Salzburg/Munich: Pustet) 203–10.

Ortwein, G. G. 1999. *Status und Statusverzicht im Neuen Testament und seiner Umwelt,* NTOA 39 (Fribourg: Universitätsverlag/Göttingen: Vandenhoeck & Ruprecht) 77–84, 287–88.

Rehrl, S. 1961. *Das Problem der Demut in der profan-griechish Literatur im Vergleich zu Septuaginta und Neuen Testament.* AeC. Münster: Aschendorff.

Wengst, K.1986. "'. . . einander durch Demut für vorzüglicher halten.' Zum Begriff 'Demut' bei Paulus und in paulinischer Tradition," in *Studien zum Text and zur Ethik des Neuen Testament, Festschrift zum 80. Geburtstag von Heinrich Greeven,* ed. W. Schrage BZNW 47 (Berlin: de Gruyter) 428–39.

———. 1988. *Humility: Solidarity of the Humiliated: The Transformation of an Attitude and Its Social Relevance in Graeco-Roman, Old Testament, and Early Christian Tradition.* Philadelphia: Fortress. Ger. 1987, tr. J. Bowden.

7. The Philippians' Encomium, applied by Paul to Christian Life in Philippi, 2:5–11

TRANSLATION

2:5a Think in this way among yourselves; b it is the way you also think "in Christ Jesus,"

6a who, while living in the sphere of God, b did not consider to be like God c something of which to take advantage, 7a but himself he emptied, b taking on the sphere of a slave;

7c born in humanity's likeness, d and, in appearance perceived as a human being, 8a he experienced humiliation for himself, 8b becoming obedient to the point of death,

8c —yes, death on a cross.

9a Therefore God has indeed exalted him most highly 9b and freely given him the name 9c that is above every name, 10a that at the name of Jesus

10b every knee shall bow—

10c of those in the heavens and those on earth and those in the world below—

11a and every language confess that

11b the Lord is Jesus Christ,

11c to the glory of God the Father.

EXCURSUS B: The Message about Jesus Christ's Humiliation and God's Exalting Him to Lordship (2:6–11)

This passage, often poetically arranged (NA[26,27]; NRSV, etc.), plus v 5, has long been the Mt. Everest of Philippians study. Excurses in Lft. 127–37; Gnilka 131–47; Collange 81–94; O'B 253–71; Walter 56–59. *Research reports:* Hübner 1987:2740–42 and Rissi in ANRW; Schenk, *Phil.* 185–213; Habermann, Battasi 62–64; R. P. Martin chronicled the history of scholarship for forty years; see further *Philippian Studies.* Our *working theory:* Paul employs in vv 6–11 an encomium the Philippians had worked out to use in mission proclamation about Christ and God in their Greco-Roman world.

I. "Traditional" Views through the Nineteenth Century

Patristic, medieval, and some later treatments usually reflect classical Christology, e.g., the two "natures" for Christ, "form *(morphē)* of God" (6a), "form *(morphē)* of a servant" (7b).[1] Many stress transformed Christians imitating Christ; others oppose imitating "Jesus' steps" (1 Pet 2:21).[2] In the 19th-cent. principle of kenosis (2:7a *ekenōsen*), Jesus voluntarily lays aside prerogatives and powers of divinity during his state of humiliation, resuming them later at exaltation.[3]

II. Modern Critical Studies

A. *Lohmeyer's Treatment.* His 1928 work (1930 commentary 90–99; summaries in Martin 1967:25–30, 38–39; C. Brown 1998) traced the title *kyrios* (Phil 2:11b) back, behind the Hellenized world of divinized heroes (Bousset [(1) Bibl. **Lord**]), to Jewish (Christian) roots in a pre-Pauline "psalm" of six Stanzas, three lines each (cf. NRSV; Hellerman 129–30). Only the words *thanatou de staurou* (8c) were added by Paul. Jewish roots, possibly "Jerusalem liturgy,"[4] but he never claimed the hymn was composed in a Semitic language (Beare 76). P. P. Levertoff retroverted it into Aramaic (W. K. L. Clark 1929:148; cf. Fitzmyer 1988:473), which Martin 1967:40–41 reprints. C. Brown 25, perhaps from "Damascus and Antioch" or a place open to "Hellenistic rhetoric" (Philippi "is not impossible"), a poem known to Paul's readers; cf. Edart 151.

B. *Other Structurings.* J. Jeremias (1963:186–87 = *Abba* 312) proposed three Stanzas, each of four somewhat longer lines, + three additions by Paul (8c, 10c, 11c).[5] Rooted in the OT. Stanza 2 is not on incarnation but the earthly life and death of Jesus as humiliation. So Mihoc 103; Martin 1967:36–38. Other analyses in Deichgräber; Hofius 1976; Jervell 1960:213, two hymns, vv 6–8 about Christ, vv 9–11 about God; Gnilka 137–38; Habermann 147–49.

The "shape" of the passage: traditionally preexistence in v 6, "descent" to the world of human life and death, then "ascent" to glory with God, a V-shaped parabola (cf. Talbert 1975, 1976):

---

[1] Schumacher 1914 defended the "mainline 'theocentric'" view, against an "anthropocentric" line in Ambrosiaster, Luther, and others, and the "radical anthropocentric" line since the 19th cent. (2:6–8 refers to a person entirely human).

[2] See J. H. Elliott, "Backward and Forward 'In His Steps': Following Jesus from Rome to Raymond and Beyond. The Tradition, Redaction, and Reception of 1 Peter 2:18–25," in *Discipleship in the New Testament*, ed. F. F. Segovia (Philadelphia: Fortress, 1985) 184–209. The 1990s "WWJD movement" also asked, "What would Jesus do?" To that, some respond, "We're not Jesus; we don't know what Jesus would do" on many of our issues.

[3] Cf. Dawe 1963:127–41; Henry 139–46; R. P. Martin 1967:63–74; C. Brown; *NIDNTT* 1:548–49; Welch; Sykes; L. J. Richard. Emily Elliott's hymn, "Thou didst leave thy throne and thy kingly crown/When thou camest to earth for me . . . , But in lowly birth didst thou come to earth/ And in great humility" (Dawe 1963:83–85).

[4] Ligier, a eucharistic hymn, relating to the *Nishmat kol hay* of the Jewish Passover (*JE* 9 [1905] 313–14), perhaps going back to Jesus in the Upper Room; Bockmuehl 145. Jervell 1960:206–8, baptismal; Edart 152–53, liturgical. See also (7) COMMENT B.3 n 31.

[5] A. M. Buscemi, *Una Sinfonia, gli Inni di Paolo a Cristo Signore*, SBFLA 48 (Jerusalem: Franciscan Printing Press, 2000): redaction by Paul and then by a disciple of his. Edart 142–49, 174–76 takes 8c and *dio kai* in 9a as redaction.

2:6–8 → katabasis ⟋ anabasis 2:9–11

A variation: v 9a may mean *"highly* exalted" to a more lofty position (as Lord) than previously:

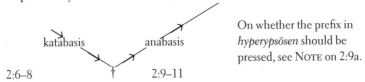

katabasis anabasis

2:6–8 2:9–11

On whether the prefix in *hyperypsōsen* should be pressed, see NOTE on 2:9a.

Others deny preexistence; the person was human from the start, exalted by God because of obedience unto death (Martin 1983: xx-xxi; Habermann 141–47; Talbert 1967).[6]

exaltation
2:9–11

2:6–8 ⟶ †

C. *Ernst Käsemann's "Critical Analysis"* (1950)[7] sees a story of salvation, not an ethical model to be imitated.[8] The "indicative" behind the "imperatives" in 2:1–4 (84). 2:5 admonishes the Philippians "to conduct themselves toward one another as is fitting within the realm of Christ" (84). Key terms come from the Hellenistic world.[9] Echoed by Bornkamm 1959a and others; contrast Schmauch 1967.

D. *History-of-Religions Backgrounds.* Roots for Phil 2:6–11 have been sought in "early Christian paraenesis and possibly from the Jesus tradition" (Hurtado 1984:126; Hawth. 78, 87, the foot-washing, John 13:1–17); in the OT (Isa 45:23 LXX at 2:10–11a); Gk. sources and other ancient religions. Possibilities can be variously arranged (Henry 38–56; Martin 1967:120–33; J. T. Sanders on NT hymns generally, 58–74; Habermann 150–55; O'B 193–98; Fee 43–44), without consensus.

1. *Iranian Zoroastrianism*—Loh.; Henry 41; Beare 75; Martin 1967:121–22; Kuschel 245; *DDD* 60. At best, a "source" now seen as something behind a "myth of the Heavenly Redeemer."

---

[6] Cf. Moule 1970; Carmignac; Howard 1978; H.-W. Bartsch 1974 ([6] Bibl.), "preexistence" is a "lie of speculation" that arose in early Christianity; Murphy-O'Connor 1976, background in Wis 2:12–13, 16–18; 3:1, 4, 8–9; 5:1–2, 4; Edart 154–55, 170, cf. 160 n 34.

[7] Cited from *JTC* 1968. Martin 1967:90–93, passim; V. Wiles 143–64; Way 88–94; R. Morgan 43–73.

[8] Morgan 43, 47–49, 72: doctrinal norms may be "undesirable," 49; an interpretation other than the ethical "will strike English-language readers as implausible," 55, but cf. 68; contrast Martin 1967:84–88.

[9] Käsemann 59–83; Morgan 59–67. E.g., *morphē* means not "form," as in classical Gk., but "mode of being" (*Daseinsweise*); *harpagmon* = "something for one's own benefit"; *morphē doulou*, "slave of Fate or the powers."

2. *Gnosticism and the Heavenly Man*/Urmensch/Anthropos *Myth*[10] — Of "historical necessity" in terms of the day. Increasingly out of favor. No full "myth" can be demonstrated prior to 2:6–11.[11]

3a. *OT: Angels: Adam and Lucifer* — Isa 14:12 ("Lucifer"), re *harpagmon* in 2:7.[12] At best, remote.

3b. *OT: Angel of the Lord* — Exod 23:20–21; Ezek 1:26–28 (Gieschen 337–39). Vollenweider 1999a:11, an "angelomorphic Christology" as "missing link" from Gk.-speaking Jewish-Christianity.

4. *OT: Adam and Christ* — Gen 1:26–27, 3:5, 5:1, "image" (*eikōn*, behind *morphē* in Phil 2:6a?); the second or last Adam, 1 Cor 15:20–22, 45–49; Rom 5:12–21.[13] Influential; not convincing to all.[14]

5. *OT/Synoptic Gospels: Son of Man*[15] — Dan 7:13; sayings of Jesus.[16] Nonsense?[17] Hawth. 78–79, with J. Ferguson 1971 ([6] Bibl.), would connect 2:6–11 with John 13:3–7 (foot-washing).

6. *OT: The Servant* — Isa 42–53 (Heb. *'ebed YHWH* = LXX *pais* = 2:7b *doulos*). Isa 45:23 LXX quoted at 2:10 is *not* from a "Servant passage." Cerfaux 1946; Jeremias, *"pais theou,"* TDNT 5:654–717 and *The Servant of God*, SBT 17; Mihoc 110–11, 126, 130. Disputed esp. by M. Hooker 1959:120–21; *NIB* 11: 503.[18] O'B 194, "insufficient"; Byron ([1] Bibl. **slaves**) 151–52; Fee 212; Bockmuehl 155–56; Hellerman 206 n 27, secondary to social context.

7. *OT: The Righteous Sufferer* — Isa 53, Pss 22, 69; Wis 2:12–20 and 5:1–7; some invoke Jewish martyr theology in the Maccabean period (cf. M. Hooker 1959); E. Schweizer 1962; 2nd Ger. ed. 5, 99–101 shifted to Jewish wisdom speculation.[19]

---

[10] Bultmann 1951 (INTRO. X Bibl.) 164; Käsemann, Bornkamm; Martin 1967:122–28; J. T. Sanders 66–69; Gnilka 143–44; Nagata 1981:39–45; R. L. Gordon, "Anthropos," *DDD* 59–62 (Bibl.). Contrast Colpe 1961, Georgi 1964b.

[11] Gnilka 143–44; U.B. Müller 112; Kuschel 245–50; Son 66–70, 120.

[12] Cf. *Ascen. Isa.* 10.29. Loh., *Phil.* 92–93; Martin 1967:157–61; J. A. Sanders 1969 ([6] Bibl.), "fallen . . . angels."

[13] Loh. 1928:21–29; J. T. Sanders 64–66; Martin 1967:128–33; S. Kim 1981:162–93, 260–67; Hurst 1986; O'B 196–97; Kuschel 251–53; *TPTA* 199–204, 241–42, 281–92 champions this view; N. T. Wright 1983 and 1986:57–62; Hooker *NIB* 11:503–506, "but greater than Adam."

[14] Fee 204 n 49, unlikely; D. H. Wallace 1966; Steenburg; Wanamaker 1987; Bockmuehl 131–33; Mihoc 108–10; Scroggs 1966:89–90, "the subtlety of the allusions . . . defies positive identification."

[15] The un-Gk. phrase *ho huios tou anthrōpou* is not found in Paul. U. Wilckens 1975 and Borsch 1992 relate "Adam and Christ" (4, above) to "(Son of) Man," which Loh. claimed to find in Phil 2:7d.

[16] Loh. 1928, re 2:7d–8a (plus the Servant); Deichgräber 130–31; Gnilka 139–40; Nagata 1981:30–31. Cullmann 1959 ([1] Bibl. **Christ**) 177–81 and Bonnard 43 combine Adam, Son of Man, and the Servant of God.

[17] So A. Vögtle, "'Der Menschensohn' und die paulinische Christologie," *Studiorum Paulinorum Congressus* (1963) 1:211, cited in Gnilka 139–40; Bornkamm 1959a:178–80 = tr. 1969:113–15; Habermann 151.

[18] Cf. Martin 1967: 182–90; Gnilka 140–41; Nagata 1981:31–33; Habermann 151–52; Seeley 50–57; Kuschel 253–55.

[19] Cf. L. Ruppert; Martin 1967:191–94; Gnilka 141–42; Heriban 407–10; Nagata 1981:36–39; K. T. Kleinknecht 189–90 (with Hofius 1976), 311–21; cf. (4) COMMENT A.1, above, on Phil 1:19; O'B 194–95.

8. *OT: Wisdom*—Prov 8; Job 28; 9:5–16; Sir 24: 5–23, esp. 8–9, 17–22; Wis 2:21–23, 3:1–4; 5:1,16; 6:12–11:1; cf. 18:15–16; *1 En.* 42.[20] Kramer ([1] Bibl. **Christ**) 121–23; Wengst 1972. Schimanowski 328–36. But 2:6–11 does not use *sophia* or *logos* (as in John 1) or treat creation.

9. *OT: Poverty*—2:7 "emptied himself," 2 Cor 8:9 "became poor *(eptōcheusen)* for your sake."[21] Economic poverty? Martin 1967:172–73 finds "little support" and rules out such a "nontechnical" sense.

10. *Judaism: The Post-Biblical Figure of Joseph* (Byron [(1) Bibl. **slaves**] 156–71), "humiliation [note the term]—obedience—exaltation," in *T. Jos.* 1.7; 10.3; 18.1 (*OTP* 1:819, 822, 823). Insufficient. *T. Jos.* seems a later document (Christian interpolations? Stoic elements, 69–94).[22]

11. *The Hellenistic World*—Scholars have ransacked classical Gk. (Lft.) and Hellenistic sources (Käsemann 1950), Greco-Roman hymnody, rhetoric (see below), and concepts like friendship (L. M. White 1990). Edart 151, more likely from a Hellenistic than a Jewish situation.

12. *Personages in the Greco-Roman World*—Henry 39–41 lists four figures well-known in the Roman *colōnia:* (a) *Heracles*, the greatest of Gk. heroes; after death exalted to deity.[23] Played a political role in Gk. "ruler cults" (Huttner). See (7) COMMENT A.5, nn 12, 13. (b) *Alexander the Great* (Lft. 111; Ehrhardt). Plut. applied the Hercules myth (above, [a]) to him.[24] The Macedonian royal family (Philip II, for whom Philippi was renamed) claimed descent from Heracles; Alexander, like Heracles, as direct son of Zeus (*OCD*³ 59). (c) *Gaius Caligula and Nero*, Roman Emperors (37–41 and 54–68 respectively). 2:11 may be directed against their claims (Bornhäuser 1933, 1938).[25] Imperial apotheosis, *RoR* (INTRO. I Bibl.) 2:227–28 (Cassius Dio 75.4.2–5.5) and, below, (7) COMMENT A.5.

13. *Social Setting in the Greco-Roman World*—Martin 1967:174 noted Bornhäuser (12c, above) and Max Maurenbrecher, Jesus literally a *doulos*, 2:7. Heriban 415–19; Cassidy 2001: 178–84. Feminist and Liberation interpretations

---

[20] J. T. Sanders 70–74; Georgi 1964b; Martin 1967:92–93, 318–19; Gnilka 142–43; Schüssler Fiorenza 1975; Nagata 1981:45–60; O'B 195–96; Kuschel 255–58; U. B. Müller 112; *TPTA* #11; Byron ([1] Bibl. **slaves**) 153–54.

[21] Dib. 77; K. Petersen 1933 (Ruth 1:21, Luke 1:53); Hofius 1976:59–60; *TPTA* 290–92, "a vivid allusion."

[22] Byron ([1] Bibl. **slaves**) considers backgrounds only in OT and Judaism. Joseph's "self-humiliation" (134–35) seems read in; "slave of God," admittedly not used re Joseph (138); "no direct exhortations of imitation" (136).

[23] Padilla; texts in Rice/Stambaugh 59–63. Cf. W. L. Knox 1948; Gnilka 138–39; Schenk 207–8; *RAC* 14 (1988) 559–82; *OCD*³ 684–86; U. B. Müller 112–13; Heracles as *sōter*, *TDNT* 7:1105; A. Y. Collins 1999:247–48.

[24] *Vit. Alex.* 1.8, *Mor* 330D: Alexander did not *(ou)* overrun Asia like a brigand, nor form the design of rending it and ravaging it as brigand's plunder *(harpagma)*, obtaining the spoils by luck, but *(alla)*, wishing to make all humanity a single people, he fashioned himself *(heauton eschēmatizen)* by wearing Asiatic dress to gain obedience *(hypēkoa)* from them. Cf. Gnilka 138–39; Schenk 207–8; Habermann 150; A. Y. Collins 1999:249.

[25] *OCD*³ 619–20, 1037–38; Martin 1967:78–81, 155–57, 222 n 3; Schenk 206–12; A. Y. Collins 1999:250–51.

reject 2:6–11 with its "mental universe of slaveholding antiquity" (S. Briggs 148).[26] Hellerman 127–56, 163: 2:6–8 is *cursus pudorum,* "a succession of ignominies," from equality with God to slave status and a socially degrading cross; 2:9–11, "reward" (154) for willing obedience.

14. *Enthronement as "Aggregation Ritual"* — 2:9–11 has been likened to ancient enthronement ceremonies[27]; cf. 1 Tim 3:16 (J. Jeremias, NTD 6th edition 1953:22–23; Quinn/Wacker 324–25; R. P. Martin 1967:33, 281). C. Strecker 59–77 relates the three-stage Christology of 2:6–11 ("form of God"; self-humbling human form, death; exaltation) to "separation, liminality, and aggregation" as "rites of passage" in cultural anthropology[28]: [1] separation out of one group or situation (here, from *morphē theou* and its status); [3] aggregation to a new status (initiation into office as cosmocrator; Käsemann). [2] is a stage "betwixt and between," a "threshold period" (Lat. *limen, liminis,* door or dwelling through which a person passes), status inversion, as slave, humiliation. Strecker 176 sees a process of "transformation" as also in Phil 3:2–21:

	Christ (2:6–11)	Paul/the Philippians (3:2–21)
Status A	Divine *morphē*	(Jewish) position of status
Separation	Renouncing privileges	the past considered as loss/crap → on account of Christ
Liminality	Humiliation, death	sufferings, death → participation in his sufferings being conformed to his death
Aggregation	Exaltation	upward call/transformation of the body, → *anō klēseōs . . . en Christō[i] Iēsou.*
Status B	Lord	Body of glory → *symmorphon tō[i] sōmati tēs doxēs autou*

For application to believers, see (12)-(14), below. The case for liminality in 2:6–11 seems forced (J. Schröter, *RBL,* http:www.bookreviews.org/Reviews/3525538693 .html).

No one background unlocks every problem in 2:6–11 (O'B 197). There are OT aspects, via the LXX and Hellenistic Judaism, and reflections of the Greco-Roman world. The history-of-religions setting is syncretistic. Nagata 1981:65 adds "the creative theological ability of the Christian community."

E. *Continuing and Conflicting Proposals.* Treatments of 2:5–11 have become increasingly hard to classify; cf. Martin 1983 and 1997. Often putative liturgical

---

[26] Cf. the commentaries by P. Perkins 334, C. Osiek 1994:242–44, Thurston 90–91; S. Wood; (7) COMMENT A.5.

[27] R. P. Martin 1976:242–43; Hofius 1976:29–34; Schenk 189; R. P. Martin 1983/1997:xxviii; J. F. Maile, *DPL* 275–78.

[28] A. van Gennep, *The Rites of Passage,* tr. M. B. Vizedom/G. L. Caffee (Chicago: Univ. of Chicago Press, 1960); V. Turner, *The Ritual Process: Structure and Anti-Structure* (Chicago: Aldine, 1969); cf. *ER* 12:382–86; T. Förster, "Victor Turners Ritualtheorie," *TLZ* 128 (2003) 703–13.

settings, *chiastic "concentric" structures,*[29] *rhetorical aspects* (Robbins; Robuck 45–48; Brucker; Krentz 1995). Cf. (7) COMMENT A.3, 4. N. T. Wright 1986 seems a counterattack toward more classical positions: "Adam Christology" (Adam corresponds to Israel, messiah, and people of God, 1991:18–40, summarized on 41), echoes of the Servant from Isa 40–45; incarnational.[30] Yet grasping "characterized pagan rulers . . . pagan gods and goddesses . . . the Philippians might have worshipped in their pre-Christian days" (89). *Literary, narrative approaches* see a "meta-story" (Martin 1997:lxxiii), often apart from historical setting and sources (R. B. Hays 1983 [(4) Bibl. **faith**]; Wright 1991:204–16; Kuschel 260–61). Fowl 1990:208, "a common narrative tradition which he shares with his audience." That the Philippians shaped?

"Hymn" has been used for 2:6–11 (Knoll 1921), along with "psalm," "song," and other terms, often loosely defined, with increasing restiveness about the imprecision. Martin reflects a consensus in the 1960s, but by 1997 debate (xliii–xlv, lv–lvi, esp. n 24; with Deichgräber 5–106). Fowl 13–19, 31–45, a "very general sense of poetic accounts of the nature and/or activity of a divine figure" (45).[31] Berger 1984a related the passage to the "encomion" form in rhetoric, praise or blame for a person (Sir 44–50) or god, as to origins, deeds, and fame.[32] Kennel 1995 questions "hymn" as a NT Gattung (christological confession, 276); Krentz 1995, under epideictic rhetoric, encomium and prose hymn; Brucker 319–20, 330–31, "epideictic" (praise), *epainos* as in Aristot. *Rhet.* 1.9.33–34, pp. 113–14, for the scope of *aretē*; Lat., *laus* (not *carmen*) *Christi* (319). Walter 57, perhaps a "Lehrgedicht" (didactic poem) about the "way" of the Son of God. See COMMENT A.3, below; (7) COMMENT B Biblio.

NOTES

2:5ab. *Think in this way among yourselves;* b *it is the way you also think "in Christ Jesus."* 5a impv., *phroneite*; 5b no vb., lit. "this (think-ye) in you (pl.) which also in Christ Jesus." *touto* parallels *ho*; "in you" parallels "in Christ Jesus" (Edart 178). P[46] Western MSS Majority Text linked v 5 to impvs. in 2:2–4 with *gar*, "for"; J. D. Price 278–79, Silva 107, 111–12. Fee 197 n 17, the unlinked text is original (asyndeton, BDF #459); *gar* (in a few MSS *oun*, "then") is secondary (NA[25–27]; UBSGNT {C}; TCGNT 613). On the vb., see NOTES on 2:2 *in that you think the*

---

[29] See INTRO. VI.B nn 2 (rhetoric) and 3 (chiasm); chiastic proposals by J. Bligh (*Bib* 49 [1968] 127–29), Manns 1976, and Lund ([3] Bibl.) are treated by J. D. Harvey 248–52. More in (7) COMMENT A.4 n 7.

[30] On *harpagmos*, Wright 1991:62–90 follows Hoover (divine equality is something Christ possessed but "did not regard as something to be taken advantage of") plus Moule 1970 (divine equality is not "getting" on the part of Jesus, but "giving").

[31] *History of research:* Deichgräber 11–18; Rese 1970; Wengst 1972:11–26; Kennel 22–46; Brucker 1–17; *WDNTECLR* 222–24.

[32] Cf. Lattke 1991 (pertinent texts; Brucker 14 n 73 adds more); Gk. texts and trs., by cult sites and in drama, in Furley/Bremer; K. Thraede, *RAC* 16 (1994) 915–46.

same thing and 1:7 *to think*; cf. 4:10 *your concern for me*. Lit., "Continue to think . . . ," + *touto*. Sölle 1965:164 = 1968:25, "Orient yourselves to this" (so M. Barth for Col 3:2 in AB 34B:395). A v.l. *phroneisthō*, Majority Text (3rd sg. pres. pass. impv., + *touto* as subject: "let this be thought . . ."; KJV "let this mind be in you"; Hawth. 76, 79–80; NRSV) is rejected by text critics (attestation inferior to *phroneite*, P⁴⁶ ℵ A B, etc.) and most interpreters (O'B 203, 255–56; Fee 197–98 n 18).

    touto. Dir. obj. See NOTES on 1:6 *Since I am confident about this point* (*auto touto*); 1:7 *. . . to think about you all in this way* (*touto phronein*); and 1:19 *This* (*touto*). Generally *houtos* (here neut.) refers back to something immediately preceding (BDAG 1.a.β and b.α; BDF #290.2,3), but may refer to something that follows (BDAG 1.a.δ and b.β; 2:6–11; BDF #290.3; Käsemann 1950:83–88; Losie 52–53). Most trs. fill it out with a noun from *phroneō*, "this mind," "attitude." The TRANSLATION *in this way* (cf. CEV) refers back (COMMENT B.3) to 1:27ff., esp. 2:2–4.

    2:5a. *among yourselves*. *en hymin* (dat. pl.); see NOTE on 1:6 *among you*; emphasis on "you all" at Philippi (1:7 bis, 8, 25). Some (Heriban 89–90) urge (1) an individual sense, parallel to "in Christ Jesus" as an individual (Joüon 91–93; Lft. 110 "in your hearts"; Edart 181–83); or (2) a social sense, one to another, reciprocally, Moule 1970:265 "towards one another"; or (3) an ecclesial sense, cf. 5b *en Christō[i] Iēsou* (the community in Philippi, "saints in Christ" 1:1). Losie: "Set your mind on this confession, in your mutual relations, on which also you set your mind when you came to be 'in Christ Jesus' (at your baptism)" (Senses 2 and 3, a community of the baptized). The TRANSLATION agrees with RSV, NABRNT, REB.

    2:5b. *it is the way you also think "in Christ Jesus."* Neut. sg. rel. pron. (*ho*), "which" (KJV, RSV) or "that" (NRSV), referring back to *touto*, "this (mind, attitude)." Since *touto* = *in this way*, since 5b introduces a further relationship "in Christ Jesus," of Philippian Christians with each other (Schenk 175–77, 185), *it is* has been added, *ho* rendered as *the way*, and a parallel vb. to 5a, *you . . . think* (*phroneite*, indic.) supplied (see below). *kai* = *also* (KJV, NABRNT); [N]RSV, NIV, REB omit. Silva 107, an intensive, "which indeed"; Caird 118, *id est*: "the disposition which must govern your common life, i.e., your life in Christ Jesus, because he. . . ." ZBG 156 omits *kai*; "in Christ Jesus" = the "mystical body" of Christ (disputed by Fee 200–1 n 32).

    Much depends on the vb. supplied in 5b. Traditionally (1) *ēn* (imperf., *eimi*, "be"), KJV, the mind "which *was* also in Christ Jesus" (NRSV-txt); justified from "the narrative that follows" (Fee 200 n 29). Or "is" (Bockmuehl 123–24; RSV 1971; NABRNT). (2) a 2nd pl., as in 5a: "which you have" (RSV 1946–59; NRSV-mg); "what you find" (REB); Loh. *Phil.* 91. (3) Some form of the vb. in 5a, "which he thought (in himself)" (Lft. 110; Ellicott 54; Plummer 41). (4) Käsemann 1950:83–84: "in the realm of Christ" + "as is fitting" (*prepei*) (Gnilka 109) or "as you think" (*phroneite*, Thüsing 1965:50) or "as it is necessary to think" (*phronein dei*). BDAG *phroneō* 3, "**develop an attitude based on careful thought**, *be minded/disposed* . . . have the same thoughts among yourselves as you have in your communion with Christ Jesus* (so CDodd, *The Apost[olic] Preaching* '37, 106f.)";

NEB-txt, "Let your bearing for one another arise out of [*phroneisthō*] your life in Christ Jesus." Orientation to Christ determines relations to each other in Christ's community. Koenig 147: "Have this mind among yourselves . . . which indeed is your new life in the realm of Christ Jesus." Final decision depends on overall conclusions (is 2:6–11 about how Christ thought?) and immediate context; see COMMENT B.3.

en Christō[i] Iēsou. See NOTES on 1:1, 13, and 26 *in Christ Jesus;* 2:1 *in Christ.* Traditionally here pre-temporal existence (as *logos asarkos*) and/or earthly life *(logos ensarkos);* Ewald 103–4 = Wohl. 114–15. For some, the historical Jesus, a model for Christians, "Your attitude should be the same as that of Christ Jesus" (NIV); cf. [N]JB, GNB, CEV. Heriban 92–95 lists four senses: (1) Ethical-paraenetic (Hawth. 75, "This way of thinking must be adopted by you . . . the way of thinking adopted by Christ Jesus"; Moule). (2) "Christological-soteriological" (Käsemann; Bornkamm 1959a:112; Martin 1967:291, "Become . . . the type of persons who, by that *kenosis*, death, and exaltation of the Lord of glory, have a place in His body, the Church"). (3) Ecclesial, "in Christ" = his body, the church; (Bultmann 1951 [INTRO. X Bibl.] 311); "as members of His Church" (Grayston 1967:91; "in the company of Christ's people," Martin 1967:71; Son 16). (4) Mystical, Deissmann ([1] Bibl. **Paul**) 1927 ed.:147–57, 193–94, 297–99; Martin 1967:70–71.

Käsemann's sense has been assailed by those advocating solely an ethical one (O'B 200–1). At 2:5b reference to the story about Jesus Christ in vv 6–11 *(inclusio* with *the Lord is Jesus Christ* at 11b, and/or *in Christ* in 2:1) is difficult to avoid. The communal, ecclesial aspect reflects the persons addressed *(among you* 5a). No "Christ mysticism" or ethical paradigm need be seen in the phrase itself in 5b. 2:5a continues the impvs. of vv 2–4; 5b recalls the bases in 2:1 for such admonitions and anticipates the narrative in vv 6–11 that grounds these and the impvs. in 2:12–14. 2:5a is about the Philippians' relations with each other; 5b, the relationship they have "in Christ" under his lordship. They *do* think this way about Christ, for they wrote vv 6–11 (see COMMENT B.1, 2); hence the *kai.* Paul applies their message to conduct among themselves.

2:6a. *who, while living in the sphere of God. . . . hos,* who (KJV-[N]RSV), "the one who," Christ Jesus (2:5b), as at Col 1:15, 1 Tim 3:16. *hyparchōn,* masc. nom. sg. pres. act. ptc., "being" (KJV, NIV), agrees with *hos. en morphē[i] theou,* "in the form" (KJV-[N]RSV) or "very nature" of God (NIV-txt). The vb. *archō* ("rule"; m. "begin") + *hypo* means (1) **exist, be present** (3:20); (2) in Hellenistic Gk., for *eimi,* "be" (BDAG). Does it imply (BDF #414.1) "'exist originally'"? "continuity with a previous state" (MM 650)? "'prior existence,' but not necessarily 'eternal existence'" (Lft. 110)? Connection with *archē,* "origin," is sensed by Binder 1987:236; Kuschel 258–59. NEB, "was his from the beginning." But such a sense "gradually . . . faded in later Greek" (MM 650). Pres. tense, in contrast to aors. in vv 7–8 *(labōn, genomenos* (bis), *heuretheis),* thus "continuing to be" (divine) during actions in the "form of a slave" and death? Collange 98; like an imperf. alongside the aors. (B. Weiss 147 n 1). Is the ptc. concessive ("though," [N]RSV); *GGBB* 220, 634–35; or causal ("precisely because he was . . . he recognized what it meant. . . . ," Moule, in Wright 1991:83 n 110). To press tense and *hyparchōn* as causal usually accompanies a traditional view, Christ as "truly God" (CEV, cf. LB), but need not, depending on how *morphē theou* is taken. *hyparchōn en* + dat. suggests to some "be wrapped or clothed in" (*TDNT* 4:751 n 52; cf. Luke 7:25; Nagata 210 and others). Ernst 65, cf. 77, used "living"; so the TRANSLATION, to avoid ontological language of "being" and remain open to varied possible backgrounds.

in the sphere of God. theou, see NOTE on 1:2 God; cf. 2:6c. *morphē theou* is to be treated with *morphē doulou* 7b, *homoiōmati anthrōpōn* 7c, and *schēmati . . . hōs anthrōpos* 7d (cf. Lft. 127–33). *morphē* occurs only here in the NT (+ Mark 16:12). Compounds include *symmorphoumai, symmorphos* at 3:10, 21. Word studies: J. Behm, *TDNT* 4:742–59; G. Braumann, *NIDNTT* 1:703–10, with *eidos*; W. Pöhlmann, *EDNT* 2:442–44; *TLNT* 520–25; Heriban 234–47.

Most church fathers saw the divine nature of the preexistent logos; a few (Ambrosiaster, Pelagius; later, Luther), the incarnate Son in his human nature (B. Weiss 145–46). Lft. 110, 127–33 (cf. below, [14] NOTE on 3:21a *will change*): "form," as in the Gk. philosophers, esp. Aristot., means intrinsic, essential, in contrast to *schēma* (fleeting, changeable "figure, shape"; outward, external accidents). Jowers: = essence, *ousia*. Contrast EGT 435–36. Lft.'s view persisted (K. Barth 61–63). Behm documented far greater variety in Gk. use (744–46): *morphē*, external, visible appearance, perceived by the senses; at 2:6, divine glory, "the garment by which His divine nature may be known" (752). Käsemann 1950:59–63 pointed to the Hellenistic world where "essence" was comprehended by "mode of existence" *(Daseinsweise)*, as in the mystery religions. (Behm 756–59 cites texts Käsemann stressed, like *Corp. Herm.* 1,12–21, HCNT #794.) Käsemann's analysis has, in turn, been questioned (e.g., Nagata 1981:179–207). In Plato, *morphē* suggests external form or appearance; in Aristot., *morphē* = *eidos*, "form," in contrast to "matter" *(hylē)*; in the Hellenistic world, "mode of existence." Schweizer, *Erniedrigung* 1955:54 n 234, invoked the OT: *morphē* = "condition." But see Jervell's criticism, 1960:230 n 220. Nagata 208 concluded at 2:6 for "a perceptible divine form by which the divine reality is vividly cognizable."

If "form," what aspect of God? Cf. Collange 96–98; Martin 1967:99–120, 1976:94–96; Habermann 110–18; Hawth. 81–84; O'B 206–11. (a) Traditionally "essence, being" *(ousia)* or nature *(physis)* (Schumacher; Henry 129; *PGL* 884–85; Heriban 234–35), reflected in Lft. 110; Hawth. 84; Gdsp., Moffatt, NIV, GNB. Little support among recent exegetes (Silva 116). (b) = *eikōn*, God's "image" (Gen 1:26,27, patristic and modern scholarship), "Adam Christology," the first man and Christ are parallel; Cullmann 1959 ([1] Bibl. **Christ**) 176; Bandstra 1966; Talbert 1967:149; Murphy-O'Connor 1976:41; Heriban 236–39; Dunn 1980:115–17; W. Eltester, *Eikon im Neuen Testament* (BZNW 23; Berlin: de Gruyter, 1958) 81; Jervell 1960:204–5, it came via Gnosticism. Cf. 2 Cor 4:4,6 (*eikōn, doxa* "glory"; AB 32A:222, 246–49); Col 1:15 (*eikōn tou theou*, AB 34B:195, 248–50). But D. H. Wallace 1966 finds the LXX evidence insufficient to equate *morphē* and *děmût*. Martin 1967:97 rejects it; similarly Habermann 115–16; *TLNT* 2:523; *EDNT* 2:443; Steenburg. (c) "Glory" *(doxa)*, in some *eikōn* texts and depictions of

God (Exod 16:1; 24:16; 33:17–23; Isa 6:3; 40:1,2; 2 Macc 2:8). Cf. Martin 1967:103–5, 109–19; Heriban 235–36, cf. 274–80; O'B 208–9, 210–11; Hellerman 131–33, "in garments of divine majesty." Isa 52:14 LXX *doxa* = Aquila *morphē* (Seeley 1994:50–51). Behm (*TDNT* 4:746, 751 esp. n 53), "the divine *doxa*," the concept Käsemann (1950:60) attacked; Hawth. 82, etc.: "glory" is inadequate.

(d) *Daseinsweise* (Käsemann, cf. Dib.75), "manner of being present, mode of existence," can apply to God or human beings, "the sphere in which one stands and which determines one like a field of force" (61, tr. from Kuschel 606 n 46). Cf. Gnilka 112–14; Bornkamm 1959a:115–16; Jervell 1960:276–81; Schenk 195–96, 200, 203, 212. (e) "Condition," "status" (Bonnard 43; Dupont 1950:502–4; Spicq 1973; Fowl 54; JB "His state was divine"). Schweizer, *Erniedrigung* 1962: 95–96, something between "visible outward form" and "essence"; OT "form and matter" or "being and appearance" go together. Martin 1967:103–4 approved. Heriban 246–47; I. H. Marshall 50. Collange 97, Nagata 207, and Habermann 117 found the evidence insufficient (cf. Jervell 1960:230 n 220); cf. Pöhlmann, *EDNT* 2:443; Schimanowski 330. (f) Habermann 111–12, "form of appearance." Edart 155–57, exterior manifestation of a real identity. (g) Appeal to *homoiōma* (Gen 1:26); 2:7c, + pl., *anthrōpōn*, not *theou* or *doulou* as with *morphē* (Habermann 116). J. Schneider (*TDNT* 5:197), "Christ changed his form," but "[t]he earthly *morphē* is also the husk which encloses His unchanging essential existence." (h) Bockmuehl (1997, *Phil.* 126–27), "something . . . perceived by the senses" (J. Behm, *TDNT* 4:745), "visual characteristics" (*Phil.* 127). Moses saw in the midst of the flame (Exod 3) a *morphē* most beautiful (*Life of Moses* 1.66 = LCL *Philo* 6:310–11); to safeguard God's transcendence (cf. Wis 18:1), Philo does not press *morphē* further. Part of a "Jewish tradition about mystical ascent" (Segal 1990 [(1) Bibl. **Paul**] 34–71, esp. 62–63; cf. Hammerich)—a category not beyond criticism. Qumran materials (*tabnit*, 4Q 400; 4QshirShabb[a]) seem remote. Later Jewish mystical texts. The lexical and contextual jumps are not persuasive. (i) *Metamorphosis* "in secret epiphanies of gods on earth" (Zeller 2001 [(1) Bibl. **Lord**] 321–24; Zeller 1988:160–63; accepted by Söding 1992b; U. B. Müller 1988:23–27; 1990: 20–26; *Phil.* 93–94). More Greco-Roman parallels in Vollenweider 1999b: Eur. *Bacch.* 4–5, 53–54, Dionysus the *morphē* of a god in human form; Lucian, *Philops.* 14; Iamblichus *Vit. Pyth.* 30; Justin Martyr *Apol.* 1.9. Frenschkowksi 1997. But Phil 2:6–11 implies more than *external* change or disguise. Instead of self-disclosure at the end of a story, the figure in 2:8 dies. Bockmuehl 1997, cf. *Phil.* 127, rejects such pagan myths but did not convince Zeller 2001:322; cf. Vollenweider 1999b, "angelomorphic Christology" (Exc.B.II. D.3b).

Given such conflicting views, Spicq cautioned against "a precise theological meaning" for *morphē* (*TLNT* 2:525). Fee 204–5 dismisses "image" and "glory"; the metaphor in 2:7b, *morphē doulou*, "determines the meaning" of 2:6a and "the reality (his being God)"; with Hawth., "a form which truly and fully expresses the being which underlies it" (MM 417; contrast Silva 115). But that statement (from Kennedy!) could take no cognizance of texts injected by Käsemann or by Spicq from the papyri. Habermann 118 settled on *Daseinsweise* (d, above), cf. Eichholz

1972 (Intro. X Bibl.)141. As Kuschel 606 n 46 put it, "Anyone who decides . . . for 'appearance' . . . runs the risk of reading into the text a contrast between changing 'external appearance' and a permanent 'inner being.' . . . Anyone arguing that this is a statement about Christ's nature" runs the danger "that such a statement about Jesus 'can be misunderstood in physical-real terms.'" Anyone for status, position (Schweizer) "will hardly find a parallel in other New Testament writings" (Gnilka 113–14). Anyone for "divine glory" (Schnackenburg 1970:315) overlooks the fact that in the hymn "the obedient one only received this status after the humbling and not before." Kuschel, Käsemann, and Translation opt for *sphere* (realm, place and relationships).

   2:6bc. *did not consider to be like God something of which to take advantage.* *hēgēsato*, aor. m. act. indic., *hēgeomai*; see Note on 2:3 *consider.* . . . Bornhäuser 1938:18–19, "'imperial' style" (cf. 3 Macc 3:15). Avoid "think" (KJV), used for *phronein.* Here + double dir. obj. (as at 3:7,8), "regard not (as) *harpagmon* the being equal with God *(to einai isa theō[i])*." Neg. *ouch* before *harpagmon,* not before the vb. (the usual location); few trs. bring this out (KJV does, "not robbery"). A "but" cl. follows, with another vb.; 6bc and 7ab go closely together (Grelot 1973, an emphatic negation, followed by a strong "but," *alla*). Carmignac made this the starting point for defending the traditional view (Gk. fathers, Vg); it was "not usurpation" for the eternal Word to be equal with God; Carmignac applied it to Jesus' earthly life.

   2:6b. *to be like God.* KJV "to be equal with God," often taken to corroborate 6a, Christ "equal with," and therefore, God (Hawth. 84). Art. infin. (*to* [neut. acc., sg.] *einai* [as at 1:23]); see Notes on 1:21 *to live . . . and to do*; 1:23 *to depart and to be with Christ*; 1:24 *to continue to stay on . . .* ; 1:29b (chart in ATR 1424). A pred. adj. might be expected, *isos* = equal + dat.; an adv. (neut. pl. *isa*) is substituted; BDF #434, an old usage; GNTG 3:21, 226, cf. Habermann 125–26; common in the LXX, esp. Job, e.g. 11:12, "be like" (Lft. 111). But "to be like" *(isa)* "is not synonymous with *isos theō[i]* = '. . . equal to God' (identity of nature)" (*TLNT* 2:229). Grelot 1972:500, "an enfeebled sense," cf. *TLNT* 2:224–25, no special emphasis on equality; "like" (Habermann 126). Grelot 1972:500 cites Nicolaus of Damascus, Augustus Caesar was "honored as a god" (*ton . . . isa kai theon timōmenon*; FGrH 90, frg. 130.97; cf. also frg. 130.117). *TLNT* 2:229–30 cites Aristot. *Pol.* 3.13.13, "like a god among human beings"; *isotheos,* "godlike," of Darius (Aeschyl. *Pers* 856), Heracles (Diod. Sic. 1.2.4 *isotheon timōn*), Pythagoras (Diod. Sic. 10.9.9, "honored equally with the gods"), and a woman from Samos (POxy 39.2891 frg. 3, col. II.4; *TLNT* 2:229 n 29); kings (Tellbe 2001:256). Caesar appears in hymns alongside the gods *(ex isou tois theois)*; honors given to rulers make them *isotheoi* (Cass. Dio 51.20). *theos* is documented for Augustus, Claudius, Titus, and Vespasian (*TLNT* 2:230 n 30). Germanicus rejected for himself acclamations "addressed to gods *(isotheous)*"; they apply to the reigning Emperor, Tiberius (edict A.D. 19; Hunt/Edgar, LCL *Select Papyri* 2 #211). One honored *philoi* "like (you would honor) a god" *(ison theō[i]*; FCG 4:347.269, ed. Jaekl, 53.357, tr. in Heen 1997:185). More in BDAG *isos, ē, on* and Heen 1997:182–87 (*terminus technicus* is involved).

Stählin (*TDNT* 3:345–48, 351–52; cf. E. Beyreuther, *NIDNTT* 2:497–98) treated "equality" as "basic . . . in Greek political and legal theory" and equality "with God outside the NT"; Phil 2:6, "equal to God by nature" (*TDNT* 3:345–48, 351–52, 353). Spicq, aware of divine honors paid to humans, saw "equality of treatment, dignity . . . recognized" (2:229, with P. Benoit, *Bibel de Jérusalem* 1956:1551; Grelot). Habermann 126–27, *gottgleiche Daseins- und Existenzweise*, but he also cites "condition," "position of worth, dignity." Heen 1997:177–96 treats *isa theō[i]/theois, ison theō[i]* (neut. pl. and sg. adv.), *isos theō[i]* (adj.) and *isotheos*; they "blurred in actual usage." Examples root "in the honorific tradition of the Greek cities" for heroes and rulers (cf. Meeks 1990:312–14), a "civic tradition" at home in Philippi. The "Judaic tradition" does *not* let mortals "think that they are equal to God" (2 Macc 9:12; cf. Philo *Leg. All.* 1.49; *Sib. Or.* 5.34, 12.86, of Nero, *isazōn theō[i]*; John 5:18). Thus two traditions; they clashed in A.D. 39–41 when Gaius Caligula attempted to place his statue as Jupiter in the Jerusalem Temple. 2:6 reflects the positive Gk. sense ("like God") and the OT-Jewish view (Jesus did *not* treat it as *harpagmon*). Phil 2:6 reflects and contrasts with Imperial cult (Bornhäuser 1938:17–19, specifically Caligula; Georgi 1991:72–75); 2:10c will offer a hidden critique of the *decurions* in Philippi who sat under the Emperor (cf. Garnsey 242–45, the local elite = the *epigeiōn* there; Heen 2004). *einai* should not be pressed ontologically, nor absence of an art. with *theō[i]*. Many take *to einai isa theō[i]* as subject acc. (RSV "did not count *equality with God* a thing to be grasped." Others follow the Gk. word order, KJV, "thought it not robbery *to be equal with God*."

2:6c. *something of which to take advantage. harpagmon* (acc. sg.). Rejected textual conjectures include *apragmon*, "free of business, toil, duty"; *pragma*, lit. "(no) matter"; and *harpagimon*, "something he should snatch up" (Habermann 95–97). From *harpazō*, "steal, snatch" (1 Thess 4:17, "caught up in the clouds"). Nouns in -*mos* denote the action of the vb. root; those in -*ma*, the result of the action (BDF #109.1, 2; cf. Vokes). *harpagmos* "act of robbing," KJV "robbery," but BDAG 1 deems this "next to impossible" at 2:6 (Fee 205; *TDNT* 1:472–73, sense a), though Lat. fathers took it as act., Vg *rapina* = "robberie" (Rheims NT). Moule 1970:266–68, "act of snatching" (see below); then *harpagmos* = *harpagē* (Heb 10:34 "plundering"; Matt 23:25 par. Luke 11:39 "rapacity"). On the "grasping" nature of pagan deities, cf. N. H. Young re Aristoph. *Eccl.* 777–83: to give is "not our custom but to take (*ou . . . alla*), so also the gods," "that they may get something."

BDAG 3, "to be like God was no rapture" (cf. 2 Cor 12:2; 1 Thess 4:17; Rev 12:5), for "Christ had it by right" (Hammerlich; Henry 24; D. W. B. Robinson 1969, Jesus rejected "being caught up" to heaven, escaping suffering), has found little support. Habermann 125, "fantasy," like L. Abramowski's "raptured" or "was beside himself" (*Drei christologische Untersuchungen* [BZNW 45; Berlin: de Gruyter, 1981] 1–17).

BDAG 2 takes *harpagmos* as pass., equal to *harpagma*, "the thing seized or stolen," though examples are lacking in non-Christian literature (Heriban 250–65; R. P. Martin 1967:135–53; Habermann 119–25). (Lat. phrases employed as shorthand expressions for each sense have confused even commentators, cf.

N. T. Wright 1991:65–69). The pass. meaning developed as [a] **booty, (a) grab,** *TDNT* 1:433 sense b. A prize already obtained (Gk. fathers), *res rapta* (pass. ptc. of *rapio;* "a thing seized," in one's possession; Wright prefers *res retinenda,* "a prize to be held on to") or a prize to be sought after (*res rapienda,* not possessed, to be grasped anew, Wright; cf. Beet 1887:123). So Vollenweider. [b] **a piece of good fortune, windfall.** *TDNT* 1:473–74 sense c; Martin's "third possibility," 1967:143–48. *res rapta* (something already possessed, by a preexistent Christ) or *res rapienda* (something yet to be obtained).

Martin 1967:134–64 traced gyrations in interpretation. Wright 81 charted ten "solutions" for *morphē,* as divine (so most) or human (e.g, Murphy-O'Connor); *to einai isa theō[i]* (usually divine equality); and *ouch . . . hēgēsato,* "abandoned" (something possessed) or "did not snatch at" something Christ did not possess. Habermann arranges solutions under *res rapienda* (dominant in Anglo-Saxon and French scholarship) and *res rapta* (esp. in Ger. scholarship). What he calls "the idiomatic sense" emerges as solution, without reference to Wright. *Word studies:* W. Foerster, *TDNT* 1 (1933) 472–74; E. Tiedtke/C. Brown, *NIDNTT* 3:601–5; W. Trilling, *EDNT* 1:156–57—indicate how rare examples are of *harpagmos.*

Verse 2:6b must be approached in light of the entire phrase, "consider *to einai isa theō[i]* something of which to take advantage." W. Jaeger 1915, like Lft. 111, called attention to texts (from Wettstein) in the *Ethiopian Story* by Heliodorus, a 3rd or 4th cent. A.D. Gk. novelist (*Aeth.* 7.20, etc.). Here *harpagma/heurēma hēgeisthai/poieisthai,* etc., means "regard something as a stroke of luck, a windfall, a piece of good fortune." Popular jargon, then a literary *topos* (Plut., *De Alex. fort.* 8; Exc.B n 24) or proverbial formula (Schumacher 2:284–85). Not *res rapienda* (the object already in the person's possession), nor *res retinenda* (it doesn't fit the nonbiblical examples).

Hoover 117–18 distinguished more sharply. (1) *harpagma* (pred. acc.) + *hēgeisthai* and other vbs. is "distinguishable from . . . *hermaion* and *heurēma*" (contra Jaeger) (117). Thus not luck or a windfall. (2) "*harpagma* and *harpagmos* were used synonymously in the Hellenistic period" ("virtually certain"). (3) Evidence from "*harpagma* in double accusative constructions . . . can be a basis for determining the meaning" of *harpagmos* at 2:6 (117–18). = "take advantage of" an opportunity, "something to use for his own advantage" (118). (2) assumes (107–8) *harpagmon* is used in the LXX with act. (Isa 61:8) and pass. meaning (Isa 42:2), and that in Eus. they are synonymous (*harpagma, H.E.* 8.12.2; *harpagmos, Comm. in Luc* 6, catenae frgs.). Later data are being used to settle NT meanings. All we have, but the data base is slim, esp. when "booty" references are set aside. Hoover concluded, 2:6 "owes nothing to scriptural antecedents" (119).

Hoover's solution (*morphē* and *to einai isa theō[i]* refer to a preexistent Christ already possessing divinity) commended itself to Habermann (121–24), though Murphy-O'Connor 38–39 and Howard 377 n 28 worked it into their view of a human Christ. Wright 1986:76–90 combined Hoover's findings with Moule 1970 (*harpagma* signifies an action; Christ "did not regard equality with God as consisting in* snatching" [266, his italics]; "not . . . getting, but paradoxically, giving," 276). Wright "combines Moule's theology and Hoover's philology" (Robuck 106).

Actually, Moule "bowed to Hoover" (Hawth. 1998:102). Wright 78: "*the attitude one will take towards something which one already has and holds and will continue to have and hold*" ("attitude," not in Hoover, from 2:5?). *ouch* negates the entire idiom (cf. Carmignac). Thus NRSV, "something to be exploited." Though Hoover's study did not of itself rule out the possibility of taking 2:6a and c in a "humanitarian sense," Wright used his interpretation to establish a preexistent God-figure as the subject. Indeed, "precisely because he was such" (*hyparchōn* as causative) (82 n 107; 83 n 110). The result "is a new understanding of God": "one . . . himself God, and who never during the whole process stopped being God," embracing incarnation and cross (84). Wright appealed to Eus. *H. E.* 5.2.2 for support (Phil 2:6 quoted, martyrs did not use martyrdom as "something to take advantage of"); but surely, Dunn objects, they did not already "possess" it, *TPTA* 285 n 87). 2:9–11 means, That is why honor (that belongs to the one God) was given to Christ. The hymn with its Adam Christology shows us love on God's part (though *agapē* is not used). To the objection that an act. sense for *harpagmos* calls for some obj. (snatched at what?), Wright points to Philippian background: "it refers, intransitively, to a particular way of life, namely, that which characterized pagan rulers and indeed pagan gods and goddesses such as the Philippians might have worshipped in their pre-Christian days" (89).

Wright's interpretation has dominated many Anglo-Saxon commentaries (Silva 118, Wright "settled" the question); otherwise in Schenk 188, 212; U. B. Müller. But renderings vary. Silva 112: "took no advantage of"; O'B 202–3, "something to be used for his own advantage"; Fee 207, "a matter of seizing upon to his own advantage"; Bockmuehl 114, "needed to take advantage of." The matter is not settled (Dunn, *TPTA* 285; O'Neill 1988 raises some valid points but his emendation adding a negative, "*not* being equal with God." is a counsel of despair). Wright's interpretation fits *morphē* and *to einai isa theō[i]* into the sense developed for *harpagmos*. Methodologically, others would prefer to determine the sense of 6a and 6c somewhat differently and then fit *harpagmos* in. Vollenweider 1999b, the "idiom" (*harpagma* + vb. of consideration + double acc.) is attested only in the 4th cent., it doesn't fit an elevated style. Lack of a scriptural background and the presence of a Gk. idiom suggest a phrase known to the Philippians, one they would not have "tied themselves in knots over" as interpreters have done (Bockmuehl 130; 131, a "Philippian tendency to use status and privilege to one's own advantage," the opposite of Christ in 6bc). Cf. Vollenweider: usurpation of equality with God by kings, rulers, and tyrants.

2:7a. *but himself he emptied. alla* (1:18d, 20; 2:4; cf. Grelot 1973; "on the contrary," Thekkekara) introduces a contrast to v 6: Christ emptied or divested self. *heauton* (obj.; see NOTES 2:3b . . . *yourselves*; 2:4a *not your own interests*) + *kenoō* (aor. act. indic. 3rd sg.) are unparalleled in Gk. LSJ lists for *kenoō* "empty, leave a place, empty out, expend"; pass., "waste away"; Phil 2:7, "make empty." Adj. *kenos* "empty" (12x in Pauline corpus; Phil 2:16 bis, "run *in vain*"). Vb., "make empty, divest, destroy," rare in the OT (only Jer 14:2 and 15:9), 5x in the NT, all in Paul, a metaphor, usually in a bad sense (1 Cor 1:17; Rom 4:14; 1 Cor 9:15; 2 Cor 9:3); cf. *kenodoxia* 2:3, "vainglory." Antonym of *pleroō* ("make full," 1:11; 2:2). *Word* *studies:* A. Oepke, *TDNT* 3:659–62, rules out "negated himself" on the basis of context; E. Tiedtke/H. G. Link, *NIDNTT* 1:546–48, Hellenistic background; M. Lattke, *EDNT* 2:281–82; *TLNT* 2: 303–10 defends the Vg *exinanivit* ("He annihilated himself," is "reduced to nothing"), even though the preexistent Lord's "personal identity is immutable." The term has a more imposing subsequent history (*NIDNTT* 1:548–49; *PGL* 743, *kenoō* II, III, rarely + *heauton*). Heriban 280–90 notes *auto-kenosis* and a metaphorical sense, either absolute (nullify; Silva 119–20) or relative ("stripped himself," Beare; "beggared himself," from 2 Cor 8:9). K. Petersen, "fixed . . . associations"; Ruth 1:21 "full *(plērēs)* . . . empty *(kenēn)*. . . . The Lord humiliated *(etapeinōse)* me"; Luke 1:53, "The Lord has sent the rich away empty *(kenous)*"; 2 Cor 8:9, though rich, Christ became poor; Phil 2:7 *ekenōsen, etapeinōsen;* cf. Schenk 205. Fee 210, "poured himself out," assuming preexistence; cf. Habermann 127–31.

Jeremias (1963:183–84 = *Abba* 309–10) claimed as background Isa 53:12, the servant "poured out himself to death" (NRSV; cf. *TDNT* 5:711 n 445; Hofius 1976). Then 2:7a refers to crucifixion, not incarnation. The LXX is, however, "his life was given over to death"; that *pais* (Isa 53) = *doulos* (2:7b) has met with resistance. Isa 53, precious to many (Fee 212), has been widely rejected as background (Hunzinger 146; R. P. Martin 1967:165–77, 182–90, xxiii–xxv; C. Brown, *NIDNTT* 1:548; *EDNT* 2:282 (M. Lattke); O'B 190, 194, 220, "insufficient to establish with certainty," 268–71; Gnilka 118; Habermann 129–30). For Bockmuehl, Isa 53:12 is "subliminal." Hooker does not even mention Isa in connection with 2:8 (*NIB* 11:508; cf. 503 and Hooker 1959). 2:7 is a general metaphor, in contrast to "enriching" or "making full" oneself.

2:7b. *taking on the sphere of a slave. morphē*, see NOTE on 6a *in the sphere of God;* the two uses of *morphē* interpret each other. *doulou*, gen. sg., see NOTE on 1:1 *slave.* Aor. ptc., *lambanō*, BDAG 1; "taking the form of" ([N]RSV, "assuming" NEB, REB). 7cd are often taken with 7a, defining "he emptied himself"; circumst. ptcs., "by taking the nature of a servant" (TC; Fee 211 "modal"), "being born like other human beings" (O'B 203) and "being found in appearance as a human being"; even aor. ptcs. of simultaneous action (Robuck 113). Then all the v deals with the incarnation. *GGBB* 630: *labōn* amplifies "emptied himself," which should be by "subtraction, not addition," but here = "emptied his glory by veiling it in humanity." Many who see a "story" opt for stages (Käsemann 70, "the sequence of occurrences in an event unified in and of itself"). An aor. ptc. can denote action prior to the main vb. (BDF #339); hence, "having taken on a servant's form, he emptied self (or poured out his life in death)." Hunzinger 156, two phases: (1) in 6–7b, from *morphē theou* to *morphē doulou*, abandoning divinity; (2) 7c–8, from human likeness to death, abandoning human existence. Cf. Fowl 54–69: Christ's exalted position (6a), but a position not taken advantage of (6bc); change of position (7ab); situated in the human realm (7cd); ultimate humiliation (8); a reversal of fortunes (9–11). Others see the ptcs. as simultaneous or identical action (BDF #339.1; Hawth. 86): emptying self was precisely Christ's taking on a servant's form, aor. for a particular moment, the incarnation. ATR 1114 invoked the "timelessness" of ptcs.; to find subsequent action in 2:7 is gratuitous. No widely agreed construal of the ptcs. in a story line. The TRANSLATION does not press antecedent action or manner.

slave. Why *doulou* in 7b before Christ becoming "human" 7cd? Suggestions vary (Martin 1967:169–96). (1) Kenotic Christology: Christ "emptied himself" of "the form of God" (6a) in taking on "the form of a *doulos.*" Michaelis 37: then Paul should have written, "Having emptied *(kenōsas)* himself, he took *(elaben)* the form of a slave." (2) "Servant of the Lord" (Isa 52:13–53:12, Seeley 1994:51– 52, noting *douleuonta* in Isa 53:11 LXX or 49:7) and (3) the "righteous sufferer" (E. Schweizer) depend on OT backgrounds (see Exc. B, II.D.6,7). (4) To make prominent a contemporary societal term (cf. Moule 1970:268; Bruce 1983:53; Feinberg; Hellerman 136–42; Exc. B, II.D.13), on social status, "deprivation of rights." D. B. Martin 1990 ([1] Bibl. **slaves**) 130–32, Greco-Roman slavery was "multifaceted," self-abasement *and* upward mobility. (5) Slavery to fate and cos- mic powers (Käsemann 1950:67, 72; Exc. B, II.C). Christ entered the realm where the cosmic, demonic forces rule (cf. Gal 4:1–9, 24–25; 5:1; Rom 8:12–23); 10c, heavenly and subterranean creatures, *doulos/kyrios* contrast; "enslavement to the evil spiritual forces" said to "rule over the destinies of people in the Greco- Roman world" (O'B 219). Cf. Gnilka 119–20; Walter 60; *EDNT* 1:352. (6) Hurtado 1984, "slave *to* God" reads in *tō[i] theō[i].* Awkward with a preexistent Christ "like God." The "Lordly Example" Hurtado wants for ethical purposes stresses obedience (8b; not present in *doulos,* A. Weiser, *EDNT* 1:352).

Actual slavery, lowest social status (4), and bondage to the ruling powers of the world (5) were concepts that the Philippians knew well, and are the likely back- grounds.

2:7c. *born in humanity's likeness.* Obj. phrase, then ptc. (as in 7a and b); *en homoiōmati anthrōpōn* ("males" would be *ho anēr;* cf. O'B 214 n 1), followed by *genomenos,* aor. ptc., *ginomai* (infin. at 1:13). BAGD II.4 = *eimi,* "be like men" (cf. BDAG 5.c). [N]RSV, "being born. . . ." (BAGD I.1.a; BDAG 1; LSJ *gignomai* I.1; cf. Gal 4:4; Rom 1:3; 1 Cor 15:37); so Joüon 300; Beare 83, Schenk 202, de- nied by Habermann 134; U. B. Müller 102 n 177. *born,* no date or place indicated. Gen. "of men," better "human beings" (NJB); "in human likeness" (NRSV, NIV, NEB, inclusive language paraphrase) loses the pl. *anthrōpōn.* Sg. *anthropou* (P⁴⁶ some church fathers) is due to Christ-Adam typology or sg. *doulou* and 7d *anthrōpos* (*TCGNT* 613); scribal error common in P⁴⁶, Silva 126. Pl. suggests "the whole human race" (Fee 213 n 94).

likeness. homoiōma (*-ma* for the result of an action). *Word field:* J. Schneider, *TDNT* 5:186–99; E. Beyreuther, *NIDNTT* 2:496–508; T. Holtz, *EDNT* 2:512– 13. Likeness, not exact identity. *isos,* equality in size or value, the external; *ho- moios,* likeness in a qualitative sense (*TDNT* 3:343; *NIDNTT* 2:496–97), but they can be interchangeable (*TDNT* 5:186–87). BAGD *homoiōma* (6x in NT) (1) like- ness (BDAG, **state of having common experiences;** Rom 6:5a, cf. 6:4 and 5b); (2) image, copy (BDAG 2.a, **state of being similar in appearance;** Rom 1:23); (3) form, appearance (BDAG 2.b); less clear, (4) (BDAG 3) Phil 2:7 and Rom 8:3, God sent "his own Son in the likeness of sinful flesh" (NRSV). To nuance Christ's identity with humanity (less than a full incarnation)? To avoid connecting Jesus with sin(ful flesh), Heb 4:15? BAGD paraphrased J. Weiss (*Earliest Christianity* [tr. 1937, repr. New York: Harper, 1959] 2:488–91): either "capable of sinning as human bodies are, or . . . only the form of a man . . . looked upon as a human being" but "in reality . . . a Divine Being." "Paul grazes . . . 'Docetism'"; "the inner being of the personality of Christ remains untouched by actual earthly humanity and sinfulness" (Weiss 490); BDAG likewise, adding to *1 En.* 31.12, as an example, Aesop, *Fab.* 140H, Hermes *homoiōtheis anthrōpō[i].*

In classical Gr., *homoiōma* "seldom" occurred (*TDNT* 5:191); "common" in papyri (5:187 n 4; MM 449 offers little). POxy 1.124.2, "from the same social rank." At times synonymous with *eikōn* (*TDNT* 2:388; *Phdr.* 250B); "*homoiōma* emphasizes the similarity," but no "inner connection between the original and the copy" (*TDNT* 5:191). In the LXX, for *děmût* and other Heb. terms, often with *morphē, eikōn, eidos, idea,* and *schēma* (Deut 4:12, 15–18, 23, 25; Isa 40:18–20; on Isa 53:3 LXX see Seeley 1994:53; Ezek 1:5, 16, 22; 8:2, 3; more in Loh. 94 n 2); sometimes "copy" or "image" (Ps 106:20), sometimes "form" (Deut 4:12, the "form" of God *not* seen at Sinai was no "copy") (5:191). Vanni suggested "perceptible expression" for LXX use. From such data arose various conclusions. Rom 8:3, came "as sinner" (Branick 1985:261–62, with Vanni); J. Fitzmyer (AB 33:485), "proneness of humanity . . . to sin." But 2:6–11 is not about sin or "the Son" who is "sent."

Those assuming a human figure (not preexistent) invoke Wis 2:23–24 (Murphy-O'Connor 1976:43–44). Christ "looked like any other man" (7d) but "was in fact only like them" (7c), "they needed to be reconciled with God . . . he did not." This reads reconciliation into 2:6–11; the interpretation of Wis 2:23–24 is dubious (Howard 1978:371–72). *homoiōma anthrōpōn* can suggest the likeness of the human race both to God and to one another.

Exact sense remains enigmatic (Heriban 295–301). O'B 225 ("full identity with the human race," but "a secret relationship" with God) sounds like a *tertium quid* (Nagata 252, "a totally different race"). Fee 213: "full humanity" but "not 'human' only." Bockmuehl 137: "the same conditions of human life as the rest of us" (sinful flesh), not *unlike* human beings (*pace* Fee 213). Silva 126, "Whatever distinctions may be posited are subject to contextual adjustments, including semantic neutralization . . . here." *homoiōma* is "a close synonym to . . . *isa* in v. 6"; 7d = "Thus, presenting Himself as no more than man" (121, but note the capital "H").

2:7d. *and, in appearance perceived as a human being.* Sometimes taken with 7c, sometimes with 8a, depending on theories of hymnic stanzas. The beginning of v 8 in KJV, RSV, etc. (UBSGNT punctuation apparatus; O'B). *kai* is the first conj. since *alla* in 7a. In the KJV-[N]RSV tradition the start of a new sentence, "And . . ." (so O'B 214 n 3). Edart 154–55, *kai* is logical, not chronological. Michaelis 38 and Gnilka 121, *kai* connects 7a *heauton ekenōsen* and 8a *etapeinōsen heauton.* The TRANSLATION takes *kai* thus, without committing to stanza divisions.

euretheis. Aor. pass. sg., *euriskō,* BDAG 2, fig. sense **discover intellectually through reflection, observation, examination, or investigation** *find, discover;*

pass. *be found, appear, prove, be shown* (to be) (Rom 7:10; Gal 2:17; 1 Cor 4:2; 15:15; 2 Cor 5:3). 2:7, "when he appeared in human form." Cf. H. Preisker, *TDNT* 2:769, sense e. NEB, "revealed in human shape," but (S. Pedersen, *EDNT* 2:82–84) no "theology of revelation." REB "found himself in human circumstances" suggests Jesus' perception of his lot rather than how others saw him. *hōs*, "as" (BDAG 3.a.γ) + pred. nom., is almost pleonastic; [N]RSV and other trs. omit. It may nuance Christ's humanity, like *homoiōmati* in 7c. *anthrōpos* = "human being" (BDAG 1.b), not the Son of Man of Dan 7:13 (Loh. 1928:38–42; rightly rejected, O'B 222 n 147, among others); probably not in contrast to God, but possibly a specific person in contrast to the human race in 7c.

in appearance. schēma, esp. since Lft. 127–33, changeable outward shape, contrasted with *morphē* (6a *sphere*) inner essential form. Michaelis 38, appearance versus essence. Further study suggested a less sharp contrast and a wider range of meanings for both terms. G. Harder, *NIDNTT* 1:703–14 treats both under "form"; Braumann 709, avoid such distinctions between outer (shell) and inner (essential character). W. Pöhlmann, *EDNT* 3:318 lists other contrasts to be avoided (e.g., Loh. 1928, nature and "history"). BDAG *schēma* 1, **the generally recognized state or form in which someth[ing] appears,** *outward appearance, form, shape.* Silva 121, 126: 7d may simply recapitulate 7b and c, the context neutralizing our efforts at semantic distinctions; Hawth. 87–88.

J. Schneider (*TDNT* 7:954–58): *-ma* (BDF #109.2) expresses result of the action in the verbal root, here *echō* (fut. *schēsō*), "what one has," Lat. *habitus*, "appearance, bearing, form, figure," even "garb." LXX, only at Isa 3:17 (corrupt in Gk.). The classical sense, also in Philo, "what can be known by observation," fits at 2:7 with *euretheis*, "mode of appearance," seen by anyone, expressing what the person is (Käsemann 1950:69; *TDNT* 7:956). *metaschēmatizō* (cf. 3:21, God "will transform the body of our humiliation" at the parousia) is sometimes brought in to suggest transformation at 2:7. But varied NT use (see NOTE on 3:21) and the context in 2:7 (not parousia) exclude that here. Pöhlmann: "the specific appearance unique to one person and unalterably associated with him" (*EDNT* 3:318, are "unique" and "unalterably" too strong? cf. *NIDNTT* 1:709, "what anyone could see"). Locative dat. (ATR 523) or dat. of respect (BDF #197; GNTG 3:220, almost an adv.). Schenk 187, with *en*, like *homoiōmati* in 7c.

2:8a. *he experienced humiliation for himself. etapeinōsen* (+ reflexive pron. obj. *heauton* as in 7a, *himself he emptied*), see NOTES on 2:3b *humiliation (tapeinophrosynē)* and 4:12 *to be brought low.* "He humiliated himself," "suffered or experienced humiliation on his part" (the social-world sense presented for 2:3) goes against "he humbled himself" in most Eng. Bibles. Loh/Nida 59 put emphasis on the person in 7a, *himself he emptied,* in 8a on being humiliated. Possibly from rhetoric, for description of a person, *habitus* of body or mind (Quint. *Inst.* 5.10.23, 28–29), in epideictic praise (Hermagenes, *Prog.* 7; *Praeexercitamenta* by Priscan [ed. Helm] 7; Lausberg #376), part of the *evidentia* or detail about a person (Quint. *Inst.* 8.3.63–65; Lausberg #813, cf. #810; *schēma* in rhetoric, see Index).

Aor. of *tapeinoō* (BDAG 2.a), **cause someone to lose prestige or status,** *humble, humiliate, abase,* "reversal of status." Within the word field (summarized in the Note on 2:3), the vb., "lower, reduce," included further senses, "lessen, disparage, minimize" (LSJ; "moral" sense, "make lowly, humble," citing Matt 23:12, along with Phld. *Vit.* p. 38J). Cf. Xen. *An.* 6.3.18, God "wills that they . . . should be brought low *(tapeinōsa)*" (LCL, *An.* 4–6, pp. 210–11); Xen. *Mem.* 3.5.4, "the glory *(doxa)* of the Athenians is brought low *(tapeinōntai)*"; Aeschin. 3.235; Plato, *Resp.* 553C, "humiliated by poverty"; *Phdr.* 254E; Menander, *Frg.* 544 (ed. T. Koch); Phld. *Rhet.* 1.2255; Anon. Oxy. 664.22. The vb. + *heauton* seems not to occur; post-NT, in patristic authors, only from Phil 2:8 and occasionally a late scholia (*PGL* 1375; *TLG* search). Numerous LXX uses, "humble, harass someone; abase oneself"; God humbles someone. On attempts to trace 8a to Isa 53:4, 7, and 8, see Seeley 1994:53. In Paul, 2x besides Phil 4:12 and 2:7: "degrading self" by working with his hands (2 Cor 11:7) and fear that "God may humiliate me before you" (2 Cor 12:21) reflect the generally negative sense in Gk. Philippians were familiar with humiliation by superiors in their social, political, and economic worlds, and knew about Jesus who experienced humiliating abasement to the point of death. Perhaps the climactic action word in their account about Christ, analogous to "he sacrificed himself" in 7a (Loh. 95), 7a connected by *and* in 7d. Like *himself he emptied*, 8a is under the *alla* of 7a, contrasting with 6.

2:8b. *becoming obedient to the point of death.* Ptc. *genomenos*, in 7c *born*, here "become" (KJV-[N]RSV). Can show manner or means, "by submitting" (TC, NLT). Aor. need not imply action prior to *etapeinōsen heauton*, nor one momentary action; "simultaneous . . . with the main verb . . . and . . . also explanatory" (Loh/Nida 60).

hypēkoos, pred. adj., "obedient," only here, 2 Cor 2:9, and Acts 7:39, but *hypakouō* words are common; see Note on 2:12 *you have always obeyed*; G. Kittel, *TDNT* 1:224–25; W. Mundle, *NIDNTT* 2:179; *TLNT* 1:446–52, background in the political arena. Perhaps Paul "introduced *hypakoē* [Rom 1:5, etc.] into the Greek language and gave it its meaning of strict obedience" (450); "primitive catechesis" likely taught believers "the meaning, and the fullness of Christian obedience" (452; bibl. in n 72; Rom 6:16–17; 10:16; 15:18; 16:19; 2 Cor 10:5–6; Phlm 21). Obedience in Greco-Roman ethics is minimized by Bockmuehl 150, but Philippians knew it in military and civic worlds (Geoffrion 38–42; 139–40; 184–87) and from Paul's kerygma (Rom 5:19), catechesis, and example. Christ's obedience to the will of God is implied (from vv 6 and 9; cf. Gal 1:4; Plummer 47; Loh. 95; Caird 122; CEV), but not stated (Heb 10:7–8 = Ps 40:6–8 LXX should not be read in). K. Barth 65, not *to whom* but *that* Christ obeyed (Martin 1967: 216–17). Beare 86, "submission to the power of the Elemental Spirits" (v 10c); Käsemann 1950:74, death subjects "men to the servitude of the powers" (Heb 2:14–15), but Jesus overcame *anagkē* (Fate). Bockmuehl 138–39 tacitly corrects notions of "obedience to demons or to death." To say "Christ was obedient to the wishes of people as well" as of God (Hawth. 89) is eisegesis (O'B 229; what people?)

to the point of death. mechri (achri in D* F G), prep. + gen., for the degree of Christ's obedience (BDAG 3, *to the point of;* cf. also 2:30). KJV "unto death" is well avoided in NRSV; Christ did not obey Death. For *thanatos* see Note on 1:20 *whether by life or by death.* Here, lit. sense (BDAG 1.b.β), often a penalty inflicted by secular courts; used of Christ at 3:10; 1 Cor 11:26; Rom 5:10; 6:3–5. Jesus' death became the content of Christian proclamation, significant through baptism and Lord's Supper. On linking it to Isa 53:7, 8 and 12 LXX, see Seeley 1994:54.

2:8c. *yes, death on a cross. death* is repeated (BDAG *thanatos* 1.d), linked to 8b by *de* (BDF #447.8, explanation or intensification, "and . . . at that"; BAGD *de* 2, "transitional," BDAG 2 **linking narrative segments, *now, then, and, so, that is***). KJV-NRSV, "even," suggests heightening, indeed shock (NIV adds an exclamation point!). *cross* = means of execution (BDAG *stauros* 1). An emphasis of Paul (3:18); cf. 1 Cor 1:18, cf. 17; Christ crucified (1 Cor 1:23; 2:2, 8; cf. Gal 3:1, 5:11, 6:12 and 14; 1 Cor 1:13, Gal 5:24). D. K. Williams 2002:26–40, Paul used it "in conflictual/polemical situations" for "rhetorical aims" (145); "his unique contribution to the traditional articulation of the death of Jesus Christ" (235–36). Paul could tell the Christ-story without using the word "cross," as in Rom (overly offensive term in the capital city? but cf. AB 33:348–49 on 3:24–25), perhaps in Philippi (cf. Martin 1967:221–22; Fee 217). *Word studies:* J. Schneider, *TDNT* 7:572–84; E. Brandenburger/C. Brown) *NIDNTT* 1:391–405; H.-W. Kuhn, *EDNT* 3:267–71. On *theologia crucis* (from Luther, contrast "theology of glory," D. K. Williams 2002:10–19), cf. A. E. McGrath, *DPL* 192–97; Dunn, *TPTA* #9; J. Becker 1993 ([1] Bibl. **Paul**) 187–239, 399–411; A. M. Madsen, *The Theology of the Cross in Historical Perspective* (Eugene, OR; Wipf and Stock, Pickwick Publications, 2006); C. B. Cousar, *A Theology of the Cross: The Death of Jesus in the Pauline Letters* (Minneapolis: Fortress, 1990). In M. Hengel, *Crucifixion: In the Ancient World and the Folly of the Message of the Cross* (Philadelphia: Fortress, 1977), crucifixion = "slave's punishment"; "parallels" involving Prometheus and Dionysus show its "harsh reality" in the world of the day. Hellerman 143–48, the nadir in a *cursus* of degradations. The gen. may indicate means or place; D. B. Wallace, gen. of "production," death "produced by . . . a cross" (*GGBB* 105).

2:8c links with 8b (O'B 229), 8a, or both, as "the extremity" of humiliation and obedience. The cross is *consequence* for a life of a certain sort, the *purpose* of Jesus' existence (Hofius 1976:60–64). Not a word about the meaning for humans (atonement, reconciliation), or descent at death to the netherworld (Loh. 96 and n 1).

2:9a. *Therefore God has indeed exalted him most highly.* A "new start . . . with *dio* and . . . change of grammatical subject . . . *ho theos*" (Holmstrand 103; *God* last mentioned 2:6 bis; see NOTE on 1:2). Two vbs., in 9a and 9b, tell what God does for Christ. *dia* + acc. *ho* rel. pron., neut. ("on account of which"; "therefore," BDF #451.5; EDNT 1:336) may show "self-evident" inference (BDAG *dio*, Rom 4:22 MSS; 15:22; 2 Cor 1:20; 5:9), have ascensive force, or introduce result (BDF #442.12, "even"; Luke 1:35; 11:49). Silva 131–32 cautions against trying for too precise a meaning. "Because of this" (NAB[RNT], cf. Gdsp., GNB) raises the question "because of what?" Christ's prior divine status? his obedience? death (Hofius 1976:3–17, 63–67)? "total self-humbling" throughout all his life (O'B 233–34)? as reward for humility (Martin 1976:100)? "merit" on Christ's part (Heriban 323–24; cf. K. Barth 66–67; Martin 1967:231–35; Feinberg 42)? humiliation/exaltation (Gnilka 125; *per aspera ad astra*, Hawth. 90, critique in Silva 127–28; O'B 235)? "Then" (CEV) implies too little. "Therefore" [N]RSV improves on KJV "wherefore." For connection with Isa 53:12 LXX, 53:23MT, see Seeley 1994:55. Edart, a (redactional) *correctio* (cf. 2 Cor 1:20, 4:13). Hellerman 209 n 68, "wholly unexpected," not (contra Oakes 2001:151–60) a natural expectation. "also" for *kai* (KJV, NRSV "God also"—someone else too? did God do something previously in the passage?) was dropped by RSV, NIV, etc. ZBG #462 calls it "stereotyped." Others (Silva 132; Fee 220 n 10) say it enhances *dio; indeed* (so TRANSLATION). Dir. obj. "him" *(auton)* in Gk. before the vb., directly after, in juxtaposition with, *ho theos.*

hyperhypsoō, only here in the NT. *hypsoō*, "lift, raise up" (20x, in Paul only at 2 Cor 11:7). *Word field:* G. Bertram, *TDNT* 8:602–20, esp. 608–9; D. Müller, *NIDNTT* 2:200–205; G. Lüdemann, *EDNT* 3:399, 410. Limited Gk. usage (but cf. Plut. *Mor.* 103F = Letter to Apollonius 103; on elevation of heroes, cf. Bertram, *RAC* 6:22–43). In the LXX *hypsoō* occurs 150x for several Heb. vbs.; *hyperhypsoō*, some 50x, usually no Heb. equivalent, for, e.g., exalting God. Bertram and D. Müller treat Babylonian and Egyptian myth, Hellenistic syncretism, mystery religions, wisdom texts (on the righteous sufferer), and apocalyptic writings. Self-abasement followed with exaltation by God appears in Luke 18:14, etc.; Jas 4:10; 1 Pet 5:6. In John, Jesus was "lifted up" on the cross and so exalted (8:28; 12:32, 34), in light of 3:14 (Num 21:8–9, where LXX does *not* use *hypsoō*). Jeremias, *TDNT* 5:712 n 446, appeals to Isa 52:13. None of these backgrounds or "parallels" need lie behind 2:9a. More pertinent may be sermons at Acts 2:33 and 5:31, God exalted Jesus at his right hand. But Ps 110:1, about God's right hand, does not use *hypsoō*. On such exaltation as "resurrection," cf. W. Thüsing, *Erhöhungvorstellung und Parousieerwartung in der ältesten nachösterlichen Christologie* (SBS 42; Stuttgart: KBW, 1979) 41–55; *TDNT* 8:612; Ps 9:13.

What of the *hyper*-prefix? KJV-NRSV, "*highly* exalted." Koine Gk. often added prefixes to weakened vbs. without necessarily any further meaning (BDF #116.1,4). Most trs. bring out *hyper-*, often with a superlative (Moule 1970:269 "the highest possible"; Collange 106, with Delling 1969) but avoid a comparative sense, "greater than he was before the incarnation" (Hawth. 91). Elative (Silva 132). Stressed by Cullmann 1959 ([1] Bibl. **Christ**) 174–81 and others (in Martin 1967:239–40). Cf. Ps 97 (LXX 96):9 (Gnilka 125) as source (Schweizer 1955:66 n 286), "Lord . . . you have been exalted far above *(sphodra hyperhypsōthēs hyper)* all the gods," in a class by yourself. Cf. Synes. *Ep.* 79.28, *hyperhypsōse ton hypsēlon.* BDAG *hyperhypsoō*, "raise . . . to the loftiest height"; NEB/REB "to the heights"; "the highest place (above)" (Hawth. 75; NIV, GNB, CEB). Cullmann: "more than exalted" him (1959:180, 217, 235). Martin 1967:239–40: "*hyper*-exalted." Cf. Hofius 27; O'B 236; Fee 221; U. B. Müller 106–7. The TRANSLATION uses *exalted him most highly.*

2:9bc. *and freely given him the name that is above every name.* Word order (*kai* before *theos*, not the vb.) and idiom *(dio kai)* discourage "*both* exalted *and* gave." *kai* in 9b can be epexegetical (Silva 128–29), in effect "by granting him." The vbs. are "coincident" aors. (O'B 237 n 26; Lenski 793 spoke of "one act"). *echarisato*, aor. m., *charizomai*, BDAG 1, **give freely as a favor, give graciously**; see NOTE on 1:29 *it has been granted by God.* RSV, NEB/REB, "bestow." D. M. Stanley 1961:98–99, "act of grace on the Father's part, a bold expression, unique in the

NT." A benefaction? Howard 1978; Caird 123, "conferred," God exalts the *man* Jesus.

onoma. No art. in D F G, Majority Text, etc. (KJV "a name"), but *to* in P⁴⁶ ℵ A B C and most interpreters. BDAG *onoma*, here not a title (3) but (1) proper name, d. in connection with God and Jesus, δ., *the Name*, but cf. BAGD I.4.c.β (= BDAG 1.d.γ.כ), in the sense of "title." In biblical theology, "name" is an important concept, name of God, "in the name of" Jesus, or to express what a person is. Cf. H. Bietenhard, *TDNT* 5:242–83 (contrast van der Woude, *THAT* 2:935–62 on the OT), H. Bietenhard, *NIDNTT* 2:648–55; L. Hartman, *EDNT* 2:519–22; each agrees *kyrios* is the name given to Jesus (273, 654, 521, respectively). So, finally, Silva 129; Hawth. 93; O'B 238, though others suggest "Jesus" (Ellicott 60; Caird 123, "Savior," as in Matt 1:21); "Jesus Christ" (Vincent 62); "Jesus Christ, the Lord" (v 11b, Jones 33); "Son" (church fathers); and *theos* (Martin 1967:235). *kyrios* carries authority, status, supreme dignity proper to God (Heriban 334). Hellerman 151, honor discourse. Fee 222–23 (cf. Hawth. 61; Robuck 121) sees intertextuality, "Jesus is Lord," Isa 45:23, and the Philippians' Roman setting ("lords many" and "lord Caesar").

that is above every name. Art. *to* repeated; prep. phrase in second attrib. position; vb. "is," supplied. *hyper* (BDAG B, + acc.) "excelling and surpassing, *over and above, beyond, more than*. . . ." On the neut. of *pas*, see BDAG 1.a and 5; NOTES on 1:3, 4, 7, etc., *every, all*. A phrase of sweeping nature; hence, "every other name" (NAB[RNT]), "all other names" ([N]JB).

2:10a–c. *that at the name of Jesus every knee shall bow—of those in the heavens and those on earth, and those in the world below—*. *hina* + two subjunct. vbs., *kampsē[i]* (10b "bow") and *exhomologēsetai* (11a, "confess"). Parallelism from Isa 45:23 LXX, where God speaks a word (LXX *logoi*), righteousness (*dikaiosynē*), that "will not return" unfulfilled: "To me every knee shall bow, every tongue shall swear" (NRSV; LXX *hoti emoi kampsei pan gonu kai exhomologēsetai pasa glōssa tō[i] theō[i]*, to God; some LXX MSS with MT, "every tongue will swear (an oath to) God," *omeitai . . . ton theon*, fut. of *omnymi*, not a vb. used in Paul). LXX goes on, differently from MT and [N]RSV, "saying, Righteousness and glory will come to him, and all who separate themselves [cf. Gal 2:12] will be put to shame; from the Lord they shall be justified and in God they will be glorified, all the seed of the children of Israel." Cf. Martin 1967:255–57; Heriban 338–51; Hofius 1976:41–55. Isa uses *hoti*, "that" (not *hina*); the fut. indic. ("will bow, will confess/swear"); and "To me . . . to God," but Phil 2:10a "in the name of Jesus" and 11 "that Jesus Christ is Lord, to the glory of God the Father."

Classical Gk. *hina* expressed **purpose, aim, or goal *in order that***, or simply *that* (BDAG 1; BDF #369; Moule *IB* 138; Bockmuehl 146; KJV, RSV), but often result (BDAG 3, *so that*; BDF #391.5; Moule *IB* 142–43; DA 325, cf. 356; Gal 5:17; Rom 3:19, etc.). Hence GNB "And so"; Fee 223: result. Purpose and result blur in NT usage (*GGBB* 473–74). Is it fut. fulfillment (at the parousia) or an outcome already now realized, at least in part (Martin 1967:266–70; O'B 239)?

kampsē[i]. Aor. subjunct., *kamptō*, classical Gk. "bend the knee to." Semitic background, (self-)subjection—"bend" (the knee), "bow" (the neck) (as in prayer) before Baal (Rom 11:4 = 1 Kings 19:18) or Israel's God (Rom 14:11 = Isa 45:23).

H. Schlier *TDNT* 3:594–95 reports "fairly common" LXX use, "always in connection with prayer," but "no occurrence of *kamptein gonu*" in Gk. sources as prayer to "official gods" (but cf. *TDNT* 1:739). For the papyri, MM 320 cite only POxy 10.1287.4, 16. The phrase here is from the LXX.

knee. gonu (12x in the NT, esp. the Synoptic Gospels, "bend the knee in respect," cf. *gonupeteō*; in Paul, 3x, above, under *kamptō*, + Eph 3:14). H. Schlier (*TDNT* 1:738–40) and J. M. Nützel (*EDNT* 1:257–58) trace oriental origins, reverencing a person or deity; LXX and rabbinic usages (Schlier 739). Greco-Roman world, "bow the knee" before various gods; Plut. *C. Gracch.* 16.5 (I, 482c); Eur. *Tro.* 1306–8; Aristoph. *Av.* 501; Soph. frg. 672; Plato *Leg.* 10.887C; Ael. Arist. 50,39. In Luke-Acts, a posture for prayer (Luke 22:41 [AB 28A:1441–42]; Acts 7:60 [AB 31:394]; 9:40; 20:36; 21:5). *pan* at 2:10b ("every") makes the reference universal.

at the name of Jesus. en + dat. of *onoma* (see 9bc) + gen. *Iēsou* (ℵ* 81 etc., "Jesus Christ," Gnilka 127 n 111). Cf. *en Christō[i]*, DA 319. Moule *IB* 78, *en* shows "accompaniment, attendant circumstances," i.e., "when the name of Jesus is spoken" (temporal, 76). But his Corrections (2nd ed., 205; cf. liturgical piety, "utterance of the Name" [Jesus] is the signal for genuflecting [Beare 86]) call *Iēsou* "possessive"; "to the name (as subject of worship)," in light of LXX evidence (Lft. 114–15; Pss 62:5 [Heb. 63:4]; 43:9 [Heb. 44:8], etc.). Critique in O'B 237, 240. Moule 1970 went back to his original "instinctive judgment" (*IB* 78), contrary to the weight of scholarly opinion: "the human name, 'Jesus,' is acclaimed as the highest name" (270). "Christ" in 11b is an "extension" of *Iēsous*, acclaimed as Lord, an "elevation . . . such that it is no longer customary to call another human child by this formerly common name" (but note Hispanic practice). See further Moule 1977 ([1] Bibl. **Christ**) 41–46.

en tō[i] onomati Iēsou lacks parallels in secular Gk. Could reflect a Christian formula in exorcisms (Mark 9:38; Acts 3:6; etc.); baptism (Acts 10:48); or prayer (John 15:16; cf. 14:13, etc.). O'B 239–40, the "efficient cause" for submission of all creatures. Or "before the Name of Jesus" (connected directly with "every knee shall bow," Knox, Moffatt, *EÜ*). Howard 1978:386 has a speculative course of development for *to onoma Iēsou*. BDAG *onoma* 1.d.γ.ℶ, "at the mention of, when the name of Jesus is mentioned"; ZBG #116; ZG 596. Not "the name, Jesus," but "the name of Jesus"; as at 9bc, *onoma* as a title, "Lord," asserted in 11b (Lft. 114; Michael 96; Martin 1967:249–50; Heriban 335–36; O'B 240; Edart 163). Worship settings make Jesus an object of praise (Lft., cited under Moule *IB*, above; Martin 1967:50–52; Bockmuehl 145) or the medium for worshiping God "through Christ" (Thüsing 1965:56; Hawth. 93; Silva 132–33). Such interpretations were brushed aside by Loh. for enthronement where Jesus becomes "Lord of the world" (1928:60; *Phil.* 97); the universe beholds Christ's triumph. Hence Käsemann struck the note that it is precisely Jesus who is identified as *kyrios* (82–83; Martin 1967:254–55).

of those in the heavens and those on earth and those in the world below. Three gen. pls., no art., connected by "and," *epouraniōn kai epigeiōn kai katachthoniōn*, inserted into Isa 45:23. Each is a compound adj. used as a noun, *ep(i)* "at" + *oura-*

nios, -on, "heavenly," from *ouranos,* 3:20; + *geios, -on,* "earthly," from *gē; kata* "under" + *chthonios -on,* from *hē chthōn,* "earth," hence "subterranean," the three spheres of ancient cosmology (J. Guhrt, *NIDNTT* 1:522–23; cf. Exod 20:4; Rev. 5:3; Ign. *Tr.* 9.1; E. Peterson 1926:159–60; Martin 1967:257–65). Each may be neut. ("*things* in heaven, in earth, under the earth," KJV, RV; Lft. 115; Carr 1981:86–89; but neut. pls. sometimes refer to persons, BDF #138.1, 263.4; Gal 3:22; Rom 11:32; 1 Cor 1:27–28) or masc.-fem. ("*beings* in the heavens, on earth, and in the underworld," [N]JB, GNB; O'B 244; CEV). Possibly creatures of the spirit-world, angels, demons, etc. (Rom 8:38–39). To avoid "things/beings," many use "in heaven and on earth and under the earth" ([N]RSV, NIV).

Most common of the three in the NT is *epouranios* (18x, 11x in the Pauline corpus, esp. 1 Cor and Eph). Pl. *hoi epouranioi,* of the gods (Theocr. 25.5; Lucian, *Dial. Deor.* 4.3; Moschus 2.21). Hence BDAG 2.b.β, "heavenly beings"; H. Traub, *TDNT* 5:541–42; H. Bietenhard, *NIDNTT* 2:196; O. Michel, *EDNT* 2:46. *epigeios* (7x in the NT, 5x in the Pauline corpus) = earthly bodies (1 Cor 15:40), "earthly dwelling" (2 Cor 5:1), "earthly things" (Phil 3:19). At 2:10, "not confined to human beings" (BDAG 1.b.β; *TDNT* 1:680–81, H. Sasse; *EDNT* 2:24, O. Michel). *katachthonios* (only here in the NT) in Gk. from Homer on, for chthonic deities (Lat. *di manes*); Zeus *katachthonios* (*Il.* 9.457); Sasse, "always *theoi* or *daimones*" (*TDNT* 3:633–34; but see below). Many see cosmic, spirit powers (Dibelius 1909; Käsemann 1950:78–79; Bornkamm 1959a:116–18; Wengst 1972:132–33, 135, 149–50; Cullmann 1949: 59, 62, 1959:227–28; cf. J. Michl, *RAC* 5:53–200; Schlier 1958; C. D. Morrison). Others stress human beings (Heriban 342–47; Carr 86–89; Hunzinger 151–54; Hofius 1976:18–55, angels in heaven, persons alive on earth, the dead in the underworld, 53; Silva 133 n 68, "[t]he least objectionable classification").

Paul elsewhere (Hunzinger 152–54; cf. U. B. Müller 108–9) contrasts *epouranios* and *epigeios* (1 Cor 15:40; cf. 2 Cor 5:1; Phil 3:19–20); *angeloi* and *anthrōpoi,* who in 1 Cor 4:9 make up "the world"; those "living" and "dead" (Rom 14:9). *katachthonioi* was a designation for the dead in the underworld (Soph. *Ant.* 75, cf. 65 and 24–25; *Ajax* 865; Aeschyl. *Cho.* 855; Lat. *manes* = spirits of the dead, *OCD*[3] 916–17). In funeral inscriptions *theois katachthoniois* = *dis manibus,* abbreviated "D.M." (in Gk. inscriptions *theta kappa;* IG index 14, p. 756; even in Jewish inscriptions, CIJ I. 287, 464, 524, etc.; Hunzinger 153 nn 45–50). The meaning is then spirits above, humans on earth, and the dead in Hades, appropriate for "the Roman milieu of Philippi" (Schenk). Cf. (Hofius 1976:25) Prophyry (according to Servius on Virgil, *Bucol.* [= *Ecl.*] 5.66), Apollo is the Sun among those above, Liber Pater (an Italian deity) on earth, Apollo among the dead below (*superos, in terris, inferos*); Apuleius, *Metam.* 11.5.1 and 25.3; *T. Sol.* 22.1, "spirits of the air, the earth, and beneath the earth" (*OTP* 1:983). *katachthonioi* for the dead lay at hand in Roman Philippi. Paul may have spoken about *those in the heavens and those on earth.* The full phrase came naturally for Christians there to describe the universe (Schenk 193; U. B. Müller 109). The TRANSLATION opts for the masc.-fem., *those in;* for *epouraniōn* (pl.), *the heavens* (several "layers," 2 Cor 12:2 "the third heaven"); *on earth* (1 Cor 8:5; 10:26; 15:47); and *in the world below*, Sheol or Hades.

2:11a–c. *and every language confess that the Lord is Jesus Christ, to the glory of God the Father.* Isa 45:23, LXX word order reversed (*pasa glōssa* after the vb.); parallels 10b (subject, vb.). + "every, all," as in 10b. *glōssa* = "tongue, language" (BDAG 2; Acts 2:11; Edart 167), "person" (2nd cent. A.D., Praise of Imouthes [= Imhotep]-Asclepius, "Every Greek *glōssa* will tell your story, and every Greek man will worship . . . Imouthes"; *PGM* 12, 187–88 = tr. ed. Betz 1:160).

2:11a. *confess.* Aor. subjunct. (parallel with the subjunct. in 10b), *exhomologēsē-tai* (P⁴⁶ א B Fᶜ some cursives; NA²⁷), but fut. indic., *exhomologēsetai*, in A C D etc. (UBSGNT; [N]JB note, "will acclaim"; Lft. 115). For indic. after *hina*, see BDF #369.2; Moule *IB* 138–39; 1 Cor 9:15, 18; 13:3; Gal 2:4. Kennedy, from Isa 45:23 (after *hoti*); Fee 218 n 2, Paul's "original subjunctive" was changed to make v 11 "a final sentence of its own"; similarly O'B 203; Edart 133 n 10.

The three gens. in 10c, *of those in the heavens and those on earth and those in the world below*, go also with *glōssa*. Hardly bowing now (v 10, aor. subjunct.) but confessing (v 11, fut. indic.) only at the parousia. Most read both vbs. as subjunct.: present acknowledgment in action and words (Käsemann), or future acknowledgment by knees and voices later (O'B 242–43, 250).

exhomologeō, from *homologeō* (2x in Rom; *homologia* at 2 Cor 9:13), 3x in OT quotes—here; Rom 14:11 = Isa 45:23; and Rom 15:9 = Ps 18:49 = 2 Sam 22:50. *homologeō* in the LXX = "praise," "thank" God (Heb. *yadah*), in many instances to confess sins. *exhomologeō*, even more common in the LXX, in the NT (BDAG 2) means **confess sins** (Matt 3:6; Acts 19:18); (3) **acknowledge,** Phil 2:11 (Isa 45:23); and (4) "confess" or **praise** God, Rom 14:11 (Isa 45:23); Rom 15:9. For those unconvinced or unwilling to believe in Jesus' lordship, "acknowledge" fits (Gdsp., TC; papyrus evidence, MM 224, legal contexts). O. Michel, *TDNT* 5:215, treats 2:11 under confession of sins, but adds 2:11 has "the sense of God's praise." Hofius (*EDNT* 2:9), D. Fürst (*NIDNTT* 1:347) favor "confess" (KJV-[N]RSV; Fee 225). O'B 246–50 notes "make a (personal) confession" (Lft. 115; Hofius) but opts for "openly declare" (250), "acknowledge" (203). "Jesus (Christ) is Lord" (2:11b; 1 Cor 12:3; Rom 10:9) is a "confession," but does Isa 45:23 present grudging acknowledgment or (Hofius 39) joyful confession (of Yahweh's sovereignty) by those who "separate themselves" or "were incensed against him" (45:24)? Is *exhomologēsetai* "open and glad proclamation"? Is Phil 2:11 a summons to do so (cf. Acts 17:30) or divine intention at "the final day"? "Openly declare," here and now by believers, and at the end by others "against their wills to a power they cannot resist" (250)? Some insert "every *intelligent* being" for those who will "proclaim openly and gladly" Jesus' reign, as if a matter of rationality (cf. Hawth. 94, citing Lft.; O'B 249; Martin 1976:101 "consentient tribute"). Bockmuehl 130, author(s) and first hearers did not "get tied up in knots" over such topics.

2:11b. *the Lord is Jesus Christ. hoti* (= quotation marks, NEB/REB) introduces *kyrios Iēsous Christos.* Nestle, through the 25th ed., used capital letters, for emphasis (cf. TC), a practice halted by UBSGNT and NA²⁶,²⁷. The TRANSLATION follows the Gk. order, pred. noun first (definite; sc. "the," *GGBB* 270), and supplies *estin* (KJV and most renderings). On *Iēsous*, mentioned at 10a, see NOTE on 1:1 *Jesus*; here, a personal name. *Christos*, see NOTE on 1:1 *Christ*; originally a title, by now a name, Jesus' *cognomen*. *kyrios* (BDAG 2.b.γ.ɔ), see NOTE on 1:2 *Lord* (acclamation-*Kyrios*). Identification with Yahweh (Capes 1992 ([1] Bibl. **Lord**) 123; better, Dunn, *TPTA* 249–60) is to be avoided. Gods and goddesses of the day *(kyrioi)* and the Emperor cult *(dominus*; Dunn 247–48) color the term. On *kyrios* in a community like Philippi "made up mainly of former pagans," cf. Zeller 2001 ([1] Bibl. **Lord**) 316–18. It challenges the Imperial cult (Hellerman 151–52). On development of this confessional formula see COMMENT A.2.

2:11c. *to the glory of God the Father*. *eis* + acc. of *doxa*, + two nouns in the gen., lapidary style, no arts. *doxa* (BDAG 3, *fame, recognition, renown, honor, prestige*), see NOTE on 1:11 *glory*, also at end of a section. *theou*, obj. gen. (unlike 1:11; Gdsp, "glorify God"). *theou patros*, see NOTES on 1:2 *God* (BDAG *theos* 3.d) and *our Father* (BDAG *patēr* 6.e), also anarthrous (BDF #257.3). Since Jesus Christ has been exalted to lordship, "Father" is needed to distinguish the God who grants lordship to Jesus. Philippians knew the phrase from Christian tradition and Greco-Roman usage (Zeus as Hercules' father whom he must obey, Diod. Sic. 4.11.1; *Zeus patēr*).

Climactic finality was lost or redirected in the Vg, *quia Dominus Iesus Christus in gloria est Dei Patris*, "because" (Rheims NT) "our Lord Jesus Christ is in the glory of God the Father" (Martin 1967: 273 n 1; *ZBG* #108 corrects Vg tendencies to make *eis* = *en*). Some (*TDNT* 3:1089; Hofius 1976:9, 54, with Jeremias; Schenk 191; U. B. Müller 110) connect 11c with 11a, "every tongue proclaim to the glory of God the Father" (NAB) or "to the glory of God the Father everyone will openly agree" (CEV). Others make 11c part of the acclamation, "'the Lord is Jesus Christ, to the glory of God the Father'"; then all three groups, the cosmos, acclaim the Father as well as the Lord Christ (E. Peterson 1926:133, 171 n 3; 1941:15–17; Georgi 1964b:275, 291). Usually 11c is set off from 11ab with a comma (so KJV-[N]RSV). 2:6–11 ends with—or Paul has added (Jeremias; Gnilka 130; U. B. Müller 110; Hunzinger 148–49)—a qualifying phrase about God's glory after asserting Jesus' lordship. Does it seek to exclude "rivalry in the godhead" (Martin 1967: 275–76)? Or is it "rhetorical proviso" (Dib. 79), a "tail-piece" (Martin 1967:272)? Or climax of the entire narrative (Fee 226; Bockmuehl 148), "revelation of a fatherhood inspiring confidence and love" (Collange 108)? May be a counterpart to Isa 45:23 LXX, ". . . every tongue shall swear/confess *to God*." Not simply "Jesus Christ is *Lord*" but "to the glory of God . . ." (Thüsing 1965:59).

For *Father*, Käsemann 1950:81–82 noted three possibilities: God as father *of the world* (Loh. 1928:61; cf. 1 Cor 8:6; OT/Jewish usage); added by Paul, who subordinates Christ to the Father at the End (cf. 1 Cor 15:28); third, Christian usage, "father *of Christ*" (2 Cor 1:3) and *of Christians* (even without explanatory "our" ["of us," Phil 1:3], 1 Thess 1:3). Thüsing 1965:46–60 built on Käsemann (1 Cor 3:21–23, 11:3, functional subordination; parallel features in Rom 15:1–13; cf. COMMENT A.5, n 10). That Christ is Lord and rules to the glory of God the Father is typically Pauline. Schenk 191 turned this to support Philippian origins for the v:

they learned it from Paul. Hardly a "kenosis of the Father" before Christology, or retreat from the world by God; rather, in conferring Kyrios on Christ," God "gains the name of Father" (Bornkamm 1959a:118).

COMMENT

A. FORMS, SOURCES, AND TRADITIONS

1. *Old Testament.* Isa 45:23 LXX (boldface italics) provides structure and content for 2:10–11: *every knee shall bow . . . and every language confess . . . to* the glory *of God.*[1] Inserted in 10c is a contemporary commonplace, *those in the heavens, on earth, and in the world below*; in 11b, a Christian creedal slogan (see 2, below). On the LXX or "Old Greek" text of 45:23, see NOTES on 10abc. The Heb. MT is about "Yahweh's Victory through Israel" (AB 20:80–84); the LXX, more about God's saving, justifying righteousness, though some are put to shame. Oakes 2001:133–37 sees LXX rewritten in 2:10–11 to present the "triumph of God, in Christ, over the Roman empire." Paul used Isa 45:23 also at Rom 14:11 to warn that "we will all stand before the judgment seat of God." At Rom 14:11 the word order is the same as Phil 2:11 (not the LXX) + *tō[i] theō[i]* from the LXX. The vb. means "confess" sins. If Phil 2:10–11 with its christological sense precedes Rom, 14:11 may be retrogressive or, better, reflect flexibility in using the OT. The Philippians probably heard Paul use Isa. 45:23 in a doxological sense or in Hellenistic-Christian Christology (Koch 1980). Wengst 1972:134–35, used at 2:10–11 to show universal homage.

In 2:9 *dio kai* some see an OT principle of reversal, "whoever humbles self will be exalted." Isa 53:12, "*Therefore* I shall allot him [the Suffering Servant] a portion with the great," and/or Dan 7:13–14 (the Son of Man, Cerfaux 1959 [(1) Bibl. **Christ**] 392; Krinetzki, esp. 314–15). But Isa 53:12 LXX reads *dia touto*; Krinetzki had to posit an independent Gk. rendering. Bruce 72 allows "echoes" of "some OT precedents" (nothing in Hays 1989 [(4) Bibl.]; cf. O'B 235).[2] U. B. Müller 106 sees Synoptic sayings like Matt 23:12, Luke 14:11, 18:14 as more influential.

On broader attempts to find behind 2:6–11 the Son of Man in Dan 7; the Servant in Isa; the righteous sufferer; wisdom; or an Adam-Christ comparison, see, with generally negative conclusions, EXC. B, II.D.4–8. Some speak of a "midrash" here (Nagata 1981:283; Bockmuehl 144–45), but outside of Isa 45:23 at 2:10–11, there is little, perhaps nothing, of direct OT wording. Efforts to equate *morphē* and *doulos* in Phil with LXX vocabulary (*eikōn* at Gen 1:26–27, *pais* in 2 Isa, respectively) are dubious. Jeremias' claim for Isa 53:12 behind 2:7a has generally

---

[1] Hengel 1983b:85 sees influence also from Ps 8:5–7 LXX; Robuck 72–73 speaks of "messianic psalms."
[2] On other Isaiah allusions in 2:6–11, none of them compelling, see Minear 1990:213; M. Hooker 1959; *Jesus and the Suffering Servant*, ed. W. H. Bellinger, Jr./W. Farmer (Harrisburg, Pa.: Trinity Press International, 1998), esp. J. R. Wagner, "The Heralds of Isaiah and the Mission of Paul."

been relegated to a subliminal level or dropped entirely; see NOTE on *but himself he emptied*. The Adam Christ comparison rests on sensing allusions, not direct OT wordings.

On OT use in Paul's churches[3] Harnack 1928a argued Paul employed it only in argument with Judaizers; or (Ulonska) only when forced to. OT words are woven in at Phil 1:19, 2:15, and 2:10–11. Paul likely instilled some knowledge of the OT among the Philippians (cf. Conzelmann 1969 [INTRO. X Bibl.] 166–70), in oral instruction, not from a written book.[4]

2. Early Christian Formulas. 2:11b *kyrios Iēsous Christos* is an older Christian confession, popular and meaningful for Gentiles (1 Cor 12:3; Rom 10:9). Cf. Cullmann 1949; J. D. N. Kelly 1950; Kramer ([1] Bibl. **Christ**) 127; on acclamations in the Greco-Roman world, Cuss 74–88, esp. 88. Not (Bultmann 1951 [INTRO. X Bibl.] 42–52, 65–72; Bousset 1970 [(1) Bibl. **Lord**] 119–52) from a "Kyrios-cult originated on Hellenistic soil"; cf. NOTE on 1:2 *Lord* (1 Cor 16:22, *Marana tha*, "Our Lord, come!" and *DPL* 562–63). From the earlier confessions, "Jesus is the Christ" and "Jesus is Lord," "Christ" developed as "Jesus' last name," not a title; *kyrios* became the decisive affirmation, a fundamental, known to Philippian Christians in, among other places, the salutation of all Paul's letters (1:2). Pertinent in a world of many *kyrioi*, including their masters in the pyramid-like system of Roman rule. In 2:10–11, *kyrios* is affirmed by persons and powers, universally, not just converts (Conzelmann 1969:64; Kümmel 1973 [INTRO. X Bibl.] 157–60). "Jesus is Lord" was connected with the resurrection (Rom 10:9), but for the Philippians more with "apotheosis" to lordship (see on 3:10; Reumann 2002:420–21).

at the name of Jesus is probably not confession or liturgical material (see NOTE on 10a). *11c*, "the glory of God the Father," sometimes taken as pre-Pauline liturgical speech (G. Strecker 1964:69, cf. n 29), is (Hunzinger 149) almost exclusively a Pauline phrase, rare in the LXX (3 Macc 2:9). Phil 1:11; Rom 15:7; 2 Cor 1:20; 4:15; 1 Cor 10:31; Rom 3:7 vary so much that it is difficult to claim a liturgical formula here (Schenk 191).

3. A Hymn? Various analyses of stanzas and strophes were noted in EXC.B, II. A–C, but 2:6–11 fits neither OT/Jewish nor Greco-Roman hymnody (II.E). Not a hymn, it "*became* a hymn" (Mihoc 123). With the decline of loosely used terms like "hymn," speculations about antiphonal arrangements and music (e.g., Gamber 1970) exit also, as does liturgical reenactment (A. F. Segal 1998:410–12 and n 21). Claims for epideictic rhetoric or 2:6–11 as an *encomion* have meet with some positive response (Basevi/Chapa; see 4, below). This fits with authorship by

---

[3] Cf. (4), above, on 1:19 (COMMENT A.1); Dunn, *TPTA* #7.2.
[4] C. D. Stanley, SBLSP 37:718–19: at best 20% of a Pauline congregation could read, a lower percentage for women; only well-to-do patrons likely had scriptural texts unless MSS came from a local Jewish synagogue.

converts in Philippi, an assertion for the Greco-Roman world about Christ and God, used in witnessing to neighbors.

2:6–11 as "story" or "narrative" and its shape (Exc. B, II.B) remain disputed. Perhaps two different Christologies (two "hymns," Jervell 212–13; Martin 1967:247–48): 2:6–8, a preexistent Heavenly Man, condescension, nothing about ascension; 2:9–11, Jesus exalted to lordship (as in Acts 2:36; 5:31; Rom 1:3–4), subordinate to the Father (cf. 1 Cor 3:21; 11:3; 15:23–28). Few favor two hymns, but we get different glimpses of Jesus. A result of Paul's converts "putting things together" for themselves? Each fits ideas in the Greco-Roman world: deities appearing on earth; mortals elevated to divinity (apotheosis). We regard 2:6–11 as one composition, but hardly a smooth unity—staccato phrases in two (vv 6–8, 9–11) or three segments (6–7b; 7c–8; 9–11). That 2:6–11 comes from the circle around Euodia and Syntyche—and 3:20–21 from Clement (4:2–3; Schenk, *Phil.* 322–27, 336–37; ANRW 2.25.4: 3303)—is unverifiable speculation.[5]

4. Literary Features. Amid numerous proposals for *chiastic structure* for Phil, 2:6–11 is itself seldom "chiasticized."[6] Wick 60 sees "chiastic tension" involving "the form of God," the cross, and "the glory of God the Father." *Chiasm* has been claimed in 10–11b by Deichgräber (Exc. B, II.B; so Hofius 1976:5, 108; Schenk 191, and others), differently O'B 248; by Fee 219 n 6 for 2:9–11, omitting 10c. Commentators scent chiasm, but with little agreement. Many *literary features* can be pointed out (Edart 129–38), some of them discussed in the NOTES. E.g., "every knee, every tongue" = *synecdoche*, the part for the whole; *homoiōmati* (7c) and *schēmati* (7d) = *homoeoptoton* (Robuck 31, contrast Lausberg ##729–31); 2:5 exhibits *asyndeton* (no connecting word). Space precludes treating Schenk's literary observations (185–90).

5. Greco-Roman Factors in the Philippians' Composition. 2:6–11 sounds Pauline, but not always precisely characteristic of Paul. Hence efforts to mark off "Paul's additions" to a pre-Pauline piece (Schenk 190–93, five possible phrases: 6c, 8c, 9c, 10c, 11c). Hence a century of discussion over authorship. By Paul or Jewish- or Hellenistic-Christian forebears in the faith? Beare 76–78, "distinctively *Christian* and Christian against a Hellenistic, non-Jewish background"; not "pre-Pauline" but "composed in Pauline circles, under Pauline influence," with themes "elaborated independently of Paul"; "best interpreted within the frame of Hellenistic (syncretistic) religious thought." Hellerman 162, "best interpreted under . . . Roman *cursus* ideology."

Composition by Christians in Philippi was developed by Schenk (173–75,

---

[5] Holloway 2001a:121–23 finds "little in the hymn that might function by way of consolation" (at best "that those who follow Christ's example will be rewarded," 123). This disconnect with so central a passage in Phil weakens his theory that Phil is a "letter of consolation."

[6] See INTRO. VI.B n 3; (5) COMMENT A.1 for Letter B. 2:6–11 is often made the center of the chiasm, but Bittasi 210 parallels 2:6–11 with 3:4–14, Paul's example. Breck 72: A = 2:5–6; B = 2:7–8b; C = 2:8c; B′ = 2:9–10; A′ = 2:11; this employs v 5 as part of the structure. Bittasi 67: A = 2:6–7a, God; B = 2:7b–8, human; B′ = 2:9, human name; A′ = 2:10–11, God.

192–93, 195, 202, 209, 336; *ANRW* 2.25.4 [1987] 3299–3308) and Reumann 1993 (contrast Walter 59). Perhaps (Deichgräber 132) a psalm such as church members in Corinth with charismatic gifts brought to gatherings (1 Cor 14:26; Schenk 194–95). A tool for missionary outreach,[7] to evangelize in Roman culture by people who lived in it, and so advance the gospel (1:5, 12, 27), reworking what they had learned from Paul in idioms of their own. On OT material in 2:6–11, see A.1, above. The NOTES indicate how words and phrases often have parallels in Paul's letters (cf. esp. 2 Cor 8:9,[8] perhaps Rom 8:3,[9] and possibly Rom 15:3–6, 7c, and 9a[10]) and also how they differ. In Phil 2:6–11, details fit a Hellenistic syncretistic (so Beare) or more specifically Greco-Roman world[11]; Hellerman 129, 161 emphasizes "the readers' social context," honor, rank, status.

For "sources" or analogues that made 2:6–11 effective witness to people in and around Philippi, see EXC. B, II.D.10, Hellenistic world, and II.D.11, Heracles (Hercules), Alexander the Great, and two Roman emperors. A. A. T. Ehrhardt noted parallels between Alexander of Macedon and Christ (II.D.11.a) and conjectured that Stoic texts about Heracles, *isa theois* ("equal to the gods") and a model ruler, stood behind both Plutarch's "On the Fortune or Virtue of Alexander" and Phil 2. Alexander was significant in Philippi, where inscriptional materials indicate Heracles cult.[12] W. L. Knox lifted up Heracles (II.D.11.b) as a model for "'Dying Hero' Christology" in the NT.[13] A "god becoming human" would have been familiar from Eur. *Bacch.* (Dionysus dishonored and imprisoned; cf. EXC. B, D.10 above); humiliation, in the tasks enjoined on Heracles (*OCD*³ 684–

---

[7] Widely assumed (O'Brien 1995, Ware 1996 [(8) Bibl.]), though evidence Pauline congregations engaged in missionary preaching is not easy to find (Ollreg 130). Cf. J. Becker 1993 ([1] Bibl. **Paul**) 241–55; Dickson 85, 142–43, 177, 259, 311–12. That 2:6–11 is by the Philippians for mission preaching, Dickson 107 n 70 calls "utterly plausible but highly speculative."

[8] "Our Lord Jesus Christ . . . became poor, rich though he was." Cf. EXC. B.II.D.9; H. D. Betz, *2 Cor 8 and 9:*62–63. A formulation originally *by the Philippians* for supporting Paul's mission and the collection for the saints in Jerusalem (cf. Reumann 1993:450–54)?

[9] "God . . . by sending his own Son in the likeness *(en homoiōmati)* of sinful flesh and as a sin offering, condemned sin in the flesh" (NRSV-mg), linked with Phil 2:7c by some through *en homoiōmati* (Cranfield *Rom.* 1:381–82). But in 2:6–8 no reference to an action by God; the figure performs every act (and makes the decisions) himself.

[10] Phrases occasionally used in comparisons with Phil 2:6–11 (see NOTE on 2:11c *to the glory of God the Father*, end, Thüsing 1965), Christ "did not please himself" (in his earthly life) as basis for the ethical impvs. (e.g., Larsson 231–35, on 2:6–8; cf. 253, 261 on 2:9–11; R. P. Martin 1967, 1997:72; Cranfield *Rom.* 2:732; AB 33:702).

[11] Typical of the Gk. attitude is Eur. *Phoen.* 504–10 (Eteocles, son of Oedipus, refuses to give up ruling Thebes, as agreed, when it is his brother's turn; JR tr.):

> I would go to the rising of the stars or sun,/ go, if I could, beneath the earth,/ to gain Power (*Tyrannis*, absolute sway), greatest of the gods./ This happy thing (*chrēston*; or, 'Power is good. It'), then, mother, I do not wish/ to yield to another but to preserve it for myself./ For it is unmanliness, whoever loses what is better/ and takes the less.

[12] Cf. H. Hendrix, *ABD* 5:315; Portefaix 98–99, 100–1; de Vos 247; Pilhofer 2:##650, 666, 679, dedicatory inscriptions to Hercules as *theos*, but the texts from S. *Mertzidēs* are dubious; cf. Pilhofer 1:10.

[13] Cf. M. Simon, *Heracle et le christianisme*, Publications de la Faculté des Lettres de l'Universite de Strasbourg, 2. ser. No. 191 (Paris: Belle Lettres, 1955) 77–118; *Le Christianisme antique et son contexte religieux: Scripta Varia*, WUNT 23 (Tübingen: Mohr Siebeck, 1981) index s.v. "Hercule."

86; Diod. Sic. 4.31–39; Apollod. *Bibl.* 2.4.12, 2.6.3; Eur. *Al.*, among other references). In Roman times depictions were popular of Heracles leading Alcestis back from the realm of the dead. Cf. Portefaix 110–12, 142–45, 147–49, Christ as slave and as "absolute ruler of the cosmos" would have spoken to people in Philippi.

The Philippians knew stories about gods descending to earth from Olympus, the toils of those born of a god(dess) and a mortal, and apotheosis, the hero elevated to some sort of divinity.[14] What Talbert 1975, 1976 called a "Mediterranean concept of the immortals" and a "katabasis–anabasis" pattern (cf. Exc. B, II.B) was available to apply to (redemptive) figures in Hellenistic Judaism (Moses; Jos. *Ant.* 4.328–30) and early Christianity (Christ). Absence of any stated soteriological effects in 2:6–11 prompted Talbert to call 2:6–11 "closer to the mythology of the immortals" pattern "than to any other in antiquity," in particular the myth of Heracles, who went, as son of Zeus, obedient *(peithomenos)* to clear away wickedness (Epict. 2.16.44); cf. Virgil's *Fourth Eclogue*; Hor. *Ode* 1.2.25–46 (Augustus as an appearance of Mercury); tradition about Romulus, who came from the gods, founded Rome, and became the god Quirinus in heaven (*OCD*[3] 1335). Such praise for Roman Emperors became common; cf. Horace, *Carm.* 2.9 as encomium on Augustus (M. C. J. Putnam in Raaflaub/Toher [INTRO. I. Bibl.] 212–38); later, the *Panegyricus* by Pliny for Trajan (Showalter [INTRO. I. Bibl.]). For this "pattern," cf. also the encomion from the 1st cent. B.C. about the physician Hippocrates (*HCNT* #793; ed. Hercher, *Epistolographi*, p. 289) "with divine nature," "from both sides of his family."

On 2:6–11 as *encomion* form (Lat. *encomium*), see Berger 1984a: #99, cf. pp. 367–68; *ANRW* 2.25.2:1173–95, 1232–39; *WDNTECLR* 145–47. Malina/Neyrey 19–63 place the form within topics in the *progymnasmata* or "how to" handbooks in composition.[15] Such "speech of praise" was an "ancient native model" for describing "personhood" (23, cf. 33). The pattern (Berger) includes (divine) origins; deeds or acts, service on earth; and fame, including any titles bestowed. Malina/Neyrey speak of "origin and birth, nurture and training, accomplishments and deeds," and "comparison" with others (23–33; texts from Quint. *Inst.* 2.4.1–12 and 3.7.10–18; Theon of Alexandria; Hermogenes; Aphthonius + scholion, pp. 220–24). 2:6–11 is the oldest NT example of *encomia* (Berger). Preexistence is part of the origins for the "god-like, prophetic messenger" who is sent in such passages. The *praxeis* (or "acts") section concentrates on the figure's death. Such encomia, beginning with "who" (2:6a), unfold "the great name" of the person. *HCNT* (##794, 795) also offers *Corp. Herm.* 1.12–15 (convincing esp. to those who think *Anthropos* speculation relevant) and *Ascen. Isa.* (Gk.) 2:33–36,

---

[14] A. Y. Collins 1999:245 cites *Od.* 17.485–87; Homeric *Hymn to Demeter*; Apollodorus (LCL 1:390–91); more in Zeller 1988:160–63. Exaltation after death is better attested in Gk. religion than in OT/Judaism (Collins 247, esp. Heracles and "hero" figures; *DDD* 785–91, esp. 787–88; "Ruler Cult," *DDD* 1342–52.

[15] Krentz 1995:59–71 is less impressed by the pattern in the *progymnasmata* for praising the gods because most examples (except for Theon, *OCD*[3] 1503–4) are later than the NT period. But cf. Quint. *Inst.* 3.7.6–9 (Krentz 56–57), with *topoi* that "clearly apply to Christological hymns."

the prophet's somewhat forced return to earth to face martyrdom. Malina/Neyrey 52, 55: Jesus' "life" exhibits encomium features. "Encomium" is, then, a likely candidate from Paul's day (not "hymn" or Schattenmann's "prose hymn"; *WDNTECLR* 224) to describe 2:6–11.

For people in Philippi the most significant factor in life historically and socially was probably Roman rule and ordering of society. The emperors Caligula (†41) and Nero (ruled 54–68) have been connected with the background of 2:6–11, as figure(s) against whom its affirmation is directed, "the Lord is Jesus Christ," not Caesar in the emerging Emperor cult (B.11.c, above). Heen 2000:193–96; 2004 suggests that "the local elite" (Hellerman 10, 24–25, 57–58, 80–100) was the target of a "hidden critique" in 2:6–11, *decurions* depicted in iconography under an effigy of the Emperor, their power elevated by association with the Imperial authority in the structures of the day. Such officials kept religious movements in their place and could bring about persecution. Christians would easily associate them with *those on earth* who one day will bend the knee to Christ. Such implications were part of universal homage to the new faith's Lord.

B. MEANING AND INTERPRETATION

1. *Complex Levels of Meaning.* 2:6–11 is a composition by the Philippians, not "pre-" but "para-Pauline" (Walter 57). Epaphroditus brought it to Ephesus when he came with aid from Philippi. House-church members there had put it together for missionary work. It would strike hearers in Philippi as an encomion about the Christians' hero-savior Lord. Possibly it came to Paul in written form, but the memorable seventy-three words could have been transmitted orally. The Philippians hoped for applause from their apostle (Schenk). Paul pondered the contents. Perhaps Christians in Ephesus (1:14–18) learned of the piece, used or debated it. Paul made just one addition (8c) as he sent the words back to Philippi in Letter B. But he turned the encomion in a new direction, as criterion about relations with each other in the house churches (2:2–5, 12–13) and with civic authorities (1:27) and neighbors. The piece took on further significance when Paul's three notes to the Philippians were redacted into a single epistle.

There are levels of meaning. (a) On the earlier slogan "Jesus Christ is Lord" and Isa 45:23, see above, A.1,2. (b) The Philippians' composition (2, below). (c) Paul's redaction and use of the piece in Letter B, particularly 2:5 (3, below). (d) Meaning in Phil as a whole. Those convinced 2:6–11 is by Paul can read (2) and (3) as how the first readers in Philippi would have heard it. If the Philippians wrote it, (3) suggests how the Philippians heard afresh.

2. *The Philippians' Encomium about Christ and God (2:6–11).* In Philippi, Roman hegemony and Caesar's dominion stood over all. Yet Paul (in prison) urged converts there to exercise their citizenship (1:27) and be partners in the gospel (1:5) for its spread (1:12, 25), in the face of opponents (1:28). They had to couch their message in language appropriate in the Roman *colonia*. The Gk. *encomion* form (Lat. *encomium*, A.5, above) was appropriate, a subcategory of epideictic rhetoric,[16] praising a people (Dionysus on Rome; D. Balch in Fitzgerald, ed., 1997: 123–44), a person (Caesar, Hippocrates, Moses), ancestors (1 Macc 2:50–64), famous men (Sir 44–50), or a deity (Zeus, Smithian Apollo). Not an *exemplum* (example to be imitated), but a profession of faith (Basevi/Chapa 343, 346, 348, 356), rhetorical, but not a hymn. Two long sentences about Christ's self-abasement (vv 6–8) and then glorification by God (9–11) (C. J. Robbins). Three parts (Berger 1984a:345; *ANRW* 2.25.2:1184–92, chart on 1193; cf. Schenk, A.4, above): origins, acts, and fame.

This encomium arose not because of a "rival gospel in Philippi" (D. F. Watson 1988b:58–59; it antedates the opponents in ch. 3), nor simply for internal usage (cf. Minear 1990:203–5, sung in Philippi), but as a response to what the Philippians had heard from Paul, in their own terms, for outreach in their world. Thus Paul's gospel (including some OT/Jewish backgrounds, 2:10b,11a) plus the Philippian environment, "Pauline" and "fitting for Philippi." This excludes an Aramaic original or ties to the mind of the historical Jesus at the foot-washing, etc. (claims usually set aside quite apart from the proposal of a Philippian provenance). It is the work of Christians who received the Spirit when they believed (Gal 3:2) and were baptized (1 Cor 12:13), who possessed God's charismata (Phil 1:29). Paul agrees generally, incorporating it in his letter.

2:6–11 can be read in terms of a divine figure entering into human existence, or a human being subsequently exalted.[17] Either construal was possible as a Philippian depiction of Christ. Christians there knew from Paul something of the man Jesus and his death, but also of Jesus Christ as Lord. Either reading was relevant in the world of *kyrioi* the Philippians faced. Each fits current notions about Caesar—as a mortal man who went around Rome in disguise, even as a slave, but divinized at death; or as already divine, something affirmed at death by fixture in the pantheon. From 6–7b the latter sense seems more likely, though with enough ambiguity for ancient listeners (and modern scholars) to sense a human figure later experiencing anabasis.

a. *The Origins of One, Godlike, Who Emptied Himself and Appeared Like a Slave (2:6–7b).*[18] The rel. pron. *who* is paralleled in other NT "hymns" like Col 1:15–20 to introduce the figure being presented. Identity unfolds in a series of glimpses into whence he came and what he's like; no name is indicated until v 10, no geographical place, ever. Those using this encomium in evangelization could preface it with "We preach (or believe in) Christ who . . ." or "I declare good news

---

[16] *WDNTECLR* 145–47. Krentz 1995:55 emphasizes Menander Rhetor (*OCD*³ 957; late 3rd cent. A.D.), who includes "hymns directed to the gods." Phil 2:6–11 is not to Christ or God, however.

[17] See Exc. B, II.B. For the latter "shape," cf. Talbert, Howard, Murphy-O'Connor. *morphē theou* (6a) is then the image of God all mortals share; 7bc = equality with God not yet possessed, for which this person does not reach out; emptying of selfhood means abasement, slavery, humiliation, and death. Then exaltation to divine honors and status. The other, more traditional shape begins with a figure already within the realm of divinity who becomes mortal and then is lifted back up to whence he had come or even higher.

[18] For 2:5, see below, 3, *Paul's . . . Use of the Encomium in Letter B.*

to you about Jesus Christ who . . . ," or a title like "The Son of God" (Walter 59),[19] or they could leave the hearers in suspense, "I'm talking about a person *who.* . . ."

The initial segment is built around two main vbs., what he *did not consider* (6b) and *himself he emptied* (7a). Each vb. is flanked by a ptc., *hyparchōn* 6a *(living)* and *labōn* 7b *(taking)*. Each ptc. has as object (in 6a object phrase) the noun *morphē* (traditionally "form"); there is balance, *inclusio,* and contrast involving "form of God" and "form of a slave." These phrases mark movement from the realm of deity to the realm of servitude. The middle line, heart of the unit, *to einai isa theō[i]* (6c, "to be equal to God"), was an ancient aim and goal.

Verse 6a seems to express state of being, a continuing state at that. The ptc., virtually an equivalent of *ōn,* "being," is the only one in 2:6–11 in the pres. tense. But neither philosophical concepts of ontology nor notions about "being *from the beginning*" are to be read in, though many have seen an ongoing implication, that *morphē theou* continues, even as this person takes on *morphē doulou.* This latter step comes only with an "emptying" of self. In contrast to 6a, vbs. and ptcs. that follow point to a series of actions, *did not consider, emptied* self, and *taking on.* . . . In 6a, *living in the sphere of God* means not static being but continuity with God.

Over *morphē* (6a, 7b) much ink has been spilled (see NOTE on *living in the sphere of God*). The two uses in 6a–7b hang together. Not technical, philosophical distinctions, but popular language average people in Philippi might use. Nuanced, not "being divine" or "being God," but "in the *morphē* of God." The NOTE suggests "mode of existence," *sphere,* or realm where a person is. The person described is in a nuanced relationship with deity, a point borne out by the other reference to God in 6bc Double references to *theos* will be paralleled and contrasted in 7cd by two references to *anthrōpos,* "human being/humanity."

The figure engages in a negative and then a positive action. He decides *against* (*ouch* goes with the vb.) "being equal to God." *morphē* (6a) avoids the bald statement, "is God." *isa* implies a weaker sense, "like God" or "godlike," the sort of thing said of benefactors and rulers in the Greco-Roman world (see NOTE on *to be like God*). The difficult (and rare) word *harpagmos* (6b) is probably to be taken as equivalent of *harpagma,* "thing seized," and the whole phrase (vb. of considering + double obj.) taken together.[20] The person being described, in the sphere of God, decides *not* to take advantage of his position, either by clutching on to what he has or by reaching out for more. A contrast to someone who did or those who do?

Instead, *himself he emptied,* by *taking on the sphere of a slave.* 7ab (note *but*) begins a contrast with the godlike status this figure had and could have used to his advantage. He emptied himself instead of making himself full(er). Of what? Honors, rank, power? "Godlike status" is what traditional interpretations have shied away from. "Riches" (in order to become poor) is suggested by 2 Cor 8:9. The at-

---

[19] A. Y. Collins 1999:240 n 32 conjectures, "We thank you, O God, for your son Jesus, who etc.," or, less likely, an address to Jesus (e.g., "We praise you, Lord Jesus Christ, who etc.").

[20] The few linguistic examples of the idiom and their late dating keep the "solution" from commanding full assent.

tempt to make it "emptied himself of life," by death (Isa 53:12, a [suffering] Servant background) is unlikely; death is mentioned specifically at 8b; therefore premature at 7a.

Verse 7a, *ekenōsen* has to do with assuming a slave's *morphē. the sphere of a slave* is the result of not taking advantage of godlikeness and, instead, experiencing abnegation of self. The outcome is serfdom. Of various interpretations (see NOTE), the most obvious to authors and hearers in Philippi would have been actual slavery, economic, social, political, in the world of the day ("slaves many" as well as "lords many"); "deprivation of rights" (Moule 1970:268). A further aspect of being a *doulos* was thralldom to fate and the ruling powers of the world (Gal 4:8,9).

The katabasis of the godlike figure, from advantaged to disadvantaged existence, by choice, was not the typical *cursus honorum* or career path of the Roman world, but a path to ignominies (Hellerman) and slavery. Malina/Neyrey see in 2:6–7b two components from the encomium form: "Jesus' genesis ('in the form of God') and his manner of life ('he did not exploit it')" (55); "comparison" *(sygkrisis)* is left to the hearers/readers to work out.

Is there an implied contrast here to Adam? Phil makes no clear reference to "the Man" of Gen 1–3. Paul contrasts Adam to Christ at 1 Cor 15:22 and 45 and Rom 5:14; perhaps Rom 1:23; 3:23; 7:7–12 (if "I" = Adam). But Pauline occurrences are scant in comparison with Jewish literature of the times; their relative importance in Paul is contested (B. Schaller, *EDNT* 1:27–28). Dunn, *TPTA* #4, uses these references to show "the dark side of humanity" and (##8.6, 9.1, 10.2) an aspect of Paul's Christology, "perhaps" to be seen in 2:6–11 (p. 203, cf. 281, 284–86). Wright 1983 is more emphatic on Adam here. Vollenweider 1999b sees any reference to Adam (Gen 3:5, "you will be like God") as problematic, preferring a different contrast (see below). Possibly the Philippians knew something about Adam from Paul. A contrast is attractive between the figure in 2:6–7b (who possesses godlikeness but is willing to let go of it) and Adam (who did not possess it, but reached out after the fruit of the tree of knowledge and then the tree of life), a Christ who did not grasp for divinity in contrast to an Adam who did. But vv 6–7b provide no overt evidence for such overtones. The OT Adam developed in Jewish traditions (Dunn #4.3) would not make sense to an audience in Philippi; one would have to explain about Adam to explain who Christ is.

The contrast preferred by Vollenweider and others is with "kings, rulers, and tyrants" who usurp equality with God. In many passages[21] a (pagan) ruler reaches for the heights but is sent crashing to earth or to the underworld by God, for attempting to be equal with God; cf. Heen's "Judaic tradition" (NOTE on 6c *to be like God*). Rulers claimed to be like God *(isotheia)*; e.g., Alexander the Great (cf. EXC. B, II.D.11.a; "the hired hand, mercenary, or robber of all nations," Curt. Ruf. 7.8.19, writing at the time of Caligula); Rome ("plunderers of the world," Tac. *Agr.* 30.4), and Imperial cult.

Roman Emperors are the foil for 2:6–11 (EXC. B, II. 10–12; Georgi 1991:33–78,

---

[21] Isa 14:12–15; Ezek 28:1–19 (Tyre); 31 (Egypt); Dan 4:20–22; 5:20, 23; 8:9–12, 23–25; 11:12, 36–39; 2 Macc 9:10–12; Jdt 3:8; 6:2,4; and *Pss. Sol.* 2.29–32 (*OTP* 2:653–54, Pompey capturing Jerusalem).

esp. 72–75, against the *princeps* in his military colony, for Paul's "alternative utopia," the *politeia* of 3:20; Portefaix; R. Horsley/Silberman; N. A. Beck 61–68, 2:11b is "a subtle anti-Roman cryptogram"). "Phil 2:5–11 is, at least in part, a subversion of Imperial public propaganda."[22] Bornhäuser 1938, the recipients of Phil were Roman army veterans who had exchanged the Lordship of Nero, the Caesar, *Divus* and *Sōtēr*, for Jesus, the Christ, their Lord and Savior (3:20).[23] "Ruler-worship," repugnant to Republican Rome, became more common under oriental influences, Emperors hailed as "god."[24] Space does not allow detailing here data for each Emperor. Philippians would have been acquainted with Caesar as a god-like figure, by apotheosis at death, during the ruler's lifetime, and as part of his origins, in the sphere of the divine. 2:6bc reflects deity-figures who ruled over them in the state (Wright 1991:89). 2:6–11 contrasts one who did not seek advantages but abased self to the level of a slave.[25]

Some speak of a "political Paul."[26] There were also "political Philippians," Christians included, aware of Caesar's lordship, the Imperator's kinship to the gods, and local magistrates in the pyramid of power and Imperial cult. Thus another reflection of "the conflicts of Paul and the Christian community with the Roman municipal authorities" (Bormann 1995:218).

b. *The Actions of This Man amid Humanity — Birth, Humiliation, Obedience, Death (2:7c–8b).* The figure from the divine sphere who eschewed godlikeness and got slavery is now described by four terse comments. Encomia took up "origins" (forebears, birth) and "accomplishments," deeds, or "acts" (Gk. *praxeis*; Berger 1984a:345, cf. 372–73; cf. "*Acts* of the Apostles"), in the Roman world" *res*

---

[22] Meggitt 1998:98 n 115, cf. 187; cf. Seeley 1994. On Imperial propaganda, cf. Zanker 1990 (INTRO. I Bibl.); A. Wallace-Hadrill, "Roman Arches and Greek Honours," *Proceedings of the Cambridge Philological Society* 216 (1990) 143–81.

[23] In Egypt the Pharaohs had for centuries been considered nearer to the gods than to mortals (Heinen). This view rubbed off on the Greeks (and eventually Romans) from Alexander the Great on. There were Hellenistic ruler cults, beginning with Alexander (*OCD*³ 59) and then Ptolemaic and Seleucid kings. Cf. *CAH* 7:7–21; *OCD*³ 1337–38; *KlPauly* 2 [1967] 1110–12; *RAC* 14 [1988] 1047–93; Heinen). Human benefactors were honored as godlike; see NOTE on 2:6c *to be like God*, Heen's "civic tradition."

[24] *CAH* 10: 481–89; *OCD*³ 1338–39; *ABD* 5:806–9 [bibl.]; L. Koep, "Consecratio II (Kaiserapotheosis)," *RAC* 3 (1957) 284–94; Leipold/Grundmann 7th ed. 1986 vol. 2, pp. 102–105; G. Bowersock 1983:171–82; S. R. F. Price 1984a (INTRO. I) and b; Heen 1997:93–122; Horsley 1997; Clauss; K. Wegenast, "Apotheosis," *KlPauly* 1:458–60; H. D. Betz, "Gottmensch II," *RAC* 12 (1983) 234–312; H. J. Klauck 2000: 250–330; D. Dormeyer, *RGG*⁴ 1:654–55.

[25] Is "slave," before "becoming *anthrōpos*" in 7cd, perhaps a reflection of Saturnalia with its inversion of social roles, by ruler and slave, in particular re Claudius who was said to be ruled by his freedmen (Heen 1997:307–11)? Reconstructing Saturnalian attitudes toward the *Princeps* is complicated, but they were a possible factor in the world of the day in connection with *doulos* and *kyrios*.

[26] N. Elliott 1994:196–97 esp., repr. in Horsley, ed., 1997:167–204, cf. 140–47, with Georgi 1991; Blumenfeld 2001; Hollingshead xv, xvii, 113–26 (*oikos*), 205–6, 208, 217–18, 240. K. P. Donfried, "The Cults of Thessalonica and the Thessalonian Correspondence," *NTS* 31 (1985) 336–56 = Horsley 215–23) reads 1 Thess against a martyrdom situation (much as Loh. supposed for Phil), stressing oaths of personal loyalty to Caesar ("royal theology") for Romans and non-Romans alike.

gestae, "deeds done."[27] 2:7c–8b has nothing about Jesus' personal achievements like miracles, teachings, or message, nothing about the kingdom of God (1 Thess 2:12), Davidic descent (Rom 1:3), or "Christ crucified" (1 Cor 1.23; 2.2; cf. Dunn, *TPTA* 210). There was certainly curiosity about hero figures. Paul's letters include more about Christ than is often supposed, and Paul could well have taught converts what he knew. But in his letters "Paul tells us next to nothing about the life and ministry of Jesus apart from its climactic finale," mainly "[f]ormulaic or allusive references . . . to recall a central theme in their shared faith" (*TPTA* ##8–10, quotations from pp. 186, 184, 212). The terseness in 2:6–8 may reflect Roman Philippi. "The kingdom" was readily misunderstood in Caesar's realm (cf. Acts 17:6–7), replaced for Paul by God's righteousness (*TPTA* 190). A royal messiah was "politically dangerous" (ibid. 184 n 8; the title *Christos* becomes a name). Reference to the cross (8c) seems an addition by Paul (see 3, below). There is little in vv 7c-8b that one can imitate, except dying.

The picture in these four lines is built around the main vb., *he experienced humiliation for himself* (8a). Philippians knew humiliation in daily life, "put in their place" by betters in the social structures of the Roman world, its hierarchy of authority, and economic networks. All could identify with a figure who suffered humiliation. Women, particularly oppressed, were attracted to Dionysus, Artemis, Isis cults, or the dignity of citizens in Paul's gospel (1:27; Portefaix 138–39; cf. Abrahamsen 1995). With the later interpretation, he "*humbled* himself," hearers would not identify, the way they could with humiliation. Vv 6–7b brought the godlike figure into slave existence; humiliations inevitably follow. Emphasis on action; he *emptied . . .* he *experienced humiliation for himself* (Loh/Nida 60, "he humiliated himself") and 8b, *death.*

The chief vb. is preceded in 7cd by two participial expressions, *born in humanity's likeness* and *in appearance perceived as a human being.* Double use of *anthrōpos* matches the two references to *God* in 6ab. 7c provides a reference to birth, as expected in an encomium, but no celestial signs or prodigies in nature, as expected in antiquity (Malina/Neyrey 26). The phrase tells less than Paul says at Gal 4:4 and Rom 1:3 — nothing of Jewish background or earthly parents. Nil about physical prowess, endowments from fortune, or "deeds of soul" found in encomia (virtues like courage or wisdom, Malina/Neyrey 28–33). Use of *genomenos* begins an *inclusio*, however, for 7c–8b, birth and death.

2:7c situates the figure within the whole human race. Neither Jew nor Gentile is mentioned. Of other classic divisions in Gal 3:28, *slave* was asserted in 7b, "male" implied (by the gender of *who*, the ptcs., and *himself*). 2:7c speaks of the figure as viewed by others. From any angle, a human being, and what slavery implies — humiliation. Many a hearer must have reacted, not "Hallelujah, what a Savior!," but "He is one with us!"

As in 6ab about deity, there is nuancing. Instead of "born a man" (cf. Gal 4:4

---

[27] J. Fitzmyer, AB 31:47–48. Cf. *Res Gestae divi Augusti*, "the Acts of the Divine Augustus" (Gk. "Deeds and Benefactions"), Caesar's achievements in the 1st per.; Paul records his, 1st per., Phil 3:2–11 (Malina/Neyrey 34–60).

or Rom 1:3), the wording is "in the likeness *(homoiōmati)* of humans," similarity, though not exact identity. Some sense Gen 1:26 (NRSV "Let us make humankind . . . according to our likeness [*kath' homoiōsin*]"), but that is God's likeness, not humanity's. Others, 2:7c avoids implying Christ was a sinner like the rest of humanity, simply "in the likeness of sinful flesh" (Rom 8:3). Or a touch of Docetism; see Note on *likeness*. Is the wording one Philippians adopted naturally, reflecting stories about demigods born to mortal women or the status claimed for a divine ruler, "born in similarity to human beings," but really something more?

Verse 7d, *in appearance perceived as a human being,* nuances what the figure was found or seen to be. Some trs. set aside *hōs* ([N]RSV; NAB). *schēmati* is more troublesome, often contrasted with *morphē* in 6a and 7b, "changeable and outward," not "inner essence"; then the humanity was impermanent and fleeting, worn as an outward covering. Better, it was what anyone could see by looking, a personage within humanity who, as a slave, experienced humiliation. (One would like to find reflection of Jesus' passion, but gospel accounts do not use *tapeino-* vocabulary there.)

Both 7c and d express the situation or condition of the figure, *born,* perceivable *as a human being.* The double description is the assumption for the action word describing his life and its outcome, "human, as he was, this slave *experienced humiliation* in his obedience, *to the point of death.*" 8b spells out the degree of humiliation: *death,* not suicide but execution; *thanatos* upon sentence by the authorities. *genomenos* in 8b matches 7c, an *inclusio* from birth as a slave to obedient death. No modifier for *thanatos,* the normal word for the end of life. Hermogenes (*Prog.* 7.40 = Malina-Neyrey 223) urged that an encomium tell the manner of a person's end, e.g., "he died fighting for his fatherland," or (Achilles) at the hand of a god (Apollo) (Malina/Neyrey 31, 223). Phil 2:8ab is the barest of NT passion references.

obedient at 8b (only occurrence in Phil) is a rare word in Paul (only at 2 Cor 2:9; the vb. is more common, the noun *hypakoē* a Pauline term). In antiquity, obedience was often praised, along with faithfulness or loyalty (*pistis*; Malina/Neyrey 166–68; Paul's terminology on p. 195). The Philippians could have known the theme from Paul's teaching (cf. Rom 5:19; Rom 1:5; Rom 10:16; 2 Cor 10:6). Here, scarcely "obedience to God" (God is not mentioned in 8b). Philippians, as military veterans, citizens, and inhabitants of a *colōnia,* would have known the concept (*obedientia, officium* = duty), a quality on which much rested in contemporary society. Is it because the concept was so obvious that nothing more is said in v 8 about to whom obedience is given? A figure faithfully obedient at his post would appeal to people in Philippi. Especially one faithful unto death. Then what?

Commentators have seen in 2:7c–8 the Suffering Servant (Isa 53) or the "righteous sufferer," but remarkably little provides a toehold, quite apart from whether people in Philippi would have perceived such overtones. The theme was also found in Plato (*Ap.* 29A–31C, *Crito* 54D, *Phaedo* 115B–118A; Hengel 1981:1–32). We get snapshots in the encomium of a human being undergoing humiliation (but no details), death (how, is not stated), in the course of being obedient (to whom unstated). Nothing about the purpose or results, like "Christ died for us" or "for our sins." Nothing about his death atoning for anything. The story line is limited to humiliation and dying. One might be reminded of Gaius Caesar putting on costumes to play Heracles or Dionysus (Philo, *Leg. All.* 79), but the impression in 2:6–8 is far more a very human person coming to a tragic end, not theatrical posturings. Did Philippians think of Heracles, whose final toil for humankind was self-immolation (cf. 1 Cor 13:3; *TDNT* 3:467)? By "this figure" or "the humiliated one," we know Jesus is meant. But vv 6–8 have not identified the person by name or place.

c. *God Exalts This Figure, Jesus, to Lordship over All — to God's Glory (2:9–11).* Enter *God*, previously mentioned only re the sphere where the humiliated figure once existed, the status-holder of whose position the one obedient unto death did not take advantage (6ab). Now for the first time the self-negating figure is identified, *Jesus* (10a), indeed *Jesus Christ* (11b). God's action is twofold: he *exalted* Jesus *most highly* and *freely gave him the name that is above every name* (v 9). The results are twofold: *every knee shall bow* and *every* tongue or *language confess* or "openly declare" the newly exalted *Lord* (10–11b) in universal acclamation. There is an addendum, typical of encomia, praise — here, for God, now designated *Father*. Thus an *inclusio*, the unit begins and ends with reference to God. If in vv 6–8 the Christ-figure was subject, in 9–11 God is, dramatically. Such is the plot line of Philippian witness to *res gestae Dei*.

Transition from humiliation to enthronement is signaled by change of subject, shift from participial style (none, but five in vv 6–8; instead four indic. or subjunct. vbs., the same number as in 6–8), and *Therefore* to indicate a fresh start. If *dio* means "because of this," we are not told why, not even "because of Christ's obedience"; only that God has swung into action. *kai* intensifies, "has *indeed* exalted him." No vbs. show "state of being;" instead a pattern: two actions, a twofold outcome (in words from Isa 45:23) about knee and "tongue," physical homage and verbal profession. As in 6–7b and 7c–8b, it amounts to a protasis (Schenk), but more certain in tone than "if" — since, indeed *because*, God has exalted Jesus, it follows that. . . . One superior to Caesar has granted status and honor, publicly acknowledged (Hellerman 148–51).

hyperhypsōsen says more about Jesus than the customary resurrection formula, "God raised him from the dead." It carries the story of Christ to exaltation, more appropriate for an audience in Philippi than "resurrection" of a body. To "lift to higher status" (*hypsoō*) fits with Greco-Roman accounts about elevation of heroes and apotheoses (see on 3:10, below; Reumann 2002). Most Eng. NT trs. bring out the prefix *hyper-*, "highly exalt," or "to the highest degree possible," in view of what follows in v 11 (lordship) and the nuancing in vv 6–8.

The encomium depicts unparalleled largess from the Father, God's act of grace (see NOTE on *and freely gave him . . .*). A *name* (really title) is shared that Jesus did not have before, even though in the sphere of God. Many see an "enthronement ceremony," as in the ancient Near East, OT, and Greco-Roman world. The title-name, *Lord*, is appropriate in Roman Philippi (many "lords," Caesar as *dominus*).

How vv 10–11b were put together is easier to describe than what some details mean. LXX wording from Isa 45:23 (A.1, above) is interlaced in 10c with three levels from ancient cosmology (10c, "those above, below, and on the earth") and in 11b with an acclamation formula (A.2, above) from the early church. The Philippians would have known these biblical and creedal words from Paul; they shared the three-story universe with most people of the day. *those in the heavens, those on earth, and those in the world below* comes from Pauline language and inscriptions in Philippi about the dead in Hades. Therefore, angels and spirits in the heavens, humanity on earth, and the dead in the underworld (see NOTE)—the universe, without enumerating "angels, rulers, and other "powers" as Paul does in Rom 8:38–39.

OT language is reapplied. Isaiah had said that one day all would yield and swear allegiance to Yahweh, even those "incensed against him." Paul used this (in Rom 14:10–11) to inculcate accountability, all will face the Judge; they will bow and give God praise and confession some day; the words of Isa provide warrant for Christian conduct. In the encomium the words are used without mentioning judgment or conduct: all will bow "at the name of Jesus" and confess Christ's lordship, for God's praise and glory (11c).

When? The easy answer is "at the parousia, when Christ comes in glory," a Pauline emphasis (*TPTA* #12) from his earliest extant letter on (1 Thess 1:9–10; 2:12, 19; 3:13, etc.; cf. 1 Cor 15: 22–28, 51–57, etc.). The Philippians knew about "the Day of Jesus Christ" (Letter A, 4:19; Letter B, 1:5,10; 2:16; Letter C, 3:20–21). But Paul's discussion of his own immediate future (1:19–26) suggested being "with Christ" at one's death. Does 2:9–11 see some expectations fulfilled *before* the parousia? Käsemann 1950 made a case for this. Philippian reflections on the grandeur of Christ's lordship could have let them see already in effect what they would obtain some day: the reign of their God and Christ over all rulers. It was an attractive vision for witnessing.

Put grammatically, does *hina* cl. at 10–11a express purpose ("that every knee should bow" and tongues "should confess", KJV-[N]RSV) or (also) result, consequences of God's action already beginning to occur? Should the subjunct. after *hina* be read in 11a or a fut. indic. (see NOTE on *confess*)? We reject result now in 10b ("so that all beings . . . bend the knee") but a fut. tense in 11a ("and every tongue will acclaim" [N]JB mg); this breaks up the parallelism for the sake of a textual variant; the scenario is difficult to envision (genuflection now, verbal confession only at the parousia). 10b as purpose and 11a result (future?) is no better. Philippian Christians would probably have emphasized the certainty of divine purpose, but added Jesus is already divine Lord whom some on earth, any of their community who have died, and heavenly beings now confess, part of a universal triumph for Christ. The encomium gives no further details, nor does Paul add any. One does not trace out the aftermath of apotheosis or enthronement, simply the degree of exaltation, here *most highly* (9a), as Lord (11b).

Bowing and various languages affirming the Kyrios fits Philippian experience; they knew subjection to Rome's rulers, and polyglot affirmation of Caesar. *at the name of Jesus* (10a) is a phrase unparalleled in secular Gk. or NT usage (see

NOTE). Baptism "in the name of Jesus (Christ)" (Acts 10:48, e.g.) reflects Luke's "name" theology.[28] But does that fit here? 1 Cor 5:4 may seem more pertinent, "assembled in the name of our Lord Jesus" (NEB, NIV), but there it likely goes with pronouncing judgment in Jesus' name (RSV; Fee, *1 Cor.* 206–8). A cultic aspect is often claimed, the risen Jesus being worshiped, or God worshiped through Jesus.[29] But there is nothing in 2:9–11 about the Christian community giving thanks for benefits from Jesus' death and exaltation. Believers are part of a broader company giving homage to Jesus "in the heavens, on earth, and in the underworld." Not "genuflecting every time the name 'Jesus' is mentioned," but submission when the title *Lord* for Jesus is perceived. Perceived in his true identity? That happens for some in the present; it will obtain for all in God's future time. Such is the fame of Christ Jesus in this encomium.

For all the high Christology (Jesus as Lord, "kyriology"), the final point is praise of God. What God has done redounds *to the glory of God the Father* (11c). The Philippians were capable of the phrase on their own, though it could stem from the closing reference to God in Isa 45:23 LXX or from Paul's own teaching. "It is not that God has stepped aside and Jesus has taken over. It is rather that God shared his lordship with Christ, without it ceasing to be God's alone" (*TPTA* 254). Cf. Thüsing 258, "the christology of Paul is theocentric" (tr., *TPTA* 255 n 113).

God the Father may be directed against Zeus as "Father" or Caesar as *pater patriae* ("Father of the Fatherland," a title of Augustus and most Emperors after Tiberius). The most direct anti-Roman claim comes in *"the Lord is Jesus Christ,"* unspoken comparison to "Gaius (or Nero) Caesar is *dominus.*" There is also contrast between gods of the day and the God from whose sphere Jesus came and who has exalted him to lordship (and *imperium*). "[T]he real theological meaning of the hymn . . . is a new understanding of God" (Wright 1986:84)—not (as in traditional Christology) one who, during the "humiliation of the incarnation and the cross," did not "stop being God," but rather the Father of the world, of Jesus, and of Christians.

3. *Paul's Redaction (2:8c) and Use of the Encomium in Letter B (2:5–11).* Paul approves the Philippians' composition by citing it, to speak afresh to issues in the house churches there. To reapply the Philippian encomium came naturally for Paul. He (and other early Christians) reapplied OT materials like Isa 45:23. The Philippians' indirect polemic against Caesar and the "civic tradition" of their world would have triggered in Paul's mind OT and Jewish stances against tyrant rulers who usurp divinity (passages cited from Vollenweider above, 2.a; Heen's "Judaic tradition" in the NOTE on 6c *to be like God*). The piece "became Pauline" as the apostle "found it useful for his own purposes" (Minear 1990:203).

Verse 8c is most frequently designated an addition by Paul, *yes, death on a cross,*

---

[28] The name = the person (cf. Fitzmyer, AB 31:265–66; H. Conzelmann, *The Theology of Saint Luke* [New York: Harpers, 1960] 177–78), "at the presence of Jesus."
[29] Cf. *TPTA* #10.4–5, "veneration," not worship of Christ. Scroggs 1993 goes too far in seeing "replacement," Jesus Christ "de facto functions in the place of Yahweh," as cosmocrator.

thanatou repeated from 8b, *de* as connective, then "cross" in the same case (*staurou*, = anadiplose), a clarifying comment or *correctio* (Edart 144–45). Paul thereby excludes any notion of self-burning, as in the story of Heracles. If "death by crucifixion" were intended in the encomium, a clearer expression might have been expected. "Christ crucified" and "the cross of Christ" were a strong emphasis in Paul's theology, esp. at this point in his career (J. Becker [1] Bibl. **Paul** chs. 8 and 12, the stage when the letter was written to Philippi from prison). The Philippians may have omitted mention of this Roman method of execution out of sensitivity to potential converts in the *colōnia*, as Paul himself does in writing Rom. But Paul adds *thanatou de staurou* to make absolutely clear the reference (and the offense, 1 Cor 1:23), without mentioning "Christ" or "Jesus" before the encomium does. In this "governing metaphor" of 2:6–11, the cross becomes culmination for "cruciform existence" (D. K. Williams 2002:145–47). The reference is "sufficient to recall a central theme in their shared faith" (*TPTA* 212), "a criterion by which he measures other would-be gospels" (ibid. 233; D. K. Williams 2002:13, "the context demanded it").[30]

To introduce the Philippians' encomium and link it with paraenesis in 1:27–2:4, Paul carefully phrased **2:5**, *Think this way among yourselves; it is the way you also think "in Christ Jesus." Think . . . among yourselves* employs *phroneite* (2:2; 1:7) from a Philippian slogan he quoted at 4:10 in Letter A, about "your concern for me." He urges them to keep on thinking thus in relationships with one another in and among the house churches. Too often *en hymin* has been individualized ("in you"), and *phronein* ("think") made "attitude" within the heart (Edart 177–85, Christ exemplifies interior attitude). Such interpretations avoid the reciprocity in the church community and social setting found in Gk. concepts of "friendship." The root *phron-* has rich connotations, including thoughtful conduct and a life with discernment. Its range of applications is suggested by *in this way* (the concerns expressed in 2:2–4 and from 1:27 on, about citizenship in *polis* and church groups). However, in view of what follows, *the way you also think "in Christ Jesus"* (*ho* 5b in relation to *touto* 5a), there is also a relationship of baptized believers[31] to Christ and God signified in *touto*. Losie refers *touto* to vv 6–11, "set your minds on this *confession*."

Correlation between *en hymin* (*among yourselves*, 5a) and *en Christō[i] Iēsou* ("*in Christ Jesus*," 5b) is carried through by use of *touto* and *ho* (*in this way . . . it is the way . . .*), repetition (understood) of the same vb. *phroneite* (but in the indic. in 5b), and *kai*: "you do *indeed* think this way in Christ Jesus." *in Christ Jesus* norms *en hymin* (cf. Martin 1997:lxxi n 66; Schenk 175–77, 2:1 and 6–11 provide the indic. for the impvs.).

In Letter B *in Christ Jesus* (5b) has referred to the ecclesial sphere of "saints"

---

[30] Other putative additions by Paul (cf. Jeremias) depend esp. on notions that they intrude into the metrical scheme of a hymn, but there has been little agreement. We are content to allow that everything in the passage except 8c comes from the Philippians.

[31] Believers are "brought into Christ through baptism" (Son 29, with many exegetes). If 2:5b functioned as a confession (Losie), was it a baptismal confession? Cf. Exc. B n 4.

and leaders in Philippi (1:1); their situation re Christ (2:1) and Paul's in mission (1:13); and "in Christ" as present life and future hope (1:26). 2:5b points to what has happened "in Christ Jesus" for their salvation (2:12), which they work out in its daily-life aspects, as slaves under the *Kyrios* Jesus Christ (2:5b, 11, *inclusio*, bracketing the whole). The confession, "Jesus Christ (is) Lord," stands over their lives and relationships to him (and God) *and to each other*. They are "minded" in certain directions by who their Lord and their God are, just as Roman citizens and other inhabitants of Philippi were stamped and oriented by Caesar's rule. The Philippians rightly comprehend Christ and God in their encomium. Now apply this relationship to themselves re one another: amid humiliations in Caesar's world, practice obedience by abnegating self in favor of others, esp. others in their faith community (2:2b–4). 2:6–11 provide the indic. about God's acts for the impvs. to the community (Söding 1995 [(2) Bibl. **love**] 183), esp. for *agapē* (2:2) to others (182); cf. 183–86 (2,3,6,8). 2:6–11 is not itself ethical summons but is used by Paul to underscore his paraenesis (Grabner-Haider 43–44).

Paul's reapplication of their encomium must have made its authors take notice. If they thought previously about implications for themselves, most likely they saw lordship for themselves, a touch of glory here and now. Paul picks up vv 6–8 in his paraenesis, before quoting their words back to the Philippians: note parallels between their humiliation (2:3b) and Christ's (8a); contrast Christ's not grasping (6bc) and their *self-interest, vainglory,* and *own interests* (3a, 4). In becoming a slave, Christ considered others to *surpass* himself (cf. 3b), putting the interests of others ahead of his own (4). The story they knew so well has implications for communal life. Paul laid the groundwork by alluding in 2:1 to aspects of the Christ story that the Philippian summation did *not* include: *agapē,* (divine) affections and mercies, and the Spirit, not criticizing the Philippians' kerygma, but motivating, with aspects of Christian experience that subsequent readers have not usually noticed to be missing in 2:6–11.

The Philippians' encomium did not suggest what the Christ event meant for believers in the church. It applied results to the cosmos (10–11). The rival with whom vv 6–11 contrast is Caesar. Paul redirects the material to help house churches in Philippi on internal relations, without forgetting connections to the *polis* and cosmos. Apply the slaveship of Jesus to yourselves and your relations with each other in *the fellowship brought about by the Spirit.* In such ways, *Exercise your citizenship in a manner worthy of the gospel of Christ* (1:27).

4. 2:5–11 *Within the Combined, Canonical Letter.* As Letter B was combined with Letters C and A, no changes were made in 2:5–11. But 2:6–11 was no longer "the center," as it was in Letter B. Chiastic schemes (Wick, Luter/Lee, etc.) to make 2:6–11 the generative heart of all Phil disagree among themselves. Such efforts blind us to how much of Paul's thought is lacking in 2:6–11 and to what 2:6–11 actually says about Christ and God, with Caesar's world as foil.

Once 2:6–11 was part of a unified document, connections were made with other passages. Within Phil, esp. with 3:20–21 (see COMMENT there). Within the Pauline corpus, with passages on "the cross," or "hymns" as a category. For some, canonical context means stressing 2:6–11 as "kerygmatic," the Christ story; for others, as "ethical," Jesus an example to be imitated. Childs 1984:329–37 regards the amalgamated three letters as a case where "the redactors have largely concealed their footprints" (336); it is in light of 2:6–11's christological confession about "ultimate victory" that Paul views his imprisonment and suffering; the letter becomes "canonically . . . a last will and testament of the martyred apostle" (337).

The importance of 2:6–11 grew over the centuries, but origins in Philippi were obscured. Only an inspired apostle could have written so grand a piece, or it must go back to the Aramaic-speaking church, closer to Jesus himself, to provide foundations for later Christology. No passage in Phil has had a greater influence than 2:6–11 in Christology, soteriology, and ethics. Debate over the vv as "story of salvation" or Jesus as exemplar continues. "Theological treatments" abound.[32] Hellenistic-Roman backgrounds for 2:6–11 have come increasingly into play, but do not solve all problems of interpretation (cf. G. Theissen 1983b:324 and 326), in a composition by people "whose life is full of experiences of lowliness and humiliation," who discovered "that Christ as joined them" (Wengst 1988 [(6) Bibl. **humiliation**] 50–51).

No passage in Phil has had more use in appointed readings at church services over the centuries than 2:5–11, as "the Epistle for Palmarum," Passion Sunday, in the *Ordo* for all three years: a theological vision for Holy Week, with the light of Easter at the end of the tunnel. Its imagery appears in hymns (cf. Minear 1990; Kreitzer/Rooke). What the Philippians wrote to proclaim Christ in their Roman world has continued to shape preaching, hymnody, Christology, and Christian life.

SELECT BIBLIOGRAPHY (see also General Bibliography and Commentaries)

Aune, D. E. 1990. "Hercules and Christ," in FS Malherbe (see Gen. Bibl., White, L. M.) 3–19.

Bandstra, A. J. 1966. "'Adam' and 'The Servant' in Philippians 2:5ff.," *CTJ* 1:213–16.

Basevi, C., and J. Chapa. 1993. "Philippians 2:6–11: The Rhetorical Ethical Function of a Pauline 'Hymn,'" in Porter/Olbricht, eds., 338–56.

Beck, N. A. 1997. *Anti-Roman Cryptograms in the New Testament: Symbolic Messages of Hope and Liberation.* Westminster College Library of Biblical Symbolism, 1. New York: Peter D. Lang.

Beet, J. A. 1887. "Thought It Not Robbery to Be Equal with God," *The Expositor*, 3rd Series, Vol. 5:115–28.

Binder, H. 1987. "Erwägungen zu Phil 2,6–7b," *ZNW* 28:230–43.

Bockmuehl, M. 1997. "'The Form of God' (Phil. 2.6): Variations on a Theme of Jewish Mysticism," *JTS* 48:1–23.

Bornhäuser, K. 1933. "Zum Verständnis von Phil 2,5–11," *NKZ* 44:428–34, 453–62.

———. 1938. *Jesus Imperator Mundi (Phil. 3, 17–21 u. 2,5–12). Vortrag vor den theolo-*

---

[32] E.g., Dawe, Fairweather, L. Richard, Sykes. Minear 1990:219 nn 21 and 25 ranks Kierkegaard highly. E. Schillebeeckx 1981:169 treats Phil in his history of the NT experience of grace. For ecumenical and interreligious concerns, cf. Laporte 1974, 1985 and D. H. Jensen.

gischen Fachschaften von Groningen, Kampen, Amsterdam (städt. Universität), Utrecht und Leiden. Gütersloh: C. Bertelsmann.

Bornkamm, G. 1959a. "Zum Verständnis des Christus-Hymnus, Phil. 2, 6–11," in his Studien zu Antike und Urchristentum, GS Band 2. BEvT 28 (Munich: Chr. Kaiser, 1959, 2nd ed. 1963) 177–87. Cited from tr. by P. L. Hammer, "On Understanding the Christ-hymn (Philippians 2.6–11)," in Bornkamm's Early Christian Experience (New York/Evanston: Harper & Row, 1969) 112–22.

Borsch, F. H. 1992. "Further Reflections on the Son of Man," in The Messiah, ed. J. H. Charlesworth et al. (Minneapolis: Fortress) 130–44.

Branick, V. P. 1985. "The Sinful Flesh of the Son of God (Rom 8:3): A Key Image of Pauline Theology," CBQ 47:246–62.

Breck, J. 1987. "Biblical Chiasmus: Exploring Structure for Meaning," BTB 17:70–74.

Briggs, S. 1989. "Can an Enslaved God Liberate? Hermeneutical Reflections on Philippians 2:6–11," Semeia 47:135–53.

Brown, C. 1998. "Ernst Lohmeyer's Kyrios Christos," in Martin/Dodd (see below) 43–73.

Brucker, R. 1997. 'Christushymnen' oder 'epideiktische Passagen'? Studien zum Stilwechsel im Neuen Testament und seiner Umwelt. FRLANT 176. Göttingen: Vandenhoeck & Ruprecht.

Carmignac, J. 1972. "L'Importance de la place d'une négation: OUCH ARPAGMON ĒGĒSATO (Philippiens II.6)," NTS 18:131–66.

Cerfaux, L. 1946. "L'hymne au Christ—Serviteur de Dieu (Phil II,6–11 = Is. LII,13–LIII,12)," in Miscellanea historica Alberti de Meyer (Louvain: Université de Louvain, 1946) 117–30, repr. In Recueil Lucien Cerfaux 2: Études d'Exégèse et d'Histoire Religieuse (BETL 7, Gembloux, 1954) 2:425–37; cf. Cerfaux 1959 ([1] Bibl. Christ) 382–83.

Clark, W. K. L. 1929. "The Epistle to the Philippians," in his New Testament Problems: Essays—Reviews—Interpretations (London: SPCK) 141–50.

Clauss, M. 1999. Kaiser und Gott. Herrscherkult im römischen Reich. Stuttgart/Leipzig: Teubner.

Collins, A. Y. 1999. "The Worship of Jesus and the Imperial Cult," in C. C. Newman et al., ed. 234–57, esp. 240–51, "Philippians 2:6–11 in Cultural Context."

Colpe, C. 1961. Die religionsgeschichtliche Schule. Vorstellung und Kritik ihres Bildes von gnostischen Erlösersmythos. FRLANT 78. Göttingen: Vandenhoeck & Ruprecht.

Cullmann, O. 1949. The Earliest Christian Confessions. London: SCM.

Dawe, D. G. 1962. 1963. The Form of a Servant: A Historical Analysis of the Kenotic Motif. Philadelphia: Westminster. Cf. SJT 15 (1962) 337–49.

Deichgräber, R. 1967. Gotteshymnus und Christushymnus in der frühen Christentum. SUNT 5. Göttingen: Vandenhoeck & Ruprecht.

Delling, G. 1969. "Zum steigernden Gebrauch von Komposita mit 'hyper' bei Paulus," NovT 11:127–53.

Dibelius, M. 1909. Die Geisterwelt im Glauben des Paulus. Göttingen: Vandenhoeck & Ruprecht.

Dunn, J. D. G. 1980. Christology in the Making: A New Testament Inquiry into the Origins of the Doctrine of the Incarnation. London, SCM; rev. ed. 1989.

———. 1998. "Christ, Adam, and Preexistence," in Martin/Dodd (see below) 74–83 = Dunn's TPTA (1998) #11.4.

Dupont, J. 1950. "Jésus-Christ dans son abaissement et son exaltation, d'après Phil., 2,6–11," RSR 37:500–514.

Eckman, B. 1980. "A Quantitative Metrical Analysis of the Philippian Hymn," NTS 26:258–65.

Ehrhardt, A. A. T. 1945. "Jesus Christ and Alexander the Great," *JTS* 46:45–51 = *EvT* 8 (1948–49) 101–10, plus "Nochmals: Ein antikes Herrscherideal," *EvT* 8:569–72. Repr. in his GS, *The Framework of the New Testament Stories* (Manchester: Univ. of Manchester Press, 1964) 37–43.

Fairweather, E. R. 1959. "The 'Kenotic' Christology," in Beare, *Phil.* 159–74.

Feinberg, P. D. 1980. "The Kenosis and Christology: An Exegetical-Theological Analysis of Phil 2:6–11," *TJ* 1:21–46.

Fitzmyer, J. A. 1988. "The Aramaic Background of Philippians 2:6–11," *CBQ* 50:470–83.

Frenschkowski, M. 1995. *Offenbarung und Epiphanie. I. Grundlagen des spätantiken und frühchristlichen Offenbarungsglaubens.* WUNT 2/79. Tübingen: Mohr Siebeck. *II. Die vorborgene Epiphanie in Spätantike und frühem Christentum.* WUNT 2/80. 1997.

Furley, W.D., and J. M. Bremer. 2001. *Greek Hymns. Selected Cult Songs from the Archaic to the Hellenistic Period.* Vol. 1, *The Texts in Translation.* Vol. 2, *Greek Texts and Commentary.* STAC 9, 10. Tübingen: Mohr Siebeck.

Gamber, K. 1970. "Der Christus-Hymnus in Philipperbrief in liturgiegeschichtlicher Sicht," *Bib* 51:369–76.

Georgi, D. 1964b. "Der vorpaulinische Hymnus, Phil. 2.6–11," in *Zeit und Geschichte,* FS Bultmann, ed. E. Dinkler (Tübingen: Mohr Siebeck) 263–93.

Gieschen, C. A. 1998. *Angelmorphic Christology: Antecedents and Early Evidence.* AGJU 42. Leiden: Brill.

Grelot, P. 1972. "Deux expressions difficiles de Philippiens 2,6–7," *Bib* 53:495–507.

———. 1973. "La valeur de *ouk ... alla ...* dans Philippiens 2,6–7," *Bib* 54:25–42.

Habermann, J. 1990. *Preexistenzaussagen im Neuen Testament.* Frankfurt: Peter D. Lang. Cf. J. D. G. Dunn, in Martin/Dodd (see below) 80 n 19.

Hammerich, L. L. 1966. *An Ancient Misunderstanding (Phil. 2,6 'robbery').* Kopenhagen, cf. *ExpTim* 78 (1967) 193–94. Cf. "Phil 2,6 and P. A. Florenskij," DVSS.HF 47.5 (1976).

Harnack, A. 1928a. "Das Alte Testament in den Paulinischen Briefen und in den Paulinischen Gemeinden," SPAW.PH 1928:124–41.

Heen, E. M. 1997. "Saturnalicius Princeps: The Enthronement of Jesus in Early Christian Discourse." Diss., Columbia Univ.

———. 2004. "Phil 2:6–11 and Resistance to Local Timocratic Rule: *isa theō* and the Cult of the Emperor in the East," in *Paul and the Roman Imperial Order,* ed. R. A. Horsley (Harrisburg, PA: Trinity International Press) 123–53. Cf. SBL "Paul and Politics Group," *SBL 2000 Abstracts,* S144.

Heinen, H. 1995. "Vorstufen und Anfänge des Herrscherskultes im römischen Ägypten," ANRW 2.18.5:3144–80.

Henry, P. 1957. "Kénose." DBSup 5, cols. 7–161.

Heriban, J. 1983. *Retto PHRONEIN e KENOSIS: Studio esegetico su Fil 2,2–5. 6–11,* Bibliotheca di Scienze Religioso 51 (Rome: LAS [Liberia Ateneo Salesiano]), esp. "Nota 2. Interpretazione del Concetto di Kenosis in Fil. 2,6–7," 400–19.

Hofius, O. 1976. *Der Christushymnus Philipper 2,6–11.* WUNT 17. Tübingen: Mohr Siebeck; 2nd ed. 1991.

Hooker, M. 1959. *Jesus and the Servant: The Influence of the Servant Concept of Deutero-Isaiah in the New Testament.* London: SPCK.

Hoover, R. W. 1971. "The HARPAGMOS Enigma: A Philological Solution," *HTR* 56:95–119.

Howard, G. 1978. "Phil. 2:6–11 and the Human Christ," *CBQ* 40:368–87.

Hunzinger, C.-H. 1970. "Zur Struktur der Christus-Hymnen in Phil 2 and 1 Petr 3," in *Der*

Ruf Jesu und die Antwort der Gemeinde (FS J. Jeremias), ed. E. Lohse et al. (Göttingen: Vandenhoeck & Ruprecht) 142–56.

Hurst, L. D. 1986. "Reenter the Pre-existent Christ in Philippians 2:5–11?" *NTS* 32:449–57; rev. as "Christ, Adam, and Preexistence Revisited," in Martin/Dodd (see below) 84–95.

Hurtado, L. W. 1984. "Jesus as Lordly Example in Philippians 2:5–11," in *From Jesus to Paul: Studies in Honour of Francis Wright Beare*, ed. P. Richardson/J. Hurd (Waterloo, Ont.: Wilfrid Laurier Press) 113–26.

Huttner, U. 1997. *Die politische Rolle der Heraklesgestalt im griechischen Herrschertum.* Hist.-E 112. Stuttgart: F. Steiner.

Jaeger, W. W. 1915. "Eine stilgeschichtliche Studie zum Philipperbrief," *Hermes* 50:537–53.

Jensen, D. H. 2001. "The Emptying Christ. A Christological Approach to Interfaith Dialogue," *Studies in Interreligious Dialogue* (Leuven) 11:5–24.

Jeremias, J. 1963. "Zu Philipper 2,7: HEAUTON EKENŌSEN," *NovT* 6 (1963) 182–88 = *Charis kai Sophia*, FS K. H. Rengstorf (Leiden: Brill, 1964) = *Abba* (1966) 308–13.

Jervell, J. 1960. *Imago Dei: Gen. 1.26f. im Spätjudentum und in den paulinischen Briefen.* FRLANT 76. Göttingen: Vandenhoeck & Ruprecht.

Jowers, D. W. 2006. "The Meaning of *morphē* in Philippians 2:6–7," *JETS* 49:739–66.

Käsemann, E. 1950 (Ger.). "A Critical Analysis of Philippians 2:5–11," in *JTC* 5 (1968), H. Braun et al., *God and Christ: Existence and Province* (New York: Harper & Row, 1968) 45–88.

Kelly, J. N. D. 1950. *Early Christian Creeds.* London: Longman, 3rd ed. 1972.

Kennel, W. 1995. *Frühchristliche Hymnen? Gattungskritische Studien zur Frage nach den Liedern der frühen Christenheit.* WMANT 71. Neukirchen-Vluyn: Neukirchener.

Knoll, J. 1921. *Christliche Hymnodik bis zu Clemens von Alexandria.* Königsberg: Harlung.

Knox, W. L. 1948. "The 'Divine Hero' Christology in the New Testament," *HTR* 41:229–49.

Koch, D.-A. 1980. "Beobachtungen zum christologischen Schriftgebrauch in den vorpaulinischen Gemeinden," *ZNW* 71:174–91.

Kreitzer, L. J., and D. W. Rooke. 1998. " 'Singing in a New Key': Philippians 2:9–11 and the 'Andante' of Beethoven's *Kreutzer Sonata*," *ExpTim* 109:231–33.

Krentz, E. 1995. "Epideiktik and Hymnody: The New Testament and Its World," *BR* 90:50–97.

Krinetzki, L. 1959. "Der Einfluss von Is 52,13–53,12 Par auf Phil 2,6–11," *TQ* 139:157–93, 291–336.

Kuschel, K.-J. 1992. *Born Before All Time? The Dispute over Christ's Origin.* Tr. J. Bowden. New York: Crossroad.

Laporte, J.-M. 1974. "Kenosis: Old and New," *The Ecumenist* 12:17–21.

———. 1985. "Kenosis and Koinonia: The Path Ahead for Anglican-Roman Catholic Dialogue," *One in Christ* 21:102–20.

Lattke, M. 1991. *Hymnus: Materialen zu einer Geschichte der antiken Hymnologie.* NTOA 19. Freiburg: Universitätsverlag/Göttingen: Vandenhoeck & Ruprecht.

Ligier, L. 1963. "L'Hymne christologique de Philippiens 2,6–11, la liturgie eucharistique et la bénédiction synagogale 'Nishmat Kol Hay,' " in *Studiorum Paulinorum Congressus* 2:65–74.

Lohmeyer, E. 1928. *Kyrios Jesus: Eine Untersuchung zu Phil 2,5–11.* SHAW.PH 1927/28,

4. Abh. Heidelberg: Carl Winter Universitätsverlag, 1928. Repr. 2nd ed., Darmstadt, 1961.

Losie, L. A. 1978. "A Note on the Interpretation of Phil 2:5," *ExpTim* 90:52–54.

Manns, F. 1976. "Un hymne judéo-chrétien: Philippiens 2,6–11," *EuntDoc* 29: 259–90, and in his *Essais sur le Judéo-Christianisme*, SBFA 12 (Jerusalem: Franciscan Printing Press, 1977) 11–42. Summary, "Philippians 2:6–11: a Judeo-Christian Hymn," *TD* 26 (1978) 4–10.

Martin, R. P. 1960b. *An Early Christian Confession: Philippians II. 5–11 in Recent Interpretation*. London: Tyndale.

———. 1967. *Carmen Christi: Philippians ii. 5–11 in Recent Interpretation and in the Setting of Early Christian Worship*. SNTSMS 4. New York: Cambridge Univ. Press.

———. 1983. = 1967 repr. (Grand Rapids: Eerdmans) with a new Introduction, xi–xxxix.

———. 1997. *A Hymn of Christ: Philippians 2:5–11 in Recent Interpretation & in the Setting of Early Christian Worship*. Downers Grove, IL: InterVarsity Press.

———, and B. J. Dodd, eds. *Where Christology Began: Essays on Philippians 2*. Louisville: Westminster/John Knox, 1998.

Meeks, W. 1990. "Equal to God," in FS J. Louis Martyn (see Gen. Bibl., Fortna, R. T.) 309–21.

———. 1991. "The Man from Heaven in Paul's Letter to the Philippians," in *The Future of Early Christianity* (FS Koester), ed. B. Pearson et al. (Minneapolis: Fortress) 329–36.

Morgan, R. 1998. "Incarnation, Myth, and Theology: Ernst Käsemann's Interpretation of Philippians 2:5–11," in Martin/Dodd (see above) 43–73.

Morrison, C. D. 1960. *The Powers That Be*. SBT 29. London: SCM.

Moule, C. F. D. 1970. "Further Reflexions on Philippians 2:5–11," in *Apostolic History and the Gospel*, FS F. F. Bruce, ed. W. W. Gasque/R. P. Martin (Grand Rapids: Eerdmans) 264–76.

Müller, U. B. 1988. "Der Christushymnus Phil 2,6–11," *ZNW* 79:17–44.

———. 1990. *Die Menschwerdung des Gottessohn. Frühchristliche Inkarnationsvorstellungen und die Anfänge des Doketismus*. SBS 140; Stuttgart: KBW.

Murphy-O'Connor, J. 1976. "Christological Anthropology in Phil. II,6–11," *RB* 83:25–50.

Nagata, T. 1981. "Philippians 2:5–11. A Case Study in the Contextual Shaping of Early Christology." Diss., Princeton Theological Seminary. Cf. *AnnJapanBibInst* 9 (1983) 184–229.

O'Neill, J. C. 1988. "Hoover on *Harpagmos* Reviewed, with a Modest Proposal Concerning Philippians 2:6," *HTR* 81: 445–49.

Padilla, M. W. 1998. *The Myths of Herakles in Ancient Greece: Survey and Profile*. Washington, DC: University Press of America.

Petersen, K. 1933. "HEAUTON EKENŌSEN, Phil 2,7," *SO* 12:96–101.

Peterson, E. 1926. 'HEIS THEOS: *Epigraphische, formgeschichtliche und religionsgeschichtliche Untersuchungen*. FRLANT 41. Göttingen: Vandenhoeck & Ruprecht.

Rese, M. 1970. "Formeln und Lieder im Neuen Testament: Einige notwendige Anmerkungen," *VF* 15:75–95.

Richard, L. J. 1982. *A Kenotic Christology: In the Humanity of Jesus the Christ, The Compassion of God*. Washington, DC: University Press of America.

Rissi, M. 1987. "Der Christushymnus in Phil 2,6–11," *ANRW* 2.25.4:3314–26.

Robbins, C. J. 1980. "Rhetorical Structure of Phil 2:6–11," *CBQ* 42:73–82.

Robinson, D. W. B. 1969. "*harpagmos*: The Deliverance Jesus Refused?" *ExpTim* 80:243–54.

Robuck, T. D. 1987. "The Christ-hymn in Philippians: A Rhetorical Analysis of Its Function in the Letter." Diss., Southwestern Baptist Theological Seminary, Fort Worth, TX.

Sanders, J. T. 1971. *The New Testament Christological Hymns: Their Historical Religious Background.* SNTSMS 15. New York: Cambridge Univ. Press.

Schattenmann, J. 1965. *Studien zum neutestamentlichen Prosahymnus.* Munich: C. H. Beck.

Schillebeeckx, E. 1981. *Christ: The Experience of Jesus as Lord.* New York: Crossroad. Dutch 1977, tr. J. Bowden. Pp. 165–77.

Schimanowski, G. 1985. *Weisheit und Messias: Die jüdischen Voraussetzungen der urchristlichen Präexistenzchristologie.* WUNT 2/15. Tübingen: Mohr Siebeck.

Schlier, H. 1958. *Mächte und Gewalten im Neuen Testament.* Freiburg: Herder.

Schmauch, W. 1967. "Das Heilsgeschehen in Christo Jesu: Zur Interpretation von Philipper 2,5–11." In ... *zu achten aufs Wort: Ausgewählte Arbeiten,* ed. with C. Grengel and M. Punge by W.-C. Schmauch (Göttingen: Vandenhoeck & Ruprecht) 38–47.

Schnackenburg, R. 1970. "Die entfältete Christologie: Christus in seiner Präexistenz, irdische Seinswesen und Verherrlichung: 1. Der Christushymnus Phil 2,6–11," in *Mysterium Salutis* III/1, ed. J. Feiner and M. Löhrer (Einsiedeln-Zurich-Köln: Benziger) 309–22.

Schumacher, H. *Christus in seiner Präexistenz und Kenose nach Phil. 2, 5–8.* Scripta Pontificii Instituti Biblici. Rome: Verlag des Päpstl. Bibelinstituts. Teil I. *Historische Untersuchung.* 1914. Part II: *Exegetisch-kritische Untersuchung.* 1921.

Schüssler Fiorenza, E. 1975. "Wisdom Mythology and the Christological Hymns of the New Testament," in *Aspects of Wisdom in Judaism and Early Christianity,* ed. R. L. Wilken (Notre Dame, IN: Univ. of Notre Dame Press) 17–41.

Schweizer, E. 1962. *Erniedrigung und Erhöhung bei Jesus und seiner Nachfolgern.* ATANT 28. Zurich: Zwingli Verlag, 1955; 2nd ed. 1962. Tr., *Lordship and Discipleship,* SBT 28 (London: SCM, Naperville: Allenson, 1960).

Schwindt, R. 2006. "Zur Tradition und Theologie des Philipperhymnus," SNTSU 31:1–60.

Scoggs, R. 1966. *The Last Adam: A Study in Pauline Anthropology.* Philadelphia: Fortress.

Seeley, D. 1994. "The Background of the Philippians Hymn (2:6–11)," *Journal of Higher Criticism* 1: 49–72.

Söding, T. 1992b. "Erniedrigung und Erhöhung. Zum Verhältnis von Christologie und Mythos nach dem Philipperhymnus (Phil 2,6–11)," *TP* 67:1–28, repr., cited from Söding 1997:104–31.

Sölle, D. 1965. "Gottes Selbstentäußerung. Eine Meditation zu Philipper 2,5–11," *GPM* = *Pastoraltheologie* 54: 154–65, repr. in *Atheistisch an Gott glauben: Beiträge zur Theologie* (Olten/Freiburg i. B.: Walter, 1968) 9–25.

Spicq, C. 1973. "Notes sur MORPHĒ dans les papyrus et quelques inscriptions," *RB* 80:38–45. Cf. *TLNT* 2:520–25.

Steenburg, D. 1988. "The Case Against the Synonymity of MORPHĒ and EIKŌN," *JSNT* 34:77–86.

Strecker, G. 1964. "Redaktion und Tradition im Christushymnus Phil 2$_{6-11}$," ZNW 55: 63–78.

Sykes, S. W. 1986. "The Strange Persistence of Kenotic Christology," in *Being and Truth: Essays in Honour of John Macquarrie,* ed. A. Kee/E. T. Long (London: SCM) 349–75.

Talbert, C. H. 1967. "The Problem of Pre-existence in Philippians 2 6–11," *JBL* 86:141–52.

———. 1975. "The Concept of Immortals in Mediterranean Antiquity," *JBL* 94:419–36.

———. 1976. "The Myth of a Descending-Ascending Redeemer in Mediterranean Antiquity," *NTS* 22:418–40.

Theissen, G. 1983b. "Christologie und soziale Erfahrung. Wissensoziologische Aspekte paulinischer Christologie," in his *Studien zur Soziologie des Urchristentums*, WUNT 19 (Tübingen: Mohr Siebeck, 2nd ed.) 318–30.

Thekkekara, M. 1992. "A Neglected Idiom in an Overstudied Passage (Phil 2:6–8)," *LS* 17:306–14.

Ulonska, H. 1963. "Paulus und das Alte Testament." Diss., Münster.

Vanni, U. 1977. "'*Homoiōma*' in Paolo (Rm 1,23; 5,14; 6,5; 8,3 (Fil 2,7): Un'interpretazione esegetico-teologico alla luce dell'uso dei LXX," *Greg* 58:321–45, 431–70.

Vokes, F. E. 1964. "Arpagmos in Philippians 2:5–11," *SE II*, TU 87: 670–75.

Vollenweider, S. 1999a. "Die Metaphorose des Gottessohn," in *Das Urchristentum in seiner literaraischen Geschichte*, FS J. Becker, ed. U. Mell/U. B. Müller, BZNW 100 (Berlin/New York: de Gruyter) 109–31; repr. in Vollenweider 2002:285–306.

———. 1999b. "Der 'Raub' der Gottgleichheit. Ein religionsgeschichtlicher Vorschlag zu Phil 2.6(-11)," *NTS* 45 (1999) 413–33; repr. in Vollenweider 2002:263–84.

Wallace, D. H. 1966. "A Note on morphé," *TZ* 22:19–25.

Wanamaker, C. A. 1987. "Philippians 2.6–11: Son of God or Adamic Christology?" *NTS* 33:170–93.

Way, D. 1991. *The Lordship of Christ: Ernst Käsemann's Interpretation of Paul's Theology*. Oxford: Oxford Univ. Press.

Welch, C., ed., tr. *God and Incarnation in Mid-Nineteenth Century German Theology: G. Thomasius, I. A. Dorner, A. E. Biedermann*. Library of Protestant Thought. New York: Oxford Univ. Press, 1965.

Wengst, K. 1972. *Christologische Formeln und Lieder des Urchristentums*. SNT 7. Gütersloh: Mohn.

Wilckens, U. 1975. "Christus, der 'letzte Adam,' und der Menschensohn. Theologische Überlegungen zum überlieferungsgeschichtlichen Problem des paulinischen Adam-Christus-Antithese," in *Jesus und der Menschensohn* (FS A. Vögtle), ed. R. Pesch/R. Schnackenburg (Freiburg: Herder) 387–403

Wood, S. 1997. "Is Philippians 2:5–11 Incompatible with Feminist Concerns?" *Pro Ecclesia* 6:172–83.

Wright, N. T. 1983. "Adam in Pauline Christology," *SBL 1983 Seminar Papers*, ed. K. H. Richards (Chico, CA: Scholars Press) 359–89, rev. in and cited from *The Climax of the Covenant* (Minneapolis: Fortress, 1991), "Adam, Israel, and the Messiah," 18–40.

———. 1986. "*harpagmos* and the Meaning of Philippians 2.5–11," *JTS* 37: 321–52, rev. in and cited from *The Climax of the Covenant* (above) 62–90.

———. 1991. "Jesus Christ Is Lord: Philippians 2:5–11," in *The Climax of the Covenant* (above) 56–98.

Young, N. H. "An Aristophanic Contrast to Philippians 2.6–7," *NTS* 45 (1999) 153–55.

Zeller, D. 1988. "Die Menschwerdung des Sohnes Gottes im Neuen Testament und die antike Religionsgeschichte," in *Menschwerdung Gottes – Vergöttlichung von Menschen*, ed. D. Zeller, NTOA 7 (Fribourg: Universitätsverlag/Göttingen: Vandenhoeck & Ruprecht) 141–76.

8. *Paraenesis* (Exhortatio, *with Further Reasons for the Comfort and Admonitions*), 2:12–18

TRANSLATION

2:12a So then, my beloved — b just as you have always obeyed, c not as in my presence only, d but now much more in my absence — e with reverence and trembling continue working out what your salvation means. 13a For the One at work in and among you is God, b both to will and to work above and beyond goodwill. 14 Keep on doing all things without complaints and wranglings, 15a that you may be unfaulted and uncorrupted, children of God who are unblemished b amid a crooked and twisted generation c in which you shine as luminaries in the world, 16a because you hold on to the word of life — that is grounds for boasting on my part, toward the Day of Christ, b that I did not run in an empty way, nor did I struggle in an empty way. 17a But — even if I am being poured out like a libation — I rejoice b at the sacrificial service of your faith, c I rejoice and feel joy with you all. 18 In the same way, rejoice, you too, and rejoice together with me.

NOTES

2:12a. *So then, my beloved.* hōste (BDAG 1.b; 1:13; 4:1), "and *(te)* so," **therefore** ([N]RSV); BDF #391 (2); Moule *IB* 144; DA 266, 411, sets off the unit; "beginning . . . a statement of consequence" (Holmstrand 106–7). Voc. pl. of *agapētos* (BDAG 2; *EDNT* 1:12), first direct address since 1:12 *adelphoi*; also at 4:1 twice. Vb. comes only at the end of 2:12, *katergazesthe*.

2:12b–d. —*just as you have always obeyed, not as in my presence only, but now much more in my absence—*. kathōs, "(just) as" (BDF #453) + hypēkousate, aor., *hypakouō* (BDAG 1), **follow instructions, obey, follow, be subject to** (see NOTE on 2:8 *obedient*, Gk. *hypēkoos*), "hear, harken" *(akouō)* + hypo suggesting subjection (ATR 634); G. Kittel, *TDNT* 1:223–24; G. Schneider, *EDNT* 3:394–95, "of a church's *obedience* when he praises their conduct," cf. 2 Cor 7:15, Phlm 21; *TLNT* 1:446–50. "Complexive" or "constative" aor., linear actions "regarded as a whole" or "repeated actions" (BDF #332), + pantote (1:4, 20, *always*). Goes with two phrases, obeyed *in my presence*, obeyed *in my absence*, parousia (see NOTE on 1:26 *through my coming again* or "being present"), apousia ("being away, absence," only here in the NT, but cf. 1:27b and 2 Cor 13:10 apōn). hōs = "as" (see NOTE on 1:20 *as always, so now*), omitted by B and a few MSS (UBSGNT, {B} level of certainty), probably by accident or "as superfluous" (TCGNT 613); Silva 141; Fee 230 n 3, to avoid implying "they might be obedient only when he was present." *hōs* repeats *kathōs* in an abbreviated way, "because" (BDF #453 [2]; Schenk 214) or "when" (*DA* 316; [N]JB, NEB/REB), without settling whether "when I was with you" or "will be with you" (Collange 110; Hawth. 99; O'B 281 "in view of my return"; contrast Fee 234 n 17). For *mē . . . monon alla nyn pollō[i] mallon,* see NOTES on 1:29bc *not only . . . but also* (*ou monon . . . alla kai* + art. infin.); for *pollō[i] mallon,* 1:23 *(for that is) much (better) by far;* for *nyn,* 1:5, 20, 30, *now,* the present moment.

Paul's *absence* is heightened by *now much more;* "all the more now" (Bockmuehl 152). *mē* (not *ouch,* Merk 183) goes with *katergazesthe* (impv.), but *presence* is being negated (U. B. Müller 115; Walter 64). In Koine Gk., *mē* could occur in declarative, temporal, and causal cls. (BDF #428 [5]; Schenk 214). Possibly understand a ptc., *mē hypakouontes* (cf. BDF #430). "Presence/absence" has been construed with what follows ("make every effort to insure your salvation, not simply as though I were with you, but all the more because I am away," Gdsp., NAB); or divided ("as you have always followed my advice—and that not only when I was present to give it—so now that I am far away be keener than ever to work out the salvation that God has given you," Phillips); or with what precedes ("as you have always obeyed—not only in my presence, but now much more in my absence—continue to work out your salvation," NIV). Word order suggests with what precedes. Some make *hypēkousate* impv., you "must be obedient," (NEB/REB; GNB, CEV). The TRANSLATION takes all of 12bcd, *kathōs . . . apousia mou* together, with dashes (Lutherbibel 1984; EÜ, cf. NIV), indicating the basis ("protasis," as 2:1 was for 2:2–5a) for the impv. in 2:12e; "Because you have constantly harkened . . . not only in my presence but now much more in my absence, continue to . . ." (Schenk 213–14, 226; 277 chart).

2:12e. *with reverence and trembling continue working out what salvation means.* Traditionally "fear and trembling" (KJV-NRSV; JB, quotation marks as "biblical language"). Exegetes dispute "Godward/manward" or "theological/soteriological" understandings in 2:12–18 (O'B 277–84).

with reverence and trembling. phobos (gen. after *meta*), only here in Phil (11x in 1, 2 Cor and Rom; vb. *phobeomai* 9x in the Pauline corpus) = **reverence, respect** (BDAG 2.b), α. toward God (Rom 3:18 = Ps 36:1; 2 Cor 7:1); β. toward human authorities (Rom 13:7, cf. 13:3; Fitzmyer AB 33:670; Eph 6:5). The Gk. word field includes a deity named *Phobos,* philosophical uses, and "awe and reverence" as "reactions to the claim of authorities and especially of the gods" (*TDNT* 9:197). In the OT (Heb. *yārē',* "tremble," *"fear,"* H. F. Fuhs, *TDOT* 6:291), of God (as numinous mystery) and in the human sphere. In the gospels and Acts at epiphanies of divine power (Mark 4:41; 9:6; 16:8 vb.). In Paul, "a correlative of faith" (confidence, 2 Cor 5:11; Rom 11:20; in exhortations, Rom 13:1–7). *tromos,* **trembling, quivering** (BDAG), in the NT only at Mark 16:8 (with *ekstasis*) and, paired with *phobos,* 3x in Paul besides Phil 2:12 (see below). *Word studies:* H. Balz/G. Wanke, *TDNT* 9:189–219; Balz, *EDNT* 3:432–34, fear "is a part of faith and characterizes Christian obedience," 1 John 4:17–18 otherwise); M. Mundle, *NIDNTT* 1:621–24; Glombitza 1959–60; Giesen; Eckert 1991.

In the LXX, note parallelism in Ps 2:11, "Serve the Lord with fear *(doulousate . . .*

en phobō[i]), and rejoice with him with trembling *(en tromō[i])*"; Isa 19:16 LXX, *en phobō[i] kai en tromō[i]*); Gen 9:2; Exod 15:16; Deut 2:25 and 11:25, *tromos* and *phobos* of Israel upon peoples everywhere; Job 4:13–14 in a night vision; Ps 54:7 (NRSV 55:5); Isa 54:14, you shall not fear, *tromos* will not draw near to thee. Gk. only, Jdt 2:28; 4 Macc 4:10. Cf. *1 En.* 13.3; 1QpHab 3.4, 4.7–8 (of the Romans); 1QS 1.16–17, 10.15–16 (cf. Pedersen 1978:17–18; Schenk 215). To some, the LXX occurrences suggest "reverence and awe" (O'B 282–84); to others, terror (Oakes 2000 [(4) Bibl. **1:19**] 255, for a Gentile Christian in Philippi "a vague reminiscence of the LXX"). "[N]o precise Heb. equivalent for . . . *phobos kai tromos*" (*TDNT* 9:199). OT senses range considerably (fear of God, holy war, moral response, H. F. Fuhs, *TDOT* 6:290–315). "Fear of the gods" also character-ized Greco-Roman religions (Statius, *Thebais* 3.661, "At the beginning of the world, fear created the gods"), though awe and reverence or piety better describe human response than does "trembling." Deidun 65 n 39: "reverential deference"; Baumert 1979, respectful awe *(Ehrfurcht)*.

In Paul, "it is not at all certain what he intends by these words" (Fee 236). Lft. 116, "a nervous and trembling anxiety to do the right." Paul arrived in Corinth "in weakness and in fear and in much trembling" (1 Cor 2:3)—psychological (after minimal success in Athens and fear at tasks in Corinth; Acts 17:16–34; 18:9–11; Fee, NICNT *1 Cor.* 93–94)? or rhetorical (L. Hartman 1974:117–18)? Christians in Corinth welcomed Titus "with fear and trembling" (2 Cor 7:15; Furnish, AB 32A:398, "evidence of their obedience"; or guilt, Paul's "severe letter" worked "reverence and respect," R. P. Martin, WBC 40:244). Eph 6:5 inserts the phrase into a *Haustafel*, a servile note from social structures; cf. 5:33 (NRSV "respect") and 5:21, "reverence for Christ" (AB 34A: 662–68, part of a "theology of fear"). A fixed OT/NT idiom ("awe and reverence in the presence of God," O'B 284) be-comes, when examined, more complicated and less obvious. Loh. 102, "Pharisaic piety" in 2:12, Dib. 83, a Jewish maxim. Glombitza 1959–60 wished to insert *"not with fear and trembling,"* as if the Philippians feared divine retribution (a "base-less" suggestion, Ware 1996:266).

An alternative understanding (traced by P. Thompson and J. H. Burn at least to the 18th cent.) argued for "respect and reverence" or "humility and concern" in behavior of community members toward each other (Michael 1924b; MNTC *Phil.* 102–3). Cf. NAB; TC. Collange 110; Martin 1976:103; Loh/Nida 67, OT expression toward God but of community relationships; Giesen, attitude toward hostile environment in Philippi. Possibly Paul had in mind an OT background, but his other references (re Titus, Paul, or an earthly master) suggest human rela-tions.

continue working out what salvation means. Impv. *katergazesthe*, linked to *So then* (12a) and *mē* in 12c. On *ergon* (vb. root), see 1:6, *a good work*, NOTE, on divine and human activity, with decision for "what Christians do as a result of their faith." *Word studies: ergazomai,* with *energeō* (2:13), G. Bertram, *TDNT* 2:635–55; H.-C. Hahn, *NIDNTT* 3:1147–52; R. Heiligenthal, *EDNT* 2:48–51; *katergazomai* only in *TDNT* 3:634–35 (G. Bertram) and *EDNT* 2:271; see also Baumert 1973:346–50; Ware 1996:264 n 8, "by their own activity to accomplish or effect their salvation." 20x in the Pauline corpus, 11x in Rom, 6x in 2 Cor. Often a negative sense (Rom 2:9 "work evil"; Rom 7:13, 18). In a positive sequence, "produce" endurance, character, and hope (Rom 5:3; cf. 2 Cor 7:11, contrast 7:10; 2 Cor 9:11; 2 Cor 4:17). Not used in discussing "works of the law" or "the person who works" for wages (Rom 4:5), but for "what Christ has accomplished *(kateirgasto)* through me to win obedience from the Gentiles" (Rom 15:18). BDAG 2, **cause a state or condition, *bring about, produce, create*** (cf. *EDNT* 2:271), has not commended itself to trs. for 2:12; cf. U. B. Müller 116. To "work out" (KJV-NRSV) is most common; in NIV, linear action, "continue to work out."

your salvation. 3rd per. reflexive, *heautōn,* between the art. *tēn* and *sōtērian,* = *your,* for classical *hymōn autōn,* "of yourselves," as in "LXX, NT, and illiterate papyri" (*GNTG* 3:42; subj. gen., Loh. 103 n 1); cf. 2:3 *yourselves.* Not "salvation of one another *(allēlōn)*" (Vincent 65), but "of yourselves"; pl., not individual by individual. On *sōtērian* see NOTES on 1:19 *deliverance* (release from jail and "eternal salvation") and 1:28 *your salvation* in contrast to *destruction* for opponents; "victory" in the contest? "Salvation" is traditional at 2:12e (BDAG 2, pres. and fut.; Osten-Sacken 1983:176–77, from the final judgment, as in Rom 10:9–10). Or "well-being" or "health" of the Christian community at Philippi (Michael 1924; *Phil.* 101–2; Beare 91; Martin 1976:102–3; Hawth. 98–99; Loh/Nida 67; Swift 245; Peterlin 68–71). Some (Silva 135–37, O'B 277–80) call this (merely) "sociological," not "theological." At issue: God's community or one's relationship to God; "individual salvation" (Ware 1996:264 "personal salvation") or a "corporate" sense. Gnilka 149, the passage is not about "the individual" but "individuals in community." Fee 234–35, "a false dichotomy" (NT salvation is "personal," never "individual," Caird 125); "an ethical text" on "how saved people live out their salvation," not "a soteriological text" about "people getting saved." (That may blur eschatology and "ethics" as part of *sōtēria.*) We conclude for *salvation,* as a common gift and task "from the first day" until "the Day of Christ" (1:5, 10; 2:16), which includes care and concern for the welfare of the community in Christ, in its present circumstances (1:28, opposition; 2:2b–4, internal needs). Who better than the Philippian believers to deal with these matters? While "deliverance" is a possible tr., the traditional rendering has been expanded as *what salvation means* (CEV "what it really means to be saved"), to show consequences are involved of the soteriological act of God in Christ (2:6–11), in contrast to the *sōtēria* that Caesar offers (N. T. Wright 2003:228).

2:13a. *For the One at work in and among you is God,* [b] *both to will and to work above and beyond goodwill.* D etc. Majority Text add *ho* before *theos,* "(the) God" *(ho theos* would then be subject), in violation of Colwell's rule (Moule *IB* 115), a pred. noun that precedes the vb. "to be" gets no art. (John 1:1; Fee 230 n 4). The TRANSLATION renders *theos* as pred. (end of 13a), then 13b (in Gk. directly after *among you), at work . . . both to will and to work. . . . For (gar)* coordinates the impv. in 12 and the indic. in v 13, "because" (O'B 284), not subordinating 13 to 12, but explanatory (*DA* 324, 330). Lft.116, "stimulus" and "corrective"; O'B, "ground for" the entire preceding exhortation, not simply Paul's absence (Bengel, *"Deus* *solus* is present with you, even though I am absent"; Collange 110, "You do not need to wait for my arrival to reform your community life . . . it is God himself, not I, who presides over this") or *reverence and trembling* (because God is Judge, Deidun 1981:65).

ho energōn (subst. ptc.) "he who is at work in" (root noted at 1:6 and 2:12, last word in Gk., "work out"); *en-ergeō*, often intrans. ("be at work, operate, be effective," as at 2:13b), or trans. in Hellenistic Gk. (*ZBG* #66; BDAG 1 and 2), as here, **work, produce, effect** + acc.; MS A adds *dynameis*, "miracles," Gal 3:5. Word studies (G. Bertram, *TDNT* 2:652–54; H.-C. Hahn, *NIDNTT* 3:1151–52; H. Paulsen, *EDNT* 1:453–54; Baumert 1973:267–83; Ware 1996:277 "*supernatural* activity") indicate no OT background; Hellenistic usage for physical or cosmic forces. Walter 65, an attribute of the Creator employed in the realm of the gift of faith. 1 Cor 12:4–6, *charismata, diakonia,* and *energēmata* correlate with *pneuma, kyrios,* and *theos,* respectively (but 12:11, the Spirit "activates" [*energei*] these things). God energized *(ho energēsas)* Peter and Paul (Gal 2:8); here, all believers. Faith "works itself out, in love" (Gal 5:6). Cf. Phil 3:21, *energeia* operate in Christ; 1 Cor 16:9 *(energēs)*. ATR 564 contrasted "in-working" (2:12) with "outworking." Lft. 116, *en-* intensifies, "works mightily." *en hymin* (pl.) reflects the tendency to repeat the prep. after a compound vb. (ATR 560; Moule *IB* 91). Is it "in you" (KJV-NRSV), internalization ("within you," TC, LB; "in your hearts," Gdsp.) and individual salvation (Ware 1996:279), or "among you," pl. and collective (Pedersen 1978:29; Gnilka 150; O'B 286–87)? Or both (Bruce 57)? Eng. "among" reflects the pl. (Loh/Nida 68). Cf. 1:6 *among you* and 2:5 *among ourselves.* Fee 238, "in/among you." The TRANSLATION offers both senses, *God is at work in and among you.*

2:13b. *both to will and to work above and beyond goodwill.* Two art. infins, *to thelein* and *to energein,* + *kai . . . kai,* "both/and, not only/but also" (BDAG *kai* 1.f, in Letter A, 4:12 and 16). Such substantivized infins. (BDF #399 [1]) were a stylistic feature at 1:21, 22, 24 and 2:6. *thelō,* BDAG 2, **have something in mind for oneself, of purpose, resolve, will, wish, want, be ready** to do something. Only here in Phil, common in classical Gk., LXX, and the NT (207x, 53x in Paul's unquestioned letters). Word *studies:* G. Schrenk, *TDNT* 3:44–62; D. Müller, *NIDNTT* 3:1015–23; M. Limbeck, *EDNT* 2:138–39. God is often the subject, indicating divine purpose, acting on human wills; may be linked, as here, with a vb. of doing *(poiein,* 1 Cor 7:36, 2 Cor 8:10, Gal 5:17; *prassein,* Rom 7:15–16; *epitelesai,* 2 Cor 8:11). Cf. Rom 7:14–25, "the divided I"; Bultmann 1951 (INTRO. X Bibl.) 223–24, 326–27; *TPTA* 472–77. *energein, work,* act, repeats the vb. used of God in 13a. Willing and doing make a unity, in Stoicism (Loh. 103, 105; Sen. *Ep.* 41.5).

above and beyond goodwill. hyper tēs eudokias (Vg *pro bono voluntate*) has been interpreted in a number of ways: "that which you wish" (Syr.); *the Philippians' goodwill* (Ambrosiaster, Erasmus, Michaelis); traditionally "God's good pleasure" (KJV-NRSV; C aeth add *autou* = his); with v 14 (Bengel; BDF #231 [2]; *TDNT* 2: 746–47 nn 32, 33), "for the sake of his [or "whose," *hou*] goodwill do all. . . ." *hyper* + gen. begins the problem. See NOTES on 4:10 *your concern for me,* echoing a

Philippian slogan; 1:7 *to think about you all;* and 1:29 *for the sake of Christ.* From "original local senses of 'over', 'above'" (M. J. Harris, *NIDNTT* 3:1196), *hyper* at 2:13 has been taken to mean "for" ([N]RSV), "according to" (NIV); *above and beyond* (BAGD 1.e); *with reference to, with (God's) good pleasure in view* (BDAG A.2); and paraphrased as "willing to obey" him (GNB, CEV). The problem deepens with *eudokia: goodwill* by human beings (see NOTE on 1:15, the "rival preachers") or on God's part? Divine *eudokia,* God's "good pleasure" (NRSV), is the dominant interpretation, but variously understood: purpose, Bockmuehl 154; the Law, Blaschke ([11] Bibl.) 397; redemptive plan, O'B 288–89; graciousness, Gnilka 150, with Eph 1:5,9; grace, G. Barth 49; love, Schenk 219, cf. 139 on 1:15–16; Fee 239–40. The equally ancient view, goodwill as "the hallmark of any Christian community," also finds support (Hawth. 101; Collange 111; earlier, Wohl. 137–38; Michael 104; BDAG 1; Baumert 1979: 7 n 4; S. F. Winter 164, "a favourable and positive attitude towards Paul"; Thurston 94 "for the good"). O'B 288 and others object that *to will and to work above and beyond goodwill* is "tautologous, even banal"; this misses the point: Philippian believers may know what *eudokia* calls for in the community but they fail to exhibit goodwill among themselves (2:2–4). Seldom asked is what "*above and beyond* God's will or plan" might mean (hence the battle over how to render *hyper*). The art. *tēs* suggests "the well-known *eudokia*"; *hyper,* a sense of benefaction (DA 320, 326).

2:14. *Keep on doing all things without complaints and wranglings.* Impv., *poieite,* used elsewhere with *to will* (see above). Neut. pl. object from *pas* (BDAG 1.d.β), frequent in Letter B (1:1, 3, 4, 7, 8, 9, 13, 18, 20, 25; 2:9, 10, 11); alliterative, *panta poieite. chōris, without,* + gen. pl. of two nouns that suggest "murmuring" by Israel in the wilderness (Exod 15–17; Num 14–17; against Moses, not God, S. F. Winter 164). Onomatopoetic like "murmur," *gongysmos* occurs only here in Paul; vb. at 1 Cor 10:10, the Israelites "complained" in the wilderness. Elsewhere in the NT, not about Israel's murmuring (John 7:12; Acts 6:1; 1 Pet 4:9). BDAG, "*complaint, displeasure,* expressed in murmuring." Silva 148. "outbursts [pl.] of complaints and arguing," against appointed leaders; Friedrich 155, Christians between Easter and the Parousia, perhaps (Oakes 2000 [(4) Bibl. **1:19**] 256–57) sensed by hearers as a reference to Israel.

dialogismos, more common in the NT (14x), has significant Gk. background, "conversation," philosophical "dialogue" (G. Schrenk, *TDNT* 2:93–98). NT use is primarily negative (1 Cor 3:20 = Ps 94:11; Rom 1:21; 14:1, "quarreling over opinions" [NRSV], the closest Paul comes to debate over disputed issues among philosophers). BDAG 2, *thought, opinion, reasoning, design,* but *in malem partem* (as above). BDAG 3, **verbal exchange that takes place when conflicting ideas are expressed,** *dispute, argument* (Luke 9:46), preferred at 2:14. Schrenk 97; G. Petzke, *EDNT* 1:308, and Gnilka 151, "doubt" (Luke 24:38; BDAG 4). D. Fürst, "questioning" (*NIDNTT* 3:821). Fee 243–44, "controversies," as in Phil 4:1–3; cf. 2:2.

The three-word phrase at 2:14 never occurs exactly in Exod or Num for Israel's murmuring against God. The case for OT coloring depends on cumulative effects from phrases that follow; see COMMENT A.1. Geoffrion 40, 118–19, 187–88 finds

Stoic background, "the good soldier of life" obeys orders without grumbling; Krentz 2003:357. The suggested biblical background has sometimes been termed "Godward" (Israel rebelled against Yahweh). Others see a "manward" sense, quarrels with or over leaders (Moses; Bonnard 51, Acts 6:1; Kennedy EGT 441, Euodia and Syntyche; Silva 144, the *episkopoi* and *diakonoi* of 1:1; O'B 292) or legal deliberations (Martin 1976:104 "litigation," cf. 1 Cor 6:1–11 and MM 151; Silva 148, a "judicial flavor," Exod 17:2, 7; Heb. *rîb*) Most trs. permit either "OT" or "communal" senses or both. Colloquially, "wrangling" (Stagg 346), "bitching." Loh/Nida 69, add "to and with one another" to both nouns.

2:15a. *that you may be unfaulted and uncorrupted, children of God who are unblemished.* Purpose (*hina* + subjunct.; Fee 244; DA 325, NRSV, "so that"), in effect a third command (U. B. Müller 118), after *continue working out* (12e) and *keep on doing . . .* (14). Possibly imperatival *hina* (Moule *IB* 144–45; Schenk 220); NEB/REB, "Show yourselves. . . ." Aor. subjunct., *ginomai*, "become," entering into a new nature or condition (BDAG 5; NIV) but usually taken as if *eimi*, "be" (BAGD II; BDAG 7–10; KJV-[N]RSV; "remain" NJB; CEV "will be"). Variant *ēte* ("be"; P⁴⁶ A D* etc.), perhaps from 1:10, or to avoid any idea that the Philippians were not yet, but were only "becoming," blameless children of God (Silva 148); Fee (240 n 1), a "'sense' variation" where scribes "mess with Paul's use of . . . the LXX." Fee 244 assumes Gen 17:1 *ginou* [2nd sg. impv.] *amemptos*; then Christians are compared with Abraham (Oakes 2000 [(4) Bibl. **1:19**] 262). ZG 597, "*live* (= conduct oneself)."

All three pred. adjs., *amemptoi, akeraioi,* and *amōma,* are alliterative (*alpha* privative, BFD #117.1; in the TRANSLATION *un-*). *tekna theou* and *amōma* reflect Deut. 32:5, *tekna mōmēta,* "blemished children." For *amōma,* neut. pl., *amōmēta* ("blameless, unblemished") is found in D F G etc. Majority Text, to make 2:15 closer to Deut 32:5 (Silva 149). Under the influence of *amōmos* in Lev, 1 Pet 1:19, and Heb 9:14, the adjs. have been said to reflect cultic use, sacrificial animals without defects, terms "from the cultic language of purity" (Newton 84–86). But a "moral and religious sense" might better describe them (cf. *amemptos* at Phil 3:6).

amemptos (NT 5x), also at Phil 3:6, *blameless* re righteousness in the Law. More Gk. background than LXX use (for 9 or 10 Heb. terms, esp. "blameless Job," Job 1:1, 8, etc.; otherwise, only Gen 17:1; Wis. 10:5; 18:21). 1 Thess 3:13 is fut. eschatological, cf. 5:23 (adv.); pres. ethical implications, 1 Thess 2:10; Phil 2:15. *Word studies:* W. Grundmann, *TDNT* 4:571–74; T. McComiskey, *NIDNTT* 2:143–44. MM 26 notes a letter (time of Augustus, BGU 4.1141.25), "Wishing your friendship, I kept myself *amemptos*"; in a marriage contract, sepulchral epitaphs, and what an apprentice has "faultlessly" written.

akeraios (*alpha* negative + *keraizō*, "not ravaged," "intact"; not *kerannymi*, "(un)mixed," *TDNT* 1:209; "in our lit. only fig. **pure, innocent,**" BDAG) 3x in the NT, 2 of them in Paul. Classical references in *TDNT* 1:209–10 (G. Kittel), BDAG; 1x in LXX, Gk. Additions to Esther 8:12ᶠ (Rahlfs 968 = NRSV Addition E, 16:6, "the *sincere* goodwill [*akerainon eugnōmosynēn*] of . . . sovereigns," Schenk 221, a virtue of rulers); further, Jos. *JW* 1.621; *Ant* 1.61; Hellenistic uses in Loh. 108 n 1;

Schenk. Matt 10:16, "innocent as doves," is probably proverbial (*TDNT*'s "sacrificial dove" is a stretch); Rom 16:19, "'guileless, unsophisticated,'" re evil (AB 33:746). Lft. 117, Michael 105–6, etc., *amemptoi* "judgment of others," *akeraioi* "intrinsic character," is now viewed as unfounded.

amōmos (NT 8x, in undisputed Pauline letters only here), from Deut. 32:5, Israel = "degenerate children" (NRSV; Heb. *mûmam*, LXX *mōmēta*, "blemished"). *Word studies:* F. Hauck, *TDNT* 4:829–31; H. Währish, *NIDNTT* 3:923, 924, 925; *EDNT* 1:73; MM 28–29. In Gk., *mōmos* = "'censure' which derives from ill-will towards another," therefore "reproach, contempt," etc., Gorgias, *Encomium of Helen* 1 = *FVS* ed. Diels 2:288. As "faultfinding personified," Momos was a literary figure ("god of reproach and blame," Suidas, *TDNT* 4:830 n 1, but no cult), used by Callimachus (*Hymn* 2.113) and Lucian (*Iupp. Trag.* 19ff.), cf. *OCD*³ 994. This sense, "reproach, ignominy," appears in the LXX (Sir 11:33). More frequently, LXX used Gk. *mōmos* for a Heb. term like which it sounded, *mûm*, "spot, blemish" (Lev 24:19–20; 21:16–23). Hence *amōmos*, "unblemished," applied to sacrificial animals (Exod 29:1; Lev, cf. *NIDNTT* 3:924), but usually for the Heb. *tāmîm*, "whole, sound, perfect." Also in LXX of God (2 Bas [2 Sam] 22:31; Ps 17:31 [18:30]); the Law (Ps 18:8 [19:7]); a faithful Israelite (2 Bas 22 [2 Sam]:24; Ps 14 [15]:2; 36 [37]:18). BDAG 56 reflects this twofold sense via the LXX: (1) cultic use (the 2 non-Pauline NT examples); (2) moral sense, the other six examples, all concerning God's people (Phil 2:15; Col 1:22; Eph 1:4, 5:27; Rev 14:5; Jude 24). Phil 2:15 thus begins a line of development applying the Gk. "moral" sense, "irreproachable, unblemished," unless (LXX sense) "unstained, unspotted," of the church community, cf. christological application of *amōmos* for Christ's unblemished sacrificial offering (Heb 9:14; 1 Pet 1:19, lamb).

children of God. Pl. *tekna*, Deut 32:5, + gen. *theou* (possession, subj., source, not obj. gen.) from the context there. Cf. Phil 2:22; 1 Cor 4:17. From *tiktō*, "bear/beget." G. Schneider, *EDNT* 3:341–42, A. Oepke, *TDNT* 5:638–39, 653. Not frequent in Paul. Usually under OT influence (here; Rom 9:7–8; Gal 4:25, 27 [= Isa 54:1], 28, 31), for members of the community in Christ (1 Cor 4:14; Rom 8:16, 17, 21; Phlm 10; *teknia*, Gal 4:19) or natural children (1 Cor 7:14, etc.). Generally Paul prefers the language of Greco-Roman legal adoption, *huiothesia*, *huios*, "sonship, son (and daughter)" (AB 33:500–2 on Rom 8:15–17; BDAG *teknon* 4.b).

2:15b. *amid a crooked and twisted generation.* Except for *amid* (Gk. *meson*, improper prep. + gen., neut. acc. sg., *mesos, ē, on*, used as adv., BDAG 1.c; BDF #215.3; Moule *IB* 85; *en mesō[i]* in D etc., EGT 441), the words come from a description of Israel in Deut 32:5, "a perverse and crooked generation" (NRSV), LXX *genea skolia kai diestrammenē* (in gen. at 2:15); cf. 32:20 "perverse (*exestrammenē*) generation." *hē genea*, classic Gk. senses, "generation" (Matt 1:17), "age" (the time of a generation, Col 1:26; Eph 3:21). LXX, usually for Heb. *dôr*, "generation, age" (*TDOT* 3:174–75). In the NT, 43x; 33x in the Synoptics, 25 for "the Jewish people in the time of Jesus," 17 for "this generation" (Matt 11:16–19 par Luke 7:31–35, etc.; V. Hasler, *EDNT* 1:241). Often, as in Deut 32:5, + some pejorative adj.: "adulterous" (Mark 8:38), "faithless" (Mark 9:19), "faithless and perverse" (Matt 17:17 par. Luke 9:41). The whole people, viewed as a solidarity in sin (F. Büchsel, *TDNT* 1:663; cf. R. Morgenthaler, *NIDNTT* 2:35–36). BDAG 2, **contemporaries.**

skolios, a, on (4x in NT), "crooked, twisting," of roads, rivers, snakes, etc., or speech, actions ("unscrupulous, dishonest"). Common in LXX (Isa 40:4 = Luke 3:5; Prov, 14 of 28 LXX examples; Job 9:20, "blameless . . . perverse"; *amemptos, skolios*). Phil 2:15 and Acts 2:40 apply Deut 32:5 ("perverse") to contemporaries of the day (*TDNT* 7: 403–8, *pace* G. Bertram, in Phil 2:15 not the Jews, but the pagan world). Limited Greco-Roman use (MM 578; Hes. *Op.* 7; *Theog.* 536; *Phaed.* 253E; *TDNT* 7:403–4, cf. 401). The Philippians would have understood "harsh masters" of slaves (*skoliois*, 1 Pet 2:18; Reicke AB 37:98; Elliott AB 37B:513–18; *TLNT* 1:387–89).

twisted, pf. pass. ptc., *diastrephō* (BDAG 2, **cause to depart from an accepted standard . . . make crooked, pervert,** in a moral sense "perverse," even "depraved" [NIV]; cf. G. Bertram, *TDNT* 7:717–19). In Deut 32:5 = Heb. *petaltol*, "crooked, crafty, perverse"; cf. Prov 6:14; 8:13, etc. Its considerable Gk. background may have made the term attractive for the LXX: Aristot. *Poetics* 5.1 1449a.36; *Eth. Nic.* 2.9.5 1109b.6, etc.; Epict. 3.6.8. *diastrophē* is "a t[echnical] t[erm] for the moral corruption of the empirical man" (7:717; Diog. Laert. 7:89; Chrysipp. *Frg.* 228–36 [v. Arnim 3.53.5ff.]). To claim "NT usage is controlled by the OT" and "Hell[enistic]-Stoic influence is exerted at most only *via* the Gk. OT" (7:718 and n 4) does not tell the full story for "the earliest appearance of the vb." in the NT at Phil 2:15. The term carried implications in the Greco-Roman world, quite apart from OT "background." Acts 13:10, e.g., "demonstrates . . . Greek influence" and biblical usage (U. Busse, *EDNT* 1:313).

2:15c. *in which you shine as luminaries in the world. en* + pl. *hois* (not fem. dat. sg. referring back to *geneas*); "within/among whom (pl.)" (KJV, RSV). NRSV ignores the pl. *phainesthe*, 2nd pl. deponent, *phainō*, BDAG 1.b, "of light and its sources *shine, flash*" (so most recent commentators and trs.), though 2.a, *appear, be* or *become visible, be revealed* is sometimes preferred (Lft. 117, Loh. 108; Martin 105; Gdsp., NASB). Kennedy EGT 442, both senses converge; Silva 146. Is the vb. indic. (Lft. 117, Loh. 108, Merk 185 n 72; Silva 146, O'B 296, Fee 246; KJV, [N]RSV, NEB-txt/REB) or (same form) impv. (Wohl. 140, Michaelis 47, Beare 92, Loh/Nida 70, Hawth. 103; LB, etc., below)? Bonnard 52 n 1: an impv. founded on an indic. In Paul, otherwise only at Rom 7:13 and 2 Cor 13:7, both "appear." Cf. *TDNT* 9:1–2 (Bultmann/Lührmann); *NIDNTT* 2:487–88 (H.-C. Hahn); *EDNT* 3:411–12 (P.-G. Müller). An impv. is awkward in a relative cl. *(en hois)*; hence a separate sentence (NEB-mg, "Shine out among them . . ."; GNB; CEV "Try to shine . . . ," conative?). The indic. is more likely: 15c stands in a *hina* cl. begun in 15a, showing purpose or which is imperatival *hina*. Hawth. 103 objects one does not remind the Philippians "of what they are already doing"; Silva 146–47 answered: the NT calls people to "become" and "act" by emphasizing "what we already are." The description provides a basis for the nearby impvs.

as luminaries in the world. hōs, "as." *phōstēres* is usually rendered as "stars" (pl.; NRSV, NJB "bright stars"; Michael, Hawth., O'B, U. B. Müller). KJV had "lights"

(RSV, Phillips, CEV; Martin). Occasionally "beacons" (R. Knox; Finlayson, with Bengel, lighthouses). Not *astēr*, "star" (in Paul, only at 1 Cor 15:41), but *ho phōstēr*, "light" *(phōs)* + the ending *–tēr* to name the agent (*GNTG* 2:364–65, cf. BDF #109.8), therefore "light-bearer," "light-giving body," of sun, moon, stars. *Word studies: TDNT* 9:312, 345–46 (H. Conzelmann); *NIDNTT* 2:490–96 (H.-C. Hahn/C. Brown); *EDNT* 3:448–49; *TLNT* 3:487–88; Str-B 3:621. Amply attested in classical Gk. (*TDNT* 9:312). Ware 1996:288 urges Isa 42:6LXX, the community as light for the Gentile world. From Dan 12:3 apocalyptic eschatology enters (Oakes 2000 [(4) Bibl. **1:19**] 263–64; at the resurrection those with under-standing "will shine like lights [*phanousin hōs phōstēres*] of heaven, and those who possess my words [*logous*] as the stars of heaven [*hōsei ta astra tou ouranou*] forever and ever"; *TDNT* 9:345–46). Hengel 1974 1:196–98 saw from Dan 12:3; Isa 26:19; *1 En.* 104:2 ("Like bright stars [*phōstēres*] in heaven, you will light up and shine") "a Jewish version of '*astral immortality*' . . . uncommonly widespread in the Hellenistic period in both philosophy and poetry as in popular belief"; cf. Aristoph. *Pax* 832–33, "we become as stars *(asteres)* when someone dies"; epi-taphs, esp. for "the wise," replacing shadowy existence in the Underworld with a place for the souls of the dead (*1 En.* 12–36; Orphic Elysian fields, Pythagorean doctrine, Plato, the Stoics, popular belief; more in Hengel's nn 579, 585; cf. Volz 2nd ed. 1934:400).

Even if Paul had Dan 12:3 and resurrection in mind, the language was mean-ingful to a Greco-Roman audience. Bormann 219 presents evidence on heroes of the Roman state as astral phenomena (the soul of Caesar exalted to heaven = a comet, Suet. *Divus Iulius* 88; Julius' star appeared over Augustus at the battle of Actium, Virg. *Aen.* 8.611; a fixed place in the heavens for those who defend *patria*, Cic. *Rep.* 6.13; more in Bormann n 38). Oakes 2002:16, "heroization of the de-ceased," esp. in northern Macedonia; see below on 3:20–21. Cf. *TLNT* 3:487. But Matt 5:14–16 ("let your light so shine . . .") and a missionary sense have exercised great influence on interpreting 2:15c. On the eschatology involved, see Com-ment B. The Translation uses *luminaries* to avoid suggesting "stars" only.

in the world (en kosmō[i], anarthrous (*GNTG* 3:175; *ZBG* #183) seems obvious, "the whole world" (BDAG 3; cf. J. Guhrt, *NIDNTT* 1:521–22; NIV "the uni-verse"; Walter 66). But with *phainesthe* (Lft. 118; JB) or with *hōs phōstēres* (Gk. word order, most trs.)? Is *kosmos* synonymous with "heaven" in Dan 12:3? Or does it denote the human race (Bengel; Loh. 109; Fee 247 n 29; BDAG 6; CEV "among the people of this world"), a deliberate change from Dan 12:3 (Fee)? H. Sasse *TDNT* 3:887 and Oakes 2000 ([4] Bibl. **1:19**) 264–66 note the debate. "The world" at 2:15 can have a broad sense (cf. 2:10, heavenly, earthly, subterranean spheres), but illumination by Philippian believers comes in the realm of human and societal relationships.

2:16a. *because you hold on to the word of life — that is grounds for boasting on my part, toward the Day of Christ. epechontes*, agreeing with *you* (pl.) in 15c (and ul-timately the *hina* cl. in 15a); ptc., *ep-echō* (א* *echontes*, prefix lost by haplogra-phy?). BDAG 1, **hold fast** + acc. *(the word of life);* so most recent interpreters (Ware 1996:290, e.g., Michael 107–8; Martin 1976:121–22; Gnilka 153; Hawth.

103–4; Silva 146; O'B 297–98; Schenk 223, Bockmuehl 159; Hooker 2002:389). BDAG also lists 2 *hold toward, aim at* + dat. and 3, *stop, stay.*

Others take *epechō* as "hold out (to others)," "hold forth" (KJV), "offer" (Gdsp., GNB, [N]JB); "proffer" (NEB); Lft. 116, 118; Vincent 69–70; Wohl. 141. Ware's detailed examination (1996:291–300; 1998) found "no instances in which the verb *epechō* means to *hold fast*" prior to the early Byzantine period (298–99; so also Oakes 2000 [(4) Bibl. **1:19**] 267–69), setting aside examples in Bauer (*T. Jos.* 15.3; Jos. *B.J.* 1.230; Plut. *Otho* 17; Diod. Sic. 12.27.3). BDAG 362 also notes *Sib. Or.* 3.340, Athenagoras 8.4, and Luke 4:42 (MS D, NA[25], *epeichon auton*, the crowds held Jesus fast). Ware presents considerable classical evidence for *epechō* as "holding forth"; directing attention to a matter (= BDAG 2); and intrans., for extension or spread of something (293–95). He concludes that, since *epechō* is used transitively at 2:16 (with *logon zōēs* as dir. obj.), only "holding forth" the word in "*missionary activity*" is possible (300). But Dickson 108–14, writing on mission in Paul, rejects Ware's conclusion and the arguments of O'B and Fee for evangelism; "eschatological faithfulness" is meant, to ensure endurance to the End; ethics, not proclamation.

On the basis of the Syr. Peshitta ("because you are to them in the place of life"), Wettstein and F. Field (*Otium Norvicense* [1864–81] 3:118–19 = *Notes on the Translation of the New Testament* [Cambridge 1899] p. 194) suggested a Gk. idiom is involved, *epechō logon* = correspond, as in Diog. Laert. 7.155; hence, "you shine . . . corresponding to life." So finally Oakes 2000 ([4] Bibl. **1:19**) 266–85, with appeal to texts from astronomy for the sense "playing the role" or "holding the position" of life (Oakes 1996 diss.:142–43). Kennedy EGT 442 had set this suggestion aside on grounds that Paul is thinking of "steadfastness in the faith." Silva 149, it deserves refutation. Ware 1996:295–97 rejects any tech. sense. The word order (*logon zōēs epechontes*) makes unlikely an idiom *epechō logon.* Poythress' examination of the evidence concludes for "holding" or "having" ("hold fast" may be a bit strong).

All in all, there seems enough evidence for including "holding forth" in future eds. of Bauer as a possible sense (LSJ 619, II). Ware too easily excludes "hold on to" something (LSJ "*have* or *hold upon*"). Fee 240, 247 includes both, "hold out/ on to"; similarly I. H. Marshall 64. Like U. B. Müller 119, Bockmuehl 158–59 opts for **continue holding fast the word of life** on the grounds of context and "the absence of comparable evangelistic usage of the verb in other early Christian texts." The Philippians, as *luminaries in the world*, are already engaged in mission (Ware 1996: 302–3, who is reduced to claiming "the threat of persecution . . . had deterred, or might deter, some members of the Philippian community from spreading the message"). At issue is their rootedness in the word (and expression of it in 2:6–11), exhibited in conduct, not just as missionaries but among themselves, in the house churches.

epechontes could be conditional (Wohl. 140 n 1); better, modal (Wohl. 141; Fee 247, "as"; NIV), or causal (NRSV "by"; JB "because"), the pres. tense stressed, "continue to hold fast." To take it as impv. (Dib. 83, Hawth. 103; NLT), needlessly multiplies direct commands (Merk 185).

word. See NOTES on 1:14 *to speak the word*; 4:15c *account.* Here, BDAG *logos* 1.a.β; *DA* 313, message, the content of what is spoken, + gen. defining it; cf. "message about the cross" (1 Cor 1:18), reconciliation (2 Cor 5:19), etc., parallel to *kērygma* (1 Cor 2:4). Cf. *TDNT* 4:114–19 (G. Kittel); *NIDNTT* 3:1110–14 (B. Klappert); *EDNT* 2:358 (H. Ritt); Schenk 223, the word of the cross. Radl 1981:78–79 *word of life*, but it occurs only here in Paul. See NOTES on 1:20 *whether by life or death* and 1:21 *to live*. Str-B 3:621 does not help much (Torah as source of life, Str-B 3:129–31; Ware 1996:301). Here, *of life* = BDAG *zōē* 2.b.α, life, from God, for believers, effected by the preaching of the gospel, now and future blessedness, Phil 4:3. Gen., obj. ("the message that brings life," Loh/Nida 71), quality (Schenk 223), origin (O'B 297–98), or epexegetical, *the word*, i.e., *life*. Again, no arts. as at 15c (Wohl. 142 n 1). For Paul, true life is present for believers in a world of death, see R. Bultmann, *TDNT* 2:866–70, present in word and faith, with concrete possibilities, + future life; 1951 (INTRO. X Bib.) 324–30, faith as "eschatological occurrence," 348–52; H.-G.Link, *NIDNTT* 2:481–82; L. Schottroff, *EDNT* 2:106–7.

eis kauchēma emoi eis hēmeran Christou. Paul shifts back to himself, the first time since 12e ("I" continues in 16b–17), abruptly, indicated by a dash (NIV), though *the Day of Christ* stands over the Philippians as well as Paul. On *kauchēma*, see NOTE on 1:26 *your grounds for boasting*, there the Philippians' grounds for glorying (including Paul's faithful ministry); here, Paul's grounds for boasting (involving the Philippians' continuing steadfastness). The first *eis* is telic, "with a view to, resulting in" (Moule *IB* 70; cf. 1:19; BDAG *eis* 4.e. for 16b, cf. 4.f; Fee 248). For clarity, *that is* has been added. *emoi*, ind. obj. (NAB "you give me cause to boast"), amounts to a possessive (NEB/REB "my pride") or tr. as the subject of a vb. from *kauchēma* ("that I can boast," NRSV; Gdsp., fut., in a new sentence, "Then I will have reason to be proud of you . . ."). The TRANSLATION paraphrases, *on my part*; avoid "*for* me" after "grounds *for* boasting."

the Day of Christ. BDAG *hēmera* 3.b.β, final judgment; see NOTE on 1:6 *the Day of Christ Jesus*; Mattern 186–92; Cruz 364–65; Radl 1981:78–80. *eis*, not *achri* (1:6 "until") or *en* ("at"); see NOTE on 1:10 *for (eis) the Day of Christ*; BDAG *eis* 2.a.β. Lft. 118 "against" = in anticipation of; archaic, but rightly suggests the Day is not yet here. TRANSLATION, *toward* to catch this sense, avoiding another "for." Paul's boast depends on his converts continuing faithful till the End. Thus Gdsp.'s "Then" (above). GNB, "If you do so . . ."; Loh/Nida 72 "conditional force," for which Fee 248 n 38 finds "no lexical or grammatical warrant." Involved is how *hoti* (16b) is construed.

2:16b. *that I did not run in an empty way, nor did I struggle in an empty way.* Explanatory *hoti, that* (most trs.; O'B 299), not "because" (Gdsp., GNB, Loh/Nida 72); Schenk 223, citing BDF #456 (2), cf. 391 (but p. 226 "weil"); *DA* 218 "because" but 324 "ambiguous" and 355 "*clarification*: corrective," 416. Aor. vbs.; Paul looks back from the standpoint of *the Day of Christ* (Vincent 70). ZG 597 (*ZBG* #253), the aor. records a fact "globally" though the action "may have occupied a long time" or was repeated.

I did not run (edramon). 2nd aor., *trechō*, run stadium footraces (1 Cor 9:24), but (BDAG 2) fig., **to make an effort to advance spiritually or intellectually, *exert oneself.*** Arena jargon, brought into religious and philosophical language (O. Bauernfeind, *TDNT* 8:227–28); of moral endeavor in Cynic-Stoic diatribe. OT prophets were runners or couriers for the Lord (Jer 23:2 LXX; Hab 2:2; Isa 52:7; Derrett 1985; Ware 1996:304–14, Paul "*a prophet of the new covenant for the Gentiles,*" the servant-figure of Isa 49; with Denis 1957b, (Roloff 1965:43); but Paul was not likely influenced by this usage (Pfitzner 49, 107). Paul employs *trechō* of "exertion" in life (Rom 9:16; cf. 1 Cor 9:26); Gal 2:2 missionary endeavor ("not running, or had not run, in vain," *eis kenon trechō ē edramon,* same phrase as here, aor. and pres.). Gal 5:7; 2 Thess 3:1 (Ps 147:15 [LXX 4]). Pol. *Phil.* 9.2 quotes *eis kenon edramon* back to the Philippians; Pilhofer 1:212–18. Word studies: O. Bauernfeind, *TDNT* 8:226–35; G. Ebel, *NIDNTT* 3:945–47; Pfitzner 1967:49, 76, 99–108, 158.

struggle. Aor., *kopiaō;* BDAG 2, **exert oneself physically, mentally, or spiritually, work hard, toil, strive, struggle.** Word studies: F. Hauck, *TDNT* 3:827–30; M. Seitz/H.-G. Link, *NIDNTT* 1:262–63; H. Fenrich, *EDNT* 2:307–8; *TLNT* 2:322–29; Pfitzner 102–3 passim. Vb. + noun *kopos,* 25x in the Pauline corpus. Common in the LXX, "work hard" (*TLNT* 2:323–25); "in the papyri and the inscriptions" (MM 352). For *kopian eis (to) kenon* (or some related form) see Job 2:9b; 20:18; 39:16; Isa 65:23, cf. 49:4 *kenōs;* Jer 28:58; Wis 3:11; cf. Ps 127 (LXX 126):1. Paul, for manual labor, self-support while preaching (1 Thess 2:9 = 2 Thess 3:8; 1 Cor 4:12). Harnack 1928b: *kopos* = hard work for the gospel, his (1 Cor 15:10) and others' (1 Cor 15:58; 2 Cor 10:15; 1 Thess 5:12). Not an athletic metaphor, "training hard" for a race (Pfitzner 102–3; Vincent 70, correcting Lft. 118; but cf. *TLNT* 2:306), it reflects Paul's background as a worker (tent-making). "Missionary labor" (1 Cor 3:8; 1 Thess 3:5); "in the Lord" (Rom 16:12), in the community (Rom 16:6), out of love (1 Thess 1:3), rating high esteem (1 Cor 16:16; 1 Thess 5:12). It allows grounds for boasting, ironic reward (proclaiming the gospel free of charge, 1 Cor 9:15–18), and eschatological reward (1 Cor 3:8). Amid hardships (*kopos* 2x in 2 Cor 11:23–27, *peristasis* catalogue), Paul found joy. Just as Gal 2:2 says "run in vain," so Gal 4:11 faces up to the fear of having labored (*kekopiaka*) in vain (*eikē*).

in an empty way. eis kenon, 2x, usually rendered "in vain." *eis* (BDAG 4.e) indicates the result of running and labor (+ *ouk, oude* "for nothing," JB, NIV) + neut. acc. sg., *kenos, ē, on,* "empty," BDAG 3, fig., **without purpose or result, *in vain*** (in the LXX, no exact Heb. equivalent); Str-B 3:621, citation on p. 220 comment l. In Paul, noted above, a frequent concern of the apostle. Here, prep. phrase with adverbial force (ATR 550; Jas 4:5). Root connection with *kenodoxia* and *kenoō* (see NOTES in 2:3 *vainglory* and 2:7 *but himself he emptied*). Cf. A. Oepke, *TDNT* 3:659–60; E. Tiedtke/H.-G. Link, *NIDNTT* 1:546–47; M. Lattke, *EDNT* 2:281; *TLNT* 2:303–8. C. J. Bjerkelund 1977 is reflected in *EDNT:* "derived from the LXX," *eis kenon* is an eschatological concept distinguishing what is "empty" and "in vain" from what God creates, does, or blesses; cf. Isa 45:18 LXX; Isa 65:23 (Edart 196 n 22, Isa 49:4); Hab 2:3 LXX; Deut 32:47 LXX. When the prophet fears that he labored vainly and for nothing, God's assurance follows about "a day of salvation" (Isa 49:4, 8 = 2 Cor 6:1–2; AB 32A:353; note at Phil 2:16 *the Day of Christ* as context). Bjerkelund 181 cites also *Midr. Rab.* VI where Isa 65, Isa 49, and Deut 32 are combined, perhaps through the theme "not . . . in vain." The OT concept involves holding fast to Torah (Deut 32:46–47; Lev 26:16–17 LXX); Paul, to the gospel (Phil 2:16 *the word of life*). A connection with (eschatological) *destruction* (1:28; 3:19) is noted, without application to Paul's congregations. Lattke cautions against tracing *eis kenon* "directly to the LXX"; *trechō* has its "origin in the language of disputation and . . . diatribe." On this OT phrase in Paul's career, see Gundry Volf 1990 ([2] Bibl. **work**):262–71 and COMMENT B.2. Paul liked to use *kenos* in parallelisms (1 Cor 15:14, "our kerygma, your faith"), with reiteration (1 Cor 15:14, 17 *mataia*). Possible reflection of *ekenōsen* at 2:7 (Bjerkelund 185–86, he "made himself one expelled or thrust out"). The TRANSLATION uses *in an empty way* to make the link.

2:17a. *But—even if I am being poured out like a libation—I rejoice* b *at the sacrificial service of your faith,* c *I rejoice and feel joy with you all.* A new sentence, not a new section (Loh. 111–12). Holmstrand 108–13 links 17–18 with 14–16, as present consequences. The TRANSLATION sets off 17a *(ei kai spendomai)* by dashes and takes 17b with 17c (*I rejoice* is moved forward in the TRANSLATION to show that *thysia* and *leitourgia, sacrificial service,* the Philippians' *faith,* are what Paul rejoices over, Walter 67). 17, along with 15c–16a, undergirds the expectation in 14–15b and 16b. Cf. Schenk 224–25. Rejoicing is specifically grounded in the Philippians' faithful response to the gospel, thus indicating Paul's labor among them has not proven "empty."

But . . . I rejoice. alla (BDAG 2) introduces a contrast after 16b ("not in vain"). Some compare 1:18 *alla kai* (BDF #448 [6], "not only this, but also"), but that depends on taking *ei kai* directly with *alla* (KJV "Yea, and if . . ."). Others combine 16b and 17 more closely, giving *alla* ascensive force (BDAG 4.b; Ware 1996:316; O'B 303, but BDAG 1.a does not fit here as at Phil 1:29; Fee calls it "questionable," 250 n 49). On *chairō*, see NOTES on 1:18c *I rejoice* and 4:10.

even if I am being poured out like a libation. ei kai (a very few MSS have *kai ei,* E F G Vg *et si*; Vincent 71, nowhere else in Paul). See BDAG *ei* 6.e, with *kai, even if, even though, although* (concessive sense in O'B 303, rejected by Fee 253 n 59). Silva 152, *ei kai* "focuses on the extremity of the condition," *kai ei* on its "unlikelihood." Silva and Fee nudge it closer to a future more vivid supposition (Burton, *MT* 100–112), but *ei* + pres. indic. = "Class 1" or "real" condition (Fee 252–53 n 58; Ware 1996:316 n 106). At issue: "am to be poured out . . ." (fut. sense; RSV, Gdsp., NEB/REB) or "am being poured out" now (NRSV; NIV; Fee)? Martyrdom (so Loh.), future as Paul writes, or present and past involvement in a struggle (1:30)? Lft. 119, Plummer 54, and others reject any notion that "the sacrifice has begun." Hence paraphrases (italics added): Silva 149, "*if matters should worsen so that* I will crown the sacrificial service [of the Philippians] by being poured out . . .'"; LB, "if my lifeblood is, *so to speak,* to be poured out. . . .'"

I am being poured out like a libation. Pres. pass. indic., *spendō,* in the NT, here + 2 Tim 4:6, "I am already (*ēdē*) being poured out as a libation" (reflecting 2:17? cf. Cook 1982). *Word studies*: O. Michel, *TDNT* 7:528–36; R. France, *NIDNTT*

2:853–55; *EDNT* 3:263; *OCD*[3] 854; *KlPauly* 5 (1975) 922–23, "Trankopfer"; U. B. Müller 121 n 282. The vb. + noun *spondē* (Lat. *libatio*) have considerable background in the Greco-Roman world, from Homeric times for "pouring out" (a portion of) a drink on the ground at meals in honor of gods, heroes, or the dead, or in cult, for Olympian Zeus (poured on the burning flesh of an animal sacrifice). Wine, milk, honey, water, or olive oil. By itself or with some other sacrifice. MM 586, libations of wine to a god, oil at a temple, "sacrifices and libations" to a deified emperor. Geoffrion 189; Krentz 2003:357, libations before battle. Rarely was blood involved but cf. Loh. 113 n 1. Seneca, forced to suicide by Nero in 65, imitating Socrates, sprinkled drops of water on slaves nearby (*Ann.* 15.64). Clodius Thrasea Paetus, suicide in 66, sprinkled blood from his open veins on the ground (*Ann.* 16.35). "Liberator" for Jupiter (Gk. *Zeus eleutherios*) may reflect Stoic notions of death as liberation, or sarcastically allude to a term Nero sometimes used of himself (on coins) (*TDNT* 7:531 and n 18). BDAG 937 cites a 2nd-cent. A.D. papyrus about a prophet of Apollo, his death a *spondē* (Denis 1957a disputes bloodshed). These incidents, later than Paul's Letter B, illustrate something of the world of the day, though there was little use of *spendō* in the cultic sphere (530; a hoplite departs for a military campaign, a woman holds a libation vessel, *OCD*[3] 854).

Others see OT background. The Gk. = Heb. *nāsak*, to pour, cultic libations (the drink offering, Num 15:5; 28:7,14, 24, 30; 29:6, etc.; Lev 23:13, 37). A practice in Israel from neighboring religions, esp. Canaanite; viewed as syncretistic in Deuteronomistic redaction (Jer 7:18 etc.) and Ezek 20:28. Michel (7:531–35) maximalizes OT/Palestinian cultic practices, later "spiritualized," esp. in Hellenistic Judaism; Phil 2:17 is modeled on sayings "of later Judaism or the Hellenistic world." The OT "drink offering" was "perhaps a secondary offering" (535); C. Dohmen, *TDOT* 9:458–59, "ancillary offerings," almost never "an independent sacrificial act." Ps 16:4, "their drink offerings of blood," refers to illicit offerings of "those who choose another god" (AB 16:86–89, Canaanite gods; cf. Isa 66:3). Thus, background in the OT and Judaism for Paul's phrase is less obvious than one might expect. Whatever Paul had in mind, Philippians could readily understand his words in light of pagan temple cult, libations in the Greco-Roman world, and perhaps Stoic thought. As at 1:21–24, Paul has no intention to commit suicide. He is already pouring himself out as libation in his missionary career and current situation. Therefore not of death (O'B 305–6), let along martyrdom (Loh., Gnilka 155), but apostolic labors and sufferings, including now prison (Michaelis 48; Denis 1957b, 1958; Collange 113; Hawth. 105–6; Ware 1996:316, Paul's *agōn*, not his death; Fee 254).

2:17b. *at the sacrificial service of your faith. epi* + dat. of *thysia*, on which see 4:18 in Letter A, *sacrifice acceptable*; + *leitourgia*, well-known from ancient Athens; + *faith* (see NOTE on 1:25). But problems: many take the entire phrase with *spendomai* in 17a (cf. Silva 151–52). What, then, does *epi* mean? (1) A "local sense," Paul's libation poured out "upon" the Philippians' sacrifice (KJV, RSV; cf. NIV "on") or "over" it (NRSV, NAB) or alongside it, as in some cult rituals like the Daily Whole-Offering (see below). (2) "in addition (to)" (Vincent 71; O'B 306–7, with Seidensticker 227–29, as in Num 28–29, the drink offering is an addition to the burnt offering or some other sacrifice; Fee 254 n 62, Oakes 2000 [(4) Bibl. **1:19**] 257–58, Num 15:5, "wine as a drink offering with [LXX *epi*, Fee 'in connection with'] the burnt offering"; so TC; NEB "to crown that sacrifice," REB "to complete" it [!]). Grayston 30 complains about "ritual language without making it quite plain what [Paul] means." Perhaps (Sir 50:14–15) an idealized Yom Kippur ritual or the Daily Whole-Offering as at Num 28:7 (AB 39:550–53). (3) Temporally (BDAG *epi* 18.b, *at the time of, together with, the sacrifice*; ZG 597; "poured out as a libation as you offer," Gdsp.; Beare 94 "*at the sacrifice*—perhaps 'to crown the sacrifice', perhaps 'to imitate it' . . ."). Interpretation of *epi* is thus tied to speculations over what ritual is in Paul's mind. Or is it a general metaphor suitable for both Jewish and Gentile worlds? The TRANSLATION takes the phrase with *I rejoice* in 17c (*chairō* + *epi* + dat., BDAG 1074; cf. 1 Cor 13:6; 16:17; 2 Cor 7:13; Rom 16:19; Wohl. 145–46; Haupt 102; Gnilka 154; Schenk 225). The *epi*-phrase is in effect causal, "I rejoice because of your . . . faith."

sacrificial service. Lit., "the sacrifice and service" (KJV, NIV), *tē[i] thysia[i] kai leitourgia[i]*; NRSV adds a second art., "the sacrifice and the offering of your faith," cf. NEB/REB. Hendiadys is a stylistic feature in Phil; see NOTES on 1:19 *tēs hymōn deēseōs kai epichorēgias*; 1:20 *my expectation and hope*; 1:25 *your progress and joy*; ATR 787; ZBG #184. Hence "sacrificial offering" (RSV), "sacrificial service" (NAB[RNT]) and paraphrases (Gdsp. "service of sacrifice"). Cultic sacrifices were familiar in the Greco-Roman world and at the Temple in Jerusalem (Loh. 113; *KlPauly* 4 [1972] 307–10). *thysia* seems fig. (BDAG 2.b), of something offered (Vincent 71; Lft. 119; "the thing sacrificed," O'B 308; cf. 4:18, the Philippians' recent gift to Paul and solidarity with him). Better: **the act of offering, as you offer your faith** (BDAG 1; Gnilka 155). Loh. 113 n 2, both act and object offered. Holloway 2001a:126 n 119, "faithful death as sacrifice," even martyrdom. Discussion is complicated by attempts to pin down specific OT/Jewish or Greco-Roman sacrifices and debate over "priestly" concepts, Paul as Levitical priest, e.g., offering up himself and the Philippians or their faith (Loh. 113–14). See (16) COMMENT B.2.d on 4:18 in Letter A (K. Weiss [(16) Bibl.], Corriveau, Newton; cf. Seidensticker) on moves away from cultic, priestly emphases to moral/ethical or theological concerns (F. M. Young, "Opfer. IV. Neues Testament," *TRE* 25 [1995] 271–72). 2:17 does not provide clarity on priests and cult offerings (Fee 251–55), but the imagery, uncertain to us, was "perfectly clear to Paul and probably reasonably understandable to the Philippians" (251). Fee reads 2:17 as the second part of an *inclusio*, with 1:27–30 and therefore the *agōn* in which both apostle and converts engage. Opinions vary in Word studies: J. Behm, *TDNT* 3:185, *thysia* at 2:17 (cf. Rom 12:1) = "what faith does," the opposite of cultic sacrifice; *NIDNTT* 3:431–32, Paul's death "as a freewill offering for the sake of the church," but not "propitiatory" (C. Brown); H. Thyen, *EDNT* 2:162, cf. Rom 15:16 and 1 Cor 9:13, Paul probably offers the "faithful practice" of the Philippians as sacrifice, his own martyr's blood the "drink offering" (Lev. 23:37) (but cf. *TDNT* 7:535 on the vb. and 4:227–28 for alternate views).

service. Similar battles exist re *leitourgia*. BDAG lists (1) **service of a formal**

or public type, (a) in ritual and cult (only at Luke 1:23 and Heb 9:21); (b) "other kinds of service to God" (Phil 2:17); (2) **service of a personal nature,** *help, assistance,* Phil 2:30; 2 Cor 9:12 (the collection). Vb. in Paul, only at Rom 15:27; noun for the agent of service *(leitourgos),* of Epaphroditus (Phil 2:25), Paul (Rom 15:16), and Roman governmental officials (Rom 13:6). *Word studies:* H. Strathmann/R. Meyer, *TDNT* 4:215–31; K. Hess, *NIDNTT* 3:551–53; H. Balz, *EDNT* 2:347–49; *TLNT* 2:378–84; *KlPauly* 3 (1969) 550; *OCD*³ 875–76 "liturgy." One must clear away later ecclesiastical use of "liturgy" and notions in biblical theology and stewardship about "the work of the people" *(laou ergon;* [Ionic] *leïtos* + the root *erg* = service or discharge of a task *for* the public). In Gk. city-states for tasks required of well-to-do citizens or done voluntarily, e.g., providing a ship for the navy for a year ("trierarchy"); a horse for war; a chorus or athletes for a festival (about a hundred opportunities annually, each eligible person undertaking the task every two or three years). By the 4th cent. B.C., the state began to take over such *leitourgiai,* but their scope expanded to "all kinds of service to the body politic" *(TDNT* 4:217), esp. in Egypt (papyrus evidence, MM 372–73), and then "service" of almost any sort, with no emphasis on *leïtos.* Thus, of slaves to masters, services friends render one another (Plut. *Mor.* 2.95E, *De amicorum multitudine* 6, whoever accepts services from many must render services to many; 10.787A, *An seni* 6, small, frequent tokens of service, not great *leitourgias);* a courtesan "servicing" three men *(Anth. Pal.* 5.49 = LCL *Greek Anthology* 1, p. 153, in Lat. so as not to offend). Many examples in *TDNT* 4:247–48. The terms were employed for cultic functions by temple employees (not just priests), for cultus was part of *polis* life. While Strathmann claims "the future belongs to this [cultic] strand by way of the LXX" (219), the varied non-cultic senses continued (Lat. *munera,* "public duties"). In Philippi, citizens and non-citizens owed *munera* of all sorts to Rome and to the *municipium,* financially and in terms of services *(OCD*³ "munus," "municipium"; perhaps through the *tribus Voltinia).* For usages in Paul's day, cf. Plut. above + 2.792E, *An seni* 17, performing services over a long period of time for one's father. Army units rendered services *(leitourgei leitourgian)* for the tribune (Polyb. 6.33.6) or were sent on "special service" assignment (10.16.5). Also for nature and bodily functions; *TDNT* 4:217, we perform many services every day for the belly, teeth, etc., Epict. frg. 23 = LCL 2:466–67. Such senses were likely familiar in Philippi. More examples and bibl. on *munera* in *TLNT* 2:378–81.

The LXX employed *leitourg-*terms some 140x in cultic legislation (Exod 28–29, Num, Chron, and Ezek 40–46), usually for *šērēt* *(TDNT* 4:219–22, a tech. usage, almost exclusively service to Yahweh). Sir 4:14, "Those who serve [*hoi latreuontes*] Wisdom minister [*leitourgēsousin*] to the Holy One" (NRSV; *šērēt* twice). Continued in rabbinic literature, but "spiritualization" of sacrifices occurred, even before Temple worship ended in Jerusalem.

The limited NT usage at times reflects OT cult (Heb 8:6; 9:21; 10:11; 1:14; Luke 1:23). In Paul, three examples reflect "popular usage": 2 Cor 9:12, Rom 15:27 re the collection; Phil 2:30, "services" by Epaphroditus, which the Philippians themselves "could not give" to Paul. Acts 13:2 is the single example of "new

Christian terminology": prophets and teachers in the church at Antioch "render-ing service to the Lord" (Fitzmyer, AB 31:497, *leitourgountōn autōn*); *TDNT* 4:226–27, "engaging in a fellowship of prayer." This leaves Phil 2:17 as singularly cultic and priestly in Paul *if* construed with *thysia* and in light of *spendomai* as cultic, "to characterise either the missionary work of Paul [his *leitourgia* estab-lished the Philippians' faith, *pisteōs* as obj. gen.] or the Christian walk of the Phi-lippians [*pisteōs* = subjective gen.]" (*TDNT* 4:227). Balz, obj. gen. (*EDNT* 2:348); Hess, Paul "offering up the obedient faith of the Philippians to God" (*NIDNTT* 3:552); Spicq, *leitourgia* = the sacrifice, in its public character, of the Philippians' Christian life (*TLNT* 2:383). Schenk 225, "voluntary accomplishment," like 2 Cor 9:12.

In summary, *thysia* and *leitourgia* had cultic applications, Greco-Roman and OT-Jewish. They also had wider non-cultic applications. No consensus about spe-cific sacrifice rituals. The Philippians likely heard *leitourgia* in light of "services" called for in the Roman Empire. Did Paul mean it that way? In the hendiadys there is no agreement on which term dominates (cf. Meyer 95 + American ed., p. 113). The TRANSLATION takes *service* as basic and, with RSV, ZBG #184, Hawth. 105, O'B 309, and others, *thysia* as adjectival.

of your faith. hymōn (pl.) is possessive. *tēs pisteōs*, subj. gen. (*TDNT*, above; NIV "coming from your faith"; GNB; Wohl. 145; Beare 94 "source"; Hawth. 105; Silva 151; Schenk 225, the Philippians' acceptance of the gospel, from which their activity in all its forms has grown; Fee 225 n 65). To take *faith* as obj. gen. ("as you offer your faith in a service of sacrifice to God," Gdsp.; NEB/REB; Vincent 71) or epexegetically (O'B 310, "that is, your faith," 272; JB) seems muddled. Is *pistis* in Paul something one can offer to God, esp. if it is a gift from God? O'B seeks to save the interpretation by "life of faith," financial assistance to Paul, mis-sion exertion, and prayer. But the previous nouns seem to refer to such things, so *tēs pisteōs* becomes tautologous. The subj. gen. reading indicates whence the positive responses of the Philippians come. *fides quae* and *qua creditor*, "faith-content that is believed" and "faith with which one believes."

2:17c. *I rejoice and feel joy with you all.* The TRANSLATION repeats *I rejoice.* In the Gk., followed by *sygchairō*, compound form of the same vb., + dat. (also in v 18; cf. 1 Cor 12:26; 13:6; Luke 1:58; 15:6). The prep. prefix is associative (ATR 627, 828). Pres. tense, possibly iterative, repeated action. Some make *chairō* and *sygchairō* fut. and conditional (CEV, "If this happens, I will be glad and re-joice with you"; JB, LB); better, the future is "experienced as joy in the present" (Conzelmann, *TDNT* 9:369). The compound vb., reasonably well attested in Gk. (BDAG p. 953), sometimes = "congratulate" (BDAG 2; MM 616; Fee 255 n 67; Vg *gaudeo et congratulor*, v 18 Rheims NT, "rejoice, and congratulate with me"); congratulations, e.g., to a *polis* on its citizens (Plut. *Mor.* 231B); Lft. 119–20; Mof-fatt; Gdsp.; R. Knox, "I congratulate myself and all of you. . . ." The rendering has died out (Gnilka 156 n 65; Wohl. 147). "I share my gladness" (Morrice 1984:76–78) is not convincing (O'B 311 n 55). Even in Letter B it is too early to take the vb. as "farewell" (*DA* 241–42); 2:12–18 is not a "farewell charge" (COMMENT A.3; even Beare 94 keeps "rejoice and share in joy" for 17 and 18).

2:18. *In the same way, rejoice, you too, and rejoice together with me. de* (not to be elided as in TR or WH; ATR 207; GNTG 2:61) is continuative (DA 327, as at 1:22, 23; 2:8). *to auto*, acc. neut. sg., *autos, ē, o,* (= *same*, BDAG 3.b), acc. of content or adverbial acc. (BDF ##154, 160; ATR 487; Schenk 226, = *hōsautos*, Rom 8:26, "likewise," RSV). As at Matt 27:44, "(In) the same way." Cf. Moule *IB* 34. For the character of the action, not its object (KJV). *chairete* and *sygchairete* could be indic. (KJV), but context and *to de auto* call for an impv. (NEB), though often disguised (you "should be glad and rejoice," RSV, NIV; "you must . . ." [NJB]). The causal idea KJV found in *to de auto* has been set aside, in part because different reasons have been seen for Paul's rejoicing and the joy of the Philippians. For emphasis *(kai hymeis) you too* has been added after the first vb., which could be rendered, "continue to rejoice. . . ."

COMMENT

A. FORMS, SOURCES, AND TRADITIONS

1. Old Testament. LXX phrases (see NOTES) dot the passage: 2:15a *children of God . . . unblemished,* 15b *a crooked and twisted generation* (Deut 32:5); 15c *shine as luminaries* (Dan 12:3); 16b *struggle in an empty way* (Isa 49:4; 65:23); 12e *with reverence and trembling* (several OT passages); 14 *complaints and wrangling* (the "murmuring" tradition in the wilderness, Exod 16:12, Num 14:2, etc.). Fee 244 n 16 urges Gen 17:1 for 15a *be unfaulted.* This mosaic is not treated by Hays 1989 or others on Paul and the OT ([4] Bibl. **1:19 OT**). Gnilka 151, "almost a catena of OT citations," yet "with a completely new sense," re the OT "wandering people of God as a type for the Christian community in its eschatological existence." Schenk 222, an "apocalyptic topos" (15c; Dan 12:3; Wis 3:7; *1 En.* 108:11–14; *2 En.* 66:7; *Ascen. Mos.* 10:9; Matt 13:43; 4 Ezra [= NRSV 2 Esdras] 7:97, 125; *2 Apoc. Bar.* 51:1–2). Edart 194–96, exodus and prophetic *topoi.* Reed, "embedded" OT language in the "epistolary argument, " hardly in context of the Heb. Scriptures, scarcely perceived by Gentile readers.[1] Fee 241–43 asks, "intentional intertextuality" or just "the overflow of a mind steeped in Scripture"? Fee suggests an earlier sermon or teaching, on which Paul draws. Scripture is part of Paul's *inventio* here (Edart 194).

Deut 32, the Song of Moses, is the centerpiece. Michael (*Phil.* 99–106) argued Paul was "comparing and contrasting himself with Moses" and his injunctions for a time when he would no longer be alive.[2] Moses predicted "you will utterly corrupt yourselves" (31:29; cf. the harsh words about Israel quoted from 32:5 at 2:15);

---

[1] DA 291–92. Reed rejects as "forced" Wick's claim for a chiastic macrostructure to all of Phil based on OT/Jewish chiasm (2 Sam 9–20, 1 Kgs 1–2, Eccl 1:3–3:15). At best, "a microstructural feature" for 2:12–18 (DA 292–93, 362–64). See further INTRO. VI.B n 3.

[2] Michael also linked Phil 1:6 ("God will perfect the good work in you") with Deut 32:4 ("the Rock, his work is perfect"), and 1:28 ("not intimidated . . . by your adversaries") with Deut 31:6 ("have no fear or dread of them").

Paul is confident the Philippians, in his absence, will "act for themselves" in working out salvation (12e). Moses promised God would be with Israel (Deut 31:8); Paul asserts God is at work among the Philippians (2:13). F. W. Beare labeled 2:12–18 Paul's "Farewell Appeal," akin to Deut 31:25–30, 32:1–5; *chairete* (2:18) suggests "farewell." Cf. Houlden 88. On Beare's "farewell address" genre, see A.3, below. Michael's picture (Paul comparing himself favorably with Moses) does not fit Moses as an otiose figure in Paul, a warning not a type (C. K. Barrett 1962:46–67; L. I. Belleville, *DPL* 620–21). As with Michael's attempt to see Paul at 1:19 as another Job, does the connection stem from Paul's text or the modern interpreter? We doubt Paul could assume "specific awareness of a link with Deuteronomy 32 on the part of his readers" (Bockmuehl 157) or that he presented himself as (another) Moses.

What Moses said negatively about perverse Israel (cf. Str-B 3:621) is applied by Paul not to Israel or (dissidents in) the church but to the pagan world. Where Moses spoke of the Israelites as "blemished children of God" (NRSV "degenerate"), Paul calls the Christian community "*un*blemished children of God." Does this mean (Collange 112) "the church takes over from Israel the privilege of being God's 'child', . . . nothing remains for Israel but to melt away into the 'perverse and straying' mass" of "the world"? (cited approvingly in Hawth. 102; O'B 294; Bittasi 80–81).[3] The passage could be a striking example of Bultmann's view that "the Jew" in the NT at times symbolizes "the world" of all human beings in their lostness. But Israel is not a topic in 2:12–18; 1:27ff. is concerned with the church in the Roman world, to which the harsh words are directed (rightly, O'B 294–95).

2:16b has led to the claim Paul saw his ministry "as modelled on, even an extension of, that of the *Isaianic* Servant of the Lord."[4] Any such use is secondary to Christ as the Servant (in 2:6–11, debated). Some appeal to Gal 1:15 (Isa 49:1, cf. 6; really Jer 1:4–5) and Rom 15:21 (Isa 52:15; so Dunn, WBC 38B:866; contrast Fitzmyer AB 33:716). "Paul, never, in his own writings, identifies himself explicitly with the Isaianic Servant"; 2:16 may hint at it (C. G. Kruse, *DPL* 870).

All in all, it is unlikely that a story about Israel runs through 2:12–18 (so F. Thielman 1994: 156–57; 1995:139–40) or that Paul instructed the Gentile Philippians on their continuity with "biblical Israel" (1994:143–44; Patte 186–87).[5] Gen 17:1, Deut 32:5, Dan 12:3; and even Isa 49:4 and 65:23 are not vv Paul employs elsewhere. The "murmuring" theme is in 1 Cor 10:1–13 a warning to the community about "sacraments." Any reconstructed story behind 2:12–18 would be about Israel's disobedience and *Unheilsgeschichte* (unholy, non-redemptive history). More

---

[3] Hawth. also has in mind 3:2, where he regards the opponents as Jews.

[4] O'B 300 n 73. Radl 1986 ([7] Bibl.):144–49, emphasizing "in vain" from Isa 49:4; O'Brien 1995; Bockmuehl 159–60. For Paul as the Isaianic servant, cf. Acts 13:47 (Paul *and Barnabas*, perhaps really Christ, Fitzmyer, AB 31:521).

[5] Ware 1996, "Philippian Christians have supplanted the Jewish nation as the mediatorial community" (286, 288, 321); "mediatorial" = for "conversion of the nations," assumed for the servant of Isa 49 (Christ in 2:5–11; Paul, in Acts 26:17; Rom 10:13–17; 15:21; then Paul's Philippian converts, Ware 1998).

likely, Paul employs "scriptural" phrases with which he was familiar, some of them almost proverbial (Thurston 97, "the furnishings of his mind").

2. The Philippians' Encomium. Connections between 2:6–11 and 2:12–18 are often noted.[6] Deidun 63–69 minimized such links; 2:12–18 is a comprehensive expression of Christian morality.

Surprisingly from a "Christ hymn," 2:12–18 has only a single reference to Christ (16b) and that to the day of judgment. Instead the talk is about God (vv 13, 15a).[7] Not Christology but *salvation* (12e) is lifted up out of 2:6–11, with fuller implications for life, till the divine judgment occurs. Obedience (2:8) comes to the fore, the first point in the section (12b *as you have always obeyed*), with *captatio benevolentiae* (Paul commends, as he reminds them of what they have said in describing Jesus). "Obedience (unto death)" could be read as the "obedience of faith" to the point of martyrdom; as a theme in OT/Jewish piety and paraenesis (Loh. 101 n 2); but also as a Roman virtue, something Philippian Christians knew well and perhaps overdid. Geoffrion 186–87 points to a political/military context of "obey." Whom you obey, matters, not just blind obedience (discernment!). Paul seeks to rouse the Philippians to maturity, to work out, in his absence, what *sōtēria* (*salvation*) means, as "emancipated clients" (Bormann 1995:206–17). God continues to work among the Philippians (2:13), till and towards *the Day of Christ* (16a). Is this a corrective (their piece ended with universal glory, but no note of judgment)? The *Day of Christ* strikes a note, responsibility, that Paul emphasized earlier (1:6, 11) for the Philippians and himself. 2:12–18 thus builds on 2:6–11 (*So, then,* 12a) but also corrects it and expands implications for daily life.

3. Structure, Rhetorical, and Literary Features. Following the indic.-mood account in 2:6–11, 2:12–18 continues the paraenesis in 1:27–2:5. 1:27 *Exercise your citizenship in a manner worthy of the gospel of Christ* stands over 2:12–18 as its impvs. treat how believers relate one to another and with the *politeia* of city and Empire. Silva 134, "Therefore, my loved ones, [. . . I call upon you once more to live as Christian citizens:]. . . ." Occasionally 2:1–13 has been taken as the unit (*heautōn*, "your own," "of yourselves," 3, 4 and 12e), but *hōste* in v 12 and the voc. mark "a fairly fresh start" (Holmstrand 106–7; see NOTE on 2:12 *So, then, my beloved*). The unit is occasionally deemed to end with v 16, with 2:17–30 the next

---

[6] Cf. how 2:1–4 anticipated 2:6–11. Obedience (*hypēkoos* 2:8; *hypēkousate* v 12b); salvation (2:12e, the theme of the "song of salvation" in 2:6–11); "empty" (2:7a *heautōn ekenōsen*; 16b *eis kenon* twice). To parallel *reverence and trembling* (12e) with the *tapeinophrosynē* (*humiliation*) of 2:3 (and 2:8 vb., U. B. Müller 115) is dubious (Merk 184). Others relate death on the cross in 2:8 to *being poured out like a libation* in 17a and *sacrificial service* in 17b, particularly if v 8 = Isa 53:12 Heb., rejected in the NOTE on 8 *but himself he emptied.* Emphasis on Jesus' "Lordly Example" (Hurtado 1984 [(7) Bibl.]; Silva 134; O'B 272–73) is common for interpreting vv 12ff. Loh. 99–100 viewed 2:12–16 as an interpretation of the Christ-psalm, analogous in structure (Larsson 263, a midrash on it)—denied by Gnilka 148 n 3, cf. U. B. Müller 114.

[7] Thus is answered the criticism that Paul quotes 2:6–11 only for the emphasis on Christ in vv 6–8 and that vv 9–11 are "throwaway" lines, playing no part in the argument. They do, in 2:12–18.

unit (Loh., but with few followers). Generally the vv have been subdivided 2:12–13, 14–16, 17–18 (Gnilka 147–56, Silva 134, O'B 271–312, Edart 188–90, though headings differ). Fee 229–58, three sentences, "General" (2:12–13) and "Specific Applications" (2:14–18), but a threefold concern: their common cause, the gospel, and Paul. G. Barth 51, it is "difficult to bring [12–18] under a common theme."

Form critically, some have seen a "farewell appeal," like that by Moses in Deut 31–32 (Michael; Beare; above, A.1) or the Lucan Paul in Acts 20:17–38 (Munck AB 31:205, citing Deut 29–30, not 32; Fitzmyer AB 31:674–76, a pastoral "last will and testament"). *WDNTECLR* 182–83 and treatments like Stauffer 1955 (INTRO. X Bibl.) 344–47 do not identify anything in Paul as a farewell address. But K. Berger treats "Testamentary Speeches,"[8] and under "Symbuleutische Argumentation" (1984a:100) lists Phil 2:16–18 as an example in communication of the "I/you relationship," and 2:15 as demarcation from others *(the twisted generation)*. Typical of testamentary addresses is awareness of judgment (2:16 *Day of Christ*; Paul and the community shrink from it). Elements listed by Fitzmyer (674, with classical Gk. examples) include for Phil 2:12–18 (1) some recollection of the relationship between Paul and the Philippians (12b, 16b–17); (5) exhortation to fidelity (12e, 14–16a); and perhaps (6) commendation/blessing (in a mutual form, 17; God's blessing, 13). Less obvious are (3) leave taking (12d *in my absence*, 17a *if I am . . . poured out*) and (4) assignment of "successors" (Timothy and Epaphroditus, 2:19–20). There seems nothing on (2) discharge of debts (unless 4:18 refers to that, in Letter A) and Paul's past services. Paul's words would seem not unfamiliar to the Philippians on the basis of Greco-Roman categories of the day.

Rhetorically, 2:12–18 are *exhortatio*.[9] Vv 12–18 develop the *propositio* about standing firm (or citizenship, 1:27, *politeuesthe*, Reed 1993:318–19, criticizing D. F. Watson); the apostle's joy, at the judgment, will rest on the Philippians' continuance in faithfully working out salvation. Geoffrion 185–90 makes 2:12–13 an enthymene ([2] COMMENT A.4). Schoon-Janßen 143 sees *diatribe* style *(antitheses*, 2:15, 17; cf. Bultmann 1910:20; impvs., 2:12, 14, and 18, Bultmann 13). Holloway 2001a:124–25 finds a *topos*, "complaining against God."[10] But according to

---

[8] 1984a:75–80. Greco-Roman examples contain admonitions from a Caesar or philosopher facing death (Plut. *Otho* 16, Do not fear, you've had a Caesar as uncle; Epicurus bade his friends to remember his teachings, Diog. Laert. 10.16) and perhaps something about what death means (Dio Chrys. *Or.* 30. 8–44, to be friend and table-companion with the king of the gods). No mention of Paul.

[9] Bloomquist 168–72; Holloway 2001a:120 for all of 2:1–30; Bittasi 74–83, 210, parallel to 3:15–16. Or *probatio* (D. F. Watson 1988b:67–71, 2:1–3:21; Brucker [(7) Bibl.] 296; Black 1995, 1:27–3:21; Snyman 328); Paul persuades "his audience to 'live a life worthy of the gospel' [1:27]" (Watson 1988b:67), with *pathos* (about himself) in 16b–18, heightened by *expolitio*, the possibility he had run/labored in vain (16b, Watson 70), emotive "elaboration," in a 1st-per. soliloquy (Lausberg ##830–42). Or *peroratio* (Edart 191–97) of the *probatio* in 2:1–11; 2:12ad = *exordium* with *captatio benevolentiae*; 12e, *propositio*, supported (13a *For*) and developed in 14, 15–16 with OT *topoi* from the exodus and prophets. Cf. INTRO. VI. B n 2.

[10] Ingratitude brings on complaining (Sen. *Ad Marc.* 12.1). One should accept someone's death "without complaint" (*Ad Marc.* 10.2), without murmuring *(murmuratione)* and grumbling (*gemens*, Sen. *Ep.* 107.9; Plut. *Ad ux.* 610E–611B) against God or fate; cf. Marcus Aurelius, *Med.* 2.3, "you should

Paul, the Philippians "always obey" (2:12b) and pray for Paul (1:19); their witness is positive about God (2:9–11). The varying opinions indicate rhetorical criticism is an inexact science (*DA* 166).

The passage is marked by literary features (Edart 188–97): *alliteration* (see Note on 2:14, Gk. *panta poieite*; 2:15, words beginning with *un-* in Eng., Gk. *a-*); *asyndeton* (no connecting particle, 2:14); *hendiadys* (14, 15a, 17b); *repetition* (16 *eis* 4x); *litotes* (16b *not . . . in an empty way*); *anaphora* (13b; the vbs. in 17c-18); and *inclusio* (2:12–18 with 1:27–30; or *rejoice* 2:17 and 1:18). Silva 135 suggested a *chiasm* in 2:12 (but then hesitated, 140–41):

you obeyed ———————— in *my* presence

in *my* absence ———————— *(you)* work out *your* salvation

Better: *in my presence, in my absence* explain *always* (Schenk 215). Schenk 218 sought to solve the meaning of *goodwill* (2:13) as God's through a chiasmus parallelism:

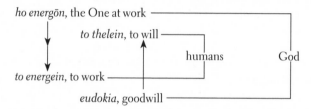

ho energōn, the One at work

to thelein, to will

to energein, to work   humans   God

eudokia, goodwill

God, in the divine loving will, energizes human willing and doing. But the chart can also be read to show that God energizes human goodwill and what lies beyond it. Language in the passage is drawn from *athletics* (16b), *friendship-letter* style (12c), *cult sacrifice* (at least at first glance, 17), and *astral imagery* (15c).

With the impvs. in 2:12–18, indic. statements are interwoven.[11] 2:12–13 expresses "the fundamental unity of indicative and imperative in Paul's thought" (Deidun 63–69; cf. Bockmuehl 154). Impvs. include (1) *continue working out what your salvation means* (12e); (2) *keep on doing all things without complaint and wrangling* (14). 15a amounts to (3) a call toward a goal, *that you may be unfaulted and uncorrupted, children of God who are unblemished* in the hostile world in which believers live; imperatival *hina* in NAB, NEB/REB. Schenk would add 15c-16, "Shine out among them" (NEB-mg, CEV) and "proffer the word of life" to the world (NEB-txt/REB), but there the indic. is to be preferred. A final impv. in v 18 is (4) *rejoice!*

---

not face death grumbling (*mē gonguzōn*) but graciously, with integrity, and from a heart thankful to the gods"; Chrysost. (PG 63.246.12–13 = NPNF 13:223), "without murmuring let us do all things." None of Holloway's classical references touch on the "farewell speech" form.

[11] On indic.-impv., cf. (5) COMMENT A.1, n 10; esp. Merk 1968:183–87.

B. MEANING AND INTERPRETATION

The (four) impvs. in 2:12–18 continue and complete the paraenesis begun at 1:27 for believers in Philippi on relationships to one another, under God, in Christian community (wrangling house churches) and relations to *polis* and Empire (at times hostile opposition). Not "self-esteem" or "self-realization," but Christian existence, in community before God and in the world (Walter 64). While primarily *exhortatio*, the vv include new reasons (in the indic.) for fidelity in the tasks ahead. The theme of *salvation* (2:12) stems from the encomium (2:6–11), the Philippians' own missionary witness.[12] Vv 12–18 see God at work (not Christology), God who vindicated the crucified Jesus continues to act among the Philippians. While praising them for obedience, Paul may hint at an overemphasis in Philippian Christianity on "obeying" (2:8, 12b). He lifts up not simply God's "glory" at the Endtime (as 2:11 did) but the specter of judgment at *the Day of Christ* (16b). In affirming the Philippians, but calling for further community-building and continued witnessing, Paul possibly reflects the "testamentary address" form (above, A.3). He weaves in scriptural language with which he is familiar, even if the Philippians may not catch it. The apostle does not appear in 2:15 as a sort of Moses (or the church as Israel). 2:12–18 will be treated for Letter B in three subsections, vv 12–13, 14–16, and 17–18 (so Holloway 2001a:123, among many); then (4) redacted into a single composite letter.

1. **Work Out What Salvation Means, Grounded in God's Continuing Work *among Us (2:12–13).** A new beginning on ethical teachings for the gospel in daily life is made with the address *So then, my beloved* (cf. 4:1), to be connected with the impv. twenty-three Gk. words later, *continue working out what your salvation means* (12e). Paul calls for *reverence and trembling* in the process, since *the One at work in and among you is God* (13a). What God works among the Philippians is *to will and to work above and beyond goodwill* (13b). 12e is a key impv., between the Philippians' account in 2:6–11 about Christ and God and a major Pauline statement in v 13 about God continuing at work. The specific warrant or grounding for 12e comes in v 13 (*For*; Schenk 213; Cruz 382–83 sees motivation only in vv 6–11; contrast Deidun 64). *salvation* is Paul's summary of the encomium, a Philippian restatement of the gospel. His emphasis is on God (as in vv 9–11). 12e–13, an impv.-indic. sequence, reverse the accustomed order (Schrage 1988:169). The introductory assumption amounts to a protasis: "if, as I affirm to be correct, *you have always obeyed. . . .*" The *always* is explained as "in Paul's *presence*" but also "in his *absence*." The sequence in 2:12–13 matches that in 2:1–11 (Schenk 217):

---

[12] U. B. Müller 114–15, 2:12–18 are not "a practical commentary on the hymn" in 2:6–11 (as Loh. 99 claimed). 2:12 connects with themes in 1:27 (Paul's presence and absence; engaging in citizenship in a manner worthy of the gospel); 2:15, facing the situation in the world stressed in 1:27–28 (Müller 118).

Assumption: 2:1 If, then, as we assume, comfort and exhortation in Christ amount to something, . . . consolation and love . . .sharing in the Spirit . . . , if affections and mercies amount to something,

[parallel]
2:12bcd Just as you have always obeyed, not in my presence only, but now much more in my absence—

Impvs.: 2:2–5a give me further joy in that you think the same thing, having the same love, together in soul, thinking one thing, nothing for self-interest, nor for vainglory . . . consider one another to surpass yourselves, each regarding not only your own interests, but also those of other persons. . . . Think in this way among yourselves.

12e with reverence and trembling, keep on working out what your salvation means,

Warrant: 2:6–11 . . . the way you also think "in Christ Jesus" . . . obedient to the point of death, . . .God has . . . exalted him . . . and given him the name.

2:13 for God is at work in and among you.

Continuing to obey and work out what salvation means will also appear in v 14, *Keep on doing all things without complaints and wranglings* (cf. also 4:9). There is no single problem or major scandal among the Philippians. Practicing the Christian life in particular circumstances, with their apostle absent, is the theme of Paul's words.

sōtēria is used here for the third time in the letter body. 1:19, in a phrase from Job, spoke of Paul's *deliverance* (from prison, with suggestion of his eternal salvation) through the Philippians' *entreaty and Jesus Christ, whom the Spirit supplies.* Human and divine elements are involved. 1:28 had a terse reference to the Philippians' *salvation* eschatologically. A firm stance on their part and God's own endtime action are involved. "Salvation" is not used in 2:6–11, though many call the vv a "hymn or song of salvation." The encomium presents high points of the kerygma. But the Philippians' composition did not assert the results of Jesus' death "for us," *sōtēria* for those who believe and confess his lordship. Paul might have used here any of a number of metaphors of salvation, like righteousness/justification (3:6–11), reconciliation, liberation, or "in Christ." With its breadth of meaning, *sōtēria* fits the encomium and the concerns he wants to put before the Philippians, in light of 1:19 and 28: *salvation,* in an encompassing sense, what happened "in Christ" and continues to occur among those who seek to live "in Christ"—in the world that put Jesus to humiliation and death. It includes the goal of the gospel and the whole Christian life (Deidun 64),[13] "the consequences of their own salvation" (I. H. Marshall 61).

---

[13] Ware sees in 2:12–18 more specifically "an exhotation *to confess and proclaim the gospel*" (1996:266, 272; "confess" from Rom 10:10). Ware's concern to provide a *command* to preach (in 2:16a) overlooks evidence listed (269) on existing Philippian participation in Paul's mission (1:5–6; 4:10–17).

Your (pl.) *salvation* focuses not on individuals "getting saved," saving "one another," or imitation of Christ (B. Weber) but on the corporate whole of believers (Larsson 264), those in the church community whose lack of consideration for others among them and concentration on their own (individual) interests have been criticized in 2:3–4. Paul thus draws attention to a deficit in the encomium: no reference to salvation as a result of God's action in Christ and its meaning for those who believe. He wants to remedy some problems in Philippian communal life. While 2:6–11 may echo in 2:12–18 (the Philippians hear their words repeated back and commended), Paul directs attention to specific implications of the gospel—not Christology, not a "saved" relationship with God, but what salvation means for life with one another, in Roman Philippi, and in relation to their apostle, Paul.

Is it just rhetoric to emphasize, almost ingratiatingly, how *you* Philippians *have always obeyed*? Readers tend not to suspect irony. Yet commentators ask, is it obedience to himself (K. Barth 69, Gnilka 148, Thielman 135; Bruce 82)? Or to God (Plummer 50; Holloway 2001a:124 n 105 and others, but, Walter 64, God is not mentioned till v 13)? Or both (I. H. Marshall 60, God, with Paul as channel for God's instructions)? Or to the *episkopoi* and *diakonoi* (1:1; Bonnard 49, de Dietrich 55–56; contrast Collange) or local leaders who assumed they were Paul's deputies (V. Wiles 68 n 106, 123 n 170), overseers in his absence. Or to the gospel (Loh.101; Beare 89, Collange 109, the faith; Schenk 216)? Paul leaves the matter open, simply echoing the encomium (2:8 *obedient*), perhaps with the implication that blind obedience was of little gain. He will not return to this term in Phil (unless *reverence and trembling* before God in 12e is equivalent, as Pedersen 1978 argued). The Philippians seem generally to have supported Paul's gospel through evangelization and support for his mission work, though (4:10) contact had slackened for a time. 2:12b is genuine commendation of the Philippians, if with some hyperbole.

One concern is Paul's *absence* and *presence*. Friendship language used these terms; letters were a substitute for presence, stating what Paul would say, were he there. But his absence, *now much more* while he is imprisoned, weighs on Paul's mind. He hopes to come again, soon (2:24). But death looms for Paul, likely before Christ comes. Here *parousia*, as "presence," refers first to when Paul was present in the past at Philippi (Michaelis 46, Martin 1976:102). Some see also 1:26, *my coming again to you*, in the future (Plummer 32; Loh. 102, Collange 110). His "forthcoming arrival" could carry a note of threat, as if "the big, bad wolf" will frighten them into submission (Collange 110)—something Paul repudiates. The real emphasis is on their maturing in his absence. They are to work matters out, under God (note the *kata* prefix on the vb.; *TDNT* 3:635, God stands behind *katergazesthai* used in a good sense; Pedersen 1978:21–22; Scheck 216; cf. Rom 8:28 NRSV-mg). "Good works" versus "righteousness by faith" is not the topic, but the fruit (cf. 1:11; Gal 5:19) that grows out of the Spirit and a faith that does not make life merely "pleasant" but finds expression in existence in the world (Walter 65).

The Philippians are to proceed *with reverence and trembling*. Often regarded as

OT language, the words also had usage in the Greco-Roman world (see NOTES). They implied a stance or attitude toward or before authority, human or divine. Not "Pharisaic, Jewish piety" (Loh. 102) or a "theology of fear." But not language strange to Philippian Christians, esp. of slave or lower classes, in their stratified society. Hence Giesen 1988: from hostile circumstances and challenges that they face; Glombitza 1959–60: human relations. In Paul's mind *reverence and trembling* were the proper stance before God (Exod 15:16; Deut 2:25; Isa 19:16), proper even for an apostle of robust faith (1 Cor 2:3), serving God and handling the message about life (Phil 2:16)—a matter of life and death, for one not yet at the goal (Walter 65).[14]

God is often overlooked in presenting Paul's thought. But the God of Israel (Dunn, *TPTA* 27–50) who exalted Jesus (Phil 2:9–11) and *is at work in and among the Philippians* (2:13a) is regularly "at the center" of Paul's theology (L. Morris 1986a [INTRO. X Bibl.]: 25–38; Hawth. 1987:24–30). Here, not *Heilsgeschichte* in the sense of God at work in creation, Israel, etc. (at best "in Christ," 2:6–11), but working for *Heil (sōtēria)* in the present time (Kertelge 1967 [(2) Bibl. **righteousness**]: 141). Paul refers to present experiences of what he calls elsewhere the varied "activities" *(energēmata)* of God who activates *(energōn,* same ptc. as at 2:13) them in every believer (1 Cor 12:6, the climax, after "grace gifts" *[charismata]* of the Spirit and "services" [NRSV, *diakoniai*] of the Lord Jesus, God "works" or "effects" them all; Fee 1994:162). Among Paul's numerous formulations, *the One at work in and among you* is unusual.

God's activities involve (13b) the Philippians' willing and doing things, in v 14 *all things, hyper tēs eudokias,* a terse, debated phrase. *to will* and *to do* are closely linked by *both . . . and;* they form a unity. God effects the will, God effects activity among believers. What is *the* (well-known) *eudokia (goodwill)* to which Paul refers? Traditionally God's (Luke 2:14; Eph. 1:5); then the prep. = "for" or "according to," and the noun "purpose" (NEB/REB; [N]JB). But at Phil 1:15 *eudokia* referred to the goodwill of Christian preachers in Ephesus; Rom 10:1, the "desire" of Paul's heart, parallel with his "prayer to God." (The vb. *eudokeō* is used more commonly of his mission work; see NOTE on Phil 1:15.) At 2:13 the case is strong (see NOTE; against traditional trs.), to take *eudokia* as *goodwill* by and among human beings (I. H. Marshall 1969:114), activated by God, expressed in communal relationships in church and *polis.* Then the prep. can be given the meaning BAGD suggests, *above and beyond* the *eudokia* that society expects.

Paul's first impv. thus has to do with working out, as citizens, aliens, or slaves of the *polis* and Empire, the further implications of what *sōtēria* means—"the health" *(sōtēria)* and *goodwill* of the community (Didier 150; Collange 109; Swift

---

[14] Cf. Bornkamm 1946, "fear" at God's presence; Bultmann, *TDNT* 6:221 and 1951 (INTRO. X Bibl.) 320–22 on "faith and fear." Ware 1996:275 contrasts "fear of *God,* before whom it is due, with fear of *men.*" Balz 1969, not to be reduced to the psychology and philosophy of the day; *Furcht,* not simply *Angst* ("dread"). Baumert 1979 speaks of revential awe. Somewhat differently, Holloway 2001a:123–24 sees all of vv 12–18 in terms of "one's duties to God": the Philippians seem guilty of "impiety," complaining against God (v 14); this and "coping with hardship in an exemplary fashion" are Holloway's "consolatory *topoi*" here in a letter of consolation.

245), *eudokia* "the hallmark of any Christian community" (Hawth. 101). The impv. (Deidun 67) "demands the Christian's continuing 'yes' to an activity which does not derive from himself, but which is nonetheless real and actual in the centre of his personality." But pl., "Christians', themselves," etc. Salvation is not only a gift but also a task to be worked out communally.

2. Do All, as Children of God, Unblemished, Luminous, in a Crooked World, until the final Day—with the Word of Life and for Paul (2:14–16). 2:14 emphasizes living out what salvation means, perseveringly and comprehensively: *Keep on doing all things,* everything mentioned from 1:27 on. Bornkamm's "singular paradox," "Because God works *all,* you therefore have to do *all!*" (1946:91) is widely cited (Gnilka 149; Merk 1968:185; Schrage 1988:8; U. B. Müller 116–17). Paradoxical for us moderns; God was expected to sustain ongoing efforts (Schenk 218). Paul's theme is actions derived from faith ("Handeln aus Glaube," Merk; Walter 66).

panta at the start of the cl. (NAB "In everything you do . . .") and the vb. are global (church and society) and ongoing, but the phrase that follows, *without complaints and wranglings,* adds specificity. Not so much a "biblical" phrase, recalling (for Paul, if not his audience) the murmuring of ancient Israel in the wilderness (Exod 15–17; Num 14–17), but one pertinent to conditions among the Philippians. Each word made sense in the Greco-Roman world, *gongysmoi* for displeasure about something, "outbursts of complaints"; *dialogismoi,* for reasonings and opinions over which there might be debate, disputes, or doubts. The OT background suggests the Philippians were malcontents, like the Israelites after the Exodus, sullen, in rebellion, against Moses and Aaron (and God), incident after incident, in the Sinai wastes. Of that there is no hint in Phil. Some see quarrels with local leaders (commentators love or loathe the *episkopoi* of 1:1) or between factions (Euodia and Syntyche, 4:2–3; Thielman 1995:142). Or (cf. "Hellenist" and "Hebrew" Christians, Acts 6:1, linguistic groups) non-Gk.-speaking proselytes (like Lydia, Acts 16) and native people, in contrast to the predominantly Gk.- (and Lat.-) speaking citizens and residents. Evidence is lacking. The strains on community and goodwill are those indicated in 2:2–4. More than that we cannot legitimately conjecture.

This second impv. is fleshed out by a series of phrases through v 16, each important but difficult to combine. Hence the long and cumbersome heading for subsection 2, above. Fee 240 n 3 overstates, that "every major motif of the letter is touched on" in vv 14–16 + 17–18—except Christ. What follows in v 15 amounts to a third impv., *that you may be unfaulted and uncorrupted, children of God who are unblemished. . . .* NEB/REB (imperatival *hina*), "Show yourselves guileless and above reproach. . . ." The alliterative adjs. (all starting with *alpha*) have been brought out by "*un*-words" in Eng. They are Gk. and OT-Jewish emphases expressing integrity, applied to the Christian community (U. B. Müller 118, with Loh. 106–7). Cf. the prayer at 1:10bc, *that you may be flawless and unfailing for the Day of Christ.*

children of God for Christians is not common in Paul (see NOTE). Here, from

Deut 32:5, the Song of Moses, from which seven Gk. words are employed (see COMMENT A.1). Paul has inserted *amid (meson)* into the citation. This divides in two the Deut material that contrasted God's faithfulness (32:4) with Israel's unfaithfulness (32:5; cf. Ps 78:8, disoriented, "not faithful to God"; Loh. 107–8; Schrage 1961:189–90). Israel as "blemished children" (LXX *tekna mōmēta,* NRSV "degenerate") has become in Paul *children of God who are* un*blemished (alpha* privative). This positive reference has been expanded and interpreted by *unfaulted and uncorrupted.* All three adjs. about *God's children* "in Christ" are cultic terms that came to have a moral sense; see NOTES on 15a for the ethical side of "without fault, without corruption, without blame."After *amid,* Paul uses the other four words from Deut 32:5, *a crooked and twisted generation* (now in the gen. case), applied not to Israel (as in Deut 32) but to contemporaries, the age or generation in whose midst Philippian Christians live (Walter 66; U. B. Müller 118). A grim picture, whether from the Heb. (NRSV 32:5 "perverse and crooked") or in Gk. ("harsh, distorted, warped, perverted"; in the vernacular today, "screwed up"); see NOTES on *crooked* and *twisted.*

Why this severe contrast between believers and unbelievers? It is *not* "church versus Israel." Anti-Semitic notions that some interpreters find (see COMMENT A.1) are not present. The "we/they" division may reflect the attitude of world-negation in early Christianity (Gal 1:4, this present evil age), part of the apocalyptic outlook; "a fair reflection of [Paul's] view of pagan society" (Fee 245, citing 1 Cor 6:9–10; Rom 1:28–30; better, 1:18–3:20). Cf. the Qumran contrast between "children of light" and "children of darkness" (1QM); Jesus' stark contrast between disciples and "this (faithless, adulterous) generation," continued in early Christian preaching (Acts 2:40; see NOTE on 15a, *amid . . . generation*). A more immediate explanation exists: the oppressive environment of Roman Philippi and what Paul has already said at 1:27–28 about *struggle* and *adversaries.* A stark contrast was indicated, their *destruction* but *your salvation, and this from God* (1:28b). The *contest* (1:29) pitted Paul and the Philippians against Roman authorities, Caesar (2:11) and his local officials. Paul points up in 2:15 the moral aspects of Christians' life together and in society, in contrast to unbelieving people around them, "an irrevocable break with certain concrete ways of life common in the world" (Schrage 1988:199), illustrated in the three adjs. about God's children. Paul sees a distance and a difference from the ways of the world.[15] In Paul's artful reworking of Deut 32, prior teaching or a sermon on church and world cannot be ruled out—or proven (cf. Fee 242–43, but not "Israel's story" or Gen 17:1 as the OT text). Paul's use of Deut. 32 provides a cryptic way of speaking about contemporary society and Rome.[16]

The contrast is further heightened by the statement, *in which* (lit. and ungram-

---

[15] Schrage 1961:189, quoting H. Greeven, "Die missionierende Gemeinde nach den Apostolischen Briefen," 62, in *Sammlung und Sendung vom Auftrag der Kirche in der Welt,* FS H. Rendtorff, ed. J. Heubach/H.-H. Ulrich (Berlin: Christlicher Zeitschriftverlag, 1958).

[16] Not noted by N. Beck ([7] Bibl.). Cf. the reference to "the arrogant kingdom" (Rome?), in Benediction 12 of the synagogue prayer *Shemoneh 'Esreh.*

matically for the people of the crooked age, "among whom," RSV) *you shine as luminaries in the world*. An impv. (NEB/REB), popular in mission preaching ("Shine . . . ," as in Matt 5:16), is less likely than an indic. that provides grounds for the daring contrast in 15ab (see Note on 15c). *luminaries* = "light-bearers," not just "stars." *hōs phōstēres* and the vb. in Dan 12:3 ("those who are understanding will shine as luminaries") could suggest, for Paul, an apocalyptic note, Endtime, the resurrection of the dead; perhaps for Jewish and Hellenistic hearers "astral immortality" (see Note on *as luminaries . . .*). The Philippians' worldview (see 2:10) included such realms beyond the terrestrial. Fee 247–48 seeks to bring in "evangelism" (16a, "hold out [to others] the word of life," plus from Dan 12:3, "those who bring many to righteousness" will "shine as stars"; dubious, after what 15b said about contemporaries in the world), but settles for the Philippians cleaning up "their internal act so that they may 'hold firm' the gospel." Not holding it fast "so that the enemy does not take it away from you" or (15c) shining as beacons to rescue people adrift, but a contrast, *luminaries* in their world, God at work among them, showing what salvation means.

2:16 indicates why Paul is confident the Philippians will *stand steadfast* in the struggle: it is *because you hold on to the word of life*, i.e., the gospel that brings life in contrast to a world of death around them that faces *destruction* (1:28). These words occasionally have been made into an impv. (NLT, "Hold tightly . . ."). More common is the "missionary sense," "hold out (to the world) the word of life" (NIV). The KJV-RSV tradition (see Note) is to be preferred (without attaching it so directly to what follows as in NRSV, "It is by your holding fast to the word of life that I can boast on the day of Christ . . ."). The Philippians hold fast to what matters, not to Paul (present or absent), but the word. Thus they can carry out their tasks in the community and in world. The church community serves as *pointer (endeixis)*, vis-à-vis its opposition, for *salvation* (2:12) and *destruction* (1:28).

Paul then tacks on a phrase that some link loosely to what precedes (KJV-[N]RSV) and others make a new sentence ("Thus [or Then] you will be my pride on the Day of Christ," NEB/REB). Our paraphrase — *that is grounds for boasting on my part, toward the Day of Christ* — supplies a summarizing subject: *that* refers to the Philippians' continuing to hold fast to the gospel and living out their salvation till the End. This sense of judgment (Cruz 364–65) and final deliverance appeared earlier (1:6, 10, though not in 2:6–11). Ethics is related to future eschatology (Schrage 1988:183). Boasting, by Paul over his favorite congregation, is reciprocal to their boasting over Paul (1:26). His converts' steadfastness (Radl 1981:79 says "faith") is what Paul will rejoice about, their solidarity with him in the gospel, support financially, and evangelization efforts,[17] including the encomium (2:6–11) for witnessing. Paul again affirms the composition sent to him. The "I/you" relationship that reappears here (last at 12ab), after the "we/they"

---

[17] Ware 1996:315 regards "the missionizing activity of the *Philippians*" as "the outworking in them of the power of God at work in *his* [Paul's] ministry," but the vv cited (like 1:6,7,14,15,29–30; 2:13) lack clear reference to God at work *through the apostle*. Ware 1998:249 better refers to "partners" in Paul's mission, his preaching "extended through the missionizing activity of his churches"; 1996:325.

contrast in v 15, will continue through 2:18 and then in the plans for future contacts in vv 19–30.

Why Philippian fidelity mattered so much is further clarified in 16b. Paul looks back over his career from the vantage point of *the Day of Christ* and God's judgment: their steadfastness to the word will show, Paul concludes, *that I did not run in an empty way, nor did I struggle in an empty way.* (*empty way* links it to 2:7, *himself he emptied.*) Paul's vocabulary strikes some as athletic imagery (fruitless training, no laurel crown); others, physical toil (a tent-maker fears crafting something poorly, *eis kenon*, fit only for rejection, Deissmann, *LAE* 317); or moral endeavor urged by philosophy teachers (let the goats eat the laurel crown awarded at the arena; you run the course in life toward virtue; Diogenes vanquished others in what is noble and good; cf. *TDNT* 8:228; Pfitzner 1967:28–35, 99–109). But pre-eminently "run/struggle" *in an empty way* ("synthetic, if not synonymous parallelism," *EDNT* 2:281) refers not to how the Philippians may "ruin their reputation through complaining" (Holloway 2001a:126) but to general stance and missionary work for the gospel (Harnack), as in Gal 2:2.[18] Paul foresees a final eschatological testing of all mission endeavor (1 Cor 3:10–15). He often used "in vain" re his labors (1 Thess 2:1, 3:5; Gal 4:11; 1 Cor 15:10) and those of believers in his congregations (1 Cor 15:58; Gal 3:4).

At Phil 2:16 ongoing involvement in the gospel is at issue, with the outcome seen only at the last Day. Hence, hold fast to the word (2:16a; 1 Cor 15:2). Apostle and congregations interrelate (Bjerkelund 1977:187), in eschatological earnestness. What such endeavor meant to Paul, Spicq sums up thus: manual labor, fatigue in missionary journeyings, blows and suffering, insults and humiliations, difficulties in exercising his apostleship, sermons and letters, and "the care of all the churches" and their varied members; "no Christian life, no apostolic ministry, without rough, persevering labors" (*TLNT* 2:329). Paul neither peddled nor expected "cheap grace" (Merk 1968:186). In this context of eschatological salvation (2:12e) and proper boasting at the judgment over mission work, what Paul says about his own prospects, including (possibly imminent) death (1:19–26; 2:17–18, 23–24, 30), is to be placed (Hoffmann 1966 [(4) Bibl.] 287). Paul sees things "from a long-term perspective" (I. H. Marshall 65), under God's judgment.

3. Rejoice, Mutually, in Sacrificial Service, out of Faith (2:17–18). In contrast to the impossible possibility of living the Christian life "in vain" or pursuing a missionary career "in an empty way," the opening *alla* in Gk. is in order: *But . . . I rejoice. . . .* It shoves aside any notion in v 16 that Paul's work with the congregation could result in failure (U. B. Müller 120). This (indic.) affirmation leads into the fourth impv., *rejoice, you too.* 2:17 seems a jumble of cultic-sacrifice pictures, not yet sorted out with much agreement on which sacrifices and intent (Paul a sacrificing priest, or the Philippians? as priest *and* offering? or faith at work in life?).

---

[18] Paul went up to Jerusalem to lay out before leaders there the gospel he proclaimed, "to make sure (*mē pōs*) that I was not running or had run in vain" (NRSV). For Paul "running (in vain)" concerns the authentic word and experience of revelation as well as God's final eschatological judgment.

Paul resumes the theme of joy (1:18; 2:5, 17). Does *being poured out* (2:17a) hark back to discussion of life or death for himself, 1:20–26? Or the theme of "suffering" (1:29)? For Bloomquist, 126–27, 168–72, suffering emerges as problematic in 2:12–18. All in all, 2:17–18 caps 1:27 and the following paraenesis, with reminiscences of the *agōn* (struggle, 1:30 and passim) *and* awareness of the gospel's gifts for the present moment. *Salvation* is to "find expression in the communal life of the group," Philippian "house fellowships" (I. H. Marshall 66).

Vv 17–18 have been put together in various ways. See NOTE on 17a for *even if I am being poured out like a libation* (so NRSV) as a correct premise about Paul's longtime apostolic, missionary experience, giving of himself (2 Cor 4:8–12; Rom 12:2), not just possible martryrdom to come (so RSV).[19] Various OT or pagan sacrifices have been claimed as background.[20] One cannot be dogmatic about who is sacrificing what, when and where (*epi*, "on," "over," "in addition to," "together with"?). Paul uses general terms, capable of varied interpretations, at the Temple in Jerusalem, temples in Philippi, or in house or family libations. The connotations of *leitourgia* in the Greco-Roman world (see NOTE on 2:17 *service*) may provide a surer starting point: civic duties *(munera)*, services in the *polis* (town; *municipium*, see NOTE on *service*). That would strike home to the Philippians. Hence, for the hendiadys in Gk., *sacrificial service*, Strack 1994:304–7 sees cultic language in the service of "Gospel/Community" and "faith," as proper "engaging in citizenship" and contesting for the gospel-faith (1:27).[21]

faith is the final Gordian knot to be loosed in the v. The Philippians' *pistis* is involved. Their faith—what they believe (exemplified in 2:6–11) and how they believe (continuingly, Paul urges)—is the source of *sacrificial service* by the Philippians. "The sacrifice" and the service may even consist "of their faith" (I. H. Marshall 65). At this Paul rejoices. It matters for their well-being (he adds, *I feel joy with you all*) and toward his own confidence at the Day of Christ. He has seen an example of it in their encomium as well as in their support for him: prayers, gifts, and their steadfast stance in Philippi against opponents.

The 1st per. sg. in vv 16–17 is not a sign of Paul's ego (as Fortna 1990 alleged). Quite apart from rhetorical aspects ("I/you [pl.]" relationships), the vv are appropriate expression of passionate involvement, concern for the Philippians (on

---

[19] Cf. Michaelis 48, Denis 1958:630–45; Collange; T. W. Manson 1939 (INTRO. VII.A): 151–52; Roloff 1965:114–15 "priestly service."

[20] Fee, "metaphors drawn directly from the sacrificial system of the OT," Paul a Levitical priest and himself the "drink offering" of Num 28:7, though what sacrifice is meant re the Philippians is less clear (p. 254 "equally uncertain"), particularly when Paul's addition "and service" *(kai leitourgia[i])* is factored in. Others: the OT cereal offering; an *"act* of sacrifice" (the Philippians then as sacrificing priests). Then how will Paul's libation sacrifice relate to or "crown" that of the Philippians, and whose "account" gets credit for what (Bruce, *Phil.* 1989:88–89)? Vincent 72, "heathen rather than Jewish sacrificial usage," something familiar in Philippians, far away from Jerusalem cult. The NOTES explore usage of *spendomai, thysia*, and esp. *leitourgia* in the Hellenistic world and the "spiritualized" sense given to such terms in some Jewish and Greco-Roman sources (E. Ferguson 1980).

[21] Ware 1996:317 holds that the weight of 2:17 "falls not upon Paul's offering, but the sacrifice and service of the Philippians." But even with 4:18, this scarcely makes the Philippians "a community of priests," with "a *mediatorial* role of Israel for the *gentiles*," as Ware goes on to claim (1996:318).

whom so many of his hopes rest), as well as a step toward "I" statements that follow (2:19, 24, 25).

From this intense feeling of joy, united in a common struggle together with believers in Philippi, Paul concludes (v 18), *In the same way* (as I rejoice), *rejoice, you too, and rejoice together with me,* the fourth and concluding impv. of 2:12–18. The words of the messenger who brought news to Athens after the victory at Marathon in 490 B.C. have often been cited, "Rejoice, we too rejoice." *Inclusio* possibilities for joy go back to 1:18 and 1:4. Holloway 2001a:126 sees "a turning point in the rhetoric of the letter": rejoicing, implied before, is now explicitly urged (2:18, 28–29; 3:1; 4:4), even as they struggle (Walter 67; 1977: 342). Hopes are high for the Philippians' exercising their citizenship as children of God and inhabitants of a Roman colonia.

4. 2:12–18 *Within the Combined, Canonical Letter.* Once Letters C (Phil 3) and A (4:10–20) were added to Letter B, 2:12–18 lost their significance as decisive conclusion of the chief paraenetic section in B. The vv were obscured when a long polemical section (3:1–21) and the "thankless thanks" (4:10–20) reshaped the four-ch. letter. Exegesis paid attention to what preceded 2:6–11 in 2:1–4; less so for 2:12–18.[22] Themes in 2:12–18 (obedience, boasting, Day of Christ, and rejoicing) could be found elsewhere in the letter. The emphasis on God (2:13) paled beside the "Christ hymn." The paradoxical vv 12–13, curious use of the OT in 15, and, for some, priestly sacrifice in 17, became the isolated areas of interest.

Addition of ch. 3 directed exegesis of 2:12–18 toward the opponents depicted there, rather than opposition in Philippi mentioned in Letter B,[23] even as the overall effect was to minimize the import of the concluding paraensis in 1:27–2:18.

2:12–18 has seldom been assigned in lectionaries (for Lent IV, Laetare, in *Perikopenbuch* Series III). The paradoxical 2:12–13 has attracted greatest interest doctrinally: "[W]orke your salvation" (Rheims 1582) seems Roman Catholic; "For it is God who worketh in you" (Geneva 1560, + 12e "(so) make an end of your owne salvation"), Protestant. Cf. Calvin 69; K. Barth 72, 73; Fitzmyer, *NJBC* 82:71; A. T. Robertson 1917:145–46; Thielman 1995:146–49.

SELECT BIBLIOGRAPHY (see also General Bibliography and Commentaries)

Balz, H. 1969. "Furcht vor Gott? Überlegungen zu einem vergessenen Motiv biblischer Theologie," *EvT* 29:626–44.

Baumert, N. 1979. "'Wirket euer Heil mit Furcht und Zittern' (Phil 2,12f.)" *GuL* 52:1–9,

---

[22] Even though some called it "commentary" on the "hymn" (Loh.). Martin 1967 has many more references to 2:1–5 than to vv 12–18 (only 3x in the index, all for v 12).

[23] W. Schmithals saw in 2:12e, "fear and trembling," a warning against the false security of those who felt they had already attained perfection (3:12–14); in the *complaints and wranglings* of 2:14, dissension brought about by those false teachers (1972:98 and 74, respectively). Cf. Hawth. 102 on 2:15 (Israel) and 3:2, there is "every reason for the church to divorce itself from Israel, from Judaism"; Collange 112.

repr. in his *Studien zu den Paulusbriefen*, SBAB 32 (Stuttgart: Katholisches Bibelwerk, 2001) 100–8.

Bjerkelund, C. J. 1977. "'Vergeblich' als Missionsergebnis bei Paulus," in FS N. Dahl (Gen. Bibl., under "Sampley, J. P.") 175–91.

Bornkamm, G. 1946. "Der Lohngedanke im Neuen Testament," *EvT* 6:143ff., repr. in, cited from his GS, Band II, *Studien zu Antike und Urchristentum*, BEvT 28 (Munich: Kaiser, 1963) 69–92, esp. 90–92.

Burn, J. H. 1922–23. "Philippians ii.12," *ExpTim* 34:562.

Clark, K. W. 1935. "The Meaning of *energeō* and *katergeō* in the New Testament," *JBL* 54:93–101.

Cook, D. 1982. "2 Timothy IV.6–8 and the Epistle to the Philippians," *JTS* 33:168–71.

Corriveau, R. 1970. *The Liturgy of Life: A Study of the Ethical Thought of St. Paul in His Letters to the Early Christian Communities*, Studia Travaux de recherche 25 (Bruxelles/Paris: Desclée de Brouwer/Montreal: Les Éditions Bellarmin) 111–17.

Deidun, T. J. 1981. *New Covenant Morality in Paul*, AnBib 89 (Rome: Biblical Institute) 63–69.

Denis, A. M. 1957a. "Versé en libation (*Phil.* II,17) =Versé en son sang? A propos d'une réference de W. Bauer," *RSR* 45:567–70.

———. 1957b. "L'Apotre Paul, Prophete 'Messianique' des Gentils," *ETL* 33:245–318.

———. 1958. "La fonction apostolique et la liturgie nouvelle en Esprit. Étude thématique des métaphores pauliniennes du culte nouveau," *RSPT* 42:401–36, 617–56.

Derrett, J. D. M. 1985. "Running in Paul: The Midrashic Potential of Hab 2:2," *Bib* 66:560–67.

Didier, G. 1955. "Le Salaire du Désintéressement (I Cor. ix, 14–27," *RSR* 43, repr. In *Désintéressement du chrétien. La rétribution dans la morale de Saint Paul.* Théologie 32. Paris: Aubier.

Eckert, J. 1991. "'Mit Furcht und Zittern wirkt euer Heil!' (Phil 2,12). Zur Furcht vor Gott als christlicher Grundhaltung," in *Die Freude an Gott—unsere Kraft*, FS O. B. Knoch, ed. J. J. Degenhardt (Stuttgart: KBW) 262–70.

Ferguson, E. 1980. "Spiritual Sacrifice in Early Christianity and its Environment," *ANRW* 2.23.2:1151–89.

Finlayson, S. K. 1965–66. "Lights, Stars or Beacons," *ExpTim* 77:181.

Giesen, H. 1988. "'Furcht und Zittern'—vor Gott? Zu Philipper 2.12," *Theologie der Gegenwart* 31:86–94.

Glombitza, O. 1959–60. "Mit Furcht und Zittern. Zum Verständnis von Philip. II,12," *NovT* 3:100–6.

Harnack, A. von. 1928b. "*Kopos (Kopian, hoi Kopiōntes)* im frühchristlichen Sprachgebrauch," ZNW 27:1–10

Marshall, I. H. 1969. *Kept by the Power of God* (London: Epworth) 122–25.

Mattern, L. 1966. *Das Verständnis des Gerichtes bei Paulus*, ATANT 47 (Zürich: Zwingli) 186–92.

Michael, J. H. 1924b. "'Work Out Your Own Salvation.'" *Expositor*, 9th Series, 12:439–50.

Newton, M. 1985. *The Concept of Purity at Qumran and in the Letters of Paul*, SNTSMS 53 (Cambridge: Cambridge Univ. Press) 60–75.

Osten-Sacken, P, von der. 1983. "Heil für die Juden—auch ohne Christus?" in *"Wenn nicht jetzt, wann dann?"* FS H.-J. Kraus, ed. H.-G. Geyer et al. (Neukirchen-Vluyn: Neukirchener Verlag) 169–82.

Pedersen, S. 1978. "'Mit Furcht und Zittern' (Phil. 2,12–13)," *ST* 32:1–31.

Poythress, V. S. 2002. "'Hold Fast' versus 'Hold Out' in Philippians 2:16," *WTJ* 64:45–53.

Radl, W. 1987. "Kult und Evangelium bei Paulus," *BZ* 31:58–75.

Schelkle, K.-H. 1956. "Der Apostel als Priester," *TQ* 136:257–83.

Thomson, P. 1922–23. "Philippians ii.12," *ExpTim* 34:429: an article by "P" in *The Journal of Classical and Sacred Philology* 2 (1855) took *meta . . . tromou* with *hypēkousate*.

Ware, J. 1998. "'Holding Forth the Word of Life' (Phil 2:16a): Paul's Mission through the Philippians," *AARSBL Abstracts 1998*, S59, pp. 248–49. 1996 Diss., see Gen. Bibl.

Weber, B. 1996. "Philipper 2,12–13. Text – Kontext – Intertext," *BN* 85: 31–37.

9. *Travel Plans for Mission and Some Paranesis*, 2:19–30

TRANSLATION

2:19a But I do expect, in the Lord Jesus, to send you Timothy soon, 19b in order that I too may gain encouragement as I come to know events affecting you. 20 For no one do I have available of like "soul," who will genuinely care for what affects you. 21 For they all seek after their own interests, not those of Jesus Christ. 22 But Timothy's proven character you know, because, as a child in relation to a father, together with me he has slaved for the gospel. 23a This man therefore I expect to send 23b whenever I shall see what results for me; this, on the one hand, at that very moment. 24 On the other hand, I am confident in the Lord that I too will soon come myself.

25a But I do consider it necessary in regard to Epaphroditus — 25b who is brother and fellow worker and fellow soldier of mine, 25c and your "apostle" and public servant for my need — 25d to send him to you, 26 since there he was, longing for you all and very troubled because you had heard that he was ill. 27a For he was indeed ill, close to death. 27b But God showed mercy on him — not just on him but also on me, so that I might not have sorrow in addition to sorrow.

28 Accordingly I am all the more eagerly sending him in order that you, upon seeing him, again may rejoice and I too be the more without sorrow. 29a Give him a continuing welcome, therefore, in the Lord with all joy, 29b and such persons hold in honor, 30a because, for the sake of work for Christ, he came close to dying, 30b having risked his life 30c in order that he might fill up what was lacking in your service towards me.

NOTES

2:19a, *But I do expect, in the Lord Jesus, to send you Timothy soon. . . . de*, a new beginning (Holmstrand 113), in contrast to 2:17 *poured out as a libation*, linked

with 1:12 *events affecting me* (Lft. 120; continuative, *DA* 327, 328). [N]RSV omit
de. "Sentence-initial" *elpizō* signals discontinuity (*DA* 118 n 187); see Note on
1:20 *hope*; here (BDAG 2) a secular not a theological sense (*TLNT* 1:482), as in
travel plans (1 Cor 16:7; Rom 15:24; Phlm 22). Yet + *in the Lord Jesus*; see Notes
on 1:1 *in Christ Jesus* and 1:2 *Lord*. "*Christ* Jesus" in Western uncials D* F G etc.
In *Kyrios Iēsous*, Fee hears an echo of 2:9–11 (262 n 9). LB and GNB, "If the Lord
is willing" (no MS evidence for omitting "Jesus"), equate *en kyriō[i] Iēsou* with
1 Cor 4:19, 16:7, *ean ho kyrios thelēsē[i]* (O'B 317), which Paul does *not* use here
(Fee 264 n 18). The phrase stands over all Paul says in v 19, for the sphere of lordship in which life functions. Schenk 228 parallels *elpizō* (2:19, 23) with *pepoitha
de en kyriō[i]* in v 24, confidence through "a living connection with the Lord
Jesus" (Gnilka 157). *in the Lord (Jesus)* provides an *inclusio*, 2:19–24. In this "contextual synonymy" (Silva 157–58) *elpizō* = "I expect. . . ." On *Timothy*, see 1:1.
Aor. infin. *pempsai* (BDAG *pempō* 1, *send* persons; K. H. Rengstorf, *TDNT* 1:398–
406; D. Müller, *NIDNTT* 1:126–28; cf. *DA* 222–23 n 254) recurs at 2:23 and 2:25
(of Epaphroditus). Paul prefers the aor. for such sending (*DA* 391; 1 Thess 3:2,5,
etc.; H. Ritt, *EDNT* 3:68). Adv. *tacheōs* (BDAG 2.a; + *pempein* at Plut. *Mor.* 612E)
= *soon*. Dat. *hymin* (not *pros* + acc. v 25) = the Philippians.

2:19b. *in order that I too may gain encouragement as I come to know events affecting you*. Purpose, *hina* (*DA* 325, cf. 411). *I too* (*kagō = kai egō*) hints the Philippians also will benefit from Timothy's coming (Ware 1996:195 n 63; Silva 156,
"the main motive"), something the Philippians requested (Meyer 98 n 1). That
assumes (cf. Fee 264–65 nn 23, 24) the Philippians need strengthening by an apostolic team member. Paul's stated purpose: that he *may gain encouragement*.
eupsycheō, **be glad, have courage** (MS A ineptly, *ekpsychō* = expire), here only in
the NT; rare but in letters of condolence ("Take heart!" *TLNT* 2:155–56) and sepulchral inscriptions (Loh. 115 n 2; POxy 1.115.2, instead of *chairein*), with *alypē*
(cf. 2:28 below; "now free from anxiety, be glad"). BGU 1097.15, "in good spirits."
A father to his son, "Write me soon *(tacheōs)* so that I may rejoice *(hina eupsychō)*"
(POxy 2860.17). *TLNT* 2:156: a military sense, "courageously" (Ware 1996:195
n 63, "take courage," amid dangers, Thuc. 6.69, 2.87, with *andria*; 2 Macc 14:18;
4 Macc 6:11, 9:23, etc.; Pollux 3.135–6); civic sense, "generosity." Schenk 229,
synonym for *chairō* (2:18; 29 *chara*), Paul "cheered" [N]RSV; "heartened") as he
comes *to know events affecting* the Philippians. Aor. ptc. *gnous* (BDAG *ginōskō*
1.a; cf. 2.a **learn**), ingressive (EGT 444; O'B 318); temporal, or even causal
(*DA* 345). On *ta peri hymōn* see Note on 1:12 *events affecting me* and 1:27 *news
about you* (same Gk. phrase); your circumstances, situation (*DA* 330; Loh. 115–
16; Schenk 234; Fee 265 "your affairs," treated in 1:27–2:18, therefore under the
theme *politeuesthe,*1:27, Schenk 229). On envoys returning messages as well as
taking them and providing "personal attestation" of what they have seen, cf.
DA 223 (n 257, papyrus letters); M. M. Mitchell 1992:653–54. But not "ambassadorial language," as at 2 Cor 2:20–21 (Bash 119–22).

2:20. *For no one do I have available of like "soul"*. . . . *gar* (as at 2:13) explains
why Timothy will be sent (*DA* 330, "explanatory"). *no one (oudena)* signals a problem (amplified in v 21) and the uniqueness of Timothy. Of those at hand (*echō*

BDAG 1.c, "have at one's disposal," not all those whom Paul knows), only Timothy is "of equal or like soul" (*isopsychos, on,* adj., masc. acc. sg.). Only here in the NT; 1x in the LXX (Ps 54:14 *anthrōpe isopsyche,* "O man like-minded"; NRSV 55:13 "my equal"). For *isos* see NOTE on 2:6c *to be like God; psychos,* 1:27d with one *soul (psychē).* Wordplay (Loh. 116; Schenk 233) on *eupsychō* in 2:19 ("well-souled, like-souled"; perhaps "gain encouragement, of equal courage") and 2:2c "together in soul" (*sympsychoi).* Joüon 1938:302, Syr. = "like my soul, like me"; Vg *tam unianimem,* Rheims NT 1582 "so of one minde." Fridrichsen 1938b, a term of social equality, cf. Ps 54:14, Aschyl. *Ag.* 1471. Jewett 1971a:348–52, "a socially collective sense" in Phil 1:27; 2:2, 19, and 20, perhaps a Philippian usage; for birth and existence in the new aeon. P. Christou (later Byzantine evidence), "courage, confidence"; "confidant" (to Paul). Fee 265 n 27 finds little favorable response to these proposals. Krentz 2003:361, "alter-ego." Normally the *iso-*part of the compound governs, here the second element does (BDF 118[1] and 120[1]). E. Schweizer (*TDNT* 9:666), in 2:19 and 20 "an echo" of "the inner man and his experience," one's "spiritual state," i.e., "courage and strength." Whether someone equal to or like *Paul* (NEB-txt "who sees things as I do"), like *Timothy* ([N]RSV, the usual view), or like *the Philippians* (Fridrichsen; Jewett) is debated (O'B 318 nn 13–15). Too compressed (Caird 128) to decide (Hawth. 110; Walter 68). Context suggests affinity to Paul and to the Philippians; v 21, Timothy is a nonpareil.

who will genuinely care about what affects you. hostis (= *hos*) for "a characteristic quality by which a preceding statement is to be confirmed" (BDAG *hostis* 2.b, cf. 3; BDF #379), "who, to be sure, by his very nature . . ." (Rom 16:4, 6, 7, 12). *merimnaō* (BDAG 2 **attend to,** *care for, be concerned about,* also at 4:6). What he will do when he arrives in Philippi, fut. sense (with Fee 266 n 30, against Silva 158, O'B 319–20, and NEB/REB, NIV; so DA 348). Dir. obj. *ta peri hymōn,* same phrase as in 19b, "your affairs" (Moule *IB* 63). Hawth. 110, citing *The Cynic Epistles* ([14] COMMENT A.3 n 15) 282 line 11 and 2 Cor 11:28 (*merimna* for all the churches), suggests "concern for the welfare of others"; cf. 2:13 *eudokia,* "goodwill." Parallels and contrasts with *zētein* in v 21 ("strive for," Bultmann *TDNT* 4:591 n 14, 592). Some appeal to Synoptic usage (O'B 319; Gnilka 158): Timothy is no Martha, "anxious" about many things (Luke 11:41); Q (Luke 12:22, 25, 26 par Matt 6:25, 27, 28, 31; [*epi*]*zētein* 12:29, 30 [Matt 6:22]) suggested to Schenk 231–32 Pauline development of Jesus' logion (≠ means not equal to, does not seek):

Q- *merimnan*	*tēn basileian*	*zētein* ≠ *psychē/sōma.*
to care about	the kingdom	to seek ≠ life/body.

Paul- *merimnan ta peri hymōn* = *ta Christou Iēsou* = *zētein ta heautōn*
to care about what affects you = the things of Christ Jesus ≠ to seek your own concerns

1 Cor 7:32, 34 *zētein ta Christou Iēsou* = *merimnan ta tou kyriou;* "seek one's own interests" (2:4), "anxious about the things of the world" (1 Cor 7:33) contrast with "care for, seek the things of the Lord/Christ Jesus." *merimnan* has an active, engaged aspect (as in 1 Cor 12:25).

gnēsiōs. Here only in the NT; adj. at 4:2; BDAG *sincerely, genuinely.* Etymologically, from *gen-esthai* (*ginomai* 1 "be born"), = "by birthright," "naturally" (KJV). Hence "spiritual parentage" (Lft. 121) or "legitimate," contrast bastard "sons" (Heb 12:8); rejected by Loh. 116 n 5; Schenk 233. Jewett 1971a:349, "a social category," citizenship; cf. (in Lft.) [Dem.] *contra Neoer* p. 1353, "citizens by nature and who share by birth in the city." From "legitimacy" developed the idea of Timothy as "the sole authorised representative of the apostle" (Collange 117; 1 Tim 1:2; Titus 1:4; Michael 114). *TLNT* 1:136–38, authentic disciple (Aristot. to Plato); a person to whom revelation is transmitted (in Isis cult). One who "efficaciously" or "effectively involves himself" (138 n 17). *genuine(ly)* covers these several aspects (so O'B, Fee; Schenk 233).

2:21. *For they all seek after their own interests, not those of Jesus Christ. gar,* continuative and explanatory, as in v 20 (*DA* 324, 330). *hoi* + masc. nom. pl., *pas* (BDAG 4.d), no noun; "all, in contrast to a part" (2 Cor 5:14b; 1 Cor 10:17; Rom 11:32 *bis*; *TDNT* 5:888). No linguistic grounds for inserting "all *the rest*" (JB) or sg. "everyone" (NAB, NIV). *zēteō* (see v 20 re *merimnan*), BAGD 2.b.α says, is here "somewhat removed fr[om] the basic m[ea]n[in]g" of "seeking"; "strive for, aim (at), desire, wish" (1 Cor 13:5); BDAG 3.b *strive for one's own advantage;* ZG 597 "be intent on." *Word studies:* H. Greeven, *TDNT* 2:892–93; H.-G. Link, *NIDNTT* 3:530–32; E. Larsson, *EDNT* 2:102–3. The conflicting dir. objects are *ta heautōn,* as at 2:4 *your own interests,* and "the (things) of Jesus Christ" (*GNTG* 3:270). Instead of *ta Iēsou Christou* (P⁴⁶ ℵ A C D etc.), B 0278 Majority Text reverse the order ("Christ Jesus," NEB/REB, CEV); MS K Cyp, simply "Christ" (Grundmann, *TDNT* 9:553 n 390, "an original *Christos*," supplemented by *Iēsous*). Let the harder reading, "Jesus Christ," prevail (Fee 262 n 11).

2:22. *But Timothy's proven character you know, because, as a child in relation to a father, together with me he has slaved for the gospel. de* contrasts Timothy with those in v 21 (Fee 268 n 37; antithesis, *DA* 137) and links 22 with 20 (Schenk 230; O'B 323; *DA* 327, 328 "continuative"). Like v 20, 22 starts with a dir. obj., *tēn de dokinēn autou. Timothy's* has been inserted for *autou,* "his." Emphasis on *proven character,* a further reason for sending him (Ewald 140–41). For *dokimē* and other terms from *dokimazein,* see NOTE on 1:10 *keep on appreciating.* Here "the quality of being approved," "(proven) character" (Rom 5:4; 2 Cor 9:13), as a result of being tested (2 Cor 2:9; 2 Cor 8:2, the "ordeal" of "the churches of Macedonia," Philippi and Thessalonica). More than Timothy's "record" (NEB/REB). Pass. suggests "what is approved," namely, his worth (GNB), faithfulness in ministry as well as faith in Christ (Grundmann, *TDNT* 2:259), his character (*TLNT* 1:360). *dokimē* came to prominence (Schenk 234; summary in *EDNT* 1:343) in controversy in Corinth as a slogan from opponents (2 Cor 13:3, demanding "proof [*dokimēn*] that Christ is speaking in" Paul); then 2:9; 8:2; 9:13; Rom 5:4, in a general sequence. Apostle, congregations (2 Cor 2:9), and Timothy all must exhibit approvedness. Timothy's character the Philippians *know* (indic., not impv. as in the Vg; R. Knox, "you must know"; but cf. *DA* 224) from the days of the founding mission (aor. in the next cl., *he has slaved;* if gnomic aor., continuing, habitual service, *DA* 224). P⁴⁶ has *oidate;* it fits Pauline style when *hoti* follows, but here + "a dir. obj. (*tēn dokimēn*), and in such cases Paul seems to prefer *ginōskō*" (Silva 159).

because, as a child in relation to a father, together with me he has slaved for the gospel. hoti recitative, "you know that" (KJV, NEB/REB; *DA* 324, 329–30), or, better, *because,* why the Philippians know about Timothy's character (NIV; Fee 262). [N]RSV and others hedge, "how . . . he has served. . . ." *as a child in relation to a father,* introduced by *hōs* (BDAG 1.b.α, indicating manner). If the vb. that follows fills out the ellipsis, *patri teknon* = "as a child serves/is enslaved to his father." *teknon* (BDAG 1.b) = "son" (cf. Luke 15:31; Rev. 12:5; *TDNT* 5:638, affectionate). See NOTE on 2:15 *children of God.* The dat. *patri* expresses relationship. Could suggest a son toiling for and with his father (Mark 6:3 par.; Caird 129), in subordination (cf. *Haustafeln,* Col 3:20; Eph 6:1), under the absolute power of the father (Roman *patria potestas*). Many invoke Paul's "spiritual fatherhood," of the community (1 Cor 4:15; G. Schrenk *TDNT* 5:1005) and of converts (1 Cor 4:17, Timothy; cf. Acts 16:1–3). So O'B 324, plus the master-disciple relationship among OT prophets (2 Kgs 2:12) and the rabbis (*b. Sanh.* 99b; Str-B 3:340–41). Further, Gutierrez; Holmberg 1978:79–81. Cf. "father–son" language in epistolary paraenesis, in the Hellenistic moralists (*DA* 173; Malherbe 1987:56–59, 73, 75; esp. 1 Thess 2:11). Paul shifts the imagery from "he was a slave to me" *(emoi)*" to "he slaved *together with me*" (*syn emoi*; BDAG *syn* 1.b, association in activity, modifying the vb., *DA* 345 and 191 n 139). Ellicott 71, *oratio variata*; ATR, intentional lack of symmetry (441, 1199). Some trs. insert *syn* into the father-son analogy (KJV-NRSV "like a son with a father"), others not (NEB/REB "working under his father"). *douleuō* (BDAG 2.c, **act or conduct oneself as one in total service to another, perform the duties of a slave, serve, obey**), not to be toned down, but in light of 1:1 (Paul, Timothy) = "worked like a slave" (Gdsp). In antiquity the slave was a "worker" (*TLNT* 1:383, n 13, derivation from Doric *dōlos* = activity). O'B 327 and others would see a reflection of *doulos* at 2:7. Work (cf. 2:25, 30) *for the gospel* (*euangelion,* 1:5; evangelism, O'B 1986: 226–27). *eis* + acc., "for its spread," not "in the gospel" (KJV/RSV; NRSV "in the work of the gospel," TC "spreading the Good News"; "preaching" it, Gdsp.; Ellicott 71; *DA* 208 n 201; 324). Paul puts Timothy on the same level with himself, with authority to use in Philippi (Loh. 117).

2:23. *This man therefore I expect to send whenever I shall see what results for me; this, on the one hand, at that very moment.* As in vv 20 and 22, initial reference to Timothy (dem. pron. *touton*; neither *men* nor *oun,* which follow, could begin a Gk. sentence). *elpizō* + aor. infin. *pempsai,* repeated from 19a. *oun,* "so, then, therefore," is "resumptive or transitional" (Moule *IB* 162–63). It resumes v 19 (O'B 325; Fee 269). Eadie 152 took *men* with *de* in v 19. But *men oun* = a transition from recommendation for Timothy to more precise travel plans. *men* thus goes with *de* in 24, "on the one hand, on the other," as at 1:15, 16–17 (*DA* 328), seldom brought out in trs. The TRANSLATION weaves it in at the end: *this* (the step involving Timothy), *on the one hand,* + *at the very moment* (Gk. *exautēs*), a term that defines *soon* in 19a. Schenk 227–28 takes the *men* cl. in v 23 concessively, re *de* in v 24 (BDR 447, 2a, note 11); in effect, "Although I expect to send Timothy . . . , I am confident . . . that I shall come soon."

2:23b. *whenever I shall see what results for me. hōs* (BDAG 8.c.α; BDF 455 [2]

[3]) + *an* (BDAG I.c.δ, *as soon as*, + subjunct.), for an event the speaker believes likely but cannot be assumed with certainty (1 Cor 11:34, Rom 15:24; *GNTG* 1:167). *aphidō*, aor. subjunct., *aph-horaō*; aspiration (*h*, rough breathing mark), though *eidon*, stem *id-*, has a smooth breathing mark (*GNTG* 2:98; ZG 597). Lit. "look away" (from the pres. to the fut.), "see ahead"; "fix one's eyes on"; **determine, see** (BDAG 2, KJV-NRSV, most tr.), then "consider, reflect on" a situation (*TLNT* 1:248). JB, "know something definite about my fate"; NJB, "make out what is going to happen to me." Dir. obj. *ta peri me* echoes 2:19b and 20; *peri* + acc.; "matters" or "circumstances" concerning me (*GNTG* 3:15 and 270), acc. of specification (DA 330); outcome of his court proceedings. *exautēs*, usually "as soon as," suggests immediate action (BDAG *at once*; Mark 6:25; Acts 10:33, etc.; only here in Paul). From *ex autēs tēs hōras*, "from the hour itself"; cf. Acts 16:18 and 33. *soon* means *at that very moment* he has news about his fate and future.

2:24. *On the other hand, I am confident in the Lord that I too will soon come myself. de* (usually rendered "but" or "and") is paired with *men* in v 23 (see above). *pepoitha*, 2nd pf., *peithō* BDAG 2.a, with pres. meaning, DA 341; "I have been persuaded, therefore I trust, am confident." JB, "I continue to trust." Participial forms at 1:6 *since I am confident*; 1:14 *having become confident in the Lord . . .* ; and 1:25 *and since I am confident of this*, with *en kyriō[i]* at 1:14; cf. on 2:19 above, *in the Lord Jesus*. Hawth. 109, deliberate change from *elpizō* in 2:19, "more certain than the expected arrival of Timothy"; Schenk 228, they are synonymous. Caird 129, not "much confidence in his own release, or he would not have needed to send Timothy." U. B. Müller, v 24 relativizes the sending of Timothy. Both expectations are "in the Lord."

hoti-recitative follows, as at 1:6, cf. 25. Fut., *erchomai* (aor. at 1:27, *come to see you*). The subject (in the vb.) is emphasized by *kai*, "too, also," + intensive pron. *autos* (ZG 597); contrast with Timothy, *kai* in addition to Timothy (DA 378, 391). *tacheōs, soon*, repeated from v 19, means (23) when Paul sees how his trial comes out. MSS ℵ* A C etc. add "to you" (*pros hymas*).

2:25. *But I do consider it necessary in regard to Epaphroditus—who is brother and fellow worker and fellow soldier of mine, and your "apostle" and public servant for my need—to send him to you. hēgeomai* (see NOTES, 2:3b *consider*; 2:6 *did not consider . . .* ; BDAG 2), aor. m. Some, a true past action, "I have thought it necessary to send you Epaphroditus" (RSV; KJV, NJB), an act already done (Rahtjen 169–70, 173). Most, = epistolary aor. (BDF 334), "I think it necessary" (NRSV, NIV, NEB); Vincent 75 (Epaphroditus carried the letter to Philippi); O'B 330; Fee 274 n 9 but "I considered . . ."; Schenk; Walter). + neut., *anagkaios, a, on*, comparative in 1:24 (BDAG 1 **necessary**) + aor. infin. *pempsai* (as at 2:19a and 23), *send to you*, at the end of the v, + *Epaphroditon* dir. obj. Instead of the dat. (*hymin* in 19a), *pros* + acc. *hymas*. Danker sees benefactor language in *anagkaion* (1982:426 and n 52). Is it "send *back*" (NIV, JB, Gdsp, LB; Schenk 235; Epaphroditus had come from Philippi)? Not *anapempsai* (Phlm 12), no *palin* (1:26; 4:4), which could suggest criticism of Epaphroditus (K. Barth 88; Gnilka 162; U. B. Müller 129; Metzner 115 n 9 denies this implication, deriving *pempsai* from *apostolos* in 25c). Absence of "back" or "again" led Bengel, Michael 122,

Martin 120, Hawth. 117, etc., to suggest Epaphroditus had been seconded to Paul "on permanent assignment," as long as Paul needed him. Contrast O'B 333 n 26; Fee 274–75 n 12. *de* connecting v 25 to 19–24 is a marker (*DA* 391; Holmstrand 114), introducing a new section through 2:30 (or 3:1, U. B. Müller 126), different from what was said about Timothy. *But* (NIV, Gdsp.), "Yet" (KJV), "Still" (NRSV), though *DA* 327, 328 sees continuity, "I feel also . . ." (NEB/REB; NAB "too"). Some omit *de* (RSV, JB). At the least, the *de* in 25 parallels *de* in 19.

2:25a. *Epaphroditus.* See M. E. Lyman, *IDB-EJ* 2:107; J. Gillman, *ABD* 2:533–34; Ollrog 28 n 119; 42, 60–61, 98–99, 192, 244; E. E. Ellis 1970–71 = 1978 ([1] Bibl.); *DPL* 182–89; H.-J. Venetz, "Stephanas, Fortunatus, Achaikus, Epaphroditus,. . . . Die Frage nach den Gemeindevertretern und Gemeindegesandten in den paulinischen Gemeinden," in *Peregrina Curiositas: Eine Reise durch den orbis antiquus*, FS Van Damme, ed. A. Kessler et al., NTOA 27 (Fribourg: Universitätsverlag/Göttingen: Vandenhoeck & Ruprecht, 1994) 13–38; Comment A.3, below, and, in B n 12, R. Harris. Mentioned in the NT only here and 4:18 (brought the Philippians' gift to Paul). A not uncommon masc. name (Lat. *Venestus*), from the goddess Aphrodite (Lat. *Venus*) (MM 230, adj.). Surname of the Roman dictator Sulla (138–78 B.C.), "favored by Venus." Krentz 2003:362, name implies fidelity to the Julian line of Emperors. Literary patron of Jos. (*Ant.* 1.8; *Life* 430; *Ap.* 1.1; 2.1, 296), perhaps Marcus Mettius Epaphroditus, a grammarian (so Thackeray, LCL *Ant.* 1–4: x–xi; *OCD*[3] 527; *KlPauly* 2:283), possibly a freedman who was secretary to Nero (*DNP* 3:1063), maybe later secretary to Domitian (*OCD*[3] 527); fancifully identified with Epaphroditus in Phil 2:25 by R. Eisenman, *James the Brother of Jesus* (New York: Viking, 1997) 791. Beare 97–98 conjectured, "Epaphroditus must have come from a Greek family devoted to her cult." Aphrodite was not prominent in Philippi (Portefaix 75–128; Bormann 1995:37–60). Upon becoming Christian, Epaphroditus did not (have to) change his name. Metzner 120 n 28, Paul in friendship regarded the name sympathetically (122). "Epaphras" could be a shortened form, but Epaphroditus is not to be identified with the Epaphras of Col 1:7; 4:12; Phlm 23 (BDF 125,1).

2:25b. *who is brother and fellow worker and fellow soldier of mine.* Three terms (from Paul's perspective) with a single art. *(ton)*; *mou* applies to all three. The Translation adds *who is* (for *ton*); *mou* is rendered *of mine*. *brother (adelphos),* regular term for "Christian" (see Notes on 1:12 and 14 *brothers and sisters*). Used of Timothy (2 Cor 1:1) and many others (chart in *DPL* 184). Ellis's semi-tech. sense (*adelphos* + art., a limited group of workers for the gospel, overlapping with *synergoi*; see Notes on 1:1 *Timothy* and 4:21 *The brothers and sisters*) is unlikely here (Fee 275 n 14; Ollrog 78 n 93). "my brother" may show personal affection for Epaphroditus (O'B 330; Bockmuehl 169–70; cf. Geoffrion 204); Metzner 122–23, the primary relationship of Paul and Epaphroditus is not "in Christ" but *philia*; *adelphos* = "(my) friend." On "brother" as a "friendship" term, cf. K. H. Schelkle, *RAC* 2:632. Would be more persuasive if *mou* attached directly to *adelphos*, or Paul employed *philos* (vb. only, 1 Cor 16:22; avoided deliberately?). To ground the relationship in *philia* overlooks what v 30 says motivated them, *work for Christ*, a point Metzner 123 recognizes when he takes *fellow worker* and *fellow soldier* to signify "for the gospel," cf. 125 (but cf., under *systratiōtēs* below, Aristot. *Eth. Nic.* 8.11. 1159b.27ff.). Paul was wary toward some aspects of Gk. friendship and patron-client relationships; see (16) COMMENT B.2.

Next, two compounds with *syn*, a characteristic of friendship-language (Fitzgerald 1996:128, 146, cf. 88; 1997: 156 n 16). Well tr. as "fellow" (Gdsp., RSV, NIV), in spite of occasional feminist objections that the Eng. word is limited to males only; *DA* 209 n 210). "Coworker" (NRSV) fits for *synergon*, but not "co-soldier." *synergos, on,* **working together with,** *helper, fellow worker,* also at Phil 4:3 for Clement and others; 1 Thess 3:2 (Timothy); 1 Cor 3:9 (Apollos); 2 Cor 8:23 (Titus); 2 Cor 1:24 (Timothy, etc.); Rom 16:3 (Priscilla and Aquila); 16:9; Phlm 1 and 24; *DPL* 184. Application to cooperation in mission work *(ergon)* is probably Paul's coinage; called by God, not simply "helpers" (Ollrog 63–72).

systratiōtēs (*nu* in *syn* assimilates to the following consonant, BDF 19), *fellow soldier* (KJV-NRSV), "comrade in arms" (NAB; cf. NJB). Of Archippus (Phlm 2). Another military/political metaphor (Phil 1:27–30; 4:1–3; Ollrog 77; Geoffrion 25, 38–42, 144). *Word family* (limited LXX use): O. Bauernfeind, *TDNT* 7:701–13; MM 613; C. Brown, *NIDNTT* 3:963–65; *EDNT* 3:314; Tellbe 2001:247–48. Considerable classical usage. Suet. *Iul.* 67; Polyaenus *Stratagems* 8.23.22; Synes. *Kingship* 13 p 126; approaches "friend" *(philos)* at Aristot. *Eth. Nic.* 8.11.1159b.27ff. Paul, it is said, used military imagery in imprisonment epistles as he looked at the Imperial Guard around him (1:13 *praitōrion;* 4:22; Fee 275). Bauernfeind 711 n 37 derived it from Paul's "zealot days" when "Hell[enistic] enthusiasts for Jewish traditions sometimes took words from Gk. military usage and . . . applied them to themselves" (cf. 2 Cor 11:2, "zeal for God"; M. Hengel 1988 [(12) Bibl.] 180); forced. To see *systratiōtēs* as one who bears the sufferings of the office of apostolic *synergos,* indeed martyrdom (Loh. 119), or for a leader in the congregation is unlikely (Pfitzner 161). Here from struggles at the founding of the church in Philippi, not just recent experiences (Ollreg 223 n 3; Chapple 1984:576; contrast B. Mayer 1987:179 n 15).

2:25c. *and your "apostle" and public servant for my need.* Two Philippian designations, marked off by juxtaposition of *mou/hymōn de. apostolos,* here only in Phil; etymologically "one sent" (John 17:16), but not on a par with the Twelve in Luke-Acts or most *apostoloi* Paul mentions (1 Cor 15:7; 1 Thess 2:7, Silvanus = Silas, Timothy; 1 Cor 4:9, Apollos; 1 Cor 9:1,6, Barnabas; Rom 16:7, Andronicus, Junia). Cf. *DPL* 47–50; *EDNT* 1:142–46; J. Roloff, *TRE* 3:463; Ollrog 80, 95–108. = an individual (2:25) or group sent by a congregation, for designated task(s), often in mission (2 Cor 8:23), like the collection project (Roloff 1965:13, 39, 209, passim). BDAG 1, *delegate, envoy, messenger* (KJV-NRSV, NIV); "representative" ([N]JB); NAB, "whom you sent." To say Epaphroditus was "equally an 'apostle' with Paul" (Martin 1976:116–17) goes too far (Silva 161); better, "commissioned and sent out with full authority to perform specific tasks of service" (117); Collange 120, "commissioned" with "delegated powers." *Apostoloi* as (a) "missionizing preachers" like Paul and (b) "representatives of the congregation appointed to special tasks" like Epaphroditus "are to be distinguished, but not basically separated" (J.-A. Bühner, *EDNT* 1:145). Brockhaus ([1] Bibl.) 115–16, "partly charismatic." J. E. Young, a category of "apostles," broader than the Twelve, those who plant and build up churches. F. Hahn 1974:54–77, esp. 56, 60–61, distinguished "apostles of the risen Christ," empowered at a Christophany of the risen Lord; the "charismatic apostle" empowered by the Spirit (2 Cor. 11–12); and Gemeinde-*apostoloi* (e.g., 2 Cor 8:23; "apostles of the churches," p. 56), akin to synagogue practice, appointing delegates to take money collected to Jerusalem. Cf. *EC* 1:107–9; *RGG*⁴ 1:637. The TRANSLATION transliterates, *"apostle"* in quotation marks (not Paul's usual usage).

leitourgos. See NOTE on 2:17 *service,* cf. 2:30 *leitourgia.* Well-known from Gk. civic life, **one engaged in personal service, aid, assistant** (BDAG 2). Background from civic officials (Rom 13:6), not cultic priests (BDAG 1.a, not b; cf. 2:17). ZG 598, "holding an official appointment, religious or secular, *public servant* (in the sense of civil 'servant'), *delegated assistant.*" Peterlin 187–202 began with a "priestly" sense, but then accepts "the secular use of *leitourgia* terminology" from which interpretation of the passage must begin (201–2). Liturgies "were one of the pillars of the economic (and political) life of every polis" (198). On the institution's evolution, see above on 2:18. The sense of "service" continued; "work for [*not of*] the people — service to the state — service to the divinity" (R. L. Fox, *Pagans and Christians* [Harmondsworth: Penguin, 1988] 55). Cf. F. Oertel, *Die Liturgie: Studien zur Ptolemäischen und Kaiserlichen Verwaltung Ägyptens* (Leipzig: Teubner, 1917). The original sense ("'office or service in a political or administrative unit'") continued in "74% of occurrences ... in the Roman period," N. Lewis, "Leitourgia Papyri Documents on Compulsory Public Service in Egypt Under Roman Rule," *TAPA* n.s. 53 (1963) 1–39. Peterlin sketches how this sometimes burdensome office worked out, often among "three or four main families" in a place, military veterans usually exempt from the task of "expending my resources for your enjoyment." It implied "relatively high social status and favorable economic standing in the community" (200). Money collected for Paul fell short of what was needed (because of opposition from Euodia or Syntyche? so 221–23); Epaphroditus likely made up the difference and paid his own travel expenses (203–5, 224). Metzner 127 makes *leitourgos* and (v 30b) *leitourgia* cultic and an aspect of friendship, but the terms do not seem *"philia* vocabulary."

Thus a term out of public life for ecclesial purposes and functions (Vincent 76; against U. B. Müller's cultic emphases, 129, cf. Schenk 237–38; Bockmuehl 170; J. N. Collins [(1) Bibl. **agent**] 219–20), *public servant.* Fee wonders (276 n 19) "how Collange [120] could have persuaded himself of a pagan background to the usage here," rather than an LXX sense from priests and Levites (cf. Newton 1985 [(8) Bibl.] 61, 63, 65–66); it's a Philippian term, *"your* leitourgos" (cf. O'B 332). + gen. of *chreia* (BDAG 2, **need, lack, want, difficulty**), object of the serving involved, the financial gift for Paul's need (4:16, cf. 19; not "request," Sampley 1980:54–55; cf. Peterman 1997:124–27, 135). Hendiadys (2:17 *sacrificial service*) here (NEB; Caird 129; Bruce 74; O'B 331) has little to commend it. Further, Danker 1982:330–31.

2:26. *since there he was, longing for you all and very troubled because you had heard that he was ill. epeidē,* "since, because" (1 Cor 1:22; 14:16; 1 Cor 1:21;

15:21). *ēn*, imperf., *eimi*, + pres. ptcs. masc. nom. sg., *epipotheō*, **long for, desire,** and *adēmoneō*, **be in anxiety, distressed, troubled,** periphrastic equivalent of the imperf. (*GNTG* 2:452), he "was-longing," [N]RSV. NIV, "he longs" = epistolary aor. in effect, a dubious step (Fee 277 n 22). The alternative: the ptcs. are adjectival (Gal 1:22, 23; *GNTG* 1:227; O'B 334 n 31), "he-was longing"; hardly an Aramaism, *pace* Loh. 119 n 3. To express this in Eng., anticipatory *there* has been added. For *epipotheō* see NOTE on 1:8 *I long for*; + *pantas hymas*; *you all,* all the believers in Philippi. Longing fits the "friendship" theme (*DA* 171). ℵ* A C D etc. add "to see *(idein)* you all"; J. D. Price 279–80; cf. Rom 1:11; 1 Thess 3:6; and 2 Tim 1:4. {C} level of certainty without *idein* (*TCGNT* 613–14); cf. Phil 1:8. *idein* is secondary (Silva 162; Fee 271 n 1, 277 n 26). P⁴⁶, "desiring to send to you *(pempsai pros hymas),*" reflects carelessness by the copyist.

very troubled. Mark 14:33, Jesus in Gethsemane ("distressed and *agitated*"; par Matt 26:37, "grieved and *agitated*"). Sometimes derived from *dēmos* + *alpha* privative, "not at home, away from home," therefore "beside oneself" (Photius; Ewald 143 n 2; Haupt 111 n 1). Lft. 123 and others accepted "the older derivation, *adēmon, adēsai,*" loathing, discontent, restlessness (Hesychius, *Etymologicum Magnum*; ultimately from *adeō*, "be sated"). Debate continues. The first emphasizes "homesickness" (LB; Barclay; Plummer 61; Martin 1976:121; Loh/Nida 82; Hawth. 117; Schenk 236; Walter 70). Strange to early Christianity (Loh. 119, but cf. Schenk 236 n 55); Fee 277 n 22, "bad psychologizing." Homesickness could lead to illness (J. Ernst 87) and depression (B. Mayer 1986:45). The second approach (Gethsemane) saw a "confused, restless, half-distracted state which is produced by physical derangement or mental stress" (Lft. 123, cf. Dion. Hal., *Ant. Rom.* 1.56); "torn by fear" (Loh. 119 n 4); "a nervous disorder" (Martin 1976: 121). Fee 277 n 24, "pure psychologizing"; "longs . . . and is distressed" = a condition going on for some time, now a factor in Epaphroditus' return. Expositors conjecture anguish as a leader in the Philippian church (he regrets not being there when local persecution has broken out, Loh. 119; U. B. Müller 129); Epaphroditus abandoned the service he was to provide for Paul (Ewald 143, cf. 23 n 1, cf. Bonnard 57); K. Barth 87 parallels John Mark's desertion of Paul, Acts 15:37, cf. 13:13 — all termed by Gnilka 161–62 sheer "fantasy." Bockmuehl 171, not shock but his "perceived inability to change a state of affairs." Frustration? But what affairs?

because you had heard that he was ill. because (*dioti = dia touto hoti*; 1 Thess 2:8; 4:6; etc.) the Philippians have heard (*ēkousate*, aor.), in the exchange of information, that (*hoti* recitative) Epaphroditus was ill (*ēsthenēsen*). *astheneō* (lit., "be weak," BDAG 1, **suffer a debilitating illness, be sick**), also at 2:27a; *asthen-*terms (*alpha* privative + *sthenos* = strength, therefore, "powerless, weak"), 83x in the NT, 49x in the Pauline corpus, esp. 1 and 2 Cor and Rom. Common in classical usage, esp. for "bodily weakness, illness"; LXX, frequent and varied uses, but not for physical illness (unless Ps 6:3 [NRSV 6:2 "languishing"]). In the gospels, common for sickness (Mark 6:56; John 4:46); in Paul here and 1 Cor 11:30 (with eschatological overtones of judgment). *Word studies:* G. Stählin, *TDNT* 1:490–93; H.-G. Link, *NIDNTT* 3:993–96; J. Zmijewski, *EDNT* 1:170–71; D. A. Black

1984, esp. 10–21, 207–14, 248–53. Issues: (1) sequence of tenses—the Philippians heard, "Epaphroditus is ill," but after an aor., *you had heard* (KJV, GNB; most render simply "you heard"); (2) when he became ill (ingressive aor., "he fell ill"): en route to Paul (Buchanan), unlikely (Metzner 124 n 35 among many); or while there, and whether he is still sickly. K. Barth 88, odd that a grown man would worry that others worried over him; but cf. the 2nd cent. A.D. papyrus letter (POxy 12.1481; Moffatt 1917), a soldier to his mother, "I was grieved when I heard that you had heard (that I was ill). For I was not seriously ill." (3) What was his illness? Something in his system from Philippi, like malaria; dangers in travel or from the authorities (Schenk 240), or persecution (Loh., Egger 64, Metzner 124; rejected by B. Mayer 1987:182 n 32, among others)?

2:27a. *For he was indeed ill, close to death. ēsthenēsen*, repeated from v 26, + *kai*, "indeed," + *gar* (explanatory, DA 324, 330; Baumert 1973:374–75, 380, "and . . . indeed"; contrast BDF 452 [3] "yes, even"). Affirms in writing the previous oral report. "For indeed" (KJV; Lft. 123; Fee 279, to persuade, as at 1 Thess 3:4; 4:10, etc.; BDF 452 [3]) explains *(gar)* and intensifies *(kai*; Loh. 120 n 1). Neut. of the adj. *paraplēsios, ia, ion* ("coming near"), used as adv. + dat. (cf. 2:15 *meson*), *close to death* (Gk. *thanatō[i]*, see NOTE on 1:20). Gen. *thantou* in ℵ² B D etc. appeals to some as the harder reading (Hawth. 114; cf. *mechri thanatou* in 2:30), but does not alter the sense. KJV "nigh unto death," rejected already by Vincent 76 for "in a way resembling death." *ho plēsion* = neighbor, + *para*, "alongside"; Wuest, *Phil* 84, Epaphroditus and death were next-door neighbors.

2:27b. *But God showed mercy on him—not just on him but also on me, so that I might not have sorrow in addition to sorrow. But* = *alla*, strong contrastive conj. (DA 328; 2:3, 7, 12, 17). Aor., *eleeō*, here only in Phil, 14x in the Pauline corpus, 9 of these in Rom. *Word family* (77 NT examples): R. Bultmann, *TDNT* 2:477–87; H.-G. Link, *NIDNTT* 2:594–98; F. Staudinger, *EDNT* 1:428–31; *TLNT* 1:471–79. In classic Gk., "pity," for someone not deserving misfortune (Aristot. *Poet.* 13.1453a 4; *Rhet.* 2.8.1385b 13–14). In "the administration of justice," one sought "to arouse the *eleos* of the judge" (*TDNT* 2:478). Stoics regarded such emotion as a sickness of soul, *pathos* or a form of *lypē* ("sorrow," see end of 2:27); for the sage, gentleness (*epieikeia*, cf. 4:5) yes, *eleos* no. Judge 1986, tensions persisted between pity and justice; in a 4th-cent. A.D. letter (POxy 1.120.16), "God will pity us" *(ho theos hēmas eleēsē[i])* is perhaps sarcastic rejection of divine pity. Otherwise in the OT: *eleos*-words 400x in the LXX, esp. for Heb. *ḥesed*, vb. *ḥānan* (noun *ḥēn*), "(show) mercy, lovingkindness, 'grace'"; cf. *charis* (Phil 1:2), *splagchna* and *oiktirmoi* (2:1). *eleos/eleein* is an attribute of God, shown in (saving) benefactions to Israel. Limited use in Paul is surprising (perhaps not, given connotations of *eleos* in the Greco-Roman world). Mainly Rom 9, 11, and 15, with a salvation-historical, eschatological sense, esp. in OT quotations (e.g., 9:15 = Exod 33:19; 9:17 = Exod 9:16; 11:30–32; 15:9). Cf. Gal 6:1; Rom 12:8, in light of 12:1. Paul "received mercy from the Lord" (1 Cor 7:25; cf. 1 Tim 1:13, 16) and must pass it on (2 Cor 4:1, "apostolic pl."). That *God showed mercy* on Epaphroditus by restoration in the face of death is singular. Cf. 2 Cor 1:9–10, rescue from death in Paul's life.

Paul adds, "divine mercy *not just* (*monon*, BDAG *monos* 2.c.α) *on* Epaphroditus *but also on me*"; *ouk . . . monon alla kai* as at 1:29; *de* could be adversative (*DA* 327); usually omitted or taken as "and" (KJV-[N]RSV, NIV) because *alla* follows. God's intervention as a mercy for Paul is explained in the *hina* cl. (purpose, blurring toward result, *DA* 325). Vb. *schō*, aor. subjunct., *echō* (1:7, 23, 30; 2:2, 20); BDAG 7.a.β, **experience something, have,** of emotions, as at 1:23; cf. *lypēn schō*, 2 Cor 2:3, "have (NRSV suffer) pain." *hina mē*, "that I might not have" (KJV-RSV "lest") is often paraphrased "(so as) to spare me" (NAB, NIV, [N]JB, NEB/ REB) or recast, God "kept me from being burdened down with sorrow" (CEV). Twice *lypē* occurs, **pain of mind or spirit, grief, sorrow, affliction** (BDAG), obj. of the vb. and of the prep. *epi* (cf. *alypoteros* in v 28). Contrasts with *chara/chairō*, "joy, rejoice," 2:28, as at 2 Cor 2:3, 7; 6:10; 7:8–9. *lypē* and related terms (some LXX use) have significant Gk. background (R. Bultmann, *TDNT* 4:313–24; H. Haarbeck/H.-G. Link, *NIDNTT* 2:419–21; H. Balz, *EDNT* 2:362–64; *TLNT* 2:417–22). "You must rejoice and grieve, for you are a mortal" (Eur. *Iph. Aul.* 31–32). To live without joy or being grieved is "to live like a stone" (Plato *Gorg.* 494A). But avoid *lypē*, even in the quest for pleasure *(hēdonē)*. Philosophers discussed *lypē* as an evil ("dis-pleasure"). Holloway 2001a:128 n 129, because Paul "earlier presents himself as indifferent to things that cause grief, including death" (4:11b–13?), would "not read too much into his words here." Deepest development of the theme comes in engagement with the Corinthians (18 of 23 instances of *lypē* terms), esp. 2 Cor 7:9–11, "worldly grief" produces death, "grief or pain for God's sake" works repentance leading to salvation; "being grieved" is a step toward joy (7:9); believers are *lypoumenoi*, sorrowing but always rejoicing, 6:10; Cf. R. Bultmann, *2 Cor.* 47–50; *EDNT* 2:364. At 2:27 *lypē* contrasts with rejoicing, without characteristically Gk. or the deepest Pauline senses. Papyri examples where persons sorrow over illness and health in *TLNT* 2:418–19 n 5. Prep. *epi* + acc. (BDAG 7) = **to, in addition to** something already present, *sorrow upon sorrow*; BDF 235 (2); 208 (2), "follow without ceasing." Dat. after *epi* (Majority Text, Lft. 124) would have the same meaning (BDAG 7, *grief upon grief*, + classical parallels). *GNTG* 2:173, "multiplicative," "sorrow times sorrow."

2:28. *Accordingly I am all the more eagerly sending him. . . .* A conclusion (*oun* BDAG 1.a, **so, therefore, consequently accordingly, then**), resuming the thought of v 25, BDF 451(1). *I am sending . . .* Epaphroditus *(epempsa auton)*, vb. at 2:19a and 23 re Timothy, epistolary aor. (*GNTG* 3:72–73; ZG 598; Schenk 241), like *hēgēsamēn* in v 25 (so most trs. and commentators; but KJV, NABRNT, "I sent"; Bonnard 57, Paul had already sent him back). *spoudaioterōs* (from *spoudaios, a, on*) is debated re (1) meaning and (2) force of the comparative ending *-terōs*. (In D* F G, *spoudaioteron* [EGT 446; Loh. 120 n 3] = Attic adv. form, BDF 102 [1].) (1) It can mean (a) *with haste*, or (b) *diligently* (Luke 7:4, 2 Tim 1:17; Titus 3:13) in line with the adj. as **eager, zealous, earnest, diligent** (2 Cor 8:17, 22 *bis*) (BDAG p. 939); "more diligently," implied "than I should have done if ye had not heard, and been disquieted by the tidings of his sickness" (Ellicott 74–75). But context may suggest (a) "more hastily than I would have done otherwise," "with greater dispatch" (Vincent); hence [N]JB, "as promptly as I can"; Hawth.

119, invoking LSJ; O'B 339; Beare 99 "somewhat prematurely." Paul apologizes for sending Epaphroditus home before he completed tasks with Paul (so Fee 280 n 38, cf. 272–73; contra Hawth. 119). Most trs. take it atemporally, to reflect eagerness on Paul's part. (2) In Hellenistic Gk., the comparative could be leveled almost to a positive or taken as a superlative (both are elative) (BDF 60, 244). Hence "very eager" (Martin 122; Collange 121), "as quickly as possible" (*TDNT* 7:566; *TLNT* 3:281 n 20; O'B 339); *GNTG* 3:30 "very zealously"; Schenk 235. Positive degree, but with an adv. added, "specially eager" (Moffatt); "particularly anxious" (Phillips). The Translation keeps the comparative (ATR 298, 665; ZG 598).

in order that you, upon seeing him, again may rejoice and I too may be the more without sorrow. hina (2:27, cf. 30), purpose. 2nd aor. pass. (deponent) subjunct., *charēte, chairō*, "rejoice, be glad" (see Notes on 1:18ab; 2:17, 18; 4:10; 1:4 *joy*). Ptc. *idontes* (act. from *eidon*, 2nd aor. of *horaō*, "see," cf. 1:27 *idōn*); circumst., in agreement with the subject of the vb. *charēte*; temporal, but not necessarily prior action (BDF 339). The effect is little changed if *idontes* is a predicative ptc. with a vb. of emotion, "that you may rejoice to see him" (*GNTG* 3:158–60). Adv. *palin* (BDAG 1.b, *again*), with the ptc., "see him again" (KJV-[N]RSV, [N]JB, NEB/REB, most trs.; Hawth. 119; Silva 162); better, with *rejoice* (NAB[RNT], GNB; Loh/Nida 84; Lft. 124; O'B 339; Fee 280 n 39, Paul puts the adv. normally before the vb.). Some omit (CEV; LB/NLT). What Paul says of himself and grief parallels the Philippians rejoicing again at their congregational apostle's recovery and return (H. Conzelmann, *TDNT* 9:369, reciprocal relationship; mutual joy characterizes friendship, Fitzgerald 1996:146). But Paul's joy (*I too = kai egō*, as at 2:19b) is nuanced. Not "I may again rejoice," implying joy at getting Epaphroditus off my hands. But "may be *alypoteros*." 1st sg. pres. subjunct., *eimi*, + pred. adj. from *alypos, on*, cf. *lypē* in v 27; *alpha* privitive, comparative degree. Lit., "not more-grieved," "without sorrow or care" (R. Bultmann, *TDNT* 4:323), a characteristic of the wise in Stoicism. This, Paul hopes to be. **free from anxiety**, BDAG p. 48, "*less anxious* (than now)," reflected in [N]RSV, NIV; "relieved of anxiety" (Hawth. 114; Silva 162) is criticized by Fee (281 n 40) for inventing "anxiety" as a lexical meaning for *lypē*. Better, "may have less sorrow" (cf. KJV, JB).

2:29. *Give him a continuing welcome, therefore, in the Lord with all joy, and such persons hold in honor. prosdechesthe*, classical Gk. "receive" someone, or "welcome" (cf. Rom 16:2). Perhaps lost sight of in *wordbook articles*: W. Grundmann, *TDNT* 2:57–58; H.-G. Link, *NIDNTT* 3:744; A. Palzkill, *EDNT* 3:162–63. But cf. Pl. *Leg.* 4.708A; Jos. *Ant.* 6.255, "receive." In KJV, RSV, GNB "receive him" may sound grudging. Moffatt, NAB, JB, NIV, NRSV went to "welcome" language. Gdsp., "a hearty Christian welcome" is a bit much. The Translation brings out the pres. tense of the impv. As in v 28, *oun* is inferential, *therefore*, here + impv. (as at 2:1–2, DA 266), "*oun*-paräneticum" (BDAG *oun* 1.b.; W. Nauck 1958:134–35). U. B. Müller 131 n 62 sees more of a consecutive sense than in v 28.

en kyriō[i] as usual with an impv.; *meta pasēs charas*, joy (1:4; 2:2; *chairō* at 1:18; 2:17, 18). *meta* + gen., circumstance attendant upon the action of the vb. (BDAG *meta* A.3.a, cf. 2:12). *all joy* (*pas* forms frequent since 1:1), "every kind of, all sorts of" joy (BAGD 1.a.β; BDAG 5). Either (W. Grundmann, *TDNT* 7:772–73) adjectivally ("with all joy," RSV; "a most hearty welcome," JB) or adverbially ("joyously," NAB). How to connect the phrases? Cf. Loh/Nida 84–85; O'B 340: *in the Lord* can go with (1) the vb., "Welcome him as the Lord would welcome him"; but Rom 15:7 is not quite analogous. *en kyriō[i]* + the impv. = "in the sphere of Christ's lordship," not "as Christ does." (2) with *meta pasēs charas*, "Welcome him as Christians joyously welcome fellow believers"; JB, Gdsp. TC. (3) *chara* + *en kyriō[i]* = "joy that is characteristic of those in the Lord," "produced by being in union with the Lord," or "such as believers should express" (but then *en Christō[i]* might be expected). (4) + *auton* ("as a brother in the Lord," O'B 340–41; GNB) and/or with the subject of the vb., you "as fellow believers in the Lord" (NEB/REB "in the fellowship of the Lord"). Fee 282, everything believers do is "in the Lord"; cf. *TDNT* 2:541, "activity or state as a Christian. . . ." The phrase adds weight to Paul's directive, as does 29b.

and such persons hold in honor. The second impv. begins with the dir. obj. (after *kai*), as at 2:20, 22, 23; in 29ab a chiasm,

vb.   *prosdechesthe*   *auton* dir.obj.

dir. obj.   *tous toiautous*   *entimious echete* vb.

toioutos, autē, outon, here noun + art. (BDAG c.α.א; ATR 771; BDF 274) = *such a person;* pl., class or group of people; Danker 1982:101, cf. 434 n 53. Impv., pres. act., *echō* (BDAG 6), **have an opinion about someth[ing],** *consider,* **look upon, view** + pred. acc. (BDF 157 [3]). Pres. tense, "continue to hold . . ." (O'B 341). The important word is acc. masc. pl. from the adj. *entimos, on,* **honored, respected** (BDAG 1.b); noun *timē,* vb. *timaō,* "honor," *TDNT* 8:169–80 (J. Schneider); *NIDNTT* 2:48–52 (S. Aalen); H. Hübner, *EDNT* 3:357–59, nil on *entimos* (cf. *EDNT* 1:458–59). In the Gk. world, for a person's possessions; then the honor paid by society to a person in the *polis,* and increasingly the individual in his/her own right. Plato distinguished "inward *timē*" from outward honors. Artistot. *Eth. Nic.* 4.3 stressed virtue (*aretē*) and being "great of soul" (*megalopsychia,* 1123b), not striving for outward honors or objects of ambition (*ta entima*) (3.19, 27, 36). But outward honor may come for inner worth. Stoics stressed such worth, but be relaxed about external tribute. In the LXX, for a variety of Heb. words (no exact Heb. equivalent for *timaō*), esp. in later writings not in the Heb. canon. Gk. senses appear in Jos., e.g. *Ant.* 2.39, Potiphar held Joseph "in highest esteem." In the NT cf. Luke 14:8, someone "more esteemed than you," + "shame" in v 9, but "precious" at Luke 7:2 (of the centurion's servant) and 1 Pet 2:4, 6 (= Ps 118:22). In Paul, Rom 12:10, Christians "preferring one another *en timē[i]*"; 13:7, give *timē* to whom it is owed in the state; 1 Thess 4:4, *timē* re one's wife, cf. 1 Pet 3:7. On honor/shame in Gk.-Roman society with great emphasis on *timē,* see Malina 1981; Malina/Neyrey 176–82 and passim; Pilch/Malina ([4] NOTE on 1:20 *disgraced*) 95–104; (3) COMMENT B.1 n 12. Schenk 238, among others, sees 2:29 seeking to strengthen Epaphroditus' authority in the Philippian congregation; cf., near the end of other letters, 1 Cor 16:16, "be at the service of such people"; 16:18 "give such people recognition"; 1 Thess 5:12–13, "respect those who labor," "esteem *(hēgeisthai)* them." 2:29a suggests there were other leaders in Philippi, besides Epaphroditus.

2:30a. *because, for the sake of work for Christ, he came close to dying.* Causal *hoti* reiterates why the Philippians should welcome their Epaphroditus. What v 27 said, 30a repeats in different vocabulary: *he came close to dying,* aor., *engizō,* BDAG 2, **draw near, come near, approach** + *mechri,* BDAG 3, **"to the point of . . .** to note degree," + *death—*as at 2:27 *thanatos—*in the gen. here. As at 2:27, a somewhat unexpected prep. equivalent (there *paraplēsion,* here *mechri;* Diod. Sic. 15.27.2; 2 Macc 13:14; more in BDAG 644). Loh. 121 n 3 thought 2:30 a play on 2:8, "obedient *mechri thanatou"*; Fee 282 n 47, the Philippians would "have heard the echo." But Christ died; Epaphroditus didn't (B. Dodd 190). Near death *for the sake of (dia* + acc.) *work for Christ.* MS C, simply *to ergon;* Lft. 124, Loh. 121 n 1, "the work," Acts 15:38, for Christian mission; "a careless omission" (J. D. Price 280). Evidence in P⁴⁶ etc. "is overwhelming" for *Christou* (Silva 163; {C} level of support, *TCGNT* 614). Some MSS add *tou* with *Christou* (D Majority Text; Price 280 prefers it), not (Fee 271 n 3) to designate Jesus "as '*the* Christ' but to conform to standard usage" of art. with both *ergon* and *Christou* (Middleton's rule, ATR 780–81). In ℵ A etc., NRSV-mg, *tou kyriou,* influenced by 1 Cor 15:58; 16:10 (Vincent 77). The *work* in 2:30 *(ergon* BDAG 2) is the gospel task. Bockmuehl 174, part of "working out what salvation means" (2:12e, you pl.), but details in his citation from Rabbi Tarfon *(m. Abot* 2.20–21) are lacking or contradicted in 2:30, e.g., the "lazy" workmen (unless 2:21?).

2:30b. *having risked his life ᶜin order that he might fill up what was lacking in your service towards me.* Ptc. *paraboleusamenos,* aor. m., *paraboleuomai* (deponent), **expose to danger, risk,** + *tē[i] psychē[i],* dat. of respect (ZBG #53) or of relation, adverbially, for an acc. (GNTG 3:239). *psychē =* "earthly life in its external, physical aspects" (Montague 17 n 5). So the best MSS (P⁴⁶ ℵ A B D etc.; conjectured in 1600 by Scaliger before this MS evidence was known; Jonge 1975, Scaliger deserves credit in NA). A different vb., *parabouleuomai,* **be careless,** have no concern for one's life, occurs in C (which also had a singular variant in 30a) Ψ etc. Majority Text (hence KJV "not regarding his life"). UBSGNT and *TCGNT* no longer report this v.l. Was *paraboleusamenos* coined by Paul? Vbs. ending in *-euein* suggest "perform as, follow the occupation of" (BDF 108 [5]), here the adj. (used as a noun) *parabolos,* "(one who is) venturesome, risking, hazarding." Deissmann *(LAE* 88) noted a 2nd-cent. A.D. inscription from Olbia on the Black Sea (MM 480; Danker 1982:426) about a lawyer: "he had risked danger *(kindynous . . . paraboleusamenos)* for the sake of friendship in legal strife (by taking cases) up to *(mechri)* the Emperors." The vb. underlying *parabolos* is *paraballō,* "throw," give or expose oneself to danger (1 Clem 55:6). At Diod. Sic 3.36.4 hunters "hazard their lives *(paraballesthei tais psychais)"*; Poly. 2.26.3, "risk everything"; 3.94.4; Ditt. *Syll.*3 762.39 = Danker 1982:77–79, "hazard body and soul." Rienecker 209 gives patristic evidence about merchants exposing themselves to death *(heōs thanatou paraboleuontai)* for gain (V. *Alexandri Acoemetae* 5

p. 660.2) and *parabolos* for a fighter in the arena (Socr. *h.e.* 7.22.12 = Migne 67.785c, cited by Scaliger; *PGL* 1008, 1009). Vincent 77 and others cite *Parabolani* in the patristic church who disregarded dangers in visiting the sick (*ODCC* 1012–13; not in *PGL*). Lees connected *paraboleuomai* with gambling, via Aphrodite as goddess of gambling; dice-players cried out "*epaphroditos*" when hoping for a lucky throw—"favorite of Aphrodite." Paul, perhaps watching soldiers play dice at his prison, applied *paraboleusamenos* "with a smile" in wordplay on his Philippian friend's name; cf. Phlm 10,11, pun on Onesimus as "useful." Epaphroditus "gambled with his life, but won because God was there" (Lees 46; Hawth. 120; U. B. Müller 132 n 68). Appeal to *kybeia* "dice-playing" at Eph 4:14 proves little (in context there, "trickery"). Silva 163 rightly questions the proposed link of Phil 2:30 to gambling; O'B shrinks the matter to one sentence (343 n 92); Bockmuehl 174 omits it.

2:30c. *in order that he might fill up what was lacking in your service towards me. hina* (cf. 27, 28), purpose but close to result (*DA* 325). Aor. subjunct., *anaplērōsē[i]* (MS B, no prefix *ana-*); root *pleroō* (4:19, *God will fulfill every need* [*chreia*, also at 2:25] *of yours*) and 2:2 (*give me further joy*), + *ana*, "fill up." *TDNT* 6:305–6 (G. Delling); *NIDNTT* 1:733–34, 736, 738, 740–41 (R. Schippers); *EDNT* 3:108–10 (H. Hübner). Among classical uses, Plat. *Tim.* 17A = take over in place of someone who is absent; compounds, *apoplēroō* and *anaplēroun;* "do completely, pay in full" (*TDNT* 6:306; MM 37). More pertinent to the Philippians than limited LXX use of the vb. BDAG puts 2:30 under (3) ***fill a gap, replace***, with 1 Cor 16:17 (cf. Loh. 121), in Ephesus Stephanas, Fortunatus, and Achaicus "have made up for your absence." Epaphroditus made up for a lack or absence on the part of the Philippians. As in 1 Cor 16:17, "the account is balanced [Letter A, 4:10–19, financial language] representatively by members of the community that is in arrears" (*TDNT* 6:306). Cf. 2 Cor 9:12, NRSV "the rendering of this ministry *(leitourgias)* supplies the needs *(prosanaplērousa ta hysterēmata)* of the saints . . ."; secular, political overtones of *leitourgia* here, in H. D. Betz, *2 Cor 8 and* 9:117–18. Col 1:24 *ant-anaplēroō* is not related to Phil 2:30.

what was lacking, on the part of the Philippians, is indicated in the dir. obj., with its two gens. *to hymōn hysterēma tēs pros me leitourgias.* On *to hysterēma,* cf. 4:11 *Not that I am referring to being in need (kath' hysterēsin); TDNT* 8:593, 595, 598–99 (U. Wilckens); *NIDNTT* 1:741 (R. Schippers), 3:952–53, 955 (W. L. Lane); *EDNT* 3:409 "deficiency"; *TLNT* 3:427–31. Rare in secular usage. In two papyrus examples (Spicq, both subsequent to MM) = "deficiency" or "delay." Examples in *Corp. Herm.* are likely later than Paul. Spicq, the six LXX instances of *hysterēma* (*TDNT* 8:595, "lack") suggest *to hysterēma* "was current in Alexandrian Koine" (*TLNT* 3:430). Hence for 2:30 (BDAG 1) **need, want, deficiency** in contrast to sufficiency (Phil 4:11) in material goods; re the collection (2 Cor 8:14 *bis;* 9:12) or Paul's own needs (2 Cor 11:9). Here (cf. 1 Cor 16:17) a representative of a church community makes up for *(anaplēroun)* the absence of the group. At 2:30 the Philippians are the ones deficient (*hymōn,* subjective gen.). *tēs leitourgias,* obj. gen., what is lacking (cf. BDF 168 [1] on this "concatenation of genitives with different meanings"; *GNTG* 3:218; Schenk 238). On *leitorurgias* see NOTES on 2:17; 2:25 *public servant.* A word from "general popular use" (H. Strathmann, *TDNT* 4:227) in the *polis* and *colōnia* of Philippi, applied for the congregation's relationship to their apostle-founder, their service toward him, its direction indicated by *pros me,* "towards me." The TRANSLATION (cf. BDAG *leitourgia* 2) shifts *your* from *to hysterēma* to *tēs leitourgias,* though the art. *tēs* can be possessive in effect. Between each art. and noun an explanatory word *(hymōn)* or phrase *(pros me)* is inserted.

COMMENT

A. FORMS, SOURCES, AND TRADITIONS

1. *Apostolic Parousia? Recommendation Form.* 2:19–24 and 25–30 exhibit certain similarities, but are not exactly parallel (cf. Schenk 227, 235; DA 219–20):

"Sending" mentioned	2:19a Timothy, *pempsai hymin*	2:25 Epaphroditus, *pempsai pros hymas*
Reason given for this concerning the Philippians	19b to know events affecting you	26 he was longing for you all and was very troubled
Praise by Paul for the person sent	22 he slaved together with me for the gospel 20 he will care for you	25 five epithets: my brother, fellow worker, soldier; your "apostle" and public servant
Additional reason	—	26,27 he was ill (twice mentioned)
"Sending" mentioned again	23 I expect to send this man	28 I am sending him all the more eagerly
Paul's own plans	24 I too will come soon	—
Exhortation	—	29 Welcome him, hold such in honor
Additional reason reiterated	—	30 He came close to dying

a. *Apostolic Parousia?* Such passages Funk 1966:217, 264–65, 269 called a "travelogue" or (1967) "apostolic *parousia,*" a form about the coming of an emissary and Paul's personal presence, authority, and power; expressed in a letter, by the person sent, and Paul's own coming. He cited no papyrus examples, but cf. Gk. letters of *philophronēsis* (friendship; "absent in body, present through letter"), *homilia* (conversation) between writer and recipient(s), and *parousia* (anticipated reunion) in Koskenniemi and Thraede 1970. Funk's form included: (1) "I write," + the author's (a) disposition in a ptc. or (b) purpose in a *hina* cl.; (2) Paul's apostolic relationship to recipients; (3) implementation expressed in terms of (a) eagerness, (b) hope to come, (c) some hindrance or delay, (d) hope to be "sent on by you"; (e) meanwhile, an emissary is being sent (i) mentioned by name, (ii) who is (credentials); (iii) purpose *(hina);* then (f) announcement of the apostle's own coming. (4) God's approval is invoked, (a) by prayer or the phrase (b) "if God wills." (5) Benefit(s) are listed (a) to Paul, (b) the recipients, or (ab) mutually. Rom 15:14–33 is the fullest version; two examples in Phil 2:19–30 + ten other fragmentary ones.[1] For 2:19–24 Funk (cf. 256, 261–62) threw in references from chs. 1:8–2:24. 2:25–30, about a Philippian associate coming home, "cannot be pressed to the same degree for structure as the passages which present the apostolic *parousia* proper" (258). The double example in 2:19–30 includes, at v 24, reference to Paul's own coming. "Neither the naturalness of the motif nor the Aristotelian doctrine of friendship accounts . . . for the significance Paul accords his presence," which invokes "charismatic . . . eschatological, power" (264, 265). 2 John 12 and 3 John 9–10, 13–14 show "presbyterial parousia" (R. W. Funk, "The Form and Structure of II and III John," *JBL* 86 [1967] 428–29). Cf. Doty 1973:36–37; R. Russell 303; J. Fitzmyer on Rom 15:14–33, AB 33:710. Claim that the form appeared esp. at the *conclusion* of letters, here Letter B (Funk 1967:263, but cf. his n 1) attracted the fire of those viewing Phil as a four-ch. unity (e.g., O'B 314–15). J. L. White 1971b:38–39 related Funk's "form" to some papyrus letters (Doty 37; White 1986a:219–20). L. A. Jervis, *The Purpose of Romans: A Comparative Letter Structure Investigation* (JSNTSup 55, Sheffield: JSOT 1991) 110–31, reduced Funk's five units to three: Paul writes, dispatches an emissary (with credentials), he himself will come (purpose, "if God wills"). Cf. *WDNTECLR* 55, 271, "travel plans"; Bittasi 179–81, travelogue.[2]

Berger 1984a:277–79 (cf. *ANRW* 2.25/2:1048, 1350) lists such passages under "Epistolaria (personal elements in letters)," including "the so-called *parousia-*

---

[1] In order of completeness, in addition to those in the adapted chart below, 1 Thess 2:17–3:13; 2 Cor 12:14–13:13; Rom 1:8–15; Phlm 21–22 (AB 34C:123); 1 Cor 4:14–21; 2 Cor 8:16–23; Gal 4:12–20; 2 Cor 9:1–5; 1 Cor 16:12.

	Rom 15:14–33	1 Cor 16:1–11	Phil 2:19–24	Phil 2:25–30
(1a) "I write," disposition	vv 14–15a	v 1		
(1b) purpose, cf. 3e.iii	none cited in Funk's charts(!)		[cf. 19b]	
(2) apostolic relationship	15b–21			
(3a) eagerness	23b		cf. 1:8	v 26a [28]
(3b) hope to come	24b	7	19,23	25
(3c) hindrance	22	8–9	[cf. 23b]	
(3d) to be sent on	24c	6b		
(3e.i) emissary named		10	19a	25
(3e.ii) credentials		3b, 10–11	20,22	25–28
(3e.iii) purpose		3b, 10–11	19b	28
(3f) Paul's coming	28b	2b, 4, 5–6	24, cf. 1:25–26	
(4a) prayer	30ff.		1:19	
(4b) *deo volente*	32	7b		
(5a) benefit to Paul	32b, cf. 24d		2:19b	30b
(5b) benefit to recipients			cf. 19b *I too*, 20	
(5ab) benefit to both			1:25–26, cf. 2:16b–18	28b

[2] Mullins 1973 preferred "visit talk" as a theme in ancient letters, like "health," "business," etc. Fee 258–59 n 1; Bockmuehl 163 took this to mean Funk's "form" does "not hold together." Mullins actually wrote, "Visit talk is an epistolary theme common to the non-literary papyri and to the NT," in Paul connected with "apostolic status and eschatology" (358). M. M. Mitchell 1992, "envoys" Paul sent (analogy to diplomatic conventions) reflect his presence, with an "intermediary role that he could not play, even if present himself" (662). Cf. Stirewalt 2003:81–84, 89–90. L. A. Johnson 2006 notes Paul's adjustment of the topos to the situation in each congregation, with a higher emphasis on epistolary presence in Corinth.

motif."[3] Cf. 302–3, Paul's "I am coming soon," like Christ's parousia (Rev 2:16; etc.), may have threatening overtones (2 Cor 10:13; 1 Cor 4:19–21; Funk's item [3f]). Is this a set "form"? Aune (1987:172–73, 190–91, cf. 210): "a *topos* or theme with a number of subordinate motifs." Cf. L. Alexander 1989; P. Trebilco, *DPL* 449–50; Edart 203, "visit talk." Such a "travelogue" has an "indirect persuasive function," Black 1995:39), to comply with what the apostle recommends (Reed 1993:320).

b. *Letter of Recommendation Form.* There is greater agreement that 2:19–30 reflects "letters of recommendation" in the Greco-Roman world (praise for Timothy, vv 20 and 22; epithets for Epaphroditus, v 25; Funk's item 3e.iii; Berger, point [5]). C.-H. Kim 1972 ([1] Bibl.) outlined the form thus: (1) introduction "concerning my child," + some petition for him; (2) credentials, praise for the person, relationship to himself; (3) what Paul wants the recipient to do. Cf. 120, 131–35 on Phil 2:29–30. Phlm, 3 John; 2 Cor 3:1 refers to such letters among missionaries of the day.[4] (Ps.)Libanius' model "letter of commendation" (*Epistolary Styles* 8, 55 = Malherbe 1977:64–65, 70–71) commanded, "Receive (*dexamenos*) this highly honored and much sought-after man, and do not hesitate to treat him hospitably . . .."; cf. 2:29–30; 4:2–3. Stowers 1986:153–65, "Letters of Mediation," papyrus, patristic examples. Aune 1987 put such commendations in the patron-client system of the Roman empire (166–67; E. Agosta, in Sampley, ed., 2003:119–22). In composing 2:19–30 Paul drew on such elements.

2. Chiasm and Other Literary, Rhetorical Features. Macro-chiastic structurings for Phil treat 2:19–30 in very different ways.[5] The attempts are unconvincing (*DA* 255, 292–93, esp. n 503; 362). Luter/Lee, Davis, and Bittasi give prominence to 2:19–30 not otherwise granted. For Letter B, note the broad chiasmus (Aspen; Pretorius 1995:280; Black 1995):

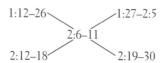

News about Paul (1:12 *ta kat' eme*, 13–19a) and expectations in prison while facing death (1:19b–26) are balanced by hoped-for news about the Philippians (2:19,

---

[3] (2) those with the writer, present situation and opponents; (3) past and future travels; (4) whom he is sending (to carry his letter?); (5) recommendation of coworkers (2:20–22); (6) requests (2:29); (7) earlier correspondence; (8) greetings; (9) actions to be carried through. "I–he–you" triangulation.

[4] Cf. Berger, ANRW 2.25/2:1328; 1984a:278; DA 221–28; Edart 200–201; Schenk 230–34; Fee 259 n 3; 262–63, 268, 2:20–22 is commendation, vv 19, 23–24 "travel narrative," though "form" is lacking and Timothy is not delivering this letter, Epaphroditus is (p. 272). Holloway 2001a:126–29, "letter of recommendation" has been overdone for 2:19–24, but he can find elements of his "consolation" theme only in Paul's use of surrogates to comfort the Philippians.

[5] Cf. INTRO. VI.B n 3. Wick 40, 51–53, 78–81, 209 aligns 2:19–20 with 4:10–20; Rolland, 1:12–26 with 2:19–3:1. Luter/Lee 98, 2:17–3:1 = the "crowning, central thrust of the letter," with no chiastic counterpart; C. W. Davis (117–22, 150, cf. 154), 2:19–30 is center point, but his divisions do not match those of Luter/Lee; Bittasi 177–218. Black 1995:31, 1:12–26 and 2:19–30 balance one another, A and A'; 1:27–2:19 = "instructions for the church," B.

20 *ta peri hymōn*) and expectations for renewed contacts. What will happen to Paul (2:23 *ta peri eme*) and what is going on in Philippi (1:27 *ta peri hymōn*) interplay.

Minor chiasms: v 29, NOTE on *and such persons hold in honor*. V 30 (Schenk 239; O'B 342):

A	for the sake of work for Christ	he came close to dying	B
	dia to ergon Christou	*mechri thanatou ēggisen*	
	paraboleusamenos tē[i] psychē[i]	*hina anaplērosē[i] to hysterema*	A′
B′	having risked his life	in order that he might fill up what was lacking	

More broadly, Schenk:

26 *he was ill* — 27 *he was ill, close to death*
30 *he came close to dying* — *having risked his life*

Schenk speculates that v 27 *mechri thanatou* may be from the Philippian hymn (of which the one-time Aphrodite-devotee may have been the author!), made more specific by the words in 30b *having risked his life* (239).

Stylistic devices are rare in 2:19–30 (D. F. Watson 1988b:72; more in 25–30 than in 19–24, Edart 199–200): "I"-form, 2:19–30 (DA 184–85); *enthymemes*, introduced by "for" or "because" to support a point (Aune 1987:173; e.g., vv 20, 21, 22, 26); wordplay (*paranomesia*, Watson 1988b:72) on *psychē* (see NOTES on 19b *eupsychō* and 20 *isopsychon*, and perhaps 30b *having risked his life*) and on *lypē* in vv 27–28; concatenation of gens., 2:30 end (NOTE). Epaphroditus' titles in 2:25 = *epitheton* (Porter, *Handbook* 580). Rhetorically, perhaps a *digressio*.[6] Then Timothy and Epaphroditus become *exempla*, "two Christ-like men" (Black 1995:39 n 38), who illustrate 1:27 or 2:6–11.[7] But are they good examples? See below. *Mimēsis* is not enjoined by Paul until 3:17. The notion of "Christ-figures" is overplayed (so even Fee 261 n 8). Paul's concern is to secure "acceptance by the Philippians" of Timothy and Epaphroditus; hence the recommendations and rhetoric "characteristic of a *culture* based on honor and shame" (Reed 1993:320, cf. 315–16 and Watson 60). 2:25–30 has almost an apologetic tone (Fee 272).

Friendship themes: presence/absence (2:24); longing and affection for friends (2:26); contrasting models (2:21 Timothy, *they all*); father and son (2:22); *syn*-words (NOTE on 2:25b); and joy (2:28, 29). Metzner makes 2:25–30 a parade example in a "letter of friendship."[8]

---

[6] So D. F. Watson 1988b:71–72; Geoffrion 145, 161; Edart 200, 203, 207; contra Garland 164, 173 (3:1–21 is the *digressio*); Witherington 75, *probatio* part 2. Yet even if "digression from the logical order of our speech" to bring in some theme "bearing on the case" (Watson 71, comparing Quint. 4.3.14), the result "underplays" the "clear epistolary structure and is difficult to fit into Paul's supposed larger rhetorical purpose" (Reed 1993:320; 228 no need for term).

[7] Hawth. 108, 114; O'B 315; Bloomquist 128–29; Edart 205–8, who (200, 207) pits rhetorical analysis against epistolary form, with exemplary function winning out.

[8] Cf. Stowers 1991 (*PT 1*):107–14; Malherbe 1986:144; DA 171; Fee 273 n 8; Fitzgerald *ABD* "Phil.";
(16) COMMENT A.2.(B). For Metzner 119, Paul and Epaphroditus emerge as a pair of friends like Demetrius and Antiphilos in Lucian's *Toxaris* [LCL *Lucian* 5:103–207]; L. M. White 1990:201–15;

There is no OT/Jewish material in 2:19–30.

Michael 112 asked whether 2:19–24 was once a separate note, appended here in canonical Phil. No. Mengel 314–16 regarded 2:25–30 as an interruption written after Epaphroditus recovered from his illness; unlikely. But "body closing" fits (Bloomquist 109–11).

3. *Epaphroditus' Role(s).* Why so much on Epaphroditus? Many try to fill in the gaps. Did he come alone or accompanied by other Philippian Christians? Was he simply a courier, bringing funds to Paul (cf. Buchanan 159; Garland 1985:151), or was he also to remain and help Paul in some way (the "'twofold mission' view," Fee 272 n 7)? Evangelization (Ollrog 98–99; previously active spreading the faith in Philippi, through the encomium quoted at 2:6–11)? Supporting Paul during imprisonment (by his presence, encouragement, securing food)? Liaison with believers in Ephesus (cf. 1:14–18; Suhl 183; cf. B. M. Rapske 1994:209–19, 236–42, and passim; Fee 276)? Contacts with those in the Praetorium (1:13) and of Caesar's household, his background a help with military, Imperial, or business groups? Legal help in presenting Paul's case (a Philippian Gentile may know Roman law better than a Jew from Tarsus)? Thus seconded to Paul on "long-term assignment"; see NOTE on 25a–d "*send* back." Had Epaphroditus, by falling ill, failed in this service to Paul (some of the money expended for his own needs?)? Or worse, deserted him? See NOTE on 26 *very troubled* (*adēmonōn*, "homesickness" or "anguishing"?). Some claim Epaphroditus was a church leader in Philippi; his duty was to be at home during tensions there (Fee 272), disunity and divisions (Peterlin), or persecution (Loh.). Rahtjen 169, he "had already returned home" before Paul writes 2:25–30 (*ēgēsamēn*, 25; *epempsa*, 28, true past tenses) and in Philippi "had been received with coolness if not hostility." Was he taken sick en route to Paul or while with him? Defenders of Rome as the place of Paul's imprisonment, to minimize travel time, claim Epaphroditus left Philippi with several other Christians (and "a considerable sum of money"; Fee 278). Taken ill on the way (preferably on the Via Egnatia, before the voyage to Italy). A colleague took word back to Philippi; the Philippians knew of his illness (v 26) before he got to Rome (thus saving one whole trip back to Philippi from Rome). Why the sick man went on instead of going home goes unexplained; concern for the "considerable sum" drops out of the calculations, though a man facing death makes the trip more difficult and the money less secure. When did he "hazard his life" at "death's door"? Wohl. 160, not in good health when he left Philippi; Mackay 169; Buchanan 158–60; Caird 100; Bruce 96.

Such matters can never be resolved from our limited evidence. Special pleadings enter into all reconstructions. We suggest Epaphroditus came to Paul as Philippian *apostolos* and *leitourgos* to bring money and aid Paul, on behalf of the Philippians, and help with work for Christ in Ephesus, for a time, like others — Stephanas, Fortunatus, and Achaicus from Corinth (1 Cor 16:17–18); Onesimus

---

Pervo, in Fitzgerald, ed., 1997:163–80), *service* in 2:30 is both "service of God" and "service in friendship." See NOTES on these terms; 2:25b *brother*, and COMMENT B.

(Phlm 13); Epaphras and Aristarchus (Phlm 23; cf. Col 1:7–8; 4:10,12). Cf. Oll-rog 93–108, not Paul's closest coworkers like Timothy and Titus but delegated for work with Paul by congregations, their authority from the gospel and their churches (Ollrog 121, 125; 183 n 101).

B. MEANING AND INTERPRETATION

Paul turns to expectations for the imminent future, as Letter B draws to a conclusion (Walter 67). The hoped-for coming here is not Jesus Christ at the Day of the Lord (1:6, 10; 2:16) but (1) Epaphroditus, a Philippian, (2) Timothy, and then (3) Paul himself, to encourage believers in Philippi (2:19b). Paul uses personal terms ("I") and travel plans, but all is ultimately *for the sake of work for Christ* (2:30a), evangelization and firming up life together of the house churches in hostile Philippi. He expects to send Epaphroditus immediately, with Letter B. He carefully (2:25–30) commends the man who brought him the Philippians' gift (4:18), now "invalided home." Next he plans to send Timothy, *soon* (2:19–23). Finally Paul is *confident in the Lord* that he *too will soon come*, his trial in Ephesus favorably ended. The order in the letter is strategic. First (2:19–23), Timothy, why appropriate and the purpose(s). Then (2:24) Paul. Only at 2:25–30 (almost 15 lines of Nestle text, compared with 9+ on Timothy and Paul), Epaphroditus' story, sickness, almost death, for Christ. Paul draws on "visit language" and letters of recommendation (COMMENT A.1). Titles vary for what read like sections in family letters (Alexander; *DA* 169): "the immediate future" (Collange 115, + 3:1 and 4:2–7); "Plans for Renewed Fellowship" (Bockmuehl 163). But mission setting, "work for Christ," and helping each other *stand steadfast* (1:27) must be kept in mind amid logistical details as people are put to the best use for the gospel.

1. *Sending Timothy to Philippi ahead of Paul (2:19–24).* A new section *(But)*, fresh hopes for Paul (v 24) after the possibility that his life might end (17). The note of joy in 2:18 continues; mutual encouragement (19b), confidence (24), rejoicing in contrast to sorrow (28). Consonant with living as citizens for the gospel (1:27), to fulfill mutual joy (2:2) and work out what salvation means—under God's working (2:12–13). Nothing overt is said in 2:19–30 about Timothy, Paul, or Epaphroditus as models or their imitating Jesus Christ in 2:6–8, though some stress them as examples (Hawth. 108, 114; Culpepper 1980:355–57; O'B 315, 349; Fee 284, but with cautions in n 8; D. F. Watson 1988b:71–72; Bloomquist 128–29; Peterman 1997:103, 118–19). Paul's recommendations re Timothy and Epaphroditus should not be made into impvs. for all Philippian Christians. There is uncertainty whether Epaphroditus' performance as *apostolos* has been exemplary (see below), question over how well Timothy succeeded in Corinth (see 1.a below), and dispute over Paul's current situation (see COMMENT on 1:14–18, some opposed his appeal to his Roman citizenship to escape punishment). These figures may not have been ideal models for Philippian Christianity. Timothy's proposed mission puts him into a situation where Philippian house churches were by

no means in agreement, with each other or with Epaphroditus. *But* at 2:19 points all the way back to 1:12, *events affecting* Paul (1:12), now *events affecting you* Philippians (2:19b) (chiasmus in the body of Letter B, COMMENT A.2).

Paul's plan *to send you Timothy soon* (2:19) is simply and directly set forth. He will depart for Philippi whenever it is clear how charges against Paul will come out (23). If death (1:20; 2:17), Timothy would bear sad tidings about Roman "justice" in Ephesus and comfort the Philippians at the loss of their apostle. If life (1:20, 25), Timothy will bring good news (cf. 1 Thess 3:6) and prepare for Paul's arrival in Philippi. Timothy is further to inform Paul about what is going on in Philippi (Banker 101–2: by a trip to Paul). Paul expects encouragement from the stance of his converts (19b). If they shine as *luminaries* for the gospel *in* their *world*, he has *not run in an empty way* or toiled in vain (2:16) as their missionary church-founder. 19b also implies the Philippians would gain encouragement (*I too* suggests "you, first of all") as Timothy amplifies what Paul has written, how *to live* means *Christ, to die, gain* (1:21). Living or dying, Paul encourages the Philippians, and they, he hopes, will encourage him.

Circumstances in Philippi prompting Paul's concern are unclear to us. There were opponents there (1:28), but evidence is lacking for severe persecution and martyrdom(s) (Loh.). Paul warned against strife, self-seeking, and claiming individual superiority over other Christians (2:1–4), but little evidence for massive disunity (Peterlin) or gnosticizing dangers in Philippi (Schmithals 1972:70–71). Beare 96–97, Paul was "not satisfied that he has a clear and true picture" of conditions. Timothy will help him learn what's what; then he can send a final message before he dies or act perceptively when he arrives in Philippi.

a. *Recommendation for Timothy (2:20–23).* This half-Gentile convert (the fourth most frequently mentioned early Christian missionary in the NT, after Paul, Peter, and Barnabas) was well-known to the Philippians. He shared responsibility in Paul's team for evangelization in the Aegean basin (Ollrog 22) and accompanied Paul on the mission into Europe (1 Thess 3:2). He had major responsibilities in Corinth in Paul's absence (1 Cor 4:17), but with fears the Corinthians would hold him in "contempt" (1 Cor 16:10–11); it was Titus who put things right (2 Cor 2:13; 7:6–7; Fee, *1 Cor.* 821–23). Phil 1:1 makes him coauthor with Paul (an honor, not necessarily joint composer), though hardly of the commendation in vv 20–22. He is *of like"soul,"*[9] with Paul and Philippian believers (Walter 68), perhaps unique in Paul's estimate (cf. NOTE on 20 and cf. v 21). His *proven character* the Philippians *know* (v 22) from previous contacts (Acts 16). Some think the Philippians requested Paul to send Timothy to them. The father-child relationship between Paul and Timothy is language of apostolic teacher and convert (see NOTE). Paul comes close to implying "he was my slave," adjusted to explain, Timothy has *slaved for the gospel together with* Paul. Thus (20, 22) two reasons for sending and welcoming Timothy, besides availability: they know his character, his record provides hope of genuine care for them.

---

[9] I avoid "soul brother" in some American commentators, repeated in others unaware of connotations in African-American communities. Timothy was the same as Paul in faith, not ethnically.

Hardest to understand is that others *all seek after their own interests, not those of Jesus Christ* (21). *all?* Realism, not romantic notions about early Christianity! Some see personal animosities, others theological differences (G. Barth 52). The rival preachers in Ephesus (1:14–18) are not meant (Michaelis 50; Walter 68). Paul criticized some in Philippi (2:1–4, 14–16). But *no one* else who cares genuinely for converts? *All* seeking *ta heautōn*, not *ta Christou Iēsou* (2:21, cf. 2:3–4)? Paul may be speaking only of those *available* to him in Ephesus to send to Philippi. Among those available, only Timothy will do. Paul could be quite critical, of self (cf. 3:12; his weaknesses), coworkers, even preachers who had the message basically correct (1:14–18). His standards were high, and on occasion Paul seemingly stood alone on issues (e.g., 2 Cor 8:16–23). The time in Ephesus was a busy period in Paul's life (Ollrog 61; see INTRO. VIII, Chart 2), people came and went. At times Prisca and Aquila may have been there; Titus and Tychicus (2 Cor 8:16–23, cf. Col 4:7–8), but there is no evidence that they fall under Paul's strictures here (Ollrog 194). The putative "others" some think came from Philippi. Was Epaphroditus meant? Philippian readers, hearing v 22, could have entertained this possibility. Some might have welcomed the dig. Or is it simply rhetorical, making Timothy look better in comparison with a sweeping but hypothetical negative example? Cf. Schoon-Janßen, diatribe style of antithesis (1991:143). We take 2:21 as an aside, to praise Timothy, by an elaborate contrast (Mengel 255–56 n 124), hitting whoever is hit, affording the insight that Paul had no one else available fit for this particular mission; too many coworkers mix up self with Christ's interests.

In v. 20b the second purpose for Timothy's trip is to *genuinely care for what affects* the Philippians. He will reliably, naturally, and authentically be concerned about whatever faces Philippian believers.[10] Of such a sort is Timothy, who is to come *at that very moment* when Paul has word from the authorities about his future.

b. *Paul Expects to Come Himself (2:24).* After poignantly treating life or death in 1:19b–26, he now says more clearly than anywhere in Phil 1–2 what he expects for himself: *I am confident in the Lord that I too will soon come myself.* Not just Timothy, but the imprisoned apostle himself.[11] In vv 23–24 *men* and *de* (Schenk 227–28; see NOTE on 23a . . . *this, on the one hand*) suggest how much emphasis there is on v 24: "Although I expect to send Timothy, I am persuaded, I believe that I also will come soon." To account for this shift, some speculate considerable time elapsed between writing 2:18 and 2:19 (Merk 1968:188, "several weeks or even months"; Paul says that he will come *soon*, a word not used in 1:24–25) or that Paul had some sign from Caesar's officials (or heaven!) that his case will be resolved favorably to Paul. We have no such clue from what he writes. He does, however, shift from *I expect* to *I am confident*, a new tone of faith, accompanied as

---

[10] See NOTE on *gnēsiōs*, going back to the Jesus tradition (Luke 12:22–30 par, trust in God, seeking the kingdom, not things for one's physical comfort); in Pauline terms, the things of Christ Jesus, anxious to please the Lord in body and spirit, not one's own interests (1 Cor 7:32–34; Phil 2:4).

[11] These words, esp. *soon*, fit Ephesus better than Caesarea (where it is doubtful Paul had expectations of being loosed on the spot) or Rome (whence the apostle, if freed, wanted to go on to Spain; Walter 68–69).

in v 19 with *in the Lord* (Jesus). Not merely, "D.V., if God wills," but "as the risen Jesus makes possible" (Schenk 228, 234). Christian confidence *en kyriō[i]* is like OT confidence in God, esp. the Psalms (Bultmann, *TDNT* 6:6). Paul puts Timothy's visit and purposes in a larger context, God's overall will and the Philippians' ongoing relations with Paul.

2. Sending Epaphroditus Now to Philippi (2:25–30). Somewhat parallel to 2:19–24 in form and content, these vv differ in their triple references to Epaphroditus' "weakness" in sickness, double allusions to his almost dying in his work, and exhortation to welcome and honor him (COMMENT A.1, above), as if the Philippians might not do so. At issue: was Epaphroditus a "dud whom the apostle sends home with pretty words or a thoroughly useful coworker whose praise Paul intends to sing before the Philippians" (B. Mayer 1987:176) or something in between? Paul's starting point in v 25 is five *epitheta ornantia*, distinguishing appellations (B. Mayer 1987:178).

a. *High Recommendations but a Necessary Step (2:25).* Unlike v 19 (what Paul expects to do *in the Lord Jesus* with Timothy), the statement about Epaphorditus comes on Paul's own (but not inconsiderable) authority, "*Necessary* (emphasis on the initial *anagkaion*) I . . . consider it . . . to send Epaphroditus *to you.*" The TRANSLATION reflects *de*, "I am confident in the Lord that I, Paul, will soon come personally. *But* meanwhile, till then, *I do consider it necessary.* . . ." In Gk., *Epaphroditus* comes right after the vb. The infin. *to send* is the same form as in v 19 (and 23; cf. 28); *to you* = prep. + acc. (see NOTE; perhaps *send you Timothy*, whom you requested; *send Epaphroditus* back *to you*—Gdsp. and others, but not derogatory)—you who may be surprised when he turns up with this letter and its news. Five terms in 25bc characterize the letter-bearer.[12]

The first three terms *(ton adelphon kai synergon kai systratiōtēn mou)* are artfully bound in a unity to express Paul's affirmation of Epaphroditus in ascending sequence. *brother . . . of mine* is low-level; *adelphos* applied to every Christian man and woman, all in Philippi (1:12), the *brothers and sisters* in Ephesus (1:14–18) including the rival preachers. The pl. is used with *mou* often by Paul (3:1); but "my *adelphos*" (sg.) is not common (of Titus, 2 Cor 2:13). It reminds the Philippians that Epaphroditus *is* a fellow Christian. Pairing came naturally with the next term (1 Thess 3:2), coworker-in-the-gospel-cause, significant colleague, no mere "helper."[13] Compounds with *syn-* are part of friendship language. The third term reflects military terminology, attractive for Philippi with its Roman army

---

[12] For Epaphroditus as carrier for Letter B to Philippi (or canonical Phil.) see Lft. 37, 122; Michaelis 51; Gnilka 162; O'B 330; and Fee 39; the subscript in MSS K 1908 and Majority Text said, "written from Rome by Epaphroditus" (*TCGNT* 618); Rendel Harris, "Epaphroditus, Scribe and Courier," *Expositor*, 5th Series, 8 (1898) 401–10.

[13] See NOTE for the dozen or more men and women to whom *synergos* is attached. For two women, a man, and others in Philippi, see 4:2–3. Chapple 1984:576, some *synergoi* in Philippi (4:3; 2:25) were *episkopoi* and *diakonoi* (1:1), and some *episkopoi* and *diakonoi* were *synergoi*, but no definite conclusion is possible on Epaphroditus; perhaps (578 n 345) *diakonos*, since he was free to be away for some time. But that assumes heads of households (= *episkopoi*) always had to be at home.

background, but also connected with *philia*: shipmates and those together in the military are, as *systratiōtai*, "friends" (Aristot. *Nic. Eth.* 8.9.1). Battling together for the gospel here likely goes back to the earliest struggles for the faith in Philippi, but also includes whatever he and Epaphroditus have been through together in Ephesus.

Sharply distinguished from the first three titles by word order, ". . . of me, but of you" (pl.), are two epithets of Philippian choice, *your "apostle" and public servant for my need*. Both have histories prior to application here. *apostolos* had limited Gk. usage for someone sent on a naval or military expedition, including colonists for a settlement, and then religious "prophets," including the Cynic-Stoic messengers of Zeus (K. H. Rengstorf, *TDNT* 1:407–11; *TLNT* 1:186–88). These backgrounds are generally dismissed for the Twelve in the gospels, or for Paul. To locate *apostolos* in "a Semitic substrate," *šāliaḥ* = one sent with a commission, post-OT, in rabbinic Judaism (Rengstorf, *TDNT* 1:413–43), is common but overdone; cf. *TLNT* 1:188–94; in *NIDNTT* contrast 1:134 (D. Müller) with 135–36 (C. Brown); bibl. in *EDNT* 1:142–43, esp. Agnew. The NOTE distinguishes various NT uses of *apostolos*, its meaning far from settled or uniform in Paul's day. Epaphroditus is an "apostle of and for the congregation," one of the "apostles of the churches" (2 Cor 8:23 = "the brothers" in vv 18, 22), appointed for some particular task, like shepherding the collection to the Christian poor in Jerusalem. Possibly this sort of *apostolos* ultimately derived from Paul and those like him (but "apostles of the Apostle" is hardly apt), or in the case of the collection as a parallel to the *šĕlîḥîm/apostoloi* from a synagogue in Thessalonica or Corinth, escorting funds to the Temple in Jerusalem, a connection not likely for Philippi. The usually discarded Gk. evidence should probably be brought back for the title "*apostolos* of the Philippian house churches." But no prefix *syn*, as with the two prior terms, for Epaphroditus is not on a par with Paul.

The climactic term is "your *leitourgos*," important for determining Epaphroditus' background. Not cultic (see NOTE).[14] The obvious background is *leitourgos* and *leitourgia* in the Gk. *polis* and Roman officialdom (cf. Rom 13:6; ambassadors, Bash 66–69); see NOTE, esp. Peterlin 281–86. Hence *public servant* as a rendering. This fits because (1) the term is a Philippian one, created by people there. (2) Epaphroditus undertakes this "office" *for* Paul's *need*, collection, delivery, and expenditure of funds to provide what Paul lacks, and service in behalf of the Philippians. (3) He functions as a *leitourgos* did in the Gk. world, undertaking personally, probably using his own resources, a task for the community, here support of their founder-apostle, Paul in need.

Further implications: the Gk. *leitourgos* was often a person of some wealth and status, a benefactor, voluntarily or by communal assignment, at times as part of a

---

[14] Some lump passages together (see NOTES on *leitourgia* 2:17 and 30) to give Paul priestly symbolism. Re Rom 15:16, "Jesus is the priest, Paul the priest's servant" (Bengel, *Gnomon* 2:361); "Paul is thinking of himself as fulfilling the function . . . of a Levite," Cranfield, *Rom.* 2:755; Thielman 1995:154 n 9. Then Epaphroditus = some sort of Levite to Paul's priestly functioning for Christ. Caird 129 protests treating Epaphroditus "as though .. ordained to a priestly office." Cf. Peterlin 195–97.

magistracy. Fulfilling the office of gymnasiarch, priest, or some *(epi-)chorēgia* (supplying a chorus for a festival; cf. 1:19), fell under "benefaction," rather than vice-versa. Cf. Danker 1982:330–31. The office had to do esp. with finances. Did Epaphroditus, as community *leitourgos*, reflect a patron's sense of duties (and client relationships) in Philippi? See (16) COMMENT on patron-client "friendship" and Paul's concern for "emancipation" from some aspects of it for the Philippians. Was Epaphroditus self-appointed, stepping forth to meet a need, supported by only some house churches or just his own household? Cf. Peterlin's reconstruction, summarized in the NOTE. Was there an "office" (*diakonos* or *episkopos*) to which his "communal service" was attached, or did it go with being head of a household? Or was the *leitourgos* created *ad hoc* in Philippi, for this particular need? One can only speculate. In any case, he was *apostolos* and *leitourgos* of the Philippian church (or a part of it), not (Bormann 1995:212–13) "brother of the congregation and servant of Paul" but "servant of the congregation and brother of Paul." Paul calls him his own brother, reminding the Philippians he is theirs too.

From such data and 4:18, Epaphroditus' story can be pieced together. He was sent from Philippi with money for Paul's support and for other services. Not just to transmit money, but to minister to Paul in prison (Calvin 81, "ambassador"; cf. Bash, 119–22); to stay and work with Paul (Chapple 577, cf. B. Mayer 1986:45). For additional tasks, see COMMENT A. 3. Possibly with others from Philippi (Fee 278, e.g.; COMMENT A.3), bearing a letter from Philippi.[15] But neither 4:18 ("gifts received from Epaphroditus") nor 2:25–30 refers to Philippians accompanying Epaphroditus to or from Ephesus.

Epaphroditus might have been among the *diakonoi* or *episkopoi* of 1:1 (cf. n 13 above). Very likely, patron or head of one of the house churches. Perhaps chosen by all the Philippian Christians or the (other) *episkopoi* and patrons, for the mission to aid Paul and stand by in solidarity with him (cf. 4:10; 1:7; Schenk 102–3; Pesch 91). Possibly he acted on his own, using his own resources. Maybe caught up in differences between Euodia and Syntyche (4:2–3), who differed over whether the Philippians should go on supporting Paul or not (so Peterlin). Epaphroditus may thus not have had united support in Philippi when he left there to go to Paul. Craddock 51, "whispering in the church" at Philippi against Epaphroditus. Hence Paul emphasizes "you all" (2:26, earlier 1:4, 7 *bis*, 8). Reference to Paul's *need* make this an ideal spot for saying "thank you" for the gift (Fee 276; Walter 71; a problem for defenders of a unitary letter). In Letter B, the focus is on the person who has brought the gift; Paul has already acknowledged it in Letter A. Paul begins with a series of terms whose "sheer number is unique" in his letters (Mayer 1987:177), to persuade the Philippians to goodwill toward one of their own, in light of Paul's necessary decision to send him home.

b. *Epaphroditus' Brush with Death, and God's Mercy (2:26–27).* Paul explains

---

[15] Cf. the three "envoys" in 1 Cor 16:17–18, an "official delegation" of coequals or a business man with two slaves (Fee, *1 Cor.* 831–32). Or a pair of representatives (Jeremias 1959), like Titus and an unnamed brother (2 Cor 8:16–19, 22–23). Or the pairs in Acts 20:4, representatives gathered at Philippi from several congregations for the (collection) trip to Jerusalem.

why he sends Epaphroditus to Philippi with his letter. Timothy and Paul are not free to travel (Hawth. 115, an initial reason of four for sending Epaphroditus). The forlorn Philippian was *longing for you all and very troubled because you had heard that he was ill* (26). Two more reasons: his illness[16] and consequences from the congregation knowing he was sick. At the least, *epipothōn ēn . . . kai adēmonōn* suggests Epaphroditus' desire for all the Christians back home and distress over a period of time. Some take this as a pres. tense, "he misses you all and is worried" (JB; NIV). The TRANSLATION adopts an adjectival construction, pointing to Epaphroditus: *there he was*, Paul observes him, *longing* (usually a positive term in Paul, as at 1:8) but *very troubled*. Two different explanations for the root meaning of *adēmoneō* and coloring from Jesus in Gethsemane have lead to a variety of renderings and explanations (see NOTE): Epaphroditus anguishes because he has abandoned his leadership post in Philippi; he has abandoned his post with Paul and run off home (v 25 then refers to what Paul thought in the past); a "quitter" (W. Barclay 1958 [(6) Bibl.]: 4).

A benign interpretation would make him homesick. But, Paul says, Epaphroditus is agitated *because* the Philippians *have heard that he was ill.* The vb. *astheneō*, "be weak," can cover many things. Schenk 240 and others see sufferings Christian missionaries faced (2 Cor 11:24–26). But would the Philippians have been surprised at that? Knowledge that the Philippians knew he was ill has gotten back to Epaphroditus. Hence he is *very troubled*, *ill* and upset, anxious over what those at home know about him. Epaphroditus, not the Philippians, was upset.

For those in Philippi Paul confirms what they had heard, Epaphroditus *was indeed ill* (27a), *close to death*. Then, in an expression uncommon for the Greco-Roman world, but not the OT, God is mentioned for the first time since 2:15, *But God showed mercy on him—not just on him but also on me* (27b), God, an often overlooked actor in Phil (but cf. 1:28; 2:9–11 and recall 2:13). The God of Israel was merciful. The Gk. world had less good to say about *eleos*, "pity." The mercy here was that Epaphroditus did not die. It is not said that he was "healed," so the door remains open to escape from danger, surviving some hazard (even winning a legal case decision, as in OT psalms), or the menaces in Pauline catalogues of dangers (*Peristasen-kataloge*; see [16] COMMENT A.4.e), like 2 Cor 11:23–28. Perhaps Epaphroditus had gotten off from a charge against him in court (something that gave Paul hope in his own case, hence v 24), like smuggling money into the prison (Walter 70), aiding a prisoner. Or Epaphroditus was "weak" and "anxious" over care for his house church or all in Philippi. The text is not specific. Most take "he was ill" to imply recovery from physical (and interrelated mental) sickness.[17]

---

[16] C. O. Buchanan, as part of a defense for Rome as place of Paul's imprisonment, locates Epaphroditus' illness en route, before he gets to Paul; Witherington 79–80, "on the Egnatian Way" but he had "gotten too far from Philippi to turn back." Forced and unnecessary. Cf. Intro VII.A and (9) COMMENT A.3.

[17] Was Epaphroditus cured miraculously? Paul did work wonders (cf. Gal 3:5; 2 Cor 12:12). Fee 279, "the gifts of healing" (1 Cor 12:9, 28, 30) were involved, unmentioned in "this theological account." Contrast Oepke, *TDNT* 3:214; Foerster, *TDNT* 7:161–62. Plummer 62, it would have been selfish for Paul to use his powers thus; Hendriksen 141.

Seldom asked is the attitude of the Philippians. Was it divine judgment, punishment for *hybris*? Perhaps punishment for sin (John 9:2; cf. 1 Cor 11:30)? Did the Philippians' attitude reflect their encomium (2:9–11): Christians partake of Christ's exaltation, heavenward, now (in terms of "perfection," 3:12–13)? Then Epaphroditus is not among the "real Christians" (cf. Culpepper 356). Ambiguity existed about what Epaphroditus' illness meant.

God's mercy was on Paul, not just Epaphroditus. How? . . . *so that I might not have sorrow in addition to sorrow* (*lypēn*, "grief, affliction"). Possibly "one sorrow after another" (Gdsp., NRSV, sorrows multiplied; "an even greater sorrow," GNB). Many commentators isolate specific griefs.[18] We do not know. Amid sorrows, real or potential, attitudes in Philippi toward Epaphroditus seem not unanimously favorable: while going to aid Paul (on his own, without support of all the house churches? *his* public service, v 25), he met with illness or some misfortune. Yet Paul is now affirming him.

c. *Joy in Sending, and the Reception of, Epaphroditus (2:28).* Paul reiterates what he said in v 25 and spells out two purposes (and possible results) in Epaphroditus' return and reception: *Accordingly I am all the more eagerly sending him in order that you, upon seeing him, again may rejoice and I too be the more without sorrow.* Again as in v 25, an epistolary aor.; what Paul wrote in Ephesus will have present-time meaning in Philippi. *Accordingly* draws conclusions out of what was said about Epaphroditus' illness and troubled longings. The emphatic term, first in the Gk. sentence, is the comparative form of a word that may mean "hastily, speedily" ([N]JB) or "eagerly" ([N]RSV, NIV, NEB/REB; see Note on tr. problems), *all the more eagerly.* Perhaps more hastily than he or I planned. But he must not be blamed by the Philippians; Paul himself judges his return now "to be necessary" (Michael 122). Paul puts up front in v 28 an eagerness, if not haste, to send the man home now.

It seems odd to say that, when Epaphroditus gets there and this letter is read, the Philippians *may rejoice* on seeing him *again.* Joy is a theme throughout the letter (1:4, 18; 2:17, 18); of course Christians rejoice when a brother comes back from the dead. Do old differences over Epaphroditus and his mission rankle, or disappointments about his illness and that he may not have carried out his tasks fully?

More perplexing are the aim and likely outcome re Paul. One would expect, that "*I too* may rejoice" (cf. 2:18; 1:18cd). Instead, a negated form of the adj. from *lypē,* "not grieved" in the comparative degree. Not, Stoic-like, "free from all anxiety." Fee questions any "anxiety" terminology (see Note on 28b, though Mullins 1973 viewed "anxiety" as part of "visit talk")." Paul looks to be *more without sorrow,*

---

[18] Epaphroditus' death on top of his sickness (Beare 98); then v 28 means, upon his recovery Paul was "free of sorrow" (Loh/Nida 84, cf. GNB, CEV); hardly what *alypoteros* means, see Note on 28 *the more without sorrow.* Or Epaphroditus' death on top of Paul's imprisonment (Vincent 76; Michael 125; Black 1984:212; Holloway 2001a:129 n 129), but Paul has not made his jailing a cause for lament (cf. 4:11; 1:12, 16b, 19). Others: letdown by coworkers (2:21; Koenig 160); opposition by rival preachers in Ephesus (1:14–17); O'B 338, captivity and adversaries. Peterlin 193–94, Epaphroditus' death on top of "discord" and a "hurtful attitude" toward Paul in Philippi (denied by Metzner 126); a dispute between opponents and supporters involving Paul himself.

not devoid of all *lypē* (he is still in prison; there are rival preachers; the situation in Philippi is a concern). How are matters *less* sorrow-laden, when Epaphroditus goes? Possible answers (Mayer 1987:186–87; cf. 1986:45–47; Metzner 115–16): (1) Paul is glad to be rid of Epaphroditus, he was not much help; Paul had to care for him rather than vice versa (Bittlinger 22–23; 88–89). Good riddance![19] This ill agrees with laurels heaped on Epaphroditus in vv 25–27 and what Paul will say in 29. (2) Paul identifies with concerns in Philippi over Epaphroditus' illness.[20] When he returns home, both they and he will be at ease on this point. (3) The congregation will rejoice at having Epaphroditus, now well, with them again. Cf. B. Mayer 1986:46; Bruce 97. But why, then, underscore the obvious in the previous part of the purpose cl. in 28 and why add 29? (4) Paul will have in Philippi a trusted coworker to deal with problems there (2:1–4; 4:2–3) and build up support for Paul in his circumstances. Cf. Beare 99; Witherington 80, "a power vacuum" in Philippi since Epaphroditus left (79, cf. 82); thus a "two-way envoy" (M. M. Mitchell 652); Loh. 120, a presbyter returns to the leaderless congregation facing martyrdom. (5) Paul is confirming a positive relation of friendship for Epaphroditus with the Philippian community. No mistrust, no need for rehabilitating him.[21] An idealized and unlikely solution. Witherington 76–82, who stresses friendship in Phil, notes nothing on *philia* in 2:19–30.

Decision is between (2) and (4) (Mayer), but some bring in the Euodia-and-Syntyche situation (4:2–3). O'B 339–40, the "cause of . . . anxiety" for the two women is Paul. Peterlin (223–24, cf. 200, 204), one of the women *diakonoi* and her house congregation withdrew (financial) support from Paul and so precipitated an "anti-Pauline lobby" in Philippi. The majority of Philippian Christians agreed to send Epaphroditus to Paul with the funds they had collected. News of his illness caused further strife at Philippi ("a failed mission"). No wonder Epaphroditus worried and Paul sent him back (prematurely) with so carefully phrased a letter. Paul was mediating between two groups in Philippi when he wrote 2:25–30, putting the best construction on how Epaphroditus had not failed in the mission on behalf of the Philippians (Mayer). Cf. Combrink 144, a "breach in the relationship between the Philippians and Epaphroditus." Much here cannot be

---

[19] Metzner 115, "Epaphroditus as disappointment who has not come up to expectations"; Bittlinger, irony; K. Barth 87–89; Craddock 51; Wohl. 155–61; Michael 118–19; Mengel 259; Peterlin 189ff.

[20] Metzner 116, citing B. Mayer 1987, criticism of Epaphroditus who could not do what was necessary because of illness; I. H. Marshall 70; cf. Hawth. 119; Silva 159, "Was Epaphroditus a consolation prize, sent simply because Timothy, whom the Philippians expected, had to stay with Paul?"

[21] Metzner 116, citing Egger 64; Ernst 88; Schenk 238; Fee 272–73, at worst "Paul is here 'covering Epaphroditus' tracks' for him." Metzner 116–19 denies any tensions between Epaphroditus and the congregation in Philippi (united, no varying house churches). Sending Epaphroditus parallels sending Timothy (in spite of *de* at 25a, *But*); 29b, *such persons hold in honor* = standard admonition, not specific address to a local problem. "Epaphroditus enjoys undivided trust in his home congregation" (118). The personal and "intensive friendship" between Paul and the congregational *apostolos* that Metzner claims (see NOTE on 2:25b) is a product of assuming Phil to be a "letter of friendship" and then applying an optimistic assessment of *philia* to Paul and Epaphroditus and the Philippians; the common bond is not Christ but the Hellenistic philosophy exemplified in Sir 6:16, "a trustworthy friend is a life-saving medicine, those who fear the Lord will find one" (131).

proven or disproved from our texts. In 4:2–3, must the blame always be heaped on the two women? Paul was not the controverted figure in Philippi Peterlin 273–74 thinks (so Bockmuehl 173). But Epaphroditus was controversial, at least to some of the Philippians, if for no other reason than that he seems to have failed in part of his mission. Hence (U. B. Müller 131), "a developing crisis" between Epaphroditus and his congregation. Paul seems relieved at seeing him go (more without sorrow), a fourth reasons for sending him home. How will Epaphroditus be received in Philippi?

d. *Commendation for Extraordinary Service (2:29–30).* To abet Epaphroditus' return home Paul issues a double injunction (a) about the Philippians' envoy specifically and (b) more broadly but pertinent: ᵃ *Give him a continuing welcome, therefore, in the Lord with all joy,* ᵇ *and such persons hold in honor.* Why Epaphroditus rates this will be elaborated in v 30. *welcome* is preferred to "receive" (KJV), which can sound grudging (see NOTE), ongoing action, "an *enduring* welcome" (O'B 340; Bockmuehl 174), over the long haul, against any presumption the Philippians might not find him acceptable. As in v 28, *oun* points to conclusions from what has been said above, and to specific paraenetic advice. On *in the Lord* (which with 2:19 frames the passage) and *with all joy,* see NOTES: Christ's lordship is the realm in which everything about (Timothy and) Epaphroditus takes place, "joy" characteristic of Christians and what they do. Schnider/Stenger ([1] Bibl.) 176, an epistolary formula of joy. The pl. "you" (understood; cf. *you all,* v 26) implies every Philippian believer

2:29b is about a class or group (of congregational leaders) whom Philippian house church members are to *hold in honor,* honor-shame aspects of Gk. culture; recognition appropriate to the city-state and the church *(in the Lord).* Thus the twin aspects of 1:27 are reflected. Paul does not add here, "Be subject to such persons" (1 Cor 16:16, not at issue here? too delicate an issue?). He strengthens the place and role(s) of Epaphroditus in Philippi, in any office he holds now or in the future, and, in endorsing leaders who exhibit qualities such as Epaphroditus has shown, however imperfectly, affirms local leaders in the face of any controversy going on in Philippi.

Why does Epaphroditus rate such honors? Paul expands on what the man has done, ³⁰ᵃ*because, for the sake of work for Christ, he came close to dying,* ᵇ*having risked his life* ᶜ*in order that he might fill up what was lacking in your service towards me.* = 27a in different language. If *mechri thanatou* in 30a (see NOTE) reflects 2:8, Christ "obedient unto death," there are intricate overtones, esp. if Epaphroditus had anything to do with the composition of 2:6–11 (Schenk 239). But no talk of *tapeinophrosynē* (humility, humiliation) or "god-likeness" on Epaphroditus' part in 2:25–30. Detractors would readily point out, he did *not* die; he was perhaps a bit arrogant in undertaking this *leitourgia;* was his illness a sign of disfavor? He *came close to dying,* but *God showed mercy on him* (27b; cf. 2:8c, 9a). That calls for honor and esteem, not by God's exalting him but the Philippians' welcoming him. Epaphroditus' brush with death is made more vivid by the phrase ᵇ*having risked his life* (see NOTE). The lexical problem is now resolved by older NT MSS discovered since 1611 and an aptly parallel inscription as well as other evidence for *paraboleusamenos*, but without notions of "gambling his life" and wordplay on (Ep-)Aphrodite/us. The most important phrase, rhetorically and theologically, is that with which Paul leads off 30ab: *for the sake of work for Christ* Epaphroditus ventured all he did. Not "for Paul" (Ollrog 192) or self, but for Christ. "The work" = the gospel cause, specifically the Pauline mission in and around Philippi and Ephesus. In his life and with his resources Epaphroditus worked out "what salvation means" (2:12e).

Epaphroditus did this ᶜ*in order that he might fill up what was lacking in your service towards me.* Traditional difficulties in understanding 2:30c are clarified by looking at 4:10–20 (O'B 344) as the body of an earlier letter. In it Paul acknowledged receipt of the Philippians' gift through Epaphroditus (4:18), making reference to "needs" (his and theirs, 4:16, 19), using language about "want" or "lack" (4:11 *hysterēsis*; in 2:30 *hysterēma*) and "filling (up)" what is lacking or needed (4:19). See NOTE on 2:30c and cross-references to ch. 4 for details. Paul carries over language from 4:10–20 in 2:25d, Epaphroditus as "*leitourgos* for my need (*chreias*)" (see above), and in 2:30c *what was lacking* (Peterlin 201–03, *hysterēma* = "shortage *of money*" for living; Ollrog 98–99, lack of other Philippians in Paul's current mission work). *fill up* is not to be vested with overtones about salvation, certainly not from Col 1:24. It simply means "make up what is lacking" in a fiscal balance-sheet, as at 1 Cor 16:17. Believers in Philippi could not provide, because of geographical distance, necessities for Paul's physical existence in Ephesus, mission liaison and "leg-work" with other Christians there, legal assistance, etc. But Epaphroditus did, as circumstances and health permitted. That, Paul lifts up, not in criticism of the Philippians but to conclude his commendation for the man going home. 2:30 parallels the accolades for Epaphroditus at the beginning of the passage (Mayer 1987:188, cf. Fabris, *Filippesi* 85):

v 25:	fellow worker	v 30:	for the sake of work for Christ
	my fellow soldier		he came close to dying,
			having risked his life
	your "apostle"		in order that he might fill up
			what was lacking
	public servant of my need		in your service towards me

Epaphroditus' ministry is cause for joy, Paul writes, seeking to persuade the Philippians (*DA* 260, cf. 227), within "friendship" categories (*TDNT* 9:166 n 166; Fitzgerald 1997:234, 1998:147, cf. 28–29). 3:1 will add, besides "welcome him" and "honor such persons," *Rejoice in the Lord.*

3. 2:19–30 in the Redacted, Canonical Philippians. Once Letter B was placed in a four-ch. epistle, 2:19–30 (a) generally diminished in importance. Specific travel, mission plans now stood in the middle of the expanded letter. Its new location has tempted some (Luter/Lee; C. W. Davis; Bittasi) to make 2:19–30 the heart of a four-ch. concentric structure, but the contents have seldom led commentators to such a view. Instead, travel plans so far from the letter's ending seemed lost in the shuffle. Funk's "apostolic parousia" form here led defenders of a four-ch. Phil to downgrade the "form," lest the vv suggest the conclusion of a shorter letter (B).

(b) Ch. 3, with its vigorous refutation of opponents, overshadowed 2:19–30 and influenced how some details in it were interpreted. For 2:20, *all who seek after their own interests, not those of Jesus Christ,* and sorrows that weigh on Paul (27b), speculations could be brought in from 3:2–21 about gnostic Christians (Schmithals; 2:20ff. = " 'divine-men' missionaries," Jewett 1970b:369, 390) or Jewish Christians. Epaphroditus would face such opponents upon return to Philippi.

(c) Relating 2:19–30 to ch. 3 encouraged the theme of "imitation" (3:17), so that in ch. 2 Timothy, Epaphroditus, Paul, and ultimately Jesus Christ are said to be models to be followed. Epaphroditus becomes a positive model in contrast to the negative (merely rhetorical?) figures in 3:2–19. Could Epaphroditus have been an effective model in Philippi? See COMMENT A.2 and B.2.

(d) Positioning 2:19–30 before, rather than after, 4:10–20 complicated the picture of Epaphroditus and the money he brought Paul. Having mentioned Epaphroditus as *leitourgos* of the Philippians *for my need* (25c) and his *service towards me* on behalf of the Philippians (30c), why does Paul not refer to their gift and express thanks then and there (Walter 71)? The problem is exacerbated by redaction that puts Paul's note about the gift *after* plans now for Epaphroditus. ·

(e) But "apostolic parousia" (2:19, 25, 28) is seldom related to Christ's parousia (3:20–21).

2:19–30 lacks doctrinal content (K. Barth 79). Attempts[22] to make ethical models out of Timothy and Epaphroditus are dubious when examined. The passage has no history in lectionary use, even for commemoration of Timothy or "St. Epaphroditus" (but cf. I. H. Marshall 74).

SELECT BIBLIOGRAPHY (see also General Bibliography and Commentaries)

Agnew, F. H. 1986. "The Origin of the NT Apostle-Concept: A Review of Research," *JBL* 105:75–96.

Black, D. A. 1984. *Paul, Apostle of Weakness. Astheneia and Its Cognates in the Pauline Literature,* American University Studies, Series 7: Theology and Religion 3 (New York/Bern/Frankfurt/Nancy: Peter D. Lang) 207–14, 309–11.

Christou, P. 1951. "ISOPSYCHOS. Ph. 2.20," *JBL* 70:293–96.

Fridrichsen, A. 1938b. "*Isopsychos* = ebenbürtig, solidarisch," *SO* 18: 42–49 (= Magno Olsen FS). repr. in his *Exegetical Writings* (1994) 221–27.

Funk, R. W. 1967. "The Apostolic *Parousia:* Form and Significance," in *Christian History and Interpretation. Studies Presented to John Knox,* ed. W. R. Farmer/ C. F. D. Moule/R. R. Niebuhr (Cambridge: Cambridge Univ. Press) 249–68.

Gutierrez, P. 1968. *La Paternité spirituelle selon Saint Paul.* EB. Paris: Gabalda.

Hahn, F. 1974. "Der Apostel im Urchristentum," *KD* 20:54–77.

Jeremias, J. 1959. "Paarweise Sendung im Neuen Testament," in *New Testament Essays* for

---

[22] Thielman 1995:158–59; Bloomquist 173–78, Timothy, Epaphroditus, Paul, and Christ as *exempla;* Witherington 81, citing O'B 344; Oakes 2001:104, 121. To Epaphroditus "as a godly example of the way the Philippians should imitate Christ" (O'B 1992:178), B. Dodd 190–95 objects that, unlike Christ, Epaphroditus in his brush with death did not die; "Paul's paradigmatic 'I' exemplifies the soteriological significance of life 'in Christ,' " not mirror images for ethics.

T. W. Manson (Manchester: Manchester Univ. Press) 136–39, repr. in his *GA*, *Abba* 132–39.

Johnson, L. A. 2006. "Paul's Epistolary Presence in Corinth: A New Look at Robert W. Funk's Apostolic *Parousia*," *CBQ* 68:481–501.

Jonge, H. J. de. 1975. "Eine Konjektur Joseph Scaligers zu Philipper II 30," *NovT* 17:297–302.

Judge, E. A. 1986. "The Quest for Mercy in Late Antiquity," in O'Brien, P. T./D. G. Peterson, ed., FS D. B. Knox ([1] Bibl. **God**, under "Morris, L."), 107–21.

Lees, H. C. 1925–26. "Entre nous," *ExpTim* 37:46.

Mayer, B. 1987. "Paulus als Vermittler zwischen Epaphroditus und der Gemeinde von Philippi, Bemerkungen zu Phil 2,25–30," *BZ* 31:176–88.

Metzner, R. 2002. "In aller Freundschaft. Ein frühchristlicher Fall freundschaftlicher Gemeinschaft (Phil 2.25–30)," *NTS* 48:111–31.

Mitchell, M. M. 1992. "New Testament Envoys in the Context of Greco-Roman Diplomatic and Epistolary Conventions: The Example of Timothy and Titus," *JBL* 111:641–62.

Moffatt, J. 1917. "Philippians II 26 and 2 Tim IV 13," *JTS* 18:311–12.

Mullins, T. Y. 1973. "Visit Talk in New Testament Letters," *CBQ* 35:350–58.

Nauck, W. 1958. "Das *oun*-paräneticum," *ZNW* 49:134–35.

White, J. L. 1971b. "The Structural Analysis of Philemon: A Point of Departure in the Formal Analysis of the Pauline Letter," SBLSP 1971 (Missoula, MT: SBL) 1–47.

Young, J. E. 1976. "'That some should be Apostles,'" *EvQ* 48:96–104.

10. *Toward Concluding Paraenesis,* 3:1

TRANSLATION

3:1a Finally, my brothers and sisters, rejoice in the Lord. b To write the same things to you does not cause me hesitation and provides steadfastness for you.

NOTES

3:1a. *Finally. loipos,* "(what) remains, (the) rest," neut. acc. sg., adv. (BDAG 3.b), + art. (BDAG *ho, hē, to* 2.f). BDAG *as far as the rest is concerned, beyond that, in addition, finally.* As adv. of sequence could refer to "the rest" of Paul's agenda (Loh., Gnilka, U. B. Müller, Hendriksen 197; cf. NAB); or "what remains" temporally (1 Cor 7:29, "from now on" [N]RSV; Phil 4:8; no art., 1 Thess 4:1; 1 Cor 1:16; 4:2); "for the future" (LSJ), "henceforth." Cavallin, "interjunctional." Can approach *oun,* "therefore," inferential (Meecham, with appeal to Modern Gk.; Loh. 123 n 1; ATR 1146; Holmstrand 117). Moule, *IB* 161–62, cites both senses; *finally* (KJV-NRSV, NIV; G. Barth 54) is "commonest" or *and so* (here; 2 Cor 13:11); ZG 598; Hawth. 122, 124, "Well, then" (Moffatt; Caird 131–32); O'B 348;

Tellbe 2001:265 n 241. Tr. is complicated by text segmentation. Does 3:1a conclude a section (2:28–30; Lft. 125; Beare 100; Collange 122; Furnish 1963–64) or
introduce what follows (Vincent 90; Loh/Nida 88)? Thrall 25–30, transitional to
"a logical conclusion" *or* to "a fresh point" (28, but hardly the point in 3:2, Bockmuehl 177). *finally* indicates Letter B is drawing to a close (resisted by Hawth.
123–24; O'B 348; but see 2 Cor 13:11; Gal 6:17; Schenk 242, *clausula epistolae*,
the close of a letter). Or *finally* in a list (cf. Thrall 29) to introduce the last of
(three) impvs. in 2:29–3:1 (*DA* 258, cf. 239–41). Black 1995, it hastens toward a
conclusion (40 n 39); "a transitional device ('furthermore')."

my brothers and sisters. See NOTE on 1:12 *adelphoi*. + *mou* (4:1); cf. *my beloved*,
2:12. J. W. Marshall 367, "to identify with and ingratiate himself to the audience,"
thus "ethos through style"; Reed, transitional marker or "marker of emphasis
(focus)" (*DA* 262 n 397).

rejoice (pres. impv.). See NOTES on *chairō* 1:18ab; 2:17, 28; 4:10; *chara* 1:4;
impv. at 2:18. Instead of ("continue to) *rejoice*" (BDAG 1; KJV-NRSV, most trs.,
comm.), *good-bye* or *farewell* (BDAG 2.a) is possible (Gdsp. tr. and 1945:174–75;
cf. *Od.* 5:205; Beare 100, 145–46; Rahtjen 171; *JBC* but *NJBC* "rejoice" in Letter
B; NEB; NRSV-mg.). Both senses in Lft.125; NEB, "farewell; I wish you joy."
D. Thomas 1996: "Pin your hopes on the Lord (not elsewhere)!" Since "farewell"
suggests the conclusion of Letter B (H. Conzelmann, *TDNT* 9:367), it is vigorously resisted (Fee 291 n 23). Analogous is 2 Cor 13:11, *loipon, adelphoi, chairete*:
RSV "Finally, brethren, farewell," but v 9 "we rejoice," + four impvs. in v 11;
hence NRSV-mg "rejoice" (so Furnish, AB 32A:581). Cf. Alexander 1989:97.
Reed finds only one papyrus letter using *chairete* at the end meaning "farewell," a
reconstructed Christian example, about A.D. 400 (*DA* 242 n 315; Sb 6.9527.17);
"farewell," in (sepulchral) inscriptions, robs joy of its force as a theme (Gnilka
165; U. B. Müller 133 n 81; Holloway 2001a:131 n 6). That *chairete* "should suddenly acquire a new meaning" here is unlikely (Bockmuehl 178). Rejoicing is a
"friendship" theme, cf. Fitzgerald 1996:127, 144; *DA* 251; 257 n 380 (papyrus letters); 259–60. Gnilka (165 n 62; Zerwick 1953), "keep up the rejoicing"; Schenk
243 notes "always" at 4:4.

in the Lord. See NOTES on *en kyriō[i]*, 2:19, 29; 4:10; + the same impv. 4:4;
BDAG *en* 4.c, close association, personal relation. The "basis for joy" is "in the
Lord—and not anywhere else" (I. H. Marshall 78). Sometimes taken as obj. of the
vb. (cf. 1:18; B. Weiss 217, contrast "boast in the flesh," 3:3; Bruce 101; O'B 350,
noting Pss. 32:11, 33:1; Fee 291; Schenk 248, rejoice in view of our risen Lord).
Usually the sphere in which Christians rejoice (Wohl. 162); i.e. (Conzelmann,
TDNT 9:369), ecclesiological; W. Kramer ([1] Bibl. **Christ**) §50b; Neugebauer
(144 n 17, against OT derivation), an "incorporative" sense; Merk 1968:188–89;
O'B 350; GNB "in your union with the Lord." Paul usually employs "*epi*, never
en, to indicate the object of *chairō*," but 1:18 is ambiguous, so possibly obj. of the
vb. here (*DA* 257–58 n 381). But contrast our NOTE on 1:18c *over this fact*. Reed,
here not "solely . . . theologically-motivated" (as with O'B 349) but "sociologi-
cally-motivated . . . by the epistolary situation" (256–57). See COMMENT B.1.

3:1b. *To write the same things to you does not cause me hesitation and provides* *steadfastness for you.* Subject infin. (no art., unlike 1:21, 22, 23, etc.), *graphein*, pres. tense. No one presses for "keep on writing." Some supply "again" as if *palin* (Witherington 86; G. Barth 54). Dir. obj. = *ta auta*, neut. pl., *autos* attrib. position, = same; see NOTE on 2:18 *In the same way (to de auto)*. *TAAUTA* was contracted in א* F G P into *TAUTA*, dem. pron. "these things" (Rahtjen 172). A common confusion; *tauta* is usually not even noted. Holloway 2001a:131 n 6, "no need (for us) to write (to you)" is "a common hortatory idiom"; 1 Thess 4:9 (AB 32B:243–44, *paralipsis*, "one pretends to pass over something one in fact mentions," BDF 495.1); 5:1; 2 Cor 9:1; etc.; Malherbe 1987:70–72, to influence conduct, not new teaching.

ta auta. Emphasis is "on 'the same things,' not on 'to write'" (Fee 292 n 30). GNB (italics added) overtranslates, "I don't mind repeating what I've *written* before"; [N]JB. What *things*? Some see communications outside this passage (DA 243; O'B 350–52):

(1) The *same things* Paul took up (a) in Philippi previously (O'B 352, teachings repeated in 3:2–11, righteousness/ justification, coming to faith in Christ; Silva 167, 171–72; Garland 1985:164–65; Pollard 62). Fields 124 n 68, "some guidelines . . . presented previously," cf. 236. Or about false teachers; cf. 3:18, people "of whom I have often told you and now tell you . . . ," but 3:18 indicates clearly he is repeating earlier teachings. If this is Paul's meaning, *palin*, "again" should have been included (Fee 292 n 30). (b) The *same things* as in previous letter(s) not now extant (Lft. 138–42, noting the pl. "letters" in Pol. *Phil.* 3.2; Vincent 91; Michael 123; Loh/Nida 89). Letter A, the "thankless thanks," 4:10–20? In Letter B, what precedes (on Epaphroditus?), or what follows? (c) *things* Paul communicated orally after the founding mission (Erasmus, cited in Beare 2nd ed. 1969; Gnilka 185). Formidable objections in Bockmuehl 179–80. (d) *things* the bearer of the letter would add orally (Martin 1976:124; Furnish 1963–64:86–87, *asphales* 3:1b = "specific, concrete" commands, like Phil 1:27). But this does not determine what these things are.

(2) The *same things* taken up in Letter B or Phil as a whole (Bockmuehl 180). (a) 3:1 *rejoice*. Objection: pl. *ta auta*, a single command (Wohl. 162 n 1; Fee 292–293); but "rejoicing" appeared earlier and often. Cf. Michaelis 52; Loh. 123–24, joy in martyrdom; Dib. 66; Hawth. 124; Merk 1968:188–89; Caird 132; Bruce 102; Walter 71; Bockmuehl 180. Schenk 242–48 links 3:1 with 4:4 in Letter B, *chairete* twice, once with *en kyriō[i]*. (b) Exhortations to humility and unity (M. Jones 1914 [INTRO. VI] 471, but his *Phil.* 48 sees previous oral or written warnings akin to 3:2ff.; Hendriksen 148, "militant unity"). (c) Warnings about dissension in the Philippian church (Lft. 125–26, e.g., 4:2–3). (d) The paraenesis as a whole in 1:27–2:18 (Holmstrand 116–17, pl. *auta*) or 2:12–18 (J. Ernst 91–92); or the plans announced in 2:19–30 (U. B. Müller 134–35). (e) Warnings about opponents in 3:2–19 (Mackay 163–64, "Judaizers," whom he wrongly finds also at 1:28, 29; 2:14–16; Gnilka 165; Collange 123; O'B 352); objections in Bockmuehl 178–79.

DA 254–55 supports reference to 3:1 from Paul's other two uses of *auta* at the beginning of a cl. (Rom 2:1; 1 Thess 2:14). Edart 217, should be sg. to refer to "rejoice" but it also occurs at 2:17–18, 29 and 4:4. Cf. P. Wick 57 (plus warning against opponents); Edart 218–19 (what follows in ch. 3 but with points of contact to ch. 2). Aspen's concentric structure took 3:1 with 2:19–30, highlighting "Epaphroditus' trials" (Pretorius 1995:280), with the sound principle not "to look outside the text to locate its referent" if one appears in the text itself.

After subject infin. + obj. *ta auta* and indir. obj. *to you (hymin)*, supply *estin.* Impers. but implies Paul *(emoi)* as real subject (*DA* 243), "I do not mind writing . . ." (Gdsp., etc.). *emoi men . . . hymin de . . .* , dats. of respect or advantage (BDF 188, 197; *DA* 252), *emoi* sharply juxtaposed with the indir. obj. *hymin. men* and *de* suggest contrast (cf. on 2:23, 24; ATR 1153); Reed, *de* is additive, not contrast (*DA* 252; *GNTG* 3:331–32). BDAG *men* 1.b, *de* is adversative, *men* "need not be translated." KJV, ". . . indeed . . . but"; [N]RSV omits *men*, takes *de* as "and." Emphasis is on the "two-part predicate adjective," the final words in each phrase (*DA* 252):

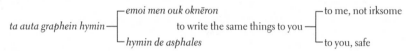

ta auta graphein hymin	⎡ *emoi men ouk oknēron*		⎡ to me, not irksome
	to write the same things to you	
⎣ *hymin de asphales*		⎣ to you, safe

Schenk 243, 248 sees a parenthetical protasis and apodosis, "If I repeat the same things for you, that is not irksome, but safe."

hesitation. oknēros, here neut. (to agree with the infin. cl., *DA* 252 n 361) nom. (or acc.) sg. + neg. *ouk.* Vb. *okneō*, "hesitate, delay" (Acts 9:38, "without delay"). Word family used in Gk., esp. in ethics (". . . fear of punishment . . . makes people hesitant [*oknērous*] towards base actions," Plut. *Lib. Edu.* 12CD = LCL *Moralia* 1:58–59). Cf. *Apophthegmata Pomp.* 204C = LCL *Mor.* 3:212–13; *TDNT* 5:166–67 (F. Hauck). In LXX wisdom literature, the slothful person (Prov 6:6, 9, "O lazybones"); 20:4; 21:25; contrast the virtuous wife, 31:27; Sir 22:1. Hence the other two NT occurrences ("possessing *oknos*," BDAG 1): the indolent servant (Matt 25:26); Rom 12:11, "not (f)lagging [*oknēroi*] in zeal or diligence." Thus Spicq, "always pejorative in the Bible" (*TLNT* 2:576). Phil 3:1, **involvement in *oknos*, causing hesitation, reluctance, *(such as)* to shrink from** (BDAG 2; ZG 598. *TDNT* 5:167, + *emoi* "irksome to me," RSV. *EDNT* 2:506, "I am not reluctant . . . ," cf. Soph. *OT* 834, "cause for trepidation." Dib. 66, "a stylistic formula" (classical evidence); Fridrichsen 1930. Hauck saw *mē oknōn graphein* ("not hesitating to write you," PElph 13.7) as an "expression in epistolary style" (*TDNT* 5:166); cf. MM 445; *TLNT* 2:577 papyri. *DA* 229–38, 23 papyrus examples where an *okneō*-term (vb., not adj. as here) is used in a request ("Do not hesitate [do not fail] to write me, knowing that without hesitation I will do it") + 10 more where writer gives a course of action ("I/we do/do not hesitate to . . . ," i.e., am/are not negligent or lazy in doing). An "epistolary hesitation formula" (COMMENT A.1): *okneō* word "plus some course of action . . . usually present in the preceding discourse," often + *graphō*, "near the closing of the letter" (238); at 3:1, " 'hesitating' . . . rather than 'burdensome, bothersome' " (304). The TRANSLATION paraphrases, *does not cause me hesitation.*

steadfastness. asphalēs, es (only here in Paul) = *alpha* privative (BDF 117.1) +

sphallō, "trip up"; "not slipping or falling," therefore (1) **firm** (Heb 6:19), or (3) **safe, secure** (BDAG). (2) *write someth.* **definite** (Acts 25:26). *asphaleia* (noun, Luke 1:4) often dominates word studies (K. L. Schmidt, *TDNT* 1:506; C. Brown, *NIDNTT* 1:663; G. Schneider, *EDNT* 1:175–76). Wide background in Gk. literature; appeal to medical vocabulary for Luke (*TLNT* 1:212–19) is problematic. Limited LXX uses (1:213 n 6, esp. in wisdom literature, Furnish 1963–64:83–84); MM 88 for papyri. 1 Thess 5:3, "Peace and security" likely reflects a Roman slogan, not Jer 6:14 (Wengst 1987 [(1) Bibl. **peace**] 77). Sometimes an act. sense, "that which makes safe" (cf. Erasmus; Luther, make certain); pass. "something to be relied on" is more common (Bockmuehl 181, *"inherently 'safe' . . . a bulwark against all manner of dangers"*); hence, "a safeguard" (NIV, NRSV), a precaution (Holloway 2001a:132). With Acts 25:26, Furnish 1963–64:84–86 argued for "definite, specific, concrete" at 3:1; "certain, dependable *knowledge*" (Acts 21:34, 22:30; 1 Clem 1:2; Phil 3[:10], with which he relates 3:1), specific warnings, contrast earlier generalities in 1:27–30 (so Collange 124, but Fee 292 n 31 finds no support for Furnish's view). Art. *to* before *asphales* in some cursives (NA²⁷; Gnilka 185 n 3, ℵ*), "the safe course" (TC), is secondary, though Tellbe 2001:264 n 241 urges it, *to asphales* = *asphaleia*, "security"—for Tellbe "the Judaizers' teaching as a safeguard or social protection." D. K. Williams 2002:149–53 claims a "political topos," the safety of the *polis*; N. T. Wright, a "coded message of subversive intrigue" (2000:175; 2003:235). Usually *oknēron* is taken as "irksome," *asphales* "assured from danger, safe," even "a guarantee" (*TLNT* 1:218). But if *oknēron* = "(causing) hesitation," then *asphales* = " 'trustworthy, unfailing'—sometimes to describe friends [LSJ 2]—or 'not liable to fall, immovable, steadfast' " (*DA* 253); Schenk 248, "serves to establish you"; 243, "strengthen." Thurston 112, "your steadying." The TRANSLATION paraphrases, *provides steadfastness for you.*

COMMENT

A. FORMS, SOURCES, AND TRADITIONS

1. *Aspects of Style in 3:1.* Edart 212, 214 finds little. But (Fee 288), 3:1(-2) is "asyndic (lacking the standard nuancing particle)." *Aposiopesis* (breaking off suddenly, to omit what is disagreeable to an audience) at the end of 3:1 (cf. Lausberg #888. 2b.α, "Such things . . . as I would hesitate [*oknēsaim'*] to mention"); (D. F. Watson 1988b:72–73), *aphodos* (transitional statement after his *digressio* in 2:19–30) and *transitio* (recalling what was said and briefly setting forth what follows) (cf. Lausberg ##849–51). In 1b, "to you . . . me" *(hymin emoi men)*, then *hymin de*, contrast, euphony and even rhythm (ATR 420). Beare 143, *ĕmoī mĕn oūk ŏknērŏn, hȳmĭn dĕasphălēs* = iambic trimeter (short syllable, then long; three measures), similarly Schenk 243; Moule *IB* 199 n 1, perhaps from an unknown Gk. source, a proverbial point, "for me no problem, for you a benefit." Hence *oknēron* and *asphales* do not fit context perfectly (Dib. 66). Reed (*DA* 251 n 359) sees an "epistolary hesitation formula": *okneō* + "to write" + a request ("rejoice")

or announcement of plans (here, send Epaphroditus and then come himself); see NOTE on 3:1b *hesitation.* None of Reed's papyrus examples uses the adj. form found in 3:1. Bockmuehl 178 was not persuaded, but D. F. Watson 2003:170–71 speaks of a "no grounds to hesitate" formula; not Mullins' "disclosure" form (Russell 304).

Some see *rejoice in the Lord* (1a) as Pauline "Psalms language," with Christ the object of rejoicing (Thielman 166–67; see NOTE on 1a, *in the Lord* as dir. obj.; Fee 291 n 27); *chairete* for *agalliaō* or *euphrainō* in the LXX, *en* instead of *epi,* Paul's regular usage. An OT explanation is unlikely; *en kyriō[i]* is a frequent, multivalent phrase in Paul.

2. The "Seam" at 3:1. Many see a break after 3:1. O'B 349 "a hinge," like 1:18; Engberg Pederson 2000:85, "a pivot" for "two halves that mirror one another."[1] Contrast D. F. Watson 2003:167–69. I. H. Marshall 77, 3:1a "has no direct connection with what precedes" and does not "seem to be connected with what follows." Some place the seam between 3:1a and 1b (Gnilka 165; Vincent 91–92; K. Barth 91, 3:1a could "be followed by 4:21f."; Collange 122). K. Lake 1914 took 3:1b–4:3 as an interpolation; Michael 1920 connected 3:1a with 3:20, making 3:1b–19 a unit. Others treat 3:1b as a redactional insert when several letter frgs. were combined.[2] Still others expand their tr.; Silva 168, ". . . rejoice in the Lord. [There is a matter, however, about which I must remind you.] Writing to you again about the same things is certainly not troublesome for me." Bockmuehl 175–77 termed 3:1 an "interim" or "unfinished conclusion," but finally decided for 3:1 as "a *general* conclusion to 2,19–30." G. H. Guthrie sees "cohesion" in 2:25–30 and 3:1–2.

We conclude that 3:1 followed 2:19–30 in the body of Letter B and can be understood in that context, without theories about redactoral insert or relegating 1a and 1b to separate letters (cf. Beare; Bornkamm; Schmithals; G. Barth; INTRO. VI.B). For what followed 3:1 in Letter B, see (15) on 4:1–9. Ch. 3:2–21 = Letter C. The same TRANSLATION of 3:1 can serve for both Letter B and the four-ch. letter. In both, 3:1 proves pivotal, but in different ways.

B. MEANING AND INTERPRETATION

1. In Letter B. Paul continues toward the conclusion of his second extant letter to Philippi, a conclusion signaled in 2:19–30 by travel plans (U. B. Müller 132–33) and 3:1a *Finally (to loipon).* Some paraenesis (now in 4:1–9) and greetings (as in 4:21–23) will round out the letter. 3:1 is closely connected with Paul's decision to send Epaphroditus home. To 2:28, *Welcome him in the Lord with all joy* and *Such*

---

[1] Bittasi 1–16 made 3:1 his starting point for finding parallel repetition in 1:1–2:18 and 3:2–4:23 (210, INTRO. VI. B n 3).

[2] Müller-Bardorff 1957–58 (INTRO. VI Bibl.) 593; Walter *Phil.* 20, 72. Edart 216–21, 3:1b was added when 3:2–16 was inserted from a separate letter; Luke was likely redactor, as for Heb (P. Garuti) and John (M.-E. Boismard).

persons hold in honor, Paul adds a third impv.: "As you do this, continue to *rejoice in the Lord."* Welcome and honor Epaphroditus, joyously (2:29a *with all joy*), in the realm where the Lord Jesus rules, i.e., the church community, *en kyriō[i]* 2:29a, 3:1a. Paul has paved the way for his return by sending Timothy on ahead and announcing that he himself plans to visit (he is personally concerned how his wishes will be carried out)—plus the implication, from Jesus' lordship, of judgment (2:16; cf. 4:4–5, "the Lord is near"; U. B. Müller 133). *my brothers and sisters* softens the tone and gains goodwill. If *to loipon* suggests "what remains" in Paul's agenda, concern about Epaphroditus is likely.

rejoice in the Lord has received diverse interpretations, depending on how *the same things* in 1b are taken. Loh. 123, joy for supposed martyrs in Philippi; rightly opposed by Gnilka 185 n 2. Joy as antidote to *these things,* esp. if *asphales* is taken as "safeguard"; joy becomes "a great safeguard to their souls" (Phillips), an attitude to "save them from the ills that plague their church—murmurings, dissensions, empty conceit, and so on" (Hawth. 124). Caird 132, "[J]oy . . . is a safeguard against the utilitarian attitude which judges people and things wholly by the use that can be made of them, and Christian joy, the exaltation of spirit that flows from acceptance of the free gifts of God's grace, is the best protection" against such things (repeated by Hawth. 124, Witherington 87). But joy "is hardly the cure for disunity caused by pride" (O'B 351), or grounds for security (Fee 293). Many a happy heresy or joyously confident Christians have split churches! Holloway 2001a:132 stresses Sen. *Ep.* 23.3, "Learn how to rejoice." Bockmuehl 181–82 links joy with God's strength (Neh 8:10; Pss 81:1; 48:2–3; 5:11, etc.); U. B. Müller 134, with the realm of God's might or reign, a sign of the kingdom of God (Rom 14:17), fruit from the Spirit (Gal 5:22; cf. 1 Thess 1:6) and expression of faith (Phil 1:25, G. Barth 55); power for the community in adverse circumstances, building up the community (*asphales* as *steadfastness*), with "revaluation of values" (Gnilka 191).

To take *in the Lord* as the object and/or ground of Christian joy is true theologically but hardly the intent here (see NOTE and COMMENT A.1). Paul is concerned with the Philippians as Epaphroditus returns. The rising crescendo of references to joy comes to a climax here[3]: joy in prayer (1:4), rejoicing in dire circumstances (1:18; 2:17), hope that the Philippians, as they progress in the joy of faith (1:25), would fill up his joy (2:2); he has urged them to rejoice together with him (2:18). Paul hopes they will rejoice when Epaphroditus returns (2:28), receiving him *with all joy* (2:29). Now for the first time the impv., "Continue to rejoice *in the Lord,"* i.e., in the church community under the Lord Christ.[4] 4:1 (the Philippians as Paul's joy) and 4:4 (3:1a repeated) also unfold the challenge, can the Philippians receive back Epaphroditus joyfully?

---

[3] Gnilka 165 speaks of the letter's *Ceterum censeo,* Paul's appraisal differs from the world's, a recommendation other than what is expected.

[4] Schenk 242–44, 248, 3:1b is parenthetical in a threefold pattern, "rejoice in the Lord" (1a), "rejoice in the Lord; always—I say it again—rejoice" (4:4); 3:2 and 4:1 = a framework of impvs. (274); Holloway 2001a:131 n 5 extends this *inclusio* to 3:1a "Rejoice *in the Lord,"* with 4:1 "stand thus *in the Lord."*

3:1b, sometimes called an *apologia* on Paul's part for repetition (Silva 171–72), is better understood as a further, irenic move by Paul, playfully to drive home *rejoice in the Lord*, with the comment, *To write the same things to you does not cause me hesitation and provides steadfastness for you*—phraseology from Gk. letters of the day, possibly in poetic meter and proverbial content (COMMENT A.1), about no grounds to hesitate at saying it again. If Paul's admonition is lived out (*DA* 254), *steadfastness* results. Furnish (1963–64:85) well saw something specific in the term, a concrete challenge to rejoice at Epaphroditus' reintegration in the Philippian community (*DA* 253). If the pl., *the same things*, is stressed, more than joy in Letter B is in view: all the paraenesis in 1:27–2:18, *exercise your citizenship* (1:27a), *stand in* oneness (27c) in the face of Roman opponents.

2. 3:1 in Redacted, Canonical Philippians. Once 3:1 was followed by the body of Letter C (3:2–21), new puzzles and interpretations resulted, e.g., for *ta auta*; see NOTE on *the same things*. *to loipon* could not be understood as *finally*, but as "Now" (Gdsp., NEB/REB), "Well, then," or "Whatever happens" (LB, NLT). *adelphoi* was taken, like *brothers and sisters* in 3:17, to contrast with menacing opponents. *rejoice in the Lord* became not the climax of references to joy in Letter B but just another example of a repetitious theme about which Paul was a bit apologetic, a problem when juxtaposed with 3:2, "Look out for the dogs." This "abrupt transition" (O'B 347) led to theories that, during a pause in dictating (a delay of perhaps some time), Paul received a frightening report about opponents on the prowl, soon to threaten Philippi. 3:1 = an "interim conclusion," followed by a new section after Paul heard "alarming news" about the Judaizers (Bockmuehl). Or "Paul stopped writing or dictating after the words *chairete en kyriō[i]*; by the time he returned to the document he had decided he must include a doctrinal discussion," on something he had communicated orally before (Silva 167). Rhetoric gives other answers.[5] It seems preferable, in the four-ch. letter, to hold to a connection with Epaphroditus (2:25–30): rejoice when receiving him in the church community, home after his vicissitudes.

3:1b functions as both summary and transition. *To write the same things* can refer back to all the references to rejoicing in 1:1–2:30, more broadly to the paraenesis (1:27–2:18) Paul has kept reiterating. The epistolary formula (not being hesitant to broach a topic) can now refer to warnings against false teachers in 3:2–19. Even if the tr. "not troublesome to me" is customary, Reed's "hesitation formula" is applicable, but *steadfastness* for *asphales* is probably harder to sustain in a letter that includes 3:2–21; the idea of a "safeguard" (NIV, NRSV), through what Paul writes against false teachers, is more attractive. Integration of 3:2–21

---

[5] D. F. Watson 1988b:76, 3:1–21 is "a further development of the proposition of the letter, namely 1:27–30" (O'B 345), i.e., paralleling developments in 2:1–11 and 12–18 of the *propositio* (2:19–30 = *digressio*). Black 1995, 3:1–4:9 = a "body subpart," against "pride in human achievements," after 1:12–2:30 on unity. Fee 286, 3:1 is a "framing device" for 3:1–4:9 as Paul returns to "their [the Philippians'] affairs."

with 3:1 loosens connection with 2:25–30 (Epaphroditus) and heightens influence of warnings and examples in ch. 3.

In lectionaries 3:1 has had no usage, little in preaching, doctrine, or ethics.

SELECT BIBLIOGRAPHY (see also General Bibliography and Commentaries)

Cavallin, A. 1941. "*(to) loipon.* Eine bedeutungsgeschichtliches Untersuchung" *Eranos. Acta philologica Suecana* 39:121–44.

Fridrichsen, A. 1930. "Exegetisches zu den Paulusbriefen, 4. Phil. 3,1" *TSK* 102:300–1, repr. In his *Exegetical Writings,* ed. C. C. Caragounis/T. Fornberg (1994) 209–10.

Meecham, H. G. 1936–37. "The Meaning of *(to) loipon* in the New Testament," *ExpTim* 48:331–32.

Michael, J. H. 1920. "The Philippian Interpolation—Where Does It End?" *Expositor,* 8th Series, 19:49–63.

Reed, J. T. 1996. "Philippians 3:1 and the Epistolary Hesitation Formulas: The Literary Integrity of Philippians, Again," *JBL* 115:63–90.

Thomas, D. 1996. "Rejoice in the Lord? Cohesion in Philippians 3:1," *Notes* 10:53–54.

Zerwick, M. 1953. "Gaudium et Pax —custodia cordium (Phil 3,1; 4,7)," *VD* 31:101–4.

LETTER C, BODY, 3:2–21

11. *A Brusque Warning: "Circumcision" and Us*, 3:2–4a

TRANSLATION

3:2 Beware the dogs! Beware the wicked workers! Beware "the incision!" 3a For it is we who are "the Circumcision," 3b the ones who serve by the Spirit of God and make our boast in Christ Jesus and do not place confidence in the flesh, 4a although I for my part have grounds for confidence indeed in the flesh.

NOTES

3:2. *Beware . . . !* Pres. impv., 2nd pl., *blepō* (here only in Phil, but 3x); "**watch** (out for," NIV), **look to** ("look out for," RSV), **beware of** (KJV, NRSV) (BDAG 5). B. Weiss 1897 (*AJT* 1:390, cf. Vincent 92, Haupt 118) and Kilpatrick argue *blepō* means "beware" only when followed by *apo* (Mark 8:15, parr., etc.) or by a dependent cl. with *mē* (Mark 13:5 parr Matt 24:4, etc.; 1 Cor 8:9; 10:12; Gal 5:15, etc.); *blepō* + acc. = *look at, consider* (BDAG 5, 6b); connection with 3:1 "is not as abrupt as is usually assumed" (148). So Caird 132–33 ("the Jews . . . as a cautionary example!"); Hawth. 125; cf. Schoon-Janßen 124–25; Garland 1985:165–66; Geoffrion 196–97; Stowers 1991:116. U. B. Müller 142 n 23 minimizes any distinction. Contrast, against Kilpatrick, Silva 172; *DA* 244–46, "Kilpatrick's 'rule' is syntactically based whereas it should be semantically (or both syntactically and semantically) based" (245), "consider" "misses the urgency of the situation" (246); Schenk 253; O'B 353–54; Fee 293 n 36; Bockmuehl 185; C. Strecker 114 n 161; Holloway 2001a:133. The polemical context calls for "beware," not just "be aware of" (D. K. Williams 2002:154–55). No examples of such triple repetition are cited from ancient rhetoric, but cf. Tennyson's "Break, Break, Break . . . O sea!" (ATR 1178); "Blow, bugle, blow . . . Blow, bugle; answer, echoes, dying, dying, dying" ("The Princess," Part IV, Song, stanza 1).

the dogs. Acc. pl., *ho kyōn, kynos*, fig., to depreciate a group. Dogs in antiquity, except for hunting, herding, and as watchdogs, were generally held in contempt, as packs of scavengers (Ps 59:6, 14); not "man's best friend" or house pets. *kynaria* (diminutive, Mark 7:27–28 par Matt 15:26–27), not "lapdogs"; allowed into the house to wolf down food on the floor, *skybala*, "garbage," 3:8. Cf. E. Firmage, *ABD* 6:1143–44, 1153; W. S. McCullough, *IDB* 1:862; G. J. Botterweck, *TDOT* 7:146–57 (unclean and loathsome animals); Str-B 1:722–26, 3:621; S. Lachs, A

Rabbinic Commentary on the New Testament (Hoboken, NJ: KTAV, 1987) 138–39. Tobit 6:2 and 11:4 are the most positive references to canines in Scripture. O. Michel (*TDNT* 3:1101–4) suggests Paul might have known the logion at Matt 7:6, "Do not give what is holy to dogs"; S. Pedersen, "perhaps" (*EDNT* 2:332); definitely so, A. T. Hanson 1987:89–97. For dogs in the classical world, cf. *OCD*³ 490; *KlPauly* 2 (1967) 1245–49; *RAC* 16 (1993) 773–828; Cynic philosophers received their name ("dog-like") from Diogenes called "the dog" for his shamelessness.

3:2 is often said to stem from application of "dogs" by Jews to "non-Jews or lapsed Jews (Mt. 7:6, 15:26–27)" (Garland 1985:167–68; Loh. 124; Fowl 1990:98); Paul then turns back on Jews or Jewish Christians in 3:2 an epithet they contemptuously used of others. For the claim that "dogs" = Gentiles in Matt 15:26 par. Mark 7:27, there is less documentation than might be supposed (Garland 167 n 92; AB 26:84 cites Phil 3:2 as primary evidence). Matt 7:6 may reflect inner *Christian* debate; H. D. Betz, Hermeneia *The Sermon on the Mount* (1995) 493–500. If "dog" was once used by Jews for opponents, and Christians employed it for outsiders, then the application to apostates and heretics in the Christian movement follows the course traced for "demonic" language by E. Pagels, *The Origin of Satan* (New York: Random House, 1995).

the wicked workers. ergatēs (here acc. pl.); cf. NOTES on 1:6 *a good work*; 1:22 *fruitful missionary labor*; 2:30 work for Christ. Cf. Matt 9:37–38 par. Luke 10:2; Matt 20:1,2,8, a term for Christian missionaries (BDAG 1.b; 2 Tim 2:15), though never employed by Paul of himself or members of his mission team. The adj. (*kakos* 1.a, "bad," in a moral sense, "evildoer"; "wicked," *DA* 322) goes integrally with the noun. (1) Some derive *tous kakous ergatas* from the Pss (Bruce 104); but Ps 5:5 (LXX 6) and 6:8 (LXX 9) are "not exactly parallel" (O'B 355 n 54); *(kakoi) ergatai* "doesn't turn up in the canonical books of the LXX." Fee 296 n 47 offers 1 Macc 3:6 and Ps 93 (LXX 92):16 Symmachus. (2) In light of Reformation theology ("justification by faith," in contrast with "the works of the Law"; Bockmuehl 188) "workers" here are connected with *erga tou nomou*, against works-righteousness. Cf. Bultmann 1910:105; O'B 356; Fee 296, who relates it to (1), they work iniquity "in trying to make Gentiles submit to Torah." Bockmuehl 188, "a deliberate pun on the opponents' claim to be doing the so-called 'works of the Law,'" a Qumran phrase (4QMMT 113, *ma'asê ha-tôrah*). So Edart 224–25. Cf. F. Watson 1986, esp. pp. 2–18 and 74–80. A solution in light of Gal and the Judaizers. (3) "Worker(s)" is missionary terminology, as in 2 Cor 11:13; Georgi 1964a = 1986:40, a self-designation of Jewish-Christian missionaries in Corinth; see COMMENT A.2, below. Paul caustically adds "deceitful." Cf. AB 32A:494–95, 48–54. Not quite parallel; Paul's apostleship is not under attack in Philippi (O'B 356; Baumbach 1971). But supported by Synoptic usage (Matt 9:37–38) and later evidence (2 Tim 2:15; cf. 1 Tim 5:17–18, Quinn/Wacker, 450–51). Cf. F. Thiele, *NIDNTT* 3:1151; *EDNT* 2:49 (R. Heiligenthal); Loh. 125; U. B. Müller 142–43; Bockmuehl 187, "a contemporary expression of Jewish piety . . . turned into . . . [a] battle standard," Torah-faithfulness in contrast to "non-observant Pauline Christianity." Roloff 1965:112 n 252, a "terminus technicus for 'missionary,'" connected via the parable of the Laborers in the Vineyard (Matt 20:1–16) with the picture of the church as "God's planting" (1 Cor 3:9); Hainz 1972:321 n 3. For development of *ergatēs* as a term for missionary preacher in early Christianity, see Haraguchi.

"*the incision.*" *katatomē*, "cutting down, mutilating (the penis)," contrasts with *peritomē* in v 3 ("cutting around," removing the foreskin [prepuce], in circumcision). Not a term elsewhere in the NT. Gk. background (H. Koester, *TDNT* 8:109–11): "incision, notch, groove" (LSJ), e.g., for a "sectional plane" (cross-cut) of a plant, tree, or stone ("face" in a quarry). Vb., cut into strips or pieces; among people beyond Scythia, when a man's father dies, kinsmen bring beasts from their flocks, slay them, and cut the meat up *(katatamontes)*, likewise *(katatamnousi)* the dead father, the pieces are mixed together for a feast (Herodot. 4.26 = LCL *Herodotus* 2:224–25). Aristoph. *Av.* 1524, "innards cut up." Hence people ready "to make mincemeat of someone" (Plato *Resp.* 6.488B = LCL *Plato* 2:18–19; cf. Aristoph. *Ach.* 300–301). Vb. = "crush" or "kill"; Xen. *Mem.* 1.2.55, "kill *(katatemnein)* oneself" = cut family ties; a speech of Demosthenes "inflicted a thousand gashes *(katatetmēke)*" (Aeschines, *In Ctes.* 212); Socrates and friends "cut up *(katatemnontes)* everything with words" (Plato *Hippias Major* 301B). Thus two backgrounds for Paul's use of *katatomē* (Koester 111): savage use of the vb.; ironic plays on words in the diatribe.

LXX use of *katatemnō* is "always for the forbidden rite of slitting the skin" (Koester 110) in pagan cult or mourning, not allowed to Israel (Lev 19:28; 21:5; Deut 14:1). Baal priests "cut themselves *(katetemnonto)* . . . until blood gushed . . ." (1 Kgs = 3 Bas.18:28; Oakes 2000 [(4) Bibl. **1:19**] 258); people "gash themselves *(katetetemnonto)* for grain and wine" (ritual self-mutilation for fertility, Hos 7:14; AB 24: 474–75 relates this to Paul's diagnosis of the heathen in Rom 1:24–25); Isa 15:2 LXX , "arms lacerated *(katatetmemenoi)*" instead of "beards shorn." Vb. more frequent in Aquila, Theodotion, and Symmachus, who also has the noun *katatomē* (Jer 48 [LXX 31]:37) for "gashes" on the hands. Cf. MM 334. In such OT references to "ritual maimings . . . abhorrent to a Jew," Koester finds additional, ironic background for Paul's turning the term against (Jewish-Christian) opponents. Blaschke 402–3, circumcision is like this forbidden pagan practice; so Edart 222–24, with Vanni 2000:59–61. Paul's own experiences and situation add other reasons for his use of *katatomē*; see COMMENT B.1, below.

For such wordplay in Eng. and Gk., see Lft. 144. Philo, *Spec.* 1.9, circumcision is "excision [or cutting off] of excessive *(perittēs* [Attic for *perissēs] ektomēn)* and superfluous pleasure"; perhaps, in Heb., Gen Rab 46.10. To reproduce it in Eng. is difficult. Vg used *concisio* (not *consisura* = cut, incision) in a play on *circumcisio* (*concisio* = a rhetorical term for dividing up of words into cls. [OED; Cic. *Part.* 19]; not in Lausberg); KJV "concision," a transliteration little used except in "church talk." With RSV, "mutilate (the flesh)" became popular. Gdsp. was blunt, "mischief-makers with their amputation." JB, "the cutters" (GNB "cutting the body"), NJB "self-mutilators." NEB/REB paraphrase, ". . . mutilation— 'circumcision' I will not call it." CEV, they "want to do more than just circumcise you." TRANSLATION, *"the incision"* keeps the wordplay, reflecting a basic classical LXX meaning.

3:3a. *For it is we who are "the Circumcision."* hēmeis is emphatic; TRANSLATION adds, "It is . . . who . . ." to bring this out (so NAB; GNB "It is we, not they . . ."). "We/us, of us" occurs in Phil 3: 17, 20, 21, all in Letter C; otherwise only in stock formulas at 1:2 and 4:20 ("God our Father"). 1st pers. pl. vb., only at 3:15; cf. *DA* 322. gar links 3a with v 2 (trs. often omit it). V 3 explains *"the incision."* Art. + pred. noun *(hē peritomē),* as thrice in v 2. "Circumcision" can be used by Paul for the Jewish rite where a male child entered into the covenant relationship (3:5, below). More frequently, for the state of being circumcised (1 Cor 7:19; Rom 2:25–26, contrast NRSV "uncircumcision" *[akrobystia,* lit. "foreskin"]; Gal 5:6, neither it nor uncircumcision counts for anything, only "faith working itself out through love"; 6:13). Already in the OT, where *peritomē* occurs only 4x (Fields 268), there were voices giving a "spiritual" (Fields 265) and even "allegorical" sense to this visible mark (for males) of the covenant (Gen 17:10–24): circumcise "the foreskin *of the heart"* (Deut 10:16; 30:6; Jer 4:4); Israel is "uncircumcised in heart," no better than other, uncircumcised, nations (Jer 9:25–26; 1 QS 5.5–6; 1QpHab 11.13). Paul reflects this sense at Rom 2:29 (NRSV), "A person is a Jew who is one inwardly, and real circumcision is a matter of the heart (Gk. simply *peritomē kardias)*—it is spiritual *(en pneumati)* and not literal." Cf. Col 2:11, *"peritomē* not made with hands" (NRSV "spiritual"). Dunn 1999:182: a Jew "'in Spirit, not in letter' (Rom. 7.6; Phil. 3.3)," "a Jew *en tō(i) kryptō(i)* (Rom. 2.29)." 3:3, abstract noun for the concrete "those who are circumcised" (BDAG 2.b). Paul could employ *peritomē* for (a) Jews (Rom 3:30; 4:9, 12a; 15:8; Gal 2:7–9) or Jewish Christians (Gal 2:12); (b) here only, Gentiles. O. Betz terms this concrete meaning "[w]hat is new in the NT" *(EDNT* 3:79); cf. T. R. Schreiner, circumcision is "Entrée into 'Newness' in Pauline Thought." Many insert some adj. ("the true circumcision," Gdsp., RSV, NJB). See COMMENT B.1 on "the Circumcision" as a title for Christians in community.

3:3b. *the ones who serve by the Spirit of God and make our boast in Christ Jesus and do not place confidence in the flesh.* 3a, "the Circumcision," is explained by a noun phrase, art. *(hoi,* masc. nom. pl.) + three subst. ptcs., *latreuontes kai kauchōmenoi . . . kai . . . pepoithotes.* Cf. BDF 269, 276; GGBB 278–86. Each ptc. + obj. or prep. phrase, one after, two before, the ptc.

latreuō (in Paul, only at Rom 1:9, 25 + 2 Tim 1:3; noun *latreia,* Rom 9:4 and 12:1), "serve, render services," in nonbiblical Greek "not very common" (H. Strathmann, p. 59, *TDNT* 4:58–65; cf. K. Hess, *NIDNTT* 3: 549–51; next to nothing in papyri or inscriptions, MM 271). Could refer to service to the gods (Eur. *Ion* 152; Plut. *De Pyth.* 26 [*Mor.* 407E]; Epict. 3.22.56; noun, Plato *Ap.* 23C, *Phdr.* 244A, etc.). In LXX, frequent (70x, esp. Exod, Deut, Josh, and Judg), noun 9x, usually of sacred cult (Heb. *'ābad,* also rendered by *douleuein,* "serve as a slave"). E.g., Exod 3:12; 7:16, "serve," in the sense of "worship," + Yahweh as object (Exod 23:25; Deut 10:12, 20) or other gods and idols (Exod 20:5; 23:24, etc.; *TDNT* 4:60–61). *leitourgein* was "wholly restricted to priestly functions"; *latreuein,* for Israel as a whole, "the inner attitude, of confident committal to Yahweh, of conduct" (61), e.g., Deut 10:12, cf. 10:16, "Circumcise, then, the foreskin of your heart"; Josh 24:18–24; spiritualized at Sir 4:14; 1 Macc 2:19, 22, contrast 1:43.

In the NT "the cultic" motif (H. Balz, *EDNT* 2:344) "is mentioned only in OT citations and references" (e.g., in Heb). In Rom, *hē latreia*, cult, was one of Israel's prerogatives (9:4); for Christians, "spiritual" or "reasonable worship" or "service" (*logikē latreia*, 12:1) = serving others in daily life (*EDNT* 2:345). Strathmann calls Rom 12:1 "the crown" of the theme's development in the Bible; in Phil 3:3 it "comprises the whole of Christian existence." Contrast Rom 1:25 ("serve [*elatreusan*] the creature [what God has made] rather than the Creator"); 1:9. *latreuō* could be rendered at 3:3b as *worship* (so most Eng. trs.; BDAG, also citing Koester 1961–62:320–21 *work as a missionary*). Fee (299 n 59) dismisses missionary service as "unlikely," but note Rom 1:9 and the "missionary" aspect of the opponents in 3:2. Fee rightly prefers "serve" (1994:752); his commentary concludes for "minister" (299–300), not far from missionary ministry.

The varied trs. of *hoi pneumati theou latreuontes* (NA²⁷) stem in part from textual problems. Some (Fee 288 n 10) see as original *hoi pneumati latreuontes* (P⁴⁶ vgᵐˢ; "who serve by [the] S/spirit," NEB "whose worship is spiritual"; REB-mg²; CEV-mg "worship sincerely") or *hoi pneumati theō[i] latreuontes* (ℵ² D* etc., "who serve God [obj. in dat.] in the Spirit," KJV; NRSV-mg); or "in spirit" (Moffatt; NEV-mg¹; REB-mg¹). The preferred text (*pneumati theou*) occurs in ℵ* A B C etc., {C}-level of certainty; J. D. Price 280–81, probability 0.63, 0.37 for the dat. *theō[i]*, 0.0 for omission of any reference to "God." P⁴⁶ is again careless (Silva 173, cf. 27). Fee (288 n 10), to "serve God" is so common (Rom 1:9, cf. 25; 2 Tim 1:3; etc.) that "it is difficult to imagine scribes deliberately changing" *pneumati* or *pneumati theō[i]* to *pneumati theou*.

pneuma can refer to the divine Spirit (BDAG 5.a; 1:19 "Spirit of Jesus Christ"; 1:27 *one and the same Spirit*; 2:1c *sharing in the Spirit*, both debated; DA 300, 306) or to "the spirit as part of human personality," a person's "very self" (BDAG *pneuma* 3.a and b, often with, and in contrast to, "flesh," as here [*en sarki* with *pepoithotes*]; 4:23 *with your spirit*). "Spirit of God" occurs at Rom 8:9, 14; 15:19 MSS; 1 Cor 2:11,12,14; 3:16; 6:11; 7:40; 12:3; 2 Cor 3:3; 1 Thess 4:8.

Since *latreuō* takes its obj. in the dat., one could render "worship the Spirit of God," but the Spirit is seldom the object of worship. Better: "serve" (Schenk 293, on the basis of Sir 4:14; cf. Koester 1962:321–22; Klijn 1965:284; Gnilka 188; Fee 1994:753 n 80). For Schenk, terminology from the "Jewish propagandists," a point rejected by U. B. Müller 144 n 30.

pneumati is commonly taken adverbially. Moule, *IB* 46, instrumental dat., "*whose service is of a spiritual (and not of a material) sort*"; GNTG 3:238–39, "dativus relationis," cf. 2:30 *tē[i] psychē[i]*. Instrumental in ATR 540, ZG 598, E. Schweizer, *TDNT* 7:131–32, with no dir. obj. for *latreuontes*, "worship by the Spirit of God" (RSV-mg, NEB-mg², REB-txt., NIV, NJB-txt.; CEV-txt "by the power of God's Spirit"); Fee 1994:753, "by means of the Spirit"; NRSV "in the Spirit of God" is locative, for "the sphere in which . . . we render proper service to God as we live in the Spirit." U. B. Müller 144 n 30, "modal." The Spirit is "an eschatological gift of salvation for the community as well as for the individual" (Hainz 1972:327 n 5), as in 1 Cor 12:13; Rom 5:5; 8:16.

Once textually *pneumati theou* is adopted, "worshiping God in the Spirit" (KJV, RSV) or "spiritually" (cf. NEB) fall to the ground. Meaning involves the relation to "flesh" in v 3 (twice in v 4) and what Paul is opposing in this definition of the church community.

and make our boast in Christ Jesus. kauchōmenoi, cf. *kauchēma* in NOTES on 1:26 and 2:16 *grounds for boasting.* Here a positive sense. As in those vv, KJV has "rejoice in Christ Jesus" at 3:3. On *en Christō[i] Iēsou,* see NOTE on 1:1 *in Christ Jesus* and subsequent uses (1:13, 26; 2:1, 5, cf. 1:13; 4:7, 21). Since *kauchomai* can be followed by *en* + dat. to indicate the object of a boast (LXX; 1 Cor 1:31, 2 Cor 10:17b [both = Jer 9:23]; Rom 2:17; 5:11; BDF 196), most take vb. and prep. phrase together, "boast (or glory) in Christ Jesus" ([N]RSV); cf. *TLNT* 2:299 n 17; Bultmann, *TDNT* 3:648–49 n 35. There is a parallelism with *pepoithotes* later in the v and contrast between *in Christ Jesus* and *in the flesh* (nn 37 and 39; Sánchez Bosch [(4) Bibl.] 191–92). The Christian boast is grounded in Christ; Bouttier 1962 ([1]Bibl. **Christ**) 136, "la raison d'être" for us. Cf. (1) Bibl. **Christ:** W. Kramer n 511 saw no ecclesial sense for "in Christ Jesus"; Neugebauer 1961: 99 n 3 related 3:3 to both ecclesiology and "the work of Christ," but *en* goes with *kauchasthai*; no "in-Christ" formula here (D. K. Williams 2002:160, with Reumann 1989b [(12) Bibl.] 135).

and do not place confidence in the flesh. Ptc. from *peithō* (BDAG 2.a, **be so convinced that one places confidence in someth[ing],** *depend on, trust in*), pf. act. with pres. meaning (BDF 341); see NOTES on 1:6 *since I am confident* and 1:14 *Having become confident in the Lord (en kyriō[i]).* The pf., *pepoitha* — "radically relying on God" (Bultmann, *TDNT* 7:7) — can be related to the word field "have faith, believe" (same stem, *pisteuō, peithomai;* O. Michel, *NIDNTT* 2: 587–606; Louw/Nida 31.82 and 85). Usually *pepoitha* + *epi* + dat. (2 Cor 1:9), but + *en* here. *ouk* negates *en sarki* (note the Gk. word order); a positive phrase can be inferred ("not in the flesh but [in Christ]"). *ouk,* rather than *mē,* reflects older practice (BDF 430; GNTG 1:231); cf. 1 Cor 4:14; 9:26; 2 Cor 4:8, 12x in the Pauline corpus.

sarx, see NOTES on 1:22 and 24 *in the flesh,* there neutral ("existence"), here pejorative (BAGD 6, "*the external . . . side of life,* as it appears to the eye of the unregenerate person, that which is natural or earthly . . . *earthly things or physical advantage*"; cf. BDAG 5). Spicq lists birth, fortune, etc as such advantages; at 3:3–6, Israelite descent, Pharisaism, zeal for the Law, and righteousness in accord with it (*TLNT* 3:237 n 35). Once *sarx* becomes the object of one's trust (at Rom 2:28, *en sarki peritomē;* cf. Gal 6:12–13), then "flesh" becomes, in Pauline use, the subject on which, and through which, Sin acts. While the Spirit "is often presented as an acting subject with and without *sarx,*" *sarx* "never occurs as the subject of an action where it is not in the shadow of a statement about the work of the *pneuma,*" as here (E. Schweizer, *TDNT* 7:126–32). Flesh becomes the base for operations by Sin, the bastion for human pride and improper boasting. W. D. Davies stressed the obvious *physical* connotation to *sarx* at Phil 3:3 ("Paul and the Dead Sea Scrolls: Flesh and Spirit," in *The Scrolls and the New Testament*, ed. K. Stendahl [New York: Harper, 1957] 163, repr. in Davies, *Christian Origins and Judaism* [Philadelphia: Westminster, 1962] 153), more "in the main stream of Old Testament and Rabbinic Judaism than in that of the sect" (182 = 177). Moehring saw at 3:3 "man as a whole," including a *moral* connotation (432). To show the radicality of Paul's position here on "flesh" (for which his ultimate term will be *skybala* 3:8, "rubbish"; Schenk 294), Moehring cited Targum of Jerusalem (ed. J. W. Etheridge) on Gen 40:23: Joseph (in prison, like Paul) put his trust in the chief butler, he "trusted in the flesh" (a mortal) instead of God (cf. Jer 17:5,7). For Paul, circumcision and its implied submission to the Law "belong to the realm of *sarx*" (436). Paul "attributes ethical conduct to the Spirit (Rom. 8:4–9)" (Bultmann 1951 [Intro. X Bibl.] 337). Westerholm 1988: 214–15 includes Phil 3:3 among passages about the Spirit as "enabler of Christian moral behavior." The moral side is not obvious as yet in ch. 3, but Paul is beginning to attack circumcision, Torah, and its kind of righteousness by lifting up *sarx* in an antithesis (cf. Schenk 294–95).

3:4a. *although I for my part have grounds for confidence indeed in the flesh.* Subordinate cl., linking the 1st pers. sg. account that follows to what Christians are in v 3. Not an independent sentence (Loh. 124, 128 n 2; KJV, RSV, NEB) or protasis to which v 8 provides the conclusion and corrective. The linking words between 3 and 4a are *confidence* (*pepoithēsin*) and *in the flesh*, repeated from v 3 (*en sarki pepoithotes . . . pepoithēsin kai en sarki*; a chiasm). Conj. *kaiper* (BDAG p. 497), **although,** often with a concessive ptc. (BDF 425.1; GNTG 1:230, 3:157); DA 326 "(even) though." *per* (B-D-R 107 n 2) gives intensive and extensive force to *kai*; "and 'in spite of opposition,'" ATR 1154; Heb 5:8, etc. Ptc., *echōn*, masc. nom. sg., with *egō* ("I," 4:11 in Letter A; 3:13; acc. *eme*, 1:12; 2:23, 27; gen. *emou* at 4:10, *mou* 24x in Phil; dat. *emoi* 10x, 1:7, 3:1, etc., plus *moi* 7x, first at 1:19), thus numerous references to himself, apart from the autobiography in 3:4b–14. NIV, NABRNT, "I myself." The Translation paraphrases, "I for my part." For ptcs. from *echō* (BAGD I.2.e.β, "*have as one's own, possess,*" BDAG 7.a.β, "characteristics, capabilities, emotions, inner possession") see 1:23 (*echōn*) and 2:2; subjunct. at 2:27 *that I might not have sorrow*; for 3:4a, ZG, "have (grounds for)" (NABRNT, cf. REB).

grounds for confidence. pepoithēsis (vb. root in v 3 *pepoitha*, "trust, confidence"), 6x in the NT, all in the Pauline corpus, esp. 2 Cor. Confidence toward God (2 Cor 3:4; Eph 3:12), confidence in other Christians (2 Cor 8:22; 1:15), and Paul in himself (2 Cor 10:2; cf. 1:15 and 3:4–6). Here, re *human* advantages (*TLNT* 3:79). Once in the LXX (2 Kings 18:19). The Gk. background is fuller (*TLNT* 3:66–79). The vb. has to do with persuasion and believing. Bultmann sees in Phil 3:4 confidence that "shapes the whole of existence," whether self-confidence and the privileges of 3:4–6 or "surrender to radical confidence in God" (2 Cor 3:4), faith in Christ v 9 (*TDNT* 7:7–8; O. Becker, *NIDNTT* 1:588–92). ZG 599, *pepoithēsis* here = *kauchēsis*, pride. For the Translation *grounds for confidence*, cf. NEB/REB "grounds" and [N]RSV "reason for confidence." The *kai* between *pepoithēsin* and *en sarki* (omitted in Western witnesses D* E* etc., deflecting Paul's emphasis, Fee 302 n 68) is rather far from *egō echōn* to take as KJV did ("I might also have confidence"; NRSV "I, too"). RSV takes it with *sarki* ("in the flesh also"; NABRNT "even in the flesh"; NJB). The TRANSLATION brings in the *kai* as "*indeed* in the flesh."

COMMENT

A. FORMS, SOURCES, AND TRADITIONS

1. *Literary, Rhetorical Features of a New Epistolary Beginning.* Three abrupt, harsh, impvs. open a new section (Holmstrand 117; "an undeniable change in *thematic organization*," DA 265; cf. Bloomquist 101). Phil shifts to a "we"-form (3a *we . . . "the Circumcision"*), a feature prominent in 3:2–21, as nowhere else in the four chs. Schenk 254–56 sees a chiasm:

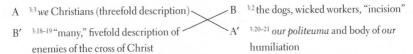

A ³:³ *we* Christians (threefold description)   B ³:² the dogs, wicked workers, "incision"

B′ ³:¹⁸⁻¹⁹ "many," fivefold description of   A′ ³:²⁰⁻²¹ *our politeuma* and body of *our*
enemies of the cross of Christ   humiliation

Circumcision, Spirit and flesh, law and righteousness are not emphasized in chs. 1–2 (or 4). Rather than positing Paul knew all along of the enemies now described or that, after writing 3:1, he got news of this threat and launched into 3:2–21, we treat 3:2–4a as (B.1) part of the body (3:2–21) of Paul's third letter to Philippi (cf. INTRO. VI.B), and then (B.2) part of the four-ch. letter.

Though "circumcision" has an OT-Jewish background, there is no OT material embedded in 3:2–4a,[1] no pre-Pauline formulas or Jesus-logia (unless Matt 7:6 or 15:26 for the "dogs" of 3:2). Paul may know terms these opponents employed, "(missionary) workers"; "(the) Spirit (of God)"; "(we are) the Circumcision." He disparages or inverts their language, as in the diatribe (wordplay, like *incision*, to make opponents laughable; antithesis, "we" and they; Schoon-Janßen 143, who sees a "potential apologia" in 3:4–6). There are significant rhetorical devices.[2]

In rhetorical and larger chiastic analyses, 3:2–4a is only sometimes treated as a discrete unit.[3] D. F. Watson 1988b, who makes 3:1–21 the third development

---

[1] That Sir 24:1–2 LXX lies behind those condemned in 3:2 (U. B. Müller 145) is speculative.

[2] *Asyndeton* (Spencer 282–83), the three cls. in v 2 lack connectives; *for* in v 3 is an exception. D. Watson 1988b:73–74 lists *epanaphora* (repetition of *blepete* in v 2); "*enargeia* or vivid description" ("dogs," "incision"); *paranomesia, peri-* and *katatomē*, BDF 488.1.b; B-D-R 491 n 4 *homoioploton*; *synecdoche*, use of a part for the whole; *metonymy* (the vice stands for the people themselves); *irony*. Holloway 2001a:133, "parsicolon" (3:2). Alliteration: *kynas, kakous, katatomē,* and *kauchōmenoi*. Spencer's "stylistics" approach lists devices passim for 3:2–4:13 (e.g., 142–43, 145–47). Edart 211, 214, *antimetabolē* (Lausberg #801), several words repeated in inverse order: *en sarki pepoithotes . . . pepoithēsin kai en sarki* (chiasm), in the middle of which is *kaiper egō echōn.*

[3] See INTRO. VI.B nn 2, 3. Black 1995, 3:2–4a is a "Warning Against Selfish Ambition" (p. 43; cf. 40–41). Bittasi 90–98, 3:2–3 is exhortation under Paul's example (3:2–16); it parallels 2:1–5 as exhortation. Luter/Lee parallel 3:1b–21 with 2:5–16 as "example and action" (criticized by Porter/Reed 1998); C. W. Davis, 3:1–4:9 with 1:27–2:18; Rolland, 3:1–4:20 with 1:12–2:30; Wick, 3:1–16 with 1:12–26, "joy, opponents, report about himself (and opponents)" (41–43, but p. 85, "Paul, imitator of Christ"; Pretorius 1998:15; cf. DA 361–64). Bloomquist 137, 178: within the *argumentatio* (1:18b–4:7), 3:1–16

within his *probatio*, terms vv 2–4a "a carefully crafted enthymene" (73; the concealed, short-cut syllogism works by contraries, "they are *katatomē*, we the *peritomē*").[4]

Garland 1985 terms all of ch. 3 *digressio* (Lausberg ##340–42, a shorter or longer excursus, optional in a speech), "a deliberate rhetorical device . . . to affect his audience prior to the direct, emotional appeal in 4:2" (Garland 173; rejected by Fields 220 n 101). (Is 4:2 more "emotional" than 3:2ff.?) Ch. 3 is then "epideictic or demonstrative discourse," repeating what Paul has taught before in Philippi (164–65). Paul seeks to regain the audience's attention, lest *taedium* set in (3:1 *oknēron*)—after the travel plans in 2:19–30? because he is going to say "the same things" (3:1, *ta auta*) as he had taught before? Schoon-Janßen 125–29 3:2–11 is *digressio*, reflecting experiences in Galatia (3:12–17 return to the actual situation in Philippi); 3:2–11 is, then, "a rhetorical trick" so the Philippians think about their claims to perfection in light of false boastings by the Jews (128).

Schenk 277–80 took the rhetorical structure H. D. Betz developed for Gal (Hermeneia *Gal.* 16–23) and applied it, not to the whole of Phil, as D. F. Watson had done (1988b:61–80, to defend the unity of the letter), but to Phil 3 as Letter C. Then Phil 3:2–3 = *exordium*; vv 5–6, *narratio*; 7–11, *argumentatio*, or perhaps a continuation of the *narratio*; or in 8–11 *propositio*; 12–14, *argumentatio*, with notes of *refutatio*; 15–21, direct *refutatio*; 4:1–3, 8–9 = *peroratio* in the same letter (279–80). Somewhat similarly, Harnisch 137: 3:2–4a *exordium*; 4b–7 *narratio*; 8–14 *argumentatio*; 15–21 *peroratio*. Edart: *exordium, narratio,* but 8–21 = *probatio*. Wick 164 concluded such rhetorical analyses do not provide "a key to understanding" but exemplify the splintering of opinions—something true also for chiastic master plans. Minimally, we can term 3:2–3 *exordium*, with v 4 a transition to autobiography (Reumann 1991a:137).

Smaller chiasms within 3:2–4a may be more convincing. E.g., a "ring composition" in verse 3 (Schenk 250, 253–54; but cf. G. Klein 1989:301 n. 39):

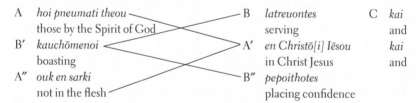

The three ptcs. relate to each other, as do "Spirit of God," "in Christ," and "not in the flesh." Or a triple chiasmus, A, B, C, and their counterparts (Schenk 253; G. Klein 1989:301 n. 39):

---

is *reprehensio* (an attempt to defuse arguments by opponents), 3: 2–4a begin this "through *negatio* argumentation;" critique in M. Müller 190–91, who finds (90–91) 3:2 + 17b, and 3:3 + 17a, bracket the unit. Holloway 2001a:133–35 cites no features in 3:3 from a "letter of consolation."

[4] Cf. (2) COMMENT A.4 n 10. Fields 229–33, the absent minor premise in this "'umbrella' enthymeme," the first of three in 3:2–21, is "There are those around who put their confidence in the flesh. They are not true people of God." M. Müller 191: major premise (3a) "We are the circumcision"; minor premise = fleshly circumcision amounts to incision; conclusion = the opponents preach fleshly circumcision. Banker 120 speaks of "propositionalization"; D. K. Williams 2002:159, v 3 is the *propositio*.

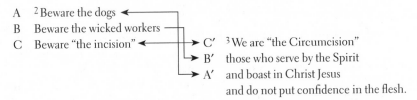

A   ²Beware the dogs
B   Beware the wicked workers
C   Beware "the incision"   C′   ³We are "the Circumcision"
                                    B′   those who serve by the Spirit
                                    A′   and boast in Christ Jesus
                                              and do not put confidence in the flesh.

Cf. Edart 213. The clearest contrast is "incision/Circumcision"; some see contrasts between "dogs" and "not flesh," or "workers" and "serve by the Spirit."

2. The Enemies in Ch. 3. Those Paul denounces so vigorously in 3:2 and tearfully in 3:18–19 have been variously identified. They should be distinguished (Reumann 1987:527–28; Holloway 2001a:134; D. K. Williams 2002:55 n 67, and others) from (a) the rival preachers in Ephesus, all of them with a correct gospel (1:14–18); and (b) the Roman authorities in Philippi, opponents *(hoi antikeimenoi)* in the struggle mentioned at 1:27–30. We shall, for accuracy and convenience, call them, from 3:18, "enemies *(echthroi)*" (of the cross of Christ). Gunther 1973:2 listed eighteen different assessments of the opponents in Phil 3; G. Klein 1989:297–301, six approaches. Two derive from other NT letters: (1) The *Judaizers in Gal* (esp. 2:14). Cf. Alvarez 292–317. Data common with Phil 3 include Law, flesh, boasting, (be found) righteous(ness), Spirit (Gal 2:16–17; 3:1–5; 5:16–26; 6:13–14), circumcision (Gal 2:3, 7–9, 12; 5:2–6,11; 6:12–15), and an outburst at 5:12, "I wish those who unsettle you would castrate *(apokopsontai)* themselves!" cf. Phil 3:3, on "the incision." (2) *The opposition to Paul in 2 Cor 10–13*. Cf. Alvarez 341; Georgi, Gnilka: Hellenistic Jewish-Christian missionaries who have turned up in Corinth, divine wonderworkers *(theios-anēr* hypothesis). Links between 2 Cor and Phil 3 include the title "workers" + a pejorative adj. ("deceitful" 2 Cor 11:13, "wicked" Phil 3:2); "Hebrew(s)" and Israelite/*ek genous Israēl* (11:22; 3:5); "glory *(doxa)* and "shame" at 2 Cor 4:2 and Phil 3:19 *(aischynē* in these two vv only in the Pauline corpus); perhaps "be confident," "boast according to the flesh" (2 Cor 10:7 *pepoitha* and 11; Phil 3:3 *kauchomenoi . . . en sarki pepoithotes*).

Among other proposals: (3) Gnostics (Schmithals, Koester); (4) agitators for a Jewish, dualistic wisdom concept (Schenk); (5) Torah legalists, perhaps from Jerusalem or Antioch (Schenke-Fischer, *Einl.* 1:1280; Lüdemann 1989a [INTRO. II Bibl.] 103–9) or "Pseudonomists," God-fearers in Philippi seeking to return to the shelter of the synagogue in the face of persecution (Suhl; cf. Tellbe); (6) two groups (Lft. 88–90, 144, 155, cf. 70; cf. Lambrecht 1985 [(14) Bibl.]199–205; Jewett 1970a 48–49; Pohill 360); (7) no reconstruction is possible (Kümmel, *Intro.* 327–28; Baumbach 1971). Further (cf. Alverez 318–40) (8) "newly converted proselytes" (U. B. Müller, from Vielhauer 1975:164; Grayston 1986:171)[5]; (9) an anti-Pauline Jewish Christian group engaged in a counter-mission (P. Stuhl-

---

[5] Cf. also Bateman (Gentiles practicing Jewish rituals, readily dismissed by Tellbe 2001:260 n 221). Munck spoke of "The Judaizing *Gentile* Christians" in Galatia (italics added, 1959 [(3) Bibl.] 87–134, though, with Loh. and Dibelius, Munck regarded the opponents in Phil 3:2ff. as Jews, 280 n 1).

macher, *Rom.* 5–6, 50–53, 123, 252–53; Gnilka 1965 and 2001:159–60, "anti-Paulinists"; F. W. Horn 1992; Alvarez 324–40).[6]

In the face of further variations, Doughty 1995 saw 3:2–21 as "a secondary insertion" (rightly criticized in M. Müller 189 n 275); others, "fictitious, hypothetical opposition," a rhetorical device (Bloomquist 131 on Lyons, cf. 120–21[7]; Witherington 84, 88). "Decontextualization" (DeSilva 1994:30) that Tellbe 2001:259 and D. K. Williams 2002:167 n 92 rightly dismiss.

Our *working view*: 3:2ff. is more than a rhetorical trick. Paul believes an aggressive Jewish-Christian missionary group stressing circumcision (and therefore the Law) loomed as a threat to Philippi. So Edart 225–26. According to 3:2–4a, they had more in common with the opponents in Galatia than with those in 2 Cor 10–13 (cf., e.g., W. Kraus 1996:339–41), but some of their emphases Paul, formally at least, shared (he was circumcised). His defense will be personal, rather than exegetical (as in Gal).

B. MEANING AND INTERPRETATION

1. *Warning, Enemies, and Ecclesiology in Letter C.* The body of Paul's third letter to Philippi—subsequently incorporated into the four-ch. epistle (see 2, below) as a "body subpart" (Black 1995:39)—begins with a "shout" (Spencer 142): 3:2, *Beware* (repeated 3x) *the dogs! the wicked workers! "the incision!"* In Letter C, this was preceded by a Prescript, much like the address and salutation at 1:1–2. R. Pesch 95 conjectures precisely the same words, though whether Timothy was co-sender for Letter C depends on its exact date. According to 2:19–23 in Letter B, Paul planned to send him to Philippi after Epaphroditus returned home (2:25–30), as soon as he knew the results of his own case in Ephesus (the outcome of his appeal to his Roman citizenship). Then, freed, Paul himself would come (2:24). Now released from prison (there are no hints of bonds in 3:2–21) but embroiled in intense interchange with the congregation in Corinth and caught up in plans for the collection, not to mention getting Onesimus home to Philemon (see Chart 2 for chronology), Paul hurriedly writes to Philippi about an impending threat. He may be influenced by his experiences with opposition in Galatia a year or two before and by the Corinthian situation (past conflicts, recorded in 1 Cor; the need to defend himself in a letter containing 2 Cor 2:14–6:13 + 7:2–4), if not as yet the full polemics of 2 Cor 10–13.

There likely was a prayer report in Letter C, much like the Prooimion now at 1:3–11. Some elements in those vv are appropriate for Letter C: e.g., the confident assertion that the God "who inaugurated a good work among you will bring it to

---

[6] Cf. (5) above. This group sought systematically to undo and redo the apostle's work in Galatia, Thessalonica, Corinth, and Philippi and, before he even got there, in Rome. A "truth squad" (from the group's viewpoint) to correct Paul's converts on Christ and salvation, "'dogging' him for over a decade" (Fee, 294).

[7] Lyons makes only passing remarks on Phil, 129 n 21 and pp. 206–7. Bloomquist 130 holds the opponents in Phil were "some kind of Jewish Christian pneumatics," but Paul's "rheteorical polemic" veils them. Cf. *DA*, "Implied Opponents" in Phil 3:1–4:1 (392–93).

completion by the Day of Christ Jesus" (1:6, not via "the workers" of 3:2); phrases about Paul's longing for them (1:8); prayers for their "perception and discernment *in every situation*" (1:9) and being "filled with the fruit of righteousness" (1:11, but not Law-righteousness, 3:6).[8]

At 3:2, Paul moves immediately into his pressing concern in the body opening or *exordium* (Schenk 279) or *prooemium* (description in Hughes, *2 Thess.* 34–35). J. Becker 1993 (INTRO. X Bibl.) 324 likens it to the "opening of the court speech," i.e., judicial rhetoric, accusations and defense.[9] Some see here an *insinuatio* (Bloomquist 129; Harnisch 137; cf. Lausberg #263–65, 280–81), not that the audience is tired (*oknēron*, 3:1 = *taedium*, as some assume), but, as in court cases, "the opposition party" may have already won over (some of) the audience (Lausberg #280.2; 438). The *insinuatio* can use humor ("incision/circumcision"); "beware, beware, beware" is a wake-up call. "Paul begins furiously and militantly to disqualify the opponents" (J. Becker 1993:324), with "the language of demagoguery" (*Rhet. ad Her.* 1.4.8; 1.5.8, cited by Betz, Hermeneia *Gal.* 44–45, on Gal 1:6–11). An impv. is not customary here (but cf. *favete linguis* in Cic. and Horace *Carm.* 3.1.2, "restrain your tongues, be silent," Lausberg #271 α), but it is fitting (*prepon*) (263, cf. 258). Literary devices (above, COMMENT A.1) involve diatribe style, contrasts, caustic humor re a term in which the opponents took pride, employed to their discredit (BDF 488 1.b). The *expolitio* (3b, end) introduces an essential point in the controversy, *not . . . the flesh* (Edart 222).

blepete (see Note on *Beware*) could be tr. "consider (the case of)" (Kilpatrick) and should be if one sees in 3:2–21 only hypothetical enemies (cf. Lyons, Doughty 1995:104). But the context, esp. the harsh dir. objs. that follow, differs from 1 Cor 10:18, "Consider the people of Israel" (NRSV), part of a reasoned argument to support a point. *Beware!* (most Eng. trs.) so rings through the passage that P[46] added at 3:18, "Beware (*blepete*) the enemies of the cross of Christ."

The three terms, *the dogs*, *the wicked workers*, and "*the incision*," have occasionally been taken to refer to three distinct classes of antagonists, an analysis long set aside in favor of one group designated by three terms (Ewald 164; Vincent 93). That Paul's aim "is not to describe the opponents, but to insult them" (Koester 1961–62:321) has often been repeated (O'B 354 n 48, e.g.). Silva 169 prefers to speak of "irony."

Beware tous kynas could have suggested a warning against Cynic philosophers,

---

[8] Possibly Letter C had no prayer section; cf. Gal and Martyn, AB 32A:81–82, Gal 1:3–5 is "in Paul's mind a prayer"; "[u]nable . . . to thank God for the Galatian churches, Paul can cause them to thank God for their deliverance in Jesus Christ" (106). In Philippi, things were not that bad, as yet.

[9] So also Edart 221–26. In debate over rhetorical genus for Phil, Schenk 278 calls Letter C "genus iudiciale"; G. Kennedy 1984, the letter as a whole is "epideictic" (1984:77); D. F. Watson 1988b, "deliberative" (59, 79–80). K.-W. Niebuhr 82–83, the polemical warnings in ch 3 are admonitions re future decision. Harnisch 135–36 agrees with Schenk and J. Becker on the juridical category, but Dormeyer 1989:152–54 says not "public legal proceedings." Admittedly, not "public law courts." Opinions differ because commentators, seeking an overall classification, emphasize particular passages or details. Better: allow for elements of one type or another at different points. The opening of Letter C strikes one as "judicial," though that may not fit all parts of Letter C, let alone Phil in its entirety.

"doggish" itinerant teachers, who came to new prominence during the Imperial period (R. A. Hock, *ABD* 1:1221–26; *OCD*³ 418–19). Their crude *adiaphoria* or shameless indifference to conventional behavior—"constant barking, scavenging, urinating, and mating in public" (*ABD* 1:1223)—made them unwelcome. Cf. Epict. 3.22; 2 Thess 3:7–12 (Paul may distance himself and Christians from Cynic irresponsibility, Malherbe 1987:99–101, 107; AB 32B:257–59). But what follows in 3:2 is specifically Jewish—one would not call wandering Cynic freeloaders "workers," and "incision/circumcision." To interpret *tous kynas* from Matt 7:6 and 15:26 par. proves unlikely (see Note). *dogs* = wild, unclean animals, street dogs, running in packs, a menace to watch out for.

For *the wicked workers* the background lies not in Scripture ("evildoers" in the Pss) or polemic against "works of the law"[10] (even in references to the Law of Moses at 3:5, 6, and 9, that phrase will not occur), but rather missionary "workers" (see Note). *ergatai* at 2 Cor 11:13 provides an analogue, workers in a mission to supersede Pauline Christianity (see Georgi, in A.2, above). Paul does not use "worker" of himself, but note the vb. at 1 Cor 4:12; to work with one's hands to support evangelization, 1 Thess 2:9; 4:11; *ergon* of Christian mission (1 Thess 1:3; 5:11; see on Phil 1:6, 22; and 2:30); noun and vb. at 1 Cor 16:10, Timothy "works the work of the Lord, as I do." May go back to Jesus (Q, Matt 9:37–38 par. Luke 10:2). But Paul indicates his disapproval of these missionaries at 3:2 by adding *wicked*, "malicious," as at 2 Cor 11:13 ("deceitful"; Loh. 125; Schenk 292). These people work to harm individuals and the congregation as a whole.[11]

The key term for understanding the nature of the enemies in Phil 3 is "circumcision"[12] (v 3) and its parody term in v 2, *"the incision"* ("playing with words" was

---

[10] K. Barth 93, with Bultmann, "'work-heroes,' who think to achieve great things by what they do"; Bockmuehl 188; further, F. Watson 1986: 2–18, 74–80.

[11] Ewald 164. Loh. 125 n 2 noted T. Benj 11.5, "I shall no longer be called a rapacious wolf . . . [Gen 49:27] but 'the Lord's worker' . . ." (*OTP* 1:828, mentioning also Deut 33:12 and Isa 42:1, cf. 11:4); *Odes Sol*. 11.20 ("all your laborers are fair, they who work good works"), 11.2,3. Scarcely a clear connection to 3:2.

[12] On *"circumcision,"* see R. G. Hall, *ABD* 1:1025–31; R. Meyer, *TDNT* 6:72–84; H.-C. Hahn, *NIDNTT* 1:307–12; O. Betz, *EDNT* 3:79–80; G. Mayer, *"mûl," TDOT* 8:158–62; Str.-B 4:23–40; O. Betz et al., "Beschneidung," *TRE* 5:716–22; F. Stummer, *RAC* 2:159–69 (166, 3:2 = Zerschneidung); N. J. McEleney 1973–74; E. P. Sanders 1983:100–4; E. Blum/E. P. Sanders/R. Goldenberg et al., *RGG*⁴ 1 (1998) 1354–58; Blaschke 19–322, OT and subsequent Jewish texts; Fields 264–72. The practice probably spread from NW Semites to Egypt (J. M. Sasson, "Circumcision in the Ancient Near East," *JBL* 85 [1966] 473–76, though not necessarily from Egypt to Israel; Blaschke 43–45, 318). Rich OT references (*ABD* 1:1025). The "LXX refers more often to circumcision . . . than does the original Hebrew" (*TDNT* 6:74). Proportionally "in the NT, esp. in P[au]l, *peritemnō* and *peritomē* are used more often than in the OT" (*TDNT* 6:81 n 68). The practice appeared among Egyptians, Edomites, Ammonites, Moabites, and Arabs (Jer 9:25–26); Blaschke 5, one seventh of men in the world today. Some OT aspects and stories never seem reflected in Paul or the NT; e.g., Exod 4:24–26, but cf. Grayston 1986:171; Blaschke 19–30. Emphasis grew during the Exile; *NIDNTT* 1:308, cites von Rad, *Genesis* 1963:196, *"status confessionis* for the exiles"; cf. Blaschke 104–5, 318–19; Esther 8:17 LXX. Circumcision came into even greater prominence for Jews when Antiochus IV Epiphanes (176–171) banned it (1 Macc 1:48, 60–61; cf. AB 41:104–60). The practice became something to die for, also when Hadrian (A.D. 117–38) placed circumcision on a par with castration (*DNP* 2:1026–27, R. Gamauf, "Castratio") as a barbaric custom, akin to murder (cf. Schürer 1 [1973]: 537–40). Hasmonean

characteristic of the diatribe, Koester, *TDNT* 8:111). Circumcision refers to the practice, going back to Abraham (Gen 17), on the eighth day after a baby boy's birth (3:5, in Paul's autobiography), when the foreskin was cut off as "sign of the covenant" between God and Israel, the sign of religious and ethnic identity. A family rite, not a Temple ceremony (*TDOT* 8:161). *katatomē* (v 2), with a different prefix than *peritomē* (*peri* + acc. "around"; *kata* + gen. "down," + acc. "in, through"), was not Paul's invention, nor anyone else's, to satirize Jewish practice. In classical Gk., the vb. meant "cut in strips," "chop up" rhetorically; the noun, "slice" of a plant or rock or "incision." Gk. use of the vb., plus LXX application of *katatemnō* for forbidden lacerations (self-mutilation to get God to do what the person wished; see NOTE) stand behind Paul's use of *katatomē* here. So does his experience with opponents in Galatia, Judaizers who insisted that Paul's Gentile converts get themselves circumcised, as some Galatian Christians likely did. Hence his outburst, Gal 5:12, "I wish they'd go castrate themselves" (wordplay on *peritomē* and *apokoptō*; BDAG 113; G. Stählin, *TDNT* 3:854–55; Blaschke 389– 90). 3:2 should not be rendered "false circumcision" (NASB), "Paul intends more than that" (Silva 169–70). The enemies *mutilitate* men. More than "hyperbole" (*DA* 311). Paul's rhetoric is boisterous, rude, and even crude. But not here aimed at Judaism itself or what Jews do in their community (so Niebuhr 84 n 29, against F. Watson 1986:76–77) but against missionaries who, in Galatia (probably in Corinth, perhaps in Ephesus), wanted to make Paul's converts really saved and

---

rulers compelled conquered men in Jewish territory to be circumcised (Jos. *Ant.* 13.257; Blaschke 320–22). In Israel and Judaism, female circumcision, as in parts of Africa, was *not* part of the covenant-entry ritual. That phallus worship was involved (cf. the Greco-Roman Priapus cult) in Gentile taunts (F. Watson 1986:76–77) depends in part on 3:19 ("belly," "shame"). Edart 224, ironically, the equivalent of pagan practice.

Criticism of circumcision in the Hellenistic world and Jewish defense of this mark of national and religious identity are important in understanding Phil 3:2–3 (*TDNT* 6:78–79; R.G. Hall, *ABD* 1:1027– 29; F. W. Horn 1996:491; Blaschke 323–60). For Greeks, to circumcise was to mutilate the body, something barbaric. Cf. Herodot. 2.37; Martial *Epigrams* 7.35,82; *ABD* 1:1027. In Greco-Roman culture there were social implications for a circumcised man. The Gk. gymnasium (even in Jerusalem) and Roman baths assumed nudity. The Jewish badge of membership in the covenant people brought stigma. Hence attempts by some Jews to restore a foreskin by a surgical procedure called epispasm; cf. 1 Macc 1:15; Jos. *Ant.* 12.241; tech. term *epispaomai*, 1 Cor 7:19, let a Christian "not seek to remove the marks of circumcision." Details in Blaschke 139–44, 350–56; R. G. Hall, "Epispasm. Circumcision in Reverse," *BRev* 8 (1992) 52–57.

In response, Jewish documents like *Jub.* and Qumran emphasized circumcision all the more. Artapanos, Jos., and Philo sought to explain it to Gentiles. Philo's *Spec. Leg.* 1–11 justifies it for the sake of cleanliness, priestly sanctification (as in Egypt), fertility, without mentioning covenant significance. Some Jews neglected, spiritualized, or rejected circumcision (*ABD* 1:1029; *TDNT* 6:79). McEleney and others align Paul with such "liberal Judaism" in the Diaspora. Blaschke 396–97, for children of Jewish-Christian parents, the practice suggested *heilsgeschichtlich* continuity (419–21). Blaschke summarizes (478–88): in Paul, for Gentile Christians, no circumcision, yet they are, soteriologically and eschatologically, fully like "Israel." On circumcision and castration, Paul reflects Greco-Roman opposition, and presents himself "as an example of the proper position" in Phil 3:2–11 (synthesis, p. 491). That circumcision brought penalties in the Greco-Roman world to Christians adopting Judaism and its bodily sign is seldom noticed by those who suggest that Philippian Christians were attracted to Judaism as a *"religio licita"* (Loh. 126 on 3:2) to *escape* persecution (Tellbe 2001:264).

blessed by adding this rite for Gentile believers. Paul turns a proud identity marker[13] for Jews back in the face of the enemies by an insult term. He also claims the word "circumcision" for his communities in v 3. It is polemical and identifies the church. M. Müller 191–94 finds a syllogism: premise ("We are the *peritomē*"), middle term, (fleshly circumcision is equal to *katatomē*), and conclusion (the opponents preach physical circumcision). Or is "We are the *peritomē*" the conclusion?

Verse 3a is a confessional statement, akin to 1 Cor 8:6 ("*for us*, one God . . . and one Lord Jesus Christ . . ."), not on Christology but ecclesiology, *For it is we who are "the Circumcision."* The words explain (*gar*), as well as counter, *katatomē*: we are not "the incision," they are. We are the (truly) circumcised (RSV, [N]JB, Gdsp., GNB, CEV add "real" or "true" for clarity). Paul claims one of Israel's sacred terms, a concept for which Jews died during the persecution under Antiochus Epiphanes. (Loh. 126 does not make the connection.) In Phil 3, "we" becomes a significant term (*hēmeis*, first time in the entire letter; then 3:17, 20, 21; vb. in 15).

"We" certainly includes Paul and any coauthor (Timothy); more fully, "we missionaries," apostle and coworkers (Harnisch 139; M. Müller 193–94, 3:17 and 2:27–30). Some would extend (and limit it) to Jewish Christians; D. W. B. Robinson 1967: believing Jews.[14] Contrast Blaschke 403 n 1614. Ulonska 1989:322–23: Paul and the opponents; but that plays into the hands of the enemies; equality for Gentiles would come only by being circumcised. A further extension: Paul and his readers in Philippi (Ewald 166; Niebuhr 1992:84 n 30; C. Strecker 114–15) or all the churches he has founded (Lincoln 90). O'Brien 359, "all Christians, believing Jews and Gentiles alike" (cf. Fee 298; Bockmuehl 191). What Loh. 127 noticed about "you" (pl.), often found previously in Phil, "we" now for the first time, and "I" (previously at 1:3, 12, 18c-26, 27, 30; 2:12, 16–25, 28; but now 1st per. sg. 3:4–14, 17–18, with the pron. *egō* at 3:4 *bis* and 13), Schenk has traced out more carefully (chart p. 274; summarized in Eng., with positive reaction, by Dormeyer 1989:47–50). There is movement from the 2nd pl. in v 2 (*blepete* 3x) to the 1st pl. in 3:3 and then the 1st sg. in vv 4–14. At 3:20–21 there will be return to the 1st pl. pron. "our" (and in concluding admonitions in Letter C, like parts of 4:1–9, "you" again). "We" and "our" should be interpreted consistently in the ch., if possible, in contrast to "the many" in 3:18–19 and those castigated in v 2; see the chiastic structure in A.1, above, and Schenk 254–56. At 3a, Schenk would put the emphasis on "we," not "the Circumcision" (with Loh. 127).

All this makes "we" Christians and "the Circumcision" synonymous and raises ecclesiological questions. "The Circumcision" fits use by Paul of "Israel terms"

---

[13] Stressed by Dunn 1990; Horn 1996:479–80, "spiritualized" at Phil 3:3; Rom 2:28–29 (504); Tellbe 2001:262 n 232 lists Jewish texts on circumcision's role in separating Jews from others.

[14] To limit 3:3a to Jewish Christians makes Paul's statement an assertion about only a portion of the church; it gives physical circumcision a value contrary to the context, hardly appropriate to Philippian, Gentile believers.

for the church.[15] These include "Israel of God" (Gal 6:16);[16] "seed of Abraham" (Gal 3:29); "sons of Abraham" (Gal 3:7); "the saints" (see NOTE on Phil 1:1); "the elect" (*eklektoi,* Rom 8:33) and "called" (*klētoi,* 1 Cor 1:1); perhaps *ekklēsia* itself, if from the *qāhāl* of Yahweh via the LXX; not to mention "remnant" (Rom 11:5) and "God's field" or planting (1 Cor 3:9). Paul at 3:2–3a has wrenched the term "circumcision" away from its sense in Judaism and given it a new meaning, esp. by the definition that follows in 3b. Some bring in Rom 2:25–29, circumcision is a matter of the heart, spiritual, not literal. Others, baptism is the Christian equivalent to Israelite circumcision (Col 2:11–13) for all who believe, women[17] and men.

P. Richardson 111–17 regards Phil 3 as "the beginning of the transpositions" from (OT) Israel to the Christian church as (new) Israel. Minear 1960:75–76, cf. 110, 3:3a is one of ninety-six "images of the church" in the NT, "a clear-cut ecclesiological designation. The church is the circumcision and therefore it is 'the Israel of God' "(Minear 1960:76; cf. Fowl 1990:99). Cf. K. W. Clark 1972. Klaiber 28–29, 3:3a "gruffly sets in antithesis to the boastful title of opposition propaganda the essential mark of Christian existence," the Spirit.[18] But "*peritomē*-ecclesiology," even when interpreted in terms of the Spirit, would have little or no place in an increasingly Gentile church after A.D. 70, a church of uncircumcised believers.[19]

To explain "the Circumcision" that Christians are, 3b follows with a definition, (We are) *the ones who serve by the Spirit of God and make our boast in Christ Jesus and do not place our confidence in the flesh.* The first ptc. may be overarching, the second and third positive and negative instances of what "serving the Spirit" involves. Perhaps "those who serve by the Spirit of God, *both* making our boast in Christ Jesus *and* not placing confidence in the flesh"; cf. JB, NABRNT. But this scarcely expounds what "serve" means, and the Spirit/flesh contrast is obscured. One should not rush to an "implicit Trinitarianism" here (Fee 302; Spirit, God, Christ Jesus), for it is the *Spirit of God* (not "worship" or "serve" *God* by the Spirit,

---

[15] Moule 1982:46–52; Dunn, *TPTA* 534. L. Rost, "Die Vorstufen von Kirche und Synagoge im Alten Testament," BWANT 4/24 (Stuttgart 1938, 2d ed. 1967) provides a starting point. Cf. J. Roloff, *Die Kirche im Neuen Testament,* NTD Ergänzungsreihe 10 (Göttingen: Vandenhoeck & Ruprecht, 1993) 117–31; W. Strack 141–76.

[16] Cf. Martyn (AB33A:574–77), "Israel" is a term the opposition "Teachers" used; Paul adds "of God" ("those who follow the standard of God's *new* creation" (576). Otherwise, P. Richardson 74–84 and others: ". . . peace on [them], and mercy *also* to God's faithful people Israel"; cf. NRSV with RSV. I.e., *two* groups blessed, instead of the church regarded now as Israel.

[17] Lieu 1994:359 claims that the relation of Jewish male circumcision and the salvation of women was first explicity raised by Justin Martyr re Gen 17:14 (*Dial.* 23.5, cf. 46.3).

[18] With J. Jervell 1977:92–93, "proper circumcision . . . means possessing righteousness from God," in the combination Spirit/righteousness/*latreia.* Cf. F. W. Horn 1996:504 on the hermeneutical relation to justification.

[19] B. Bagatti, *The Church from the Circumcision: History and Archaeology of the Judaeo-Christians* (SBF Smaller Series 2; Jerusalem: Franciscan Printing Press, 1971), has remarkably few references to "circumcision." Cf. Dunn, *TPTA* 531–32.

as in later MSS). One must work with three parallel ptc. phrases that are not like 2 Cor 13:13 in order and content.

The unusual phraseology of *serve by the Spirit of God* tempted later scribes to change it (see NOTE on text). "Spiritual worship"—whatever that means—has long had attraction, but worship is not the topic here. The vb. means *serve*. The usual sense for *pneuma theou* holds, "(the) Spirit of God." *by the Spirit of God* is instrumental dat., "by (means of) God's Spirit," or "in the sphere of, dominated by, the Spirit"—not "in the Spirit of God," a tr. that suggests either "with God's attitude" or somehow caught up into God's Spirit. It carries one step further the ideas of 1 Cor 12 about receiving the Spirit at baptism (v 13), in the church community (v 12), and confessing Jesus (v 3). That step is living with, led by, the Spirit (Rom 8:9, 14) in daily life. It involves an ethical sense that more than one commentator has sensed.

What throws many readers off track is that *latreuontes* has no dir. obj. here. Not "serve God," as piety might expect (so a corrector in MS ℵ, followed by KJV, RSV-txt, and others). Not cultic service to God (Rom 9:4), or even serve God by preaching the gospel (correct though that is, Rom 1:9). Here "service" means the "conduct side" in OT use of *latreuō*, as in Rom 12:1–2, service to others.[20] This means a more open view of *latreia* than the "workers" of 3:2 likely espoused. They and Paul did not disagree on the need to do mission, but differed over the message (fleshly circumcision or not), and whom to serve, with what. Circumcision (and Law) as "boundary-marking ritual" for ethnic Israel was, in Dunn's analysis, what went wrong with Jewish covenant theology, "circumcision as the focal point for . . . privileged distinctiveness" (N. T. Wright's "national righteousness"; Dunn, *Rom.* WBC 38A: lxxi–lxxii; Tellbe 2001:262). Paul's definition for the church was less restricted on serving others, but it had a firm position about "flesh" as the opposite of "Spirit" and where one puts one's trust.

The second church-defining phrase in 3b, *and make our boast in Christ Jesus*, is to be taken closely with the final one, *and not place confidence in the flesh*. The first is positively put, the second has a negative (*not*). They are part of a fuller contrast, for *not . . . in the flesh* also goes with *by the Spirit* in the earlier phrase. *sarx* stands in antithesis to *pneuma* (Dunn, *TPTA* 65). A "Spirit/flesh" contrast will run through what follows, even though *pneuma* does not occur again in Phil. The closely related *en Christō[i]* theme replaces it; see NOTE on 1:19 *Jesus Christ, whom the Spirit supplies*. Sand 1971 ([4] Bibl.) 135 and others see a further contrast between "those who *place confidence in the flesh*" and "those who *serve by the Spirit of God*." To anticipate: flesh (3b, 4a), Paul's "advantages" in vv 4b–6, "gains" that really amount to "loss" (7), righteousness that comes from the Law (9), on the one hand, contrast with Spirit (3b), in Christ Jesus (3b), knowing Christ, gaining Christ (8), be found "in him" (9), and righteousness that comes through faith in

---

[20] Hawthorne 127, though taking the vb. as "worship," concludes the Spirit "is at work in the depths of human nature, profoundly transforming a person's life so as to promote a life of love and service, so as to generate a life for others"; cited approvingly by W. Strack 315 n 161.

Christ, on the other. Tannehill 115 called the contrast (between "boasting in Christ Jesus" and "trusting in flesh") "a heading for what follows."

At 3:3b, *boast* is used in its positive Pauline sense, what one can take pride in and properly make grounds for confidence, i.e., not self, but God or, here, Christ. Specifically, the "Christ event" of cross and resurrection. Cf. 1 Cor 1:30–31; Gal 6:14.

The final phrase contrasts *flesh* with *Spirit* and *Christ*, and parallels *boast* with *place confidence*. "The dogs" boast and put their trust in the circumcision of the flesh. Not so we. *pepoithotes*, "trust, reply on," is a pointer to the "faith" language that will appear in v 9. *sarx* implies Paul's negative judgment on human existence. *sarx* denotes the whole person, human life destined for demise and destruction before God, not something on which real life and future hopes can be built. It collapses in the crunch of judgment, before God's righteousness. *sarx* amounts to "rubbish" (v 8), debit or loss in the ledger of life.

As an ecclesial term, *"the Circumcision"* had little place in a later church increasingly Gentile (uncircumcised), divorced from its OT/Jewish heritage. Not so for Paul. Jesus was "the circumcised Messiah" (Jervell, Luke 2:21).[21] Gal 5:11 states a surprising charge against Paul: "if I am still preaching circumcision *(peritomēn eti kēryssō)*, why am I still being persecuted?" "Paul seems to *restate* in his own words something which in fact was held against him" (H. D. Betz, *Gal.* Hermeneia 268–69). Cf. Martyn, ". . . if, on occasion, I am preaching, as part of the gospel message, that one should be circumcised [*eti* = "in addition to," something Paul is said to add "from time to time"], as some wrongly report to you [added by Martyn], why am I being persecuted to this day? My preaching circumcision [of Gentile converts] would amount to wiping out the scandalous character of the cross" (AB 33A:475–76). Some hold the charge is totally false (e.g, Chrystost.; Mussner, *Gal.* 359). Others think Acts 16:3 (Paul circumcised Timothy) provided a basis; cf. Gal 2:3–5, with its textual variants (NEB, e.g.): Titus was not compelled but (willingly? accommodatingly?) accepted circumcision. Still others, Saul in his pre-Christian days was a Jewish missionary for circumcision (Burton, ICC *Gal.* 286; Schoeps [Intro. X Bibl.] 219; Bornkamm ([1] Bibl. **Paul**) 12; Donaldson 1997:275–84. esp. 282) or, as a Christian, advocated circumcision before he changed his mind about the rite (cf. Schlier, KEK *Gal.* 238 n. 4). Borgen 1982:37–46, Paul taught the need to overcome the desires of the flesh (cf. 5:19–21), "the spiritual essence of circumcision."[22] The basis could also be the claim (Phil 3:3a), "We are 'the Circumcision,'" something Paul taught prior to the appearance of opposing teachers in Galatia.

Rom 15:8–9 has also been brought into the picture, "I tell you that Christ has become, and is *(gegenēsthai)*, 'minister' [or servant] to the Circumcision' *(diakonon . . . peritomēs)* on behalf of the truth of God," a "doctrinal declaration"

---

[21] J. Jervell, *The Unknown Paul* (Minneapolis: Augsburg 1984) 138–45; cf. Acts 16:3; 21:21; and 7:8, with Luke 1:72–73; Jervell, *Apg.* (KEK 1998) 234, 524–26. With some reservations, J. Fitzmyer, *Luke* (AB 28) 58–59; cf. AB 31 (1998) 372; Blaschke 439–41, 489–90.

[22] Martyn (AB 33A:476 n 30), with Dunn and others, thinks this line of interpretation implausible.

(Michel, *Röm.* 358) about grace to all and the priority of the Jews (Käsemann, *Rom.* 385). It applied to Jesus' historical ministry (cf. 1:3; 9:5; he was a Jew), looking back to OT promises fulfilled, and to his present ministry as Risen One for all, including Gentiles (Käsemann, *Rom.* 385–86). Phil 3:3 reclaims "circumcision" for Gentile Christians in Paul's churches (W. Kraus 336–41).

Paul's bold ecclesiology, "We are the Circumcision,"[23] has often been overlooked, with *peritomē* viewed as a Jewish rite with no meaning for Paul. Philosemitism made recent scholarship reluctant to attribute such a claim to Paul. Post-Pauline anti-Semitism kept Christians from considering "circumcision" in any positive sense even for a supersessionist church. At issue in Paul's day was Christian identity in a Roman *colonia*, not via Jewish circumcision, but through Christ in a community with a heritage and the Spirit.

There is attached in 4a a personal reference to Paul's own heritage and situation, a concessive cl. (not a hypothetical statement), an *expolitio* (Edart 213; elaboration with variation; Lausberg #830, 842): *although I for my part have grounds for confidence indeed in the flesh.* Paul's credentials will be detailed in vv 4b–6. Some would take 4a with 4b (Phillips, "If it were right to have such confidence, I could certainly have it, and if any of these men thinks he has grounds for such confidence I can assure him I have more"). Better: 4a goes with v 3, which it reiterates closely, repeating *in the flesh* as key phrase, varying the ptc. (*popoithotes*, "place confidence") with a noun phrase, *echōn pepoithēsin* ("have grounds for confidence"). The repetition Tellbe 1994:119 n 81 calls "emphatic," and, with the final phrase in 3:3, it presents "the real nerve of the controversy" (Harnisch 139). *pepoithēsis* = be persuaded, a term of rhetorical significance (D. K. Williams 2002: 164–65, with S. N. Olson). For those circumcised, "flesh" was likely a positive term. Tangibility, fleshly circumcision, provided in covenant theology an outward sign of inward grace. Paul's pres. ptc. *echōn* could suggest "continue to possess." It is *indeed (kai) in the flesh* that Paul sees grounds for confidence he once treasured and the enemies still do.

As the defining point in 3:2–4a, *circumcision* suggests the real theme is initiation (C. Strecker 114–16). For Jewish males, *peritomē* signified entry into Israel. Paul claims the term for all those who believe in Christ. They need no surgical procedure *in the flesh* to initiate them more fully into salvation. They are *in Christ* and have *the Spirit* through baptism (1 Cor 12:13; Gal 3:2–3, 26–27).[24] A controversy over initiatory ritual looms in the rest of ch. 3. Nothing further is needed from the *wicked workers* for the boast and confidence of those with the new existence in Christ and its system of values.

---

[23] Eph 2:11, "You Gentiles in the flesh, who are called 'the uncircumcision' (*akrobystia*, foreskin) by those who are called 'the circumcision' (*peritomē*)." Cf. Blaschke 404; Marcus 1989:78–80, "epithets hurled . . . by members of the opposite group" in Rome and elsewhere; in Phil 3:3, *peritomē* is "taken up . . . and worn proudly" (80).

[24] J. Becker 1993 ([1] Bibl. **Paul**) 324–30, "the baptismal act is never mentioned" in Phil 3, but "the whole conduct of life" that will be presented in 4:4b–21 roots "in baptismal language," 330; U. B. Müller 144.

2. Phil 3:2–4a in the Redacted Letter. When 3:2–21 moved into a single epistle to Philippi, many of the meanings noted above continued. Some specificities were lost, however, as Paul was now presented writing from prison, not yet having dispatched Epaphroditus (or Timothy) to Philippi (they are then part of the "we" in v 3a) or having expressed thanks for the Philippians' gift to him (4:10–20). Our working theory allows interpretation of 3:2–21 to draw on more of the total material as known by the Philippians (since 4:10–20 was sent as Letter A, and all of 1:1–3:1 plus 4:1–9, 21–23, were in Letter B) than does the theory of a four-ch. letter, where Paul has not yet written ch. 4, and the Philippians have not heard any of its contents.

The biggest problem is why Paul suddenly took up the topic of "enemies" at this point.[25] The simplest answer is that at this time Paul got word enemies were nearing Philippi or had it targeted for their work. After dictating 3:1, during a pause overnight or perhaps an enforced delay of some duration, he heard the opponents, if not already in Philippi, were likely soon to menace the church there. If opponents he had crossed swords with in Galatia, he starts off abruptly, with frank warnings about the sort of people he goes on to describe. Or, less dramatic, as he thought about events in Galatia and Corinth, he deemed it wise to provide a word of caution ("Look at, consider") for the Philippians about what could happen there; then Paul's own cogitations, rather than a specific external group about whom he has received news, are behind 3:2–21.

Locating 3:2–21 within a single letter has had the effect of moving attention away from the contents of 3:2 and 18–19 so as to identify these enemies with either the "rival preachers" of 1:15–17 or those opposing the Philippians at 1:28 (enemies already in Philippi) or both. Treating ch. 3 as part of a four-ch. letter can complicate or simplify identification of "the dogs." The temptation is to unify all references to opposition in Phil 1–4. Proponents of a single-letter theory cannot be said to have come to any greater unanimity on who the opponents of Paul were than have critics who favor two or three letters.

When 3:2–21 is directly connected with what precedes, the triple use of *blepete* at 3:2 has been viewed as fitting "naturally into the progression of the discourse as the fourth in a series of present tense imperatives," (2:29) *prosdechesthe, echete entimous,* and (3:1) *chairete* (DA 260). The first two concern treatment of Epaphroditus, the third life in community generally, and the last (*blepete* 3x) takes up a menace to the congregation. Others see a pattern of four vbs. in closing paraenesis, as at 1 Cor 16:13, but the four here are not different terms (as there) but *chairete* + *blepete* thrice. Connection with 3:1 has also led to debate over what "the same things" *(ta auta)* in v 1b refer to. Some say "rejoice" at 1a + 2:17–18, 29 (DA 254–56; anaphoric interpretation). Others give *ta auta* a cataphonic sense: "the

---

[25] Redactoral theories can claim that the ed(s). (probably in Philippi) inserted the polemical material at this point to reflect the fact that all was not well with Philippi — there were hostile opponents threatening Paul's beloved congregation and the apostle responded in slashing terms. The section on "the heretics" was placed between the bulk of the less severe Letter B and cordial Letter A (see INTRO. VII.B). The polemic was surrounded by admonitions to joy (3:1; 4:1, 4).

same things" refer to what follows, the warnings in 3:2, things Paul had taught earlier. Or "the same" as Epaphroditus and Timothy were to report orally when they arrived. O'B 352: = 3:2–11. Or *ta auta* can be taken to refer to both "the duty of rejoicing" and treatment of "the dissensions" (Lft. 126–27). Interpreters have sought to soften the abruptness of 3:2ff. in a unified letter: Loh. 122–24, through the opponents as previously mentioned persecutors who cause martyrdom; U. B. Müller 1975:205–11, form-critically ("Rejoice!" and "The Lord is near," 3:1, 4:4–5, point to a eucharistic celebration, a Maranatha with joy, as in Acts 2:46, and 3:2 an "anathema" fencing the table against false teachers, like Matt 7:6 and Did 9:5; contrast Mengel 300–2); and, more recently, by appeal to rhetorical features and letters of friendship.

All in all, treatment of 3:2–21 within a single letter has heightened the problem of why this outburst; it has complicated, without solving, the identity of the enemies; and lost sight generally of an ecclesial sense to the assertion, "We are the Circumcision."

For obvious reasons, 3:2–4a has had no use in lectionaries and little in preaching.

SELECT BIBLIOGRAPHY (see also General Bibliography and Commentaries); additional bibliography on "Circumcision" above in Comment B.1, n 12.

Baldanza, G. 2006a. "Il culto per mezzo dello Spirito (Fil 3, 3)," *RivB* 54:45–64.

Blaschke, A. 1998. *Beschneidung: Zeugnisse der Bibel und verwandter Texte.* TANZ 28. Tübingen/Basel: Francke Verlag. Diss., Heidelberg 1997–98 (K. Berger).

Borgen, P. 1982. "Paul Preaches Circumcision," in *Paul and Paulinism: Essays in Honour of C. K. Barrett*, ed. M. D. Hooker/S. G. Wilson (London: SPCK) 37–46.

Campenhausen, H. F. von. 1954. "Ein Witz des Apostels Paulus und die Anfänge des christlichen Humors," in *Neutestamentliche Studien für Rudolf Bultmann . . . 1954*, ed. W. Eltester, BZNW 21 (Berlin: Töpelmann, 2nd ed. 1957) esp. 190.

Clark, K. W. 1972. "The Israel of God," in *Studies in New Testament and Early Christian Literature*, ed. D. E. Aune (FS A. Wikgren; NTTS 33, Leiden: Brill) 161–69.

Ellis, E. E. 1975. "Paul and His Opponents," in *Christianity, Judaism, and Other Greco-Roman Cults*, FS Morton Smith, SJLA 12, ed. J. Neusner (Leiden: Brill) 1, *New Testament*, 264–89.

Ferguson, E. 1988. "Spiritual Circumcision in Early Christianity," *SJT* 41:485–97.

Fiore, B. 1990. "Invective in Romans and Philippians," *EGLMBS* 10:181–89.

Hanson, A. T. 1987. *The Paradox of the Cross in the Thought of St Paul* (JSNTSup 17; Sheffield: JSOT Press), "Who Are the Dogs?" 79–97.

Haraguchi, T. 1993. "Das Unterhaltsrecht des frühchristlichen Verkündigers. Eine Untersuchung zur Bezeichnung *ergatēs* im Neuen Testament," ZNW 84:178–95.

Horn, F. W. 1996. "Der Verzicht auf die Beschneidung im frühen Christentum," *NTS* 42:479–505.

Jervell, J. 1977. "Das Volk des Geistes," in FS. N. Dahl (Gen. Bibl., under "Sampley, P. J.") 87–106.

Kilpatrick, G. D. 1968. "BLEPETE, Philippians 3 2," *In Memoriam Paul Kahle*, ed. M. Black/G. Fohrer, BZAW 103 (Berlin: A. Töpelmann) 146–48.

Klaiber, W. 2000. *Gerecht vor Gott: Rechtfertigung in der Bibel und heute.* Göttingen: Vandenhoeck & Ruprecht. Tr., *Justified before God: A Contemporary Theology* (Nashville: Abingdon, 2005).

Lieu, J. 1994. "Circumcision, Women and Salvation," *NTS* 40:358–70.

Luter, A. B. 1988. "Worship as Service: The New Testament Usage of *latreuō*," *CTR* 2:335–44.

Marcus, J. 1989. "The Circumcision and the Uncircumcision in Rome," *NTS* 35:67–81.

McEleney, N. J. 1973–74. "Conversion, Circumcision and the Law," *NTS* 20:319–41.

Minear, P. S. 1960. *Images of the Church in the New Testament.* Philadelphia: Westminster.

Moehring, H. R. 1968. "Some Remarks on *sarx* in Phil 3,3ff." TU 102, *SE* IV:432–36.

Olson, S. N. 1985. "Pauline Expressions of Confidence in His Addressees," *CBQ* 47:282–95.

Robinson, D. W. B. 1967. " 'We Are the Circumcision' (Phil 3:3)," *ABR* 15:28–35.

Schrage, W. 1983. "Israel nach dem Fleisch," in *"Wenn nicht jetzt, wann dann,"* FS H.-J. Kraus, ed. H.-G. Geyer et al. (Neukirchen-Vluyn: Neukirchener Verlag) 143–51.

Schreiber, S. 2001. "Cavete Canes! Zur wachsenden Ausgrenzugsvalenz einer neutestamentlichen Metapher," *BZ* 45:170–92.

Schreiner, T. R. 1986. "Circumcision. An Entrée into 'Newness' in Pauline Thought." Diss., Fuller Theological Seminary, Pasadena, Calif.

Ulonska, H. 1989. "Gesetz und Beschneidung. Überlegungen zu einem paulinischen Ablösungskonflikt," in *Jesu Rede von Gott*, FS W. Marxsen, ed. D. A. Koch et al., 314–31.

Vanni, U. 2000. "Antigiudaismo in Filippesi 3,2? Un ripensamento," in *Atti del VI Simposio di Tarso su S. Paolo Apostolo*, ed. L. Padovese, La Chiesa e la sua storia 14 (Rome: Antonianum) 47–62.

12. *Saul the Pharisee, Paul "in Christ": Autobiographical Instruction on Law, Righteousness, Resurrection, and More*, 3:4b–11

TRANSLATION

3:4b If any other person supposes he has confidence in the flesh, I do to a greater degree. 5 With reference to circumcision, circumcised on the eighth day; from the race of Israel, from the tribe of Benjamin; a Hebrew born from Hebrews; as to Law, a Pharisee; 6 as to zeal, a man persecuting the church; as to righteousness, the righteousness called for in the Law, one who was blameless. 7 Whatever things were gains for me, these I have come to consider a loss because of Christ. 8a Fur-

thermore, I do indeed therefore continue to consider that all things are a loss
b because of the surpassingness of knowing Christ Jesus my Lord, c because of
whom I experienced loss of everything, d and I consider all these things crap, e in
order that I may gain Christ 9a and be found in him, b not having my righteousness
that is from the Law c but the righteousness that comes through faith in Christ, the
righteousness that is from God, d on the basis of faith 10a to know him and the
power of his resurrection and participation in his sufferings, b while being conformed to his death, 11 if, hopefully, I am to attain the resurrection from the dead.

NOTES

3:4b. *If any other person supposes he has confidence in the flesh, I do to a greater
degree. ei* + pres. indic. *(dokei), egō mallon,* no vb. Class I (simple particular) condition (BDF 372; GGBB 450–51, 663, 685, 689–94; 706, indef. *tis* may seem not
particular; 711,"if" invites dialogue). Reality, "I can all the more" (NAB[RNT]),
not "could" (NEB; Ewald 168). Indef. pron. *tis, ti* (BDAG 1.b.α.ℶ; BDF 301) +
allos (1.d), *any other* (person). *dokeō* (BDAG 1.a) = **think** (KJV, many trs.), **believe, suppose, consider;** even "thinks he has a right to" (NAB) or "claims" (NEB/
REB; NJB). + infin. (subject acc. unexpressed; the same as the subject of *dokei*;
BDF 396). To avoid "he," NRSV has "If anyone else has reason to be confident";
GNB[2] "If any of you. . . ." *pepoithenai,* 2nd pf. act. infin., *peithō*; see NOTES on 3:3
place confidence in, 4a *confidence indeed in the flesh, en sarki* repeated in 4b. The
apodosis = *egō,* 1st per. pron. as in 4a, + *mallon,* "more" (KJV-NRSV), "rather," "to
a greater degree"; see NOTES on 1:9 *more and more;* 1:12 *actually;* 1:23 *much;* 2:12
more.

    3:5. *With reference to circumcision, circumcised on the eighth day; from the race
of Israel, from the tribe of Benjamin; a Hebrew born from Hebrews.* Seven items follow, no *men* or *de*; as in inscriptions, "syntactical economy" (Hellerman 124,
162).

    (1) *circumcision (peritomē,* v 3a), dat. of reference, BDF 197, or respect, GNTG
3:220; Moule *IB* 46, possibly "quasi-local," see p. 44. *oktaēmeros, on,* "eight" (*okta-,*
GNTG 2:286) + masc. adj. from *hēmera* = day, hence "an eight-day-er" (ATR 657;
cf. 549–50; cf. Acts 28:13 "on the second day [*deuteraioi*]"). = "when I was a week
old" (GNB); Gen 17:12; Lev 12:3; Luke 2:21. *Jub.* 15.11–14, a male child not
circumcised on the eighth day "has broken my covenant" (*OTP* 1:86). Because
peritomē is stressed, *circumcised* is added in tr. The next three items use the prep.
ek + gen. (BDAG 3.b), **from** for "origin, as to family, race, city, people . . ." (ATR
598), usually rendered "of."

    (2) *genos* (gen. *genous*), **nation, people** (BDAG 3), race (NABRNT, NJB,
NEB). [N]RSV, NIV, "of the people of Israel," suggests Gk. *laos,* which could
include proselytes (Caird 135); racial descent is meant (O'B 370). *Israēl* =
gen., apposition, "race of Israel" (NABRNT, [N]JB; Roetzel 1997, esp. against
N. T. Wright 1991, would avoid "race" as a modern concept). Josh 4:14; 11:21
(COMMENT A.1.e, n 12), and Jdt 9:14 (Fields 273–77) are far-fetched. The pa-

triarch Jacob ("Israel," Gen 32:28; 35:10), then those descended from him (W. Gutbrod, *TDNT* 3:383–84; G. Harvey 228, 231, 255–56, 271–73).

(3) *(ek) phylēs Beniamin*, "of the tribe of Benjamin," youngest son of Jacob, Gen 35:18, here Benjaminite descendants, one of the (twelve) tribes of Israel (K.-D. Schunck, "Benjamin," *ABD* 1:671–73; Str. B 3:286–88). Fields 277–82 connects Num 13:9, spies from each tribe, with "do not fear them" (14:9; Phil 1:28), but the vbs. differ *(phobeomai, pturō)*. On *phylē*, cf. C. Maurer, *TDNT* 9:245–50; N. Hillyer, *NIDNTT* 3:870–73. In Gk. for subdivisions in the Doric and Ionic communities; in Athens and other city-states, for political districts; eventually for Lat. *tribus*, "tribe," for wards into which Rome was divided (*TDNT* 9:245–46; *NIDNTT* 3:870), enrolled by geographical regions, not blood kinship. Pilhofer 1:123–27, it reflects the *tribus Voltinia* in which citizens in Philippi (and Rome) were enrolled. On *phylē = tribus*, *OCD*³ 1178–79, 1550–51. For Paul's first four expressions in 3:5, Pilhofer 134, 151 offers Roman parallels known to Philippian readers; see COMMENT B.1, below.

(4) *Hebraios ex Hebraiōn*, "a Hebrew (born) of Hebrews" ([N]RSV). Noun 4x in the NT, two of them here; "a few times" in the LXX Pentateuch (Gen 40:15; 43:32; Exod 1:15), more frequent "in the deuterocanonical and apocryphal books" (references in Fitzmyer AB 31:347). Used for the Israelite and Jewish people, often by themselves in contrast to Gentiles. "Jew" could be derogatory (but cf. the cautions in G. Harvey 6–7); "Hebrew" was preferred in Hellenistic Jewish literature (4 Macc, Jdt, *Sib. Or.*, Philo, Jos.; BDAG 269–70; J. Wanke, *EDNT* 1:369–70). Cf. Philo, *Moses* 2.32 (= HCNT #797); synagogue inscriptions, *(tōn) Hebraiōn*, in Rome and Corinth (Deissmann, *LAE* 16 n 7; *TDNT* 3:374–75; Hengel 1983b:15; Levinskaya [INTRO. II] 162–66, 183–84). Fields 282–87 (with Silva 176) implies Paul was "pure-blooded" and "orthodox." 2 Cor 11:22 ("Are they Hebrews? So am I?") suggests a term of eminence in Hellenistic-Jewish apologetics that (Christian) missionaries employed (Georgi 1964a:41–46). From Acts 6:1 a linguistic aspect (but cf. G. Harvey 270): *Hebraios* = an **Aramaic-speaking** Jew (BDAG 2); also Hebrew-speaking? Cf. Acts 21:40; 22:2; 26:14; cf. John 5:2, etc. Not Hebrew, "undoubtedly" Aramaic (AB 31:701). Nonetheless, O'B 371–72 concludes Paul "spoke Aramaic (or Hebrew) as his mother tongue" and "had special connections" with Palestine (cf. Hengel 1983b:9–11; Unnik 1962). But (Hengel 1974) avoid making Saul from Tarsus too Hebraic or Hellenistic. To give him "Hebrew Palestinian parentage" (*TDNT* 3:390) "looks like strapping Paul into a Lukan straitjacket" (Fee 307 n 14). On Jer. *Vir.* 5; *ad Philomena* 23 (Saul's parents were moved from Gischalis in Galilee to Tarsus by the Romans), see K.-W. Niebuhr 107–8; Riesner153. Possibly born in Tarsus, he studied in Jerusalem (Acts 22:3; with Unnik 1962, cf. Conzelmann, *Acts* 186; Fitzmyer, AB 31:704; Jervell, *Apg.* 542–43; Riesner 154, 268). Likely bilingual, Gk. his first language; Acts 6:1, *Hebraioi*, "Jews who, while able to speak Greek, knew a Semitic language *also*"; *Hellēnistoi*, (Jews) "who spoke *only* Greek" (AB 31:347; C. F. D. Moule, "Once More, Who Were the Hellenists?" *ExpTim* 70 [1958–59] 100–2). To claim "a Hebrew to the fullest extent" reads too much in (E. J. Goodspeed 1945:175–76; GNTG 1:10; U. B. Müller 148 n 43). *Word studies: TDNT*

3:358–59 (von Rad), 365–69 (K. G. Kuhn), 372–75, 388–91 (W. Gutbrod); *ABD* 3:95 (N. P. Lemche); *NIDNTT* 2:305–6; 309–10 (R. Mayer); G. Harvey 104–47.

(5) *as to Law, a Pharisee*. *kata* + acc., next three phrases (BDAG B.6, "denoting relationship to someth[ing], **with respect to, in relation to**"; 1:12; cf. 1:20; 2:3; 4:19), *as to* ([N]RSV). 3x, noun (without art.) + noun (or adj. phrase) for the standard Paul attained. Here the *Law* of Sinai (BDAG 2.b), as at 3:6,9. No art., in the style in vv 5–6. Attempts to distinguish "law" and "the law" in Paul produce "no firm rule" (BDF 258,2; Moule *IB* 113; *GNTG* 3:177; O'B 373 n 38; Dunn, *TPTA* 132–33). *nomos* could = "principle," "norm" (BDAG *nomos* 1; Rom 3:27; 8:2; Gal 6:2, though Dunn 634–58 sees Torah even there) or refer to Roman *lex* (*TDNT* 4:1025–35, H. Kleinknecht/W.Gutbrod, 1065–78 on Paul; *NIDNTT* 2:438–39, H.-H. Esser, 444–47). H. Hübner, *EDNT* 2:471–77, brings out the range of meanings for *tôrâ* (instruction, teaching, covenantal law), while cautious on legal(istic) connotations of the shift to *nomos* in the LXX that C. H. Dodd stressed (1935 [(2) Bibl. **righteousness**] 25–41).

nomos in the Greco-Roman world was (Sonntag 18–29) the way to righteousness; politically, as *sōtēr*, it preserves, delivers, and brings wholeness to society. Written *nomoi* by Draco, Solon, and other law-givers in Athens were the instrument for life together in the *polis* (7–17). The norm for law was *dikaiosynē*; law defined the righteous person (*Eth. Nic.* 1129a 31–b1, etc.). Righteousness is doing the law (Plato, "the law of God" incites people "to do righteous acts," Diog. Laert. 3.79, LCL tr. R. D. Hicks, 1:347). On these themes, + "friendship," in Aristot. *Eth. Nic.*, see Sonntag 32–46; *nomos* is the way to a qualitatively better life, 47–52. Good law-givers help the *polis* and every type of *koinōnia* share in a good life and happiness (Aristot., *Pol.* 1325 7–10). Law aided the rise of culture (52–89) and civilization, bringing *sōtēria* (deliverance) to cities and individuals (91–94; Aristot. *Rhet.* 1360a 17–23; Plato *Resp.*, Sonntag 95–104). Such positive senses, not without parallels in the OT (109–28), were possible for Gk. hearers re Phil 3:6 and 9 (107–108; 180–83). Sonntag makes no connection with Phil 3:21, Christ as *sōtēr*.

Pharisaios shows Paul's loyalty to the Law and rigor in observance. Word studies: Baeck; R. Mayer/H. F. Weiss, *TDNT* 9:11–48; D. Müller, *NIDNTT* 2:810–14; G. Baumbach, *EDNT* 3:415–17; *Early Judaism and its Modern Interpreters*, ed. R. A. Kraft/G. W. E. Nickelsburg (Philadelphia: Fortress/Atlanta: Scholars Press, 1986) 69–72 (G. G. Porten); A. J. Saldarini, *ABD* 5:289–303; Deines 2001:503, "the fundamental and most influential religious movement within Palestinian Judaism between 150 B.C. and A.D. 70," with "*a particular relationship to the Law*" (492–93). Fields 287–90 attempts connection with Num 6:21 (*kata nomon*), but Nazarites do not relate to Pharisees. Almost 100x in the NT; Phil 3:5, the only example outside the Gospels and Acts (there only in Jerusalem; of Paul at 23:6 and 26:5). Most treatments of Pharisees stress their origins (probably 2nd cent. B.C.); "separation" from the unholy; written *and* oral law, applied in daily life; openness to newer ideas like resurrection; communal life. More recent analysis stresses political origins (conflict with later Hasmonean rulers; not necessarily opposed to Herod or Roman rule), a movement to change society (Baumbach 1971:416;

Saldarini, *ABD* 5:301–2). Neusner 1979: the Pharisees moved away from politics, into piety, before 70 C.E., probably during the reign of Herod the Great; Hollingshead 18–21 dates this after the destruction of the Temple. Their 6000 or so members followed various occupations (not just urban artisans or lay scribes), usually in Palestine (Riesner 152). Jos. saw them as a Hellenistic philosophical school like the Stoics (*Vita* 12). Overman doubts many claims about Pharisaism; 3:5 boasts about confidence re the Jewish Law, not a claim to have been a Pharisee. Deines supports more traditional views. While there were no Pharisees in Philippi, Paul did not explain the term at 3:5. His urban social status fits with Pharisees, as does concern for communal purity (294–95; 1 Thess 4:1–7; 1 Cor 5:1,7; cf. P. J. Tomson [(8) Bibl.] 97–103, 51–53, "a Hellenistic Pharisee").

3:6. *as to zeal, a man persecuting the church. . . . kata* + acc. Could be periphrasis for the adv. (BDAG *kata* B.5.b.β), *zealously* (cf. 2:3). Usually (BDAG B.6) *as to*, or "so zealous that" (GNB; cf. CEV). *zeal* in a positive sense (BDAG *zēlos* 1), *ardor,* "religious fervor" (NJB), 2 Cor 9:2; John 2:17 = Ps 69:9; Rom 10:2; 2 Cor 11:2. The prototype in Israel was Phineas (Num 25:1–18) who killed a man from the tribe of Simeon and a Midianite woman having sex (perhaps in a tent sanctuary, v 8), a blow against idolatrous impurity; he stayed a plague and "made atonement for the Israelites"; the deed was "reckoned as righteousness" to Phineas (Ps 106:28–31; cf. Gen 15:6). Fields 290–301 adds Judg 20:28; 1 Chron 6:50; Ps 119 (LXX 118):137–44 (COMMENT A.1.e, n 15). Sirach 45:23–24 ranks Phineas "third in glory" after Moses and Aaron for zeal. Other heroes of zeal: Elijah (1 Kgs 18:36–40; 19:10–18, etc.); Jehu (2 Kgs 9–10); Josiah (2 Kgs 22:1–23:30); Dinah's avengers (Gen 34). A Maccabean theme (e.g., 1 Macc 2:26, 54), zeal for the Law, against idolatry and lack of circumcision (1 Macc 2:44–46). The "strictest guardians of ancestral institutions, without pity toward those who undermine them in any way" (Philo, *Spec.* 2.253); "the echo of or response to divine zeal" (Dunn, *TPTA* 350; O. Betz 1977:59). But it is "anachronistic" to see before 68 C.E. "members of a sect called Zealots," political revolutionists against Rome (D. Rhoads, *ABD* 6:1045, cf. 1043–54; O. Betz 1977:59; Hengel 1988:159, 168–71). At Phil 3:5 neut. acc. (*zēlos*; 2 Cor 9:2; GNTG 2:126), not masc. (*zēlon,* א² D¹ etc. Koine MSS). *Word studies:* TDNT 2:877–78 (A. Stumpff); *NIDNTT* 3:1166–68 (H.-C. Hahn); *EDNT* 2:100–1 (W. Popkes); Dunn, *TPTA* 350–53, with Hengel 1988: 146–228; Smiles.

diōkōn tēn ekklēsian credentials Paul's *zeal.* + *theou* in a few MSS, "(church) of God." First use of *ekklēsia* in canonical Phil, but see NOTE on 4:15 (Letter A, *church* as local congregations). Where such assemblies existed, there was the "church universal" (BDAG *ekklēsia* 3.c, citing 1 Cor 6:4; 12:28). Paul knew geographically regional churches (Gal 1:22–23; 1 Thess 2:14), not yet a "worldwide" concept; O'B 377. *Word studies:* TDNT 3:506–9 (K. L. Schmidt); *NIDNTT* 1:301 (L. Coenen); *EDNT* 1:412–13 (J. Roloff); Hainz 1972:229–32; 234; 250–51. W. Schrage, "Ekklesia und Synagoge," *ZTK* 60 (1963) 178–202: a Christian self-designation that arose in the Hellenistic-Jewish circle around Stephen; Paul developed it in polemical antithesis to *synagōgē,* so identified with Jewish nomism as to be of little use for Christians (cf. Schrage, *TDNT* 7:829; cf. 821–22: *CIJ*

2.1404:3–5 a synagogue was built "for reading the Law and for teaching of the commandments"; Jos. *Ap.* 2.175; *Ant.* 16.43). Roloff (*EDNT* 1:412) objects, "*ekklēsia* never occurs in Paul's letters where a tone critical of the law can be detected"; true for 3:5–6, but scarcely vv 7–8a. Hollingshead 11, 28–29 n 59 claims Jews borrowed *ekklēsia* from political assemblies to refer to the synagogue. Ascough 2003:72–76, *ekklēsia* re voluntary associations.

persecuting. Ptc. pres. act., *diōkō* (BDAG 2, **persecute**). Gal 1:13, "violently (or excessively; Hultgren 1976) persecuting the church of God"; 1:23; cf. 4:29; 1 Cor 15:9; Acts 9:4–5, etc. Subst. ptc. (*GNTG* 3:151), no art. ([N]RSV "a persecutor"). Pres. tense, iterative action (ZG 599), a "quasi-name" (ZBG 371). Some supply "I was . . ." (Gdsp., [N]JB). NLT overtranslates, "harshly persecuted." CEV understates, "made trouble for the church." *Word studies:* A. Oepke, *TDNT* 2:229–30; G. Ebel, *NIDNTT* 2:805–7; O. Knoch, *EDNT* 1:338–39.

(7) *as to righteousness, the righteousness called for in the Law, one who was blameless. kata* + acc., *dikaiosynē* (BAGD 2.a, *righteousness*, "fulfilling the divine statutes . . . the *practice of piety* originating from . . . uprightness"; BDAG 3.c; 3.b will not do). See NOTE on 1:11 *righteousness*; one of the four cardinal Greco-Roman virtues ("justice"); God's vindicating righteousness in the OT and the call to act uprightly under the covenant. Pre-Pauline Christian uses of *dikaio-* terminology were continued by Paul, who developed the theme soteriologically, christologically, eschatologically, and ethically. At 1:11, *fruit that results from righteousness,* the outcome of justification, fruit that "comes about *through Jesus Christ.*" Such teaching Paul likely set forth during the founding mission in Philippi, as part, perhaps the heart, of his gospel. At 3:6 righteousness *tēn en nomō[i],* "in the Law" attrib. position, "righteousness, the kind that is in the Torah," the Law of Moses, revealed from God, the guiding star for Pharisees. *kata* + acc. might be adverbial (Paul related to the Law "righteously," BDAG *kata* B.5.b.β); better, like 5e, *kata = as to,* Saul's standard "the righteousness that is (called for) in the Law." In covenant structure, not how a person becomes righteous (as in GNB, "a person can be righteous by obeying the commands of the Law") or "legalistic righteousness" (NIV), but election of Israel by the God of the Exodus and a person's entry into the Sinai covenant by birth within Israel and, for a male, circumcision as a sign of belonging. *(hē) dikaiosynē hē en nomō[i]* = the upright and just conduct God calls for as human response; cf. 9b, *hē dikaiosynē hē ek nomou,* righteousness that arises out of the Law. 3:6b is on "staying in" the covenant relationship, not "getting into" it; maintaining, not making, righteous(ness) (E. P. Sanders, *PPJ* 544–45). *en nomō[i],* not instrumental (as in GNB; Blank 1968:221) or even "rooted in the Law" if that implies a "right" relationship with God stems from obeying the Law (see O'B 378–79, a distinction between *en* and *ek*). Nonetheless Sanders' "covenantal nomism" is "reductionistic," "misleading" (Carson 543–48). "Covenant" is not used here by Paul (elsewhere, the [old] Mosaic *diathēkē* versus a new covenant in Christ featuring the Spirit, Jer 31:31; 2 Cor 3:6–18; Gal 4:24, cf. 3:15–18; 1 Cor 11:25; Rom 9:4 "covenants" with Israel; 11:27). He knows the structure of the covenant, its pattern of indic. ("I am the Lord your God who brought you out of the land of Egypt," Exod 20:2) and impvs. (Exod 20:3–17) or stipulations. See P. A. Reimann, "Covenant,

Mosaic," M. Weinfeld, "Covenant, Davidic," *IDBSup* 188–97; G. Mendenhall/ G. Herion, "Covenant," *ABD* 1:1197–1202. Phil 3:6 = the Mosaic Law set within God's covenant with Moses and Israel and its sign of circumcision.

Paul dares to say of himself *genomenos amemptos* re this standard of righteousness. *ginomai,* aor. m. ptc.; like *eimi,* "be," + nom. (BAGD II.1; BDAG 7; perhaps even "show oneself"). Often omitted in trs. (KJV-[N]RSV). Others, "I was (blameless)" ([N]JB, GNB), aor. A subst. ptc. in the TRANSLATION, *one who was blameless. amemptos* = "blameless" or "faultless" (Gen 17:1; Ps 15:2a); cf. 1 Thess 3:13; NOTE on Phil 2:15 *unfaulted.* Gk. examples in *TDNT* 4:572–73 (W. Grundmann). In Job LXX, common (Fields 302–3), but "no direct equivalent in Heb."; *NIDNTT* 2:137, 139, 143–45 (T. McComisky) and 3:923–25 (H. Währisch). The Pharisaic claim is not "to be sinless" (Espy 165–66; "scrupulosity" characterizes Pharisees on the Law). When a person "missed the mark" or the whole nation did, Judaism had a divinely given system of Temple sacrifices to expiate sin, and prayer and repentance (T. R. Schreiner 1985:260–61). Paul claims he lived up to what the Law called for, as did others. John Hyrcanus "wished to be righteous and did all things with which he would please God" (according to Pharisaic teaching); the Pharisees declared him "altogether virtuous" (Jos. *Ant.* 13.289–90, but cf. 292). Pss. Sol. 9.4–5 (*OPT* 2:660, from Pharisees): doing right is "in the works of our hands," "the one who does what is right saves up life for himself with the Lord." O. Betz 1976 cites Isa 56:1, "Do what is right, for soon my salvation will come." Qumran saw some as "perfect in everything . . . revealed about all the law" (1QS 8.1; cf. 1.8–9).

Thus not an impossible term for a Jew in covenant relationship with God. Not ironic (Gnilka 2001:142), not blameless "only at times," not "*I thought myself* blameless" (Goguel 1934:258–59; Espy 162, nn 6, 47). For Paul "an objective fact, as incontestable as his circumcision," etc. (Espy n 6). Phil 3:6 was the starting point for the idea that Paul *kept* the Law, suffered no crisis of conscience, and maintained a "robust conscience"; "the introspective conscience" of later Western theology (Augustine and Luther) led interpretation astray (as if Judaism and "the East" were never introspective); so Stendahl 1963 = 1976:78–96. But cf. E. P. Sanders, *USQR* 33 (1978) 175–87; Käsemann 1971b; D. O. Via, Jr., "Justification and Deliverance: Existential Dialectic," *SR* 1 (1971) 204–12; Espy. Problematic are Stendahl's imprecision on "conscience" and what is being defended, originally, "salvation history"; Reumann 1982 ([2] Bibl. **righteousness**) ##213, 216 and p. 119 n 128; Espy 162–67). Stendahl held (re Jewish hopes that if all Israel obeyed Torah for a single day, messiah would come) that Israel *as a whole* failed to fulfill the Law (Rom 2–3; Gal 3:10–12); Paul could conclude that the Law was no longer valid, one must abandon this route in favor of Christ (1963:200–2 = 1976:80–81). *blameless* reflects Pharisaic "separation" from Gentiles and many less observant Jews (Dunn, *TPTA* 349–50).

3:7. *Whatever things were gains for me, these I have come to consider a loss because of Christ. alla* ("But whatever . . . ," RSV; "Yet," NRSV), in brackets (NA²⁷; P⁴⁶, ⁶¹ ᵛⁱᵈ, ℵ* A G lack *alla*; B D ℵ second corrector, TR include it). Some (K. Barth 96) sense "But" is needed here; hence scribes added it. Asyndeton (BFD 462, 494) is not uncommon in Paul (3:17; 4:2). Cf. Silva 182. *alla* and *hatina* begin and end with *alpha*; hence omission or addition; on "longer" and "shorter readings," see on 3:12b *or . . . justified.* "But" is an addition (Fee 311 n 1; Schenk 265, with Michaelis, Hawth., U. B. Müller 151 n 55, among others), though a "correct" one. Omitted in TRANSLATION.

The v is constructed around a double or triple contrast re objects for confidence listed in 3:5–6:

hatina	ēn	moi	kerdē
tauta	hēgēmai	dia ton Christon	zēmian

Neut. pl. *hostis, hētis, ho ti,* "whoever, whatever," often equivalent of *hos, hē, ho* (BDAG *hostis* 3); 2:20 *who,* 1:28 *This.* Characteristic qualities in a class of things (*hostis* 2.b); thus Vincent 99; NEB/REB "all such assets"; cf. ZBG #215. BDF 293 the two "no longer clearly distinguished in the NT" (*GGBB* 343–45). Here, anaphoric, for what Paul has just enumerated (ATR 698). Pl. (for seven items) like *kerdē* (n. pl.). Fee 315 n 9, "whatever [other] things" might be added, e.g. (Rom 9:4), Israel's "adoption, glory, the giving of the Law, and worship." In the major cl., *tauta* ("these") refers to these same things. *ēn* (imperf. *eimi,* 3rd sg. with a neut. pl. subject = "were") contrasts with *hēgeomai,* pf. tense (BDAG 2, **think, consider, regard**), Phil 2:3, 6, 25; also 3:8ab, + a double acc., "consider them [to be, but no *einai* as in 8a] loss." *hēgēmai* here (BDF 341), not a pres. meaning (NIV); KJV/RSV, past tense "I counted"; pf. "I have come to regard" (NRSV, NABRNT, JB). Of Paul's Damascus Road "conversion" experience (Dib. 68, Michaelis 55, Michael 144, Gnilka 191, etc.)? Bruce 118, "not particularly"; an aor. would be called for. Räisänen 1987:409, interpretation "in retrospect." Byrnes 179–80, a conviction that continues.

gains . . . a loss. kerdē . . . zēmian, a second contrast. On *to kerdos, -ous,* see NOTE on 1:21 *gain;* vb. at 3:8e. Pl., the (seven) things listed (B. Weiss 238 n 1), in contrast to "one great loss" (O'B 385). Cf. *TDNT* 2:888–91 (A. Stumpff), commercial "damage," moral or spiritual "ruin," legal "disadvantage"; *TLNT* 2:157–60, *zēmia* and *kerdos* were paired in business and the diatribe, a contrast found also in the Rabbis; see Str-B 1:749–50; 3:622, as in *'Abot* 2.1 (*APOT* 2:694). D. K. Williams 2002:175 saw rhetorical terminology; better, commercial background (NIV "profit"; NEB/REB "assets"); "assessed in the light of business objectives" (Bockmuehl 204–5). *zēmia* = **damage, disadvantage** (JB), loss (KJV-NRSV), even **forfeit.** Not OT terms. Common in Gk. sources, e.g., Aristot. *Eth. Nic.* 5.4.3–6 (*TDNT* 2:888–89 as 5.7.1132 b 2ff.), the "mean" between gain and loss. Some see Mark 8:36 parr (Luke 9:25), "What will it profit people if they gain *(kerdēsē[i])* the whole world and forfeit *(zēmiōthē[i])* their life?" (Bruce 118; O'B 390–91, though the "antithesis was common in the Judaism of the day," Collange 128–29; *'Abot* 2.1 above). Bonnard 63, tr. in *TLNT* 2:159 n 9, "profits were not just wiped out," "losses; their mathematical sign changed from plus to minus." A third possible contrast: *moi* and *dia ton Christon* (B etc. read *moi ēn,* less parallel, possibly a chiasm [A = *moi;* B = vb. *ēn;* B′ = vb.; A′ = *dia ton Christon*]; less likely textually). Dat. of advantage (BDF 188; Hawth. 135; O'B 384 n 8), "gain to me, "KJV; "my profit,"

NIV; or "whatever gains I had" ([N]RSV), rather than dat. to express a judgment, "in my estimation" (CEV). *dia* + acc. (BDAG B.2.a) shows why advantages paradoxically become loss. RSV/NIV *"for the sake of* Christ" (KJV "for Christ"). Hawth. 136 objects to Christ benefiting by Paul's decision and preferred "because of the *fact* of Christ" (Damascus Road!). Silva 182: "unnecessary"; "for the sake of" implies Christ as goal (v 8 is in view, Paul "gains Christ"); similarly O'B 385. Or *"because of* Christ" (NRSV; Fee 315 n 8; ATR 583–84). *dia* + acc. (also in 8a and 8b) is causal here (*DA* 324) for Saul's great reversal in values.

3:8a. *Furthermore, I do indeed therefore continue to consider that all things are a loss. alla menounge kai* (Fee 317 n 15), "but, therefore, indeed, also." P⁴⁶ ℵ* etc. omit *kai* "to simplify" (Thrall 11–16, esp. 15); B D etc. lack *ge* (Vincent 100; Loh. 131 n 27); Ewald 172 would omit all three. Initial *alla* (BDAG 3) can mark "transition to someth[ing] new," after "a settled matter" (Rom 8:37) or (ATR 1185–86) present "an accessory idea . . . confirmatory and continuative." BDF 448,6, introduces "an additional point in an emphatic way"; *men* (no contrasting *de*) + *oun* + *ge* emphasize or correct (BDF 450,4) in an affirmative direction (*IB* 163–64). Unlike classical Gk., at the start of a sentence (Rom 9:20; 10:18; Luke 11:28; Thrall 34–36). *kai* strengthens the cumulative effect (cf. 1:18a *alla kai*); DA 327. ATR, "vernacular koine" (1145), with "climactic force"; " 'I go,' says Paul, 'so far as to consider all things to be loss' " (1148). Since KJV, "yea" or "yes" has been used (NEB); "more," in NEB, NIV, NRSV. "Not only (that), (but) . . . ," JB, GNB. No tr. can pick up every nuance in this introduction to a repetition of v 7 that heightens it in two ways: now *hēgoumai* is pres. tense, "I do consider" or "continue to consider" (O'B 386) things enumerated in vv 5–6 to be (*einai*, infin. in indir. discourse, GNTG 3:137) *loss* (see NOTE on v 7); secondly, *panta*, "all things," for *tauta* in v 7; "all things" (BDAG *pas* 1.b.β, subst.) means "everything" ([N]RSV) attached to circumcision, Law, righteousness, etc.; Lft. 148. *kai* = "also now still" (Schenk 264), in the face of "the enemies."

3:8b. *because of the surpassingness of knowing Christ Jesus my Lord.* The basis for 8a. *dia* + acc., expanding on *dia ton Christon* in 7. As in v 7, *dia* is debated ("for the sake of" or "because of Christ"); cf. Lft. 148; Michael 145; Fee 317 n 18. Once the causal sense is agreed upon (with Schenk 305; Sanders, *PPJ* 485), comparison enters through knowledge that "surpasses" or "excells"; knowing Christ "renders everything else worthless in comparison" (Michael 145). *to hyperechon*, ptc., pres. tense, *hyperechō*; see NOTES on 2:3 *surpass* (social-world background) and 4:7 *exceeds*. Subst. neut. sg., an abstract noun (BDF 263,2), more concrete than *hyperochē* (GNTG 3:14). + gen. (as at Rom 2:4; 2 Cor 8:8). Some supply a noun, "surpassing worth" (RSV), ". . . value" (NRSV), ". . . greatness" (NIV), or make it a noun (KJV "excellency"). *surpassingness* catches the abstract noun form. Some take the gen. with *to hyperechon* as hendiadys (Vg *eminentem scientiam*; "surpassing knowledge," NAB; contrast Vincent 100) or in apposition (GNB "what is so much more valuable, the knowledge . . ."); ZBG #140, "the 'surpassing good' which *is* the knowledge of Christ" (so Fields 238 n 23); or gen. of comparison, "the excellence of Christ which passes understanding" (cf. 4:7?). Delling (*TDNT* 8:524 n 5), subj. gen., the excellence that knowledge of Christ produces.

knowing. gnōsis (gen.), only here in Phil; vb., 1:12 *come to know*; 2:22 *Timothy's proven character you know*. Nowhere else does Paul use "knowledge of Christ Jesus" (but cf. 3:10a "to know him"; 1 Cor 2:2; 2 Cor 5:16); "knowledge *of God*" at Rom 11:32; 2 Cor 2:14; 4:6; and 10:5. 2 Pet 3:18, "knowledge of our Lord and Savior Jesus Christ," may reflect Phil (Koperski 1996:5–6). BAGD *gnōsis* 2, Christian *knowledge*, supernatural, revealed, even "mystical" knowing; cf. BDAG 2. More than "intellectual knowledge." *Nomen actionis* (Schenk 305), "knowing," Gdsp., [N]RSV, NIV, etc. Does background lie in the OT (*yāda'*, *da'at*, *TDOT* 5:448–81, by "hearing")? Or in the Hellenistic world (by "seeing," Gnilka 2001:144; cf. Gärtner 1967–68), more specifically in Gnosticism (H. Jonas, *The Gnostic Religion* [Boston: Beacon, 2nd ed.1963] 31–47; *ABD* 2:1033–39)? Or both (Gnilka 2001:144–45)? In *wordbook treatments*, Bultmann (*TDNT* 1:689–719) stressed Gnosticism (710), but noted LXX use of *ginōskein* as a further presupposition for NT usage; E. D. Schmitz (*NIDNTT* 2:394), "gnostic myth" and Qumran use of Heb. terms (397); C. Brown added a note (401) against reading in later Gnostic ideas. Dupont 1949 ([2] Bibl.) found OT roots (esp. in apocalypticism). Eng. commentaries favor the OT as source and often seek to exclude Gnosticism (Fee, *Phil.* 318 n 21). Ger. commentaries are often open to more than OT-Jewish background (e.g., Gnilka 192–93; U. B. Müller 152). A "Gnostic Redeemer myth" was set aside as a source for 2:6–11 in Exc.B., II. D. 2, but more than "OT" versus "Gnosticism" is involved in 3:8b. If "Jewish," is it Palestinian (Aramaic-speaking) or Hellenistic (Greek) Judaism? O'B 388 mentions Hellenistic mysticism (Dib. *Phil.* 69) or "an amalgam of Hellenic and Hebraic ideas" ("a new, creative fusion" issuing in "a distinctively *Christian* synthesis," Beare 115).

Koperski 1996:20–65 lists four proposals on *gnōsis Christou*: (A) *Hellenistic mysticism*, beholding the deity, with resulting transformation of the beholder (cf. 2 Cor 3:18; 4:6). Dibelius, R. Reitzenstein 1978; Michael 152, mystery religions. Wikenhauser ([1] Bibl. **in Christ**]) 140–41, "Hellenistic mysticism" or "gnosticism," without transformation at the vision of God or absorption into the deity. Bultmann, "Gnosis," *JTS* 3 (1952) 10–26. H. A. A. Kennedy, *St. Paul and the Mystery-Religions* (New York: Hodder & Stoughton 1913), both mystery religions and OT "knowledge of God." Schmithals 1972:92; Koester 1961–62; Tannehill 118–19. (B) *OT/ Jewish background*—D. Deden, "Le 'Mystère' paulinien," *ETL* 13 (1936) 405–42, connected "knowledge" with "wisdom." Dupont 1949 ([2] Bibl.), knowledge of God, "being known by God," knowledge of Christ, nonmystical; Jewish (biblical) context, "of the essence of Christianity." But "knowledge *of Christ*" is not a Jewish term; it reflects polemics with "the religion of the Law" (36). J. T. Forestell 1956 responded: perfection (vv 12, 15) is knowledge; for Christians, perfection is "charity" (*agapē*, Col 3:14); knowledge is connected with love (Col, Eph), *gnōsis* "equivalent to the intellectual content of faith" (129). Cf. Ahern; Martin 1976:130–31, 133; Hawth. 138; Byrnes 188–89. (C) *Martyrdom* (Loh. 133–35) will bring a special grace, revelation, nearness to the Lord, superabundance (*hyperechon*) of knowledge. Few have followed this view. (D) *Several influences*—Beare (above); Houlden 104, cf. 101, 102: "embryonic" Gnosticism and Judaism. Bockmuehl 205–6, a "buzzword" in the Greco-Roman world, with Pauline usage in "the Jewish tradition." Koperski, "biblical wisdom terminology and imagery" (293–321); it "enables the believer to perceive the power of God which has already triumphed in Christ" (321). In Paul's day, *Gnosis* (in Ger. often distinguished from full-blown later *Gnostizismus*) meant gnostic influences in early Christianity and the Christianizing of Gnosis (K. Rudolf, *ABD* 2:1037). Much depends on who "the enemies" were, whose term it may be here. D. K. Williams 2002:185–86, not Gnostic or from opponents, "a personal relationship with Christ."

Christ Jesus the Lord, obj. gen., + *mou* = "my Lord" (personal attachment [Foerster, *TDNT* 3:1092] or personal fellowship [Grundmann, *TDNT* 7:784]). On *Christ Jesus* see 1:1; on *Lord*, 1:2. *tou Christou* in P[46, 61], B echoes the art. in v 7; "Jesus Christ" in A K P. *hēmōn* in A P for *mou* echoes "our Lord Jesus Christ," but disrupts 1st sg. in vv 4–14. Collange 129 rejected as "unlikely" a subj. gen., "knowledge which Christ has of us" (cf. Gal 4:9, "be known by God"; Phil 3:12; Vallotton, *pistis Christou* as subj. gen.); cf. Dunn, *TPTA* 380.

3:8c. *because of whom I experienced loss of everything. . . . di' hon*, acc. rel. pron. masc. sg., "on account of whom." New sentence in (N)RSV, "For his sake. . . ." *ta panta*, from 8a, here + art. (BDAG *pas* 4.d.β) , "*all things, the universe*," as at 3:21; better, "a summation of what precedes *all this*." Vb. *ezēmiōthēn*, aor. pass. 1st sg., *zēmioō* (noun in 8a) BDAG 1, **suffer damage/loss, forfeit, sustain injury,** *for whose sake I forfeited everything*. Lose property, rights, athletic victories, through some fault or infraction of the rules; NAB "forfeited everything." KJV-NRSV, "suffer loss" (cf. "sufferings" in 10a? but different Gk. words are involved); TRANSLATION *experienced loss*. Pass. + acc. for thing(s) lost (BDF 152,2). Some see in the aor. a single definite past time, like Damascus Road (Rienecker 211). Schenk 307, *passivum divinum* (BDF 130,1; 313; 342,1), God made everything in Saul's life worthless through Christ's appearance to him.

3:8d *and I consider all these things crap. . . .* Vb. as in 8a. *kai* is omitted in NEB/REB, NIV. LB/NLT demote *kai hēgoumai* to a ptc., "counting it." As at 8a, + double acc. Supply *panta* (8a), *all these things*, an expansion of *tauta* in v 7. Infin. *einai* (8a), "consider all things *to be* a loss," is added in 8d by P[61 vid] א[2] A D[2] etc., Koine MSS. The other acc. is *to skybalon*, **useless or undesirable material that is subject to disposal, refuse, garbage;** LSJ "dung, manure; refuse, offal"; vb. *skybalizō* = look on as dung, treat contemptuously. Pl., to agree with *panta*. KJV, "dung" (NEB-mg); most trs., "refuse" (ERV/RSV), "rubbish" (NIV, NRSV, etc.), or "garbage" (CEV). Gk. popular speech (Gnilka 2001:146), in somewhat more literary usage. Similarity to *to skōr, skatos*, "dung, excrement" (cf. Eng. "scatology"; not connected with "shit" from the Old Eng.) accounts for *Etym. Magm.* (10th–12th-cent. compilation from earlier lexicons), "what is given forth through the entrails"; "bowel movement and urine," Alex. Aphr. *Problemata* 1.18; "probably what Paul meant" (MM 574; Jos. *JW* 5.571, LCL tr. *Jos.* 3:377). Also found in medical writers. Another explanation: "something 'dog-thrown,' that which is tossed to the dogs" (*kysibalon ti on, to tois kysi ballomen*), in the lexicon *Suda* (or *Suidas*, Lat. "Fortress"), end of the 10th cent., from earlier works; folk etymology; cf. *skorakizō*, "treat contemptuously," from (*ball'*) *es kyrakas*, "(throw) to the ravens." "Leavings, scraps" after a meal (for the dogs? Wettstein; Lft. 149 compares 3:2 "dogs"); Leonidas (of Tarentum, 3rd cent. B.C.; a Cynic?) was so poor a mouse would not taste "even of his leavings *(skybalou)*" from dinner *(Anth. Graec.* 6.302.6 = LCL *Greek Anthology* 1:462–63); cf. 6.303.4). "Leavings" (ashes) of a person, sepulchral epigram (ibid. 7.382. 2 = LCL 2:204–5). Leavings or gleanings from a crop (MM, who also report *Skybalos* as a proper name, "Scraps"?). Plaut. *Truc.* 2.7.5, lines 555–58, is often cited, he "takes his own property for dung . . ." (LCL tr., P. Nixon, *Plautus* 5 [1938] 280–81). A third possibility (F. Lang, *TDNT* 7:445): *skybalon* from the sea, "flotsam, jetsam" (Achill. Tat. 2.11.5); fishermen netted a "half-eaten man, a much lamented relic *(skybalon)* from a sea voyage" *(Anth. Graec.* 7.276.2 = LCL 2:150–51). At least since Dib. 69, pessimistic inscriptions on a cup (in the Louvre) from the trove of silver found at Boscoreale, near Pompeii (destroyed A.D. 79), have been quoted: "A skeleton pours a libation on bones lying on the ground" *(TDNT* 7:445); *tout' anthrōpos*, "This (is what happens to) a person"; "Live piously, you scraps *(eusebou· skybala)*." The only other biblical example of the noun is Sir 27:4, "When a sieve is shaken, the refuse *(kopria)* appears; so do a person's faults *(skybala anthrōpou)* when he speaks" (NRSV); AB 39:356, a person's "filth" shows up the way ox-dung does when grain is sifted. Schenk 265: not so much what is disgusting (hence excrement) but what miscarries. Climactic in Paul's list, just as in 3:2 *katatomē* was climax on the enemies ("incision," not "dogs," has the most sting, Fee 319). Rightly, K. Barth 98: "filth, dung [*Kot*], excrement . . . something which, once thrown away, is never touched again nor even looked at . . . *no* going back to"; 8d is "syntactically the key to all that follows, up to and including v. 11." Schenk compares *sarx* (v 3) and *koilia* ("belly" in 3:19; Mark 7:19, from the stomach into the privy) and suggests the opponents used the term *skybala*. R. Hays 1989 ([2] Bibl.) 122 (n 3 on euphemisms, compared with "Elizabethan frankness") favors "crap" (so Fowl 2005:153 n 35). Boers 1993:99, "Shit with being a Jew," a sentiment balanced in Paul by Rom 9:3–5.

3:8e. *in order that I may gain Christ. . . . hina* + subjunct., purpose, continued in 9a, *be found in* Christ. *kerdainō* = *gain, make one's own* (BDAG 1.b); cf. commercial "gains" *(kerdē)* and "loss" in v 7; Schlier *(TDNT* 3:673), "win something" (Matt 25:16, etc., KJV). Here not "win converts" (1 Cor 9:19–22). Schoder, NAB, "that Christ may be my wealth" catches accounting overtones. Aor. (likely in such a construction) suggests a fut. goal (at the eschaton) and excludes a process of repeatedly gaining Christ.

3:9a. *and be found in him. kai* suggests hendiadys, "that is," so that 9a explains 8e (Fee 320); BDF 442,9, epexegetical; Silva 183–84, "[What do I mean by 'gaining' Christ? I want] to be found in union with Him . . . ," but Silva divides vv 7–8 from 9–11. Aor. pass. subjunct., *euriskō* (BDAG 1.b), "*find* . . . Pass. *be found* [KJV-NRSV], *find oneself*"; "to *project* a possible realm" *(DA* 411). Schenk 307, = to be; 328 "receive my place in his realm of lordship"; 1 Cor 15:12. Walter 73, 79, "show myself in Christ as one who does not possess a righteousness of my own." In Gdsp. "united to him" and NEB "incorporate in him," perhaps baptismal imagery. Moffatt 1912–13, "be found at death," on the basis of Epict. 3.5.5–8 (JR tr.), "disease and death must overtake (*katalabein*; cf. Phil 3:12–13) us. . . . What do you wish to be doing when overtaken (*katalēphthēnai*)? . . . May . . . I be overtaken (*katalēphthēnai*) attending to . . . my own (moral) purpose (*proaireseōs*). . . . I wish to be found (*eurethēnai*) doing these things"; "the true meaning" (Michael 148). Hence, at the judgment (O'B 392; Loh. 136; Edart 239; cf. 2 Cor 5:3). But Dib. 69, a present experience, since Damascus Road, "Christ-mysticism," "Christ in me and I in him" (not a phrase in Paul, Loh. 136; at best, cf. Gal 2:20). Michaelis 57, fellowship begun at Damascus Road; Siber (Exc.A Bibl.) 111–12 n 53. Fee 320–21, an "'already but not yet' eschatological perspective"; U. B. Müller 154; I. H. Marshall 90, "unveiling in the future of a relationship that already exists." See COMMENT B.2.

in him. en Christō[i]; see NOTES on 1:1,13; 2:1; 4:7, 19, 21. Personal relationship? *TDNT* 4:1075, Gutbrod; whoever is in Christ has (the better) righteousness (Friedrich 9th ed. *Phil.* 118, 16th ed. *Phil.* 162). Salvation-history? Neugebauer 1961 ([1] Bibl. **in Christ**) 129. A realm, including the church, where Christ is Lord? *TDNT* 2:541 (A. Oepke); U. B. Müller 154. Not baptismal but future (Blank 1968:235 n 77, now via faith-righteousness). Schenk 307, not a formula but spatial assertion of Christ's realm of lordship (see his rendering of *eurethō* above). Against notions the believer awaits God's judgment at ease "in Christ," Schenk 308 argues *Christos* is never combined with the parousia theme (only "ad hoc," Phil 1:6, 10; 2:16); the parousia title is "Lord" (*Maranatha*). At the end time, not "in Christ" but "with Christ." W. Kramer: with the *pistis*-formula, local sense, "realm of the Lord," for the present messianic interim kingdom (1 Cor 15:28; [(1) Bibl. **in Christ**] §§35 and 36, pp. 140, 141, 143). But Phil is such an exception to Kramer's categories that he must posit a late date for the letter (n 500, contrary to Schenk's Ephesian setting) and explain the "ad hoc" examples as reflection of "Christ" being used more frequently than "Lord" in Phil (n 497, 21:5 ratio). 1:23 raised the possibility of dying and being with Christ before the final coming. Bultmann refers to baptism; not mystical but ecclesiological, eschatological, and ethical (1951:311, 327–39, cf. 337); cf. Schrage 1961:80; Klaiber 1982:94–95, 182–90, justification, "in Christ," and the community.

3:9b. *not having my righteousness that is from the Law.* . . . *echōn*, circumst. ptc. (BDAG *echō* 1), *having*, "possess." Masc. nom. sg., with subject in vbs. of 8e and 9a, "I," Paul. *mē*, + ptc. (DA 351), *not having*, negates the obj., "righteousness from Law." Concessive ("though I have no righteousness of my own," NEB-mg) or causal ("in Christ because I have . . . righteousness from God," O'B 393, 416) or modal (O'B 393; mode or manner for being in Christ, BDF 418,5). Pres. in relation to aor. vbs. *kerdēsō, eurethō*, "gain," "be found" at the final fut. judgment, or a present experience, or both? Usually a pres. ptc. is said to be contemporaneous with the time in a main vb. (GGBB 497–98, 614–15; BDF 339,2,3, note variations), but battles have been fought over how righteousness/justification and "being in Christ" relate (O'B 415–17). Is having God's righteousness fut., present, or both?

On *dikaiosynē*, see NOTE on 1:11 *righteousness*. At 9b OT-Jewish background, *tēn ek nomou*, second attrib. position, that which "comes from [doing] the Mosaic

Law" (cf. NRSV, NIV) or is "based on (observance of) the Law" (cf. RSV, NAB[RNT], Gdsp.). *ek* + gen. (BDAG 3.c; cf. 3:5), origin or source for this kind of righteousness. Ziesler 1972 ([2] **righteousness**) 188–89 made an overly sharp distinction that the noun is "ethical," the vb. "forensic"; critique in Reumann 1982:##100, 101, 103, passim; Fitzmyer #382. 9b can be "ethical," righteous deeds from doing what the Law commands, "Paul's own moral achievement" (which he then disavows) (O'B 394), but 9c is God's saving or justifying righteousness *(ek theou)*; cf. 1:11. Because of *ek theou* in 9c, almost always tr. "righteousness" (from God or from Law), reflecting the tech. term "righteousness of God" (Stuhlmacher, *Rom.* 29–32), not here "justification"; but NAB(RNT), "a justice of my own," Lat. Vg *iustitia Dei*, R. Knox, "justification." Fee's claim ("the noun . . . does not [ever!] mean 'justification,' as though it were primarily a forensic term," 322 n 35) reflects later dogmatic distinctions in Eng., though a single root lies behind each, Heb. ṣdq, Gk. dikaio-. Excluding "forensic" aspects (law court, judgment) requires an exegetical tour de force, given emphasis on the final judgment (1:6, 10; 2:16; 3:9a; noted esp. in O'B 392–93). In 9b, *tēn* occurs only with the prep. phrase in attrib. position (BDF 272, cf. 285,2); the possessive adj. *emēn*, fem. acc. sg. from *emos, ē, on*, occurs before the noun, "*a* righteousness that is *my own*" (cf. GNTG 3:191; ZBG 180). Emphasis on "*my* own" (efforts, JB; grounds for boasting in the flesh, 3:3) and *ek nomou* characterize the first type of righteousness. Cf. Koperski 1996:192–201.

3:9c. *but the righteousness that comes through faith in Christ, the righteousness that is from God. . . . alla*; NAB omits, as do GNB and CEV, which, however, insert (italics added), "I *now* have . . . ," "God accepted me *simply* because of my faith in Christ." One can supply *echōn* from 9b, "(having) the kind of righteousness that is *dia pisteōs Christou*, that is *ek theou*." So NAB, "The justice I possess . . ."; NEB-mg; GNB. *dikaiosynēn* + art. twice, *tēn dia pisteōs Christou, tēn ek theou dikaiosynēn. ek theou* for source or origin, "from God"; NAB, GNB; NEB/ REB, "given by God"; Aguilar 203, cf. Rom 4:3 = Gen 15:6, "reckoned (by God)," *passivum divinum.* How does this differ from righteousness *ek nomou*, if the Law was given by God (Rom 9:4)? *my* = based on my obedience to, observance of, what the Law says. Covenant setting, as gift, seems minimalized. Doing all the Law is emphasized (Gal 3:10–12) as means for fully "getting into," as well as "staying in," the Mosaic relationship to God. In Phil 3, for Gentiles, getting circumcised.

How does *ek theou dikaiosynē* come about for the person "in Christ"? Answer: *dia* + gen. of *pistis* (see NOTES on 1:25 . . . *faith*; 1:27d . . . *the gospel faith*; and 2:17b . . . *your faith*, vb. at 1:29b *to continue to believe on him*) + the gen. *Christou.* (1) *through faith in Christ*, RSV, NRSV-txt; NIV, NAB(RNT), (N)JB, NEB/REB; church fathers (Harrisville 1994), Reformation writers. *pistis* is "*trust, confidence, faith* in the active sense = 'believing' in relig[ious] usage"; *Christou* obj. gen. (BDAG *pistis* 2.b.β; so, among many, D. K. Williams 2002:180 n 129; Aguilar 202). From time to time as alternative, (2) *Christou* as subj. gen., i.e., Christ's own believing or show of faith, trust, and confidence. *pistis* = "faithfulness" (therefore "his obedient sacrifice," Thurston 129). KJV, "the faith of Christ" (perhaps gen. of source); J. Haussleiter, *Der Glaube Jesu Christi und der christliche Glaube* (1891;

cf. W. Grundmann, *TDNT* 9:552 n 383); Vallotton 88–89; Collange 131, "Christ's faith (i.e. work) . . . justifies us, and this faith subsequently arouses man's faith (*'epi tē pistei,*' at the end of the verse)"; Lampe, in Sampley, ed. 2003:506. Vallotton: God's trust and confidence in man for final salvation and the faith Jesus exercised historically and now exercises as Christ. P. E. Davies, *JBL* 80 (1961) 194, termed this "scarcely recognizable as Paul's forensic term." But a host of scholars endorse it in one form or another (NRSV-mg.; Hays 1983 [(4) Bibl. **faith**] 139–91 and the "Yale School"; Hooker 1989, the only possible meaning; NIB 11:528, but cf. 530–31). At times related to the quests for the historical Jesus; cf. L. E. Keck, *A Future for the Historical Jesus* (Nashville/New York: Abingdon 1971; repr., Philadelphia: Fortress 1981), how Jesus trusted; in liberation theology, J. Sobrino, *Christology at the Crossroads* (Maryknoll, NY: Orbis 1978) 79–145. Vanhoye 1999: "faithfulness of Christ" is a weak alternative; "trustworthiness" fits better. At times, related to Jesus in the "hymn" at Phil 2:6–8 and the imitation of such faithfulness by Paul and others (e.g., O'B 399–400; *GGBB* 114–16). Contrast J. D. G. Dunn 1997; *TPTA* 379–85; literature on p. 335; I. H. Marshall 91 calls it "improbable." Some term *(tou Iēsou) Christou* a gen. of authorship (T. F. Torrance, "One Aspect of the Biblical Conception of Faith," *ExpTim* 68 [1956–57] 111–14, "our vicarious Believer"). Or a gen. of quality (Hultgren 1980, Semitic, equivalent of an adj., giving an attribute), faith is identified with God's justifying act in Christ, proclaimed in the gospel and made effective for those who believe it. Or (G. Taylor 1966), like *fidei commissum* in Roman inheritance law, for property held in trust for two successive heirs (Abraham, Christ, then the Gentiles). But altered by Paul (S. K. Williams 1980:275) and, according to Boers 1993:107–8, "polysemous," virtually untranslatable (101 n 16), "a new condition, the justification of the Gentiles by faith . . . announced by Abraham," the "*sach*-critical basis" for recasting all understandings of justification. Arguments for the subj. gen.: (a) other passages use *pistis* + gen., "the faith of our father Abraham" (Rom 4:12, cf. 16; 3:26 "the person who has the faith of Jesus," NRSV-mg). But the gen. can express a variety of ideas (BDF 162–68); context determines. While Abraham "believed God, and it was reckoned to him as righteousness" (Rom 4:3; Gal 3:6 = Gen 15:6), we lack instances in Paul or the gospels where Jesus is the subject of the vb. "believe." (b) *pistis* = "faithfulness." D. W. B. Robinson 1970:76, G. Howard 1973–74:213, "fidelity," "reliability" is the normal meaning in Gk. and the LXX. Others, God in the OT is faithful to self and the divine promises. God's fidelity and Jesus' faithfulness. Cf. Rom 3:5 *theou dikaiosynē* (contrast "our unrighteousness," *hē adikia hēmōn*), starting point for seeing God's righteousness as a quality or attribute, God's faithfulness within loyalty to the covenant (with Abraham, Gal 3:6–22); so A. Schlatter, *Gottes Gerechtigkeit* (1935), tr. S. S. Schatzmann, *Romans: the Righteousness of God* (Peabody, MA: Hendrickson, 1995) 76–80; Stuhlmacher's summary, xiv–xvi. But 3:22 and 26 do not mean "the faith that Jesus presented to God" or "the faithfulness by which he completed his obedience," but faith in Jesus and not "the works of the individual" (94, 101, 104).

Grammatically, *pistis Iēsou Christou* could mean "Jesus' own faith/faithfulness," but such an interpretation "faces the insuperable linguistic objection that Paul never speaks unambiguously of Jesus as faithful (e.g., *Iēsous pistos estin*) or believing *(episteusen Iēsous)*, while he certainly speaks of individuals believing in Christ" (Silva 187). Gal 2:16, *dia pisteōs Iēsou Christou* and *ek pisteōs Christou* are explained by "we have believed in Christ Jesus *(eis + acc., episteusamen)*." Hays: saying the same thing here thrice about "belief in Christ" is redundant; Paul "would benefit from the judicious application of a red pencil" (184 n 80); hence a second meaning (as in NRSV-mg, ". . . the faith of Jesus Christ. And we have come to believe in Christ Jesus, so that we might be justified by the faith of Christ"). But rhetorically this triple repetition is on precisely the point at issue in Galatia, faith in Christ versus "the works of the law" (3:11–12). What seems "unnatural" to us should not "lead us to assume, falsely, that an alternative interpretation is preferable" (Silva 187 n 31). At Gal 2:16 Dunn sees a triple antithesis between *pistis Christou* (+ "we have believed") and "works of the law," mentioned 3x. Hays' argument revolves around "the narrative structure of Paul's gospel," said to provide a fuller account of the story of Jesus Christ, esp. in Phil 2:6–11. But 2:6–11 has no reference to Jesus believing, only obeying, *hypēkoos*, not *pistis*. The "obedience of faith" is part of Paul's understanding of *pistis* (Rom 1:5; 16:26; so esp. Bultmann, *TDNT* 6:205–6, 217–18; 1951:314–17), but the roots are different *(pist-, hyp-akou-)*, and in most vv faith, believing, trust, fidelity are in the picture *(pisteu-*terms), not obedience. Note also the relation of *pistis*-terms to "persuasion" *(peithō;* see NOTES on 1:6,14,25; 2:24; 3:3 and 4); persuading hearers to faith in Christ is involved (BDAG *pistis* 2.d.α). We find a good case for the obj. gen. at 3:9, "faith in Christ." Cf. Matlock; B. W. Longenecker, ed., 2002: 54–57; Byrnes 204–9; the campaign for the subj. gen. may have peaked.

"Faith in Christ" is the means by which persons respond to the kerygma, come into the grace of justification/righteousness, and find themselves "in Christ." One can call it individualistic, part of a small-group context in house churches, in danger of becoming mere intellectual belief (Jas 2:19). "Christ" as object of faith must be spelled out through terms like "crucified" and "risen." The pros and cons of "Christ's faith" (subj. gen.) are not always carefully examined. Historical Jesus or risen Christ? Did Paul, let alone the Philippians, know (or care) about how Jesus thought and acted during his Palestinian ministry? 2:6–11 is not about this ministry but a (pre-incarnational?) relationship with God, slave-like existence in humiliation, and death (and cross). If believing in Jesus is set aside, what sort of "response" do supporters of the subj. gen. assume? Ethical (impvs. from Jesus' teachings)? Sacramental (baptism)? Is salvation *ex opere operato*, i.e., efficacious in that Jesus does the believing, trusting, and being faithful for us? The varied positions and unanswered questions under the slogan "the faith of Jesus Christ" do not suggest the position has been tested the way "faith in Jesus Christ" has been over the centuries. The passage is complicated by a second reference to *pistis* in 9d that leads on to v 10.

3:9d. *on the basis of faith. epi* + dat. (BAGD II.1.b.γ; BDAG 6) "**basis for a state of being** [like being justified, *dikaiosynē*], **action** [to count all as loss], **or result** [to know Christ]"; hence **on;** cf. Acts 3:16 ("by faith in his name [*epi tē[i] pistei*] . . ." NRSV); "on the condition of faith" (Lft. 150), "on the ground of faith" (Meyer 131);

"based on faith" (NRSV, NAB, [N]JB). Schenk 313, causal (BDF 235,2, cf. 3:12 *eph' hō[i]*; BDAG *epi* 6.c; Aguilar 204, but recall Fitzmyer on Rom 5:12, where *eph' hō[i]* means "with the result that" (AB 33:413–17; *NTS* 39 [1993] 321–39).

pistis in 9d has been assigned all the meanings claimed by commentators at 9c, and then some. (1) Faith that has Christ as its obj. (B. Weiss 250; Fee 325–26, repeating the sense of *dia pisteōs Christou* "in slightly different language, so as to reinforce its point"). (2) Subj. gen., "Christ's faith(fulness)"; more difficult here (no *Christou*). *tē[i]* denotes "renewed mention" of "Christ's *pistis*" (O'B 400). (3) Some favor subj. gen. in 9c but obj. gen. in 9d. O'B, 9c "through the faithfulness of Christ and which is based on faith" (382), 9d "man's answering response" (400). Bockmuehl 211, "*two* kinds of faithfulness," the "objective ground of righteousness" in the "instrumental faithfulness *of* Christ" and "the subjective mode of its acceptance" in "the responding faithfulness of the believer." That seems to get rid of a redundant second reference to faith, but Fee asks, tellingly, "how the Philippians could possibly have caught on to such a radical shift of subject and object in a clause that seems so clearly designed to repeat the first for emphasis" (325 n 45). For Fee, *tē[i]* is "anaphoric, referring back to Paul's faith in the preceding clause," not ours (cf. BDF 489, 491, parallelism by use of the same term). (4) Silva, in 9d *pistis* is "the act of counting as loss all those things that may be conceived as grounds for self-confidence before God" (187–88; O'B 400, "plausible"). Cf. Lft. 150. Can *dia pisteōs* and *epi tē[i] pistei* be distinguished? Gnilka 194 n 57, the first is "the cause [*Ursache*]," the second "the ground" on which the result rests. Loh. 137 n 2, "an act of God for the individual" and "the individual becoming endowed with this wonder"; faith is a miracle, eschatologically, from God, like the "revelation of righteousness in Christ" at the end of days; the first phrase sees faith "sub specie dei et Christi," the latter also "sub specie animae" (under the aspect of God and Christ, under the aspect of the soul); Schenk 313 adds, "Not 'God and the soul'" as in Western individualistic tradition, but the community. Thus (Loh.) *dia pisteōs Christou* is analyzed by the double phrases *ek theou . . . epi tē[i] pistei*. Walter 79–80 finds human belief in Christ and fidelity on the part of God; "one complex idea" (Eadie 186), though Paul nowhere else uses *epi* + faith.

(5) An ancient construal connects *on the basis of faith* with what follows in v 10 (Gk. fathers, Erasmus, Hofmann; Ewald 177–78). Chrysost. (PG 62:265:56–59 = NPNF 13:235–36), "'By faith that I may know Him.' So then knowledge is through faith." Alternatives: *epi tē[i] pistei* goes with *dikaiosynēn*; then *tēn* should be repeated before the prep. phrase (to indicate it modifies "righteousness"). Or with *echōn*, supplied after *alla* in 9c, "but (having) the righteousness that comes through faith in Christ, the righteousness that is from God, (having it) on the basis on faith"; then *epi* provides a "solemn emphasis" at the end of v 9 (so Meyer 131; B. Weiss 251 n 1). Bengel 680–81 took the whole with "I consider" in 8d and connected 9d with 10. On the connection of 9d with 10, cf. Westcott; Hendriksen 166–67; Collange 131, who finds here a "definition—'faith is . . .' (*epi tē[i] pistei tou . . .*')." For prep. phrases + art. infin. in the gen. to show purpose, Hofmann noted 2 Sam (Bas. B) 6:2 (*en anabasei tou anagagein*) and Isa 10:32 (*en hodō[i]*

tou menai); each differs from the MT. Some argue by structural analyses that 9d goes with 9c, not 10a (Schenk 250–51, 310; cf. Banker 132; Fee 321 n 34, repetition, not chiasm):

9b	A	*mē echōn emēn*			
	B		*dikaiosynēn*		
	C			*tēn ek nomou*	
9c	D				*alla tēn dia pisteōs Christou*
	C′			*tēn ek theou*	
	B′		*dikaiosynēn*		
9d	A′	*epi tē[i] pistei*			

Two kinds of righteousness, "from Law" and "from God," emphasizing "righteousness through faith in/of Christ." Silva 185, this chiasm is "possible" (likewise O'B 394). Fee 321–22 (matching three-part phrases, more convincing in his Eng. than in Gk.):

9b	I. a.	*mē echōn emēn dikaiosynēn*
	b.	*tēn ek nomou*
9c	c.	*alla tēn dia pisteōs Christou*
	II. a.	*tēn . . . dikaiosynēn*
	b.	*ek theou*
	c.	*epi tē[i] pistei*

This pairs "from the Law" and "from God" (I b, II b), "faith" in I.c and II.c (parallel or contrast?), but at the cost of putting the second kind of righteousness in I c as well as in II abc. Many sense chiasmus in the two kinds of righteousness (Plummer 74); perhaps most agreement is on a broad chiasm (Loh/Nida 101; Reumann 1982 [(2) Bibl. **righteousness**] #110; see COMMENT A, below),

9b	(a)	righteousness of my own		(b)	from Law
9c	(b′)	through faith in Christ		(a′)	righteousness from God

That leaves 9d as a non-chiastic pendant, possibly to introduce v 10.

3:10a. *to know him and the power of his resurrection and participation in his sufferings.* Art. infin., gen., *tou gnōnai*, usually taken to express purpose (BDAG *ho, hē, to* 2.d.β.ɿ; BDF 400). On *ginōskō*, see NOTES on 1:12; 2:22; 3:8b *knowing*; here, aor. act. (ingressive aor? Hawth. 143). But purpose is disputed, in part because of debate whether it goes with 9d "on the basis of faith" or is parallel to the *hina* construction in 8e–9a ("in order that I might gain Christ and be found in him") or ultimately goes back to "I consider" in 8d; in part because the neut. sg. art. in the gen. + an infin. is rare in Paul. He preferred *eis* (or *pros*) + art. infin. in the acc. (ATR 990, cf. 1002, 1067, 1088; Moulton, telic [final] force is notably absent, *GNTG* 1:216–18). Rom 6:6c is the other probable instance of purpose; some (BDF 400,8) take it as epexegetical, explanatory of the *hina* cl. at Rom 6:6b. Phil 3:8e–9a, "so as to know Christ . . ." expands on "gain Christ and be found in him." Moule, *IB* 128–29, "may be final" or "or consecutive, expressing the result of the previous conditions," "so as to know . . ."; similarly Phil 3:21, "by the power . . ." or "so that. . . ." Eng. trs. sometimes suggest purpose, "that I may know him" (KJV/RSV) or add a vb., "I want to know him" (NIV, NRSV). NLT, "As a result, I can really know Christ," abbreviates LB, which connected v 10 with 8cd, "Now I have given up everything else — I have found it the only way to really know Christ." *GNTG* 3:136, cf. 141–42, saw result in 10a (even if *hōste* is not used) and suggested for *gnōnai* a ptc. or gerundive, i.e., "knowing Christ"; cf. Gal 3:10, "doing everything" = Deut. 27:26), hence *ZBG* #392, "Semiticizing."

The first dir. obj. of *gnōnai* is *auton*, Christ, the obj. of faith in 9c. The second acc., connected by (epexegetical) *kai*, is *tēn dynamin tēs anastaseōs autou*. On *power* (BDAG *dynamis* 1 **power, might, strength, force, capability;** infin. at 3:21), cf. W. Grundmann, *TDNT* 2:284–317, esp. 316; O. Betz, *NIDNTT* 2:601–6; G. Friedrich, *EDNT* 1:355–58; and the NOTE at 4:13 (Letter A), God as "the One who strengthens *(endynamounti)* me." Extensive classical Gk. background (*TDNT* 2:285–90), for "capacity," "ability," or "potency in contrast to *energeia,*" which denotes operative power (Aristot. *Metaph.* 8.8 1049b.24; cf. Phil 3:21), an all-pervading force dynamically at work in human life and the cosmos (so Stoicism), through various gods and acts of power (*dynameis,* miracles). For God as *dynamis,* cf. Eur. *Alc.* 219; Plat. *Cra.* 404E. In contrast to *dynamis* in the world of nature, the OT presents a God of power and might at work in history (e.g., the Exodus), as well as in creation (Deut.-Isa; *TDNT* 2:290–94). In apocalyptic writings, the power of God in the last times to come (*NIDNTT* 2:602). Cf. Deut 3:24, "O Lord God, you have only begun to show your servant your strength and your power" (LXX *dynamin,* text in *TDNT* 2:292); doxologies like 1 Chr 29:10–12, "Yours, O Lord, are the greatness, the power, the glory . . . the kingdom," cf. Matt 6:13 NRSV-mg). God's power at work in Jesus is vividly expressed in the gospels via miracles, but also via Jesus' word or teaching. After Easter, power continues through the Lord Jesus (1 Cor 5:4); Rom 1:4, "Son of God with power *(en dynamei)* according to the s/Spirit of holiness by resurrection from the dead" (*EDNT* 1:357). Fitzmyer (AB 33:229–30, 235), *en dynamei* may be Paul's addition, for power with which the risen Christ is endowed "to energize human beings who turn to him as the risen Lord." Jesus = *theou dynamis* (1 Cor 1:24); the gospel = the power of God for salvation for everyone who believes (Rom 1:16). Christ "lives by the power of God" and "we will live with him by the power of God" (2 Cor 13:4, within the Pauline paradox of power and weakness). Paul knew divine power in his apostolic ministry and life (2 Cor 12:9; Rom 15:19, etc.). God's power will raise believers (1 Cor 6:14; 2 Cor 4:14; Phil 3:21 fits here). In the present, the gospel message works in word and power and the Holy Spirit (1 Thess 1:5; 1 Cor 2:4b, 4:19–20). 3:10a, "the power of Christ's resurrection" has usually been interpreted to mean "the risen *Kyrios* brings it about that Paul — and every Christian — will be 'found in him,'" but Fitzmyer 1970:208 rightly notes *power* "includes a reference to the origin of that influence in the Father himself" (1 Thess 1:10; 1 Cor 15:15; Rom 1:20; 9:17 = Exod 9:16).

his resurrection. anastasis (here acc.; BDAG 2.a) + *anistēmi* ("stand up, rise") form one NT word field for resurrection. (The other is *egeirō,* 1 Thess 1:10; Gal 1:1; 1 Cor 6:14, etc.). *anastasis* of Jesus Rom 1:4 (with *en dynamei*), 1 Cor

15:21. "Resurrection of the dead" (*anastasis nekrōn*, pl.) is what opponents deny and Paul proclaims (1 Cor 15:12,13, 42; Rom 6:5). Vb., "Jesus died and rose" (*anestē*, 1 Thess 4:14, unusual act. voice; cf. 4:16; Rom 14:9). Usually, "God raised Jesus" (1 Thess 1:10) or pass., Jesus "was raised" (by God; 1 Cor 15:4, 20). A. Oepke, *TDNT* 1:368–72, in the Gk. world "resurrection" was impossible; at best, an isolated event in stories about the physician Aesculapius or Apollonius of Tyana. Upon dying, one faces a shadowy existence in the abode of Hades; at times notions of the "immortality of the soul" or "transmigration of souls" (Plato *Resp.* 10, the myth of Er). But cf. Zeller 2002. Resurrection of the body is not found in most of the OT, only in late texts like Isa 26:19 and Dan 12:2. Samaritans and Sadducees rejected it. Hellenistic Judaism spiritualized it, sometimes accepting the Gk. view of immortality of the soul. A. F. Segal 1998 places Paul "firmly within the Jewish apocalyptic-mystical tradition" (400). Paul's reference to "Jesus and the Resurrection (*tēn anastasin*)" in Athens met with scorn. To L. Coenen in *NIDNTT* 3:259, 275–78, C. Brown has added 259–75, history-of-religions and OT data, esp. 278–79. R. Martin-Achard's approach, which Brown reflects, appears in *ABD* 5:680–84, + G. W. E. Nickelsburg on early Judaism and Christianity (684–91). Resuscitations, by Elijah and Elisha (1 Kgs 17:17–24; 2 Kgs 4:31–37; 13:20–21), must be distinguished from bodily resurrection, as must accounts of a mortal being "translated" to heaven (Elijah, 2 Kgs 2:1–15; Enoch, Gen 5:21–24, Heb 11:5). "Resurrection-restorations of the people of God" (Hos 6:3; Ezek 37; Isa 53:10–12; *ABD* 5:681–82) came to be applied to Jesus (1 Cor 15:4 "according to the scriptures"). *EDNT* 1:88–92 (J. Kremer); O. Cullmann 1958 (Exc.A Bibl.); R. E. Brown, *The Virginal Conception and Bodily Resurrection of Jesus* (Paramus, NJ: Paulist, 1973); P. Perkins, *Resurrection: New Testament Witness and Contemporary Reflection* (Garden City, NY: Doubleday, 1984). 3:10, *tēs anasteōs*, the gen. may be subj. or source or origin (Hainz 1972:97), similarly *autou*, the power which comes to Paul and other believers is from Jesus as risen Lord. If obj. gen., power that leads to a resurrection like his. In either case there is room for God (cf. Fitzmyer; Bockmuehl 214) effecting Jesus' resurrection, that of believers, and the life of those "in Christ" between the two resurrection events. Possibly gen. of apposition, "the power that his resurrection is" (Montague 1961:124; Vincent 104). Survey in *NIDNTT* 3:297–305 (C. Brown); tensions exist between resurrection as present possession and future goal, *TDNT* 1:371.

and participation in his sufferings. koinōnian (P⁴⁶ ℵ* A B etc.). ℵ² D etc. TR add *tēn*; NA²⁷ prints the art. in brackets. The art. means a third dir. obj. after "to know," not a compound object ("the-power-of-Christ's- resurrection"-and-"participation-in-his-sufferings," hendiadys, zeugma). This second *tēn* is secondary (Hawth. 129, 144, Fee 311 n 2; contrast Silva 195). In Phil, Paul often uses two nouns with one art. (1:7 *defense and confirmation*; 1:19 *entreaty* and supplying of the Spirit); 1:20 *hope and expectation*). Somewhat related is lack of *tōn* before *pathēmatōn* in the same MSS (P⁴⁶ ℵ* B); *koinōnian pathēmatōn autou* is quite understandable without arts. *tēn* before *koinōnian* is reflected in KJV and NRSV ("the power of his resurrection and the sharing of his sufferings"), obscured in NEB, cf. REB, and RSV ("may know him and the power of his resurrection, and may share his sufferings").

participation. koinōnia. See NOTES on 1:5 *sharing (in the gospel),* 2:1 *sharing in the Spirit.* Here, "have a part in or share in" (+ gen.), BDAG *koinōnia* 4, ***participation***, as at 2 Cor 8:4; Phlm 6; perhaps 1 Cor 1:9; 2 Cor 13:13; 1 Cor 10:16; 2 Cor 1:7. KJV "fellowship," NJB "partake of." Baumert 2003 ([2] Bibl. **sharing**) 210–11, 502, 510–12, revelation of his sufferings and consolation as Paul, with Christ, bears sufferings. 3:10 would not at first surprise Philippians who knew *koinōnia* in societal and friendship contexts (see Wolter 1990:544–46, 553–54), but *what* Paul shares in here, might. Hearers might have expected "participation in the community of Christ" or "sharing in Christ's (risen) life" or a closer relationship with God's son (1 Cor 1:9).

sufferings. BDAG *pathēma* 1, ***suffering, misfortune.*** See NOTE on 1:29c *but also keep on suffering for his sake* (vb. *paschō*); considerable Gk. background, in COMMENT B.2, on 1:28b–30. Paul's kerygma involved the death of Christ, possibly his sufferings; his teaching in Philippi, likely suffering for believers (1:29). W. Michaelis, *TDNT* 5:930–35, "the *pathēmata* of Christ are the same as His *thanatos*" (chiasm equating *pathēmata autou* and *thanatō[i] autou,* Michaelis, *Phil.* 58). W. Grundmann found the chiasmus unconvincing (*TDNT* 7:788 n 106). According to Michaelis 5:932, Paul elsewhere uses *pathein* not for Jesus but the sufferings of Christians. 2 Cor 1:5 *(ta pathēmata tou Christou)* is disputed, cf. 6 "the sufferings of you and us": Furnish AB 32A: 110, 118–20, "the Passion Narrative," a gospel tradition behind Phil 3:10; R. P. Martin WBC 40:9–10, "messianic sufferings" by "those associated with him in the messianic age," cf. Col. 1:24. 2 Cor 1:5 could mean our "sufferings *for* Christ" (obj. gen., E. Schweizer, *TDNT* 5:931–2); ditto 3:10 (obj. gen.; *TDNT* 6:434). Or obj. and subj. gen. ("Christus-leiden") or "sufferings *en Christō[i]*" (Siber [EXC. A Bibl.] 112 n 54 for references). B. Gärtner, *NIDNTT* 3:719–26, a "mystical union" of Christ and church. J. Kremer, *EDNT* 3:1–2, cf. 51–52: 2 Cor 1:5, possibly "difficulties experienced by Paul for Christ's sake" (with Michaelis), "more probably Jesus' own suffering," yet Phil 3:10, daily experience of afflictions and power as "the way to become one with Christ . . . ," p. 2. Cf. Schenk 320, polemical against the enemies' view of *koinōnia.* Thus reference to (1) Jesus' passion is by no means assured. 10a may refer simply to (2) his death (Michaelis). O. Betz 1990:207–8 suggested derivation from Isa 53:5; cf. Bockmuehl 215. From Pauline use of *pathēmata* generally and the "I"-context here, (3) apostolic sufferings or those of Christians generally (1:29). Participation can also involve baptism; Rom 6:4 (U. B. Müller 160, "past dying with Christ," "present dying with Christ in suffering"; Tannehill 117). The COMMENT on 1:28–30 noted Loh.'s emphasis on martyrdom and Walter's on suffering as joy. For Walter (*Phil.* 80–81), participation in Christ's sufferings points to participating also in his resurrection; thus, Jesus' death for us (Gal 3:13–14) has ongoing meaning for believers.

3:10b. *while being conformed to his death.* . . . *symmorphizomenos,* pres. m.-p. ptc., *symmorphizō,* only in Christian writings, ***grant*** or ***invest w[ith] the same form as,*** here pass. + dat., *be conformed to, take on the same form as* (BDAG). Two variants (not in NA) may be ignored: *symmorphoumenos, give* or *take on the same form; synphorteizomenos* "burdened (together with others) by his death." Paul possibly coined *symmorphizomenos* (ATR 150), *-izō* ("to make, become") + noun or adj. (*GNTG* 2:407; BDF 108,3). Cf. 3:21 "be conformed" *(symmorphon)*; NOTES on *morphē*, 2:6 and 7 *sphere*. *Word studies:* TDNT 7:787–88 (W. Grundmann), 5:932 (W. Michaelis); G. Braumann, *NIDNTT* 1:705, 707 ("the death of Christ acquires a *morphē* in the death of the apostle"; *EDNT* 3:287–88 (W. Pohlmann); Byrnes 223–30, patterning and participating. Its obj. *tō[i] thanatō[i] autou* = the death of Christ on the cross (BDAG *thanatos* 1.b.β; *autou* as with *resurrection* and *sufferings*). Exact sense may be clarified by a chiasmus:

10a	A	the power of his *resurrection*	B and participation in his *sufferings*
10b	B′	being conformed to	A′ if somehow I may attain to the
		his *death*	*resurrection* from the dead (v 11)

So Hawth. 145; Schenk 251, 320–21; Fee 313, 329; U. B. Müller 158–59; Bloomquist 180; Wolter 1990:543. O'B 407 relates *symmorphizomenos tō[i] thanatō[i] autou* to all of 10a and not just its last phrase. Some press details in *symmorphizomenos* so that *syn* suggests a "corporate bond," Paul, Christ, and the Philippians (Fields 239–40); middle voice, strive "to make the effects of that death an ever-present reality within himself" (Hawth. 145); pass. voice, "Paul's *being conformed*" (by God) (O'B 408); pres. tense, continuing, daily renewal (O'B 408). The ptc. refers to Paul, the subject of the infin. *gnōnai* (10a, "that I may know him," acc., a sense construction) or the subject in 9a ("that I may be found in him," parallel to *echōn* in 9b, "not having"). The ptc. is circumst., modal (Fee 333 n 65), the manner by which Paul will come to know Christ's power and fellowship, "by becoming like him in his death" (NRSV; JB, "by reproducing the pattern of his death"), causal, or (better) temporal, *while*; NEB/REB "in growing conformity to his death").

3:11. *if, hopefully, I am to attain the resurrection from the dead.* "I shall attain to (*katantēsō*, fut. *katantaō*, BDAG 2.a *arrive at, attain (to)* + *eis*) the resurrection of the dead," connected to 3:10 by *ei pōs. if* (BDAG *ei* 6.n.β) + enclitic particle *pōs* ("somehow, in some way, perhaps"), in Paul only here, Rom 1:10, 11:14; a hoped-for event, amid uncertainty; simple particular condition (BDF 371,1; 372, 1b). In the LXX, *ei pōs* at 3 Kgdms 21:31 (1 Kgs 20:31); 4 Kgdms (2 Kgs) 19:4; Jer 28:8 (51:8); Baumert 1973:392–95 (with BDF 375) an expression of expectation. In all six cases, hope and doubt seem involved. R. E. Otto 326–28 plays the doubt and uncertainty off against "a great expectation." At 3:11 the vb. form could also be (aor.) subjunct. (ZG 599; Koperski 1996:280), deliberative use, "if after all I am to attain . . ." (*GNTG* 1:187,194; cf. ATR 1017, possibility, with *skopōn* implied, "looking to see, considering if," cf. 1421; *skopete* at 3:17). Schenk 321 n 452: fut. indic., but 3:12 will have aor. subjunct. *(ei katalabō).* Many see *pōs* suggesting "doubt or uncertainty in the apostle's mind" (Loh/Nida 106; Koester 1961–62: 323; Collange 132 and Michael 154, Paul distrusts himself, not God; Siber [EXC. A Bibl.] 118; Mengel 266 n 156); KJV "If by any means"; "if possible," RSV; "somehow" (NIV, NRSV). Eng. trs. reflect this uncertainty via "might" (KJV), "may attain" ([N]RSV), or advs., "if only I may finally arrive" (NEB). Martin 1976:136, any doubt refers "to the way in which" resurrection will be Paul's, by martyrdom or otherwise. Cf. O'B 413; Byrnes 231–32. Silva 192 finds no support for "means or method" in *pōs*. BDF 375, *ei* in "expressions of expectations," Acts 27:12; 8:22; Phil 3:12 (*ei kai katalabō*, "to make it my own," NRSV). Cf. also Gundry Volf ([2] Bibl. **work**) 254–60: no doubt is involved; Schenk 321. Hence Gdsp., "in the hope of attaining . . ."; NAB "This I do hope. . . ." Bruce 119, "a clause of purpose," attainment of which "is not altogether within the subject's power." Cf. 2 Cor 5:3, "if (it is) indeed true (*ei ge*)," re our heavenly dwelling, or "presupposing, of course" (Furnish, AB32A:267, with Thrall 86–91). Doubt and hope are caught rather well by the popular (grammatically bad) Eng. idiom *hopefully*, a weaker expression of "I hope."

The obj. after the vb. + *eis* (place or goal, Acts 16:1; Schoder 21, "arrive at the resurrection from the dead"; fig., Acts 26:7, cf. 1 Cor 14:36; Eph 4:13; more in BDAG p. 523) is not *anastasis* (10a) but a double compound, *ex-ana-stasis* (Hippocrates, "getting up"; Polyb. 3.55.4). Most see no difference (*TDNT* 1:371; *NIDNTT* 3:259; cf. *anistēmi* and *exanistēmi*, Mark 12:19 parr; Acts 15:5). Owen, "*resurrection out of* or *from the dead*," for martyrs or the just, prior to the general resurrection (cf. Rev. 20:4). Michael 154 said *exanastasis* was "employed in the Mystery Cults," without adducing evidence. Perhaps rhetorical variation. Hellenistic Gk. liked to add prefixes to strengthen words (*ZBG* 484; Silva 195). Bockmuehl 218, *ex-* is "intensifying" (without evidence or telling what is intensified; cf. Lft. 151). *tēn* is repeated to show *ek nekrōn* is attrib., "the resurrection which is from (the) dead" (*GNTG* 3:221), "almost pedantic" repetition (Moule, *IB* 109). Subst. use of the adj. "dead," BDAG *nekros* 2.a. Usually tr. "resurrection from the dead." KJV "resurrection of the dead" reflects TR, *tōn nekrōn*; JB; Rom 1:4, 1 Cor 15:42. F G, *tōn ek nekrōn* is an odd error, "of those from the dead." *ek nekrōn* suggested to Lft. 151 the resurrection also of Jesus from the dead (1 Pet 1:3; Acts 4:2); Silva 195, difficult to sustain.

COMMENT

A. FORMS, SOURCES, AND TRADITIONS

1. *Literary, Rhetorical, and Related Features.* 3:4b–11 is a *narratio*, with a *propositio* in 9–11 about knowing, gaining, being found in Christ (Reumann 1991a:137).[1]

---

[1] Cf. INTRO. VI.B n 2 and (11) COMMENT A.1, esp. Schenk (280–83, 3:5–6 an encomium of self-recommendation); Harnisch 137 (4b–7 *narratio*, 7 *propositio*; 8–14, *argumentatio*). Edart 213, 226–41, 274, 4b–7 *narratio* with *gradiatio* (progressive anadiplosis, Lausberg #623), 8–11 *probatio*, with *propositio* in 7b. Holloway 2001a:136–40 does not relate 3:4–11 to letters of consolation; Y. W. Smith does, plus an OT lament form, unconvincingly. Fields stresses "rhetoric" (55–69, 165–224), with OT "background," in 3:1–4:1, "Paul as model," for community esp. in Black theology (336–73): 3:1, *aphodos* and *transitio*; 3:2–4a, first enthymeme (see [11] COMMENT A.1 n 4); 3:4b–6, historical *exemplum*; 3:7–16, contemporary *exemplum*; 3:17–19, second enthymeme; 3:20–21, third enthymeme; 4:1, reiteration. The Philippians' "value emphases" are said to be informed by Aristot. *Rhet.* ("happiness," noble birth, good reputation [*eudoxian*], and virtue, pp. 205–11). Fields 202–4 sees Roman Philippi charged with "animosity toward the Jewish people." D. F. Watson 1988b, 4b–16, "an example of trust

Black 1995:43 takes 3:4b–11 as a unit ("Paul's Past and Present Values Contrasted") within 21 vv of *refutatio*. Few follow Loh. 131 on six double- and tricolons in 3:7–11. See further, 2 and 3 below.

Macrochiastic treatments of all four chs. are in conflict, unhelpful re units in ch. 3.[2] For smaller chiasms see the NOTES on 9d and 10b (for vv 10–11; Reumann 1982 [(2) Bibl. **righteousness**] #110). Delling (*TDNT* 8:501 n 86) claimed a seven-membered series in vv 5abcde–6ab, with 2 accents each + end rhyme (*Pharisaios, amemptos*). Schenk 250, 280 headed his structure (below) "With reference to circumcision, circumcised on the eighth day":

A   *ek genous Israēl,*
  B   *phylēs Beniamin*
    C   *Hebraios ex Hebraiōn,*
A′   *kata nomon—Pharisaios,*
  B′   *kata zēlos—diōkōn tēn ekklēsian,*
    C′   *kata dikaiosynēn—tēn en nomō[i]—genomenos amemptos*

But do A-B-C and A′-B′-C′ really match or contrast? Should circumcision be separated from the other six items? Fields 286 n 99 sees *a Hebrew . . . from Hebrews* as central in 3:5–6. Better is O. Betz's arrangement of two pairs of three (1977:55–56; cf. earlier B. Weiss 233–35):

v 5 Descent:	circumcised on the eighth day
	origins from the people of Israel, tribe of Benjamin
	a Hebrew born from Hebrew parents
5e–6 Accomplishments	as to Law, a Pharisee,
	as to zeal, a persecutor of the church,
	as to righteousness that comes about through the Law, blameless

O'B 368–69 structures the seven items on a slant as Schenk does; but with Betz, structure and content are "thoroughly Pharisaic."[3]

Schenk noted encomium style in 3:5–6, with asyndeton, continuing the "I"-style of 3:4 (one can supply *egō eimi* at 5a, Gdsp., "I was circumcised . . ."). 5–6 have positive importance, not just appositional (Ewald 169) to 4b ("I, to a greater degree") or 7 (things that had been gains for me). The credentials are prerogatives

---

in the righteousness of Christ versus the righteousness of the law"; vv 7–8 = *regressio* (Lausberg #798) and *transplacement*, to explain comparison between Law-righteousness and Christ-righteousness by "the repetition of *hēgēmai . . . zēmian, hēgoumai . . . zēmian* ["consider a loss"], *ezēmiōthēn* ["experienced loss"], *hēgoumai* ["consider"]; transplacement also in v 9, the antithesis *not . . . righteousness that is from the Law but the righteousness . . . through faith in Christ . . . from God.*

[2] Cf. INTRO. VI.B n 3. Bittasi 98–113, Paul's example parallels Christ's (2:6–11): identity in the flesh rejected, identity in Christ affirmed.

[3] Cf. Schenk's examples (282–83) of multi-membered rhetorical statements in Jewish propaganda: Jos. *JW* 2.135; *Pirke Aboth* 3.19 (APOT 2:701–2); Rom 2:17–20, Jewish advantages before Paul's critique in vv 21–28: 17–18, the heritage of the Jew; 19–20, tasks in the Gentile world. Schenk notes terminological ties to Phil 3. Fitzmyer, 2:17–24 is rhetorical diatribe (AB 33:315); Torah and circumcision become "God's word *tout simple*" and God's will, leading to national pride (Dunn, WBC 38A:117). But the assertions of Israel's prerogatives are positively meant by Paul.

in which Saul once vaunted, perhaps in letters recommending him to synagogues in Damascus (Acts 9:2). Hellerman 121–27, 162–63: Paul's Jewish *cursus honorum* (birth, status, 5a–d), acquired honor (achievements, 5e–6). Cf. Duling 2003:233–40.

3:7 is constructed around several contrasts (see NOTE). Schenk's double chiasm for vv 9 and 10, accepted in more modest forms for 9bc and 10ab, is preceded in 8e–9a by yet another structure.[4] At best, a few words, phrases, or cls. in a-b-b'-a' sequence, not macrostructures.

2. Agendas and Influences. In Paul's *inventio* of material for 3:4b–11 they include the following.

a. *The "I"-form.* Begun at 3:4a, it continues through v 14.[5] Not egocentric (Fortna) but inevitable in autobiography (Lyons, a "formerly-now" contrast, 146–52; "*before and after,*" Léon-Dufour 1974:152) and literary style (Spencer) when dealing with opponents and giving personal testimony to religious experiences (S. F. Winter 175–76, "Paul's story"). Paul's "I" is both polemical and paradigmatic (B. Dodd 180–95). "Imitation" of Paul is not mentioned, as it will be in 3:17. *synkrisis* is employed in 3:4–11, rhetorical "comparison."[6] "Chiasms" may simply reflect comparison between Saul and Paul, "before and after" Christ, and Paul compared with the enemies in 3:2, who contrast with "we/us" in v 3. In the comparison, both options are made attractive; vv 5–6 are not caricature of Saul's Judaism. Not "bad versus good," but something good compared with something better. Yet a decisive turning point (7–8a), toward what is clearly better. What Paul formulates very personally (as at 1:21–26) has a programmatic dimension (as at 1:29–30), to draw the Philippians as co-participants into his sufferings. *synkrisis* was meant to persuade (cf. Vollenweider 1994 [(4) Bibl.]). The effort by Malina/Neyrey 55 to see comparison with Christ in 2:6–11 (genesis, manner of life, "deeds of soul," noble death, and "subsequent fame and fortune") does not hold up well; if anything, there are contrasts. 2:6–11 has nothing on Jesus as a Hebrew, of Israel, let alone his tribe (cf. Heb 7:14), or his relation to the Law (cf. Gal 4:4)— as might be expected in a composition by Philippian (not Jewish) Christians.

---

[4] The structure:

8e	A	*Christon*	
	B	*kerdēsō*	The two vbs. and two references to Christ make the X or
9a		C *kai*	>-form, with "and" as the crossover point (Schenk 250, 309–
	B'	*eurethō*	10). Burnes 184, 198; cf. 13–14:
	A'	*en autō[i]*	

Chiasm as a tech. term is actually postclassical (Lausberg #723 n 2), 4th cent. A.D., its background shaky (J. W. Welch 1981; Di Marco 1993; I. H. Thomson 1995; *WDNTECLR* 93–96).

[5] Schenk 260–63, 274. Some form of the 1st per. pron. appears in vv 4b, 5, 7, and 9, + vb. or ptc. forms referring to "I" or "me" in these and every other v. *DA* 367 charts uses of "I" language in Phil.

[6] Stowers 1991:115–17; B. Dodd 181 n 39; Malina/Neyrey 52–55, "encomiastic comparison *(synkrisis)*"; Harnisch 135–36; above, (4) COMMENT A.4. Features noted above for *synkrisis* apply here: interrelations with praise *(enkomion)* and blame ("incision, circumcision"); comparison, in 4b, *I, to a greater degree (mallon)*; the sequence of two kinds of righteousness, the "loser" mentioned first (that *from Law*).

In 3:11–14 notions of exaltation for Paul will be muted or eschewed, contra
2:9–11.

b. *Kerygma about Christ's Death and Resurrection and the "Jesus Story."* No
creedal formulas like 1 Thess 4:14 or 1 Cor 15:4, no use of OT texts. But cross and
resurrection[7] stand behind what Paul writes. (See 10–11, *thanatos, (ex)anastasis*).
Some see *Phil 2:6–11* behind what Paul says in 3:8–11, with *pistis Christou* in 9c
as link, "Christ's faith(fulness)"; see NOTE on *faith in Christ* (Hays and others).
Usually Jesus is taken as model of faith(fulness) and humility; Paul is humble, not
cocksure about attaining to the resurrection.[8]

Christ as model in a "story" could be pushed even further. 3:8b, *gnōsis Christou*, as subj. gen.,[9] = "the superlative way in which Christ Jesus my Lord had
knowledge" (8b), i.e., his "mind" in 2:5–6; in the story would follow his
faith(fulness) (9c); sufferings and death (10); and resurrection (10a, cf. 11). One
might tease out a fuller "story" from his being circumcised, living under the Law,
and future parousia (3:20–21). This sequence—knowledge, fidelity, obedience
unto death, resurrection, lordship, and future, transforming coming—parallels
later creedal assertions and orthodox notions of faith as *notitia* (knowledge), *fidu-
cia* (faithfulness), and obedience. But it assumes two dubiously subj. gens. and
reads in much. 3:8–11 say nothing about "humility" *(tapeinophrosynē)*, nothing
about the "mind" *(phronein)* of Christ (of Christians, later in 3:15, 16, 19). Not
the inner workings behind Jesus' "career path," whether pre-incarnate or during
earthly ministry, but how Christ caused a reversal in Paul's story. The Christ story
is subservient to the "I"-account, as catalyst for Saul's reversal in values. B. Dodd
191–94, "Most elements of the Christ story in 2.6–11 are arguably inimitable";
Paul does *not* argue that the Philippians should receive circumcision as Christ's
example and Paul's might suggest; in what Paul says, "Christ is not portrayed as an
example" for any point in his self-presentation.

c. *Critique of the Philippians' Encomium in 2:6–11.* Paul accepted their "story
of salvation," but added *death on a cross* at 2:8c. 2:12ff. corrected the "hymn" by
emphasis on *the day of Christ* (2:16) and judgment. Not Christology but *salvation*
(2:12e) and implications for daily life till the parousia, including whom you obey
(2:12b). See (8) COMMENT A.2. 3:20–21 and 4:5b, *The Lord* (Jesus) (is) *near* (a

---

[7] N. T. Wright 2003:227–33 is forced to argue that Paul, in writing 2:6–11, omitted his usual emphasis
on "resurrection" because the Caesars, against whom he writes, did not claim resurrection. If so, Paul
mutes his gospel to fit their rhetorical claims of apotheosis (exaltation) instead of resurrection!

[8] O'B, Christ in 2:5–11 is "the supreme example of humility"; 3:9c = "the faith[fulness] of Christ";
3:11, "Paul's 'humble admission of his own . . . unworthiness' " (Plummer 75). Fee, "the example of
Christ" in 2:5–11 is "a paradigm for Christian life" (227); "being conformed" in 3:10b recalls 2:6–11
(333–34); Fee favors "faith in Christ" over a subj. gen. (324–25). Bloomquist 180, "depiction of the
Christ type in Paul's present experience"; Fowl 1990:98–100, "the precedent provided by Christ [as
examplar]." Bockmuehl 206: "the great doctrinal affirmations of 2.6–11 . . . shape the deepest realities
of Paul's own life and self-understanding," including "the instrumental faithfulness *of* Christ in his
self-humbling death" (211). Silva 178 rejects the subj. gen. at 3:9; "(a call to) sanctification" links
1:27–2:18 with 3:10. On story, narrative in Paul, cf. B. W. Longenecker, ed. 2002, esp. 133–71.

[9] See NOTE on *knowing*; Vallotton, Collange; *gnōsis* and *gnōnai* could be taken as complementary, as
some take *dia pisteōs Christou* and *epi tē[i] pistei*.

parousia reference), provide another element missing in 2:6–11. The striking new note in 3:8–11, compared with 2:6–11, is *resurrection*, Christ's (3:10a) and ours or at least Paul's (11). Is this a place where the theology of the Philippian "hymn" was vulnerable? It ignored OT-Jewish bodily resurrection and implications for believers. Greeks had problems with the resurrection and its meaning (witness 1 Cor 15). Some hoped for "the isles of the blessed," Elysian fields (Peres 75–81), or a heavenly city (120–21). The enemies in Phil 3 may have stressed resurrection as a life-form already present for "true Christians." Paul begins his definition of "knowing Christ" in v 10a with a reference to *the power of his resurrection*, something not heard in Letters A and B. Those who see 2:6–11 as linchpin for all of Phil seldom note *(ex)anastasis* in 3:10–11 but its absence in 2:6–11 (Reumann 2002).

d. *The "Enemies" Introduced in 3:2.* Cf. O'B 413; Bockmuehl 195, 219; even Fee ("alleged 'opponents' . . . are not mentioned throughout this narrative," 336 n 72, but 3:6 = "the kind of righteousness that Judaizers would bring one to," 310, cf. 323). Schenk 250–51 allots to the "Jewish agitators" or "wisdom teachers" some fifty Gk. terms,[10] notably (two kinds of) *righteousness* in 3:6, 9.[11] 3:9b *ek nomou* = "getting (fully) into righteousness" through circumcision and taking on the nomism of a "righteous proselyte" in Israel. "The enemies" help explain the two kinds of righteousness here.

e. *Israelite, OT Tradition?* Fields 236 claims in Paul's "historical *exemplum*" (3:4b–6) a trajectory of *Israelite, OT tradition*. Not persuasive in methods or data.[12] Relations between "Israel's story" and Paul's "I"-account (2.a, above) are better explored by Hofius 1986 and Theissen 2002, esp. re Rom 9–11.[13]

f. *Prior Status and Liminality in the Transformation Process for Paul and the*

---

[10] E.g., "gains" (v 7); "knowledge" (8b), "crap" (8d); "righteousness" (8b); "to know," "the power of the resurrection," and "participation" (10a); "being conformed" (10b); and "resurrection" (*exanastasis* in 11). In vv 12–13 and 15, "already obtaining" (maturity or perfection). Schenk's examples are not all equally convincing.

[11] Schenk 295–303 follows E. P. Sanders (*PPJ* 199–200) on the *gēr sedeq*, the "righteous [or true] proselyte," who accepts circumcision and is obligated to obey the whole Law, versus a second kind of righteousness (9c) where what is new and basic is "Christ risen from the dead" (Schenk 305, 311–12, 314; *anastasis autou* specifically in 10a). Rom 10: 3 parallels Phil 3:9, Israel's righteousness from the Law and God's righteousness "on the basis of faith." The first is "covenantal nomism," (national) pride in "the righteousness of the covenant-keeper" (Dunn WBC 38B:588–89); Smiles 284–85, "activism" for the Law.

[12] From OT passages (computer search), Fields picked out one reference for each item Paul notes about himself: Gen 17:7 (12–14); Josh 11:21, cf. Phil 3:19, pp. 276–77; Num 13:9; Num 25:6–11; Ps 119 (LXX 118):137–44. (For *a Hebrew . . . from Hebrews* and *as to Law*, Fields 282–90 cites mainly NT data.) These five passages are treated in light of "relevant Jewish-exegetical techniques" (305–30), for Fields the seven tests Hays 1989 proposed in seeking "echoes" of Scripture in Paul (see above, [4] COMMENT A.1). The yield is often meager. To save the case, Fields appeals to a possible lectionary (324 n 161), for a "small number of Jews" and "Jewish believers in Philippi" (318, 328), assuming Philippian Christians understood Paul's terminology (317) and use of the OT tradition (339).

[13] On Phil 3:9 and Rom 10:3, see A.2.b, above. Saul/Paul serves as a prototype for Israel's coming to faith (O. Hofius, "Das Evangelium und Israel: Erwägungen zu Römer 9–11," ZTK 83 [1986] 320). Theissen 2002 parallels what Paul says here in 1st per. sg. form and what he says in Rom 9–11 about Israel; hence, "Paul the Called as Model for the Salvation of Israel in Rom 11," including the analogy of "life from the dead" (11:15, resurrection).

Philippians. C. Strecker treats 3:2–21, like 2:6–11, in light of "rites of passage" ("separation" from a prior status, "liminality," final "aggregation" to a new status, V. Turner). See Exc.B, II. D.14 (not convincing on 2:6–11). 3:2–4a does suggest rites of passage, initiation: *circumcision* for Jewish males, baptism for all Christians; see (11) COMMENT B.1, final paragraph. Taking ch. 3 as "past, present, and future" is common.[14] Paul presents a "complete transformation of person and value system." 3:4b–6 = past status in Judaism ("pre-liminal"). His about-face means inversion or destruction of old values (*gains* have become *a loss because of Christ*), repeated in v 8, old values gone but his new and final status ("the body of glory") not yet achieved. The reversal is universalized (*all things* a loss), the contrast sharpened by use of the offensive word *crap.* The new existence = *knowing Christ Jesus* (repeating *because of* Christ Jesus, 8c), communion with Christ, all that Heb. *yāda'* (to know) and Gk. friendship imply; "in Christ" = participation, in a vertical and horizontal Communitas of Jews and Gentiles. Paul is taken into the field or realm where the power of Christ's resurrection is at work, into a Communitas of suffering, including death. Final "aggregation" is hinted at in v 11, *resurrection from the dead.* Cf. Rom 6:3–11, baptism as death and future resurrection with Christ. *gnōsis,* suffering, death, and resurrection are typical initiation themes. The principles apply to all believers. 3:12–21 will treat the uncompleted character of the transformation process and ultimate, final, aggregation (postliminal, vv 20–21). The schema works well for Saul/Paul.[15] It is less satisfactory for the Philippians. They never possessed the Jewish status described in 3:4b–6, though Pilhofer offers Greco-Roman counterparts to all the points Paul lists (B.1, below).

3. *The Enemies and Law, Righteousness/Justification, Faith, and Christ.* These topics have each been proposed as master theme for 3:4b–11, as well as "knowledge," *koinōnia* (B.1, below), or eschatology (3:12–21). All are part of Paul's theology. They relate also to "the enemies" in Letter C (A.2.d, above); see (11) COMMENT A.2 (more like Paul's opponents in Galatia than those in 2 Cor 10–13); (12) A.2.d. What 3:4b–11 adds is debated, because evidence is indirect. But the group is on Paul's mind as he writes.

a. *Righteousness/Justification.* "The key term in Philippians 3:4–11."[16] On translating *dikaiosynē*-terms (3:6b, 9b, 9c), see NOTE on 1:11a *righteousness;* cf.

---

[14] Bengel, Gnomon on 3:7; Schenk 305, 314, 322, "The Beginning: call through the risen Christ," "the Present (Time) as Christian Existence," and "Perfection as the Goal"; Fee 305–51, "No Future to the Past," "the Future lies in the Present," "the Future is also Future."

[15] It poses an alternative in the debate whether Paul was "converted" or "called." Some reject "conversion" to avoid any "change of religion" on the part of Saul (Stendahl 1976:7–23, "Call Rather Than Conversion"; cf. B. Roberts Gaventa, *From Darkness to Light: Aspects of Conversion in the New Testament,* OBT 20 [Philadelphia: Fortress, 1986] 17–51, esp. 29–33; Hoerber). Yet "conversion" existed in antiquity, even among philosophers (Malherbe 1998; AB 32B:305, passim). It fits Paul (Segal): "initiation process," transformation from old to new status; Paul's entire Christian ministry in a state of liminality; Reumann 2005; A. E. Martínez: religious alternation or resocialization.

[16] J. C. Beker, "Paul the Theologian," *Int* 43 (1989) 361. Houlden 96–102 and Reumann 1982 "give the impression that *righteousness* is the most important term in interpreting the whole of Phil 3:2–11" (Koperski 1996:191 n 3, a view she opposes, see d, below). Cf. also Hultgren 1985:12–46, 82–124; on Phil 3:9, 33–34, 93.

Houlden 98. Sacchi views "justification" as a new, more complex way of understanding "righteousness" within salvation. Fee 326 n 47 would limit 'justification'" to *dikaiōsis* (Rom 4:25, 5:18), "forensic 'justification,'" of which he finds "no hint" in 3:3–9. Contrast Lenski 843, on 3:6, "forensic, as always"; Plevnik 1986. Fee overlooks "the Day of Christ" (1:6 etc.) and "the Grand Assize" (O'B 392; 3:19–21). *dikaiosynē* in Paul is neither wholly and always forensic, nor without the law-court/final judgment aspect. Silva 184–89 finds place for "justification (righteousness through faith)," but (189–93) stresses "sanctification" (v 10, though *hagiazō*-terms do not appear) and "glorification" (v 11, via Rom 8:17), from an *ordo salutis* (not just Calvinist, cf. Rom 8:30, etc.). Re "righteousness" and "in Christ" see O'B, *Phil.*, Appendix E, pp. 415–17, and his 1992 overview.

On *dikaiosynē* in Paul, see NOTE on 1:11 *righteousness*; ABD 5:752–54, 757–68. It is both gift "from God" (3:9, Bultmann 1964) and power (3:10, Käsemann 1969). For all the debate over *pistis Christou*, 3:9 is an "unambiguous instance . . . of a justification 'pronounced' on the basis of the believer's faith" (9d) (Cosgrove 1987:667 n 34). Righteousness/justification rooted for Paul in the OT; for his auditors, in Roman Imperial cult, celebrating an upright and life-giving world order, *dikaiosynē* as God's beneficent righteousness.[17] It involves a process or continuum, from past event (Christ's cross, Rom 3:24) and the time when a person hears the kerygma and believes (Rom 5:1,9; and is baptized, 1 Cor 6:11), to present-time, ongoing implications (Gal 2:16), and future fulfillment at the final judgment (Rom 3:30; Gal 5:5; Ziesler [(2) Bibl. **righteousness**] 208–9). Though Phil 3 "lacks . . . the present side of justification" (no ptc. like *dikaioumenoi* in Rom 3:24), that aspect may be assumed; the enemies emphasize precisely that, via circumcision (Reumann 1982 [(2) Bibl. **righteousness**] 111, against O'B 393 n 69, which does not reckon with the context). Communal, corporate, or cosmic aspects of righteousness/ justification go unstated, because Paul is writing in the "I"-form. Likewise missing (Fortna) but certainly to be understood is the term "grace" (in Phil, only at 1:7; vb. 1:29; 2:9; but cf. "from God" in 9c; cf. Blank 1968:237).[18]

b. *Faith. pistis* (9c, 9d) may be grouped with righteousness/justification (Aguilar 202–4) or regarded as a separate theme. In contrast with *ek nomou* (righteousness *from the Law*) in 9b (and 6a), it is the means for believers to appropriate righteousness from God, through faith in Christ (obj. gen.; if subj. gen., faithfulness, the decisive attitude and stance on Christ's part that brings God's saving righteousness). Bockmuehl, "*two* kinds of faith in relation to God's righteousness revealed in Christ," that of Christ on the cross, and that of the believer (211). Koperski 1996:227–29, faith in 3:2–9 is "relying on Christ for final salvation" (with *pepoitha* thrice in vv 3–4 and *kauchōmenoi*, "glorying" in 3) and hence "the strongest concern" in the passage. "Faith in Christ" changed Paul's life. It is even more

---

[17] Blumenfeld's "Political Reading" of Rom (302–414) relates *dikaiosynē theou* to the kingdom or *politeia* in heaven (Phil 3:20), *dikaiosynē pisteōs* to the "political locale" in Philippi; Paul works alongside the Roman Empire, "upholding" it and "making it last." Blumenfeld 440–45 contrasts his view with Stowers 1994 ([3] n 14).

[18] Gnilka 2001:151, 158 defends "the declaring righteous of the sinner" *sola fide, sola gratia*, and refers to 1 Cor 15:10, "by God's grace I am what I am," as implicit in Paul's "turn" to Christ.

important when *epi tē[i] pistei* in 9d is taken as the basis for knowing Christ (v 10) and/or as the opposite of all the things Paul has renounced in vv 5–6 (Silva 187–88; O'B 400).

c. *Law. nomos* (3:5e, 6b, 9b) = the Law of Moses. Affirmed for Saul (vv 5,6) but not part of the righteousness from God through faith in Christ (therefore in contrast to *pistis*; if a subjective gen., then Jesus, not just Paul, stands opposed to the Law as means for salvation and life). E. P. Sanders calls 3:6–9 "the only passage in which Paul unambiguously says that there *is* a righteousness which is actually obtainable [!] by law" (63 n 132), setting forth, like 2 Cor 3:4–18, "the old dispensation and the new" (137–41), leading to Sanders' oft-quoted conclusion: the plight of all humanity, Jews included, is that they are not "in Christ"; what is wrong in Judaism "is that it is not Christianity" (*PPJ* 554, 552; expanded in *PLJP* 1985:47. The Law and circumcision are no longer the way of "entry to the 'in' group . . . those who would be saved"; for "proper Christian behaviour" it is the Spirit (Gal 5:22) and "general hellenistic moral summaries (Phil 4:8)" that matter (but cf. Rom 13:8–10; 1 Cor 9:8–9). "The law was good," now it is a loss (Phil 3:7–8; Sanders 1986:77–80).

Notions of development in Paul's view of the Law[19] do not always factor in Phil 3, though Wilckens sees Phil as already in contrast with the hostile estimate in Gal.[20] Räisänen's claim that Paul was ambiguous and confused about the Law (it is abolished, but he has by no means broken completely with it) applies less to Phil than to comparisons of Gal with Rom.[21] Equality of Jew and Gentile (a Pauline concern) does not account for Paul's attitude toward the Law in Phil 3.[22] Nor are there in Phil 3 expectations of an "eschatological pilgrimage" to Jerusalem (R. D. Kaylor) when Gentiles will learn Torah (Isa 2:2–4 = Micah 4:1–3). Rather, a Christ/Torah antithesis[23] that has to do with "community identification," righteousness as a "membership term," two kinds of righteousness expressing "mutually exclusive boundary markers, rival ways of determining the community of

---

[19] Among others, J. Drane, *Paul* (New York: Harper & Row, 1976) 61–77, 132–36; Hübner 1984b:55–57, 63–65, 136–7: an earlier quite negative view in Gal, a more positive one in Rom 7–8; Westerholm 2004:165–69.

[20] 1982a, "Statements on the Development of Paul's View of the Law," in *Paul and Paulinism*, FS C. K. Barrett [London: SPCK] 17–26; 1982b, "Zur Entwicklung des paulinischen Gesetzesverständnis," NTS 28:154–90, esp. 178, is a fuller presentation.

[21] Räisänen, the problem lies in "a Christological failure" on the part of Israel (1983:176); cf. N. T. Wright and Donaldson. Critique of Räisänen in T. E. van Spanje, *Inconsistency in Paul?* (WUNT 2/110; Tübingen: Mohr Siebeck 1999); Westerholm 2004:170–77.

[22] As if "Torah excludes, so no Torah"; cf. N. T. Wright 1991, esp. ch. 7, but without treatment of Phil 3; the indictment is ultimately against Israel, "the nation as a whole" has failed to "keep the Torah as a whole," 146; in the "renewed covenant," "the badge of membership in faith," 156.

[23] So Donaldson 1997:165–86, with charts on the several construals. Not, for Donaldson, as in W. D. Davies 1948, Christ replaced the Law at Damascus Road, something in part prompted by Paul's "uneasy conscience" (63, 66), so that Torah is set aside (Rom 10:4), distinctions between Jew and Gentile eliminated (Gal 3:28; Davies 67), and the Gentile mission follows. Nor does Donaldson see Israel as under a curse (Gal 3:10 = Deut 21:23) for not keeping all the Law (so Wright). Indeed, "the curse" which applied to Jesus (as "hanged on a tree," Gal 3:13) is not the root for Paul's Christ/Torah antithesis.

salvation," by Torah or by Christ.[24] The survey on law by Hollingshead 50–72 (esp. in Rom 5) (and Spirit), with, among others, Snodgrass, and J. C. Beker 1980:164–65, stresses "spheres of influence" for *nomos*, spatial and sociological as well as temporal and apocalyptic. Westerholm 2004 surveys old and "new perspective(s)," esp. 401–4, 408–39. In such ways references in Phil 3 have become part of some larger studies on Law.

d. *Christology. Christos* or a pron. occur 10x (vv 7, 8b,c,e, 9a, 9c, 10a thrice, 10b, the most frequent referent after Paul ("I, me"). From the phrase *knowledge of Christ Jesus my Lord* (8b), Koperski sought to show that vv 7–11 provide "one of the strongest christological statements in Christian Scripture," stronger than 2:6–11 (1996:1). Christ appears in wisdom categories.[25] Pate 2000 argues that Paul used the wisdom theme to separate Christ as God's wisdom from Law. Byrnes 237–44 stresses "the whole Christ" as mediator. Treatments of Pauline Christology make relatively little of Phil 3:7–11.[26] With its emphasis on cross (3:18) and parousia (20–21), the case for it is good (Reumann 1991a). Its "high" nature stems from what Christ does (death, resurrection), his role as basis for Paul's shift in outlook over gains and loss (7, 8c), Christ as surpassing (8b), object of faith (9c) and knowledge (10a), in whom one aims to be found (9a).

We shall let these themes in 3:7–11 unfold as Paul brings in each topic.

B. MEANING AND INTERPRETATION

1. *Saul's Credentials: Heritage in Israel and Achievements (3:4b–6).* Paul has not forgotten the enemies in 3:2 (A.2.d, above) as he continues Letter C with the "I"-form begun in 4a, *I . . . have grounds for confidence indeed in the flesh.* His autobiographical narrative (through v 14) repeats language of 4a in 4b, on confidence in something fleshly (like circumcision). Paul asserts credentials in contrast with those who threaten Philippian Christians, using the rhetorical device of comparison (*synkrisis*, above 2.a): whatever they claim, *I do to a greater degree. any other person* (sg.) does not seem to have a specific individual in mind, let alone anyone now in Philippi ("any of you," GNB[2], is for inclusive language). Anyone who might appear in Philippi from the enemies of the cross of Christ. Paul addresses Philippian believers, not opponents over OT interpretation as in Gal 3–4 (esp. 3:6,11; Gen 15:6, Hab 2:4), to persuade via personal history and example. It

---

[24] Donaldson 171–73, with U. Wilckens, "Die Bekehrung des Paulus als religionsgeschichtliches Problem," in *Rechtfertigung als Freiheit: Paulus Studien* (Neukirchen-Vluyn: Neukirchener, 1974) 11–32; Wilckens stresses apocalyptic material and soteriology, Donaldson "covenantal nomism" and ecclesiology.

[25] Wis 7:7–10; Job 28:15–18, 42:7–8 and 17a, LXX addition, Job "will rise [*anastēsesthai*] with those whom the Lord raises up [*anistēsin*]"). But it cannot be demonstrated "with certainty that Paul had the example of Job in mind" (more plausible if Phil 1:19 = Job 13:16 LXX); wisdom seems brought in from 1 Cor 1:30 and elsewhere.

[26] E.g., Soards 1999 ([7] Bibl.) 90, 95; *NJBC* #82:48–54; B. Witherington, *DPL* 100–15, oriented to "story"; Hawth. *Philippians* (Word Biblical Themes) 41–59; F. J. Matera, *New Testament Christology* (Louisville: Westminster/John Knox 1999) 120–34.

is not theoretical (*"might* trust in the flesh," KJV). The person(s) in 3:4b "think(s) himself/themselves (entitled) to trust" (ZG 599) in circumcision of the flesh. *flesh* embraces all Paul mentions about "natural descent of the Israelites . . . Pharisaism, zeal for the law, legal righteousness," "in the last analysis anything outside Christ" (E. Schweizer, *TDNT* 7:130–31 and n 255); it reflects the flesh/Spirit contrast of 3:3b (*TDNT* 6:428). In "more than . . . autobiography [cf. Collange 129; Lyons 153] . . . Paul sets forth a stronger argument (*argumentatio firmior*) than that of his opponents."[27] He delineates "more fully his own position, not theirs" (133; cf. 178–79, existence "in Christ" as superior to that "in the flesh"). "Personal testament" (M. Müller 187–88, 203–4), not form-critically (K. Berger 1984a:75–80; cf. Acts 20:18–35), but autobiography as an "ethics of example" (cf. *T. Benj.* 3.1, cf. 4.1, *OTP* 1:825–26), with *inclusio* (Müller), 3:2 + 3:17b ("observe those who live according to the example you have in us"); 3:3 + 3:17a ("join in imitating me"). Vv 5–6, *via contrario*, are *not* what the Philippians are to imitate.

Paul lists (3:5–6) seven advantages or *gains* as a Jew[28] to support his claim in 3:4b (Banker 123). The list provides "an encomiastic comparison *(synkrisis)*" (Malina/Neyrey 52), self-praise of Paul and what is best in Israel, true of a true Jew, but aimed at the enemies of 3:3 and their vauntings. Whatever they claim, Paul can claim more. Variously arranged (A.1), the catalogue includes four items in the inheritance of any Jewish male (one particular to Saul, his tribe), then three accomplishments where he had "advanced in Judaism beyond many among my people of the same age" (Gal 1:14). Terms go unexplained, perhaps used when Paul told his story during the founding mission. He appears an "exemplary Jew" (K.-W. Niebuhr 1992:81–109; Walter 77).

(1) *circumcision on the eighth day*, an obvious starting point, is the issue raised by the enemies (3:2, 3a). Paul was not circumcised "more" than any opponent, but his parents carried out the rite at the time appointed in the Law (Lev 12:3). He conformed from the beginning (K.-W. Niebuhr 105) with what God ordained for Israelites. Not a convert. But was circumcision necessary for Gentile believers, in a church where there is "no longer Jew or Greek" (Gal 3:28)?

The first four items can each be paralleled by a phrase Roman citizens might use for their heritage (Pilhofer 1:126–27). As counterpart of circumcision, the *toga (virilis)* can be claimed, chief garment of a free-born Roman male.[29] In a

---

[27] Bloomquist 130, Cic. *Inv.* 1.51.96. Not *argumentatio infirmior* (M. Müller 190 n 280) unless 3:5–7 is seen as "less strong" than 3:8–11. W. Deming (Sampley, ed., 2003: 390, 397, 397) sees a Stoic framework in 3:5–8 and "indifferent things."

[28] *Israel* and *Hebrew(s)* are used (not *Ioudaios* 1 Cor 1:22–24, etc., or "Judaism" Gal 1:13, etc.), perhaps because the enemies used the terms, like the opponents in 2 Cor 11:22. *Ioudaios* could be a reproach in Gentile applications (3 Macc 3:3–7; R. Mayer, *NIDNTT* 2:310), though adopted by Jews in the Diaspora (W. Gutbrod, *TDNT* 3:369–71), occasionally in "books of the Apocrypha and Pseudepigrapha originating in Palestine," not at Qumran, seldom in the Rabbis (*EDNT* 2:194).

[29] Hellerman 12–14, 126, 201 n 51, public expression of elite status. Description in *OCD*³ 1533. The *toga praetexta* for highborn boys had a purple border (part of Lydia's livelihood? Acts 16:14). Given as a symbol of citizenship in an annual religious ceremony on March 17 to 15–18 year olds (*KlPauly* 5:879–80). In eastern provinces the Gk. *himation* or *pallium* remained common.

Roman *colonia* this was familiar as "badge of membership" for citizens, as was the ceremony of "entry into the forum" (*tirocinium fori*).

Paul took a risk in mentioning his circumcision. The enemies are trying to persuade people to this practice. "Paul is circumcised, why not you?" But evidence is lacking they made an issue of Paul personally. As a point of truth, he states *circumcised on the eighth day* was part of his heritage. It will make his testimony more telling when he later speaks of the change that took place in his values and denies circumcision is needed for "perfection" (3:12–15).

The next three phrases, (2) *from (ek) the race of Israel,* (3) *from the tribe of Benjamin,* and (4) *a Hebrew born from (ex) Hebrews* continue Saul's "generation or genesis" in terms of "ethnic group, clan, and ancestry" (Malina/Neyrey 53). Lft. 146 saw here "an ascending scale" ("a progressive argument," W. Gutbrod, *TDNT* 3:390); K.-W. Niebuhr 107, *from Hebrews* is the climax of "people-tribe-family." For *genos, race,* not "people" (which could include proselytes), makes Paul's point (with Loh. 129, among others; cf. NOTE). *Israel* recalls the "adoption" (Rom 9:4, a Greco-Roman term) or election of Jacob's descendants (Rom 9:11–12; 11:5; 11:28b; *TDNT* 3:360). The counterpart for a Roman citizen was *civis Romanus;* for Paul (Acts 22:25–28, cf. 16:37–38), "born a citizen." (3) *tribe of Benjamin* parallels the *tribus Voltinia* for Philippian citizens (see NOTE). His name "Saul" came from Israel's first king, a Benjaminite (1 Sam 9–31). The climactic (4), *a Hebrew born from Hebrews,* lifts up a term employed by Jews, of Paul and his immediate and ancestral forebears. Like *tribe of Benjamin,* a term proselytes could not truthfully use. It helps imply Saul of Tarsus once studied in Jerusalem (Acts 22:3; 23:16, his sister presumably lived there now), that he spoke Aramaic, but not necessarily that he was of Palestinian parentage; see NOTE. He was "a full-blooded Hebrew . . . socialized . . . to the customs of his family, clan, and ethos" (Malina/Neyrey 53; Hengel 1991:26–27 minimizes the Diaspora side; K.-W. Niebuhr 106–8 is more nuanced). Family background, with genealogy, was important in Judaism, and not just for priests (Jos. *Vit.* 1.1–6). The counterpart Roman term for family identity (Pilhofer 1:126–27) was *(Cai) filius,* "son (of Caius)" (or whoever).

The final three phrases move to Saul's "manner of life (*anastrophē* [Gal 1:13])" (Malina/ Neyrey 53), what he accomplished re goals of a good Jew. (5) *as to Law—a Pharisee,* first and foremost the Mosaic Law, the norm in accord with which (*kata*) Paul sought to walk, "in, with, and under" which "the Pharisee lives" (O. Betz 1977:57). The degree of conformity was as *a Pharisee:* intensely studying Scripture, adhering to extended oral Law for "modern times," a Pharisaic *talmîd ḥākām,* disciple scholar, trained likely in Palestine (Hengel 1991:27, against Strecker 1976:482 n 10). In Acts, Paul is "a son of Pharisees" (23:6), belonging to "the strictest sect of our religion" (26:5).[30] He fits into Sanders' "covenantal no-

---

[30] Which wing of the Pharisaic movement? Jeremias 1969b, Saul was a follower of Hillel; Hübner 1973 and Haacker 1971–72 and 1975, the school of Shammai (more restrictive views; Hillel was "liberal" and later normative, R. Goldenberg, "Shammai, School of," *ABD* 5:1158; 3:201–2 on "Hillel"). That the Lukan Paul studied "at the feet of Gamaliel" (grandson of Hillel) in Jerusalem (Acts 22:3; cf. *NJBC* 79:18) supports the Hillelite proposal, as may Paul's exegetical methods (Jeremias). Paul and Hillel agreed on resurrection and Gentile missions (Pes. 8.8 [H. Danby, *The Mishnah* (Oxford: Oxford

mism," though how much *nomos* and how much "covenant" is difficult to say.[31] Pharisees (O. Betz 1977:57–58) were a group "separated" (cf. Qumran, 1QS 5.1 "kept away" from sinners), a community set apart for the service of the Law. Open to new impulses often minimally attested in Scripture (resurrection, Phil 3:10; Acts 23:6–8; 24:15); likely to seek converts (cf. Matt 23:15). Unlike the Sadducees and later Zealots on Rome—lackeys and armed guerrillas, respectively—the Pharisees' stance fitted Paul's position (appeal as a citizen for release from prison, see on 1:14–18c; exercise of citizenship, 1:28a; but Caesar is not Lord, 2:11).

(6) *as to zeal, a man persecuting the church.* Saul held to the Law zealously, treating with rigor those "soft" on Torah. *zēlos* has a positive background (see NOTE). Israel's God showed zeal (a "jealous" God), though other Gk. words were used for Heb. *qin'āh* (A. Stumpff, *TDNT* 2:878–79; Exod 20:5; Deut. 4:24; Ezek 38:19; Isa 9:7 "the zeal of the Lord of hosts"). Heroes exhibited zeal from Phineas on, leading to "zeal for the Law" in Maccabean times and Paul's day, but not yet identified with avowedly political Zealots (references in NOTE). Zeal for the Law was an integrating feature in Pharisaism (O. Betz 1977:59; cf. Hengel 1988:146–228; *TPTA* 350–53), at times expressed "in a physically violent way." Donaldson 1989:284–92, zeal for Torah led Saul to see Christ as a rival way to membership in the people of God; the contrast is "ecclesiological"; Deines 2001:494–99. But Hultgren 1976:102, the message about Jesus "provoked Paul's response as a perse-cutor." Can message and community be separated? Cf. Gal 1:14, zeal for ancestral traditions (Law and the community of Israel). At 3:6a *zeal* is flanked by references to *the Law* in 5e and 6b, ultimately "zeal for God," who gave the Law (Acts 22:3). Malina/Neyrey 53 compare being "truly loyal to God ('zeal' = 'piety')" with "tradi-tional virtues or 'deeds of soul'" in an encomium.[32]

Saul showed *zeal* for Torah by *persecuting the church.* *ekklēsia* needs no expla-nation (used earlier, in Letter A, 4:15). Here any synagogue or house assembly in Palestine or Syria that he targeted; for the Philippians, their house churches under pressure by the authorities in their Roman *colōnia* (1:28; 1 Thess 2:2). Paul uses the same vb. for his actions in Gal 1:13, 23, and 1 Cor 15:9. See NOTE for texts

---

University Press, 1932) 148], circumcision as conversion from death to life). Contrast M. S. Enslin, "Paul and Gamaliel," *JR* 7 (1927) 360–75. But use of Deut 27:26 in Gal 3:10 is characteristic of the school of Shammai (Hübner). *zeal* and *persecuting the church* (Phil 3: 6) reflect the rigor of Shammai (Haacker 10), on the model of Phineas (Haacker 1975:14–15, 20; Ps 106:30–31). O. Betz 1977:59–60 inclines to Paul as a Shammaite; so also Donaldson 1989:278, with L. Gaston, "Paul and Torah," in *Antisemitism and the Foundations of Christianity*, ed. A. T. Davies (New York: Paulist, 1979) 61; S. Kim 1981:41–44; Hübner 1984b:44 n 16; J. Becker 1993 ([1] Bibl. **Paul**) 39–41. Data are lacking for a conclusive decision; *DPL* 504–6; Hengel 1991:28, "an idle" question.

[31] For varieties of "covenantal nomism," cf. *Justification and Variegated Nomism*, ed. D. A. Carson et al. As a term, "covenantal nomism" is judged "reductionistic" and "misleading" (543–48), the poles "getting in" and "staying in" in need of nuancing; the schema too easily pits "covenant theology" against "merit theology." "Covenant and Law were so bound together that they were essentially syn-onymous" (Smiles 298, cf. 291–92; E. J. Christiansen, *The Covenant in Judaism and Paul: A Study of Ritual Boundaries as Identity Markers*, AGAJU 27 [Leiden: Brill, 1995]).

[32] In the Gk. world, *zēlos* = commitment to a person, cause, or goal (A. Stumpff, *TDNT* 2:877–78); Aristot. *Rhet.* 2.11 1388a 32–1388b 2 (LCL *"Art" of Rhetoric*, tr. J. H. Freese, 243).

about "Paul the persecutor." He "played only a subsidiary role" against Stephen and the Hellenists, but when criticism continued of the Law and temple, "he took the initiative and brought about a 'pogrom'" against conventicles in Jerusalem and Damascus (Hengel 1991:63–86; Hultgren 1976:105–10, "incomparable zeal," but not "violently").[33] Paul does not "depict his activity as persecutor *from a Christian perspective*" in 3:6a (Thiessen 1987 [INTRO. VII.A Bibl.] 234–432; 242 cited, italics added). 3:6 raises the question of zeal for goals, conduct as the way toward them, and ultimately "the End" (cf. K.-W. Niebuhr 109).

(7) The climactic point: Paul = *one who was blameless* re the standard of *righteousness called for in the Law*. This self-description has stung many commentators, and not only Protestants, as outrageous. "Righteous because blameless!" (Lenski 843); who can be faultless? Cf. Calvin 92–93; Melick 130; Hawth. 134. Gnilka 191: "human striving to make oneself righteous before God," in antithesis to v 9. Cf. Mark 10:20 parr. Protests about *blameless* were attacked by Sanders as a caricature of Judaism (1977:33–59).

Within the Mosaic covenant, *righteousness* (see NOTE) is the type of conduct called for as response to God's choice of Israel and a man's entry into this covenant relationship through circumcision. One stays in this communal/national relationship by living in accord with what Torah teaches—for Saul, in its Pharisaic elaboration. Like Hyrcanus, earlier Pharisees, and Qumranites (see NOTE), Saul felt doing so was possible. Rabbis in the Tannaitic literature viewed the covenant as unconditional; Israel was to obey (Sanders 92–97); obedience was not burdensome but duty and delight (110–11; cf. Ps 119). In this literature "righteous(ness)" (*tsadaq* in Sanders' transliteration) is "fairly rare" (except in the phrase *ger tsedeq*, see below), often meaning "alms, charity." Doing righteousness does not earn but "*preserves* one's place in the covenant" (198–205). From such sources (plus Sir, *1 En.*, Jub., Ps. Sol., and 4 Ezra) Sanders drew his pattern for "covenantal nomism" (442): God chose Israel, maintains this election, and has given the Law to be obeyed; obedience is rewarded.[34] When this covenant relationship is broken, means were provided for atonement; "all those who are maintained in the covenant by obedience, atonement, and God's mercy . . . will be saved."[35] While Sanders' analyses have rightly been criticized at points,[36] they suggest the widespread sense among Jewish groups of Paul's day about human ability to "walk the walk"

---

[33] Lüdemann 1989 (INTRO. II Bibl.) 93, 115, on historicity; not psychologizing the impact on Saul to explain "Damascus Road," as E. J. Goodspeed did (*Paul, a Biography* [Philadelphia: Winston, 1947] 10–19).

[34] The doctrine of "merits of the fathers," *zekut 'abot*, which played a role in Reformation criticism of medieval Catholicism, is adjudged by Sanders 183–98 to refer to "historical rewards," not the final judgment. Does that make it more likely or palatable? Cf. Westerholm 2004:343–51.

[35] The "pattern" in the Dead Sea scrolls may vary somewhat, emphasizing "knowledge" of God, grace, the "nothingness" of mortals, and God's gracious righteousness, but there is the same obedience to the community's rules for "staying in," 316–21.

[36] Cf. T. R. Schreiner 1985; Deidun 1986 (Pauline exegesis and Lutheran theology need not be kept entirely apart); Westerholm 1988, 2004; Thielman 1989; Seifrid 1992 ([2] Bibl. **righteousness**) 71–77, 255–70, 171–76 on Phil 3:2–11; Walter 78–79. Laato, while generally affirming Sanders' work, stresses an anthropological approach: "Paul criticizes Judaism . . . for boasting in self-righteousness," which

God wills. Commands in Torah are "not too hard for you"; providentially "very near . . . for you to observe," they mean life (Deut 30:11, 14–16; cf. 1 John 5:3). In Saul's Pharisaic self-assessment, Dunn (*TPTA* 349–50) sees "a separation both *of* Judaism *from the other nations* and *within* Judaism *from other Jews.*" That Paul and some Jews of the day "could have thought of themselves as 'righteous' . . . and 'blameless'" puts a question mark to notion that Israel was still "in exile" and under the curse of Deut 27:26 (= Gal 3:10) (so N. T. Wright 1991:137–56, "Torah brings the curse for Israel, because Israel has not kept it").[37] Paul's audience in Philippi may at first have thought of *dikaiosynē* at 3:6 as one of the virtues, "justice." "The Pharisee pursued righteousness; the Greek, virtue" (A. Schlatter, *Geschichte Israels* [3rd ed. 1925] 150). Being *blameless* was no impossibility among Greeks; "unblamed by friends," "faultless justice" (Plato *Leg.* 11.924A and 12.945D; W. Grundmann, *TDNT* 4:572). A goal in friendship or moral progress was to live "without a blemish" (Danker 1982:354, in decrees of honor; MM 26 [BGU 4.1141.35], "I kept myself blameless"; sepulchral epitaphs). The list in 3:5–6 assumes Paul and his readers "share a common index of honor, . . . socially agreed upon as bestowing worth, respect, and prestige" (Malina/Neyrey 53). Now what?

2. The Great Reversal in Paul's Life Because of the Risen Christ (3:7–11). The contrast to Saul's heritage and accomplishments comes in vv 7–8, former *gains* are now *loss* ("marketplace metaphors," Ascough 2003:118–22) *because of Christ.* The "because" phrase occurs 3x (7, 8b, 8c, *dia* + acc.). Encounter with the risen Lord proved utterly decisive for the zealous *Pharisee.* Paul gives up "Jewish covenantal privileges" (Räisänen 1987:409). *All things* past are now assessed as *crap* (8d). While 7–8d could be a separate unit, virtually all commentators go on with 8e–9a, two purpose cls. (*hina* + subjunct.) attached directly to the main cl. in 8d. Another purpose cl. follows in 10a, using a different construction (art. infin., *to know Christ*), concerning the present and the final *resurrection.* 9bc(d), about *righteousness* and *faith*, some would take parenthetically (e.g., Schenk 250–51, 328, explanatory). But *righteousness* (twice in 9bc) also appeared in Saul's credentials (6b), as did *Law* (5e, 6b, and now 9b but with *ek*, not *en*). Cf. also *faith* (9cd) and *confidence* (4b). The new term is *Christ* (7, 8b, c, e, 9a, 10a, 10b, including pronouns), whose *death* is mentioned (10b) but even more his *resurrection* (10a).

How do these themes relate in Paul's theology (A.3, above) and to the enemies, who were perhaps responsible for some of the terms here (A.2.d)? In a "past/ present/ future" sequence, *resurrection* and *knowing* have both present and future aspects. Others see "before" and "after," 4b–6 and 7–11, respectively, but there is carryover, as well as contrast, between Paul's life in Judaism and his new life "in Christ." Rhetorical analyses find within Paul's *narratio* a proposition in v 7 or in

---

arises "even from covenantal nomism" (209–10). On Phil 3:3–9, see 202–8. Thurén 146–47 speaks of "a more balanced post-Sanders era"; cf. 168–71, 183 on Phil 3. Cf. Westerholm 2004:226–35.

[37] Critique of Wright, among other places, in D. A. Carson, "Summaries" 546 n 158, in Carson et al. 2001, noting J. M. Scott, ed., *Exile: Old Testament, Jewish, and Christian Conceptions*, JSJSup 56 (Leiden: Brill, 1997) and C. C. Newman, ed., *Jesus and the Restoration of Israel: A Critical Assessment of N. T. Wright's Jesus and the Victory of God* (Downers Grove: IVP, 1999).

9–11 (A.1, above). 3:7 marks a turning point in the narration. 8e–11 treat the meaning of "gaining, knowing, and being found in Christ," not least in terms of righteousness/justification. The passage is written to meet many agendas (A.2, above).

The "great 'But'" (K. Barth 96) that one might expect at the start of v 7 is uncertain textually (see NOTE; brackets in NA[27]); we omit it. *I have come to consider* is the first of three examples of *hēgeomai*, here pf. tense ("I learned to regard as loss," at some past time, RSV), with pres. implication ("I now consider loss," NIV). It remains Paul's judgment in 8a (pres. tense *I . . . continue to consider*) and 8d, with *skybala* as obj., climactically (*I consider all these things crap*; Schoon-Janßen 149). Terms escalate on what Paul depreciates as *loss*: *these things* (v 7, referring back to the sevenfold listing in vv 5–6); *all things* (8a *panta*); 8c *ta panta*, *everything*; 8d implied, *all these things*, i.e., whatever else might be dragged in by the enemies as grounds for boasting. The contrasts within v 7 (Gk. in the NOTE) are:

whatever things (in vv 5–6)	*were*	*gains*	*for me*
these	*I have come to consider*	*loss*	*because of Christ.*

The vbs. contrast past and present. *gains/loss* was a common contrast, esp. in finance (profits, debits; plus and minus; cf. 4:15, 17, 18), coming over into Judaism (but not the LXX), and in a saying of Jesus (Mark 8:36, hardly a direct influence here; cf. Koperski 1996:161 n 66 for literature). *for me* (Saul) stands in contrast to *because of Christ*, the first reference to the Lord Jesus in Letter C since the salutation (cf. 1:2; in the redacted letter, since 2:30 and 3:1). Not "loss *for (the sake of)* Christ" (KJV, RSV), as if Saul sacrificed his past glories for Jesus, but (NRSV) the One *because of* whom Saul changed his view on what mattered to him. The experience that made him Paul, apostle and missionary, includes "Damascus Road" but also subsequent development, unfolded in contacts with others in Christ, baptism, study of Scripture, and life together in the communities of Christ (1 Cor 15:8–11; Gal 1:15b–23). Harnisch 141–42 separates 3:7 from 3:8–11 as *propositio*, "a brief summary of the matter to be proved" [Lausberg #289], "the intellectual core . . . of the *narratio* . . ." [#346]; then 8–11 becomes *argumentatio*, an *amplificatio* of the thesis in v 7. But v 7 does not summarize, it contrasts with, the narration in 4–6; 8a and 8d repeat the "thesis," while amplifying not just v 7 but more specifically *knowing Christ Jesus* (8b) and what it means to *gain Christ and be found in him* (8e, 9a). Fee 317 finds Paul's "thesis sentence" in v 8.

Verse 8a is repetition of 7b, *alla* plus a cumbersome plethora of particles and conjunctions, brought out in the rendering, *Furthermore I do indeed therefore continue to consider all things as loss* (see NOTE on textual variants and problems with nuance). After the *peripateia* in v 7, the "about-face" continues; after years of mission work and conflict with opponents, its significance abides. Escalation to *all things* has been noted. Some think *all things* = items listed in 5–6 and referred to in v 7 (Vincent 100; Schenk 264); or just *Law* in its cultic form (rejected in Schrage 1961:94 n 93); others, "absolutely everything" (G. Barth 60), even Paul's "Roman citizenship, material possessions, or an assured position in the world" (O'B 387). *panta* could be rhetorical hyperbole (Thurén 2000:32–33), in a pattern of antitheses (7a/b; 8a/b), "perhaps based on the style of the diatribe" (DA 261–62 n 395, from Schoon-Janßen 143). But the line of argument, Paul's theological consistency, and stance on benefactions from Philippian Christians and "status" in a *colōnia* of the Empire suggest he does mean "everything."

Two more *dia* constructions follow: 8b *because of the surpassingness of knowing Christ Jesus my Lord*, 8c *because of whom I experienced loss of everything*. 1st per. narrative, with expanding application. Such "knowing" (further discussed in 10a) ought to characterize every Christian. A shift from (auto)biography to exemplary discourse ("Paul's biographically unique 'I' in 3:3–7 becomes in 3:8ff. a general 'I,'" J. Becker 1993 [(1) Bibl. **Paul**] 326; denied by Harnisch 142 n 24). Application to the Philippians is not yet explicit, as in v 17 (voc. and impvs.). Only in retrospect, upon rereading, is Paul's story paradigmatic.

After the "semantic intensification" of v 7 in 8a (Koperski 1996:151–57, "because" language as "motivating constructions"), there is a shift to "knowledge terminology" in 8b and 10a, which provides a framework for what follows. *loss* will appear only once more, in 8c; *gain*, only in 8e. Why *gnōsis*? Paul's unusual phrase, *knowing Christ Jesus my Lord* (debate continues over its backgrounds) likely stems from the thought-world of Pauline opponents (Schmithals 1972:91–92; Schenk 305–6); for its multiplicity of backgrounds, see NOTE. "Wisdom" revealed from God is involved—with OT roots, Jewish applications, Hellenistic mysticism; even personal acquaintance with important people and god(s), "I know so and so"—a "buzzword" in the world of the day. Making *Christ Jesus my Lord* the object of such knowledge marks the phrase as Christian and individualistically personal, whether of Paul, the enemies, or every believer. Christ is the Lord "through whom God brings salvation, justification and righteousness" (D. K. Williams 2002:177, with Reumann 1991a:134). *surpassingness* involves comparison with *all things* Paul listed as *loss* and with *gnōsis* he had in, with, and under the Law. "I, to a greater degree," (4b) may still be in the picture. The closest passage in Paul (Schenk 305) is Gal 4:8–9.[38] As in Gal, Phil 3:5–11 treats circumcision, Law, righteousness, faith, and knowing. Paul writes in the face of opponents encountered in Galatia, who, he thinks, menace Philippi with a word dear to the Gk. world,

---

[38] To ex-pagans: "Formerly, when you did not know God *(eidotes)*, you were enslaved to beings that by nature are not gods. Now, however, that you have come to know God *(gnōntes)*, or rather to be known by God *(gnōsthentes)*, how can you turn back again to the weak and beggarly elemental spirits?" (NRSV). Jews "were enslaved to the elemental spirits of the world" (4:3) through the Law "ordained by angels" (3:19), Law not "direct from God" but via *angeloi* as mediators, angels in Paul's references usually not on the side of God and good. Cf. Martyn, AB 33A:357, 366–70, 388–89, the Law has "two voices," Sinaitic and promise. Against "the Teachers" (as Martyn calls them), Paul states boldly, "God played no part in the genesis of the Sinaitic Law" (367). Paul's rhetoric is not simply "comparison *(synkrisis)*"; the Law is inferior (368). The opponents in Galatia offered knowledge of God and the divine will through the Law, including, crucially, circumcision. Paul's "rhetorical self-correction" is that what matters is "to be known by God," thus "correcting the teachers' religious message" (Martyn 411, 412–14; H. D. Betz, *Gal.* 215–16, "gnostic" flavor, but cf. Philo, *Cher.* 115). "Being known by God"— the *extra nos*, outside and beyond us (Schenk 305)—here in antithesis to "knowing God," is typical of Paul (1 Cor 8:2–3; 13:12; cf. 2 Cor 4:6), not in Phil, but cf. 3:12, " Jesus Christ has made me his own." Knowledge *of Christ* is an escalation on "knowing God."

gnōsis, introduced for further amplification. What he has, not dependent on Law and circumcision, surpasses what the enemies may offer.

In 8c Paul reiterates his point with another *dia* cl.: *because of whom I experienced loss of everything*. Christ is the turning point. "God's action in Christ alone provides salvation and makes everything else seem, in fact, actually *be* worthless" (*PPJ* 485). *everything* from the past becomes a minus, a deficit. "Loss" is vividly illustrated at Acts 27:10 and 21, of cargo, ship, and lives by shipwreck. The pass. voice *(ezēmiōthēn)* may imply it was God's doing in Paul's case. We have little idea what he lost in prestige, material goods, friends, or family when he turned to Christ; only catalogues enumerate the cost of ministry for Christ (e.g., 1 Cor 4:10–13; 2 Cor 11:22–29, how he suffered, though *Hebrew, Israelite,* and *descendant of Abraham*). Losses were not just for a moment on Damascus Road; the bill kept coming in for years thereafter.

As culmination ("the nucleus" statement, Banker 127), 8d repeats the assertions of vv 7 and 8a in stronger terms: *I consider all these things crap*. The climactic word *skybala* is offensive, just as *katatomē* was in v 2 (see NOTE on *the incision*). The NOTE discusses trs. like "rubbish" and "dung" ("shit," an expletive in Eng. nowadays, shock value gone, but unlikely in public reading of the NT). *crap* includes "excrement" and anything "deceitful, useless, or empty" (*Webster's Third*; *OED* 3:1117–18, since 15th cent. for chaff, later dregs, rubbish, nonsense; excrement first in the 19th cent.). What Saul once treasured turns out to be *skybala*.

Purpose cls. show what rejection of Law and circumcision means for Paul in positive terms. "Christ" (8bc, 9a, 10) and "(to) know" (8b, 10a) frame what is said about "righteousness." The two *hina* constructions, 8e *in order that I may gain Christ* and 9a *and be found in him*, depend on the assessment (vv 7, 8a, and 8d) about *gains* and *loss*, and ultimately on the vb. *I consider* (Koperski 1996:163). There is a parallelism (O'B 392), with possible chiasm:

hina	A	*Christon*	B	*kerdēsō*	*that*	A	*Christ*	B	*I may gain*
kai	B'	*eurethō*	A'	*en autō[i]*	*and*	B'	*be found*	A'	*in him*

O'B credits Schenk 250, whose structuring is somewhat different (A.1, above). The eschatology is debated (see NOTES). Gaining *Christ* may finally occur only at the Day of the Lord. Similarly with *be found in him*, if *eurethō* implies "found at death" (Moffatt, Epictet. 3.5.5–8). But Paul does not normally use "in Christ" of the parousia and thereafter (Schrage). Hence 9a may mean "found united to" (Gdsp.) or "incorporate in" Christ now, at baptism (Rom 6:3–5; 1 Cor 6:11, the righteousness/justification reference strengthens the case, *ABD* 5:759e), or simply "be in Christ's realm of lordship." Not an *en Christō[i]* "formula" but where Paul finds his place to be, now and at the End. Though the word is not used, baptism hovers behind the passage, from v 3 on (*circumcision* as rite of entry; *the Spirit*; cf. 1 Cor 12:13; Gal 6:15; 3:27–28; J. Becker 1993 [(1) Bibl. **Paul**] 330). If Paul's life "in Christ" began at Damascus Road, then "gaining Christ" is not entirely future. If at the beginning of 9a *and* is epexegetical, *be found in him* explains what *may gain Christ* means, or even corrects it. The latter possibility is heightened in that, while *gains/loss* language may have been appropriate in vv 7–8c, at

8e Paul is "somehow caught in the web of his rhetoric"; he says *gain Christ* but "does not mean . . . a personal profiting from Christ" (Hawth. 139–40). 9a is better put; cf. Gal 4:9 ("know God, be known by God") and Phil 4:18–19, shift from financial to cultic terms. *gain Christ,* a phrase perhaps from the opponents, may flow out of Paul's earlier language. Christ is now "the plus" in Paul's life. But 9a "tends to . . . correct the inappropriateness of the terminology" in 8e (so, finally, Koperski 1996:166). The overall eschatology—future in 8e, present status in 9a (Harnisch 144)—is best taken as "already but not yet" (Fee 320–21). Paul is "in Christ" now, a personal relationship under Christ's lordship, but realized only in part; to be perfected at the final Day, when Paul (and others) will be "with Christ" (U. B. Müller 154). Further light will come as Paul uses a characteristic theme, faith-righteousness (9bc), and then faith-knowledge of Christ (9d–10).

Verse 9bc, *not having my righteousness that is from the Law but the righteousness that comes through faith in Christ,* though called (grammatically) "parenthetical"[39] or a "foreign body," is highly important (Walter 80), a basic, perhaps the clearest, part of Paul's argument in 3:7–11 (Koperski 1996:168–69). Paul characterizes antithetically (N. Schneider 105–7) two kinds of righteousness, Law-righteousness and "the God-kind of righteousness (Rom 1:17)" (A. T. Robinson 1917:192) or "righteousness by faith." 6b referred to *righteousness . . . in the Law* that can permit understanding oneself as *blameless,* a point that practically demands return to the matter later on, as does reference to *Law* in 5e (picked up in 9b). Paul is brief here, for probably he dealt with righteousness (and Law) in his earlier oral teaching at Philippi.[40] "The enemies" have now made the term their own (Schenk 309–11), as the Teachers in Galatia did. What *dikaiosynē* means in distinction to Gk. notions (a cardinal virtue) and the enemies' use follows.

In Paul's cascade of thoughts, 9bc go very closely with *gaining Christ* and being *found in him* (8e, 9a) not because of a *righteousness* of my own (emphasis on *my,* something I can possess) but because of or by means of *the righteousness that comes from God.* Contrasts appear for the two kinds of righteousness (chiasm, end of the NOTE on 9d): *my* and *faith in Christ, from the Law* and *from God.* The latter contrast invites attention to 3:6b, *righteousness called for in the Law (en nomō[i]),* explained there as "staying in" the Mosaic covenant relationship by obedience to Torah. 9b shifts to *ek nomō[i],* parallel to the phrase in 9c *(hēn ek theou dikaiosynēn);* cf. 1 Cor 1:30 *apo theou dikaiosynē; dikaiosynē theou,* a possibly tech. term, *ABD*

---

[39] Gnilka 195; Sanders *PPJ* 501; Schenk 309. "Parenthesis" for 3:9b–d at least since Dib, not as peripheral but a grammatically independent thought inserted into the context (BDF 458, 465). The form is independent, the contents belong to the unity of the section. An important assertion in contrast to *the righteousness called for in the Law* (6), indeed the heart of Paul's contention (Gnilka 2001:159), so significant that he breaks the sentence structure to bring it in (139–40). Gnilka 159, cf. 155, accepts the rendering, "As my righteousness, I do not want to have that which comes out of the Law, but that which comes through faith in Christ" (BDF 285.2).

[40] Gnilka 195; cf. righteousness/justification formulas in early Christianity, like Rom 3:25; 4:25; 1 Cor 1:30 for presenting the meaning of the death of Christ, Reumann 1982 [(2) Bibl. **righteousness**] ##58–76), prior to any encounter with opponents in Galatia; Paul's experience was part of his witness (Gal 2:15–21).

5:758, 2.b). 6b and 9b mean conformity to what the Law requires as a way of staying in the covenant, esp. for those seeking the fullest kind of relationship with God that the opposing teachers offer. If the first contrast involves *my* righteousness and *pistis Christou* in the sense of Christ's believing or faithfulness (subj. gen.; interpretation [2] in the NOTE), the contrast is total; Christ does for me whatever is involved in *pistis*. But an obj. gen. (see NOTE, interpretation [1], my *faith in Christ*) is preferable here, indicating how one responds to Christ and the righteousness that comes from God through Christ's cross, "getting in" and "staying in" a right relationship with God. God takes the initiative (with Israel, the Exodus; cross); God elects, one says in retrospect; but the involvement of people is called for, in the case of the Christ event by believing, trusting, and obeying Christ. Paul's kerygma and pattern of life in Christ have been upset, however, by those who demand circumcision for baptized Gentiles to attain true and full life. The background for Paul's use of *dikaiosynē* here (E. P. Sanders *PPJ* 199–200; cf. Schenk 302–3) seems to lie in the Jewish concept of the "righteous proselyte." Converts to Judaism or the kind of Jewish Christianity promulgated in Galatia and threatening at Philippi were to take on themselves all the Law, including circumcision—a rite involving my flesh versus my believing in Christ my Lord, Mosaic Law versus Christ as God's means to deliver through Jesus' death (v 10). A stark contrast. Paul's gospel collides with the system of missionaries whose program is not good news (cf. Gal 1:6–7). Issues will be sharpened in what follows. 9b suggests righteousness in conduct; 9c, saving, justifying righteousness from God; 3:15–17 will (re)turn to matters of conduct. On the ch. as a whole, cf. *ABD* 5:763.

The eschatological question continues in 9bc. 8e–9a offer present and future eschatology ("already, not yet"). Such a description also fits references to righteousness/ justification.[41] *dikaiosynē* is a term of continuity ("God who justifies," Rom 8:33), involving "initial acceptance by God" and "God continuing to exercise his justifying righteousness with a view to the final act of judgment and acquittal" (Dunn, *TPTA* 386). Of adjs. used to characterize Paul's views (Dib. 69; K. Barth 99), "forensic" or "juridical" are pertinent, for God's judgment at the End and a verdict moved up through faith to the present. "Mystical" (union) applied via the "in Christ" theme (*TPTA* 393–95) is not always helpful.

Repetition in 9d of *faith* has led to all sorts of theories about *pistis* and the relation of *epi tē[i] pistei* to what precedes and follows. The NOTE outlines five construals. The subj. gen. is urged sometimes for 9c "Christ's faith(fulness)," and in 9d the believer's response—too clever a solution for Paul's readers to have grasped. Better: "the *(tē[i])* faith" just mentioned—redundant in theories about Christ's believing (Hays 1983 [(4) Bibl.] mentions 3:9 only in a list of passages assigned by *TNDT* 6:204 n 230 to the obj. gen. sense for *Christou*). But if 9c = *faith*

---

[41] Based on the Christ event in the past (Rom 3:25), continuing in the preaching of the gospel (Rom 3:21, 24) and experienced in the present by believers from the outset of their new life (1 Cor 6:11; Rom 5:1, cf. 6:7). There is clearly a future side (Gal 5:5; Rom 3:30; 5:19), above all at the final judgment ("Day of the Lord" references).

in Christ, 9d has a clear function with v 10 (construal [5] in the NOTE): *on the basis of faith,* the believing trust in Christ just mentioned, 10a *to know him and the power of his resurrection and participation in his sufferings* b *while being conformed to his death. . . .* Faith grounds knowing Christ, crucified and risen. *tēn dia pisteōs Christou . . . dikaiosynēn, epi tē[i] pistei* is a striking reference to righteousness/ justification—and more—pronounced on the basis of faith. The "more" involves knowing Christ re two specific events in the story of Jesus and their implications for believers.

We rest v 10 on 9d (*"to know* Christ" depends on *faith in Christ;* knowledge *"by means of pistis,"* D. K. Williams 2002:186), and behind that on *righteousness* by faith (9bc), and ultimately on the assessment Paul made in vv 8a and 8d (*I consider* past heritage and accomplishments as *loss,* Christ as *gain* for me). This helps explain how the infin. in 10a has sometimes been regarded as parallel to the two *hina* cls. in 8e and 9a (*in order that I may gain Christ and be found in him,* with which *to know* Christ is coordinated, Koperski 1996:170–77; cf. Moule, *IB* 128– 29; RSV) and has sometimes been regarded as loosely explanatory of 8e and 9a or a result of being in Christ, justified (NLT), or even a new sentence, stating in different words Paul's real concern (NEB/REB). Paul can shift sentence structures (anacoluthon). But *hina* at 10a would break the intimate connection with *epi tē[i] pistei.* The art. infin. in the gen. avoids that.[42] The purpose aspect may be less pronounced than in the *hina* construction.

Earlier Paul spoke of *knowing Christ Jesus* (8b), possibly a phrase from the enemies. Now he indicates more fully what is known. At most, three dir. objects, *him* (= Christ), *the power of his resurrection,* and *participation in his sufferings.* But the last two, with a single art., are a closely structured hendiadys, "the power-of-Christ's-resurrection-and-sharing-in-his-sufferings." You cannot have one without the other. Some would make this phrase appositional to *him,* Christ both risen and suffering; Gdsp.; cf. Moffatt. But why the sequence *resurrection,* then *sufferings*? An impossible order in any story of Jesus, it is straightened out in 10b–11, *death* then *resurrection*; cf. Koester 1961–62:323 n 4. *pathēmata* (see NOTE on *sufferings*) more likely refers to the apostle's sufferings (and those of other Christians, 1:29, the Philippians) than to the historical Jesus' passion. Then "the power of Christ's resurrection" provides "the ability to endure suffering for Christ's sake" (O'B 404; cf. K. Barth 104; Loh. 138–39, martyrs, contrast Siber 114 [Exc. A Bibl.] n 61); or to know Christ "*in* the power of his resurrection" (Moffatt, cf. Gdsp.) transforms a person, inner subjective experience (Hawth. 143–44); or resurrection-power = spiritual activity of the exalted Christ in the earthly life of Paul and every believer (via baptism and incorporation in the body of Christ, Gnilka 196; or as an ethical paradigm). Still others, a power operative in the past, present, and future (Forestell 124), related to baptism (Beare 122–24) or subjective experience (Vincent 104). Dramatically put, "The righteousness of God . . . has raised us from the dead with Christ. That is where you begin; and then you set

---

[42] Cf. other instances of noun (in a prep. phrase) + the infin. (3:21 *kata tēn energeian tou dynasthai auton;* 1 Cor 9:10; 16:4 with *axion;* 2 Cor 8:11; Rom 15:23; 1:24; 8:12; 1 Cor 10:13).

about dying in order to attain the resurrection of the dead" (Synge, *Phil.* 2nd ed. 1958:43). "To know Easter means . . . to be implicated in the events of Good Friday" (K. Barth 103). More in Koperski 1996:178–79. All these attempts to make sense of the resurrection-sufferings sequence avoid the possibility that the order is dictated by the enemies; so, in varying forms, Schmithals; Martin 1976:134; Siber (Exc. A Bibl.) 111, 115–22; Bouwman 85–86; Collange 131, and esp. Schenk. The enemies put emphasis on "resurrection power" and *koinōnia* therein, likely also "being conformed" to that. They start with *resurrection*, followed by *koinōnia* (Paul adds *"in sufferings,"* against their understanding of participation); 10b–11 correct the sequence, *death*, then *resurrection*, normal in narrative and Paul's theology.[43]

A clash over *resurrection* is apparent. The enemies stress it as a present experience (Christians "already raised," perhaps through baptism). Paul adds *autou, his* resurrection, of Christ. Ours will come later (vv 11, 20–21). In so doing, he tacitly fills a gap in the encomium by the Philippians (2:6–11). 2:8 mentioned Christ's death but went directly to exaltation (2:9–11), without the basic kerygmatic theme, "God raised Jesus from the dead." Problems with Jesus' bodily resurrection and implications for believers were endemic to Paul's congregations in Macedonia and Greece.[44] Converts in Greco-Roman Philippi failed to understand or emphasize the resurrection of Christ and so were vulnerable to opponents stressing the term and "perfection now" (vv 12–14), rather than progressing but arriving at the goal only at the End. Gnilka 197, Schenk 321–22, Harnisch 145–46 note Paul's polemical concern here.

From the Jesus story, vv 10–11 pick out his *death* (10b) and *resurrection* (10a), not how he believed or any detail in his life, like circumcision or being under the Law, points to which Paul could have alluded (Gal 4:4–5, AB 33A: 389–90, 406–8). The "I"-account continues through 9b (*my righteousness*) and 11 (*"I"*), implying my knowledge and participation, but shaped by phrases likely from "the enemies." He takes up points from the kerygma, some unstressed in Philippian belief (*resurrection*), some like *sufferings* very real in their situation. *power* and *participation* are sometimes overlooked. The first is a word about potency, ultimately from God, regularly connected with Christ in Paul, power shown in the raising up of Jesus and impacting believers now (see NOTE on *dynamis*). The vb. root appeared in Letter A for God strengthening Paul (4:13). If used by the opponents, it was likely in the phrase "power of resurrection," but *his* ties it to Jesus'

---

[43] Cf. Rom 10:8–10, "confess with your lips" followed by "believe with the heart," because of the sequence in Paul's source (v 8 = Deut 30:14 mouth, heart); then in 10:10 he gives the proper order, "believes with the heart and so is justified . . . confesses with the mouth and so is saved." Similarly at 1 Cor 10:16, "blood . . . body" (usually in eucharistic formulas "body," then "blood," 11:24–25), reversed to attach a comment on "body of Christ" as "church."

[44] Besides the Lukan account about preaching Jesus and "the resurrection" in Athens (Acts 17:31–34), cf. 1 Thess 4:13–5:11, where Christians had problems when the first few of their community died; Corinthians boggled over whether there is any resurrection of the dead (15:12, traditionally taken to imply Gk. philosophical rejection of resurrection; more likely, overrealized eschatology, "we are already raised," as in 2 Tim 2:18). Cf. Thurston 125.

resurrection. Implications for believers will come in v 11 (Paul's hope *to attain the resurrection from the dead*) and in v 21 (future transformation of Christians corporately at the parousia is attributed to the active expression of the risen Christ's operative power).[45]

koinōnia is important in Paul (Phil 1:5; 2:1; vb. at 4:15; compounds at 1:7 and 4:14), though not the theme of Phil. It was a concept widespread in the world of the day, familiar to Philippians and useful to "the enemies," a word as vague and enticing as "fellowship" nowadays. *koinōnia* could fit Sanders' reinterpretation of "justification" as "eschatological *participation,*" his contrasting term to "covenantal nomism" (*PPJ* 502–8; discussion in Reumann 1982 [(2) Bibl. **righteousness**] ##217–22, cf. 408). At 3:10a, it introduces a jarring note: "participation in *sufferings.*" The 1st per. narrative refers to Paul's involvement in *pathēmata,* such as he often catalogues (2 Cor 11:23–27, e.g.); then the Philippians' sufferings (1:28) and those of other Christians (2 Cor 1:5–7; 1 Thess 2:14; Gal 3:4; 1 Cor 12:26; Rom 8:18). *his* sufferings can suggest (see NOTE) Jesus' "passion" (references in Paul are sparse) or "sufferings of the Messianic age" (Col 1:24; Jewish sources early enough to influence Paul are not certain). To the jargon word *koinōnia,* Paul has attached "sufferings," and to that *autou* for the same emphasis (christocentric) as in *power of his resurrection;* possible "sufferings for him." The sequence in the Jesus story will be set forth chronologically in 10b–11. Wolter 1990 connects the apostle's sufferings with Christ's destiny in suffering ("Leidensgeschick Jesu Christi") and the community as participant in the apostle's destiny in suffering via friendship terms.[46] 10a and 10b relate closely (see above, discussion of *his sufferings* and *his death*). 3:11 relates and contrasts with 10a through the word *resurrection.* Cf. the chiasm (NOTE on 10b, cited in Eng.):

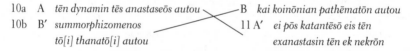

10a   A   *tēn dynamin tēs anastaseōs autou*   B   *kai koinōnian pathēmatōn autou*
10b   B′   *summorphizomenos*   11 A′   *ei pōs katantēsō eis tēn*
         tō[i] thanatō[i] autou   *exanastasin tēn ek nekrōn*

A and B form one integrated object phrase with just one art. *(tēn),* and so should not be too sharply sundered. B′ A′ are both are "I" statements. The linked words vary: *anastasis* has an additional prefix in A′; in B B′ *sufferings* and *death* are related but are not synonymous; *participation in his sufferings* has a broader meaning than Jesus' passion, as sufferings of the apostle (and other Christians). But B′ involves Paul's being conformed to *his death.* ABB′A′ connections here are not a perfect fit; chiasms do not always match. Disparities may stem from *dynamin tēs anastaseōs, koinōnia, symmorphizomenos,* and *exanastasin* as terms from the enemies (A.2.d, above). Paul works with, but counters, their language.

---

[45] Two corollaries of Jesus' resurrection (Nickelsburg, *ABD* 5:689) are apparent: expectation of an imminent parousia (Phil 3:20); the final resurrection of all Christians (3:21, moderated for Paul at 1:21–25); the Spirit of the risen Christ at work (Rom 6 and 8) is missing.

[46] Clitarchus, *Sent.* 90, "Consider *(hēgou)* the misfortunes of friends as your own, but share *(koinōnei)* your own good fortunes with friends" (H. Chadwick, ed., *The Sentences of Sextus,* TS 5 [Cambridge: Cambridge Univ. Press, 1959] 80).

In 10b, Paul's autobiography picks up afresh, *being conformed to* Christ's *death*. The language reflects baptism, though *baptisma* is not used; cf. Rom 6:3–4, "baptized into his death"; 1 Cor 6:11, "washed"; ABD 7:759,e. Baptism points toward, in the future, being "united with Christ in a resurrection like his" (Rom 6:5). God's power is the common factor (1 Cor 6:14). Some try a link with Phil 2:6–11, via Christ's *death*, but *resurrection* and *righteousness* are lacking there; *faith* too, unless it simply means "obedience" (2:8). It is too much to claim Paul's "own former motivation of pride [in 3:5–7] has given way to one of Christ-like humility" (Bockmuehl 216); *tapeinophrosynē* terms do not appear in ch. 3 till and only at v 21. *being conformed* means by God, the One behind *resurrection*, 10a, as well as justifying *righteousness*, 9c, in an ongoing process throughout Paul's life in Christ. NRSV's "by becoming like him in his death" may obscure resurrection-power at work before the parousia; cf. 2 Cor 4:10–11.[47] Better, *while being conformed to* Christ's *death*, one finds God's power is at work, in Jesus' resurrection and as the effective factor in ours to come.

3:11 points to that future resurrection. The vb. *attain*, "arriving at" this event on the Last Day, is in keeping with pressing on to a goal in vv 12–14.[48] Efforts have been made to give *exanastasis* in v 11 a different sense from *anastasis* in 10a[49]; the NOTE finds only rhetorical variation in the terms, a verbal distinction from the language of the enemies. The most difficult phrase is *if, hopefully* (see NOTE; indic. with *ei; pōs*, "perhaps," "somehow").[50] Some see no uncertainty or doubt (O'B 411–14); Paul's hope is sure and certain; Gnilka 197, a polemical distinction from the opponents, a factor overlooked by Forestell). Koester 1961–62:323–24, against those who think their resurrection has already occurred. But total elimination of uncertainty for *ei pōs* is hard to pull off. Others find the uncertainty over *how*, not *that*, Paul will attain to resurrection from the dead; events between now and the End are uncertain (Motyer 170; O'B 413: martyrdom? will Paul live until the parousia? Morlet 133). Still others, distrust of himself (Vincent 106), plus humility (Hawth. 148; Silva 192–93). R. E. Otto (cf. Thurston 128–29) revived the unlikely theory of a first resurrection for martyrs; "*real* doubt . . . in Paul's mind

---

[47] M. Byrnes provides a detailed study of the 1st. sg. passage in Phil and the 1st pl. segment in 2 Cor (power belonging to God, death "at work in us," our future resurrection).

[48] Paul never makes an "I" statement like Luther's Small Catechism, "I believe that . . . Jesus Christ . . . the Holy Spirit [or God] . . . will raise me up" (Creed, Third Article), even at Phil 1:20–26. 2 Cor 4:13–14 may come closest.

[49] Lft. 151, 3:11 = the resurrection of Christ and those who rise with Christ *ek nekrōn* (Luke 20:30; 1 Peter 1:3; Acts 4:2); 10a *anastasis* (of the dead) (1 Cor 15:42; John 5:29) = the general resurrection of both good and bad. Few accept the distinction; it doesn't fit 10a (his *anastasis*). Others, the reality of (bodily) resurrection "from among the physical dead" (Gnilka 197; Martin 1976:135), or resurrection just for martyrs (Loh. 138–42), or directly after the individual's death (cf. 1:23 "with Christ," but *not* "resurrection," Volz 2nd ed. 1934:270; more in O'B 414–15, with Gnilka). Siber (Exc. A Bibl.) 119–20 rejects all these efforts.

[50] Edart 239–41, 263–64 calls *ei pōs* . . . a *dubitio* or expression of uncertainty (Lausberg #776–79), contrast the certitude of 1:23; 3:20–21. 3:11 = a redactoral addition to Letter B (an unneeded proposal).

about his maintaining his confession in his impending death" (330).[51] Beare 125–28, attainment of blessedness for Christians at the Parousia.

Some uncertainty, perhaps in contrast to cocksureness of opponents, should be permitted the apostle, who in 1:19–26 anguished over *life* and *death*, with *expectation and hope*, as well as concern about being put to *shame* (1:20, which Otto might have invoked even more). Distrust of self or humility seem read in. *pōs* cannot bear the sense of "somehow" interpreted as "in what way" rather than of "indefiniteness" (Silva 192). It does carry a note of expectation, expressed by the idiomatic *hopefully*, a wistful expression not as strong as "I hope." Involved also may be *certitudo* on Paul's part, but not *securitas*.[52]

Verses 10b–11 tilts eschatology toward "the future perspective" (Rogahn 125–29; Koperski 1996:180–88). 10b anchors the believer's relation to future resurrection in presently being conformed to the crucified Christ. That is so whether behind this "morphization" of the individual one sees baptism and its implications ("with Christ" in the water, "in Christ" throughout life, "with Christ" fully after the parousia and judgment); participationalist language (*koinōnia*-justification); a "pattern" of experience based on Christ's, applicable to believers (Koperski 1996:266–75)[53]; or the idea of "daily resurrection" (Baumert 1973:396, realized eschatology).

3. *Phil 3:4b–11 in the Redacted Letter.* Many meanings presented above for Letter C continued in the canonical four-ch. document, though some features are obscured. "The enemies" and the great reversal in Paul's life should be all the more important in a single letter, for they take over so completely that he delays his paraenesis and thanks for the gifts from Philippi.

In actuality, treating 3:4b–11 within a longer letter has often diminished the overall importance of vv 4b–11. Koperski 1996:2 sought to show that "Phil 3:7–11 is fully as strong (if not stronger) a christological claim as the hymn" in 2:6–11. But 3:7–11 does not occupy a place anywhere near the towering influence of 2:6–11. *Law* and *righteousness* end up as less significant, because *nomos* occurs in Phil only at 3:5,6,8 and *dikaiosynē* at 3:6 and 9 plus 1:11 (adj. at 1:7 and 4:8). Treatments on "Paul and the Law" or righteousness/justification regularly focus on Gal and Rom, with little attention to the few references in four-ch. canonical

---

[51] Otto distinguishes (in n 20) his view from Loh. 138–42, a "preconceived and unproven thesis" (cf. Mengel 178–83). Otto's supporting data (Wis 3:8; Col 1:24; Acts 7:59) scarcely provide much certainty for a special resurrection of martyrs (Matt 27:52–53; Rev 20:4–5) on Paul's part. Contrast Bockmuehl 89, 217: Paul has no separate category for martyrs (so above, on 1:23, Exc. A.6). Otto's view does not work for Letter C (no evidence that Paul is imprisoned). In a four-ch. letter it ill accords with the overall outlook in 1:19–26 and 2:24.

[52] On "certainty" and "security" in later theology, cf. J. Schniewind, "Gewissheit—Nicht Sicherheit" (1935), repr. in his *Zur Erneuerung des Christenstandes*, ed. H.-J. Kraus and O. Michel, Kleine Vandenhoeck-Reihe 226/227 (Göttingen: Vandenhoeck & Ruprecht, 1966) 33–44; Bouttier 1966 ([1] Bibl. **in Christ**) 37.

[53] Perriman would see personal meditation, not a statement about all believers (contrast Peterlin 86; D. K. Williams 2002:196 n 186), and death, not rapture.

Phil.[54] This heart of Letter C becomes in the canonical epistle a complicated passage with many themes and agendas, often unrelated to other parts of Phil. Some find unity by imposing themes or patterns on the passage (Silva: justification, sanctification, glorification for 3:9–11; Fee, past, present, and future), not wrong, but more precise than ch. 3 is.

Treating 3:4b–11 in a unified epistle has lifted up or (over)emphasized certain elements in light of the rest of Phil. Paul writes from prison (1:12–14), facing possible death. That allows closer linkage of *participation* in Christ's *sufferings* (3:10a) with Paul's "suffering in my imprisonment" (1:17, NRSV; Gk. *thlipsin*) and suffering by Philippian Christians at the hands of local opponents (1:28–29, *paschein*; we assume carryover of the latter, even if in an earlier letter). Hence Loh. and R. E. Otto claimed Paul looked to, or feared for, his own constancy as he faced martyrdom that would bring him resurrection in advance of nonmartyrs (rejected above, as by most who treat Phil as a unity). *koinōnia* at 3:10a has provided support for that theme as central in the letter. But 3:10 is the most difficult of all the examples from the word-family (see NOTE on 1:5) to integrate.[55] *participation in . . . sufferings* is often passed over; it does not readily fit with *partnership* (in the gospel) or financial sharing. Or is it a neglected key? If no likeness to Christ in sufferings or death, no conformity to his resurrection life.

For many interpreters, 2:6–11 influences 3:4b–11 in specific ways. See A.2.b, above, on points from "the 'story' of Jesus" in the "hymn" (better: encomium, a term also applied to 3:4–11, A.2.a, above) claimed in 3:8–11 (Bloomquist, Fowl 1990, Bockmuehl; and some who reject *pistis Christou* as subj. gen., Silva, O'B, and Fee). The case is weakened by failure to build 3:8–11 into this "story." Hays 1983, e.g., dealt with Gal; 1997 with Rom; for Phil he relied on Hooker 1989:331–33, who heard an "echo of Philippians 2" in 3:7–11, in the vb. "consider" and a pattern of "'interchange' between Christ and the believer." Not the "joyous interchange" *(fröhlicher Wechsel)* of Reformation theology (Christ's righteousness and human sin, humans gladly give up the latter in exchange for the former), but an "'interchange' of experience." The "echo" suggests *pistis Christou* at 3:9c "ought to refer to the obedient self-surrender of Christ," for Paul "abandoning every-

---

[54] It is worthwhile beginning Paul's views on justification with this astutely theological, experiential self-description, rather than the exegetical passages in Rom or polemical narrative in Gal; cf. Reumann 2006.

[55] Aspan finds a "call to *koinonia*" in 1:3–11 and 4:2–9, but 3:10 is for him part of a separate letter (pp. 179–80, 217–28, 238 chart, 264–70; 282–87; summary in Pretorius 1995:280–82. Geoffrion 83–104 makes *koinōnia* more political, linked to the *politeuma* of 3:20. Neither makes much of 3:10 (at best, Geoffrion 44). Swift, "the Philippians' partnership in the gospel" (1:5) is "the central theme of the epistle" (237), but ch. 3 is "closely associated with chapter 2" (247), no reference to 3:10. Wick's concentric analysis at one point calls *koinōnia* "the basic theme of the entire letter" (p. 14, esp. in 1:5 and 7), but it seems to end up a "subordinate theme" (concerning community and unity) to Christ's attitude in the "hymn" and the "call to joy" (142–51); summary in Pretorius 1998:17–21. *koinōnia* plays no role in Wicks' "Einheit A" blocks that match 1:12–26 and 3:1–16 (pp. 41–43).

thing . . . in order to win the prize"; it amounts to "conformity to those attitudes which led Christ to submit to death" (332).[56]

Vocabulary links between 2:5–11 and 3:4–11 are more limited than often assumed. Of the list above in A.2.b, *kyrios* is so common a title that little can be rested on it; 2:11 explains how Jesus came to be so acclaimed in the cosmos; at 3:8 it is personal, *Christ Jesus my Lord*. As to *euriskō*, Jesus "being found as a mortal" (2:7), Paul "found in him" (3:9), are scarcely parallels; see NOTE on varied uses of the term. At 2:7 *morphē* = "form of God" and "form of a slave"—or, better, *sphere*—while 3:10 *symmorphizomenos* applies to our being conformed to, or "adopting the form" (Bockmuehl) of, Christ's death, not dual forms of his "person." The vb. *hēgeomai*, Hooker's starting point (3:7, 8a, 8d), expresses what Paul has come to regard as gains or loss; at 2:6, something Christ did not consider "being equal with God" to be. Garland 1985:171 n 103 cites commentators who parallel "Christ's self-emptying and Paul's account of his own self-emptying"; but Paul does not set Law and circumcision aside in order to resume them later, as Jesus apparently does with whatever he gave up in becoming human. Better (N. T. Wright 1991:88) Paul understood Israel and such things "in a new way." Some work with broader ideas than just vocabulary. Thus Bouttier 1966 ([1] Bibl. **in Christ**) 17; or Wick 72:

Hymn: be in the form of God	3:2–11	Jewish descent
be like God		righteousness according to the Law
not consider it robbery (*hēgeomai*)		consider it a loss (*hēgeomai*)
exaltation over all		gain Christ (or participation in the resurrection)

To Wick, 3:10b–11 is practically synonymous with 2:5–11, expressing the right "mind" needed (73). But Wick 41–43 lists a similarly impressive set of words and themes to connect 3:1–16 with 1:12–26 in his chiastic concentric structure for the entire letter (e.g., "death," in a report about himself, involving "opponents" and "joy").

In relating 2:6–11 and the opponents of ch. 3, one cannot (cf. Summey 1999:179–80) claim the enemies derived their views from a radical (mis)interpretation of the "hymn" (esp. if an encomium by the Philippians that these enemies may not even have known). But Paul could be concerned about the Philippians' theology in 2:9–11, which ends with cosmic adoration of the *Kyrios*: his beloved Philippians were vulnerable to a message promising them access to the heavenly realm apart from suffering, without the future general resurrection, exaltation without suffering, physical death, and bodily resurrection at the parou-

---

[56] Cf. Hooker's "Interchange in Christ," *JTS* 22 (1971) 349–61; "Interchange and Atonement," *BJRL* 60 (1978) 462–81; "Interchange and Suffering," in *Suffering and Martyrdom in the New Testament*, ed. W. Horbury/B. McNeil (Cambridge: Cambridge Univ. Press 1981) 70–83; "Interchange in Christ and Ethics," *JSNT* 25 (1985) 3–17. The master thought is "Christ entering into our experience and we into his." Christ is representative (new Adam), not substitute; like us that we might become like him (Irenaeus, in a behavioristic mode). Hays is concerned to preserve the *extra nos* quality of salvation, "outside ourselves"; "narrative" theology versus that which is "experiential-expressive" (Hays 1997:56). Cf. Dunn, *TPTA* 383 n 200 and 384 n 209; and 1997:78–79, critique on "interchange."

sia and last judgment. Cf. Koester 1961–62:321; Fowl 1990:99; B. Dodd 178–80. These concerns will come to light in 3:12–21.

The contents of 3:4b–11 are a response, autobiographical and theological, instructing the Philippians, in the face of threatening enemies. Saul the Pharisee describes himself along with Paul the Christian *(en Christō[i])*. There is continuity as well as contrast in the person, his heritage, and commitments.[57] Past and present experiences are best seen in the terms *Law* and *righteousness*, used of both Saul and Paul. Paul discards *Law* as a way of entry for Gentiles via *circumcision* or the means for being *blameless* or perfected. *Righteousness* remains important, not what the Law calls for; rather it comes from God through faith in Christ, saving righteousness or justification. Being raised by God was the crucial step for Jesus; it will be for believers, at the End, *from the dead*. Meanwhile, between Christ's resurrection and ours, life means conformity to Jesus' *death* and participation in *sufferings* for Christ, not resurrection as a present possession.

3:4b–11 is significant in treatments of Paul's life (J. Becker 1993 [(1) Bibl. **Paul**]) and for certain themes (J. Becker, beyond "election" and "the cross," "justification," Paul's "functional Christology"; *to know Christ* 3:10a). Little used in traditional Western lectionaries. The *Ordo* gives the vv more exposure than at any time in lectionary history (Lent 5 Year C, 3:8–14; Revised Common Lectionary, 3:4b–14; Proper 22 [27 in some numberings]).

SELECT BIBLIOGRAPHY (see also General Bibliography and Commentaries)

Aguilar Chiu, J. E. 2003. *La justificación y el Espíritu en Pablo*. European University Studies, Series XXIII Theology, Vol. 713. Bern/New York, etc.: Peter D. Lang. Diss., Inst. Pontifico Biblico 2000 (Vanhoye).

Ahern, B. M. 1960. "The Fellowship of His Sufferings (Phil. 3,10)—A Study of St. Paul's Doctrine on Christian Suffering," *CBQ* 22:1–32. Cf. his "In Phil 3,10–11," *VD* 37 (1959) 26–31.

Baeck, L. 1927. "Die Pharisäer," repr. in *Paulus, die Pharisäer und das Neue Testament*. Frankfurt am Main: Ner-Tamid Verlag, 1961. Pp. 39–98.

Betz, O. 1976. "Rechtfertigung in Qumran," in *Rechtfertigung*, FS Käsemann, ed. J. Friedrich et al. (Tübingen: Mohr Siebeck/Göttingen: Vandenhoeck & Ruprecht) 17–36.

———. 1977. "Paulus als Pharisäer nach dem Gesetz. Phil 3,5–6 als Beitrag zur Frage des frühen Pharisäismus," in *Treue zur Thora. Beiträge zur Mitte des christlich-jüdischen Gesprächs*. FS G. Harder, ed. P. von der Osten-Sacken, Institut Kirche und Judentum bei der Kirchlichen Hochschule Berlin, 3 (Berlin) 54–64.

———. 1990. "Die Übersetzung von Jes 53 (LXX, Targum) und die Theologia Crucis des Paulus," in his GS, *Jesus: Der Herr der Kirche, Aufsätze zur biblischen Theologie*, WUNT 52 (Tübingen: Mohr Siebeck) 2:197–216.

Blank, J. 1968. "Phil 3,6–11," in *Paulus und Jesus: Eine theologische Grundlegung*, SANT 18 (Munich: Kösel) 214–22, 231–38.

Boers, H. 1993. "Polysemy in Paul's Use of Christological Expressions," in *The Future of*

---

[57] On biographical and theological alienation in what some called the "two halves" of Paul's life and his "status change," yet continuing "identity," see Gremmels.

Christology, FS L. E. Keck, ed. A. J. Malherbe/W. A. Meeks (Minneapolis: Fortress) 91–108.

Bultmann, R. 1964. "*DIKAIOSYNĒ THEOU*," *JBL* 83:12–16.

Byrnes, M. 2003. *Conformation to the Death of Christ and the Hope of Resurrection. An Exegetico-Theological Study of 2 Corinthians 4,7–15 and Philippians 3,7–11*. Tesi Gregoriana Serie teologia 99. Rome: Pontificia Università Gregoriana.

Carson, D. A., P. T. O'Brien, M. A. Seifrid, eds. 2001. *Justification and Variegated Nomism. Volume I. The Complexities of Second Temple Judaism*. WUNT 2/140. Tübingen: Mohr Siebeck/Grand Rapids: Baker Academic. *Volume 2. The Paradoxes of Paul*, 2004.

Cosgrove, C. H. 1987. "Justification in Paul," *JBL* 106:653–70.

Deidun, T. 1986. "Having His Cake and Eating It. Paul on the Law," *HayJ* 17:43–52.

Deines, R. 1997. *Die Pharisäer: Ihr Verständnis im Spiegel der christlichen und jüdischen Forschung seit Wellhausen und Graetz*. WUNT 101. Tübingen: Mohr Siebeck. Review essay, J. Meier, *CBQ* 61 (1999) 713–22.

———. 2001. "The Pharisees Between 'Judaisms' and 'Common Judaism,'" in Carson et al., eds. (above), *Justification and Variegated Nomism* 1:443–504.

Di Marco, A.-S. 1993. "Rhetoric and Hermeneutic—on a Rhetorical Pattern: Chiasmus and Circularity," in Porter/Olbricht, eds., 479–91.

Donaldson, T. L. 1989. "Zealot and Convert: The Origin of Paul's Christ-Torah Antithesis," *CBQ* 51:655–82.

Duling, D. C. 2003. "'Whatever Gain I Had . . .': Ethnicity and Paul's Self-Identification in Philippians 3:5–6," in FS Robbins (Gen. Bibl., s.v. "Sisson") 222–41.

Dunn, J. D. G. 1997. "Once More, *PISTIS CHRISTOU*," *PT* 4: 61–81.

Espy, J. M. 1985. "Paul's 'Robust Conscience' Re-examined," *NTS* 31:161–88.

Fitzmyer, J. A. 1970. "To Know Him and the Power of His Resurrection; Phil. 3:10," *Mélanges biblique en homage au R. P. Béda Rigaux*, ed. A. Descamps/A. de Halleux (Gembloux: Duculot) 411–25; cited from repr. in Fitzmyer's *To Advance the Gospel: New Testament Studies* (New York: Crossroad, 1981) 202–17.

Forestell, J. T. 1956. "Christian Perfection and Gnosis in Phil. 3,7–16," *CBQ* 18:123–36.

Gärtner, B. 1967–68. "The Pauline and Johannine Idea 'To Know God' Against the Hellenistic Background," *NTS* 14:209–31.

Goguel, M. 1934. "*Kata dikaiosynēn tēn en nomō[i] genomenos amemptos* (Phil. 3,6). Remarques sur un aspect de la conversion de Paul," *JBL* 53:257–67.

Gremmels, C. 1974. "Selbstreflexive Interpretation konfligierender Identifikation am Beispiel des Apostels Paulus (Phil. 3,7–9)," *Theologische Existenz heute* 182:44–57.

Haacker, K. 1971–72. "War Paulus Hillelit?" *Das Institutum Iudaicum der Universität Tübingen* 106–20.

———. 1975. "Die Berufung des Verfolgers und die Rechtfertigung des Gottlosen," *TBei* 6:1–19.

Harrisville, R. A. 1994. "*PISTIS CHRISTOU*: Witness of the Fathers," *NovT* 36:233–41.

Harvey, G. 1996. *The True Israel. Uses of the Names Jew, Hebrew and Israel in Ancient Jewish and Early Christian Literature*. AGJU 35. Leiden: Brill, repr. 2001.

Hays, R. B. 1997. "*PISTIS* and Pauline Christology: What Is at Stake?" *PT* 4:35–60.

Hengel, M. 1988. *The Zealots*. Edinburgh: T&T Clark. Ger. 2nd ed. 1976.

Hoerber, R. G. 1996. "Paul's Conversion/Call," *ConcJour* 22:186–88.

Hooker, M. D. 1989. "PISTIS CHRISTOU," *NTS* 35:321–49, repr. in her *From Adam to Christ* (Cambridge: Cambridge Univ. Press, 1990) 165–86.

Howard, G. 1973–74. "The 'Faith of Christ,'" *ExpTim* 85:212–14.

Hübner, H. 1973. "Gal 3,10 und die Herkunft des Paulus," *KD* 19:215–31.

———. 1984b. *Law in Paul's Thought.* Edinburgh: T & T Clark.

Hultgren, A. J. 1976. "Paul's Pre-Christian Persecutions of the Church: Their Purpose, Locale and Nature," *JBL* 95:97–111.

———. 1980. "The *Pistis Christou* Formulation in Paul," *NovT* 22:248–63.

———. 1985. *Paul's Gospel and Mission: The Outlook from His Letter to the Romans.* Philadelphia: Fortress.

Jeremias, J. 1969b. "Paulus als Hillelit," in *Neotestamentica et Semitica,* FS M. Black, ed. E. E. Ellis/M. Wilcox (Edinburgh: T & T Clark) 88–94.

Käsemann, E. 1969. "'The Righteousness of God' in Paul," in his *New Testament Questions of Today* (Philadelphia: Fortress) 168–82.

———. 1971b. "Justification and Salvation History in the Epistle to the Romans," in his *Perspectives on Paul* (Philadelphia: Fortress) 60–78. Ger. 1965.

Kaylor, R. D. 1988. *Paul's Covenant Community: Jew and Gentile in Romans.* Atlanta: John Knox.

Klaiber, W. 1982. *Rechtfertigung und Gemeinde: Eine Untersuchung zum paulinischen Kirchenverständnis.* FRLANT 127. Göttingen: Vandenhoeck & Ruprecht.

Koperski, V. 1995. "The Meaning of *dikaiosynē* in Philippians 3:9," *LouvStudies* 20:147–69.

———. 1996. *The Knowledge of Christ Jesus My Lord: The High Christology of Philippians 3:7–11.* CBET 16. Kampen: Pharos.

Laato, T. 1995. *Paul and Judaism: An Anthropological Approach.* South Florida Studies in the History of Judaism 115. Atlanta: Scholars Press.

Léon-Dufour, X. 1974. "When a Witness Speaks. In the Epistle to the Philippians," *Resurrection and the Message of Easter* (New York: Holt, Rinehart and Winston) 151–55 (French 1971).

Malherbe, A. J. 1998. "Conversion to Paul's Gospel," in Malherbe et al., eds., *The Early Church in Its Context,* FS E. Ferguson, NovTSup 90 (Leiden: Brill) 231–44.

Martínez, A. E. 2002. "Filipenses 3:4–11 y la conversión de Pablo como proceso de resocialización," *Apuntes* 22:44–63.

Matlock, R. B. 2000. "Detheologizing the *PISTIS CHRISTOU* Debate: Cautionary Remarks from a Lexical Semantic Perspective," *NovT* 42:1–23.

———. 2002. "'Even the Demons Believe': Paul and *pistis Christou,*" *CBQ* 64:300–18.

Moffatt, J. 1912–13. "Found in Him," *ExpTim* 24:46.

Neusner, J. 1979. *From Politics to Piety: The Emergence of Pharisaic Judaism.* New York: KTAV.

Otto, R. E. 1995. "'If Possible I May Attain the Resurrection from the Dead' (Philippians 3:11)," *CBQ* 57:324–40.

Overman, J. A. 2002. "Kata Nomon Pharisaios: A Short History of Paul's Pharisaism," in *Pauline Conversations in Context: Essays in Honor of Calvin J. Roetzel,* ed. J. C. Anderson et al., JSNTSS 221 (London/New York: Sheffield Academic Press) 180–93.

Owen, J. J. 1864. "Examination of Philip. III.11 and Rev. XX.4," *BSac* 21:362–83.

Pate, C. M. 2000. *The Reverse of the Curse. Paul, Wisdom, and the Law.* WUNT 2/114. Tübingen: Mohr Siebeck.

Perriman, A. 1991. "The Pattern of Christ's Sufferings: Colossians 1:24 and Philippians 3:10–11," *TynBul* 42:62–79.

Plevnik, J. 1986. "Recent Developments in the Discussion Concerning Justification by Faith," *TJT* 2:47–62.

Räisänen, H. 1983. *Paul and the Law.* Philadelphia: Fortress.

———. 1987. "Paul's Conversion and the Development of his View of the Law," *NTS* 33:404–19.

Reumann, J. 2002. "Resurrection in Philippi and Paul's Letter(s) to the Philippians," in *Resurrection in the New Testament*, FS J. Lambrecht, ed. R. Bieringer/V. Koperski/ B. Lataire, BETL 165 (Leuven: Univ. Press) 407–22.

———. 2006a. "Justification by Faith in Pauline Thought: A Lutheran View," in *Rereading Paul Together: Protestant and Catholic Perspectives on Justification*, ed. D. E. Aune (Grand Rapids: Baker Academic), 108–30.

Robinson, D. W. B. 1970. "'Faith of Jesus Christ'—a NT Debate," *RTR* 29:71–81.

Roetzel, C. 1997. "No 'Race of Israel' in Paul," in *Putting Body & Soul Together*, FS R. Scroggs, ed. V. Wiles et al. (Valley Forge, PA: Trinity Press International) 230–44.

Rogahn, K. W. 1975. "The Function of Future-Eschatological Statements in the Pauline Epistles." Diss., Princeton Theological Seminary.

Sacchi, P. 2001. "From Righteousness to Justification in the Period of Hellenistic Judaism," *Henoch* 23:11–26.

Sanders, E. P. 1986. "Paul on the Law, His Opponents, and the Jewish People in Philippians 3 and 2 Corinthians 11," in *Anti-Judaism in Early Christianity, Vol. 1, Paul and the Gospels*, ed. P. Richardson/D. Granskou (Waterloo, Ont.: Wilfrid Laurier Press) 75–90.

Schreiner, T. R. 1985. "Paul and Perfect Obedience to the Law: An Evaluation of the View of E. P. Sanders," *WTJ* 47:245–78.

Smiles, V. M. 2002. "The Concept of 'Zeal' in Second-Temple Judaism and Paul's Critique of It in Romans 10:2," *CBQ* 64:282–99.

Snodgrass, K. 1988. "Spheres of Influence: A Possible Solution to the Problem of Paul and the Law," *JSNT* 32:93–113.

Strecker, G. 1976. "Befreiung und Rechtfertigung: Zur Stellung der Rechtfertigungslehre in der Theologie des Paulus," in FS Käsemann (above, under "Betz, O.," 1976) 479–508; repr. In Strecker's *Eschaton und Historie: Aufsätze* (Göttingen: Vandenhoeck & Ruprecht, 1979) 229–59.

Taylor, G. M. 1966. "The Function of *pistis Christou* in Galatians," *JBL* 85:58–76.

Theissen, G. 2002. "Röm 9–11—eine Auseinandersetzung des Paulus mit Israel und mit sich selbst: Versuch einer psychologischen Auslegung," in I. Dunderberg et al., eds., *Fair Play*, FS Räisänen (Gen.Bibl,, under Hooker, M.), 311–41.

Thielman, F. 1989. *From Plight to Solution: A Jewish Framework to Understanding Paul's View of the Law in Galatians and Romans.* NovTSup 61. Leiden: Brill.

Ulrichs, K. F. 2007. *Christusglaube. Studien zum Syntagma pistis Christou und zum paulinischen Verständnis von Glaube und Rechtfertigung* WUNT 2/227 (Tübingen: Mohr-Siebeck).

Vanhoye, A. 1999. "*Pistis Christou*: fede in Cristo o affidabilità di Cristo?" *Bib* 80:1–21.

Welch, J. W., ed. 1981. *Chiasmus in Antiquity: Structures, Analyses, Exegesis.* Hildesheim: Gerstenberg.

Westcott, F. B. 1913. *St Paul and Justification: Being an Exposition of the Teaching in the Epistles to Rome and Galatia.* London: Macmillan.

Williams, S. K. 1980. "The 'Righteousness of God' in Romans," *JBL* 99:241–90.

Wolter, W. 1990. "Der Apostel und seine Gemeinden als Teilhaber am Leidensgeschick Jesu Christi: Beobachtungen zur paulinischen Theologie," *NTS* 36:535–57.

Zeller, D. 2002. "Erscheinungen Verstorbener im griechisch-römischen Bereich," in FS J. Lambrecht, ed. R. Bieringer et al., 1–19.

13. *Paul and the Philippians: Running Toward the Goal, but Not Perfected, 3:12–16*

TRANSLATION

3:12a I do not say that I have already had success, ᵇ or that I have already been justified or am already perfected; ᶜ but I run in pursuit if I also may successfully take hold, ᵈ the way I was successfully taken hold of by Christ Jesus. ¹³ᵃ Brothers and sisters, I, for my part, I do not consider myself to have taken hold successfully. ᵇ But one thing I do say: unconcerned about the things that lie behind but stretching out toward the things that lie ahead, ¹⁴ I run in pursuit toward the goal at the finish, for the prize, to be called upward by God, in Christ Jesus. ¹⁵ᵃ As many, then, as are "perfected," let us think in this way; ᵇ and if you think differently about something, this too God will reveal to you. ¹⁶ Only, with respect to what we have attained, let us continue in the same course.

NOTES

3:12a *I do not say that I have already had success.* Elliptical *ouch hoti*; supply *legō*, "I do not say that" (BDF 480,5; GNB), as at 4:11 and 17, to introduce a clarification (*DA* 416). Schenk 262, an appellative sense, as at 3:18 ("I used to say to you . . . and now say [to you]"), implied also at 3:4 and 13 (p. 260). NEB/REB supply *estin*, "It is not that." 12a corrects any misunderstanding from what preceded. *lambanō* (here, aor. *elabon*), at 2:7b, aor. ptc., *taking on the sphere of a slave* (influence on 3:12 is unlikely). Here (BDAG 8) **enter into a close relationship, receive, make one's own, apprehend** (by grasp) or **comprehend** (with the mind); *receive* (the prize), ZG 599; BDAG 10.b, 1 Cor 9:24–25. Tr. is difficult; no dir. obj. (a trait throughout v 12); wordplay on *katalambanō*-forms in 12c and d. The obj. relates to what Paul pursues (*diōkō*), what he is not (*justified* or *perfected*), or has not taken hold of (*katalabō*). Can one object fit all these statements? Hence "this" in (N)RSV, etc., or "it" (NAB[RNT]). Proposals (cf. O'B 420–21): (1) vv 8–11 (Vincent 107; Bruce 122); (2) knowledge of Christ (3:8b, 10a; Hawth. 151); (3) Christ (3:8b, 10a; BDAG *lambanō* 8; Dib. 70); (4) righteousness (3:9bc; note *dedikaiōmai* in P⁴⁶ D, 12b, below; Klijn 1965:281); (5) resurrection (10a, 11; Lütgert 10–14; Michael 156–57, against opponents who think they are already raised; Greenlee; Perriman [(12) Bibl.]). (6) the prize (*brabeion* 14; Chrysost.; Bengel; Beare 128; CEV "reached my goal"). The prize may then be "bliss of the messianic kingdom" (Meyer 135–36) or the crown of life (1 Cor 9:24–25; cf. Delling *TDNT* 4:7). (7) (moral or spiritual) perfection (12b, 15a; LB). (8) martyrdom (Loh. 144, see below on 12c and COMMENT A.2). (9) Paul intended no object, just "attaining"

(EGT 457), "to suggest something incomplete" (Collange 133; Haupt 137, formally Paul means *skopos* in v 14, materially *sōtēria*; Gnilka 198; Schmithals 1972:70–71). Trs. that avoid an object in Eng. use "attained" (KJV), "obtained" ([N]RSV), or "succeeded" (GNB), none with wordplay on *katalabō* (12cd).

Pf. tenses *(dedikaiōmai, teteleiōmai)* follow the aor. *elabon,* so some distinguish (lack of) past achievement or results and (what is not) present reality (ATR 845, 901). *ēdē* (*already, now, by this time;* see NOTE on 4:10b *now at last;* DA 316) + aor. is often rendered by a pf. ("Not that I have already attained"), and the pf. given its pres. sense (NRSV-mg, "am perfected"). For Lft. 152, *elabon* pointed to "a past epoch," Paul's conversion (Loh. 144) or (Vincent 107) his "entire past up to the time of writing," an "effective" aor. for "the whole course of events" (Loh/Nida 108; Baumert 1973:391). The TRANSLATION "have success" will connect with *katalambanō*-forms that follow. Du Plessis 195 emphasizes the 1st per. sg., not the (gnomic) aor., "Not that I actually did the taking (or secured the attainment)."

3:12b. *or that I have already been justified.* Between *ēdē elabon* and *ē ēdē teteleiōmai,* P⁴⁶ D* Western MSS read *ē ēdē dedikaiōmai* (pf. tense), "I have already been justified" (by God); cf. *dikaiosynē* 9bc; F G *dikaiōmai,* "I am already being justified"; G* after *ē ēdē teteleiōmai,* as if explanatory, "or already have reached the goal, being justified"; see NA²⁷; UBSGNT; UBS⁴ no apparatus on this lemma. Full data in Aland 1991, 3:586–88. In papyri like P⁴⁶ scribes tended to omit rather than add material; so E. C. Colwell, "Scribal Habits in Early Papyri," *Papers Read at the 100th Meeting of the Society of Biblical Literature, December 28–30, 1964,* ed. J. Philip Hyatt (Nashville: Abingdon, 1965) 370–89, repr. in Colwell's *Studies in Methodology in Textual Criticism of the New Testament,* NTTS 9 (Leiden: Brill/Grand Rapids: Eerdmans, 1969) 106–24; J. R. Royse, "Scribal Tendencies in the Transmission of the Text of the New Testament," in *The Text of the New Testament in Contemporary Research: Essays on the Statis Quaestionis: A Volume in Honor of Bruce M. Metzger,* SD 46 (Grand Rapids: Eerdmans, 1995) 238–52, esp. 242–47. Usually the justification cl. is set aside as an addition; TCGNT 614–15; Price 281, "some pious copyist" felt "the Divine side of sanctification [sic] was left too much out of sight" (EGT 457) or added it by analogy with 1 Cor 4:4 (*ouk en toutō[i] dedikaiōmai,* Gnilka 198 n 75) or to compensate "for the lack of any objects . . . in this verse" (Hawth. 148, unless omitted by homoioteleuton, *-ōmai* ending on both *teleioō* and *dikaioō;* Edart 233 n 5, though 3:2–16, Letter B, stresses justification). López, *dedikaiōmai* and *diōkō* provide attractive paronomasia, "I do not, on account of being received, consider myself justified, but pursue . . ." ("not credible" syntax, Silva 204 n 54). Metzger, "addition of the clause destroys the balance of the four-part structure of the sentence" (TCGNT 615, presumably *elabon, teleleiōmai, diōkō* [what of *katalabō?*], and *katelēmphthēn;* from Loh. 143?), to which Silva 204 retorted that "omitting the clause destroys a five-part structure." Silva 203–4, "[t]he most striking textual variant of P⁴⁶ in Philippians"; omission is either deliberate "because of its apparent theological difficulty" (fut. reference, Paul is regarded as teaching only "present justification"; cf. Fee 333 n 1) or accidental (homoioarcton, *ē ēdē*). Baumert 1973:400–401, *dikaiosynē* was in Paul's mind from v 9 on. Loh. 142 n 1, "ancient . . . but secondary" (so finally Silva; {B}-level in UBSGNT).

But objections must be considered (David Noel Freedman) against automatic preference in NT text criticism for the shorter reading ("mantra: LECTIO BREVIOR POTIOR"). Often otherwise in OT studies; cf. P. K. McCarter, Jr., AB 8:5–11; 8:56–57 on 1 Sam 1:22–24; 8:168 on 9:3. Freedman cites Exod 20:5 par Deut 5:9, cf. Exod 34:7 (include "and upon sons of sons"); Ezek 28:13 (nine precious stones) compared with Exod 28:17–20 and 39:10–13. In Pseudepigrapha texts, bored scribes often shortened the text; cf. *OTP* 1:93–94; 2:180. "Let the shorter reading prevail, there has been dittography," should be balanced by awareness the longer reading has sometimes been truncated by haplography, as here. For the NT, cf. J. K. Elliott, *The Greek Text of the Epistles to Timothy and Titus*, SD 36 (Salt Lake City: Univ. of Utah Press, 1968) 6–7 (contrast G. D. Fee, *JBL* 89 [1970] 505–6); J. M. Ross 1983 ([2] Bibl.), and K. Elliott/ I. Moir, *Manuscripts and the Text of the New Testament: An Introduction for English Readers* (Edinburgh: T&T Clark, 1995) 33. AB 6:428, 431–32, "called into question in recent times"; cf. 410, "subjectively determined"; E. J. Epp, "Issues in New Testament Textual Criticism: Moving from the Nineteenth to the Twenty-First Century," in *Rethinking New Testament Textual Criticism*, ed. D. A. Black (Grand Rapids: Baker Academic, 2002) 17–76, esp. 25–30, cf. 107 n 9, 129, 132, 145. Preference for a shorter text cannot be applied "when the short text can be explained by homoioteleuton fault or other . . . errors" (T. Baarda, e-mail 8/19/02).

or am already perfected. *ēdē* (12a) + *ē*, disjunctive particle, *or.* *teteleiōmai*, pf. m.-p. of *teleioō*, BDAG (2) **bring to an end, to its goal** or **to accomplishment,** 2.e.α "make someone perfect" (Heb 10:1; 7:19), pass. "become perfect." D. K. Williams 202–5, completion, not perfection. BDAG 3 prefers a mystery religions background, **consecrate, initiate,** pass. "*be consecrated, become a teleios*" (adj. at 3:15a). In Paul, vb. also at 2 Cor 12:9 ("power is made perfect [*teleitai*] in weakness"). *teleios* (adj. 3:15a; 1 Cor 2:6; 14:20; 13:10; Rom 12:2) may be a tech. term for a mystery cult initiate (BDAG 3) or contrast with "babes," i.e., "full-grown, mature, adult." P[46] has *teleiōmai* (pres.); 104 *tetheamai*, "have beheld"; 1985 omits *ē ēdē*; Edart 261, redactoral addition.

perfected. Traditionally *teleios* was taken as "moral perfection" (Pietism, John Wesley, Roman Catholic interpretation of Matt 5:48 and 19:21 as "evangelical [gospel] counsels of perfection"); cf. R. N. Flew (COMMENT n 5, below) vii, ix, xi–xv; the comments by Castelli 13 are revealing. In reaction, *teleioun* in Hebrews was said to mean "wholeness" in contrast to what is fragmentary. For perfection in Heb, see D. Peterson 2–19. Reitzenstein and the history-of-religions school saw initiation into the mystery cults and resulting mystical union with a deity. From here it was but a step to *teleios* as a Gnostic term (Bultmann 1951 [INTRO. X Bibl.] 177, 180–81). Preisker 130–34 saw an eschatological NT "*telos*-faith," with the kingdom of God as goal and end. Against appeals to "Hellenistic religiosity," Du Plessis sought a "Semitic interpretation" via the LXX (Heb. *tāmîm*, Gk. *amemptos*, "an echo of the O.T. doctrine of righteousness," 33); O. Michel, Meyer KEK *Heb.* (1966) 225–29. But (Peterson 23–30) the LXX evidence is very limited, often cultic. Du Plessis: an OT sense of totality; one becomes *tāmîm* by total submission to God's will, absolute dependence, devotion in service, and "an unimpaired relationship with Yahweh" (241, cf. 96, 101–2; Eccl. 12:13, p. 63). In Paul, *teleios* denotes "the totality of the plenitude of redemption experienced by all who are converted to Christ" (242–43). At Phil 3:12 (Du Plessis 195–96), "Not that I . . . have already been made perfect" contrasts with ultimate eschatological resurrection.

Delling (*TDNT* 8:49–87, *telos* [3:19]; *epiteleō* [see NOTE on 1:6 *bring it to completion*]; and *teleios*, 3:15) documents (pp. 67–84) a considerable background in Gk. philosophy ("the perfect man" attains *phronēsis* or "firm, true views," Plato; perfect virtue in Aristot.; Stoicism; Philo; Holloway 2001a:141 n 50) and limited usage in the LXX (somewhat more at Qumran, "whole" and "without blemish"). Delling, 3:12 = "I have not yet [sic] reached the full and final thing" that comes "only in the resurrection"; polemical contrast to what Saul thought he had as a Pharisee, "the whole" (p. 84; cf. Philo, *Leg.* 3.74). On "perfection" and "knowledge" at Qumran, cf. B. Rigaux, "Révélation des mystères et perfection à Qumran et dans le Nouveau Testament," *NTS* 4 (1957–58) 237–62; pp. 249–50 on Phil 3:12–15, knowledge of Christ (v 8) allows a person to be counted among the *teleioi* (with Bonnard 69, perfection founded on the unique righteousness of God in Christ), though not yet perfect, v 12 ("relative perfection"?). *Word studies:* R. Schippers, *NIDNTT* 2:59–66; H. Hübner, *EDNT* 3:342–45; J. Y. Campbell, *IDB K-Q* 730; W. W. Klein, *DPL* 699–701, "relative perfection" possible in this life, esp. Col-Eph; "ultimate perfection" only in the age to come, 3:12–14. R. N. Flew (COMMENT, n 5, below) re 3:12–14, Paul distinguished "absolute perfection . . . reserved for the future . . . and a relative perfection ["a contradiction" in terms, p. xiii] . . . realizable by himself and his converts" (52). Peterson 37–41, Phil 3:12, 15 = terms of Paul's opponents, promising perfection. H. W. Attridge, Hermeneia *Heb.* 83–87, "hints of a special, Gnosticizing use" in Phil.

Whatever one decides on "Gnosticism," mystery cults existed in Paul's day, at Eleusis (near Athens); Dionysus cult (pertinent to Philippi; Pilhofer 1:100–5), with initiation rites (cf. *OCD*³ 1017–18, with U. Bianchi, not Reitzenstein). "Become an initiate, one consecrated" cannot be excluded at 3:12, at least for Paul's hearers; rare in Eng. trs., but Schoder 33, an echo of ancient mystery religions. Usually rendered, "perfection" (KJV, RSV, etc.), often with later notions of moral perfection; esp. possible if a claim by opponents. To "reach the goal" (NRSV-txt, NJB) in the footrace is stadium imagery. The TRANSLATION *am already perfected* brings out the pres. aspect of the pf. tense, and the pass. (sc. "by God"?). Loh. 144 saw perfection with martyrdom; Wis 4:7, 13, "the righteous *(dikaios)*, though they die early *(teleutēsai)*, will be at rest . . . being perfected *(teleiōtheis)* in a short time"; Philo, *Leg.* 3.74; Pfitzner 147–48 added 4 Macc 7:15 ("death has perfected *[eteleiōsen]*" Eleazer), plus martyrdom texts in Eus. *HE* 6.2.12; Ign. *Eph.* 3.1. To grasp (the prize, *katalabō*, 12c) means "arriving at the gate of perfection . . . personal resurrection" for the martyr (144). So Loh.; see COMMENT A.2.

3:12c. *but I run in pursuit, if I also may successfully take hold.* de, in most trs. *but* (contrast GNB); occasionally a new sentence (CEV), in contrast to 12ab. *diōkō* (3:6a, *persecuting the church*), BDAG 1, **move rapidly and decisively toward an objective, hasten** [*TDNT* 2:229], **run, press on.** *run in pursuit* (of a goal), cf. "persecute." On Stoic "striving," cf. Engberg-Pedersen 1995a: 280–82. 12c + *katalambanō*, cf. Herodot. 9.58 (enemies "pursued [*diōkteoi*] until overtaken [*katalamphthentes*]"); Sir 11:10; Prov. 28:20; Luc. *Herm.* 77 ("pursued and failed to catch"); Lam 3:1. D. J. Williams, a chariot race (260–62; cf. Lft. 152–53). Esler 2005, esp. 379–81, uses (vase) paintings as visual evidence for a runner looking back. Bauernfeind (*TWNT* 8:232), "only with reservations" can Paul's athletic metaphors be considered a model.

if = ei + aor. subjunct., *katalabō*, the vb. in 12a + *kata-* (BDAG *katalambanō* 1, **make someth[ing] one's own, win, attain**); compound at 1 Thess 5:4; Rom 9:30; 1 Cor 9:24. Baumert 1973:399, *kata-* suggests intensity. Is there connection with Stoic *katalēpsis*, "complete grasp of the truth which cannot be dislodged by reasoning" (Engberg-Pedersen 1995:262 n 11)? For *ei* (never *ean* in Phil.) + subjunct., cf. 3:11 *ei . . . katantēso*; BDF 368, 375; DA 348. Class III condition (Rienecker 212, citing ATR), "But, if I (should) attain, I run in pursuit." Many see a deliberative question ("am I to attain?") carried over into an indir. question (BDAG *ei* 5.b.β, "*I press on (to see) whether I can capture*"; ATR 916; BDF 368,4; Gdsp.). Thus it expresses "an uncertain expectation associated with an effort to attain something" (ZBG 403, supply "to try [if I can . . .]", cf. 349). See on 1:22 *what, then, shall I choose?* within the options listed at 1:21 *to live*, conditional sentence with (deliberative) question. For 3:12, NEB/REB, NABRNT; ZG 599, "in hope that I may possess it." Some then speak of purpose or aim ([N]RSV, "to make it my own"; NIV; GNB). ZBG 127, "I pursue that perchance I may lay hold . . . ," but (129) others of a final sense. Tentativeness is seen in JB ("trying to capture"); NJB ("the attempt"); CEV ("struggling to take hold of the prize"). ℵ* D* etc. omit *kai* (haplography, either homoeoarcton, *kai kata*, or homoeoteleuton, *ei kai*); so in effect most trs. DA 327, *kai* here and in 12d indicates "an 'addition' relation," functioning as an adverb (not coordinating). How to render? With *ei* (BDAG 6.e; cf. 2:17), *even if, even though*; with *katalabō*, "even attain"; with the subject in the vb., "if even I, I also, should attain." Cf. Fee 338 n 2 on "receptor language" problems. In our tr. *also* links *elabon* with *katalabō*, *had success* and *successfully take hold*. Baumert 1973:401 cf. 384, *kai* here and in 12d expresses a reciprocal relation, "I on my part, Christ on his part."

3:12d. *the way I was successfully taken hold of by Christ Jesus. katelēmphthēn*, aor. pass. indic., *katalambanō* (12c). Trs. often match wordings in 12 (apprehend/am apprehended, KJV; make it my own/has made me his own, [N]RSV; capture/have been captured, Gdsp., JB; win the prize/ has won me to himself, GNB). We connect 12d with 12a via 12c *successfully take hold*. Shift from act. (in 12c) to pass. (12d) is a device of which Paul is fond; cf. 1 Cor 8:2–3; Gal 4:9; 1 Cor 13:12. *kai* is omitted by D^gr E^gr G (EGT 456; haplography, double homoeoarcton, *kai kata*) and not usually reflected in trs. (KJV "for" is an exception). *hypo* + gen. (BDAG A.a.α), agent after the pass. voice. *Iēsou* is omitted by B D^(2) etc., brackets in UBSGNT, NA^27, and NAB(RNT); omitted in NEB/REB, CEV, LB. "Jesus Christ" in a few MSS and versions (UBSGNT^4; Gdsp.). Decision "is nearly impossible to call" (Fee 338 n 3).

eph' hō[i] (BDAG *epi* 6, cf. *epi* at 3:9; + rel. pron. *hos, hē, ho* 1.k.δ) is usually taken as "because" (NRSV; Moule *IB* 50, cf. 132). *DA* 324–25, all six uses in Phil = "basis" or "cause," here "on the basis of Christ's taking hold of him." But (cf. Baumert 1973:386–91, against "because"), Fitzmyer's CD-Rom research on *eph' hō[i]* (see NOTE on 4:10 *on which*) suggests for Rom 5:12 result, not cause; for Phil 3:12d, with NIV, "take hold of that for which Christ Jesus took hold of me" (1993:330, 338–39). So Fee 346 n 31; Bockmuehl 221; Hooker NIB 11:533; Fowl 2005:160; cf. Walter NTD 82. Sometimes recast with Christ as subject (NIV; [N]RSV, etc.). Possibly 12d provides the object cl. for 12c, but what of the three preceding vbs.? *epi* + dat. after *katalambanō* needs proving; is an acc. *(ekeino)* to be supplied, to which *eph' hō[i]* refers? So apparently NIV (but cf. Thielman 194–96). 12d thus indicates result and serves as a corrective. = "with regard to which (fact)," or "*the way I was successfully taken hold of by Christ Jesus.*

3:13a. *Brothers and sisters, I, for my part, I do not consider myself to have taken hold successfully.* Voc. *adelphoi,* the first dir. address in 3:2ff. (also at 3:17); *adelphoi mou* last at 3:1, next at 4:1. On tr., see NOTE on 1:12 *brothers and sisters. egō* + pres. m.-p., BDAG *logizomai* 3, **hold a view . . . think, believe, be of the opinion.** See NOTE on 4:8 *ponder.* KJV, a commercial sense ("count"); most use *consider.* "Focal indicators" *(adelphoi, egō, emauton)* lead up to *kateilēphenai* (*DA* 392), infin. (*GNTG* 2:137, pf. act. of vb. in 12c and d, "to have taken hold," BDAG *katalambanō* 1) + subject acc. (BDF 406, *emauton,* "myself," from *emautou, ēs*). Nom. in classical Gk; NT often the acc. (*GNTG* 1:212); ATR 1037–39, acc. of general reference; cf. *GGBB* 192–97. Acc. + infin. perhaps an LXX influence (*EDNT* 2:355); cf. Rom 3:28; 6:11; 14:14. Lack of pred. noun is unusual (BDF 406,2); cf. the double acc. at 1:7 NOTE. *logizomai* middle voice + *emauton* seems redundant (ATR 811), but the sense is clear. Schenk 260, cf. 328–29, 1st sg. vb., initial *egō,* and *emauton* stresses "I" (Paul) in contrast to others; "I, *for my part, I. . . .*"

ou was expanded to *oupō,* "not yet," in P61vid א A D* etc.; *oupō emauton* in 629; more in UBSGNT, which rates "not" {C}-level of certainty; J. D. Price 281, probability of 0.78 for *ou.* Metzger assigns *oupō* to "copyists who considered Paul . . . too modest in his protestations" (*TCGNT* 615). Many trs. have "yet" (e.g., NIV). Silva, decision is "immaterial . . . context injects the nuance 'not yet.'" But there is a difference: "Paul said 'not' because he is speaking eschatologically" (Fee 338 n 5), not "making it his own" before the parousia. *ou* was too strong for scribes; it was weakened to "not yet," with disastrous consequences (Schenk 260–61).

Again, no dir. obj. in Gk. (so KJV, NABRNT). Some add "it" ([N]RSV, NIV, etc.) or supply "the finish line" (NAB); "the prize" (Loh/Nida); Martin, full knowledge of Christ, the blessedness of the resurrection still to come; Silva 199–200; O'B 417 "this ambition."

3:13b. *But one thing I do say: unconcerned about the things that lie behind but stretching out toward the things that lie ahead. . . . hen de* is verbless, like 4:5b (ATR 1202). Many insert "I do" (KJV-[N]RSV; BDF 481,1) or "I say" ([N]JB, NEB/REB). Schenk 260–61, 329, "I say to you" (3:18, the Philippians in contrast to opponents). "I focus on," Hawth. 148; Holloway 2001a:142 n 52 *kateilēpha,* "I have firmly in hand." Fridrichsen 1934 proposed an adv., *en de* (BDF 203, 481), "but thereby" (?). I. Heikel (*TSK* 101 [1934–35] 316) inserted *men* to balance *de* in 13b, "I think I have still not made him [Christ] my own, but at least one thing" (Gnilka 199 n 80; BDF 481). Fridrichsen 1944, *hen de* is an abbreviated interjectional cl.; cf. the novelist Xen. *Eph.* 5.3; "But one thing I do do." *de* is adversative (DA 327, 328). Edart 242, *correctio*. Cf. 1:27 *This point only (monon)*; 3:13 Gdsp., "only. . . ." LB took *hen* as dir. obj., "but I am bringing all my energies to bear on this one thing: Forgetting the past."

unconcerned . . . but stretching out . . . . Two ptcs. + *men* and *de*, "on the one hand, on the other" (BDAG *men* 1.a.α; cf. 1:15, 16–17; 2:23–24; 3:1b, contrast, DA 328; Edart 261 sees redaction):

ta men opisō epilanthanomenos,	unconcerned about things that lie behind,
tois de emprosthen epekteinomenos.	but stretching out toward things that lie ahead.

epi-prefix on each vb. epi-lanthanomai, here only in Paul, compound or simple form, "forget," + acc. of the thing (BDF 175). *EDNT* 2:30, *be unconcerned about/ neglect.* NAB/Schoder, "give no thought to." Not amnesia, but what Paul concentrates on. *ep-ek-teinomai* (double prefix; nowhere else in the Bible), **stretch out, strain** (oneself, m.) + dat., *"toward the (goal) that lies before (me)"* (BDAG p. 361); "stretching myself forward" (ATR 807).

the things that lie behind . . . the things that lie ahead. Adv. in attribut. position after neut. pl. art., subst. use (BDF 215). *opisō* means "behind," of place, "where?"; therefore, "the part of the course already covered" (BDAG 1.a). Perhaps Paul's heritage and achievements in Judaism (3:4b–6). *emprosthen* (BDAG 1.a), **in front, ahead,** what lies ahead; cf. BDF 214,1. Some see a chariot race (at the Circus in Rome); Lft. 152 quotes Bengel, Verg. *Georgics* 3.106; Bröse; but Lft. adds "equally appropriate to the foot-race . . . Paul's usual metaphor" (1 Cor 9:24). Pfitzner 140–41, the runner strains "toward the goal with outstretched empty hands," but ought "to keep his eyes fixed on the goal before him." On footraces, see *OCD*[3] 206–7. Can be temporal ptcs., "while."

3:14. *I run in pursuit toward the goal at the finish, for the prize, to be called upward by God, in Christ Jesus.* Main cl., introduced by 13b. Repeats *diōkō* from 12c, + two prep. phrases, *kata skopon* before, *eis to brabeion* after it. (Ptc. *diōkōn* in a few MSS.) *kata* (BDAG B.1.b, + acc.) is local (ATR 608), place, "extension . . . **toward, to, up to,**" "run (over the course) *toward the goal.*"

the goal at the finish. skopos (BDAG: **goal, mark**), here only in the NT; vb. at 2:4a *regarding,* 3:17 "look out for." Classical background includes a mark on which one fixes the eye or at which one aims, a goal in life; Polyb. 7.8.9; E. Fuchs,*TDNT* 7:413–14. Galen 1.387, 10.162 (cf. Baumert 1973: 395, against BDAG *diōkō* 1 *"toward the goal"*) reflects a medical meaning, intention, "a process or manner of healing of incised wounds" (*Webster's* 3rd, 1176, meaning 5); R. Alpers-Gölz, *Der Begriff* skopos *in der Stoa und seine Vorgeschichte,* Spudosmata 8 (Hildesheim: Olms, 1976). In the LXX, God set Job up "as his target" (Job 16:12; cf. Lam 3:12, a mark for God's arrow; Wis 5:21). Such "arena" language was common in the diatribe. The "Christian's course has a mark or goal," which Paul pursues in the obedience of faith (*TDNT* 7:414). In track language, the finish mark or tape; in life generally, the goal; hence *the goal at the finish*.

the prize. eis (*epi* in D G Koine MSS; cf. EGT 458; perhaps influenced by *epekteinomenos*) + *brabeion*, 1 Cor 9:24, "prize" in a race. Edart 261 calls it redactoral. BDAG b, fig., "*the prize that is the object of* (and can only be obtained in connection with) *the upward call*," assumes *tēs anō klēseōs* that follows is subj. gen. From *brabeus*, umpire or official at games/vb. *brabeuō*, "order, rule, control"; cf. Col 3:15. On the *-eion* ending, see *GNTG* 2:344; BDF 111,5, the prize awarded. E. Stauffer (*TDNT* 1:638–39), "the goal beyond this age," resurrection. A. Ringwald (*NIDNTT* 1:648–49) treats victor's prizes in Gk. sports and *brabeion* in LXX and Jewish sources under Gk. influence (Wis 10:12); Phil 3:10–14, not "ethical perfection" but resurrection ("martyrs" implied, Rev. 20:6; Loh.'s influence? See Comment A.2). W. Stenger (*EDNT* 1:226) distinguishes Phil ("the goal of the Christian race [of life] has not yet been reached") and 1 Cor 9:24 (everyone is challenged "to a strenuous and methodical Christian fulfillment of life," without saying "only *one* will win the prize"; cf. Conzelmann, *1 Cor.* 162). A. A. T. Ehrhardt, "An Unknown Orphic Writing in the Demosthenes Scholia, and St. Paul," *ZNW* 48 (1957) 101–10, an Orphic frg. speaks of crowns (pl.; one for each race?); he stresses the "presiding authority . . . in whose presence the contest was held and in whose name the prize was given," i.e., "a god, an emperor or a civil magistrate" (110; cf. Pfitzner 13–14, 86–87).

to be called upward by God. tēs anō klēseōs can be subj. gen. (BDAG above; "the prize for which God has called me homeward," NIV, etc.; O'B 433; Silva 202); or epexegetical (ZG 600; "apposition or definition," O'B 431; NEB, "the prize that is God's call to the life above"; GNB; perhaps KJV-[N]RSV); or obj. gen., "the prize which has the object of being called up by God (to the victor's platform)." Vincent 110, "a genitive of belonging," i.e., "The prize is attached to the calling and involved in it"; Gnilka 200. Fee 349 (the "sense is easier to sort out than its grammar") suggests "'result-means' (the call is the means that has brought about the promised result, the prize)." K. L. Schmidt (*TDNT* 3:492), a tech. Pauline term, calling by God in Christ. Vincent 111, "*act* of calling," something continual for the person(s) called. Cf. Rom 11:29; 1 Cor 1:26; 1 Cor 7:20. The vb. *kaleō* is more common in Paul, but does not occur in Phil, nor does *klētos*, "called." *Word studies* build on the vb.: L. Coenen, *NIDNTT* 1:275; H. Bietenhard, 2:188 on 3:14); J. Eckert, *EDNT* 2:243; Lincoln 9–32, 87–134. The Translation paraphrases, *to be called.* . . .

upward. anō, adv. in attribut. position, modifies *klēsis*; = "above," here "upward(s)" (BDAG 2; RSV, NRSV-mg). Some see two worlds, "above" and "below" (as in John 8:23; Col 3:1–2; F. Büchsel, *TDNT* 1:376–77). Philo (Gnilka 200), "those craving wisdom and knowledge *(epistēmēs)* . . . have been called upwards *(anakeklēsthai)* . . . those who have received [God's] down-breathing *(katapneusthentas)* should be called up to Him *(anō kaleisthai)*" (*Plant.* 23; LCL *Philo* 3:224–25); U. B. Müller 169 adds *Her.* 70, "the mind *(dianoias)* . . . stirred . . . by heavenward yearning, drawn . . . upward *(anō . . .)*" (LCL *Philo* 4:316–17). *3 Bar.* 4.15 is irrelevant (J. Beutler, *EDNT* 1:112; U. B. Müller 169 n 146). In a three-story universe, *anō* = "heavenward" (NIV); "heavenly call" (NRSV, cf. Heb 3:1, Vincent 111). KJV, "high calling" (called on high?). Some see a track judge calling the victor up to winner's pedestal at the Olympic games; Collange 134, the *Hellanodikai* "had a herald announce the name of the victor, his father's name and his country"; the judges gave the athlete his palm branch (cf. Daremberg-Saglio, *Dictionnaire des antiquités grecques et romaines* III,1:60–64; I,1:148–50, "Agonothètes"; Smith, *Dictionary* 590, 32, 830–32, 166–68). D. J. Williams 262, "the presiding magistrate" summons the winner. For Collange, God is the agonothete (= *brabeus*), Christ his herald. So Martin 1976:139; Hawth. 134–35; Bruce 121 (the Emperor, in Rome), 123. Older commentators (in Vincent 111) envisioned God summoning the runners *to* the race. Some object to any race-course background (Silva 202): evidence is lacking for *kaleō* at Olympic ceremonies; "*klēsis* has such a theologically charged nuance for Paul" that "call" should exclude stadium imagery. Similarly Fee 349 n 49; Bockmuehl 223, though attracted to the Philo references above. *tēs aneglēsias* in one late cursive (1739), "(the prize) of irreproachability" (Origen; Hawth. 148; Fee 338 n 7), is patristic speculation. See COMMENT A.3.

by God, in Christ Jesus. tou theou en Christō[i] Iēsou has many minor textual variants. The calling comes from and belongs to God (gen. of source or subj. gen.). *in Christ Jesus* (see NOTES on 1:1, 13, 26, etc.) can be construed with (1) *diōkō* (pursuit "in Christ"); (2) *klēseōs* (Lft. 153; O'B 433, the sphere in which the summons is given; Fee 350, locative, in Christ's death and resurrection); (3) *theou* (instrumental *en*, Michaelis 59; Collange 134; Schenk 309; "through Jesus Christ"; TC). See COMMENT B.1. The TRANSLATION leaves open the several possibilities.

3:15a. *As many, then, as are "perfected," let us think in this way. hosoi*, subject pron., masc. nom. pl., *hosos, ē, on* (BDAG 2 "as many as"); neut. pl. 5x at 4:8, *whatever things*. . . . Many trs. make a rel. cl. out of *hosoi oun teleioi* and begin with *phronōmen*, "Let those of us who are mature be of the same mind" ([N]RSV; REB). Some render as if *pantes* ("All of us who are mature," NIV, GNB, JB). No vb. (like *esmen*); BDF 128,2. *oun* (see NOTE on 2:1 *then; oun paraeneticum,* BDAG 1.b) + hortatory impv. *phronōmen* mark a shift from "I" to "we." *teleioi*, "perfected" (masc. nom. pl., *teleios, a, on*), provides continuity with 3:12b, "not that I am already perfected" (*teteleiōmai*). Adj. 19x in the NT, 5x in Paul's undisputed letters; see NOTE on 12b. Applied to God (Matt 5:48b), God's will (Rom 12:2), and "the complete" that will come at the End (1 Cor 13:10). For 3:15a, either (BDAG 2ab) **full-grown, mature, adult,** in contrast to a child; 1 Cor 14:20; 1 Cor 2:6, contrast "infants" at 3:1; so Bauer (1902 diss.), reflected by G. Delling in *TDNT* 8:76, among others; Phil 3:15 (N)RSV, NIV, etc. Or (BDAG 3) **a cult initiate,** tech. term from the mystery religions; Schoder 23, "All of us then who have been initiated." Cf. Col 1:28 ("the mystery, Christ in you"); BDAG takes 1:28 as (4) "***perfect, fully developed*** . . . in a moral sense," KJV, "perfect in Christ," E. Schweizer, EKK *Col.* 111; AB 34B:267–68. Du Plessis 196–98, Paul and all the Philippian Christians are in "a state of perfection" (3:15), yet Paul still remains "in the flesh" (1:23); 3:12 and 15 show "distinct discernment between the present redemptive state and its future consummation" (197). Delling (*TDNT* 8:76) took 3:15 as "mature," as did Schippers (*NIDNTT* 2:62). Hübner (*EDNT* 3:343), perhaps "*(the) complete/mature ones*." D. Peterson 40 opts for irony, "those who think that they have obtained perfection." Apart from KJV ("as many as be perfect") and JB, most Eng. trs. employ "mature" (NABRNT "perfectly mature"), but for Paul's audience and if terminology from opponents, "initiate" cannot be excluded. Moffatt 1916, "perfect" misleads, "mature" is "less objectionable," someone on the right road, making progress; cf. Epict. *Enchir.* 51, "a mature man who is making progress (*hōs teleion kai prokoptonta*) . . . now is the contest, the Olympic games are already present . . . live as one who wishes to be a Socrates" (LCL *Epictetus* 2:534–35). Michael, *teleioi* "was used in the Mystery Cults" and later "of baptized Christians as distinguished from catechumens" (*PGL teleios* C.3]; perhaps "tending to acquire some such meaning even in Paul's day" (165). Thus philosophical, athletic, and mystery-religions senses are all possible. To render "*perfected*" allows for a mystery cults sense and "perfected in years," in keeping with 3:12b.

let us think in this way. phronōmen, hortatory subjunct.; vb. frequent in Phil, see 1:7, etc. Moffatt 1916: "let this be our point of view." D. Sölle's rendering at 2:5 works well here, "Let us orient ourselves to. . . ." The TRANSLATION uses *think*, as in most *phroneō* passages in Phil; so (N)JB, NEB/REB, CEV; but KJV-(N)RSV "be . . . minded"; "attitude" in NAB(RNT), etc. Indic. *phronoumen* in ℵ L etc., (N)JB-mg, "We who are called 'perfect' all think in this way." *touto*, dir. obj. or adverbial acc.; neut. sg. from *houtos*, as at 1:7; 2:5 *in this way* (JB). Some trs. try to help readers: "thus minded" (KJV, RSV), "of the same mind" (NRSV, cf. 2:2; 4:2), or "this attitude" (NAB[RNT], etc.), "such a view of things" (NIV). See COMMENT B.1, below.

3:15b. *and if you think differently about something, this too God will reveal to you. ei* + 2nd pl. pres. act. indic. *phroneō* (also in 15a; in pairs as at 2:2 and 4:10). *apokalypsei* in apodosis is fut. indic. Class I condition: if at any time such different thinking occurs, God will provide a revelation about it. Adv. *heterōs*, only here in the NT, but adj., gen. pl., at 2:4 *other persons*. Hence, "otherwise" (KJV, RSV); "differently" (NRSV, NIV, NEB/REB), or (with the vb.) "a different attitude" (Gdsp., NABRNT, GNB). Lft. 153 suggested "at fault," "amiss," a "euphemism for *kakos*," something "bad"; Silva 206–7, citing LSJ "*otherwise than should be, badly, wrongly*" (Epict. *Diss.* 2.16.16; Jos. *Ant.* 1.26); 3:15b "the wrong frame of mind." *differently* than the persons in 15a or Paul in 12–14 or the views set forth from 3:4b on (H. W. Beyer, *TDNT* 2:703). *ti*, from *tis, ti*, enclitic, indef. pron. (see NOTE on 2:1 *something*) can be dir. obj. or adv. acc., "in some way." Many trs. omit, but NAB, "If you see it another way"; Schoder, "If in any point. . . ."

reveal. apokalyptō, a Pauline term. In the Pauline corpus as many times (13) as in the rest of the NT; 9x in the acknowledged letters. (Noun *apokalypsis*, 13 out of 18 NT examples, 10 in acknowledged letters, none in Phil.) Used for the righteousness and wrath of God being revealed (Rom 1:17,18), glory and judgment to be revealed (Rom 8:18; 1 Cor 3:13). The Son revealed to and through the apostle; the Faith revealed when Christ came (Gal 1:16; 3:23; AB 33A:157–58 "apocalyptically to reveal"; 362, "invasively revealed"). Cf. "things God has revealed to us through the Spirit" (1 Cor 2:10), revelations when (house) churches assemble

(1 Cor 14:10). BDAG places Phil 3:15 under *apokalyptō* b, revelation of transcendent secrets, with Gal 1:16; 1 Cor 2:10; 14:30. A. Oepke (*TDNT* 3: 563–92), "revelation of the living God" in the OT and in Christ, but Gk. religion too had revelations. *NIDNTT* 3:310–16 (W. Mundle); *EDNT* 1:131 (T. Holtz); *TLNT* 2:247–50. U. B. Müller 171–72 distinguishes ecstatic revelation in the Corinthian letters from Phil (concrete direction from God on something specific, 3:15b *ti*, perhaps re the false teachers); with D. Lührmann 1978 ([3] Bibl.) 41–43; *touto* refers to vv 2–14; Paul places his theology under the criterion of God's revelation, God's righteousness from which there is no retreat. Beare 131, Paul "is ready to wait until God opens the minds of the others to the truth as he has expounded it"; against Loh. (martyrdom). The revelation will be *to you* Philippians *(hymin)*, whom Paul addresses (13a *adelphoi*), pl. like the subject in *phroneite* 15b. *kai* has adverbial force (*DA* 327, an "addition" relation); in most trs. with *touto* (*this too*, NRSV); some omit (Gdsp., GNB). Understandings vary: NAB, "God will clarify the difficulty to you"; NJB, "God has yet to make this matter clear to you."

3:16. *Only, with respect to what we have attained, let us continue in the same course.* Tersely worded. *plēn* (conj.; cf. 1:18b + *hoti, Simply that.* . . . ; 4:14, NOTE on *Anyway*). BDAG 1.c, **only** ([N]RSV, etc.), **in any case, on the other hand, but** (CEV), *however* (BAGD, GNB). KJV "Nevertheless," (N)JB "Meanwhile." Breaks off discussion to single out what is important (ATR 1189; BDF 449,2; Thrall 20–25; J. Blomqvist 75–100, esp. 82, a "modifying" use); "to correct possible misunderstandings" (*DA* 329), cf. 1 Cor 11:11. Holmstrand 120 n 75, "a closing-marking function," it begins "a modified final appraisal."

what we have attained. Aor. (a tense rare in the passage, *DA* 398), *phthanō*, 1st pl. (P[16] has 2nd pl.). BDAG 3 **come to or arrive at a particular state, attain.** Except for Matt 12:28 par Luke 11:20, all NT examples are in Paul (5x): 1 Thess 2:16, 4:15; 2 Cor 10:14; Rom 9:31, mostly eschatological. All examples except 1 Thess 4:15 involve a prep. phrase (G. Fitzer, *TDNT* 9:90–91). Like Rom 9:31, + *eis* + acc., here neut., rel. pron. *hos, hē, ho.* For *(touto) eis ho ephthasamen,* the whole an acc. of reference, *with respect to what we have attained.* It relates to what follows, the enigmatic *tō[i] autō[i] stoichein,* "let us hold true/fast to what we have attained" ([N]RSV, cf. NIV, Gdsp.). What have we have attained? Fitzer: "the Gospel of righteousness by faith in Christ . . . also the *regula ac norma* of conduct." Some stress conduct, even without the textual variant on a rule *(kanōn)*; REB, cf. NEB. But (Fitzer n 19) Loh. 149 put his finger on the problem: "the relative clause speaks of the point already attained, whereas the main clause speaks of the 'rule' *(kanōn)* whereby it is reached." V. Hasler (*EDNT* 3:422), the background is "those who are more perfect" striving "enthusiastically for a higher level of fellowship in suffering with the crucified Lord"; the apostle "admonishes them to hold to his own example and be content with what they have already *attained.*" Grammar and lexicography set limits within which interpretation takes place, usually with some reconstruction of the situation and the reader's thematic preferences. Textual variants suggest uncertainties from early times.

let us continue in the same course. tō[i] autō[i] stoichein, P[16,46] ℵ* A B etc. (10 witnesses in Aland 1991:592). Expanded in TR by *kanoni* after *stoichein,* agreeing with *autō[i]* ("walk by the same rule") + *to auto phronein* (2:2, "let us mind the same thing," [N]KJV; haplography or dittography -*ein*); so ℵ² Ψ 075 Byzantine MSS, list in UBSGNT; Aland 1991:589–90 lists 493 witnesses. Gal 6:16 was an influence, "As many as will walk according to this rule *(hosoi tō[i] kanoni toutō[i] stoichōsousin)*, peace . . . be upon them." Some Gk. MSS (D G etc.), Vg, and other versions move *to auto phronein* to the fore, before *tō[i] autō[i] (kanoni) stoichein*; so R. Knox, (N)JB-mg. J. D. Price gives it 0.52 probability, 0.30 for TR, 0.10 for simply *tō[i] autō[i] stoichein*. UBSGNT 615, {B}-level of certainty for *to[i] auto[i] stoichein*, "The variety and lack of homogeneity of the longer readings make it difficult to suppose that the shorter reading . . . arose because of homoeoteuton" *(stoichein/phronein)*. The longer readings = an "obviously secondary attempt to make sense of Paul's otherwise laconic clause," Fee 352 n 6.

stoichein (infin.) is imperatival, akin to the hortatory subjunct. in 15a *phronōmen*, *let us think . . . let us continue*, or, as a 2nd per. command, "continue on. . . ." Edart 235 compares the Heb. infin. abs. An old Gk. use of the infin. (BDF 389; GNTG 1:179, cf. 204 and 3:78; *chairein* in a Gk. letter, "greetings," Acts 23:26; IB 126). One can supply a vb. of saying or an impersonal vb. *(dei, chrē*, BDF 389) but need not. Cf. Rom 12:15 *(chairein . . . klaiein*, rejoice . . . weep). Holmstrand 120 counts the infin.-as-impv. construction "not unproblematic," but finds no real alternative. *stoicheō* was originally a military term, "be in a *stoichos*, rank or series," but it came to have fig. uses like "agree" (Delling, *TDNT* 7:666–67; Geoffrion does not treat it); Pfitzner 152 paraphrases, "not swerve from the course in which we were running"; therefore, "stay in your lane." All five NT instances are "fig., **to be in line with a pers[on] or thing, considered as standard for one's conduct, *hold to*, *agree with*, *follow*, *conform*"** + dat. (BDAG 946). Cf. Acts 21:24; Rom 4:12; Gal 5:25 and Gal 6:16. Long equated with *peripateō*, "walk," for ethical conduct (Loh. 149), like *politeuesthe* at Phil 1:27 (rather than *Exercise your citizenship*). Delling argues for distinct meanings in each NT instance of *stoicheō*; 3:16 = "(let us) remain in one and the selfsame thing." That it always takes an obj. in the dat. in the NT makes it different from intrans. vbs. like *peripateō*. So also *systoicheō* (Gal 4:25), a variant at 3:15 in F G. *NIDNTT* 2: 451–52 (H.-H. Esser), "living accordingly to definite rules." E. Plümmacher, probably military background and use in honorific inscriptions (so Delling 667), backgrounds fitting for Philippi; 3:16, "*hold true to, stay in agreement with* what has been (spiritually) attained" (*EDNT* 3:278). The TRANSLATION brings out the pres. impv. as linear action (ATR 1081; GNTG 3:75), *let us continue*; 1st pl. inferred from 16 *ephthasamen* and 15a; NABRNT has in effect a 2nd pl., "continue on the same course." Either is possible, "us" or "you" (Holmstrand 121).

in the same course. BDAG *autos, ē, o* 3.b, **the same**; cf. 1:30 *the same contest*. Scribes early added *kanoni*, "rule" (Gal 6:16, "the standard" of the new creation, articulated in 6:15). Many trs. insert "rule(s)" at 3:15 (KJV, [N]JB-mg, GNB). (N)RSV, NIV, NEB, hold fast or live up to what we have [already] attained; LB "obey the truth you have." Racetrack imagery in NABRNT, CEV, "continue on the same course." Collange 132, 135, "walk boldly" or "let us go on" + *tō[i] autō[i]* "in step" ("the same" as the vb. in a military sense implies?). To tr. *in the same course* fits track imagery but also direction in life and thought.

COMMENT

A. FORMS, SOURCES, AND TRADITIONS

1. *Literary, Rhetorical, and Related Features.* "Paul's Greek" in 3:12–16, Hawth. 149 remarks, "is difficult," its meaning often ambiguous; see NOTES. There is nothing from OT Scriptures in the vv, no kerygmatic or creedal phrases, unless "in Christ Jesus" in v 14.

a. *The Autobiographical "I"-form.* Begun at 3:4b, it continues through v 14 (vbs. 1st sg., ptcs. agreeing, 9x in 12–14; *egō* and "myself" in 13a; *DA* 367 chart). Paul reflects on experiences in Christ. The voc. *brothers and sisters* appears in 13a, the first time in 3:2–21; "we/us" and "you" (the Philippians) take over in 3:15–16 (+ 17). Spencer pictures a camera moving "from a close-up of the opponents [3:2–3] to a close-up of Paul [4–14], to a close-up of the Philippians [15–16]."

b. *"The Enemies."* Some phrases and themes in 3:12–16 stem from "the enemies" (18–19), introduced in 3:2–4a.[1] Sumney 1999:180–84 allows the claim that "circumcision leads to a higher level of spiritual achievements" (184), a considerable admission; it ties 3:2 to 14 (*anō*, "higher level"), *teteleiōmai* (12b) and *teleios* (15a) form an *inclusio*. Fee tends to dismiss "mirror readings" but here Paul's "disclaimers" ("not perfect yet") may reflect "Judaizers" and "the idea that Torah observance makes one 'more complete' in Christ" (341–42; cf. Koester 1961–62; Rigaux 1957–58 [in NOTE on *perfected*], a circumcised person, with knowledge of revealed mysteries and true to Torah, can reach perfection). Some see a second group in 3:12–16, different from those in 3:2–4a, further described in vv 18–19 (so Lincoln 93–95; Friedrich 1962:120, "Gnostics").

c. *Imagery from a Race.* Likely on foot, not chariots: *I run* (12c, 14); *for the prize* (14; 1 Cor 9:24–25 a crown of laurel, see NOTE on 4:1 *crowning wreath*); *toward the goal at the finish* (14, the "post . . . on which the runner intently fixes his gaze," Pfitzner 139; finish line, NAB; pylon). Some limit racing terminology to v 14 (Fee 340). O'B 429 sees the athlete's "manner of running" in what precedes (419; 13b). It begins (Beare 128; Caird 141; Collange 133; Loh/Nida 109; Dupont 1970:180–81) in v 12 (*elabon* 12a, "obtain a prize"; *teteleiōmai* 12b, "reach the winning-post," Dupont 180). 13b, "forgetting what is behind, straining toward what lies ahead," fits an athlete, oblivious to other runners, straining every nerve (TC), lunging toward the finish tape ("with outstretched, empty hands," K. Barth 107). The call *upward* (14) may announce the victor who steps up onto the winner's pedestal. Is v 16, *what we have obtained*, one's position on the track, laps completed? Pfitzner 78–81 warns against overdoing it, Paul's athletic metaphors as a moral struggle (life a race to be won, "to the swiftest, victory"), Christianity an *agōn* (boxing, footrace) against others toward a heavenly prize. Overemphasis

---

[1] Schenk 251 lists "I have already received" or *had success* (12a); "I am already perfected" (12b); "I press on," that I may "take hold" (12c); perhaps "I have been taken hold of" (12d) and "myself, taken hold of" (13a); more definitely "the upward call of God" (14); "perfect" (15a); "God will reveal it to you" (15b). Perhaps "we have attained" (16). They claim "perfection."

plunges some interpreters into a position (the need for moral effort to attain salvation) for which they criticized Judaism. The overall imagery is appropriate for a Greco-Roman city (Spencer 201); but the prize for Christians was not given in a Philippian stadium by officials of a Roman *colonia* (Pilhofer 1:152, cf. 28–29).

d. *Literary Structure and Features.* Loh. 142–43 claimed in v 12 four rhythmic lines, in 15–16 three two-liners; this attracted no following. Fee 339–30, 3:12–14 = two sentences, each with *diōkō*, the second reinforces and clarifies the first; each has a disclaimer (O'B 418) about "not having arrived" (3:12ab, 13), an indication about what Paul is pressing toward (12cd, 14), and a reference to God and/or Christ (12d, Fee 340, "a 'divine passive' . . . toward something Christ has already 'taken hold' of him for)." One can also parallel *hypo Christou Iēsou* and *en Christō[i] Iēsou*, the latter at the end of 14 an abbreviated repetition and reminiscence of "taken hold of by Christ Jesus" in 12d (Schenk 309). Fee regards the second sentence (13–14) as "much easier to grasp," the sports imagery better understood than terms used in v 12. Because terms in v 12 came from "the enemies" (n 1, above)?

Rhetorical treatments of 3:12–16 exhibit little agreement.[2] Concentric, chiastic analyses of Philippians shed little light.[3] Proposals for chiasm within these vv are rare (unlike much of Phil).

But cf. 3:15ab (imperfect chiasm)

a   *hosoi oun teleioi* ——————→ b   *touto phronōmen*
b′   *ei ti heterōs phroneite* ——→ a′   *kai touto ho theos hymin apokalypsei*

There is *wordplay* (*lambanō* 12a, *katalambanō* 12cd, 13a, act. and pass. voice; cf. Baumert 1973:400; n 474). *Words repeated in pairs: diōkō* (12c, 14); *ēdē* (12a and b); *teteleiōmai* (12b) and *teleioi* (15a); *phronein* (15a, 15b); "by" and "in Christ Jesus" (12d, 14). Contrasting ptcs., beginning with *epi-, epilanthanomenos* and *epekteinomenos* in 13b. *Irony* is likely with *teleioi* (15a, Lft. 153; Lincoln 93–94); see B.2, below.[4]

---

[2] See INTRO. VI.B n 2; (11) COMMENT A.1, on 3:2–4a; (12) COMMENT A.1, on 3:4b–11. Fields 229; Black 1995:44; Reumann 1991a:137, vv 12–14 *argumentatio*, 3:15–21 direct *refutatio* of those in v 2, via paraenesis in 15–16. Harnisch 146–49: *argumentatio* in *refutatio* form (12–14), with 15–16 the "upbeat" to the *peroratio* (15–21), rousing the audience against the opponents (*indignatio*). Holloway 2001a:140–42 finds a *correctio* (Lausberg #784–86), vv 13–14 amplify v 12, and 15–16 are concluding exhortation. Edart 241–43, 274, 3:12–14 = *probatio* (12ab *subpropositio*; 13 *concessio*); 15–16 laconic *peroratio* of Letter B.

[3] See INTRO. VI.B n 3; (11) COMMENT A.1, n 1. No proposal seems to treat 3:12–16 as a discrete unit. Wicks takes 3:1–16 with 1:12–26 (43, 85–101); *touto phronōmen* is related to 2:5 (98), and perfection (3:12b, 15a) to 4:18 (*memyēmai*), with *teleios* a tech. term from the mystery cults (95). See B.3 below. Bittasi 98–99, 113–20, 3:13–14 continue on Paul (parallel to Christ in 2:6–11); 3:15–16 is exhortation.

[4] Edart 234–35 has a complex theory: Letter B (3:2–16), on justification by faith, includes three redactoral additions (257–75) before A and B were combined: 12b *ē ēdē teteleiōmai*; 13b *ta men opisō epilambanomenos, tois de emprosthen epekteiomenos*; 14 *to brabeion.* Together with 3:11 ([12] COMMENT n 48), 3:12b introduces a note of eschatological uncertainty, *not already perfected* (contrast 1:23; 3:20–21). In 3:13b,14, athletic metaphors stress lack of achievement or imperfection. They heighten what Letter B (by Luke?) has said, but qualify the topos of the "Stoic sage" and his possible achievements

2. *Martyrdom as Perfection?*[5] Loh. 1928 argued that *the* theme throughout Phil is martyrdom. In 3:12–16, he stressed martyrdom for Paul (imprisoned in Caesarea) and for Philippian Christians. Cf. Loh. 1927b, his HNT commentary on Rev (1926, 2nd ed. 1953); his pupil G. Fitzer on *martys* (1928 diss.). For Loh., martyrdom became a hermeneutical principle; Jewish and Christian martyrs were lumped together, as were suffering and confession or witness (1927:233). Dornseiff argued that Christian "martyrs" arose out of Isa 43–44, esp. 43:9–13, "You are my witnesses" (vv 10, 12; cf. 44:8); Israel was chosen by God to witness and suffer. Judaism was a "religion of martyrdom" (W. Bousset, *Die Religion des Judentums im späthellenistischen Zeitalter*, HNT 21 [Tübingen: Mohr, 2nd ed. 1926] 374). Christianity elevated this, with Jesus Christ as "the faithful (and true) witness" (Rev 1:5; 3:14). Martyrs combine "the blessedness of suffering" and the "joy of

---

that Edart 93–113 sensed in 1:12–30, the gospel as a "new wisdom." These hypotheses are not convincing.

[5] *Literature on Martyrdom* (see also Exc. A.6): R. Asting, *Die Verkündigung des Wortes im Urchristentum: dargestellt an den Begriffen "Wort Gottes," "Evangelium," und "Zeugnis"* (Stuttgart: Kohlhammer, 1939); T. Baumeister, *Die Anfänge der Theologie des Martyriums*, Münsterische Beiträge zur Theologie 45 (Münster: Aschendorf, 1980); K. Berger 1984a:333–40, cf. 303; 1984b:1248–56; G. W. Bowersock, *Martyrdom and Rome* (Cambridge: Cambridge Univ. Press, 1995); D. Boyarin, "Martyrdom and the Making of Christianity and Judaism," *JECS* 6 (1998) 577–627; *Dying for God: Martydom and the Making of Christianity and Judaism* (Stanford: Stanford Univ. Press, 1999); N. Brox, *Zeuge und Märtyrer*, SANT 5 (Munich: Kösel, 1961); H. von Campenhausen 1936 (Exc. A Bibl.); F. Dornseiff, "Der Märtyrer, Name und Bewertung," *ARW* 22 (1923–24) 133–53; E. Esking, "Das Martyrium als theologisch-exegetisches Problem," in *In Memoriam Ernst Lohmeyer*, ed. W. Schmauch (Stuttgart 1951) 224–32; H. A. Fischel, "Martyr and Prophet. A Study in Jewish Literature," *JQR* 37 (1947) 265–80, 363–86; G. Fitzer, *Der Begriff des* martys *im Judentum and Urchristentum* (diss. Breslau, 1928); R. N. Flew, *The Idea of Perfection in Christian Theology: An Historical Study of the Christian Ideal for the Present Life* (London: Oxford Univ. Press, 1934); W. H. C. Frend, *Martyrdom and Persecution in the Early Church* (Garden City, NY: Doubleday, 1967); A. Gelin, "Les origines bibliques de l'idée de martyre," *LumVie* 36 (1958) 123–29; E. Günther, *Martys. Die Geschichte eines Wortes* (diss. Hamburg 1941); "Zeuge und Märtyrer," *ZNW* 47 (1956) 145–61; J. W. van Henten, *The Maccabean Martyrs as Saviours of the Jewish People: A Study of 2 and 4 Maccabees*, JSJSup 57 (Leiden: Brill, 1997); ed., *Die Entstehung der jüdischen Martyrologie*, StPB 38 (Leiden: Brill, 1989); ———/ F. Avemarie, *Martyrdom and Noble Death: Selected Texts from Graeco-Roman, Jewish, and Christian Antiquity* (London/New York: Routledge, 2002); K. Holl, "Die Vorstellung vom Märtyrer und die Märtyrerakten in ihrer geschichtlichen Entwicklung," *Neue Jahrbücher des klassischen Altertums* 33 (1914) 521–66, reprinted in Holl's *Gesammelte Aufsätze zur Kirchengeschichte* 2 (Tübingen: Mohr Siebeck, 1928) 68–102; W. Horbury/B. McNeil, eds., *Suffering and Martyrdom in the New Testament*, FS G. M. Styler (Cambridge: Cambridge Univ. Press, 1981); E. Kellermann, "Das Danielbuch und die Märtyrertheologie der Auferstehung," in van Henten, ed., 1989:51–70, "Anhang: Das Erscheinungsbild der Märtyrer in den frühen jüdischen Texten," 71–75; S. Lieberman, "The Martyrs of Caesarea," *Annuaire de l'institut de philologie et d'histoire orientales et slaves* 7 (1939–44) 395–446; "Roman Legal Institutions in Early Rabbinics and in the Acta Martyrium," *Texts and Studies* 57–111 (1944), repr. 1974; E. Lohmeyer 1927b (Exc. A Bibl.); T. W. Manson, "Martyrs and Martyrdom," *BJRL* 39 (1956–57) 463–84; J. S. Pobee, *Persecution and Martyrdom in the Theology of Paul*, JSNTSup 6 (Sheffield: JSOT, 1985); A. M. Schwemer, "Prophet, Zeuge und Märtyrer. Zur Entstehung des Märtyrerbegriffs im frühesten Christentum," *ZTK* 96 (1999) 320–50; K. Stendahl, "Martyr. Ordet och Saken. En Forskningsöveersikt," *STK* 27 (1951) 28–44; H. Strathmann, "Der Märtyrer," *TBl* 37 (1916) 337–43, 353–57; H. W. Surkau, *Martyrien in Jüdischer und Frühchristlichen Zeit*, FRLANT NF 36 (Göttingen: Vandenhoeck & Ruprecht, 1938); W. Wischmeyer, *RGG*[4] 5 (2002) 862–66.

proclaiming." But (Brox 147–49) can one make "witnessing" a "mark" of Israel, like election? *martys* appears in 43:9–13 only at vv 10 and 12, and then as "witnesses," not "martyr." 41:21–29, to which Loh. also appealed, lacks the term. Thus, Loh. called Deutero-Isaiah "creator of the idea of martyr in Judaism" (234), but evidence is hard to come by, even in Isa 53 (a text filled with problems). Isaiah has witnesses for God but not martyrdom; Judaism, martyrs (2, 4 Macc) but not called "witnesses" (Brox 149). According to Loh., "witness" and "martyr" continued in the NT. Mark 13:10 par Matt 10:17 (1927:244), Jesus' disciples testify to governors and kings (this need not mean martyrdom). von Campenhausen 1936: martyrdom was first developed as a theme by Christians, without going back to the OT.

In Phil, Loh. (*Phil.*148) asserts, Paul writes "as a martyr to martyrs" from prison (1:12, 20–24; imminent death seems more likely on Roman or Ephesian hypotheses than in Caesarea, Acts 26:32). Some Philippians, likely leaders (143, 148), are imprisoned. Proud of their martyr-consciousness, these witnesses regard themselves as "perfect" (143); they are full of grace and knowledge, receiving revelation from God. Martyr-pride threatens to bring division in the community. "Pursuit" involves the totality of the believer's life; martyrdom is its continuation (Loh. 146)[6]; believer and martyr are bound together by the images of running and growth from child to adult (1 Cor 2:6; 3:1–2). Faith and knowledge, imperfection and perfection are not an either/or but a process of growth (cf. 148). Were all believers in Philippi "grasped" (12d) by "perfection"? No. Note *hosoi* in v 15 and the impvs. (in 15b and 17). Some are *teleioi*, others are urged to think and walk as they do. In 15a, "we" unites Paul and other *teleioi*-martyrs, whose perfection comes, finally, when they receive the "call from God," homeward, as proof of salvation (149). 15b, "if you (2nd pl.) have a different mind," refers to martyrs in Philippi: they regard their perfection as an absolute; Paul regards it as relative, "not yet" (148–49). At whatever point in the race or pursuit one is, what matters (3:16) is that perfection come, whether at the parousia (4:5) or death (150). 3:17–21 will attack *outside* agitators (for Loh., Jews); 12–16 handle the *internal* threat ("martyrdom as perfection") more gently (150).

Reactions to Loh. were mixed.[7] Brox separated "witness" terminology in the NT and Christian "martyrdom," a later phenomenon (232). If *martys* was a title

---

[6] Loh. invokes Luther, "The nature of a Christian exists not in what he has become but in becoming " (cited by Beare 131), and Chrysost., "It is characteristic of one who is *teleios* not to consider himself *teleios*" (Bockmuehl 226).

[7] K. Holl regarded Jewish martyrs as forerunners of Christian martyrs; from 1 Cor 15:15, "martyrs of God" (a mirror-reading deduced from "falsewitness of God") were, through the Spirit, eyewitnesses of Christ's resurrection (Acts 6:15; 7:55–56; 22:15, 20; Rev 11:3; cf. Conzelmann, *1 Cor.* 265–66). Similarly, Surkau. Asting 711 asserted a direct line from *martys* as "proclaimer" to *martys* as "witness by blood" (in death). Flew 411 n 2 regarded "Lohmeyer's theory" as "not proven." E. Günther, with Strathmann (1916; *TDNT* 4:477–520, Ger. 1942), emphasized "apocalyptic witness" for the NT. Stendahl 1951 suggested NT data on the rise of the title "martyr" be separated for investigation from a biblical theology of martyrdom. Esking saw in Protestant exegesis a move from "word" and confession to "martyr." Is there, then, a (catholic) "sacramental" fellowship of sufferings with Christ? The connection of martyrs and prophets was pointed up by Fischel 1947. T. W. Manson supported roots in Isa 43, as did Gelin.

for martyrs in the NT period, why a gap of 50–60 years before it appears in this sense re Polycarp (martyred A.D. 156)? Martyrdom assumes death, not simply sufferings, so Ignatius (233–37). The Christians term came not from the philosopher as witness (Epictet.), but from witness in words and by deed. Perhaps "witness of the sufferings of Christ" (1 Peter 5:1) suggests imitation (39), but *martys* in the NT does not yet mean "martyr" (Brox; AB 37B:818–20). G. Delling (*RGG*[3] 5 [1961] 335) declared Loh.'s view "generally set aside." Frend 1965 pointed to Jewish origins for martyrdom in Christianity, but the church's conflict involved the Roman Empire (vii, ix, 104–26, 160–69 on the crisis of A.D. 64; "Lord Caesar or Lord Christ?" 70–138; 210–35 and passim). Frend has little about Paul, less on Philippi (85–87, 95–99, 158–59). *martys* is simply assumed to mean "martyr." Loh. is mentioned (582) only for his 1928 article. Frend's volume became standard. Cf. Baumeister 1980. Horbury/McNeil, Pobee, and Schwermer reflect a "consensus position" on martyrdom.

A "new look" in martyological studies has come in van Henten, Bowersock, and Boyarin, challenging roots in early Judaism and the extent of martyrdoms in NT Christianity. van Henten (1986; rev. 1997) questioned the date and historicity of materials in 4 Macc and even 2 Macc.[8] 4 Macc may reflect the Gk. *epitaphios logos* (oration at a tomb, as in praise for Athenians fallen for their *polis*; cf. Berger 1984a:346), as late as A.D. 70–135. Criteria for "Jewish martyrs" involve a government hostile to Jewish piety and religion; readiness to die for Torah; persecution to force Jews to renounce their religion; martyrs die for their faith and expect eternal life with God (16; cf. van Henten 1997:8). Kellermann lists some fifty-one motifs in Jewish martyr-texts (71–75), references in Phil for six of them,[9] though none in 3:12–16. Features claimed by Loh. (Spirit, grace, revelation) are *not* present.

Bowersock 1995 argues more radically against "martyrdom" prior to Christianity; it arises later, in confrontation with the Roman Empire. In Rabbinic Judaism the term for martyrdom, "*qidduš ha-shem* (sanctification of the name), does not occur until after the Tannaitic period" (9). The heroic stories in 2 Macc 6:18–7:41 do not occur in 1 Macc; the second of them may be a later insertion in 2 Macc (Bowersock 10–12). 4 Macc material is likely even later (79). Rev 1:5, 3:14, and 2:13 = witness, not martyr. Likewise Acts 22:20 (75–76). The martyrdom of Polycarp provides "the first attested example of word and act together" (17). Martyrdom as witness was thus a post-NT development. Martyrologies involve court scenes and records. Bowersock's analysis further undermines Loh.'s theory on Phil. Confrontation with the Roman Empire may fit Paul's day; a "civil role," involving pride in the *polis* (47, 50, 56), can be seen in 1:28. But there is little or no Jewish background in the Philippian church; no appeal to alleged OT-Jewish

---

[8] Van Henten 1989 shows the variety of views on Jewish martyrologies: there is a diachronic tendency (p. 19), development from Isa 53 on; and a synchronic one, Jewish and Christian materials influenced the other, 261; cf. 241–44. For texts, see van Henten/Avemarie 2002.

[9] Kellermann #(22), martyrs are encouraged to endure torture and carry on (Phil 1:14); (23) martyrdom as an athletic contest (2:16; add 3:12–14, *diōkō*?); (25) joy in suffering (4:4); (27) martyrdom as a military battle, God vs. Satan (4:3); (44) spiritualized meaning of martyrdom as sacrifice (2:17); (49) the martyr taken up into heaven after death (1:20, 23; 3:10). But are all these vv are really about "martyrs"?

roots for martyrdom need be made. *martys* does not occur in Phil, even for "witness"; no hint of legal hearings (but cf. Acts 16:19–24, 35–39). Evidence falls short of Bowersock's criteria. There is witnessing, without the term *martyreō*, but (*pace* Loh.) no martyrs.

Boyarin (1998 combines parts of chs. 1 and 4 from his 1999 book, cited here; cf. S. Lieberman, his teacher) sets aside Frend's thesis, that Christian martyrology is a "prolongation and succession" of Jewish martyrology (127–30), and accepts Bowersock's view that martyrdom had nothing to do with Judaism or Palestine but is something new in Late Antiquity, a Roman cultural product then borrowed from Christians by Jews. Christianity and Judaism were interrelated movements with cultural interchange (93–95, 114–17, 7–11). Loh. goes unmentioned.

This secondary literature seems unaware of K. Berger 1984a,b (van Henten 1997:7 is an exception), treating the deaths of John the Baptist, Jesus, and, in Acts, Stephen, James, and "the passion of Paul" form-critically. Berger concludes, "[I]n Hellenistic pagan Acts only the legal process is presented, in Jewish reports only the suffering and death," but both lines are reflected in NT data (1984a:338). Loh. is nowhere cited, or Phil. On this approach too, exit Lohmeyer's martyriological reading of the epistle.

3. The Upward (Heavenly) Call. The climactic 3:14, "the prize of the heavenly (or upward) call of God in Christ Jesus" ([N]RSV), raises many issues. We exclude a call "homeward," to the world above, *via martyrdom* (Loh. 147; see 2, above). The gen. *tēs . . . klēseōs* has been variously explained (see NOTE on v 14); *anō* may be taken as "upwards," to a higher level, or (in light of 3:20 *en ouranois*) as "heavenly." For *anō* + "call(ing)," O'B 431–33 (cf. Bockmuehl 222–23) lists three interpretations: (1) "The prize" (*to brabeion*) is "the upward call" (*klēseōs* as gen. of apposition or definition); calling and prize are the same thing (Fee 349 n 47; NEB). Cf. Philo, *Plant.* 23 (see NOTE) and Lincoln 93–94; the unusual sense for *klēsis* comes from opponents who locate the upward call to heavenly existence already in this life. (2) Athletic imagery: the victor is called up to receive the prize (by the *Hellanodikai* and officials at the games; Collange and others in NOTE). The call brings the prize (Fee 349 n 47). O'B 433, it "may be correct" if *klēsis* can mean the call to the victor's pedestal (concrete evidence is lacking); allusion to the games is fanciful (Fee n 49). (3) O'B, most trs.: *klēsis* = God's act of calling to salvation; *tēs klēseōs*, subj. gen. (NIV, many commentators). The prize is what "is announced or promised by the call," i.e., "everlasting life," "full and complete gaining of Christ." *klēsis* has its normal sense in Paul, *anō* = "heavenward." The call is "initial summons"; the prize, what it announces; meanwhile, "Run!" Fee 349 regards "call" "from the perspective of its completion rather than its beginnings"; the prize is "tangible evidence that the goal of God's call has been reached." Bockmuehl 222–23 objects; with Müller, he notes Philo, where "the spirit-filled soul is . . . 'called up (*anō kleisthai*) to' God" (*Plant.* 23; see NOTE). But Bockmuehl declines making too precise an interpretation.

Other solutions: the call = *entry* into the race; divine election to be "in Christ" or, in Paul's case, apostleship and grace (Rom 1:5); initial call (Damascus Road) or more likely mission throughout Paul's career, Gal 1:15; not completed till the goal is reached, at the parousia or the individual's death. Many see the outcome in a heavenly *politeuma* (3:20), "Jerusalem above" (Gal 4:26); cf. Lincoln 101, 18–27. Less frequently an *interim kingdom* on earth is read in; cf. 1 Cor 15:24 (between the parousia and "then come the rest," NRSV-mg). Portefaix 138–54 urges "celestial citizenship" (see below on 3:20–21). Alexarchus is said to have founded a town about 316 B.C. on Mt. Athos, some fifty miles south of Philippi (J. Ferguson, *Utopias of the Classical World* [London 1975] 108–12, 124ff.), named Uranopolis, "City of Heaven" (Ath. 3.98D; Strab. 7 frg. 35; Pliny *NH* 4.10.37). Portefaix 153–54 assumes that this was "known in Philippi," including anecdotes on egalitarian status for women in Uranopolis. Subsequent commentators have not endorsed speculations about Uranopolis with regard to 3:12–16, 20–21.

The TRANSLATION *I run in pursuit toward the goal at the finish, for the prize, to be called upward by God . . .* tries to keep open some of these possibilities. In terms of Paul's "I"-account, it reflects his call as apostle, still in pursuit of this calling. Metaphors about a runner continue: called to the course, in the race, eyes on the prize, called up to the victor's pedestal. *upward* may eventually be defined to include a heavenly *politeuma* (3:20), but for now one runs the course in Caesar's world. Paul runs thinking of *brothers and sisters* in Philippi, who are also called to run, in the same contest as Paul.[10] See further, B.1, end, below, on the v.

B. MEANING AND INTERPRETATION

1. I, Paul, Continue the Race Toward the Goal (3:12–14). With ellipsis (*I do . . . say* is supplied) and asyndeton (no "and" or "but"), a new section, on the heels of all Paul has said about himself in 3:4–11 concerning Law, his faith-righteousness, and resurrection hope. Lack of a connective points to a "clarification and a proposition [eventually in v 14] referring back to what has gone immediately before" (Holmstrand 119). The "I"-form, through v 14, asserts what existence means for Paul as one who believes in and knows Christ, in "the language of 'Already' and Not yet'" (D. K. Williams 2002:195). Just as there was a negative picture of Saul the Pharisee and then a positive one of Paul "in Christ" (3:4b–6 and 7–11, respectively), there will now be a negative presentation, what the apostle has *not* attained (3:12–13a), then a positive one, how he runs toward the goal (vv 13b–14).[11] There was a "great reversal" in values because of Christ (3:7). There will be a great fulfillment for the Pharisee who was "taken hold of by Christ Jesus" (3:12d). Perfection is *not* his, even now in Christ, the way it *will be* one day, with Christ. This holds for every Christian—existence means tension between what has already been received and what still lies ahead.

---

[10] Holloway's diagnosis (2001a:142) is curious: the "fundamental problem at Philippi" was "a backward looking emphasis on the mission and not a present and forward-looking emphasis on Christ." Eschatology at fault?

[11] "Negative/positive pattern," cf. Schenk 309; Dupont compares 3:4–16 with Rom 1:18–ch. 5 and 7:7–8:39.

As to aim(s) in 3:12–16, some hear a *polemical* tone against people who claim to have "taken hold" and "been perfected" (Loh. 143; Schmithals 1972:93–94; Koester 1961–62; Baumbach 1971:302–3; O'B 418), "the enemies" in 3:2–3, or the Pharisaic Jew described there from Paul's earlier days. Some claim only theoretical enemies (the negative) in ch. 3 but Paul as model (Stowers 1991:109, 116; Ernst, RNT *Phil.* 100). Sumney 1999:181–82 minimalizes polemics (contrast Schenk, COMMENT A.1.b above). Others see *clarification*, to prevent misunderstanding of vv 4–11. All has been turned about for him, but he has not attained the final goal. He spoke with tentativeness about attaining the resurrection of the dead (in v 11), so it is advisable to say more robustly what he does press forward toward. Caird 141, Paul corrects the "book-keeping terminology" about "profit and loss" in v 7. He clarifies his position against notions that "to know Christ" means to have arrived (at perfection) and opposes any and all who think they are now *teleioi* and make similar claims.

Verse 12 has five vbs., never a dir. obj., no nouns except at the end, *by Christ Jesus*. ("I" is expressed by vb. endings, not a pron. in v 12.) The two initial vbs. will be reiterated later: *elabon* (*I have . . . had success*) by *katalambanō* twice in 12cd and also in 13a, wordplay brought out in the TRANSLATION through *successfully take hold; teteleiōmai* (*I am . . . perfected*), by *teleioi* in v 15 ("perfected"), explained by what is said within this *inclusio*, esp. the imagery of running a race, a metaphor introduced in v 12 by *I run in pursuit* ("keep on running," CEV; NABRNT).

The abrupt, objectless vbs. are the bane of commentators. The first could simply mean "I (have not) received"; "take hold of" mentally (recall the *phronein*-vbs., 2:5, etc.), "take hold of" with the hands (a trophy, for example), or "make one's own." But *what* has Paul not grasped? The vb. that piggybacks on *elabon*, *katalambanō*, does not help much. It can mean "make one's own," "attain," or in track-talk "win" (1 Cor 9:24). In classical and LXX texts (see NOTE on 12c) the combination "run" and "overtake" might have been proverbial. "I run," Paul says, "to overtake . . . ," but what? Some light comes when Paul employs a favorite device, a shift to the pass., "be overtaken by, *was successfully taken hold of* (*katelēmphthēn*), *by Christ*"; see NOTE on 12d for other examples. *by Christ Jesus* begins an *inclusio* completed with *in Christ Jesus* in v 14. Thus, for all the attention given the "I"-form and the racing metaphor, Christ begins to emerge in v 12 as the key figure, with God (14, 15b), in the passage. Inclusion of *justified*, though not finally as in the Last Judgment, goes well with acts of God and Christ.

teteleiōmai is similarly abrupt and multifaceted. To "reach a goal" (NRSV-txt.) could fit a footrace. But "bring to completion" at the Day of Christ Jesus (1:6) pushes the sense toward future eschatology (Fowl 2005:160, his [proper] end). A long tradition of (moral) "perfection" language rings in the ear from Gk. philosophy, the KJV, and Christian piety, though Paul says, "I have *not* yet reached perfection" (NEB/REB). Note "yet," a nefarious adv. that creeps into many a rendering, commentary, and sermons, from the textual variant *oupō* in v 13 and/or *ēdē* in 12a and b (Gdsp. and JB with *elabon*). On grounds that Paul, in spite of his plain words, must have expected to become *teleios* (cf. 15a) during his lifetime on earth, "yet" has abetted the notion of "real saints" reaching perfection soon and spurred people on to greater efforts. Fee 338 speaks strongly against such optimism in his textual note on 3:13a. Our NOTE on 12b (word studies on *teleioun*-terms) documents battles over "absolute" and "relative perfection."[12] BDAG 3, "become consecrated, initiated," is a choice that few in Anglo-Saxon scholarship have followed at 3:12b, with its mystery-cults or "gnostic" connotations. But given the religions and language to which the Philippian audience was no stranger (see NOTE on 12b) and Paul's use in Letter A of *memyēmai* at 4:12c (see NOTE on *I have had my initiation experience* and COMMENT, a "mystery-cult term," possibly ironic), one cannot exclude the sense here. Our TRANSLATION, not that "I am already perfected," is open to it; such cults offered perfection to initiates.

Various objects have been proposed for the first four vbs. (the fifth is pass.). Too many. To insert "this" or "it" masks the problem. The NOTE on 1:12a lists options: Christ, knowledge of him, righteousness, future resurrection; in vv 12–14, the prize, perfection, or even martyrdom. Paul could have had different terms in mind with different vbs. Possibly he omitted any obj. because his attaining is incomplete; so is any list. To that extent, "all of the above" could apply, summarized as "Christ and his benefits," of which Paul had a foretaste but did not fully possess or have at his disposal.[13] The abrupt vbs. and their uncertain objects did not arise out of thin air. If Paul were being autobiographical, we could expect him to be more precise. The question of aim (noted above) and slogans from "the enemies" (A.1.b) shape Paul's language (see below). On one level, Paul is engaged in *self-correction*. Talk about "profit and loss" (3:7) or his reserve about himself in the final resurrection (3:11) might be misunderstood. So Paul shifts in 12d to the pass. voice to bring in God or Christ as agent, not just "I." Paul "could have simply exchanged boasts" (Garland 1985:171) about his union with Christ and shown "an even greater sense of superiority than he had as a Pharisee" (Caird 141). Without using "boast" here (cf. 3:3), Paul corrects possible misunderstandings by clarifying what was said previously. "I"-talk is corrected by *hypo Christou Iēsou* in 12cd. "Countinghouse language" about gains and losses (3:7) is balanced by what amounts to "assets under development but not yet matured." Justification as a past and present experience, triggered by reference to faith-righteousness (3:9bc), is seen to have a "not yet" side in the future.

A second level of application concerns *Judaism and what Paul has said about his life in Pharisaism* (3:4b–6). Any boasting over life "in Christ" (vv 7–11) is balanced by the theme "not yet" (cf. Caird and Garland above). This may be critique of the view in Judaism about the attainment possible under the Law (see NOTE on 12b, citing Delling; Philo, *Leg.* 3.74; Rigaux on Qumran). *diōkō* in 12c "to describe his religious pursuits as a Christian" echoes 6a on "his pre-Christian reli-

---

[12] "Relative perfection" was popularized by R. Brown in contrast to the view of the "Secessionists" in 1 John who taught freedom from sin (AB 30:79–83, 257–58, 430–31, 521, 530; *The Community of the Beloved Disciple* [New York: Paulist, 1979] 124–27).

[13] E.g., resurrection: the believer is joined with Christ in his death, to walk in newness of life, but not yet raised the way Christ is (Rom 6:4). Righteousness/justification: the sinner is reckoned righteous, lives righteously, and even is "filled with the fruit of righteousness" (1:11), but has not yet attained the final verdict at the Day of the Lord (confirmation of an earlier declaration).

gious pursuits as a persecutor" (*DA* 310). In 3:4b–6, Paul did not trash his years in Judaism; in 3:12–16, any comparison is mixed, pro and con. He avoids notions that he has "arrived fully" now. There is contrast with what Saul once thought, but also a likeness to Israel "on the way" in the wilderness years (cf. 1 Cor 10:1–13).

Another level of meaning has to do with *all Christians* (Dupont, among others). Philippian believers are to benefit from Paul's example and how he now runs. They had no "great reversal" from Pharisee and Torah to life "in Christ" but have had reversals in religious belief (whatever the background in each household) and change in Lords (from Caesar or other deities to Christ). They face questions of suffering (even if no "martyrdom" theory from Loh. holds for leaders in prison) and resurrection (absent in their credo in 2:6–11, but prominent at 3:10a, 11). Above all, there is the issue of perfection, attaining the goal now, laying hold on Christ fully. Such emphases could arise out of Paul's teaching—the present aspect of justification, the sacramental side of baptism as "died and risen with Christ," Paul's use of "initiation" language as at 4:12b. Admonitions like 1 Cor 14:20 ("be *teleioi* in your thinking") could lead to perfectionist attitudes in Philippi, as in Corinth (so Thielman 1995:197).

More specifically, 3:12 reflects *the language of opponents*. Statements atypical of Paul (the emphasis on human achievement, though balanced by 3:12d, *taken hold of by Christ Jesus*) "may simply have been occasioned by the opponents' particular ideologies" (*DA* 137), perfectionism that they taught. The link with 3:2–4a suggests a claim that, for Christians, circumcision adds a grasp on "success," perfection. Terms and ideas unparalleled earlier in Phil can be accounted for as phrases from those whom Paul combats. Even commentators who deplore "mirror readings" allow that reflections of teachings not by Paul (or developed from him among the Philippians) appear in v 12. Dir. objs. may be lacking because Paul does not know their claims exactly or does not want to mention them precisely. The vbs. are what Paul negates. Of the possible dir. objs. listed above, Paul shares all of them with "the enemies," though differing, e.g., over "when" for resurrection (now or to come) and a future side of righteousness/justification. The clear, closing thought in the v is *successfully taken hold of by Christ Jesus*; here "the call of God upward" (v 14) reaches Paul (Grundmann, *TDNT* 9:552 n 376).

Ample markers in 13a indicate a new beginning.[14] Paul articulates his goal emphatically through a final formulation in v 14. He could hardly lead up to the point in 13b–14 more plainly; it is like a ship or airline announcement, "Attention all passengers, hear this." Paul softens it with an affectionate address, *adelphoi*. The negative *ou*, with *logizomai* (as in 12a, where a vb. of saying must be supplied), denies the claim of having attained or become perfect. Later scribes weakened the word with *oupō*, "not yet," suggesting that what Paul is denying will soon be his; LB/NLT-txt, "I am still not all I should be" (but, implication, will be

---

[14] Holmstrand 119: *Brothers and sisters* in initial position; emphasis on the speaker, *I for my part . . . myself* (*egō* and *emauton*), in contrast to what others say about perfection (so Schenk 328–29), "metapropositional *ou logizomai*," "I do not consider," in effect reiterating *I have come to consider* and . . . *continue to consider* in vv 7–8a (*hēgeomai*).

shortly), cf. GNB-mg. Instead of the widely quoted formula about eschatology, "no longer/not yet" (Merk 190), one should say here, *"no longer* what I was, but *not* in this life *what I shall be* (at the parousia)."

But one thing I do say (13b) heralds Paul's announcement. The terse Gk. has prompted many expansions (see NOTE). "Just one thing" (NABRNT) catches it nicely. Paul offers a conviction derived from his gospel, logical consequences (Schenk 261, in connection with *logizomai*) from the Easter gospel of the risen Lord (as at Rom 8:18, Rom 6:11, 2 Cor 11:5, 1 Cor 4:11). 3:13a shifts to the pres. tense, which will predominate all the way through v 21 (aor. in vv 16 and 21 in dependent cls., fut. in 16 and 21 about what God or Christ will do). Paul is speaking to the present, not of the past as in 3:4b–6, 7, 8c or future (as in Fee's formulation for vv 12–14, "The Future Lies with the Future"). Paul talks about himself in the here and now. He uses imagery from athletic games, begun in 12c with *run in pursuit*, like *take hold* (of a trophy), language that may have come originally from those who think they run and have already obtained (12a).

Paul's statement uses the same main vb. in 3:14 as in 3:12c, *I run in pursuit*, with two carefully balanced subordinate ptcs. in 13b, "on the one hand, on the other": *unconcerned about the things that lie behind, but stretching out toward the things that lie ahead.* Here the "autobiographical" and the "stadium-metaphor" levels collide. *In a race* the athlete cannot forget or be unconcerned about how much ground has been covered (Lft. 152) if s/he is to pace him/herself for the distance. The runner will respond when rivals are catching up.[15] The first line also fits with Paul's *experience in life.* He has not forgotten his time in Judaism (vv 4–6b detail features from it). He has not forgotten circumcision (enemies now demand it for those in Christ, 3a). But he is *unconcerned* about such things; they are "losses," not "assets" (7), "crap" (8c). Thus (*pace* O'B 428–29), *the things (that lie) behind* refer in 3:4b–16 to Paul's past in Judaism (Martin 1976:139; H. Marshall 96; Witherington 95; Walter NTD 82). Hawth. 153 sees further the wrongs Paul did persecuting the church. Martin includes "past achievements as a Christian apostle." Many prefer such a view. Vincent 109, "his *Christian* course already traversed," as Paul may itemize it in a *peristasis* catalogue like 2 Cor 11:23–28. Beare 130; Caird 143; Gnilka 199; Michael 161–62. Collange 134 and Loh/Nida 111 include both. The value of the phrase is its contrast with what follows.

Paul pictures himself *stretching out toward the things that lie ahead.* Track imagery dominates over autobiography. Commentators see the runner straining toward the finish line, conjecturing how close he may be to the goal (see NOTE). Do "outstretched, empty hands" (Pfitzner 140) mean a hand stretched out to grasp "the goal" (Hendriksen 173) or should we hear Toplady's hymn line, "Nothing in my hand I bring, Simply to Thy Cross I cling" ("Rock of Ages," against John Wes-

---

[15] A footrace, not chariots (not to keep an eye on other chariots could prove fatal), Krentz 2003:352. Jones 57 recalls, re looking back during a race, the dire results in the story of Atalanta, who was promised to the man who could defeat her in a footrace. After several suitors were defeated, Hippomenes won her by dropping golden apples during the race that she stopped to pick up (references in OCD[3] 199).

ley's notion that a believer could go through life without sinning)? "What lies ahead" gets less conjecture than *the things that lie behind* because v 14 spells out what is before the runner, mostly in "stadium" terms. For Paul theologically "the End, parousia, resurrection, judgment, the Kingdom, life and glory, immortality" (1 Thess 4:13–5:11; 1 Cor 15:48–53; Phil 3:20–21; Rom 8:18–23, 30–39; *TPTA* 294–315); cf. the hopes expressed in Phil 1:19–26; 2:23–24. More immediately, he hopes to come to Philippi, travel to Jerusalem with the collection for the poor saints there, and then his Spanish mission, via Rome. If he is still jailed in Ephesus (3:2–21 within a unified letter), those hopes hold, once he sees how things turn out in court (2:23–24).

The denouement for 3:12–16 and all of 3:2ff. thus far comes in v 14: *I run in pursuit toward the goal, for the prize, to be called upward by God, in Christ Jesus. diōkō* is part of an *inclusio* with 12c. The point (13b *hen de*) is running in pursuit, again linear action; "I continue my pursuit" (NABRNT). 3:12 was a v of vbs., 3:14 is a concatenation of nouns, six of them, with just one vb. All three of the noun phrases that surround *diōkō* — *kata skopon, eis to brabeion,* and the gen. *tēs anō klēseōs* — fit the racecourse metaphor, but can also have meanings in Paul's apostolic career, particularly "call" *(klēsis)*, where some make the theological side determinative. Clearly theological contents appear immediately after *klēseōs*: "of God" and the phrase "in Christ Jesus," again climactic, like *by Christ Jesus* in v 12. The complexities of "the upward call" have been discussed in COMMENT A.3. There is "stadium" language, Paul's story, and theological conclusions drawn from the gospel of God in Christ, for the Philippians, against "the enemies."

The first phrase, *toward the goal at the finish (kata skopon),* esp. with *I run,* refers to the finish line at a track meet. It could also refer in Gk. to one who watches out for (in a good sense, cf. 3:17 *skopeite*) or watches over a city, and then a goal or target at which one aims (see NOTE), a goal that controls life; cf. Plato *Gorg.* 507D, "This goal seems . . . necessary for the person who sees it to live, and who strains *(synteinonta)* toward it for himself and the *polis,* in order that justice may be present and self-control"; Gk. text and further references in *TDNT* 7:413–14; for *skopos* in Stoic philosophy, see Alpers-Gölz (in NOTE). There might have been such connotations to *kata skopon,* but the sense of stadium finish line takes over as the passage goes on; hence our TRANSLATION. But further reflection asks about the goal in life for Paul and other believers. Thus Fee 348: "the eschatological consummation of what is 'already' his in Christ." Or, better, what is promised, and meanwhile mission.

The second phrase is *for the prize (eis to brabeion).* Again, athletic jargon: a wreath of wild olive or celery branches for a winning runner, familiar in Philippi for champions at the games and awards for civic benefactors (see on 4:2 *crowning wreath, stephanos*). Paul uses *brabeion* in an athletic setting at 1 Cor 9:24, "all compete, but only one receives the prize." Here at 3:14 Paul is the only runner mentioned, a model, with the implication that whoever crosses the finish line will gain the prize. His point: we're not at the goal; no prize as yet.[16]

---

[16] Less likely interpretations: "the call" is synonymous with *brabeion,* or is the call to enter the race, or a "call upward" (to heaven), issued but not yet fulfilled.

The third phrase, *to be called upward by God (tēs anō klēseōs tou theou)*, is the most disputed. One approach is "called up to the winner's pedestal," by the judges or a herald, at Gk. games to receive the prize; see NOTE for evidence. The chief objection is that no text is extant using *kalein*, let alone with *anō*, in such a context. A second approach comes in texts from Philo (see NOTE) where "called up to God" occurs (*Plant.* 23); "heavenward yearning" and being "pulled upward" (*Her.* 70).[17] "Paul's Jewish Christian opponents or the group likely to succumb to their teachings in the Philippian church were using this sort of language in their claims to an exalted status," they "have received the upward call already in this life." Cf. 2 Cor 3:12–18 on Moses and glory in the claims of opponents there. So Lincoln on Paul's "unusual use of *klēsis*" at 3:14. Schenk 303–4 went further,[18] but his mix of Qumran, Philo, and *Joseph and Aseneth* with Philippi is well rejected by U. B. Müller 170.[19] Behind the "upward call" there may be a case in Philo texts for Jewish-Hellenistic (Christian) speculations; Lincoln is more convincing than Schenk or Müller.

A third approach to *called upward* is strictly biblical: "call" = the summons from God to faith and responsibility, for an individual like Paul or a people (Israel, "the saints" in Corinth, Philippi, etc.). They are "chosen" or "elect." See NOTE on *klēsis* and COMMENT A.3.(3). But to see this as (part of) the background does not settle whether 3:15 means (a) initial, or (b) continuing, or (c) a future, special call "above," and whether (i) for Paul or (ii) all Christians. Clearly, Paul is meant. If what is true for Paul is true for every believer, the "upward call" holds for all the Philippians addressed in vv 15–16. When does this call occur? Paul had an initial calling to believe in Christ and to serve as an apostle (Gal 1:1, 15–16); it involved revelation (1:12 *apokalypsis*). That call continued throughout his mis-

---

[17] So Gnilka 200; U. B. Müller 169; Bockmuehl 223. Lincoln 93–94 used the *De Plant.* material to relate such ideas to the way Paul used *anō* for "the heavenly dimension" (Gal 4:26) and *klēsis* as "the divine initiative in bringing a person to faith." In the Philo passages, those who are heavenly plants, "who have received the divine spirit, are called up to God." Of Moses in particular, it is said, God "called him up above" (Lev 1:1, *anekalese*).

[18] Schenk adds Philo *QE* 2.46 (LCL p. 91): "The calling above (*anaklēsis*) of the prophet" (Moses, to Mt. Sinai and the glory of the Lord; Exod 24:12, 15–16) "is a second birth better than the first"; "the calling above" is "divine birth." Schenk relates the *anō* at 3:14 with *(ex)anastasis* at 3:10a and 11; 3:14 = Jewish "conversion terminology" (circumcision assumed for a convert?). Cf. 1QH 3.19–20, ". . . Lord . . . you have lifted me up to an everlasting height," cf. 21–22 to "fellowship with the angels" (tr. García Martínez p. 332 = Col. xi. 19–20, 21–22); 1QH 11.11–12, p. 353 = Col. xix.12; 1QH 15.17, ". . . [from] flesh you have raised [up] his glory" (p. 323 = Col. vii.21), "resurrection" describes exaltation to fellowship in the sphere of divine life. Such dualistic wisdom Schenk finds also in the Hellenistic-Jewish conversion story, *Joseph and Aseneth*. Aseneth "will be renewed and formed anew and made alive again" (*Jos. Asen.* 15.5 = OTP 2:226; cf. 15.12 = OTP 2:227). She finds "mysteries of the Most High revealed" to her. Schenk thinks the opponents reflected such language in presenting resurrection as entrance now into heaven, with sacramental initiation (circumcision?). To such views, some in Philippi succumbed. Euodia and Syntyche (cf. below, on 4:2–3), Schenk supposes, were on the way to becoming Aseneths!

[19] *Jos. Asen.* 15.5 refers to re-newal (as in OTP), not "upward-newal" (*herauferneuert*, Schenk; i.e., *ana*, not *anō*). "Conversion as 'ascent into the heavenly world'" needs better evidence. 3:14 cannot be understood apart from polemical argumentation by the apostle, who is oriented to an "upward call"; opponents remain in the realm of "earthly things" (cf. 3:19), including the Law as part of what lies behind Paul.

sionary labors. But now, as nowhere else, he speaks of a call "upward" *(anō)* that has to do with *the goal at the finish* and *the prize*, which are not simply to be equated, though Paul's Gk. interrelates them. Cf. A.3, end, above. If the upward call is understood solely in "track" terms, then it may be virtually the same as the prize; *brabeion* = called up to the winner's stand to receive the wreath (NEB/ REB). But more is implied by "call," and the prize too may suggest more, though not an ascent now into the heavenly realms, apart from the future resurrection (2 Cor 12:2–4 is not in view). If the call is that of Paul to apostleship and "the race" in mission life, then the prize and the term "upward" provide something further: at the finish line, the goal—death or the parousia, when winners are crowned— resurrection-exaltation. If the call upward is more specific than Paul's being called to faith and service, as we think it is, then *klēseōs* is a subj. gen.; God's call upward leads to the prize—Christ, acceptance at the final judgment, and (the crown of) life. 3:20–21 will fill out the picture. Paul does not use the term "heavenly" in 3:14; what follows in 15–16 (17–19) continues to be oriented to the running of the race here and now.

diōkō in 14 and 12c emphasizes that Paul keeps on running. That is what he commends to the Philippians. His experience with congregations caught up in speculations about the Endtime is that they stopped daily tasks and work in this world (1 Thess 4:13–5:11; 2 Thess 3:10, counted Paul's in AB 32B). From Corinth Paul knew problems with the resurrection (1 Cor 15) and how gifts of the Spirit could disrupt daily life; hence 15:58, abound in the work of the Lord. Philippi was different from either Thessalonica or Corinth, but Phil 3 faces up to disruptive threats to the congregation's life. Paul's continued running, pressing on, was meant to model the ongoing task for each believer and the whole community. Keep on in what for them? Worship (3:3), evangelization (a Philippian emphasis), right teaching and living, support for others financially, engagement as citizens or sojourners in the *polis*, Caesar's and God's. 3:15–16 will be marked for the first time in Letter C with impvs. Paraenesis is part of "running." From God comes the call.

The final phrase in v 14, *in Christ Jesus,* is a signature piece in Paul's major as- sertion against claims of perfection. It can be taken with *I run* or with *called up- ward* or with *God.* If the last, it is God "*through* Christ Jesus." If with the vb. *diōkō,* the *sphere* in which Paul runs (relationship with his Lord, an ecclesial sense). If with "calling," agent (perhaps Christ as herald at the games), but also *content,* Christ's death and resurrection. "In Christ" exhibits, as usual, a range of options. In context here, it goes with *successfully taken hold of by Christ Jesus* in v 12d (Schenk 309: the event of calling through the risen Jesus that grounds Christian existence). The race is run totally "in Christ," till at the End we are with Christ.

2. You, Philippians, Think and Continue Likewise (3:15–16). To all his beloved converts (S. F. Winter 174), the *brothers and sisters* at v 13a, Paul now speaks as apostle-founder and teacher of their house churches, in light of what he has said autobiographically, in the face of potential enemies. Paraenetic consequences are drawn, indicated by *then* (*oun*, first and only time in Letter C); "we" (15–16), not

"I" (4b–14); impvs. (15a, 16) (Holmstrand 119). A rhetorical shift, though critics disagree whether 15–16 are part of a peroration or a refutation through v 21 (n 2, above). All this suggests (Holmstrand) a conclusion for the unit that began at 3:2, in the body of Letter C.

3:15a seems straightforward, *As many, then, as are "perfected," let us think in this way. teleioi*, usually rendered "mature," has, like *I am* (not) *already perfected* in 12b, a mystery-religions background; hence "initiated" into whatever the enemies of 3:2–3 were peddling, in light of 12–15 on "perfection" as arrival now at the goal, already in this life. *think* reintroduces a familiar vb. (see NOTE on 4:10); here, to what shall we be oriented? How shall we think among ourselves? What is our concern? *in this way (touto)* points to what Paul means. The real problems are, Why *As many as?* All Philippian believers or a particular group (Baumbach 1971: 303; Montague 131–32)? Does Paul identify with the *"perfected,"* in spite of 12a about *not* being among those who claim perfection?

let us think shows goodwill toward the Philippians. No gruff 2nd per. command. Paul identifies with them.[20] He can include himself because he has recounted how he thinks/runs/lives in Christ. *in this way* refers not to what follows but back to what Paul has said: (a) he continues to "press on" ("run the race," Bockmuehl 226); (b) fulfillment is future, not perfection now. Behind vv 12–14 lies what Paul recounted in vv 4b–11 on his experiences with the Law, knowing Christ, faith-righteousness, and the resurrection to come. Righteousness/justification is pivotal (Reumann 1989:24–25); for Paul, *dikaiosynē* involves both pres. (realized) and fut. aspects.

As many . . . as are "perfected" is, or modifies, the subject of the main vb., *us*, Paul and those in Philippi. Some see the entire community infected with perfection-fever, even Euodia and Syntyche. Others envision the Philippians standing firm against potential threats, literary composites in a gallery of possible menaces. The truth lies somewhere in between. *hosoi*, "whoever (of us)," lays down a principle that applies whenever *teleios* crops up.

We regard Paul's use of *teleioi* as ironic. Opponents claim, "I am already perfected." Paul denied this for himself in 12b. He invites any in Philippi who profess or feel this way ("attracted by the perfection propaganda," Grayston 40) to think the matter through as he has done. *teleios* has the sense that BDAG 3 prefers; cf. Col. 1:28 and 1 Cor 2:6. To indicate its origins and ironic use by Paul, *"perfected"* is put into quotation marks.[21] Irony is not inappropriate for Paul,[22] even as pastor

---

[20] All three impvs. here are softened: *stoichein* (16, [*let us*] *continue*) is an infin., instead of a 2nd pl. In 17, 2nd pl. "be," the initial word has a prefix *sym-*, "co-imitators"; NRSV "join in imitating me."

[21] Cf. Lft. 153, who compared 1 Cor 8:1, "We all have knowledge," an opponents' slogan; Beare 130–31 cites Haupt 142, an oxymoron, "in the Christian vocabulary **perfect** can only mean 'conscious that we are not perfect'" (cf. Aquinas, *Phil.* 105: "Think what I think, i.e., that I am not perfect") ; Koester 1961–62:322–23; Gnilka 201; Collange 122, 135 considered reading the indic. *phronoumen*, "Is not this how all we who are 'perfect' think?" (ironic); Silva 205 "a touch of irony"; Lincoln 99–100; D. Peterson 40; O'B 435 n 89; Fee 353 n 10; Harnisch 148–49; Peterlin 84.

[22] E.g., 2 Cor 11:19–20; 1 Cor 4:8; Phil 3:19 "god"; litotes as ironic understatement, 3:1b.

(contra Ernst, RNT *Phil.* 104, whose sense of *Seelsorger* should be compared with "the philosophical tradition of pastoral care" in Malherbe 1987 and AB33).

An alternative gives *teleioi* at 15a a sense that can include Paul, namely "(spiritually) mature." Then Paul denies he is "perfect" (12b) but is "adult" in his Christianity (1 Cor 14:20, perhaps 1 Cor 2:6). Thus NEB/REB, NRSV (mg in v 12). Some take 12b as an athletic metaphor, "It is not that . . . I have already finished my course" (NAB, though Schoder had "perfection," echoing the mystery religions, and "initiated") or "reached the goal" (NRSV-txt; NJB). There are in these interpretations no quotation marks; *teleioi* does not come from opponents.[23] If *teleioi* = "mature" or adult, the sentence becomes a truism, with little reference to 12–15. But Paul *is* refuting something, polemically, using irony, though with surprising gentleness in v 15 (as in 1:15–17). That "something" is the claim to be "already perfected," here via circumcision and Law.

Any chiasm linking 15a with 15b (COMMENT A.1.d) is inexact.[24] In amplification of 15a, Paul presents in 15b a condition regarded as true, a situation God will address among the Philippians. In recent (primarily Eng.) commentaries that reject polemic or opponents here, the interpretations vary and generally trivialize.[25] For *heterōs* Silva (see NOTE on 15b *otherwise*) sees "negative overtones," "if you are thinking *wrongly*. . . ." Not minor matters but "the right Christian mindset (*phronein*)," cf. Bockmuehl 226–27, as at 2:1–4 and 4:2–3. "Friendship" has been offered as an explanation, but the *philia* is curious.[26] "Imitation" (3:17) carries an idea of "sameness," to be the same as the person imitated (here Paul), not notions

---

[23] For "mature" in v 15, cf. Michael 164–65 (but see our NOTE on 15a); Bruce 124, 126; O'B 436–37; Bockmuehl 225–26; Caird 143–44, 3:15–16 exhibits "two radically different interpretations": Paul's "mark of a mature Christian" leads to either (a) the notion "That's Paul's conviction but we all have different levels of understanding," in accord with the individual's conscience; or (b) if there are matters on which you hold "unsound opinions," "God will lead you to see the truth," meanwhile we must live together "by that one standard we all share." For good reasons, Caird objects to (a) as "modern individualism," but (b) may not be much better when Paul's convictions are considered.

[24] *let us think* + an obj. *(in this way, touto)* and *if you think* + an obj. *(about something, ti)* suggest one crossover, but the other leg of the X would link *As many, then, as are* "*perfected*" with *this too God will reveal to you.* Those claiming to be *teleioi* need a revelation from God. The b and a′ segments (on the right of the X) are related, in parallel, by the use of *touto.*

[25] O'B 437–40 , *ti,* "something," = "*minor* issues . . . inadequacies or inconsistencies" (cf. Hooker NIB 11:534) compared with a "primary concern" of "basic thinking and striving" (*touto* in 15a). *apokalypsei* is then rendered "will make it plain to you" (NEB/REB), i.e., remove the inconsistencies and any "aberration" in minor matters, even though O'B thoroughly summarizes the "theologically-important word-group," *apokalyptein,* revelation, in the NT. As analogy for 3:15, Eph 1:17–18 is scarcely minor matters. Fee on the "surprising qualification" in 15b (357): the tenor is "almost nonchalant—a kind of 'throw away' sentence—which makes one think that no great issue can be in view" (358). For 3:15b (nonpolemical), cf. 1 Cor 14:37–38. But if no opponents, why have the words at all?

[26] Fee 358–59: "'patron/client' friendship" but no hint of "superior to inferior"; Paul deals here not with "specifics" but "generalities." "Here is the offer of friendship; they may freely disagree with him at points"; if so, "Paul trusts God to bring them up to speed." Witherington 96 makes nothing of 3:15 under "friendship." In Fitzgerald ed. 1996, *phronein* is a possible "synonym for friendship" (110, but why then *apokalypsis* to remedy minor disagreements?). Bockmuehl (cf. 34–35): "possible" here, but Paul's relationship with the Philippians may look "rather too anachronistically 'laid back'" (226).

of pluralism, variety, and tolerance.[27] Paul is serious that the Philippians march as he does. Attempts to avoid all opposition and polemics in 3:15 turn 15b into minor matters and nonchalance.

Let Paul speak here "with a touch of irony but gentleness" (Hawth. 155). 15a recommends thinking the way just presented from Paul's own experience. The admonition seeks the goodwill of his Philippians (and subsequent readers).[28] The apostle could be surprisingly tolerant.[29] But "recognition [in Phil 3:15] of how far from being perfected one still is" (*TPTA* 495) is *not* a trivial area. 15b deals with (some) Philippians thinking/acting differently from with what Paul has just outlined, acting wrongly on some points. Yet he is optimistic about God's revealing things to them. They are recipients of a revealed gospel Paul brought to them. God continues to work among them (1:6; 2:12–13) until the Day of Jesus Christ (1:10–11). How will this revelation on some concrete matter *(ti)* take place? Most likely "through the Spirit's activity within the ongoing life of the community," in the house churches, at corporate gatherings, through prophets (Bockmuehl 227–28; I. H. Marshall 98). Note the pl., *to you.* Not an individual becoming convinced, but the corporate group, discerning and testing. Such communal revelation may contrast with (private) revelations of opponents who claim already to have attained perfection. Paul and God's revelation, past experiences and promised future insights, counter that. Cf. O'B 438 n 122; Bockmuehl 227; Harnisch 148–49, v 15 = revelation at the End, shortcomings revealed at the judgment, thus a threat, to make those who think differently ponder matters all the more seriously now. *How* God will reveal remains somewhat open; *that* God will, is certain. Under this revelation, in continuity with what he knows in Christ, Paul places his experience and theology, which stresses justification but not perfection now, life in Christ but not resurrection in the present (cf. Lührmann, cited in the NOTE).

Paul concludes with a "punch line" (Weidmann 254): *Only, with respect to what we have attained, let us keep on in the same course* (16). *Only* serves to sum up and correct what might be misunderstood. Emphasis is not on differences within the community, but likeness, to Paul (developed in 3:17, imitating Paul; cf. Castelli); not revelation or being "perfect," but continuing onwards, till called

---

[27] So Castelli 21–22, 81, 86–87, 95–97, 116–17, contrary to what, in a feminist, egalitarian outlook, one might wish to find. *Mimēsis* (imitation) always includes "a hierarchical relationship," "privileged status of" and "authority" for, the "model," "valorization of sameness over against difference" (16). "Christians are Christians insofar as they strive for the privileged goal of sameness . . . . Difference has only negative connotations in the mimetic community"; to resist "the mimetic relationship . . . has dire consequences."

[28] Cf. at 1:15–17 how he dealt with "rival preachers" in Ephesus, but with this difference: the "rival preachers" proclaim the right gospel; here, people who stress circumcision (3:2–4a) and resulting perfection (3:12–14) understand the gospel benefits amiss, esp. re eschatology and anthropology. They regard themselves as *already* recipients of (full) knowledge about Christ, final righteousness, the risen life, and perfection; not so, Paul.

[29] Cf. Rom 12–14; R. Jewett, *Christian Tolerance: Paul's Message to the Modern Church* (Philadelphia: Westminster, 1982). But be wary of reducing the apostle's comments to "unessentials" (Dunn, WBC 38B *Rom.* 801).

upwards at the End, *on the same course* (racetrack image) as Paul has sketched in his own career.

Commentators who see no polemic in 3:12–16 vary as they continue their polemic against "mirror reading." Fee 360 n 37 plays off Hasler against Plümmacher (*EDNT* 3:422 and 278) over *what we have attained.* The phrase may reflect athletic idiom ("the point at which a runner has arrived on the course"); eschatology (as in other NT uses of *phthanō*); or a "rule" or "principle," from *stoichein* + *kanoni* ("rule") in many later MSS (see textual NOTE). Among possibilities for *what we have attained* are faith-righteousness (3:9bc; Garland 171) and resulting perfection/imperfection (Fitzer, cited in NOTE); "being Christian" (too general); "knowledge of Christ" (8b, 10a; Meyer 144, Koperski 1996); belonging to Christ (Walter, NTD 84); sharing Christ's suffering and the power of his resurrection (v 10; Schütz 231). "Living the gospel" (Fee 360 n 36), "moral conduct," was illustrated by Meyer 145 with a chart where B = *what we have attained* (after beginning in Christianity at point A):

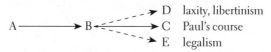

To move toward D or E would not *continue . . . the same course.* This fits Corinth or Galatia, but is difficult to find in Phil 3:16 (legalism of the Judaizers? Gnostic libertinism?). Emphasis on "behavior" is common (Fee 360 n 36; Caird 145). Then a new note has entered (Jones 81; Gnilka 202): pride *(hybris)* on the part of the perfect who have attained the goal leads to laxity. This has been connected with a lifestyle in which each acts in accord with what each knows and believes (references in Gnilka 202; an individualistically subjective understanding of the v). Gnilka appeals for some objective norm and progress. Beare 131–32, "differences of insight" exist among Christians, but "we must live by the highest level that we have been able to grasp" and "not fall back from **the point which we have already reached.**" I. H. Marshall (98), a "Christian level of insight." Plummer 80, "we must never cease striving to make advance." It is not the assumption of polemics that makes for difficulties (*pace* Fee) but Paul's terse Gk. and the fertile minds of expositors reading in ideas they find congenial.

Clearly, Paul puts the matter into the laps of his hearers/readers. Either Paul's view of existence or some alternative extreme (S. F. Winter 175). His relationship with Philippi and Letters A and B suggest a community grounded in the gospel from the outset and progressing in faith. 3:8–15 speaks, in a new situation where enemies threaten, of Christ (and knowing him), faith-righteousness, and resurrection-hope. Such indics. imply impvs., the gospel includes ethics. Paul and his converts have attained much; they have not obtained all.

The Philippians are to *continue on. stoichein* ("move in ranks, fall in step") is appropriate for a Roman colony with military veterans and honors for those who maintain civic standards and piety. "Sameness" is valued (Castelli on *mimēsis*.) To an extent, Paul is not telling the Philippians "anything new in this letter" (Fee 361); he affirms what they have already attained. New or fuller are clarification and expansion on eschatological teachings and the situation of the Christian (anthropology) "between the times" in the face of a threat that prompted 3:2ff. with its violent outburst against "the enemies." Paul here rallies "wavering Philippian Christians . . . disturbed by schismatic teachers" (Martin 1976:141). Fee, who has disparaged polemic in 3:12–16, explains that "in the face of opposition and some internal dissension," some Philippians "have lost their vision for and focus on their crucified and risen Lord" (361–62; 3:18 enemies of the cross; but resurrection is part of the problem).

in the same course is so compressed *(tō[i] autō[i])* that it invited explanation by adding "rule" *(kanoni)* from Gal 6:16 (where the reference is to the new creation, 6:15, not some law) and repetition of a phrase from Phil 2:2 involving *to auto* and *phronein* (the vb. in 15a and 15b). Many feel the additions "capture the meaning here in an appropriately Pauline manner" (Bockmuehl 228), but Fee 361, esp. nn 39, 40, correctly sets aside all notion of "some external 'rule' that he and they have in common"; Fee prefers for "what we have already attained" what is "exemplified in the gospel" (352 n 6; 361). Paul's message to the Philippians, after his No to the enemies' perfectionism now, is "Keep on."

3. Phil 3:12–16 in the Redacted Letter: Progress, but Not Perfected. This subsection in Letter C continued much of the meaning sketched above after 3:2–21 was combined with Letters A and B. Reciprocal influences between 3:12–16 and chs. 1, 2, and 4 are less than for other parts of ch. 3, because of the singular contents and vocabulary in 3:12–16.

The vv are relatively immune from attempts to relate everything in Phil to 2:6–11. Wick 73 links only *touto phronōmen* at 3:15a with *touto phroneite* at 2:5.[30] Luter/Lee 1995:92–94 tied 3:1b–21 to 2:5–16 only by broad themes. Meager links compared with those found between 2:6–11 and 2:1–5 or 2:12–18. But could the perfectionism Paul battles in vv 12–16 have been a danger among the Philippians because of their theology as expressed in the encomium they composed? Paul corrected the thought of the "hymn" (encomium) by adding 2:8c and emphasis on salvation and future eschatology in 2:12–18. Some Philippians, viewing Christ as example for themselves, may have paralleled their suffering with his, and their exaltation ("the upward call," to heaven, 3:14) with his. "Glory" (2:11; 3:19, 21) for them = transformation (3:21), knowledge of Christ (3:8b, 10a), experiencing the divine power (3:10b, 21), perfection—now. "Perfection" was a term "in the air" in Gk. philosophies and mystery religions (Thielman 1995:199). Peterlin 82–88 allows that perfectionism existed among some of the Philippians. Baptism (being raised to new life) lent itself to "already possessing the new life and resurrection" (so in Corinth; Rom 6:1–4). One need not posit Schenk's idea of a "heav-

---

[30] For his Einheit A (1:12–26 and 3:1–16), Wick draws in 3:17 "Paul, an imitator of Christ." But Paul is not perfected (*Unvollendete*, 96–100). "Perfection" represents language from the mystery cults (95–96; with BAGD). 3:12–16 is related to 2:6–11 thus: the person who is *teleios* is not one going through cultic rites but who humbles self in the world and takes on the form of a slave; the initiate (96) is Christminded (*phronein* 96, 171).

enly ascent" or Lohmeyer's martyrdom experience for an elitist group. "The enemies" taught that we become *teleioi* by circumcision, like Jesus Christ in the flesh and then in his heavenly exaltation. Paul criticized such perfectionism because he felt the Philippians were vulnerable to its blandishments and needed to be lined up (*stoichein*, 3:16) against such a menace, a defect to which 2:6–11 could lead to anthropologically.

In *Phil 1–2*, the theme of "running in pursuit toward the goal at the finish" (3:12c, 14) can be connected with "progress" or "advance" (1:12, 25). Athletic metaphors mesh with the *agōn* motif at 1:30, the contest or struggle in which Paul and the Philippians engage against adversaries. Absence of dir. objs. with the vbs. in 3:12–13 has led to many proposed solutions (see NOTE on 12a); some involve chs. 1–2. For example, "Christ" interpreted in light of 2:6–11; nearing the finish line in a race and Paul's expectations in 1:21–24; cf. 2:24. If Paul is in prison (1:13), he seems closer to the finish line of his life than if 3:12–16 were written after he was out of jail. The expansion of Paul's words in 3:16 include an addition from 2:2, "think the same thing," and thus the theme of *unity* (and the problem at 3:16 of disunity; Black 1995:41).

Ch. 4 may also influence interpreting 3:12–16. Impvs. (3:15a and 16) continue in 4:2–9. Schenk suggests Euodia and Syntyche need to be told to "think the same thing" (4:2) as Paul because they have fallen for ideas of the false teachers about perfection and a heavenly ascent. More convincing: 4:5 (the nearness of the parousia) fits with Paul's emphases in vv 12–16. A possible solution for the meaning of *touto* in 3:15a appears in 4:8: *whatever things are true*, etc.—*these things ponder* (4:8; the vb. is not *phroneō*, 3:15, but *logizomai*, 3:13). Readers pondering what Paul calls them to in 3:15 get at 4:8 a specific list of praiseworthy virtues appropriate in Greco-Roman Philippi.[31]

3:12–16 was seldom assigned in lectionaries until revisions of the *Ordo* appointed 3:4b–14 for Lent 5 C as well as for Proper 22 (27) in Year A. Thus helps on preaching the pericopes have dealt with vv 12–14 since 1992 or so. There have also been hymns and gospel songs invoking the imagery of 3:14, such as "We're on the Upward Trail," "I'm pressing on the upward way." Perhaps the most famous sermon ever preached on Phil 3 was John Wesley's "Christian Perfection" in 1741,[32] on how believers can achieve sinlessness, freedom from outward sins and sins of the heart. This emphasis on perfection for truly "sanctified people" characterized Wesleyanism, Holiness groups, and the Keswick movement ("let go" of your own efforts toward godliness, "let God" do the work of sanctification). On battles over perfection, cf. Thielman 1995:209–14, I. H. Marshall 98–99, and various ecumenical discussions.[33] G. A. Turner captions the vv

---

[31] Many of the connections between 3:12–16 and Phil 1–2 and 4 are possible also on partition theories, for the vv would have been received and heard by the Philippians prior to (or in) Letter C.

[32] Repr., among other places, in *The Works of John Wesley, Vol. 2, Sermons II*, ed. A. C. Outler (Nashville: Abingdon, 1985) 96–121.

[33] E.g., Methodist-Roman Catholic, Denver Report (1971), ##7, 50, 52–53; Dublin Report (1976) #22; Honolulu Report (1981) #18, repr. in *Growth in Agreement*, Ecumenical Documents II, ed. H. Meyer/L. Vischer (New York: Paulist/Geneva: WCC, 1984), pp. 308–9, 318–19; 345, and 371–72.

"Perfection: Achievement or Aspiration?" (*The Wesleyan Bible Commentary* [Grand Rapids: Eerdmans] 5 [1965] 474; cf. his exegesis of 3:10–15 in *Asbury Seminarian* 29:9–14).

SELECT BIBLIOGRAPHY (see also General Bibliography and Commentaries); Literature on "Martyrdom" is in n 5.

Bröse, E. 1920–21. "Paulus durch Virgil kommentiert. Zu Phil. 3,12–14," *TSK* 93:78–82.

Castelli, E. 1991. A. *Imitating Paul: A Discourse of Power.* Literary Currents in Biblical Interpretation. Louisville: Westminster/John Knox.

Dibelius, M. 1914. "*Epignosis aletheias,*" in *Neutestamentliche Studien,* FS Henrici, ed. A. Deissmann/H. Windisch (Leipzig: Hinrichs) 178–89, esp. 184–86.

Du Plessis, P. J. 1959. *TELEIOS. The Idea of Perfection in the New Testament.* Kampen: Kok.

Dupont, J. 1970. "The Conversion of Paul and its Influence in his Understanding of Salvation by faith," in *Apostolic History and the Gospel,* FS F. F. Bruce, ed. W. W. Gasque/R. P. Martin (Grand Rapids: Eerdmans) 176–94.

Fridrichsen, A. 1934. "Exegetisches zum Neuen Testament," *SO* 13–14:38–46.

———. 1944. "HEN DE, zu Phil. 3,13," *ConNT* 9:31–32.

Greenlee, J. H. 1990. "Saint Paul—Perfect but Not Perfected: Philippians 3:12," *Notes on Translation* (Dallas) 4:53–55.

López Fernández, E. 1975. "En torno a Fil 3,12," *EstBib* 34:121–23.

Metzner, R. 2000. "Paulus und der Wettkampf: Die Rolle des Sports in Leben und Verkünkigung des Apostels (1 Kor 9.24–27; Phil 3,12–16)," *NTS* 46:565–83.

Moffatt, J. 1916."Expository Notes on the Epistle to the Philippians," *Expositor,* 8th Series, Vol. 12:347–49.

Peterson, D. 1982. *Hebrews and Perfection: An Examination of the Concept of Perfection in the 'Epistle to the Hebrews.'* SNTSMS 47. Cambridge: Cambridge Univ. Press.

Weidmann, F. W. 1997. "An (Un)Accomplished Model: Paul and the Rhetorical Strategy of Philippians 3:3–17," in FS R. Scroggs ([12] Bibl., under Roetzel, C.) 245–57.

Wiederkehr, D. 1963. *Die Theologie der Berufung in den Paulusbriefen.* Studia Friburgensia, N. F. 36. Freiburg: Universitätsverlag. Pp. 188–93.

Lutheran-Roman Catholic, *The One Mediator, the Saints, and Mary,* Lutherans and Catholics in Dialogue VIII, ed. H. G. Anderson/J. F. Stafford/J. A. Burgess (Minneapolis: Augsburg, 1984), esp. ##76–83, 91–98, and 103 in the Common Statement; *Joint Declaration on the Doctrine of Justification* by the Lutheran World Federation and the Roman Catholic Church (Grand Rapids: Eerdmans, 2000), ##28–30.

14. *The Pauline Model versus Enemies of Christ's Cross: Future Change, Proper Glory, 3:17–21*

TRANSLATION

3:17a Imitators together of me, continue to become, brothers and sisters, 17b and take note of those who live in this way, as you have us as example. 18 For many live lives, about whom I have often spoken to you but now speak even with tears, as the enemies of the cross of Christ. 19a Their final goal — is destruction; b their god, the belly, c and their "glory," in what is shameful; d those whose concern is earthly things. 20a For our governing civic association exists in the heavens, b from which indeed we eagerly await the savior, the Lord Jesus Christ, 21a who will change the body of our humiliation to the sphere of the body of his glory, b in accord with the action of his ability also to put all things into subjection to himself.

NOTES

3:17a. *Imitators together of me, continue to become, brothers and sisters. ginesthe,* impv., 2nd pl. pres. m.-p. (BDAG *ginomai* 5 "become" or 7 "[turn out to, show oneself to] be" [KJV, NAB] + pred. nom.). *adelphoi,* voc., makes it less abrupt; *brothers and sisters* (3:13; H. D. Betz 1967: 152 from a redactor). *symmimētai mou,* initial and emphatic, "fellow-imitators of me" (obj. gen., BDAG; DA 209 n 210). *syn* does more than strengthen *koin-* in the stem (Baumert 2003 [(2) Bibl., **sharing**] 394); "join" ([N]RSV, NIV), "be united" ([N]JB, "Unitedly become imitators" (Jeh. Wit.). *symmimētēs,* in Gk. literature only here, in Phil the only term from the *mimeomai* word-family (11 NT examples, 8 in the Pauline corpus). Vb., 2 Thess 3:7,9; Heb 13:7; 3 John 11. *mimētēs,* 1 Thess 1:6 ("imitators of us and of the Lord"); 2:14 ("imitators of the churches of God in Christ Jesus . . . in Judea"); 1 Cor 4:16 ("be imitators of me") and 11:1 ("Be imitators of me, as I am of Christ"); Eph 5:1 ("imitators of God"); Heb 6:12; and 1 Pet 3:13. *mimēsis* was important in classical antiquity (cf. E. Auerbach, *Mimesis: The Representation of Reality in Western Literature* [Princeton Univ. Press 1953, 3rd ed. 1971] e.g., 44–49), but not a term in the NT or early Christian literature in BDAG. The compound may be coined by Paul (Plato *Plt.* 274D has *symmimeomai*). Only 5x in Paul, but much has been made of "imitation" (COMMENT A.3).

of me. gen. *mou,* not dat with *syn.* (1) Some dismiss *syn* as tautologous (Michaelis, *TDNT* 4:667 n 13, *Phil.* 61; cf. U. B. Müller 173 n 162); GNB, "Keep on imitating me." (2) "imitators together with me (of Christ)"; Bengel; Plato *Plt.* 274D, A and B join together in imitating C; McMichael; Gnilka 202–4; Pollard

63; Hooker 1989 ([12] Bibl.) 332–33 = 1990:176–77; 2002:387 n 31. (3) *syn* = "with (others)": NIV, "Join with others in following my example," those mentioned in 3:17b, Christians or churches (cf. 1 Thess 2:14) elsewhere, or the *teleioi* in vv 15–16. Ellicott 93; Meyer 145; Melick 142; Thielman 199; Joüon 307–8. (4) *syn* = "together," stressing unity; (N)JB, TC; NEB "Agree together"; Beare 135; Collange 136, Hawth. 160, O'B 445–46, Fee 364–65; U. B. Müller 173; De Boer 177–79; H. D. Betz 1967:145–53, esp. 151–52 n 6; A. Schulz 1962:313–14; Hopper 143; *GGBB* 130. Lft. 154, "Vie with one another in imitating me." But re (1), the *syn*-prefix seems Paul's own addition in an emphatic position at the start of the sentence. (2) His usual construction is *mimētai* + gen. (1 Thess 1:6; 2:14; 1 Cor 4:16 and 11:1 *mimētai mou ginesthe*). Phil 3:17 repeats it, with a prefix. (3) 17a makes no reference to "others." To refer it to 17b overlooks *kai*, a different vb. *(skopeite)*, and different obj. Fee 365 n 10, "the least likely of all" suggestions. We adopt (4), the majority view, without emphasizing disunity. The TRANSLATION follows Gk. word order: pred. phrase, impv., voc.

imitators. Some seek "imitation" in the OT (Tinsley 1960) or Jewish thought (I. Abrahams, "The Imitation of God," *Studies in Pharisaism and the Gospels* [2d Series,1924, repr. New York: KTAV 1967]; Kosmala; Gulin; Schoeps 1950). Tinsley: Jesus, as "the way," imitated "the 'Way' of Israel" and Israel as *imitator Dei*; Paul's "ways in Christ" (1 Cor 4:17) continued this, plus *mimēsis* of Paul himself (134–65); "imitation of Christ" becomes "the distinguishing characteristic of Christian ethics, spirituality, and worship" (7). Contrast De Boer 29–41; H. D. Betz 1967: 4 n 2, 27; Castelli ([13] Bibl.) 27–28; Hopper 65, 74, 183. Lindars separated imitation of God and of Christ, treating the former with reserve for Christian ethics. The word family (W. Michaelis, *TDNT* 4:659–63) is decidedly Gk. LXX use is "very rare," only in books under Gk. influence. Though 4 Macc. 9:23 and 13:9 speak of imitating martyrs, it "cannot be understood as a t[echnical] t[erm]" re martyrdom, 663 (versus Loh. 151 n 2). Cf. Hopper 82–89. The terms become more common in the Pseudepigrapha, Philo (Platonic influence, Hopper 89–96), and Jos. (*TDNT* 4:664–66; *T. Benj.* 4.1; *Let. Arist.* 188, 210, 280, 281), perhaps reflecting "Hellenistic-ruler theology," references in 664 n 8. For the rabbis, Str-B 1:372–73; 3:605; M. Buber, "Nachahmung Gottes," *Werke* 2 (1964) 1053–65, but Gk. influences are likely (W. Bauder, *NIDNTT* 1:490–91; M. J. Wilkins, *ABD* 3:392). Some (Kosmala, with Buber) see a "paradox": the invisible God is to be imitated by humans (1st cent. A.D.? Midrash *Sifra* on Lev 19:2, Abba Saul, "This is my God, and I will be as He"; De Boer 42, with Schoeps 1950: 286–87; contrast Betz 1967:96–98, 2nd cent.). Rabbinic influence on Paul is unlikely (Betz 101). Evidence is stronger in Hellenistic Judaism, esp. Philo (A. Schulz 1962:213–21; De Boer 46–50; Betz 1967:93–95, 130–36; Wild 1985:128–31; B. Mack, "Imitatio Mosis," *StudPhilon* 1 [1972] 27–55). Thus no significant OT background; in Jewish sources the roots are Gk. (A. Schulz 1962:213–25; H. D. Betz 1967:84–101).

3:17b. *and take note of those who live in this way, as you have us as example. kai* + *skopeite*, impv. (BDAG) **look (out) for, notice** (+ acc.); see NOTE on 2:4 *regarding.* Here a good sense, not like Rom 16:17, "Keep an eye on those who cause dissensions," possibly a gloss from Phil 3:19 (Bultmann, *TLZ* 72 [1947] 202) or frg. similar to 3:17–19 (AB 33:745). *skopos* (3:14 *the goal at the finish*) is probably not an influence on 3:17b. For *skopein* as "look at critically," E. Fuchs (*TDNT* 7:414–15) offers some 12 classical passages (two LXX examples, Esth 8:12g, 2 Macc 4:5) 3:17b, hold "before one as a model on the basis of inspection" (415); cf. Aristoph. *Eq.* 80–81. D. K. Williams 2002:212 contrasts *blepete* in 3:2.

those who live in this way. Subst. ptc., pl. pres., *peripateō*, BDAG 2.a.γ, fig., "**conduct one's life, *comport oneself, behave, live*** as a habit of conduct"; 3:18 (1:27a *politeuesthe* was often treated as if *peripateite*). Gk. *pateō* (often compounded, *peri*), "walk (around)"; cf in philosophy, the Peripatetic School, from walks *(peripatoi)* outside the walls of Athens. But "conduct the walk of life" is rare in Gk. (1x at Phld. *Peri Parrhēsis* p. 12). In the LXX *(peri)pateō* sometimes (24x) for Heb. *hālak*, religious/ethical "walk" (before God), e.g., Gen 17:1, cf. 5:22, 6:9; esp. in the Deuteronomistic history, 1 Kgs 2:4; 3:6; 8:23, 25, etc.; also "walk with God" (F. J. Helfmeyer, *TDOT* 3:388–403, esp. 392–95). LXX may avoid literal tr. of *hālak* "because it found it too naïve" (G. Bertram, *TDNT* 5:943); thus *euaresteō* at Gen 17:1, "Be well-pleasing before me." *NIDNTT* 3:933–34, 943–44 (G. Ebel), "walk" in the Dead Sea scrolls. Rabbinic usage, *hǎlākā'* (Jastrow 353). In Paul and John, *peripatein* = "the walk of life." 2 Cor 12:18 (NRSV), "conduct ourselves . . . take [walk in] the same steps." Most trs. prefer dynamic-equivalence, "live, act," or "follow" (from *akoloutheō* in the gospels?). In Paul, + a) *en* + dat., for the sphere or condition of the walk (Rom 6:4); b) *kata* + acc., for a norm (Rom 8:4); c) associative dat. (2 Cor 12:18; Gal 5:16); d) adv., "worthily" (1 Thess 2:12), "honorably" (Rom 13:13a); or e) some comparison, here with "the many" (18) who walk as "enemies of the cross of Christ" (R. Bergmeier, *EDNT* 3:75–76). *houtō* (NA²⁷, only here in Paul) fits d) above; usually *houtōs* 4:1, + "movable *sigma*," BDF 21. With what precedes (BDAG 1; *DA* 323; "thus like me," Paul) or what follows (BDAG 2 **in this way, *as follows;*** "them which walk so as ye have us for an ensample," KJV). See NOTE on 4:1 *in this way.* The matter is complicated by how one takes the *kathōs* cl. and the referents of *us.*

as you have us as an example. *kathōs* can be causal, BDF 453,2; BDAG 3 *since, in so far as;* see NOTE on 1:7 *It is indeed right . . .* (no *houtōs* as correlative); 17b is then argumentative (Silva 212), undergirding "imitate me" and "look for others" (like Paul; cf. Fee 366; De Boer 179 n 269; Merk 1968:191; B. K. Dick [(1) Bibl.] 118). Or correlative, with *houtō* (BDAG *kathōs* 1; O'B 448–49; De Boer 180–81; "those who walk in the way our example has set for you"). *echete* (BDAG 2.b, *have someone as an example*) + obj. + pred. acc. (BDF 157,1), *typon hēmas* (= *us*). Paul alone? Hawth. 160–61; Merk 1968:191; Silva 212; Moffatt, "the example you got from me"; LB "my example"; cf. Dick ([1] Bibl.) 117–18. Hawth. 161, "we/us" for "I/me" (Rom 1:5, etc.); Moule *IB* 118–19; W. Lofthouse, "Singular and Plural in St. Paul's Letters," *ExpTim* 58 [1946–47] 179–82; a literary pl. is frequent in Gk. authors (BDF 280). 3:17 then differentiates Paul and others, "*imitators* of me" but "*mark and follow* those who walk" in accord with Paul's pattern. Apostolic authority against conflicting views (*TDNT* 4:668, contra De Boer 184–87)? If "us" is a real pl., who else is "determinative example"? Loh. has little support for Paul, the *adelphoi*, and "the perfect" (v 16), who face martyrdom (152 n 1; Michaelis, *TDNT* 4:667 n 14; De Boer 180). Such factors may enter into interpretation, but not necessarily into a tr.

example. typos has a host of classical meanings (only 4x in the LXX). *Word-books:* L. Goppelt, *TDNT* 8:246–59 and 1982 ([8] Bibl.); H. Müller, *NIDNTT* 3:903–7; G. Schunack, *EDNT* 3:372–76; *TLNT* 3:384–87, "In ethics, . . . a model, hardly different from an example"; in inscriptions, papyri, 4 Macc 6:19, Strabo 4.1.12, and Philo. BDAG *typos* 6.b: *example* or *pattern* in the moral life Cf. 1 Thess 1:7 (for 1:6, see NOTE on 3:17a, *Imitators together*); 2 Thess 3:9; Titus 2:7; 1 Peter 5:3. Paul thus uses *typos* in two passages with *mimeomai* (*EDNT* 3:373). He is "example to the community" (*TDNT* 8:249). His *didachē* too in Rom 6:17 (*TDNT* 8:250; *TLNT* 386), possibly a gloss (*EDNT* 3:374, so Bultmann), but Fitzmyer (*Rom.* AB 33: 449), a "succinct baptismal summary" from Paul. 1 Thess 1:6–7, the community = "a *strikingly formed model (typos)* for believers" in Mace-donia and Achaia (Schunack 373), in that they accepted the word and lived in faith and obedience to the Lord, amid persecution. Phil 3:17, "those who live as you have a *prefiguration* in us"; "the pattern of a life fulfilled in the future," life formed by Christ (Schunack 373; cf. Gnilka 203–4). Cf. Baumert 2003: ([2] Bibl., **sharing**) 393–94, ethical *Vorbild.*

3:18. *For many live lives, about whom I have often spoken to you but now speak even with tears, as the enemies of the cross of Christ. gar* (BDAG 2, cf. 1), **marker of clarification,** explaining (cf. 3:3a and 20; *DA* 324) why the Philippians should imitate Paul and take note of those about them. *polloi*, masc. pl., *polus, pollē, polu* (BDAG 2.a.β.ℵ, subst.), "much, many"; "a countable number" (*DA* 314, like 1:14 "the majority"). *peripatousin*, same vb. (BDAG 2.a.γ) as in 17b ptc. ("live *lives*," not mere existence). *pollakis* ("often, many times"; Rom 1:13; 2 Cor 11:23, 26, 27ab). Alliterative paronomasia *(polloi . . . peripatousin . . . pollakis). hous* (masc. acc. pl. *hos, hē, ho*), obj. of *elegon* (and *legō*); Eng. requires a prep. ("of whom," KJV-[N]RSV; *about*). BDAG *legō* 3, *speak, report. hous* anticipates *the enemies of the cross of Christ, tous echthrous* acc. (antecedent incorporated into relative cl. with "identity of case," ATR 718), "Many live whom I tell you (are) enemies of the cross . . ." (*GGBB* 183; D. B. Wallace, *GTJ* 6 (1985) 91–112). The TRANSLATION supplies *as* for a link. Imperf. *elegon, + pollakis*, repeated past action, "I used to mention them often" (Jeh. Wit.); most Eng. trs., with KJV, use a perf. tense, "I have told you." *legō* could be linear, "am telling you now" (NIV "say again"). *de* is adversative (*DA* 327), in contrast with *pollakis, often . . . but now. kai, even,* with *klaiōn*, ptc., *klaiō* (BDAG 1, *weep, cry*). Circumst. ptc., manner ("weeping"), equivalent of adv. cl. (BDF 418), *with tears* ([N]RSV; "with tears in my eyes," NJB, NEB). Cf. 2 Cor 2:4. K. H. Rengstorf (*TDNT* 3:722), *klaiōn* is not of "theological significance"; Lft. 155, grief because "they degraded the true doctrine of liberty."

the enemies of the cross of Christ. tous echthrous, acc. pl., subst. use of adj. *ech-thros, a, on*, "hostile," + gen. for object of enmity (BDAG 2.b.γ); cf. Acts 13:10; O. Linton, *ConBNT* 4 (1936) 9–21. *enemies* in most Eng. Bibles (TC, "living with enmity"). Personal enemies (Gal 4:16; Rom 12:20) or (OT influence) enemies of Israel and of God; hostile to God (Rom 5:10; cf. 1:30), the attitude of all men and women by nature (Rom 8:7–8; 11:28, NRSV-mg corrects NRSV). *Wordbooks:* W. Foerster, *TDNT* 2:811–15; H. Bietenhard, *NIDNTT* 1:553–55; M. Wolter, *EDNT* 2:93–94. *the cross of Christ* is the polemical heart of Paul's gospel (1 Cor 1:18; Gal 6:12). Thus personal opponents, in theological terms. P⁴⁶ adds *blepete, beware of* them, tying vv 18–19 to triple *blepete* in 3:2 (Fee 362 n 1) and *skopeite* in v 17; critics are not persuaded. *tous* (often omitted in trs.) substantivizes the adj. and makes the group definite ("the enemies," KJV, [N]JB). For *tou Christou*, see NOTE on 1:1, *in Christ Jesus*; as at 1:27a *the gospel tou Christou*, the art. need not be pressed. On *cross*, see NOTE on 2:8c *yes, death on a cross. stauros* (BDAG 2, not just 1) represents an esp. striking way of setting forth in a Roman *colōnia* the death of Jesus; + *tou Christou*, an abbreviated reference to the salvation event. Against Christians "who . . . spurn the cross by their manner of life" (J. Schneider, *TDNT* 7:576). "One who has been *philos*, but is alienated" (Ammonius, 2nd-cent. A.D. grammarian, LSJ, in Geoffrion 153–54); D. K. Williams 2002:225, once "associated with the church in some way." Apostates (Loh. 153; denied by Schneider 576 n 31). But *many*? In classical usage, *echthros* could refer to outside adversaries.

3:19a–d. *Their final goal—is destruction;* ᵇ *their god, the belly,* ᶜ *and their "glory," in what is shameful;* ᵈ *those whose concern is earthly things.* Four characteristics, linked with v 18 by *hōn*, gen. pl., rel. pron. *hos, hē, ho,* "of whom," "whose" (KJV); repeated with 19b, but not c or d. In most trs., a new sentence, often with "Their" ([N]RSV, NIV); or recast as "They are doomed to destruction" (Gdsp., NEB/REB, [N]JB). CEV links 18–19a, "And now with tears in my eyes, I warn you again that they are headed for hell!" Then 19a is something Paul previously told the Philippians. Supply "is" for phrases a, b, c, as the TRANSLATION does for 19a. 19d shifts the construction. Nouns in 19a, b, c, and d each have several possible meanings, depending on who one thinks the opponents are (OT-Jewish, Gnostic backgrounds?). Tr. involves historical reconstruction, final decision only after conclusions about "the enemies"; see COMMENT A.4.

3:19a. *Their final goal—is destruction; to telos.* Cf. *teteleiōmai,* NOTE on 3:12b *I am already perfected* (which Paul denied), and *teleioi,* 3:15 *"perfected"* (language from "the enemies"); mystery cults background. Here, BDAG 3, *end* (of the world, cf. 1 Cor 15:24; of the Law, Rom 10:4, 3:19; of sinners, Rom 6:21; KJV-[N]RSV); *goal* (cf. Rom 10:4; if at 3:19a, ironical); *outcome* (cf. LB "Their future . . ."); *destiny* (NIV, cf. [N]JB). G. Delling, "end result, final destiny" (*TDNT* 8:55, cf. R. Schippers, *NIDNTT* 2:61; H. Hübner, *EDNT* 3:348, 2 Cor 11:15, their *telos* "will be in accord with their deeds"). Final judgment holds devastating results for the enemies. But *telos* may have a positive sense; cf. related terms in 3:12 and 15. Koester 1961–62:326, the opponents claim to have achieved a final goal, "already perfected" *(teleioi).* Cf. Corp. Herm. 1.26, "consummation *(telos)* for those who have *gnōsis,* to be in god" *(theōthēnai;* W. Scott, *Hermetica: The Ancient Greek and Latin Writings which Contain Religious or Philosophic Teachings Ascribed to Hermes Trismegistes* (Oxford, 1924–1936, repr. 1985), 2 [1924] 67, brackets the last word). Probably "a double meaning . . . their claim to have achieved the *telos* earns only destruction in the last judgment" (Koester 326). O'B 455 tepidly endorses this "play on words"; Gnilka 206; Martin 1976:145, Paul denies "their 'realized' eschatology"; Lincoln 95; Fee 370 n 34 (but not from opponents; contrast Schenk 251, 286–87). On *apōleia*, see NOTE on 1:28b *destruction* (for authorities in Philippi who oppose the gospel); **annihilation, ruin** (BDAG 2), complete or in process. Rare in secular Gk., common in the LXX, an OT ring (A. Oepke, *TDNT* 1:396–97). Loh/Nida 116, "Paul's usual word" for "the opposite of 'salvation.'" Hence "perdition" (ERV/ASV; R. Knox; Collange 119), "end up in hell" (GNB).

3:19b. *their god, the belly*; *ho theos* (+ *hōn*, lit. "whose god"), 17x in Phil, often of "God our Father" (see NOTE on 1:2). Here, fig., **nontranscendent but...worthy of reverence or respect,** *god* (BDAG *theos* 4.b; but cf. 1, **transcendent being,** 1 Cor 8:5. Gal 4:8), gods [pl.] of the pagan world out of which many of Paul's converts have come (E. Stauffer, *TDNT* 3:92 n 142; cf. W. Foerster, 3:1091). Hence no capital G (exceptions: KJV, NABRNT, TC). Cf. N. T. Wright's plea for "god" in *The New Testament and the People of God* (Minneapolis: Fortress, 1992) xiv–xv. Pred. noun (*estin* understood) = *hē koilia*, lit. "hollow," the abdominal cavity, where food is digested, hence **belly, stomach** (BDAG 1) or (2) the mother's **womb** (Gal 1:15 = Jer 1:5). CEV, "They worship their stomachs." Cf. Eur. *Cyc.* 334–35, Cyclops says, "I offer sacrifice ... to this belly (*gastri*) of mine, the greatest of deities" (Gk. in Loh. 154 n 1). *Wordbooks:* J. Behm, *TDNT* 3:786–89; S. Wibbing, *NIDNTT* 1:169; F. G. Untergassmair, *EDNT* 2:301; Sandnes 2002:24–93, Greco-Roman data, esp. Epicurean (cf. De Witt), banquets as "opportunities for the belly"; 97–132, a *topos* in Jewish-Hellenistic sources. Like 3:19b, other Pauline uses reflect teachings of opponents ("heretics," *EDNT* 2:301): 1 Cor 6:13a, "Food for the stomach (*koilia[i]*), and the stomach (*koilia*) for food," perhaps parallel to "the body for fornication" (13b); Rom 16:17–18, "those who cause dissensions ... serve ... their own appetites (*tē[i] heautōn koilia[i]*)," see NOTE above on 3:17b *skopein* re Phil 3:17–19. Interpretations of *koilia* reflect differing views on "the enemies":

(1) Excesses at table, gourmet tastes, gluttony. On luxurious eating in the Greco-Roman world, cf. Smith, *Dictionary* 303–9; Sandnes 2002:79–93. Classical texts on those who worship or are enslaved to the belly, "stomach-deities" (Ath. 97C), in *TDNT* 3:788 n 11; *PGL* 759. *TLNT* 1:293–95, those who would rather fill their bellies than work or are "nothing but a belly" (cf. Titus 1:12, they "live to eat"; 3 Macc 7:11, Jewish apostates "for the belly's sake transgressed the divine commandments," Bockmuehl 231, but cf. [2] below). Lütgert; Dib. 71 (Philo references); Beare 136; Schmithals 1972:109; Michaelis 62; Loh. 154; Str-B 3:622, cf. 189 n. β, "epicures"; Eur. *Cycl.* 335 (above), the "belly ... greatest of deities" — perhaps a proverb (Eastman [(1) Bibl.] 200 n 5). Cf. Fee 372; Bockmuehl 231. At the *agapē*-Lord's Supper in Corinth, the rich feasted on delicacies before workers or slaves could get there (1 Cor 11:17–22, 33–34, G. Theissen 1982 121–74). Oakes 2000:260–61, Christians who reverted to pagan cult to meet economic needs.

(2) (Over)scrupulosity about foods (Jewish food laws). So the church fathers (*TDNT* 3:788 n 14; Hawth. 166), though some saw idolatry, luxurious eating and drinking (B. Weiss 284). *TDNT* 3:788, food laws, "bitter scorn on the Judaizers with their belly god." Ewald-Wohl. 206–7 nn 1,2 and K. Barth 113, food laws +

circumcision in 3:2; Bonnard 71; Hawth. 166; Feine 1916 (INTRO. VII.A) 26–28; Gunther 1973:98; Koester 1961–62:93. Contrast Fee 372 n 39. Sandnes 2002:145–46, "nowhere in Graeco-Roman or Jewish sources" does "belly" refer to people "devoted to Jewish customs in general and dietary laws in particular," in patristic sources "rarely" (219–62).

(3) Sexual immorality. *koilia* includes the womb and (19c in some interpretations) the genitals; the male sex organ in the LXX (Ps 131:11; Sir 23:6; *TDNT* 3:786, Mearns 198–99; Moiser 1997). Dismissed by Fee 371 n 36, but cf. 1 Cor 6:13 (cited above; "sexual license," their "appetites" are "god," Bruce 130). "Rebels from the holy laws" minister "to the delights of the belly *(gastaros)* and the organs below it" (Philo *Virt.* 182 = LCL *Philo* 8:275). Epictet., we "think of ourselves as bellies *(koiliai)* . . . as genitals *(aidoia)* . . . because we have appetites" (1.9.26). Martin 1976:145: "immorality" based on "their false anthropological notions." Schenk 287–88 equates *koilia* with *kardia* (Sir 19:12, 51:21); the agitators in Philippi were Jewish wisdom teachers (a view rejected above). Many combine (1) and (3), self-indulgence in food/drink and sex (O'B 456 n 72; cf. *DA* 303). Sandnes 2002, gluttony in eating and sexual activity after banquets (145, 154). "Self-love" *(philautia* in Aristot. on friendship) characterizes such people (151–52; for Philo, Cain [*Det.* 32–34] and Onan [*Post.* 180–81] exemplify self-love). Belly-worshipers are "self-loving citizens," unreliable in battle or for the common good (163).

(4) A pointed way of referring to "flesh." Sandnes 2002:77, in Epicureanism, hedonism re "the hunger of the *sarx*." Cf. Collange 138. Koester 1961–62:326–27, "'flesh' that is to pass away"; Paul sneers at a "catchword of the opponents, which expressed their claim of identity with the Divine: 'This, your high religious claim of Divine union, is in fact nothing but the belly, which has no part in the future world.'" Gnilka 205–6, "belly" intensifies "flesh"; Klijn 1965: 283; *EDNT* 2:301, with "earthly" in 19d; Caird 147; Lincoln 96; O'B 456. Given Paul's "flesh-Spirit" contrast (Gal 5:16–25; Rom 8:3–9a; Phil 3:3), conduct "not guided by the Spirit" (Silva 209–10).

(5) Collange 138 was "tempted to take it as: 'They have their eyes fixed on their own navel: their god is themselves!'" But is there any evidence that *koilia* = *omphalos*, "navel"?

(6) Loh. 154, "for those who despise martyrdom the highest concern is . . . their own physical life." "Quite outside the history of the term" *koilia* (Behm, *TDNT* 3:788 n 15; Michaelis 62).

Explanations (5) and (6) find little support. (1) and (3) and perhaps (4) make the enemies hedonists or libertines; (2) and perhaps (4), legalists. Some hold evidence is lacking to determine what *koilia* meant (Fee 372; Bockmuehl 231; Edart 249–50).

3:19c. *and their "glory," in what is shameful;* *hōn* (19b) goes with *doxa* as well as *ho theos;* it is clinched by *autōn* at the end of 19c, "of them" = their (BDF 297); cf. Heb. *'ăšer . . . lô,* but also a Gk. construction (Gal 3:1 v.l. *hois . . . en hymin;* GNTG 2:434–37). Vb. *(estin)* is understood.

"*glory.*" *doxa;* see NOTE on 1:11 *glory;* 2:11; 4:19, 20; 3:21, Christ's "glorious body." BDAG 3, **fame, recognition, renown, honor, prestige;** here, an oxymoron, "*whose prestige is in their disgrace.*" DA 308, either "They glory in what is shameful" or "That which is worthy of praise to them is in their shameful conduct." G. Kittel, classical Gk. "repute" or "honor," as at 1 Thess 2:20; 2:6 ("praise"); 1 Cor 11:15; 2 Cor 6:8, etc. (*TDNT* 2:237). H. Hegermann (*EDNT* 1:345), failure to seek *doxa* from God (Rom 2:7–8). Fits shame/honor culture of the day. Kittel kept this use (*TDNT* 2:237) distinct from *doxa* as "the divine mode of being" (so Reitzenstein 1978, OT *doxa* interpreted as the nature of deity in texts from Hellenistic mysticism and the magical papyri, *TDNT* 3:252). For influence of Hellenistic mysticism on BDAG (*doxa* 1.a), see NOTE on 1:11 *glory*. Koester accepted "participation in the Divine" (Corp. Herm. 1.26); 19c, the enemies claiming "achievement of *doxa*" (1961–62:327). Martin 1976:145, "glorying," i.e., boasting (cf. 3:3), by "charismatic figures . . . a special breed of Christians who had 'arrived'" at a "nirvana state" (already raised). Cf. Lincoln 96. O'B 457, possible; Fee 373 n 45 criticizes the jump from "glorying" to "boasting," and introduction of "charismatic figures" (from 2 Cor?). Loh. 154–55, *doxa* from martyrdom, a direct route to transfiguration. Hawth. 166 proposed for 19bc, "Their god is the belly and (the) glory in their shame," i.e., food laws and circumcision (see below on *aischynē* [2]); Jewish missionaries deify these emphases. Silva 212, the analysis is "solecistic"; Sandnes 2002:144 n 31, "artificial." The TRANSLATION puts *glory* in quotation marks, to flag its ambiguity, possibly ironic.

what is shameful. aischynē, BDAG 2, *shame, disgrace*; in Paul, only at 2 Cor 4:2 ("shameful things one hides"). See NOTE on 1:20 vb. *I shall not be disgraced in any way* (shame culture). Bultmann (*TDNT* 1:189–91) brings out background in LXX and Judaism, esp. shame brought on by God's judgment. 3:19 + Rev 3:18 ("shame of your nakedness") suggests "play on the sexual sense of *aischynē*" (Gen 2:25, contrast 3:7; Ezek 16:36–37; 23: 10, 18; H.-G. Link, *NIDNTT* 3:562–64). Cf. also 1 Cor 11:6; 14:35. In the LXX, *aischynē* sometimes (8x) renders '*erwâh*, "nakedness," *pudenda*, uncovered sexual organs, of which one should be ashamed (Gen 9:22,23; Exod 20:26; Lev 20:17, etc.). *aischynē* has an objective sense "disgrace"; subjectively, a "feeling of shame" (*EDNT* 1:42–43). Some render "what they should [*or* ought] think shameful" ([N]JB, cf. REB, GNB). *what is shameful* can mean "shameful to them" or have an objective sense.

If *aischynē* = *pudenda*/private parts (Bengel; Hawth. 166), then (1) sexual looseness, immorality involving the genitals (Vincent 117; Dib. 71; Beare 136; Schmithals 1972:110–11; Bruce 130; Loh/Nida 117; Pohill 369; C. S. de Vos 272) or (2) the male sex organ circumcised (K. Barth 113; cf. Ewald-Wohl. 205; Hawth. 166; Mearns 198 [contrast Fee 373 n 43]; Edart 251). But (objection) Paul never speaks so disparagingly of circumcision (for Jews; for Gentile Christians, see on 3:2 and 3a); so Michaelis 62; Bruce 130, 132; de Vos 272. Koester 1961–62:327 denied equation of "shame" with *pudenda* (against R. Bultmann, *TDNT* 1:190). Silva 210 notes "lack of lexical evidence" for circumcision here.

(3) *aischynē* = "the experience of God's judgment," contrast "glory" and "shame" as in Isa 45:24–25 (Gnilka 205, cf. 1965:275–76). *aischynthēnai* = ashamed at the judgment (Gnilka 67 n 24 lists examples); O'B cites Pss 34:26 (vb.); 70:13 (vb.); Isa 30:3,5; 45:16 (vb.); and Mic 7:10; Oakes 2000:259–60, Hos

4:7, Jer 2:11–13, cf. Rom 1:23. Silva 210: objective disgrace, parallel to *apōleia* in 3:19a. Koester 1961–62:327: "disgrace," without emphasis on the judgment. Jewett 1970b:381 objected to fut. divine judgment (no vb. here, *autōn* suggests immortality now); O'B 457 n 81 shrugs this off as "not decisive." Fee 373 n 43, "what is shameful" involves present immoral behavior," but he reopens the door to fut. judgment by suggesting wordplay with "glory" in 3:21 and Hos 4:7 as background, "I will make your glory *(doxa)* into dishonor *(atimian)*" (cf. LXX; NRSV, "They changed their glory into shame." Sir 4:21 in Fee is harder to assess.

(4) Some combine with (3), judgment, the idea that the opponents claimed already to possess heavenly qualities, through circumcision, and so avoid judgment (Lincoln 96; cf. O'B 457).

(5) Related to (3) is Loh.'s martyrdom interpretation: *aischynē* = "disgrace" or "shame" for *lapsi* (apostate Christians), the opposite of the divine glory destined for the martyr (155–56). Michaelis 62 counters, *aischynē* at 3:19 is not to be explained by *ouk aischynthēsomai* at 1:18.

Some commentators (Fee, Bockmuehl) "plead ignorance" on exactly what terms in 3:19 mean. Criticism rules out some options, like (5). Oakes 2000:260, an OT theme, no particular OT text.

3:19d. *those whose concern is earthly things. hoi ta epigeia phronountes.* No *kai* or *hōn.* Subst. ptc., nom. pl., pres. act., *phroneō,* BDAG 2, **set one's mind on, be intent on,** a signature term in Phil (4:10; 1:7, etc.). From KJV on, "mind" as noun or vb.; Gdsp., "absorbed in earthly matters"; as at 3:15a, orientation (U. B. Müller 179; O'B 457); what concerns these people.

earthly things. Neut. pl., *epigeios, on,* 2.a; subst., **worldly things.** See NOTE on 2:10, . . . *those on earth.* . . . ZG 600, "whose thoughts are earth-bound." Cf. Lincoln 96–99; H. Sasse, ". . . earth is the place of sin, *epigeios* acquires a subsidiary moral sense" (*TDNT* 1:681); cf. Rom 8:3–13 (U. B. Müller 179). E. Schweizer, *TDNT* 7:131; G. Bertram *TDNT* 9:232, cf. Phil 3:3, 4a, "confidence in the flesh," people whose "thinking is governed by earthly powers," those of "this age"; Bultmann 1951 (INTRO. X Bibl.) 254–59; Böttger 255. Determined by "the earthly sphere of sin" (O'B 458), regularly (Koester 1961–62 328) "in contradistinction to *ouranios*" (3:20 "in the heavens"). Thus a "temporal and transient character" (2 Cor 5:1; cf. 1 Cor 15:40); "values that pass away, having neither divine origin nor eternal quality." Paul sarcastically judges opponents' religious claims, possibly a slogan about earthly/heavenly things (Jewett 1970b:378–89; Schenk 251, 290–91; Rom 8:5, 7; Sir 9:16–17). Fee 374 rejects this twist (n 47) but allows they "have abandoned the pursuit of the heavenly prize, in favor of what belongs *only* to the present scheme of things"; O'B 458 allows the possibility. Schenk went further: "things on earth, things in heaven" suggests a *topos,* well enough known to be ridiculed—Diog. Laert 1.34, "You know things in the heavens *(ta epi tou ouranou)* but cannot see things at your feet" (JR tr.); of Claudius, Sen. *Apocol.* 8.3; John 3:12. 3:19d conceals a warning under its mockery: what the enemies regard as "gains" (v 7), "perfection" (vv 12, 15, 18), and "heavenly citizenship" (v 20) is really "loss" (7–8), "crap" (8), "earthbound and destined to pass away," like *sarx.*

The construction is explained as (1) "a disconnected nominative with exclamatory force" (Lft. 156, "Men whose minds are set on earthly things!"), a cry of disappointment ("with tears"), to climax Paul's description. (2) A *"logical* subject of what precedes" (Meyer 148; O'B 458). NAB, "I am talking about those who are set upon the things of this world." (3) With 3:18, *polloi,* "For many walk—those who mind earthly things— . . ." (Ellicott 95; ATR 413; Schenk 290), one expects a qualifying phrase with *peripatousin.* Michaelis 62: anacoluthon (BDF 468), but not with *polloi.* (4) In "apposition to what precedes" (Vincent 117–18; BDF 136,1; 137,3; Loh/Nida 117).

3:20a. *For our governing civic association exists in the heavens. . . . hēmōn,* "of us"; gen. *hēmeis,* 3:3, 3:17 (acc.); 1st pl. last at 3:15 *let us think.* Strong emphasis for which attrib. position *(to gar hēmōn politeuma)* "was not sufficient" (BDF 284,2). In contrast with "they, them," the "many" (3:18), and initial gen. in v 19 *(hōn,* "of them"). It anchors *gar* (postpositive; usually "causal and explanatory force," KJV "for"; *DA* 324, 356; NAB "As you well know"), but here (*ZBG* 472) opposition, "destruction is the end of the worldly, but our . . ." ([N]RSV, etc.; "by contrast," NEB/ REB; ZG 600, "on the other hand"). *hyparchei,* ptc. at 2:6, see NOTE *who, while being in the sphere of God.* BDAG (1), **really be there, exist, be present, be at one's disposal,** not simply equivalent (2) to *eimi;* "lies in heaven." NAB recasts, "we have our citizenship in heaven."

in the heavens. Only use of *ouranos* in Phil, but cf. 2:10 *those in the heavens (epouranios).* BDAG 2, **transcendent abode,** the dwelling-place of God (in Gk. thought and the OT). Paul's "view of heaven" (11 references in acknowledged letters; *EDNT* 2:545) is associated more with final eschatology than creation (1 Cor 8:5). *Word studies:* H. Taub/G. von Rad, *TDNT* 5:497–536, esp. 507–9, and 532–33; H. Bietenhard, *NIDNTT* 2:188–96; U. Schoenborn, *EDNT* 2:543–47; J. F. Maile, *DPL* 381–83. Pl., a Semitism (Heb. *šāmaîm*) via the LXX, though several heavens may also be involved (2 Cor 12:2; N. Turner 1980:202–5, 308–12). Pl. like *ta epigeia* (19d), but regarded as a collective sg. to which *ex hou* refers (so Dib. 70; Böttger 258; Hawth. 171; in the NT, "almost always in the sing. with *ek,*" *TDNT* 5:513; Baumgarten [(2) Bibl.] 79), *ex hou* does not connect with *politeuma* (Loh. 158; *TDNT* 5:523 n 207). The *politeuma* is "in heaven and, therefore, still to come" (Koester 1961–62:330; Gnilka 206), but Lincoln 101–2, "The believer *now is,* in this present world, a citizen of the heavenly commonwealth" (101). Böttger 259, the "not yet" of Christian existence but (Gal 4:26) *politeuma* is the power determining that existence.

governing civic association. politeuma. Vb. *politeuomai,* "be a citizen"; m.-p., "be/live as a free citizen; administer, govern," etc. (LSJ); see NOTE on 1:27a *Exercise your citizenship* and (5) COMMENT A.4.a. BDAG, **commonwealth, state.** *Wordbooks:* H. Strathmann, *TDNT* 6:516–35, esp. 535; H. Bietenhard, *NIDNTT* 2:801–5; U. Hutter, *EDNT* 3:129–220; *TLNT* 3:124–33; Peres 133–41.

Appeal is often made to Jewish *politeumata* (Hawth. 171; O'B 468; Bockmuehl 233; W. Kraus 1996:344; D. K. Williams 2002:230–31; contrast Blumenfeld 294 n 18; Sonntag 171 n 565). Cf. *Let. Arist.* 310; Jos. *Ant.* 12.108 (LCL *Josephus* 7:55); *CPJ* 3.1530A; SEG 16.931; CIG 3.5361; Appelbaum, CRINT (INTRO. II n

3) 1:427–30, 438–40, 451–54. 2 Macc 12:7, "the whole community (*politeuma*) of Joppa" (AB 41A:429 the whole "citizenry"), but Lüderwitz 188 n 15, as in classical usage, "the ruling class," those responsible for a decree against the Jews (NRSV "done by the public vote of the city" = "according to the official [*koinon*] vote of the city"). Evidence for *politeuma* as a Jewish political entity within a city does not hold up. Not a public institution with rights of citizenship (Lüderwitz 204); see (5) below. Classical evidence becomes determinative for this NT *hapax legomenon*.

At the present stage of research there is considerable agreement that (1) support is lacking for *politeuma* as "home" (Ruppel; critique in Böttger 252 n 72; Lincoln 99; Silva 214 n 66; O'B 460; Fee 378 n 17). (2) "Citizenship" (*Bürgerrecht*; J. C. De Young 125; Schwemer 2000:299–36) is only weakly attested (Böttger 252; Lincoln 99 and n 56; O'B 460; Fee 378 n 17). (3) Moffatt's "colony of heaven" (on earth, in Philippi) no longer attracts serious adherents (Lincoln 99; O'B 460; Fee 378 n 17, "the believers' *politeuma* is in heaven, not on earth"). (4) Böttger, "state," with political power, officials, a constitution (*politeuma*). From "interplay between 'constitution' and 'state,'" Lincoln 99–100 suggested the "admittedly awkward rendering—'For our state and constitutive government is in heaven'"; Philo (*De Op. Mundi* 143–44; *De Agr.* 81, the ideal realm "determines the quality of the lives of those who belong to it") is background for "the Jewish Christian teachers" in Phil 3 (p. 97). O'B 460, Roman Philippi, governed by the *ius Italicum* (461, with Lincoln 100; Fee 378–79, a "true 'commonwealth' . . . in heaven," without renouncing "their common citizenship in the earthly "commonwealth' of Rome"). Hence Bockmuehl 233, "a political entity ('state')" with "active participation of the individuals who belong to it." So Blumenfeld 294 n 18; Sonntag 172; Jung 312 n 213, political, with a social aspect.

(5) Lüderitz concluded that *politeuma* in a Gk. *polis* referred to a smaller, ruling council, not the whole *politeia*, all the people, or even all the citizens; and to voluntary associations for cultic, social purposes and mutual support among ethnic aliens. MM 525 compared our word "community." (6) Evidence is strong for *politeuma* as a civic association, like a *thiasos* or *collegium* (Ascough 2003:77–78, 146–49, voluntary associations). Attractive as political aspects are and the (pretentious) glory of a (Christian) state or kingdom (in heaven), for house churches the local club or association lay much closer at hand (Alvarez 339, *collegia licita*). Cotter 1993:101–4, the *episkopoi* and *diakonoi* (1:1) were officers of such a civic entity, but bawdy socializing and pursuit of honors in *collegia* are out of place in "God's *politeuma* where the *cursus honorum* includes only the names of the faithful" (104). (7) Perhaps used by "the enemies" in ch. 3, for their group with "perfection now." See COMMENT A.4, below; Perkins 1991: *PT* I:94.

How to tr. *politeuma* at 3:20? Some reflection of "state, constitutive government," etc., seems needed, but also the social world of clubs, guilds, and (religious) associations. Therefore "civic association." It exercises some control over members (not with, or over, the state, *polis* or Empire), so *governing* (us, its members). *our governing civic association* is awkward. It lacks the homiletical attraction of a "colony of heaven," but is truer to lexical findings: less than "the state," yet civic, with a place in the public world of the day; like an association or club but with governance over members; it is in heaven, where its Lord is.

3:20b. *from which indeed we eagerly await the savior, the Lord Jesus Christ. ex +* gen. sg., masc. or neut., *hos, hē, ho* (BDAG 1.c.β.ℵ), "from which" ("whence" KJV; "from there" NRSV), a sense construction (Radl 1981:89): the sg. refers to *ouranois*, masc. pl.; cf. Acts 24:11. Vb., 1st pl., *apekdechomai*, "await eagerly"— *dechomai*, 4:18 *I have received* + double prep. prefix. In Paul (6x), of eschatological waiting (Rom 8:19, 23, 25; 1 Cor 1:7; Gal 5:5), here, the return of Christ (Grundmann, *TDNT* 2:56). Cf. E. Hoffmann, *NIDNTT* 2:238–46, esp. 245; M. E. Glasswell, *EDNT* 1:407. *kai, indeed,* can express addition (*DA* 327); KJV "also," "and" ([N]RSV, NIV, [N]JB). On *the Lord Jesus Christ,* see NOTES on 1:2 and 4:23; variations at 3:8; 2:11, 19; full list in *TLNT* 2:350 n 58. With anarthrous *kyrios,* any appositives (BDF 254.1; 268.2) can dispense with the art.; *GNTG* 3:206.

the savior. sōtēr. Cf. 1:19 *deliverance* (*sōtēria,* "salvation" at 1:28b and 2:12). Vb. *sōzō,* 1 Thess 2:16; 9x in 1 Cor (e.g., 1:18, 21); 2 Cor 2:15; Rom, 8x. The noun ending *–tēr,* one who saves (*nomen agentis*), is an old form (BDF 109,8), a title of deities in the Gk. world. In the NT, BDAG (a) of God (Luke 1:47; Pastoral Epistles 6x, cf. J. D. Quinn, AB 35:304–15); (b) of Christ, in Paul's acknowledged letters, here only (Eph 5:23; Pastorals 4x). At 3:20, not necessarily "*a* savior" ([N]RSV, etc., capitalized "Savior" to compensate), for it goes with *the Lord Jesus Christ* (anarthrous, see above); Fee 380–81 n 23, "a variation on 'Colwell's rule'" (Moule, *IB* 15–16). *Word studies: TDNT* 7:1003–21 (W. Foerster); *NIDNTT* 3:216–21 (J. Schneider/C. Brown); Diaz y Diaz; *EDNT* 3:326–27 (K. H. Schelkle); *TLNT* 3:354–56; Cullmann 1959 ([1] Bibl. **Christ**) 238–45. Jung, pagan literary sources (45–122) and inscriptions (123–72; for Philippi, Pilhofer 2:664,2 a falsified text); Ascough 2003:158–60, patron deity in voluntary associations.

In the Gk. world, a common title for a god who delivers, frees, protects, preserves, or heals a *polis* and its citizens (examples in wordbook articles; Cuss 63–71; Schofield; Jung 96–111, esp. Zeus). Then for Seleucid and Ptolemaic kings in Hellenistic ruler cult (*TLNT* 353, esp. n 43; cf. Bringmann; Jung 46–52, 58, 131–33), e.g., Ptolemy I Soter, often with "benefactor" (Nock 1951); Danker 1982:324–25, bibl. in n 371. In Roman Imperial cult (Jung 138–40) increasing use, though not an official title (not "Caesar Soter"). "Savior of the world" at times (Priene, 9 B.C., Augustus, cf. *TLNT* 3:353 and n 44). Lat. *salvator,* rare on coins (*TDNT* 7:1011). *Salus,* a personified virtue, "the safety and welfare of the state" (Jung 173–76; *OCD*³ 1350, cf. Gk. *sōtēria*). Foerster 1010–12 takes up the Emperor as benefactor, in a coming "Golden Age" (Verg. *4th Ecl., sōtēr* does *not* occur), though "No one felt the new age was heaven on earth" (*TDNT* 7:1010 n 42, citing M. I. Rostovtzeff). Some see this in 3:20 (fut., "not yet"), no savior "god" or new age now on earth. *sōtēr* was used of gods and goddesses (Leda, Isis), deified human beings (Heracles; ruler cult), and mortals whose achievements benefited the community (AB 35:308; Herodot. 7.139.5; Plato *Resp.* 5.463B; Dem. *Or.* 18.43): a physician, like Asclepius, savior and healer (Dio Chrys. *Or.* 77; more in *TDNT* 1007 and n 15); politicians, statesmen (1007–9) through deeds for the *polis;* e.g.,

Aratus of Sicyon (died 213 B.C.), "common father and *sōtēr*" of his city-state (Plut. *Aratus* 14.3 and 24, *Vit.* 1047A and 1033D = LCL *Lives* 11:32–33, 11:96–97 "preserver"). *sōtēr* did not make a person a deity. Used of one responsible for some achievement and of his legate/lieutenant (Pompey and a subordinate; *TDNT* 7:1008); for Philippian hearers, Christ as God's legate?

In the LXX (AB 35:308; Jung 177–238; Heb. *yš'*) of God (Isa 45:15 and 21; cf. 35:4); or human beings as "savior" (Judg 3:9, 15, etc., "deliverer"; Neh 9:27, "saviors who saved them," LXX 2 Esd 19:27, "you gave them saviors and you saved them . . ."). Gk. Additions to Esther, for Mordecai (8:12n Rahlfs; NRSV Addition E 16:13). An anointed leader ("messiah," Zech 9:9 LXX, Isa 49:6, 2 Esd 13:26). In the Apocrypha, all uses are of God (Wis 16:7; 1 Macc 4:30, etc.). See also *Pss. Sol.* 3.6; 8.33; 16.4; 17.3 *Sib. Or.* 1.73; 3:35 (God, *TDNT* 7:1014). For Qumran, *TDNT* 7:1014 found no equivalent; Jung 290–61, little; cf. 1 QS 11.12. In Philo, under Hellenistic influence (Jung 239–61). Rabbinic references in Str-B 1:67–74; *Tanhuma b.* 12e, of the messiah. Loh. claimed "savior" is "a term . . . in almost all religions and lands, of every age, in Orient as in Occident" (159; cf. *ER* 13:418), the background in Near-Eastern Redeemers, rather than Hellenistic sources. Hawth. 171, the "substance" for Paul is in the OT; Koester 1961–62:330 n 5, an apocalyptic sense from the OT.

Bultmann 1951 (INTRO. X) 78–79 thought *sōtēr* common in primitive Christianity, esp. re final eschatological deliverance; cf. *TDNT* 7:992–94 and 1016. But (Fee 381 n 24) not exclusively for future eschatological salvation, thus correcting the notion (Hawth. 172, Collange 140) that "salvation" refers (only) to "what yet remains to be done," "justification" (only) to past action (overinterpretation of Rom 5:9). Some see 3:20b as "nontechnical," from "salvation" (Phil 2:12; 1 Thess 1:10, etc.); Dib. 93; Gnilka 207; Beare 137; O'B 462–63; K. H. Schelkle, *EDNT* 3:326; U. B. Müller 181. For others it roots in Hellenistic ruler-cults and Roman Emperor worship (Fee 380, used "for the Philippians' sakes," *sōtēr* "a common title for Caesar"); cf. Bornhäuser 1938 ([7] Bibl.); Perkins 1991: *PT I*:93–94; Witherington 99–102; Bockmuehl 235; Jung, emphatically. N. Beck ([7] Bibl.) 56–58 notes no anti-Roman cryptogram here. "Savior" was prominent later (against Imperial cult?) in the "fish" symbol, *ichthus*, an acronym for *Iēsous Christos Theou Huios Sōtēr*, "Jesus Christ, God's Son, Savior." *sōtēr* was used sparingly by Paul, not (Hawth. 172) because Paul was "reluctant to use such a common term of someone so unique as Christ." It was appropriate for "Philippi, where the Emperor was regarded as 'saviour'" (O'B); the Philippians would grasp it (Fee 381). One cannot be confident they would have known OT usage ("God our Savior").

3:21a. *who will change the body of our humiliation to the sphere of the body of his glory. hos*, as at 2:6. Fut. act., *metaschēmatizō* (BDAG 1) **change the form of . . . transform, change.** *Wordbooks*: J. Schneider, *TDNT* 7:957–58; G. Braumann, *NIDNTT* 1:708–10, W. Liefeld 3:864; J. M. Nützel, *EDNT* 2:419. Numerous classical usages, only one LXX example (*TDNT* 7:957), 4 Macc 9:22, the first of seven martyred brothers, "as though transformed (*metaschēmatizomenos*) by fire to immortality. . . . [23] 'Imitate me (*mimēsasthe me*), brothers,' he said. . . ." Other NT uses (2 Cor 11:13, 14, 15; 1 Cor 4:6), all in Paul, do not help at 3:21a.

Some appeal to *morphē* at 2:6a, 7b (*the sphere of God* and *of a slave*, contrast *schēma*, 7d, *in appearance*) and *metamorphoō*, "transform, transfigure" (Jesus' "transfiguration," Mark 9:2 par. Matt 17:2, not at Luke 9:29; 2 Cor 3:18, believers "changed into his likeness"; Rom 12:2, "transformed by the renewal of your mind"). Thus *TDNT* 4:756 (J. Behm): *metamorphousthai*, physical transformation (759), *metaschēmatizesthai*, "become different" (756, cf. 7:957). Views vary. Some reflect Lft. 127–33, esp. 130 (Gk. philosophy, not the pertinent Hellenistic usages; see [7] NOTE on 2:6a *living in the sphere of God*). Some take *metaschēmatizō* as "change the outward fashion', that is, 'the sensible vesture in which the human spirit is clothed'" (rejected by O'B 464). Loh., transfiguration for martyrs; contrast *TDNT* 7:957 n 6 (J. Schneider): it applies to all Christians; Michaelis 64. Traditionally "change" (KJV, RSV, etc.). NAB, "give a new form to," "transform" (NIV, NRSV; Fee 382, stressing Phil 2:6–8); "transfigure" ([N]JB, NEB/REB; Jesus' transfiguration, only momentary, temporary change?). *How* does "vindication" (Bockmuehl 236) occur? By change now (2 Cor 5:1–10; O'B 464)? By resurrection at the parousia (1 Cor 15:42–57, 52–53)? Only believers alive then (Lincoln 102) or deceased believers as well (Bruce 134)? See COMMENT B.3.

the body of our humiliation. to sōma tēs tapeinōseōs hēmōn, "the body of the humiliation of us." On *sōma*, see NOTE on 1:20 *through my own self*; BDAG 1.b., **the living body** (or person, Hawth. 172; cf. Gundry 1976 [(4) Bibl.] 1–3, 50, 165, 200, 228), contrasted with "the body of [Christ's] glory." *Wordbooks*: E. Schweizer, *TDNT* 7:1061 and *EDNT* 3:323; *NIDNTT* 1:236 (S. Wibbing). Jewett 1971a:252–54, polemic against "heretical libertinistic theology." *sōma + hēmōn* pl. = "a collective singular" (O'B 464), not like "body of Christ," the church, but the body of each individual Christian in the "we"-group (Gundry 1976 [(4) Bibl.] 220). NIV, REB, etc., "bodies."

tapeiōseōs. See NOTES on *tapeinoō*, 2:8a *he experienced humiliation on his part*; 4:12a *to be brought low* (economically); *tapeinophrosynē*, 2:3b *humiliation*. *TDNT* (W. Grundmann) 8:5, 10–11 14–15 (Philo), 20–21; *NIDNTT* 2:259, 263 (H.-H. Esser); *EDNT* 3:335 (H. Giesen). In the Gk. world, *tapeinōsis* was negative ("base, ignoble") but also a virtue (modesty, moderation, self-depreciation); *TLNT* 3:370, citing S. Rehrl, 26ff., but cf. (6) NOTE on 2:3b *humiliation* re Rehrl; positive senses for *tapeino*-words, later in the NOTE on *humiliation*, Plato, *TLNT* 3:370 n 5. BDAG *tapeinōsis* 1: **humiliation** (Polyb. 9.33.10; Plut. *Mor.* 2.149A; Epict. 3.22.104 in NOTE on 2:3b); Acts 8:33 (= Isa 53:8 LXX); Jas 1:10; cf. *EDNT* 3:355; (2) **lowliness, humility, humble station,** Luke 1:48 (= 1 Sam 1:11, "the low estate of his handmaiden," RSV; "powerlessness" rather than "mental attitude," L. T. Johnson, *Luke* 42; Jung 267, Mary at God's beck and call). A socioeconomic sense of "humiliation" is apparent, more than with *tapeinophrosynē*. The gen. (like *doxēs* which follows) is attribut. and descriptive (ATR 496; RSV "our lowly body"; NRSV-mg "our humble bodies"; GNTG 2:440, cf. 1:74 and the note on 235–36). Others claim a Hebraism (W. Grundmann, *TDNT* 7:788 n 103; ZBG #41; GNTG 3:214; Edart 246). BDF 165, a gen. of quality (O'B 464; Michaelis 63). Fee 382 n 28, gen. "expresses 'belonging.'" *hēmōn* not with "body" (NJB "this wretched body of ours"; KJV, RSV, GNB) but with "humiliation" (Fee 382 n 28, "the body that belongs to our humiliation"). Body is "the locus of present suffering and weakness" and "humiliation" in the world; not itself "vile" (that would call for *sarx*, not *sōma*; cf. *TDNT* 7:1061 n 383). So NRSV-txt, Moffatt, NEB. Grundmann (*TDNT* 8:21) reads in "humiliation in death."

   to the sphere of the body of his glory. symmorphos, on, similar in form (BDAG; NT, otherwise only at Rom 8:29); neut. sg. acc., agreeing with *sōma*. On the adj., cf. *TDNT* 7:787 (of Agamemnon, becoming like the Gk. gods, Heraclitus, *Hom. All.* 77); G. Braumann, *NIDNTT* 1:705, 707; W. Pöhlmann, *EDNT* 3:287–88, "transformation of being and essence" or "change of . . . form [cf. 2:443, point 4 under *morphē*] which constitutes one's identity." Some trs. add an infin. (RSV "to be like"; NABRNT "to conform with"; "to resemble," Gdsp.) or take it with *metaschēmatisei* (U. B. Müller 183; JB "transfigure . . . into copies"; NJB ". . . into the mould of . . ."). Later scribes added a purpose (or result) cl. (first in the 7th-cent. corrector of D, etc., Majority Text [545 witnesses in Aland 1991 3:594–95]): *eis to genesthai auto,* "in order that it [our vile body] may be fashioned like unto his glorious body," KJV; NIV; textual evidence is strongly against the addition (lacking in ‭א‬ A B D, etc.). Some treat *symmorphon* as parallel to *metaschēmatisei;* NEB, ". . . will transform the body belonging to our humble state, and give it a form like that of his own resplendent body"; REB, etc. NIV (cf. CEV) moves it ahead of 21a, "who, by the power that . . . will transform. . . ." Most keep the Gk. order ([N]RSV, etc.). Opinions vary on pressing the prefix *syn* ("same," "similar"? exactly like or akin to?) and on *morphē* (ontological? a "sphere"? see NOTES on 2:6a and 7b). Fee 382–83 sees ties with 2:6–11; O'B 464–65, with 3:10, *symmorphizomenos.* Bockmuehl 235–36, echoes of 2:5–11, 1 Cor 15.

   the body of his glory. tō[i] sōmati, dat. with *symmorphon,* or associative dat. (BDF 194,2; ATR 528, hardly instrumental). In Paul, *sōma* shows "continuity between the present and the future" (Fee 383). *doxēs* parallels "of humiliation." On *doxa,* cf. and contrast 3:19c, NOTE on their "glory." BDAG 1.b, *radiant, glorious body.* Loh. 160–61, "eternal uniting" of the martyrs "with the Lord"; contrast Gnilka 79, Michaelis 64. Gieschen ([7] Bibl.) 338–39 speculates about a "preincarnate Form of God," a "body of the Divine Presence," a *gigantic* body," but not *cosmic.* More likely related to Hellenistic mystery religions (U. B. Müller 183; cf. 2 Cor 3:18), but here in fut. terms, as at 1 Cor 15:49. Kotsidu notes *doxa* as a term of honor for Hellenistic rulers. Debated: is *doxēs* a Semitism? descriptive (ATR 496) or gen. of "quality" (O'B 464 n 131; GGBB 86–88)? *autou* with *sōmati* ("his glorious body," NRSV-mg.) or *doxēs* ("the body of his glory")?

3:21b. *in accord with the action of his ability also to put all things into subjection to himself. kata* + acc., "*in accordance with* and *because of* are merged" (BDAG *kata* B.5.a.δ, "the norm is at the same time the reason"); cf. Phil 4:11 *being in need.* At 1 Cor 12:8 *kata to pneuma = dia* + gen. Fee 383, "in keeping with," not instrumentality ("by the power that," NIV, etc.); Fee 1994:481 n 24, "the 'norm' or 'standard' in keeping with which something is done." *tēn energeian* (BDAG **the state or quality of being active, working, operation, action,** of transcendent beings), see NOTE on 2:13a (ptc.) *For the One at work . . .* and 2:13b (infin.) *both to will and to work* (there, of human activity; 2:13a, God energizing, G. Bertram,

TDNT 2:653). Here, Christ's action. Possibly language of "liturgical confession" (Hawth. 173). KJV, "the working whereby he is able to . . ."; most trs. use "power" ([N]RSV, NIV, etc.); NJB "the working of the power which he has." O'B 466, *energeia* = "power to work effectively," but p. 286 hardly justifies it. Expanded phrases in Col 1:29; Eph 3:7; 1:19 have influenced interpretation of the noun here (the only one in the undisputed letters), assuming "Paul meant what later passages add." Though *dynamis* does not appear at 3:20b, "power" may reflect *tou dynasthai auton*, subst. infin. in gen. (*tou* = BDAG *ho, hē, to* 2.d.β.ב), + subject acc. (*auton* = Christ), lit., "(the fact that) he is able." The root *dyna-* (*dynamis* [3:10 power] and *dynamai* [here only, in Phil]) spills over into *energeia* in some interpretations (ZG #392, "his power enabling him . . ."). The infin. may modify (GNTG 1:218–19, with ATR 996) or be a real subst. (ATR 1061), in a consecutive or final sense, "power so that he can . . ." (BDF 400,2; GNTG 3:141, "power by which he can . . ."; O'B 466, n 143, Hawth. 173, Schenk 326). Or be epexegetical (Moule, *IB* 129, "power, namely his ability to . . ."). Sometimes *tou dynasthai auton* emerges as if an attrib. ptc., "power that enables him . . ." ([N]RSV, NIV, etc.). [N]RSV etc. subordinate v 21b as the means by which Christ transforms our bodies, but others make it parallel to 21a or primary (NIV; CEV, ". . . Christ has power over everything, and he will make these poor bodies of ours like his own glorious body") or even into a separate sentence (JB). Hawth. 173 (cf. O'B 466), Christ will achieve this goal (in 3:21a) "by the outworking of his ability to. . . ."

also to put all things into subjection to himself. Another infin., *hypotaxai*, aor. from *hypotassō*, BDAG 1.a, **to subject, subordinate.** Backgrounds in military use, the citizen and the state (Rom 13:1,5), and in codes about superior and subordinate in a household (Col 3:18; Eph 5:21, not in the acknowledged letters, but cf. 1 Cor 14:34). Cf. G. Delling, *TDNT* 8:39–42; R. Bergmeier, *EDNT* 3:408; *TLNT* 3:425, n 11, accepting the place God has assigned, one's rank in society. 3:21b echoes Paul's treatment of Ps 8:6b (LXX 7b) in 1 Cor 15:27 (*hypotaxai* + "all things," in 3:21 with art. *ta panta*, BDAG *pas* 4.d.β, for *the universe*, the whole of creation).

to himself. autō[i] ("subject all things *to him*"), א* A B D* etc., = Christ, the subject of the infin. Should be reflexive (Back 183), with a rough breathing mark, *hautō[i]*, as WH urged.; cf. GNTG 2:180–81; Moule, *IB* 119; BDF 64,1 and GNTG 3:41 are dubious. Many MSS read *heautō[i]* (א² D² L Ψ etc.). TCGNT 615–16 shows a committee majority for the unaspirated "prevailing Hellenistic usage," a minority for the rough breathing. In effect, *autō[i]* functions as a reflexive (BDAG *heautou*, Intro. 1.a). Cf. GTNG 3:41; ZBG 210. Price 282–83 gives *heautō[i]* 0.55 probability (0.39 for *autō[i]*; 0.06 for *autō*) and finds *hautō[i]* improbable (though, on the basis of MS 81, UBSGNT had it in its 1st and 2nd eds., but not the 3rd). Most trs. have a reflexive ("to himself," [N]RSV, Gdsp., NEB/ REB). NIV paraphrases, "under his control"; JB omits. *kai* before *hypotaxai* is often ignored (Gdsp., NEB/REB, NIV, etc.); "even" in KJV/RSV, NJB, "also" in NRSV. Fee 384 sees a "final word of assurance to the Philippians": "In keeping with the same power by which he will transform their present bodies that are suffering at the hand of opposition in Philippi, Christ will *likewise* subject 'all things'

to himself, including the emperor himself and all those who in his name are causing the Philippians to suffer." Emphasis (Froitzheim 241–42) is on soteriology and
the *kyrios-sōma* relationship for believers.

COMMENT

A. FORMS, SOURCES, AND TRADITIONS

1. Literary Features. The NOTES (cf. Edart 244–46) indicate alliterative paronomasia (3:18); ironic wordplay (19a *final goal*, 19c *"glory,"* 19b *god*); jarring contrasts (*goal, destruction; god, belly; "glory," what is shameful* in 19; *me, us* in 17 and
20–21, the *many* in 18–19, "them" in 19c and "us"; *earthly* in 19d, *the heavens* in
20; "lowly" and "glorious" in 21); cliché, 3:19d; antitheses, 3:21 (*DA* 137), perhaps from the diatribe style (Schoon-Janßen 143, 149–50; Reumann 1984:599, +
parataxis, vv 20–21). Much has been made of positive and negative models
(Schoon-Janßen 142); how "friends," in contrast to "enemies," behave (Stowers
1991:117; Fitzgerald, *ABD* 5:321; Minear 1990:211; Geoffrion 197, "insiders and
outsiders"). Hence (Schoon-Janßen on 3:2–11) example from Paul's prior conflicts, e.g., in Galatia (146–59, 159–61, 164–65). Tellbe 1994:103–5, 116–20;
2000:261–67 (cf. Hansen 196–98) reconstructed a situation where the Gentile
Philippian Christians were tempted to adopt Judaism, so as to be regarded as legal
in Roman society.[1] Such models are not *"the* key" (*DA* 260–61 n 391, contra
Stowers). Paul creates "boundaries of identity" for himself, readers, and other
Christians, in contrast to the enemies described (261 n 394). Reed 291 sees "a
personal hortatory letter" with "background" and "petitions" — "indicative" and
"imperative"; opinions vary on the pattern.[2] The "positive and negative exampla"
in 3:17–18 ease transition from 15–16 to 17–18, which lacks any connective word
(*DA* 262).

Rhetorical analyses abound for 3:17–21, but scarcely agree.[3] Similarly with

---

[1] The ghost of *religio licita*, Bockmuehl 190–91. On its history and repudiation in NT studies, see
R. Maddox, *The Purpose of Luke-Acts* (Edinburgh: T&T Clark 1982) 91–93; P. F. Esler, *Community
and Gospel in Luke-Acts: the Social and Political Motivations of Lucan Theology* (SNTSMS 57; Cambridge: Cambridge Univ. Press, 1957) 211–14; (5) COMMENT A.3, n 13.

[2] Reed 291 lists 3:18–21 as "background" and 4:1 as petition ("Stand firm!"); Schenk 256–59, 4:1–3
after 3:2–21 (all in his Letter C); more specifically, 3:17 is "petition," 3:18–21 "background" and contrast.

[3] See INTRO. VI.B n 2. Fields 229, 3:17–19 = "Second Enthymeme" (cf. 3:2–4a; [2] COMMENT A.1,
n 10 on the device), 3:20–21 Third Enthymeme. Vv 17–19 (major premise) "The people of God walk
in dependence upon Jesus Christ and not on the flesh"; (minor premise) "Those who walk in the flesh
are enemies of the cross of Christ"; (conclusion) "Therefore, beware or consider those who walk in the
flesh" (243). 3:20–21 (major) "Citizens of heaven are transformed by Jesus," admittedly missing;
(minor) "We are citizens of heaven . . ."; (conclusion) "We will be transformed" (247–48). Differently,
Banker 154. Bloomquist 135–36, 3:17–4:7 as *exhortatio* concludes the *reprehensio*. Garland 160–62,
"rare" terms in 3:20 (*politeuma*) and 1:27 (*politeuesthe*) mark 1:27–4:3 as a structural unit; unlikely
(Schoon-Janßsen 118, cf. 139–41; *DA* 364–65 n 82). D. F. Watson 1988b:75–76, 3:17–21 = the third

chiastic-concentric treatments.[4] More simply, "Paul's rheorical strategy is . . . to reverse the *values* of his opponents" (D. K. Williams 2002:217–18).

OT material: perhaps 19c (Hos 4:7; *DA* 291), but glory and shame, common OT terms, were also widespread in Gk. culture. Ps 8:6 [LXX 7] echoes in 3:21; see NOTE and B.3 below.[5] Sources: hymnic frg. in vv 20–21? (2, below); "imitators" theme (v 17; 3, below); slogans from "the enemies" (4, below).

2. A Hymnic Fragment in 3:20–21? Loh. 150–51 took 3:20–21 as "a festive song of praise" in "the style of an OT psalm." (Vv 18 and 19 were also two-liners, v 17 a three-line sentence; cf. [13] COMMENT A.1.d.) For subsequent trends see Reumann 1984. The "somewhat tentative vote" in 1984:604 was for a hymn,[6]

> Our commonwealth is in the heavens,
>   from which we await a savior, Jesus,
>   who will transform our lowly body
>   to conform to his glorious body,
>   in accord with his power by which he is able
>   also to subdue all things to himself.

Akin to 1 Cor 15 (esp. vv 21–22, 44b–45) in apocalyptic content, it could have arisen among Corinthian Christians who, from Paul's teachings, sang of Christ transforming us. But (605 and n 85) evidence for 3:20–21 as hymnic "is not as impressive" as for 2:6–11.

Since then there has been a retreat at 2:6–11 from "hymn," often toward "encomium" (above, EXC. B, II.E), applied in Phil 3 more to vv 5–6 ([12] COMMENT B.1; Berger 1984a:344–46) than to 20–21. Encomiastic elements in 3:20–21 in-

---

development in 3:1–21 of the *probatio* (2:1–3:21); vituperation of the opponents, Paul's "life of trust" (to be emulated); "*topos* of eschatological hope of resurrection" in "what may be a hymn," 20–21. Black 1995:41, 43, 48, 3:17–21 "True and False Teachers Contrasted" within the *refutatio* of 3:1–21. Schenk 279–80, 3:15–21 is "direct *refutatio*"; Harnisch 148–51; Edart 246–47, 252–54, for Letter A, *peroratio*. Brucker ([7] Bibl.) 297, 332–33, 3:17–21 = *conclusio* for 3:1–21. Bittasi 120–39 follows Fiore 1986:87–88, a hortatory letter of friendship (contrast Reumann 1996; Holloway 2001a:31 n 120). Fiore 1986:189 n 77 calls v 17 the "command"; 18–19, contrast; and 20–21 "gnomic saying and elaboration." Though some call 3:17–21 "paraenetic" (Wick 104–5; Banker 146, "hortatory"), Brucker's argumentative (symbouleutic) unit is crowned in 20–21 with epideictic material (330–31, 334; Jung 310, 315). Holloway 2001a:143 finds "consolatory value" in 3:17–21 primarily in pursuit of Christ as "a source of joy independent of . . . successes in the gospel mission."

[4] See INTRO. VI.B n 3. Wick pairs 3:17–21 (his b[2]) with 1:27–30 (b[1]), both on conduct and "opponents"; cf. Edart 252; Bittasi 120–39, 210, 3:17–4:1. Luter/Lee, 2:12–16 parallels 3:17–21 (p. 94); they highlight "themes that do not fit into their chiastic outline" (Porter/Reed 225). Some see a minor chiasm in 3:18–19 (S. F. Winter 198 n 99).

[5] The point has shifted from *God* subjecting "all things" and "enemies" under *Christ's* feet in 1 Cor 15:25 to *Christ* subjecting "all things to *himself*." See n 45 below.

[6] Clues include *hos* at 3:21, perhaps *ex hou* in v 20 (Güttgemanns 1966:243); a seemingly rhythmic style, but no precise agreement on "stanzas"; antithetical style (the heavens, earthly things); unusual vocabulary ("savior," *metaschēmatisei*, humiliation); and possible differences from Paul's theology elsewhere (at the parousia *Christ* transforms Christians then alive). But each point has been disputed. Cf. O'B 467–71.

clude the origins of the Savior (from his homeland above) and his accomplishments (*praxeis;* his operative power and glory will change the bodies of those
who belong to him to be like his, subjecting the universe to himself). The deeds of
others—the enemies or Caesar—pale by comparison (cf. Malina/Neyrey 55). A
Philippian audience would have found such features familiar from encomia of
the day, on which they modeled their witness to Christ in 2:6–11. Links with
2:6–11 do not suffice to posit a "third stanza" of the "Christ hymn."[7] The content,
in context (opponents), augments 2:6–11 and at points corrects deficiencies in the
Philippians' encomium; see B.3 below.

3. Imitators and Example (3:17). Paul asks all the Philippian believers to *continue to become imitators together of me (symmimētai mou)* and to *take notice of
those who live in this way, as you have us as an example (typon).* From this and four
other instances of *mimeomai*-terms in Paul's acknowledged letters, much has been
made of a Pauline pattern of "imitation" (overview in Probst [(1) Bibl.] 286–90;
history of recent interpretation, Reumann 1989b [(12) Bibl.] 18–22; a different
summary in D. K. Williams 2002:213–14): Paul imitated the Christ figure in 2:6–
11 (and God, Eph 5:1; but cf. AB 34A:555–56, 588–92); converts are to imitate
Paul, Timothy, and Epaphroditus (O'B 254–55, 262; Edart 254); 3:17–21 = "true
and false models."

The theme is Gk., not from the OT.[8] Sometimes related to "following Jesus"
and discipleship in the gospels (*akolouthein, mathētēs;* Ger. *Nachfolge* = discipleship, *Nachahmung* = imitation). But in Paul *akolouthein* occurs only for the rock
at 1 Cor 10:4, *mathētēs* not at all. Schulz 1962 separated the two concepts, ethics
being the one link between discipleship (with Jesus) and membership in the body
of Christ (195–97; 269–70; 288–89); "following Jesus" and "imitating Christ"
were identified with each other only apart from and after Paul; cf. John 13:14–15
(foot-washing); 1 Peter 2:21 (*hypogrammon;* pp. 298–300, 177–79). Similarly
Hopper 167–81. H. D. Betz 1967 sought to connect one concept in Palestinian
Judaism and another in Hellenistic mystery religions,[9] with likeness in intentions,
in ethical responsibility (with Schulz), through the developing concept of faith,
belief in the exalted Christ (42–43).[10] N. A. Dahl saw a "Conformity Pattern":
"Just as Christ, so you also" ("Form-Critical Observations on Early Christian

---

[7] Lincoln 88, the vv "suit the apostle's purposes"; Lambrecht 1985:203–4, it draws on 3:10–11 and
1 Cor 15:25–28, as well as 2:6–11; Bittasi 133–35.

[8] See NOTE on 3:17a *imitators.* Cf. Hopper. Byron ([1] Bibl. **slaves**) 129–31 appeals to Jewish writings
influenced by Hellenism. Occasional use in late LXX books is under Gk. influence.

[9] The OT and Judaism provided no influences on Paul re *mimētēs* (Betz 84–101), there is no direct
connection for the Synoptic concept of *Nachfolge* with the OT (43–47); one cannot appeal to a "Hebraic background" behind the two concepts.

[10] Critique of Betz in M. Hengel, *The Charismatic Leader and His Followers* (1968; tr., New York:
Crossroad, 1981): Pauline "*mimēsis Christou* (cf. I Cor 11,1) relates primarily to the sufferings of
Christ and not to concrete 'following' by Jesus' disciples," though believers share "a common destiny
with Christ" (62).

Preaching," in his *Jesus in the Memory of the Early Church* [Minneapolis: Augsburg, 1976] 34).

The other term in 3:17, *example*, is often overlooked. *typos* (see NOTE) has considerable Gk. background but little LXX usage.[11] Classical data in *TDNT* 8:246–48. A. Lumpe[12] shows how *exempla* (examples, models, patterns, prototypes) were a necessary part of rhetoric (Lausberg #19, 24, 29, 410–16, index p. 659—the quest of speakers for good illustrations). Examples might come from myth, history, drama, parents and forebears, superiors in government, sometimes with encomiastic *synkrisis* (the hero appears greater by comparison). In the OT, cf. Mal 2:6,8; Hos 4:13b–14; Pss 78, 105; Ezek 20:4b–39; 1 Macc 2:51–60; Sir 44; Neh 9:6–37. In the NT, cf. Acts 7:2–53; Heb 11 ("by faith"); John 13:15 (Jesus washed the feet of the disciples as example); on 1 Pet, cf. AB 37B:110–11, 526–28 and passim. In Paul, "example" and "imitation" appear together in two of the four *mimētēs* passages (1 Thess 1:6–7; Phil 3:17). Paul's use of *(sym)mimētēs* stems from the Gk. world, whence it infiltrated Hellenistic Judaism.[13]

Michaelis (*TDNT* 4) avoids *imitatio Christi* or a mystical relation to the risen Lord; Christ is a figure of authority to whom obedience is due (672–73; *Phil.* 61). Contrast Fiore 1986:164–87, esp. 165–68.[14] Michaelis: (1) 1 Thess 2:14 and 1:6–7 express "simple comparison" between persecuted churches in Judea and Thessalonica, and between the Thessalonians and Paul (666–67, 670). Fiore 1986:184–85 agreed. (2) Phil 3:17 and 2 Thess 3:7, 9 mean recognizing Paul's authority and being obedient (Michaelis 667–68). Fiore 185–86, authority and obedience are "specification of the Pauline model to be imitated"; 3:17 = walking "behind the Pauline model." (3) Michaelis 668–69 saw obedience at 1 Cor 4:16 (to commands; note "teaching" 4:17) and 11:1 (Christ and Paul in a "chain of tradition," 11:23); Fiore (168–84) is Paul "apostolic example," imitation of Christ "mediated by imitation of the community's father." Fiore added Gal 4:12, "Become as I am" (*ginesthe hōs egō*; no *mimeomai*-term).

D. M. Stanley agreed with Michaelis that Gk. literature provided "no real parallels to Pauline usage" (1959:859–60 = 1963:371); "Jesus' earthly career is rarely

---

[11] Only 4x, for two different Heb. words at Amos 5:26 and Exod 25:40 (*tabnît* there is usually rendered *paradeigma*); 3 Macc 3:30, the "form" of a letter; 4 Macc 6:19, see NOTE. Goppelt (*TDNT* 8:248, 258–59) brings in Philo's usage re philosophical speculations on hermeneutics in Hebrews.

[12] "Exemplum" (Gk. *paradeigma, hypodeigma*), *RAC* 6 (1966) 1229–57; cf. Berger 1984b:1145–48 and 1984a:28–31, deliberative rhetoric, and 330–73, esp. 373; bibl. in M. Mitchell 1992 ([9] Bibl.) 39 n 93.

[13] *mimēsis* arose perhaps in Gk. drama or philosophy (Kosmala 1963; Schulz 1962:206) or cult (Gulin; H. D. Betz 1967:48–53; Hopper 22–36, mystery religions) and was spread by the Hellenistic ruler cult (*TDNT* 4:664 n 8).

[14] Michaelis is said to react "against the *imitatio Christi* of the Catholic tradition" (Stanley 1959:373 = 1963:861–62; Kurz 1985:103). Catholic tendency toward *imitatio*-language is often shared by Anabaptist (Mennonite) and Free Church, pietist traditions; contrast Lutheran and Reformed theology. But recent scholarship scarcely follows denominational lines. For ecumenical dialogue, see Reumann 1989b ([12] Bibl.). Stendahl claimed that Paul, as the (unique) Apostle to the Gentiles, does *not* speak for general Christian experience (1976:75, 45–46; cf. *IDB* 1:418–31; Pfitzner 150, not "an exact paradigm for every believer"). For an opposing view, see Everts 164–66, 188–94.

a model for Christian behavior" (cf. 877 = 389). Stanley 1984 was more critical of Michaelis. W. P. De Boer 209–11 argued for deliberate imitation (e.g., at 1 Thess 2:14), *imitatio Christi* is "emphatically present" in 1 Cor 11:1 (p. 211). E. Larsson, *Nachfolge* (of Jesus) and *Nachahmung* (of Paul) are identical, possible through baptism; "imitation" becomes sacramental (cf. "image" behind 2:6, NOTE on *living in the sphere of God*, interpretation [b] for *morphē*; Larsson 230–75; Crouzel 23).

"Paul as teacher" was the emphasis in D. M. Williams (1967): a pedagogical pattern. Just as a rabbi lived Torah, so Paul lived Christ. In a martyr situation (with Loh.), Christ's life (2:6–11) provided pattern for Paul in 3:4–11 (great renunciation, suffering). W. S. Kurz, the NT keeps "following Jesus" and "imitating Christ" separate "on a literary level," but they refer to "a common *res* ('reality, phenomena')" in "*pedagogical* practice" (1985:122–23 n 2), on Greco-Roman pedagogical principles (Fiore). "Kenotic" (Phil 2:7) applies to Paul re ch. 3, "self-emptying models" are relevant for "Christians of any age" (121).

Fiore 1986 (also in Sampley, ed., 2003:228–57; cf. O'B 445–46) focuses on the *function* of *personal* example in the Pastorals (168–87). Classical examples (*paradeigmata*; 26–163; cf. also Hopper 11–64) occur in (a) rhetorical treatises (Aristot. *Rhet.*; Cic. *Inv.*, Quint. *Inst.*) and handbooks. Pupils imitated teachers as "living voice" among authors read for models, including *encomia* (p. 37; cf. 105; cf. Phil 3:5–6). Protreptic discourse might hit false teachers and addressees on "actions and attitudes which militate against what is useful for them" (p. 40; cf. Phil 3:17–19). (b) "Kingship literature" (45–78; OCD³ 807), e.g., Plut. *Ad principem ineruditum* and *Prae. ger. reip.* (*Mor.* 779c–782 and 798–827, LCL *Plutarch's Moralia* 10:49–71 and 155–299). (c) "Official letters" from the Hellenistic period (a superior instructs a subordinate on conduct in office, 79–84). (d) Hortatory letters, Seneca (84–100), "letters collected under the names of Socrates and the Socratics" (101),[15] esp. *Ep.* 28 (pp. 101–63). The letters fuse *bios* or life-example and *logos* or exposition (131); treatment of Socrates lacks the "autobiographical perspective" (134) in Phil 3. Largely "prototypes, to urge imitation" (137), with negative examples (the sophists), as well as positive (150–53), re, e.g., *autarkeia* (cf. Phil 4:11); *paideia* imparts the teacher's *phronēsis* ("sensibleness") to pupils.

Though critical of Michaelis, Fiore likewise concentrates on 1 Cor, not chronological development of Paul's references (167). Paul calls for obedience that "will result in imitating . . . concern for the common goal ([1 Cor] 10:33)" (168). The gospel is "the matrix of generation" for doctrine and lifestyle (180 n 53, *not* Paul's own particular way of life "for imitation"). So even 1 Cor 11:1, "Be imitators of me," with its "rider," *kathōs kàgō Christou* (181–82); Paul exercises "a gospel ministry which declares verbally what Christ declared dramatically" in his death on behalf of the weaker brothers and sisters (8:11), specifically "preaching the cross" and "self-effacement for the common good" (182). On Phil 3:17, little is said about *symmimētai* and *typon*. The striving "toward the goal of perfection" in

---

[15] Included in *The Cynic Epistles*, by A. J. Malherbe (SBLSBS 12; Missoula, MT: Scholars Press, 1977).

3:4–6, Paul "goes on to relativize" (3:7–11) "in light of Christ" (185). "Perfection" is language used by "the enemies" (12 and 15), not by Paul of his days in Judaism. 3:4–6 are not "part of an example offered for imitation" (188).[16]

Feminists have raised questions about imitating Paul (and Christ). Does *mimētai mou ginesthe* bespeak "the same boasting and arrogance" for which Paul criticized the Corinthians (Adele Reinhartz)? Paul's "egocentric exhortation to imitate him" contradicts "his own command to self-humiliation" (Jo-ann A. Brant 285). In no Gk. descriptions does "the author or narrator declare himself a worthy model, as Paul does" (Reinhartz 395). A process is involved (396; Brant 295), after baptism (Brant 286, 289), involving authority (apostolic authority, Reinhartz 397, 399, 401, 403). "Once the imitator acknowledges Paul's authority, he or she shares in the power of that authority," "progressing from immaturity to maturity" (Brant 295); it is "teleological rather than ontological" (298). In Phil, the end is unity (Reinhartz 400, sharing in a common attitude; Brant 297, acting "with a common purpose").

Much more critical is Castelli ([13] Bibl.; the background is "imitation of the saints" in Catholic piety, set "in a hierarchical relationship of power" [13], and feminist, postcolonial concerns about power [133 and passim]): "mimesis functions in Paul's letters as a strategy of power" (15) that is often bad news for those subservient. The mimesis Paul inherited (59–87, 16, cf. 86) was (1) "always . . . a hierarchical relationship" (e.g., Plato *Tim.* 67–70); (2) it presupposed "valorization of sameness over against difference," "unity and harmony" over against diffusion and discord; (3) "the authority of the model plays a fundamental role in the mimetic relationship" (God, king, teacher, parent as model), to "shore up" power relations in a hierarchy that valued sameness and privileged position (116–17). In Phil 3:17, the *adelphoi* either join in imitating Paul or are enemies of the cross of Christ. People today value difference, not sameness; hierarchy and power are political issues; we need some other reading of imitation (cf. 134–35). *mimēsis Paulou* is not benign (cf. 18, 101, 103, 112–13). Castelli's attention to "textual effect rather than the textual meaning" is a corrective to Fiore's neglect of the power dynamic (B. Dodd 26–29).

We take Phil 3:17 in the context of his letters, chronologically (Hopper 184–87). 1 Thess suggests the terminology was Paul's own, not forced on him by opponents. He and his mission team (Silvanus and Timothy, 1:6) and the Christian

---

[16] The pseudepigraphical, fictional Socratic/Cynic letters fit the Pastorals but not Phil 3; they are not cited by Doughty 1995 (for whom Phil 3 is deutero-Pauline) or by those who regard the opponents as hypothetical or fictitious (Lyons 120–21; cf. Bloomquist 131). Other views: C. M. Proudfoot, "Imitation or Realistic Participation?" *Int* 17 (1963) 140–60, "suffering with Christ" (in Phil 3:10–11) is "*participatio Christi*" and not "*imitatio Christi*" only" (160). Everts treated Phil 3 in light of P. Ricoeur's idea of "testimony"; Phil 3 shows the superiority of the life in Christ. D. B. Capes, "*Imitatio Christi* and the Early Worship of Jesus" in C. C. Newman et al., eds. (Gen. Bibl.) 294–95, "aspects of Jesus' life which could not be imitated were 'liturgized,'" i.e., "they became hymns and practices . . . used to exalt God and Christ in worship" (297). Is Phil 2:6–11 then a hymn, not ethically imitatable? Grabner-Haider 20–21, an "Urbild-Abbild Schema": Paul is prototype for believers, who shall become duplicates or images of him in their life.

communities in Judea (2:14) were examples for Thessalonian Christians, in proclaiming the gospel and facing suffering (as in Philippi, 2:2). The Thessalonians
were in turn examples for Achaia and Macedonia (including Philippi) in receiving the word and letting it sound forth to others (1:7–8). The tiny house churches
needed examples. But "deliberate imitation" is not the point (Fiore 1968:184).[17]

Paul needed to urge the Corinthians to "be imitators of me" (1 Cor, not 2 Cor,
because of intensity of feelings between opponents and Paul). 1 Cor 4:16 means
to "embody the life of the cross" (S. E. Fowl, DPL 429; 1:18, 23; 2:2) in communal
life (B. Sanders; cf. Betz 1967:155–57; Fiore 1986:178–80). 1 Cor 11:1 repeats
mimētai mou ginesthe at the end of a section (10:23–11:1) on what is beneficial
and upbuilding in matters of meat and drink, internal "edification" of the body of
Christ, a theme since 8:1. Be like Paul in firmness and flexibility. Then 11:1b,
kathōs kàgō Christou, usually "Follow my example, as I follow Christ's" (NEB),
"as I copy Christ himself" (Phillips); Schulz 1962:285–86, 308–9; Stanley
1959:874 = 1967:385, in a hierarchical structure; Hopper 135–40; Michaelis:
obedience. Jesus while on earth? How much did Paul (or the Corinthians) knew
about that?[18] The simplest and boldest solution for 11:1b takes it not "as I also
[imitate] Christ"—there is no vb., 11:1a mimētai is a noun—or even "as I also
(am) (an imitator) of Christ," but "as I (am + gen. of possession, belong to) of
Christ" (B. Dodd 28–29, 187–88). In 1 Cor, Christou is often "an identifier of
one's Christian status"; cf. 1:1; 1:12 egō de Christou, "I belong to Christ" (NRSV);
3:23; 4:1; 7:22; 15:23 hoi tou Christou; cf. 2 Cor 10:7 (from opponents?); Gal 3:29;
and 5:24.

Phil 3:17, mimētai mou ginesthe, is in line with Paul's previous letters, in situations involving congregational upbuilding and opponents (cf. Merk 1968:190). It
adds the prefix syn, to get the hearers mindful of working together, along with
Paul. Commentators (cf. Fowl, DPL 430) warn against modern notions of trying
individually to be like "the original" in as many ways as possible—resulting in arrogance. Paul is more specific than simply "Live a Christ-cruciform life." In Phil

---

[17] 1:6 "imitators of us and of the Lord" (kai tou kyriou, kyrios, not "Jesus") may "concentrate attention
on the central features of the Christ event" (E. Best, HNTC Thess. 77–78) or refer to how we (Paul)
"received the word" (from the Lord, 1 Cor 11:23; Gal 1:1), as you did from us. Stanley 1959:866 =
1967:377 called it an "afterthought"; others, a corrective like 1 Cor 15:10 (not I, but the grace of God);
so Hopper 105. If "deliberate imitation," some claim the roots of Christian conduct lie in "the example
of the Lord himself" (De Boer 121). Better: the presently active Lord Jesus Christ, who "has chosen
you" (1:4; Betz 1967:144; Malherbe, AB 32B:114–15, 126–27, "a theological point," not "moral hortatory convention," not "conscious commitment to imitation"). See n 28 below. 1 Thess 2:14 parallels
conduct in the face of suffering by converts in Judea and in Thessalonica (Best, Thess. 109–23; Hopper
108–21; AB 32B:164–65, 172–79, an authentic part of Paul's letter).

[18] De Boer 158–69 is typical of this approach. For Fiore, see above. Betz 1967:161–62 takes 11:1b in
light of Rom 15:1–3, we, the strong, "ought to put up with the failings of the weak and not please ourselves," but ". . . please the neighbor for the good purpose of building up the neighbor," like Christ who
"did not please himself." The imitator of Paul and Christ "thinks in accord with Christ Jesus" (15:5,
phronein . . . kata . . .). Merk 1968:129–30, 11:1b is christological grounding for 11:1a and the oikodomē theme, as in 8:11. Cf. Probst ([1] Bibl.) 288–90.

3:17 *mou* picks up the 1st sg. language from 3:4 on. The *paradeigma* continues to be Paul; the "I" is paradigmatic.

4. Again, the Enemies. In vv 17–21 some phrases are attributable to the *enemies of the cross of Christ* (3:18, first described in 3:2–4a).[19] Fee sees Christians who "have taken Paul's view of 'justification by faith' to a libertine conclusion" (375).[20] With the polemical phrases in 3:19, a case for libertinism, "gnosticizing" or not, is difficult to exclude; a case for Jewish aspects exists, but not convincing in all details (so de Vos 271–73; Sandnes 2002, "belly-worshipers" is not Jewish). No theory listed in (11) A.2 has convinced a majority of commentators.[21]

3:2–21 hangs together versus the threat of one group of enemies, not two. Paul counters aspects of their teaching and style through his autobiography, Jewish heritage (with hazards for Christians like Law and circumcision) and his experience "in Christ" (where eschatological misinterpretation of what is to come can wrongly be taken as present possession).

A segment of the Philippian congregation may have moved on its own into emphasis on "perfection now," attaining the goal "above" in their church group "below" (3:12–18), its dynamic from Paul's gospel as they understood it (cf. 2:6–11). Paul deals gently with the (would-be) *teleioi* in vv 15b–16,[22] unlike those in 3:2–4a. He tolerates, rather than castigates. The *enemies* and the readers in Philippi must be distinguished (Alverez 325–26).

A more distinct threat involves outsiders, teaching what Paul has encountered in Galatia and/or Corinth. With blunt warnings, he contrasts them with the Pauline model for Christian existence, while addressing those in the Philippian congregation who might tend, or were already moving, in such directions.[23] Paul has spoken *often* to the Philippians about such people (v 18); thus habits long present in Philippi. C. S. de Vos 262–75 sets 3:2–21 within "conflict with the . . . civic

---

[19] Schenk 251 and passim lists *final goal* and *destruction* (3:19a); *god* and *belly* (19b); "*glory*" (19c, 21a), and thinking *earthly things*; "the *politeuma* that exists in the heavens" (20a; others like Gnilka 210 claim only *politeuma*; cf. Böttger 245, 247; Cotter 1993:101).

[20] Attempts to derive more of 3:20–21 from the enemies, like transformation of Christians now (Gnilka 210; Lincoln 102; cf. Spörlein 170), "runs into the fact that these slogans appear so late in the argument, without clear correctives, that any nuancing by Paul [i.e., by redaction like 2:8c] is scarcely apparent" (Reumann 1984:605; applauded by Fee 379 n 17). But Paul's correctives have appeared in 3:12–15, emphasizing *in the heavens* and the fut. tense, *will change.*

[21] That includes the trend toward a rhetorical composite (Lyons, Bloomquist, Witherington). An extreme example appears in S. W. Winter; cf. M. Hooker 2000:525, 529–30, 534–35 on Phil; NIB 11:525, 534–35. Winter sees in 3:18–19 a "highly polemical description of Judaism written for . . . the Philippian congregation" (181), Judaism becomes a "form of paganism" in this "rhetoric of reversal" (213). Cf. also D. K. Williams 2002:218–20, cf. 244–52.

[22] Hardly Epicureans (Bloomquist 132–33). Peterlin 81–82 n 14 sees a group with the "Good Life" syndrome.

[23] Compare and contrast Peterlin 78–81, who separates "the readers" from "the opponents," but finds a "tendency to perfectionism" in some of the Philippians (88) and ends up making Euodia and Syntyche the focus of disunity in Philippi (123–28). Jewett 1970b:382 cf. 377, the heretics in 3:18 carry "to logical conclusion some of the tendencies which were merely latent in the congregation as a whole." Duncan (*IDB* 3:789), "retrograde tendencies" in Philippi.

community,"[24] following the Christians' withdrawal from traditional and Imperial cult.[25] Paul wants them to change allegiance, as "citizens of a new empire," one "at war with the one in which they live" (283, 287); this is correct on civic aspects,[26] overstated on "war."

To sum up: Jewish-Christian missionaries, such as Paul dealt with in Gal, were criticized in 3:9–11 for their positions on Law, faith, and righteousness; in 3:12–19 for illusions of perfection through adherence to the Law, via circumcision (and food laws), in contrast to the Pauline paradigm. Libertinistic trends, whether from gnosticizing or indigenous influences, or even from the Pauline message itself, are directly criticized. If there were groups in the Philippian house churches moving on their own away from Paul's preferred model, they are indirectly called to account as the apostle speaks about *enemies* of the heart of his gospel. The converts in Philippi face dangers from opponents like those in Galatia, those in Corinth, and from themselves, as well as from governmental authorities.

B. MEANING AND INTERPRETATION

1. *Continue Imitating the Pauline Model, Together (3:17).* The impv., "Show yourselves to be *imitators together of me*," follows two exhortations in vv 15 and 16. After the 1st per. account of how Paul came to be "in Christ" and runs toward the goal in Christ Jesus, he urged Christians in Philippi, some of whom thought they were "perfected," *let us think in this way* (15a, the way outlined from his own example) and (v 16) *let us continue in the same course.* 3:17 shifts to 2nd pl., but again strikes the note of continuing on (pres. tense, repeated action). Persevere, amid challenges of the world. The command is softened by *brothers and sisters,* a term of affection, also at 3:13. Paul speaks to all the congregation (Merk 1968:190). Some see the "family of Christ" exchanging information (*DA* 169, as in "family letters," L. Alexander 1989). But more is involved: (four) commands 2nd pl. from the apostle-founder in 3:15–17, the first in Letter C since the triple *blepete* in v 2 (*DA* 411).

The initial and emphatic concept is *symmimētai mou,* be Paul's *imitators,* a notion not strange to Gk. ears, a Gk. theme with no significant OT counterpart (see NOTE and COMMENT A.3). Not derived from "following Jesus" (discipleship during his earthly ministry; the word families are different in Gk., as in Eng., though Ger. connects *Nachfolge* and *Nachahmung*). To imitate a model, in nature, art, teaching, rhetoric, was widespread in Gk. theory and practice. From the Hellenistic world the concept entered into Diaspora Judaism, as in Philo, and eventually rabbinic channels; to imitate Yahweh is not typical of the OT, it develops only

---

[24] de Vos, "idolatry [from OT/LXX use of "shame(ful thing)" for an idol, cf. 1 Cor 10:7], gluttony, and illicit sexual activity" in 3:18–21 are practices likely to occur in a *collegium* or *thiasos.*

[25] Bittasi 137–39, like Wick and others, relates 3:17–4:1 to 1:27–30.

[26] Voluntary associations (*thiasoi,* etc.) in the NT period and esp. in Philippi were stressed by Beare 9 (cf. now Pilhofer 1:102–3, 149–50; index: *thiasoi, collegium*); Cotter 1993:98–101, Paul often spoke against them, with their boisterous socializing (cf. Sandnes 2002) and emphasis on giving honors and prestige.

later in Judaism (Buber). Various types of Greco-Roman literature used personal examples (see NOTE, esp. Fiore 1986), though no exact parallel to "imitate me" appears in classical sources (or Jewish). There are dangers to imitating, esp. in our culture today (mass replication of an original); COMMENT A.3. The dangers make some wish for a different term in tr. (cf. I. H. Marshall 100–2). Imitation tends toward sameness, being like an authority figure in a hierarchy (Castelli [(13) Bibl.]). The model has the power, though it may be shared with those seeking to imitate the model (cf. 3:21, note "subjection *to himself*"). Handle *imitatio* with care. A "Christ figure" can be manipulated (Moiser 1977, Christ was male and celibate; clergy imitate him; Crouzel 24).

Yet for Paul (cf. NOTE) what alternative was there, to communicate with an audience hundreds of miles from where Jesus lived and Christianity began, in a world of few and scattered Christians and an ascended Lord—except to point to those who brought the message and lived by it? What option but to include themselves and other churches as examples and embodiments of the gospel?[27] How this dynamic operated in the Pauline mission before he came to Greece, we cannot tell. Possibly rabbi-teacher and pupils were a parallel. In 1 Thess, Paul refers to himself and colleagues as persons whom the Thessalonians were imitating in the way they received the word and exemplarily passed it on to others.[28] So also the assemblies in Judea; the Thessalonian house churches are compared with them (2:14) for imitation in persecution and suffering.

Phil 3:17a agrees in wording with two uses of *mimētai mou ginesthe* at 1 Cor, where Paul calls converts to his stance and orientation: 1 Cor 4:16, re the cross of Christ (as at Phil 3:18) and manner of life. At 11:1 (and Phil 3) how one lives when issues of conduct arise (perhaps involving food and food-laws). 11:1b, *kathōs kagō Christou*, not imitation by Paul (alone?) of Christ, but "as I belong to Christ," something true of all Corinthian Christians (7:22), not just one clique (1:12) (B. Dodd). One change at Phil 3:17a prefixes *syn* to *mimētai*, a new compound in Gk. This puts the term *together* over the Philippians' imitation of himself, all together in matters at hand.

Verse 17b, the last impv. in ch. 3, *take note of those who live in this way, as you have us as example*, continues such language with *typos* (see NOTE on *example* and COMMENT A.3). Less emphasized than *mimēsis* in later *imitatio* piety, it occurs with *mimētai* also at 1 Thess 1:6–7. Again a word of Gk. stamp, common in rhetoric and education. For Philippi, Alexander the Great might be an example

---

[27] Paul appeals elsewhere to revelation (of God in Christ), Scripture (LXX version of the Hebrew Law, prophets, and writings), Christian tradition and creed (oral teaching and confessions like "Jesus Christ is Lord"), experience, and "the resulting 'mind of Christ.'" Phil 3 refers to future revelation (v 15), but not Scripture (so Phil generally), credo, traditions, or Jesus' teachings. Or apostleship (not at issue) or "false apostles." The argument is couched in terms of Paul's experiences "before" (3:4b–6) and "after" Christ (3:7ff.), re righteousness/justification, faith, Law, and lifestyle till the final resurrection and "perfection" then. Paul is paradigm.

[28] 1:6, "imitators of us—*and of the Lord*," not the Lord (Jesus) receiving the word, but the One on whom the message centers, from whom messengers and the Thessalonians stem by divine election (1:4); see n 17 above.

(Bohm). Examples also appear Scripture: God acts faithfully in salvation history, even though the chosen people disobey (Neh 9, Acts 7; Sir 44 and Heb 11 enumerate those who kept faith). Jesus as example (John 13) is less common in the NT than supposed. Phil 2:6–11 does not use *typos*, or nearby vv *imitatio* terms. Some import "humility" into ch. 3 from 2:3, cf. 2:8, (O'B 447, who then must defend Paul against *not* expressing humility in placing himself on a pedestal); but *tapeino*-vocabulary does not occur in ch. 3 till v 21 and then in a different sense.

Who is *example* in 17b? *us* refers at least to Paul, in parallel with 17a (a literary pl.; Hawth. 160–61; see NOTE). A literal pl. makes Paul less egotistical (O'B 447); others see and do things Paul's way, examples when he is not present. Minimally Timothy. Perhaps Epaphroditus, though his image in Philippi was tarnished (cf. on 2:25–30); it may have been appropriate not to mention him. Some see Paul's "team of associates" (Lincoln 95; Fee 365 n 14); others, Philippian leaders (Bockmuhl 229) like the *episkopoi* and *diakonoi* of 1:1 (De Boer 181–82; Merk 1968:191; contrast Hainz 1972:220) or specifically Clement, Euodia and Syntyche (4:3). Paul could have in mind people and churches elsewhere, e.g., Thessalonica. Perhaps phraseology is intentionally open. When you grasp the pattern, fill in names of those who fit it.

Paul sets forth a method: *take note of*, observe carefully, even critically, people for reflection of Paul's gospel. They can be models only after inspection. This fits (Fee 366) for itinerants on the Via Egnatia claiming religious credentials that might impress house church members. The emphasis is on conduct, how they *live* or act, not "letters of recommendation" (2 Cor 3:1–3).

What criterion is indicated by *in this way*? In what follows, NEB/REB reverse cls. in 17b to get indic. and impv., "You have us for a model: imitate those whose way of life conforms to it." Lenski 866 brought out the corporate side *(syn-)*: "In Philippi many walked so as to serve as an example together with Paul. All these imitate each other and are to keep doing this . . . their very imitating is to be imitated." The Pauline example can be seen in others besides Paul.

For content and specifics, note what was said previously: "imitators together *of me*" (17a) implies all Paul said in vv 4ff. (Merk 1968:190–91, content from 3:8ff. and 12ff.). Paul "in Christ" contrasts with the best in Pharisaic Judaism on Law, righteousness, and object of faith (Christ, not Torah, vv 9–11). Contra opponents in Galatia, a contrast on justification (Reumann 1989b [(12) Bibl.], imitate Paul's "righteousness by faith"). Also on future-resurrection hope and likely sufferings now (vv 10–11)[29]; press on, no pretense of being "perfected" or at the goal (vv 12–14), think this way (15a *phronein*), hold a firm course (v 16; cf. 4:1). What opposes the Pauline model becomes clearer in vv 18–19.

2. In Contrast to the Enemies of the Cross of Christ (3:18–19).

A biting description and condemnation follow of unnamed persons who provide an antithesis to the Pauline model in 3:14–17. Some see mere rhetorical examples (Black

---

[29] Oakes 2001:103–28, Paul models "the right attitude to have under suffering," with "confidence in God's sovereignty" (2002:126).

1995; Fiore 1986:69, 72, 146–53, esp. 187–88; O'B 422). Fee 367 (over)states that "nothing . . . in the letter has quite prepared us for some of this."[30] Major debate rages over these *enemies of the cross*, their relation to 3:2–4a and Philippi.

For connects 3:17 and 18. Paul explains and gives a reason for his appeal to imitate the Pauline model (B. Weiss 281 n 1; Merk 1968:191–92; Fee 366–67). Some escalate *many* to mean "numerous" opponents (O'B 451), others "a countable number" (DA 314), in a church of perhaps only thirty members (de Vos 261). Are they outside Philippi (Fee 369) or in the city (O'B 452–53, "close enough . . . to present 'a tempting model for Christian existence,'" Jewett 1970b:376)? Gnilka 204, people in congregations founded by Paul in Greece and Asia Minor, but not an "anti-Pauline front." *many* may be rhetorical (Silva 212), but suggests the threat is serious. The *polloi* rival *those who live in* the *way* Paul has set forth in 17b (*peripatein* in each instance, "walk," act); contrast *(continue in) the (same) course* in v 16. How the *many live* (church fathers added, "badly, not rightly," B. Weiss 281 n 1) will be described in 3:19 *"the enemies of the cross of Christ"* (acc.) their *concern is earthly things* (nom.), abrupt, syntactically incorrect, anacoluthon (Koester 1961–62:325 n 2; Gnilka 204 n 104; Fee 368 n 26).

Paul has *often spoken* to the Philippians about these people (alliteration in Gk., "the *lot* of them, how they *live*, *lots* of times." Perhaps in his preaching in Philippi (Merk 1968:192) or in (lost) letters (Ewald-Wohl. 204 n 2) or both (O'B 451). H. C. G. Moule, "the mischief" was "in the air" at a "very early" time in Philippi (CGT *Phil.* 71). CEV suggests the warning about judgment and destruction was part of the initial missionary message (1 Thess 1:10, "the wrath to come"); Paul "often warned" about people "living as enemies of the cross of Christ"; now he adds the four further phrases in v 19, *with tears*, i.e., great emotion. Caird 149, "frustration, because . . . his teaching . . . has been distorted." Fee sensed "the language of parents to children" (369 n 27), "I often told you," appropriate in a figure of authority. "I *now speak*" *(legō)* reflects how the letter was to be read aloud in Philippi (DA 134, but cf. 136–37; Schenk 253, as at Gal 5:2, *ide* = NRSV "Listen!"), the apostle speaks authoritatively through letter and messenger.

enemies of the cross of Christ (18) overarches four characteristics (19) in a new sentence (so Fee 362, but numbering [1] to [5]). The sequence, *ad hoc* (?), is artful: the most devastating point *(destruction)* comes first (19a); 19d provides the full subject for 18–19. *enemies* means people hostile to Christ, personal enemies to Paul but on theological issues (see NOTE). Not "enemies of the lordship of an exalted Christ" but hostile to *the cross*, a concentrated way of saying Christ suffered and died for sins, past, present, and ours (1 Cor 1:23–2:2, 8; 2 Cor 5:14–15; Gal 6:12, 14; *TPTA* 208–23, 232–33; Weder 217–24),[31] antipathy to atonement. The Philippians' theology in 2:6–11 ignored the cross; they were vulnerable here. The

---

[30] Perhaps if one assumes a single letter, with glowing praise of the Philippian church in 1:3–11 (O'B 452); less so if a disunited church (Peterlin); not surprising if the vigorous body-opening in Letter C at 3:2–4a is recalled.

[31] Collange 137 sees in 3:18 intersection of the cross re Law (Gal), the cross and wisdom (1 Cor), and cross and reconciliation (Col-Eph). But Col and Eph are later or deutero-Pauline. Reconciliation and wisdom do not occur in Phil. Better: in Letter C, Paul expounds the "election theology" of 1 Thess

enemies fail to apply implications of the cross to practical behavior (Schmithals 1972:106; Silva 211, "Doctrinal Polemics"; *TDNT* 7:576, quoted in the NOTE). Thus GNB (italics added), "many whose *lives* make them enemies of Christ's death on the cross." For Paul, ethics roots in theology (Furnish 1968); *peripatein*, in *phronein* and life in Christ, faith, righteousness, and everything discussed in 3:4b–16. The cross grounds lifestyle for Paul and all Christians. A legalistic way of life (food laws, circumcision) perverts the cross of Jesus Christ (Gal, esp. 6:12–14), just as a libertinistic style or "overrealized" eschatology empties the cross of meaning (1 Cor). A self-understanding that affects all of life is at issue (Weder 222 n 382).

The four descriptive phrases in v 19, *Their final goal — is destruction;* b *their god, the belly,* c *and their "glory," in what is shameful;* d *those whose concern is earthly things,* have each many interpretations (see NOTES).[32] Possibilities were narrowed down in COMMENT A.4. The items can be read in a libertine or "Gnostic" manner, with links to 1 Cor and parts of 2 Cor (some make connections with 2 Cor 10–13, likely written after Phil C, see Chart 2, INTRO. VIII; Paul may have known earlier of this opposition taking shape in Corinth). Or in a Jewish-Christian or Jewish way, with links to Gal, esp. Phil 3:2–4a. Neither view, no one theory on opponents in Phil 3, dominates scholarship currently. One need not give up or settle for a fictional composite of imagined enemies. The threat is real to Paul; he writes a drastic warning.

The enemies in ch. 3 are (1) not the same as groups mentioned in 1:15–17 (rival preachers in Ephesus) or 1:28 (the authorities in Philippi), both in Letter B. (2) 3:2–21 is to be treated as a unity (so G. Barth 69, among others). (3) Some terms in v 19 likely come from these enemies or are colored by their use (see COMMENT A.4). (4) The enemies contrast with the Pauline example (3:4b–17) and with the Christian community now and to come (3:20–21). (5) *politeuma* (3:20a) casts a political tone over many interpretations (our Lord and Savior versus Rome's Caesar), but the NOTE suggests also a civic-social side, smaller councils in a *polis*, associations, *collegia, thiasoi.*[33] (6) Quite possibly, in Philippian house churches, some converts of Paul or subsequently of the Philippians, on their own or under outside influences, tended toward things the apostle warns about here. (7) The critique may aim at dangers Paul saw in the Philippians' encomium (2:6–11): exaltation, rather than cross or resurrection; for Christ, why not for us now too? Triumph, not suffering; the body already redeemed. "Life above" was an attractive goal. When they heard about circumcision and the Law (from Paul himself? from other types of Christians?), they saw this rite and what the Law says about food and

---

"more profoundly" through "reinterpretation in light of the theology of the cross" (J. Becker 1993 [(1) Bibl. **Paul**] 329).

[32] Sandnes 2002:145 sees the four phrases "closely related," but focus on "belly" overwhelms other items.

[33] Sandnes 2002:149–53 brings out the significance of (Epicurean) "belly-devotees" as "self-loving citizens" whose selfishness is "detrimental to good citizenship" (77). Conduct at symposia, including sexual license, is documented vividly (79–93); the body is important for "citizens of the heavenly *politeuma*" (160–62).

purity as the way to "transformed existence." (8) What the enemies were against, *the cross of Christ*, goes to the heart of Paul's gospel and the cruciform lifestyle the Pauline example embodies. The enemies reject how Jesus' "sacrifice of atonement by his blood" justifies (Rom 3:25), frees from Sin and Law, and brings peace, access to God, and hope of sharing God's glory in the future (Rom 5:1–2).

For the enemies (and possibly some Philippians), *their final goal (telos,* 19a) was the prize or promised destiny of which Paul spoke in 3:12b, 15. But they thought they had already arrived (like those in 1 Cor 4:8–13). Paul knew that he had *not* already *had success,* been *"perfected,"* or *taken hold successfully* of all the gospel ultimately will bring at the End. On these delusions, a single word— *destruction.* Punctuating with a dash reflects the terse original. "Destruction" or "annihilation" is the opposite of "salvation." Cf. *apōleia* at 1:28 (Letter B) for the fate of the adversaries there. Portrayal of the enemies thus leads off with the outcome. Their fate puts them in the same class as adversaries the Philippians already know, the city authorities. For as many as, among the house churches, think themselves *"perfected"* (15a), Paul suggests, "Think again." 19a is far more blunt than the initial impvs. in 15–16.

Why such a grim outcome for the *enemies?* 19bc provide the most specific descriptions of what is wrong: *their god, the belly, and their "glory," in what is shameful.* Bad "theo"-logy and doxology. A false object of worship goes with wrong notions of glory normally expected at the End (cf. 3:21; so, regularly in biblical thought, in contrast to earthly shame), but sometimes in Paul (2 Cor 4:6; 3:18) and more definitely for the enemies, expected now. *what is shameful (aischynē)* may be clearer than *belly.* Honor/shame contrasts were rife in the Greco-Roman world. In biblical eschatology, at final judgment glory will be changed to shame or vice versa; cf. 3:21; NOTE on *what is shameful* (3). To interpret as sexual immorality or circumcision identifies *what is shameful* with the genitals; circumcision, from context (*belly,* a dubious connection with "penis"; ultimately from 3:2–3). Then the opponents saw themselves possessing glory now, through circumcision. More likely is sexual immorality. "Idolatry" (cf. 19b "god") would scarcely be apparent to the Philippians from OT use of *aischynē* as a euphemism for idols (Hos 9:10 or Jer 3:24–25; contra de Vos 273 and Oakes 2001:147), but *aischynē* was "heavily loaded with sexual connotations" (de Vos 272; Cotter 1993:93; *TDNT* 1:189–90). *belly* is even more debated. As "stomach," it could allude to gluttony ("I can eat all I want") or ascetic food laws ("I will not partake of what is forbidden by Torah"). It could suggest sexual appetites; circumcision (a more doubtful connotation); or amount to saying the enemies deify "flesh" (cf. 3:3, 4a), the opposite of "God." See NOTE on *belly,* interpretations (1)–(4), the hardest of the terms in v 19 to pin down. Behavior is clearly involved; it may also involve a concept of God (and therefore "doctrine").

The most revealing phrase may be 19d, *those whose concern is earthly things,* the belated subject (expounding the *many* in v 18) and needed explanation about *the enemies of the cross of Christ. phronein* has run through the relationship and correspondence between Paul and the Philippians. He here employs the vb. for a second time in Letter C, in contrast to 3:15a (*let us think [phronōmen] in this way*), i.e., according to the Pauline model. *earthly things* means the sphere of flesh and sin, contrasted with what is *in the heavens* (3:20–21), a contrast between God ("above") and a sinning creation; cf. in the Fourth Gospel "above/below"; Jas 3:15–17; in Paul, Gal 4:25–26; De Young 118–34; Lincoln 95 and passim. The contrast is temporal, as well as locational. The awaited savior will come in the future; change in our body, of ourselves, is fut. tense. The enemies have taken a future expectation, perhaps wrongly conceptualized, and claim perfection has come about in their *politeuma* here and now. What erroneous eschatology produced in Corinth, or in Galatia an erroneous way of attaining the goal via Law and circumcision, Paul here confronts. The enemies' outlook, orientation, theology, and praxis are wrong. Their fate is clear. (For more on 3:18–19, the enemies, see COMMENT A.4, end). But what does Paul's model imply for Christians on earth?

3. Our Association in the Heavens and the Savior to Come: Christian Existence Now and Finally (3:20–21). 3:20–21 may be a hymnic frg. (reexamined in COMMENT A.3; criteria remain unresolved). Hymn features do not come through as strongly for 3:20–21 as for 2:6–11 (Reumann 1984). Seeing 2:6–11 as an encomium has diminished support for 3:20–21 as a hymn. Vocabulary links proposed between the passages (e.g., Hawth. 169; Lincoln 88) suggest Paul writes with the Philippians' encomium at 2:6–11 in mind (cf. Silva 214)—but not uncritically. "Sources" in v 21 may include liturgical, confessional material (Martin 149; Hawth. 173; Gnilka 209; Siber [Exc.A Bibl.] 122–26; Baumgarten 1975:76–77; Lincoln 89) and Paul's earlier interpretation of Ps 8:6 in 1 Cor 15:27 (below, n 45). He writes with *the enemies* in mind. This response to the *many* of 3:18 (Fee 376) provides a *conclusio*, a rousing climax, and expression of hope (Jung 309).

for suggests cause (why *those whose concern is earthly things* face *destruction* at the judgment) and contrast (with "us").[34] Antithetical, it motivates (Merk 1968:192). The opening word in Gk., *our* (cf. "we" later in the vb.) recalls 3:15a (*let us think in this way*, Paul and the Philippians, including those *"perfected"*) and 17b (*as you have us as an example*, Paul, Timothy, and all who provide "the Pauline example"). *our (politeuma)* applies to all (true, here Pauline) Christians. The NOTE on *governing civic association* treats *politeuma*. Much rests on assessing sources for a word found nowhere else in the Bible.[35] An explanation from Jewish political enclaves in Greco-Roman cities like Alexandria does not hold up. Nor do "homeland" ([N]JB), "citizenship" (NIV), or "colony of heaven" (Moffatt's genius phrase dies hard, as Fee 379 shows, "Paul's language will not quite allow the translation," but "the point of the imagery comes very close"). A political sense is attrac-

---

[34] Radl 1981:91–93 connects 3:20–21 with 3:15–17, as grounds for the impv. in v 17, thus minimizing contrast with 18–19; but admittedly vv 20–21 function within 3:15–21 somewhat the way 2:6–11 does within 2:1–12.

[35] Schwemer 2000, Phil 3:20 closely connects with Gal 4:26, "Jerusalem above"; behind both is Ps 87 (LXX 86) 4–7 LXX (Mother[-city] Zion, where the Most High registers the peoples, as dwelling [*katoikia*]). Paul, she claims, must have taught the Philippians about the heavenly city and citizenship (232), a "mother-city" and register of citizens (see Phil 4:3). But *politeuma* occurs only at 3:20. Against "citizenship" as the sense, Jung 312–13 n 214 remarks that in such interpretations "*savior* plays no role."

tive vis-à-vis the Roman state (Fee 379, 384), but must be qualified by actual use of *politeuma* (see esp. Lüderitz, earlier Sherwin-White 1963:184–85, in the NOTE). Alongside the political sense (as in *TDNT* 6:519–20), M. Müller puts a Hellenistic sense, as *terminus technicus*, for an association of people from a geographical region (E. Berneker, *KlPauly* 4 [1972] 979), cultic societies, or Gk. and Roman corporations organized away from home (Niebuhr 95; Philo, *Spec.* 1.51, proselytes join a new godly [*philotheō(i)*] *politeia*). If *the enemies* employed *politeuma* for their gathering of converts, it meant an association within the society of a Greco-Roman city, where their version of "heaven on earth" took form— governed by beliefs and praxis of the missionaries, probably not incorporated legally but a *politeuma* in parlance of the day.[36]

our governing civic association (awkward but explained at the end of the NOTE), emphasis on "our," *exists*, Paul says, *in the heavens*. There it "really exists," present in the realm where God dwells (pl. as in Heb. and Pauline use), the heavens whence Christ came (1 Cor 15:47) and will come (Phil 3:21b). Elsewhere he says our habitation (*oikētērion, oikodomē*, the *oikia* that supplements our earthly body) is "in the heavens" (2 Cor 5:1–5; cf. AB 32A: 291–99, with reference to Phil 3 on p. 295), so a *politeuma* in heaven is quite Pauline. This *politeuma* is norm for the lives of believers. 1:27 spoke of Christians exercising citizenship in Empire and *polis* (Fee 378–79, 3:20 = Paul's "second play on their Roman citizenship"). But 3:20 is not concerned with Rome; it speaks against *the enemies* and their *politeuma* concept. Features of these enemies in ch. 3 cannot fit Roman officials or the Emperor. Here Paul emphasizes the future and "the heavens," at 1:27–28 life here and now in the setting of Roman Philippi. 3:20–21 speaks against *enemies* who may turn up and influence Christians in Philippi. The *politeuma* in heaven speaks of what is already so for believers. What is "not now" appears in 20b–21 (with Fee 376–77), consonant with Paul's autobiographical picture in 3:12–14.

Christians *eagerly await* the parousia of *the Lord Jesus Christ*. The vb. reflects an eschatology of waiting (see NOTE); the word and the fut. tense in 21 (*will change*) combat a fully realized eschatology. Phil does not describe the heavenly *politeuma*, nor precisely how believers are to conduct themselves (*not like the enemies but like Paul*). He grounds this life in the Lord and his power, described in v 21 (M. Müller 202). *kai (indeed)* intensifies the emphasis on heaven.

savior, here only in Paul, is applied to Christ. *sōtēr* had a prominent background

---

[36] Re *politeuma* as a term from the enemies, unused by Paul elsewhere, one may ask what word(s) he might have used on his own. Perhaps "kingdom" (*basileia*) (*TDNT* 6:535; O'B 460, with D. M. Stanley 1961:106; Schenk 324). "Kingdom of the heavens/of God" suggests a realm in the heavens, but some in Corinth may have taken Jesus' beatitudes (in Q; 1 Cor 4:8, reflecting Matt 5:3 and 6 parr.; J. M. Robinson, *Int* 16 [1962], esp. 79–86) to imply it was already breaking in or was now here. If Paul's experience at Thessalonica provides any criterion (Acts 17:7), he could have written, "*Our basileia is in the heavens*" (*the enemies* talked of one on earth). *ekklēsia* seems unlikely here. The house churches are on earth, in Philippi and elsewhere (Phil 4:15); Paul does not speak of an *ekklēsia* in the heavens (contrast Col 1:18 and Eph 2:5–6 and Bockmuehl 234). "House(hold)" might have been used by Paul, certainly for house churches (*oikos* at Phlm 2; Rom 16:5); cf. *oiko-, oikia* words in 2 Cor 5:1–5 (see below) for the heavenly habitation and "tent" to be put on by Christians at death. Paul uses none of these terms but one strange to his own usage, likely influenced by opponents.

in the Greco-Roman world (Jung: a Hellenistic honorific, received into the NT), esp. in Hellenistic ruler cult and for Caesar.[37] Also for human benefactors and deliverers in the Hellenistic and Heb. worlds (OT "judges" in particular); see NOTE.[38] Perhaps from *the enemies*, though it could have been a common Christian title that Paul happens not to employ elsewhere (Bultmann 1951 [INTRO X Bibl] 79). This seems one place in 3:20–21 where there is an anti-Caesar overtone (Loh. 1919; O'B 462 n 120; esp. Fee 380 and Bormann 1995:218–19; more in NOTE; Jung is cautious, 312 n 213). Thus a term out of the Greco-Roman world of the day, here aimed at teachers who claim a savior with whom their converts are now united in their *politeuma. savior* relates to "salvation" (2:12); Christ is agent of salvation, who delivers and judges.[39] Judgment, missing in 2:6–11, is an area where Paul has concerns about Philippian theology in their encomium. Here, concern that some may take *salvation* to involve circumcision and ascetic rules and suppose salvation is fully present now, no parousia needed, no resurrection (3:10–11) or heaven to come. The future soteriological functions of Christ, "the shaping prototype" (J. Becker 1993 [(1) Bibl. **Paul**] 420) need to be clarified.

3:21a turns to a specific role of the savior at the Day of Jesus Christ (cf. 1:6, 10; 2:16; missing in 2:6–11), namely, he *will change the body of our humiliation to the sphere of the body of his glory.* Absolute christocentricity, something even clearer in 21b, where a function traditionally God's is attributed to Christ. This fits ch. 3, Christ prominent and dominant: he, not Torah (3:9); the object of knowledge (3:10); Christ's cross (3:18). Yet God hovers in the background, the One who calls ("in Jesus Christ," 3:14) and who will reveal (15a) what those "perfected" need to know. *metaschēmatisei* tells what Christ will effect at the parousia, he *will change* us (cf. 1 Cor 15:51). This tr. avoids analogies to "transfiguration"[40] or attempts to link this vb. with *schēma* at 2:7.[41] In the Philippians' encomium 2:9–11 is proba-

---

[37] Jung 9–20 objects to History-of-Religions approaches where NT *sōtēr* is a "counterterm," countering Caesar, esp. in cult (Bousset); or represents "rejection of the same title for Asklepios"; or stands against a Gnostic "Redeemer Myth" (Staerk). Jung does not sufficiently set *sōtēr* at 3:21 in the context of Philippi's *Romanitas* (309–16, esp. 311) and its Caesar cult. Oakes 2002:138–39, "Almost every element" in 3:20–21 "recalls Rome and the emperor"; 2001:138–47 finds comparison in 3:20–21 with the Emperor in (a) the political and ethical context; (b) *sōtēr* as a military leader who saves (29); and (c) connection with "power" in 3:21, transforming "his people into his likeness" (E. R. Goodenough, "The Political Philosophy of Hellenistic Kingship," *Yale Classical Studies* 1 [1928] 55–102, esp. 100 and 89).

[38] Jung 314 specifically compares Aratus of Sicyon (cited in NOTE) and Sulla (Plut. *Sulla* 34.1).

[39] Bultmann 1951 (INTRO X Bibl.) 78–79; 1 Thess 2:19 and 2 Cor 5:10, yet alongside God as judge, 1 Cor 4:5 and Rom 14:10). Jung 316 maintains that the savior in 3:20–21 neither destroys nor judges, but that overlooks the context in 3:19.

[40] As with Jesus, Mark 9:2 parr., *metemorphōthē*, a vb. Paul does use at 2 Cor 3:18 and which Rom 12:2 applies to a present transforming renewal in believers; see NOTE on 3:21a and AB 33:641, "a complete metamorphosis of thinking, willing, and conduct"; Doble, "will transform our body characterized by humility"; Engberg-Pedersen 2000:125, "transfigured self-abasement."

[41] Or *symmorphon* in 3:21 with *morphē* at 2:7, in what are often later ontological interests, signaled by the term "transform" (examples, e.g. in W. Pöhlmann, *EDNT* 3:288, in the NOTE on *to the sphere of . . .*), matters unsolvable on the basis of vocabulary.

bly on Paul's mind, about Christ's exaltation, a state where *the body of his glory* provides analogy for Christians' hopes about themselves.

The Gk. adj. often linked to 2:6 and 7 is *symmorphon*, rendered (in line with our treatment of *morphē* there) as *to the sphere of*. Textual additions since at least the 7th cent. A.D. (see NOTE) and trs. (e.g., NEB) expand this modifier that means "having a similar or same form" as "the body of Christ's glory." This "similarization," making us like Christ in body, will occur *(metaschēmatisei)* under the working power of Christ (21b), either "in the heavens" (20a) or in "mid-air" when Christ comes (cf. 1 Thess 4:17)—regardless of where one supposes the future, completed kingdom will be (1 Cor 15:24–28), "above" or a "renovated earth" or new Jerusalem (a question Paul does not answer, so pictures from the Book of Revelation or elsewhere have often been imported). Others interpret *symmorphon* with the help of Phil 3:10 *(symmorphizomenos, while being conformed to his death)* as a process now going on, re cross and sufferings, a process under the power of the crucified and risen Christ (A. F. Segal 412–13). All this background makes advisable a tr. that suggests *the sphere* where Christ rules and his power is at work as the locus of the change to come.

Contrasted antithetically (N. Schneider 118) are *the body of our humiliation* (which refers to Christians) and *the body of his glory* (referring to Christ). *humiliation* and *glory*, often taken as adjectival (RSV "lowly" and "glorious"), show the sphere or realm to which each body belongs. *tapeinōseōs*—not "humble," "lowly," or "vile," but, as in 2:3 and 8, "humiliation"—means here our human state in contrast to promised future glory. *glory* refers to Christ's risen, radiant state, characteristic of the kingdom of God (1 Thess 2:12; 2 Cor 4:6); it has a bite, against the "glory" the enemies find in earthly, shameful things (3:19c). *our* and *his* go with these two nouns, not with "body." We live in *tapeinōsis* now, Christ in glory. *body* refers to Christ as an individual and to each individual believer, *sōma* (sg. but corporate) for those in Christ as a collectivity, Christ and the redeemed as a body. "Christ possesses transfigured corporeality . . . into which Christians are changed" (J. Becker 1993 [(1) Bibl. **Paul**] 384); destinies "are linked by the word 'like' (vs. 10, 21)" (330). While lacking apocalyptic detail found in 1 Thess 4:13–18, 3:20– 21 is broadly apocalyptic (Siber [Exc. A Bibl.] 122–34; Baumgarten 1975:76–82). No specifics about a "spiritual body" (1 Cor 15:44) or the imagery of 2 Cor 5:1–5, 8.[42] Nor does Paul take up here "present transformation" (2 Cor 3:18; morally, Rom 12:2). The aim is different: future change, over against completed present transformation (Back 179–84). He provides a glimpse, akin to Rom 8:29 and 1 Cor 15:49, of parousia and future life. Change will apply to all the faithful raised from the dead (cf. 3:10–11) and those alive at the Day when Christ comes (J. Becker 1993 [(1) Bibl. **Paul**] 423).[43]

---

[42] J. N. Sevenster 1961 ([4] Bibl. **suicide**) 68–75 contrasts notions of the body as a burden, as in Seneca's attempt to console Marcia *(de Consolatione)*, "a shell, a prison" (24.5; 25.1; not cited by Holloway 2001a).

[43] In composite treatments 3:21 may not always receive its due. Cf. *DPL* 808–10 ("the resurrection body of the believing community"); *TPTA* 294–315, 468, 487–93; M. J. Harris, *Raised Immortal: The*

On what *action* or "working" *(energeia)* does the coming change depend? It will happen *in accord with*, because of, the effective operation for us of Christ's being able *also to put all things into subjection to himself.* On Christ's ability to act as cosmocrator or ruler of all rests the hope of Christians for changed bodies, in the sphere of his glory (Baumgarten 1975:81).[44] Christ's *energeia* effects change in resurrection bodies and far more in the universe. At 2:13, God was *the One at work (energōn) in and among you* (13a). At 3:21b the doing is entirely Christ's. He is to *put all things into subjection to himself.* Appeal to this greater *energeia* assures hearers Christ can do a lesser thing with (and for) them.

In the final five Gk. words of 21b, Paul quotes from both Ps 8:6 and himself at 1 Cor 15:27, in a treatment about the End.[45] Two words are brought over from 15:27 into 3:21 (*put into subjection* and *all things*, art. added), but with a significant change. In 1 Cor 15:23–28 God subjects "the powers" and Death ("all things") to Christ; in 3:21b Christ subjects the universe to himself.[46] Phil 3:21b is Christocentric, while 1 Cor 15:27, in using Ps 8:7, remained with the OT sense of God subjecting all things; in the Psalm under the feet of humans, in 15:27 to the Son.[47] The neut. pl. *ta panta* is universally inclusive, so Fee suggests "subjection" in 3:21b could mean *destruction* for "enemies of the cross of Christ" (3:19a; cf. 1:28). This contrasts with 2:10–11 where all in the cosmos end up acknowledging, in homage, Christ as Lord. 3:21 preserves the universal outlook of 2:9–11, but with future eschatology, at the Day of the Lord; it speaks of "subjection" as the encomium did not (again, an indirect critique of it). *ta panta* could include the Emperor and the opponents of 1:28. 3:21ab represents a positive answer to any uncertainties after Paul's phraseology in 3:11 on attaining to the resurrection of the dead. In this way, Letter C ends on a positive note, for all the grim warnings with which 3:2 began. Overall, the passage is shaped versus opponents. It has to do with the eschatological existence of Christians now as well as at the Day of Christ (Froitzheim 158–69), corresponding theologically to gracious justification out of faith (*iustificatio impiorum* or justification of the impious is inauguration of the *resurrectio mortuorum*, resurrection of the dead, 234). Treatments of Pauline eschatology sometimes put 3:21b in an overall picture as "the last act in the drama

---

Relation Between Resurrection and Immortality in New Testament Teaching (Grand Rapids: Eerdmans, 1974) 108–14 (summary in O'B 465 n 137). See also n 48 below.

[44] See NOTE. Many trs. read in "power" from Col and Eph, from *tou dynasthai*, or from 3:10, the power of Christ's resurrection, shown in righteousness/justification (Reumann 1989b:138–39). But the word *dynamis* is not there, so the TRANSLATION avoids "power."

[45] The psalm celebrates God's glory (8:2, "above the heavens") and how God crowned human beings with glory (8:5). 1 Cor 15:24–48 (Ps 8:7 LXX + 110:1) tells how at the final resurrection Christ reigns, enemies under his feet, God subjecting them (as in Ps 8:6). Then the Son will also be "subjected to the One who put all things into subjection to him, so that God may be all in all" (15:28; v 24, "he hands over the kingdom to God the Father"). Cf. Fee NICNT *1 Cor.* 752–59.

[46] 3:21 differs with 2:9–11, where God is the subject. The phrase "under the feet" is omitted at 3:21, but the *autou* from it ("*his* feet") could have led to the difficult *autō[i]*, "to Christ."

[47] It is probably too subtle to think Paul's use of *ta panta* in 3:21 was influenced by "all his enemies" in 1 Cor 15:25 and that this suggests *the enemies of the cross of Christ* in 3:18. Ps 110:1 (= 15:25) is not quoted in Phil 3.

of cosmic redemption" (Caird 149).[48] Paul finalizes in Jesus current notions of *politeuma* and *sōtēr*, so that savior and salvation become one (Jung 348–49); the emphasis is on "a completely new form" of Christ and Christians "with one another" (314). N. T. Wright 2003:229–36: transformation at the parousia; continuity and discontinuity anthropologically with the body; and, he adds, political confrontation with Caesar.[49]

4. *Phil 3:17–21 in the Redacted Letter:* Imitatio, Enemies, and Final Glory.

Once these vv were read within Phil 1:1–4:23, effects appeared in several areas, though much of the meaning sketched above for Letter C continues.

a. A greater tendency to associate 3:20–21 with 2:6–11, if not as a "third stanza" to "the hymn," at least as linked by vocabulary and ideas. 2:6–11 was thus enhanced as "the center" for the entire letter (Wick and many others). Usually 3:20–21 is seen as a development of ideas there, not a supplement or critique, so that the unity of the four chs. was considered enhanced too. O'B 444: "striking parallels with 2:6–11" with "particular attention to the second half of the humiliation-exaltation theme." Garland 1985:159, "the distinctive vocabulary of 2:5–11 pervades *all* of chap. 3." We argued that 3:20–21 is little akin to 2:6–11; the ideas of 3:20–21 contrast (parousia, future change, not just present acclamation of Christ; a different stance toward powers and forces in the universe with reference to Christ, namely subjugation, perhaps destruction of them). It thus supplements or corrects deficiencies in 2:6–11.

b. 3:17, *imitators . . . of me* and *us as example,* led to extension of the *imitatio* theme to 2:6–11 ("imitation *of Christ*"), though *mimēsis*-vocabulary and *typos* do not occur in or around 2:6–11 and imitation of Christ had to be read in from 1 Cor 11:1. This led to Christ in 2:6–11 being viewed as example to be imitated, and then, because of 3:17b *(us as examples),* to Timothy (2:19–24) and Epaphroditus (2:25–30) as models.[50] Usually *ethical* exemplars. The moral side comes to the fore also in seeing "bad models" in 3:19, *enemies of the cross of Christ.* Esp. in Anglo-Saxon treatments; contrast Gnilka; Mengel; G. Barth; U. B. Müller 113 is nuanced on the hymn, cf. 173–74. *imitatio* of Paul and "the Pauline example" should be recognized where the concepts occur, but not expanded throughout the letter as a whole.

c. Placing *enemies of the cross of Christ* (3:18) in a four-ch. letter led to efforts to combine them with 1:28 ("the opponents" also doomed to *destruction*) and/or

---

[48] Cf., e.g., Siber (Exc. A Bibl.) 122–34; Gnilka 78–79; G. Vos 1961; L. Kreitzer, *DPL* 256–65, esp. 264; *TPTA* 294–315; J. Plevnik, *Paul and the Parousia. An Exegetical and Theological Investigation* (Peabody, MA: Hendrickson, 1997) 170–93; Witherington 1994:186–204; and n 43 above.

[49] Wright speaks of living in the colonia, not yearning to go back to Rome, *and* of the emperor coming from Rome to deliver from local difficulties (230–32; cf. "the imperial rescue from the Thracians" (Collart [Intro. I] 249–51), living "in the present as members of the world that is yet to be," sitting "loose to the privileges of empire" (235).

[50] So Hawth., Caird, Egger, Swift, D. F. Watson 1988b:69–70, Fee, Witherington, Bockmuehl 148, I. H. Marshall, Fowl 1990:92–95, 101; O'B, Timothy and Epaphroditus as "two Christ-like examples," as well as Christ himself; Garland 1985:163; Black 1995:38–39; Thielman 129, 151, among others. Contrast Martin 1976:91–93 on 2:6–11; Collange 94, and many who, while treating Christ as model, recognize 2:19–30 as mission or travel reports.

1:15–18 ("the rival preachers"). Cf. Gunther 1973; (12) COMMENT A.2.d and (14) A.4. Such blending has scarcely helped pin down the meaning of terms in 3:19, except *destruction* (3:19a, 1:28, a sense regular for *apōleia* in Paul). There is little reason, even on a single-letter hypothesis, to think 3:2–21 bursts out as it does about a group Paul has spoken of in a relatively positive way at 1:16 and 18 or the group mentioned negatively in 1:28. The apostle predicted at 1:28 *destruction* for those currently intimidating Philippian Christians; in 3:2–19 he refers to a future menace that rates *destruction* (3:19a) on totally different grounds (Law, circumcision, etc.). Opposition groups should not be homogenized into one set of enemies of the cross.

d. Fusion of 3:2–21 with 4:1ff. encouraged regarding 4:1 as the conclusion of 3:17–21 (K. Barth 117; Hooker NIB 11; Thurston 135)—our *politeuma* exists in the heavens, therefore, *stand steadfast in the Lord* (possible also on partition theories, Gnilka, Collange, Walter). A four-ch. epistle makes the move more likely; see NRSV paragraphing. 3:17–21 (+ 4:1) may be called the "second peak" in the letter, along with 2:6–11 (+ 2:12) (M. Müller 202–4).

e. The fullest ecclesiology in Phil comes in an *inclusio* of church images in 3:3 "We are the Circumcision" and 3:20 "Our *politeuma* is in the heavens" (structurally analagous, W. Kraus 1996:343). On 3:3, *peritomē*-ecclesiology, see (11) COMMENT B.1, from Israel and the prophets ("true circumcision") for Gentile Christians. 3:20 balances this with an analogy to political, civic associations of the day.[51] By itself the first image runs the danger of arrogance and anti-Judaism. The second makes the Christian *politeuma* future and otherworldly. Together, they remind the house churches of Philippi of an "Israel" heritage and that they do not yet possess *politeuma* or *savior*, the way "the enemies" claimed "perfection" via circumcision for their local associations. Ecclesiology makes claims but needs reservations at points until the Lord comes.

3:17–21 was used in traditional lectionaries (Book of Common Prayer, Lutheran) for Trinity 23 (Pentecost 24), when the Epiphany season was short, often read with Matt 22:15–22 ("Render unto Caesar"); cf. Fendt 1931 207–9. In the *Ordo*, 3:17–4:1 (or just 3:20–4:1) is read on 2 Lent C, with Luke 9:28b–36 (the Transfiguration).

The most significant theme in 3:17–21 for later theology, ethics, and piety, is *imitatio* and *example* (3:17); see COMMENT A.3. The second most important may be ecclesial images in 3:20 and 3:3; see COMMENT A.2 and B.3, B.4.e. The "profiling" for opponents in 3:18 was one of the earliest warnings about deviations, if not heresies, in Christianity (COMMENT A.4).

SELECT BIBLIOGRAPHY (see also General Bibliography and Commentaries)

Back, F. 2003. *Verwandlung durch Offenbarung bei Paulus*, WUNT 2/153 (Tübingen: Mohr Siebeck) 179–84.

Becker, J. 1971. "Erwägerungen zu Phil 3,20–21," TZ 27:16–29.

Böttger, P. C. 1969. "Die eschatologische Existenz der Christen. Erwägungen zu Philipper 3:20," ZNW 60:244–63.

---

[51] Minear 1960 ([11] Bibl.) 60–61, 3:20 is a "minor image" of the church; W. Kraus 1996:341–46.

Bringmann, K. 1993. "The King as Benefactor. Some Remarks on Ideal Kingship in the Age of Hellenism," in *Images and Ideologies. Self-definition in the Hellenistic World*, ed. A. Bulloch et al. (Berkeley: Univ. of California Press) 7–24.

Cotter, W. 1993. "Our *Politeuma* Is in Heaven: The Meaning of Philippians 3:17–21," in FS Hurd (Gen. Bibl., under Krentz, E. M., 1993) 92–104.

De Young, J. C. 1960. *Jerusalem in the New Testament: The Significance of the City in the History of Redemption and in Eschatology* (Kampen: Kok) 125–28.

Díaz y Díaz, J. 1965. "Die Wortgruppe *sōzein, sōtēria, sōtēr* in den neutestamentlichen Briefen, diss. Heidelberg.

Doble, P. 2002. "'Vile Bodies' or Transformed Persons? Philippians 3:21 in Context," *JSNT* 86:3–27.

Jung, F. 2002. *SŌTĒR. Studien zur Rezeption eines hellenistischen Ehrentitels im Neuen Testament.* NTAbh N.F. 39. Münster: Aschendorff.

Karrer, M. 2002. "Jesus, der Retter *(Sōtēr).* Zur Aufnahme eines hellenistischen Prädikats im Neuen Testament," *ZNW* 93:153–76.

Kotsidu, H. 2000. *TIMĒ KAI DOXA. Ehrungen für hellenistische Herrscher im griechischen Mutterland und in Kleinasien unter besonderer Berücksichtigung der archäologischen Denkmäler.* Berlin: Akademie Verlag.

Lambrecht, J. 1985. "Our Commonwealth Is in Heaven," *LS* 10:199–205.

Lüderitz, G. 1994. "What Is the Politeuma?" in *Studies in Early Jewish Epigraphy*, ed. J. W. van Henten/P. W. van der Horst (Leiden: Brill) 183–225.

Moiser, J. 1997. "The Meaning of *koilia* in Philippians 3:19," *ExpTim* 108:365–66.

Müller, U. B. 1975. "Prophetische Gerichtspredigt bei Paulus," *Prophetie und Predigt* (Gen. Bibl.) 175–214.

Nock, A. D. 1951. "*Soter* and *Euergetes*," in *The Joy of Study*, FS F. C. Grant, ed.S. E. Johnson (New York: Macmillan) 127–48, repr. in Nock's *Essays on Religion and the Ancient World I/II*, ed. Z. Stewart (Cambridge: Harvard Univ. Press, 1972) 720–35.

Reumann, J. 1984. "Philippians 3.20–21—a Hymnic Fragment?" *NTS* 30: 593–609.

Ruppel, W. 1927. "*Politeuma*. Bedeutungsgeschichte eines staats-rechtlichen Terminus," *Philologus* 82:268–312, 433–52.

Sandnes, K. O. 2002. *Belly and Body in the Pauline Epistles.* SNTSMS 120. New York: Cambridge Univ. Press.

Schofield, M. 1999. *Saving the City. Philosopher-Kings and Other Classical Paradigms.* London/New York: Routledge.

Schwemer, A. M. 2000. "Himmlische Stadt und himmlisches Bürgerrecht bei Paulus (Gal 4,26 und Phil 3,20)," in *La Cité de Dieu/Die Stadt Gottes: 3. Symposium Strasbourg, Tübingen, Uppsala 19–23 September 1998 in Tübingen*, ed. M. Hengel et al., WUNT 129 (Tübingen: Mohr Siebeck) 195–243.

Spörlein, B. 1971. *Die Leugnung der Auferstehung: eine historisch-kritische Untersuchung zu 1 Kor 15.* BU 7. Regensburg: Pustet. Pp. 165–70.

Staerk, W. 1933. *Soter I. Die biblische Erlösererwartung als religionsgeschichtliches Problem.* BFCT 2/31. Gütersloh: C. Bertelsmann. *Soter II. Die Erlösererwartung in den osterlichen Religionen. Untersuchungen zu den Ausdrucksformen der biblischen Christologie.* Stuttgart/Berlin: Kohlhammer, 1938.

imitation (*symmimētai*, 3:17): S. Siegel, *EncJud* 8:1292–93; S. E. Fowl, *DPL* 428–31; U. Luz, "Nachfolge Jesu I.5," *TRE* 23 (1994):685; G. Strecker, *EC* 1 (1999) 851; D. Sim, *RGG*[4] 6 (2003) 4–6. Cf. Note on *imitators* and Comment A.3.

Betz, H. D. 1967. *Nachfolge und Nachahmung Jesu Christi im Neuen Testament*, BHT 37 (Tübingen: Mohr Siebeck) 145–53.

Bohm, C. 1989. Imitatio Alexandri *im Hellenismus. Untersuchungen zum politischen Nachwirken Alexanders des Großen in hoch- und späthellenistischen Monarchien.* Quellen und Forschungen zur Antiken Welt, 3. Munich: Tuduv.

Brant, Jo-Ann A. 1993. "The Place of *mimesis* in Paul's Thought," *SR* 22:285–301.

Buber, M. 1946. "Imitatio Dei," *Mamre: Essays in Religion,* tr. G. Hort (Melbourne: Melbourne Univ./London: Oxford Univ. Press) 32–46. Originally in "Kampf um Israel" (Berlin 1933).

Crouzel, H. 1978. "L'Imitation et la 'Suite' de Dieu et du Christ dans les premiers Siècles chrétiens ainsi que leurs sources gréco-romains et hébraïques," *JAC* 21:7–41.

De Boer, W, P. 1962. *The Imitation of Paul: An Exegetical Study.* Kampen: Kok/Grand Rapids: Eerdmans.

Fiore, B. 1986. *The Function of Personal Example in the Socratic and Pastoral Epistles.* AnBib 105. Rome: PBI.

Gulin, E. G. 1925. "Die Nachfolge Gottes: Versuch einer religionsgeschichtlichen Skizze," *Studia Orientalia* I (Helsingfors) 35–50.

Hopper, M. E. 1988. "The Pauline Concept of Imitation." Diss. Southern Baptist Theological Seminary, Louisville.

Kosmala, H. 1963–64. "Nachfolge und Nachahmung Gottes. Teil I: Im griechischen Denken," *ASTI* 2:38–85. "II. Im jüdischen Denken," *ASTI* 3:65–110, repr. in his *Studies, Essays and Reviews* (Leiden: Brill, 1978).

Kurz, W. S. 1985. "Kenotic Imitation of Paul and of Christ in Philippians 2 and 3," in *Discipleship in the New Testament,* ed. F. F. Segovia (Philadelphia: Fortress) 103–26.

Lindars, B. 1973. "Imitation of God and Imitation of Christ," *Theology* 76:304–402.

Longenecker, R. N., ed. 1996. *Patterns of Discipleship in the New Testament.* McMaster NT Series. Grand Rapids: Eerdmans. Esp. G. F. Hawthorne on Phil.

McMichael, W. F. 1893–94. "Be Ye Followers Together of Me: *Symmimetai mou ginesthe*—Phil. III.17," *ExpTim* 5:287.

Merk, O. 1989. "Nachahmung Christi: zu ethischen Perspektiven in der paulinischen Theologie," in *Neues Testament und Ethik,* FS Schnackenburg, ed. H. Merklein (Freiburg/Basel/Wien: Herder) 172–206.

Moiser, J. 1977. "Dogmatic Thoughts on Imitation of Christ," *SJT* 30:201–13.

Reinhartz, A. 1987. "On the Meaning of the Pauline exhortation: '*mimētai mou ginesthe*—become imitators of me,' " *SR* 16:393–403.

Sanders, B. 1981. "Imitating Paul: 1 Cor. 4:16," *HTR* 74:353–63.

Schoeps, H. J. 1950. "Von der imitatio dei zur Nachfolge Christi," *Aus frühchristlicher Zeit. Religionsgeschichtliche Untersuchungen* (Tübingen: Mohr Siebeck) 286–301.

Schulz, A. 1962. *Nachfolgen und Nachahmen. Studien über das Verhältnis der neutestamentlichen Jüngerschaft zur urchristlichen Vorbildethik,* SANT 6 (Munich: Kösel) 308–14. Cf. 1967, *Unter dem Anspruch Gottes. Das neutestamentliche Zeugnis von der Nachahmung.* Munich: Kösel.

Stanley, D. M. 1959. " 'Become Imitators of Me': Apostolic Tradition in Paul," *Bib* 40:857–77, repr. with editorial changes in Stanley's *The Apostolic Church in the New Testament* (Westminster, MD: Newman, 1967) 371–89.

———. 1984. "Imitation in Paul's Letters: Its Significance for His Relationship to Jesus and to His Own Christian Foundations," in *From Jesus to Paul,* FS Beare, ed. P. Richardson/J. Hurd (Waterloo, Ont.: Wilfrid Laurier Press) 127–42.

Tinsley, E. J. 1960. *The Imitation of God in Christ: An Essay on the Biblical Basis of Christian Spirituality.* Library of History and Doctrine. London: SCM/Philadelphia: Westminster.

————. 1972. "Some Principles for Reconstructing a Doctrine of the Imitation of Christ," *SJT* 25:45–57.

Waetjen, H. C. 1963. "Is the 'Imitation of Christ' Biblical?" *Dialog* 2:118–25.

Wild, R. A. 1985. "'Be Imitators of God': Discipleship in the Letter to the Ephesians," in *Discipleship* (cited above under "Kurz") 127–43.

Williams, D. M. 1967. "The Imitation of Christ in Paul with Special Reference to Paul as Teacher." Diss., Columbia Univ.

Wolbert, W. 1981. "Vorbild und paränetische Authorität. Zum Problem der 'Nachahmung' des Paulus," *MTZ* 32:249–70.

15. *Concluding Paraenesis (with Letter Closing), 4:1–9*

TRANSLATION

4:1 And so, my brothers and sisters, beloved and longed for, my joy and crowning wreath, in this way stand steadfast in the Lord, O beloved. 2 Euodia I exhort and Syntyche I exhort to think the same thing in the Lord. 3a Indeed, I am asking you also, my faithful partner, assist them; b for these women, in the gospel cause, engaged in a struggle, together with me, along also with Clement and my other co-workers. c Their names are written in the book of life.

4 Rejoice in the Lord always. I shall say it again, rejoice. 5a Let your patient steadfastness be known to all sorts of people. b The Lord is near. 6a Do not continue to be anxious about anything; b instead, in each instance, let your requests be constantly made known toward God by prayer and entreaty, with thanksgiving. 7 And the peace of God that exceeds all understanding will keep guard over your hearts and minds in Christ Jesus.

8 Finally, brothers and sisters, whatever things are true, whatever honorable, whatever just, whatever pure, whatever lovely, whatever appealing, if there is any excellence, and if anything worthy of praise—these things ponder. 9a What things you indeed learned and received and heard and saw in my life, these things continue to do, b and the God of peace will be with you.

NOTES

4:1. *And so. hōste*, + *adelphoi mou agapētoi mou* + impv. (*stēkete*). See NOTE on 2:12a *So then, my beloved. hōste* draws consequences from what precedes, 3:17–21 (EGT, Rienecker), 3:1–21 (Holmstrand), or 1:27–2:30; see COMMENT B.1 and 5. The six terms of address and shift to the impv. suggest "a fairly clear new start" (Holmstrand 122; DA 266; Loh. 163). *brothers and sisters.* See NOTE on 1:12 (here

+ *mou* as at 2:12), transitional, as often (*DA* 262 n 397; 378). Paul can use sibling terms "to apply pressure"; cf. Phlm 7, 20 (Aasgaard 517).

beloved. 2x in 4:1; cf. 2:12. *agapētos,* "beloved," is in Wischmeyer's tradition-history ([2] Bibl. love 1983, 1986) interchangeable with *adelphos;* esp. at the start of a passage (2:12; 4:1); without actual kinship ties (as at Phlm 1), it seems not to occur prior to Paul (BDAG *agapētos* 2 cites POxy 2.235.2, letters uncertain). Hence (Wischmeyer) a dual heritage: (1) sporadic OT and (Hellenistic-)Jewish references to those loved and chosen by God (Isa 41:8; Dan 3:35 LXX, etc.; *TDNT* 4:42–43; Rom 11:28; 1:7; 1 Thess 1:4), a community of elect and beloved brothers and sisters "in the Lord." Not just "affection," the apostle can admonish his "beloved children" (1 Cor 4:14, etc.). (2) Non-Jewish influences: (a) as address from Ptolemaic times, in private letters (Koskenniemi 105); (b) Greco-Roman concepts of "friendship" (*JAC* 7 [1964] 169, 174; also the Pharisees, Jos. *JW* 2.166 = 2.8.14, "affectionate to one another [*philallēloi*]"; Qumran). Thus a community of brotherly-sisterly friendship-love.

longed for. epipothētos, from vb. at 1:8 *I long for* and 2:26 *longing for you all. TLNT* 2:58–60, "ardent desire" in most NT passages (Phil 2:26), but "tender affection" 2 Cor 9:14; Phil 1:8 ("I cherish you") and 4:1. Friends yearn to be with friends and rejoice together; a term of endearment in letters (Stowers 1986:61, 65, 83, 99; 1991:109; Fitzgerald 1996:148–49, 154–55; *DA* 171).

my joy and crowning wreath. chara (see NOTE on 1:4 *with joy;* 1:25; 2:2, 29). *stephanos,* in Phil, only here. Eschatological tone (1 Thess 2:19–20, Phil 1:26, 2:16; Radl 1981:80–81). *mou* could be objective, "a crown of joy for me" (GNB "How happy you make me . . ."). BDAG *stephanos* 1 **wreath, crown;** fig. 2, "as **adornment or source of pride**"; hence GNB "how proud I am of you!" Christianity criticized Hellenistic crowns given on various occasions (Tert., *De corona* [CSEL 70]; W. Grundmann, *TDNT* 7:615–36, esp. 624, 635; C. J. Hemer, *NIDNTT* 1:405–6; H. Kraft, *EDNT* 3:273–74). OT use was "slight in comparison": Isa 28:5; wisdom literature (Prov 12:4; 17:6); apocalyptic materials; Gk. use infiltrated Judaism Exact background is unclear here. Gks. had crowns of laurel, olive, ivy, or oak (*TDNT* 7:616–17), used (Krentz 2003:362) in cult for priests, altars, and even sacrifices (cf. Acts 14:13 "garlands"), at oracles, processions, and feasts. As a sign of salvation and protection (Tiberius, laurel crown as defense against lightning, Pliny *NH* 15.134–35; mystery cults, "Mithras is my crown"). Prominent in athletic games, the army, civic-political and private life (for joy, at weddings, symposia; sorrow, on the dead or gravestones); see *TDNT* 7:617–24. Athletes ran "to receive a perishable wreath" (1 Cor 9:24–27); Paul and the Philippians engage in an *agōn,* he is a "runner for the gospel"; see NOTES on 1:30 *the same gospel* and 2:16 *I did not run* and *struggle.* Not *diadēma* (for royalty). Pfitzner 104–7, 153–54 rejects Deissmann's proposal for 4:1 (*LAE* 373), a golden crown presented to a sovereign at his parousia in some eastern city; "Paul claims the faithful as his own crown on the day of the Lord." Loh.'s martyr crown (164–65) is read in from Rev 2:10, 3:11, cf. 4:4; Paul's *stephanos* is for "apostolic work." Dubious is "the crown of the Mysteries" (105; cf. H. Kraft, *EDNT* 3:274). 4:1, "a symbol of joy and honour without recalling the athletic image" (Pfitzner 153). For military imagery Geoffrion 206–7 (cf. Pfitzner 157–64) notes Jos. *JW* 7.14; 1.231; Dem. *Cor.* 83–86; cf. *TDNT* 7.620–21. Political leaders were recognized for contributions to the *polis* (Pfitzner 106, Geoffrion 206–7; Dem. *Cor.* 83–86); wreaths for civic service, public benefaction, and *aretē* (Danker 1982:468–71). *TDNT* 7:620: politicians wore wreaths when orating at the Attic assembly; Emperor and state officials, in the processional relief on Augustus' Ara Pacis in Rome; Roman officials in Philippi (Bormann 1995:193–99) on occasion. Wreaths to crown achievement were thus familiar.

in this way stand steadfast in the Lord. stēkete, see Note on 1:27 *that you stand steadfast* (same form) . . . ; pres. impv., "continue . . . to stand firm" (NAB). *houtōs*, "thus" (RSV), *in this way* (NRSV), can point backwards to what precedes (BDAG 1; Fee 388–89; *DA* 323; Banker 157 "on the basis of all that I have told you"; S. F. Winter 166, = 3:17–21; cf. *And so* above; Holmstrand 122), or what follows (BDAG 2; Loh. 163, Hawth. 178), or both (Silva 217, O'B 476; Geoffrion 203 n 153, "recapping" and "introducing some specific applications before closing"). *without further ado, just, simply* (BDAG 4). *in the Lord* (Christ; Geoffrion 203 tries to bring in God), see Notes on 1:2 *Lord* and 2:19, 29, and 3:1. The realm or sphere where the firm stance takes place (*DA* 257–58, n 381).

O beloved. Final *agapētoi* is omitted by some (mostly Western) MSS. B 33 sy add *mou*, as in 4:1. Scribes thus moved in contrasting directions (Silva 218). Were some vocatives redactoral?

4:2. *I exhort. parakaleō* (contracted), 2x. Cf. *paraklēsis*; Note on 2:1 *comfort and exhortation.* BDAG 2, *appeal to, urge, exhort, encourage* + acc. of person; Bjerkelund 1975 ([5] Bibl.), "exhort" (but his "formal" "parakalo-periods" or sections are overdone, Fee 391 n 33). As in private petitions (Mullins 1962 [(2) Bibl.] 49; *DA* 272; Edart 283, 285–86 lettre de demande). Common in Pauline paraenesis (*DA* 173; 1 Thess 2:12; etc.). Trs. vary: "beseech" (KJV), "entreat" (RSV), "urge" (NRSV), "plead with" (NIV), "beg" (NEB). S. R. Llewelyn (*NewDocs* 6:145–46, following D. Hartman's diss.) terms *parakalō* less courteous and more humble than *erōtō* ("I ask," 4:3); then the two women are subordinated more than the person addressed in v 3.

Euodia. A good Gk. name (Pilhofer 240); inscriptions (Lft. 158; MM 263; *NewDocs* 4:178–79). *eu*, "well," + *hodos*, "way, road"; vb. *euodoō*, "go well" (3 John 2), "succeed" (Rom 1:10); thus "Success" or "Prosperous Journey" (Fee 390). Some later MSS read *Euōdian* (EGT 464; Alford; Fee 390 n 29 on interchange of *omicron* and *omega*), cf. 4:18 "fragrance" (Martin 1976:152). Schenk 273 conjectures Luke used "Fragrance" here in presenting the woman from Lydia in Acts 16; "quite impossible," Lüdemann 1989 (Intro. II Bibl.) 181–82. A man's name (Grotius; KJV "Euodias") lacks inscriptional support; *autais* in v 3 requires two fem. names in v 2 (Lft. 158). She is named in "the first word in the clause" (*DA* 382; cf. 2:19b Timothy; 25 Epaphroditus).

Syntyche. Gk., "with luck," "Lucky," from Tyche, "Dame Fortune" (Lat. *Fortuna*), a deity governing human affairs, prominent as traditional Gk. gods and goddesses declined in importance, esp. after the 4th cent. B.C. (*OCD*³ 1566; Fee 390 n 30 emphasizes Tyche's fickle nature). Male derivatives include Tychicus

(Acts 20:4; Col 4:7); Eutyches (Acts 20:9), and Fortunatus (1 Cor 16:17). On the accent see ATR 235. Sometimes taken as a man, to get a husband and wife. Schenk's proposal ("Child of Fortune" at 4:3 is "source" for the girl with a "spirit of divination" at Acts 16:16–18) is to be rejected. Peterlin 127 n 143 reports the name *Syntyche* in a 2nd-cent A.D. inscription from Lydia in Asia Minor.

to think the same thing in the Lord. to auto phronein (infin. with force of a command, DA 349), as at 2:2 *think the same thing*; NOTES on 1:7 *to think* and 4:10 *your concern for me* and *you were long intent,* a Philippian phrase and "friendship" term. Assuming the two women quarreled, *phronein* here has been taken (ZG 601) as "agree together" (NEB), "live in harmony" (TC), be friends (Fitzgerald 1996:146), or "be reconciled," Vincent 129; Banker 160. NRSV went back to KJV's "be of the same mind"; CEV, "stop arguing." *in the Lord,* see NOTE on 4:1. With the two names, "sisters in the Lord" (GNB). Or how they are to agree "together in the Lord" (REB) or "in union with the Lord" (TC). Or with *I exhort* (cf. 1 Thess 4:1; etc.; cf. DA 267). Most likely (*en kyriō[i]* with a command) for the ecclesial sphere where the Lord Jesus rules.

4:3a. *Indeed, I am asking you also. nai,* **indeed** (*kai* in TR; "And," KJV/RSV) can confirm a previous assertion (ATR 1150), emphasize by repetition (BDAG *nai* c), or introduce a further point (Phlm 20; NRSV, etc.; "Yes, and . . ."). *erōtaō* (DA 267–68), here only in Phil., otherwise in Paul only at 1 Thess 4:1 (with *parakaloumen*) and 5:12; *ask, request,* often introducing an impv. (BDAG 2; Deissmann 1909 ([1] Bibl.) 195–96, 290). See NOTE on 4:2 *I exhort,* "ask" is "more courteous," addressed to (social) equals (Hartman). *kai* before *you* (sg., *se*) = *also,* a further request beyond that in 4:2 (DA 327).

my faithful partner. Voc. of *syzygos* (*syn* = with + *zygos* = yoke, fig. at Acts 15:10, Matt 11:29–30; Rev 6:5 "a pair of scales") + *gnēsios* (NOTE on the adv., 2:20 *genuinely*). *synzyge* in ‭א‬ᶜ A etc. makes the etymology plainer, not assimilating the *nun* (BDF #19). Reversed word order, *syzyge gnēsie,* in K L etc. Older views in B. Weiss 299–300. (1) A *proper name, Syzygos,* many commentators (Wohl. 217; Vincent 131; Michael 191, Gnilka 166; Ollrog 28) and trs. ([N]JB, NRSV-mg, etc.). + *gnēsie,* "truly called Syzygus" (Lft. 159), "who really is, in fact and name, 'fellow-in-yoke'" (Meyer 162; Ellicott 99; Str-B 3:623)—wordplay like "Onesimus/useful" (Phlm 11). Occasionally, Gnesios as a proper name (Lft. 159). Against "Syzygus": no instance to date in Gk. or Lat. (BDAG p. 954), but cf. similar compound names like Syndromos, Symmachos, Symphrōnes (TDNT 7:749); Kennedy 465 claimed "Zygos" as a Jewish name (Jastrow, Dict. 384). Fee 393 n 44, "the qualifier 'genuine' almost totally disqualifies it as a proper name."

As (2) a *common noun,* the Gk. compound presents complexities. For *zygos* (masc. or neut., BDAG), see G. Bertram/K. Rengstorf, TDNT 2:896–901; vb. *heterozygeō,* "unevenly yoked, mismated" (2 Cor 6:14), classical Gk. *zeugnymi.* Is *syzyg(i)os* (adj.) pass., "yoked together" (the usual understanding; Eur. *Hipp.* 1147), or act., "yoking together" (Stob. *Ecl.* 2.54, cf. Poll. 3.38)? "Spanned together" in a common yoke "is not found" (TDNT 7:748). Bound together in marriage = *syzygia,* couple, copulation; *hē syzygos* (fem.) = wife (Eur. *Alc.* 314); *synzygeis,* 3 Macc. 4:8, "husbands" (NRSV); Mark 10:9 "what God has joined together" *(synezeuxen)*. Hence (2a) "the true yokefellow," Paul's wife (Clem. Al. *Strom.* 3.53.1; MS D Lat. *delectissime conjunx*; Origen, *Comm. in ep. ad Rom.* 1.1); adj. = lawful (wife) (BDAG *gnēsios* 1). (2b) From a yoke or pair of animals (LSJ *syzygia*; Eur. *Hipp.* 1131), in Judaism (loanword *zûg*, Jastrow 383) "couple, pair" for messengers sent by twos from Jerusalem to diaspora synagogues (*šᵉlûḥîm*; A. Schlatter; K. Rengstorf, *apostolos*, TDNT 1:417; Jeremias 1959 [(9) COMMENT B.2.a] 136–37). Jesus sent out pairs of messengers (Mark 6:7; Luke 10:1); continued in Acts (Paul and Barnabas, 13:1; Paul and Silas, Barnabas and Mark, 15:40; Judas and Silas, 15:32; perhaps Andronicus and Junia[s], Rom 16:7); Phil 4:3, the "reliable yoked-colleague" = Silas (Jeremias 140; Delling, *TDNT* 7:749–50, esp. n 12). Fee 392–94, companion "in itinerant ministry," here Luke. Bormann 1995:216, Delling is one-sided, it is a patron/client relationship (cf. Dion. Hal., *Ant. Rom.* 2.10.4, pp. 202, 204).

(3) Most common, *syzygos* = "comrade" (Eur. *IT* 250, Orestes and Pylades; Aristot. *Pol.* 945; Bormann 1995:216, within yet against the patron–client structure), even "brother" (Eur. *Tro.* 1001). *syzygeō*, soldiers standing in one rank (Polyb. 10.23.7; cf. Arr. *Tact.* 7.2, 8.2); Lat. *commilito*, comrade in arms (Cic.); gladiators, yoked in pairs, fight each other, each *syzygos* to his opponent (*JHS* 34 [1914]:19). Fitzgerald 1996:149, via "yoke," relates 4:3 to friendship; Plut., *De Am. mult.* 93E, famous pairs under the "yoke [or bond] of friendship" *(zeugos philias)*, like Achilles and Patroclus. Cic., friendship is "sweetest . . . 'yoked together with' *(coniugavit)* congeniality of character" *(Off.* 1.58; *Oxford Latin Dictionary*, ed. P. Glare, 1968–82, vb. *coniugo*, "form a friendship"). Hence 4:3 = "genuine friend" (1996:151; Hom. *Il.* 13:701–11, two heroes fight "shoulder to shoulder" as comrades; 1997:33). 4:3 *gnēsie* = "tested" *(TDNT* 7:749), "loyal" (NRSV, NIV), "faithful" (GNB, cf. 1 Tim 1:2, BDAG 1), "much beloved" *(TLNT* 1:296; "true," 297, background in NOTE on 2:20 *genuinely)*; "tried and tested, true" (Fitzgerald 1996:158).

Trs. vary from lit. "yokefellow" (KJV, RSV, NIV) to "comrade" (Gdsp., NEB/REB), "teammate" (LB/NLT); "Syzygus" in marginal notes. The TRANSLATION uses *my faithful partner*; close relationship to Paul, without prejudging the person's identity (no connection with *koinōnia* as "partnership").

assist them. Impv., 2nd sg., pres., m., *syllambanō*, BDAG 4, **help by taking part w[ith] someone in an activity** (lit. 'take hold of together'), *support, aid, help,* + dat., fem. pl., 3rd per. pron. Most trs., "help." Delling *(TDNT* 7:762), "pastorally to Christian concord" (v 2 assumes conflict). DA 269 n 419, "assistance," no discord implied; PMich 8.485.9, 2nd cent. A.D., requests a friend to act as mediator, "I beseech *(parakalō)* you" that you be "not only be a helper *(boēthos)* . . . but a good pilot *(kybernētēs)*"; further examples (like POxy 4.744.6–7) with *erōtō* and *parakalō* to request assistance (in PMich 8.487.6–12, with *synlabou*), often material aid. Michael 192 and O'B 481 deduce, from *syn* and pres. tense, that the women tried to adjust differences but found the task none too easy.

4:3b. *for these women, in the gospel cause, engaged in a struggle, together with me.* . . . Asyndic, no connective. *haitines*, fem. pl. rel. pron., "these women" ([N]JB, CEV); see NOTE on 2:20 *who*; BDAG *hostis* 2.b, for "a characteristic quality, by which a preceding statement is to be confirmed"; in effect, causal, "seeing that, since" (ATR 728; ZG 601); [N]RSV "for." *gospel cause, euangelion* (BDAG 1.a; see NOTE on 1:5 *gospel* and 2:22), *nomen actionis*, evangelization (*TDNT* 2:729; O'Brien 1986:227), promoting the gospel (NAB[RNT]), its "spread" (GNB), "in the cause of the gospel" (NEB/REB). *synathleō*, aor., **contend/ struggle along with** + dat. *moi*; BDAG: *they fought at my side in (spreading) the gospel.* See NOTE on 1:27d *engage together in the struggle*, athletic, military connotations, but not here stressed (Pfitzner 119, even with *stephanos* 4:1). The struggle began when the congregation was founded (Michaelis 65; Ewald 214; Gnilka 166; Ollrog 107). Fitzgerald 1996:128, a *philia* term, friends "engage in mutual enterprises." Not "contended with," "against," Paul; hence RSV "side by side with me"; "were a help to me" (JB).

along also with Clement and my other coworkers. meta + gen., *along with.* Not *kai . . . kai,* "both . . . and," but *along also with . . . and. meta kai* is sometimes pleonastic (BDF 442.13; [N]RSV and others omit); occurs in the papyri (Deissmann 1909 [(1) Bibl.] 64 n 2; 265–66; ATR 612). Lft. 159 suggested *meta kai Klēmentos* with *syllambanou,* "I invite Clement also, with the rest of my fellow-labourers . . . to aid in this work of reconciliation" (158)—awkward (Vincent 132; O'B 482); "coworkers" suggests mission involvement, not reconciling Euodia and Syntyche. *Clement* = Gk. form of a fairly common Lat. name. Not the author of 1 Clem. or the "foreign secretary" of the church in Rome (Herm. *Vis.* 2.4.3). Bockmuehl 240 notes Valerius Clemens in a 2nd-cent. A.D. list of members of the Silvanus cult at Philippi (*CIL* 3.121, Pilhofer 1:108–12 on the cult; 2:170–75, No.163/L002). Perhaps an army veteran, retired in the Roman *colōnia.* Zahn supposed he was the jailer of Acts 16, married to one of the women in 4:2 (Pilhofer 1:237 n 9).

my other coworkers (tōn loipōn synergōn mou). See NOTE on 2:25b . . . *fellow worker.* Here, helpers at the founding of the church in Philippi, too numerous to name. Fitzgerald 1996:128, 146, *syn*-compound, mutual enterprises, so in the orbit of friendship. For *loipōn* see NOTE on 1:13 *and to all the rest*; here, adj. (BDAG 2.a, **other**), with an "et cetera" quality. Two MSS (א P[16]) read *tōn synergōn mou kai tōn loipōn,* "my fellow-workers and the others" (NEB-mg), two groups. Silva 223 gives it consideration. *TCGNT* 617, "scribal inadvertence"; Fee 385 n 4, "patently secondary." {B} level in UBSGNT.

4:3c. *Their names are written in the book of life. hōn* ("of whom") joins *names* (BDAG *onoma* 1, "proper names") to the *other coworkers, Clement, Euodia,* and *Syntyche.* Deissmann, *LAE* 121, a formula (BGU 432 II. 3). Supply "are" (KJV-[N]RSV) or "written" ([N]JB, CEV). No art. with either *book* or *of life*; Apollonius' canon (Moule, *IB* 114–15), or because the phrase follows a prep. (GNTG 3:180). *zōē* (BDAG 2.b.β) = life of believers; see NOTE on 1:21 *whether by life or death. hē biblos, book,* only here in Paul; cf. Acts 19:19, etc.; *to biblion* in Paul only at Gal 3:10. For 4:3, cf. Rev 3:5; 13:8, "(the) book of (the) life"; 21:27; 17:8; 20:12, 15; 22:18–19, 4x; Bockmuehl 242 excludes Rev 22:19). Likely a papyrus book or scroll (ZG 601). OT phrasing has been claimed (Bruce 139, esp. apocalyptic, Bittasi 144 n 149): Ps 69:28 ("the book of the living," LXX 68:29; Ps 56:8, LXX 55:8; 87:6, LXX 86:6;138:16 LXX; Exod 32:32; Isa 4:3, 34:16; Mal 3:16–17; Dan 12:1; Ezek

13:9; cf. *En.* 47:3, *OTP* 1:35; *APOT* 2:216, "registers of actual Israelite citizens" in the OT; see below); *1 En.* 104:1,7; 108:3,7; *Jub.* 30:19–23 (heavenly tablets); 1QM 12:2; 4Q180 1:3 (cf. AB 28A: 863–64). No example contains the exact two words at Phil 4:3. Brinktrine, 1 Sam 25:29, "the bundle of the living" (AB 8:390), gets no support. Some passages (Dan 12:1, Rev) have an apocalyptic tone. In the Jesus-tradition, Luke 10:20, "names written in heaven" (AB 28:860 "a heavenly register of favored people"). *Bibl. on heavenly books* is extensive; see M. Rissi, "Life, Book of," *IDB K-Q* 130; L. Koep, "Buch IV (himmlisch)," *RAC* 2:725–28, listing the righteous elect or the wicked destined for destruction (Dan 7:10) or fut. events (Ezek 2:9–10; Rev 10:8–11); Str-B 2:169–76. Note registers of citizens in Israel (the result of a census?) or Jerusalem (Ezek 13:9; Ps 87:6), including family lists and genealogies (Gen 5:1; Jer 22:30); cf. G. Schrenk, *TDNT* 1:620 (Neh 7:5–6, 64; 12:22–23); or a civic register for citizens in the Roman *colōnia* (and God's heavenly commonwealth, cf. 3:20). So Caird 150; Hawth. 181; Pilhofer 1:130–34, archives of the *tribus Voltinia*, documented also in Aquae Sextiae (Aix-en-Provence) and Nemausus (Nîmes). Cf. F. Schulz 1942–43 (INTRO. II n 3); J. F. Gardner, "Proof of Status in the Roman World," *BICS* 33 (1986) 1–14; M. Hengel/U. Heckel 1991:7, n 61, on birth registration; Schwemer 2000 ([14] Bibl. 230–32. At 4:3, not a list of those who have died for the faith (so Beare 145; Michael 193) or of martyred leaders (Loh. 167), for Euodia, Syntyche, and Clement are included (O'B 483 n 41, but cf. K. Barth 119 and U. B. Müller 194).

4:4. *Rejoice in the Lord always. chairete*, impv. as at 3:1 with *en kyriō[i]*; see NOTES on *rejoice* and *in the Lord.* Also after *I shall say it again (erō*, fut. indic. *legō*, equivalent of a hortatory subjunct., ZG 601; ZBG #341, "let me say it anew"). As at 3:1, Gdsp. has "Goodbye," NEB (but not REB) "Farewell." See COMMENT B.3.a. Alliterative *pantote* (with the initial *chairete en kyriō[i]*) and *palin* (with *erō*) appeared earlier; see NOTES on 1:4 *always* (+ 1:20, 2:12) and 1:26 *through my coming again to you* (also 2:28, *that you . . . again may rejoice*). Bengel suggested *pantote* with the second *chairete*, "always, I say again, rejoice," *palin erō* is parenthetical; fut. for the present (EGT 466); Loh. 167–68 n 3 found no analogous examples, yet KJV, etc. treat *erō* as a pres. R. D. Webber ([2] Bibl. **joy**) 355–57: a communal disposition from "the new . . . situation created by the risen Lord."

4:5a. *Let your patient steadfastness be known to all sorts of people.* Impv., 3rd sg. aor. pass., *ginōskō*; see NOTE on 1:12 *come to know.* DA 386 does not press the aor. Here, "be evident" (NIV, JB), "obvious" (NJB), "manifest" (NEB). Be "learned, perceived, recognized" (BDAG *ginōskō* 2, 4, 7, respectively) or "detected" (*TDNT* 1:703) scarcely fit with the dat. (indir. obj., not *hypo* + gen.) *anthrōpois* (BDAG *anthrōpos* 1.c, *associates, people*; KJV/RSV "men"; omitted in NIV, etc.). *pasin*, see NOTE on 1:9 *discernment in every situation*; BDAG *pas* 1.a.β, "every kind of, all sorts of," appropriate re "the way in which Christians and non-Christians should live together" (W. Bauder, *NIDNTT* 2:258). Some recast: Gdsp. "Let all men see"; GBB "Show. . . ."

patient steadfastness. Adj. *epieikēs, es*, here substant. (after the art.), neut. for an abstract noun (BDAG *ho, hē, to* 2.b.γ); cf. Phil 3:8 *to hyperechon*; Rom 2:4, etc. = *hē epieikeia* (2 Cor 10:1; Acts 24:4; Vg *modestia* at 4:5), a topic discussed in Aristot.

Eth. Nic. 5.10 1137a 31–b 27 and elsewhere. Sonntag 32–43 relates it to *diakaio-syne* and law (and friendship, 43–46) as something that improves on or betters legal justice. The neut. adj. is classical, found in the "higher *koine*" (BDF 263 [2]; ZBG #140; GNTG 3:14; Moule *IB* 96). From *epi* + *eikos*, neut. ptc. of *eoika*, "be fitting." The noun and adj. are difficult to tr.; Moffatt "used six different translations for seven occurrences" in the NT (*TLNT* 2:34 n 1; chart in L. Marshall 306). Cf. Riley; Spicq 1947; Duchatelez; d'Agostino; L. H. Marshall 305–8, graciousness; "magnaminity" is not quite right. Dictionary definitions = "clemency, benevolence, moderation, fairness, mildness"; in Bible trs., "lenience, clemency, indulgence" (*TLNT* 2:34). BDAG 371, **yielding, gentle** [cf. NRSV, etc.], **kind, courteous, tolerant,** for 4:5 *your forbearing spirit* (cf. RSV); JB "tolerance"; NJB "good sense." Dickson 272, "a weighty, 'catch-all' term." No fixed Heb. word behind the 16 LXX examples. Harnack 1920, clemency on the part of a ruler, whether God or king. Preisker, *TDNT* (Ger. 1935), applied this to Christ (2 Cor 10:1, his "meekness and gentleness [*epieikeia*]"); royal majesty (Phil 2:5ff.), complemented by gentleness; his heavenly authority allows him to display clemency. Paul and Christians, with "a heavenly calling" (Phil 3:20) "associated with the divine *doxa*," can and must display *epieikeia*. Because "the Lord is at hand" and the final *doxa* will soon be manifest, "they can be *epieikeis* towards all men in spite of every persecution" (4:5), exhibiting the "earthly counterpart of the heavenly glory" (*TDNT* 2:589–90). Cf. W. Brauder, *NIDNTT* 2:256–59; *TLNT* 2:34–38; Dacquino: a condescending attitude by one superior but open to all that is praiseworthy. Leivestad ([6] Bibl.), however, brought Wis 2:19 into the discussion, on "the righteous sufferer," thus undermining the notion that *epieikeia* characterizes a person of authority and power, a superior showing clemency to inferiors. At Wis 2:19, the enemies of the righteous man say (NRSV), "Let us test him with insult and torture, so that we may find out how gentle he is *(ten epieikeian autou)* and make trial of his forbearance" (cf. 2 Tim 2:24). 2:19 (Leivestad 158) "has no connexion with the indulgence of a ruler [Preisker brought in "son of God" at Wis 2:13, cf. 16, but "son of God" could fit any loyal Israelite]; *epieikeia* here signifies "a humble, patient steadfastness . . . able to submit to injustice, disgrace, and maltreatment without hatred and malice, trusting God in spite of all of it" (Rienecker 214).

Thus (H. Giesen, *EDNT* 2:26) it may reflect (a) the "benevolence of the sovereign" (Harnack; Acts 24:4, Governor Felix; 1 Peter 2:18, the masters of slaves); or (b) from Wis 2:19, "weak" human believers (2 Cor 11:30; 12:9; 13:3, Paul!) in whom God's power is revealed (2 Cor 10:1; Phil 4:5); 1 Tim 3:3, the *episkopos*; Titus 3:2, Christians, gentle and showing courtesy to everyone, subject to rulers and authorities. Cf. Jas 3:17 (AB 37A:274). Dickson 262–75 relates *epieikes* to 1 Thess 4:11–12 ("live quietly, mind your own affairs, behave properly toward outsiders"), where he claims a rabbinic *siman* or device calling attention to a body of material (*topos*?; contrast AB 32B:246–60); 4:5 "may recall a whole set of traditions about what it means to express 'graciousness' toward an unbelieving and, at times, hostile civil society," thus an "ethical apologetic" (Dickson 274–5).

How to render 4:5, where the exegetical tradition often missed the sense

(Leivestad [(6) Bibl.] 158 n 4)? Spicq, *sympathique équilibre*, "friendly equilib-rium, friendly well-balanced character" (*TLNT* 2:38, but literature on *philia* in Paul makes nothing of *epieikēs*). Dickson 273, "humanitarian regard." Giesen, *forbearance* (*EDNT* 2:26). It clearly reflects the social setting of Philippian Chris-tians in their struggle in the Roman *colōnia. patient steadfastness* relates to 1:27. They would have known the *clementia Caesaris* (bibl. in *TLNT* 2:35 n 9) and citi-zens' fitting respect for social norms (*TLNT* 2:36–37 and n 16). Non-Christians and Christians are called to this Gk. virtue of balance and amiability, but with dif-ferent motivation.

4:5b. *The Lord is near.* Vb. supplied. The *kyrios* (last at 4:1, 2, and 4) is Jesus. *engus* is an adv. of time, *near*, referring the parousia (BDAG 2.a; Vincent 133–34; Pilhofer 131; in *TDNT*, Preisker, 2: 331, 590; A. Oepke, 5:868; K. G. Kuhn, 4:469; Radl 1981:94–98, traditional formula; political connotations, Popkes 2002:854–55). Pred. use of the adv. as in classical Gk. (*GNTG* 3:226), "not far from the ad-jective idea" (ATR 546). Gdsp., "is coming soon" (GNB, LB); "will soon be here" (CEV). Alternative: near to hear prayers, provide help (DA 272, 295), assuming *ho kyrios engus* stems from (Caird:151: "are a quotation" of) Ps 145:18, "The Lord is near (LXX 144:18 *engus kyrios*) to all who call on him . . . ," prayer and divine protection (145:19–20; Phil 4:7; Oakes 2000:261). Cf. also Ps 34:18 (LXX 33:19); 119 (118):151; 31:20. Calvin 118–19, "give help," not "judgment"; God's hand is "everywhere present." Loh. 168–69, eschatological (Maranatha, 1 Cor 16:22, prayer for the parousia, as in NRSV-txt) *and* "the nearness in which the martyr approaches Christ through suffering" and so a transition to prayer in 4:6 — but Paul understood 5b eschatologically. C. H. Dodd's support for "reminiscence" here of Ps 145:18, in a context he termed "not eschatological" (1933–34 [Exc. A. Bibl.] 112), fits his downplaying "futurist eschatology." Cf. Michaelis 67; D. M. Stanley 1973 ([2] Bibl. **prayer**) 106; Hawth. 192 ("intentionally vague . . . the Lord who will come again is presently very near in his Spirit"). W. Kramer ([1] Bibl. **Christ**) n 360, "primarily . . . the parousia (cf. 3.20f.)," as commonly with "Lord" (n 497), "nearness" of the Lord then (n 639). Baumgarten 205–8, 4:5 is spatial, "the concrete present activity of Christ"; Yahweh in the Ps. is now none other than the Lord Jesus. Reversal of the LXX word order, placing *kyrios* first, in-dicates high christological emphasis. Contrast Radl 1981:95. Chapple 1992, Paul is "quoting or alluding to" three Pss vv, now applied to Jesus; not "Christian escha-tology" but "biblical piety" (160). The "prayer argument" finds support in 4:6 *prayer*, but petitions could include *Marana tha!* for the parousia. Most exegetes decide for the parousia, from references (in Letter B) to the imminent Day of the Lord (1:6, 10; 2:16, qualified only slightly by Paul's possible death before that day, 1:18b–26); and 3:20–21, the Savior awaited from heaven. Cf. Rom 13:12, "the Day [of the Lord] is near *(hē de hēmera ēngiken)*"; Zeph 1:7, 14, *engus hē hēmera [tou] kyriou;* Jas 5:8. Some opt for both a (pres.) spatial and a fut. (temporal) refer-ence (Collange 141; Bruce 142–43; Hawth. 182; O'B 489). Fee 408 contrasts Phi-lippian suffering "at the hands of those who proclaim Caesar as Lord" and fut. vindication from their Lord.

Does the asyndic 5b go with (i) 5a and even 4, as eschatological grounding for the impv(s).? LB, NLT, "Remember that the Lord Jesus is coming soon"; Lft. 160; Loh. 168–69 (martyrs); Gnilka 169; Martin 1976:155; more in Fee 407 n 33. Or (ii) with v 6 (new paragraph)? "The Lord is near; have no anxiety," NEB/REB; Chrysost.; Michaelis 66–67; cf. Caird 151). Or (iii) with both 5a and 6? Vincent 133; Silva 223, "[After all, remember that the coming of] the Lord is near. So let nothing worry you . . ."; Collange 144; Fee 407 n 35, "intentional double entendre"; 408 n 39, motivation for 5a.

4:6a. *Do not continue to be anxious about anything. merimnaō* (see NOTE on 2:20 *who will genuinely care about what affects you*); here (BDAG 1) **have anxiety, be anxious, be (unduly) concerned.** Beare 146 "be fretful"; NRSV, [N]JB "worry." Pres. impv. + neg. *mē*, stop being concerned; NAB "Dismiss all anxiety . . ." + neut. acc. sg., *mēdeis* (2:3a *nothing*), as at 1:28a *not . . . in any way*; subst. (BDAG 2.b.β, acc. of inner object, *not . . . at all*; or acc. of respect or reference, "anxious about," Moule *IB* 34; or as if a cognate acc., *mēdemian merimnan merimnate, IB* 32, lit. "anxious about no anxiety").

4:6b. *instead, in each instance, let your requests be constantly made known toward God. alla* (BDAG 1.a), first particle since *hōste* (4:1), in contrast to neg. in 6a. *gnōrizesthō* (thirteen words later), 3rd sg. pass. impv. (cf. *gnōsthētō* in v 5a), pres. tense; repeated, continuing action; *gnōrizō*, see NOTE on 1:22 *I do not know.* Bultmann cites Philo re God (*TDNT* 1:718), but not involving prayers. *pros ton theon* (BDAG *pros* 3.a.ζ), place or person "toward(s)" whom one prays, 2 Cor 13:7; 2 Cor 1:18, etc.; Acts 12:5. Thurston 145 claims Semitism, "the god," not pagan deities. The subject of the sg. vb. is neut. pl. of *to aitēma*, "request," rare in the NT (Luke 23:24; 1 John 5:15; vb. *aiteō*, 1 Cor 1:22; Col 1:9; Eph 3:3, 20). Several requests, "individual petitions which constitute a prayer" (G. Stählin, *TDNT* 1:193; cf. Loh. 170 n 2). *en panti* (neut.), not with noun that follows (*tē[i] proseuchē[i]*, dat. sg. but fem.). See NOTES on 4:12c *in every situation* and 1:18b *in every way* (*panti tropō[i]*). BDAG *pas* 2.a.β, *in everything* (KJV-[N]RSV), *in every respect* (LB, CEV); or (as if with *tē[i] proseuchē[i]*) "in every form of prayer" (GNB); contrast Schenk 246 n 31.

by prayer and entreaty, with thanksgiving. Three types or aspects of prayer, the first two in the dat. (instrumental, ZG 601; KJV-[N]RSV, NIV; Moule, *IB* 45, accompaniment; GNTG 3:241, associative., the means by which). *proseuchē* = "prayer comprehensively," in contrast to petitionary prayer ("requests"); see NOTE on the vb. in 1:9 *I am praying. entreaty* (Gdsp.), see NOTES on 1:4 *entreaty* and *making entreaty* (*deēsis*; "supplication," 4:6 KJV-NRSV) and on 1:19 *entreaty for* Paul's deliverance from prison; NIV "petition." Loh. 170, "virtually indistinguishable"; U. Schoenborn (*EDNT* 1:286–87), *proseuchē* = "general request," *deēsis* "special request." The third term, obj. of *meta* + gen. (BDAG A.3.a, **attendant circumstance,** of "moods, emotions, wishes, feelings"; cf. 2:12, 29), is *eucharistia,* "rendering of thanks, thanksgiving." Only here in Phil; vb. at 1:3 *thank;* a Hellenistic term; "the proper mode of eschatological vigilance" (*TDNT* 9:414; Col 4:2; cf. 1 Thess 5:6, 10, 16–18; 1 Cor 16:13).

As in 9ab (see below), *Do not continue to be anxious* and *let your requests be constantly made known* can be taken as conditions ("if"), protasis before the apodosis in promise form in v 7 (*kai* = "then"); Merk 1968:195; U. B. Müller 195, 199; M. Müller 142; Snyman 332: cause (in 4:2–6 and 8), effect (vv 7, 9). Jewett 1971a:325 saw "no condition whatever attached" to v 7.

4:7. *And the peace of God that exceeds all understanding will keep guard over your hearts and minds in Christ Jesus.* *kai,* first such linking word since 4:1 (6b *alla* = contrast), has "a kind of consecutive force" (ATR 1183); "so," "then" (Gdsp. NEB, CEV). *peace* (BDAG *eirēnē* 3), see NOTE on 1:2 *peace*; cf. *the God of peace,* 4:9. In contrast with the *pax Romana* (Wengst 1987 [(1) Bibl. **peace**]; Popkes 2002:854). Krentz 2003:363 notes a statue base in Philippi to the *Quies Augusti* ("the quiet of Augustus"). Not simply OT *šalôm*, but peace with God (*pros ton theon,* end of v 6), through Christ (Thüsing, Schenk; cf. NOTE on 1:2), an outcome of prayers. *tou theou* is "probably subjective" gen., i.e., "the peace that God has and gives" (ATR 499), not adjectival ("the peaceful God," E. Stauffer, *TDNT* 3:111–12). Most trs. are quite lit., but cf. "God's (own) peace" (NAB, GNB). CEV "God will bless you with peace. . . . And this peace will control the way you think and feel." MS A, etc. read "of Christ," "a liturgical alteration" (Fee 402 n 10).

Ptc. *hyperechousa,* second attribut. position after *hē,* agreeing with *eirēnē,* is from *hyper-echō* (BDAG 3, ***be better than, surpass, excel***); 2:3, see NOTES on *surpass* (social-world background) and 3:8 *surpassingness.* The prefix *hyper* (+ acc.) suggests comparison, "more than" (ATR 477, 629, cf. 800), "'exceeds' what we can grasp or think" (Delling, *TDNT* 8:524). Dir. obj., acc. of *nous,* BDAG 1.b, "***understanding, mind*** as the faculty of thinking." H. J. Rose, "The *Clausulae* of the Pauline Corpus," *JTS* 25/49 (1924):17–43, proposed *hyperechousa pantos noos* (gen.) or *panta noun hyperechousa* ("St. Gregory Nazianzen and Pauline Rhythm," *HTR* 26 [1933] 323–24); no one thinks Rose improved on the MSS. *nous* occurs only here in Phil, for the reasoning power in each person, practical perception rather than an "academic mind." In Paul's picture of human beings under Sin, *nous* is, like flesh, turned away from God (Rom 1:28; 7:23, 25), but can through the Spirit be "renewed" (Rom 12:2; 2 Cor 2:16), playing a role in prayer (1 Cor 14:14–15, 19). Cf. Bultmann 1951 (INTRO. X Bibl.) 211–14, one's "real self"; Dunn, *TPTA* 73–75, "the thinking I," a bridge-term (already found in Hellenistic Judaism) to the Greco-Roman world.

will keep guard over your hearts and minds in Christ Jesus. Fut., *phroureō,* "guard" (2 Cor 11:32); "hold in custody, confine" (Gal 3:23); "keep" or even "protect" (cf. 1 Pet 1:5); thus 3 of 4 NT examples are in Paul. *Wordbooks:* only in *NIDNTT* 2:134–35, H.-G. Schütz, with *phylassō.* 4x in the LXX, not for "any original Heb. word in the text" (134). Rienecker 215, a military term; Geoffrion makes nothing of this; Krentz 2003:363. MM 677; BDAG 3, including Soph. *OT* 1479, "May a god *(daimōn)* guard/guide you." From 2 Cor 11:32, etc., Riesner 88 thinks "guard from the inside," not the outside. On impv. v 6 + *kai* + fut. indic. as a Semitic type of conditional sentence, "(If you) make your requests known . . . , then the peace of God will guard your hearts" (result; K. Beyer 238–55; BDF 442 [7]; Rienecker 215), see above, end of NOTE on 6b. Heckel ([17] Bibl.), esp. 266–68, argues for the "wish-character"of the fut. indic.

your hearts and your minds. Twin objects (hendiadys, Bultmann 1951 [INTRO. X

Bibl.] 213; Edart 282), each with the possessive *hymōn. kardia*, see NOTE on 1:7 *heart.* The center of each person from which thoughts and affections flow (Jewett 1971a:326), "the innermost part of the person," "the experiencing, motivating I"; if "characteristically Hebrew," also "equally Greek" (Dunn, *TPTA* 74–75). Bultmann 1951:220–23, synonymous with *nous*, note the Hellenistic *ta noēmata* that follows. Pls., of a group, in contrast to the Semitic sg. at 1:7 (*GNTG* 3:23). *to noēma,* only 6x in the NT, five of them in 2 Cor (2:11; 3:14; 4:4; 11:3, all pl. and negative; 10:5, "We take every thought [sg.] captive to obey Christ"). Frequent in Gk., little used in the LXX; = "the result of the activity of the *nous,*" "what is thought" (J. Behm, *TDNT* 4:960–61; G. Harder, *NIDNTT* 3:123, 125, 128; W. Schenk, *EDNT* 2:470). To this negative picture of human beings (Bultmann 1951:213), Phil 4:7 is an exception: "thoughts which proceed from the heart of Christians" (*TDNT* 4:961). A few Western MSS read *sōmata,* "bodies"; P[16] (reading not certain), *noēmata kai ta sōmata,* "your hearts and your bodies" ([N]JB-mg). Loh. 172, "bodies" fits "martyrdom." Silva 228 is somewhat open to *sōmata* (haplography). Fee 402 n 1, "bodies" reflects 1 Thess 5:23 *(to pneuma kai hē psychē kai to sōma).* Or *sōma* in Phil 3:20–21.

in Christ Jesus (P[46] adds "Lord"). See NOTE on 1:1 and subsequent uses of *en Christō[i] (Iēsou).* KJV "through Christ Jesus" implies *dia* + gen.; cf. Gdsp. GNB takes it with the vb., "will keep . . . safe in union with Christ Jesus." = the realm or sphere where Christ reigns.

4:8. *Finally, brothers and sisters, whatever things are true, whatever honorable, whatever just, whatever pure, whatever lovely, whatever appealing, if there is any excellence, if anything worthy of praise—these things ponder. to loipon adelphoi,* see NOTES on 3:1 *Finally, my brothers and sisters* (at 4:8, without *mou*). Some see closure (GNB "In conclusion"); but Gdsp., NEB/REB "(And) now . . ."; ATR 1146, almost *oun*; cf. Thrall 25–26, 28. Six neut. pls. are introduced by *hosa* (then two *if* phrases), summed up by *tauta* (*these things,* anaphoric, resumptive, ATR 698) + an impv. 2nd pl. m. from *logizomai* (BDAG 2 **think (about), consider, ponder, let one's mind dwell on**). Usually *hosos, ē, on* has a correlative *posos* or *tosoutos,* "how many, so many," BDAG 2; here the dem. pron. sums up, as at Rom 8:14; Gal 6:12, cf.16; Gk., not a Semitism (K. Beyer 171, 175). For repetition of *hosa* rhetorically, see Appian, *Liby.* 117 #554, "whatever things were excessive and foolish and fastidious"; three times in Liban. *Or.* 20, p. 443.1. Vb. *estin,* only in the first *hosa* cl., 3rd sg. with neut. pl. subject (BDF #133); omitted thereafter in the TRANSLATION, *whatever* [things are] *honorable,* etc.

logizomai, in the Pauline corpus 34x, esp. Rom (19x) and 1 and 2 Cor, usually "reckon"; Phil 3:13 *consider.* H. W. Heidland (*TDNT* 4:284–92, esp. 289), an "emotional ring" from the LXX (Ps 140:2 [LXX 139:3]; Jer 11:19), beyond the commercial (*TLNT* 1:83 n 75) and political usages in Gk. Paul does not customarily summon readers to reflection at the end of an epistle, as here; but cf. "think things through" (2 Cor 10:7, 11). To expound Phil 4:8 (and 1 Cor 13:5) in light of Zech 8:17 (J. Eichler, *NIDNTT* 3:825) is scarcely obvious. H.-W. Bartsch, "*thinking* as a reasoning process" here comes "more clearly into focus" (*EDNT* 2:355).

In Stoic virtue lists, cf. (Schenk 315) Sen. *De tranq. anim.* 3.4, "the meaning of justice *(quid sit iustitia)*, of piety *(quid pietas)*, of endurance, of bravery, of contempt of death, of knowledge of the gods" (LCL *Moral Essays* 2:224–25); Cic. *Tusc.* 5.23.67 (Loh. 174 n 1), "all that is lovely *(pulcra)*, honourable *(honesta)*, of good report *(praeclara sunt)* . . . is full of joys," ultimately "from rectitude *(ex honestate)*" (LCL 141:493); 43, "every good thing *(bonum)* is joyful *(laetabile)* . . . glorious . . . praiseworthy *(laudabile)* . . . right *(honestum)* . . . the happy life . . . with rectitude *(honestate)*." From synagogue liturgy, the Beraka *'amat wĕ-yaṣṣîb* (Loh. 174 n 1), after the Shema, "True and trustworthy . . . ," sixteen adjs. (8 pairs) about Deut 6:4. On *virtue (and vice) lists,* cf. R. P. Martin, *NIDNTT* 3:928–32; J. T. Fitzgerald, *ABD* 6:857–59 (ancient Near East to post-NT); C. G. Kruse, *DPL* 962–63; T. Engberg-Pedersen, in Sampley, ed., 2003, 608–33. For tables of NT virtue lists, see Preisker 146–47; Dunn, *TPTA* 662–64; for Gk. terms, Wibbing 99–100. On Stoicism, see *OCD*[3] 1446, *DPL* 715, Engberg-Pedersen 1995a and 2000. Connections with Sen., Lft. 270–333; Sevenster 1961 ([4] Bibl. **suicide**) 152–56.

true. Like all six adjs. that follow, neut. pl., pred. after *estin.* From *alēthēs, es,* BDAG 2, **true**; Bultmann, *TDNT* 1:248 "upright." 1:18 *in truth,* in contrast to hypocritical pretense. Here a Greco-Roman moral sense *(TLNT* 1:82–83 n 75, "true [honest]"); Sevenster 1961 ([4] Bibl. **suicide**) 154, from popular moral philosophy." Not "religious truth," in contrast to lies, or "doing the truth" (John 3:21; Loh. 174), but what is true/honest/genuine (Gnilka 220). Schenk 316 contrasts "imposters" (2 Cor 6:8; cf. Rom 3:4). Cf. Prov 1:3 LXX, "understand true justice"; wisdom in a life rationally determined (Wis 1:6, the "true overseer of the heart"; cf. 12:24; 15:17); reliability, in contrast to what is merely imagined. In virtue lists, 2 Cor 6:6; Eph 5:9.

honorable. Neut. pl., *semnos, ē, on,* BDAG b, **honorable, worthy, venerable, holy, above reproach.** No other examples in Paul's acknowledged letters; adj. and noun in the Pastorals for church leaders (1 Tim 3:8, NRSV "serious"; Titus 2:2, 7 "gravity") and the life of Christians (1 Tim 2:2, "dignity"); vb. in Acts for devout (13:43, 50) worshipers (16:14; 18:7, etc.). Considerable Gk. background (W. Foerster, *TDNT* 7:191–93; Spicq, *TLNT* 3: 244–48): august qualities in a person that call forth respect, awe, and reverence; cf. Wibbing 102–3. Applied also to a court or council, a city, or dinner club. In decrees, dignity in men or women, nobility, an admirable nature. Lat. *honesta* (Cic. *Tusc,* cited above). Epict. 1.16.13; 3.20.15; Lucian, *Encomium Patriae* 1. P. Fiedler *(EDNT* 3:238), "that which is exalted as part of the divine realm (the numinous)" in people. Little LXX use (chiefly in Prov, 2 and 4 Macc), but Philo and Jos. parallel Gk. usage *(TDNT* 7:193–94). Spicq, "what is noble" re "bearing and attitude," "comportment in general," "even collective behavior" *(TLNT* 3:246). Use grows in 1 Clem. (6x) and Herm. (7x) (Schenk 316). J. Quinn, *Titus* (AB35) 282–91, details the coloring from the Roman Principate *(sebastos,* Acts 25:21,25,27 = Lat. *augustus),* so that "the earliest Christian documents regularly" avoided "the terminology." Phil 4:8 and the Apostolic Fathers are exceptions. See below, COMMENT A.1.a

just. See NOTES on 1:7 *it is right* and 1:11 *righteousness (dikaiosynē,* one of the four cardinal Gk. virtues). Here, a moral sense; BDAG *dikaios, a, on* 2, "that which

is **obligatory in view of . . . justice.**" 4:8 is "altogether Greek" (*TLNT* 1:323 n 16).
In the Delphic commands (inscription from Melitopolis; SIG 1268.23; *LAE* 311
n 1; Wibbing 102; Vögtle 181), "do things just!" *(prasse dikaia)*. Schrenk (*TDNT*
2:187–88), "social conduct described in conventional expressions" of Hellenistic
virtues, but "inconceivable that Paul should not be using *dikaia* for action in
accordance with the will of God." Cf. Prov. 1:3, cited in NOTE on *true*. Ziesler
([2] Bibl. **righteousness**), the adj. in Paul always reflects ethical use, the vb. is
"forensic" (32–36; 79–85, 136–41), an overstatement (Reumann 1982 [(2) **righteousness**] ##41, 100–1, 103–5, 119, 138, 382, etc.; cf. Schenk 316 n 408). *just*
not re *dikaiosynē* at 3:6, 9 (Letter C) or 1:11, but "one virtue among others" (Wibbing 102). Eph 5:9 is similar.

   pure. hagnos, ē, on (BDAG b, *pure*), cf. NOTES on 1:1 *saints (hagiois)* and 1:17
not with a pure motivation (adv. *hagnōs*). Moral, not cultic (Loh. 172), ethically
"pure, undefiled" in conduct (H. Balz, *EDNT* 1:22). Only 11x in the LXX (esp.
Prov, 2 and 4 Macc, 5x for a Heb. term, Loh. 174 n 4); e.g., Prov 15:26. In civic life,
"blameless discharge of office" (F. Hauck, *TDNT* 1:122). Schenk 317 notes 2 Cor
7:11 ("guiltless") and 11:2 ("chaste," i.e., morally pure). D. F. Watson 1988b:77, a
topos, purity *(hagnos)*, 2:15 "is reiterated"; the supposed *topos* does not use *hagnos*.

   lovely. prosphilēs, es, only here in the NT. *pros + phileō*, act. sense in classical
Gk., "loving" (Ewald 223), NT "loved." BDAG: *pleasing, agreeable, lovely, ami-
able;* Dib. 73. G. Delling, *TDNT* 8:77 n 60, not re God, but could be used for
something "(most) dear to the gods" (Diod. S. 2.49.2; more in BDAG). More
common in the Koine than in the LXX (only 3x, Loh. 174 n 5: Esth 5:1b, an LXX
addition, NRSV Esth [Gk.] 15:5; Sir 4:7 and 20:13). Jos. *Ant.* 1.258 and 17.149.
MM 552, papyri and epitaphs; Dib. 73 and Gnilka 221 cite the adv. in an inscription from Pergamon, "pleasingly to his brother and to us and to all the others."
From its stem, "friendship language." Aquinas 116, perhaps from Aristot. *Eth. Nic.*
8, "things *prosphilē*" = "leading to material friendship" (Reumann 1996:104).

   appealing. adj. *euphēmos, on.* Here only in the Bible (for the noun see below).
Thoroughly Gk. *eu* = well + *phēmi* = say; act. sense, "well-speaking, fair sounding" or pass., "well-spoken of, well-reported." BAGD, "auspicious, well-sounding,
praiseworthy, attractive, appealing"; BDAG *commendable.* Men. *Frg.* p. 194,
"speech that is well-sounding" or "of good repute"; MM 266–67, 4:8 " shows earlier associations" of "auspicious sounding," rather than (later), "good reputation,"
a view echoed in *GNTG* 2:287. Hard to translate adequately. The Delphic commands (see NOTE on *just*) included, "Be *e]uphēmos*" and "practice *euphēmian*"
(Wibbing 101–2). Loh 174 n 5 reported a sense of "acclamation" (E. Peterson
1926 [(7) Bibl.]). Jos. *Ap.* 2.248, "auspicious (or respectable)." M. Aur. *Med.* 6. 18,
vb. = "commend." Paul uses the noun in a catalogue of hardships:

   in *(dia)*   A honor *(doxēs)* and   B dishonor *(atimias)*

(2 Cor 6:8)   B' ill repute *(dysphēmias)* and   A' good repute *(euphēmias)*

Furnish, AB32A:346, "defamed and praised." The chiasm continues, B' "imposters", A' "true" (cf. 4:8 *alēthēs*). Martin 1976:159 chooses for 4:8 "speaking well"

over "well spoken of," calling Moffatt's "'high-toned' . . . just right." To tr. as "gracious" (RSV, NEB-txt) may too easily suggest "grace." REB, "attractive"; NRSV,
"commendable." Loh. 174–75 claimed *hagna, prosphilē,* and *euphēma* reflect
Jewish thought; contrast Schenk 317 n 413 and the Gk. background of the latter
two. [N]JB, "everything we love and honor."

if there is any excellence. ei tis (supply *estin*) recalls 2:1, *If . . . as we assume.* Here
too, a statement of reality; "since" may be too strong a tr. NEB/REB, GNB, etc.
omit *if.* To add "to (or in) them" (the six items), summarizing prior to *tauta,* would
subordinate the six to *excellence,* which Paul does not do. Cf. Fee 416 n 13. *aretē,*
BAGD 1, "moral excellence, virtue," is a central theme in Gk. ethics. BDAG:
**uncommon character worthy of praise, *excellence of character, exceptional
civic virtue.*** O. Bauernfeind, *TDNT* 1:457–61; H.-G. Link/A. Ringwald, *NIDNTT*
3:925–28 (Gk. philosophers; Qumran is deemed "similar to the Stoic writers");
Danker 1982:318. "Something fitting or pleasing," hence "eminence" (Bauernfeind 458). Could refer to a god's demonstration of power (*Il.* 9.948) or a hero's
valor or merit (Xen. *An* 1.4.8; Jos. *JW* 3.380). Socrates moved *aretē* from the *polis*
to an individual's excellence in striving toward the good (Plato *Prt.* 329–30; *Ap.*
25D). Plato: *aretē* overarches *sophia,* wisdom; *andreia,* courage; *sophrosynē,* prudence; *dikaiosynē,* justice (*Resp.* 4.433, 442B–D; Cic. *Off.* 1.24.29). Aristot. took
virtue as a "permanent pattern of behavior" in a person (*hexis; Eth. Nic.* 2.4–5
1106a 14ff,), a mean between extremes (1107a). For the Stoics, an end in itself,
in accord with which one should live (references in *NIDNTT* 3:926). The four
cardinal *aretai* were expanded at times into longer lists, often antithetically, virtues and vices (*ABD* 6:857). Chrysipp. (*Frg.* 129. 43–44; Loh. 175 n 1 and others),
"Virtue . . . is the perfection and peak for the particular nature of the individual."
"Pursue fame, praise (you sg.) virtue" (Delphic commands). Philo added faith
and prayer to the cardinal virtues (H. A. Wolfson, *Philo: Foundations of Religious
Philosophy in Judaism, Christianity, and Islam* [Cambridge: Harvard Univ. Press,
1948] 2:200–78).

No Heb. term corresponds to *aretē.* Isa 43:21 (and 42:8,12; 63:7) LXX use pl.
aretai for God's praise or praiseworthy deeds (Heb. *tehillâh*); 43:21 is quoted at
1 Pet 2:9 (BAGD *aretē* 2,3; BDAG 2 **manifestation of divine power,** *miracle*).
Hab 3:3, *aretē* = Heb. *hôd,* God's "glory"; Zech 6:13 "the Branch" will receive
aretē, "(royal) honor" (Bauernfeind 460 "fame"). Most LXX examples reflect Gk.
senses: 2 Macc 6:31; 4 Macc 7:22, 9:8; etc.; *TDNT* 1:459; *NIDNTT* 3:926. In
Wis., *sophia* teaches the four cardinal virtues (8:7; cf. 4:1; 5:13; Wibbing 103
n 121). 2 Pet 1:3, God's "glory and *aretē*" (RSV "excellence"); 1:5, a "chain of
virtues," human *aretē,* "goodness," NRSV; J. H. Neyrey, AB 37C:154–55, 156,
speaks of honor-shame terminology. Phil 4:8 reflects this extensive Gk. background. Hardly "an echo" of LXX usage (Bauernfeind 460); better, cf. Cic. *Tusc.
Disp.* (above). Paul has commended "a notion inherent in the culture of his day"
(Sevenster 1961 [(4) Bibl. **suicide**] 154).

Is *aretē* a seventh virtue (so Bauernfeind), or does it stand over the other six
(examples of what "virtue" is)? Is it (with *epainos*) one of "two general heads," intrinsic character and subjective estimation? So Lft. 162; cf. Haupt 166, *aretē* =

"inner quality" and *epainos* ="what finds acknowledgment, general approbation," questioned by Schenk 318. Lft 162 paraphrased, "'Whatever value may reside in your old heathen conception of virtue, whatever consideration is due to the praise of men.'" *ei tis* is likely rhetorical variation for *hosa*, not indication Paul subordinates the first six items to *excellence*.

and if anything worthy of praise. (ho) epainos = **praise, approval, recognition,** to humans from other people or God (BDAG 1), or to God (1:11, NOTE on *praise*, classical Gk. sense of "praiseworthy" for 4:8). *tis*, masc., agrees with the noun but is often taken as "any*thing*" ([N]RSV, etc.) that partakes of "praiseworthiness" (BAGD 2, Sir 39:10; MM 227, examples not analogous). Western witnesses (D* F G etc.) added *epistēmēs*, gen., "understanding, knowledge" (a virtue in *Herm. Vis.* 3.8.5 and 7; cf. *Cebes* 20.3), "praise of understanding." Vg *laus* + in some MSS *disciplinae*; hence, Rheims NT, "if any praise of discipline," [N]JB-mg, "everything there is of knowledge" or "of discipline." Silva 230 (who earlier suggested "praiseworthy deed," "New Lexical Semitisms," *ZNW* 69 [1978] 253–57) claims scribes were unfamiliar with "the passive sense 'worthy of praise'" and added an object to its active sense; Dib 73, because Stoics (see below) spoke disdainfully of praise. Preisker (*TDNT* 2:586–87), "a concept of civic life," recognition in the community (cf. *Plato* 287A; *Leg.* 6.762E; Epict. 2.1.34–36, etc.). Stoicism sought to free individuals from desire for such praise (Epict. 1.18.22, etc.; M. Aur. *Med.* 4.20). O. Hofius (*EDNT* 2:16), Roman authorities commended "worthy citizens through a public record or through inscriptions." Hence "complementary address, panegyric" (LSJ *epainos* 2) in rhetoric (Lausberg #61.3.a, p. 33). In the diatribe, *epainos* and *aretē* are often combined (Wibbing 103).

4:9a. *What things you indeed learned and received and heard and saw in my life, these things continue to do.* As in v 8 *(hosa)*, a relative, neut. pl., begins the sentence *(ha,* from *hos, hē, ho).* Acc., obj. of four aor. vbs., summed up by *tauta (these things;* BDAG *houtos* 1.a.ε), obj. of impv., *continue to do.* Rel. pron. not repeated as *hosa* was in v 8. *prassete,* 2nd pl. pres. act., *prassō,* **do, accomplish,** BDAG 1; NEB/REB, NIV "put into practice." Repeated action (NRSV). Wordbooks — C. Maurer, *TDNT* 6:632–38; H.-C. Hahn, *NIDNTT* 3:1155–58; G. Schneider, *EDNT* 3:145–46 — indicate a "colourless word" for human actions, often a "negative judgment" on what is done (Maurer 635); "the activity . . . rather than its successful outcome" (ibid. 633–34). In Paul, negative sense at 1 Cor 5:2 (cf. 2 Cor 12:21; Gal 5:21); Rom 1:32–2:3 (cf. *TDNT* 6:636; Dunn, WBC *Rom.* 38A:81). Neutral sense, 1 Thess 4:11; 2 Cor 5:10; and Rom 9:11. Positive sense, Acts 26:20 (O'B 511; Luke is fond of the term); Rom 2:25; Phil 4:9; perhaps 1 Cor 9:17.

learned and received. Aor. act. 2nd pl., *manthanō* (BDAG 1 **learn** through instruction); see NOTE on 4:11 *For I have learned* (by experience); here from what Paul preached and taught in Philippi (cf. Rom 16:17 "*didachēn* which you learned"). *paralambanō,* from rabbinic use a tech. sense, **receive** (and then pass on) an oral tradition (BDAG 2.b.γ, 1 Cor 15:3; 11:23, etc.; so Loh. 176; O'B 509–10, but contrast K. Wegenast, *Das Verständnis der Tradition bei Paulus und in den Deuteropaulinen,* WMANT 8 (Neukirchen: Neukirchener Verlag, 1962), 114 and Collange 147). BDAG, like BAGD, 3.b, *receive, take over,* implying "agreement or approval," 1 Cor 15:1. J. C. Beker 1980 (INTRO. X Bibl.) 123, *"believing* acceptance of the gospel tradition."

All four vbs. are preceded by *kai,* a point of style (ATR 1182; BDF 460 [3] "polysyndeton," abundance in a staccato fashion). Tr. as "and" to connect vbs.; RSV, NIV omit the first one, before *emathete.* KJV took this *kai* with the next one as "ye have both learned and received"; cf. 2:13b NOTE; 4:12, 16; that relates these vbs. to Paul's teaching (and *heard and saw in me,* to his example, Schenk 318). Correlative *kai . . . kai* could be claimed twice, "both learned and received" and (GNB) "both from my words and from my actions." Initial *kai* can also be taken with *ha,* "which things also," referring to *tauta* in v 8 (O'B 508); then Paul taught and modeled the six or eight things just mentioned. Or the first *kai* may be adversative (Schenk 270, 330; "But those things which . . ."). O'B 508 objected, but cf. BDAG *kai* 1.b.η, 1 Cor 5:2; 2 Cor 6:9. This makes the Christian standards in v 9 (teaching and the apostle as model) the norm for the Hellenistic ethic set forth in v 8 (so Merk 1968:196–97). Final interpretation involves segmentation of the four vbs. and the relationship of v 9 to v 8. The TRANSLATION renders the first *kai* by *indeed.*

heard and saw in my life. Aor., *akouō* (1:27, 30; 2:26). *eidete,* aor. *eidon,* 1:30 (ptc. 1:27, 2:28). See NOTES on 1:27b and esp. 30 *you saw* in my life and *of which you are now hearing* in my life (*en emoi,* as here). *en emoi* follows *saw,* but some infer it with the other three vbs. (O'B 511); [N]JB: "learnt from me and have been taught by me and have heard or seen that I do." The Philippians saw (and heard) what Paul's Christianity was like when he was in Philippi and heard from others (Timothy and Epaphroditus) what it was like earlier, subsequently, and elsewhere.

4:9b. *and the God of peace will be with you.* See 4:7 *And the peace of God* (chiasm with 9b) for earlier references to *theos* and *eirēnē* (1:2). Cf. "the God of hope" (Rom 15:13, etc.); "God of peace" (1 Thess 5:23, etc.), which occurs (Deichgräber [(7) Bibl.] 87–105) mostly in a prayer-wish toward the end of a letter. Here and 2 Cor 13:11, fut. indic. (*estai,* cf. 4:7 *will keep guard*) and so a promise of blessing. In the OT, God gives peace (Num 6:26; Ps 29:11; Isa 26:11; Judg 6:24 "the Lord is peace"); "God of peace" specifically only in T. Dan 5.2 ("be at peace, holding to the God of peace"). G. Delling 1975, "God of peace" arose out of OT-Jewish usage ("the Lord be with you," "peace be with you") as a prayer-wish; similarly Stuhlmacher 1970 ([1] Bibl. **peace**) whose links for Paul with "reconciliation" and the eschatological power of "peace" are questioned by G. Baumbach, "Das Verständnis von *eirēnē* im Neuen Testament," in *Theologische Versuche* 5 (Berlin: Evangelische Verlagshaus, 1975) 43–44. W. Foerster (TDNT 7:195), a reflection of 1 Cor 14:33, where "(God of) peace" contrasts with "disorder" (*akatastasia,* disobedience, revolt); then 4:9 would point toward "subjection to the unity of the community." Sometimes rendered freely, "God who gives peace" (Gdsp., GNB, CEV, cf. TC); *TLNT* 1:432, "who alone creates peace."

"(God of) peace" would not have sounded strange to Philippian ears. The Emperor Augustus was called "the guardian of peace" (*eirēnophylax*), who "transcends human nature in all the virtues"; he ended warfare and brought order out of disorder (Philo, *Legat.* 143–47). The Emperor's *Res Gestae* (13, 25, 26) said he pacified land and sea. Antony conferred the title "peace-maker," *eirēnopoios*, on Julius Caesar (Dio Cass. 44.49.2). Caesar "seems to provide great peace for us"; no wars, brigands, etc., even if he cannot bring peace from earthquakes or envy (Epictet. 3.13.9–10). Cf. *TLNT* 1:437–38 n 65. Paul may apply an epithet expected in Philippi for Caesar. For citizens "surrounded by acclamations of the *Pax Augusti,*" Paul's *euangelion* is "in contrast to the 'gospels' of the imperial ideology" (Tellbe 2001:203, italics removed).

with you (pl.). BDAG *meta* 2.a.γ.א, as at 2 Cor 13:11. Some take 9a as protasis with 9b its conclusion: "(if you) continue to do these things . . . , then *(kai)* the God of peace will be with you" (Schenk 270–71, 330; cf. NOTE on 6b, end). Cf. "Then" for 9b in NAB[RNT], Gdsp., [N]JB; TC, but without a conditional structure. See COMMENT B. 3 and 4 against a conditional construal.

COMMENT

A. FORMS, SOURCES, AND TRADITIONS

1. *Historical, Literary, and Rhetorical Factors in the Text-Segmentation of 4:1–9.*

a. Much is *Greco-Roman,* almost nothing OT/Jewish (*the book of life* 4:3c, *The Lord is near* 4:5b do not exactly repeat any one OT verse). Jesus-tradition lies behind 6a. 4:8 is a "virtues list," a form widespread in the Gk. world, perhaps (J. Quinn, *Titus,* AB 35:290–91) "a Roman Christian catechetical list" from Paul's "own missionary catechism (Phil 4:9)." Might it be a *Philippian* catechism (cf. their encomium at 2:6–11)? Then v 9 is an affirmation ("such things you indeed learned from me") but also a corrective ("*ponder* your list, *do* what the Christian tradition sets forth, which norms your virtues"). 4:6 may be a wish-prayer (Loh. 170; Wiles 1974:286–89). 4:7 and 9b reflect liturgical blessings (Wiles 202–3).

b. *Literary devices,* esp. in 4:8–9.[1] Cf. NOTES and Edart 277–82 (esp. assonance, alliteration); 4:3, enthymeme.[2] 4:2–3 may reflect "letters of mediation" (n 17 below; M. Müller 144). Some see cause and effect in 4:6 and 7 ("If you do not continue to be anxious but pray, then God's peace will keep you . . ."; Schenk 245–46, 249); and in 2–6, and 4:8–9 (Snyman 332) ". . . ponder these things . . . continue to do these things, and the God of peace will be with you" (Schenk 318, 330 on 4:9 Edart 287, "if . . . , then"). Thus (Synman) "logos" and "pathos" (*brothers and sisters, joy and crowning wreath*). Fee 401, 413 and Fitzgerald, ed., 1996:48–52, 157–60 note friendship themes in 4:8–9; Paul seeks to correct and elevate their views.

---

[1] Hawth. 185–86, echoed by Weima 192, mentions (ep)anaphora (repetition of *hosa* and *ei tis*); asyndeton; polysyndeton *(hosa)*; and homoioteleuton *(-ete)*; Watson 1988b:77 adds the "accumulation effected by *diallage*" [interchange], synonymy (Lausberg #674).

[2] Assumed premise: those who advance the gospel should be helped; minor premise: Euodia and Syntyche did so; conclusion: Euodia and Syntyche must be helped (Snyman 431).

c. *Text-segmentation*—Most divide 4:1 ("stand fast"); 4:2–3 (Euodia and Syntyche); 4:4–7 ("rejoice," patient steadfastness; not anxious; pray!); 4:8–9 (virtues to reckon with, things to do) (O'B). Vv 4, 5, and 6–7 can be treated separately (I. H. Marshall 107).

d. Segmentation is a problem for those who take *Phil as a unity.* Holmstrand 124 speaks of "diverse character"; Bockmuehl 237, "[c]ommentators differ widely over the argument." What Eadie said of Phil generally (p. xxxi), "[W]e can never know what suggested to the apostle the order of his topics," applies particularly to "the ethical miscellany" in 4:2–9 (239). Swift 249, who claimed "Philippians is one of the most systematically structured epistles in the New Testament," took 4:1 as conclusion to chs. 2–3; 4:2–9 is headed "Walk in unity and steadfastness" (though *peripateō* is used only at 3:17 and 18). Like most, Swift rejected "martyrdom" (Loh.) as a unifying theme (251 n 4). Similarly with "joy" (4:4). Or *koinōnia* (Aspen, "have the same mind in the Lord" [4:2] = *koinōnia* [1:5], pp. 265, 285; then the "schism" between the two women is "the specific concern of the letter," 289; cf. Pretorius 1995:280). Geoffrion 202–9, 4:1 (*inclusio* with 1:27) aims to strengthen self-identity, esp. through "pathos" terms of direct address; 4:2–23 is "an extended epilogue," 4:1–9 "not . . . recapping," but "further exhortation" (211 n 177).

e. Most defenders of a *unified Phil* refer simply to *"final exhortations" in 4:1–9.* Some see "culmination" of the entire letter (Garland 1985:171), re Euodia and Syntyche; Peterlin, "The Focus of Conflict"; Paul wrote 1:27–2:4 with "this quarrel in mind," Caird 149; Mengel 280; Dahl 1995:4; Black 1995:44; Kittredge 92; denied by O'B 474 and Witherington 104. Defenders of a single letter differ whether the unit is 3:2–4:1 (Mengel 260, 281; U. B. Müller 185–86) or 3:2–4:3 (Bockmuehl 257; Fee 385; Witherington 104); whether 4:2–23 is the concluding unit (U. B. Müller 192, cf. Silva 220) or 4:4–23 (Fee 399–400, a "genre" of concluding "staccato" paraenesis, as at 1 Thess 5:12–22 [Edart 286–87]; 1 Cor 16:13; 2 Cor 13:11; cf. n 22 below; 4:4–7 and 4:8–9 become "final" and "transitional" to the "final" and "first" concern of a unified letter, the thanks in 4:10–20, Fee 401–2). I. H. Marshall, no "clear structure and logic," any more than in Prov.; he links his five subunits in 4:1–9 with "the situation of the church" in Philippi (107), esp. historical reconstruction of what was going on with Euodia and Syntyche (see 2, below).

f. *Rhetorical analysis* provides no agreed solution on how 4:1–9 relate to the rest of the letter or its vv are to be divided. The most common designation is *peroratio.*[3]

---

[3] Cf. INTRO. VI.B n 2. Watson 1988b:76–77, *repetitio* (esp. of the proposition in 1:27–30) within the *peroratio* of 4:1–20. Reed 1993:321, Paul is not just recapitulating but advances new materials in 4:3, 5–9. Cf. O'B 474; Schoon-Janßen 126–29, 142–43; Snyman 328–29; Black 1995:48, 4:1–9, *peroratio*; Witherington 104; Bloomquist 137, 183–87. Pretorius 1998:4–5 notes the lack of agreement. Edart 282–88, 303–309, *peroratio* (like 3:17–21; really a second *peroratio*, but not redactoral), with *conquestio* (to win sympathy, Lausberg #439, 258, 1219; pathos, joy, imitation; 4:1, 4:7), a *recapitulatio*. Bittasi 139–51, 210, exhortation to communal unity, joy and peace, with virtues relativized in relation to Paul.

g. Endeavors at *concentric, chiastic analysis* likewise vary.[4]

h. For 4:1–9 in *separate letters,* based on contents, literary and rhetorical structure, see charts in Garland 1985:155; Bormann 1995:110, 115; Wick 30. Some theories about *two letters* put 4:1–9 in Letter A[5], others in polemical Letter B.[6] Gnilka (10, 219): 4:2–7 goes with the epistle from prison (1:1–3:1a + 4:10–23), but 3:1b–4:1 + 8–9 = the polemical letter; 4:8–9 are redactoral. Similarly P. Fiedler (*EDNT* 3:238), 4:8–9 are transition to Deutero-Pauline thought (Gnilka 223). J. Becker 1993 ([1] Bibl. **Paul**) 310 puts 4:8–9 with 3:2–21 in Letter B, 4:1–7 with Letter A.

i. *Three-letter theories* never associate 4:1–9 with Letter A (4:10–20). In one pattern (Schmithals 1957/1972) 4:4–7 goes with 1:1–3:1 (Letter B), 4:1–3 and 8–9 with polemical Letter C (3:2–21).[7] Others shift vv 8–9 to Letter B, with only 4:1–3 in Letter C.[8] Rahtjen assigned all of 4:1–9 to the polemical Letter C.[9]

j. We believe that *4:1–9 can be construed with Letter B.* The vv will be so treated in B.1–4 below; then, in B.5, in light of ch. 3 in the four-ch. letter.

k. Holloway 1998 argues 4:6–9 is a unity on grounds that 4:8–9a is a consolation using an "Epicurean technique of *avocatio-revocatio*"; vv 6–9 console re Paul's imprisonment and the Philippians' struggle.[10] Edart 308 n 24 questions these conjectures.

l. Elements of a *letter closing* appear in 4:1–9, though proponents of a unified Phil minimize them. Berger 1984a:141–42 lists the exhortation to joy (4:4), prayer

---

[4] Cf. Intro. VI.B n 3. 4:1–9 has been related to 1:3–11 (Aspen 230, 283–87), to 1:12–2:4 (Luter/Lee 92), to 1:27–30 (M. Müller 175–76), and 2:1–18 (Wick 106–23). C. W. Davis aligns 3:1–4:9 with 1:27–2:18, with 2:19–30 central (so also Bittasi, but 4:2–9 parallels 1:12–26).

[5] Michael xi–xii: 1:1–3:1a, 4:2–23; 3:1b–19 is an interpolation, though by Paul; Gunther 1972:86–88.

[6] Friedrich (NTD 126–28, 167) assigned 3:1b–4:9 to B; 1:1–3:1a, 4:10–23 = letter A, from prison; so also Suhl 149–61.

[7] Schenk 242–49, 269–73; Koester, *Intro.* 2:132–33 ("perhaps"; 1961–62 is less clear); Bornkamm 1962 (Intro. VII.B Bibl.) 4:4–7 (B) and 4:1–3, 8–9 (C); Marxsen, *Intro.* 62; Schenke-Fischer, *Einl.* 1:126; G. Barth 11; R. Pesch 92–93, 107–8; Byrne, *NJBC* #48:8–9.

[8] Vielhauer 1975:160, followed by Marxsen *Einl.* (4th ed. 1978:7); Fitzmyer, *JBC* #50.8. Collange (8, 12) put 4:2–7 in Letter B and 4:1, 8–9 in C; so also Ollrog 28 n 116; B. Mayer; Perkins 1991 *PT I*:89.

[9] Cf. Perrin-Duling, *Intro.* 2nd ed. 173–74, and Bornkamm (1962 [Intro. VII.B Bibl.], rev. in *Geschichte und Glauben* II [VII.B. Bibl.]:197). Beare took 4:2–9 with 1:1–3:1 + 4:21–23, the final of three letters (3:2–4:1 was regarded as an interpolated fragment, from earlier in Paul's career, 1959: 4–5, 24–26). So also Murphy-O'Connor in *Dictionnaire de la Bible, Supplement* 7 (1966) 1211–16; Peifer. *Other suggestions:* Müller-Bardorf 1957–58 (Intro. VI Bibl.) Letter B ran 1:27–2:1b, 4:1–3, 2:19–30 (3:1a), 4:4–7, 21–23; 4:8–9 go in C with 3:2–21. P. Benoit (*Les Épîtres de saint Paul aux Philippiens . . . Éphésiens* [Paris: Cerf, 3rd ed. 1959] 19), B = 1:1–2:18, 3:1–4:1 and 8–9; C included 2:19–30 and 4:2–7. Walter 1978 ([5] Bibl.) put 4: (4) 5–7 (8–9) in B, and 3:2–4:1 (2–3) in C. His 1998 commentary (20, 93, 95) locates 4:4–7 in B (4:4 and 3:1 are doublets), 4:1–3 with 3:2–21 in C; 4:8–9 could go with either B or C.

[10] The technique (see Cic., *Tusc.* 3.15.33) directs the mind away from what disturbs (*avocatione*), back to contemplation of pleasure (*revocatione*). So Epicurus, modified in Cicero's critique as a *revocatio* or calling back to the cardinal virtues (3.17.37). This technique, popular in the world of the day (Sen., *Ad Poly.* 5.8 and 12–13; Plut. *De tran. an.* 468F–69D), Paul is said to employ here: *bona cognitare,* think on good things. Paul himself modeled this (1:12–21; 1:30; 4:9a).

(v 6), effect on outsiders (5a), and promises (vv 7, 9b). See NOTES and COMMENT on 3:1 and 4:8 *Finally* and on the promises at 4:7 and 9b (Heckel [(17) Bibl.] 288–98, esp. 293, "Friedenswunsch"). M. Müller 139–43 would distinguish these two vv from 4:23, which is a benediction (and from 4:19 as "conductive divine comfort"), partly on the grounds that 4:7 and 9b are introduced by *kai*.[11] Weima 191–201, 4:8–9 is part of a letter closing (cf. also his review of Müller, *RBL* 1 [1999] 350).

2. Dramatis Personae: Euodia, Syntyche, and Others in 4:2–3. The cast of characters includes two women in Philippi,[12] Euodia and Syntyche, who *engaged in a struggle* for *the gospel cause*, together with Paul, *along with Clement and . . . other coworkers* of Paul. Someone who is addressed as *my faithful partner* (Gk. *gnēsie syzyge*) is asked to *assist them to think the same thing in the Lord*. See NOTES on the two women with Gk. names, the Lat. Clemens, all Gentiles, and why a tr., not a proper name "Syzygus," has been chosen for the helper Paul appoints.

Interpreters have speculated for centuries about these four persons, and what is wrong between Euodia and Syntyche. Reconstruction of the situation is needed before one can tr. *syllambanou* (v 3, "help, mediate between") or *gnēsie syzyge*. Is *faithful partner* to resolve a personal dispute, straighten out a congregational quarrel that threatens church unity, perhaps over supporting Paul's mission work, or nip in the bud a menacing heresy? Does *to auto phronein* in v 2 mean "live in harmony" (TC) or "stop arguing with each other" (CEV)? *think the same thing* as Paul, or as the other woman does ("agree with one another"), or as the rest of the Philippians think? We see *to (hyper Paulou) phronein* as a phrase of the Philippians ("concern for, solidarity with, Paul"; Schenk 65, a *topos* from Hellenistic political life), in the letter that accompanied their gift, a phrase Paul repeated in Letter A (4:10, see NOTE on *your concern for me*) and then in B at 1:7 (see NOTE on *to think*) and 2:2,5, and here. Some think Paul had 4:2–3 in mind when he wrote 1:27–2:4 (above, 1.e; Caird, etc.), others that he heard about the issue only after he dictated 1:27–2:4 and paused at 3:1. Mengel 279–80: if Paul had it in mind, why not mention it at 2:1–4? Fuller news came only later, 314–15. Agouridis 82ff., Paul pretends not to know as much as he does, so as not to seem to support one woman or her party over the other. The very use of names is unusual for Paul ("pastoral confrontation," Garland 1985:172; from "friendship," friends mentioned by name, enemies not, Fee 389–90, with P. Marshall 341–48). Paul's habit is to omit the names of opponents (Gal 2:12 "certain people"; 5:10; 6:12; 1 Cor 4:18; 5:1, etc.; Rom 16:17). He names individuals near the close of a letter (1 Cor 16:12, 15–18; lists of greetings, Rom 16).

a. For *Euodia and Syntyche* some (bad) guesses may be excluded. With

---

[11] *kai* could indicate an apodosis ("then"); cf. Weima 88–90, *kai* instead of adversative *de*, indicates "the closing section of the letter begins . . . with" material preceding the peace-wish or benediction; cf. 191.

[12] Women have long been given prominence in the Philippian church; Rhijn, W. D. Thomas, Adinolfi, Abrahamsen 1987, Agourides, Malinowski, Gillman 1990, Koperski 1992a, Pollard 1993, Trebilco, Luter 1996, Ascough 2003:134–38, Thurston 19–22.

F. M. Gillman (*ABD* 2:670–71): not male, not symbolic figures (Tübingen School, Hegelian analysis, for Jewish and Gentile Christianity) reconciled by the "unifier" (*syzygos*), Peter (Hainz 1972 [(2) Bibl. **sharing**] 217 n 1); not allegorical (Carls). Is Euodia (or Syntyche) to be equated with Lydia in Acts 16:14–15, 40? *hē Lydia* could mean "the woman from Lydia" (where Thyatira was located, Acts 16:15); her proper name in Phil 4:2. Usually denied (Michael 188; Bruce 115; O'B 478; Fee 390 n 28; Bockmuehl 17, 239; U. B. Müller 192), but still defended (Hawth. 179; cf. Pilhofer 1:234–40, the woman in Acts 16 is historical, had a house in Philippi, but not a citizen or of the nobility; de Vos 256–58: a freed slave [*libertata*], dealing not in *murex* or marine purple but "garments dyed with the madder root, the so-called 'Turkey Red'"; Sterck-Degueldre 137–38). Meeks 1983:57, they are among "merchant groups who were metics in Philippi." Walter 1998:91 speculated Syntyche was a slave to Lydian Euodia; both convert to Christianity and are "sisters in Christ." Syntyche protests, "How in the church can you give me commands?" A spat ensues. Much too speculative.

b. *Role(s) of Syntyche and Euodia in the Philippian Church*. Malinowski, courageous during the founding mission[13] but not "ministers"; contrast F. M. Gillman, *ABD* 2:671. Unlikely they were a pair of independent missionaries (D'Angelo 76; cf. Osiek "Phil." 1994 2:246–47; Kittredge 107–8), let alone lovers (cf. D'Angelo). Not in dispute with Paul (but with each other), else he would not appeal to them individually (Bockmuehl 239). Authority for women in Paul's churches fitted some Greco-Roman cultural norms (see n 15 below). The *ecclēsiai* stamped their leaders with countercultural equality (Gal 3:28; Cotter 1994). Yet Christian women must have felt tensions with their families, former religions, and among themselves, (Gillman 1990).

c. *Specific duties or office* depend on how socioeconomic status and church organization are reconstructed (cf. [6] COMMENT B.3, *Social Setting*; Reumann 1993a and 1993b [(1) Bibl. **overseer**] on method). If women of substance, heads of households (Lydia; cf. Peterlin 124–25), each was a patron with clients (cf. Bormann 1995:187–217, Paul desired "emancipated clients," worked out in 4:10–20; *syzyge* may reflect their status, 216), each a leader in a household *ekklēsia*, perhaps preaching, leading worship, overseeing finances and house-assembly policies, providing validity with the authorities (Hawth. 179; Meeks 1983:57; Reumann 1993b:86–90). Bockmuehl 238 adds "administration, hospitality, or oversight." In terms of 1:1, they could have been *diakonoi* (Portefaix 138 n 13; Peterlin 106–18, 123) or *episkopoi* (see [1] Bibl. **overseers,** Lemaire 1971:102–3; Witherington 108; *not* monepiscopacy, Hainz 1972:218; I. H. Marshall 108; Sterck-Degueldre 241–42 n 150; contrast de Vos 255 n 80). If two house church leaders, division between Euodia and Syntyche and their claques was a serious matter.[14] The two

---

[13] Further mission labors seem involved, Pfitzner 161; cf. U. B. Müller 191. *coworkers, in the gospel cause* (4:3) includes subsequent "progress of the gospel," in and around Philippi (1:5, 12, 25; see NOTES there; for Loh. an ongoing *agōn*; Witherington 106; Dickson 141–43).

[14] On house churches in Philippi and surrounding territory, see (1) COMMENT B.5.a; L. M. White, "Paul and Pater Familias," in Sampley, ed. 2003, 457–87, esp. 466–68.

women may have had major voices in any "co-ordinating committee" (Chapple 1984:558–59) for the house churches of Philippi. That earlier leaders were now jailed or martyred, and Euodia and Syntyche were "emergency" replacements (Loh. 167) is unlikely (Hainz 1972:216 n 3).

Traditionalist, masculine readings have often obscured 4:2–3. For a century or so, there has been appreciation of a relatively greater freedom that women in Macedonia possessed[15] and more recently of the impact from the Pauline baptismal formula with its equality for female and male (Gal 3:28; Martyn, *Gal.* AB 33A:374–83). That Syntyche and Euodia went to court before Roman judges depends on applying 1 Cor 6:1–8 here (B. W. Winter 1994; Peterlin 127–28); *gnēsios syzygos* in 4:3 could then be a Christian arbiter, in place of the pagan judge.

d. Euodia and Syntyche may have provided *support for Paul in his mission work*. Several times the Philippians sent him aid (4:15–16; [16] COMMENT B.1). In (1) Fleury's reconstruction of a legal, business partnership with Paul, Lydia is the *syzygos* whom Paul now asks to reconcile Euodia and Syntyche. (2) In Sampley's "consensual *societas*" (= *koinōnia*, 1:5; [2] COMMENT B.2) the Philippians supported him as "their apostle." When Paul was imprisoned, people felt he had let them down at his end of the bargain. Therefore a "rift" and "breach" (Capper). Richter Reimer 128 refers to Abrahamsen's contrast (1987:17–20) of the obedient (but fictional) Lydia with Euodia and Syntyche as missionary rivals to Paul. L. M. White broadened the notion of a "contractual society" into (3) aspects of *philia*, including benefaction and patronage: Euodia and Syntyche had a falling out over whether to continue to support Paul (1990:214 n. 59). Cf. Bormann 1995:206–24. Peterlin 124–25, these "ladies of rank" long contributed to support for Paul, though Epaphroditus was chiefly responsible for the gift of which 4:10–20 speaks; conflict between the two women was serious for the unity of the Philippian church, in part because of the possibility of litigation in civic courts (174–75; Capper 194–96). In such ways financial involvement of Euodia and Syntyche in the Pauline mission has been interpreted.

e. *Clement*, sometimes regarded as dead when Paul writes (because of 4:3c *the*

---

[15] Lft. 55–57 (based on inscriptions and Acts 16) claimed women in Macedonia had a higher social position "than in most parts of the civilised world." B. Witherington, *Women in the Earliest Churches*, SNTSMS 59 (Cambridge: Cambridge Univ. Press, 1988) 107–8 and *ABD* 6:957–61 (bibl.), "in terms of personal, property, and educational rights the women of . . . Macedonia faired better than the women of Greece or Judea, but in terms of political rights Roman women were at a disadvantage when compared to . . . Macedonian women. . . . In terms of roles and status in religious settings, women in . . . Macedonia had more possibilities than Greek or Roman women in general" (6:958). Cf. F. M. Gillman 1990. I. H. Marshall 110–11, "the more liberal attitude of the Macedonians" might have prevailed in the early church but for "Jewish influence." L. M. White 1995:257 n 70 cautions: Lightfoot's claim needs "critical discussion"; Portefaix "blurs the literary setting with the real sociographic situation at Philippi"; all the "evidence collected by Abrahamsen," "demonstrating the popularity" [of the Diana cult] for women, "or even egalitarian tendencies in funerary cult, is not the same as claiming an overall social prominence of women in other arenas of social life." How "Macedonian" was the Roman *colōnia* in Paul's day? Cf. further K. Traede, "Frau," *RAC* 8 (1972) 197–269, esp. 227, 230; G. Schrot, *KlPauly* 2 (1967) 608–10; *DNP* 4 (1996), B. Wagner-Hasel 634 and R. Albrecht 630–40.

book of life; Beare 145; K. Barth 119) or no longer in Philippi (Hainz 1972:219), likely was alive and significant. Other *coworkers* may go unnamed to avoid any resentment (in case Paul failed to mention every name, Hainz 1972:219). On other Clements, see Lft. 168–71.

3. What Was at Issue Between Euodia and Syntyche? (a) A *spat between women*; "they're like that." A male-chauvinist view. (b) A petty *personal difference* (Bock-muehl 239, Peterlin's attempts to find disunity are "overkill"). Tension between two friends (Dahl 1995:14); cf. 2:1–4 (Dahl 9–10). (c) From 2:3–4, *self-interest*, not considering the other (woman) to surpass you (one has more status), even "vainglory" (Hainz 1972:218–19). Their split threatens the entire Christian community. 4:2–3 brings into the open the concern Paul had during all (four) chs. (Garland 1985:172; B. W. Winter 1994:99–101; Black 1995:16–17, 30–31, 44–45; Peterlin 12–15, 102–3). P. Oakes, in the *agōn* "some who suffered little, due to greater wealth and status, were failing to help financially those who were poorer and of lower status" (2001:220; *eritheia* 2:3 = concern for one's own social advantage; *kenodoxia* = pride in one's high [social] position). (d) Euodia and Syntyche differed over *some aspect of their diaconal ministry* (Gnilka 166), perhaps *financial support for Paul* as missionary (which one?; L. M. White 1990:214 n 59; Fee 389 n 26; contrast Bockmuehl 239–40). (e) *Doctrinal reasons* (ch. 3). (1) One or both may have opened her house to *alien teachers* (gnostics, Schmithals 1957:338 = 1972:114; Schenk 272, 2:6–11 possibly arose out of such a syncretistic circle; 304, they accepted the teachings of Jewish agitators); cf. (13) COMMENT on 3:14 and n 17. Dismissed by most (Gnilka 166: a trace of the old Tübingen school). (2) The women moved toward *Judaism* (Lydia's former faith), to escape suffering (cf. Fee 289, 306; Tellbe 1994, Judaism as a *religio licita*).

(f) The dispute involved *attitudes toward Roman authorities*. The *agōn* in 1:30 (Paul in prison, the same struggle as the Philippians face with the Imperial system) is hinted at in 4:3 *engaged in a struggle*, during the founding mission (1 Thess 2:2; cf. Acts 16:19–40) and subsequently. 4:1, *stand steadfast (stēkete)*, repeats 1:27, on confrontation with Roman officials in Philippi. 4:1, 2, 4, "in the Lord (Jesus Christ)," uses a title that contrasts with Caesar as Lord in Imperial cult (see NOTE on 2:11). At 4:5 *ho kyrios engus* could oppose the overshadowing presence of Caesar Kyrios. Followers of the Lord Jesus had ample occasion to debate how to respond to Kyrios Caesar, in their varied socioeconomic backgrounds— citizen, retired soldier, metic, slave (oppressed or of "the family of Caesar"). See B. 1, below.

4. The Man Asked to Aid Euodia and Syntyche in 4:3. He remains unidentified after centuries of speculation (B. Weiss 299–300). The adj. *faithful* is masc. (*gnēsie*, not *gnēsia*); no evidence Paul was married at this time (at best, a widower; 1 Cor 7:8; cf. Fee, *1 Cor.* 288 n 7), so eliminate *Paul's wife* as a guess ("yoked in marriage"; Lydia, in Clem. Al, Origen, Erasmus, Renan, among others). *Syzygus* would be an otherwise unknown Philippian Christian, but the name has not turned up from antiquity. We may forget *Peter* (Tübingen School, 3.e, above);

Christ (who helps all to bear their yoke, Matt 11:29; K. G. Wiesler, *Chronologie* [Göttingen: Vandenhoeck & Ruprecht, 1848); the *husband* or *brother* of one of the women (patriarchy! Chrysost., Zwingli; cf. Ewald 216–17; the spouse of a contestant is scarcely the ideal mediator); or the chief *bishop* among the *episkopoi* at Philippi (Luther, Ellicott 99). To conjecture *a name in a lost letter* (Schmithals 1957:306 = 1972:76–77 n 47) multiplies entities without telling us who is meant. The "the *entire Philippian church*" (Houlden 110; Hawth. 180; Motyer 202; Silva 222; contrast Fee 393 n 46) or "*any individual* in the church who hears the letter being read" (I. H. Marshall 109) provides no specific mediator(s) ("everybody's business is nobody's business"). Paul does bring the entire community into the picture, but not as *syzygos*. The Philippians knew who the *faithful partner* was (Gnilka 167; G. Barth 71); we do not (Ascough 2003:126–27).

Proposals include *Epaphroditus* (who took Letter B to Philippi, see on 2:25–30); *Timothy* (who was to follow him soon afterward to Philippi, 2:23); *Silas* (Acts 16:19, 25, 29; 17:1, Paul's associate in the founding mission, last mentioned in Acts at 18:5; no evidence he was with Paul in Ephesus, unmentioned in Phil); and *Luke* (assuming a connection with Philippi and his authorship of the "we" sections in Acts; cf. Phlm 23).[16] *Barnabas* (Eadie 243; Michael 190) is unlikely (he and Paul had split up, Acts 15:38–40; Gal 2:13). Possibly a member of Paul's mission team (Thdrt., Pelagius), or someone among his beloved Philippians (Ollrog 182–83).

Epaphroditus we think most likely. Sometimes excluded because he was with Paul as he dictated the letter and it would be awkward for Epaphroditus as messenger to read these words publicly in Philippi (Fee 394 n 46). Or unlikely, given the feeling (noted on 2:25–30) he had failed in his mission and was returning home under a cloud. Yet Paul dealt very graciously with him in 2:25–30. *faithful partner* might be a further, daring commendation, identifying with, and reestablishing, him at home. If Euodia and Syntyche were split over continuing support for Paul, Epaphroditus could "help them" with personal observations on how the work was advancing in Ephesus. If they differed on relations with the Roman authorities, Epaphroditus was in an almost unique position to explain why Paul had invoked his Roman citizenship during legal proceedings.

Address of an unnamed person as *gnēsie syzyge* fits with letters of friendship. M. Müller 144 cites Ps.-Dem. *Typoi epistolikoi* No. 1 and 32/33; a *topos*, not a full "letter of recommendation" or of "mediation."[17] 4:2–3 includes other "friendship

---

[16] For *Luke*, see Ramsay 1896:358; T. W. Manson 1939 (INTRO. VII.A Bibl) 199; Hájek; Fee 394; Bockmuehl 13, 241. For *Silas* (Silvanus), Jeremias 1959 ([9] COMMENT B.2.a) 137; Bengel, Wesley; Delling, *TDNT* 7:749–50. For *Timothy*, Schmithals 1957:306 = 1972:76–77 n 47; Collange 143; Friedrich, *NTD* 16th ed. 168; Schenke-Fischer *Einl.* 128; Schenk 272. For *Epaphroditus*, Marius Victorinus; Grotius, and others, in B. Weiss 299; Lft. 158; cf. Jones 65; Witherington 106–7; Thurston 141.

[17] On "letters of mediation," see Stowers 1986:153–65, 178, subdivided into (a) "letters of introduction" or "recommendation" (later, the *parathetikē* or "entrusting" letter, Ps.-Lib. 8, also called "introductory," Malherbe 1977:65 = 1988:69), reflected in 2:25–30 (about Epaphroditus); and (b) the "intercessory" letter; cf. C.-H. Kim 1972 ([1] Bibl.) on Phil 2:29–30 and 4:2–3 as commendation (121, 122, 128–29); the "formula" includes (a) introduction ("I am asking you, my faithful partner");

language."[18] "The recommended person is often the carrier of the letter" (Stowers 1986:153; Demetrius' and Libanius' model letters[19]). Epaphroditus may or may not have read Paul's letter in each house church, but he was present to add comments and carry out the requested task with Euodia and Syntyche, ahead of Timothy and Paul. Paul entrusts him with the assignment as a fresh chance in "the work of Christ" (2:30), appropriate for a leader in the congregation, *episkopos* or *diakonos* (1:1; B. Mayer 62), yet with a certain independence and maturity as *coworker* (Ollrog 182). He is invested by Paul with new life through the epithet *faithful partner*. The gospel works with individuals in community through trust and new opportunities.

B. MEANING AND INTERPRETATION

Following the travel plans in 2:19–30 for Epaphroditus, Timothy, and Paul, about coming to Philippi, Letter B moved toward concluding paraenesis with 3:1, *Finally*; the impv. *rejoice* (or "fare well"), and assertion *that to write the same things* (about joy and exercising citizenship as Christians in Philippi, 1:27) provides *steadfastness* for believers. Now in 4:1–9, all of which can be construed with Letter B (COMMENT A.1.h–j), Paul reiterates and expands his exhortations and admonitions, quite specifically about individual Philippians in vv 2–3. 4:7 and 8–9 indicate that the letter is drawing to a close (above, A.1.l). For a possible chiastic structure in Letter B, see (5) COMMENT A.1. Links to earlier themes in Letter B appear in 4:1–9 as part of the paraenesis:

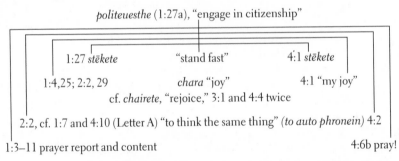

politeuesthe (1:27a), "engage in citizenship"

1:27 *stēkete*	"stand fast"	4:1 *stēkete*
1:4,25; 2:2, 29	*chara* "joy"	4:1 "my joy"
	cf. *chairete*, "rejoice," 3:1 and 4:4 twice	

2:2, cf. 1:7 and 4:10 (Letter A) "to think the same thing" *(to auto phronein)* 4:2

1:3–11 prayer report and content   4:6b pray!

Links with 3:2–21 will be treated under 5, below, on the redacted, four-ch. letter.

(c) desired action ("assist them"), and (b) credentials ("these women . . . engaged in a struggle . . . , their names are written in the book of life"; cf. [9] COMMENT A.1.b). Stowers 156, 4:2–3 asks "the community to support the two women"; his examples include the name of the person recommended or for whom a third party is being asked to perform a favor. On letters of petition, see NOTE on 4:2 *exhort*.

[18] *to auto phronein, synēthlēsan*, the use of "yoke" in connection with "genuine friend," *Il.* 13.701–11, cited in the NOTE on 3a *my faithful partner*; Fitzgerald, ed., 1996:88, 128, 150–51; 155–56, Paul's "incredible frankness" in his appeal; 158, "genuineness" is a mark of friendship.

[19] Ps.-Dem. *Typoi epistolikoi* 2, "So-and-so, who is conveying this letter to you, has been tested by us and is loved on account of his trustworthiness . . . . Indeed, you, too, will praise him to others when you see how useful he can be" (Malherbe tr. 1977:31 = 1988:33).

1. Stand Steadfast! (4:1). The verse reflects 1:27c (Holmstrand 122), *Exercise your citizenship in a manner worthy of the gospel of Christ* (1:27a). Continue this stance! *And so* marks a new beginning but draws consequences from what was said in 1:27–2:30 and 3:1, including 2:6–11 (esp. 2:2 "one mind" and 2:5, Holmstrand 122). *in the Lord* indicates where and under whom this stance is to be carried through: in the community of the Lord Jesus Christ.[20]

Several terms of address exhibit affection—*my brothers and sisters, beloved and longed for, my joy and crowning wreath, . . . O beloved*—some possibly added when the warnings of 3:2–21 were inserted, but no voc. can be shown to be redactoral. *adelphoi mou* is common address, 3:1a and elsewhere in Phil. That they are Paul's *joy*, now and at the last judgment, continues use of *chara* in the letter. *my . . . crowning wreath* is new, vivid language familiar in Philippi for honors granted those who serve society well. The Christian community there will be Exhibit No. 1 for Paul at God's judgment, as to the fruitfulness of his mission work (2:16). The epithets seek the goodwill of the Philippians (Geoffrion 204), as he turns to a delicate matter about two leading Philippian Christians in vv 2–3. Christian identity is underscored: God's *beloved* (OT election concept, plus the bonding of Gk. friendship concepts); on *brothers and sisters* see NOTE. Phil 4:1, "a fairly self-contained entity" (Holmstrand 123), is "strategically placed recapitulation . . . of Paul's argument going back to the political/military theme . . . in 1:27" (Geoffrion 202). It is not about the parousia (3:20–21) but the relation of Paul and the Philippians (Radl 1981:81).

2. Help for Euodia and Syntyche in the Philippian Community (4:2–3). Paul names two women in Philippi who need *to think the same thing.* The point has been addressed to all Philippian Christians at 2:2b; cf. also 2:2d, "thinking one thing," i.e., unity. The vb. is a leitmotif, in Letter A (a Philippian slogan about concern for "their apostle" Paul, 4:10); in B (1:7, how Paul thinks or is concerned about them; 2:5, how they are to "think . . . among themselves," the way they "also think 'in Christ Jesus'"). At 4:2 an ecclesial locus is indicated by *in the Lord*, for Christ's sphere of dominion. Use of actual names, as often toward the end of a letter, has been discussed in COMMENT A.2. Interpretation and even trs. reflect a reconstructed situation in Philippi about which we cannot be certain (A.2, above) and views on women in the church and leadership. If tradition sometimes denigrated women (*Euodia* and *Syntyche* taken to be men), some recent treatments go beyond the evidence and sound conjecture.

The two have good Gk. names. He addresses them equally, with frankness (Sampley ed. 2003:311–12), *Euodia I exhort . . . Syntyche I exhort,* in alphabetical order. To tr. *parakalō* "I beg" or "plead" sounds more desperate than "entreat." There is probably some note of authority in *I exhort,* compared with 3a to the mediator he selected, *I am asking you. . . .* But one cannot conclude thereby that Euodia and Syntyche were socially inferior or ecclesially subordinate to the man

---

[20] 2:13 spoke of God "at work in and among you," the encomium of both God and Christ, but as usual *kyrios* = Jesus, as at 2:11, 19, 21, 24, 29; and 3:1, "the Lord" Jesus Christ.

in 3a, or that one woman was slave to the other. Neither Euodia nor Syntyche can be identified with Lydia in Acts 16 with certainty (see A.2.a), though "Lydia" may suggest a social-economic level for Euodia and Syntyche (L. M. White 1995: 244–46, 257–61).

Paul first praises them: *in the gospel cause,* they *engaged in a struggle (synēthlēsan), together with me.* This vb. also occurred at 1:28, *those who stand steadfast in one and the same Spirit, engage together in the struggle (synathlountes) for the gospel faith.* . . . Athletic and military language, but also for the philosopher's struggle toward virtue and for the common endeavor of friends. Here, struggle to establish the Christian faith in Philippi when the Pauline mission first arrived (Acts 16:12–40), an *agōn* with insulting treatment and suffering from the outset (1 Thess 2:2). The struggle continued, an *agōn* with the Roman authorities (Phil 1:30) in which Paul and the Philippian Christians engage even as he writes.

The two women may have opened their homes to Paul's missionary team (cf. Lydia in Acts 16) and provided legal cover as benefactors and patrons, even speaking up publicly in defense of the gospel. They likely provided financial support, along with other Philippians, for Paul's further work. The picture at Phil 1:3–6, 12, 25 of Philippian involvement in the advance of the gospel suggests a role in evangelization, perhaps using the Philippians' encomium now found at 2:6–11; cf. COMMENT A.2.b. Malinowski argues *synēthlēsan* at 4:3 ("RSV "labored with me," not *kopiaō,* "toil [in mission]") does not prove Euodia and Syntyche preached or presided at worship, but cf. *euangelion* (as an action term) and pairing the women with *Clement* (see NOTE and COMMENT A.2.e) and *other coworkers* (*synergos,* 2:25 of Epaphroditus), whose *names are written in the book of life.* This is Paul's further tribute to them. Whatever OT overtones there were in Paul's mind—perhaps eschatological, a book for judgment day—people in Philippi would have been reminded of civic registers for citizens of the *polis, tribus Voltinia,* and perhaps for resident aliens, lists by the authorities of each legally classified group, part of life in a Roman *colōnia.* Could there have been a list for subversives, enemies of the state? Euodia and Syntyche had their names in God's book *of life* in Christ eternally (cf. 1:20–21).

Euodia and Syntyche were influential among the house assemblies of Philippian believers, leaders of some sort; see COMMENT A.2.c; 1:1, "deaconesses" (Portefaix, Peterlin) or "overseers" of a house church in Philippi (Reumann 1998 [(1) Bibl. **overseer**] 107). No guarantee they personally led prayers, Scripture reading, preaching, teaching, or the Lord's Supper; we do not know who presided at the meal in Corinth, Philippi, or elsewhere in this period. Roles in finance, hospitality, and coordination of the house churches made it important that they "think alike."

Why Paul writes as he does has led to much speculation. See COMMENT A.3. Likely Paul was aware of the matter as he wrote 1:27–2:5, though we need not make "the Euodia-Syntyche affair" *the* issue toward which the entire letter is leading; see COMMENT A.1.e. Engberg-Pedersen 2000: 312–13 n 3 judges such views "overbold and one-sided," incautious mirror-reading. 2:2–4 may be our best guide to what was wrong. Why not immediately after 2:1–4 take up the case of the two women? Because he wanted to use the Philippians' encomium (2:6–11) as a corrective to general failings, typically Gk., of self-interest, glory-seeking, and claims to surpass others. He thus lays a foundation for 2:12–18 and 4:2–9, advice for individuals near the close of a letter (Gnilka 165).

In light of 1:27–2:5, the nub of the problem was status on the part of Euodia and/or Syntyche; they seek their own interests in contrast to those of others; social (economic, political) advantage, pride. See COMMENT A.3.c. Possibly (P. Oakes 2001) one or both failed to help poorer believers, of lower status, in their own household(s) or some other house church. Rivalry among the upwardly mobile was common. Differing opinions over how to relate to Roman authority (A.3.f) go with different types of house churches, some more attuned to allegiance to Caesar, obedience to customs, conformity to society. Whether Paul should have invoked his Roman citizenship while jailed in Ephesus, and attitude toward the Caesar cult in Philippi, could have been involved. Strong evidence for the case developed in A.3.f, above, is 1:28, on *adversaries* who *intimidate*, in the *agōn* over the gospel (local Roman authorities in the *colōnia*).

Paul's *faithful partner* who will *assist* Euodia and Syntyche (see COMMENT A.4 above and the NOTE on *gnēsie syzyge*) is some partner in mission, comrade, or brother in Christ. If a Philippian named Syzygus, we know only his unique name. Of all the guesses, Epaphroditus is most likely (Lft. 158; older commentators in Meyer 101, including J. C. K. von Hofmann, who regarded Epaphroditus as the scribe as well as bearer of the letter). The suggestion takes on new interest when Paul's generous treatment in 2:25–30 of this somewhat discredited Philippian is recalled. No one else would be in as good a position to present in Philippi Paul's stance re the Roman authorities (yes and no) and to expand on the Apostle's reaction (yes and no) to the Philippians' encomium, which he has used to correct some aspects of their common life; see COMMENT B on 2:1–4 and 2:12–18. Paul recommended Timothy for work in Corinth (1 Cor 16:10–11). He commends Epaphroditus at 2:25–30 and here.

Euodia and Syntyche are *to think the same thing* as Paul (Marchal 148–49), what he set forth in 1:27–2:5; as one another, to the extent they differ over mission support, attitude toward the authorities, or some other issue; and as the rest of the Philippians, if that is at issue. To this end the *faithful partner* (Epaphroditus) is to *assist them*. Perhaps (cf. the prefix in *syn-lambanein* and the pres. tense) the women had tried to work things out together by themselves; more likely the vb. implies "work *with* them."[21] What help they need, is not stated. "Help in their common work" has been suggested (Watts, who saw no quarrel; contrast Beet), but that overlooks *to auto phronein*. Reconciling views, if not persons, seems involved. To this end the matter is raised in a letter to be read aloud, in public, in all the house churches. To this end *Clement* and *other coworkers* are brought into the picture, though it is too much to say that Paul is asking the entire congregation to undertake the task. Paul brings others to the task of helping.

---

[21] Did Paul know the procedures reported at Matt 18:15–17 for dealing with some fault in the community, first *adelphos* to *adelphos*, then a committee, then the local *ekklēsia*?

3. Rejoice and Pray! Ethical Living and Eschatology, and Peace (4:4–7). Seven sentences, from two to twenty Gk. words long, one after another, no connecting word except *alla* (6b) and *kai* (7). These miscellaneous exhortations—mostly ideas previously expressed in Phil (*rejoice* v 4), even *epieikes* in 5a, if "patient steadfastness"—is scarcely a genre.[22] Some seek thematic unity: "joy," vv 4–7 (Moffatt 1897–98); martyrdom (Loh. 167–72); "the peace of God" and "the God of peace," 4:4–9 (Motyer 205–13); peace + joy, 4:4–9 (Melick 148); "threefold expression of Jewish piety—rejoicing in the Lord, prayer, and thanksgiving" (Fee 402–3). None of these does justice to the range of Paul's words in 4:4–7, aphoristic dicta but linked at points. The thoughts may relate to 4:2–3 (Euodia and Syntyche) and Letter B generally.

a. V 4, *Rejoice*, twice repeated, seems unconnected with 4:2–3 (new paragraph in many trs.) but echoes 3:1 (+ *my joy* in 4:1). 3:1 and 4:4 enclose in Letter B what has been said about standing firm in 4:1 and Euodia and Syntyche in 4:2–3. 4:3 begins "rejoice *in the Lord*" (like 3:1) for the sphere of joy (Webber [(2) Bibl. **joy**] 355–56); *pantote . . . chairete* can mean "rejoice *always*" (Bengel). But most explain the repetition as a point that needs reiteration, what with Paul in prison, struggle and possible conflict in Philippi; or a reflection of Paul's infectious hilarity in Christ. J. R. Harris saw a parallel in Aeschylus' *Eumenides*.[23] Harris suggested Paul, having read or seen this "religious appeal for concord and unity among Athenian citizens," reflected its repeated use of *chairete* for his Philippian hearers.[24] Phil 4:4 may therefore echo *Eum.* 1014, and 3:1 line 997, perhaps a commonplace. "Fare well" is an apt wish for Paul to his faithful partner, so that Euodia and Syntyche and the entire community get along well. Thus is reopened a possible double meaning for *chairete*, though *chara* 4:1 suggests "joy, rejoice" as primary sense.

b. In the third short sentence (5a), *Let your patient steadfastness be known to all sorts of people*, to *epieikes* is difficult to tr. Its considerable Gk. background includes "what is fitting," "magnaminity," in Aristot. "reasonableness." One interpretation (see NOTE) stresses the clemency of a ruler like Caesar. Another, use for the righteous sufferer in Wis 2:19. Christians in Philippi would have known about

---

[22] So Fee 400: like 1 Thess 5:16–22, where Paul had strung together at least eight such terse cls., which begin "rejoice, pray, give thanks." Fee counts all of 5:12–22. 5:23, a wish-prayer about believers being kept completely till the parousia, somewhat parallels Phil 4:7. Fee's other examples (1 Cor 16:13; 2 Cor 13:11) are much briefer. Do two or so examples make a genre? Cf. A.1.e, above.

[23] This final drama in the trilogy about Orestes (produced 458 B.C.) concludes with a reconciliation scene between the Athenian people and the Eumenides or "gracious ones" (really Erinyes or "furies," who represent retribution and vendetta). Athena leads the Erinyes, now guardians for her city, in procession to a place assigned them under the Areopagus. The chorus sings (lines 997–98), *chairete, chairet' en aisimiaisi ploutou/ chairet' astikos leōs . . .* "Farewell"—or it is "May you fare well"? as in LCL, tr. H. W. Smyth—"in duly divided wealth, fare well people of this city." Athena begins her speech *"chairete"*; in line 1014 the chorus responds, *"chairete, chairete, d'authis, epei diploizō . . . ,"* "Fare well, and again fare well, I say it twice. . . ." Verrall's tr., cited by Harris. Lft. noted the passage (160).

[24] Philo tells how he saw an audience carried away at a performance of a play by Euripides; *Prob.* 141–44 = LCL *Philo* 9:90–93.

the alleged benevolence of their rulers, and from experience the need for forbearance, patient enduring of insults and persecution, and a steadfastness amid humiliations by the world. A balance or amiability was called for, not insisting on rights but pressing on in the face of opposition. Exemplified in Paul's treatment of Epaphroditus (2:25–30; K. Barth 121). Schenk 244, the first of several consequences from rejoicing.

The Christians' *epieikes* is to be made *known to all sorts of people;* that means turning toward others. Bockmuehl 244, "how *other people* are to experience the Christian's joy in the Lord" (Bengel, rejoicing in the Lord produces true equity or justice toward the neighbor and a legitimate "freedom" or even "carelessness" about one's own affairs). Such *epieikes* is to be made obvious to all, Christians and non-Christians. Schenk 244, friendship with a missionary aspect, as in 2:15–16 ("shine as luminaries"). Cf Rom 12:17 (U. B. Müller 194), ". . . what is noble in the sight of all." Dual citizenship in church and civic community (1:27) continues to play out in Paul's letter.

c. The shortest statement is 5b, *The Lord* (Jesus) (is) *near.* With 5a or 6a or both (references in the NOTE), it undergirds ethics with eschatology: because the Lord is near, exhibit patient steadfastness, stop being anxious about everything. The parousia sense (Merk 1968:195–96; Collange 144; Gnilka 169) fits Paul's eschatology and references in Phil to "the Day of Christ" (cf. 1:6, 10; 2:16; so, among many, Grabner-Haider 66–67, 86–87). The fut. coming of the Lord, to judge and vindicate, stands over all communal life, as well as over the cult of Caesar who also claims lordship (cf. COMMENT A.3.f). But this corporate sense does not remove responsibility on the part of each individual, as Paul's discussion of his own life and death (1:18d–26) and enjoinder to his *faithful partner* (4:3) make clear.

The second, less likely interpretation of the Lord's nearness as "presence," in part reflecting C. H. Dodd's "realized eschatology," invokes Ps 145:18 ("near to all who call upon him") or the nearness Paul experienced from fellowship *en Christō[i]* (4:7) and joy *en kyriō[i]* (4:4) (Michaelis 67). Baumgarten (see NOTE) sees early Christian apocalyptic material received through "the Hellenists" at Antioch (pp. 43–53), which Paul "demythologizes" and "de-apocalypticizes" to present Christology or ecclesiology.[25] 4:5 is an eschatological warrant for conduct. Fee 407–8, after examining "intertextuality" with Ps 145:18, concludes for an eschatological sense; it reminds "a suffering congregation . . . of their sure future, despite present difficulties," esp. "their suffering at the hands of those who proclaim Caesar as Lord."

d. *Do not continue to be anxious about anything* (6a) is brief and in Gk.alliterative, *mēden merimnate.* A saying by Jesus in Q (Matt 6:35 par Luke 12:22), "Do not worry (*mē merimnate*) about (your) life," may be reflected (yes, Fee 408; "an

---

[25] Paul moves from the "*Mare-Kyrios*" category (*Maranatha*) to "statements about practical conduct" (Kramer [(1) Bibl. **Christ**] #47; e.g., 1 Thess 3:12–13). But the three words in 4:5b lack the content of Kramer's examples about conduct. Radl 1981:97, anticipatory joy prior to the Lord's coming. Edart 304–9 sees Stoic thought: using language familiar in Philippi, Paul exhorts to peace now; his emphasis on faith in God and union with Christ excludes possible confusion with Stoic ideas.

echo," O'B 491; no, Loh. 169, who saw Matt 10:19 behind 6a, when they hand you over for trial, "do not worry [mē merimnēsēte]"—Loh.'s martyrology interpretation). Schenk 231 saw the Jesus-logion in developed form at 1 Cor 7:32, 34 (see NOTE on 2:20 *who will genuinely care for you*). The vb. is at home in Paul; cf. 1 Cor 12:25, members have "the same care for one another" *(to auto hyper allēlōn merimnōsin)*; Phil 2:20, Timothy = one "who will genuinely care about what affects you." 4:6 suggests a negative side, undue concern, anxiety—worry about "hostility from the Philippians' neighbors and . . . persecution," O'B 491. Good advice re the opponents of 1:28–29 and Euodia and Syntyche.

e. Directly coupled to 6a is 6b, *instead (alla), in each instance, let your requests be constantly made known toward God by prayer and entreaty, with thanksgiving.* See NOTE on the parallelism of vb. form with 5a, *Let your patient steadfastness be made known,* repeated action in each, and the unusual turn of phrase *toward God* (not just a dat. "to God"), in contrast with "to all sorts of people" in v 5. Beyond our struggles is "a Thou outside and above the one who prays" (Kleinknecht, *TDNT* 3:119). The paraenesis sounds general but could include prayer when tackling the un-likemindedness of Euodia and Syntyche or daily encounters with neighbors and officialdom in Philippi. The NOTES try to sort out *requests, prayer* (1:9), *entreaty* (1:4), and *thanksgiving* (1:3). Petitions to God *(proseuchē* and *deēsis,* a hendiadys, Schenk 246) and rendering of gratitude are included. O'B 492 suggests, with Loh. 167, that Paul himself breaks into prayer here: "In everything [I pray] may your prayers . . . come before God."

V 6b is linked with 6a, "not anxiety, but prayer." 6ab connected with 5b ("The Lord is near, so stop worrying and pray . . ."). 6ab could also be protasis for v 7 as conclusion or apodosis (see NOTE on 6b, end; cf. also 9ab): if you stop being anxious and pray, then God's peace will keep guard over you. Moffatt: "Never be anxious, but always make your requests known . . . with thanksgiving; so shall God's peace . . . keep guard." The NT scholar-preacher, James Stewart, of Edinburgh, called 6a (1937–38) good Stoicism ("keep calm, be passionless"), but asked, Who can obey that? Paul brings God in, through prayer (6b); hence peace, perspective, and power for living. Anxious cares and prayer go together like fire and water (Bengel). But a conditional construal of vv 6–7 (LB, "If you do this you will experience God's peace") compromises the promise-character of v 7 (peace will keep guard). Paul urges what seem impossible impvs., but asserts unequivocally what God will do.

f. The longest sentence in 4:4–7 is v 7, *And the peace of God that exceeds all understanding will keep guard over your hearts and minds in Christ Jesus.* An indic.-mood statement (like 5b)—hence *in Christ Jesus* for the relationship and realm involved, not *in the Lord*—in the fut. tense (hinting of the final judgment?), but with implications for the present. Not a prayer-wish, as later liturgical use made it (5, below, end, the Votum). The Philippians knew peace from God through the gospel (e.g., in Paul's message about righteousness from God, Rom 5:1) and the salutation in Phil 1:2 (and every Pauline letter). Readers in Philippi would compare and contrast it with the *pax Romana* of Caesar (Popkes 2004), even if Paul had some sense of OT *šalôm* in mind.

This peace surpasses all human *understanding*, all the reasoning and thought men and women can muster. *nous* was a term employed for the self engaged in perceiving and thinking about all that one encounters. It produces *noēmata* (later in the v), literally "things thought." The tendency was, even among Philippian Christians, to think of oneself as superior to others; Paul corrected this at 2:3b, with the same vb. as here, "consider one another to surpass *(hyperechontas)* yourselves." Coupling *noēmata* with *kardias* as anthropological terms, *hearts and minds*, led to taking *nous* as the result of thought, i.e., understanding. God's peace goes beyond the grasp of humans, even in their wildest dreams or deepest logic.

The phrase, *will guard*, may have been suggested by guards at Paul's current prison. For military veterans at Philippi, if Christians, God's peace, not Caesar's *pax*, will garrison and secure their innermost person. 4:4–7 are rounded out with *in Christ Jesus*, balancing *in the Lord* at 4a. V 7 provides a promise[26] pertinent to Euodia and Syntyche and life generally in the church community of Philippi. The "dawn of the age of joy overthrows the restless cares associated with human thought, because with it the peace which passes all understanding is granted to the Christian [better, Christians]" (Deissner, *TDNT* 4:631). The promise (4:7) creates pathos (Synman 334).

4. Take Account of the Best in the "Pagan" World of the Day, Keep Doing What Has Come to You Through Paul, God with You (4:8–9). These noble vv seem repetitious. *Finally* in v 8 duplicates *to loipon* at 3:1. The doubled *ei tis* construction in v 8 ("if there is any[thing] . . .") echoes 2:1 ("*If, then . . .*"). V 9 is, like v 7, a fut. promise, this time *the God of peace* (instead of *the peace of God*) *will be with you. ponder* and *continue to do* are akin to impvs. to the community in vv 1, 4, 5, and 6, and in v 3 to individuals. As in vv 6b and 7, the opening impvs. may be protasis, the final cl. beginning with *kai* the conclusion (see NOTE on 9b at the end). New in 4:1–9 is listing some eight virtues from the Greco-Roman world (v 8); for "imitation of Paul" (9a) cf. 3:17.

Appeal to *literary structure within vv 8–9* is often made,[27] but the "patterns" are inexact, broken, and do not agree with each other. At issue: how to relate v 8 with v 9. O'B 499 (cf. Bockmuehl 249) finds 4:8–9 "not logically connected with the previous sentence." Fee 413 claims "the 'stuff' of friendship" (Bockmuehl 249, an "unsupported suggestion") and (419) *imitatio*, broader than just connection with *philia* in Gk. philosophy and ethics. Analysis remains uncertain.

Reflective, rather than repetitious, of Letter B earlier, 4:8–9 is the concluding paraenetic unit in 4:1–9, the body closing of Letter B, with only greetings and benediction to follow (now at 4:21–23). Bockmuehl 249, cf. 254: "practical impli-

---

[26] Cf. T. Dan 5:2, "You will be at peace, since you will have with you the God of peace, and contention [*polemos*] will have no hold over you" (Bockmuehl 255).

[27] Loh. 172 found "four-liners" in both vv 8 and 9, as he had found three-liners in 1:27–2:11 ([5] COMMENT A.1, n 1; [6] COMMENT A.3); six virtues in two sequences of three (172–73; Gnilka 218–19; cf. U. B. Müller 197, certainty is not possible). O'B 501 laid out the vv in pairs of terms. Fee (413 n 5) lists in columns (a) the six virtues in v 8, paralleled by the four vbs. in 9a; (b) the two *ei tis* phrases, with *en emoi*; and (c) *tauta logizesthe, tauta prassete.*

cations . . . for Christian life in Roman Philippi." More specifically, 4:8–9 reflect the *agōn* the Philippians faced as Christians in a Roman *colōnia*, with "dual citizenship" (1:27); pertinent to Euodia-Syntyche, esp. if the women differed over status and conformity to their culture and Caesar's rule.

Paul presents favorably virtues hailed in the Greco-Roman world. See NOTES on v 8 for similar passages in Sen. and Cic.; Lucian of Samosata (2nd cent. A.D.), a commendation of "whatever things *(hosa)* are noble and divine" (*Encomium Patriae* 1); further HCNT #782. Bockmuehl stresses later patristic usage of such terms. Hellenistic aspects are borne out esp. in *prosphilē* (nowhere else in the NT), *euphēma* (nowhere else in the Gk. Bible), and *aretē* (see NOTES on *lovely, appealing,* and . . . *excellence*). The last two virtues seem "pagan," so devoid of "inherent morality" that Fee takes "if" as a "double proviso," namely, "*if* anything is excellent, *if* anything is praiseworthy" in them (419, 416 n 13); cf. Bockmuehl 251. This forced interpretation goes with an attempt to claim (almost all) the virtues as "biblical" because the terms were sometimes used in the LXX (see NOTES on each).[28] The LXX examples usually occur in later (wisdom) books reflecting Hellenistic influence, with no underlying Heb. term. Against notions of Jewish influence on such a catalogue of virtues, see esp. Wegenast 113–14; it is not Torah-related, but "current coin in popular moral philosophy, especially in Stoicism" (cf. O'B 502). E.g., *whatever* (is) *just* in v 8 is to be understood in moral terms of the day for social conduct, not from "righteousness" as an attribute of God's character (Rom 3:5), let alone God's saving righteousness (Phil 3:9), as Fee 417–19 and others suggest. Paul "assumes a certain consensus in ethical judgment"; in the *polis* and human relationships, people know "what is good" (Delling, *TDNT* 8:30 n 20, Rom 2:14–15; 1:32). But Paul has not taken over "a current list from a textbook of ethical instruction . . . the virtues of the copybook maxims" (so Beare 148). No list extant exactly parallels v 8; *prosphilē* and *euphēma* appear in no known virtues-catalogue (Fee 416 n 15). V. 8 ignores three of the four "cardinal" virtues (self-control, prudence, courage; only "justice") and reduces *dikaia* (and *aretē*) to one item among (six) others, without giving *excellence* preeminence. Paul seems to be composing *ad hoc* (Fee 416–17).

Why this list at the close of Letter B? We argued that in Letter A (4:10–20) Paul accepted some aspects of friendship and its patron-client system in the Greco-Roman world, but also sought to correct, and extricate himself from, other aspects of the Philippians' view of *philia*. With the Philippians' encomium about God and Christ (2:6–11), Paul accepted their summary, inserting just one phrase (2:8c), but he subtly corrected it at points and applied it to their own communal relationships (2:1–4, 12–18). Now in 4:2–3 he deals with Euodia and Syntyche. If their difference had to do with typically Gk. interests like status, relation to inferiors, and "selfish ambition" or how Christians relate to the *politeia* of Caesar and

---

[28] For attempts at "biblical" or "Pauline" senses for the six terms, cf. Loh., Michaelis 68–69 (contra Dib.), and Fee 415, who claims Jas 3:13–18 as "the closest parallel . . . in the NT" (James as "one of the least hellenized documents in the NT" n 11, is questionable; cf. L. T. Johnson, *James* AB 37A:27–29, 287–88).

socioeconomic, political life in the *colōnia,* Paul is dealing critically with what was dear and customary to many Philippians. Is he completely against their culture? In v 8, Paul affirms aspects of moral and civic life of the day. Were some of the eight terms esp. precious to Euodia or Syntyche? The apostle lifts up good and positive factors in the heritage of Philippian Christians and their non-Christian neighbors. He links things "good in themselves and beneficial to others" (O'B 503) that hold for Roman citizens and subjects and can apply also for carrying out their citizenship in the gospel (1:27). Perhaps (Michael 201–2) Paul is answering a Philippian question: "What shall be their attitute to pagan ethics?" Had persecution blinded them "to what was good in the pagan life by which they were surrounded?"

The *structure of v 8* (and likewise v 9), after a final introductory word (*to loipon,* GNB "In conclusion" for all of Letter B), plus the direct address, *brothers and sisters* (as at 3:1 and 4:1, thus rounding out the section), has been indicated in the NOTES: relative cls., resumptive word (*these things*), and impv., an order that could be reversed in tr., "Fill your minds with those things that are . . . ," "Put into practice what . . ." (GNB). *ponder* and *do* should not be contrasted too sharply as "thought" and "action" (Bockmuehl 254–55). The first suggests "'take into account,' rather then simply 'think about'" (Fee 415). Both are continuing processes (pres. tense). Paul wants the qualities enumerated in v 8 to be put into practice, not just contemplated.

The virtues are Hellenistic, not "biblical." (1) *whatever things are true* means things honest and genuine, "true in fact" (MM 21), not deceptive, available to all quite apart from the gospel (Rom 1:18, 25); not intellectual but moral. (2) *honorable* might mean "with the honor given to the gods" (Michael 203; *TDNT* 7:191); in people, qualities that call forth veneration; a gravity that is the mean between obsequiousness and stubbornness (Aristot. *Rhet.* 2.17.4; *Eth. Eud.* 2.34). Hence (W. Barclay, *Phil.* 78–79), things that have "the dignity of holiness" upon them, Matthew Arnold's "nobly serious." Bockmuehl 252, "noble" with "an aura of the sublime." Hence "inspiring, worthy of respect." (3) *just* is less connected with Paul's doctrine of justification than with the cardinal Hellenistic virtue of justice. Michael 203, "Paul was probably thinking of . . . Roman law and government." (4) The ethical sense of *pure,* "undefiled," "not besmirched" (Fee 418), could point to "domestic purity," including sexual chastity, in the household (Michael 204; Bockmuehl 252; 2 Cor 11:2) and conduct generally. These last two terms could suggest "duty faced and duty done" (Barclay, *Phil.* 80) in civic life (see NOTE on *pure*).[29] (5) The biblically rare term *prosphilē* suggests things beloved, attractive (Moffatt), *lovely.* (6) The even rarer *euphēma,* "well spoken of" by people (cf. 2 Cor 8:6), points to things *appealing,* "winsome" (Barclay). Dib. 73, "a purely societal value," approbation or commendation (*Let. Aris.* 191; M. Aur. *Med*

---

[29] Preferable to D. F. Watson 1988b:77 (NOTE on *pure*) or deSilva 2000:294 n 16, that Paul's use of "the terms *impurity* and *unrighteousness* . . . as synonyms shows the virtual identification of purity codes with ethical conduct in the early church (see Rom 6:19; 2 Cor 6:6; Gal 5:19: Phil 4:8; 1 Tim 4:12; 5:2)."

6.18). (7) Moral *excellence*—the Gk. construction is varied for rhetorical purposes by use of *ei tis*—is the term most clearly Hellenistic. In Aristot., *aretē* referred to ethical virtues that can be acquired by doing them ("practice makes perfect"). Virtue is not an emotion or potentiality but a state of mind (*hexis*, "habit"), a mental state; e.g., being *dikaios*, "just," out of which the person does *dikaia* ("just things") and becomes just. Every virtue is, according to its essence, a mean between extremes (of excess and of defect), but according to its excellence it is an extreme (*Eth. Eud.* 2). The development of "cardinal virtues" (see NOTE on *if there is any excellence*) meant that *aretē* stood over the four, or however many one lists. Not so here. Paul does not ask if there is anything excellent (or praiseworthy) in the category of *lovely* or *admirable* (so Fee 418–19), but brings in any moral feature readers might propose, wisdom or prudence (knowledge, perception, and discernment appear at 1:9–10, but not *sophia* or *sophrosynē* in Phil.) or courage (*andreia* is implicit in "standing firm" against opponents). Here character of excellence, worthy of praise, such as might be singled out in the *polis* for civic honor (BDAG). (8) *epainos*, "approval, praise," is closely related. It "would appeal to the Philippians who . . . were proud of their citizenship in the empire" (Martin 1976:159). To see (7) and (8) as interior qualities in a person that gain approval in society relates them to an "honor" culture.

Alongside this Hellenistic list in v 8 of things worth pondering, Paul refers in v 9 to things in his own life and message that the Philippians *learned and received and heard and saw*, things they are to keep on doing. The vbs. are about the Philippians' experience with Paul, his kerygma and teaching, heard, received as oral traditions, and learned in this way, and Paul's conduct and way of life, seen first-hand. His "way of life" was a "theology of the cross," a cruciform lifestyle, as letters he was writing to Corinth in this period make clear (Chart 2, INTRO. VIII; J. Becker 1993 [(1) Bibl. **Paul**)] chs. 7 and 8).

Some take 4:9 to elaborate v 8: the virtues are things the Philippians learned from Paul (O'B 508; cf. 499; Bockmuehl 254, for them, "biblical" virtues). Paul then modeled Gk. values for the Philippians! Fee 414 properly rejects such a reading; *ha* in v 9 does not have as its antecedent the preceding *tauta*, two words earlier in v 8, but looks to the *tauta* that follows in v 9 (grammatically more likely). Paul in v 9 thus puts the Hellenistic morality of v 8 into perspective. *kai* may have an *adversative* sense (Merk 1968:196–98; Schenk 270, cf. Phil 3:15 "But (*kai*) if some of you have a different attitude," GNB). Without driving so sharp a wedge between vv 8 and 9, we take v 8 as a call to reflection over norms in the world of the day that Christians too can practice; for this process, the apostolic tradition and the apostle himself serve as criteria (v 9). In this way, discernment over things that matter (1:10) can be carried through (U. B. Müller 196–98). In this way, what salvation means is worked out in daily life (2:12). So Merk 1968:196–97, the basis *for the believer* not in reason or Gk. anthropology (Lohmeyer's "natural morality," 173) but in the relationship with God "in Christ" and its eschatological grounding.

A promise in 9b rounds out the closing paraenesis and letter body. To say "ponder . . . do, *and the God of peace will be with you*" could suggest a result (Bockmuehl 255): divine presence at the end depends on carrying through the tasks of dual citizenship during life on earth. But Paul has emphasized in 2:13 God as "the One at work in and among you . . . both to will and to work (*thelein, energein;* cf. 4:8, 9 *logizesthe, prassete*) above and beyond goodwill (*eudokia,* such as was found in the society of the day)." God who is with them, in Christ the Lord, will continue to be with them. *Pace* Fee 421, there is no talk in 4:1–9, and little in Letter B or in Phil generally, of the Spirit or of "transformation." There is repetition, esp. when the benediction at 4:23 is factored in, in Letter B just three vv later (4:9 → 4:21–23; cf. A.1.l, above):

4:7 "And the peace of God . . . will keep guard over your hearts and minds";
4:9 "And the God of peace will be with you";
4:23 "The grace of the Lord Jesus Christ be—and is—with your spirit."

The three assurances parallel the three admonitions to rejoice (3:1; 4:4 *bis*). They vary in formulation, reflecting Paul's usual liturgical benediction at the end of the letter (4:23) and his frequent references to *the God of peace* (4:9) near the close of a letter (U. B. Müller 199; 1 Thess 5:23; Rom 16:20; cf. 2 Cor 13:11). Phil 4:7 is then a "playful" formulation phrased re Paul's Roman custody ("keep watch") and *the peace of God* needed in Philippian Christianity re: Euodia and Syntyche, with and in contrast to the *pax Romana.* The fut. tense is part of the eschatological motivation (U. B. Müller 196) for Christian life now, within Caesar's realm, to which Letter B has summoned the Philippians.[30]

5. 4:1–9 in Redacted, Canonical Philippians. Once Letter A (4:10–20, its body) and Letter C (3:2–21, its polemical core) were inserted into Letter B, ch. 4:1–9 came to be treated in terms of what now preceded and followed it, no longer "final paraenesis" but "attached admonitions" (Berger 1984a:160). Connections throughout 4:4–9 to Euodia and Syntyche (4:2–3) and "dual citizenship" diminished in importance or were lost from sight. Defenders of the unity of a single letter pressed to find logic and coherence for the nine vv in their new context; see above, A.1.d–g. *hōste* (4:1) came to be taken as "therefore" (KJV-NRSV); *stand steadfast* was directed against false teachers in 3:2–3, 18–21 (so Webber [(2) Bibl. joy] 316), rather than the Roman *adversaries* (1:28). M. Müller sees 4:1 *(hōste)* pointing back to the peak in the letter in ch. 3 (along with 2:6–11) where Paul sets forth what eschatological existence means (147, 185–86). The vocatives in 4:1 = signs of endearment in light of "heavenly citizenship," 3:20–21.

Failure of *Euodia* and *Syntyche* to *think the same thing* (4:2–3) was seen less as reflection of communal failings in Philippi (2:2–5) and rather as a spat between two women, often blamed for all that was wrong or as the only blot on an otherwise idyllic church. When the two women were made the "focus of conflict" (Peterlin, ch. 6), 4:2–3 were related not to the rest of 4:1–9 but, in light of 4:10–20, to a difference of opinion about continuing support for Paul: one woman and her

---

[30] Paul's "Christ-believers do live in the present world (cf. especially 4:5a and 8). But even here the text is shot through with forward-looking references" like 4:3 and 5b (Engberg-Petersen 2000:99).

house-congregation withdrew support, leading an "anti-Pauline lobby" (223, cf. 228). Or (one of) the women may have opened (her) their house-assembly to the false teachers in ch. 3 (if Jewish teachers, to put themselves under Judaism as a "legal religion," Fee, Tellby; or Gnostic teachers, Schmithals). Euodia and Syntyche were variously interpreted (A.2, above), re support for Paul (A.2.d), as to the issue between them and Paul or, more likely, between the two women (A.3, above). For a unified letter, any difference over relating to Hellenistic culture has been little considered (in spite of 4:8), and a difference re Imperial authorities, never. Personal differences (3.b) or self-interest (3.c) became likely, with unanimity the theme in vv 2–3 (Silva 220).

Phil 4:4–7 can be read in the redacted letter much as in Letter B (above, 3). To the theme "rejoice!" nothing is added in 3:2–21 or 4:10–20. That "The Lord is near" (4:5b) is nudged toward the fut. parousia by 3:20–21, but some supporters of a unified Phil still take it to refer to the Lord's nearness to hear prayers and bless believers; or in both senses (space and time; O'B 488–89). Gentleness (5a), living without anxiety (6a), and prayer become more difficult to relate to anything specific in Philippi (unless *to epieikes* in contrast to the "enemies of the cross of Christ" in ch. 3) and so were related to Jesus' character (via 2 Cor 10:1) and teaching (Matt 6:35 par) and the biblical tradition of prayer, respectively.

On *peace* from God in v 7, 3:2–21 adds nothing, unless a foil in language about the "dogs" (3:2) and "enemies of the cross" (3:18). The problem (see B.3) is how to pull together the themes in 4:4–7. Silva 223, "joy and anxiety"; Fee, "rejoicing in the Lord, prayer, and thanksgiving," to which could be added eschatology and ethics. K. L. Berry ([16] Bibl.) related 4:4–7 with 4:11–13: Paul exemplifies not being anxious; he makes requests known to God (Fitzgerald 1996:123).

Verses 8–9 present the same problems in a four-ch. letter as were outlined for Letter B, how to combine the list of Hellenistic (civic) virtues (cf. Silva 229) and Paul's teaching and apostolic lifestyle. With 3:17–20 in the picture, doing what the Philippians have seen in Paul can be contrasted with what they've perceived in the false teachers (3:17, "the example you have in *us*," Paul and others), sometimes tied to *philia*. Fitzgerald (1996:155, "Christ as model friend," 2:6–11) suggests Euodia and Syntyche are being asked "to have the *homonoia* [unity] that friendship entails"; peace "can only exist when they cease from strife and become friends"—overstated (cf. Bockmuehl 249). Far more from the Gk. world than *philia* is involved. Paul does not make doing such virtues the condition for God's peace, but uses apostolic teaching as criterion and eschatology as motivation for the ethical life. I. H. Marshall 116–17 warned against the "tidy system" of thinking that to "trust in God and do his will" brings blessing, but people who quarrel "will not experience God's blessing." That is hardly Paul, let alone 4:8–9.

A model from Stoicism has been employed by Engberg-Pedersen 2000 (33–44; cf. 287; chart, p. 34) to elucidate Paul's thought and practice in Phil: I → X → S. In the "I"-stage, the individual is concerned with fulfilling individual desires (egoism). The X-stage involves, in Stoicism, reason; in Paul, God and Christ. The S-stage is a resulting moral stance or altruism within a group or community and in relations outside the group (the result of change or conversion; the person adopts the group's identity and ethical schema). In Paul, "a human being will belong simultaneously at both the I- and S-levels" (36).[31] This model is applied to Phil as a whole (81–130), but fits chs. 3 and 4 particularly. The "I" stage stands out—Paul's call (3:4–14); his joy (e.g., 4:4); self-sufficiency (4:11–13). Phil 1–2 are "mainly concerned with how to handle the present world"; in 3–4 "the general drift is . . . in the direction of the other world" (99, but a passage like 4:5–9 reflects both points, n 30 above). (Fut. fulfillment, beyond the S-stage, may not be brought out by this model.[32]) This Stoic model of existence, the Christ event, and Paul's own experiences and insights undergird what he says, emphasizing for Christians the heavenly *politeuma* (3:20) *and* living "in a *politeuma* in the proper way here *on earth*" (125). Community formation is shaped by "friendship" and "righteousness through Christ faith (3:6–9)."[33]

In church lectionaries, Phil 4:4–7 was used over the centuries as Epistle for the Third Sunday in Advent (Roman Missal) or Fourth Sunday (Book of Common Prayer, Lutheran lectionaries);[34] continued in the Roman *Ordo* for Advent III Year C, in spite of the assignment of 4:6–9 also for Pentecost XIX Year A (4:4–13 Lutheran, Episcopal lectionaries, 4:1–9 Revised Common Lectionary). From the opening words of 4:4 in Lat., the Sunday when 4:4–7 was read was often called Gaudete, " 'Rejoice!' Sunday." Cf. Bengel's summary on Phil, *Gaudeo*, "I rejoice,"

---

[31] Engberg-Pedersen 36 refers to "Luther's idea of being *simul iustus et peccator*, when this is given a proper, naturalistic interpretation" (as above). But elsewhere he talks of "sinlessness" (re Rom 6:1–8:13) or of the Philippians as attaining S, a "life of mutual love and 'self-absement' " (125), like a "Stoic utopian community of sages" (126).

[32] Perhaps more accurate are the four stages in G. M. Styler, "The basis of obligation in Paul's christology and ethics," in *Christ and Spirit in the New Testament*, FS C. F. D. Moule, ed. B. Lindars et al. (Cambridge: Cambridge Univ. Press, 1973) 175–87, esp. 176: A, the accomplished act of Christ; B, the beginning of belief and baptism (conversion); C, the continuing Christian life; and D, the last Day, final judgment and salvation.

[33] P. 126, *Christou* subjective gen. The case for Paul's "essential connection to Stoicism" (330 n 13) rests not only on Engberg-Pedersen 1995 but also his monographs, *Aristotle's Theory of Moral Insight* (Oxford: Oxford Univ. Press, 1983) and *The Stoic Theory of Oikeiosis* [orientation]: *Moral Development and Social Interaction in Early Stoic Philosophy*, Studies in Hellenistic Civilization 2 (Aarhus: Aarhus Univ. Press, 1990). It is not simply a matter of Stoicism in Philippi (Engberg-Pedersen illustrates his model also with Gal and Rom) but of Stoicism in Paul. From Stoic ethical tradition Engberg-Pedersen would give coherence to Paul's letters through "the logic of paraklesis" (105), at the expense of a disconnect with "the indicative" (or theology), hoping that such Stoic language makes sense as an option today. But our fragmentary knowledge of Stoicism may be a problem (J. A. Harrill, *CBQ* 63 [2001] 744); Paul may be only superficially Stoic. See further the reviews of Engberg-Pedersen 2000 in *RBL* 9/2/2002 (on line at www.bookreviews.org) from the SBL "Hellenistic Moral Philosophy and Early Christianity Section" in 2000 (S110), by J. T. Fitzgerald (Intro.), K. L. Gaca (Stoicism), H. W. Attridge (Gal), S. K. Stowers (Rom), and V. P. Furnish (Phil), plus a response by Engberg-Pedersen. Furnish is critical of the lack of "attention to Paul's apostolic self-understanding and specifically theological claims." It is unclear how, for Engberg-Pedersen, "perfection" in 3:12–16 relates to "sinlessness" (Rom 6–8) or Paul as a model who has *not* himself "reached the goal" (115) and the Philippians with regard to "S" (90, 95, 114; 122–25 offer almost too many possible answers).

[34] Hence treatment in Fendt 1931:28–30; v 5, "The Lord is near," is a "liturgical detour" from Paul's eschatological sense of the parousia, to suggest (in the lectionary) the imminence of Jesus' birth at Christmas.

gaudete, "rejoice ye" in the Lord. 4:7 has been employed as "the Votum" after the sermon, esp. in the Lutheran tradition (Schenk 248, Paul has a fut. indic. vb., not a wish-form). In discussions of women in the church 4:2–3 (COMMENT A.2.a-d and n 11) and of Hellenistic material in Paul's ethics 4:8–9 have been prominent. In such ways 4:1–9 has had ongoing influence.

SELECT BIBLIOGRAPHY (see also General Bibliography and Commentaries)

Abrahamsen, V. 1987. "Women at Philippi: The Pagan and Christian Evidence," *Journal of Feminist Studies in Religion* 3:17–30.

Adinolfi, M. 1975. "Le collaboratrici ministeriali di Paolo nella lettere ai Romani e ai Filippesi," *BibOr* 17:21–32.

Agouridis, S. C. 1980. "The Role of Women in the Church of Philippi," *BBS* 1 n.s. 2:84; Gk. in *DeltaBibMel* 9 (1980) 77–85.

Beet, J. A. 1883–84. "Did Euodia and Syntyche Quarrel?" *ExpTim* 5:179–80.

Brinktrine, J. 1963. "Eine biblische Parallele zum 'Buche des Lebens," *TGl* 53:130–31.

Bugg, C. B. 1991. "Philippians 4:4–13," *RevExp* 88:253–57.

Carls, P. 1995. "Wer sind Syzygos, Euodia und Syntyche in Phil 4,2f.?" *PzB* 4:117–41.

———. 2001. "Identifying Syzygos, Euodia, and Syntyche, Philippians 4:2f.," *JHighCrit* 8:161–82.

Chapple, A. 1992. "'The Lord Is Near,' (Philippians 4:5b)," in D. Peterson/J. Pryor, eds., *In the Fullness of Time: Biblical Studies in Honour of Archbishop Donald Robinson* (Homebush West, NSW: Lancer) 149–65.

Cotter, W. 1994. "Women's Authority Roles in Paul's Churches: Countercultural or Conventional?" *NovT* 36:350–72.

Dacquino, P. 1961. "La gioia cristiana (*Fil.* 4,4–9)," *BibOr* 3:182–83.

d'Agostino, F. 1973. "Il tema dell' epieikeia nella s. Scrittura," *RTM* 5:385–406.

Dahl, N. A. 1995. "Euodia and Syntyche and Paul's Letter to the Philippians," FS W. A. Meeks (Gen. Bibl., under L. M. White 1995) 3–15.

D'Angelo, M. R. 1990. "Women Partners in the New Testament," *Journal of Feminist Studies in Religion* 6:65–86.

Delling, G. 1975. "Die Bezeichung 'Gott des Friedens' und ähnliche Wendungen in den Paulusbriefen," in *Jesus und Paulus*, FS W. G. Kümmel, ed. E. E. Ellis/E. Grässer (Göttingen: Vandenhoeck & Rupecht) 76–84.

Duchatelez, K. 1979. "L'epieikeia' dans l'antiquité grecque, paienne et chrétienne," *Communio* 12:203–31.

Gillman, F. M. 1990. "Early Christian Women at Philippi," *Journal of Gender in World Religions* 1:59–79.

Hájek, M. 1964. "Comments on Philippians 4:3—Who Was 'Gnésios Syzygos"?" CV 7:261–62; "Bemerkung zu Phil 4:3," *Theologickà Prihloha* (Krestanska Revue) 31 (1964) 113–14.

Harnack, A. von. 1920. "Sanftmut, Huld und Demut in der alten Kirche," in *Festgabe J. Kraftan* (Tübingen: Mohr) 113–29.

Harris, J. R. 1923–24. "St. Paul and Aeschylus (Phil 4:4)," *ExpTim* 35:151–53.

Holloway, P. A. 1998. "*Bona Cognitare*: An Epicurean Consolation in Phil 4:8–9," *HTR* 91:89–96.

Luter, A. B. 1996. "Partnership in the Gospel: The Role of Women in the Church at Philippi," *JETS* 39:411–20.

Malinowski, F. X. 1985. "The Brave Women of Philippi," *BTB* 15:60–64.

Moffatt, J. 1897–98. "The History of Joy; a Brief Exposition of Phil. 4.4–7 (R.V.)," *ExpTim* 9:334–36.

Pollard, J. P. 1993. "Women in the Earlier Philippian Church," in *Essays on Women in Earliest Christianity*, vol. 1, ed. C. D. Osburn (Joplin, MO: College Press) 262–66.

Popkes, W. 2004. "Philipper 4.4–7: Aussage und situativer Hintergrund," *NTS* 50:246–56.

Rhijn, C. H. van. 1903. "Euodia en Syntyche," *ThSt* 21:300–309.

Riley, L. J. 1948. *The Nature, History, and Use of* Epikeia *in Moral Theology.* Washington, DC: Catholic Univ. of America Press.

Spicq, C. 1947. "Bénignité, mansuétude, douceur, clémence," *RB* 54:321–39.

Sterck-Degueldre, J.-P. 2004. *Eine Frau namens Lydia. Zu Geschichte und Komposition in Apostelgeschichte 16,11–15.40.* WUNT 2/176. Tübingen: Mohr Siebeck.

Stewart, J. S. 1937–38. "Old Texts in Modern Translation: Philippians iv.6,7 (Moffatt)," *ExpTim* 49:269–71.

Thomas, W. D. 1971–72. "The Place of Women in the Church at Philippi," *ExpTim* 83:117–20.

Trebilco, P. R. 1990. "Women as Co-Workers and Leaders in Paul's Letters," *Journal of the Christian Brethren Research Fellowship* (Wellington, New Zealand) 122:32.

Verhoef, E. 1999. "*Syzygos* in Phil 4:3 and the Author of the 'We-sections' in Acts," *JHighCrit* 5:202–19.

Vögtle, A. 1936. *Die Tugend- und Lasterkataloge im Neuen Testament,* NTAbh 16:4–5 (Münster: Aschendorff) 177–88.

Watts, J. C. 1893–94. "The Alleged Quarrel of Euodia and Syntyche," *ExpTim* 5:286–87.

Wibbing, S. 1959. *Die Tugend- und Lasterkataloge im Neuen Testament und ihre Traditionsgeschichte unter besonder Berücksichigung der Qumrantexte,* BZNW 25 (Berlin: Töpelmann) 99–103.

LETTER A, BODY; CANONICAL PHILIPPIANS BODY CONCLUSION, 4:10–20

16. *Friendship, Thanks, and God, 4:10–20*

TRANSLATION

4:10a I greatly rejoiced in the Lord b that you have now at last revived your concern for me, c a concern on which you were long intent, but lacked opportunity to show it.

11a It is not that I mention this out of need, b for I have learned to be content with whatever I have.

12a I know how even to be brought low with few resources;

b I know how also to abound with much.

c I have had my initiation experience in every situation and all circumstances,

d both to get my fill and to go hungry,

e both to abound and to suffer lack.

13 I am strong, able to tackle everything, through the One who strengthens me.

14 Anyway, you did well in sharing together with me in my affliction. 15a But do you indeed know, you Philippians, that b "at the beginning of the gospel," when I departed from Macedonia, c no church had shared with me in "an account of giving and receiving" except you alone? 16 And that, even in Thessalonica, more than once, you sent me something for my needs?

17 It is not that I am seeking alms. I am rather seeking the profit that accumulates to your account. 18a I have been paid in full and I abound. b I am filled full, because I have received from Epaphroditus what you sent—c a fragrance with aroma, a sacrifice acceptable, well pleasing, to God. 19 My God will fulfill every need of yours, in accord with the divine riches, gloriously, in Christ Jesus. 20 To our God and Father belongs glory forever and ever. Amen.

NOTES

4:10a. *I greatly rejoiced in the Lord. . . . de* connects v 10 with what preceded, "and" or "but" (KJV); in [N]RSV, "(correctly) untranslated" (Fee 428). Lft. 163, *de* "arrests a subject which is in danger of escaping"; Hawth. 196, "for rhetorical effect." O'B 516 n 7 rightly doubts such significance; "simply . . . transition." Similarly Schenk 39, 67, as at 1:12 (beginning the letter body). Walter 96, *de* is a redactor's addition when Letter A was inserted into the Phil B and C.

I rejoiced. echarēn, 2nd aor. pass., dep., *chairō* (see NOTE on 1:18 *I rejoice; chara* 1:4 *with joy*), a major theme in Phil (Bengel; COMMENT A.4.c, "epistolary rejoicing formula"). A true past tense, *I rejoiced* when you again showed concern for me (KJV, NRSV-mg; Loh. 178; Gnilka 171; Schenk 67; O'B 516; Silva 235; Berry 109 n 11; Fee 428 n 17); not epistolary aor., "I rejoice" (RSV, NRSV-txt; Bruce 126; Hawth. 196; see NOTE on 2:28 *I am sending*; BDF #334). Upon receipt of good news in papyrus letters; White 1986: No. 103B (BGU 2.632, line 10, "When I learned that you were well, I rejoiced exceedingly"); No. 28.10–11; No. 93.3–6, COMMENT A.3 n 32 below.

chairō/chara, "rejoice/joy," connects etymologically with *eucharisteō*, "give thanks" (Schenk 43,58; joy at "the rendering of thanks" to God, Deut 16:13–15, 12:6–7; Conzelmann, *TDNT* 9:363), and with *charis*, "grace," "grace-gift" *(TDNT* 9:393); see NOTES on 1:2 *grace*; 1:7 *this gracious opportunity*. But "joyful thanks" reads more in than Paul says. *echarēn* begins a series of 1st per. sgs. (6x in vv 10–13, plus 3 more in vv 17–18); cf. 3:4b–14 and the prayer report in 1:3–11, "I thank my God . . . I pray. . . ." Schenk 57–58 compares Phlm 7.

greatly. megalōs, only here in the NT, but in the LXX and papyri (Loh. 178 n 4). Pol. *Phil.* 1.1, "I rejoice together *(synecharēn)* with you greatly *(megalōs)* in our Lord Jesus Christ," may echo Phil 4:10; cf. INTRO. VI.A. On joy in letters at news, cf. Koskenniemi 55–57. R. Funk 1967 ([9] COMMENT A.1.a) 426, "functional equivalents of the *eucharistō* thanksgiving periods" in Paul; "not impossible as a letter opening," but no example of *echarēn lian* (or variation) as a letter opening can be "dated with certainty earlier than A.D. 100"; Schnider-Stenger ([1] Bibl.) 176.

in the Lord. en kyriō[i]; see NOTES on 1:2 *Lord* and 1:14 *in the Lord*. + *chairete* at 3:1 and 4:4; see NOTES there. Usually "in the Lord" + impv., "in Christ" + the indic. But "in the Lord" + indic. at 1:14; 2:19 ("hope in the Lord Jesus"), and 24 ("confident in the Lord Jesus"). It characterizes an activity or state as Christian (3:1, 4:4; A. Oepke, "*en*," *TDNT* 2:541) and may have ecclesiological significance (H. Conzelmann, "*chairō*, etc.," *TDNT* 9:369), relations in church under the Lord (Jesus Christ). Joy at how communal life is being worked out (G. Delling, *TDNT* 6:266). No note here of suffering as bond between Paul and his Lord *(pace* Loh.). Bouttier 1962 ([1] Bibl. **Christ**) 88 sees Paul's apostolic consciousness; Neugebauer 1961:143–44, historical, creaturely existence, not eschatological joy. Kramer ([1] Bibl.) #50, context: apostle and church.

4:10b. *that you have now at last revived your concern for me. hoti*, in Eng. trs. since Tyndale, = *that* (BDAG *hoti* 1.e.), "I rejoiced at the fact that. . . ." Or "because," "for" (BDAG *hoti* 4; *chairō*, p. 1075, it "gives the reason"); Hawth. 196; O'B 517, "the sole ground, or the more immediate reason"; Fee 428 n 21. Vg *quoniam*. Schenk 67, the first of two reasons to rejoice, with 10c.

you have . . . revived. anethalete, 2nd aor. act., *anathallō*. BDAG, **cause to be in a state** [delete the comma, F. W. Danker, e-mail 11/4/02] **identical with a previous state, *cause to grow/bloom again.*** (1st aor. *anethalate* in P46 D*, perhaps rightly; *-ete*, 2nd aor. ending, was a newer substitute; BDF ##72,75.) *thallō* = "grow, flourish" + prep. prefix *ana-*, "again"; GNTG 2:295–96, "causative force," grow *up*, Ewald 1908:209 = 1923:225. Nowhere else in the NT. Is it factitive, "cause to grow or bloom again" (Sir 50:10), + *to hyper emou phronein* ("your concern for me") dir. obj.? Or intrans., "grow up or bloom again" (Eus. *Praep. Ev.* 5.34.14) + acc. of respect (BDF #160) or of reference (Moule *IB* pp. 33–34)? BDAG allows either *you have revived your care for me* or *you have revived, as far as your care for me is concerned.* Eng. trs. prefer the former ([N]RSV), the Philippians *(you)* as acting subject; Paul writes from the Philippians' standpoint (Gnilka 173). For the intrans.: Baumert 1969; Gnilka 173; Martin 1976:161; O'B 518; for the causative: Ewald 1908:211 = 1923:227. Hawth. 197, it "makes little difference." But are the Philippians "revived again" (Tyndale, Geneva Bible), or their care for Paul (KJV, NEB)?

   your concern for me. phronein; see NOTE on 1:7 *to think.* With Schenk 102–3, *to hyper emou phronein* is a phrase from the Philippians; it echoes through the correspondence, 2:2 *bis,* 5; 3:15 *bis,* 16, 19; 4:2, and 4:10 *bis. phronein* = think or feel, *be concerned about* a person (BDAG *phronein* 1), often + *peri* (Wis 14:30; classical sources). In the NT, only here and at 1:7 + *hyper,* "in behalf of, about" + gen. (BDAG *hyper* A.1.δ: "think of me = care for me, be interested in me"; cf 3, "think **about, concerning**"; GNTG 3:270). *your* (KJV, most trs.) derives from the 2nd pl. vb., "you revived (your) care for me." 2 Macc 14:8, "genuinely concerned for the interests of the king" (*hyper* + gen. pl. *phronōn*), a *topos* in Hellenistic politics (Schenk 65) and friendship (cf. 1 Macc 10:20, the king's friend; LXX [Gk.] Esther 8:12b = NRSV Addition E 16:(1) = AB *Daniel, Esther, and Jeremiah,* by C. A. Moore, 232,234, those "loyal to our government," lit., thinking our things). Gk. art. infin., like 1:21, "To live [*to zēn*] (means) Christ" (ATR 1065–66); cf. 1:24, 2:6; GNTG 3:140. At 4:10b we take *to . . . phronein* as acc. dir. obj. of the causative vb. *anethalete.* The art. is "anaphoric," to point up something well known to both parties, previously done and now revived (BDF #399.1). MSS F G, *tou . . . phronein,* gen., final or purpose cl. (BDF #400), "(so as) to care for me," or (BDF #101, p. 52, under *thallein*) "as far as your care for me is concerned."

   Some view the phrase *to hyper emou,* lit. "the (phrase) 'for me,'" as obj. of *phronein,* taken epexegetically, ". . . that you have again blossomed, to (be able to) be intent about the 'for me' [what is best for me]." Ewald 1908:210 = 1923:226; Bengel, *to hyper emou* is equivalent to *ta para hymōn* 4:18, the things from you, NRSV "the gifts you sent."

   now at last. ēdē pote, troublesome to tr. Adv. of time, **now, already, by this time** (BDAG 1) + enclitic particle, of the past, *once, formerly;* of the fut. *once, at last;* combined, **now at length** (BDAG 434), *now at last* (BDAG 856). Rebuke (KJV now at the last; NEB after so long . . . now)? So Chrysost. and others (B. Weiss 324–25). Loh/Nida 139, Paul is not chiding the Philippians for delay. Cf. Rom 1:10. *ana-* in *anethalete* could suggest "again," cf. vv 15–16 (Ewald 1908:209–10 = 1923:225–26). Baumert 1969, 2001 Nachtrag (p. 116), not temporal but *offentsichtlich,* "obviously, apparently."

   4:10c. *a concern on which you were long intent, but lacked opportunity to show it. ephroneite,* imperf. of vb. in 10b, "you were (repeatedly) concerned," + *ēkaireisthe,* "you (repeatedly) had no opportunity" (NRSV adds, "to show it"). *de* (postpositive), *but*, joins the vbs. *kai* before the first vb. is explicative (BDAG *kai* 1.c) or adjunctive, "indeed." NEB contrasts, "you did care about me before . . . , it was opportunity that you lacked."

on which. eph' hō[i], omitted in [N]RSV, etc., is variously rendered (KJV "wherein"; Moffatt "for"; NKJV "though"). *epi*, "on, upon," + dat., rel. pron. *hos, hē, ho*, masc. or neut. sg. Cf. Phil 3:12d (NOTE on *the way* . . . ; NRSV "because"); 2 Cor 5:4; Rom. 5:12 (NRSV "because"). BDAG *epi* 6.c at end and *hos* 1.k.δ suggest in all four passages *for, indeed*, or *for the reason that, because*; "a commercial metaphor" is possible in the first three (Danker 1967–68, 1972). At 4:10 (Baumert 1969; Meyer 174–75) (1) "because" is common; BDAG; BDF #235.2, 294.4; Silva 233; *DA* 325. But (Baumert 1969:257) for what does "because you were concerned" provide the basis? Paul's joy (already explained in the previous *hoti* cl.)? the reblossoming of the Philippians (out of concern for Paul)? See (6) below. (2) *eph' hō[i]* = "to be sure" (NRSV), "indeed," "of course" (Bockmuehl 258); "you were indeed concerned" (RSV), as if a *men/de* contrast, but you "lacked opportunity." But *eph' hō[i]* is not equivalent to *men*, nor necessarily a contrast with the often untr. *de*. (3) Turner, GNTG 3:272; Baumert 258, a time-contrast, "Your concern came very late (I indeed thought you have forgotten me?), but *then* (I recognized) you had never forgotten me," cf. R. Knox tr. Danker 1967–68:434 n 4 is perplexed at Turner's "temporal" classification. Knox was translating the Vg, the basis of a fourth rendering (Baumert). (4) Lat., *gravisus sum autem in Domino vehementer quoniam tandem aliquando refloruistis pro me sentire, sicut et sentiebatis: occupati autem eratis* (note the colon); 1582 Rheims NT, "And I rejoyced in our Lord exceedingly, that once at the length you have reflorished to care for me, as you did also care: but you were occupied." *eph' hō[i]* = *sicut*, "as" (was Jerome perplexed?) Cf. ZBG #127; Fitzmyer 1993 NTS:322–23; AB 33:413–14. (5) *eph' hō[i]* is a noun phrase with its rel. pro. antecedent suppressed; BDF #294.4; ZG p. 601, ZBG §129; Thrall 94, "with regard to which"; therefore, ". . . for which thing you were concerned," care for Paul. Moule *IB* 132; O'B 518; Bockmuehl 260. Baumert 258 objects, *phronein* then has one construction in 10b (*hyper* + gen.) and another in 10c (*epi* + dat.). Variety in usage, but in the same v? Baumert 1973:387 takes *phronein* in a classical sense, with *mega*, "think great(ly), take pride" (LSJ *phroneō* II.2.b, with *eph' hō[i]* as a relative, "at which"); wordplay on *phronein* + the acc. (*to hyper emou*, to think on the "for me" or care for Paul) and *phronein* + *epi* (be proud at this); the former (10b) gives the grounds for the latter. Cf. Ewald 1908:210 = 1923:226. It has little support; Silva 233 n 10.

(6) Some question "because" for *eph' hō[i]*. Lyonnet 1955, no evidence *eph' hō[i]* = *hoti* until after the NT period (first *perhaps* in Appian of Alexandria, *Sicelica* 4.1.2–4 [2nd cent. A.D.]; then Damascius *Vita Isidori* 154, 6th cent.; Syntipus 124/25, 127/28, 10th cent.). Fitzmyer (AB 33; *NTS* 39 [1993] 321–39) examined previously uncited instances of *eph' hō[i]* (CD-Rom, *TLG*). For "causal use," (1) above, examples claimed in BDAG (p. 365) do not hold, only the three late examples above (*NTS* 39:331–32, cf. AB 33:415). Rom 5:12 means ". . . with the result that all have sinned"; Phil 3:12d, "that for which Christ Jesus took hold of me" (see NOTE on 3:12). 4:10, " 'you have revived your concern for me, for whom

you were once indeed concerned, but lacked the opportunity'; or possibly 'with regard to which' (i.e. *to hyper emou phronein*) you were once concerned" (*NTS* 39:331); Fee 430. With Glombitza 1964–65:137 and Moule *IB* 132, the phrase refers back to *emou*, "me" (Paul), though in *NTS* 333 n 58 Fitzmyer inclined toward Danker 1967–68:434, *hō[i]* as a neut., referring to *phronein* (or *to hyper emou*, in the sense of v 18, *ta par' hymōn*, the Philippians' gifts), "in the matter in which you were concerned." Danker's "binding contract" with "the aspect of a *nomos*" is scarcely relevant to Phil 4:10, unless a "law" of friendship and reciprocal obligations (see COMMENT A.2). TRANSLATION: *on which.*

you were long intent. Imperf., continuing past action, *ephroneite* (10b infin.; see NOTE on *your concern for me*). Schenk 44, conative, "you tried to show your concern. . . ." The NOTES indicate varied senses for *phronein*. 1:7, feeling as well as intellect, hence *phronein* + *hyper* or *epi* = "care in thought and act for . . ." 1:7 and 4:10 (G. Bertram, *TDNT* 9:233). How one's life is directed; NRSV Rom 8:5 "live according to the flesh" or Spirit (H. Paulsen, *EDNT* 3:439); hence 2:5, lit., "Think (live) in this way among yourselves, the way you do in (relation to) Christ Jesus"; 3:19 "setting their minds on earthly things," instead of heavenly ones. A further dimension is ecclesial: "the Kyrios and . . . the body of Christ determine one's *phronein* concretely" (Paulsen ibid.); "Phil 1:7 speaks of Paul's own commitment to the church," 4:10, "feeling on the church's part toward the apostle." 2:2; 3:15, 16; and 4:2 have to do with church unity. *phronein* may relate to friendship (COMMENT A.2, below), but the ecclesial context must not be overlooked.

you had no opportunity. Imperf. m.-p., dep. (cf. BDF #307) *akaireomai* (BDAG **lack an opportunity**), in NT and early Christian literature only at Herm. *Sim.* 9.10.5. A Hellenistic derivative from *kairos*, "time," + *alpha* privative (BDF #117.1); adj. *akairos, on,* **untimely, ill-timed,** contrast *eukairos* (2 Tim 4:2, NRSV "favorable or unfavorable"). *eukaireō*, "have good opportunity, leisure; spend time on," is accepted Koine; *akaireomai,* **have no opportunity, have no time,** condemned by later lexicographers (Phrynichus, Photius; GNTG 2:390; cf. Louw/ Nida 67.7). P. Marshall 164 n 151, "may imply a lack of finance" among Philippian Christians.

4:11a. *It is not that I mention this out of need.* Lit., "Not that (*ouch hoti*) because of lack (*kath' hysterēsin*) I speak (*legō*)." Elliptical for *ou legō hoti . . . ,* "(I do) not (say) that I speak out of poverty"; or supply *estin* (GNTG 3:303, "(It is) not that. . ."; "my meaning is not that. . . ." *ouch hoti* is used at 3:12 (see NOTE), 2 Cor 1:24, etc., and Phil 4:17. ATR 1165–66; BDF #480.5, under ellipsis of *legō*; but common enough that the "ellipsis was probably never present to the mind" (Goodwin/ Gulick #1519). Here for *written* communication (BDAG *legō* 2.f; 1 Cor 6:5, etc.); oral style in dictation, assuming the letter will be read aloud. Cf. *legō* at 3:18. 4:11 renderings vary: "speak" (KJV), "complain" (RSV), "mean" (Phillips), "allude to" (NEB), "refer to" (NRSV).

"I say" + adv. expression (*kath' hysterēsin*) is not uncommon in Paul (BDAG *legō* 1.b.ε). *kata* + acc. (BDAG B.5.a.δ; NOTE on 1:20 *In accord with . . .*) merges *in accordance with* and *because of,* re some norm or reason; *as a result of, on the basis of,* Phlm 14. On *hysterēsis*: U. Wilckens, *TDNT* 8:592–601, esp. 599;

W. L. Lane, *NIDNTT* 3:952–56, esp. 955; BDAG, **lacking what is essential, need, lack, poverty,** Mark 12:44, the widow in her penury (par. Luke 21:4 *hysterēma*, used at Phil 2:30). Paul is not speaking out of such poverty. Lack of joy (Ewald 1908:212 = 1923:228)? Paul claims ample joy "at the sharing of his church in his present distress (4:14)" (Wilckens, *TDNT* 8:599). Beet 1889b:175, my gratitude "is not a beggar's thanks for charity," repeated in Jones and Hawth. 197. Then Paul is not saying thank you. His financial condition remains tantalizingly vague; see COMMENT B.2.a.

4:11b. *for I have learned to be content with whatever I have. egō*, "I," + *gar* (*for*, postpositive) + *learned (emathon)*; then a subordinate cl., *en hois eimi*, lit. "in (things, circumstances, situations in) which I am"; *autarkēs einai* completes the main vb., "(I have learned how) to be content." *autarkēs* (BDAG **content, self-sufficient**) is an important term in Stoic, Cynic, and other philosophies. Rienecker 216, *egō* is "strongly emphatic"; Turner, *GNTG* 3:37, "without much emphasis." Was *egō* added so *gar* can be in postpositive position? Or to anticipate, what "I, Paul, have come to know in my circumstances"?

learned. See NOTE on 4:9 *you learned*, "learn by experience" (BDAG *manthanō* 3, **come to a realization . . . less through instruction than through experience or practice, learn, appropriate to oneself**). Proverbial Gk. wordplay, *emathen aph' hōn epathen*, "one learns from what one suffers" (Herodot. 1.207; Aeschyl. Ag. 177; Philo *Somn.* 2.107; Heb 5:8, Jesus "learned [obedience] by what he suffered"). ATR 834–35, an "effect" or "resultant" aor., B. Gildersleeve the "upshot" aor.: Paul states his finding after experiencing various circumstances. Hawth. 198, "constative" aor.; "for linear actions . . . completed," regarded as a whole (BDF #322.1). The infin. *(einai)* is complementary, classically correct after *manthanō*, "learn how" (*GNTG* 1:229; ATR 1040–41). The subject of the infin., normally acc. (lit., "I learned me to be . . .") need not be expressed; *autarkēs*, pred. nom., as with "to be" (*GNTG* 3:146); BDF #405.1, *manthanein* is related to "be able"; not acc. and infin. *en hois* truncates *en toutois en hois*, "in these (things) in which I am" (ATR 721). Neut. pl. *hois* = situations or circumstances where Paul undergoes his learning experience. Cf. BDAG *eimi* 3.c, + prep. *en, in the situation in which I find myself.* Glombitza 1964–65:136–37 takes *hois* as masc., "among which people I too live," those who share distress (v 14) and help (v 15).

content. autarkēs, *es* (only here in the NT), noun *autarkeia* (2 Cor 9:8, 1 Tim 6:6 "godliness . . . with *contentment*"). *autos* (self) + *arkeō*, "suffice, be enough," therefore "be satisfied, content." At 4:11, "self-sufficient" (NEB "find resources in myself") or "content" (KJV, [N]RSV). In the LXX, adj. only (5x; noun not at all), but "a central concept in ethical discussion from the time of Socrates . . . a well-worn term in ordinary usage" (G. Kittel, *TDNT* 1:466–67). Word studies: B. Siede, *NIDNTT* 3:727–28; EDNT 1:179; Louw/Nida 25.83,84; 75.6.

In classical Gk., economic and political self-sufficiency, in household *(oikos)*, village, *polis*, or larger unit, often associated with independence *(autonomia)* and rights *(themis)* (A. Mannzmann, *KlPauly* 1:777–79). Later, living with internal freedom *(autarkeia* a synonym for freedom) in communities (philosophical groups, social clubs, and the mystery religions) or as an individual. "I am free to do anything" (1 Cor 6:12) may reflect this background (H. Conzelmann, *1 Cor.* 108–10). The self-sufficient person *(autarkēs)* appears in philosophical contexts, esp. in connection with "happiness" (Ebner 339); the ideal was existence not dependent on others, sufficient to oneself, independent and therefore free (cf. H. Schlier, *TDNT* 2:487–96); the individual (generally male) sought self-control over the inner life, liberation from external circumstances. Heroes like Odysseus, thinkers like Socrates and Diogenes the Cynic exemplified *autarkeia* and freedom. Socrates, "a man of great independence *(autarkēs),*" asked, "How many things can I do without?" (Diog. Laert. 2.24; LCL tr. R. D. Hicks). Distinguish things under our control *(ta eph' hēmin)* and things not; pray the gods for contentment (Epict. 1.1.13). Not "property brings security," but freedom from possessions leads to virtue (Plut. *De Vitando Aere Alieno* 3 = *Mor.* 828C = LCL 10:321, "On Borrowing"). Cf. Antisthenes (Diog. Laert. 1.15; 6.11–13); P. Wilpert, *RAC* 1:1040; Ebner 339–40.

This ideal was variously implemented (Berry 111–14, bibl. in n 26; Ebner 338–45; P. Wilpert, *RAC* 1:1040–48). Plato, self-sufficiency was attainable on the moral level; resources for the good life lay within; nothing else, not even friends, is necessary. Aristot., community; parents, children, wife, fellow-citizens, a few virtuous friends *(Eth. Nic.* 1.7.6–7, cf. 1.9; 9.9–12), a moderate amount of material possessions (10.7.4, 8.9). Epicurus, the best way to make a person happy is to eliminate desires; plain, simple food, absence of pain (Diog. Laert. 10.130–31). Cynics attracted attention for public austerity: freedom from externals *(autarkeia)* and all desires and affections *(apatheia;* Diog. Laert. 6.37; Xen. *Mem.* 1.2.14); rejection of the world included family, etc.; through *askēsis* (discipline) and *ponos* (acceptance of hardship; *OCD³* 186–87). Later Cynics like Bion (ca. 325–255 B.C.) and Teles were less strict (Ebner 339–40).

Stoics (cf. R. Bultmann 1956:138, 185–86; *OCD³* 1446): "life in accord with virtue" is the goal; virtue suffices for happiness (Sen. *Ep.* 85.1); to possess one virtue is to possess all (Diog. Laert. 7.125, on Zeno). Develop inner resources, be detached from externals, so that inward tranquillity is not affected by external circumstances. The Stoic can stand serene, accepting whatever comes from fate, nature, or destiny. Cf. LCL *Seneca ad Lucilium, Epistolae Morales* 2:309, tr. R. M. Gummere): "So the wise person will develop virtue (ethical perfection),

if he may,	in the midst of riches,	if not,	in poverty;
if he can,	in his own country,	if not,	in exile;
if he can,	as commander,	if not,	as a soldier;
if he can,	healthy,	if not,	sickly.

Whatever fortune he experiences, he will accomplish something memorable out of it." Unlike Aristot. (some material goods), Stoics made inner tranquillity enough. Plut., *De virtute et vitio,* "On Virtue and Vice" *(Mor.* 101DE), sounds close to Phil 4:12:

You will be content *(autarkēs)* if you learn *(mathē[i]s)* what is the honorable and good *(to kalon kagathon).* You will live luxuriously *(tryphēseis)* amid poverty and be like a king, and you will love the unencumbered life of a private citizen not less than that of military or civic office. You will not live unpleasantly if you become a philosopher, but will learn how *(manthēsē[i])* to live pleasantly anywhere and from any resources. Riches will gladden you, in that you can benefit many people; poverty will gladden you, in that you can be without anxiety about many cares; and reputation will gladden you in that you are honored, and obscurity, in that you are unenvied. (LCL *Moralia* 2:101, tr. F. C. Babbitt, cf. p. 93)

Stoic self-sufficiency could reject *philia*; between the unwise, friendship disappears once the want *(chreia)* is removed; the wise *(sophoi)* are "self-sufficient *(artarkeis)*" and do not need friends (so Theodorus, in Diog. Laert. 2.98); Sen., the wise *can* do without friends, but *need not* (*Ep.* 9.5). Cf. Aristot. *Eth. Nic.* 9.9.4–7: most people think of friends in terms of usefulness or pleasure, the happy person does not; a good friend can be a recipient for beneficence, so that one can find pleasure in good deeds (good company stimulates good deeds; "learn what is good by associating with the good," Theognis). But did the average Gk. distinguish among the views of the various schools (Ebner 338–39)? Engberg-Pedersen 1995a:262–63 allows that "by Paul's time" *autarkeia* "need not have any philosophical overtones at all." There was also a weaker, everyday sense of "sufficiency" (Kittel, *TDNT* 1:466; Ebner 338 n 43). E.g., "sufficient water" (Jos. *Ant.* 2.259 = 2.11.2); LXX Sir 40:18, NRSV-mg; Prov 30:8 "what suffices *(ta autarkē)*"; Sir 5:1, 11:24, 31:28, etc. Papyrus examples in MM 93 ("enough heat" for a bath house).

Does 4:11 reflect this popular meaning of "sufficient" (T. Nägeli, *Der Wortschatz des Apostels Paulus: Beiträge zur sprachgeschichtlichen Erforschung des Neuen Testaments* [Göttingen: Vandenhoeck & Ruprecht, 1905]) or the philosphical sense of "self-sufficient"? BDAG 152, "perh[aps] *self-sufficient.*" MM, "Paul could use the technical words of thinkers in their own way." In this "meteor fallen from the Stoic sky," Fee 431–32 sees "common parlance for 'contentment'"; Philippians would have recognized the term. Others claim something different in Paul "because he has learned Christ" (K. H. Rengstorf, *TDNT* 4:410); cf. B. Siede, *NIDNTT* 3:728. G. Kittel (*TDNT* 1:467), "in a new light" as "part of *eusebeia*" (1 Tim 6:6); for Phil 4:13, cf. Marcus Aurelius (Emperor A.D. 161–80), *Med.* 1.16.11, "self-sufficient in everything"; but these texts are later; note the independence of Paul's apostolic office, and dependence on "the One who enables" him (Gnilka 175; Ferrari 276). *autarkēs* in 4:11 is far from popular philosophical opinions (Loh. 180; cf. Priero 1961, 1962:62). Not within "the technical Stoic idea of *autarkeia*" (Malherbe 1996:125), but of "friendship"; the Philippians' letter "expressed their desire, as Paul's friends, to meet his needs" (139; cf. Malherbe 1990:254 and n 44); he seeks to move beyond utilitarian aspects to "a yet higher level of discussion that even dispenses with *philos* and *philia*" (139).

4:12. *I know how even to be brought low with few resources; I know how also to abound with much. I have had my initiation experience in every situation and all circumstances, both to get my fill and to go hungry, both to abound and to suffer lack.* Paul expounds what *be content* (v 11 *autarkēs*) means in various circumstances via a "peristasis catalogue" or list of situations, circumstances, and hardships (Gk. *peristasis*, circumstance, danger, a term in philosophers, rhetoricians, and others); see COMMENT A.4.e; Fitzgerald 1988:33–46; Ebner, Ferrari. Examples: 1 Cor 4:8–16, esp. 9–13; 2 Cor 11:23–29; cf. 2 Cor 12:10; 4:7–12; 6:4–10; Rom 8:31–39. Loh. claimed two three-line stanzas in 4:12–13 (178, 180–81, cf. Friedrich 173). Other structural/ rhetorical analyses in Schenk 30–39; Silva 232 n 9; Egner 334–38; Ferrari 273–75; U. B. Müller 203. At points such analyses, though inconclusive, may affect word meanings.

4:12a. *I know how even.* . . . Perf. act. *oida*, from *eid-*, "I have seen, therefore I know," 2x in 12ab; 4:15 "you know"; 1:16 (aor. ptc.), 19 ("I know," see NOTE), and 25. Knowledge through experience (Ewald 1908:212 = 1923:228), not revelation (*ginōskein*); (BDAG 4) **come to know** or **understand how** (1 Thess 4:4), **can, be able** (+ infin.) (Seesemann, *TDNT* 5:117); NAB "I am experienced." Six infins. follow, in contrasting pairs; with the first two *oida* is repeated. *kai* before each infin. may mean more than "and." Many take *kai . . . kai* as correlatives, ". . . both how to be abased, and . . . how to abound," etc. (KJV). In 12 a and 12b, *kai* comes between *oida* and the infin.: lit., "I know how both to be abased, I know how also to abound." ATR 1181 called it "adjunctive," "also." BDF #444.3, "peculiar," the first *kai* = "even." BDAG *kai* 1.f, "both/and, not only/but also," citing Phil 2:13 ("both to will and to do"), is misleading: at 4:12 each *kai* introduces a single infin., the second *oida* intrudes. See also 4:16 NOTE, *kai en Thessalonikē[i] kai hapax kai dis*. Some trs. (RSV) ignore *kai . . . kai* in 12a, and in 12b, d, and e express it as a connective, "and." The TRANSLATION follows BDF (above).

to be brought low with few resources. Negative and positive terms are grouped in an a-b, b-a, b-a pattern. Not negatives alone (1 Cor 4:9–13; 2 Cor 11:23–29, 12:10), or positives (Rom 8:31–39), or hardships first, then positive qualities, then pairs akin to Phil 4:11 ("honor and dishonor," etc.; 2 Cor 6:4–10). The first two infins. occur also at 12e (*perisseuein*) and 2:8a (*tapeinousthai*, NOTE on *he experienced humiliation* . . . ; cf. *tapeinōsis* 3:21 NOTE on *the body of our humiliation* and *tapeinophrosynē* 2:3b NOTE on *in humiliation*. BDAG *tapeinoō* classifies 4:12 with (4) OT usage (humble oneself under God, "*discipline, constrain, mortify* oneself"; cf. E. Schweizer, *Lordship* [(7) Bibl.] 1960:61–64, 114–15), traditionally at 4:12, "be abased," KJV, RSV. Michel: as for Christ at 2:8 (*TDNT* 4:655). Loh.181 noted economic poverty (cf. Jas 1:9), then martyrdom (in contrast to rich in the gifts of salvation). Grundmann (*TDNT* 8:17–18) doubts martyrdom here; Paul was "humble (*tapeinos*) when face to face" (2 Cor 10:1, "demeaned" by critics, Furnish, AB 32A:456, 460–61); Grundmann equates *tapeinousthai* with *hystereisthai* at 4:12, "be in need," in contrast with "have plenty"; 12a = "live in poor circumstances, in want." Loh/Nida 141: not "live humbly," but a contrast to being prosperous; W. Barclay, *NT* 1969, "I know how to live with less than enough." Economic deprivation, not humility as a Christ-like virtue. Cf. *TLNT* 3:369–71; Wengst 1988 ([6] Bibl. **humiliation**) 46–47; O'B 523; Oakes 2001:96.

4:12b. *to abound with much. perisseuein* + *oida kai* repeated from 12a. Pres. act. infin., also at 4:12e; cf. 1:9, NOTE on *grow*; 4:18a *I abound*; 3 of the 4 examples in Phil are thus in Letter A. BDAG *perisseuō* 1.b.α: *persons have an abundance, abound,* are *rich;* Louw/Nida 57.24 "possess an overabundance"; "have plenty" (NEB, NRSV). Of economic goods. See NOTE on 4:12a *be brought low.* G. Schneider, *EDNT* 3:77, contrasts "salvation possessions" (1:9) and 4:12, economic resources for food, lodging, etc., of a missionary (cf. 1 Cor 15:58) or prisoner. 12e, with "be in need." Baumert 1973:300–10, a favorite word of Paul. Material aid from the Philippians is involved in Paul's *autarkeia* and "abounding"; 4:18, *I abound (perisseuō) . . . because I have received . . . what you sent* (Berry 115 n 34, "economic abasement and abundance . . . rather than spiritual conditions"). In abundance and in poverty, Paul is content.

4:12c. *I have had my initiation experience.* Pf. pass., *myeō,* here only in the NT. Is it a general term or (BDAG) a "t[echnical] t[erm] of the mystery religions **initiate (into the mysteries)**"? Patristic interpreters (B. Weiss 329) favored "be tested, practiced, taught in, accustomed to" (Vg "instructed"); "initiate in a mystery religion," appears with Erasmus in the 16th cent., then Grotius, though *myeō* is common in the Gk. Fathers for Christian inititation (and instruction; *PGL* 887). Used of initiation into a mystery cult (G. Bornkamm, *TDNT* 4:828); cf. 3 Macc 2:30. Lft. 164 noted this sense. Evidence is limited: (1) Plut. *Mor.* 795E (*An seni* 24 = LCL 10:141, tr. H. N. Fowler), "a neophyte *(myoumenos) . . .* and initiator *(mystagōgōn)*"; (2) Alciphron (A.D. 200) *Epist.* 2.4; (3) Ign. *Eph.* 12.2 "fellow initiates *(symmystai)*" of Paul, said to reflect Phil 4:12 (W. Schoedel, Hermeneia *Ign.* 73). Some evidence exists for a non-tech. sense. KJV "I am instructed"; Silva 234–36, parallel to *oida.* Bornkamm, the Plut. passage shows *political* connections, Alciphron = "instruct"; cf. also Palatine Anthology 7.385 (LCL *The Greek Anthology,* tr. W. R. Paton, 2:206–7). Loh. 182, initiation in martyrdom, a view not compelling; e.g., Ferrari 447 n 444. Bornkamm decides for a "general" sense, concrete stresses and gifts of daily life where Paul experiences the power of Christ. *EDNT* 2:444–45, a mystery-religions term "to describe the power of Christ operative in the apostle." Priero 1962:62–63, Paul has disciplined himself (middle voice) and learned (cf. Vg *institutus sum*).

in every situation and all circumstances. en panti kai en pasin, "in" + dat. sg. and pl., neut., *pas, pasa, pan,* **any and every, every,** used as a noun (BDAG 2.a.β). Either place ("everywhere" KJV; "in all places") or time ("any time, all the time"). Trs. may combine local and temporal (TEV). ATR 117–18, *en panti* 12x (1, 2 Thess, 1, 2 Cor), *en pasi(n)* 5 or 6x in the Pastorals; together at Phil 4:12. Moule *IB* 75 compares 1 Cor 15:28, "all in all" *(panta en pasin).* 2 Cor 11:6, NRSV "in every way and in all things *(en panti . . . en pasin)."* 4:12 is adverbial, "repetition for . . . emphasis" (B. Reicke, *TDNT* 5:889). [N]RSV, "in any and all circumstances," fits the *peristasis*-catalogue form; Moffatt, "all sorts and conditions of life."

4:12d. *both to get my fill. kai* + *chortazō,* only Pauline occurrence. (BDAG) **feed, fill,** pass. **be satisfied,** of animals or human beings; NT chiefly in feeding miracles (Mark 8:4, 8; Ps 132 [LXX 131]:15). From *chortos,* feeding-place, fodder for animals, + *azō* as verbal suffix. Originally depreciatory (Plato *Resp.* 9.586A; human beings "foddered"; Athenaeus 3.99F–100B, LCL 1:428–31); later, equivalent to *esthiō* "eat" or *korennymi* "satisfy, glut" (Lft. 164; *GNTG* 2:405). Cf. *NIDNTT* 1:743–44 (J. G. Baldwin); *EDNT* 3:470–71. Loh. 182 n 3, the term is frequent, no need to see influence from Jesus' beatitude, ". . . you will be filled (*chortasthēsesthe*)," Luke 6:5 par Matt 5:6. Physical, economic, further defined by the next term (U. B. Müller 203).

and to go hungry. Pres. act., *peinaō*; infin. *peinan*. BDAG 1, lit. **hunger, be hungry.** In Paul, 5x (1 Cor 11:34, cf. 21; 1 Cor 4:11, *peristasis* catalogue; Rom 12:20 = Prov 25:21). In Gk. philosophy (L. Goppelt, *TDNT* 6:12–22), the well-organized state should prevent hunger (Plato *Leg.* 9.936BC); as the gulf grew between rich and poor, Stoicism taught *enkrateia*, moderation in food (Sen., *Ad Lucilium Epistulae Morales* 17.9; 18.6–11), sharing bread with the hungry (ibid. 95.51–53). In the OT, hunger could be a judgment (Deut 28:47–48; Isa 8:21) or a humbling to wake people up (Deut 8:3); the future hope, people "will neither hunger nor thirst" (Isa 49:10). Hence Jesus' beatitude and the "eschatological banquet" theme (Isa 25:6). Goppelt (p. 19) connects 12a "be abased" with 2:8, Christ "humbled himself"; 4:11–13 is "'philosophically' formulated," but Paul does not represent Stoic ascetic discipline (or gnostic initiation) but "the poverty in which the beatitude [Luke 6:21] is worked out in faith" (p. 21, cf. 20). But 4:10–20 is not Christocentric; influence from Jesus' beatitude on 4:12 is dubious. Others see an economic meaning (contrast with *perisseuein, chortazesthai,* and the gifts from Philippi, vv 15b–18). Cf. W. Bauder, *NIDNTT* 2:265–68; H. Balz, *EDNT* 3:64. Neither ascetic fastings (A. Fridrichsen, "Zum Stil des paulinischen Peristasenkatalogs," *SO* 7 [1928] 27) nor *imitatio Christi* in salvation history, but conditions in daily life, food in short supply, a concrete fiscal, economic situation of the apostle (Ferrari 277; Furnish AB 32A:518; R. P. Martin WBC 40:380).

4:12e. *both to abound* (*perisseuein*, 12b, contrasting with) *and to suffer lack.* Material abundance and dearth of resources, both matters of indifference (Hauck *TDNT* 6:61). *hystereō*, pres. m.-p.; in classical usage, "wanting, lacking something," often pass. dep. Gk OT, "having a deficiency," lack (Ps 23 [LXX 22]:1; Sir 51:24, AB *Sir* 578). NT, **lack . . . go without, come short of** (BDAG 5.b); Mark 10:21, Luke 15:14; Rom 3:23; 1 Cor 1:7. With *perisseuein* at 1 Cor 8:8, re foods (idol-meats). Stoic parallels in U. Wilckens (*TDNT* 8:597 n 25), esp. Epict. 3.5.7; 3.5.9; 3.10.8; 4.4.34. *Wordbooks*: U. Wilckens, *TDNT* 8:592–601, the fullest treatment; W. L. Lane, *NIDNTT* 3:952–56, esp. 955 top; *EDNT* 3:409; *TLNT* 3:427–31.

4:13. *I am strong, able to tackle everything, through the One who strengthens me.* Some MSS add *Christō[i]*, " through Christ which [sic] strengtheneth me" (KJV; Majority Text, second corrector in א, D² etc., lacking in א* B D* etc., the shorter reading has strong external witness; O'B 513 note b, but 527 "the One who so strengthens Paul is Christ"; Hawth. 193 note b; Fee 434; Edart 289 *lectio brevior*). UBSGNT and *TCGNT* do not even report the addition. Cf. Silva 23. Some suggest Christ as quickening Spirit; E. Schweizer, *TDNT* 6:418 n 568; F. Prat 1926–27 ([1] Bibl. **in Christ [Jesus]**) 2:291–94. Gk. "the One who strengthens me" is God.

I am strong, able to tackle everything. Neut. acc. pl. (*panta*) + *ischyō*, no subject pron. Root *ischy-* = "power, strength, capacity," therefore "be strong, able." Here, **have power, be competent, be able (to do) all** (BDAG 2.a; Banker 180, "cope with every situation"). Trs. often supply an infin. "to do," or take *panta* as acc. of reference, "I am able (with respect to) all things." W. Grundmann, *TDNT* 3:397–402 and *Der Begriff der Kraft in der neutestamentlichen Gedankenwelt* (BWANT 60; Stuttgart: Kohlhammer, 1932), put 4:13 under "be able," to show Christ as "the source of all Paul's capacity in face of the reality of human life" (398). G. Braumann (*NIDNTT* 3:712–14, more classical and LXX background), under God's strength/power and human weakness. H. Paulsen (*EDNT* 2:208), it "orients the power of the apostle to the gift provided in Christ" (13b *endynamounti*). To avoid any idea of arrogance on Paul's part, some limit *all things* to those mentioned in v 12 (B. Weiss 330). But Loh/Nida 143, all situations, all conditions. Meyer 1889:178, "there is *nothing* for which Paul did not feel himself morally strong." Fee 435–36 sees in this an "unfortunate history of interpretation"; cf. COMMENT B.2.b.

through the One who strengthens me. Subst. ptc., *endynamoō* (BDAG 1, **strengthen**), masc. (unless neut., *pneuma* understood, "the Spirit who strengthens me"), dat. after *en.* + dir. obj. *me.* Compound vb., *en* + *dynamoō/dynamai*, cf. *dynamis* in NOTES on 3:21 *the power that enables* and 3:10 *power.* *-oō* vb., causative sense, "the one who makes me able"; BDF #148.3. The prefix *en-* may suggest intensity (Moule *IB* 88). Hawth. 201, Christ at 4:13 because *endynamai* is used elsewhere of Christ, but the references are all deutero-Pauline (Eph 6:10; 1 Tim 1:12; 2 Tim 2:1, 4:17). The excursion (*TDNT* 2:313) into *Religionsgeschichte* (*PW* 11:2116), invisible spiritual power said to pervade objects (*ER* 11:470, an Iroquois or Huron version of *mana*, *ER* 7:284–87; *RGG*[4] 5:722–23), Grundmann himself set aside for "fellowship between Christ and man," a "personal relationship" O. Betz, *NIDNTT* 2:601–6, the "work of the exalted Christ in the lives of individual believers." H. Paulsen, *EDNT* 1:451, Stoic character in 4:11–13, but "the decisive element is . . . Christ as the *dynamis* of God," empowering the apostle and present in the apostle's proclamation." *TDNT* 2:316–17, in Paul's apostolic work, divine power present in "human and earthly existence" marked by weakness (2 Cor 13:4a; 1 Cor 1:25; 2 Cor 12:9–10; 2 Cor 4:7).

en has varying trs.: "through" (KJV, NEB, NRSV); "in" (Moffatt, RSV); "by" (TEV); even "thanks to the strength God gives me" (Knox). BAGD, *en* III.1.b, causal or instrumental, means by which something happens (LXX *en* + dat. for the Heb. prep. *bᵉ*; BDF #219; GNTG 1:104, 2:463–64), specifically "with pers[ons]: *with the help of*," not listing 4:13; BDAG *en* 5.b and 6. Moule *IB* 77: either extended use of *en*, instrumental, "by" or "through," or like "in Christ" (p. 80); see NOTE on 1:1 *in Christ Jesus*, where 4:13 could relate to interpretation (5) at 1:1, the "existential," (6) the "dynamic," or (8) the "inclusive personality" view, discussed in the NOTE. Loh. 182–83, (4), martyrdom overcomes "all oppositions . . . through divine power." Older exegetes (B. Weiss 331) debated *objective* power in Christ (Meyer; *TDNT* 2:541) or *subjective* fellowship with Christ (de Wette). Bouttier 1962:87, Neugebauer 1961:128 (both [1] Bibl. **Christ**) see "apostolic consciousness," one side of which is our weakness (2 Cor 13:4b); the other side (Phil 4:13), one can "do all" via Christ, the power of God (1 Cor 1:24). But 4:13 may not belong with *en Christō[i]* passages (no "formula"); NOTE on 4:19 *in Christ Jesus*.

4:14. *Anyway, you did well in sharing together with me in my affliction.* Some see a minor break here (NA[26]); others, a new paragraph (RSV, NIV, NAB); or the conclusion to vv 10–14, new paragraph at v 15 (UBSGNT, NRSV). Moffatt set off v 14 from both 10–13 and 15–20, all in the same paragraph. Paragraphing affects how the opening word, *plēn*, is rendered, an adv. used as conj. (in Paul 5x, 3 of them in Phil); see NOTES on 1:18 *Simply that* and 3:16 *Only*. BDAG *plēn* 1.c. puts 3:16, 4:14, and perhaps 1:18 under **only, in any case, on the other hand, but,** to emphasize "what is important"; Fee 437 agrees; UBSGNT, NRSV. *plēn* can also mean (1.e) **only, but,** "passing to a new subject" (so NA[26], RSV), from Paul's sufficiency in Christ to Philippian sharing with him. Etymology is disputed: from *pleon* = "more," or *plēsion* = near by (GNTG 2:331). ATR 1187 cited classical usage as a conj. with *hoti* (Phil 1:18), "to single out the main point" at the end of an argument; repeated by BDF #449.2 re Phil 3:16,1 Cor 11:11 (where *plēn* does not occur), Eph 5:33 (where *hoti* does not occur). Turner, GNTG 3:338, Paul's use is "peculiar," like the LXX "pleonastic *only*. . . ." Thrall 20–24 traced development of this "linguistic phenomena" in Koine Gk.; at 4:14 *plēn* "functions as a balancing adversative." Balancing what? Paul's sufficiency in Christ with the Philippians' gift? Against *plēn* lifting up what is important: Philippian sharing was not a topic of the "I" statements of 11–13; perhaps it goes back to their revived concern, v 10. Schenk 41, a "progressive," not adversative, sense (NRSV "in any case").

you did well. **kalōs epoiēsate** = aor. act. indic. 2nd pl., *poieō* (BDAG 5.d, *do*) + adv. (BDAG *kalōs* 4.a, *well*), common in the papyri (Berry n 38; DA 278 n 457): "do what is right, act rightly, you do well (in doing something) if . . ." ; idiomatic equivalent of "please. . . ." Fee 438 n 7 offers the slang expression, "You did good." GNTG 1:228, + complementary ptc., usually aor. (as in 14b), "the normal way of saying 'please' in the papyri," classical as well; cf. GNTG 3:158–59). 3 John 6, "You will do well to send them on"; Acts 10:33; 2 Peter 1:19. H. Braun, TDNT 6:477, groups 4:14 with NT vv where *poieō* = do good to the neighbor, render mutual aid. A request formula or instructions, often introducing the body of a papyrus letter, J. L. White 1986:208; "please," "kindly," MM 522–23. Ebner 361, *captatio benevolentiae.*

in sharing together with me. **sugkoinōnēsantes.** Supplementary ptc. with *kalōs epoiēsate*, regularly aor. and nom.; lit., "you did well by sharing . . ."; NRSV "it was kind of you to share. . . ." *syn* + *koinōneō*, only here in acknowledged letters (plus Eph 5:11); simple vb. 4x (see Phil 4:15). *sugkoinōnos* once (see NOTE on 1:7 *sharing . . . with me*). *koinōnia*, 3x in Phil (see NOTE on 1:5 *sharing*; history of *koinōn*-terms, *koinōnia* as a fellowship theme, use by Paul prior to Phil). 4:14 = "give a share, go shares with"; BDAG *sugkoinōneō* 1.b, **be associated w[ith] someone in some activity, be connected,** here willingness to share in Paul's afflictions (Hauck, TDNT 3:807; Baumert 2003 [(2) Bibl. **sharing**] 65–66, 502, 508, 525, their gift ties them to his affliction). The TRANSLATION brings out *syn-* by *together*.

Suggs 1984 ([2] Bibl. **sharing**) made 4:14 his starting-point on *koinōn*-language in 1:5–7 and 4:10–16. On *mou*, see the next phrase.

in my affliction. thlipsis, dat. after vb. compounded with *syn*. Also at 1:17 (NOTE on *trouble*). BDAG 2, **inward experience of distress, *affliction, trouble*;** or (BDAG 1) distress from outward circumstances like eschatological tribulations (Mark 13 parr); in Paul, *difficult circumstances* (2 Cor 8:13; financial "pressure"; "a hard time," AB 32A:407); 4:14 *show an interest in (someone's) distress.* But 4:14 may not be solely "outward circumstances" (cf. 11b–12, *I know, I have learned to be content*). Eschatology may be part of the picture (O'B 529 n 101, but eventually relegated). An important Pauline term (20x in the acknowledged letters, 9 of them in 2 Cor). H. Schlier (*TDNT* 3:139–48) amalgamates references so that "the constant tribulation of Israel in the OT has become the necessary tribulation of the Church" and of "exemplarily the apostles" (143). Paul's *thlipsis* is something in which the Philippians share. Rightly, there are "afflictions of different kinds" (7 kinds in Rom 8:35), external and internal (146–47). Similarly, R. Schippers, *NIDNTT* 2:807–809, within "God's plan of salvation." J. Kremer (*EDNT* 2:151–53), "the *thlipsis* of persecution as eschatological *thlipsis*," but "afflictions . . . not limited to persecution." Positive meaning comes from association with Christ, cross and resurrection (cf. 3:10); hence future joy, present rejoicing, 4:10 (cf. Schrage 1974:145–46). To render "hardships" (JB, NAB), "difficulties" (Gdsp.), "troubles" (TEV) aligns the term with vv 11b–12. Gnilka 176 and O'B 529 n 106 rightly reject Loh.'s notion (183–84) of martyrdom for the Philippians. Fee 438 n 9 sees little "eschatological significance."

mou. Obj. gen. or possession. Before *thlipsei*, as at Phil 2:2 *(mou tēn charan)*; *GNTG* 3:189. Unemphatic form to make the personal reference less obtrusive? Or to emphasize the Philippians' "personal relation to the Apostle" (H. A. A. Kennedy, EGT 471; O'B 529 n 106)? They share in Paul's distress by empathy, their gift(s) (cf. 4:10, 15–18; Meyer 178), and their distress. *mou* can also be construed with the ptc., "share together *with me* in distress"; *koinōneō* words often take their object in the gen. (BDAG *koinōneō* 1.a; DA 209 n 210; 1 Cor 9:23; Rom 11:17; Phil 1:7 *sharing . . . with me in this gracious opportunity of mine*). Schenk 44, Phil 4:14 *sygkoinōnēsantes mou* parallels v 15 *ekoinōnēsen moi*; Hawth. 193, O'B 515 (italics added), ". . . partners *with me*. . . ." The TRANSLATION takes *mou* both ways, *with me in my affliction.*

4:15a. *But do you indeed know, you Philippians, that . . . ?* 15 and 16 form one long sentence in Gk., RSV. Most trs. make 15 and 16 separate sentences (KJV, NRSV). Apparent structure: "you know" *(oidate)* + two *hoti* cls., "that . . . no church shared with me . . . except you" 15; "that . . . you sent help . . . more than once" 16. But various construals exist. After *oidate, de kai (But . . . indeed),* + voc., "O Philippians," before the first *hoti* cl. *de* is omitted in P⁴⁶ D* etc. (not noted in UBSGNT or TCGNT) as superfluous with *kai* (Hawth. 194; cf. Silva 23). A new paragraph in UBSGNT, NRSV, but NA²⁶, RSV, etc., begin the paragraph with v 14. *hoti* could mean "because" (Ewald 1908:214 = 1923:230; contrast Meyer 178–79). *that* is preferable.

oidate. See NOTE on 4:12 *I know.* 2nd pl., with *hymeis,* "*you* know" or "you yourselves . . ." (NEB). An indic. statement is trite, condescending. Impv. in Wohl.'s added note to Ewald 1923:233. Better, a question on what the Philippians now need to recall. For *oidate* as a Pauline cliché, see COMMENT A.4.c.

Philippēsioi. Voc., set off by commas, though trs., KJV through NRSV, treat it as nom. (same ending), "you Philippians know." Normally *Philippeus* or *Philippēnos* in sg., "person from Philippi" (so Steph. Byz.; inscriptions). Paul uses a Lat spelling, found nowhere else in Gk. literature (Pilhofer 1:116), to reproduce the official title of the Roman colony (INTRO. I; Ramsay 1900; *GNTG* 2:337; Pilhofer 2:#004, cf. index 881). Hawth. 203, for Gk. a monstrosity. Paul flatters the Philippians by using their (proud) term, likely from their note to him. Church Fathers (B. Weiss 335; J. H. Michael 219; Hawth. 203) saw it ameliorating rebukes in 11–13, 14. Others (O'B 530–31), no rebuke, *Philippēsioi* expresses "affectionate gratitude." Similarly with *kai:* with vb. ("you know also") or (cf. Moule *IB* 167) *hymeis*, "you also know . . . ," "you as well as I," not "you as well as others" (O'B 530; Vincent 147; Hawth. 203). *de* seems transitional, possibly with a note of contrast (cf. BDAG *de* 4, but 4:15 is not listed); *kai*, "you also," like me; *hoti* for the content of what they know. The TRANSLATION has *But* for *de*, indeed for *kai*.

4:15b. *"at the beginning of the gospel," when I departed from Macedonia.* Temporal phrases, variously interpreted. Lit. (KJV, RSV) "(the) beginning" (*archē*, BDAG 1.a, **commencement of something**, *when the gospel was first preached*). On *gospel* see NOTE on 1:5; the content of good news and the "action aspect of sharing in missionary proclamation" (*nomen actionis*; TDNT 2:729; BDAG *archē* 1.a, above; *euangelion* 1.a.β, *"beginning* (of the proclaiming) *of the gospel"*). No qualifying phrase like "gospel of God"; one of 23 such examples in Paul, including all 9 in Phil (G. Friedrich, *TDNT* 2:729). Cf. Mark's title, "The Beginning of the Gospel of Jesus Christ"; *1 Clem.* 47:2 (reflection of 4:15?), Paul "wrote to you *en archē[i] tou euangeliou*," either "in the beginning of his gospel" in 1 Cor or, more likely, in the beginning of his missionary work in Philippi (Hartke 1917 [INTRO. VII.B] 55); Lft. 165: 2 Thess 2:13, reading *ap' archēs*; Pol. *Phil.* 11.3, "you were his letters in the beginning [*in principio*]" (cf. 2 Cor 3:2). G. Delling, *TDNT* 1:482, "the first period of Paul's evangelistic activity" (forget prior work in Acts).

when. hote + aor. indic. *exerchomai* (BDAG 1.a.α.ℵ) + *apo*, temporal and geographical (Loh. 184). *from Macedonia* (Acts 16:12, the province), 13x in Paul, 1 Thess 1:7–8; 4:10; 2 Cor 2:13; 7:5, etc.; Macedonia supported Paul's work (2 Cor 11:9) and the collection (2 Cor 8:1; Rom 15:26). The *when* cl. may be epexegetical (explanatory), defining the first phrase: "the beginning of the gospel" = "when I left Macedonia" (Meyer 179). Others give *exēlthon* a pluperf. sense, "when I had left Macedonia," or take it as if "when I began my mission in Macedonia" (cf. Haupt; discussion in Ewald 1908:214 = 1923:230).

Proposals (Hawth. 204, in light of Gal 1:15– 2:1 and missionary journeys in Acts 13–16, which brought Paul and his team to Philippi) include

(1) the view (traditional) that Paul speaks *from the standpoint of the Philippians* (diplomatically); "the beginning of the gospel among them"; Hawth., *in their vicinity*; NIV "in the early days of your acquaintance with the gospel"; cf. Vincent 147; Michaelis 72; Bruce 127; U. B. Müller 240; O'B 532, their partnership in the

gospel (Phil 1:3–5) "from the first day until now," "linguistic parallels" with the prayer report (in Letter A or Letter A helped shape what is now at 1:3–11).

(2) *Paul began preaching the gospel only in Macedonia, and that in the 40's.* Cf. J. Knox 1950 (INTRO. VIII) 87. Suggs 1960 ([2] Bibl. **sharing**), "the beginning of the ministry at Philippi" or "in Europe"; 1:5, the Philippians were associated with him from the outset; the Thessalonians were the "first fruits" of this missionary endeavor (2 Thess 2:13). This sets Acts aside, but accepts 2 Thess; "the beginning" is work *in* Macedonia, not when Paul *left* the province. G. Lüdemann 1984 (INTRO. VIII) 103–7, Paul with the Philippians carried out an independent mission in Thessalonica and Corinth (chronological chart, Lüdemann 262–63; but 137 n 193 rejects use of Phil 1:5 to interpret 4:15). Critique in U. B. Müller 204 n 80; Riesner 1998:269–71.

(3) *Earlier preaching was of no importance; the start that mattered is indicated in 4:15,* a new continent, a message now of God's grace, Glombitza 1962; 1959:140; see NOTE on Phil 2:12). Glombitza 1964–65: 4:10–20 = thanks for the Philippians' loyalty and support in the task. O'B 531–32 rejects this on the basis of Acts; Paul previously preached a "joyful message of grace."

(4) Proclamation *begins when Paul leads his own program* of evangelization, not as Barnabas' assistant (Acts 13–14). *apo Makedonias* was the starting point for this (Gnilka 177). A "decisive turning point in his career" (E. Meyer, *Ursprung und Anfänge des Christentums* [Stuttgart/Berlin: Cotta, 1923] 3:80, cf. 428). Cf. Loh. 184–85; Pilhofer 1:246. Collange 152 endorses both (1) the Philippians' standpoint, and (4) Paul's own view, mission activity for which Paul "was entirely responsible." O'B 532, this "places too much weight on the gospel mission as being Paul's."

Given such views, NRSV paraphrased, "in the early days of the gospel" (with Moffatt). R. Knox reversed the cls., "when I left Macedonia in those early days of gospel preaching." But does *archē* mean "early days"? Hawth.: "none of the suggestions is completely satisfactory," (4) is "perhaps the best." Loh., "a somewhat loose manner of speaking," the Philippians and Paul know from their common knowledge. Perhaps the phrases were originally in the Philippians' letter, "the beginning of the gospel" for them in Philippi and how Paul went forth, with their aid, which began in Macedonian Thessalonica (v 16)?

4:15c. *no church had shared with me in "an account of giving and receiving" except you alone.* The Philippian house churches are an *ekklēsia* (term not used in 1:1b but to be understood there). Phil 3:6 (see NOTE) gives a *ekklēsia* broader sense. 4:15 = the total Christian community in Philippi and environs (BDAG *ekklēsia* 3.b.β). Later, "other churches" (2 Cor 11:8, 12:13) helped support Paul's mission. *No church . . . except you* compares the Philippians at this time with house churches at Thessalonica or Beroea. + fem. nom. sg., *oudeis, oudemia, ouden,* "no, not one." Indir. obj. *moi,* NRSV "with me," between the adj. and noun, lit., "not-one to-me church shared . . . ," a striking juxtaposition. *ekoinōnēsen,* aor., *koinōneō* (BDAG 2, *give/ contribute a share*), we tr. as a pluperf. (Ewald 1908:215 = 1923:231). See NOTES on 1:5 *sharing*; 1:7 *sharing*; and 4:14 *share.* Sometimes Eng. uses "partnership" language, anticipating commercial terms that follow, ". . . partners in payments and receipts" (NEB; cf. BDAG 552; Baumert 2003 [(2) Bibl. **sharing**] 55–56, 274, 502, 507–8, 524), though not a legal contract (Fleury, Sampley; contrast L. M. White 1990; Berry 118–19). Hauck (*TDNT* 3:808), a "two-sided meaning," give (Paul) a share in, and (have a) share with Paul.

A Pauline principle applies (Gal 6:6; Hainz 1982 [(2) Bibl. **sharing**] 62–89, cf. *EDNT* 2:303), "Let the person who is being instructed in the word share in all good things with the one who teaches"; share physical goods with those teaching the gospel. Fellowship through sharing, but not giving up all one's possessions (as in Acts 2–5, in some Gk. societies or communes). This "*koinōnia* principle" (cf. *EDNT* 2:304) means (I) community through common participation (Phil 1:5, in the gospel); (II) *koinōnoi*, persons who share in something in common; (III) *koinōnein*, have or keep fellowship through reciprocal giving and receiving shares (Phil 4:15); (IV) Phil 4:17, *sugkoinōnein, sugkoinōnos* (1:7), common sharing, in the apostle's grace or suffering. 4:15 can refer to duties (Gal 6:6, support the teacher), but Hainz 112–15 doesn't link it with "business terms" and "mercantile metaphor"; rather, reciprocity in giving and receiving. Can be linked to *philia,* "friends share everything in common" (H. D. Betz, *Gal.* 304–6); thus a Pythago-rean maxim applied to educational praxis in the Galatian churches. On Hainz, see Reumann 1994 ([2] Bibl. **sharing**) ##25–27; Baumert 2003 ([2] Bibl. **sharing**) 12, 14, 499–509, 526; on Gal 6:6, 139–40, 502, 505–6. Such friendship had three components (Ebner 356–59; COMMENT A.2 and 5): (1) place or locale ("friends dwell *together*," Aristot. *Eth. Nic.* 9.10.5–11.6 (1171a 5–1171b 28); (2) a moral aspect (here, 4:14 "share in affliction"); (3) finances (next phrase).

in "an account of giving and receiving." eis (+ acc.), for the dat. BDAG *eis* 4.g. Papyrus parallels include POxy 2.275.19, 21 (A.D. 66) = MM 379, the story of an apprentice and his father, vividly reconstructed in J. D. Crossan, *The Historical Jesus* (HarperSan Francisco 1991) 20–29, esp. 28–29. The phrase reappears in Phil 4:17 *eis logon hymōn;* see NOTE on *to your account. logos,* here acc. sg. (NRSV "the matter"; BDAG *logos* 1.a.ε); tech. sense (financial) computation, reckoning (of accounts); BDAG *logos* 2.b, "*settlement of a mutual account* (lit., 'of giving and receiving,' 'of debit and credit')." Long known from classical sources, new promi-nence from the papyri (Deissmann *LAE* 117; H. A. A. Kennedy 1900–1901); cf. Plut. *Mor.* 11B; Dion. Hal. 5.34.4; papyri in MM 379. H. Ritt, *EDNT* 2:359, 7.e, 4:15 = tech. usage, "settling accounts."

giving and receiving—tech. terms, rare in the NT. *dosis,* only here + Jas 1:17. From the vb. *didōmi,* "gift" (Jas 1:17 KJV) or (BDAG 2) (act of) **giving** (Jas 1:17 NRSV); with *lēmpsis, dosis* = "debit" (bookkeeping entry, something given out). *lēmpsis,* "receiving," in a ledger "credit," here only in the NT; *lambanō,* fut. dep. *lēmpsomai* (BDF #101, p. 53; GNTG 2:106, 246–47). *dosis* was "very common in financial transactions," for "installment, tax payment"; papyrus texts in MM 169, examples with *lēmpsis* noted. Usually *dosis,* the action of giving, is distinguished from *doma,* "gift." On *lēmpsis,* see MM 374. Both terms in Epict. 2.9.12, "what one receives and what one pays out" (LCL 1:271). Sir. LXX 41:21, "receiving and giving," *APOT* 1:468, v 19; AB 39:481; Sir 42:7 "Both giving and receiving, (put) everything in writing." Heb. counterpart terms (*mattah wĕloqaḥ*; rabbinic *mesā' ûmattān* for giving/receiving) in Str-B 3:624; the commercial language extended to human relations, God's judgment, and "give-and-take" in discussion between teacher and pupils. Lat., *ratio acceptorum et datorum* (Cic. *Amic.* 6.58). *KlPauly* 2:151–53; *EDNT* 1:349; Collange 148, "a profit-and-loss account." Hawth. 204–5, 4:15 = "the financial gift of the Philippians" *and* "the receipt they received back from the apostle acknowledging its safe arrival" (in two earlier communications?); cf. 4:18 "paid in full."

In the "two-way transaction" (Martin 1976:165) Paul is usually seen providing "spiritual" goods, instruction in faith; the Philippians, physical goods, money (F. Hauck, *TDNT* 3:808; Loh. 185, citing 1 Cor 9:11; Gnilka 177–78; contrast Schenk 63). *eis logon doseōs kai lēmpseōs* as friendship language appeared Wettstein (Cic. *Amic.*); developed by P. Marshall 1–34, 157–64; applied to this passage by Ebner 346–56. Inscriptional evidence (Pilhofer 1:147–52) moves away from friendship. 2:#213, a bequest to build a fountain in the Forum; 2:#87, gifts for gladiatorial games; 2:#306, 2:##700–3, honors for a benefaction; 2:#202, cf. 203, all illustrate the *do-ut-des* principle: honors come for gifts and attainment. "Giving and receiving" characterized *collegia* and other *socities*, e.g., a bequest for roses on one's grave (the Rosalia festival), a banquet in one's memory (2:#91; Pilhofer 1:104, at Philippi in connection with Dionysus; Silvanus, 1:108–13, 2:##163, 164, and other cults). Thus *logos doseōs kai lēmpseōs* was a "constitutive principle" of society in Philippi. Paul appeals to Christians, with their *politeuma* in heaven, not to invest in fountains or festivals but Paul and mission.

except you alone. Lit., "if not you (pl.) only," *ei mē hymeis monoi*; picks up "you Philippians" (15a, an *inclusio*). *ei* + neg. *mē*, "if not, except" (BDAG *ei* 6.i.α; *mē* 1.a.α; BDF #376; 428.3). Adj. nom. pl., *monos, ē, on* (adv. form at 1:27,29; 2:12,27 *monon*) "only, alone" (BDAG *monos* 1.a.γ, "pleonastic," after a neg.). Not a Semitism (K. Beyer 128). KJV downgraded it to "but ye only"; Phillips, NEB with *ekklēsia*, "the only church/congregation"; Moffatt left out *monoi*, "no other church but yourselves." [N]RSV, "except you only/alone," reflect all the Gk. words, pleonastic or not.

4:16. *And that, even in Thessalonica, more than once, you sent me something for my needs?* The second thing of which Paul reminds the Philippians. See NOTE on 15a *But do you indeed know* . . . ? We divide vv 15–16 into two short sentences, with KJV, NRSV. *hoti*, as in 15a, depends on *oidate*: "you know . . . *that* . . . you sent (help) . . ." (Gnilka 178; Collange 152; Hawth. 205; Schenk 39; U. B. Müller 205; etc.), not "because" (Haupt 174; Bruce 128; O'B 535, etc.). Silva 241 takes v 16 as argumentative ("Why, even when I was still in Thessalonica . . ."). *epempsate*, aor., *pempō*, "send"; see NOTES on 2:19,23; 2:25,28. *eis*, the goal or end for which the Philippians sent gifts (BDAG *eis* 4.d). As obj., (1) the preferred reading (NA²⁶/UBSGNT) is *eis tēn chreian moi*, "for the need to me"; supply a dir. obj., "what was necessary" (BDAG *pempō* 2); NRSV, "you sent me help for my needs." {C} level, in ℵ B Gᵍʳ K etc., Majority Text. (2) *eis tēn chreian mou*, gen. "of me," "for my need"; Dᶜ L P etc., scribal replacement for an unexpected *moi*. KJV "unto my necessity." (3) *tēn chreian moi* = dir. and indir. obj., "you sent me what I needed"; so P⁴⁶ A Dᵍʳ* etc. Thus *eis* was omitted very early (P⁴⁶), by haplography (ΔΙΣΕΙΣΤΗΝ, Silva 241) or deliberately to provide a dir. obj. (*TCGNT* 617). Cf. RSV "you sent me help." (4) Dᵍʳ* aram Ambrosiaster Augustine, *mou* but no *eis* (cf. [2] above), "you send (something for) my need" or "what was needed of me." We omit some maverick readings. Price 283–84 gives (1) 65% probability; (2) 13%; (3) 17%; (4) 5%. Cf. Silva 23. Read (1), but little rides on the matter.

chreia = *want, lack, need* (BDAG 2). See Notes on 2:25c . . . *public servant for my need* and 4:19 *need*. Debate over how real Paul's needs were (Drummond, Lambert) is now seen within "a social context of reciprocity" (*DA* 279 n 458) and friendship. Ebner 352–53 makes *needs* his starting point to discuss *philia*, as the Epicureans did. Many friendships were based on needs and usefulness (Aristot. *Eth. Nic.* 8.3.1–4 [1156a 6–31]; [16] A.2.(A).(2); Ebner 352; cf. Schroeder; Aristippus, Diog. Laert. 2.91; Plut. *Mor.* 51B = *Quomodo adul.* 5 = LCL 1:277). "True friendship seeks after . . . virtue as a good thing, intimacy *(synētheia)* as a pleasant thing, and usefulness *(chreia)* as a necessary thing" (*Mor.* 94B = *De Amicorum Multitudine* = LCL 2:53, tr. F. C. Babbitt). Cic. recommends a person who "will be a source of both pleasure and profit *(usui)* to you" (*Fam.* 13.10.3 = LCL *Letters to His Friends*, tr. M. Cary, 3:43). Cf. Xen. *Mem.* 2.6.21. Friendship based on utility is fitting for unequal partners (Aristot. *Eth. Nic.* 8.8.6 1159b 12–13), like father/son, those older/younger, rich/poor, etc. (8.7.1 1158b 11–12; 8.8.6 1159b 13–14; Comment A, below, n 19). When a friend is in need, the partner gives something; "payment" may be in various "currencies," like money for teaching (8.8.6 1159b 14–15; Plato *Prt.* 9.1.5 1164a 22–27). "Need" *(chreia)* thus expresses an aspect of Gk. *philia* and its reciprocal relationships.

Thessalonica. A city larger than Philippi, to its SW, where Paul went after the founding mission in Philippi (Acts 17:1–15; cf. 1 Thess 2:1–2). *kai*, following *hoti*, with *en Thessalonikē[i]* = "even" or "also" (KJV, [N]RSV, NEB). *en* (not for *eis*, cf. BDF #218) is brachylogy (condensed expression) for "(when I was) in Thessalonica" (Loh. 186 n 3). *kai hapax kai dis*, then = "both . . . and"; 2:13 *both to will and to work*, 4:12, the final 4 infins.; BDF #444.3; GNTG 3:335. ATR 1183, "even . . . both . . . and. . . ." Cf. Fee 445. Or the first and second *kai* are correlatives, "both in Thessalonica and once or twice . . ." (L. Morris 1956; U. B. Müller 205 n 84). *hapax* (BDAG 1) **once**; *dis* **twice.** Variously understood: "two different times" (Banker 185); "more than once" (Lft., Hawth 205). Cf. "not once but even twice" (Dion. Hal. 8.56.1); "once or twice" (Aelius Aristides 36.91); *kai hapax kai dis*, Anna Comnena, *Alexias* [A.D. 1148] 3.3, ed. Reiff 1.102.17, "more than once" (*The Alexiad* [London: Kegan Paul, 1928] 78); Herodot. 2.121.2; Plato *Gorg.* 498E, *Phdr.* 63D, 63E. LXX: 1 Kgdms (1 Sam) 17:39, "once or twice *(hapax kai dis)*"; 2 Esd 23 (Neh 13):20, "once or twice"; 1 Macc 3:30, "more than once *(hapax kai dis)*" (AB *1 Macc* 249, 251). *hapax kai hapax*, Judg 16:20 (B text); 20:30,31; 1 Kdgms 3:10, 20:25. 1 Thess 2:18 is an exact Pauline parallel, "again and again" (NRSV). Cf. *1 Clem.* 53:3, "' again and again *(hapax kai dis)*,'" with Deut 9:13–14 LXX, but the Heb. has no such phrase. Titus 3:10, NRSV "first and second admonition."

G. Stählin (*TDNT* 1:381), *hapax kai dis* = "repeatedly"; so *DA* 315. L. Morris

1956, *again and again, more than once* (so BDAG *hapax* 1). Not a Latinism *(semel iterumque)*, likely (Morris 205) a "Septuagintism," (208) "Both (when I was in Thessalonica) and more than once (in other places)." E. Best *(Thess.* 126) "several times" ("twice" is too weak, "repeatedly" too strong). Thus not lit. "once and twice," or limited to Thessalonica. Several times aid was sent to Paul elsewhere (Corinth—and now, after a gap, Ephesus, Gnilka 178; cf. O'B 535–36). Hawth. seems to restrict it to "more than once" in Thessalonica (193, 205; Dickson 206). Tillmann 1931:160 thought Paul was correcting himself, "once, no, twice."

4:17. *It is not that I am seeking alms. I am rather seeking the profit that accumulates to your account. ouch hoti,* elliptical, as at 3:15 and 4:11; see Notes there. Supply *legō,* "I do not say that . . ." or *estin* (GNTG 3:303), *It is not that . . .* ; or lit. (KJV-NRSV), "Not that . . ." (KJV *hoti* causal, "Not because"). A "disjunctive negative" (ATR 1166), one thing denied to assert another.

epizētō (twice). *zēteō,* contract vb., "seek" (see 2:21) + *epi* to concentrate the action on some object (GNTG 2:312). In Paul here and Rom 11:7, **wish (for)** (BDAG 2.a), with a note of demand (G. Delling, *TDNT* 6:265 n 10; cf. H. Greeven, 2:895). Paul does not seek *to doma,* a/the gift (cf. v 15c *dosis,* "giving"); *alms,* cf. B.1 (Fleury); Beet; B.2.d, below. Grotius: *epizētein to doma,* "seek interest" (Loh. 186 n 4; Sampley 1980:54; Ebner 333; Berry n 56, "demand interest payment"; contrast Fee 447 n 34). *rather* (BDAG *alla* 1) Paul seeks "fruit" (KJV, RSV), *profit* (NRSV), abounding to the Philippians' *account; ton karpon,* see Note on 1:11 *fruit,* agricultural, then metaphorical or commercial senses. Cf. 1:22 *karpos ergou,* "fruitful labor" in missionary endeavor. 4:17 *karpon . . . eis logon hymōn* = **advantage, gain, profit** (BDAG *karpos* 2) for the Philippians' account *(logos,* BDAG 2.b, as at 4:15, obscured in NRSV "matter of giving and receiving"). As in Jewish texts, the result of an action is its "fruit" (Heb. *pĕrî,* "interest," "retribution"; *t. Pe'a* 1.2–4, *b. Qidd.* 40a; Str-B 3 624–25; 1:466, works of love provide capital [reward] in heaven and fruit [interest] in this world). Philippian converts would know the commercial sense from farm produce (Danker 1972:93, 112), hence "profits" generally. MM 321 reported "no example of *karpos* = 'profit,' 'credit'" to match H. C. G. Moule 1897:88, "the *interest . . . accruing* to your *credit*" (Chrysost.; cf. B. Weiss 343 n 1). But MM cited *karpeia* as "profits" and *karpizetai,* to profit. Hence many opt for *karpos* as "profit" (Hawth. 206; Gnilka 179, contrast Bormann 1995:152–55, ethical-paraenetic; O'B 538; Mott 61–64; P. Marshall 159, *karpos* "is often used of the profit to be gained in a business transaction," no evidence cited, but see pp. 9–12). Cf. Cic., "fruit" *(fructus)* from friendship (*Amic.* 9.30–31):

> Although many and great advantages did ensue from our friendship [that of Cicero and Scipio Africanus], still the beginnings of our love did not spring from the hope of gain. For as men of our class are generous and liberal, not for the purpose of demanding repayment—for we do not put favors out at interest, but are by nature given to acts of kindness—so we believe that friendship is desirable, not because we are influenced by hope of gain, but because its entire profit is in the love itself *(omnis eius fructus in ipso amore inest)* (LCL tr. W. A. Falconer, *De senectute, De amicitia . . . ,* p. 143).

Ebner 354–55 compares 4:17, Paul contrasts "interest" (*doma*) he might get with "profit" (*karpon*) for the Philippians' account. Cic. contrasts "demanding repayment" (*exigamus gratiam*) and "fruit" (*fructus*, used metaphorically); a "spiritual" gift stands behind the term "fruit," the love (*amor*) that characterizes friendship. The fruit of friendship "grows" (9.30); in 4:17 *karpon* "abounds" or "accumulates" (*pleonazonta*).

ton karpon, "fruit/profit," is modified by *ton pleonazonta*, ptc., second attribut. position, masc. acc. sg. *pleonazō* (BDAG 1), **be/become more** or **great, be present in adundance, grow, increase.** Rom 5:20; 2 Cor 4:15; 2 Cor 8:15 = Exod 16:18. Phil 4:17 "fruit that increases" superlatively, superabounds (G. Delling, *TDNT* 6:264). If financial, "profit that *accumulates* to your account" (*eis* functions like a dat., ATR 594.) But BDAG cites no evidence for *pleonazō* in a financial sense. But commentators see a business term (W. Bauder, D. Müller, *NIDNTT* 2:131; Martin 1976:167). O'B, "no certain evidence" but "the figure of compound interest" derives from "surrounding expressions." For background, cf. B. W. Frier, "Interest and Usury in the Greco-Roman Period," *ABD* 3:423–24 (bibl.).

4:18a. *I have been paid in full.* Tech. term, *echō* (lit. "have," so KJV) + prep. prefix *apo*, **be paid in full, receive in full**, 'provide a receipt for a sum paid in full' (BDAG 1; papyrus texts in *DA* 279 n 459, often at opening or close of a letter). LXX, Gen 43:23 (receive money); Num 32:19 (receive an inheritance). Plut. *Mor.* 334A = LCL 4:425 "receive full pay." Deissmann 1909 ([1] Bibl.) 229 and *LAE* 110–12 argued from the papyri, ostraca, and inscriptions that *apechō*, sometimes (as in 4:18) with *panta* as dir. obj., occurred in receipts, (full) payment has been made. Applied also to Matt 6:2,5,16 par Luke 6:24. MM 57, examples "might be multiplied almost indefinitely"; the "*perfectivizing*" *apo* prefix gives the pres. tense a past meaning, "I have received. . . ." Therefore "Paid in full" for the Philippians' account; CEV, "I have been paid back everything, and with interest." Deissmann carried the day, but cf. Loh.186, Soph. *Ant.* 498. *de* is "slightly contrastive" (Fee 450), not adversative; it signals a new unit (Banker 187).

and I abound. kai perisseuō, 1st sg. pres. act. indic. See NOTES on 4:12b *abound with much* and 12e, in contrast with *suffer lack*. The third occurrence in 4:10–20; it gilds the lily after *apechō*, "I have received full payment, and more" (RSV). Great abundance (older trs.; Phillips "I am rich"), or a commercial note (CEV "and with interest"). BDAG *perisseuō* 1.b.α, 4:12 and 18a = *have an abundance, abound, be rich.* Hauck (*TDNT* 6:61), "very modest improvement" financially but "more than abundance" of "riches . . . in Christ." Loh. 186, martyrdom, as in 12a.

4:18b. *I am filled full, because I have received from Epaphroditus what you sent.* P[46] (2495) vg[ms] add *de* after *peplērōma*; less abrupt style or contrast, "I do not seek the gift . . . but I have everything" (B. Weiss 345 n 1; Meyer 183; cf. Silva 23). *plēroō*, see NOTE on 1:11 *you have been filled with*; also at 2:2 and 4:19. Words in the climax of Paul's prayer report in 1:9–11 also occur in 4:10–20:

1:11	peplērōmenoi—	4:18	peplērōmai; 4:19 plērōsei
	karpon (dikaiosynēs)—	4:17	karpon (ton pleonazonta eis logon hēmōn)
1:9	perisseuē[i]—	4:12	perisseuein (twice); 4:18 perisseuō
1:11	eis doxan—	4:20	doxa

Some use these data to argue for the unity of Phil, or an *inclusio*, or 4:10–20 as body closing or summary of major themes. If 1:3–11 and 4:10–20 are in Letter A, the words stand even closer. Some terms may come from what the Philippians earlier wrote to Paul. The same word may be employed differently in 4:10–20 (financial connotations) than in 1:9–11. *peplērōmai* (4:18) refers to Paul; 1:11, to the Philippians. 1:11 = filled with certain qualities; 4:18, *well supplied* in physical resources or money (BDAG *plēroō* 1.b; G. Delling, *TDNT* 6:294 n 49, "profane use in Phil. 4:18"). 4:18 (gifts brought by Epaphroditus) is not eschatological like 1:11 (fruit at "the Day of Christ"). 4:18, no need to take *peplērōmai* and *perisseuō* as hendiadys, "I am abundantly filled," or supply *charan*, "filled with joy" (B. Weiss 345 n 1). The three vbs. are clarified by *dexamenos* (Ewald 1908:218–19 = 1923:235); that the three move to a climax is uncertain (Loh. 186–87).

dexamenos. Aor. m. ptc., *dechomai* (BDAG 1; papyrus texts in *DA* 278 n 460), "having received the things [gifts] from you." Circumst. ptc., cause ("because I have received"); or time, antecedent action ("after I had received the gifts, I was full and well supplied") or contemporaneous (Rienecker 217, "I received them and was well supplied"). Most trs., "having received" (KJV, RSV), or paraphrase ("now that I have received . . . what you sent" NEB, NRSV). Fleury, "receive news or assurance" about the Philippians (LSJ).

para + gen., twice, *from Epaphroditus*, "from you." Cf. BDAG *para* 3.a.β; Moule *IB* 51–52; with vb. of receiving, for whence something originates. *Epaphroditus*, see NOTE on 2:25. *what you sent*, Gk. *ta par' hymōn*. Neut. acc. pl. art., no noun; prep. phrase as a noun substitute, "the things from (beside) you." BDAG *para* 3.b.β.ℵ; NRSV "the gifts you sent." GNTG 3:15, papyrus examples, sg. *to para* + gen., money paid by someone; pl. *ta para* + gen., "something sent."

4:18c. *a fragrance with aroma, a sacrifice acceptable, well pleasing, to God.* Three phrases from cultic sacrifice ("borrowed directly from the LXX," Fee 451, but also found in the Greco-Roman world). (1) Taken usually in apposition to *what you sent.* Or (2) referred to the whole action of the Philippians. Or (3) the Philippians themselves (J. Fleury). Or (4) with *peplērōmai* to refer to Paul (Loh. 187–88; acc. of respect, stylistically *zeugma*, elliptically linking ideas [BDF #479.2]); Gnilka 179 n 154, "impossible." Ebner 334, 361–62, Paul, a cultic mediator in the process, presents the gift of the Philippians to God on their behalf. COMMENT B.2.d, below, prefers (2).

a fragrance with aroma. osmēn euōdias, acc. of *osmē*, **odor** (BDAG 2, fig.), + gen. sg. of *euōdia*, **aroma, fragrance**, gen. of quality (BDF #165); or a Hebraism, *euōdias* like an adj., "fragrant offering" ([N]RSV). The precise phrase occurs in Gen 8:21, "the Lord God smelled the pleasing odor" (NRSV; Heb. *rēaḥ hannîḥōaḥ*) of Noah's sacrifice of animals and birds after the flood. Thus to mollify a deity is age-old; cf. *Gilgamesh* xi.159–60 (*Ancient Near Eastern Texts* [Princeton: Princeton Univ. Press, 3rd ed. 1969, p. 95). Cf. Exod 29:18,25, 41 ("a pleasing odor" of a ram); Lev 1:9,13,17 (livestock, birds); 2:2,9,12 (grain offering of flour, with frankincense); 3:5 + LXX 11 and 16 (sacrifice of well-being [NRSV] or peace-offering [RSV], sheep or goats + a covenant meal); Lev 4:31; 6:15,21; 8:20,27; 17:4,6; 23:13,18; cf. 26:31, etc; Num 15:3 (animals as burnt offering, freewill offering, at festivals or to fulfill a vow, "to make a pleasing odor for the Lord," plus a grain offering). Walter 99 adds Ps 141:2 (incense offering). Ezekiel warns against the "pleasing odor" *(osmēn euōdias)* of sacrifices to idols (6:13; 16:19; 20:28); some day God will accept Israel "as a pleasing offering *(en osmē[i] euōdias,* 20:41)." Sir 50:15, the high priest offers "a pleasing odor *(osmēn euōdias)* to the Most High"; Sir 38:11, a sick person offers "a sweet-smelling sacrifice *(euōdian).*"

"Spiritualization" of animal/grain/temple sacrifice was a growing factor *(NIDNTT* 3:427–28). Amos 5:21–22 and Lev 26:31 challenged notions Yahweh feeds on the scent of cultic offerings. God prefers steadfast love, not sacrifice; knowledge of God, not burnt offerings (Hos 6:6; cf. 1 Sam 15:22). Cf. Dupont ([2] Bibl.) 2nd ed. 1960:40–42. The LXX kept the anthropomorphic "pleasant odor to the Lord" (yet cf. G. Dautzenberg, *EDNT* 2:90). The rabbis changed *(han)nîhōah* to *nûhat,* "good pleasure" (A. Stumpff, *TDNT* 2:809; cf. Str-B 3:625, 605, and 497). In Sir 24:15, Wisdom says, ". . . like choice myrrh I spread my fragrance *(osmēn)*"; Philo, *Somn.* 1.178; Sir 39:14; T. Levi 3:6, "a rationalized bloodless offering." Qumran (Gnilka 179–80) abandoned physical sacrifices and offered up "a pleasant aroma" through prayer *(rēah nîhôah)* (1 QS 8.7–9). Not "the flesh of burnt offerings" or "the fats of sacrifice," but prayer and "correctness of behaviour" (9.4–5; cf. 10.6) (tr. García Martínez 12, 13). Cf. G. Vermes, *The Dead Sea Scrolls: Qumran in Perspective* (Philadelphia: Fortress, 1977) 180–81; *ABD* 5:8–9 and 5:870–91, esp. 882–85 and 891 ("absence of real sacrifices in the ancient sense" among Christians); H. Wenschkewitz, *Die Spiritualisierung der Kultusbegriffe: Tempel, Priester und Opfer im Neuen Testament* (Angelos-Beiheft; Leipzig: E. Pfeiffer, 1932); R. Reitzenstein 1978; J. Behm, *TDNT* 3:186–89; in (8) Bibl., P. Seidensticker 44–120, R. Corriveau; E. Ferguson; D. Georgi 1965/1992 (INTRO. VIII) 64–66; Bormann 1995:156–58, re 4:18.

Sacrifices and the odor of burning flesh and grain were also known from temples of the Greco-Roman world. Diod. Sic. 1.84.6, *euōdia* of incense, but no precise parallel to *osmē euōdias* in pagan ritual. Rejection of animal sacrifice was common in Greco-Roman philosophical circles. On "spiritualization" in Gk. cult, see J. Behm, *TDNT* 3:187–89; P. Seidensticker 1–43.

History-of-religions background was stressed by E. Lohmeyer 1919b, "Von göttlichen Wohlgeruch" (SHAW.PH 10,9; Heidelberg: C. Winter; summary and further lit. in G. Delling, *TDNT* 5:493–95; Corriveau [(8) Bibl.] 86–90). Smell was of great importance in antiquity, "considered to contain, quite literally, a lifegiving force" (O. Flender, *NIDNTT* 3:599), "the bearer and producer of divine life" (Loh. 1919b:13). Cf. Sir 24:15; Tobit 6:8 and 8:2–3, odor drives a demon away. Corriveau 86–90, the "perfume image" developed into an ethical symbol (Sir 39:13–14; Bormann 1995).

In Paul, cf. Eph 5:2, Christ "gave himself up for us, a fragrant offering and sacrifice to God" *(osmēn euōdias)*; 2 Cor 2:14–16 moves from (a) the death of Christ as "a sacrifice whose fragrance is pleasing to God" (NEB) to (b) the apostles as aroma or odor of life or death to others. Cf. A. Stumpff, *TDNT* 2:808–10; G. Delling, *TDNT* 5:495; O. Flender/C. Brown, *NIDNTT* 3:600–1. Some see Paul as incense-bearer in a triumphal procession akin to those of Roman Emperors; others transfer "divine fragrance" to the apostles; others see sacrifice; others

connect "aroma of Christ" with *Christos* from *chriō*, "anoint" (with a fragrant oint-
ment; cf. John 12:3). References in Dautzenberg, *EDNT* 2:90–91. V. P. Furnish
(AB 32A:176–77, 187–88), the apostles are prisoners in a procession; no sacrificial
imagery; they disseminate the gospel throughout the world; "the apostles themselves" are "*the aroma of Christ*"; like Wisdom in Sir 24:15 (cited above; cf. *2 Bar.*
67.6), "knowledge of God" is fragrant. Corriveau 90–97, multiple senses, but not
"sacrificial allusions." S. Hafermann, *Suffering and the Spirit* (WUNT 2/19;
Tübingen: Mohr Siebeck, 1986) 43–51, a cultic term for sacrifice but in the wisdom tradition.

osmē euōdias in 4:18 has usually been seen as cultic imagery, from the OT/
LXX, perhaps christologically (via Eph 5:2 and 2 Cor 2:14–16). But the OT prophets, the LXX, and what becomes rabbinic Judaism had moved from a crass sense of
the aroma of burnt offerings mollifying God to concern for knowledge of and
obedience to God. The smell of animal sacrifices was also known to Greeks and
Romans, as was critique of such offerings. For Paul, the apostles give off "the
aroma of Christ" (2 Cor 2:15) among those with the gospel for salvation or a stench
of death for those perishing. See further COMMENT B.2.d.

a sacrifice acceptable. thysian (acc.), modified by *dektēn*, "acceptable." *to God*
is to be understood with it. On *thysia* see NOTE on 2:17 *the sacrificial service of* the
Philippians' *faith*. 4:18 is fig. (BDAG *thysia* 2.b), "the life of Christians as a self-
offering to God" (cf. Rom 12:1); Phil 2:17. 4:18, "the gift of the community" =
"acceptable sacrifice" (J. Behm, *TDNT* 3:182). "All that faith does . . . becomes
thysia. . . . Life is a sacrifice—the direct opposite of . . . cultic sacrifice" (3:185).
At 4:18, Paul's work, communal relations with Paul, or the Philippians' gift to him
(C. Brown, *NIDNTT* 3:431–32, who refers to "Paul the priest" [Rom 15:16] for
Phil 2:17; H. Thyen, *EDNT* 2:162, "his work" is "a priestly service" [1 Cor 9:13],
the Philippians' gifts are "pleasing *sacrifices*" [4:18]). But Hawth. 207, sacrifices of
animals, birds, and grain were replaced by "a crushed and humbled spirit"
(Ps 50:18–19 LXX) as the sacrifice God prefers.

acceptable, dektos, ē, on, in Paul here only + 2 Cor 6:2 (= Isa 49:8 LXX); in the
NT, Luke 4:19 (= Isa 58:5) and 24, and Acts 10:35. All of these examples except
Luke 4:24 mean "acceptable to God" (*EDNT* 1:285). Grundmann (*TDNT* 2:58–
59), "in the LXX . . . sacrificial cultus," but steadily spiritualized (Jer 6:20; Prov
16:7 LXX, cf. 15:8). Corriveau ([8] Bibl.) 113–14 emphasizes "acceptable *to God*"
and the "spiritualization process."

well pleasing, to God. euareston tō[i] theō[i]. to God goes with *acceptable* as well
as with *well pleasing* and likely also *a fragrance with aroma*. Dat. with each adj.
euarestos, from *areskō*, to "please," + *eu* = well. W. Foerster (*TDNT* 1:456–57), in
NT usage, acceptable *to God*, usually re *future* conduct as a *goal* acceptable to
God (Rom 12:1–2; 14:18; 2 Cor 5:9; Col 3:20). Only at Phil 4:18 retrospective
("having received . . . an acceptable sacrifice"). Corriveau ([8] Bibl.) 114 concurs;
"God's attitude toward human behaviour," as though Paul said, "I accept your gift
as if it were a gift offered by God, before God, and to God'" (Georgi 1965/1992
[INTRO. VIII] 65–66; the last point not verifiable from the text, Bormann 1995:156).
Apoc. Ab. (17–20), "you (my God) have made this offering to yourself through

me." *euarestos* only 2x in the LXX (Wis 4:10; 9:10), no claim to cultic background. G. Stählin (*TDNT* 6:756 n 61), "be pleasing to God" corresponds to "be blameless" (*aproskopon einai,* cf. Phil 1:10, NOTE on *unfailing*); moral conduct, not cultic practice, at the Day of Jesus Christ. *euarestos* is paraenetic (*EDNT* 2:74; cf. H. Bietenhard, *NIDNTT* 2:816–17).

4:19. *My God will fulfill every need of yours, in accord with the divine riches, gloriously, in Christ Jesus. God* was the final word in v 18; *fulfill* occurred in 18b, *I am filled full* ; Philippian *need* picks up on Paul's *need* in v 16. Even prons. connect: "*my* God" with 1st per. vb. forms, vv 10–13, 17–18; "*your* every need" with *you* Philippians v 15; 2nd pl. vbs. in 10, 14–16, and the Philippians' *account* in v 17. Links to the prayer report (1:3–11): *my God,* see NOTES on 1:3 and 1:2 *God; will fulfill,* see NOTE on 1:11 *you have been filled;* for *every,* note *every, all,* and *always* in 1:3–4; *gloriously,* see NOTE on 1:11 *glory;* for *in Christ Jesus,* the NOTE on 1:1 *in Christ Jesus.* Some see v 19 as an *inclusio* (Dalton 101) with 1:1–11. For structure in 4:19, see COMMENT A.5. On God as Paul's "patron," G. P. Wiles 103; Berry 121. *de* links 4:19 with 18; adversative "but" (KJV; Martin 1976:168; Gnilka 172) or connective "and" (Vincent 151; Loh/Nida 148; O'B 545, God's "approval of their offering"; [N]RSV). Moffatt, NABRNT ignore *de.* JB "In return."

will fulfill. plērōsei, fut. act. indic., *pleroō, fill (full)* (BDAG 1.a; see NOTES on 1:11 and 4:18), in P⁴⁶ ℵ A B D² Majority Text; KJV, "my God shall supply all your need." The great uncial MSS and P⁴⁶ justify such a tr. The Philippians have paid Paul fully what they owe him; now his God will supply their needs. Is such a *do-ut-des* concept ("I'll do this so that you'll do that for me") unworthy of Paul's theology? The sting is removed for many by calling this a promise, based on Paul's own experience, enabled for all things through the One who strengthens him (v 13). So Loh., Merk 1968:200, Mengel 284, U. B. Müller 207, Bruce, Silva, Fee, Bockmuehl, Walter.

The Western Text (not in UBSGNT or *TCGNT*) has *plērōsai,* acute accent on the penult; aor. opt., wish (BDF #384), "May God supply . . ." ; D* F G etc., Lat. (Vg *impleat;* R. Knox "So may he, the God I serve, supply . . ."). Thus the Gk. Fathers in general; Chrysost. (PG 62:292.46, 55–56 = LNPF 13:252, n 1) *chreian,* "need," with word play on "every grace (*charin*)" or "every joy (*charan*)," variants not in MSS. Opt. in Erasmus, the Luther Bible, Grotius, etc.; or fut indic. treated as if an opt. (B. Weiss 347 n 1; G. P. Wiles 101–7, fut. indic. as a wish-prayer). So Hawth. 208, Schenk 51–54 (rejected by O'B 545–46): (1) Paul uses the opt. 31x. But 14 of these are the phrase *mē genoito,* "May it not be" (BDF #65.2); opt. of wish only at Rom 15:5, 13 (*plērōsai*); 1 Thess 3:11–12 (3x), 5:23; Phlm 20; 4x in 2 Thess, 3x in 2 Tim. See BDF #384; *GNTG* 3:118–22. (2) Some of these examples occur near the close of a letter, "asking God to do something favorable for his friends and using precisely the same formula that appears here in 4:19" (1 Thess 5:23; Rom 15:5; 2 Thess 3:16). Perhaps Rom 15:13; 1 Thess 3:11–13, concluding a letter frg. (cf. E. Best *1, 2 Thess* 31–35). (3) Phil 4:23 "implies the optative *eiē* ('may it be')." See (17) NOTE on 4:23 (opt., analogy to papyrus letters); (17) COMMENT A.2 (epistolary, not liturgical), B.4; and (1) COMMENT B.6. *The grace of the Lord Jesus Christ be—and is—with your spirit* offers both invocation of God and certainty of the divine promise. Commentators (without always probing the question) elsewhere usually favor the opt. 1 Cor 16:23, AB 32:366; G. D. Fee, *1 Cor* 839 n 39. 2 Cor 13:13, R. P. Martin WBC 40:506, "hope of blessing *(Segenswunsch)* rather than a promise *(Segensverheissung)*"; AB 32A:581, "be," although 13:11 has a fut. indic. Gal 6:18, a (conditional) blessing ("those who will follow this rule"), akin to the synagogue Birkat-ha-Shalom (H. D. Betz, *Gal.* 321–22). Rom 15:13, prayer-wish. But it is far from certain one can infer from Phil 4:23 the same vb. form for 4:19. Cf. 2 Cor 13:11, God "will be *(estai,* fut. indic.) with you all," 13:13 (fut.) indic. or opt. must be supplied; 1 Cor 16:23–24, "My love [is] with you all in the Messiah Jesus," "The grace of our Lord Jesus [be] with you" (AB *Eph* 34A:816 n 1).

(4) Hawth. prefers the opt. of wish because "material, physical needs are exclusively under discussion here," as in v 16; to exclude "spiritual needs," fut. eschatology, and "heavenly recompense." Most commentators are less one-sided (e.g., O'B 546; Silva 240). (5) Theological reasons (Hawth. 208): the opt. "(1) does not have Paul saying what God will or will not do, (2) allows God the freedom to be God, to fulfill our needs or not as he sees best . . . (3) wards off disappointment or disillusionment when material, physical needs are not met, and (4) keeps one from having to make excuses for God . . . pushing off the fulfillment of needs until the eschatological day." Splendid apologetics and pastoral concern, but did Paul see "needs" and eschatology that way? O'B 546, for Paul, God, out of limitless resources, "will meet all their needs through Christ Jesus, both now and in the future consummation." (6) In G. P. Wiles (101–7; 4:19 under intercessory "wish-prayers"; 1:4, 9–11 is a "prayer *report*"), "form" becomes a matter of content and even feel, not grammar and structure. O'B 546, "formal similarities with the Pauline wish-prayers" but (like 4:7 and 9) should be placed under "declarations rather than prayers" (cf. Wiles 33–38. esp. 36, and 101). (7) Schenk 67 prefers the opt., in reaction to Ewald-Wohl. 1908:219 = 1923:235–36, that v 19 is a promise that goes closely with v 18 (not 20). God is not "obligated to step in and . . . fulfill all your needs." No "irrefragable certainty" (Loh. 189). Petition is a human activity that only the future, in God's free grace, can answer.

The textual variant, not "significant for translators," turns out to involve theological and pastoral issues. Wish or promise? Textual evidence favors the fut. indic. Cf. Silva 23, 241; O'B 516, early scribes were "embarrassed" by the indic. Fee 449 n 2, O'B and others divest the original fut. indic. "of its contextual roots for the sake of 'pan-liturgism.'" We must let Paul say what the oldest and best MSS contain.

every need of yours. chreian (acc. sg.); see NOTE on 4:16 *my needs.* (a) Physical needs, here and now, as in the Lord's Prayer ("our daily bread" = sustenance) (Hawth.); (b) spiritual, likely fut. eschatological fulfillment; or (c) both (Meyer 184; B. Weiss). *every* (fem. acc. sg., *pas, pasa, pan,* frequent in Letter A; see NOTES on 1:1 *all the saints;* 1:3,4,9; 4:12,13,18) perhaps abetted the textual shift from "God *will* satisfy your *every* need" (indic.) to "*May* God satisfy . . ." (opt.).

in accord with the divine riches. kata + acc. (cf. BDAG *kata* 5; see NOTE on 1:20 *in accord with . . .*), not merely "from" God's wealth but "in a manner that befits

His wealth" (Michael 226). *ploutos* (BDAG 2) = **earthly goods,** then, as here, *wealth, abundance.* Usually masc.; neut. at 2 Cor 8:2 (in most MSS) and here; cf. also Col 1:27, 2:2, in Eph 4x (BDF #51.2; *GNTG* 2:157). On riches in Gk. philosophical groups and the Bible, cf. F. Hauck, W. Kasch, *TDNT* 6:318–32; F. Selter, *NIDNTT* 2:840–45. Paul applies *ploutos* terms, "fulness of goods," to God, Christ, the apostles and their gospel, and the church. Re deity, in expressions not seemingly found in Gk. or earlier biblical sources, "the riches of [God's] glory" (Rom 9:23), "the riches of [God's] kindness, forbearance, and patience" (Rom 2:4); cf. Eph 2:4, 1:7. The TRANSLATION uses *divine riches* to avoid "his" for God.

Seen paradoxically in the impoverished figure of Jesus Christ: "though rich, for your sakes he became poor, so that by his poverty you might become rich" (2 Cor 8:9; cf. Phil 2:5–11); "rich *(plouton)* unto all that call upon him" (Rom 10:12 KJV; NRSV "is generous"; cf. Col 1:27 and 2:2). Paul and his coworkers, though poor, make many rich (2 Cor 6:10, *peristasis* catalogue) through preaching and witness. Those who hear and heed become rich (2 Cor 8:9; Rom 10:12, cited above). Corinthian Christians are "enriched" in Christ (1 Cor 1:5), "already rich" (1 Cor 4:8, irony, possible eschatological misunderstanding of beatitudes in Luke 6:20–21 par Matt 5:3,6), while the apostles go about hungry and impoverished. God's plan implies, through Israel's "stumbling," "riches for the world," "riches for the Gentiles," plus Israel's eventual inclusion (Rom 11:12). "O the depth of the riches . . . of God!" (Rom 11:33). In light of God's "generous act" in Christ (2 Cor 8:9) Paul asks his churches to contribute to the collection for the saints, as the churches of Macedonia have "in a wealth of generosity on their part" (2 Cor 8:2). Theologically (H. Merklein, *EDNT* 3:114–17) the word group throws "God's mercy into relief." In Phil 4:19, christological motivation ("in Christ Jesus") and enrichment for selfless giving in light of 2 Cor 9:11, "you being enriched (pres. ptc.) in every way for your great generosity, which will produce thanksgiving to God through us." Cf. Boobyer in (2) COMMENT A.2, n 4.

For a Pauline "theology of riches" (cf. Di Marco 1977), H.-M. Dion 1966 traced "the riches of God's own glory" and "the riches God offers" to (a) the OT (Neh 9:17; Ps 103:8; Jonah 4:2; Num 14:18 NJB "rich in faithful love"; Exod 34:6); (b) Qumran; and (c) Philo. Such sources lack Paul's precise phraseology. *TDNT* 6:327–29 traced it to "a new and radically eschatological view" from Christ in the Synoptics. Dion added "the paschal experience of the primitive church" (148). But note also God as "benefactor" in the Greco-Roman world (Danker 1982:425–26) and friendship concerns about wealth and sharing. Paul took an important step in emphasizing God's riches, the Benefactor who meets the needs of Paul and the Philippians.

gloriously. en + *doxa* dat. sg. (no art.). On *doxa,* see NOTE on 1:11 *glory;* cf. 4:20. BDAG 1.b, **brightness, splendor, radiance,** *glory, majesty, sublimity* (of God), cf. Rom 9:23, but the entry has been criticized as influenced from theories about Hellenistic mysticism. Cf. G. Kittel, *TDNT* 2:247–48, "*Doxa* as the Divine Mode of Being"; S. Aalen *NIDNTT* 2:45–48; H. Hegermann, *EDNT* 1:344–47; R. B. Gaffin, Jr., *DPL* 348–50. *en doxē[i]* at 4:19 is a "teaser" (Martin 1976:168); it can be construed in different ways. The Gk. art. *to* is not repeated after *ploutos,* which would make *en doxē[i]* attribut., "in accord with God's riches which is marked with glory"; ATR 783, omission is possible, cf. 1:1 "the saints (who are) in Christ Jesus." Or adjectivally, "riches in glory" = God's "glorious riches" (Phillips; Bengel, others, in B. Weiss 347 n 1, who rejects it; Hawth. 207; NAB "magnificent riches"). Or (Fee 454 n 16; adopted in the TRANSLATION) adverbially, "My God will gloriously satisfy your every need . . ." (Calvin; others in B. Weiss 348; Meyer 185, a modal definition; Ewald 1908:219 = 1923:236; Collange 153, *en* = a Heb. adv. form; Beare 156). Or with *en Christō[i] Iēsou*, instrumentally, ". . . by Christ Jesus, gloriously" (Meyer 184). Is it temporal? J. C. K. von Hofmann, God will fulfill all their need *"in that He gives them glory,"* but "hidden from the world" (rejected by Meyer 184 n 4). Michaelis 73, "in the glorious age to come," at the parousia (O'B 548–49; Gnilka 180). Or local, as a place (ATR 586), heaven or "glory-land" (cf. Lft. 167); Fee 453 n 16, the "'glory' in which God dwells." Martin 1976:169 sees "an anti-perfectionist polemic" against opponents in ch. 3; "the life of the Christian *hic et nunc* is never called 'glory' in Paul" (but cf. 1 Cor 2:7–8; 12:26b; and 2 Cor 3, esp. v 18); few detect any polemic in 4:19. The polemic in Hawth. 208–9 against *"any* futuristic meaning" (italics added) reflects desire to keep the needs in v 19 material and physical only, a prayer-wish, not a promise.

in Christ Jesus. See NOTES on *en Christō[i] Iēsou* 1:1; *in the Lord* 4:10a; 4:13 *the One who strengthens me* (MSS add "Christ"); also 4:21. Earlier exegetes saw here objective grounds for what is promised through Christ, rather than subjective fellowship with Christ (B. Weiss 348–49; Meyer 185; Ewald 1908:219 = 1923:236; Loh. 189). Gnilka 180, *doxa* is the life "opened through Christ Jesus" (cf. Martin 1976:168). Hawth. 209, with the vb.: one is filled up in Christ (cf. Col 2:9–10; 1 Cor 1:5) because "the treasures of God are . . . made available in Christ." O'B 549, "the sphere in which God's supplying takes place or . . . instrumental . . . 'through Christ Jesus.'" Silva 237, "His riches [*ploutos*] in glory [which become ours] in union with Christ Jesus!" (A baptismal sense?) Schenk's chiasm relates *in Christ Jesus* to *my God* (40, 49–50). Neugebauer ([1] Bibl.) 89–90 connects it with *riches* (cf. 1 Cor 1:5). Similarly W. Kramer [(1) Bibl. **Christ**] #36a, n 509. Did hearers (or Paul) have or demand exact clarity on the phrase?

4:20. *To our God and Father belongs glory forever and ever. Amen.* Its balanced structure

| Gk. | *tō[i] de theō[i]* | *kai patri hēmōn* | *doxa* |
| | *eis tous aiōnas* | *tōn aiōnōn* | *amēn* |

was noted by Loh. 188 and Schenk 40,55, but not all relate v 20 to v 19 as closely as they did. *de* may contrast God, the originator of all gifts, with Christ the mediator in 19 (B. Weiss 349). Schenk, *de* presents a conclusion, like *ouch hoti* vv 11 and 17; 20 = "Yes, to God our Father, belongs. . . ." Most trs. ignore *de*. KJV "Now"; RSV "And"; NJB "And so." No vb. in the Gk. Trs. supply *eiē*, opt., but some understand *estin*, indic., "To God is the glory" (Ewald 1908:220 = 1923:236; Schenk 54; Hawth. 209; O'B 550). The salutation (1:2) also lacks a vb. (see [1] COMMENT, B.6), as does the benediction at 4:23 (see [17] NOTE and COMMENT A.2). "is" suggests glory already belongs to God. One does not say, "Thine be the kingdom and the power and the glory"; Matt 6:13 *estin.* Similarly 1 Peter 4:11, "is" (Kittel, *TDNT* 2:248; BDF #128.5); Rom 1:25 *(estin).* (Rom 11:36, 16:27, Gal 1:5, vb. must be supplied.) The dat. may be indir. obj., "May glory be to God . . ."; or dat. of possession, "belongs to" (BDF #189; so the TRANSLATION).

To our God and Father. theos (BDAG 3.d; here dat.); see NOTE on 1:2 *God. patēr* (BDAG 6.c.β; dat.); see NOTE on 1:2 *our Father. God* 23x throughout Phil., *Father* for the deity only here, 1:2 (gen. + *hēmōn*), 2:11 *theou patros.* Here, one art. *(tō[i]),* the nouns connected by *kai. (ho) theos (kai) patēr hēmōn* also at 1 Thess 1:3; 3:11,13; Gal 1:3; 1 Cor 1:3; 2 Cor 1:2; Phlm 3; and Rom 1:7; i.e., esp. in salutations and prayer wishes. The art. (BDAG *ho, hē, to* 2.j.β) can be taken with *theō[i]* only; then *kai patri hēmōn* is epexegetical: "To God, that is, to our Father" (B. Weiss 349 n 1; Hawth. 209; Loh/Nida 150; [N]JB). More commonly *kai* coordinates two nouns with one art., "to our God-and-Father" (Loh/Nida; [N]RSV). KJV sounds like two gods, "unto God and our Father." *Father* likely emphasizes adoption as God's children (Rom 8:23; Gal 4:5). *hēmōn* is the first use of the 1st per. pl. pron. in 4:10–20 (no 1st pl. vb. forms). Likewise 1:1–11 except for *God our Father* in the salutation. Schenk 54–55, "the *mou* of the sender and *hymōn* of the recipient" come together in prayer or doxology. In this "Our Father" and a "Gloria in Excelsis," all questions are surmounted (Loh. 190; Hawth. 209).

glory. doxa; see NOTES on 1:11 *glory* and 4:19 *gloriously,* for OT background and ideas of "radiance," "splendor," and "honor." If "be" is supplied, then *fame, recognition, renown, honor, prestige* (BDAG *doxa* 3) fit best; if "is" or "belongs to," then glory in the sense of *brightness, splendor, radiance* (BDAG 1). *hē* with *doxa* suggests the (well-known) glory that characterizes the God of Israel now revealed in Christ (2 Cor 4:6). 4:20 is thus active acknowledgment, "the extolling of what is," God's nature or the "divine mode of being" (G. Kittel, *TDNT* 2:248; Rom 11:36, 16:27). Cf. Hawth. 245; Hegermann, *EDNT* 1:345. Doxological, perhaps liturgical, of ultimate Jewish origin. Schenk 54, 67 sees God's creative, saving power (cf. Kittel, *TDNT* 2:244, *doxa* as "power" in the LXX). Such statements may occur in Paul at the close of a section (Rom 1:25; 9:5; 11:36; Gal 1:5), or the end of a letter. The TRANSLATION opts for *glory* as an existing characteristic of God, in which believers acquiesce. What God is and possesses, we affirm.

forever and ever. aiōn (123x in the NT, 22x in Paul's acknowledged letters), only here in Phil (*aiōnios* = "eternal" not at all). Reflects the Jewish "two ages," this present (evil) age and the coming (glorious, new) age (Gal 1:4; Rom 12:2 NRSV-mg; 1 Cor 1:20, etc.), related to God as "king of the ages" (1 Tim 1:17). *eis ton aiōna,* lit. "for the age," "forever" (1 Cor 8:13 "not ever"; 2 Cor 9:9 = Ps 111:9 LXX [112:9]); pl., *eis tous aiōnas,* "for the ages," "forever" (Rom 1:25; 9:5; 11:36); *eis tous aiōnas tōn aiōnōn,* "for the ages of the ages," "forever and ever" (KJV; Gal 1:5; Phil 4:20). BDAG classifies NT uses under past times, time to come (Phil 4:20), and a segment of time ("this age," "the coming age"). Word studies: H. Sasse, *TDNT* 1:197–209; J. Guhrt, *NIDNTT* 3:826–33; T. Holtz/H. Balz, *EDNT* 1:44–48; Louw/Nida 67.143, 41.38, (for 4:20) 67.95.

For Gk. readers, *aiōn* might suggest a "timeless eternity" (contrast *chronos,* "time"), with backgrounds in Gk. philosophy; cf. Plato *Tim.* 37D; Philo *Mut.*

Nom. 267 = LCL Philo 5:279. From Hellenistic philosophy and Zoroastrian concepts, "periods in world history," *aiōnes* ruled by more-than-human "powers" (cf. Phil 2:10c; 1 Cor 2:6–8, rulers of this age, 15:24, and Rom 8:38; Sasse 197–98; Guhrt 827).

OT "eternity formulas" existed about God, "throughout all generations to come" (Exod 40:15; cf. Isa 13:20), "from eternity to eternity" (1 Chron 16:36); cf. Deut 15:17; Isa 40:28 "the everlasting God." Apocalyptic writings, including Qumran, expanded the importance of *'ôlām* for the future. Imagery spread of a present evil age under hostile powers and a glorious age to come under God in (rabbinic) Judaism and early Christianity (*NIDNTT* 3:828–29; *EDNT* 1:44–45). For Paul Christ's death and resurrection were "the turn of the ages," but he does not develop the schema systematically. Probably traditional phrases from (Hellenistic) Jewish Christianity, likely liturgical, but strange for Gk. hearers. They evoke God's grandeur in the promised future, without fixed definition. Cf. *TDNT* 1:198–200; *NIDNTT* 3:831; *EDNT* 1:45–46, esp. 4.c), 47; Heckel 2002 ([17] Bibl.) 307, 318.

Amen. amēn, Gk. transliteration of Heb. meaning "so be it," a response to prayers and benedictions. In Phil only here (some MSS at 4:23, see NOTE there); 10x in acknowledged letters. Responding with "Amen" to a thanksgiving is attested in 1 Cor 14:16 and 2 Cor 1:20, Christ is God's "Yes" (Gk. *nai*), through whom "we say the 'Amen' to the glory of God" (AB 32A:136); cf. Rev. 1:7 *nai* and *amēn* (NRSV "So it is to be. Amen"). In the OT, *'āmēn* attested to what is said in a doxology and associated one with it. Cf. Deut 27:15–26; Neh 8:6; 1 Chron 16:38. In the synagogue, a response to doxologies and blessings, though seldom to prayers, to make the words one's own. Similarly Qumran. LXX (17x) rendered Heb. *'āmēn* with an opt. of wish, *genoito* ("May it be so"); 8x transliterated as *amēn*. At the close of 3 Macc (7:23), 4 Macc (18:24), and Tobit (14:15). *Word studies:* H. Schlier, *TDNT* 1:335–36; H. Bietenhard, *NIDNTT* 1:97–98; H.-W. Kuhn, *EDNT* 1: 69–70; Str-B 3:456–61; Louw/Nida 72.6; Loh/Nida 150, "surely this is true," "this is certainly the way it should be"; Heckel 308–13, 318. *amēn* entered Christian worship and piety as the response of hearers. 4:20 is Paul's own act of piety after an assertion about God, for his hearers in Philippi to make their own, appropriate "at the conclusion of a word of assurance" (4:19–20) (*TDNT* 1:337). Thus the eschatological aspect of the promise is confirmed (Loh. 189).

COMMENT

A. FORMS, SOURCES, AND TRADITIONS

1. *Phil 4:10–20 as Letter A from Paul.* Only loosely connected to 3:2–4:9. Paul delays clear appreciation for the Philippians' gift till here in Phil and then puts it oddly. Why? In 1914, Symes (INTRO. VI) 39 isolated 4:10–20 as a separate letter in a sequence of five. 4:10–23 was then often connected with chs. 1–2 in a *two*-letter sequence (Gnilka, Friedrich; Letter B = 3:1–20, [parts of] 4:1–9). In the 1950s,

proposals for *three* letters gained ground, 4:10–20 (or -23) the first of three.[1]
Garland 1985:141 heard a "crescendo of voices" against the unity of Phil. Among
Ger. critics, partition theories dominated; unity theories continued in the Anglo-
Saxon world. Engberg-Pedersen 2000:316 n 18 sees "a recent trend" to one letter, in light of Wick's "thematic blocks." Or because proponents of multiple letters
do not "agree on the number of 'letters' or on precisely what sections" (Hawth.
xxx). There has been a trend away from historical reconstruction, to take documents "as received." Rhetorical criticism and emphasis on friendship have been
used to support unity, but each can also fit partitioning. Any verdict is unproven
(Reed, DA).

4:10–20 is best read as the body of Letter A but must also be treated as part of a
four-ch. letter. Childs 333–37, though emphasizing a "canonical approach," concluded that in Phil "the case for the partition theory is the stronger"; "a new historical dimension is recovered" for Paul as well as "the intention of those editors
who gave the book its shape" (335). Reasons for a separate letter in 4:10–20 include contents, ancient references to "letters" (pl.; INTRO. VI.A), and the break at
3:2. The case for (three) letters is cumulative.

(1) (a) Paul *three times mentions receiving a gift or gifts* (of money) *from
the Philippians:* 4:14–19 is clearest; cf. 1:5–7 (sharing); 2:25–30 (Epaphroditus
provided services the Philippians could not). But no out-and-out "thanks."
(b) *Thrice there is a signal a letter is drawing to a conclusion:* 4:7 ("the peace of
God . . . will guard your hearts . . ."), 4:9b ("the God of peace will be with you");
4:19–20 ("My God will satisfy every need of yours. . . . To our God and Father
belongs glory . . .").[2]

(2) There seems *a break between 4:9* ("Keep on doing . . . and the God of peace
will be with you") *and 4:10* ("I rejoiced in the Lord . . ."). See NOTES on 4:10 *de*
(cf. 1:12 as start of a letter body) and 4:10 *I rejoiced* (such expressions occur in Gk.
letters at that point, as in Phlm 7).[3]

(3) *Two rather different references to Epaphroditus* (Rahtjen 172–73): 4:18, the
messenger who brought the gift from the Philippians to Paul; 2:25–30, much-
praised, with Paul long enough to assist him (2:25,30b), fall deathly ill (26b,27),
hear Christians in Philippi knew of his illness; he was distressed over this (26b) but
recovered enough to go home (28). Do 2:25–30, then 4:18, fit together well in one
letter?[4]

---

[1] Cf. INTRO. VI.B.2; DA 137–40, 409–18, "at least 4:10–19," 409. Childs 333, Benoit, Müller-Bardorf
(INTRO. VI), Beare (4:10–20 = Letter B), Schmithals 1957, Rahtjen, Georgi 1962:62–66, Koester,
Fitzmyer 1968, Bornkamm 1962 (INTRO. VII.B), J. L. White 1972, 1984, Collange, Vielhauer 1975,
Marxsen 1978, Schenke-Fischer, *Einl.* 125, G. Barth, F. F. Bruce 1981, D. Patte 1983:164–69, Schenk
1984; Pesch 1985, Byrne 1990, Simonis, Bormann 1995.
[2] Each may go with a different letter, unless Paul is repetitive. Pesch 1985:52–53: 4:19–20 goes with A;
4:7, with B; and 4:9b with C. Similarly Bormann 1995:161. We take 4:7 and 9 as part of Letter B.
[3] Cf. Rahtjen 173; *JBC* 50:7 "a fresh start at 4:10"; *NJBC* 48:4,7,29; Pesch 1985:4. On the "disclosure
formula" of 1:12 and the expression of joy in 4:10 as body openings, see J. L. White 1971a ([2] Bibl.)
95; 1986:20. The counterclaim sees *de* in 4:10 as insignificant; "joy" reoccurs here one more time.
[4] Rahtjen: in a single letter some of the "glowing adjectives" from 2:25–50 should appear at 4:18 as a
final affirmation; so also Pesch 55–56; Bormann 1995:153–54.

(4) 4:10–20, with a conclusion in 4:19–20, is *not part of the same letter as chs. 1–2* (which moves toward a close at 2:25–30, 3:1), *nor of a letter in 3:2ff.* with its harsh tone of urgency (Rahtjen 173; G. Barth 75, and others). The vv are *not likely a P.S. in Paul's own hand* (Bahr 1968; Hawth. 194; Rahtjen 173) nor *a summary of themes from 1:1–4:9*; instead new topics (Paul's independence), earlier ones (false teachers) omitted, words used differently (e.g., *koinōnia*).

(5) The vv *fit well as a brief appreciation* for the Philippians' gift (4:18) soon after the arrival of Epaphroditus (Rahtjen 173; Collange 5; JBC 50:7; cf. Beare 4, 150; G. Barth 12, 75; Pesch 59–60). For alternatives, see A.3, below.

(6) These 11 vv, plus an opening (like 1:1–2) and closing (perhaps 4:21–23), are *like typical papyrus letters of the day*, in length, style, and even phrases (4:10, "I rejoiced").[5]

(7) *Lack of direct thanks* is eased by *prompt acknowledgment* in Letter A of the safe arrival of the gift. Possibly Paul wrestled with whether he should accept this financial support, esp. if he was not yet imprisoned. He asserts his independence (4:11 *autarkēs*) and his dependence on the Lord (4:13), not on the Philippians.

(8) The *problem* disappears over *how late* in a four-ch. letter *this expression of "thankless thanks"* (3, below) comes; *in Letter A it is the main item of contents.* If 1:3–11 was part of A, vocabulary links between 1:9–11 and 4:10–20 (NOTE on 4:19) stand close. The phrase "danklose Dank" arose prior to consideration of 4:10–20 as the body of a separate letter.

(9) *The varied imagery*—commerce and finance (vv 15–18a), cultic sacrifice (18b), (Stoic) philosophy (11–12), church tradition (20) and personal faith (13,19)—*makes for a vivid little letter*, without influences from 2:5–11, opponents in 3:2–21, or (dis)unity in 1:27; 2:1–4, 14.

(10) Application of *the "friendship" topos works especially well for 4:10–20* (Berry 1996). *philia* marks the relationship. On the philophronetic style, cf. Pesch 61–64 and A.2, below.

(11) 4:10–20 (Letter A) is *a key to understanding the sequence and much of the contents in the later Letters B and C.* The Philippians may assume Paul is patron and they the "clients," or vice versa (they the patron)—dangers with which Letter A deals. This relationship will prove an undercurrent for Letter B, if not also C (Bormann 1995).

(12) 4:10–20 (Letter A) is also *a key to understanding the redaction of the canonical letter*, an undertaking likely carried out in Philippi. Editors made this initial note the climax of the canonical epistle, emphasizing the particular relationship of the Philippians to the apostle (see INTRO. VII.B, Bornkamm 1962; Bormann 1995:187–218).

To defend the unity of Phil some trace themes through all four chs.[6] or lift up the

---

[5] Phlm has 25 vv; Letter A, 14 to 23 vv; 44 lines of NA text compared with 28 (46 if Phil 1:3–11 is included).

[6] E.g., joy (Bengel, Schoon-Janßen 157); unity (Black 1995); disunity (Peterlin); suffering (Bloomquist); martyrdom (Loh.), friendship (L. M. White 1990; Stowers 1991); *koinōnia* (O'B 1978 [(2) Bibl. **sharing**]; "partnership," Swift; Engberg-Pedersen).

Christ hymn (2:6–11) as central (Fowl 1990, Wick), with vocabulary ties to 4:10–20. Such claims prove less persuasive upon examination.[7] The references in 4:10–20 are the starting point in a series of letters, out of a relationship of giving and receiving.

Rhetorical criticism has been used to claim *unity* for all four chs.[8] But analyses vary.[9] Gamble 1977:145–46 claimed Paul delayed 4:9–23 so he could write the words in his own hand, a conjecture far from certain.[10] "[S]ystematic application of rhetorical categories to Philippians is methodologically suspect" (Reed 1993: 315).[11] "[R]hetorical analysis is incapable of providing incontrovertible proof for or against [a unitary view of Phil]" (Engberg-Pedersen 1995a:257 n 4). Cf. Schoon-Janßen 141–43; Bormann 1995:130–32.

In various *chiastic analyses* of Phil (cf. INTRO. VI.B n 3), 4:10–23 has been paired with 1:1–11 (P. Rolland) or 1:3–11 (Edart; cf. Dalton for links); 4:10–20 with 1:3–11 (Luter/Lee; Bittasi), with 1:3–26 (C. W. Davis), and with 2:19–30 (Wick). No "incontrovertible proof" is produced by macrochiasms. Our conclusion: 4:10–20 = the body of Letter A.

2. *Elements in the* Philia Topos *Throughout Philippians.* Since the mid-1980s, Phil has often been called a "letter of friendship,"[12] with a friendly relationship

---

[7] Joy and *koinōnia* involve the Philippian gift to Paul. Joy (cf. D. F. Watson 2003:174) runs through all Paul's letters to Philippi; *koinōnia* is used in different ways, beginning with 4:10–20. As he writes 4:10–20, the "hymn" was a composition just received from Philippi via Epaphroditus. The Stoic sense of *tapeinousthai* in 4:12 (Paul *brought low with few resources*) need not derive from Christ's humiliating self in 2:8 *(etapeinōsen).* "Unity" terms do not appear in these eleven vv. "Thinking on Paul" (4:10, *to hyper emou phronein*) we take as a *Philippian* slogan that will reviberate through later letters.

[8] Engberg-Pedersen 1995a:257 n 4, a sign "the tide is turning" against partition theories; cf. Ebner 331–32 n 2, can categories of speech be applied to letters? Probst ([1] Bibl.) 50–54; Jegher-Bucher.

[9] See INTRO. VI.B n 2. Swift, 4:10–20 is an "epilogue" paralleling the "prologue" in 1:3–11. D. F. Watson 1988b: 87, 4:10–20 = *adfectus* (appeal to pathos in the audience) within the *peroratio* of 4:1–20. But (Synman 330) negative pathos or *indignatio* for opponents "is absent"; throughout 4:1–20 there are *ethos* and *logos* as well as *pathos,* as modes of persuasion (Synman 330). Watson forced "New Testament material into categories of classical rhetoric" (330). Schoon-Janßen 142: "too schematic." Black 1995, 4:10–20 = *narratio;* Bloomquist, 4:8–20 is *peroratio;* Robuck ([7] Bibl.), 4:1–20 = *petitio.* Edart 295–302, 309–19: in his Letter A, 4:10–23 parallel 1:3–11, the *exordium,* but are a *subscriptio* (like 1 Thess 5:27–28; DA 277–78, in Paul's hand) and *peroratio;* vv 11b and 17 are *propositiones,* with *correctio* in 10–13 and 14–19; 12–13, *probatio;* 15–16 *narratio;* 18–19 *probatio;* 20 doxology. Similarly, Bittasi 151–67: 4:10–20 parallels 1:3–11 ("thanks"), part of a *peroratio,* divided 4:10–14, 15–19; 20, doxology.

[10] Gamble used Rom 16 as analogy. Bahr 38–39, Rom 12:1–15:33 is autograph (AB 33:638, "lacks any real convincing evidence"). On 16:1–20ab in Paul's own hand, cf. Fitzmyer, AB 33:63. Cf. on Phil, Black 1995:47 n 50; Weima 1994:123–24; Holloway 2001a:155–56. This move by defenders of a single letter recognizes how singular 4:10–20 is. Holloway 155–60 scarcely relates 4:10–23 to "letters of consolation."

[11] Cf. Reed 1993:324; C. J. Classen (in Porter/Olbricht, eds., Gen. Bibl.) 288: "rhetoric (oratory) and epistolography were regarded as two different fields in antiquity" (288), each flexibile; cf. 289–90, 324. Similarly, Black 1995.

[12] L. T. Johnson 1986; Perkins 1987, but not 1991; Stowers 1991, but not 1986; L. M. White 1990, a *topos;* esp. Fitzgerald 1992; Witherington; Fee 2–7, 439–47, passim; Bockmuehl 34–38; Schenk 1984:62–65 re 4:16, Phil 4:10–20 reflects the *Freundschaftskonzept;* Pesch 1985:63–64. Klauck 1991

(philophronēsis) between writer and recipient(s).[13] The concept includes "guest friendship" *(xenia); philia* in Greco-Roman philosophy and life, esp. in Aristot.; and development in the city-state, broader political, economic worlds, and the Roman Empire.[14] Examples of "the friendly *(philikē) letter*" appear in handbooks (Ps.-Demetrius, Ps.-Libanius, Demetrius *De elocutione*),[15] though comparison cautions against terming Phil a "letter of friendship" (Reumann 1996:88–89).

In Phil, the greatest concentration of friendship terms occurs in 4:10–20 (see NOTES). Though scholars speak of "friendship" as a or the key to Phil, they by no means agree. D. A. Black, "Section Headings in Philippians," *Notes* 8 (1994) 12 n 46, denies (against L. M. White 1990) that friendship *"defines* the theology of Philippians"; it plays a subordinate role. D. F. Watson 2003:175–76 vacillates between "letter of friendship" and friendship *topoi*. Phil is not a "friendly letter" but a "family letter" (L. Alexander; cf. Perkins SBL1987SP 512 n 19). *philia* and *amicitia* had a range of meanings and overtones in classical sources; see (a) below. We shall conclude that elements in the friendship *topos* appear, but not all is explained by *philia*. Paul seems to wish to extricate himself from aspects of its culture.

a. *The Pervasive Theme of "Friendship" in Antiquity.* In Eng, we use " 'friendship' mostly of subjective feelings among individuals"; in Gk., *philia* had "a larger, objective meaning" (F. M. Schroeder 36 n 2; cf. Konstan 8–18). The determination of Antigone to bury the corpse of her brother Polynices comes out of "binding family obligation," not personal "liking." Friendship involved mutual relationships, in household, extended family, city-state, and other cities, and later the Empire. Friendship today stresses private relations and personal values; classical *philia* was

---

took this in a communal direction ("the church as a fellowship of friendship"), as did Ebner: Paul moves beyond a *topos* of friendship between himself and the Philippians to *koinōnia* of apostle and community with God. Cf. Schoon-Janßen 1991:136–38; M. Müller 152–67; Bormann 1995:164–70; Walter 98. Survey in Reumann 1996.

[13] Cf. [1] COMMENT A (opening) and B.1.

[14] Cf. G. Stählin, *philia, TDNT* 9, esp. 151–54; *xenos,* 5:1–36; U. Luck, *TDNT* 9:107–12, *philanthrōpia;* H. Bietenhard, *NIDNTT* 1:686–90; O. Hiltbrunner et al., "Gastfreundschaft," *RAC* 8:1061–1123; *OCD3* 611–13, 72. G. Herman, *Ritualised Friendship and the Greek City* (Cambridge: Cambridge Univ. Press, 1987): from Homer on (6), an "extensive network of personal alliances" linked "together all sorts of apolitical bodies (households, tribes, bands, etc.)"; "webs of guest-friendship" were "a powerful bond between citizens of different cities" (29). Ritual involved some act of favor *(euergesia,* 47–48), pledges *(pistia),* including a handshake *(dexia),* exchange of objects and oaths; sometimes letters (Isoc., *Letter* 7.13). *xenia* with its idealism (loyalty) and instrumentality (reciprocity) (120–21) served as a "primitive credit system" (94). A factor in Greco-Roman life, it entered into early Christianity as "hospitality" *(xenia,* cf. Phlm 22). R. P. Saller, *Personal Patronage under the Early Empire* (Cambridge: Cambridge Univ. Press, 1982): patron–client relations continued, much as in the Roman Republic, often in an "asymmetrical" relationship involving Emperor, Imperial aristocracy, and local officials as *amicitiae inferiores* (9–15). Patronage was a "lubricant" for administrative machinery, and friendship-networking significant. Plut., *Prae. ger. reip., Mor.* 798A-825F = LCL *Moralia* 10:155–299, shows how a public official could bestow *beneficia* to friends. Cf. H. Hutter, *Politics as Friendship* (Waterloo, Ont.: Wilfrid Laurier Press, 1978); S. N. Eisenstadt/L. Roniger, *Patrons, Clients, and Friends: Interpersonal Relations and the Structure of Trust in Society* (Cambridge: Cambridge Univ. Press, 1984).

[15] Malherbe 1988:16–19, 33, 69, 75; Stowers 1986:58–60; cf. Thraede 1970:125–45.

more a public relationship, with reciprocal political, economic, and social aspects. Political coloring is emphasized by Hutter (n 14, above) and Jegher-Bucher 15 (*amicus Caesaris*, party adherent). *philia* is not a middle term between A. Nygren's motifs in *Agape and Eros* (London: SPCK, 1952).

TDNT 9 (Ger. 1973; G. Stählin) 151–54 presents personal friendship as an ideal, between a pair of men, emphasizing duty, even unto death, for the friend's sake. For "Friendship in the Philosophical Traditions," see Fitzgerald, ed., 1997. In biblical books,[16] Phil offers "the richest Pauline treasure of friendship" (A. C. Mitchell 1997:233); note 1:6–11, 21–27; 2:2, 6–11, 17–18, 25–30; 3:18; 4:1–3, 10–20. Cf. Stowers 1986:58–78, esp. 60; Malherbe 1986:144, 154; L. M. White 1990:206, 211; P. Marshall 113, 151, 157–64. West concentrates on dying for friends (INTRO. VI.B n 5). P. Marshall 1–34 (Greco-Roman Conventions of Friendship and Enmity): friendship is giving to get a reciprocal return; there is obligation to return a gift; not to do so meant refusal of friendship or breaking it. Notions of trustworthiness (Gk. *pistis*) and gratitude (Gk. *charis*; cf. Konstan 1997:81) he related to the different forms of *philia* sketched by Aristot. and others, including debate over the place of money in relationships among friends. These concepts Marshall 157–64 applied to Phil 4:15, the "account of giving and receiving." That Paul is here "drawing upon familiar notions of friendship" became an "open sesame" to apply elsewhere in Phil and to claim all four chs. are a "letter of friendship."

In the Greco-Roman world *philia* had many nuances. We may list[17] treatments by (1) *Pythagoras*. (2) *Aristot.* (*Eth. Nic.* 8 and 9, *Eth. Eud.* 7),[18] who was mediated, popularized, through later interpreters, syncretistically (Schroeder 35). Types of friendship are variously based,[19] often on virtue, pleasure, or usefulness

---

[16] A. C. Mitchell 1997; Klauck 1990; for *1 and 2 Thess*, Malherbe 1987:68–71 and AB 32B:243, where for 1 Thess 4:9, in the absence of the words *philia* or *philos* in Paul, the link is made via *philadelphia*; *Gal*, H. D. Betz, *Gal.* 1986:32, 221–33 [on 4:12–20], 298–99 [on 6:2], and 304–5 [on 6:6]; *1 and 2 Cor*, P. Marshall; and *Rom* 5:6–8, Cranfield *Rom.* 1:265; Klauck 1991:9–10. For a description of friendship imagery, as assessed, often negatively, from a feminist viewpoint, see Marchal 34–50; it is often intertwined with military imagery, 50–64, and is by no means benign.

[17] Important treatments in Fitzgerald, ed., 1996; Konstan 1997; *OCD³*. See further *Philippian Studies*.

[18] *Eth. Nic.* tr. T. H. Irwin, LCL *Aristotle* 19 (1985); *Eth. Eud.*, H. Rackham, 20 (1926):198–477; relation of the two versions is debated. Cf. also *Pol.*, *Rhet.*, and *Mag. mor. OCD³* 165–69, esp. (24). Konstan 67–82. Sonntag 43–45, political relevance of friendship for *homonoia* (concord) among citizens, a task of the laws (1155a22ff.); 32–43 on *epieikeia* (fairness, equity; cf. Phil 4:5 *patient steadfastness*), re justice and law. A. W. Price, *Love and Friendship in Plato and Aristotle* (Oxford: Clarendon, 1989) 198, friendship "best preserves cities from faction," "grounded on mutual knowledge and shared virtues." Joubert 38–40, the "magnificence" of the "great-souled man" (*Eth. Nic.* 4). West 75–83 finds three elements: friends share, for the sake of the other, and for the *polis*.

[19] Type of *philia*

Type of *philia*	Constitution (*politeia*)	Parallel in household (*oikos*)
according to merit (*kat'axian*)	kingship	father–son relationship
(perversion: little *philia* or justice)	tyranny	Persian father and son (slave)
according to virtue (*kat' aretēn*)	aristocracy	husband–wife
(perversion: *philia* of a lesser degree)	oligarchy	domineering husband or rich wife
according to equality (*isoi*)	timocracy, based on property	brothers (equals except in age)
(perversion: much *philia* but low level)	(no property qualification).	

(*Eth. Nic.* 8.3.1–4; see NOTE on 4:16 *needs*). True *philia* based on virtue is "character friendship." He thus questioned pleasure and utility in friendship. Is friendship "altruistically or egotistically motivated"?[20] (3) *Later Epicurean, Stoic, Skeptic, Cynic schools.* Cf. the views on "self-sufficiency" in the NOTE on 4:11 content (*autarkēs*). (4) *Epicurus.* (5) The *Roman Antiquities of Dionysius of Halicarnassus.* (6) *Greek romances.*[21] (7) *Plutarch.* (8) *Neo-Pythagoreanism.* (9) The *papyri and inscriptions* reflect practical *philia*, often utilitarian.

Lat. sources may be particularly important for Roman Philippi. (10) Marcus Tullius *Cicero* (106–43 B.C.) left 931 letters (many to friends; cf. Probst [(1) Bibl.] 85–89) and a treatise *Laelius: De amiticia (Amic.).*[22] His eclectic views grounded *amicitia* in nature (*Amic.* 6.20) and *amor* or love (*Amic.* 27.100; cf. 9.30–31; NOTE on 4:17 *profit*). *benevolentia* (14.49–50), *constantia* (17.62–64), *fides* (18.65), and *justitia* provide the basis for friendship (Fiore 1997:60–62). Self-interest (e.g., using friends to gain public office) must be renounced; we ought to love the other as ourselves (*Fin.* 1.20,67; *Amic.* 10.34; 17.64 19.67; 16.56–17.61). Politics could produce a calculating approach, but "friendship is greater than a calculus of equality" (Fiore 64). In relations of unequals (client–patron) and equals (friend-to-friend), a "chain of obligations" was established (mutual reciprocity, gift for gift, 66). One "primes the pump," even with the gods (Fiore 1997:67). The system held society together and made it run (cf. Mott), "a mechanism by which individuals could work through the highly stratified Roman society" (Fiore 70). A friend = "anybody who shows you some goodwill, or cultivates your society, or calls upon you regularly" (*Handbook* 16). To further such connections, one might write "friendly letters" (cf. Traede 1970:27–37), offering advice or recommending someone. Many client–patron links are possible, but (so Aristot., not the Stoics) there are not many with whom you share your life (*Ben.* 6.34). (11) Lucius Annaeus *Seneca* (ca. 4 B.C.–A.D. 65), *De beneficiis* (7 books, on benefits), is esp. pertinent for Philippi.[23] Sen. treats

---

[20] Schroeder 41, self-love does not contradict altruism; for "utility friends" versus "goodness friends," cf. Sterling 208. Space precludes even listing bibl., but cf. A. W. Price (n 18 above).

[21] Best known of famous pairs of friends were Phintias and Damon, two Pythagoreans. When Phintias was condemned to death, Damon took his place in prison; at the hour of Damon's execution, Phintias returned to die for his loyal friend; the tyrant forgave them both and asked to be part of their friendship (Diod. Sic. 10.4.3–6; LCL tr., C. H. Oldfather, 4:57–59; "Damon and Pythias" in later versions). *Lucian* (A.D. ca. 120–ca. 200) has a Greek and a Scythian, Toxaris, tell stories (in an *agōn* or *synkrisis*) to prove his nation's concept of friendship is superior. Demetrius who joined his friend Antiphilos in jail has often been cited re Acts 16:26–28: when they could have escaped, they did not try to flee; Demetrius was "able to be satisfied with little"; cf. Phil 4:11–12. Pervo 165, cf. 179–80, sees parody of Greek views on male friendship. West 123–28 is more positive.

[22] OCD[3] 1558–64; *Amic.*, LCL *Cicero* 20, W. A. Falconer 1923; *Laelius, on friendship*, tr. J. G. F. Powell (Warminster: Aris & Phillips, 1990). Cf. *Handbook on Electioneering* (LCL *Cicero* 28, *Letters to Quintus*, etc., tr. D. R. Shackleton Bailey), perhaps by Marcus' brother Quintus, on how ties of friendship and of patron with clients served a candidate for political office (Fiore 1997:69–73). Konstan 1997:122–36.

[23] Bormann 1995:171–81. OCD[3] 96–98; LCL *Moral Essays* 3, tr. J. W. Basore, 1935. Konstan 1997:127–28, 137–40. Seneca's brother Gallio, proconsul of Achaia, heard Paul's case (Acts 18:12). Some of Seneca's letters (cf. Probst [(1) Bibl.] 91–96) deal with *amicitia* (LCL tr. R. M. Gummere,

benefits *apart from* friendship or *only on the margin* of *amicitia*. Every *officium*—duty, obligation, service, "reciprocal personal relationship"—places demands on both giver and recipient (*De ben.* 2.18.1). The person who receives a benefit is obligated to respond, likely with a bigger gift or benefit in return. This makes the original benefactor a beneficiary, obligated to continue with a further, larger gift (1.4.3; cf. Diod. Sic. 1.70.6), in a "most honorable contest" of outdoing benefits with benefits (1.4.4). Do not give with a view toward receiving (1.1.9–10),[24] yet a benefaction is a debt to be paid (1.4.5); "he who does not repay a benefit sins" (1.1.13). To repay a gift is essential; not to do so breaks loyalty (*fides*; *Ep.* 81.12). Note language of "capital" and "interest" (cf. Phil 4:15–17): "a man is an ingrate if he repays a favour without interest" (*beneficium . . . sine usera*, *Ep.* 81.18 = LCL 2.281). To express gratitude can meet the obligation (*Ep.* 73.9, "acknowledgment itself constitutes payment," LCL 2:109). Whoever receives a benefit is in a position of power: gratitude and giving more benefits to the benefactor (1.4.5) obligate that person to an even greater future gift (1.4.4) and formal friendship (*amicitia*; 2.18.3,5). The schema also applied to relations with the gods (cf. Mott 64–65). But (Bormann 1995:232–34) *beneficia* for Sen. involve relationships *not yet* ones of friendship. He treated *amicitia* separately in *De ben.* Book 6. Benefits may lead to friendship, but the two are not the same. In the *beneficium* structure, money or something else is freely given from A to B (3.19.1), not on legal demand but as a gift useful in the situation (4.29.2). Beneficence is an ethical act, assuming the worthiness of the recipient (4.29.3). B must reciprocate (1.1.9), with prompt thanks (2.22–25), giving more than B received (2.18.5), avoiding ingratitude or vanity. For application to Phil 4:10–20, see below, B.2. (12) *OT-Jewish background* is limited (Stählin, *TDNT* 9:156; cf. 154–59; *TDNT* 5:8–15, 19–20). (13) Fullest reflection among Jewish writers occurs in *Philo* (*TDNT* 9:158–59; Sterling), perhaps an infuence on Paul (Klauck 1991:8–9; H. D. Betz, *Gal.* 221). (14) *Philia* involved *social networks* for business and government. G. Herman (above, n 14) describes how guest-friendship (*xenia*) worked; Saller (above, n 14), how such connections were significant among the upper classes in the emerging Roman Empire. Konstan 1997:135–37, *amicitia* is almost client-ship. Cf. Meeks 1983; *Semeia* 56 (1992), ed. L. M. White, esp. 3–38, "social links within the urban environent"; influences from the Roman patronage system came into Christian communities. Fitzgerald 2003:320–31 provides a good "brief history" of this "highly vibrant social institution."

In summary: a pervasive theme in antiquity, but *philia, xenia,* and *amicitia* car-

---

Seneca *Ad Lucilium Epistolae Morales*, 1918), esp. *Epp.* 3, 9, 81; for 6, 40, and 94; see Malherbe 1985:64–65, 69–71, 127–28. Cf. also Sevenster 1961 ([4] Bibl. **suicide**); Malherbe, ANRW 2.26.1:277–78; H. D. Betz, *Gal.* 221 n 14; and Thraede 1970. Joubert 40–51 expounds "benefit-exchange" in Sen. as "part of a long tradition"; on how the process worked, pp. 70–71.

[24] Cf. "It is more blessed to give than to receive," Acts 20:35, references cited in Fitzmyer AB31:682 include Sen. *Ep.* 81.17, "A person errs who receives a benefit more gladly than he repays it" and the proverb implied in Thuc. 2.97.4, "Give rather than take."

ried a variety of meanings in the Gk., Hellenistic, and Roman worlds. Views differed whether those truly wise need friends; if so, few or many; and what the relationship was primarily to be. Friendship obtained esp. among the aristocratic elite, most frequently between individuals of somewhat equal rank. In the Roman Empire there was widespread and probably increasingly pragmatic and utilitarian use of *amicitia*. The Gk. concept penetrated Hellenistic Jewish circles. Seneca's "benefactions" are not specifically set within *amicitia*. At many points, a patron–client relationship; networking. Not "*the* concept of friendship," but aspects, themes, or, in ancient terms, *topoi* of *philia/amicitia* in what Paul writes and reflects.

b. *Philippians, Especially 4:10–20, "a Letter of Friendship"?* Do these *topoi* make 4:10–20 (or all of Phil) a "*letter* of friendship"? So esp. Fitzgerald, *ABD* 5:320–22; for 4:10–20 (Letter A in a three-letter sequence), Schenk 1984, Pesch 1985; for all of Phil, L. T. Johnson 1986, L. M. White 1990.[25] Among aspects in Paul's letters,[26] "enmity" (P. Marshall) was attractive for those defending the unity of Phil: Phil 3 (on enemies) could be part of a letter of friendship (Fitzgerald 320). But friendship themes can be used in partition theories (Pesch; Bormann, perhaps Capper). L. M. White 1990 and Stowers 1991 saw Phil as "a paradigm of friendship" (paraenesis characterizes friendly letters, Malherbe 1987:69–70). White related this to Phil 2:6–11 (a presumed "Jewish [Aramaic?] *Vorlage*"), in light of which Paul presents "a communal idea of virtue in Christ Jesus, a Pauline adaptation of the Hellenistic moral paradigm of *philia* . . ." (201; cf. Lucian's *Toxaris*). But in 4:10–20 bonds of friendship have "become strained either by Paul's or Epaphroditus's situation" (214); a house-church patron, perhaps Euodia or Syntyche, "decided no longer to support Paul" (n 59); see (15) on 4:2–3 and Comment B.1, below. White used "friendly" as an adj. attached to "hortatory letter" (206).[27] L. M. White 1990 was the commentator Stowers cited in 1991 in reversing his earlier position (1986:60) to hold now, "Scholars of ancient letter writing have long identified Philippians as a letter of friendship (*philikos typos*)" with "a massive, almost overwhelming number of connections with ancient, especially Greek, friendship motifs" (1991:106–7).[28] 2:6–11 "would

---

[25] M. M. Mitchell 1991:14 and n 50 criticizes the tendency to create genres from "ambiguous sentences" in ancient handbooks without defining the classification and often without demonstrating such a category in actual usage. "Letter of friendship" is not a form-critical category with which point-by-point comparison can easily be made for Phil. Fitzgerald 2003 sees many aspects of friendship, without using the term "letter of friendship."

[26] Hospitality (Phlm 22; Rom 16:23; Acts 16:15); patronal relationships (Rom 16:2, Phoebe as benefactor, BDAG *prostatis*); recommendations; giving, receiving (Phil 4:14); enmity (Gal 4:16) in contrast to *philia*.

[27] Critique of White, esp. on 2:6–11, in Bormann 1995:227–29 n 14.

[28] Stowers (109–10) listed presence/absence, yearning to be with friends (1:7–8; 4:1; 2:26); common projects (*koinōnia*, suffering; 1:7; 2:17–18; 4:14); giving and receiving (4:15); "one spirit" (1:27); thinking the same things (2:2); and living in a manner governed by the heavenly commonwealth (3:20) in contrast to enmity (ch. 3); and "antithetical models" of friends and enemies (1:15–17, where "envy" and "rivalry" occur, not "enemies"; 3:1–21, where "enemies" appears at 3:18, but "friends" does not).

have recalled . . . stories about those who gave up their own lives for their friends" (119, *Toxaris*). "Philippians is best read as a hortatory letter of friendship" (107, 121). Ebner (see 5.b, below) moved beyond friendship between Paul and the Philippians to include God in a triangulated relationship—not just morality, but ecclesiology and "theology" in its technical sense (363–64). Paul in 4:10–20 reshapes conventions of *philia*; the letter's literary integrity might need to be reopened.

Grounds for regarding Phil as "letter of friendship" need reconsideration (Reumann 1992; Ascough 2003:139; Holloway 2001a:31 n 120; Bittasi 125–26).

(1) Friendship *topoi* and semantic fields related to *philia* are better supported than usage by Paul of a literary category, *epistolē philikē*. So Berger 1984b:1329; L. T. Johnson 1986.

(2) A "friendly letter" marked by paraenesis (Malherbe ANRW 2.26.3:278–93; 1987:69–70) was foundational for L. M. White 1990, Stowers 1991, and Fitzgerald 1992. But is "paraenesis" sufficient criterion to identify a letter of friendship? Paraenesis occurs in many genres. Is the relationship here between friends, or teacher and pupils, founding father and community, apostle and church? Malherbe's term in AB 32B:81–86 is "pastoral paraenesis." Phil 4:10–20 involves more than moral teaching.

(3) Absence of *philia* terms in Paul has been variously explained. Theologically, the Gk. theme was too anthropocentric, not Christocentric (J. N. Sevenster 1961 [(4) Bibl. **suicide**] 178–80). Sociologically, Paul desired to avoid status implications of patronal friendship (E. A. Judge 1974, "Paul as a Radical Critic of Society," *Interchange* 16:191–203). *philos* had undesirable Epicurean connotations (Malherbe 1987:104; Stowers 1991; West 18). Instead of friendship, the apostle preferred the fictive relationship of *adelphoi* through baptism (Klauck 1991; contrast Fitzgerald 2003:331–32). An "intimate, person-to-person" style was not appropriate for a corporate group (Stirewalt 2003:89). Agreed, friendly relations with Paul are "strained" (L. M. White); Paul opposes some aspects of *philia/amicitia* with which the Philippians operated (Ebner); hence he never uses *philia*.

(4) Evidence that *church fathers* like Chrysost. spoke of Phil as an *epistolē philikē* has not been adduced. Cf. Reumann 1996:100–105, also on Aquinas and Melanchthon; Edart 312 n 24.

(5) Customary Gk. "rules of friendship" (e.g., *philia* involves males of equal social status) are lacking in Paul and the NT generally (Berger 1984a:156). Instead, Paul criticized notions of friendship in Augustan culture and politics; Georgi 1991; Bormann 1995; B.1.a.(3).(d), below.

(6) The social-world sense of *philia/amicitia* and its networking make one ask, Could Paul use this theme? It does not fit his apostolic self-understanding. A "society of friends," Greco-Roman style, is not Pauline ecclesiology (Klauck; Ebner; contrast Fitzgerald 2003:334).

(7) The concept of "benefits" in Seneca's *De beneficiis* seems particularly pertinent to 4:10–20 in a Roman colonia (Bormann 1995:171–81), more so than friendship.

(8) Hence some opt for Phil as a "family letter" (Perkins SBL1987SP; L. Alexander 1989; cf. J. L. White 1986: ##102–5)[29] or an "administrative letter" akin to 2 Cor 8 and 2 Cor 9.[30]

In Conclusion: Friendship themes appear in 4:10–20 (and elsewhere in Phil), from Greco-Roman *philia, amicita,* and "benefits," but that is not reason for calling the unit or all of Phil "a letter of friendship." A *topos,* not a *Gattung,* is involved (Berger 1984b:1329; Edart 312 n 24). Black 1995, elements of the *topos* are present, but "friendship plays a subordinate and supporting role in the macrostructure of the letter" (20 n 16; cf. 44 n 46). How the concepts that are present function in these vv will be presented in B.1, below.

3. *4:10–20 as "Thankless Thanks."* In 4:10–20 Paul acknowledges gifts from Philippi but never in Phil expresses thanks with a vb. like *eucharistein* (1:3, "I thank *my* God . . ."). Why? The oxymoron "danklose Danke" has been used at least since 1876.[31] Commentators offer various explanations on why no direct assertion of appreciation.

(1) *"Cultural contrast."* Moderns (at least in the 19th cent.) may overdo courtesy ("Danke schön, Bitte schön"). Cf. L. Alexander 1989:98; Silva 231; Peterlin 214–15 nn 35, 36.

(2) Paul was *embarrassed* at receiving gifts. C. H. Dodd 1953:71–72: "he hated taking" money (1 Cor 9:15–18) and "can scarcely . . . acknowledge" it was welcome. So he piles up "technical terms of trade, as if to give the transaction a severely 'business' aspect," typical of "a well-to-do-*bourgeois*" of the day. So Martin 1976:161.

(3) Paul was *upset they have disobeyed his principle* not to accept help from his congregations (1 Cor 9:14–18 renounces the right to support asserted in Gal 6:6; he would rather die than accept support). So C. O. Buchanan 161–63; cf. Martin 1976:161; Hawth. 195, "violation of his strict instructions not to send him assistance"; Collange 149. Some say Paul accepted gifts from converts when working elsewhere, not while with them; V. D. Verbrugge, *Paul's Style of Church Leader-*

---

[29] Exler 1923: "familiar letters" to family and friends; Koskenniemi 1956:10ff. L. Alexander 1989, the schema (derived from PMich 8.491, 2nd cent. A.D.; White #104B) does not cover 3:1–4:20 (p. 94), where Paul is said to provide "a 'sermon-at-a-distance'" (99). For 4:10–20, appeal is made to POxy 12.1481 (2nd cent. A.D.; White #102, Theonas to his mother); this analogue explains little about the contents of 4:10–20. The claim limps that thanks can occur at the end of a letter, for the five-and-a-half lines in POxy 12.1481 before Theonas' "thanks" are hardly comparable to the 191 (lines of NA text) in Phil prior to 4:10–20. The "thanks" (lines 6–9) occur proportionally just about where in Letter A what is now 4:10–20 would have been located (after 1:1–2 or 1:1–11).

[30] H. D. Betz, *2 Cor. 8 and 9:*139, cf. 93 n 27; 118 n 229; evidence on "letters of commendation to accompany royal envoys" (*epistolē systatikē*) pp. 129–39. Phil 4:10–20 *could* relate to such a category, but the apostle was no royal administrator, issuing ukases and decrees. Congregational situations seldom permitted this. Paul's eschatological outlook did not allow "administration" the place modern churches grant it. Stirewalt 2003 appeals to "official correspondence," also undercutting the friendship category.

[31] Vincent 146 and Mengel 283, from C. Holsten in 1876. The phrase has led to "the image of the 'unthankful apostle'" (Merk 1968:187 n 86). Cf. Thielman 1995:234.

ship Illustrated by His Instructions to the Corinthians on the Collection (San Francisco: Mellen Research Univ. Press, 1992) 118–27.

(4) O. Glombitza 1959 ([8] Bibl.), 1962, and esp. 1964–65: Phil 4:15 reflects *a fresh start* in Macedonia; prior preaching scarcely counted; see NOTE on 4:15b "*at the beginning of the gospel," when I departed from Macedonia.* The Philippians participated with Paul; 4:14, "You have already participated when you wished to share in my affliction." *kalōs epoiēsate* amounts to "thanks" not (137–38) for the Philippians' gift but the fruit derived from his preaching to them. The "account of receiving and giving" = sharing in the gospel and responding to it. No need to thank them that the gospel has flourished; simply glorify God for their sacrifice (4:18). This reading sidesteps lack of thanks by emphasizing common involvement in the gospel. O'B 530–32 rejects it; U. B. Müller 200 reflects it somewhat: Paul is more interested in the givers than the gift and rejoices over their involvement for the gospel.

(5) Sometimes a *previous letter* of thanks is conjectured. So J. H. Michael 1922–23 (INTRO. VI); 1928 MNTC 209; E. F. Scott, *IB* 11:121; cf. Collange 149 and INTRO. VI.A.

(6) A *thank you* lies buried behind (a) 4:10 *I greatly rejoiced . . . that you have now at last revived your concern for me . . .* (O'B 517; "rejoice" [*chairō*] connects with *eucharistō*; Schenk 43). Or (b) 4:14 "you did well . . ." (*kalōs epoiēsate*) = "Thank you for . . ." (Loh. 183 n 1; Schenk 43, among others). See NOTE on 4:14 *it was kind of you* and (4) above, Glombitza; F. F. Bruce 129. Or (c) 4:18 *I have been paid in full,* a commercial way of saying "Payment received, thank you." See NOTE on *apechō de panta.* (d) 1:3–5 (O'B 58–61; I. H. Marshall); or 1:7, tr, "because I have you in my heart"; or possibly 1:7b–8, tr. "you all being participants with me in grace" (Glombitza, [4] above) and "I long for you all." Allusions to Philippian gifts are not impossible in 1:3–11, but clear thanks are missing (DA 198–202). Some say that Paul waited till 4:10–20 so as to give prominence to an "expression of thanks" there (Bruce 123; Bockmuehl 258).

(7) From the commercial aspects (6c above; 4:15–17; Ascough 2003:149–53, marketplace language, as in voluntary associations) some assume Paul had a *business arrangement* with Lydia (Fleury) or a Roman *legal contract* with the Philippian congregation to be their evangelist (Sampley) or received *loans* from the Philippians (Hermesdorf). No "thank you" needed, simply terminate the arrangement or make a statement about the account currently. See B.1 below.

(8) The most promising solution appeals to *philia. Relations between friends did not call for a statement of thanks.* Friend helped friend. Getting a benefaction obligated responding with a (greater) gift; the receiver becomes a benefactor in turn. See above, A.2.a.(11), Seneca. G. W. Peterman applied such "first century social conventions" to 4:1–20 (1991:261; 1997:74–83), esp. a papyrus letter dated 29 August, A.D. 58, to a physician Dionysios, from a well-educated man named Chairas, perhaps also a physician, PMert 1.12:[32] (1) "verbal gratitude is misplaced among

---

[32] line 1. "Chairas to most beloved (*philōtatō[i]*) Dionysios, / 2. many greetings and continued / 3. health. When I got your letter, / 4. I was as joyous (*pericharēs*) as if / 5. I were really at home (*en tē[i]*

those who are intimate"; (2) material expression of gratitude is required that is "equivalent (*ta isa* l. 11) to the affection received . . ."; (3) verbal assertion acknowledges debt or intention to repay (Peterman 264, cf. 1997:77; Sen. *De. Ben.* 2.24.4). Twenty-five other letters (1991 n 14; 1997:78) mention "receipt of goods or favors by private individuals," 265, among them White 1986:#102 (Theonas) and Stowers 1986: p. 69 (POxy 42.3057). Peterman finds that (1) in only four of the 26 documents is a "thank you" expressed.[33] (2) The *"obligation to repay"* is a "social expectation" (267; 1997:79). In POxy 42.3057 (1st-2nd cent. A.D.; some claim it is the earliest Christian letter on papyrus outside the NT), Ammonius writes to his "brother" Apollonius, thanking him for a letter, traveling bag, etc. (1997:80–82):

> the cloaks I received not as old ones, but as better than new if that's possible, because of the spirit (in which they were given). But I don't want you, brother, to load me with these continual kindnesses (*philanthrōpiais*), since I can't repay them — the only thing we suppose ourselves to have offered you is (our) feelings of friendship (*philikēs diatheseōs*). (POxy 42.3057, pp. 144–45, lines 5–11, tr. P. J. Parsons, who remarks, 144, it is "temerarius to look for a Christian context").

After an unsolicited gift, Ammonius asserts confidence in Apollonius and mentions his own current distress. Peterman notes parallels to Phil. Was expectation of material response a burden ("load me with," *barunein*)? Ammonius was unable to meet "this social expectation." (3) Verbal thanks as a debt appears in five other papyri, usually in a closing line, "Write me about what you want." Cf. Ps.-Demetrius' "thankful (*apeucharistikos*)" letter (Malherbe 1977:39 = 1988:41),

> I hasten to show in my actions (*ergō[i]*) how grateful I am to you for the kindness you have showed me (*euergetēsas*) in your words. For I know that what I am

---

idia[i]), for without / 6. that (joy of being in one's own place) there is nothing. I can neglect writing / 7. you with great thanks (*megalas eucharistias*), / 8. for it is to those who are not friends that with words one must / 9. express thanks (*dei gar tois mē philois ousi dia logōn eucharistein*). I am confident / 10. that I can persevere (or "gain strength," after an illness?) with some degree of serenity, and will be able, if not / 11. to give you an equivalent gift (*ta isa*), to render / 12. some little return for your affection (*philostorgia[i]*) to me." H. I. Bell/C. H. Roberts, *A Descriptive Catalogue of the Greek Papyri in the Collection of Wilfred Merton, F. S. A.* (London: Emery Walker Ltd., 1948) 50–52 = White 1986:#93 = Stowers 1986:61–62. From Egyptian Oxyrhynchus or Hermopolis. Cf. White (145 n on lines 6–9), "verbal thanks . . . are an inadequate expression of intimate friendship," but a gift is expected in response. Stowers 61, a "commonplace that friends need not verbally express their thanks." "Deeds are the proper medium" of response, not writing (Peterman 1991:263). One acknowledges indebtedness and states intention to repay. An enthymeme is suggested in 1997:76. J. R. Harrison ([1] Bibl. **grace**) 84 sees in PMert 12 "a critique of the benefaction system" as reciprocity.

[33] PLugd. Bat. 42.23–24 (2nd cent. A.D.), a woman writes her sister, until she can visit in person, to thank her (*eucharistēsō*) for clothing; *charin* or *charis soi* in PMich 483.3–5a; 498.4–7a; and POxy 6:963.line 2.

doing is less than I should, for even if I gave my life for you [hyperbole?], I would still not be giving adequate thanks *(charin)* for the benefits I have received. If you wish anything that is mine, do not write and request it, but demand a return. For I am in your debt.

Ps.-Libanius 57, the *eucharistikē epistolē*," "For many other gifts am I grateful *(charin ginōskō)* . . . but especially for that matter in which you benefitted me above all others" (Malherbe 71 = 75). In 4:10–20 "verbal expression of gratitude from Paul should not be expected" (Peterman 268). Joy (v 10) comes not at receipt of a gift but for a letter, as in PMert 12 ("like being at home"). Nor "should it be expected that Paul would owe a material return to the Philippians." He has "not become socially obligated by accepting their gifts. Rather . . . they have been elevated to the unique place of partnership in the gospel." So Peterman, but how did the Phiippians perceive it? Finally (270) no pledge by Paul to repay should be expected, but he does "promise them a reward" (v 18a, God as Benefactor). He responds "in keeping with the thankless thanks practiced in the first century Graeco-Roman world" (cf. 1997:121–61, esp. 157–60).

Peterlin 208 found Peterman's application "somewhat stretched." Cf. Bassler 1991:76–79. Bormann 1995:187 n 2, the tone of delay in 4:10 and Paul's response in vv 11–13 must be brought in. Capper 208 n 33 pronounced Peterman 1991 "relevant" to his own approach but augmented it. These critiques assume disunity and a rift at Philippi. At issue is the sequence of supposed events and how *philia* enters in.

This explanation from *philia* appeals to elements in the friendship *topos*, esp. Seneca's on benefits, without assuming a "letter of friendship" form. K. G. Evans did not find much on "letters of friendship" in the papyri. Peterman augments PMert 12 with 25 other letters. PMert 12 involves educated letter writers (a physician and his peer). Did the Philippian house churches include persons (leaders) of such status and outlook (Epaphroditus?; Peterlin 135–70; 185–205)?

Conclusions: Some proposed solutions are of little or no value, (2) embarrassment, (3) anger the Philippians have disobeyed Paul's rule. Others carry elements of truth: (1) cultural contrast, (4) praise for involvement in the gospel's spread. There *could* have been a previous letter (5), perhaps (6) hints of thanks in 1:3–11, though no overt "thank you." In B.1 we shall discard (7) the legal, business explanations. Friendship (8) provides the most promising explanation.

4. Forms Within 4:10–20. For materials to write the body of Letter A (*heuresis*, Lat. *inventio*) Paul drew on the situation at hand *(stasis)*, including renewed Philippian financial support, against the background of the friendship *topos*. "*I/me" language* occurs in virtually every v except 20, "the 'I'-style of a personal confession" in 12–13 (O'B 522); "you" (pl.) in vv 10, 14–19. *Commercial, fiscal terms* are frequent in 15–18, perhaps *legal language* (10c, *eph' hō[i]*; 15c *koinōnia*). Some financial figures were originally *agricultural* (v 17 "fruit/profit, growing/ accumulation"; the Philippians' "blossoming" or "reviving," 10); Philippi was a market town (Peterlin 136–39; Oakes 2001:42–50). *Philosophical terms* appear (*autarkēs*, v 11), and the vocabulary of *friendship* (cf. A.2, above); *cultic* terms at the end of v 18; a *mystery religions* vb. in 12c, *I have had my initiation experience.* Imagery is thus surprisingly varied. On stylistic features cf. NOTES and Edart 288–93 (alliteration, etc.)

a. *The OT.* seems reflected in 4:18c, *a fragrance with aroma, a sacrifice acceptable, well-pleasing, to God* (Gen 8:21; Exod 29:18; Ezek 20:41; Isa 56:7, etc.).[34] Loh. 1919b saw a broader history-of-religions background. Sacrifices were part of daily life in Roman Philippi. The Gk. *en doxē[i]* in 19 can be taken as a Heb. adverb, *gloriously*; *amēn* (20) is a Heb. word transliterated into Gk.; *forever and ever* may root in OT "eternity formulas" (see NOTE).

b. *Early Christian Formulas.* Likely liturgical, these provide wording in vv 19–20. In the *doxology* at 4:20 (U. B. Müller 207; WDNTECLR 140–41) some see two halves (NOTE; Loh., Wiles), "To our God and Father (belongs) glory/ forever and ever. Amen"; or (1) One to whom praise is ascribed (in the dat.), (2) word of praise, and (3) temporal phrase, usually an "eternity formula" (O'B 549), + "Amen." Fee 452 n 11 is unpersuaded; cf. R. Deichgräber ([7] Bibl.) 25–40. 4:19 seems Paul's own formulation, with traditional (Pauline) elements; see NOTES.

c. *Epistolary Style and Situation.* From a letter by the Philippians likely came the spelling *Philippēsioi* at 4:15; 4:10 *to hyper emou phronein, concern for me,* a Philippian slogan about Paul; *"the beginning of the gospel"* and *Macedonia.* At 4:10, R. D. Webber ([2] Bibl. **joy**) 141–54 spoke of an *epistolary rejoicing formula* (see NOTE on 1:4 *with joy*), "one piece of evidence in favor of regarding Phil. 4:10–20 as a separate letter." 4:10bc (Webber 152) falls "into the style of oral discourse." J. L. White 1971 (above, n 3) claimed a five-part "introductory formula" to express joy; Mullins 1972 ([1] Bibl.) 384–85 was not persuaded. Cf. Peterman 1991; DA 273–80 (a secondary feature). 4:14 *kalōs epoiēsate* was common in the papyri (see NOTE). 4:18 *apechō* is commercial idiom, "paid in full." *oidate* 4:15, "you know," is typical of Paul's epistolary style.[35]

d. *Apologetic, Diatribe.* Schoon-Janßen 143–44 explored possible *apologetic* (self-justification against real opponents) versus a *dialogical diatribe style* (polemic against an imaginary opponent) in Phil.[36] Note the "antitheses" in 4:11–12, objections and rebuttal in 4:10–13, 16–17.[37] Schoon-Janßen 158–61 concluded 4:17 is not apologetic against "perfectionists" (3:15) in the congregation. U. B. Müller 203 sees traces of the diatribe style and elements of the friendship theme.

e. *Peristasis Catalogue.* This occurs in 4:12–13 (Gk. *peristasis* = (adverse) circumstance, difficulty, hardship, danger. *Peristasenkataloge* = passages where the

---

[34] F. Thielman 1994:156–58, 286 n 49 and 1995:237, Paul understood Philippian generosity as partial fulfillment of prophecies like Isa 56:7 and 60:7. But (DA 291 n 499) Paul has not "reflected on the original [OT] context"; so "allusions," the words are "part of his idiolect rather than his rhetoric."

[35] Cf. 1 Thess 2:1,2,5,11; 1 Cor 12:2, etc., as well as "Do you not know . . . ?" (*ouk oidate*), esp. in 1 Cor (3:16, etc.).

[36] On diatribe, cf. Bultmann 1910; repr. 1984; S. K. Stowers, *The Diatribe and Paul's Letter to the Romans* (SBLDS 57; Chico, CA: Scholars Press, 1981); Schmeller 422–23; WDNTECLR 127–29.

[37] 4:16 "You sent me help" is Paul's assertion; 17a "Not that I seek the gift" responds to the view that Paul *did* seek gifts; 17b "I seek profit for your account" = basis for the rebuttal.

writer "enumerates the different strokes of Fate, the *peristaseis* over which he boasts as victor" (Bultmann 1910:19). Or "Leidenskatalog," list of sufferings; "tribulation lists."[38] NT examples in NOTE on 4:12. Phil 4:12 catalogues vicissitudes both bad and good; not just adversities (Fitzgerald 203).[39] An established form in Paul (*WDNTECLR* 347; Bormann 1995:192–96). In the Greco-Roman world (Fitzgerald 47–116, cf. 203–5; Ebner 387–97; Bormann 192–93) examples include the (suffering) sage who plays a role in the divine plan with serenity (Plato *Resp.* 361E–362A, "the just man . . . scourged," racked, bound in chains, eyes burned out, "and, finally . . . crucified"). E.g., Socrates, Diogenes, Cato, Odysseus, and esp. Heracles (Ebner 388). *peristaseis* reveal what a person is (Epict. 1.24.1), serene amid calamities, with virtues like endurance; persevering at tasks, contempt for Fortune, victory over adversity, discipline, invincibility, rationality, consent to sufferings, conformity to God's plan (Fitzgerald 115).

In Paul (cf. D. Fredrickson, "Paul, Hardships, and Suffering," in Sampley, ed., 2003, 172–97), *peristasis* catalogues (Fitzgerald 1988:204–7) show (a) serenity and endurance; (b) a model; (c) attribution of hardships to God; (d) *autarkeia* or sufficiency from what Paul has learned; (e) triumphant certainty of victory (Phil 4:13; cf. Berger 1984a: 228.3, classical analogues); hence (f) joy. Some "hardships were provided by the churches to whose care he devoted himself" (206; 2 Cor 11:28); Phil 4:11–13, problems with his beloved Philippians.

Attempts to distinguish pagan and Christian *peristasis* catalogues (Gnilka 174–76; contrast Engberg-Pedersen 1995:262 n 10) and appeals to Jewish-OT backgrounds (cf. Schrage 1974) do not hold up well (Berger 1984a:228; cf. Bormann 1995:193). Ebner 395–96 sees consequences of the Christ-event worked out theologically in Paul's catalogues. His lists suggest a distancing; congregations cannot presume on "friendship" with the apostle. *philia* serves "as a provisional catalyst to bring believers into a relationship with the real 'business partner,' namely God," who enables "a life that is *autarchēs*" (396). For Phil 4:11–13 cf. esp. 2 Cor 11:23–33 and 12:10 (within 12:1–10). 4:11–13 strikes a jarring note for Paul's "favorite church," singular among his *peristasis* catalogues in so fully accepting Hellenistic views.[40] The almost churlish intrusion, "I am content, I know, I can do all things," without you, redefines the problem of friendship.

---

[38] On the term, Fitzgerald 1988:33–46; see NOTE on 4:11b *content*. Furnish, AB 32A:280–83, 354–55, 535–39, "catalogue of hardships"; Martin, 2 *Cor.* WBC 40:83. *History of research:* Fitzgerald 1988:1–32; Ebner 1–7; Ferrari 23–80, with critique of Fitzgerald. Berger 1984a:225–28 recognizes the *Peristatenkataloge* as one of the "epideictic gattungs."

[39] Connections exist with the diatribe, possibly with Judaism (W. Schrage 1974; K. T. Kleinknecht 1984), perhaps with Augustus' *Monumentum Ancyranum* (A. Fridrichsen, "Peristasenkatalog und Res Gestae," SO 8 [1929] 78–82, cf. 7 [1928] 25–29) and Imperial propaganda (Georgi 1964a, Bormann 1995), not to mention sufferings (2 Cor).

[40] Loh. proposed a strophic form; Jeremias 1958 ([3] Bibl.) 146 =1966:277), a chiasm of six infins., so A. Di Marco, "Der Chiasmus in der Bibel IV," *Linguistica Biblica* 44 (Jan. 1979) 28:

```
4:12   a    tapeinousthai          b    perisseuein
       b'   chorazesthai           a'   peinan
       b    perisseuein            a    hystereisthai.
```

Exact structure remains debated (references in NOTE on 4:12).

5. The Overall Structure of 4:10–20.

a. *Schenk.* The letter body has a threefold construction (Schenk 46; space limitations prevent sketching his text-linguistic analysis, 29–67[41]; cf. O'B 522); each part appears several times:

A. *Thanks* for the Philippians' gift, vv 10, 14, and 18; see n 41. Then a sideglance,

B. *Economic relations with the Philippians,* 10c "you tried to continue your action of solidarity with me [conative imperf.], but had no opportunity"; 15–16 you shared several times.

C. *Theological elucidations,* 11–13, esp. 13b, "the One who strengthens me"; 17 "profit (from God) that accumulates to your account"; 19–20, "God's creative actions" (*doxa = schöpferische Heilsmacht*), acclamation v 20 for God's causing Philippian support of Paul to "blossom" (10), as also in the future, "fruit/interest growing in your account," v 17.

O'B uses Schenk sparingly. Silva found it overly complex. Ferrari 444 n 413, "too starkly linguistically oriented."[42] U. B. Müller 201 accepts the new beginnings at vv 10, 14, and 18, but other features dominate "elements of a letter of thanks."[43]

b. *Ebner.* In 331–64 he broke new ground, connecting friendship, money, *koinōnia,* and *autarkeia.* He offers a different structuring of 4:11–13 than did Schenk and sees a larger chiasm in v 18:

A	Recipient (Paul)	B	Giver (Epaphroditus)
	the receipt, v 18a		18b *para Epaphroditou*
B′	Giver (the Philippians)	A′	Recipient (God)
	18b *ta par' hymōn*		18c sacrificial terminology

Schenk eliminated the sacrificial terminology (18c) from prominence, made only Paul a recipient (God is as well), and undervalued Epaphroditus as mediator. 4:19–20 is a prayer-wish that his God will respond to the needs of the Philippians. Paul becomes a "giver" through his prayers, God takes the place of Paul in a "friendship-koinonia" (362, cf. Ebner's n 161). Ebner charts what mutual obligation and participation in a common goal meant for *philia* in world of the day:

Common Point of Reference
(e.g., grief, money)

koinōnia	FRIENDSHIP	Quality
Person A	Quality/Relationship	Person B
dosis/giving	Commercial language	*lēmpsis*/receiving

---

[41] The three steps in Paul's "thanks" are (a) 4:10 *I rejoiced,* (b) 14 "you did well," (c) the receipt v 18, "Paid in full"; similarly Thielman 1995:234. Chiastic structures in vv 19–20 and in vv 17–18; below, n 88.

[42] The "thank you" is not as pronounced as Schenk claims. "Theology" is clear in v 13 (not 12), only indirectly in 17; v 19 is as God-related as v 20. Is Paul shifting attention to God in more vv than Schenk's "theological" ones? 4:19 is more likely a future assertion than a wish-prayer (see NOTES). The friendship *topos* focuses too narrowly on Paul as recipient; it needs to be broadened by attention to "benefits" (Bormann) and a sharper critique by Paul of the Philippian idea of *philia* (Ebner).

[43] Peterlin 213 saw a series of statements, clarifications, and decisions in 4:10–19; Fee 425, 3 acknowledgments (10a, 14, 18), each with qualifiers (10b, 15–16, 19), a Pauline qualifier (11–13, 17), + the doxology in 20.

4:11–13 with its *"autarkia* catalogue" (360–62) is "almost discourteous" in a letter of thanks (Friedrich 127). Such self-sufficiency and *philia* were "opposites *per se"* (360).[44] Paul thereby dampens the Philippians' zeal for their kind of *philia* (with its views on money and benefits depicted in the chart above) in two corrective steps, each introduced by *ouch hoti* (vv 11, 17; "theological elucidations"). The first (11–13) asserts Paul's personal sufficiency, so vigorously that a counterstatement is needed in 14–16 (introduced by *plēn, Anyway*). V 14 is *captatio benevolentiae,* "you did well" (Lausberg #227a). These vv, 11–16, deal with the *past.* The second (17–19) deals with the *future.* In 17, Paul functions not as "partner" *(koinōnos)* but banker who credits them with profit and interest, and cultic "middleman" who "presents their offerings for them" ("I, Paul, am filled with sweet aroma," the fourth possibility in the NOTE on 4:18a *a fragance with aroma . . . to God;* see B.2,d below). Paul presents the Philippians' gift to the real recipient, God (Ebner 333–34; cf. his chiastic structure noted above). *philia-koinōnia* shifts to "sacrifice-koinonia," from relations between human beings to relations of humans with God. Paul changes the paradigm from Greco-Roman friendship (chart above) to the real partner in *koinōnia,* God, who will take Paul's place, the One who alone can fulfill *every* need, who enables Paul too (v 13). Just as God gives Paul power for all things (13), so God will fulfill the Philippians' "every need"(19). Paul disconnects the *philia* link between congregation and himself, transforming it so that the Philippians see God as direct partner. Vv 11–16 free the Philippians from the moral obligations of Hellenistic friendship, for *autarkeia* and connection with God (19). His pastoral concern is *koinōnia* with God (364). He stands the Gk. concept "on its head" (cf. Hooker NIB 11:548):

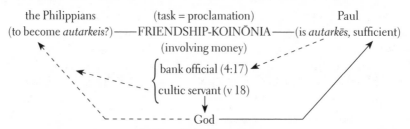

the Philippians   (task = proclamation)   Paul
(to become *autarkeis?*)——FRIENDSHIP-KOINŌNIA——(is *autarkēs,* sufficient)
                       (involving money)
                       { bank official (4:17)
                       { cultic servant (v 18)
                              God

Paul thus put into practice the principle of Gal 6:6 (stressed by Hainz): he had shared the gospel with them, they shared material support with him for its advance, in a "koinonia of friendship." In the face of what the Philippians think *philia* means, Paul asserts his independence of them; his sufficiency is based on God. Apostolic authority may be a factor here (cf. Schenk). The proper goal is *koinōnia* with God. Their kind of *philia* leads to celebration of the self "if not shifted 'as a sacrifice pleasing to God' into friendship with God." Philippi is no exception to a policy on financial support articulated in Corinthians, but "an early point in the line of development" to which Paul now cautiously returns in 4:10–20 (364).

---

[44] Recall discussions over how many, if any, friends the self-sufficient person needed (above, A.2.a.(2); cf. A. W. H. Adkins, "'Friendship' and 'Self-Sufficiency' in Homer and Aristotle," CQ 13 [1963] 30–45).

c. *Bormann.* In 1995:136–60, with aspects of Schenk's analysis, he applauds (223 n 9) the "change in perspective" (Reumann 1993) that asks about *Philippian* contributions to Paul's mission, literary style, thought, and theology. This includes what they taught Paul about "friendship" and how he reacted to it. See B.1, below, on how Paul takes up Philippian understandings, critically.

In summary: no agreed structure for 4:10–20, but interesting proposals abound. Ebner will be particularly important in the following interpretation.

B. MEANING AND INTERPRETATION

1. Historical Situation: Prior Relationships Between Paul and the Philippians. Paul drafted 4:10–20 with themes from the friendship *topos* in mind (A.2, above) and language from business, agriculture, cultic sacrifice, and philosophy, plus a doxology and *peristasis* catalogue (A.4, above). No "letter of friendship" format (A.2.b), but he had to note a gift just received from Philippi through their congregational *apostolos*, Epaphroditus, part of a history of friendly relationships with the Philippian house churches (A.3). 4:10–20 is the body of Letter A in a sequence of three, written from Ephesus. Letter A contains no evidence (unless 1:7b) that Paul was jailed, though he faced affliction (4:14) in his ministry. After examining the setting for Letter A in (1) (a) and (b), we treat its meaning (2, below), then (3) 4:10–20 in the redacted letter.

a. *Proposals on the Situation.* We reject notions that Paul married Lydia of Thyatira (Acts 16:14) and that she is the "true yokefellow" of 4:3, see NOTE on *my faithful partner.*

(1) *J. Fleury* claimed *a business agreement by Paul with Lydia* explains how fiscal support from Philippi (4:15) does not contradict declarations Paul worked to provide self-support (1 Thess 2:9; 2 Thess 3:9; Acts 20:34–35), accepting no money from those to whom he preached (1 Cor 9:15–17; 2 Cor 11:7; 12:14). *(sug)koinōnein* and *ekoinōnēsen* in 4:14–15 are associated with *koinōnia* meaning a consensual society in material things *(giving and receiving)*. Lydia, a dealer in purple cloth in Philippi, and Paul the tentmaker, who settled in her home (Acts 16:15), began a business enterprise that brought him payments after he left Philippi. The "account" in Phil 4:15 is earthly bookkeeping, legal background in the *ius italicum* of Roman Philippi. Paul was a Roman citizen; Lydia need not be to form a *koinōnia*. Fleury reconstructs the legal evolution of this sort of *societas* for an agreed purpose, with a common treasury and record of expenditures and income *(logos doseōs kai lēmpseōs)*. Twice in Thessalonica Paul received money for his needs *(chreia,* 4:15). A partner could ask for this (2 Cor 11:8 *opsōnion,* NRSV "support"; in the papyri, "provision money, pay, salary," MM 471–72). In 4:17 he further exercises his right: "Not . . . alms, but I request the revenue increasing in your account."[45] In v 18, Paul issues a receipt, dissolving the society; he has been paid enough. *I have received* (18) refers to news through Epaphroditus about affairs among the Philippi-

---

[45] Fleury distinguishes *doma* in v 17 from *dosis* in v 15; cf. MM 168–69; v. 15 is an "installment" due, v 17 a handout for a beggar (Beet).

ans. Paul calls the Philippians "a fragrant offering," etc. (cf. 2 Cor 4:6; Eph 5:2; Ezek 20:41). "I have been paid, in learning through Epaphroditus what is happening among you, a perfume of pleasant odor, an agreeable sacrifice that pleases God" (p. 58). Phil 4 fits Paul's policy: not paid by any congregation, he drew on earnings with Lydia. She may be the *syzyge* (4:3, coworker) Paul asks, as community leader *(maîtresse)*, to work for peace between Euodia and Syntyche.

Fleury's explanation (Paul as a sharp entrepreneur, living off accumulated capital and growing interest account) has little support. Some reject biographical use of Acts (Sampley 1980 says "corpus harmonization"); others, the venturesome use of Lydia references. Was the brief period (16:12) in Philippi sufficient to produce profits to pay him in Thessalonica, Corinth, and now Ephesus? Fleury ignored eschatological factors (a business partnership with the parousia approaching?) and mission support from Philippi/Macedonia. How did such "a stray piece of correspondence" (Capper 202) about financial arrangements with Lydia get into a letter to the Philippian *ekklēsia* (4:15; "you" pl. is frequent)? The view is "fanciful" (Capper 201). Fleury "fails to note the flow of 4:10–20" (Sampley 1980:59). Statements about "installments due," an end to the legal association, and then tidings from Philippi as a "fragrant sacrifice" are too abruptly joined. 4:18 is a receipt, not termination of a contract. But Fleury drew attention to the Roman legal world whence Sampley proposed an explanation.

(2) *J. P. Sampley* (1977, expanded in 1980; cf. [2] COMMENT B.2; NOTES on 1:5 *koinōnia*; 1:7 *sygkoinōnous*) envisioned a consensual *societas* between Paul and the Philippian church, "equal partners in living and preaching the gospel"; Paul is "their representative" whom they "support for his evangelistic endeavors" (1980:61). Paul also had *societas* arrangements with Philemon (Phlm 17; pp. 79–81) and Peter, James, and John (Gal 2:9, 1980:21–50).

Such a *societas* (Sampley 1980:11–20) was founded on mutual trust and reciprocity (17); equal partners agreed on goals; as long as "the parties remain of the same mind," it continued. A partner *(socius)* "was entitled to remuneration 'for expenses properly incurred.'" Death of a partner dissolved the relationship, as did "lost commitment to the original goal or aim" (16). Paul, aware of "newfound unity with the pillars at the Jerusalem conference via the norms and patterns of the consensual *societas*," applied the model in Philippi, a partnership "in Christ for preaching the gospel" (51), with "giving and receiving" (4:15). 4:18 is a receipt for the *doma* ("gift" *and* "payment," p. 54); *chreia* at 4:16 (and 2:25) means "request" as well as "need" (55; Witherington 131 is rightly critical). Cf. also 1:3 and 5 (p. 61) and "have the same mind" *(to auto phronein,* 4:2; 2:2, cf. 2:5 *phronein* and 2:6–11; 3:15; the *societas* endures as long as the partners remain *in eodem sensu,* of the same mind, 15). In Philippi there was trust enough to form a *societas,* but this was "not an all-pervasive model of the Christian community" (111–12). Paul never includes Christ or God as partner(s) in the *societas,* but it is in their service (112). This contract form was a "social framework in which Christians could creatively fulfill their mutual obligations" and "accomplish their mission." A. C. Wire suggested as book title *Roman Partnership Contracts in Paul's Letters* (*JBL* 101 [1982] 468).

Reactions: Koenig (ACNT 1985:135–36, cf. 176–77) was positive. Capper 200–7 affirmed the contractual language and use of *phronein*, but 4:10 suggests "a rift had set in" (207)—healed when the Philippians again sent funds (4:10). 1:12 hints at another breach: Philippians grumbled "that they had 'backed a bad horse' . . . tied down . . . by the Roman authorities and unable to preach" (209). Paul holds his imprisonment is no "breach of contract"; it serves the cause "through the whole Praetorium," with fearless preaching by others. His decision in 1:22–26 (further ministry *for their sakes*, 210) calls on them to "keep their part of the contract" (211). For Capper, 4:10–20 is the key to chs. 1–2 (3:1–4:9 do not "figure in the analysis"), "two closely related pieces of correspondence" or "two parts of a single letter" (200).

For questions on Sampley's proposal, see (2) COMMENT B.2. It makes Philippi the only group with a *societas* relationship, yet 2 Cor 11:9 speaks of *Macedonian churches* that supported Paul. (Peterlin 177–79). Capper's attempt to move from contractual *societas* to "*nascent canon law, grounded in the binding authority of Paul's apostleship*" is unlikely for the A.D. 50s (Bormann 1995:181–87, 196). Cf. Fee 436 n 4; 438 n 8; 441 n 13; Ascough 2003:120 n 46; D. M. Sweetland, *CBQ* 44 (1982) 689–90; Koperski 1992a:286–89. Relations between Paul and the Philippians are more flexible than legal understandings in a *societas* theory. Berry 118, "the language . . . is used with reference to the broader range of social relationships encompassed by *philia* and *amicitia.*" There is a Philippian side of things, not just a pattern imposed by Paul (Bormann 187). Hansen 2003:182–89, what "sounds like a Roman *societas*" is "a metaphor" for Paul's relationship with the Philippians (and God); friendship becomes the key (198–204). Sampley's view was superseded by application of "friendship" (L. M. White 1990; Peterman 1997:124–27; Dickson 202–4).

(3) The *philia topos* is discussed in (2) COMMENT B.2 and (16) COMMENT A.2.

(a) A. *Malherbe* 1990: just as there was correspondence between Paul and Thessalonica prior to 1 and 2 Thess, so with Philippi. Epaphroditus likely brought a letter to Paul "in addition to the contribution from the Philippians"; in 2:25–30, Paul sends him back to Philippi bearing Paul's letter to them. 4:10–11 may reflect phrases from a letter from the Philippians (Malherbe 257 n 44). See COMMENT A.4.c, above; for reconstruction of the letter from Philippi, B.1.b, below. To it Paul responds in 4:10–20. He will also pick up elements from it re Epaphroditus in Letter B.

(b) L. M. *White* 1990: friendship offers a better explanation than the "quasilegal" contractual *societas* for paraenetic, moral materials in Phil at 2:6–11 and elsewhere. 4:10 appeals to "reciprocal affections" (*I rejoiced* at *your concern for me*), but Paul's disdain of his financial distress in 4:10–12 points to strains with the Philippians (1990:214). White suspected "one or another of Paul's house church patrons" (Euodia? Syntyche?) no longer wished to support Paul (1990:214 n 59) because he was in jail, unable to evangelize. "The bonds of friendship had become strained" (214; Peterlin sees disunity through all four chs.). In 4:11–13 Paul *critically* assesses the Philippians *philia* concept (Bormann 1995:166–70, 231).

(c) L. *Bormann* 1995:171–81: Seneca's presentation of *beneficium* (COMMENT

A.2.a.11) is more likely than even the *philia topos* as background for the self-understanding of the Roman Philippians. This puts an edge on ideas the Philippians
likely held; cf. also Mott and (d) below.

(d) White's *philia* included "patronage/benefaction *(euergesia)*" (211); "house
church patrons and *"patron–client relations"* (214 n 59); Paul as "spiritual patron,"
the Philippians as "economic patron" (215 n 59). Bormann 187–205 contrasts the
patronage system for Philippi with *philia*.[46] "Patronal friendship" had an appearance of equality, but was not so in fact (P. Marshall 144). The patron system ran
through the Roman state, from Princeps down, to conquered peoples. Philippi
reflected this system (199): (1) The *colōnia* was under the patronage of the Julio-
Claudian house, the line of reigning Emperors.[47] (2) Many settlers were military
clients of the Princeps. (3) The citizens were Imperial clients, a tie confirmed by
an oath to Caesar. (4) Freedmen[48] were also part of the Imperial client system. The
system leased land to ex-military and other "householders" of Caesar.[49] (5) While
Benner spoke of "denatured clientele,"[50] Bormann sees attempts under the Principate to reconstitute older structures of patronage.[51] "Patronage is a father-son relationship, a partnership, not brotherhood or friendship" (Bormann 205).

Bormann draws on this patron–client relationship, idealized in Dion. Hal., for
4:10–20 and all of Phil (206–24). The Philippians' gift to Paul is a *beneficium*

---

[46] See E. Badian, *Foreign Clientelae (264–70 B.C.)* (Oxford: Clarendon, 1958, repr. 1984); A. Momigliano, "Cliens," "Patronus," *OCD*[3] 348 (rev.), 1126–27 (rev.); M. Gelzer, *The Roman Nobility* (Oxford: Blackwell, 1969), Saller (above, n 14); for application to the NT, E. A. Judge, beginning with
"The Early Christians as a Scholastic Community," *Journal of Religious History* 1 (1961) 6–7 and
2:128–30; P. Marshall 143–47; J. Elliott 1987; P. Lampe 2003. West 11 underestimates patronal relationships (cf. 17, Judge 1974, above COMMENT A.2.b.[3]). Ascough 2003:153–56 sees patrons in voluntary associations; cf. McCready.

[47] While there is no evidence of a distinct *patronus* for the city in the Julio-Claudian period (27 B.C.–
A.D. 68), a 2nd-cent. inscription (CIL 3.7340; Pilhofer 2: #031, cf. 004) refers to C. Oppius Montanus
as *patronus col(oniae) [et f]lam(en) divi Aug(usti)*. Bormann infers that the Princeps was patron for
Philippi in this period (cf. BCH 57 [1933] 341 n 5), a situation going back to the victory of Octavian in
31 B.C. and the soldiers he settled there. Philippi = "Rome in miniature" (D. Medicus, "Coloniae,"
KlPauly 1 [1964] 1248–50).

[48] An inscription (*BCH* 58 [1934] 449–54, Nr. 1 = Pilhofer 2:#282) from the time of Tiberius names
three freedmen, formerly slaves of Caesar (cf. Phil 4:22, "those of Caesar's household"; clients, Bormann 1995:198–99).

[49] This fits well with "soldiers and veterans," *familia Caesaris*, rural laborers and peasants in and around
Philippi; Peterlin 136–70; Oakes 2001:42–50; contra Meeks 1983, who underplays agriculture around
Philippi and views *clientela* as "internal ties" but "friendship" as external; Bormann 1995:199 n 155;
de Vos 245, 260; Oakes 2001:14–18, 29–35, 42–54, 59–76.

[50] H. Benner, *Die Politik des P. Clodius Pulcher: Untersuchungen zur Denaturierung des Client-
wesens in der ausgehenden römischen Republik*, Historia: Einzelschriften 50 (Stuttgart: Steiner-Verlag-
Wiesbaden, 1987). Publius Clodius Pulcher ("Pretty Boy") manipulated the patronage system in the
tumultuous events of 68–52 B.C.

[51] As in Dionysius of Halicarnassus' *Ant. Rom.* 2.9–11: the *plebs* (people) chose a patron (2.9.2) to
provide protection, so that good deeds and positive relations among citizens can develop
(philanthrōpous, syzygia = unity, justice, etc.); patron and client engaged in a "contest of good will"
(agōn tēs eunoias). Dionysius sanctified the patronage system but kept his distance from Hellenistic
philia-terminology.

(Sen.), voluntary in contrast to an *officium* (cf. *charites* in Dion. Hal. *Ant. Rom.* 2.10.2). Paul responds in ethical-philosophical discourse (4:11–13), theological interpretation (v 18), and social conventions of the day. Assumed is a relationship of exchange (208): they send him support; what he provides goes unstated. Bormann 208 sees key "retarding factors" in vv 11 and 17 ("not that I . . .") and the prayer in 19–20 that God will fulfill their need. Paul rejects the gift as "support of a religious hero"; his image is "itinerant preacher" without identifying with the role. So as not to jar etiquette totally, v 14 expresses appreciation. No proportionate thanks because of the affliction in which he finds himself. Paul does not want to increase his indebtedness. He puts the exchange between himself and the congregation within a relationship with God (unlike Sen.); hence the cultic theme in v 18. Sharing with Paul (v 15) reflects a Philippian view of the patron-client relationship, as did their development of *episkopoi* and *diakonoi* for such tasks (210–11, with Reumann 1993a:449–50). Paul was in need. His clients show solidarity with him, their "patron" (212–13), sending, with the gift, Epaphroditus, to aid Paul in his legal proceedings (213; the Philippians had connections with freedmen of Caesar, 4:22).

Paul fulfilled his role as patron of the Philippian church[52] by (1) preaching, representing their common concern, the gospel, and (2) visits to Philippi (2:24; 2 Cor 7:5–6, Ephesus to Corinth, via Philippi). There is a "contest in good will" (Dion. Hal. *Ant. Rom.* 2.10.4), with gifts beyond usual norms (4:18). The Philippians applied the client system they knew well, leading to what Paul deals with in 4:10–20 and 2:25–30, the gift and their representative (212). Paul's goal (Bormann 217) is "emancipated" clients, in conflict with the surrounding Roman world (217–24). He was in trouble with the authorities in Philippi (1 Thess 2:2) and would be soon, if not already, in Ephesus for his bold and open preaching (*parrhēsia*, Phil 1:12–17, 20). Likewise the Philippians (1:27–30). The Julio-Claudian house (Nero, A.D. 54–68) as patron in Philippi gave the controversy "additional brisance" (220).[53] In the Roman city of Philippi, converts organized for mission around the *euangelion* that opposes *euangelia* or "good tidings" about the Emperor. Thus they were "in conflict with the official religio-political ideology of the early Principate, in the period of the Julio-Claudian dynasty, with its social-economic and power-legitimating aspects" (224). Bormann, in moving away from *philia* to patron–client aspects, assumes a positive connection between Paul and community, unlike a final scenario proposed.

(4) *D. Peterlin* 1995: no rosy picture of friendship (227) but *disunity* throughout

---

[52] Fee 444–45 takes Paul as client of Philippian patronage. For White 1990, Paul is spiritual patron; the Philippians, his economic patron. Joubert distinguishes "benefactor" from "patron," the latter more characteristic of Roman social control than civic benefaction in the earlier Greek world (17–69). Thus, re the collection (esp. in Gal and 1 and 2 Cor, noting in 4 n 15 possible involvement of the Philippians, with Reumann 1993a), Paul is benefactor of the Jerusalem Church in this project, though the Jerusalem leadership functioned as "initial benefactors" (6–8). P. Lampe 2003:500–5.

[53] Bormann sees this clash illustrated in charges against Paul at Acts 16:20–21 ("customs not lawful for Romans"), but holds the picture is Luke's work, not historically reliable.

all four chs.[54] Philippian believers sent money to Paul in Thessalonica several times, perhaps also in Beroea; in Corinth and perhaps Athens, with other Macedonian churches (175). Never full support, except for a time in Corinth when the "salary" *(opsōnion)* from churches in Macedonia permitted full-time evangelization (Acts 18:5; 2 Cor 11:8–9). Not continuous gifts (175–77), but spontaneous, frequent at first, then drying up until the revival mentioned in 4:10. Peterlin 181–84 finds Philippi a relatively well-to-do church ("extreme poverty," 2 Cor 8:1–5, is hyperbole). Disunity in Philippi (Peterlin 19–132; cf. 2:1–4) came to the fore in the collection for Paul. It was really *"the gift of Epaphroditus"* (180, Peterlin's italics)[55]; he took the lead and made up for the shortfall (180–81).

Why so small a collection for Paul, after so long and positive an association?[56] There was "external pressure" from "pagan environment (1:27–30), possibly . . . social ostracism" (Peterlin 219; cf. Bormann, [d] above; Oakes, economic pressures). An incipient "perfectionist streak" existed (ch. 3). Paul was not fulfilling his mission; he was a failure, indeed as a Christian (219–20); is suffering compatible with real Christian faith (220)? "Confusion," not "heresy." People took sides, often with house-church leaders (2:2–4), "polarized" around Euodia and Syntyche, who had "personal dislike of each other . . . before the controversy" (221); "an anti-Pauline lobby" existed in some house churches, 223, 224).[57] Money for Paul was a lightning rod for local issues. Power among leaders without humility marked the struggle (Agourides [(15) Bibl.] 1980). Epaphroditus "offered . . . to take the collected money, stay with Paul, attend to his needs . . . at his own expense, and in this way make up for what was lacking in the Philippian church's financial ministry to Paul" (224). A church majority commissioned him for the task. He delivered the money and news of Philippi (after no contact "for quite some time," 224). Paul wrote them with "considerable . . . unease (4:10–20)" (226), not taking sides. Impartiality marks 4:10–20.

(5) *Observations.* Such efforts at historical reconstructions, whether for Letter A (Bormann, perhaps Capper 200) or a single letter (Sampley, L. M. White, Peterlin), ask if relations were harmonious and friendly (Sampley, White) or marked by disunity (Peterlin). A relationship of equals (in *philia*, White) or superior and inferior (Bormann)? Which Gk. and Lat. documents best explain 4:10–20 and prior relationships—the papyri and epistolary theorists (Malherbe, J. L. White, Stowers); Roman law (Fleury, Sampley); friendship texts (L. M. White), Seneca for

---

[54] Peterlin traces the supposed course of events re Epaphroditus (2:25–30; 185–205) and "Paul's Attitude toward the Gift" in 4:10–20. Pp. 135–70 provide a detailed picture of the "social composition" of the several house churches. Acts 16 is used with confidence; Lydia, the slave girl, the jailer, Luke, and Clement (Phil 4:3) appear, as well as peasants and soldiers (above n 49), and the banking elite and aristocracy *not* likely to be found in the church.

[55] Sent through him in cash or as a draft Epaphroditus cashed when he got to Paul (Hermesdorf 252–56).

[56] Peterlin assumes Rome, five years between the Macedonian "salary" when Paul was in Corinth and his arrival in Rome. On the Ephesian hypothesis, a year or two since the gifts in Thessalonica and Corinth.

[57] Wealthy Christians financed most of Paul's missionary tours (E. A. Judge 1961 [above, n 46]: 128–31).

beneficia and Dion. Hal. *Ant. Rom.* (Bormann)? Views vary on the use of Acts (Fleury uncritically, Peterlin favorably, Bormann is negative), other sections of Phil (2:5–11, L. M. White; ch. 3, Peterlin), and Euodia and Syntyche (trouble-makers? L. M. White, Peterlin). The solutions of Fleury and Sampley are un-likely. Friendship and patron–client relations deserve further consideration.

b. *The Situation Assumed for Letter A in This Commentary.* Paul writes his first extant letter to Philippi, from Ephesus, in A.D. 54. The body of this Letter A was 4:10–20, acknowledging the Philippians' gift. It had a salutation (1:1–2 or similar) and a prayer report (1:3–11 or some form of it), followed by brief greetings and a benediction (cf. 4:21–23). After the founding mission (Acts 16:11–40), converts in this "little Rome" had shared the gospel at home and supported Paul and his team through financial gifts, several times in Thessalonica (4:16), possibly Beroea and Athens, certainly Corinth, where other Macedonian churches helped also (2 Cor 11:7–9; cf. Acts 18:5). For this work the Philippians developed a structure of *epis-kopoi* and *diakonoi* within and among the house churches (1:1). There were con-gregational *apostoloi*, like Epaphroditus (4:18; cf. 2:25–30), commissioned for specific tasks. Paul kept in touch through coworkers (Timothy, 1 Thess 3:2,6; Phil 2:19–24) and letters (1 Thess the first extant example). Brief letters accompanied gifts to Paul or were sent separately, with news and/or asking advice (cf. Malherbe 1990; B.1.a.[3][a], above, for Philippi).

There was a gap in communications after Paul left Corinth (no money sent, 4:10), because he was on the move so much.[58] Ephesus proved a "wide door" open for the gospel (1 Cor 16:8–9). Paul hoped to journey through Macedonia on his way to Corinth at Pentecost in A.D. 54. How and when the Philippians got in touch again and learned of his needs go unstated. Perhaps through freedmen of Caesar, businesspeople in their travels, networking of peers, contact through Paul's coworkers (Timothy? Erastus?), or a note from him now lost.

In Philippi, some money was gathered to aid Paul. It was sent via Epaphroditus (4:18), who made the brief trip to Ephesus likely by sea. He provided services for Paul the Philippians could not (2:30), and then fell sick,[59] after Letter A was writ-ten. 4:10–20 do not suggest problems with Epaphroditus' health[60] or reflect a quarrel between Euodia and Syntyche (4:2–3).

Revived Philippian support for Paul arose not from legal arrangements or a Roman contractual *societas*, but earlier practices, now that opportunity has come again. In line with friendship conventions of the day, Paul does not say thanks, outright. Philippian *philia* structures were on Paul's mind, as he tries to work shy of their view about their relationship. He *is* their apostle and founding father, they

---

[58] According to Acts 18:18–19:1 he sailed for Syria, via Ephesus, landed at Caesarea, and "went up" probably to Jerusalem (18:22); after visiting "the Galatian region," he arrived in Ephesus which be-came the center for work in the province of Asia, a ministry of more than two years (18:10).

[59] On Epaphroditus' roles, see (9) COMMENT A.3. That he was taken sick en route to Paul (C. O. Bu-chanan) was argued to support Rome as place. The traditional view is that Epaphroditus became ill while with Paul.

[60] The "affliction" in 4:14 is Paul's, see NOTE on 4:14 *mou*. It is not evidence he was in prison, cf. Müller-Bardorff (INTRO. VI) 596–97.

his beloved believers. He rejoices that they tangibly express solidarity with him (vv 10, 14–16), but asserts independence (vv 11–13), several times qualifies the argument (vv 11, 17), and points theologically to God (14, 18b–20). He avoids implications the Philippians would draw of a reciprocity of equals (L. M. White), a scheme of benefaction, himself as benefactor or patron, them as clients (Bormann), or vice versa. We do not know exactly Philippian understandings of the situation, but 4:10–20 brings out facets of it. *Their note to him,* accompanying the money gift, likely included the following ideas:

> The Philippians *(Philippēsioi), episkopoi* and *diakonoi* and saints in the church there of Christ Jesus, to Paul: grace to you and peace from God our Father and the Lord Jesus Christ.
>
> We give thanks to God upon hearing of your work in the gospel and your afflictions and needs *(chreiai).* Our concern *(phronein)* for you has blossomed, to supply what you lack with this gift sent through Epaphroditus [4:10, 18]. We have lacked opportunity for some time to show concern. At the beginning of the gospel and when you left Macedonia, we shared with you, both in Thessalonica and several times elsewhere, in an account of giving and receiving. Now, please (= you do well to) accept this gift. We seek fruit that grows in our partnership and in our account of giving and receiving.
>
> The brothers and sisters greet you. The grace of the Lord Jesus Christ be with you. Amen.

Speculative, but its themes and phrases help account for Paul's wording at points in Letter A.

2. Phil 4:10–20 *as the Body of Letter A.* Paul's aim is to respond to the gift the Philippians sent through Epaphroditus (4:18). Relations between congregation and apostle and Paul's present situation in Ephesus are sketched above, in B.1.b, with the Philippians' note reconstructed that accompanied their gift; see also INTRO. VIII, Chart 2. Paul writes very soon after Epaphroditus' arrival; friends were to respond promptly to a gift (Berry 109–10). Some things learned from Epaphroditus about Philippi will show up only in Letter B. If Phil 1:7b as now phrased was in Letter A, Paul is "in bonds," but 4:10–20 does not say so. He faced afflictions but was not yet jailed.

a. *Paul Joyfully Acknowledges the Renewed Contact (4:10).* The key phrase is *your concern for me (to hyper emou phronein).* Its vb. will echo through all Paul's letters to Philippi. A slogan of congregational solidarity with their apostle (Schenk), it has led to a gift of money sent through Epaphroditus, a converted Gentile, likely leader in a house church there.[61] The Philippians commissioned him their envoy *(apostolos,* 2:25) to bring the funds to Paul and aid his mission amid affliction that

---

[61] So Peterlin (above, B.1.a.[4]). Pilhofer 1:240 and Walter 97 conjecture Euodia, the Lydian woman of Acts 16:14–15, 40, led the financial appeal for Paul. Some see her in dispute with Syntyche on the issue.

preaching Christ often brought (1 Thess 2:2). He could not report things were perfect in Philippi, for there were pressures from the Roman world around them, threats toward unity within the church (see Letter B), a disappointing response in the fund appeal for Paul. Epaphroditus likely came at his own expense (perhaps on a business trip to Ephesus), possibly adding money to the purse, making up in personal services what the Philippians had failed to arrange otherwise to do (so Peterlin). Paul has reason to write cautiously. He reflects their standpoint (Gnilka 173) and phrases at times, often agreeing, sometimes correcting.

Paul begins with a conventional formula of rejoicing (like Phlm 7; see NOTE on 4:10 *I . . . rejoiced*), enhanced by *greatly* or "enormously" and *in the Lord* (Jesus, as at 1:2) for the realm where Christ rules, the church, where Paul's joy occurs. The Lord brought him joy by moving the Philippians to this gift for the gospel (Schenk 61). The joy is "un-Stoic" (Bengel; K. Barth 127, Fee 428 n 20).[62] Some time had passed since they sent a gift; *now at last*, "at long last," hints at this. "You *lacked opportunity . . .* " (given his travels) is not the whole truth.[63] Paul prayed for the growth of the Philippians (1:9–11). The happy news is that their concern for him has blossomed again (agricultural term, see NOTE). "They do remember me." Prayers answered. Their support signals new growth among them, they are *revived.* Philippian springtime! Paul is here a diplomat, gracious but firm at points (in vv 11–13). Language will zigzag between affirmation of "his favorite congregation" and a tone distancing himself, even reproof. Much rides on the gift from Philippi, for "if the Philippians forgot him, their faith would be in danger," but (Berry 110) "they remembered him, and more importantly, the gospel that he had proclaimed among them."

b. *Paul Asserts His Independence (but Dependence on God's Power) (4:11–13).* A new beginning, with a phrase that will also occur in v 17, *It is not that . . . ;* a "disclaimer" (Hawth.; cf. Peterlin 213). (Merk 1968:198 would put 11–13 in parentheses, but 11–13 are more than an aside.) Paul is explaining his position (U. B. Müller 202). He speaks not *out of need* (11a), from dire straits financially. The Philippians' letter had probably used *needs*, suggesting they thought Paul was in poverty. Some think, in need for some time (Michaelis 70; Gnilka 174). Others see no "shortage of money" (JB; Vincent 143; Loh/Nida); perhaps he had recently inherited family property, from which he planned to pay for his appeal to Caesar (Ramsay 1896:310–13; Hawth., "Possibly"). We do not know Paul's exact financial state as he wrote Letter A.

4:11b–12 asserts a proposition (Edart 290–91), 1st per. sg. (4 vbs. reflect experiences as a mission-spokesman for Christ): *I have learned, I know how, I know how, I have had my initiation experience*, in a variety of situations. These are enumerated in 6 Gk. infins., a "catalogue of happenings," dangers, tribulations, experi-

---

[62] Weima calls 4:10–20 a "joy expression" in a unified epistle. *DA* 280–82 is rightly critical that the theme proves "a single letter theory."

[63] Perhaps there was poverty in Philippi. No one to deliver the gift. Paul did not need help. To ask for aid could be misunderstood by detractors. Paul wanted gifts to go to the appeal for Jerusalem (O'B 519). But none of these reasons can be fully supported.

ences of peril. On the *"peristasis* catalogue," see above, A.4.e and the NOTE on v 12, a form esp. in the Corinthian correspondence. 1 Cor 4:9–13 has the term "go hungry" *(peinōmen)* that appears in Phil 4:12. 2 Cor 4:8–9 is most similar, "afflicted in every way but not crushed; perplexed, but not driven to despair; persecuted, but not forsaken; struck down, but not destroyed. . . ." Faith endures such situations and will triumph (Rom 8:35–39).

The *peristasis* or "circumstances" catalogue was thoroughly Gk. On vicissitudes of the wanderer or (suffering) sage, how he perseveres, credentials, place in the divine scheme of things, a path "to the stars, through perseverance."[64] The form often used antithetical terms (wealth/poverty) in apologetic statements, at times against opposition (1 Cor 4:10; 2 Cor 11:23–28) or in self-justification (2 Cor 12:10). The form may have appealed to Paul because of parallels to the OT "righteous sufferer" (K. T. Kleinknecht) and the apocalyptic idea that God vindicates those who hold fast amid sufferings (Schrage 1974). The Greco-Roman world made connection with God's will and plan; the wise individual, coping with hardships, will exhibit endurance, serenity, and self-sufficiency through discipline; provide a model; and express certainty of victory and joy amid tribulations—features Fitzgerald 1988 finds in Paul's lists. A person shows what he really is. "When the going gets tough, the tough keep going."

Phil 4:12 includes bad circumstances (hunger) and good ones (abundance) that may be disastrous for lifestyle. *be brought low with few resources/abound with much; get my fill/go hungry; abound/suffer lack* may reflect actual experiences, but are not so specific as 2 Cor 11:23–28 ("three times I was beaten with rods"). Perhaps chiastically arranged (Jeremias 1958 [(3) Bibl.], Di Marco 1977), these infins. go with three "I" vbs. (above), the whole under the umbrella statement in v 11b, *I have learned to be content (autarkēs) with whatever I have.* Artfully arranged, elevated prose, not hymnic, possibly put together previously (structurings in A.4.e). God, *the One who strengthens me*, is the origin of the result that Paul is *content* and *strong, able to tackle everything* (Schenk, Ebner, O'B), in all sorts of areas *(every situation and all circumstances)*, food, creature comforts, or finances. Paul asserts confidence in himself as sustained by God who empowers him.

His learning process was in "the school of hard knocks," under divine tutelage. *I have learned how* (11b *emathen*), not by book-learning or revelation, but through cumulative experiences. As in proverbs, "Learn through sufferings" (wordplay on *epathen*, cf. v 14 *affliction*). The next two vbs. (12ab, *oida*) imply "know how," through experience, "learn to cope." The final vb. (12b, *memyēmai*) could reflect mystery-cults, divine revelation from above, "I have been initiated, by some rite . . . ," but many trs. ([N]RSV, NIV) prefer "I have learned." If the mysteries echo, the vb. is ironic (Bornkamm *TDNT* 4:828). NEB, ". . . very thoroughly initiated into the human lot with all its ups and downs." *I have had my initiation experience* keeps the experiential aspect and avoids "learn a secret." Not an esoteric rite

---

[64] Lat. *ad astra per aspera,* motto of the state of Kansas and the British Royal Air Force. The Russian dissident Andrei Sakharov printed them on the door of his study during exile in Gorky (Nizhny Novgorod) 1980–86.

of entry, but moments of learning in daily life, through public happenings, building attitude and outlook. Not through a routine of *askēsis* or discipline, like a Gk. sage (contra Fitzgerald 205; Paul never uses that term).

4:11–13 tells *what* Paul has learned (to be *strong, able to tackle everything,* 11b) and *how* (through *the One who strengthens me,* v 13). The key word is *autarkēs,* "content" (see NOTE on its Gk., Stoic background as "self-sufficiency"; Engberg-Pedersen 1995:101; Edart 309–12, not just a friendship term, Malherbe 1996). For Plato, resources within for the good life; Aristot., a few good friends. Epicurus and the Cynics: austerity; self-sufficiency, happiness attained by eliminating possessions and the desire for them, often an itinerant life, as a hippie-like beggar. Stoics: happiness through virtue and inner tranquility, detached from external circumstances. Debated were whether one could be *self*-sufficient or needed friends to practice friendship on, expressing generosity by giving them benefits. Paul and the Philippian Christians knew the term *autarkeia,* if not all the philosophical views. He uses the word family also at 2 Cor 9:8 (see NOTE), abundance for the Corinthians, in every circumstance; God is enabler, be content and independent. Phil 4:11 says Paul possesses *autarkeia* now, contrary to any impression of dire need. His pointed assertion the Philippians would understand from a pagan values-system.

How can 4:13 assert ability to do *everything*? Lit. "I can all things," expanded in the TRANSLATION to bring out the root meaning, *I am strong.* Adding an infin., "able to do all things," makes Paul sound like a superman, Stoic self-sufficiency plus braggadocio as in W. E. Henley's "Invictus," "I am the captain of my own soul." Traditional trs. are "misleading to the point of being false" (Hawth. 200–201, who prefers "power to cope with," "competent to handle" such situations). O'B 526 restricts "all things" to tasks of the apostolic office (cf. Martin 1976:164) and six situations mentioned in v 12 (so U. B. Müller 203). That minimizes *en panti kai en pasin* (12c). Paul may, rhetorically, in another "all/every" statement,[65] not have every last thing imaginable in mind. To avoid such misunderstandings, the TRANSLATION supplies *able (ischyō) to tackle* (or "handle") *everything* (*panta* is prominent at the start of the v).

Paul speaks thus because the divine Empowerer, God, strengthens and makes him able, acting in his life and the experience of Christians. Reference to the Spirit is unlikely (not a theme in Letter A). Later scribes inserted *Christō[i]* (cf. Merk 1968:199). *en* suggests to some "in Christ," but which function of the *en Christō[i]* "formula"? God is *the One who strengthens me* (Moule IB 77; cf. *en theō[i]* in 1 Thess 1:1; 2:2). The Gk. *peristasis* form sometimes made connections to the divine. In Paul, cf. 1 Cor 4:9–13; 2 Cor 4:8–9; 2 Cor 6:4–11. "God" occurs at 4:18,19, 20; "in Christ Jesus" only at v 19 ("the Lord" in 4:10, probably Jesus).[66] For some, 2:6–11 is a factor, but even there God is the subject of 2:9–11. Hence

---

[65] With *panta* in v 13, compare the two phrases cited in 12b, and perhaps the phrase in v 18, *apechō de panta,* as well as the use of *pas* in 1:1,3,4,7,8,9, discussed in the NOTES there.

[66] In other possible parts of Letter A, cf. "God" in 1:2,3,8,11; "[Jesus] Christ" at 1:1,2,6,8,11; 4:21,23.

the Father, though Paul, if pressed, might say God working through Christ (and the Spirit).

Paul thus asserts independence (from the Philippians!) just after acknowledging their gift. Vv 11–13 *distance him from what the Philippians imply with their gift* and their ideas of "friendship" (A.2, above). *philia* meant acknowledging a gift promptly (as Paul does) but then a (bigger) gift in response. Paul was in no position to do that. He never traded gift for gift in a "contest of good will." Avoid getting caught up in such a reciprocal relationship, even with Philippi. It would prove endless, blunt his apostolic authority and freedom, and eventually color the concept of God and the Christian faith with *do ut das*, "I give this in order that you will give that."

The Philippians had a view of benefits akin to that in Seneca (A.2.a.[11] above). Paul speaks of contentment and upholds his independence to "ensure that the Philippians" do not view "support of Paul in a way that enhanced their own status . . . superior to Paul as his patrons. Since Paul was self-sufficient, he could not be viewed as dependent on them as their client or employee" (Berry 115; cf. Fee 444–45). Bormann 1995 sees Paul in danger of becoming their patron, the way Philippi understood the Emperor to be its patron. Christian clients were shifting from Julio-Claudian rulers and their appointees to the apostle as patron. "Concern for Paul" motivated them. They sent money to him. Should he not be glad? That's how the system works!

Paul distances himself by the *autarkeia* catalogue in vv 11–13 (Ebner). (a) He is not destitute or asking for money (11a). (b) He asserts independence through what he has learned by experience. (c) Dependence on God explains whence his help comes, suggesting a model for the Philippians, a new paradigm (see charts in A.5.b from Ebner), the Philippians' understanding is "stood on its head." He hopes they move from reciprocity in "giving and receiving" (the Philippian expectation) to *koinōnia* under God, without strings of a friendship-benefits approach. From 4:10–13 we can expand the chart below. This relationship of the Philippians with God is not yet specified, but 1:3–11 indicates what Paul prays for them; 4:11–13 suggests that they too should become independent, like Paul.

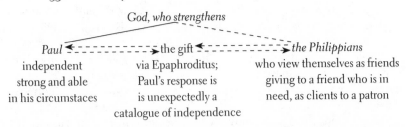

The *peristasis* (or *autarkeia*) catalogue (vv 11–13) is theological elucidation about God at work (Schenk, above, A.5.a); the ptc. *who strengthens me*, significant (Deidun 1981 [(8) Bibl.] 341). "God works not only the beginning, but also the continuation, of the Christian life" (Schrage 1961:72–73). More must be said about the past (4:14–16) and the future (17–19), in light of Paul's present outlook here.

c. *Recalling Past Sharing as Context for the Current Gift (4:14–16).* Has Paul poured too much cold water on the Philippians' reblossomed concern for him?[67] After the harsh words in 4:11–13, a new beginning: language shifts from "*I*" (Paul as subject, vv 10a, 11–13) to *you*-(pl.), the Philippians, specifically addressed in v 15, though Paul does not disappear (*sharing . . . with me* twice, 14,15; *my affliction,* 14; etc.). Vv 14–16 narrate their past relations as context for the recent gift (v 10b; Müller 204; cf. Schenk 44).[68] Paul skillfully weaves points together in an uneasy situation, not disunity at Philippi (Peterlin) but Philippian views on friendship, patronage, and benefits. In v 14, he (a) returns to the subject of v 10, the Philippians' *sharing together with* Paul; this soothes any negative reaction to 11–13 ("Paul doesn't care about our renewed concern for him"). Then (b) he undergirds their sharing for the gospel (1:5) by jointly recalling past support (vv 15–16), an ameliorating gesture. Lest the Philippians think Paul is "buttering them up" for another gift, he will make another course adjustment or clarification in 17–19, toward a "transfer of roles" from what the Philippians expect (see A.5.b, charts). In this narrative[69] some phrases may come from the Philippians' cover note for the gift (A.4.c lists phrases; B.1.b reconstructs their note). He reflects a Philippian viewpoint through their language (quotation marks in the TRANSLATION). They contributed more than money to Paul and what he writes.

The opening word in v 14 (Gk. *plēn*) points back (Gnilka 176) to the topic in 10a, revived concern for Paul. It marks progression after 11–13, a contrast to the catalogue there and the independence asserted by Paul, but not in an adversarial way (no *de* in the Gk.). In idiomatic Eng., *Anyway* (NRSV "In any case"). *you did well,* a cliché in papyrus letters (White 1986:212), expresses goodwill, *captatio benevolentiae,* commendation, the way friends speak. It "comes as close to saying 'Thank you'" as Paul ever does in Phil.[70] Sending an unsolicited gift, Paul acknowledges, "was . . . appropriate . . . in his difficult situation *(en thlipsei)*," (Berry 116).

Friendship language enters in v 14, *sharing together (synkoinōnēsantes)*; vb. re-

---

[67] Some keep the apostle on an even keel. O'B, e.g., "neither rebuking nor giving faint praise . . . ," but v 14 "shows that the apostle does not want his readers to draw the wrong conclusion from" vv. 11–13 (530, 527). Michael 219 and Hawth. 203 better reflect the bumpy path of the passage. 4:14 is a "second onset"; (U. B. Müller), a "disclaimer" (Peterlin), anticipating Philippian misunderstanding of vv 11–13. Paul "qualifies what he has just said" (Berry 111).

[68] Paragraphing is difficult (see NOTE). 4:14 can be regarded as a separate "swing" paragraph between 11–13 and 15–18. The TRANSLATION takes it with 15–16 (with RSV, contrary to NRSV). 17 clearly begins a new subsection (same opening as v 11, *It is not that . . .*).

[69] *narratio* is justified (Black 1995; Edart 298–99), though not for all of 4:10–20. In 14–16 the term *conquestio* or positive feelings might be applied, within an *adfectus,* esp. if 11–13 is *indignatio* or negative pathos for opponents (the Philippians!); cf. D. F. Watson 1988b, Snyman; Bloomquist 188 makes 10–14 the *conquestio.* Cf. A.1, above. Fee 440 sees the narrative in 15–16 as "an 'inclusio' around the theme of friendship" (partnership giving and receiving): A = 15b, B = 15c, A' = 16.

[70] Hawth. 202, with Martin 1976:164. Loh. 183 n 1, the gift was a significant expression of "thought for Paul" (*to hyper emou phronein* v 10); he could acknowledge they "think" of him *(denken)* but not "thank" *(danken)* them for the gift. Schenk 42–43 takes *kalōs* with the following ptc., "you did well in sharing."

peated without prefix in v 15, *no church had shared with me,* key terms from the word field of *philia* (B.1.a.[3]; NOTES on *koinōnia* terms at 1:5; 1:7; 4:15c). Paul had likely presented in Philippi his principle of sharing (Gal. 6:6): those instructed in the word are to support their teachers financially (Hainz 1972:62–89, 112–15; NOTE on 4:15c). For Paul, a gift of love (Hainz 1972:225–26), not a legal category (consensual *societas*) or *"an account of giving and receiving"* (4:15; cf. Berry 118), the way the Philippians thought in categories familiar to them, friendship and benefits (Ebner 358–59; A.5.b, first chart). Philippian readers might have expected after 4:14, "You did well in together sharing with me your gift of money." But a surprise follows.

They share together, Paul says, *in my affliction,* as "partners in trouble *(thlipsei)*" (Hawth. 202). Some couple suffering and grace, 4:14 with 1:7 (Loh. 183; O'B 530 n 107). But Paul does not mention *charis* at 4:14, just "distress" (NRSV), here afflictions that accompany missionary work, in Philippi, Thessalonica, and Ephesus, not aspects of the End but (cf. 2 Cor 1:4; 7:4) afflictions amid which we are consoled by God and find joy (cf. Gnilka 17; Rom 5:3–5). Afflictions will become clearer in Letter B, in Philippi (1:27–30) and for Paul (1:12–14, in jail).

The Philippians share in *Paul's* affliction by "thinking on him" *(phronein,* 4:10), empathy and solidarity, their slogan *(phronein hyper Paulou)* come to life again. By their gift, just arrived (v 10). In the person of their envoy, Epaphroditus, for mission work at Ephesus. Through prayers of the Philippian congregation, mentioned in the prayer report of their note to him. In news that Epaphroditus brought about Philippi (cf. 1 Thess 3:7, a congregation's faith amid *thlipsis* encourages Paul). In the "hymn" now embedded in Phil 2:6–11, of which Paul heard through Epaphroditus, their tool for evangelization in the Roman colony, proof of their growth in the faith. But 4:14 is specifically *sharing together in my affliction.* Together in the face of the troubles that come when you preach and live the message about Christ.[71] Paul wants the Philippians to think of sharing in this *peristasis,* affliction from following the gospel, rather than "sharing" in their value system of *philia* and benefits for what they have bestowed on him.

Continuing between rebuke and an outright "thank you" (Hawth. 203), Paul presents a narrative in 15–16 on how the Philippians *shared* with him in the past. It details what Paul acknowledged in v 14, Philippian participation with him for the gospel and resultant suffering. The dir. address, *you Philippians,* is unusual. The only parallels are a rhetorical rebuke ("you foolish Galatians," Gal 3:1 NRSV) and "frank speech" ("O Corinthians," 2 Cor 6:11) after a *peristasis* catalogue (6:4–10). *Philippēsioi* may express "affectionate gratitude," but as a Gk. form of the *Latin* name of the *colōnia,* it pays tribute also to the Roman heritage of the church in *Colonia Augusta Julia Philippensis* (as renamed by Augustus in 31 B.C.). It reflects the Julio-Claudian patronage system in the Principate (cf. Bormann 1995; B.1.a.[3][c]), from which he seeks escape. An irenic (and ironic) gesture.

Vv 15–16 take up two points, each introduced by *that* (Gk. *hoti*), points *you*

---

[71] If Paul is already imprisoned, it follows for Loh. that some Philippian Christians were imprisoned too, but nothing of this is stated in 4:10–20. Both points are dubious for Letter A.

Philippians as well as I, Paul, know (Hawth. 203). The first *kai* in v 15 = *indeed.* But (for *de*) indicates transition from the most recent sharing to earlier examples (Loh. 184 n 1). We take 15–16 as two parallel questions. Cf. the formula "Do you not know . . ." and cliché-like use of *oidate* in 1 Thess. This avoids the impression of pedantic repetition. The questions tease out implications of past events for the present situation, a matter perhaps under dispute among Philippians.

First implication, they were unique (*you alone*) among churches in contributing to the Pauline mission.[72] Both time (*"at the beginning of the gospel"*) and place (*Macedonia, Thessalonica*) are mentioned. But Paul's "loose way of speaking" (Loh. 185) leads to problems. *en archē[i] tou euangeliou* has different interpretations, summarized in the NOTE on 15a. We rejected solution 2 that Paul's career can be traced only to beginnings at Philippi; likewise 3, only work from Philippi on counted; even 4, Philippi as "turning point" (cf. the vision in Acts 16:9–10), Paul in charge of his own program.[73] Instead, it is a phrase from the Philippians (hence quotation marks) about when the gospel preaching began among them and spread in Thessalonica and elsewhere. *when I departed from Macedonia* does not mean gospel preaching and Philippian financial support began only when Paul left that Roman province, but rather no church except Philippi contributed to the Pauline mission in Thessalonica and probably Beroea. In Corinth, he could have received further gifts from the Philippians (see on v 16, below).[74] The narrative is complicated by Paul's use of the Philippians' phrases (*archē* of the gospel, Macedonia; see the reconstruction of their letter, B.1.b; did they mean they shared with Paul "at the beginning" *and* "when he left their province"?). Paul is threading his way through what they wrote and their understanding of friendship and *beneficia.*

Note two details in v 15: (i) The Philippian household gatherings form a *church. ekklēsia* in Letter A is an identity to be assumed in Letters B and C, even if the word does not appear in 1:1–2. Did the Philippians employ *ekklēsia* in their letter? Possibly. (ii) Their relationship with Paul is in *an account of giving and receiving,* "a credit and debit ledger," tech. phrase in business and commerce (see NOTE). Money was a part of friendship (COMMENT A.2 and 5), in what friends have in common. In Ebner's "friendship *koinōnia*," the *financial* goes along with *locale* (where friends "dwell together") and a *moral* component (NOTE on 15c). An *account of giving and receiving* was a "constitutive principle" of society in Philippi (Pilhofer 1:147–52, inscriptional evidence). This phrase, likely from the Philip-

---

[72] *you alone* in 15c fits Thessalonica; it may be polite exaggeration for Achaia. Dickson 207–8, contra Reumann 1993a:440–42, would make the Philippians unique in supporting Paul in Corinth (2 Cor 11:8 then becomes "rhetorically loaded exaggeration"); unconvincing.

[73] Paul testifies in Gal 1:15–16 that he was called as missionary to the Gentiles from the outset. The work in Antioch (Syria and Cilicia, 1:21–24; 2:11–14) and Galatia is not written off, for "Christ crucified" was preached and the Spirit was at work there (Gal 3:1–5; 6:14–15) (U. B. Müller 204 n 80).

[74] Aor. *ekoinōnēsen* in v 15 as a pluperf., *had shared with me,* is preferable to taking *exēlthon* as a pluperf. (O'B 533, among others), which seems to push "the beginning of the gospel" to the period after Paul's Macedonian ministry, and, against the assertion in v 16, exclude the mission in Thessalonica from financial *koinōnia.*

pians, Paul picks up. Having received, he is to give in turn to them, and not just "spiritual" goods (see NOTE on *giving and receiving*) in a "two-way transaction." Paul had proclaimed the gospel to the Philippians, "they reciprocated in the form of financial contributions" (Berry 119). Now what? See 4:17–19.

Second implication: Paul and the Philippians know they had sent financial aid for his needs in Thessalonica, etc. (v 16). Thus the point in v 15 is made more precise. The two *hoti* cls. are parallel (Ewald 1908:215 = 1923:231; Gnilka 178), *do you know . . . that . . . ? And that . . . ?* The second further defines the first. Paul specifies when they first sent him a gift (see NOTE on 4:16 *and that . . . more than once*): *in Thessalonica*, soon after he left Philippi and began preaching in that seaport, the largest city in, and capital of, the province of Macedonia. But how often and where else? (A question signaled by use of "etc." in the summary of v 16 above.) The matter hangs on the idiom *hapax kai dis*, the *kai* before it, and another *kai* before *in Thessalonica*. See NOTES. Minimally "once and a second time in Thessalonica"; maximally, "in Thessalonica and repeatedly in other places" (L. Morris 1956), Beroea and Corinth (2 Cor 11:8–9; Suhl 103–7).[75] Aid from Philippi probably fell short of Paul's needs (e.g., Gnilka 178; Collange 152; Hawth. 205); hence "we (had to) work night and day" in Thessalonica to support the mission team and not burden the congregation there (1 Thess 2:9; AB 32B:148–49).[76] Gifts ended when the apostle left Greece. They resumed only in Ephesus, not without dissension in the Philippian house churches, Epaphroditus' making up for the slack (Gnilka 178; Peterlin).

Gifts in Thessalonica were *for* Paul's *needs* (lit., sg.), living expenses while evangelizing. *chreia* will also appear in v 19 for the needs of the Philippian Christians. The term connects with friendship, on the usefulness (*chreia*) of a friend (see NOTE). To be a *philos* of B could be profitable for A, and in turn for B with the exchange of gifts. In some theories of friendship (Aristot.), *philia* based on utility implied *unequal* partners, a patron–client relationship. The Philippians' view implied a return from him for their needs in the future. They may have seen him as their patron, a position in Greco-Roman life that made him uncomfortable (cf. Bormann 1995). Or they as patron, Paul their client, inappropriate to apostleship (cf. Hainz 1972: 225–26) and the independence articulated in vv 11–13. Apparently Paul was only now catching on to implications of the *philia* system as it operated in a Roman colony. Unsure how the Philippians thought, he may have feared his words might suggest he was fishing for another gift from them. In the few lines that follow he addresses such questions.

---

[75] The TRANSLATION takes the first *kai* as *even* with *in Thessalonica*, to indicate how early the practice of financial support for Paul from Philippi began, and the numerical idiom as *more than once* (a conservative rendering). The latter phrase is set off by commas to suggest the several gifts need not be confined to Thessalonica.

[76] Dickson 204–13 makes Philippi even more of a "turning point" for Paul on finances. Hospitality from Lydia (Acts 16:15) and Philippian gifts "more than once" in Thessalonica led him to adopt a "rigid 'no-maintenance' policy"; "private labour" and such "private funding" allowed him "completely to forego his apostolic right" to support from hearers (211). The Philippians uniquely, not other Macedonian churches, aided him later (in Rome, 207–8).

d. *Payment and Repayment (4:17–19)*. Paul begins afresh, though with the same words as in v 11, *It is not that I . . . ,* + a 1st sg. vb. Another disclaimer (Hawth. 205; Peterlin 213) or clarification, here against possible charges he was *seeking alms* like a beggar. His praise of the Philippians' support (vv 15–16) could be misconstrued as hinting at another gift. Paul must clarify the "two-way transaction" implied in *"an account of giving and receiving"* (15). The matter is delicate. Aristot. urged not appearing eager for benefits, yet not rude when something is offered (*Eth. Nic.* 9.11.6). But more is involved than diplomacy. Some Christians at Philippi, as Paul likely knew, had not supported funding him (L. M. White 1990, Peterlin). Their understanding of benevolence was at risk; how God who both loves and judges operates in life. Paul will bring God into the picture in ways Philippian *philia* did not include.

Paul proceeds antithetically: a negative statement about himself (17a), a positive one about the Philippians (17b; Berry 119); a *propositio* (Edart 290–91). In v 18 he reiterates his sufficiency, in light of the gift just received from Philippi, using language from the *autarkeia* catalogue in v 12. Then a shift to God and divine riches in v 19, the Benefactor who *will fulfill every need*. The transition is made via three phrases at the end of v 18 from language of cultic sacrifice. Literary shape for 4:17–19 is disputed.[77] We take v 17, like v 11, as the start of a new subsection, a "disclaimer" (Peterlin) or "qualifier" (Fee 425). *ouch hoti* (v 17) is more a text signal than *de* in 18 (or 19). 4:19 with its fut. indic. vb. is the climax of the subunit.[78]

In Paul's critique of Philippian *philia*, a "transfer of roles" will occur. He speaks not as "partner" but like a bank official in 17b. Financial terms continue in v 18, before giving way to phrases from temple sacrifice at 18c. Paul seeks to disconnect Philippian ideas of friendship in favor of "friendship/sacrifice koinonia" (Ebner, A.5.b). *philia* themes continue in 4:17–19, but Paul as pastor-theologian brings about a change in perspective.

To any accusation he solicited the gift from Philippi or wanted future handouts, Paul responds, *It is not that I am seeking alms*. This parallels v 11 (Schenk 44–46, O'B 536–37) in using (1) *ouch hoti* to introduce a correction, about need in v 11, in 17 notions he was "keen on" (Phillips; cf. NEB, Hawth., O'B) getting gifts from

---

[77] Schenk's chiasm is open to discussion, though the B-C-C′-B′ part is accepted by Ebner:

17c	A	the profit that accumulates to your account
18	B	I have been paid in full
	C	and have more than enough
	C′	I am fully satisfied
	B′	now that I have received from Epaphroditus the gifts you sent
	A′	a fragrant offering, a sacrifice acceptable and pleasing to God

Ebner (see A.5.b) is to be preferred on recipients (Paul, God) and givers (Epaphroditus, the Philippians), mediators, and God. Schenk 46–47 takes v 17 as "theological elucidation" for vv 14–16. But how theological is v 17?

[78] Cf. U. B. Müller 207 n 91, who criticizes Schenk 51–52 for ignoring "not only the future but also the function of v 19 in context. V 19 indeed intends to take up and unfold the eschatological thought in 4:17," about the profit that accumulates in your account.

their "account of giving and receiving." (2) 1st per. vbs., *mention* (4:11) and *seek* (v 17). Greater preciseness (3) comes with *out of need* (v 11) and *alms* (v 17, *to doma*, lit. "the gift") as antonyms. What Paul denies in each case is grounded in a positive cl. that follows: 4:11, *for I have learned to be independent* . . . ; 17 *rather (alla) I am seeking* (vb. repeated) *the profit that accumulates in your account.* (4) A verbal link between negative and positive cls.: in 11 and 12e *out of need* (v 11 *kath' hysterēsin*) and *suffer lack (hystereisthai)*; in 17 repetition of *I am seeking (epizētō)*. (5) 11–13 and 17 end in a participial expression about God and God's activity as high point, v 13 *through the One who strengthens me,* 17 (profit) *that accumulates [i.e., from God's bounty] in your account* (O'B 537 n 158, God "multiplies the compound interest to the Philippians' account"). The passages differ in that vv 11–12 describe *conditions* in Paul's life and v 17 an *aim* in his work and conduct (O'B 536 point 4).

Why an impression Paul asked for gifts? Some suggest a request in prior correspondence (cf. Michael xxi–xxii; Collange 149). *you did well* (4:14 and in the Philippian note) could suggest "a request for support, either explicit or implicit, from Paul to the Philippians" (Berry 116 n 38). More likely Paul fears the praise in vv 14–16 about earlier gifts might trigger ideas that he seeks future handouts. Hence the TRANSLATION renders *doma* as *alms*, as if Paul were a beggar (so Beet).[79] It covers past as well as future "begging" that some sense, more than "gift" but not as specific as "(interest) payment," the sense for *doma* some read in from context (Gnilka, Sampley, Berry, cited in the NOTE on 17ab). We assume a gift, sent voluntarily, not without some friction in Philippi, not based on a contract (Sampley) or as salary (so D. J. Dungan, *The Sayings of Jesus in the Churches of Paul* [Philadelphia: Fortress, 1971] 29 n 205; contrast Hock 1980 [(1) Bibl. **Paul**] 92), within "the context of friendship" (O'B 537), of which gift-giving was a part. Cf. above A.2; P. Marshall 1–13; Mott 61–64; Bassler 1991:17–35 on beggars and benefactors. A friend gave out of *philia*; the recipient was to return the favor or gift with a larger one, with interest. Berry 119–20: "benefits to friends were often considered investments which one would receive back with interest." Paul calls a halt by saying that he does not solicit gifts of any kind.

What does Paul seek? 17b, in financial language called forth by the Philippians' phrase in v 15 *(an account of giving and receiving)*, says he wants to build up the account of which they had spoken: *I am rather* (than seeking alms for myself) *seeking the profit that accumulates in your account.* Emphasis on *your,* pl., the last word in the sentence; obj. gen., an account for you. *profit* (see NOTE) originally had an agricultural sense, "fruit," in Heb. and Gk., then commercially "profit" or "interest." The ptc. "growing" fits fruit in the orchard or funds in a bank account. Paul accepts the Philippians' gift, to build up *their* bank account. He seeks a more favorable balance or bottom line for them. How, will be explained in vv 18–19.

---

[79] Some object that *epizētō to doma,* "I seek (not) the gift," cannot refer to the most recent one, otherwise Paul should have used the perf. tense, "I have not sought the gift"; Ewald 1908:217–18 = 1923:234 claimed Gk. love of concrete expression. Cf. NIV. The def. art. draws attention "to each particular instance of a gift being sent to him," O'B 538; cf. A.1.(1) (a) above.

Future profit, in heaven? Mattern ([8] Bibl.) 167 compares in Jewish thought "God's eschatological account book." Or blessings now, on earth? Or both? Pres. and fut. "goods" can both be termed "eschatological," the one "futurist," the other "realized" or "inaugurated" since the Christ-event. Because of material contributions the Philippians have made to Paul? *philia* would expect a positive payback in this life, tangible goods.[80] Gnilka 179 and others seek to avoid crass implications by referring the "fruit" to the coming Day of Christ (cf. 1:10–11), a result not of financial contributions but their concern for Paul (*phronein* 4:10). "The more they practice and are busy with this *phronein*, the greater will the *karpos* be on that day." O'B 539, it is "unnecessary to choose between a future reward and a present recompense" because the ptc. (pres. tense) implies "compound interest that accumulates all the time" through "God's blessing in their lives by which they constantly grow in the graces of Christ until the parousia." Such questions will run through the rest of the passage.

Ebner (354–55; cf. Berry 119–20) sees the "change in perspective" (noted above) already coming into play, "koinonia friendship" instead of the Greco-Roman *philia*. Not pecuniary gifts, but "fruit" or "interest" for their account. Will Paul make a transfer to their account, consonant with certain aspects of *philia*? Cf. Cic., *Amic.* 64, a friend prefers advancement of friends to his own advance; Paul is acting like such a friend. But he will point them to the final reckoning at the parousia when God judges. How will the Philippians' account grow until that day? Paul was scarcely in a position to make a big gift to them. That would only prime the pump for more exchanges of the type he was seeking to scotch (where "I give in order that you will give in response"). The answer in v 19 is that *God* provides; the underlying premise is the biblical adage that God ensures growth.[81] Perhaps the Philippians would bring a more specific background: when you give to someone, that person's prayers of thanks to God rise heavenward and ensure blessings for the giver (*oratio infusa*, Boobyer, [2] COMMENT n 2). This theory of "thanksgiving" and God's "glory" (2 Cor 9:12b–14) could apply to 4:17–18. In any case, Paul adds "the eschatological dimension to their 'solidarity relations'" (U. B. Müller 206).

V 18 bears out what v 17 implies. *I have been paid in full* is a business-receipt form; it assures the Philippians they have discharged all the obligations attached to *philia*. If a principle is present from Gal 6:6 (paying the teacher materially for spiritual goods), Paul is crossing that off too, they have amply taken care of him. "Account closed."[82] 18a builds on and clarifies what Paul said previously (I seek not alms, I have been, in fact, paid in full), not a new theme indicated by *de*.

---

[80] Walter 99 recalls how in clubs and societies of the day members made contributions for some "religious, political, or private purpose," like proper burial in a *collegia tenuiorium* (burial society).

[81] Cf. Hos 14:8, God is "like an evergreen cypress; your fruit [NRSV paraphrases the Heb. as *your faithfulness*] comes from me." Fruit comes from God (Hos 2:8). Cf. H. Leroy, "*auxanō, auxō*," *EDNT* 1:178; cf. *TDNT* 8:517,91; *NIDNTT* 2:128–30.

[82] If Paul took pen in hand anywhere in Letter A, this phrase would be most appropriate (Gnilka 179; Mengel 283; U. B. Müller 206), but that lies beyond proof. Cf. also A.1 n 10 above and (17) COMMENT, Intro.

As evidence he has been *paid in full* and need not "seek alms," v 18 repeats *and I abound,* as in the *autarkeia* catalogue of vv 11b–13; there he employed the vb. twice (12b *abound with much; abound and to suffer lack* 12e). Three times in the body of Letter A may seem excessive, but Paul dwells on the positive side. He adds (18b), *I am filled full,* not merely with joy (true as that may be, v 11) but with resources for his work from the Philippians (as 18b goes on to make clear), solidarity again with Philippi because their *concern for* him revived (v 10).[83]

This is so *because I have received from Epaphroditus what you sent.* The "I" statements in 18a are possible *because* Paul received money from Philippi. If Paul knows of discord there, esp. over a gift for him, he graciously overlooks it. Enough that he referred to the long gap in gifts from them in v 10 and refuted suggestions he was in dire need (v 11) and had solicited gifts (v 17). Some see dispute over supporting Paul (L. M. White, Peterlin) in two phrases side by side, *from Epaphroditus* and "things *from* you" (double use of *para*). Epaphroditus likely had a major role in assembling the purse for Paul, coming at his own expense to provide personal services. His role is not elaborated, as it will be at 2:25–30. Here simply, the envoy has arrived safely with the gift that Paul is acknowledging (he is not as yet ill, else Paul would have noted it here).

Three phrases follow, ostensibly describing *what you sent* in language that seems drawn from cultic sacrifice, *a fragrance with aroma, a sacrifice acceptable, well pleasing, to God.* The final *tō[i] theō[i]* goes with all three expressions, well pleasing to God, a sacrifice acceptable to God, a fragrance with aroma for God. A sudden shift from banking terms to "the language of religion" (Hawth. 206), OT language of sacrifice.[84] The NOTES identify possible backgrounds for each cultic phrase. To pin down in the OT what *a fragrance with aroma* suggested to Paul, let alone the Philippians, is impossible.[85] Behind the figure was the ancient Near Eastern idea that the odor of a burnt offering was redolent to the deity (Exod 29:18). The second phrase contains a common word for *sacrifice (thysia)* + the adj. *acceptable* or "welcome" to God. It is so general that commentators find it difficult to cite a specific (OT) reference; Sir 35:6 LXX may come closest.[86] The

---

[83] The NOTE on *I am filled full* points out interweaving of "fullness" and related themes in Letter A and a possible *inclusio.* Paul is *filled full* by their gift (4:18) and prays that they may be "filled full" with "fruit of righteousness" (1:11; cf. 4:17 "fruit that accumulates to your account"). Paul "abounds" (4:18, cf. 12) and prays the Philippians' discerning love may "abound" (1:9). The "fulfillment theme" will be crowned in v 19 with the promise God *will fulfill* the Philippians' needs (as God has Paul's, 4:19, cf. 11–13), and that *gloriously* (v 19; cf. 1:11 God's glory), for *glory* belongs to God (v 20).

[84] Banking and animal sacrifice were related in antiquity in that temples served as repositories for money and savings accounts; see NOTE on 1:1 *slaves* and "sacred manumission decrees"; COMMENT on 1:1–2; *ABD* 6:369–82, esp. 371 (W. A. Ward) and 381 (S. G. Cole). The shift in metaphor may not have been abrupt for ancients.

[85] Noah's sacrifice of birds and animals (Gen 8:21); some offering at the Jerusalem temple (Fee 451 "the burnt offering"); Israel itself as an eschatological offering to God (Ezek 20:41); or a day when sacrifices by foreigners would be accepted at Yahweh's altar (Isa 56:7) have been suggested (B. Weiss 345).

[86] Schenk 48 cites Loh. 187 n 4 for Sir 32 (35):9; NRSV 35:8–9, "The offering of the righteous enriches the altar, and its pleasing odor rises before the Most High. The sacrifice of the righteous is

third phrase, *well pleasing*, turns out, when examined, not particularly cultic (see NOTE on *euareston*; O'B 541–42). Corriveau ([8] Bibl.) 114 sees a moral sense (Rom 12:1), "almost exclusively a New Testament word . . . used of God's attitude toward human behaviour."

The three "cultic" phrases thus begin with one clearly OT *(osmēn euōdias)*; then a noun *(thysian)* found in all ancient religions but with a very general adj. *dektēn*; last of all a word *(euareston)* not from OT or LXX but the NT and there of ethical behavior. The first six words, *a fragrance with aroma, a sacrifice*, are "cultic" but the next three, *acceptable, well pleasing*, are not. Much depends on how God is envisioned, "sniffer of sacrifices," nourished on their savor, as in ancient religion generally, or one seeking moral response in the ethical life, not needing animal or grain sacrifices. Parts of Judaism had long "spiritualized" cultic sacrifice (see NOTE on *a fragrance with aroma*). Paul could have OT sacrifices at the Jerusalem temple in mind, or a broader sense his once-pagan addressees in Philippi shared. He could use "fragrant offering" (2 Cor 2:14–16, cf. Eph. 5:2) as a metaphor; the aroma in 2 Cor 2 likely refers to the apostles and/or their dissemination of the gospel throughout the world. 4:18c is less cultic than often supposed and could apply to people as well as money. No specific OT background, but familiar in Philippi from the constant burnt offerings to gods of the classical pantheon or "the genius of Caesar," as the Imperial regime legitimated itself through state religion (Walter 99, cf. Bockmuehl 266).

To what do these cultic or moral/ethical phrases in 18c refer? The NOTES list four possibilities. (1) Most common is *what you sent*, the gift of money from Philippi. NRSV, "the gift you sent, a fragrant offering . . . to God"; Vincent 150; Hawth. 206; O'B; Sampley 57, Corriveau ([8] Bibl.) 113; Bormann 1995:156. Then the Philippians' sacrifice is a gift Paul has transferred to God, or the gifts to Paul have value in God's sight. Berry 120, "Paul is not the only or the ultimate recipient of their gift. Their gift involves . . . also their relationship to God. . . . [I]t is a sacrifice pleasing to God (4:18). Paul goes on to say that God will respond to their sacrifice (in v. 19)." O'B 542, the "financial support . . . is *likened to* an acceptable sacrifice," TEV, ". . . like a sweet-smelling offering to God." But there is no word for "like," such as Gk. *hōs*, in the text.

(2) *The total action of the Philippians*, remembering Paul, collecting money, and sending it via Epaphroditus. Money symbolizes ties of *philia* and love. The relations of apostle and congregation are an offering and sacrifice to God.[87] This fits Paul's argument well, to move the Philippians beyond the money gift, to a broader context of *koinōnia* under and with God.

(3) *The Philippians*. Paul calls them a sacrifice with fragrant aroma, etc. J. Fleury; see NOTES on 18c *have received* and *a fragrance with aroma* and COM-

---

acceptable . . . ," but the context in 35:1–5 is keeping the Law as proper sacrifice. The limited NT use (5x) of *dektos*, "acceptable," usually refers to acceptable times or once to a person acceptable to God (Acts 10:35).

[87] Theories (1) and (2) specifically bring God in. Any explanation must assume that the closing phrase in 18c "to (or for) God" is part of the picture.

MENT B.1.a(1). Often overlooked, for good reasons. It fails to note "the flow of 4:10–20" (Sampley). Its glowing *captatio benevolentiae* is ambiguous ("Is Paul calling for our martyrdom?"). Paul directs them to God, a point on which Fleury's proposal is weak.

(4) Refer the phrases to *Paul*. Loh. 184 connected 18c with the vb. *peplērōmai* in 18a:

18a I have everything and am rich; I am filled *(erfüllt)* —

   since I received your gift from Epaphroditus —

18c with *(von)* a sweet aroma, lovely sacrifice, to God pleasing

Three accs. of respect after the vb.; cf. *karpon* at 1:11, "filled with fruit of righteousness" (Loh. and our TRANSLATION). 18c = "I have come to fulfillment as an acceptable sacrifice," in martyrdom; "acceptable to God" at the day of his perfection, in martyrdom (cf. 2:17). Filled with lovely fragrance through the gift of the Philippians, Paul "knows that he is sanctified as a sacrifice and with him also the Philippians' gift" (188). Gnilka curtly dismissed the interpretation; see NOTE on 18c. Corriveau, "obviously forcing the text," to avoid "applying the terminology to the gift."

Loh. wove into his interpretation *Paul as priest* bringing an offering (the gift and himself) to God (188). K. Weiss developed this, in light of Rom 15:16 and Phil 2:17, as "a priestly self-understanding" on the part of Paul (Weiss 358). The community was the (holy) temple *(naos)* of God (1 Cor 3:16–17; etc.); his apostolic office, priestly sacrificial service. Paul as "Israelite priest" is "possible" (Bockmuehl 266). Contrast W. Strack 317–18. O'B 542, 18c "is part of . . . NT teaching about all Christians being a new priesthood" (1 Pet 2:9, etc.), a corporate priesthood of the people of God, not Paul's priesthood. R. Corriveau ([8] Bibl.), from Vatican Council II: the daily life of the Christian is worship of God; Christians share in Christ's "priestly function of offering spiritual worship for the glory of God and the salvation of humanity" (*Lumen Gentium* #34; ed. Abbott, p. 60). Phil 4:18b (111–17) is part of a letter frg. from Ephesus acknowledging the gift from Philippi, its sacrificial terminology from "late Jewish wisdom literature" (like Sir). It shifts attention to God (114). Their deed is proof of love. Paul is not a priest at Phil 4:18 (Rom 15:16, *hierourgounta* means "minister," preaching the gospel, 148–55); its "cosmic liturgy" is the Christian community (115–16), not liturgical worship but "sacred service" (*leitourgia* in a Gk. *polis*), like almsgiving in 2 Cor 9:12, pp. 97–105), the "overflow of praise and thanksgiving to God" for gifts received (cf. Boobyer; for Corriveau via Georgi 1965 [INTRO. VIII] = 1992:62–67, 103–7, 116–17). Paul's sacrificial terminology suggests how gifts lead to glory for God and God's glory is reflected in the gifts.

For M. Newton ([8] Bibl.)—who treated 4:18c and its context[88] in terms of

---

[88] Fishing in the sea of the LXX, Newton claims, e.g., that *doma* in 17 ("gift," *alms*) "refers to those gifts that are offered in the Temple," like the wave offering of Lev 7:30. In *karpos* (fruit, *profit*, or interest in 17) Newton detects wordplay on *karpōma*, "burnt offerings" (Num 28:2). 17 *in your account*, Gk. *logos*, is related to *logizomai*, in the LXX "the crediting of sacrificial offerings on behalf of the donors

cultic piety, as "at Qumran [10–51] . . . a systematically worked out Temple/purity scheme" (though "no such system is to be found in Paul")—"Paul as priest to the Christian community" (60–70) suggests ministry in priestly terms, as a liturgical task and willingness "to accept a martyr's death" (61–62; without citing Loh). Paul "receives gifts like a priest which he then offers up as an acceptable and pleasing sacrifice" (67), in the church/temple of God (purity required). O'B's critique is specific and on target: "Newton's understanding of the terminology is confused and not sufficiently controlled by the text of vv. 17 and 18" (537 n 163; cf. 540 n 187; 541 n 188).

How to sort out this welter of interpretations for 18c?[89] The words must fit Paul's response, acknowledging the Philippians' gift, in light of their view of friendship and its benefits. He directs the Philippians away from "giving and receiving" in human terms to a relationship that includes God. In the *philia* context, commercial language is not surprising; shift to sacrificial language is, though only the first half or so of 18c is demonstrably cultic. Cultic aspects diminish, in favor of the moral/ethical (Corriveau) or theological *(to God)* in 18c. It is unlikely Paul applies the three phrases to the Philippians (view [3] above) or to himself ([4] above; grammatically contrived, overly abrupt, and too exclusive). (On the redacted letter, when 2:17 is factored in, see B.3, below.) The most widespread explanation is the gift from Philippi, *what you sent* ([1] above). But this plays directly into Philippian views about "an account of giving and receiving," a position from which Paul is trying to extricate himself and them. Such praise would escalate the level of ongoing giving between friends, something Paul sought to break in 18ab.

The semi-cultic phrases of 4:18c, in context of Letter A, best fit (2) above, *the Philippians' solidarity with and concern for Paul*, lifted up in v 10. What they sent reflects negative factors in relations (the gap in sending money, possible dispute and half-hearted response on the present gift) and positive ones (their care for Paul; they have blossomed afresh, v 10; Paul rejoices). If "bonds of friendship" were "strained" (L. M. White) or there was a "rift" or "breach" (Capper) in the past, now there are differing expectations of what friendship means in the church, a community of saints who need to grow (1:1,9–11), bring God and the divine riches into consideration, and look to the future as well as the past and present.

Just as 4:17 paralleled 11–13, and 4:18 reiterates something of 11b–12, so 19 *(My God will fulfill every need of yours, in accord with the divine riches, gloriously, in Christ Jesus)* parallels the assertion about God in v 13, *I am strong, able to tackle everything, through the One who strengthens me.* Its personal confession, *My God*, reflects the personal experience in v 13. *will fulfill* (see NOTE on textual variants) is fut. indic., promise (KJV, [N]RSV), not opt. of wish, "May God supply . . ." (U. B. Müller 207, citing Merk 1968:200; Mengel 284; Neugebauer 1961:89–90,

---

(Num. 18:27, 30 . . .)." Even *dexamenos* in v 18 *(have received)* is given a cultic background; Exod 29:25 LXX (MS A), Moses "received" the wave offering, Gk. *aphorisma*, "set apart," the way Paul views himself in Rom 1:1.

[89] Bormann 1995:158–60 rejects all notions of the Philippians' material gifts producing eschatological or spiritual gain for them. Their ethical accomplishment in supporting Paul is not met by a counter-accomplishment of his part, but by their being brought into a fuller relationship with Paul's God.

etc. in the NOTE). V 19 completes the thought begun in v 17, but poses problems. Does Paul guarantee God will take care of every want of which a person could think, esp. physical? Some therefore make it exclusively future-eschatological (G. P. Wiles, R. P. Martin 1976:169); others allow present material needs (Hawth.). Both seem involved (Fee 452–53). Paul expresses his strong faith, based on personal experience. To be *autarkēs*, content, keeps one from asking for self-indulgent luxuries. There are hazards in any statement about the power of God (Hawth. 208): Paul is confident about what God *can* do, but not rash about what God *will* do. Yet v 13 struck just such a confident pose, "All things I can (do) or am strong for (doing). . . ." Either way, "catch-22": the promise may sound too strong, a prayer-wish can sound wishy-washy. Paul learned about God in prayer and experience (Schenk 52–53). Hence he could preach with boldness and make assertions about himself (as in v 13) and the Philippians (v 19). He *prayed* for their continuing growth (1:9–11), he *knew* their revived loyalty and generosity (10–16, 18ab); he *knew* God's munificence, the grounds for what is now offered.

V 19 uses traditional phrases, *in Christ Jesus, gloriously,* and *in accord with the divine riches,* to respond to a Philippian emphasis on *need,* in the argument Paul developed for the situation.[90] Philippian needs (see NOTE on *every need of yours*) include growth until the parousia *and* their being proven *flawless and unfailing* at *the Day of Christ* (1:10–11).

Reference to *divine riches* (see NOTE) points to a "theology of riches" in Paul. God by nature is rich in goodness and goods, righteousness and resources, mercy and manifestations of the divine nature. This has ample background in the OT; in the Greco-Roman world, God as "benefactor" (Danker 1982:426) or "patron" (G. P. Wiles 1974:103; Berry 121). This God will meet your every need. As the chiastic structure (see n 101) suggests, God's benefiting activity occurs *in* the sphere of *Christ Jesus,* through the Christ-event, implications continuing in the community of Christ. Relations between Paul and the Philippians are to be viewed "in Christ Jesus." Its eschatological nature, climaxing in parousia and judgment, is suggested by *gloriously* (*en doxē[i],* see NOTE). Not a place, "glory land," not a tirade against "realized eschatology," but Paul's usual "future reservation," reservations about "glory" here and now, even for believers. Fulfillment is at the end, on the Day of the Lord. Thus are addressed ongoing concerns in a process of giving and receiving till the end. God, not Paul, is the patron the Philippians need (cf. Berry 121; divine-human reciprocity in Mott 64–67). How God works is powerful incentive to keep on in the Christian life, "God is able to provide you with every blessing in abundance, so that by always having enough of everything, you may dare abundantly in every good work" (2 Cor 9:8). For this ethical sense, God's promise (v 19) is the eschatological side to what the Philippians do, in 17 *the profit that accumulates in* their *account* (U.B. Müller 207). God brings the increase, not Paul.

---

[90] The chiastic structure envisioned by Schenk 49 = O'B 544 contrasts Philippian *need* with God's *riches* (C,C′) and relates *my God* and *in Christ Jesus* (A, A′) as the source and sphere of the action. Linking B *will satisfy* and B′ "in glory" or *gloriously* strikes the fut. eschatological note and climax needed, whether solely at the parousia or now too.

Is Paul a priest or mediator in the process? Not in Letter A. 4:19 has nothing on "purity" (as occurred in 1:10) or on Paul as martyr sacrificing his life (Loh.). K. Weiss overdoes the theme for Paul from other passages, making Paul "cultic middleman." The gift to Paul is ultimately from God, the Benefactor will respond out of *the divine riches*. Corriveau's emphasis on worship in daily life through generosity and participation in the spread of the gospel is well taken. There remains to add only an outcry of praise to complete the argument and the body of the letter.

e. *Doxology (4:20). To our God and Father belongs glory forever and ever. Amen.* This splendid conclusion for the body of Letter A goes closely with v 19. Thought centered on God in vv 13, 18c–19, and now 20, plus the divine bountifulness in v 19. The nature of the God Paul knows as Father, who, out of sovereign largesse, supplies needs, causes him, as a good Jew (3:4b–6) and a believing Christian, to burst forth in OT style with a doxology.

V 20 completes Paul's treatment of friendship. Philippian *philia* included benefits. He dealt critically with the notions that he should respond with a bigger gift by examining the relationship of apostle and church (not "friend with friend"). Paul parallels his experience of dependence on God (11–13) and a similar experience hoped-for on the part of the Philippians. He points to God in his circumstances and for the Philippians in whatever is to come, in their "account" with God. Their expectations and his own he draws together in an expression of praise to God. The chart of reciprocal relations (above, 2.b, in connection with 4:11–13,) can be completed thus:[91]

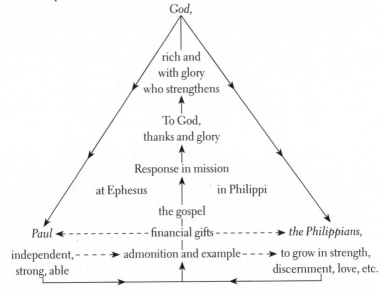

To the rhetorical question, "What do you have that you did not receive? And if you received it, why do you boast as if it were not a gift?" (1 Cor 4:7, NRSV), he can

---

[91] The chart explicates more fully what Fee 444 speaks of as a *"three-way bond,"* Paul, the Philippians, and Christ (or Gospel or God).

only respond with thanks, confessing God's goodness (Schenk 55) The Philippians are to join in this response.

V 20 has them affirm together God's glory, the first time in the body of Letter A that *our* has occurred. As in the only other example in Phil (1:2 *God our Father*), sender and recipients of the letter are brought together as senders and recipient of the gift, an *inclusio*. The doxology reflects early Christian liturgical tradition but with a structure of its own (see NOTE on 4:20; COMMENT A.4.b; cf. Gal 1:5). (1) *To our God and Father* (Phil 2:11; 1:2) praise is ascribed. Paul and the Philippians are God's adopted children, who can (in Christ) say *Abba* for a fatherhood beyond what creation offers. See NOTE on reasons for supplying "is," not "May glory be. . . ." Glory already *belongs* to God; as in Matt 6:13 and 1 Pet 4:11, believers simply affirm it. Indic. as in v 19. (2) The word of praise is *glory*—light, brightness, magnificence that characterize the divine nature, made known in creation, then in saving actions, above all in Christ, salvation that continues to be felt in the life of believers, a splendor that is God's uniquely. While in some passages *doxa* is "conferred in . . . Christ Jesus" (Danker 1982:426), here it is the Father who is object of joyful asseveration. Letter A is not particularly Christo-emphatic. (3) *forever and ever* points to endless ages beyond our own, through which glory runs. Not "eternity" in contrast to "time." The Philippians likely knew from Paul of biblical, apocalyptical "ages," including the new age come with Christ. *our God and Father* may be directed against the Emperor as "Father of the fatherland" (Witherington 132). *our God*, not Caesar, is our patron (Walter 100).

"*Amen*," Heb. though it is, was known to Paul's churches as a way to make one's own what was just affirmed. Not clients applauding a patron, but redeemed believers praising the God they know. Apostle and church, separated by the miles, speak together, of God.

3. 4:10–20 *Within the Redacted Canonical Letter.* When Letters A, B, and C were combined into canonical Phil (see INTRO. VII.B), (a) what difference did the new context make? (b) The vv must also be read in their "second setting" (Gnilka 14–18), the four-ch. context. The outline and much of B.2.a–e hold for the redacted letter (3.b.[1]–[5]), but there are shifts in meaning.

a. *The New Setting: Some Differences and Emphases.* We now read Phil 4:10–20 in relation to the preceding three and a half chs., something avoided in B.2. Most commentaries treat the vv thus, often stressing the "Christ hymn" (2:6–11) or false teachers in ch. 3. But 4:10–20 is not Christo-emphatic; it speaks of God (4:13,19,20) far more than Christ. The false teachers, so vivid in 3:2, 18–19, are not apparent in 4:10–20. But some words in 4:10–20 can be read aware of occurrences in earlier chs., "joy" (v 10 *I rejoiced*), *phronein, koinōnia, doxa*. Some approaches particularly stress vocabulary links.[92] To place 4:10–20 within the context of the entire letter does not solve all exegetical problems; it often makes decisions more complex.

---

[92] Wick sees *koinōnia* as the theme of all Phil (142–51), but regards 4:10–20 (which has *koinōn*-terminology) as chiastically parallel to 2:19–30 (which does not) (his sections e² and e¹, pp. 51–54); the hymn influences all his six sections (78–81); Epaphroditus and Timothy are then called models of the

(1) In the redacted letter Paul is *in bonds, despairing at times of life.* All four chs. are from an apostle in prison. If in Rome, pathos is heightened because readers understand that Paul will soon be martyred there. For the redactor (about A.D. 90), Paul had been dead for several decades. Such factors cast a martyr theology over 4:10–20. Loh. assumed this for the historical Paul.

(2) He is therefore *"the suffering and dying Paul"* (Gnilka 16). The anguish of 1:23 casts its spell over 4:10–20; this makes 4:13 ("I can do all things through the One who strengthens me") more of a conundrum. 2:17 (Paul's "poured out as a libation") may color how the cultic phrases about "a sacrifice acceptable . . . to God" in 4:18 are read (the "Paul as priest" question).

(3) The passing reference to *Epaphroditus* at 4:18 must now be read in light of his illness and Paul's plea to welcome him back to Philippi in 2:25–30.

(4) There is more tendency to perceive *Paul as example.* Letter A suggested (4:11b–13 and 19) the Philippians perdure as Paul does, in dependence on God. 3:17 strengthens this by "imitation" language. But we are wary of seeing in 4:10–20 Christ, Epaphroditus, or others as examples (cf. Wick in n 92 above); the content does not indicate this.

(5) The *"I" form*, so prominent in 4:11–13, 17–18ab, etc., can now be seen as a continuation, not anticipation, of that style in 1:19–26 and 3:4b–14. Is Paul's *peristasis* catalogue to be read more directly in light of assertions about his experience of righteousness from God in 3:9–10?

(6) *Financial and commercial terms* in 4:17–18ab are more difficult now. Should they be submerged after their prominence in Letter A, or do they now startle all the more? Is *koinōnia* language in Phil to be read with the financial sense in 4:14–15 as starting point (Suggs [(2) Bibl. **sharing**), or will 4:14–15 seem odd after the more "theological" uses in 1:5 or 2:1?

(7) The problem of 4:10–20 as *"thankless thanks"* remains in the redacted letter, compounded because these vv come so late in the document. The best solution is still along the lines of Gk. *philia*: friends need not use *eucharistein* or any direct expression of thanks to friends.

(8) *Delay* in mentioning the Philippians' gift (only near the end of the final ch.) exacerbates the problem. Paul did not acknowledge receipt of the gift promptly. Discussing it has lower priority among his aims. Was he ashamed to talk about money (C. H. Dodd)? Does *de* mean in 4:10, "O yes, I didn't want to forget to say. . . ." (Lft.)? Old explanations (A.3, above) may be reopened.

(9) Acknowledgment (or thanks) so late in the epistle reopens the question of *mission strategy* that touched off proposals like Fleury's (B.1.a.[1]), that Paul never accepted money from congregations, or that Philippi was an exception to this rule. Such questions are heightened in the composite document.

(10) Emphasis on *friendship*, differing concepts of it, *harmony and conflict* in Philippi or with Paul may be blurred when all of Phil is considered, *less* clear

---

proper disposition, which the Philippians in 4:10–20 are to model. In such ways the rough places are made smooth by structural theories of unity.

when all four chs. must be explained at once, rather than as development of events and feelings in a series of letters.

The redactor who put Phil together likely did not foresee all the resulting questions. Fidelity to Paul meant not letting his words perish, the apostle continues to speak in a new configuration, with possibilities that extend into the history of exegesis.

b. *4:10–20 as the Final Major Section of Philippians.*

(1) *Paul joyfully acknowledges the renewed contact (4:10)* — The apostle concludes his letter, from Ephesus, A.D. 55, by taking up a topic, the gift from the Philippians, perhaps hinted at in 1:5 *(sharing in the gospel)*, 1:6 (the good work among them), and 1:7 *(phronein)*. He came close to the topic in 2:25–30, on Epaphroditus, who brought the gift. The injunction at 3:1, *rejoice in the Lord,* could have led directly into 4:10, *I greatly rejoiced in the Lord . . . .* But the warnings of 3:2–21 intervened for reasons indicated in (11) and (12) COMMENT B.2; (13) COMMENT B.3, and (14) COMMENT B.4. More admonitions followed (4:1), to Euodia and Syntyche (4:2–3) and the whole congregation (4:4–9). Now Paul gets to the gift, welcome in his imprisonment but a problem: What do the Philippians, in their friendship code, expect from him? *de* (omitted in the TRANSLATION), which connects v 10 to what precedes, marks a transition to a new topic.

The apostle writes in better spirits than in 1:20–26 (life or death) or ch. 3 (agitated warnings). *I greatly rejoiced* (at the revived expression of Philippian concern through the gift). As in 3:1 and 4:4, *in the Lord* (Jesus Christ) denotes the sphere where this joy occurs, in Paul's ecclesial relationship with the Philippians, mutually in and under the Lord. It points away from "friendship" toward Christian *koinōnia. now at last* is a touch of rebuke. The gap in contact has become longer than if he had written immediately upon receipt of the money. Enough time has elapsed for news of Epaphroditus' arrival (in Ephesus) and of his illness to get back to Philippi and for Epaphroditus to be distressed that they know about it (2:26), not to mention delay in completing what was becoming a longer and longer letter with the polemical warnings in 3:2–21. But in prison, conditions for correspondence were not easy.

Paul does not apologize for his delay, but refers to *your concern for me (phronein), a concern on which you were long intent.* to *hyper Paulou phronein* was a Philippian phrase, for solidarity with Paul in mission (so Schenk and others). The vb. occurs throughout Phil (10x, the heaviest concentration of occurrences in the NT); references to "thinking the same thing" (see NOTE 1:7) and "thinking one thing" (2:2) provide a broader scope than "concern for Paul" and call for reconsideration of how their "friendly concern" has worked out.

4:10–20 zigzags first in one direction, then another. Positively, revival of Philippian concern. Negatively, past delinquencies, "You tried to show concern" (*were long intent* on it), excused (*you lacked opportunity*; Paul was traveling, they lacked a messenger). Philippian interest in Paul may have cooled, amid differences of opinion in the house churches of Philippi (L. M. White; Peterlin, real disunity). Hence Paul put off acknowledging a gift that poses difficult questions on relations with those who would be his friends, perhaps patrons.

(2) *Paul asserts his independence (but dependence on God's power) (4:11–13)* —
Paul begins anew, to counter a charge against him: *It is not that I mention this out
of need . . .*, out of poverty or dependence on the Philippians for a livelihood. In
their view he is an impoverished client, they, the well-to-do patron. Such an asymmetrical relationship would skew ties between apostle and congregation even worse
than Gk. *philia* or Roman *beneficia*. Paul responds with a catalogue of experiences
on how he copes in situations bad, good, or indifferent, before concluding with a
ringing declaration about God as *the One who strengthens* him (v 13). The abruptness here is not like the impassioned triple impvs. at 3:2, "look out for . . ."; 4:11–13
are a calculated part of an argument to refute possible misunderstanding and to set
the Philippians straight about the man for whom they were concerned. Among
friends the words might seem discourteous. In the redacted letter they are the more
surprising after talk about *adelphoi* who are his "joy and crown" (4:1), for whom he
longs (1:8), etc. Why this device at 4:11–13 that distances him from them?

How could the notion have arisen that Paul proceeds *out of need*? B.2.b, above,
presented speculations by commentators (who often assume a single letter). For
the redacted letter a further scenario is possible. Paul's delay in writing back about
their gift may have prompted Philippians to ask, Why no acknowledgment? Was
Paul dissatisfied? Is his situation, jail, legal expenses (or bribes) worse than we supposed? (Just as Paul had heard the Philippians knew of Epaphroditus' illness, so he
could have heard of their questions about his lack of response.) The bold assertion
in v 13, *I am strong, able to tackle anything*, goes badly with the image of "the suffering and dying Paul" (3.b.[2] as in 1:19–26). How does 4:11–13 fit into the letter
as a whole?

Paul says he has learned to be independent and content in various situations;
through the God who empowers him he is able to tackle anything. The form is a
peristasis catalogue (B.2.b and A.4.e). By the time of a single letter to Philippi,
Paul would have composed many or all of the "catalogues of tribulations" now
found in 1 and 2 Cor.[93] In 4:11b–13 (*I have learned to be independent . . . through
the One who strengthens me*) he frames six antithetical infins. and five "I" statements about experiential learning within opening and closing assertions on his
independence and God's power. Repeating *abound* (12b,e, also in v 18) strikes the
note Paul wishes, abundance. 1st per. assertions point to what Paul has come to
know through experience in his Christian life. The unit is framed by a declaration
of independence (*autarkeia*) in 11b and a theological assertion about God in v 13,
points of emphasis in this diamond-shape of experience, on results in the apostle's
life with God as the cause or ground for coping:

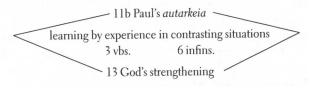

11b Paul's *autarkeia*

learning by experience in contrasting situations

3 vbs.   6 infins.

13 God's strengthening

---

[93] The later Phil is dated, the more experience Paul has with composing *peristasis* catalogues.

The artful arrangement was impressive for ancient hearers as for today. The outcome, as in Gk. catalogues about the sage or righteous sufferer, is contentment with what God gives, leading to independence from the world. Emphasis on God is emphatic; the God Paul experienced, decisive.

4:11b–13 serves to distance Paul from Philippian ideas of friendship, patronage, and exchange (gift for gift, ever a bigger gift in response). Content with what God provides, Paul serves notice that their notion of *philia* must be altered. He opposes the principle of religiosity in Lat. formulas, *do ut des* ("I give in order that you may give [to me]") or *da ut dem* ("Give in order that I give [to you]") (Bormann 1995:69). He points to God who ultimately (4:18b–19) will be the One to whom Paul (and the Philippians) look at the denouement of their lives and of the universe. Greco-Roman friendship is being reshaped toward Christian *koinōnia* by insistence on God who reverses *do-ut-des* concepts. In the redacted letter, this reversal fits with depiction of salvation through Christ in 2:6–11, but Paul chooses in 4:11–13 and most of 4:10–20 to make his argument in terms of God (the Father, v 20), rather than Christology. Later scribes added, "I can do all things through *Christ* who strengthens me" (see NOTE on v 13; cf. KJV).

The Philippians should learn to live as Paul does, in complete dependence on God. Paul as model is more apparent in the redacted letter (cf. 3:17), though the "I" statements in 4:11–13 restrict the example to Paul. Some of what he testifies to about *need* and God will be repeated in v 19 with respect to the Philippians. Perhaps abundance was particularly pertinent in Roman Philippi: be dependent on God where there is plenty; this may be harder than enduring hunger. Prosperity can be a temptation too! The problem of Paul sounding like a spiritual superman in v 13 ("I can do all things . . .") remains in a unified epistle (cf. Hawth. 200–1; O'B 526). The TRANSLATION *able to tackle everything* and B.2 attempt a solution. Paul's is the language of faith, grace experienced in everyday existence, with resulting discernment and practical knowledge. Would that the Philippians could come to this point in their reblossoming and growth!

How can Paul the prisoner, facing death (ch. 1), speak so boldly in ch. 4? The soliloquy in 1:19–26 expected deliverance; he would come to Philippi again (2:19 and 26; 2:24). Perhaps, as the letter was being written, he had assurance that all would go well (a vision? Epaphroditus' legal skills? use of his Roman citizenship?). Yet little in the epistle prepares for the confident assertions of 4:11–13. Perhaps 2:13, God *at work in and among you*. Better yet, Paul's autobiography, his "faith journey" in 3:4–14, the great reversal, Paul found "in Christ," with *the righteousness that comes through faith in Christ, from God*. The life of justification involves, amid *sufferings, the power of the resurrection* (from God). Paul has not yet reached the goal, *the resurrection from the dead* or becoming like Christ, but he presses on. He wants the Philippians to imitate his experience with faith-righteousness (Reumann 1989b; [12] COMMENT on 3:17, Bibl.). In the redacted letter the autobiographical "I" passages, 4:11b–13 and 3:4–14, should be read together. The bold words of 4:11–13 are less startling to readers who know his experience of justification in Phil 3 than to those imbued with the etiquette of friendship.

(3) *Recalling Past Sharing as Context for the Current Gift (4:14–16)*—A new

tack, after the uncouth words in 11–13: a narrative about past relationships and the money the Philippians shared in earlier days for mission. V 14 recaptures their goodwill again by returning to the subject of v 10, the gift. He commends them, *you did well in sharing together with me.* But somewhat surprisingly "sharing *in my affliction*" (14). In Letter A, *sharing* and *affliction* were new elements, but not in Phil as a whole.[94] *sharing together with me* (14) had a financial sense in the Philippians letter (and Letter A), *koinōnia* as "going shares with someone," part of friendship where "all things are in common." In the unified letter, 4:14 is to be seen in light of four earlier occurrences, which give (above, 3.a, point 6) a more Christian sense to *koinōnia*. Sharing the gospel (1:5), grace (1:7), the Spirit (2:1, and Christ's sufferings (3:10) give so Christian and theological a connotation to *koinōnia* that the Philippian understanding, as part of friendship, is obscured. *koinōnia* moves out of the Philippians' friendship orbit; their view of *philia* must be reshaped along Christian lines.

Sharing *in my affliction* (v 14) is not what the Philippians expected. In the redacted letter, Paul's *affliction* includes his imprisonment (1:13, etc.). The Philippians shared in affliction by also facing opposition for their gospel stance (1:27–30), perhaps imprisonments (Loh., of the leaders). The *narratio* in 15–16 reminds them (v 15) that they had been unique in contributing to his mission team (*no other church*) and how often they sent aid to Paul. They saw "an account of giving and receiving" as a part of friendship. Paul must deal with its implications.

(4) *Payment and Repayment (4:17–19)*—Vv 17–19 are a disclaimer so that 15–16 are not misunderstood. Paul is not *seeking alms*, but *profit that accumulates* in the Philippians' account. The vv point to God as the power of the future who *will fulfill every need* of the Philippians. See 2.d on the argument. Its flow can be depicted, like 11b–13, in a diamond shape:

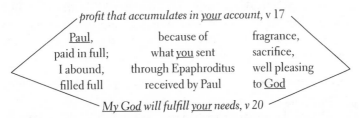

Suspicion that Paul seeks alms may have fed on his delay in responding to the Philippians' gift: was he dissatisfied? No, their gift satisfied all expectations (stated as minimal in vv. 11–13) and closes out financially the friendship relation they assumed. In the redacted letter, passing reference to Epaphroditus in 4:18b is dominated by the high praise in 2:25–30. This may obscure the earlier endeavor of Epaphroditus hinted at in 4:18 (*I have received from Epaphroditus . . .*), that he personally led the fund-raising. His role is diminished if Euodia and/or

---

[94] Some phrases are repeated from the Philippians' note that accompanied the gift, reconstructed above in B.1 (B); this letter of theirs is to be assumed for the redacted letter too.

Syntyche (or the *episkopoi* and *diakonoi* of 1:1) were responsible for the latest fund-gathering.

Re the three seemingly cultic phrases in 4:18, "Paul as priest" is somewhat more plausible in the full letter, in light of Phil 2:17. The total letter reinforces the fut. indic. of 4:19, *God will fulfill every need*; note 4:9, "... will be with you"; 4:7, "... will guard"; 3:21, the Savior "will transform"; 3:9–11, God will bring about our resurrection. For v 19, *doxa* in the full epistle (cf. 1:11; 2:11; 3:21) supports an eschatological sense for *gloriously* but with connotations for this life (cf. 3:19). *riches*, characteristic of a patron or benefactor in Hellenistic thinking, was in Paul's experience God's riches (4:13) to justify and *fulfill every need*.

Paul has redefined the playing field for "friendship." No longer himself and the Philippians, reciprocally, in "an account of giving and receiving" according to conventions of Hellenistic *philia*, Roman *amicitia*, or *beneficia*. God is in the picture as One who settles up accounts and blesses caring concern and mission endeavor. He hopes the Philippians will achieve, *through the One who strengthens* believers, the independence he knows. The summary chart (2.e, above) holds for 4:10–20 in the letter as a whole.

(5) *Doxology (4:20)* — The words are suitable for the entire letter, of a piece with 4:7 and 9. Paul and the Philippians join here as "church" (4:15) in common praise. Let the people of God say *Amen* to what they should know and live by in daily experience. The usual greetings and a benediction will round out the epistle (4:21–23).

Phil 4:10–20 has had no great impact on doctrinal or ethical themes in Christianity, even in "stewardship" (but cf. Bassler 1991:17–36, 75–80; possible blessings for givers that sacrificial offerings might amass from God?[95]; "works-righteousness?"[96]). As a preaching text, 4:10–20 or segments of it have not had major usage in ancient pericopes and only limited use recently (*Ordo*, 4:12–14, 19–20, Year A, Pentecost 20; Revised Common Lectionary dropped everything after Phil 4:9). 4:13 is probably the v most preached on in 4:10–20; cf. Beet 1889, "the Christian secret."

SELECT BIBLIOGRAPHY (see also General Bibliography and Commentaries)

Bahr, G. J. 1968. "The Subscriptions in the Pauline Letters," *JBL* 87:27–41.

Baldanza, G. 2006b. "La portata teologica di *osmē euōdias* in Fil 4,18," *Laurentianum* 47: 161–85.

Bassler, J. 1991. *God and Mammon: Asking for Money in the New Testament*. Nashville: Abingdon.

Baumert, N. 1969. "Ist Philipper 4,10 richtig übersetzt?" *BZ* 13 (1969) 256–62, repr. in his *Studien zu den Paulusbriefen*, SBAB 32 (Stuttgart: Katholisches Bibelwerk, 2001) 109–16.

Beet, J. A. 1889. "The Christian Secret," *Expositor*, 3rd Series, 10:174–89.

---

[95] R. Garrison, *Redemptive Almsgiving in Early Christianity*, JSNTSup 77 (Sheffield: JSOT Press, 1993).

[96] "Gift exchanges" continue to be part of "traditional/oral" class cultures in America. Cf. Thielman 1995:240–42.

Berry, K. L. 1996. "The Function of Friendship Language in Philippians 4:10–20," in Fitzgerald, J. T., 1996, ed. (General Bibliography) 107–24.

Danker, F. W. 1967–68. "Romans v.12. Sin under Law," *NTS* 14:434–39.

———. 1972. "Under Contract: A Form-Critical Study of Linguistic Adaptation in Romans," in *Festschrift to Honor F. Wilbur Gingrich*, ed. E. H. Barth/R. E. Cocroft (Leiden: Brill) 91–114.

Di Marco, A. 1977. "La 'ricchezza' in S. Paolo. Lessico e teologia paolina," *Laurentianum* 18: 70–115.

Dion, H.-M. 1966. "La notion paulinienne de 'Richesses de Dieu' et ses sources," *ScEccl* 18:139–48.

Dodd, C. H. 1953. "The Mind of Paul," repr. in his *New Testament Studies* (Manchester: Manchester Univ. Press) 67–128.

Drummond, R. J. 1899–1900. "Note on Philippians iv. 10–19," *ExpTim* 11:284, 381.

Elliott, J. H. 1987. "Patronage and Clientism in Early Christian Society: A Short Reading Guide," *Forum* 3,4 (Dec., 1987) 39–48.

Evans, K. G. 1997. "Friendship in the Greek Documentary Papyri and Inscriptions: A Survey," in Fitzgerald, J. T., 1996, ed. (Gen. Bibl.) 181–202.

Fiore, B. 1997. "The Theory and Practice of Friendship in Cicero," in J. T. Fitzgerald, 1996, ed., (Gen. Bibl.) 59–76.

Fitzgerald, J. T. 1997a. "Friendship in the Greek World Prior to Aristotle," in Fitzgerald, J. T., 1997, ed. (Gen. Bibl.) 13–34.

———. 2003. "Paul and Friendship," in Sampley, J. P., ed., 2003 (Gen. Bibl.) 319–43.

Fitzmyer, J. A. 1993. "The Consecutive Meaning of *eph'hō[i]* in Romans 5.12," *NTS* 39: 321–39.

Gamble, H. 1977. *The Textual History of the Letter to the Romans: A Study in Textual and Literary Criticism* (SD 42; Grand Rapids: Eerdmans) 94, 145–46.

Glombitza, O. 1964–65. "Der Dank des Apostels. Zum Verständnis von Philipper iv 10–20," *NovT* 7:135–41.

Hermesdorf, B. H. D. 1961. "De apostel Paulus in lopende rekening met de gemeente te Filippi. Een vraag en een veronderstelling," *TvTh* 1:252–56.

Kennedy, H. A. A. 1900–1901. "The Financial Colouring of Philippians iv. 15–18," *ExpTim* 12:43–44.

Klauck, H.-J. 1990. "Brotherly Love in Plutarch and in 4 Maccabees," in *Greeks, Romans, and Christians*, FS Malherbe (cited in Gen. Bibl., under White, L. M., 1990) 144–56.

———. 1991. "Kirche als Freundesgemeinschaft? Auf Spurensuche im Neuen Testament," *MTZ* 42:1–14.

Konstan, D. 1997. *Friendship in the Classical World*. Key Themes in Ancient History. New York: Cambridge Univ. Press. Bibliography essay 174–76.

Lambert, J. C. 1899–1900. "Note on Philippians iv .10–19," *ExpTim* 11:333–34.

Lyonnet, S. 1955. "Le sens de *eph' hō* en Rom 5,12 et l'exégèse des Pères grecs," *Bib* 36:436–56, repr. in Lyonnet's *Études sur l'épître aux Romains* (AnBib 120; Rome: Instituto Biblico, 1989) 185–202.

Malherbe, A. 1990. "Did the Thessalonians Write to Paul?" in FS J. Louis Martyn (Gen. Bibl., under Fortna, R. T.) 246–57.

———. 1996. "Paul's Self-Sufficiency (Philippians 4:11)," in J. T. Fitzgerald, 1996, ed. (Gen. Bibl.) 125–39; in slightly different form, in *Texts and Contexts: Biblical Texts in Their Textual and Situational Contexts*, FS L. Hartman, ed. T. Fornberg/ D. Hellholm (Oslo: Scandinavian Univ. Press, 1995) 813–26.

McCready, W. O. 1996. "EKKLĒSIA and Voluntary Associations," in *Voluntary Associations in the Greco-Roman World*, ed. J. S. Kloppenborg/S. G. Wilson (London/New York: Routledge) 59–73.

Mitchell, A. C. 1997. "'Greet the Friends by Name:' New Testament Evidence for the Greco-Roman *Topos* on Friendship," in J. T. Fitzgerald, 1997, ed. (Gen. Bibl.) 225–62.

Morris, L. 1956. "KAI HAPAX KAI DIS," *NovT* 1:205–208.

Mott, S. C. 1975. "The Power of Giving and Receiving: Reciprocity in Hellenistic Benevolence," in *Current Issues in Biblical and Patristic Literature*, ed. G. F. Hawthorne (Grand Rapids: Eerdmans) 60–72.

Pervo, R. L. 1997. "With Lucian: Who Needs Friends? Friendship in the *Toxaris*," in J. T. Fitzgerald, 1997, ed. (Gen. Bibl.) 163–80.

Peterman, G. 1991. "'Thankless Thanks': The Epistolary Social Convention in Philippians 4:10–20," *TynBul* 42:261–70.

Priero, G. 1961. "'Autarco'—Epistola ai Filippesi 4,11," *PaCl* 40:693–96.

———. 1962. "Didici . . . sufficiens esse *(emathon . . . autarkes einai)* Nota a Phil 4,11," *RivB* 10:59–63.

Ramsay, W. M. 1900. "On the Greek Form of the Name Philippians," *JTS* 1:115–16.

Reumann, J. 1997. "Philippians and the Culture of Friendship," *Trinity Seminary Review* 19:69–83.

Rolland, B. 1974. "Saint Paul et la pauvreté: Ph. 4:12–14, 19–20," *AsSeign* 59:10–15.

Schmeller, T. 1987. *Paulus und die "Diatribe." Eine vergleichende Stilinterpretation.* NTAbh 19. Münster: Aschendorff.

Schrage, W. 1974. "Leid, Kreuz, und Eschaton: Die Peristasenkataloge als Merkmal paulinischer theologia crucis und Eschatologie," *EvT* 34:141–95.

Schroeder, F. M. 1997. "Friendship in Aristotle and Some Peripatetic Philosophers," in J. T. Fitzgerald, 1997, ed. (Gen. Bibl.) 35–58.

Sterling, G. E. 1997. "The Bond of Humanity: Friendship in Philo of Alexandria," in J. T. Fitzgerald, 1997, ed. (Gen. Bibl.) 203–24.

Weiss, K. 1954. "Paulus—Priester der christlichen Kultgemeinde," *TLZ* 79:355–64.

White, L. M., ed. 1992. *Social Networks in the Early Christian Environment: Issues and Methods for Social History.* Semeia 56. Atlanta: Scholars Press.

LETTER CLOSING, 4:21–23

◆

17. *Epistolary Postscript (Greetings, Benediction), 4:21–23*

TRANSLATION

²¹ᵃ Extend greetings to every saint, in Christ Jesus. ᵇ The brothers and sisters who are with me greet you. ²²ᵃ All the saints greet you, ᵇ but especially those of Caesar's household. ²³ The grace of the Lord Jesus Christ be—and is—with your spirit.

NOTES

4:21. *Extend greetings. aspasasthe,* 2nd pl. aor. m. impv, *aspazomai,* **greet** ([N]RSV), *welcome* with fondness, endearment; impv. *remember me to* (BDAG p. 144, 1.a). NEB, REB, NJB: "give my greetings to"; KJV "salute" (cf. "salutation"). 3x in 4:21–22; 7 of 60 NT uses are in similar greetings (e.g., 1 Thess 5:26; Roller [(1) Bibl.], Tabelle 7; Francis/Sampley ##65, 69, and 254).

H. Windisch, *TDNT* 1:496–502: an act of greeting (Luke 1:27,29) may involve embracing, kissing, offering the hand, or prostrating oneself; "the embrace of greeting" (Acts 20:37); "with a holy kiss" (1 Thess 5:26; 1 Cor 16:20b; 2 Cor 13:12; Rom 16:16 [*not* "kiss of peace"]). Cf. Gamble 1977 ([16] Bibl.) 75–76; S. Blank, *IDB* 3:39–40, OT; M. Hunt, *ADB* 4:89–92, NT. Paul may have first seen the great significance of a greeting in writing as well as in person; epistolary, not liturgical (P. Trumer, *EDNT* 1:173; Schnider/Stenger ([1] Bibl) 122–23, following K. Traede 1968–69, esp. 153). Paul's greeting shows the document is not a private affair; it is for all (1 Thess 5:28; Phil 4:21) and strengthens personal friendship (Windisch 496). In the pre-Christian period such greetings were not common and never lengthy like the list in Rom 16 (496, reflecting Exler 111–12 and Roller 67–68, statistics on pp. 472–74 n 312). Windisch's analysis (*TDNT* 1:500–502), reflected in Mullins 1968 (see COMMENT) and O'B 552–53, lists [1] Impv., usually *aspasasthe,* asking (a) readers to greet certain persons (Rom 16) or (b) greet all community members (Phil 4:21a *panta hagion*), or (c) the whole congregation to greet one another (1 Cor 16:20, etc.); (d) sg. *aspasai.* [2] Indic., 3rd sg. or pl.

(aspazetai, aspazontai); (a) individual Christians send greetings (1 Cor 16:19, etc.), or a group with the writer (Phil 4:21b *hoi syn emoi adelphoi*); (b) particular groups greet a particular group (Phil 4:22b *hoi ek tēs Kaisaros oikias*); (c) the whole church greets those addressed (Phil 4:22a *pantes hoi hagioi*; 2 Cor 13:12); (d) "ecumenical greetings" by "all the churches" (Rom 16:16); (e) autograph greetings, "I, Paul, write this greeting with my own hand" (1 Cor 16:21). Those Paul instructs here to *extend greetings* are likely leaders (Vincent 153) in the Philippian house churches or (Caird 154) "the church meeting"; see COMMENT. Not "greet each other" (Ewald 220 = Wohl. 236–37).

to every saint. Acc. sg., *panta hagion* (BDAG 2.d.β, subst. use, *believers* consecrated to God); NOTE on 1:1 *the saints*, (1) COMMENT B.5.a. *every: pas* is frequent in Phil; see NOTES on 1:1 *all*; 1:4 *all of you*; 1:7 and 8 *you all*. Here, *panta* + sg. noun without art. = *every, each* (BDAG *pas* 1.a.α, "scarcely different" from "the pl. 'all'"). Some take it as equivalent of a pl., "all the saints" (NIV; grammatically unjustified, Fee 457 n 7). Others find a distributive sense for *panta* (see NOTE on 1:9 *in every situation*; Schnider/Stenger [(1) Bibl.] 122), "each and every saint." Thus NEB/REB, TEV, "each one of God's people." Loh. 191, "every" is a sign of commonality; "saint," of equality; Paul has no notion of highly valued "martyrs" and those not yet tested (as in Loh.'s martyrdom theory, which is generally rejected).

in Christ Jesus. See NOTES on 1:1 *Christ, Jesus*, and *in Christ Jesus*. (1) COMMENT B.5.a takes *in Christ Jesus* at 1:1 as (1) instrumental or causal (*how* they are holy) and (2) *where* they exist as holy people, namely "incorporate in Christ Jesus" (NEB), i.e., ecclesiologically. In 4:21 many link *en Christō[i] Iēsou* with *panta hagion*, "every saint in Christ Jesus" (RSV; Vincent 153, to distinguish from OT saints; Martin 1976:169; Hawth. 214; O'B 553 n 9; Gk. word order); cf. 1:1, sense (1) above. Others, with *aspasasthe*, NEB "Give my greeting, in the fellowship of Christ, to each of God's people." Thus Ewald 220 = Wohl. 237; Dib. 96, cf. 1 Cor 16:19, Rom 16:22; Lft. 167; Loh. 190; Fee 458. Not in attribut. position (as in 1:1, *tois ousin*) after *panta hagion* (but that phrase is anarthrous). Ecclesiological, (2) above, in 1:1; 4:21a means, "Greet in the Christian community each and every saint." The TRANSLATION reflects these two possible interpretations by setting off *in Christ Jesus* with a comma.

The brothers and sisters who are with me, "the with-me *adelphoi*." *syn* (BDAG 1.a.γ), in attribut. position, "together with" (W. Grundmann, *TDNT* 7:782). *adelphos* = a member of the Christian community, see NOTES on 1:12 *brothers and sisters* (voc.), 1:14. NRSV "friends," for variety in inclusive language, misleadingly undergirds the "friendship" theme and may not suggest believers are involved. With Paul in the city of his imprisonment (Ephesus); does it include groups mentioned in 1:15–16 who proclaim Christ out of differing motives? Others assume a smaller group than *all the saints* in 22a (O'B 553–54), members of his missionary team, like Timothy (1:1) (or Luke, O'B thinks, assuming Rome; similarly Hawth. 214, assuming Caesarea); I. H. Marshall 124). Still others (Schenk 71), coworkers, not imprisoned with Paul (as Loh. 191 thought) but with access to Paul (Gnilka 181)—as well as others. Schenk includes "contact persons from other congregations like Onesimus," the "Corinthian delegates," and Epaphroditus, distinct from the local congregation (in v 22a). E. E. Ellis, *Pauline Theology* (Grand Rapids: Eerdmans, 1989) 97 (cf. Stirewalt 2003:95 n 60) includes "those who brought gifts to Paul from the church at Philippi." But did others accompany Epaphroditus?

greet you. aspazontai, see NOTE above, *Extend greetings*; Windisch's sense [2](a). *you* pl., all the Philippians. As in 21a and 22a, vb. first, emphatic, "They greet you, those who are with me."

4:22. *All the saints greet you.* Vocabulary repeats from 4:21 for this second group. See NOTES on 4:21 *to every saint*; 1:1 *the saints*. = the church in Ephesus, including groups mentioned in 1:15–16 with their differing motives in preaching Christ. Loh. 191 saw a certain distance between Paul's immediate group and "all the saints" (Caesarea was not a congregation founded by Paul). *greet*, as in 21b, stands first, followed by *you* (pl.) for those in Philippi; then the subject.

but especially those of Caesar's household. A third group sends greetings (supply *aspazontai*), or, out of the total congregation, one particular segment. *malista, most of all, above all, especially, particularly* (BDAG 613); only here, Gal. 6:10, Phlm 16 in Paul's acknowledged letters. H. D. Betz (*Gal.* 311), "epistolary cliché." E. R. Richards ([1] Bibl.) 164 n 168, a "particularizing function."

those of Caesar's household. Art. *hoi* (masc. but including women) + prep. phrase in attribut. position (BDAG, *ho, hē, to* 2.e) *ek tēs Kaisaros oikias*. Edart 291 notes alliteration (*k*) and assonance (*oi*). *ek* (+ gen.; BDAG 3.b), "belonging . . . overshadows . . . origin"; BDF #437, used for *en* to denote "membership." *oikia*, "(members of) the house(hold)," refers to people (slaves or freed) in the Imperial service, "not members of the emperor's family or relationship, but servants at his court" (BDAG *oikia* 3). Identifiable in texts by addition of "Caes(aris) ser(vus)" or "Aug(usti) vern(a) [house-born slave]" and for freedmen "Aug(usti) lib(eratus)" or ". . . l(ibertus)" (Weaver 2–3, cf. 53). Oakes 2001:65–66 sees (at least some of) the *liberati* as Roman citizens; so also C. S. de Vos 1999:251–52, 257–58, 260; Witherington 23; Fee 162.

Caesar. Originally a proper name, Gaius Julius Caesar (cognomen); Luke 2:1; BDF #5(3). Later a title, "Emperor"; Luke 3:1; Acts 17:17; chs. 25–28; only here in Paul. At this time, Nero Caesar (Lat.) or *Kaisar* (Gk.) ruled (A.D. 54–68). Phil 4:22 shows no political confliction over the term. *Word studies:* J. Knox, *IDB* A–D:478; J. D. G. Dunn, *NIDNTT* 1:269–70; B. W. Jones, *ABD* 1:797–98; E. Stauffer, *Christ and the Caesars: Historical Sketches*, tr. K. and R. G. Smith (Philadelphia: Westminster, 1955) 138–41, Nero; cf. 192–204, "Paul and Akiba."

Caesar's household. Lat. *domus* or *familia Caesaris.* Some in the 19th cent. (Lft. 171) assumed "powerful minions of the court, great officers of state, or even blood relatives of the emperor" in Rome. Fee 459–60, Paul's " 'fifth column' within the very walls of the emperor's domicile" (contrast Witherington 135). Cassidy 2001:166, 202–3, through Caesar's staff Paul learned about Nero's debauchery. 4:22b was taken to include Flavius Clemens (cf. Phil 4:3) and his wife Flavia Domitilla, cousins of Emperor Domitian (ruled A.D. 81–96), she a granddaughter of Vespasian; he was executed and she banished for "atheism" (possibly conversion to Judaism or Christianity) (cf. Suet. *Dom.* 15; Dio Cass. 67.14; Eus. *H.E.* 3.18.4). This claim led some to charge anachronism; assault followed on the genuineness of Phil (by F. C. Baur and others). See B. Weiss 354 and Mengel 121–24. In response, Lft. wrote on "Caesar's Household" (*Phil.* 171–78, cf. 22 and 170): *domus Caesaris* included innumerable slaves and freed persons, as well as courtiers, in Italy and the provinces. Lft. 172 listed Lat. titles of household members.

Subsequent research affirmed that the "extended family of the Roman emperor" included *servi* and *liberati* (slaves and freed), like the *familia* of any Roman clan. Members did all sorts of managerial and servile tasks on the Emperor's estates and in government administration (list in Weaver 3). From this "family" the Roman civil service developed. Notions of their upward mobility (Meeks 1983:63; citing Weaver, perhaps esp. true for women, 170) and prosperity are sometimes overdone (Meggitt 126–27; n 255). That "those of Caesar's household" were couriers for Paul's letters (S. R. Llewelyn, "Sending Letters in the Ancient World: Paul and the Philippians," *TynBull* 46 [1955] 337–56) is very uncertain. *Word studies:* O. Michel, *TDNT* 5:133, esp. n 12; D. J. Kyrtatas 1987 ([1] Bibl. **slaves**), "Christianity and the Familia Caesaris"; J. F. Hull, "Caesar's Household," *ABD* 1:798; A. Weiser, "*Kaisar*," *EDNT* 2:236 (4:22 probably "slaves and freedmen in Ephesus"); P. Weigandt, *EDNT* 2:495; Tellbe 2001: 244–45.

Hawth. 215 (Paul writes from Rome) mentions "soldiers stationed in the barracks"; applicable also to Caesarea or Ephesus. But was the army part of the *familia Caesaris*? Deissmann, "simple Imperial slaves, petty clerks, employed perhaps at Ephesus in the departments of finance or of crown lands" (*LAE* 160, 238 n 3). Gnilka 182, reassurance to the Philippians that their apostle had support in Ephesus from Christians in contact with him (ditto Schnider/Stenger [(1) Bibl.] 127); a "link . . . between the Christian members of the imperial staff on government service at the place of Paul's imprisonment and the citizens of Philippi" (Martin, 1976:170; O'B 554; Bockmuehl 270). I. H. Marshall 125 conjectures "a Philippi prayer-meeting" group gathered "in some government office." Ellis 1989 (cited above in Note on 21b) 139–43, a house church.

4:23. *The grace of the Lord Jesus Christ be—and is—with your spirit.* Closing benediction as in each acknowledged letter of Paul (*The grace of the* [or *our*] *Lord Jesus* [*Christ*]) + 2 Thess, Col, Eph, the Pastorals, Heb, and even Rev; Comment A.2, below; Gamble 1977 ([16] Bibl.) 66; Schrenk 71. No vb. in Paul's seven letters. *with your spirit*, only here and Phlm 25, instead of "with you (all)." See Notes on 1:2 *grace* and *Lord Jesus Christ* (here, gen. of origin, BDF #162), a development of Jewish Christian tradition in the Hellenistic Gentile-Christian church (Kramer [(1) Bibl. **Christ**] #66c). Paul inherited the term and used *grace* regularly at the opening and conclusion of his letters (BDAG, *charis* 2.c). In salutations, it is "from God our Father and the Lord Jesus Christ"; in the final blessing, "the grace of the Lord Jesus (Christ)." See Comment B. 4 for explanations on this shift. *Lord* (BDAG *kyrios* 2.b.γ.ℵ) is a title; *Jesus*, a personal name; *Christ*, more likely title than name. Juxtaposition with *Caesar* in v 22 suggests *Kyrios Iēsous Christos* as title, cognomen, and supernomen. SB 8:9668 (PFouad 21, A.D. 63) has *hē charis tou kyriou* of Nero (J. R. Harrison 2003 [(1) Bibl. **grace**] 88).

As vb., supply (see [1] COMMENT B.6) either indic., "is" (*estin*), "will be" (*estai*, 4:9b), or an opt. of wish (*eiē*). Most insert the latter, ". . . be with your spirit" (cf. KJV, [N]RSV). But is it a "pious wish" or a "declarative [indic.] statement"? Some, esp. in discussions of liturgy, argue for the latter, "The grace of the Lord Jesus (Christ) *is* with you . . ."; so van Unnik 1959 ([1] n 40) 292, 290–91 on Phil 4:9; C. F. D. Moule, *Worship in the New Testament* (London: 1961), repr. as *Worship in the New Testament Church*, Ecumenical Studies in Worship 9 (Richmond: John Knox, 1962) 78–79; G. Delling 1962a ([2] Bibl. **prayer**) 75. Gamble 1977 ([16] Bibl.) 66–67 dismissed van Unnik's appeal to "the certitude of Paul's faith" as evidence for the indic., and Delling's paralleling of 1 Cor 16:24a ("the grace of the Lord Jesus [is] with you") with 16:24b ("my love [is] with you in Christ Jesus"). According to Gamble, Paul's "grace-benediction is neither wish nor statement; it is a blessing, and as such it incorporates aspects of both," a wish "qualified by confidence of its effectiveness" (66–67). Cf. the closing formula in a papyrus letter, a wish, usually *errōso* ("fare well"); the greeting he takes as a blessing, not a declaration (opt. in 1 Pet 1:2; 2 Pet 1:2; Jude 2; and Dan 4:1 LXX; to be understood in Paul). The TRANSLATION offers both possibilities.

with your spirit. meta + *tou pneumatos*, gen. sg., + "of you" (*hymōn*) gen. pl. Instead of *your spirit* (distributive sg., Fee 456 n 1), "with you all" (*meta pantōn hymōn*) occurs in some 536 MSS (‭ℵ‬ᶜ K L Ψ; most minuscules; list in Aland 1991:597–98). But 53 MSS that read "with your spirit" provide "distinctly superior attestation" (*TCGNT* 617, P⁴⁶ ℵ A B etc.). Other letters sometimes have "with your spirit" (Gal 6:18, Phlm 25, cf. 2 Tim 4:22); sometimes "with you all" (1 Cor 16:24, 2 Cor 13:13, etc.). See COMMENT A.2, below. Metzger deems *pantōn* "scribal substitution of a more familiar termination for a benediction" (*TCGNT* 617, but cf. Silva 242). Most modern trs. ([N]RSV, NEB/REB) have "with your spirit," without noting the variant. So also commentators (Hawth. 212, 216, "with your spirit" means "with you each one").

with. Association, accompaniment (BDAG *meta* A.2.a.γ.ɔ). Common at close of Pauline letters; also Phil 4:9. *hymōn* pl., all Philippians (v 22 *you all*), each and every one is to be greeted (v 21).

spirit. Not the Holy Spirit but "a part of the human personality." BDAG *pneuma* 3.b, "the Christian possesses the (divine) *pneuma*"; *pneuma* characterizes "a believer's inner being." Cf. NOTES on 1:27 *in one and the same Spirit*; 1:19; 2:1; and 3:3 re God's Spirit; Jewett 1971a:167–75. E. Fuchs, *Christus und der Geist bei Paulus: Eine biblisch-theologische Untersuchung* (Leipzig: Hinrichs, 1932), "the Christian 'I,'" determined by God's Spirit. Bultmann 1951 (INTRO. X Bibl.) 205–209, the "willing and knowing self," an "orientation of the will," led by the divine Spirit. E. Schweizer (*TDNT* 6:389–451, esp. 434–37), interrelatedness of the divine Spirit and anthropological *pneuma* reflects uncritical adoption of Jewish use; "the new I" of believers, which, however, perishes if they cease to be Christian (435). Cf. Jewett, "the divine spirit apportioned to the individual Christian" (182), derived from enthusiasts in Thessalonica, but employed in Paul's "homiletic benediction"; 451–53, summary. Against Jewett's claim (1971a:184) that "the tradition which shaped this formula did not distinguish between the divine spirit and the spirit which a man could possess," contrast Fee 461 n 23. U. Schnelle, the Spirit received through baptism (*Neutestamentliche Anthropologie: Jesus—Paulus—Johannes,* Biblische-Theologische Studien 18 [Neukirchen-Vluyn: Neukirchener, 1991] #3.4, esp. pp. 55–57). But W. G. Kümmel, *Römer 7 und die Bekehrung des Paulus* (Leipzig: Hinrichs, 1929), repr. in *Römer 7 und das Bild des Menschen im Neuen Testament,* TB 53 (Munich: Kaiser, 1974) 33: more likely "the inner person" than a specifically Christian sense. J. D. G. Dunn, "that dimension of the human person by means of which the person relates most directly to God" (*TPTA* 76–77, *NIDNTT* 3:693). Walter 101, "the whole person . . . after his 'spiritual' side"; I. H. Marshall 125, "grace operating in our spiritual nature." Many different senses!

At 4:23, *your spirit* is not "the inner nature of man" in contrast to "the regenerate nature of those who are in Christ" (Michael 230), nor "one spirit" that animates the Philippians (Beare 158, "team spirit"); nor a hope that the Spirit or Christ may grace them (cf. Burton *Gal.* 362, on 6:18). It is (Jewett 183–84) "traditional," possibly liturgical, from the Hellenistic church. Each Christian's through baptism, God's *pneuma* thus apportioned to one and all (1 Cor 12:13). Unity is stressed through *spirit* in the sg., individuation through *your* (pl.).

Amen. See NOTE on 4:20 *amen.* KJV, NKJV, NRSV-mg; P⁴⁶א A, most minuscules; J. D. Price 284–85: a very high a degree of probability. But enough MSS lack *amēn* that *UBSGNT* assigns its omission a {B} level of certainty; if original, its absence in so many early MSS is difficult to explain; copyists likely added it as reflection of familiar liturgical usage (*TCGNT* 617). Ewald, doubtful but appropriate for the Philippians to add (220 = Wohl. 237). Yet Hawth. 212, 216 calls it "strongly attested," "either Paul's own response to the benediction . . . or the affirmative response of the congregation to the divine promise on which the hoped-for blessing rests." Cf. O'B 555; Bockmuehl 271. Lft. 167 and others, in brackets or a note. Does a *letter* include a congregation's response or what a liturgical officiant and congregation might in later times say together? Recent commentators generally omit it on textual grounds (e.g, Silva; Fee; Güting).

COMMENT

Paul's "conclusion structure"—greetings 4:21–22 and a benediction 4:23—was common in NT letters, fixed in Paul's practice by the time he wrote Phil. The greetings expand the farewell wish in some pre-Christian letters. The benediction might stem from liturgical usage in the Hellenistic church. Some MSS add "amen" as response to v 23. Vv 21–23 reflect Paul's situation and the warmth of his relations with the Philippians (cf. *DA* 395). Some claim he wrote these 34 Gk. words with his own hand (Gamble 1977 [(16) Bibl.] 94, 145–46 includes 4:10–20; so O'B 552; cf. [16] COMMENT A.1 n 9 and n 83, and below, n 10), but this is unprovable.

A. FORMS, SOURCES, AND TRADITIONS

Letters of introduction, recommendation, or petition (cf. Kim [(1) Bibl.]) might close with a "good-bye" (*errōso* or pl. *errōsthe*, as in Acts 15:29) and the date (Roller 69 [(1) Bibl.]; J. L. White 1986:194) or simply "fare well" (*eutychei*) (White 195; examples in Stowers 1986:61–63; Stirewalt 2003:49), shifting to the sender's own hand as a sign of authenticity (Schnider/Stenger [(1) Bibl.] 131, 135–67; J. L. White 1984:1740–41; royal letters, Stirewalt 2003:49; n 10, below). Parae-netic letters used "fare well" (Stowers 1986:98–103, 110–12, 129–31; even letters of rebuke, 135–36; or comfort, 146). Family letters often greeted family and friends by name (Stowers 22; White 1986:196; Stowers 1986:72–76), at times with *aspa-zomai* (Phil 4:21–22).[1] A wish for the recipients' health might come at the letter's close: "you would favor me by taking care of your body [or yourself] to stay well" (J. L. White 1986:200–201; #28.37–39; 34.31–32; 55.19–22, pl.). Later (about A.D. 50–200) a prayer form took over, "I pray [or wish] that you are well" (White 202, examples in n 59).[2] Conclusions should reflect degrees of friendship between writer and recipient (Julius Victor, 4th cent. A.D., *Ars Rhetorica*, 27 [Malherbe 1977:61 = 1988:65.8–9]). Terms for such a section in a Pauline letter vary.[3] Se-mitic letter forms seem no direct influence; cf. ([1] Bibl.) Taatz; Fitzmyer 1974:217. Rhetoric is not an influence on the "epistolary postscript" (D. F. Wat-son 1988b; F. W. Hughes 66; Bittasi 175–76). Consensus on terms is lacking, but agreement that, after the doxology (4:20), greetings and a benediction follow. No greetings by name, no statement that Paul writes in his own hand (as in 1 Cor 16:21).

1. Greeting (aspasmos) Form. *TDNT* 1:500–2; see NOTE on 4:21 *Extend greet-ings*. Mullins 1968 provided papyrus examples, the form outlined thus:

		greeting vb.	person(s) greeted	person(s) greeting them	
anaphora	⎧	21a *aspasasthe* impv.	*panta hagion*	(Paul via some in Philippi)	
(Edart	⎨	21b *aspazontai* indic.	*hymas*	*hoi syn emoi adelphoi*	⎫ homoi-
291, 293)	⎩	22 *aspazontai* indic.	*hymas*	*pantes hoi hagioi*	⎭ teleuton

---

[1] E.g., "Greet Thermion" (White 1986: #85, line 16 = PLond III 893, A.D. 40), or "Thermouthas sends you very many greetings" (ibid. #100.15–16 = PMich III.201, A.D. 99). DA 284–85; Murphy-O'Connor 1995a ([1] Bibl.) 98–99. WDNTECLR 167 dates the shift to the "greeting formula" to the "1st cent. B.C.E."; 269–70, closing formulas.

[2] Closing wishes are distinguished from formulas that conclude the letter body (*ta de loipa*, White 204–7, esp. 207; cf. Phil 3:1 *to loipon*).

[3] Murphy-O'Connor 1995a ([1] Bibl.), "conclusion"; Doty, Vielhauer 1975:346, "closing," with a "health wish" and farewell, often preceded by a greeting, + a benediction form (Doty 27, 39–43), in-cluding "doxology." Boers 1975–76:140, doxology, greeting, and benediction. J. L. White 1984:1740, the doxology was not a standard part; contrast his earlier "letter pattern" (1972:71, 112). So also J. L. White 1986. "Eschatokoll" was employed by Roller ([1] Bibl. 68–71, 191–93); EKK *Phlm.* 51; Schnider/Stenger ([1] Bibl.) 75.

Cf. *DA* 284–285. 2nd per. type in 21a ("Extend-ye greetings to every saint"), 3rd per. in 21b, 22 (the *adelphoi*/all the saints/those of Caesar's household greet you). Mullins called *those of Caesar's household* an "identification phrase," like "I, Alexander your father" (POxy 7.1067). But that equates *those of Caesar's household* with *all the saints* and misses the force of *especially*.

Schnider/Stenger ([1] Bibl.) 108 distinguish (1) a "charge" *(Auftrag)* to those addressed to greet others (4:21a); (2) "communication" *(Ausrichtung)* of greetings through the writer to addressees (4:21b,22); (3) the writer greets the addressees. 4:23 = Paul's benediction. Thus charge and communication plus "benediction." Normally after closing paraenesis (Phil, 2:12–18; 3:1; 4:1–3, 4–7, 8, 9), possibly after an "apostolic parousia" (2:19–30; chart on p. 75, cf. p. 112).

In Phil the greetings-charge precedes communication of greetings, as in 2 Cor, Rom, 2 Tim, and Heb. Injunction to extend greetings bridges the sender's absence until presence *(parousia)* is possible (p. 120). Greetings are for every Philippian, but none is named by name. Nor are individuals with him identified. Gnilka 181 relates this to 2:21 (all except Timothy "seek their own interests, not those of Jesus Christ"); to call them "brothers and sisters" at 4:21b is conciliatory. Reference to those of *Caesar's household* (colleagues of some in Philippi) is meant to be reassuring (Gnilka 182; Schnider/Stenger [(1) Bibl.] 127). The Christological closing (23) is found also in 1 Thess 5:28; Phlm 25; and Rom 16:20b. No summary of what Paul has earlier written (as in Gal 6:11–19 and 1 Cor 16:21–24).

2. Benediction Form. L. G. Champion ([1] Bibl.; not in *WDNTECLR*) distinguished the *benediction form* (4:23) in Paul's letters from the salutation wish (Phil 1:2, *Grace to you and peace from God our Father and Lord Jesus Christ*). Ten examples occur at the end of letters (supply "be" or "is"; "you" is always pl.)[4]; similar formulas elsewhere[5] usually involve God as subject, see NOTES and COMMENT on Phil 4:7 and 9.

Champion detected (pp. 19–24) (1) certain *characteristics* in benedictions: (a) God or Christ, with attributes or activities ascribed through a ptc. (Phil 4:7 God's peace "surpassing all understanding"); (b) a closely connected gen. (4:9 God of peace); (c) full titles ("God our Father and Lord Jesus Christ" Phil 1:2; "our God and Father" 4:20, doxology); (d) the opt. mood (Rom 15:5,33; 1 Thess 3:11,12; 5:23, etc.) or fut. indic. (Phil 4:7,19). (2) *Vocabulary* often stands out ("the God of peace" Phil 4:9; "glory for ever and ever" Phil 4:20). From "a general religious vocabulary" Paul inherited (p. 23) but might alter; "well known" to hearers, but not yet fixed. *Origins* (Champion 45–90): with Dibelius, from public worship (pp. 13, 16–17, 25–34). When read at gatherings of Christians, "a substitute for" Paul's "presence and voice"; perhaps only for a "narrower circle which met for the Lord's Supper." But 4:21–23 could have been heard by all (W. Bauer 1930 ([1] Bibl. **overseer**) 1930:62–63 = 1967:208). Champion's liturgical *Sitz im Leben*

---

[4] 1 Thess 5:28; 2 Thess 3:18; Rom 16:20; Gal 6:18; Phil 4:23; Phlm 25; Col 4:18; 1 Cor 16:23–24; 2 Cor 13:13 [14]); Eph 6:24.

[5] Rom 15:33; 2 Cor 13:11; Phil 4:9; 2 Thess 3:16; Rom 15:13; Phil 4:7.

(cf. Loh. 1927c [(1) Bibl.]) was accepted widely. Cf. Loh. 191; Gnilka 182–83; Martin 1976:170; O'B 554–55; in studies on worship, G. Delling 1962a ([2] Bibl.) 75; by form critics (Vielhauer 1975:67, a blessing, leading into the eucharistic service).[6] Somewhat differently, G. J. Cuming: 4:23: the conclusion (prayers, kiss, the "grace") of nonsacramental worship.

Attack on liturgical origins for benedictions and similar material came in W. Schenk 1967 ([2] Bibl.), without discussing 4:23. C. Westermann, *Blessing in the Bible and the Life of the Church*, OBT (Philadelphia: Fortress, 1978) 68–101, was cautious (96–98) in light of Schenk's conclusion (92) that "the greetings at the beginning and end of NT letters are not specifically early Christian liturgical blessing-formulas, but are concrete intercessions with Christian content, in epistolary form." Cf. G. Friedrich 1956 ([1] Bibl.), critical of Lohmeyer 1927c on "worship-origins"; K. Berger 1984a:144, 313. Schnider/Stenger ([1] Bibl.) 132–34, not liturgical but epistolary, a modified form of the closing greeting in ancient letters, connecting writer and addressees in a wish for the latter's well-being, perhaps + something in the writer's own hand. In Gk. letters, behind *eutychei* (lit., "farewell") lurked a religious note (*Tychē*, "Forture"). Hence DA 286, 289: not a "benediction" from liturgy (cf. Weima 84–87), but a *"closing grace wish"* of epistolary nature. "Benediction" is fixed in much usage, but it can well be placed in quotation marks.

What did Paul add, in developing the blessing-wish? Schnider/Stenger 133 suggest influence from blessing-wishes at the conclusion of paraenesis in Judaism.[7] Possibly "Paul creates his own epistolary closing expression" from Gk. use of "the verb *rhōnnymi* to end a letter" (DA 286; BDAG 908–9, **be in good health, farewell,** Acts 15:29). The Philippians "would have noticed the contrast between Paul's grace wish and the typical words for physical well-being" (287). 4:23 is specifically christological. Formulas in Pauline paraenetic sections (Phil 4:7, 9 etc., n 3 above) have God as subject. Thus Paul employs both OT-like formulations and christological examples. In 4:23, "grace" and "Christ" may be taken together (Schenk); see B.4, below.

---

[6] Further, G. Bornkamm, 169–79, "The Anathema in the Early Christian Lord's Supper Liturgy, " in his *Early Christian Experience* (New York: Harper & Row, 1969); J. A. T. Robinson, "The Earliest Christian Liturgical Sequence?" *JTS* NS 4 (1953) 38–41, repr. in Robinson's *Twelve New Testament Studies*, SBT 34 (London: SCM, 1962) 154–57; W. Kramer ([1] Bibl. **Christ**) #20, pp. 90–93; and U. B. Muller 1975:201–2.

[7] E.g., 2 Macc 2:16–18, lit., "You will therefore do well to keep the days [of the feast of Tabernacles]." But even if *kalōs oun poiēsete* is an epistolary formula, is this very convincing as a blessing-wish? The claim that it is involves the hope that God "will soon have mercy on us and will gather us from everywhere under heaven into his holy place" now that Judas Maccabeus has rescued and purified the temple. On this forged letter, see J. A. Goldstein, AB 41A: 157–67, 187–88, who dates it to 103–102 B.C.E.

B. MEANING AND INTERPRETATION

1. With Which Letter to Philippi Does the Epistolary Postscript in 4:21–23 Go?
The majority of—but not all—interpreters who opt for two or three letters relate
4:21–23 with the long letter (Phil 1–2; 3:1, parts of ch. 4), that is, the first of two
letters sent by Paul, or the second of three.[8] But J. L. White 1972, 1974[9] and
Schenk 68–75 relate 4:21–23 to 4:10–20 (Letter A in a three-letter sequence). Occasionally 4:21–23 is connected with 3:2–21 (cf. Schnider/Stenger [(1) Bibl.])
Arguments are rather delicately balanced. Space limits here preclude presentation. We conclude from our analysis that 4:21–23 likely goes with *Letter B*, but
something similar would have closed out each letter to Philippi. So, e.g., Houlden
115.

2. A Charge from Paul to Extend Greetings to Every Philippian Christian
(4:21a). Paul begins the letter closing—for Letter B (see 1, above), but something
similar stood in Letters A and C; also appropriate for the entire document—with
a request that certain locals (leaders) greet all the believers in the house churches
for him *in Jesus Christ*. This follows the general structure of "philophronesis"
(*DA* 284; Weima 39) in personal letters of the day; in Paul's earliest extant letter,
"Greet all the brothers and sisters with a holy kiss" (1 Thess 5:26; 1 Cor 16:20b,
perhaps in Letter A to Philippi). It was natural for the apostle (imprisoned, Phil
1:13–14) to speak thus with his beloved Philippians; an implied embrace bridges
forced absence by a sense of presence that apostolic letters sought constantly to
convey. *you* (21b,22,23; individualized, to *every saint*) and "I" (21b *me*), the apostle who writes (perhaps in his own hand),[10] are placed under the rubric *in Christ*.
    Why no "holy kiss" as in 1 Thess, 1 Cor, 2 Cor 13:12, Rom 16:16? The kiss is
more literary than liturgical (see NOTE on 4:21; Traede 1968–69), not leading into
a service of word or sacrament,[11] but intensifying the greeting. Warmth may readily be assumed for Paul with the Philippians, his "joy and crown" (4:1). But

---

[8] So (for two letters) Michael, Friedrich, Gnilka, Doty; for three letters, usually after 4:4–7, Collange;
G. Barth; R. Pesch (each letter, A and C, like B, would have had concluding greetings); Byrne *NJBC*.
Fitzmyer *JBC* (after 4:4–9). *DA* 146 charts various views on the assignment of 4:21–23 under partition
theories and a redactor (283).

[9] On the basis of a "pattern" from Heb 13 in F. V. Filson,"Yesterday": *A Study of Hebrews in Light of
Chapter 13*, SBT 2/4 (London: SCM 1967) 22–24, noted by Houlden 115–20 and Hawth. 213 but
used to prevent 4:21–23 from being assigned to a letter frg. within Phil. Cf. H. W. Attridge, *Hebrews*
405; C. E. B. Cranfield, "Hebrews 13:20–21," *SJT* 20 (1967) 437–41, and Jewett 1969 ([1] Bibl.) But
see now Schnider/Stenger ([1] Bibl.) 75 for connecting 4:21–23 with *4:20 and 4:10–19* or with one
unified letter (so Houlden and Hawth.).

[10] All proposals about Paul's "penning a personal closing in his own hand" in Phil—whether 4:21–23,
4:10–20, 4:10–23 (Gamble [(16) Bibl.] 1977; Murphy-O'Connor 1995a:113), 4:9b–23 (Weima 191–
94), or 3:1–4:23 (Bahr)—are "quite speculative" since Paul makes no reference here to "his own hand"
(*DA* 283 n 474).

[11] See n 6 above. H.-J. Klauck 1982:346–62, Probst ([1] Bibl.) 353–56, and Murphy-O'Connor
1995:108, among others, conclude against Bornkamm's liturgical sequence of holy kiss, anathema,
and promise of grace.

"friendship letters" provide no reason to expect a kiss. The "exchange of kisses" is appropriate "where there are tensions within a church" (Murphy-O'Connor 1995a [(1) Bibl.] 108. Intermediates who pass on Paul's greeting could, if they wish, add a holy kiss to their embrace as circumstances suggest, some whom Paul knows personally, others "new members" who have joined the community since he was last there.

One should not make too much of the fact that no Philippians are singled out by name here (cf. Collange; Martin 1976). Rom 16 is exceptional. 1 Thess names no individuals at 5:26–28, nor do 1 Cor 16:19–24, 2 Cor 13:12–13, Gal 6, or Phlm 23–25. Paul has (earlier in Letter B) mentioned Euodia, Syntyche, and Clement and addressed a *faithful partner* (Syzygus, NRSV-mg), 4:2–3. 4:21–22 shows even-handedness, not lack of affection. Each is to be warmly embraced. Possibly deliberate strategy to counter any divisiveness within or between house churches. If Euodia and Syntyche, as house-church leaders, were at odds (see NOTE and COMMENT on 4:2–3) and if in Letter B appeal to them was followed by 4:8–9 (continue to do what the Philippians learned, received, and heard from Paul and saw in him and then a statement about *the God of peace*), the greeting he now sends to *every saint* would speak profoundly to any fractures in the community. Letter B thus addresses any dissension with emphasis on commonality and equality. The four-ch. letter shows an even broader, more positive sense of "all" and "every" in the Philippian church.

Not "greet *one another*," as in 1 Cor 16:20, etc. Instead "responsible leaders" (Beare 157) are to *extend* (my) *greetings to every saint*. Possibly all at a "church meeting" asked to greet each other for Paul (references in NOTE on *Extend greetings*). Not "each to one another" but "Paul to everyone." Most likely the leaders mentioned at 1:1 (assigned to Letter B, above), the *overseers* and *agents*, are to carry out this task (Hawth. 213–14, contrast Martin 1976; O'B 552, "probably"; Witherington 134, contrast Fee 457 n 6; Gnilka 181, contrast Murphy-O'Connor 1995a:105). Are Euodia and Syntyche (as *episkopoi*?) to embrace each other and believers in other house churches? Cf. Bockmuehl 268. Effective strategy, when one does not know precisely where the fault lines lie! Abetting a comrade's task (Syzygus) to help these women to reconcile?

in Christ Jesus can be taken with *every saint* or the vb. *Extend greetings* (i.e., in a Christian way). See NOTE. Neither interpretation should be closed off. One is a saint "in (and by) Christ Jesus." Greetings are extended "in (and by) Christ." The greeting, involving grace and peace from God, is a communal expression: here is "church." Cf. W. Grundmann, *TDNT* 1:105–108, 9:552; from a cultural anthropology perspective, B. Malina 1981:143–52. The TRANSLATION sets off the words with a comma, to suggest the overarching emphasis on *in Christ Jesus*. It brings together recipients, apostolic commission to greet them on Paul's behalf, and the churchly sphere for this warm embrace that reminds them of Paul's fervent wish to be there himself.

3. Greetings Communicated by Those with Paul (4:21b–22). Paul's greetings (4:21a) are expanded by Christians in Ephesus. "(They) *greet*" begins the cls. in

21b and 22a and is implied in 22b. The dir. obj. is the same each time, *you* (pl., 21b, 22a, implied in 22b), all the members of the Philippian house churches. Three groups greet them: *the brothers and sisters who are with me; all the saints;* and *those of Caesar's household.* Schenk 68 sees an A-B-B′-A′ structure in 4:21–23 that suggests this chiasmus:

A Extend greetings to every saint in   B The brothers and sisters . . . with
    Christ Jesus   me greet you
B′ All the saints greet you, but especially   A′ The grace of the Lord Jesus Christ,
    those of Caesar's household   with your spirit

On *Christ* (A) and *grace* (A′), see below, under 4, below. B/B′ implies that *all the saints* (22a, B′) refers to the local congregation(s) (in Ephesus), including a group within it (*those of Caesar's household,* 22b), while those with Paul (B) denote his coworkers (Schenk 70–71). Thus (1) Paul's colleagues (21b), (2) the local congregation (22a), and (3) a group within it that is particularly anxious to send greetings or important for the Philippians to hear of and from. Michael 229, "the Philippians would understand" who is involved, even if we must guess.

(1) *The brothers and sisters who are with me* (21b) in Ephesus do not then include the local house churches there (22a will refer to them) or reflect all the tensions of 1:14–17; 1:27–28; 2:1–4; or 4:2–3. These *adelphoi* were not in jail with Paul, but were free to go about daily work and mission tasks. Exactly who these coworkers or helpers were depends on where one locates Paul's imprisonment. For *Rome,* one can produce the fullest list, ten names (Lft. 167, cf. 10–12). Some limit the total much more (Bockmuehl 269, the names are "very few in number").[12] For *Ephesus,* C. R. Bowen (INTRO. VII.A) attempted to fit all ten persons mentioned for Rome into the Ephesian period (pp. 119, 124–32), but that is unlikely. Proponents of Ephesus usually limit the number of persons involved. Michael 229: Prisca and Aquila, Timothy and Apollos. Michaelis 74 thought Epaphroditus would name them in his oral report to the Philippians. Gnilka 181, "closer coworkers." Schenk 71, coworkers on Paul's staff plus people sent from other congregations to Paul, like Epaphroditus; Onesimus, on behalf of Philemon, representatives from Corinth going back and forth to Ephesus (see INTRO. VIII, Chart 2). Thus a circle of coworkers, intimates, and congregational representatives in Ephesus, "*adelphoi* with me."[13]

What then of 2:20–21? *No one do I have available* [with me? overall?] *of like "soul" who will genuinely care for what affects you. For they all seek after their own interests, not those of Jesus Christ.* Imperfect Christians existed on Paul's mission team as well as in his house churches. 2:20–21 could be hyperbole to exalt Timothy (see NOTES and COMMENT there). Alford 195, "colleagues in the ministry"

---

[12] For *Caesarea* the list is more limited. Cf. Hawth. 214; Loh. 191, those (unenumerated) colleagues imprisoned with Paul there. For *Corinth* more names (and different ones) are possible than for Caesarea.

[13] Is the addition of *sisters* justified here in an Eng. rendering? Yes, if local house churches were involved. But if, as we have concluded, lists of mission workers are meant, the case is more problematical. We can leave the possibility open, based on general use of the term *adelphoi* by Paul, inclusively.

might lack the quality of being *isopsychon* (KJV "likeminded") but still be *adelphoi*; i.e., without Timothy's dedication of mind or soul. Gnilka saw a conciliatory note in use of *adelphoi* here after 2:21. Hendriksen 211 applies 2:21 to people who disappoint Paul (Demas, 2 Tim 4:10), those who did not want to go to Philippi for Paul (as Timothy will, Phil 2:19–24), and gospel-workers without proper motives (1:15–17; pp. 135–36). We conclude, with Gnilka, that a routine greeting may mask tensions within the circle of apostolic assistants and friends; Paul is gracious in not naming names at 2:20–21 or 4:21.

(2) *All the saints* in 22a refers to the local congregation(s) where Paul is, a larger, broader group than in 21, less fully and "professionally" involved in mission than the first group. Ephesus was a Pauline center (Acts 18–20; 1 Cor 16:8, cf. 15:32; 1 Tim 1:3, 2 Tim 1:18; 4:12), but also a place for other types of Christianity, Jewish, Johannine, and John-the-Baptist "fringe Christians" (J. Fitzmyer, AB31:642; cf. [3] COMMENT n 25). We may picture Jewish-Christian and Gentile house churches, some gathered by Paul and his mission team over a twenty-four to twenty-seven months' stay, A.D. 53–55, toward the end of which Letter B was written. Those in v 22a form the largest group, but the entity in 21b–22 about which we may know the least.[14] Phil 1:13–18 (see COMMENTS there) suggests, from "the Praetorium," people in the governor's palace and perhaps the Imperial Guard, and two differenly motivated groups of preachers in Ephesus.

(3) The final group is a particular segment of the community in Ephesus, *those of Caesar's household* (4:22b). Possibly a house church made up from the *familia Caesaris*, slaves and/or those who have gained freedom in the Emperor Nero's lower-level civil-service bureaucracy. The gospel likely penetrated such social structures even before the current crisis when the Imperial Guard was coming to know about Paul's imprisonment for Christ (1:13). Not (see NOTE on 4:22 *those of Caesar's household*) high-level courtiers in Rome; members of the *domus Caesaris* could be in provincial cities like Ephesus, working at all sorts of tasks and trades, slaves and former slaves.[15] Not soldiers in the Imperial Guard (so Hawth.; cf. Michaelis 75).[16] Rightly, Walter 101: "Imperial administrative officials (of the Prov-

---

[14] Walter 101, noting the doubling of subjects with the vb. *aspazontai* (21b *the brothers and sisters*, 22a *All the saints*) asks, Is it likely that "the holy ones" would not be *adelphoi*, or vice versa, the *adelphoi* not *saints*? Thus a redactoral combination of greetings from two different letters. But which letter each went with is impossible to tell.

[15] Weaver, with Lft.: a "new 'estate' or status group," an *ordo liberatorum et servorum principis* (5), "in the hierarchy of Roman Imperial society," staff in personal service to the Emperor in Rome (6) and administrative staff "in a wide variety of departments" throughout the Empire, including Ephesus (7, cf. 9); "receipt and payment of funds under the emperor's control" and "public services such as aqueducts, libraries, the post, roads, public works and buildings, and Imperial enterprises such as mines, marble quaries, and the mint" (7). Functions, grades, and occupations are listed on pp. 7, 8, 227–81. As reigns of Emperors grew shorter, freedmen had a growing "sense of belonging . . . to an increasingly institutionalised Familia Caesaris," including "'Imperial' freedmen" (45). *familia Caesaris* in a "general collective sense" is admittedly a term not found in the ancient sources (299–300).

[16] The best military connection for the *familia* involves (Weaver 83) the *corporis custodes*, the Emperor's personal bodyguard in the Julio-Claudian period, recruited from Germanic tribes, organized as

ince of Ephesus)." Beare 158, some may have been Macedonians or Thracians, perhaps even from Philippi.

The *oikia Kaisaros*, now householders of the God revealed in Christ, may be lifted up in 22b so that (1) the Philippians know Paul has contacts with, and good friends among, converted servants of Caesar. A reassuring "glimpse into the cell of the prisoner" (Gnilka 182). (2) Those of Caesar's family were "especially interested in the Christians at Philippi" since they might "know many of the believers in the Roman city of Philippi" (Hawth. 216; this argument works best for Ephesus because of geographical proximity and inscriptional evidence, Fee 459 n 13). Links involved *Romanitas* ("Roman-ness"), imperial employment, and social networking.[17]

Slaves and freedmen and freedwomen of Caesar could have formed a club or association *before* becoming Christian (Michaelis 75). Deissmann, *LAE* 441, "common membership" in the *Kaisaros oikia* provided "a principle for forming a congregation" (house church), in contrast to "freedmen of various private owners at random" coming together and forming a religious group.[18] Background in Caesar's family and government service, as well as conversion to Christianity, gave the group in Ephesus an identity and possible link to Philippian Christians.

4. Paul's Closing "Benediction" (4:23). *The grace of the Lord Jesus Christ be—and is*[19]—*with your spirit* follows Paul's usual style and agrees verbatim with Phlm 25 (other references in n 4). It lifts up "Christ alone" (only 2 Cor 13:13 is triadic) but (with Phlm) has *with your* (pl.) *spirit* (sg.) instead of "with you" (equivalent in meaning, J. Kremer, *EDNT* 3:282). A.2, above, concluded that such final "benedictions" are not of liturgical origin (contra Champion and others) but reflect epistolary usage (Schenk, Berger, Schnider/Stenger [(1) Bibl.]). They develop the "fare well" (good fortune, *Tychē*) found in some Gk. papyrus letters. The religious note in Paul is Christocentric, with his distinctive word *grace*. This closing may stamp, as the writer's own, all that has been said in the letter (Moffatt 1931 [(1) Bibl. **grace**] 141, "authentication").

The blessing functions as both wish and statement ("Grace is with you"); see NOTES on v 23. Not communal esprit de corps but the Holy Spirit God gives to each believer at baptism and to the church community (2:1). Divine grace must

---

collegium Germanorum. This "Swiss guard" would scarcely have been involved in Ephesus or Caesaria, only in security for the Emperor himself.

[17] Connections of *familia Caesaris* with Philippi are stressed through inscriptions (Augustus' freedmen at Philippi, Bockmuehl 270) and, more speculatively, through Lydia and purple dye as an imperial monopoly (Witherington 137, with G. H. R. Horsley, *NewDocs* 2:28).

[18] Cf. the "synagogue of the Freedmen," Acts 6:9, slaves liberated from the Imperial household; *TDNT* 4:266 n 9.

[19] See NOTE on 4:23 for the two possible trs. Among factors that enter into a decision are (a) the "performative" nature of language (contrast J. L. Austin, *How To Do Things with Words* [Oxford: Clarendon, 1962] with A. C. Thiselton, "The Supposed Power of Words in the Biblical Writings," *JTS* NS 25 [1974] 283–99 and *NIDNTT* 3:1123–43, bibl. 1145–46) and (b) questions of liturgy and ministry (cf. Schenk 1967 [(2) Bibl. **prayer**] 21–32, 133–40; C. Westermann, "Die Frage nach dem Segen," *Zwischen den Zeiten* 11 [1957] 244–53; Heckel).

continue to be with this "apportioned spirit," to sustain and enrich. *spirit* is a term from OT/Jewish anthropology, used in the Hellenistic church, in light of the Spirit God gives to those who believe. No notions of "the soul" in any Gk. sense or a human being's natural "inner personality . . . as contact-point" (Hendriksen 213); rather, the "I" or "mind" of the person in Christ (*TDNT* 4:509; Fuchs, Bultmann, Schweizer, cited in the NOTE). *spirit* (sg.) recalls the concern of Letter B with unity in the church at Philippi; *you* (pl.) reflects emphasis in v 21 on *every* saint at Philippi (Hawth. 215; O'B 555, but *pneuma* as "a distributive singular" does not mean sheer individualism or that each receives a piece of the Spirit).

Commentators see an *inclusio* over 4:23 and 4:21 or 4:23 and 1:1–2.[20] This works for *grace* in 4:23 (the final word is *hymōn*, "spirit *of you*") and 1:2, *grace to you*. . . . Gk. letters regularly began with reference to the addressee and ended with "fare (you) well" or "good-bye (to you)." It holds for Letter B (and others) and so cannot be used as an argument for the unity of canonical Phil. 4:21 and 23 may be more impressive: *every saint* and *your spirit* balance each other, as do *in Christ Jesus* and *the Lord Jesus Christ*. Cf. B.3 above, Schenk's chiastic structure, items A and A'. Jesus Christ stands over the communications process, including greetings and closing, between Paul and the Philippians.

Little significance should be attached to the shift from *Christ Jesus* in v 21 to *Jesus Christ* in v 23. Though hearers probably thought of *Jesus* and *Christ* as names (see NOTE on 4:23), *Christ* may still retain something of its original character as a title of exaltation (cf. Grundmann, *TDNT* 9:542–43), though they interchange with little or no distinction in sense (so within Phil 1:15–26 and 3:7–14).[21] See above, NOTE on 1:2 *Lord Jesus Christ*.

In 1:2, *grace* and peace are *from God our Father and the Lord Jesus Christ*; in 4:23 *grace* is solely *of the Lord Jesus Christ*. Why this consistent shift in Pauline letters, from a "binitarian" form (the Father and Christ) in salutations to a "unitary" one (Christ alone)? 4:23 may be a succinct and penetrating formulation of the experience of grace, in light of a fuller statement used at the start of a letter. Liturgical usage might be invoked, but many are wary of these claims (see NOTE on 1:2 *grace and peace*; [1] COMMENT A and B.6; COMMENT on 4:21–23, A.2). Such claims simply shift the question to why liturgically a binitarian salutation (at the start of a worship service?) but a unitary benediction (at its conclusion?). Better: note the origins (see NOTE on 1:2 *grace and peace*; [1] COMMENT A, oriental epistolary forms, and B.6): to an inherited formula from Judaism, "grace and peace (from God)," followers of Jesus, perhaps Paul himself, added the christological phrase. The letter-ending blessing-benediction ("the/our Lord Jesus Christ") is a Christian (Pauline) formulation. Schenk 71–73 suggests that God performs the

---

[20] Fee 461, the "grace and peace . . . from God the Father and the Lord Jesus Christ" in 1:2 are now distinguished as "the peace of God" (4:7, cf. 9) and "the grace of our Lord Jesus Christ" (4:23).

[21] W. Kramer ([1] Bibl. **Christ**): Paul prefers *in Christ Jesus* at the end of sentences (4:21); it is often used "to define the Church" (*every saint*). But putting 4:21 under "theological argument" is questionable (#36a,b, nn 503, 510, and 508 respectively, not 509 as in his index). Likewise the claims "that in the Pauline corpus *Jesus* has the same meaning as *Christ*" (p. 201) and the OT/Jewish concept of messiah "is completely unrecognized by the Gentile Christian church of the Pauline period" (p. 214).

divine role through Christ but one must not thereby identify Christ and God (cf. Silva 43, on 1:2). Murphy-O'Connor 1995a:100–101, God is "ultimate source"; Christ, "the power of God" (1 Cor 1:24).

"The grace of God" was a common expression in Judaism (Loh. 191), in the OT, and Qumran writings (H. Conzelmann, *TDNT* 9:383–91). "The grace of Christ" is a significant shift. But apart from these concluding benedictions, Paul speaks of the grace of Christ only twice (2 Cor 8:9, Gal 1:6). "Christ" is a metonym for "gospel." The nine Pauline benedictions present this metonym, *pars pro toto*, a part for the whole: the real subject "God" is contained in the term *grace*. God is presupposed in speaking of the action of the Risen One in the interim until the parousia. The gen. is not subjective (as if Christ provides grace to be "with you"), but epexegetical or explanatory, grace is God's bestowal that consists of actions through the risen Lord, Jesus Christ. This fits (Schenk 73) practice in Paul's day of prayer to God, through Christ. On solidarity with God, see NOTE on 1:7c *this gracious opportunity*. To this extent, it is not "binitarian." Schenk 74–75 would render *charis* not by *Gnade* ("grace") but in the Hellenistic sense of "favor" or "gift." Paul's prayer wish in 4:23 becomes, "I wish for you that each individual of you experience ever anew how God turns to him [or bestows himself on each of you] in friendly fashion [*freundlich*] through our Lord Jesus Christ." Cf. P. Stuhlmacher on Phlm 25, "With such a blessing-greeting the letter goes back to its introduction" and proves "a communication, the sign, foundation, and perspective" in "God's encounter with men and women through and in Christ" (EKK *Phlm.* 56).

To Moffatt's eloquent contention (1931:142) that Paul's "last word to any church was 'grace'" and that Paul "allows nothing to stand alongside of 'grace,' nothing, that is, of a conventional phrase like Farewell," we must add, nothing except God, God acting through Christ.[22]

Phil 4:21–23 has had little or no use in lectionaries and preaching. For greetings, Rom 16 and Phlm 23–24 are far more detailed.

SELECT BIBLIOGRAPHY (see also General Bibliography and Commentaries)

Cuming, G. J. 1975–76. "Service-Endings in the Epistles," *NTS* 22:110–13.

Güting, E. 1993. "Amen, Eulogie, Doxologie: Eine textkritische Untersuchung," in *Begegnungen zwischen Christentum und Judentum in Antike und Mittelalter*, FS H. Schrenckenberg, ed. D.-A. Koch/H. Lichtenberg SIJD 1 (Göttingen: Vandenhoeck & Rupecht) 133–62.

Hofmann, K.-M. 1938. *Philema Hagion*. BFCT 2/38. Gütersloh: C. Bertelsmann.

Mullins, T. Y. 1968. "Greeting as a New Testament Form," *JBL* 87:418–26.

Thraede, K. 1968–69. "Ursprünge und Formen des 'Heiligen Kusses' im frühen Christentum," *JAC* 11–12:124–80.

Weaver, P. R. C. 1972. *Familia Caesaris: A Social Study of the Emperor's Freedmen and Slaves*. Cambridge: Cambridge Univ. Press.

---

[22] So Thielman 1995:239. Fee's effort (461–62) to place the "central focus on Christ" draws more on other parts of Phil (like 1:21) than on Paul's closing formulation. Bockmuehl finds "Amen" at 4:23 (in some MSS) "the only fitting coda to Paul's epistle of joy."

benediction, blessing: F. Horst/H. Köster, "Segen und Fluch (AT, NT)," *RGG*³ 5 (1961) cols. 1649–52; H.-G. Link, *NIDNTT* 1:206–15, esp. 206 and 213–14 on *aspazomai*; K. H. Richards, "Bless/Blessing," *ABD* 1:753–55; W. J. Urbrock, "Blessings and Curses," *ABD* 1:755–61; H. U. Steymans/J. T. Fitzgerald, "Segen und Fluch (AT, NT)," *RGG*⁴ 7 (2004) cols. 1132–36.

Heckel, U. 2002. *Der Segen im Neuen Testament. Begriff, Formen, Gesten. Mit einem praktisch-theologischen Ausblick.* WUNT 150. Tübingen: Mohr Siebeck.

GENERAL INDEX

Technical terms, like "anaphora," are usually defined or illustrated in the first occurrence cited.

INDEX OF AUTHORS

This index helps indicate where full bibliographical data are given for an author, usually in the first page listed. It does not include Bible translations (see pp. xxii–xxiii) or translators of LCL volumes.

INDEX OF SCRIPTURE AND OTHER ANCIENT TEXTS

PSEUDEPIGRAPHA OF THE OLD TESTAMENT